D1289254

INTERNET LAW: CASES & PROBLEMS

James Grimmelmann
Professor of Law
Cornell Tech and Cornell Law School

Seventh Edition © 2017 James Grimmelmann
ISBN 978-1-943689-03-3

www.semaphorepress.com

Copyright and Your Rights

Printing A Paper Copy

If you would like to have a printed copy of the book in addition to the electronic copy, you are welcome to print out a copy of any part, or all, of the book. Please note that you will find blank pages throughout the book. We have inserted these intentionally to facilitate double-sided printing. We anticipate that students may wish to carry only portions of the book at a time. The blank pages are inserted so that each chapter begins on a fresh, top-side page. Printed copies of the full book are also available through Amazon.com.

Finding Aids and Annotations

Finally, please note that the book does not include an index, a table of cases, or other finding aids that are conventional for printed books. This is because a Semaphore Press book, in pdf form, can be searched electronically for any word or phrase in which you are interested. With the book open in Adobe Reader, simply hit control-f (or select the "find" option in the "Edit" pull-down menu) and enter the search term you want to find. We also enable Reader's commenting features in our pdf books, so you can highlight text, insert comments, and personally annotate your copy in other ways you find helpful. If your copy of Reader does not appear to permit these commenting features, please check to make sure you have the most recent version; any version numbered "8" or higher should permit you to annotate a Semaphore Press book.

For my parents.

INTERNET LAW: CASES AND PROBLEMS

INTRODUCTION 9

CHAPTER 1: BACKGROUND 17
A. Computer Technology 17
    Technical Primer: Computers 17
    Technical Primer: The Internet 27
    Columbia Pictures Indus. v. Fung 36
    Internet Applications Problem 39
B. Theory 40
    Code 2.0 40
    The Future of the Internet..44

CHAPTER 2: JURISDICTION...51
A. Cyberspace...51
    A Declaration of the Independence of Cyberspace................................51
    The Problem of Perspective in Internet Law 53
    Law and Borders 55
    Unwilling Avatars 58
    Voyeur Dorm L.C. v. City of Tampa 61
    Voyeur Dorm L.C. v. City of Tampa 62
    National Federation of the Blind v. Target Corp. 63
    Dead Aim Problem 67
B. Territoriality..68
    Dow Jones & Co. v. Gutnick 69
    Mahfouz v. Ehrenfeld 75
    Note on the Dormant Commerce Clause...77
    Overstock.com v. New York State Dept. of Taxation and Finance.............79
    Diplomatic Mission Problem 82
C. Enforcement 83
    SPEECH Act...83
    Note on Extradition 84
    Google Inc. v. Equustek Solutions Inc. 85
    Digital Borders..91
    SeaHaven Problem 95
    Gambling Treaty Problem 96
D. Personal Jurisdiction and Venue 97
    Burdick v. Superior Court...99
    Penguin Group (USA) Inc. v. American Buddha 107
    United States v. Auernheimer...111
    Too Damn High Problem 116
    FloodZone Problem 116

CHAPTER 3: SPEECH...119
A. Defining "Speech"...119
    United States Constitution, Amendment I..119
    Texas v. Johnson 119
    Bland v. Roberts 120
    Bland v. Roberts 122

Note on First Amendment Tiers of Scrutiny 123
Packingham v. North Carolina 124
Note on Cryptography 130
Bernstein v. U.S. Dept. of Justice...135
Note on the Press..141
B. Harmful Speech 144
It's Complicated 144
Blu-Ray Problem 146
Note on True Threats 147
Restatement (Second) of Torts [Defamation] 149
Restatement (Second) of Torts [Emotional distress].............150
Snyder v. Phelps...151
Restatement (Second) of Torts [Privacy Torts].....................153
Pennsylvania Right of Publicity...154
Gawker Media, LLC v. Bollea...155
People v. Marquan M. 159
United States v. Petrovic..164
Revenge Porn Problem 168
C. Pornography 168
Pornography Law Primer 168
CDA Negotiation Problem 170
Reno v. American Civil Liberties Union 171
CPOEA Problem...176
D. Filtering...176
Center for Democracy and Technology v. Pappert....................176
United States v. Keith 185
E. Section 230 186
Restatement (Second) of Torts [Defamation] 187
Communications Decency Act § 230 187
Zeran v. America Online, Inc...188
Jones v. Dirty World Entertainment Recordings LLC 195
Doe v. MySpace, Inc. 206
Doe No. 14 v. Internet Brands, Inc..209
People's Front of Judea Problem 211
Section 230 Reform Problem..212

CHAPTER 4: PRIVACY 215
A. The Fourth and Fifth Amendments..215
Fourth and Fifth Amendment Overview....................................215
Note on Warrant Jurisdiction 217
Note on United States v. Jones 218
Riley v. California 219
United States v. Warshak...231
United States v. Apple MacPro Computer 238
Coffeeshop Problem..242
B. Wiretapping 242
Wiretap Act...243
O'Brien v. O'Brien..246
Stored Communications Act..249
Ehling v. Monmouth-Ocean Hospital Service Corp. 253

Pen Registers and Trap and Trace Devices 258
Note on technical Assistance 260
C. National Security..261
Liberty and Security in a Changing World...............................262
Other Surveillance Programs...268
Legal Challenges to NSA Surveillance..................................270
Zipper Problem..272
D. Anonymity..273
Stored Communications Act...274
Jukt Micronics Problem 274
Doe I v. Individuals, Whose True Names are Unknown 275
E. Consumer Privacy..280
In re DoubleClick Inc. Privacy Litig....................................280
In re Google, Inc. Privacy Policy Litig. 286
In re Snapchat, Inc. 296
Cookie Monster Problem..302
F. An International Perspective..303
Data Protection Directive...303
European Union: ECJ Invalidates Data Retention Directive 306
Google Spain SP v. Agencia Española de Protección de Datos 308
Schrems v. Data Protection Commissioner............................314

CHAPTER 5: ACCESS TO COMPUTERS 323
A. Contracts 323
CX Digital Media, Inc. v. Smoking Everywhere, Inc....................323
Nguyen v. Barnes & Noble, Inc. 330
Smurfberry Problem 335
ProCD, Inc. v. Zeidenberg 336
Krustilu Problem 337
SeaSells Problem 337
B. Computer Misuse Statutes 338
Computer Fraud and Abuse Act..338
United States v. Morris 340
United States v. Nosal [I] 342
United States v. Nosal [II] 349
C. Trespass to Chattels...351
Restatement (Second) of Torts [trespass] 352
Intel v. Hamidi 352
Note on Spam 359
Wireless Router Problem 361
LineJump Problem 361

CHAPTER 6: TRADEMARKS & DOMAIN NAMES......................................363
A. Trademark Basics...363
Multi Time Machine, Inc. v. Amazon. com, Inc. 364
Tiffany (NJ) Inc. v. eBay, Inc. 373
Happy Fun Ball Problem...379
B. Domain Names..380
Title 15, United States Code...381
Taubman Co. v. Webfeats 383

Drunk Kids Problem 388
ICANN and the Domain-Name System 388
Uniform Domain Name Dispute Resolution Policy 392
Flexegrity Problem 394
Curt Mfg., Inc. v. Sabin 395
Arista Records, LLC v. Tkach 399

CHAPTER 7: COPYRIGHT 405
Copyright Overview 405
A. The Exclusive Rights 407
Copyright Act [Exclusive Rights and First Sale] 407
Capitol Records, LLC v. ReDigi, Inc. 408
Note on RAM Copies 414
Perfect 10, Inc. v. Amazon.com, Inc. 415
American Broadcasting Co. v. Aereo, Inc. 419
Music Locker Problem...422
B. Licenses 422
Field v. Google Inc. 423
Vernor v. Autodesk, Inc..428
MIT License 433
GNU General Public License (GPL) 434
Jacobsen v. Katzer 438
C. Fair Use 443
Copyright Act [Fair Use]..443
Note on Sony v. Universal (Fair Use) 444
A & M Records, Inc. v. Napster, Inc. 445
Katz v. Google Inc...449
Perfect 10, Inc. v. Amazon.com, Inc. 453
Bubonic Plagiarism Problem 456
D. Direct and Secondary Liability..457
Perfect 10, Inc. v. Giganews, Inc. 457
Note on Sony v. Universal (Contributory Infringement) 461
A & M Records, Inc. v. Napster, Inc. 462
Metro-Goldwyn-Mayer Studios Inc. v. Grokster, Ltd......................466
Cachet Problem 471
Rip-Mix-Burn Problem 472
E. Section 512 473
Copyright Act [Section 512] 473
Friday Problem 478
Lenz v. Universal Music Corp. 478
Perfect 10, Inc. v. CCBill LLC...484
Section 512 Compliance Questions...488
Materials on Content ID 489
Mangle Problem 496
F. Digital Rights Management 497
Note on Digital Rights Management 497
Note on the Motivation for Anti-Circumvention Law.......................498
Copyright Act [Anti-Circumvention]..499
Universal City Studios, Inc. v. Corley 500
Universal City Studios, Inc. v. Reimerdes 502

Section 1201 Problems 508
Note on DMCA Exemptions 509

CHAPTER 8: PATENT 511
Alice Corp. v. CLS Bank Int'l 511
Soverain Software LLC v. Newegg Inc. 519
Function Media, L.L.C. v. Google 524
Apple v. Motorola 528
Apple v. Motorola 530

CHAPTER 9: PRIVATE POWER 533
A. First Amendment Limits 533
Cyber Promotions, Inc. v. American Online, Inc. 533
Zhang v. Baidu.com Inc 537
WikiLeaks Problem 544
CurrenC Problem 546
Spam Posse Problem 546
B. Antitrust 547
Note on Antitrust Law and Economics 547
United States v. Microsoft Corp. 549
LiveUniverse, Inc. v. MySpace, Inc. 556
Google Maps Problem 562
C. Network Neutrality 563
Verizon v. FCC 563
Note on Administrative Law 567
Note on Telephone Regulation 569
Broadband Internet Regulation: A Brief History 573
Note on Wireless Regulation 583
Note on Interconnection 585
Protecting and Promoting the Open Internet 587
Dissenting Statement of Commissioner Ajit Pai 596
DoubleNet Problem 601
The punchline? 602

CHAPTER 10: BEYOND THE INTERNET 603
A. Virtual Property 603
Kremen v. Cohen 603
United States v. Aleynikov 609
Bragg v. Linden Research, Inc 614
Note on Bitcoin 626
United States v. Ulbricht 629
Digital Currency Regulatory Guidance 632
Slot Machine Problem 634
Post.Mortem Problem 635
Davy Jones Problem 635
B. Defective Software 636
Kennison v. Daire 636
Pompeii Estates, Inc. v. Consolidated Edison Co. of N.Y., Inc. ..637
Rosenberg v. Harwood 640

Houston Federation of Teachers, Local 2415 v.
Houston Independent School District..643
NCIC Confidential Problem..649
C. Litigation 650
Arista Records, LLC, v. Does 1–19 650
In re Bittorrent Adult Film Copyright Infringement Cases 653
Baidoo v. Blood-Dzraku...660
Griffin v. State 663
Chace v. Loisel 668
Florida Standard Jury Instructions 669
Courthouse Technology Problem 670
D. The Physical World 671
Guns, Limbs, and Toys: What Future for 3D Printing? 671
Hackers Remotely Kill a Jeep on the Highway – With Me In It ...677
Beware the Listening Machines 678
Fact Sheet – Small Unmanned Aircraft Regulations................679
5thWheel Problem 681
Coda...682

INTRODUCTION

Welcome to Internet Law.

Innocuous as that sentence may sound, it conceals two controversial assumptions. The first is that Internet law is a coherent subject of study; the second is that "Internet law" is the right name for it.

DOES INTERNET LAW EXIST?

If you flip through this book's table of contents, you will see topics jurisdiction, free speech, privacy, torts, contracts, criminal procedure and criminal law, trademark, copyright, antitrust, telecommunications law, and more. This diversity is characteristic of the field. It also requires us to ask whether this is a field worth studying.

In 1996, Judge Frank Easterbrook was asked to speak to a conference at the University of Chicago Law School on "The Law of Cyberspace." His remarks, which bore the title "Cyberspace and the Law of the Horse," have become famous for throwing down a gauntlet at the feet of the assembled scholars. He questioned whether it made sense to talk about "cyberspace law" or "computer law" or "Internet law" at all.

> When he was dean of this law school, Gerhard Casper was proud that the University of Chicago did not offer a course in "The Law of the Horse." He did not mean by this that Illinois specializes in grain rather than livestock. His point, rather, was that "Law and ..." courses should be limited to subjects that could illuminate the entire law. ...
>
> Dean Casper's remark had a second meaning – that the best way to learn the law applicable to specialized endeavors is to study general rules. Lots of cases deal with sales of horses; others deal with people kicked by horses; still more deal with the licensing and racing of horses, or with the care veterinarians give to horses, or with prizes at horse shows. Any effort to collect these strands into a course on "The Law of the Horse" is doomed to be shallow and to miss unifying principles. Teaching 100 percent of the cases on people kicked by horses will not convey the law of torts very well. Far better for most students – better, even, for those who plan to go into the horse trade – to take courses in property, torts, commercial transactions, and the like, adding to the diet of horse cases a smattering of transactions in cucumbers, cats, coal, and cribs. Only by putting the law of the horse in the context of broader rules about commercial endeavors could one really understand the law about horses.
>
> Now you can see the meaning of my title. When asked to talk about "Property in Cyberspace," my immediate reaction was, "Isn't this just the law of the horse?"*

To this day, "the law of the horse" is a code phrase among scholars for the idea that there's nothing new here, that studying Internet law is nothing more than an exercise in applying unrelated bodies of law to the Internet, with no unifying doctrines

---

* Frank H. Easterbrook, *Cyberspace and the Law of the Horse*, 1996 U. CHI. LEGAL F. 207, 207–08 (1996).

or truly distinctive insights. Almost since Easterbrook sat down at the end of his talk, scholars have been debating whether he was right. During your study of Internet law, you should be asking yourself whether the subject really does "illuminate the entire law." As a starting point, here are some possible responses to the question.

- *Easterbrook Was Right*. Internet law is necessarily a patchwork. Maybe the effort spent learning a little antitrust law and a little privacy law and a little First Amendment law would be better spent learning one of them in depth. Perhaps this course is best understood as a sampler platter: a bit of each so you can have a better sense of what else there is to know about.

- *Internet Issues Overlap*. The same simple few facts may raise copyright, contract, and criminal issues. The way you analyze one will affect how you analyze the others. Or, a problem may require a difficult characterization: should we think of this as a free-speech matter, a telecommunications question, or an antitrust issue? Again, you will need to draw on multiple bodies of law and put them into conversation with each other.

- *The Internet Is Too Important to Ignore*. Lawyers need to handle the problems their clients bring to them. Increasingly often, those problems involve the Internet. Family law changes when children's Facebook pages become admissible evidence; securities law changes when people do worldwide fundraising from a webpage. To counsel clients effectively, lawyers need to have a clear picture of how the Internet works and what people are doing with it.

- *Some Law Is Internet-Only*. When Easterbrook spoke in 1996, Internet law was largely a blank slate. Today, that is no longer true. Major pieces of legislation, such as the 1998 Digital Millennium Copyright Act, have created important bodies of Internet-specific law. Some of these doctrines are likely to surprise you – they've certainly surprised lawyers who didn't expect that law online might not be the same as law offline.

- *There Are Patterns in Internet Law*. Even when doing Internet law just consists in applying familiar doctrines to online activities, some problems crop up again and again. It can be harder to tell precisely where a tort took place, for example, when the plaintiff, the defendant, and the computers they used to communicate are all in different countries. This is a problem for copyright, for defamation, for taxation ... and so on. By studying how different bodies of law have been applied to online activity, you can gain a feel for how other bodies of law might apply to Internet facts.

- *Maybe the Internet Does Change Everything*. Easterbrook's analogy assumes a world in which most torts and transactions don't involve horses. Nor did horses radically transform American society. But the Internet is changing how we live, think, write, love, fight, do business, and think of ourselves. Some of those changes may go so deep that they call into question basic assumptions on which areas of law are based. Studying the ways in which our legal system has tried to grapple with those changes may give you a handle on what else may be coming.

These are only possibilities. Perhaps you will agree with one or more. Perhaps you will reject them all.

"INTERNET" AND "CYBERSPACE"

Judge Easterbrook didn't mention "Internet law" in his presentation. Instead, he discussed the "law of cyberspace." That term carries a lot of baggage, and there's a reason this book generally avoids using it. The word "cyberspace" was popularized by the science fiction novelist William Gibson to describe a new *place* created by worldwide computer networks. Here is a description of it from his 1984 novel *Neuromancer*:

> On the Sony, a two-dimensional space war faded behind a forest of mathematically generated ferns, demonstrating the spacial possibilities of logarithmic spirals; cold blue military footage burned through, lab animals wired into test systems, helmets feeding into fire control circuits of tanks and war plans. 'Cyberspace. A consensual hallucination experienced daily by billions of legitimate operators, in every nation, by children being taught mathematical concepts ... A graphic representation of data abstracted from the banks of every computer in the human system. Unthinkable complexity. Lines of light ranged in the nonspace of the mind, clusters and constellations of data. Like city lights, receding. ...*

The idea that networked computers would create a wholly new place with its own geography, imagery, and laws of physics was nearly irresistible for science-fiction novelists and Hollywood filmmakers. While some movies, like *WarGames* (1983), were "realistic" in the sense that they showed computer users typing commands and looking at the results on their screens, others, like *The Matrix* (1999), imagined that the future of computing would involve highly immersive virtual realities.

Meanwhile, it was apparent to many lawyers and scholars that computers were posing interesting legal issues, such the copyrightability of software and liability for defective computer systems. Looking ahead, many also expected that computer networks (and eventually and especially the Internet) were going to raise questions about some seemingly fundamental legal concepts.

For example, consider jurisdiction. If two people across the globe from each other could interact instantaneously and profoundly with each other, perhaps it made more sense to say that their interaction happened "in cyberspace" rather than in the country either one of them was in. And if so, then wouldn't it follow the most appropriate body of law to apply would be a new body of "cyberspace law" that was specially adapted for the new physics and customs of cyberspace?

Thinking of new laws in terms of "cyberspace," however, emphasizes a particular vision of the form those laws would take. It suggests that cyberspace is somewhere separate and apart from the rest of the world, that when you go online you really are *going* somewhere and leaving your offline home behind. It suggests a kind of simple territoriality for law: cyberlaw applies in cyberspace, just as Swedish law applies in Sweden. And it creates a sharp division between offline and online conduct and laws.

With the benefit of hindsight, it hasn't turned out that way. As the Internet has grown in importance, it has increasingly permeated daily life. Rather than being a place people go to leave their regular lives behind, the Internet is something they welcome into their lives in innumerable ways. In addition, the science-fiction novelists got at least one thing very wrong. For most people, there is no one "cyber-

---

* WILLIAM GIBSON, NEUROMANCER 51 (Penguin 2000).

space." Instead, there are all sorts of things online, and the way we experience them varies enormously. Shopping for shoes on eBay is a different experience from having a video chat on Skype, and the legal regimes involved take account of those differences.

This casebook, therefore, deals with "Internet law" rather than "cyberspace law" or "cyberlaw." Judges, lawyers, and clients use the Internet, not cyberspace, and the book reflects that reality. At the same time, it is important to think about the role that the idea of cyberspace has played in shaping Internet law. Some doctrines still bear its traces. There are also important debates about how strongly Internet law should resemble offline law, and in the course of this book, we will engage with many of them.

THEMES OF THE BOOK

This book emphasizes five major themes in Internet law: *code is law*, *governmental control*, *intermediary power*, *equality*, and *generativity*. These themes run throughout the subject. Sometimes one or another is more prominent; at other times they intertwine. Being alert to them makes it easier to recognize recurring patterns in how lawyers and judges deal with Internet issues.

- The first theme, *code is law*, is the most profound and pervasive. Everything that happens online is mediated by computers. This affects how law applies to online behavior: substituting computers for people has subtle and far-reaching consequences.

- The second theme, *governmental control*, is a perennial question of law and politics: how much of people's lives are visible to governments, and how far can governments go in dictating what people do? As people do more and more online, governmental power increases in some ways and decreases in others.

- The third theme, *intermediary power*, examines the fact that the computers that make up the Internet are owned by – and controlled by – a variety of entities, including websites, network providers, and search engines. By deleting content or making it more prominent, they can shape who sees what online.

- The fourth theme, *equality*, considers whether the gains and the pains of the Internet are spread evenly throughout society, or whether they land more on some people than on others. Some observers have celebrated the Internet as a great leveler of differences among people and nations; others have worried about a "digital divide" that excludes the poor.

- The final theme, *generativity*, examines the extraordinary level of innovation and creativity that are typically attributed to the Internet. The book explores what features of the Internet might be responsible for this outpouring of expression, and what consequences it has for law and policy.

Each chapter raises questions about two or more of these themes. Keep alert for them as you read; they will help you connect the dots between different doctrines.

This is not a "hide the ball" casebook. The subject is hard enough without introducing artificial difficulties. The notes and questions following each case are meant to help you think through the legal questions faced by the court, the implications of its holding for future cases, and the policy issues lurking in the background. You do not need to have the correct answer (indeed, many questions have no single "correct" answer), but it is important to consider them all.

Some sections of this book contain statutory excerpts. The questions following them are especially important. Statute-reading is a critical legal skill, but it is hard work and it takes practice. The questions are intended to give you a guided walk-through of the process, helping you develop your mental agility as you flip between definitions, applications, and exceptions.

You may also have noticed that most sections contain one or more problems. They are an integral part of this casebook, and they are designed to be hard but doable. Some of them introduce doctrinal or factual twists not covered in the cases and notes. Others require you to exercise negotiation, counseling, and strategic skills. They are all drawn from real problems faced by real people, and if they were able to find good solutions, you can too. Do not be afraid to draw on what you have learned outside of this course.

Finally, despite all these dire warnings, this casebook is meant to be fun. It is almost impossible to flip through a newspaper or browse a website without coming across an Internet law issue. By the time you finish with this book, you will be able to spot these issues, put them in context, and impress your friends with your real-life knowledge. I have tried to select cases with vivid, memorable facts; Internet law has no shortage of them. I have enjoyed every minute of teaching the subject and preparing this casebook; I hope that you will enjoy your time with it, too.

NOTE ON THE EDITING

I have emphasized readability over strict adherence to the text of the sources being quoted. An ellipsis ("..."). may indicate the omission of anywhere from a few words to multiple pages. I have corrected typos and other obvious but trivial mistakes without specifically marking the change. I have freely omitted, edited, and moved citations to improve readability. I have also frequently removed quotation marks, along with the citation to the source being quoted. Footnotes in cases are numbered as in the original. Judges' names are for the most part standardized as "Lastname, Title" – except for the United States Supreme Court's traditional formula: "Justice Lastname delivered the opinion of the Court." The formatting of statutes has been standardized, even when they are being quoted.

NOTE ON THE TYPE

The body text is set in Miller by Matthew Carter. Miller is a Scotch Roman, a robust and unpretentious style popular in the 19th century. Headings and URLs are set in Matthew Butterick's Concourse, a modern design based on W.A. Dwiggins's classic sans-serif Metro. The code samples are set in Paul Hunt's Source Code Pro, an open-source fixed-width typeface designed specifically for programming.

GIVING BACK

I am proud to be part of the Internet law community, to which I owe debts of the kind that can never be repaid, only honored. One third of the net revenues received from sales of this edition of *Internet Law: Cases and Problems* will be donated to the Electronic Frontier Foundation (EFF). In the EFF's own words:

> The Electronic Frontier Foundation is the leading nonprofit organization defending civil liberties in the digital world. Founded in 1990, EFF champions user privacy, free expression, and innovation through impact litigation, policy analysis, grassroots activism, and technology

> development. We work to ensure that rights and freedoms are en-
> hanced and protected as our use of technology grows.

I interned at the EFF during law school, and many of the ideas in this casebook grew from seeds planted that summer. That said, this book's contents are independent of the EFF and its mission – as they are of all outside influence. The EFF and I have no control over each other, and we don't necessarily share the other's views on any particular issue.

ACKNOWLEDGMENTS

In addition to designing a fairer casebook business model, my editors at Semaphore Press, Lydia Pallas Loren and Joseph Scott Miller, did me the great favor of holding this book to their own high standards. Colleagues and friends who gave helpful suggestions include David Abrams, Sarah Ames, Marc Blitz, Annemarie Bridy, Anupam Chander, Bryan Choi, Danielle Citron, Richard Chused, Ralph Clifford, Ed Felten, Michael Froomkin, Andrew Gilden, Eric Goldman, Ellen Goodman, Joe Gratz, Michael Grynberg, Robert Heverly, Dan Hunter, Gus Hurwitz, David Johnson, Meg Leta Jones, Kate Klonick, Molly Land, Susan Landau, Greg Lastowka, Lyrissa Barnett Lidsky, Evan McLaren, Christina Mulligan, Beth Noveck, Ken Rodriguez, Brian Sites, Eric Tamashasky, Jon Weinberg, and Tal Zarsky. Aislinn Black, who knows more Internet law than many lawyers, was generous with her wisdom.

I am grateful to the students in my Internet Law courses at New York Law School and the University of Maryland, on whom I tested earlier versions of this book. Their judgments about what worked and what didn't made this book what it is. The book would also not have been possible without the hard work of my research assistants at New York Law School: Catherine Baxter, Cynthia Grady, James Major, Dominic Mauro, and Joseph Merante. Their diligence and imagination helped turn a sprawling packet of cases into a focused casebook. Very special thanks to Linda Torosian and Mary Herms.

PERMISSIONS

I am grateful to the authors and publishers who have given permission to reprint portions of their books and articles in this casebook.

- LAWRENCE LESSIG, CODE 2.0 (2006) is available under a Creative Commons Attribution ShareAlike 2.5 Generic license. A human-readable summary is available at http://creativecommons.org/licenses/by-sa/2.5/ and the full text at http://creativecommons.org/licenses/by-sa/2.5/legalcode. CODE 2.0 is available in PDF form at http://codev2.cc/download+remix/Lessig-Codev2.pdf. The author has waived the ShareAlike license condition as to this casebook.

- JONATHAN ZITTRAIN, THE FUTURE OF THE INTERNET - AND HOW TO STOP IT (2008) is available under a Creative Commons Attribution Non-Commercial Share-Alike 3.0 United States license. A human-readable summary is available at http://creativecommons.org/licenses/by-nc-sa/3.0/us/, the full text at http://creativecommons.org/licenses/by-nc-sa/3.0/us/legalcode. The author has waived the ShareAlike and NonCommercial license conditions for this casebook. THE FUTURE OF THE INTERNET is available in PDF form at http://futureoftheinternet.org/static/ ZittrainTheFutureoftheInternet.pdf.

- Excerpts from Mary Anne Franks, *Unwilling Avatars: Idealism and Discrimination in Cyberspace*, 20 COLUM. J. GENDER & L. 224 (2011), are used with permission of the Columbia Journal of Gender and Law.

- Excerpts from Jack Goldsmith and Timothy Wu, *Digital Borders*, LEGAL AFFAIRS (Jan. 2006), are used with permission of the authors.

- Excerpts from Adam Thierer and Adam Marcus, *Guns, Limbs, and Toys: What Future for 3D Printing?*, 17 MINN. J. SCI. & TECH. L. 805 (2016), are used with permission of the authors and the Minnesota Journal of Science and Technology.

- Excerpts from Elizabeth E. Joh, *Policing Police Robots*, 64 UCLA L. REV. DISCOURSE 516 (2016) are used with permission of the author.

CHANGES IN THE SEVENTH EDITION

The changes for the seventh edition are comparatively minor, compared with previous updates. There are five new principal cases and materials; eight have been removed to make room.

- In the Jurisdiction chapter, the Supreme Court of Canada's opinion in *Equustek v. Google* replaces the opinion below.

- In the Speech chapter, *United States v. Packingham* is new. *Ashcroft v. Free Speech Coalition* has been removed, and there is a new note on First Amendment tiers.

- In the Privacy chapter, the excerpts from CALEA have been replaced by a note on technical assistance, *United States v. Apple MacPro Computer* replaces *United States v. Doe*, and the materials on Patriot Act section 215 have been removed.

- In the Trademark chapter, *Panavision v. Toeppen* and *PETA v. Doughney* have been cut, and sections B and C have been combined into a streamlined Domain Names section.

- In the Beyond the Internet chapter, *Houston Federation of Teachers v. Houston Independent School District* is new. The Bitcoin materials have been gently streamlined, and now use Illinois guidance on money transmission compliance rather than FinCEN guidance. And the Litigation section has absorbed *Arista Records, LLC, v. Does 1–19* and *In re Bittorrent Adult Film Copyright Infringement Cases* from the Privacy chapter.

As usual, there are numerous smaller tweaks and new questions throughout. If you have comments on the casebook or suggestions for how it could be improved in a future edition, I welcome your thoughts.

James Grimmelmann
July 11, 2017

CHAPTER 1: BACKGROUND

The first of the five major themes of this book is how law changes when computers – rather than people – make and enforce decisions. It is arguably *the* central question in all of Internet law. Although he was not the first to focus on the question, Professor Lawrence Lessig gave the most influential answer to it: "code is law." By this, he meant that computer software (or "code") could do some of the same work that law ordinarily does in controlling people's conduct. This chapter explores the idea in two ways: a technical primer on how computers and the Internet work, and readings on how regulation changes when computers rather than people carry it out.

A. Computer Technology

This section provides a technical primer on computers and the Internet, with an emphasis on the fundamentals that recur in case after case. As you read the fact section of an opinion, it may help to try to fit the court's discussions of the particular technologies at issue in a given case into the framework provided here.

TECHNICAL PRIMER: COMPUTERS

Bits and Data

It's a cliché to say that computers reduce everything in the world to ones and zeros – but it's also true. In a very real sense, a modern computer is just a complicated electrical circuit. So compare it to a much simpler circuit: a flashlight. We could say that the flashlight "remembers" one piece of information: whether the switch is on or off. When the switch is on, current flows through the bulb and it lights up the night. When the switch is off, no current is flowing, and the flashlight stays dark.

This is a single *bit*: a piece of information that can be either 1 or 0. A flashlight is a one-bit computer. With two flashlights, we could store two bits, with ten flashlights, we could store ten bits, and so on. A computer uses smaller wires and has many many more of them, but the basic principle is the same. The presence or absence of electric current can be used to represent the values 1 and 0, respectively.

Once you have bits, you can describe anything and everything. Numbers are a good starting point. Take, for example, the number 42. To represent it using bits, we write it down in base 2, also known as *binary*: 101010. (That's a 1 in the 32s place, plus a 1 in the 8s place, plus a 1 in the 2s place, or 32 + 8 + 2 = 42.) So we need six bits to store the number 42: that's six flashlights, or six tiny wires inside a computer. For historical reasons, computers almost always group bits into sets of eight, called *bytes*. In this system, 42 would be stored as 00101010. (The first two bits are zeros in the 128s and 64s place; the last six are exactly the same as before.)

Using one byte, therefore, we can represent any positive integer from 0 (that's 00000000) up to 255 (that's 11111111). From here on, other kinds of numbers are easy. Larger integers just take more bytes: 46,105, for example, is 10110100 00011001. Negative numbers need one more bit: we could say that 1 means "the rest of this number is positive" and 0 means "the rest of this number is negative." For smaller numbers, we could use bits to the right of the decimal point as well as to left of it.* For really big and really small numbers, we could use bits to store an exponent, just like in scientific notation.

One particularly nice consequence of using binary to represent numbers is that it takes surprisingly few bits to write down even very large numbers. One bit can stand for either of two different numbers: 0 or 1. Two bits can stand for any of four different numbers: 00 is 0, 01 is 1, 10 is 2, and 11 is 3. Three bits can stand for eight different numbers, four bits can stand for sixteen, and so on. Thirty-two bits (i.e. four bytes), are enough to represent any integer from 0 to 4,294,967,295. Adding more bits increases their descriptive power exponentially.

Numbers are useful for calculating, but for communicating, we really need letters and other familiar symbols like @ and $. The most familiar way of storing, or *encoding*, letters as numbers is a system colloquially known as ASCII.† Capital A is 65, capital B is 66, and so on through capital Z, which is 90. Lower-case a is 97, lower-case b is 98, and so on again. ASCII uses other values for other commonly used characters: such as 32 for a space and 64 for the @ sign.

Using ASCII, it's possible to convert arbitrary text into bits and vice versa. Each of the numbers it uses is small enough to fit in a single byte. So, for example, capital A is 01000001 in bits. "Hello!" would be the numbers 72 101 108 108 111 33, or, in bits, 01001000 01100101 01101100 01101100 01101111 0100001. When you open an email containing those bits, your computer converts them back into letters and displays "Hello!" on the screen.

ASCII is the most familiar way of storing text in a computer, but hardly the only one. The Unicode standard – an ambitious system for representing every writing system in use by humans, from Tibetan to emoji – defines an encoding named UTF-8, which represents each character using as few as one or as many as four bytes. (Common characters like Q take one byte; uncommon ones like 💀 take more.) If you've ever received an email liberally decorated with â€œ and similar gibberish, you've seen what happens when different encodings collide. Someone sent you a message in UTF-8, but your computer interpreted it as ASCII. The same bits – 11100010 10000000 10011100 – stand for " when interpreted as UTF-8 but for â€œ when interpreted as the most common version of ASCII.

What about images? Suppose we wanted to store this admittedly crude picture of a face:

Once again, the strategy is to look for a way of breaking something down into bits. We start by overlaying a grid on the face:

---

* Useless Fact #1: technically, the term should be "radix point." It's not a "decimal" point because we're not in base 10 anymore.

† Useless Fact #2: ASCII is short for "American Standard Code for Information Interchange." There are actually numerous variations on ASCII; this section uses the most familiar one, which goes by the official name "Windows-1252."

Now, for each box in the grid, we ask whether the face contains more black or more white. The boxes that are more than half black we make *all* black; the boxes that are more than half white, we make *all* white:

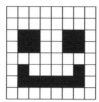

Every box, or *pixel*, is now either all-black or all-white. If we call each black pixel 0 and each white pixel 1, *each pixel corresponds to a single bit*. If we read off the first row of pixels, we get 11111111, since every pixel is white. The second row is the same, but the third row is 10011001 because the tops of the eyes show up as 1s. If we repeat for each row of pixels, the entire face is 11111111 11111111 10011001 10011001 11111111 10111101 10000001 11111111. There you go: an image has been turned into bits, suitable for storing in a computer. To be sure, the drawing has become even cruder. But by using a smaller grid with smaller pixels – for example, by using a camera with more megapixels – we can smooth out the edges until the difference has become unnoticeable.

Interesting images are rarely black-or-white. But another approximation lets computers represent shades of gray. Instead of using a single bit for each pixel, use several. Here, for example, is a three-bit way of encoding the brightness of each pixel. We divide the spectrum from white to black into eight evenly-spaced shades, so that the difference in brightness from each one to the next is the same. Then, we can approximate any shade between black and white by finding it on the spectrum and picking the one out of the eight colors that is closest to it in brightness. All that remains is to convert the eight representative colors to bits: 000 is all white, 001 is a very light gray, 010 is a slightly darker gray, and so on through 111, which is all black.

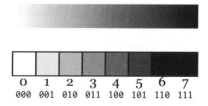

A similar technique makes it possible to represent colors. All colors are made up out of a combination of red, green, and blue light. So instead of encoding a color using a single intensity value, we can encode it using three, one for each primary color:

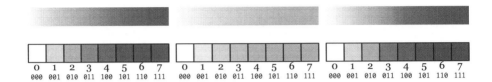

In practice, it is common to use one byte each for red, green, and blue, for a total of 24 bits – enough to describe 16,777,216 different colors, more than the human eye is capable of distinguishing.

One more example: sound. A sound wave is a vibration in the air. So consider a (simplified) wave:

First, we can slice the sound wave up by time, into a series of discrete intervals. The most common ways of representing sounds in computers uses 44,100 slices, or *samples*, per second, since this was the frequency used for CDs. Imagine that each of these slices is 1/44,100 of a second long:

Now, within each sample, we need to say how loud the sound wave is at that instant in time. We'll take the *average* loudness in that 1/44,100 of a second:

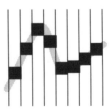

Finally, we round off, or *quantize*, the height of the sound wave within each sample the same way we rounded off the shape of the face within each pixel and the intensity of each color:

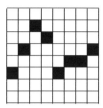

The first sample has a loudness – a height – of 3 units, the second a loudness of 5, and so we can represent these eight samples as the sequence of numbers 3 5 7 6 3 4 4 5. These numbers can, of course, be turned into bits by writing them out in binary, just like we did above.

We have now seen how to *digitize* words, images, and sounds: to represent them using bits in a digital computer. The same techniques work for other media. A video, for example, is just a sequence of images together with an accompanying soundtrack – but we already know how to encode both images and sounds.

Hardware

Some computers look familiar: they have a keyboard, screen, headphone jack, and so on. Other computers, like the one inside a pacemaker or a car engine, look radically different. But they all share a common design. Every useful computer contains at least two kinds of physical components, or *hardware*: a *central processing unit*, or *CPU*, that is capable of carrying out various computations, like addition and division, and *memory*, which stores data for use by the CPU.

Think of a memory chip as a large wall of storage lockers, each of which can hold some bits. To store bits in memory, the CPU needs to pick a locker to put them in; to get the bits out again for later use, the CPU needs to remember which locker it used. A very simple memory chip, for example, might have 256 locations, each of which can hold one byte. Each location has an identifying number, like the number on the front of each storage locker. So if we stored the digitized image of a face from above in memory, it would look something like this:

Location	Value
0	11111111
1	11111111
2	10011001
3	10011001
4	11111111
5	10111101
6	10000001
7	11111111

Location	Value
...	

Here, the face is stored in locations 0 to 7 (for technical reasons, it is more convenient for computers and programmers to count starting at zero).

It should be no surprise that these addresses can also be encoded using bits. They're just numbers, after all, and we already know how to encode numbers. So each location in memory has an address encoded in binary, from 0 (00000000) up through 255 (11111111). Here's the same depiction of the memory containing the face, this time with the addresses in memory given in binary, the way the computer itself would refer to them.

Location	Value
00000000	11111111
00000001	11111111
00000010	10011001
00000011	10011001
00000100	11111111
00000101	10111101
00000110	10000001
00000111	11111111
...	...

So to get the first byte of the face out of memory, the CPU asks for the byte stored at location 00000000 (binary for 0). To get the last byte of the face, the computer asks for the byte stored at 00000111 (binary for 7).

Computers have used a stunning variety of technologies to store data. Hard drives magnetize small portions of a spinning disc; USB flash drives store tiny electric charges. Older computers stored data as glowing spots on TV screens, as marks on a paper tape, and even as sound pulses traveling through liquid mercury. Indeed, any technology that can create either of two different physical states and then reliably tell them apart will work as memory. The ways in which data is physically encoded and stored can be remarkably complicated: data might be stored in multiple physical locations within a device (to provide redundancy in case of damage), or moved around to different locations (to speed up repeated access to it), or compressed (to reduce the amount of storage needed), or encrypted (for privacy and security), or all of the above.

There is a difference in common usage between short-term *memory* and longer-term *storage*. The former is faster but loses track of the information it is storing when the power goes off; the latter is slower but capable of storing information for much longer. Many computers that you are familiar with have both: so laptops often have RAM ("random access *memory*") to hold the programs and documents you are working with, and a hard drive for storing them when you close the lid. However, modern storage technologies like the flash memory used in smartphones and USB thumb drives blur this distinction: they are as fast as "memory" but retain information long-term like "storage."

So much for memory. Now for the CPU. The CPU's job is simple. A program consists of a list of instructions – we will see how in a moment – so the CPU takes the first instruction and carries it out, then takes the next instruction and carries it out, then takes the next instruction and carries it out, and so on forever. These instructions tell the CPU what to do with the data. For example, consider addition: an instruction might instruct the CPU to add 3 and 9.

That may not sound particularly useful, because we already know the answer is 12. Rather, a more useful program would be capable of adding different numbers, not just 3 and 9. So instead of directly referring to two numbers, an ADD instruction could refer to two locations in memory – say 204 and 180 – and tell the CPU to add their contents. The CPU would ask the memory to tell it what number is stored in location 204 and what number is stored in location 180, and then add *those* numbers together. To keep track of the result for the next step of the program, the CPU will then usually store the answer back in memory, at yet another location specified by the instruction.

The memory and CPU are the heart of a computer. Almost everything else is a *peripheral*: something attached to the computer so that it can receive data from the outside world or do something useful. A keyboard is a peripheral for typing text in: when you push a key, the keyboard sends a signal to the CPU telling it which key you pressed. A screen is a peripheral for displaying information: the CPU (typically with the aid of a sidekick processor dedicated to graphics) sends a signal to the screen telling it which pixels to turn on and how bright to make them. A fingerprint scanner is an input device that receives one kind of information; a webcam is an input device that receives a different kind. Indeed, from this perspective, even an Internet connection is just another kind of peripheral: it's a device that the computer can send information to and receive information from. The computer doesn't know what lies beyond – only that some bits went out and other bits came in.

Software and Object Code

Just as bits can be used to represent numbers and characters, they can also be used to represent *instructions*: the smallest individual operations that a computer can carry out. On the ARM CPUs used in the iPhone and in billions of other devices, for example, the bits 0100 represent the "ADD" instruction that adds two numbers together, and the bits 0000 represent the "MUL" instruction that multiplies two numbers. Put a sequence of these instructions together and you have a program in *object code* (sometimes called "machine language"), that is, a program written in a format that the computer can recognize and act on.

In other words, a program is also a form of data. After all, each instruction in object code is made up of bits.* Since we know how to store bits in memory, this means we can also store computer programs in memory. Indeed, this is exactly what modern computers do. The CPU doesn't just retrieve from memory the data

---

* So, for that matter, is a program written in source code. The difference is that the bits in source code represent letters and symbols for a program that will have to be compiled into object code, rather than representing instructions the CPU is directly able to carry out.

the program works on. It also retrieves from memory the program itself, one instruction at a time.*

The point that programs are both the instructions that tell a computer what to do and a kind of data that can be stored in a computer was first articulated by the British mathematician Alan Turing in 1936. His insight is responsible for the fact that modern computers are *general-purpose* devices, capable of carrying out all kinds of tasks, including ones their designers never dreamed of. To put the computer to a new use, just write a program, load that program into the computer's memory, and tell the CPU to get to work running it. Instead of needing to build a different computer for each possible use – one for playing *Tetris*, one for writing emails, one for calculating averages, and so on – it suffices to build a single computer.

Put another way, provided the computer's hardware is sufficiently powerful (and Turing showed that even an extraordinarily simple computer is good enough), all of its "smarts" come from the programs, or *software*. By loading a different program, or *application*, into a computer, we can make it play *Tetris*, or write emails, or calculate averages, or anything else we can express precisely enough to put into a computer program. As in the legend of the golem, a computer is an inert lump of matter which is animated by the words we put into it.

Programming Languages and Source Code

If she wanted to, a programmer could write object code by hand, choosing individual bits to describe the operations she wants the computer to carry out. In the early days of computing, this *was* programming. Unsurprisingly, it was difficult, tedious, and error-prone. In response, computer scientists developed *programming languages*, formal artificial languages for writing programs. These languages are much closer to natural human languages, like English and Wolof, in that they are written using familiar alphabets and symbols, rather than ones and zeros, and are designed to be easier for humans to read. But they are like object code in that they are intended to express each idea completely unambiguously, so that each program does exactly one, completely predictable thing.

As an example, consider the process of averaging two numbers. If asked to describe averaging, you might say "Add the numbers together, and then take half of the result." This is an *algorithm*, a step-by-step process for carrying out a calculation. Your informal plain-language description of it makes perfect sense to English speakers, but it's just a bunch of gibberish to a computer. If you turn on a computer and type "Add the numbers together, and then take half of the result," nothing useful will happen.

A computer programmer's job consists of translating informal descriptions like this one into a sufficiently precise series of statements that a computer could execute them. Here's what she might write if she were using the popular Python language:

---

   * If the CPU had an interior monologue, it might go something like this:

       Hey memory, can you look up an instruction for me in location 480? `0100`, got it, thanks! Let me see, `0100` means add, so I need to add two numbers. Hey, memory, can you look up some data for me in locations 204 and 180? 3 and 9, got it, thanks! Let me see, 3 plus 9 equals 12. Hey, memory, can you put the number 12 in location 184? Thanks!

       Hey memory, can you look up an instruction for me in location 484? `0000`, got it, thanks! Let me see, `0000` means multiply ...

```
def average (x y):
   sum = x + y;
   return sum / 2;
```

The first line of this brief program says what it does: defines ("def") a function named average which computes something based on two numbers named x and y. The second line corresponds to the first half of our informal description: it adds ("+") up x and y, then stores the result ("=") in another number named sum. The third line corresponds to the second half of our informal description: it takes half of sum by dividing ("/") it by 2, then announces ("return") that this value is the answer we're looking for. The point of expressing it this way is that each individual step, like + and /, corresponds to something so simple that the computer is already capable of carrying it out. A program assembles these elementary steps, one by one, into a more complicated, and usually more interesting, whole.

Having defined average in terms of simpler steps like + and /, the programmer is now free to treat it as a simpler step when defining other functions, like a homebuilder who puts floorboards down on top of the beams she put in place yesterday. She could write average(2,4) + average(10,20) and the computer would correctly answer 18. Now, average is just one function, while modern operating systems like Windows contain millions of functions, but the basic principle of using functions to build other functions is the same.

There are thousands of programming languages, which are useful for different purposes. The same algorithm may look quite different when written out in different languages. Here is a version of average in the commonly-used C language:

```
int average (int x, int y)
 {
 int sum;
 sum = x + y;
 return sum / 2;
 }
```

The details are slightly different, but this should be recognizable as a close relative of the Python version. On the other hand, here is a version of average written in the less-commonly-used Scheme language:

```
(define average
 (lambda (x y)
       ( / (+ x y) 2)))
```

This version may look extraordinarily different from the previous two, but does the same thing: averages two numbers. Some programmers – although probably a distinct minority – would even consider the Scheme version simpler and more elegant than the Python and C versions.

A program written in a human-readable programming language like Python is called *source code* to distinguish it from the object code that a computer runs. But this raises a complication. Source code is closer to being suitable for a computer to carry out than an English description of a program would be, because source code is formal and precise. But there is still a difference. "def average (x y)" is an arbitrary string of characters as far as the computer is concerned, just like "Add the numbers together." The computer is looking for 0100, not "def" or "add".

Thus, when a programmer writes source code in a human-intelligible programming language like Python, C, or Scheme, she must then transform this source code into something that the computer can act on. The most common way to do this is for her to write a special-purpose program, called a *compiler*, that reads source code and translates it into object code. This translation is possible because programming languages are precise enough that the meaning of a program is fully specified.[*]

Operating Systems

In theory, one could write a program that takes complete control of a computer and tells it everything to do. This is how old-school 8-bit Nintendo cartridges work: each game contains a complete program that is responsible for every pixel on the screen. But this is incredibly cumbersome for more complicated programs. If you want to write a program to keep track of your knitting patterns, for example, the last thing you want to do is write software to recognize individual keypresses or for drawing the title bar at the top of the window. And if each program stands completely alone, the only way to switch from one to another is to turn the computer off and on again – not exactly convenient when you want to look up a citation in one window and then type it into a brief in another.

Thus, modern computers run an *operating system*: a program that takes care of the administrative details so that the *applications* – programs to carry out useful tasks the user cares about – can focus on their particular jobs. Popular operating systems include Apple OS X, Microsoft Windows, and Linux. Cell phones are computers, too: their operating systems include Apple iOS and Google's Android. An operating system starts running when the computer turns on and never stops. Even when an application is running, the operating system is waiting in the wings, ready to step in if the application needs help or tries to misbehave. Typically, an operating system offers its services to applications through a set of *application programming interfaces* (or "APIs"): functions that an application can call on if it wants to carry out some specific task, such as creating a window, playing a sound, or drawing a line to the screen.

Operating systems are so ubiquitous that it's easy to overlook just how many problems they solve. A typical operating system does all of the following:

- *Hardware independence*: Computers come in all kinds of configurations and work with all kinds of hardware: they have different hard drives, CPUs, screens, graphics cards, game controllers, cameras, and network connectors, to name just a few. The operating system frees applications from having to worry about the precise details of the hardware, making it possible to write an application that will run on hundreds of different devices.

- *Powerful features*: If you are writing a quiz game for the iPhone and would like to add a phone-a-friend feature, you don't need to write from scratch the software to make a phone call. Instead, you can just send an `openURL` message with the telephone number to dial to a `UIApplication` object. What might have taken tens of thousands of lines of source code if you had to write them yourself can be done in two, thanks to the APIs that iOS makes available to applications.

- *Consistent look and feel*: Microsoft Windows looks different than Apple OS X does. That's because the Windows APIs draw windows and menus in a different way than the OS X APIs do. Every program on Windows will be

---

[*] For a brainteaser, ask yourself how it's possible to write a compiler. Isn't the source code for the compiler useless unless the compiler already works?

displayed in a similar way just because it runs on Windows and uses the Windows APIs. This consistency helps users orient themselves.

- *Multitasking*: Once you have an operating system to play traffic cop, you can run multiple programs at the same time. The point of a "windows" metaphor, or a list of "open apps," is that each program is running, independently, and the user can switch between them at will. When a new message arrives, the operating system routes it to your chat program, not your word processor.

- *Multiple users*: An even more sophisticated version of multitasking involves letting more than one person use the same computer. Your personal computer rarely does this, but you interact regularly with computers that do. A web server, for example, is typically designed to interact with many different users simultaneously: Gmail wouldn't work well if only one person could use it at a time.

- *Security*: Because computers contain all kinds of sensitive and valuable data, from love emails to tax returns, it's important to keep them secure. The operating system typically plays a significant role in keeping data private and in protecting data from accidental or deliberate destruction. When you connect your computer to the WiFi network in a coffee shop, the operating system prevents other people from installing their own software on your computer or from snooping through your hard drive.

Jonathan Zittrain, whose book *The Future of the Internet* is excerpted below, has compared this typical computer design to an "hourglass." The operating system sits at the narrow neck. Above it is a wild profusion of applications doing all kinds of jobs. Beneath it is a wild profusion of hardware with all kinds of technical details. The operating system provides a standard layer that ensures a common experience for all those applications on all that different hardware.

TECHNICAL PRIMER: THE INTERNET

You may have heard of the metaphor of the Internet as a "cloud": big and opaque. In this section, we will systematically look inside the cloud to see how things work. What we will find may be less complex than you may have feared.

Networks and Protocols

Computer networks come in all shapes and sizes. There are networks between computers in the same room; there is a network that connects the International Space Station to earth. There are computer networks for cell phones, networks for playing video from your computer on your TV, even networks that connect a wireless mouse to your computer.

The key to every single one of these networks is the idea of a *protocol*: a specification that describes how computers should use the network to communicate. You can think of a computer protocol as being like a diplomatic protocol: when two delegations meet, there is a precise order of formal greetings, handshakes, and statements. It may look bafflingly formal to an outsider, but the diplomats use it to communicate important information to each other about their countries' respective concerns.

Similarly, when two computers communicate, the protocol specifies every aspect of the technical process. A simple communications protocol along a wire might say, for example, that a message of binary 1s and 0s should be encoded as a series of electrical pulses of 500 nanoseconds each, with a 1 being a pulse at 1.5

volts and a 0 being a pulse at 0 volts. The sending computer turns the 1s and 0s into an electrical signal on the cable; the receiving computer looks at the voltage on the cable and turns it back into the 1s and 0s.

The enormous diversity of computer networks is possible because for each physical medium, there are different protocols designed to take advantage of that medium's characteristics. The idea is similar to the way that different kinds of roads have different traffic rules. You can drive faster on a highway than in a parking lot; you can drive different kinds of vehicles on a city street than on a bicycle path; you drive on the right side of the road in some countries and the left side in others.

It is common to call a physical medium connecting two computers together with an appropriate protocol a *network link*. Here are some common (and less common) network links:

- Ethernet is a widely used protocol for local-area networking (e.g., within a building, rather than cross-country). Its physical medium is most often "category 5 cable," a set of plastic-wrapped wires with a phone-like plug at each end. The Ethernet protocol specifies how computers connected by an Ethernet cable should "talk" by turning the information they want to send to each other into electrical pulses, how quickly they can talk, and what to do if two of them start talking at the same time.

- Many computers use WiFi for their local-area networks. Here, the physical medium is electromagnetic radiation, i.e. photons zipping through the air at the speed of light. Each computer using WiFi has a small radio transmitter/receiver. The WiFi protocol tells the radio transmitter on what frequencies to broadcast and listen, how loudly and for how long to transmit, and what to do if someone else starts transmitting at the same time.*

- Your cell phone also contains a radio, as do cell phone towers. Again, the physical medium is electromagnetic radiation. Instead of using WiFi frequencies and transmission rules, however, the phones and towers use protocols with names like EDGE, EVDO, and UMTS to specify how they should transmit information to each other.

- Internet signals can be carried over traditional copper or modern fiber-optic phone cables; the DSL and GPON standards, respectively, provide protocols for doing so. Cable companies use DOCSIS to do the same over cable connections. If you remember dialup, it used the PPP protocol to provide Internet access by having your computer make a phone call to a local phone number, and encoded the data transmissions as audio (which is why picking up another extension and making noise would generally destroy the connection).

- Fiber-optic "backbones" provide long-distance connections on land and via undersea cable. They are engineered for super-high transmission speeds, using highly specialized protocols .

- Computer data can even be transmitted via carrier pigeon. Here, the pigeon is the physical layer, and the protocol specifies that data should be transmit-

---

* A standard wireless router has both a WiFi-compatible radio and an Ethernet-compatible jack. It translates messages that come in along the Ethernet link into WiFi radio signals, and vice-versa.

ted by writing digits on a piece of paper wrapped around the pigeon's leg and secured with duct tape.*

Inter-Networking and the Internet Protocol

The next complication is that not every computer is on the same small local network. Your computer has a direct network connection to only one or a few others. The overwhelming majority of computers in the world do not have direct connections to each other, and it would obviously be impossible to try. How do we use the diverse networks we have in order to build up something like the Internet, where it is possible for computers around the world to communicate? This is the problem of inter-networking, and the answer lies in something called the Internet Protocol, or IP.

The first key idea of IP is *routing*. Suppose that you want to download an MP3 from Amazon's MP3 store. There isn't a wire that directly connects your computer to Amazon's computer. Instead, the information making up the MP3 is passed along from one computer to another – computers that are directly connected (by a wire or other network link) – until it reaches you. In essence, Amazon's computer hands off the MP3 to a computer that is connected to it and is slightly closer to you. That second computer hands off the MP3 to a third, which hands it off to a fourth, and so on until it is handed off to a computer that is directly connected to yours, which hands it off to you. Computers that participate in the process are generally called *routers*.

Each handoff is, in essence, a computer-to-computer copy. The computer making the handoff transmits a complete copy of the data in the file to the next one. As soon as the receiving computer acknowledges that it has received all the data, the sending computer knows that it can delete its own copy. Transmitting information through the Internet thus requires making as many transient intermediate copies as there are computers in the chain from the original sender to the final recipient.

Along the way, the data will travel over many different kinds of network links. It might start out on Ethernet inside Amazon's data center, then be transmitted along backbone links until it reaches your local area, then travel on a fiber-optic cable supplied by your phone company, and finally reach your computer via WiFi inside your home. All of these network links have one thing in common: they can be used to carry IP messages.

This is a truly profound idea. Network engineers would say that IP is *layered* on top of these various network links. The goal of any of the lower-level link protocols listed above is to create a network that is capable of carrying IP messages. Once that is accomplished, the IP message can be carried from computer to computer across multiple different networks: Ethernet, backbone, WiFi, etc. The message itself does not change in any significant way, even though the different link protocols will encode it in radically different ways on different networks.

This is why IP is called the *Inter*-net Protocol. It is designed to enable *inter*-networking: the tying together of different networks. IP plays the crucial role of giving these diverse networks a single common technical language. Indeed, this is where the *Inter*-net gets its name: it was an experiment in inter-networking that was so wildly successful that it became "the" Internet rather than just "an" Internet.

---

* No kidding. *See* D. Waitzman, *A Standard for the Transmission of IP Datagrams on Avian Carriers* (1990) (RFC 1149), http://tools.ietf.org/html/rfc1149.

Routing and Addressing

But how do the computers along the chain know where to send the data? They may only be connected to a few other computers, but the data could potentially be going to any of the billions of computers on the Internet. How do they decide which of their neighbors to pass the data along to?

The answer is that each computer on the Internet has a unique *address*, called an "IP address" (named after IP, of course). An IP address is a 32-digit binary number; by convention, they are written as four decimal numbers separated by periods. For example, here are the IP addresses of a few well-known computers:

apple.com	17.172.224.47
google.com	172.217.6.206
nytimes.com	151.101.193.164
mit.edu	104.79.147.28

Every message is carried in the electronic equivalent of an envelope with the IP address of its destination stamped on the outside. When a router receives a message, it examines the IP address on the message. If that IP address is the router's own address, then the message has reached its destination and the process is done. Otherwise, the router examines a large database called a "routing table," which tells the router what the next intermediate destination should be for any possible ultimate destination. For example, a router's routing table might say that all messages for google.com and apple.com (which are on the West Coast) should be given next to its neighbor A, but that messages for nytimes.com and mit.edu (which are on the East Coast) should be given to its neighbor B.

Each router has its own routing table. The process of constructing them is one of the most complicated and intricate aspects of keeping the Internet functioning. At a high level of generality, what happens is that individual routers tell each other what computers they know how to get messages to. The information gradually propagates throughout the Internet, until – in theory – every computer knows how to reach every other computer.

Packet-Switching

The next complication is that most messages are too big to send all at once in this fashion. Instead, they are broken down into smaller *packets* (sometimes also called "datagrams"). Each packet is sent separately, like a jigsaw puzzle that is broken down into individual pieces, each of which is sent in a separate envelope to the same destination. Along the way, they may travel by different routes, depending on factors like temporary congestion in some parts of the Internet, or routers coming on- or off-line and thus becoming available or unavailable to pass packets along.

Packet switching may seem counterintuitive, but it has some notable advantages. One is that it is much more efficient than the alternative of "circuit-switching," i.e., holding a dedicated connection all the way from sender to recipient open for the entire duration of the transmission. Circuit-switching commits to a single chain of computers from source to destination, but packet-switching allows the transmission to respond to moment-to-moment changes in the Internet, taking advantage of faster routes and avoiding sudden traffic jams. Packet-switching also avoids tying up the intermediate computers when there is no data flowing; think of a streaming concert video, where the flow of information will last for hours, but is much less than the full capacity of any of the routers along the way. In addition, as we will see shortly, packet-switching can be very resilient to errors.

These three big ideas – routing, addressing, and packet-switching – collectively characterize the Internet Protocol. As its name suggests, IP is central to how the Internet works. Indeed, "the global network in which computers communicate using IP" comes very close to being *the* technical definition of the Internet. We will see throughout the this book how these technical features have important consequences for the law.

Reliable Transport

IP is not the only protocol that matters on the Internet. Instead, network engineers commonly speak of a *protocol stack* of multiple protocols in use at one time. The "stack" metaphor captures the idea that these protocols are *layered*: ones at higher levels take advantage of the services offered by the ones at lower levels to do their jobs. Here is a simplified view of the protocol stack used by a typical home computer:

- Application (e.g. email, web, etc.)
- Transport (TCP)
- Network (IP)
- Link (Ethernet)
- Physical (category 5 cable)

We started off by discussing the physical and link layers. Then we saw how the network layer – IP – ties different networks together into a single Internet with world-wide addressing and routing. Now it is time to move up again.

The next layer above IP in the protocol stack is the transport layer, and the most common protocol there is TCP, the "Transmission Control Protocol."* It has several jobs, but the most significant is "reliable transport": that is, making sure that every piece of a message reaches the destination. IP is a so-called "best efforts" protocol; routers will do their best to make sure that packets get where they should, but they make no promises. Bad stuff regularly happens that causes packets to be lost. Sometimes a router is congested, with too much incoming traffic, and it needs to start "dropping" packets in order to cope, like an overworked mail carrier tossing some envelopes in the river. At other times, transient conditions, like electrical interference or a bug in a router's software, can cause a packet to be scrambled so badly that the data in it is unrecoverable.

TCP deals with all of these problems through good bookkeeping. The sender and the receiver each maintain a list of the individual packets making up a transmission. As the receiver receives each packet, it checks off that packet on its list and informs the sender that it has. If the receiver realizes that it is missing a packet – for example, because it is receiving more recent packets without having received an older one – it asks the sender to retransmit the missing packet. Meanwhile, the sender is keeping track of which packets the receiver has acknowledged.

---

* TCP is not the only transport protocol. Not every application needs to ensure that every single packet is delivered. A live voice chat, for example, is better off letting the audio cut out for a fraction of a second than waiting for seconds for every last bit to arrive. Multiplayer video games often prefer to minimize transmission delay so that players can respond more quickly to each other. These and other applications often use their own, specialized transport protocols. They have in common with TCP and with each other that they all depend on IP: each of them uses IP to transmit its packets, they just do different things with the results.

If too long a time passes without an acknowledgment from the receiver, the sender assumes that something has gone wrong and initiates retransmission on its own.

This is why packet-switching can be surprisingly more error-resistant than sending an entire message at once. It is true that, as with a jigsaw puzzle split among ten thousand envelopes, there are more ways for something to go wrong. But if a few packets go missing, TCP sees to it that just the missing ones are re-transmitted, rather than needing to start the entire message from scratch. To continue the analogy, if a few puzzle pieces are missing, it's easier to resend just the missing ones than to mail the entire puzzle again. Similarly, because the packets are smaller, they are less likely to suffer an error than a larger message would be. A single jigsaw piece can be mailed in an ordinary envelope; the entire assembled puzzle will require a special oversize padded mailer.

TCP is also responsible for "flow control": the process of determining how fast the sender slings packets through the Internet toward the receiver. If you have a good fiber-optic connection, you would obviously prefer to send packets faster than if you are connecting through a slow satellite connection. Put another way, TCP automatically adapts on the fly to the amount of available bandwidth between sender and receiver. (The actual algorithms it uses to do so all involve clever communication between sender and receiver, and have been tuned over the years to values that seem to work well.)

Here, we can see another advantage of layering. TCP can completely ignore the details of the underlying network. It doesn't need to know whether its running on a WiFi network or on Ethernet or whatever. It can delegate all of those details – along with the details of routing – to lower-layer protocols. TCP is only responsible for reliable transport and flow control, so it can focus on doing its job well. Unsurprisingly, this helps make TCP simpler than if it also had to do all of these other jobs. Computer programmers would say that layering is a kind of "modularity": separating out different functions into smaller pieces makes them easier to get right.

Applications

At last we arrive at the part of the Internet you are probably most familiar with: applications. These are the programs that actually do things, like email, web browsing, and instant messaging. They use TCP/IP* and other lower-level protocols to move data back and forth, and then do interesting things with it.

The first important detail here – one you are likely already familiar with – is the idea of *clients* and *servers*. A server is a computer that has a particular resource or that does a particular job. For example, the computer that stores your law school's webpage is a server, unsurprisingly called a "web server." Other common servers you probably use on a regular basis include email servers like Yahoo! Mail and your school's email, e-commerce servers like the iTunes Music Store, and chat servers that tell you whether your friends are online.

A client is a computer that connects to a server to get information or have the server do something for it. If you look at your law school's webpage, your computer is the client. It sends a message over the Internet to the web server, asking for the webpage; the server responds with a message that contains all the information making up the webpage. The process is similar with other servers. By convention, information that goes from a client to a server is *uploaded*; information that goes

---

* The two were designed simultaneously and are so frequently used together that they often go by this combined acronym.

the other way, from server to client, is *downloaded*. When there is no clear distinction between which computer is the server and which is the client – and particularly when there are numerous computers acting both like clients and like servers – the relationship is said to be *peer-to-peer*.

Applications often have their own protocols, layered on top of TCP/IP and the other lower-level protocols. When one computer sends an email to another, it uses a protocol named SMTP to tell the receiving computer whom the message is from, whom it is for, what its subject is, and what its contents are. BitTorrent is a publicly published protocol for exchanging complete files. Skype uses a secret protocol to exchange voice messages. Games use their own protocols to update players' computers on what everyone else is doing.

Like a computer, the Internet also has an hourglass architecture. This time, IP provides the narrow neck in the middle. Above it are millions of different applications. Beneath it are all kinds of different physical networks. Like an operating system, IP provides a standard middle layer that ties the different physical networks together into a common network capable of supporting any number of applications, even ones that no one has thought of yet.

The Web

Perhaps the single most important application on the Internet today is the World Wide Web or "web." The web actually consists of two closely related standards. The first is a protocol, the Hypertext Transfer Protocol (or "HTTP"), for sending webpages from servers to clients. The second is a format, the Hypertext Markup Language (or "HTML") for encoding a rich experience with images, hyperlinks, and interactivity using nothing but raw text.

Let us start by considering the process of obtaining a webpage from a server. Your web browser (e.g. Internet Explorer, Firefox, Chrome, or Safari) is a program designed to request web pages from servers and display the results. Suppose, for example, that you want to read the latest technology headlines from the New York Times, so you type "nytimes.com" into the the address bar of your browser. It uses TCP to send a message to the New York Times server at nytimes.com. In response, the New York Times server will send back a message containing the webpage itself. The rules of the road for this process – e.g., how the client describes the web page it wants, and how the server explains whether that web page is available or not – are governed by HTTP. If you have ever seen a webpage that displays the message "Error 404 not found," then you have seen HTTP at work. 404 is the error code used by HTTP to signal that the webpage the client asked for does not exist.

What you have obtained from the server is not yet a webpage, only a long text file. You can examine the details by going to any webpage and selecting the "View Source" command in your browser.* What you will see is a set of instructions for displaying the webpage you are looking at. This is the actual, literal data that was sent from the server to your computer; your web browser is then able to transform the data it into the webpage you see. (When people talk about "the source" of a webpage or "the HTML" for the page, this is what they are referring to.)

Try this, for example, at your favorite news site or blog. Pick a headline, and then try to find it in the page's source. You should be able to pick it out, along with a lot of things between angle brackets, i.e. "<" and ">" called *tags*. These tags are

---

* In most browsers, this is available under the "View" menu.

the instructions, which your browser turns into visible formatting in the webpage it displays to you.* Here is some simple HTML:

```
<li>I agree. We <b>have</b> been here before, as the <a
href="http://nytimes.com"> New York Times</a>
recognizes.</li>
```

When displayed by your browser, this text will look more like this:

I agree. We **have** been here before, as the <u>New York Times</u> recognizes.

What's different between the source and the displayed version? First, the `<li>` tag, which stands for "list item," tells your browser that what follows should be formatted as a bulleted item in a list. The matching `</li>` tag (which has a slash before the `li`) marks the end of the item. Second, the `<b>` tag tells your browser to format the following text as bold, up until the matching `</b>` tag marks the end of the boldface segment. And third, the `<a>` tag, or "anchor," specifies that the following text is a hyperlink. If you click on it, your browser loads the web page it points at, in this case the New York Times's homepage. How did your browser know which new webpage to load? It uses the location specified inside the `<a>` tag, following the "`href`"† – in this case, "`http://nytimes.com`".

One last HTML tag is worth explaining: `<img>`. Here is an example:

```
Yes, I've seen it, but I have no idea where they got the
name from: <img src="http://james.grimmelmann.net/images/
grimmelman-mosaic.jpg"/>
```

This will turn into the following in a browser:

Yes, I've seen it, but I have no idea where they got the name from:

Here, the `<img>` tag tells the browser that it should display a particular image in that position. The image isn't sent as part of the webpage itself. Instead, your

* Not every tag has visible consequences. In Chapter 6, you will encounter "meta tags," which carry information about the page (intended to be used by search engines), and which are not ordinarily shown to normal web users. You can inspect them, however, by using the View Source command.

† "href" is a less obvious abbreviation than some of the others; it is short for "hypertext reference."

browser, when it sees an `<img>` tag, sends an additional request to the server with the image. (Here, that server is `james.grimmelmann.net`, and note that the server where the image comes from need not be the same server as the one where the webpage came from.) The browser then drops the image into the place on the page where the `<img>` tag was. You can think of the tag as being a kind of placeholder for the image, one that includes instructions for how to fill in the place with a specific image.

The Domain-Name System

Another application is especially important to the functioning of the Internet. The domain-name system converts human-readable names (like google.com and icanhascheezburger.com) into the IP addresses used by computers.

When you look up a domain name – say, espn.go.com – what really happens? The process works hierarchically, from right to to left. Any URL, such as http://espn.go.com/nba/, can be broken down into three parts. The http:// at the start is a protocol identifier, which indicates that this is a request for a web page. The go.espn.com in the middle – everything up through the next slash – is the domain name that identifies the server from which you're requesting the web page. And the "nba/" part (everything following the slash) identifies to the server which particular web page you are asking for.

The general rule is that if your computer (e.g., your web browser, when you type a URL into the address bar) asks a domain-name server to look up a domain name, it will tell you the IP address of the computer with that domain name if the server knows. If the domain-name server doesn't know about that particular domain name, the server will give you the IP address of another domain-name server that can help you. That is, it will either help you or respond with the technical equivalent of "I don't know, but here's someone who might." Here's a simplified example:

(1) You start by asking the "root name server" what it knows about espn.go.com. The root name server "understands" the last part of the address, here go.espn.com. It tells you that another computer – the so-called "top-level domain (TLD) name server" for all .com sites worldwide – can help, and gives you the IP address for the TLD name server.

(2) You ask the TLD name server for .com what it knows about espn.go.com. This server "understands" the second part of the address, here espn.go.com. It tells you that another computer – the name server for go.com – can help, and gives you the IP address of this other name server.

(3) You ask the name server for go.com what it knows about espn.go.com. This server "understands" the third part of the address, here espn.go.com. It gives you the IP address for espn.go.com directly. Armed with the IP address, your computer can now directly contact espn.go.com.

This process could in theory be iterated repeatedly, although in practice it rarely continues for more than a few steps.

COLUMBIA PICTURES INDUS. V. FUNG
710 F.3d 1020 (9th Cir. 2013)

Berzon, Circuit Judge: ...

I. CLIENT-SERVER VS. PEER-TO-PEER NETWORKS

The traditional method of sharing content over a network is the relatively straightforward client-server model. In a client-server network, one or more central computers (called "servers") store the information; upon request from a user (or "client"), the server sends the requested information to the client. In other words, the server supplies information resources to clients, but the clients do not share any of their resources with the server. Client-server networks tend to be relatively secure, but they have a few drawbacks: if the server goes down, the entire network fails; and if many clients make requests at the same time, the server can become overwhelmed, increasing the time it takes the server to fulfill requests from clients. Client-server systems, moreover, tend to be more expensive to set up and operate than other systems. Websites work on a client-server model, with the server storing the website's content and delivering it to users upon demand.

"Peer-to-peer" (P2P) networking is a generic term used to refer to several different types of technology that have one thing in common: a decentralized infrastructure whereby each participant in the network (typically called a "peer," but sometimes called a "node") acts as both a supplier and consumer of information resources. Although less secure, P2P networks are generally more reliable than client-server networks and do not suffer from the same bottleneck problems. These strengths make P2P networks ideally suited for sharing large files, a feature that has led to their adoption by, among others, those wanting access to pirated media, including music, movies, and television shows. But there also are a great number of non-infringing uses for peer-to-peer networks; copyright infringement is in no sense intrinsic to the technology, any more than making unauthorized copies of television shows was to the video tape recorder.

II. ARCHITECTURE OF P2P NETWORKS

In a client-server network, clients can easily learn what files the server has available for download, because the files are all in one central place. In a P2P network, in contrast, there is no centralized file repository, so figuring out what information other peers have available is more challenging. The various P2P protocols permit indexing in different ways.

A. "Pure" P2P networks

In "pure" P2P networks, a user wanting to find out which peers have particular content available for download will send out a search query to several of his neighbor peers. As those neighbor peers receive the query, they send a response back to the requesting user reporting whether they have any content matching the search terms, and then pass the query on to some of their neighbors, who repeat the same two steps; this process is known as "flooding." ... Once the querying user has the search results, he can go directly to a peer that has the content desired to download it.

This search method is an inefficient one for finding content (especially rare content that only a few peers have), and it causes a lot of signaling traffic on the network. The most popular pure P2P protocol was Gnutella. StreamCast ... used Gnutella to power its software application, Morpheus.

B. "Centralized" P2P networks

"Centralized" P2P networks, by contrast, use a centralized server to index the content available on all the peers: the user sends the query to the indexing server, which tells the user which peers have the content available for download. At the same time the user tells the indexing server what files he has available for others to download. Once the user makes contact with the indexing server, he knows which specific peers to contact for the content sought, which reduces search time and signaling traffic as compared to a "pure" P2P protocol.

Although a centralized P2P network has similarities with a client-server network, the key difference is that the indexing server does not store or transfer the content. It just tells users which other peers have the content they seek. In other words, searching is centralized, but file transfers are peer-to-peer. One consequent disadvantage of a centralized P2P network is that it has a single point of potential failure: the indexing server. If it fails, the entire system fails. Napster was a centralized P2P network, as, in part, is eDonkey ... .

C. Hybrid P2P networks

Finally, there are a number of hybrid protocols. The most common type of hybrid systems use what are called "supernodes." In these systems, each peer is called a "node," and each node is assigned to one "supernode." A supernode is a regular node that has been "promoted," usually because it has more bandwidth available, to perform certain tasks. Each supernode indexes the content available on each of the nodes attached to it, called its "descendants." When a node sends out a search query, it goes just to the supernode to which it is attached. The supernode responds to the query by telling the node which of its descendant nodes has the desired content. The supernode may also forward the query on to other supernodes, which may or may not forward the query on further, depending on the protocol.

The use of supernodes is meant to broaden the search pool as much as possible while limiting redundancy in the search. As with centralized P2P systems, supernodes only handle search queries, telling the nodes the addresses of the other nodes that have the content sought; they are not ordinarily involved in the actual file transfers themselves. Grokster's software application was based on a P2P protocol, FastTrack, that uses supernodes.

III. BitTorrent protocol

The BitTorrent protocol, first released in 2001, is a further variant on the P2P theme. BitTorrent is a hybrid protocol with some key differences from "supernode" systems. We discuss those differences after first describing BitTorrent's distinguishing feature: how it facilitates file transfers.

A. BitTorrent file transfers.

Traditionally, if a user wanted to download a file on a P2P network, he would locate another peer with the desired file and download the entire file from that peer. Alternatively, if the download was interrupted – if, for example, the peer sending the file signed off – the user would find another peer that had the file and resume the download from that peer. The reliability and duration of the download depended on the strength of the connection between those two peers. Additionally, the number of peers sharing a particular file was limited by the fact that a user could only begin sharing his copy of the file with other peers once he had completed the download.

With the BitTorrent protocol, however, the file is broken up into lots of smaller "pieces," each of which is usually around 256 kilobytes (one-fourth of one megabyte) in size. Whereas under the older protocols the user would download the entire file in one large chunk from a single peer at a time, BitTorrent permits users to download lots of different pieces at the same time from different peers. Once a user has downloaded all the pieces, the file is automatically reassembled into its original form.

BitTorrent has several advantages over the traditional downloading method. Because a user can download different pieces of the file from many different peers at the same time, downloading is much faster. Additionally, even before the entire download is complete, a user can begin sharing the pieces he has already downloaded with other peers, making the process faster for others. Generally, at any given time, each user is both downloading and uploading several different pieces of a file from and to multiple other users; the collection of peers swapping pieces with each other is known as a "swarm."

B. BitTorrent architecture

To describe the structure of BitTorrent further, an example is helpful. Let us suppose that an individual (the "publisher") decides to share via BitTorrent her copy of a particular movie. The movie file, we shall assume, is quite large, and is already on the publisher's computer; the publisher has also already downloaded and installed a BitTorrent "client" program on her computer.[4]

To share her copy of the movie file, the publisher first creates a very small file called a "torrent" or "dot-torrent" file, which has the file extension ".torrent." The torrent file is quite small, as it contains none of the actual content that may be copyrighted but, instead, a minimal amount of vital information: the size of the (separate) movie file being shared; the number of "pieces" the movie file is broken into; a cryptographic "hash" that peers will use to authenticate the downloaded file as a true and complete copy of the original; and the address of one or more "trackers." Trackers, discussed more below, serve many of the functions of an indexing server; there are many different trackers, and they typically are not connected or related to each other.

Second, the publisher makes the torrent file available by uploading it to one or more websites ("torrent sites") that collect, organize, index, and host torrent files. Whereas Napster and Grokster had search functionality built into their client programs, the standard BitTorrent client program has no such capability. BitTorrent users thus rely on torrent sites to find and share torrent files. There is no central repository of torrent files, but torrent sites strive to have the most comprehensive torrent collection possible. ...

Lastly, the publisher leaves her computer on and connected to the Internet, with her BitTorrent program running. The publisher's job is essentially done; her computer will continue to communicate with the tracker assigned to the torrent file she uploaded, standing ready to distribute the movie file (or, more accurately, parts thereof) to others upon request.

A user seeking the uploaded movie now goes to the torrent site to which the torrent file was uploaded and runs a search for the movie. The search results then provide the torrent file for the user to download. Once the user downloads the torrent file and opens it with his BitTorrent program, the program reads the torrent

---

4 The client program is the software application used to access the P2P network. Unlike Grokster or Napster, which were "closed" systems that permitted only authorized client programs to connect to their networks, BitTorrent is an "open" system, permitting the use of any number of client programs, nearly all of which are free.

file, learns the address of the tracker, and contacts it. The program then informs the tracker that it is looking for the movie associated with the downloaded torrent file and asks if there are any peers online that have the movie available for download. Assuming that publishers of that movie are online, the tracker will communicate their address to the user's BitTorrent program. The user's BitTorrent program will then contact the publishers' computers directly and begin downloading the pieces of the movie. At this point, the various publishers are known as "seeders," and the downloading user a "leecher." Once the leecher has downloaded one or more pieces of the movie, he, too, can be a seeder by sending other leechers the pieces that he has downloaded.

A final few words on trackers. Although no content is stored on or passes through trackers, they serve as a central hub of sorts, managing traffic for their associated torrents. The tracker's primary purpose is to provide a list of peers that have files available for download. ...

Because trackers are periodically unavailable – they can go offline for routine maintenance, reach capacity, be shuttered by law enforcement, and so on – torrent files will often list addresses for more than one tracker. That way, if the first (or "primary") tracker is down, the user's client program can proceed to contact the backup tracker(s).

INTERNET APPLICATIONS PROBLEM

Familiarize yourself with the following:

- Jason Kottke's blog
- Gmail
- Amazon.com
- Skype
- Twitter
- Facebook
- Google
- YouTube
- World of Warcraft
- Snapchat
- Target Cartwheel
- Pokémon GO

You don't need to sign up for accounts or to use these applications, but you should be at least passingly familiar with them. They provide a useful range of examples. Do your best to answer the following questions for each of these applications:

1. What can you do using this application?
2. Do you need to install special software to run this application, or can you use it from your web browser? If you need special software, what kinds of devices is the software available for?
3. Does the application require that you and other users both be online at the same time? If so, how does the application figure out that you're both available?
4. How does the message get from your computer to someone else's (or vice-versa)? Is it stored anywhere along the way? Who could listen in or read it if they wanted?

5. How – in a very general sense – is the content encoded? Is it human-legible? Does its quality suffer in transit?

6. Are there servers somewhere that assist in making the application available? If so, do they store the content, or do they merely assist in making connections? Could you make connections without the assistance of a server? Who's in charge of keeping those servers running, providing them with electricity, and so on?

7. Do you need an account to post content? To receive it? How much information about yourself do you need to give up in order to participate?

8. Who's allowed to post content, and of what sort? Is this an egalitarian medium, or one in which only a few people speak and the vast majority only listen?

9. What happens "under the hood?" Is there a flow of information that you can describe in general terms, or does something so mysterious happen that it might as well be magic?

B. Theory

LAWRENCE LESSIG
CODE 2.0
121–26 (Basic Books 2006)

There are many ways to think about "regulation." I want to think about it from the perspective of someone who is regulated, or, what is different, constrained. That someone regulated is represented by this (pathetic) dot – a creature (you or me) subject to different regulations that might have the effect of constraining (or as we'll see, enabling) the dot's behavior. By describing the various constraints that might bear on this individual, I hope to show you something about how these constraints function together.

Here then is the dot.

How is this dot "regulated"?

Let's start with something easy: smoking. If you want to smoke, what constraints do you face? What factors regulate your decision to smoke or not?

One constraint is legal. In some places at least, laws regulate smoking – if you are under eighteen, the law says that cigarettes cannot be sold to you. If you are under twenty-six, cigarettes cannot be sold to you unless the seller checks your ID. Laws also regulate where smoking is permitted – not in O'Hare Airport, on an airplane, or in an elevator, for instance. In these two ways at least, laws aim to direct smoking behavior. They operate as a kind of constraint on an individual who wants to smoke.

But laws are not the most significant constraints on smoking. Smokers in the United States certainly feel their freedom regulated, even if only rarely by the law.

There are no smoking police, and smoking courts are still quite rare. Rather, smokers in America are regulated by norms. Norms say that one doesn't light a cigarette in a private car without first asking permission of the other passengers. They also say, however, that one needn't ask permission to smoke at a picnic. Norms say that others can ask you to stop smoking at a restaurant, or that you never smoke during a meal. These norms effect a certain constraint, and this constraint regulates smoking behavior.

Laws and norms are still not the only forces regulating smoking behavior. The market is also a constraint. The price of cigarettes is a constraint on your ability to smoke – change the price, and you change this constraint. Likewise with quality. If the market supplies a variety of cigarettes of widely varying quality and price, your ability to select the kind of cigarette you want increases; increasing choice here reduces constraint.

Finally, there are the constraints created by the technology of cigarettes, or by the technologies affecting their supply. Nicotine-treated cigarettes are addictive and therefore create a greater constraint on smoking than untreated cigarettes. Smokeless cigarettes present less of a constraint because they can be smoked in more places. Cigarettes with a strong odor present more of a constraint because they can be smoked in fewer places. How the cigarette is, how it is designed, how it is built – in a word, its architecture – affects the constraints faced by a smoker.

Thus, four constraints regulate this pathetic dot – the law, social norms, the market, and architecture – and the "regulation" of this dot is the sum of these four constraints. Changes in any one will affect the regulation of the whole. Some constraints will support others; some may undermine others. Thus, changes in technology may usher in changes in norms, and the other way around. A complete view, therefore, must consider these four modalities together.

So think of the four together like this:

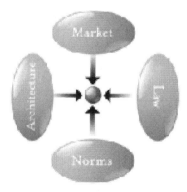

In this drawing, each oval represents one kind of constraint operating on our pathetic dot in the center. Each constraint imposes a different kind of cost on the dot for engaging in the relevant behavior – in this case, smoking. The cost from norms is different from the market cost, which is different from the cost from law and the cost from the (cancerous) architecture of cigarettes.

The constraints are distinct, yet they are plainly interdependent. Each can support or oppose the others. Technologies can undermine norms and laws; they can also support them. Some constraints make others possible; others make some impossible. Constraints work together, though they function differently and the effect of each is distinct. Norms constrain through the stigma that a community imposes; markets constrain through the price that they exact; architectures constrain through the physical burdens they impose; and law constrains through the punishment it threatens.

We can call each constraint a "regulator," and we can think of each as a distinct modality of regulation. Each modality has a complex nature, and the interaction among these four is also hard to describe. [F]or now, it is enough to see that they are linked and that, in a sense, they combine to produce the regulation to which our pathetic dot is subject in any given area.

We can use the same model to describe the regulation of behavior in cyberspace.

Law regulates behavior in cyberspace. Copyright law, defamation law, and obscenity laws all continue to threaten ex post sanction for the violation of legal rights. How well law regulates, or how efficiently, is a different question: In some cases it does so more efficiently, in some cases less. But whether better or not, law continues to threaten a certain consequence if it is defied. Legislatures enact; prosecutors threaten; courts convict.

Norms also regulate behavior in cyberspace. Talk about Democratic politics in the alt.knitting newsgroup, and you open yourself to flaming; "spoof" someone's identity in a MUD [Multi-User Dungeon, a kind of early, text-based virtual world], and you may find yourself "toaded"; talk too much in a discussion list, and you are likely to be placed on a common bozo filter. In each case, a set of understandings constrain behavior, again through the threat of ex post sanctions imposed by a community.

Markets regulate behavior in cyberspace. Pricing structures constrain access, and if they do not, busy signals do. (AOL learned this quite dramatically when it shifted from an hourly to a flat-rate pricing plan.) Areas of the Web are beginning to charge for access, as online services have for some time. Advertisers reward popular sites; online services drop low-population forums. These behaviors are all a function of market constraints and market opportunity. They are all, in this sense, regulations of the market.

Finally, an analog for architecture regulates behavior in cyberspace – code. The software and hardware that make cyberspace what it is constitute a set of constraints on how you can behave. The substance of these constraints may vary, but they are experienced as conditions on your access to cyberspace. In some places (online services such as AOL, for instance) you must enter a password before you gain access; in other places you can enter whether identified or not. In some places the transactions you engage in produce traces that link the transactions (the "mouse droppings") back to you; in other places this link is achieved only if you want it to be.

In some places you can choose to speak a language that only the recipient can hear (through encryption); in other places encryption is not an option. The code or software or architecture or protocols set these features, which are selected by code writers. They constrain some behavior by making other behavior possible or impossible. The code embeds certain values or makes certain values impossible. In this sense, it too is regulation, just as the architectures of real-space codes are regulations. ...

On Governments and Ways to Regulate

I've described four constraints that I've said "regulate" an individual. But these separate constraints obviously don't simply exist as givens in a social life. They are neither found in nature nor fixed by God. Each can be changed, though the mechanics of changing them is complex. Law can have a significant role in this mechanics, and my aim in this section is to describe that role.

A simple example will suggest the more general point. Say the theft of car radios is a problem – not big in the scale of things, but a frequent and costly enough problem to make more regulation necessary. One response might be to increase the penalty for car radio theft to life in prison, so that the risk faced by thieves made it such that this crime did not pay. If radio thieves realized that they exposed themselves to a lifetime in prison each time they stole a radio, it might no longer make sense to them to steal radios. The constraint constituted by the threatened punishment of law would now be enough to stop the behavior we are trying to stop.

But changing the law is not the only possible technique. A second might be to change the radio's architecture. Imagine that radio manufacturers program radios to work only with a single car – a security code that electronically locks the radio to the car, so that, if the radio is removed, it will no longer work. This is a code constraint on the theft of radios; it makes the radio no longer effective once stolen. It too functions as a constraint on the radio's theft, and like the threatened punishment of life in prison, it could be effective in stopping the radio-stealing behavior.

Thus, the same constraint can be achieved through different means, and the different means cost different amounts. The threatened punishment of life in prison may be fiscally more costly than the change in the architecture of radios (depending on how many people actually continue to steal radios and how many are caught). From this fiscal perspective, it may be more efficient to change code than law. Fiscal efficiency may also align with the expressive content of law – a punishment so extreme would be barbaric for a crime so slight. Thus, the values may well track the efficient response. Code would be the best means to regulate.

The costs, however, need not align so well. Take the Supreme Court's hypothetical example of life in prison for a parking ticket. It is likely that whatever code constraint might match this law constraint, the law constraint would be more efficient (if reducing parking violations were the only aim). There would be very few victims of this law before people conformed their behavior appropriately. But the "efficient result" would conflict with other values. If it is barbaric to incarcerate for life for the theft of a radio, it is all the more barbaric as a penalty for a parking violation. The regulator has a range of means to effect the desired constraint, but the values that these means entail need not align with their efficiency. The efficient answer may well be unjust – that is, it may conflict with values inherent in the norms, or law (constitution), of the society

QUESTIONS

1. Consider a familiar problem: littering. How can law deal with littering? What can markets do to reduce littering? How do social norms affect whether people litter or not? And can you think of any architectural factors that encourage or discourage littering?

2. Lessig also calls attention to the interactions among modalities. How can software substitute for law? How can software make law more effective? How can software undermine legal control? Try to give an example of each.

3. Although he famously summed up his theory with the phrase "code is law," Lessig makes the point that software *isn't the same* as law. Instead, he de-

scribes computer software as a kind of "architecture." Why does he use that word? How accurate is the metaphor?

JONATHAN ZITTRAIN
**THE FUTURE OF THE INTERNET
AND HOW TO STOP IT**
2–4, 70–74, 80–82, 90, 96–97 (Yale University Press 2008)

INTRODUCTION

The Apple II was quintessentially generative technology. It was a platform. It invited people to tinker with it. Hobbyists wrote programs. Businesses began to plan on selling software. Jobs (and Apple) had no clue how the machine would be used. They had their hunches, but, fortunately for them, nothing constrained the PC to the hunches of the founders. Apple did not even know that VisiCalc [the first spreadsheet program] was on the market when it noticed sales of the Apple II skyrocketing. The Apple II was designed for surprises – some very good (VisiCalc), and some not so good (the inevitable and frequent computer crashes).

The iPhone is the opposite. It is sterile. Rather than a platform that invites innovation, the iPhone comes preprogrammed. You are not allowed to add programs to the all-in-one device that Steve Jobs sells you. Its functionality is locked in, though Apple can change it through remote updates. Indeed, to those who managed to tinker with the code to enable the iPhone to support more or different applications, Apple threatened (and then delivered on the threat) to transform the iPhone into an iBrick. The machine was not to be generative beyond the innovations that Apple (and its exclusive carrier, AT&T) wanted. Whereas the world would innovate for the Apple II, only Apple would innovate for the iPhone. (A promised software development kit may allow others to program the iPhone with Apple's permission.) ...

In the arc from the Apple II to the iPhone, we learn something important about where the Internet has been, and something more important about where it is going. The PC revolution was launched with PCs that invited innovation by others. So too with the Internet. Both were generative: they were designed to accept any contribution that followed a basic set of rules (either coded for a particular operating system, or respecting the protocols of the Internet). Both overwhelmed their respective proprietary, non-generative competitors, such as the makers of stand-alone word processors and proprietary online services like CompuServe and AOL. But the future unfolding right now is very different from this past. The future is not one of generative PCs attached to a generative network. It is instead one of sterile appliances tethered to a network of control.

These appliances take the innovations already created by Internet users and package them neatly and compellingly, which is good – but only if the Internet and PC can remain sufficiently central in the digital ecosystem to compete with locked-down appliances and facilitate the next round of innovations. The balance between the two spheres is precarious, and it is slipping toward the safer appliance. For example, Microsoft's Xbox 360 video game console is a powerful computer, but, unlike Microsoft's Windows operating system for PCs, it does not allow just anyone to write software that can run on it. ...

It is not easy to imagine the PC going extinct, and taking with it the possibility of allowing outside code to run – code that is the original source of so much of what we find useful about the Internet. But along with the rise of information appliances that package those useful activities without readily allowing new ones, there is the increasing lockdown of the PC itself. PCs may not be competing with information appliances so much as they are becoming them. The trend is starting in schools, libraries, cyber cafés, and offices, where the users of PCs are not their owners. The owners' interests in maintaining stable computing environments are naturally aligned with technologies that tame the wildness of the Internet and PC, at the expense of valuable activities their users might otherwise discover. ...

THE GENERATIVE PATTERN

I have termed this quality of the Internet and of traditional PC architecture "generativity." *Generativity is a system's capacity to produce unanticipated change through unfiltered contributions from broad and varied audiences.* Terms like "openness" and "free" and "commons" evoke elements of it, but they do not fully capture its meaning, and they sometimes obscure it.

Generativity pairs an input consisting of unfiltered contributions from diverse people and groups, who may or may not be working in concert, with the output of unanticipated change. For the inputs, how much the system facilitates audience contribution is a function of both technological design and social behavior. A system's generativity describes not only its objective characteristics, but also the ways the system relates to its users and the ways users relate to one another. In turn, these relationships reflect how much the users identify as contributors or participants, rather than as mere consumers.

Features of a Generative System

What makes something generative? There are five principal factors at work: (1) how extensively a system or technology leverages a set of possible tasks; (2) how well it can be adapted to a range of tasks; (3) how easily new contributors can master it; (4) how accessible it is to those ready and able to build on it; and (5) how transferable any changes are to others – including (and perhaps especially) nonexperts.

Leverage: Leverage makes a difficult job easier. Leverage is not exclusively a feature of generative systems; non-generative, specialized technologies can provide leverage for their designated tasks. But as a baseline, the more a system can do, the more capable it is of producing change. Examples of leverage abound: consider a lever itself (with respect to lifting physical objects), a band saw (cutting them), an airplane (transporting them from one place to another), a piece of paper (hosting written language, wrapping fish), or an alphabet (constructing words). Our world teems with useful objects and processes, both natural and artificial, tangible and intangible. Both PCs and network technologies have proven very leveraging. A typical PC operating system handles many of the chores that the author of an application would otherwise have to worry about, and properly implemented Internet Protocol sees to it that bits of data move from one place to another without application authors having to worry on either end. A little effort can thus produce a very powerful computer program, whether a file-sharing program or a virus comprising just a few lines of code.

Adaptability: Adaptability refers to how easily the system can be built on or modified to broaden its range of uses. A given instrumentality may be highly leveraging yet suited only to a limited range of applications. For example, TiVo is greatly leveraging – television viewers describe its impact on their lives as revolutionary – but it is not very adaptable. A plowshare enables one to plant a variety of seeds; however, its comparative leverage quickly vanishes when devoted to other tasks such as holding doors open. The same goes for swords (they really make poor plowshares), guns, chairs, band saws, and even airplanes. Adaptability is clearly a spectrum. Airplanes can transport people and things, or they can be configured to dust or bomb what lies below. But one can still probably count the kinds of uses for an airplane on two hands. A technology that affords hundreds of different, additional kinds of uses beyond its essential application is more adaptable and, all else being equal, more generative than a technology that offers fewer kinds of uses. The emphasis here is on uses not anticipated at the time the technology was developed. A thick Swiss Army knife may have plenty of built-in tools compared with a simple pocket knife, but many of those are highly specialized.

By this reckoning, electricity is an amazingly adaptable technology, as is plastic (hence the historical use of "plastic" to refer to notions of sculptability). And so are the PC and the Internet: they can be endlessly diverted to new tasks not counted on by their original makers.

Ease of mastery: A technology's ease of mastery reflects how easy it is for broad audiences to understand how to adopt and adapt it. The airplane is not readily mastered, being neither easy to fly nor easy to learn how to modify for new purposes. The risk of physical injury if the modifications are poorly designed or executed is a further barrier to such tinkering. Paper, on the other hand, is readily mastered: we teach our children how to use it, draw on it, and even fold it into paper airplanes (which are much easier to fly and modify than real ones), often before they enter preschool. The skills required to understand many otherwise generative technologies are often not very readily absorbed. Many technologies require apprenticeships, formal training, or many hours of practice if one is to become conversant in them. The small electronic components used to build radios and doorbells fall into this category – one must learn both how each piece functions and how to solder – as do antique car engines that the enthusiast wants to customize. Of course, the skills necessary to operate certain technologies, rather than modify them, are often more quickly acquired. For example, many quickly understand how to drive a car, an understanding probably assisted by user-friendly inventions such as the automatic transmission.

Ease of mastery also refers to the ease with which various types of people might deploy and adapt a given technology, even if their skills fall short of full mastery. A pencil is easily mastered: it takes a moment to understand and put to many uses, even though it might require a lifetime of practice and innate artistic talent to achieve Da Vincian levels of leverage from it. The more useful a technology is both to the neophyte and to the expert, the more generative it is. PCs and network technologies are not easy for everyone to master, yet many people are able to learn how to code, often (or especially) without formal training.

Accessibility: The easier it is to obtain access to a technology, along with the tools and information necessary to achieve mastery of it, the more generative it is. Barriers to accessibility can include the sheer expense of producing (and therefore consuming) the technology, taxes, regulations associated with its adoption or use, and the secrecy its producers adopt to maintain scarcity or control.

Measured by accessibility, paper, plowshares, and guns are highly accessible, planes hardly at all, and cars somewhere in between. It might be easy to learn how to drive a car, but cars are expensive, and the government can always revoke a user's driving privileges, even after the privileges have been earned through a demonstration of driving skill. Moreover, revocation is not an abstract threat because effective enforcement is not prohibitively expensive. Measured by the same factors, scooters and bicycles are more accessible, while snowplows are less so.

Standard PCs are very accessible; they come in a wide range of prices, and in a few keystrokes or mouse-clicks one can be ready to write new code for them. On the other hand, specialized PC modes – like those found in "kiosk mode" at a store cycling through slides – cannot have their given task interrupted or changed, and they are not accessible.

Transferability: Transferability indicates how easily changes in the technology can be conveyed to others. With fully transferable technology, the fruits of skilled users' adaptations can be easily conveyed to less-skilled others. The PC and the Internet together possess very strong transferability: a program written in one place can be shared with, and replicated by, tens of millions of other machines in a matter of moments. By contrast, a new appliance made out of a 75-in-1 Electronic Project Kit is not easily transferable because the modifier's changes cannot be easily conveyed to another kit. Achieving the same result requires manually wiring a new kit to look like the old one, which makes the project kit less generative.

Generative and Non-Generative Systems Compared

Generative tools are not inherently better than their non-generative ("sterile") counterparts. Appliances are often easier to master for particular uses, and because their design often anticipates uses and abuses, they can be safer and more effective. For example, on camping trips, Swiss Army knives are ideal. Luggage space is often at a premium, and such a tool will be useful in a range of expected and even unexpected situations. In situations when versatility and space constraints are less important, however, a Swiss Army knife is comparatively a fairly poor knife – and an equally awkward magnifying glass, saw, and scissors.

As the examples and terms suggest, the five qualities of leverage, adaptability, ease of mastery, accessibility, and transferability often reinforce one another. And the absence of one of these factors may prevent a technology from being generative. A system that is accessible but difficult to master may still be generative if a small but varied group of skilled users make their work available to less-sophisticated users. Usually, however, a major deficiency in any one factor greatly reduces overall generativity. This is the case with many tools that are leveraging and adaptable but difficult to master. For example, while some enjoy tinkering in home workshops, making small birdhouses using wood and a saw, most cannot build their own boats or decks, much less pass those creations on to others. Similarly, there are plenty of examples of technology that is easy to master and is quite adaptable, but lacks leverage. Lego building blocks are easy to master and can produce a great range of shapes, but regardless of the skill behind their arrangement they remain small piles of plastic, which largely confines their uses to that of toys.

The more that the five qualities are maximized, the easier it is for a system or platform to welcome contributions from outsiders as well as insiders. Maximizing these qualities facilitates the technology's deployment in unanticipated ways. ...

Generativity's Output: Innovation

To those for whom innovation is important, generative systems can provide for a kind of organic innovation that might not take place without them. ...

Non-generative systems can grow and evolve, but their growth is channeled through their makers: a new toaster is released by Amana and reflects anticipated customer demand or preferences, or an old proprietary network like CompuServe adds a new form of instant messaging by programming it itself. When users pay for products or services in one way or another, those who control the products or services amid competition are responsive to their desires through market pressure. This is an indirect means of innovation, and there is a growing set of literature about its limitation: a persistent bottleneck that prevents certain new uses from being developed and cultivated by large incumbent firms, despite the benefits they could enjoy with a breakthrough.

We have already seen this phenomenon by anecdote in the first part of this book. ... The telephone system was stable and predictable; its uses evolved slowly if at all from its inception in the late nineteenth century. It was designed to facilitate conversations between two people at a distance, and with some important exceptions, that is all it has done. The change it has wrought for society is, of course, enormous, but the contours of that change were known and set once there was a critical mass of telephones distributed among the general public. Indeed, given how revolutionary a telephone system is to a society without one, it is striking that the underlying technology and its uses have seen only a handful of variations since its introduction. This phenomenon is an artifact of the system's rejection of outside contributions. In the United States, after the law compelled AT&T to permit third-party hardware to connect, we saw a number of new endpoint devices: new telephone units in various shapes, colors, and sizes; answering machines; and, most important, the telephone modem, which allows the non-generative network itself to be repurposed for widespread data communication.

We saw a similar pattern as the Internet overtook proprietary networks that did not even realize it was a competitor. The generative Internet is a basic, flexible network, which began with no innate content. The content was to appear as people and institutions were moved to offer it. By contrast, the proprietary networks of CompuServe, AOL, Prodigy, and Minitel were out beating the bushes for content, arranging to provide it through the straightforward economic model of being paid by people who would spend connect time browsing it. If anything, we would expect the proprietary networks to offer more, and for a while they did. But they also had a natural desire to act as gatekeepers – to validate anything appearing on their network, to cut individual deals for revenue sharing with their content providers, and to keep their customers from affecting the network's technology. These tendencies meant that their rates of growth and differentiation were slow. A few areas that these networks consigned to individual contribution experienced strong activity and subscriber loyalty, such as their topical bulletin boards run by hired systems operators (called "sysops") and boasting content provided by subscribers in public conversations with each other. These forums were generative at the content layer because people could post comments to each other without prescreening and could choose to take up whatever topics they chose, irrespective of the designated labels for the forums themselves ("Pets" vs. "Showbiz"). But they were not generative at the technical layer. The software driving these communities was stagnant: subscribers who were both interested in the communities' content and technically minded had few outlets through which to contribute technical improvements to the way the communities were built. Instead, any improvements were orchestrated centrally. As the initial offerings of the proprietary networks plateaued, the Internet saw developments in technology that in turn led to developments in content and ultimately in social and economic interaction: the Web and Web sites, online shopping, peer-to-peer networking, wikis, and blogs. ...

Generativity's Input: Participation

A second good of generativity is its invitation to outside contribution on its own terms. This invitation occurs at two levels: the individual act of contribution itself, and the ways in which that contribution becomes part of a self-reinforcing community. On the first level, there is a unique joy to be had in building something, even if one is not the best craftsperson. This is a value best appreciated by experiencing it; those who demand proof may not be easy to persuade. Fortunately, there are many ways in which people have a chance to build and contribute. Many jobs demand intellectual engagement, which can be fun for its own sake. People take joy in rearing children: teaching, interacting, guiding. They can also immerse themselves in artistic invention or software coding. ...

The Generative Pattern

Generative technologies need not produce forward progress, if by progress one means something like increasing social welfare. Rather, they foment change. They solicit the distributed intellectual power of humanity to harness the leveraging power of the product or system for new applications, and, if they are adaptable enough, such applications may be quite unexpected. To use an evolutionary metaphor, they encourage mutations, branchings away from the status quo – some that are curious dead ends, others that spread like wildfire. They invite disruption – along with the good things and bad things that can come with such disruption.

QUESTIONS

1. What is the difference between the way Lessig describes computers and the way Zittrain describes them?

2. Zittrain wrote *The Future of the Internet* before Apple added an App Store for the iPhone. How generative is the iPhone now?

3. Does generativity have a downside?

CHAPTER 2: JURISDICTION

The Internet is a global network, so questions of jurisdiction are more or less inevitable. Indeed, one could argue that every Internet issue is, at heart, jurisdictional. A computer network brings together people in different places; its *point* is to bridge geographic divisions. When those divisions are national or state borders, the network raises jurisdictional issues just by being a network.

This chapter introduces the book's second major theme: governmental power over the Internet. In the 1990s, many thinkers argued that the Internet would necessarily lead to a collapse in governmental authority. They have been challenged by others who claimed there was nothing inevitable about this transition, and by others who believe that the Internet enables governments to extend their grasp into more aspects of life than ever before. Jurisdiction has been the legal battleground for these debates; after all, jurisdiction is what connects a court's government-given power with its ability to say what the law is.

Each section of the chapter explores a different facet of jurisdiction. The first section asks whether the Internet itself is a jurisdiction, a place that could have laws of its own. The second section explores *prescriptive* jurisdiction: which countries have authority to make laws regulating online activities that cross national boundaries. The third section takes up *enforcement* jurisdiction: when countries can make those laws stick against people outside their borders. And the fourth section considers *adjudicative* jurisdiction: when, under United States law, a court will have personal jurisdiction over a defendant. The chapter is all about conflict. There is the conflict between Internet users and the governments who disapprove of what they're doing, of course, but also conflicts between different governments with different policies.

A. Cyberspace

The readings in this section begin with academic and activist perspectives on the idea that the Internet is somewhere else entirely, a place where traditional laws don't apply and traditional governments have no power. As you read them, try to figure out whether "here" versus "there" is even the right question to be asking. *Voyeur Dorm* (the two opinions are from the District Court and Court of Appeals in the same case), *Target*, and the Dead Aim problem then put the seemingly abstract question of place on the Internet into more concrete legal settings.

JOHN PERRY BARLOW
A DECLARATION OF THE INDEPENDENCE OF CYBERSPACE
Feb. 8, 1996

Governments of the Industrial World, you weary giants of flesh and steel, I come from Cyberspace, the new home of Mind. On behalf of the future, I ask you of the past to leave us alone. You are not welcome among us. You have no sovereignty where we gather.

We have no elected government, nor are we likely to have one, so I address you with no greater authority than that with which liberty itself always speaks. I declare the global social space we are building to be naturally independent of the tyrannies you seek to impose on us. You have no moral right to rule us nor do you possess any methods of enforcement we have true reason to fear.

Governments derive their just powers from the consent of the governed. You have neither solicited nor received ours. We did not invite you. You do not know us, nor do you know our world. Cyberspace does not lie within your borders. Do not think that you can build it, as though it were a public construction project. You cannot. It is an act of nature and it grows itself through our collective actions.

You have not engaged in our great and gathering conversation, nor did you create the wealth of our marketplaces. You do not know our culture, our ethics, or the unwritten codes that already provide our society more order than could be obtained by any of your impositions.

You claim there are problems among us that you need to solve. You use this claim as an excuse to invade our precincts. Many of these problems don't exist. Where there are real conflicts, where there are wrongs, we will identify them and address them by our means. We are forming our own Social Contract. This governance will arise according to the conditions of our world, not yours. Our world is different.

Cyberspace consists of transactions, relationships, and thought itself, arrayed like a standing wave in the web of our communications. Ours is a world that is both everywhere and nowhere, but it is not where bodies live.

We are creating a world that all may enter without privilege or prejudice accorded by race, economic power, military force, or station of birth.

We are creating a world where anyone, anywhere may express his or her beliefs, no matter how singular, without fear of being coerced into silence or conformity.

Your legal concepts of property, expression, identity, movement, and context do not apply to us. They are based on matter. There is no matter here.

Our identities have no bodies, so, unlike you, we cannot obtain order by physical coercion. We believe that from ethics, enlightened self-interest, and the commonweal, our governance will emerge. Our identities may be distributed across many of your jurisdictions. The only law that all our constituent cultures would generally recognize is the Golden Rule. We hope we will be able to build our particular solutions on that basis. But we cannot accept the solutions you are attempting to impose.

In the United States, you have today created a law, the Telecommunications Reform Act, which repudiates your own Constitution and insults the dreams of Jefferson, Washington, Mill, Madison, DeToqueville, and Brandeis. These dreams must now be born anew in us.

You are terrified of your own children, since they are natives in a world where you will always be immigrants. Because you fear them, you entrust your bureaucracies with the parental responsibilities you are too cowardly to confront yourselves. In our world, all the sentiments and expressions of humanity, from the debasing to the angelic, are parts of a seamless whole, the global conversation of bits. We cannot separate the air that chokes from the air upon which wings beat.

In China, Germany, France, Russia, Singapore, Italy and the United States, you are trying to ward off the virus of liberty by erecting guard posts at the frontiers of Cyberspace. These may keep out the contagion for a small time, but they will not work in a world that will soon be blanketed in bit-bearing media.

Your increasingly obsolete information industries would perpetuate themselves by proposing laws, in America and elsewhere, that claim to own speech itself throughout the world. These laws would declare ideas to be another industrial product, no more noble than pig iron. In our world, whatever the human mind may create can be reproduced and distributed infinitely at no cost. The global conveyance of thought no longer requires your factories to accomplish.

These increasingly hostile and colonial measures place us in the same position as those previous lovers of freedom and self-determination who had to reject the authorities of distant, uninformed powers. We must declare our virtual selves immune to your sovereignty, even as we continue to consent to your rule over our bodies. We will spread ourselves across the Planet so that no one can arrest our thoughts.

We will create a civilization of the Mind in Cyberspace. May it be more humane and fair than the world your governments have made before.

Davos, Switzerland
February 8, 1996

QUESTIONS

1. This is the single most influential essay in the history of Internet law. What accounts for its instant appeal? How well has it aged?

2. What is Barlow's argument? Beneath the soaring rhetoric, what is he arguing for and what is is he arguing against? What does "independence" mean in this context?

3. Freedom of thought and freedom of speech are central for Barlow. Why does he believe that they are so important – and so at risk – on the Internet?

ORIN S. KERR
THE PROBLEM OF PERSPECTIVE IN INTERNET LAW
91 GEO. L. J. 357 (2003)

In the 1999 science fiction thriller *The Matrix*, Keanu Reeves plays a computer hacker named "Neo" who learns that the reality he has known since birth is merely a virtual reality created by a computer network known as the Matrix. The *real* Neo lies in a semicomatose state attached to the network, to which he and others have been connected by advanced computers that have taken over the world and sap energy from humans while occupying their minds with virtual reality. Neo ends up joining the rebel forces trying to destroy the Matrix, and the movie jumps several times between the virtual world inside the Matrix and the real world outside of the Matrix. The movie presents us with two different realities, two existing worlds. The first reality is the virtual world that we experience inside the Matrix, and the second is the "real" world that we experience outside the Matrix.

In addition to being a fun movie, *The Matrix* points out an important problem that arises when we try to understand the nature of computer networks in general and the Internet in particular. Like Neo confronting the Matrix, we can think about the Internet in two ways, virtual and real. The virtual perspective is like the perspective inside the Matrix: it accepts the virtual world of cyberspace as akin to a reality. Of course, unlike Neo, we know all along that the virtual world that the computer generates is only virtual. But as we try to make sense of what the Internet is, to understand what we experience online, we might decide to treat that virtual world as if it were real.

I will call this virtual point of view the internal perspective of the Internet. The internal perspective adopts the point of view of a user who is logged on to the Internet and chooses to accept the virtual world of cyberspace as a legitimate construct. To this user, a computer connected to the Internet provides a window to a virtual world that is roughly analogous to the physical world of real space. The user can use her keyboard and mouse to go shopping, send mail, visit a chat room, participate in an online community, or do anything else she can find online. The technical details of what the computers attached to the Internet actually do "behind the scenes" don't particularly matter. What matters is the virtual world of cyberspace that the user encounters and interacts with when he or she goes online.

We can also understand the Internet from a different perspective. Like Neo when he is outside the Matrix, we can look at the Internet from the point of view of the physical world, rather than the virtual one. I will call this the external perspective of the Internet. The external perspective adopts the viewpoint of an outsider concerned with the functioning of the network in the physical world rather than the perceptions of a user.

From this external viewpoint, the Internet is simply a network of computers located around the world and connected by wires and cables. The hardware sends, stores, and receives communications using a series of common protocols. Keyboards provide sources of input to the network, and monitors provide destinations for output. When the Internet runs properly, trillions of zeros and ones zip around the world, sending and receiving communications that the computers connected to the network can translate into commands, text, sound, and pictures.

From the external perspective, the fact that Internet users may perceive that they have entered a virtual world of cyberspace has no particular relevance. These perceptions reflect the fact that software designers often garnish their applications with icons, labels, and graphics to help novices understand and use them – for example, by writing e-mail programs so that e-mail looks and feels like postal mail. These superficialities have no deeper meaning from the external perspective. What matters is the physical network and the technical details of how it works, not the easily manipulated perceptions of Internet users.

Both internal and external understandings of the Internet should ring true to most of us. The Internet *is* a physical network, and it *can* create a virtual world for its users that can appear sufficiently realistic to its users to make a plausible claim for equal footing with the physical world. But the key for us is that by generating a virtual reality, the technology in a sense leaves us with two Internets, rather than one. We have an external version of the Internet, and also an internal one. One is physical, the other virtual. ...

Why does this matter to lawyers and to the nature of Internet law? It matters because legal outcomes depend on facts, and the facts of the Internet depend on which perspective we choose. This is a very practical problem. The basic task of a lawyer is to apply legal rules to facts – to apply law to an understanding of reality. In the case of the Internet, however, two competing understandings of reality exist. ...

All of this may seem rather abstract, so an example may help. Consider what happens when an Internet user surfs the web. Imagine that an Internet user opens up a web browser and types in "www.amazon.com," and moments later the homepage of Amazon.com appears on the viewer's screen. ...

This is easy from an internal perspective. The user has visited Amazon.com's website, going to Amazon.com's home on the Internet. The user has visited Amazon.com's virtual store much like a person might visit a store in the physical world, traveling from one point in cyberspace to another. ...

From an external perspective, however, the event appears quite different – and significantly more complicated. Behind the scenes, the simple act of typing "www.amazon.com" into a web browser triggers a series of responses from different computers connected to the Internet. The browser begins by sending out a request across the Internet to a special type of computer known as a Domain Name System (DNS) server. The browser's request asks the DNS server to translate the letters of the website address "amazon.com" into an "Internet Protocol" or "IP" address, which is a series of numbers that computers connected to the Internet understand as an address akin to a phone number. The DNS server will respond that "www.amazon.com" translates into the IP address "207.171.184.16." The user's browser then issues another request, this time directed to "207.171.184.16," asking it to send a set of data files back to the browser. Amazon.com's computer will receive the request and then send data back to the browser. The browser will receive the data and display it on the user's screen. The resulting images and text appear in the form of the Amazon.com webpage that the user requested.

Notice that the internal and external perspectives have produced two different accounts of the same event. One model of the facts follows the virtual perspective of the user, and another model follows the behind-the-scenes perspective of how the Internet actually works. From the internal perspective, visiting Amazon.com resembles visiting a store. The user types in the address, and a moment later is paying a virtual visit to Amazon.com's site. From the external perspective, visiting Amazon.com resembles calling Information and asking for Amazon.com's phone number, then dialing the number and asking the representative to send you the latest Amazon.com catalog. The single event of surfing the web produces two set of facts, one internal and the other external. As a result, when we need to apply law to the act of visiting a website, we can apply that law to two different sets of facts, which can produce two different outcomes.

QUESTIONS

1. When you and I have a Skype videochat, what is happening from the internal perspective? How about from the external perspective?

2. Kerr's essay is in some respects a response to Barlow's. What would Kerr say about Barlow's argument that "cyberspace" is inherently independent?

DAVID R. JOHNSON AND DAVID POST
LAW AND BORDERS
THE RISE OF LAW IN CYBERSPACE
48 STAN. L. REV. 1367 (1996)

... I. BREAKING DOWN TERRITORIAL BORDERS

A. Territorial Borders in the "Real World"

We take for granted a world in which geographical borders – lines separating physical spaces – are of primary importance in determining legal rights and responsibilities. Territorial borders, generally speaking, delineate areas within which different sets of legal rules apply. There has until now been a general correspondence between borders drawn in physical space (between nation states or other political entities) and borders in "law space." For example, if we were to superimpose a "law map" (delineating areas where different rules apply to particular behaviors) onto a political map of the world, the two maps would overlap to a significant degree, with clusters of homogeneous applicable law and legal institutions fitting within existing physical borders. ...

Physical borders are not, of course, simply arbitrary creations. Although they may be based on historical accident, geographic borders for law make sense in the real world. Their logical relationship to the development and enforcement of legal rules is based on a number of related considerations.

Power. Control over physical space, and the people and things located in that space, is a defining attribute of sovereignty and statehood. Law-making requires some mechanism for law enforcement, which in turn depends on the ability to exercise physical control over, and impose coercive sanctions on, law-violators. For example, the U.S. government does not impose its trademark law on a Brazilian business operating in Brazil, at least in part because imposing sanctions on the Brazilian business would require assertion of physical control over business owners. Such an assertion of control would conflict with the Brazilian government's recognized monopoly on the use of force over its citizens.

Effects. The correspondence between physical boundaries and "law space" boundaries also reflects a deeply rooted relationship between physical proximity and the effects of any particular behavior. That is, Brazilian trademark law governs the use of marks in Brazil because that use has a more direct impact on persons and assets within Brazil than anywhere else. For example, a large sign over "Jones' Restaurant" in Rio de Janeiro is unlikely to have an impact on the operation of "Jones' Restaurant" in Oslo, Norway, for we may assume that there is no substantial overlap between the customers, or competitors, of these two entities. Protection of the former's trademark does not – and probably should not – affect the protection afforded the latter's.

Legitimacy. We generally accept the notion that the persons within a geographically defined border are the ultimate source of law-making authority for activities within that border. The "consent of the governed" implies that those subject to a set of laws must have a role in their formulation. By virtue of the preceding considerations, those people subject to a sovereign's laws, and most deeply affected by those laws, are the individuals who are located in particular physical spaces. Similarly, allocation of responsibility among levels of government proceeds on the assumption that, for many legal problems, physical proximity between the responsible authority and those most directly affected by the law will improve the quality of decision making, and that it is easier to determine the will of those individuals in physical proximity to one another.

Notice. Physical boundaries are also appropriate for the delineation of "law space" in the physical world because they can give notice that the rules change when the boundaries are crossed. Proper boundaries have signposts that provide warning that we will be required, after crossing, to abide by different rules, and physical boundaries – lines on the geographical map – are generally well-equipped to serve this signpost function.

B. The Absence of Territorial Borders in Cyberspace

Cyberspace has no territorially based boundaries, because the cost and speed of message transmission on the Net is almost entirely independent of physical location. Messages can be transmitted from one physical location to any other location without degradation, decay, or substantial delay, and without any physical cues or barriers that might otherwise keep certain geographically remote places and people separate from one another. The Net enables transactions between people who do not know, and in many cases cannot know, each other's physical location. ...

[*Power*] But efforts to control the flow of electronic information across physical borders – to map local regulation and physical boundaries onto Cyberspace – are likely to prove futile, at least in countries that hope to participate in global commerce. Individual electrons can easily, and without any realistic prospect of detection, "enter" any sovereign's territory. The volume of electronic communications crossing territorial boundaries is just too great in relation to the resources available to government authorities. ...

By asserting a right to regulate whatever its citizens may access on the Net, these local authorities are laying the predicate for an argument that Singapore or Iraq or any other sovereign can regulate the activities of U.S. companies operating in Cyberspace from a location physically within the United States. All such Web-based activity, in this view, must be subject simultaneously to the laws of all territorial sovereigns.

[*Effects*] Nor are the effects of online activities tied to geographically proximate locations. Information available on the World Wide Web is available simultaneously to anyone with a connection to the global network. The notion that the effects of an activity taking place on that Web site radiate from a physical location over a geographic map in concentric circles of decreasing intensity, however sensible that may be in the nonvirtual world, is incoherent when applied to Cyberspace. A Web site physically located in Brazil, to continue with that example, has no more of an effect on individuals in Brazil than does a Web site physically located in Belgium or Belize that is accessible in Brazil. Usenet discussion groups, to take another example, consist of continuously changing collections of messages that are routed from one network to another, with no centralized location at all. They exist, in effect, everywhere, nowhere in particular, and only on the Net.

[*Legitimacy & Notice*] Territorial regulation of online activities serves neither the legitimacy nor the notice justifications. There is no geographically localized set of constituents with a stronger and more legitimate claim to regulate it than any other local group. The strongest claim to control comes from the participants themselves, and they could be anywhere. And in Cyberspace, physical borders no longer function as signposts informing individuals of the obligations assumed by entering into a new, legally significant, place. Individuals are unaware of the existence of those borders as they move through virtual space. ...

II. A NEW BOUNDARY FOR CYBERSPACE

Traditional legal doctrine treats the Net as a mere transmission medium that facilitates the exchange of messages sent from one legally significant geographical location to another, each of which has its own applicable laws. But trying to tie the laws of any particular territorial sovereign to transactions on the Net, or even trying to analyze the legal consequences of Net-based commerce as if each transaction occurred geographically somewhere in particular, is most unsatisfying. A more legally significant, and satisfying, border for the "law space" of the Net consists of the screens and passwords that separate the tangible from the virtual world.

Many of the jurisdictional and substantive quandaries raised by border-crossing electronic communications could be resolved by one simple principle: conceiving of Cyberspace as a distinct "place" for purposes of legal analysis by recognizing a legally significant border between Cyberspace and the "real world." Using this new approach, we would no longer ask the unanswerable question "where" in the geographical world a Net-based transaction occurred. Instead, the more salient questions become: What procedures are best suited to the often unique characteristics of this new place and the expectations of those who are engaged in various activities there? What mechanisms exist or need to be developed to determine the content of those rules and the mechanisms by which they can enforced? Answers to these questions will permit the development of rules better suited to the new phenomena in question, more likely to be made by those who understand and participate in those phenomena, and more likely to be enforced by means that the new global communications media make available and effective.

Treating Cyberspace as a separate "space" to which distinct laws apply should come naturally. There is a "placeness" to Cyberspace because the messages accessed there are persistent and accessible to many people. Furthermore, because entry into this world of stored online communications occurs through a screen and (usually) a password boundary, you know when you are "there." No one accidentally strays across the border into Cyberspace. To be sure, Cyberspace is not a homogenous place; groups and activities found at various online locations possess their own unique characteristics and distinctions, and each area will likely develop its own set of distinct rules. But the line that separates online transactions from our dealings in the real world is just as distinct as the physical boundaries between our territorial governments – perhaps more so.

QUESTIONS:

1. How would Johnson and Post respond to Judge Easterbrook's claim that the law of the Internet is no different from traditional law? Is this the same response Barlow would give?

2. Have Johnson and Post adopted an internal perspective on the Internet, an external perspective, or neither?

MARY ANNE FRANKS
UNWILLING AVATARS
IDEALISM AND DISCRIMINATION IN CYBERSPACE
20 COLUM. J. GENDER & L. 224 (2011)

I. CYBERSPACE IDEALISM: PARADISE? ...

As many scholars have described it, the creation of cyberspace is only the most recent of human attempts to create a utopia. The utopian drive is certainly not new: it can be observed in rhetoric about the New World, the Wild West, Communist Russia, cults, and any number of hippie communes. ...

It is not difficult to see why cyberspace, especially in the early days of the internet, would incite such utopian fervor. As noted by numerous writers, cyberspace provides a heady opportunity to escape one's physical boundaries, both geographical and personal, in a more extreme way than ever before. In cyberspace, as the saying goes, "no one knows you're a dog." Or a woman, or a Jew, or overweight, or deaf, or whether you're in Arkansas, or Massachusetts, or St. Petersburg. At its most basic level, cyberspace seems to allow people to control who they want to be and to go wherever they want to go. ...

II. UNWILLING AVATARS: THE FALL

Cyberspace idealism unsurprisingly appeals to individuals who feel their life experiences have been restricted by their physical identity: by their social status, their age, their gender, or their physical appearance. Going online allows these individuals to experience a certain kind of positive disembodiment. One's "real" race, gender, age, and social status need never be disclosed in cyberspace, and so negative stereotypes that may attach to any of those attributes can be avoided in a way not possible in real life. Particularly for historically marginalized groups, the power to re-create oneself and control the public representation of one's identity through avatars can be liberating.

What happens, then, when individuals are not in control of their online embodiment? What if one is embodied against one's will, in places that one never chose
to enter, in ways one never consented to be shown, in graphic and vicious detail for
all the world to see and which may be impossible to erase? We would surely describe that experience as a profound loss of liberty, the very antithesis of the freeing process of avatar creation. A world populated by an increasing number of unwilling avatars, reduced to their physical characteristics, caricaturized, ventrilo-
quized and under attack, looks much more like hell than paradise.

A. Bringing in the Women ...

Sayani Chakraborty had never been a member of Orkut, a social networking
site similar to Facebook and MySpace, but she discovered that someone had created a profile of her on the site and used it to send offensive messages to her family
and friends. Someone created a similar profile for a schoolgirl in Delhi, complete
with obscene photographs and the girl's home address and telephone number. The
profile came to light after her family began receiving calls asking to speak with the
girl and referencing the Orkut profile. Eventually, two men came to her home
claiming that the girl had invited them over for sex. ...

.Kathy Sierra is a programming instructor and a game developer who runs a
blog called Creating Passionate Users. This blog is centered on discussions about
"designing software that makes people happy." ... Sierra began receiving death
threats in the comments section of her blog. Someone wrote about slitting her
throat and ejaculating; another posted her photo alongside an image of a noose
with a caption: "The only thing Kathy has to offer is that noose in her neck size."
On an external site, a user posted a manipulated photo that appeared to show
Sierra with underwear across her face, struggling to breathe. The picture was captioned: "I dream of Kathy Sierra . . . head first." Sierra canceled several speaking
engagements and suspended her blog in the wake of the threatening posts. ...

Nicole Catsouras was eighteen years old when she died in a horrific car accident. On October 31, 2006, she and her father had an argument, and he confiscated the car keys as punishment. Later that day, Nicole snuck out, taking the car
keys with her. Fifteen minutes later, she crashed into a freeway tollbooth at a speed
of over 100 miles per hour. The collision mangled her body, nearly decapitating
her. The police photographs of the accident were leaked and published online. The
gruesome images began to appear in chat rooms and fetish websites where users
would discuss, among other things, how Nicole "deserved" what happened. A My-
Space user posted the pictures along with sexualized commentary about Nicole;
another created a fake profile of Nicole that included a close-up of her remains.
Someone posted the Catsouras' home address and encouraged others to harass the
family. Nicole's parents received numerous pseudonymous emails and text messages that included the photos, along with vicious captions. They attempted to
convince web site owners to take down the pictures, but met with little success:
"We've asked them to please take down the pictures, and they've said, 'No, I don't
have to because I've got my First Amendment rights,'" says Nicole's mother, Lesli
Catsouras. Nicole's family uploaded a memorial video of Nicole on YouTube, hoping that it would help show that they "are a family with real hearts, and it hurts
what people are doing." A number of vicious and sexist pseudonymous comments
were posted on YouTube in response, including the following: "she got what she
deserved . . . you wanted equality, fine, fuck that stupid cunt . . . hahahaha, she got
what she deserved" ....

B. Cyberspace as a State of License

Part I noted the similarity between the way cyberspace idealists describe cyberspace and the way John Locke describes the state of nature as one of perfect liberty. The examples given above tell a very different story. They paint a world in which only certain individuals enjoy the mythic degree of liberty and freedom from physical restraints touted by cyberspace idealists, while others experience a loss of liberty and a re-entrenchment of physical restraints already unequally imposed upon them in the offline world. Women targeted by cyber harassment experience restrictions in liberty both in cyberspace and out of it. They experience new levels of objectification, confronting reductions of themselves to sexualized body parts in message boards, chat rooms, social networking sites, and Google searches. Women who have been targeted by cyber harassment avoid certain sites to avoid being attacked; they close down email accounts that have been flooded with abusive and obscene messages; they shut down blogs; in some cases, they withdraw from what were lucrative and vibrant online presences. The losses of liberty follow them offline, as well: they face harassment and slander stemming from online attacks in their workplaces and schools, leading them to quit or change jobs and universities; they change their daily routines for fear of being stalked or physically assaulted; they are sometimes stalked, assaulted or even killed by their online harassers. ...

Locke writes that when mankind finds itself unable to preserve the state of nature, it necessarily must establish the rule of law. If individuals abuse their liberty by exercising power in arbitrary and self-interested ways that threaten the security of the whole community, the community will slide into a state of war. In a state of war, anyone at any time might be deprived of his or her liberty and possessions. To avoid this outcome, the community collectively establishes a central authority and rules to regulate disputes. This necessarily involves giving up some of what Locke considers to be "natural rights" (e.g., the right to personally punish someone who has wronged you). But it also results in liberty for more people and security for most of one's other rights. Security for the general public – not just for the strongest or most aggressive – is the basis for the forfeiture of some individual power. Put another way, rules ensure a measure of equality for all.

The same can be said of regulations of speech on the internet. New legal regulations regarding behavior in cyberspace might indeed mean, in some sense, that some individuals will no longer have the same degree of "liberty" they had previously. It would mean, for example, that cyber harassers could no longer attack women with impunity. But the freedom to harass is an exercise of license, not liberty, and as such is hardly defensible in the first instance. The effects of such license, moreover, are that women as a group suffer a loss of liberty relative to men as a group. Regulation and reform are necessary to balance the equation and create a cyberspace that maximizes liberty for all groups. ...

III. NO EXIT: THE DOUBLE-EMBODIMENT EFFECT ...

A final point to note is that the effects of unwilling online embodiment are potentially even more pernicious and long-lasting than real-life harassment. This is due to four features of cyberspace that exacerbate the impact of harassment:

1. Anonymity: The increased opportunity for harassers to attack their target anonymously, making it difficult if not impossible for the targets to engage in self-help or legal remedies;

2. Amplification: The capacity for harassers to quickly find a wide audience for their harassment, including users who will join in the harassment;

3. Permanence: Online attacks, which often include personal information about their targets, such as home addresses and telephone numbers, are very difficult to erase from the web;

4. Virtual Captivity/Publicity: The options to avoid or exit situations in which cyber harassment occurs are extremely limited. Whereas specific acts of real-life harassment are often restricted to one place (for example, being harassed on the street does not necessarily impact one's experience in the workplace), the effects of cyberspace harassment can manifest much more readily. Particularly if the online attack is indexable by a major search engine like Google, it is accessible to almost anyone (the target's co-workers, fellow students, clients, children) almost anywhere (at her place of work, her school, her home, her doctor's office).

QUESTIONS

1. According to Franks, what is wrong with Barlow's vision of an independent Internet?

2. Would Franks be satisfied with the kinds of online self-governance Johnson and Post think will develop?

3. Does the Internet also have an upside for minorities? What does anonymity – "On the Internet, no one knows you're a dog" – have to do with it?

VOYEUR DORM L.C. V. CITY OF TAMPA
121 F. Supp. 2d 1373 (2000)

[Voyeur Dorm operated a web site at http://www.voyeurdorm.com. The site featured 24-hour live video feeds from a house at 2312 West Farwell Drive, in a residential neighborhood of Tampa, Florida. Those videos showed the lives of the "residents" of 2312 West Farwell: five women who were under contracts with Voyeur Dorm specifying that they were employed to appear on a "stage and filming location," with "no reasonable expectation of privacy," for "entertainment purposes." The nature of those purposes could be gleaned from the descriptions on the voyeurdorm.com website, which stated, "The girls of Voyeur Dorm are fresh, naturally erotic and as young as 18. Catch them in the most intimate acts of youthful indiscretion." Subscribers paid $34.95 a month for access to the web site. The address of the house was not listed on the web site, and the activities inside the house were not visible from outside.

The city of Tampa brought an action against Voyeur Dorm to enforce its zoning code, which prohibited "adult entertainment" uses in residential areas (including the area where the house is located). Section 27-523 of its zoning code defined "adult entertainment," in relevant part, as:

Any premises . . . on which is offered to members of the public or any person, for a consideration, entertainment featuring or in any way including specified sexual activities, as defined in this section, or entertainment featuring the displaying or depicting of specified anatomical areas, as defined in this section; 'entertainment' as used in this definition shall include, but not be limited to, books, magazines, films, newspapers, photographs, paintings, drawings, sketches or other publications or graphic media, filmed or live plays, dances or other performances distinguished by their display or depiction of specified anatomical areas or specified anatomical activities, as defined in this section.]

Bucklew, District Judge: ...

Plaintiffs argue that their use of the premises does not satisfy all the elements of the definition of an adult use because it is not a premises "on which is offered to members of the public or any persons, for a consideration, entertainment featuring or in any way including specified sexual activities. . . ." (emphasis added). Plaintiffs argue that no member of the public was ever offered for a consideration any adult entertainment on the premises. Instead, the viewing of the activities of the residents by the members of the public "takes place in virtual space, via a global computer network comprised of computer servers primarily located in a office building in downtown Tampa and on other computer servers located throughout the world. Any actual viewing of any computer rendered digital images of the residents takes place in the homes and offices of subscribers to the Voyeur Dorm web site." Accordingly, Plaintiffs contend that their use of the premises does not constitute an adult use. ...

Accordingly, this Court must apply the plain and unambiguous language of the City Code and may not read language into it that does not appear on its face. There is no language in the City Code that expressly states a requirement that the members of the public paying consideration be on the premises viewing the adult entertainment. The plain language of the City Code includes any premises "on which is offered to members of the public or any persons, for a consideration, entertainment featuring or in any way including specified sexual activities. . . ." The premises at 2312 West Farwell Drive is clearly a premises on which is offered to members of the public for consideration entertainment featuring specified sexual activities under the plain meaning of the City Code. To construe the City Code otherwise would require that this Court read language into the City Code requiring that the members of the public be present at the premises.

VOYEUR DORM L.C. V. CITY OF TAMPA
265 F.3d 1232 (11th Cir. 2001)

Dubina, Circuit Judge: ...

Voyeur Dorm argues that it is not an adult use business. Specifically, Voyeur Dorm contends that section 27-523 applies to locations or premises wherein adult entertainment is actually offered to the public. Because the public does not, indeed cannot, physically attend 2312 West Farwell Drive to enjoy the adult entertainment, 2312 West Farwell Drive does not fall within the purview of Tampa's zoning ordinance. We agree with this argument.

The residence of 2312 West Farwell Drive provides no "offer[ing] [of adult entertainment] to members of the public." The offering occurs when the videotaped images are dispersed over the internet and into the public eye for consumption. The City Code cannot be applied to a location that does not, itself, offer adult entertainment to the public. As a practical matter, zoning restrictions are indelibly anchored in particular geographic locations. Residential areas are often cordoned off from business districts in order to promote a State's interest. It does not follow, then, that a zoning ordinance designed to restrict facilities that offer adult entertainment can be applied to a particular location that does not, at that location, offer adult entertainment. Moreover, the case law relied upon by Tampa and the district court concerns adult entertainment in which customers *physically attend* the premises wherein the entertainment is performed. Here, the audience or consumers of the adult entertainment do not go to 2312 West Farwell Drive or congregate anywhere else in Tampa to enjoy the entertainment. Indeed, the public offering occurs over the Internet in "virtual space." While the district court read section 27-523 in a literal sense, finding no requirement that the paying public be *on the premises*, we hold that section 27-523 does not apply to a residence at which there is no public offering of adult entertainment. Accordingly, because the district court misapplied section 27-523 to the residence of 2312 West Farwell Drive, we reverse the district court's order granting summary judgment to Tampa.

QUESTIONS

1. Who is right about the statutory construction of section 27-253, the District Court or the Court of Appeals? Which result makes more sense in terms of the policies of Tampa's zoning code?

2. What would John Perry Barlow say about this case? Is it true that the adult entertainment took place in "virtual space" beyond Tampa's power to regulate?

3. What would Orin Kerr say about this case? What does Voyeur Dorm look like from the internal perspective? From the external perspective?

4. What would David Johnson and David Post say about this case? Which of their four bases for regulation are present here?

5. What would Mary Anne Franks say about this case? Do the dueling opinions speak for everyone whose lives it touches?

6. A state statute prohibits "engaging in masturbation or lewd exhibition of the genitals in the presence of a minor under the age of 16." D sends a text message with a photograph of his erect penis to M, who is 14. Guilty?

NATIONAL FEDERATION OF THE BLIND V. TARGET CORP.
452 F. Supp. 2d 946 (N.D. Cal. 2006)

Patel, District Judge: ...

BACKGROUND

Target operates approximately 1,400 retail stores nationwide, including 205 stores in California. Target.com is a website owned and operated by Target. By visiting Target.com, customers can purchase many of the items available in Target stores. Target.com also allows a customer to perform functions related to Target stores. For example, through Target.com, a customer can access information on store locations and hours, refill a prescription or order photo prints for pick-up at a store, and print coupons to redeem at a store.

Plaintiffs allege that Target.com is not accessible to blind individuals. According to plaintiffs, designing a website to be accessible to the blind is technologically simple and not economically prohibitive. Protocols for designing an accessible internet site rely heavily on "alternative text": invisible code embedded beneath graphics. A blind individual can use screen reader software, which vocalizes the alternative text and describes the content of the web-page. Similarly, if the screen reader can read the navigation links, then a blind individual can navigate the site with a keyboard instead of a mouse. Plaintiffs allege that Target.com lacks these features that would enable the blind to use Target.com. Since the blind cannot use Target.com, they are denied full and equal access to Target stores, according to plaintiffs. ...

On February 7, 2006 plaintiffs filed this action in Superior Court of California for the County of Alameda. On March 9, 2006 defendant removed the case to federal court. Defendant now moves to dismiss the complaint for failure to state a claim. Defendant claims that [the Americans with Disabilities Act, 42 U.S.C. section 12182, ("ADA")], covers access to only physical spaces. Since Target.com is not a physical space, defendant asserts that the complaint does not state a claim under these laws. ...

DISCUSSION

I. MOTION TO DISMISS

A. ADA

Title III of the ADA prevents discrimination against the disabled in places of public accommodation: "No individual shall be discriminated against on the basis of disability in the full and equal enjoyment of the goods, services, facilities, privileges, advantages, or accommodations of any place of public accommodation by any person who owns, leases (or leases to) or operates a place of public accommodation." 42 U.S.C. § 12182(a).

"Discrimination" under the ADA encompasses the denial of the opportunity, by the disabled, to participate in programs or services, and providing the disabled with separate, but unequal, goods or services. *See* 42 U.S.C. § 12182(b)(1)(A)(i-iii). To ensure that the disabled have full and equal enjoyment of the goods and services of places of public accommodation, the ADA requires "reasonable modification" of "policies, practices, and procedures," the provision of auxiliary aids to ensure effective communication with the disabled, and the removal of architectural and communications barriers. 42 U.S.C. § 12182(b)(2)(A)(ii-iv). The ADA thus, departs from certain anti-discrimination statutes in requiring that places of public accommodation take affirmative steps to accommodate the disabled.

Defendant contends that Target.com is not a place of public accommodation within the meaning of the ADA, and therefore plaintiffs cannot state a claim under the ADA. Specifically, defendant claims that the complaint is deficient because it does not allege that "individuals with vision impairments are denied access to one of Target's brick and mortar stores or the goods they contain." However, the complaint states that "due to Target's failure and refusal to remove access barriers to Target.com, blind individuals have been and are being denied equal access to Target stores, as well as to the numerous goods, services and benefits offered to the public through Target.com." Plaintiffs' legal theory is that unequal access to Target.com denies the blind the full enjoyment of the goods and services offered at Target stores, which are places of public accommodation.

Defendant contends that even if Target.com is the alleged service of Target stores, plaintiffs still do not state a claim because they fail to assert that they are denied physical access to Target stores. Although a plaintiff may allege an ADA violation based on unequal access to a "service" of a place of public accommodation, courts have held that a plaintiff must allege that there is a "nexus" between the challenged service and the place of public accommodation. Under Ninth Circuit law, a "place of public accommodation," within the meaning of Title III, is a physical place.[3] The Ninth Circuit has declined to join those circuits which have suggested that a "place of public accommodation" may have a more expansive meaning. *See Carparts Distribution Ctr., Inc. v. Automotive Wholesalers Assoc. of New England, Inc.*, 37 F.3d 12, 19-20 (1st Cir. 1994) (holding that "public accommodations" encompasses more than actual physical structures and includes the defendant insurance company); *Doe v. Mutual of Omaha Ins. Co.*, 179 F.3d 557, 559 (7th Cir. 1999) (noting, in dicta, that a "place of public accommodation" encompasses facilities open to the public in both physical and electronic space, including websites).

In *Weyer v. Twentieth Century Fox* Film Corp., 198 F.3d 1104 (9th Cir. 2000), plaintiff sued an insurance company for offering a policy that allegedly discriminated against people with mental disabilities. The Ninth Circuit adopted the reasoning of the Third and Sixth Circuits, finding that there was "no nexus between the disparity in benefits and the services which . . . [the insurance company] offers to the public from its insurance office." *Id.* at 1115. The court noted that although an insurance office is a place of public accommodation, an insurance company administering an employer-provided insurance policy is not a place of public accommodation.

Similarly, the Eleventh Circuit in *Rendon v. Valleycrest Prod., Ltd.* held that the telephone process for selecting contestants for "Who Wants to be a Millionaire" discriminated against people with hearing and other physical disabilities. 294 F.3d 1279, 1280-81 (11th Cir. 2002). The court found that the studio where the show was filmed was a place of public accommodation and that competing on the show was a privilege provided by the place of public accommodation. Thus, the court held that by using a discriminatory process for screening potential contestants, defendant was denying disabled persons equal enjoyment of a privilege (competing on the show) of a place of public accommodation (the studio). *Id.* at 1284-85; *see also Ford v. Schering-Plough Corp.*, 145 F.3d 601, 612-13 (3d Cir. 1998) (holding that plaintiff failed to allege a nexus between the place of public accommodation and the insurance benefits offered by the employer); *Stoutenborough v. National Football League*, 59 F.3d 580, 583-84 (6th Cir. 1995) (affirming the dismissal of a claim under Title III because the challenged service, the live telecast of a football game, was not offered by a place of public accommodation, the stadium).

Defendant argues that the above-cited cases stand for the proposition that the ADA prohibits only discrimination occurring on the premises of a place of public accommodation, and that "discrimination" is limited to the denial of physical entry to, or use of, a space. Each element of defendant's argument will be addressed in turn.

1. Off-Site Discrimination

The ADA prohibits discrimination on the basis of disability "in the full and equal enjoyment of the goods, services, facilities, privileges, advantages or accommodations *of* any place of public accommodation." 42 U.S.C. § 12182(a) (emphasis added). The statute applies to the services *of* a place of public accommodation, not services *in* a place of public accommodation. To limit the ADA to discrimination in the provision of services occurring on the premises of a public accommodation

---

3 The examples listed by the ADA as examples of places of public accommodation provide support for the notion that such an entity must be a physical place. They include: inns, Hotels, restaurants, motion picture houses, auditoriums, bakeries, laundromats, museum, parks, zoos and health spas. *See* 42 U.S.C. § 12181(7)(A)-(L).

would contradict the plain language of the statute. To the extent defendant argues that plaintiffs' claims are not cognizable because they occur away from a "place" of public accommodation, defendant's argument must fail.

2. *Physical Access*

According to defendants, in order for plaintiffs' claim to be actionable under the ADA, the "off-site" discrimination must still deny physical access to Target's brick-and-mortar stores. Relying on *Rendon, Access Now v. Southwest Airlines*, 227 F. Supp. 2d 1312 (S.D. Fla. 2002) and *Stoutenborough*, defendant argues that the nexus theory applies only to the denial of physical access to a place of public accommodation, and thus plaintiffs' claim that Target.com (rather than Target stores) is inaccessible, is not legally cognizable. However, consistent with the plain language of the statute, no court has held that under the nexus theory a plaintiff has a cognizable claim only if the challenged service prevents physical access to a public accommodation. Further, it is clear that the purpose of the statute is broader than mere physical access – seeking to bar actions or omissions which impair a disabled person's "full enjoyment" of services or goods of a covered accommodation. 42 U.S.C. § 12182(a). Indeed, the statute expressly states that the denial of equal "participation" or the provision of "separate benefit[s]" are actionable under Title III. *See* 42 U.S.C. § 12182(b)(1)(A).

Defendant's reliance on *Rendon, Access Now and Stoutenborough* to support this proposition is misplaced. In *Rendon*, the court held that the plaintiff stated a claim by alleging that an off-site telephone screening process discriminated against the disabled who sought to enjoy a privilege (being a contestant on a television show) offered by a place of public accommodation (the studio). *Rendon* neither states nor suggests that a plaintiff proceeding under the "nexus" theory must plead denial of physical access to a place of public accommodation. On the contrary, the court held that tangible barriers restrict the disabled individual's right to access the physical space while intangible barriers "restrict a disabled person's ability to *enjoy* the defendant entity's goods, services and privileges." *Id.* at 1283 (emphasis added).

In *Access Now*, the court held that plaintiff failed to state a claim under the ADA because plaintiff alleged that the inaccessibility of southwest.com prevented access to Southwest's "virtual" ticket counters. "Virtual" ticket counters are not actual, physical places, and therefore not places of public accommodation. Since there was no physical place of public accommodation alleged in *Access Now*, the court did not reach the precise issue presently in dispute: whether there is a nexus between a challenged service and an actual, physical place of public accommodation. ...

In *Stoutenborough*, the court found that there could be no Title III liability because the National Football League, the lessor of a public stadium, was not the entity that offered the challenged service. In the words of the Sixth Circuit, "[t]he televised broadcast of football games is certainly offered through defendants, but not as a service of public accommodation. It is all of the services which the public accommodation offers, not all services which the lessor of the public accommodation offers which fall within the scope of Title III." *Stoutenborough*, 59 F.3d at 583. Similarly, defendant contends, like the lessor in *Stoutenborough*, the owner in the present action (Target corporation) is the party through which Target.com is offered and thus a Title III claim is not actionable. *See* 42 U.S.C. § 12182. However, it is clear from the face of the complaint that many of the benefits and privileges of the website are services of the Target stores. Unlike in *Stoutenborough*, where the "service" was offered by a separate party leasing the public space, the challenged service here is heavily integrated with the brick-and-mortar stores and operates in many ways as a gateway to the stores.

The case law does not support defendant's attempt to draw a false dichotomy between those services which impede physical access to a public accommodation and those merely offered by the facility. Such an interpretation would effectively limit the scope of Title III to the provision of ramps, elevators and other aids that operate to remove physical barriers to entry. Although the Ninth Circuit has determined that a place of public accommodation is a physical space, the court finds unconvincing defendant's attempt to bootstrap the definition of accessibility to this determination, effectively reading out of the ADA the broader provisions enacted by Congress. In *Rendon*, even though the disabled individual did not contest the actual physical barriers of the facility in question, the Eleventh Circuit found that Title III was implicated because a "discriminatory procedure that deprived [the individual] of the opportunity to compete to be a contestant . . . *at* a place of public accommodation" was utilized. *Rendon*, 294 F.3d at 1281 (emphasis added) (internal citations omitted). Similarly, in the present action, plaintiffs have alleged that the inaccessibility of Target.com denies the blind the ability to enjoy the services of Target stores. The Ninth Circuit has stated that the "ordinary meaning" of the ADA's prohibition against "discrimination in the enjoyment of goods, services, facilities or privileges, is 'that *whatever* goods or services the place provides, it cannot discriminate on the basis of disability in providing enjoyment of those goods and services.'" *Weyer*, 198 F.3d at 1115 (emphasis added). Defendant's argument is unpersuasive and the court declines to dismiss the action for failure to allege a denial of physical access to the Target stores. ...

QUESTIONS

1. Where is target.com? Is it a "place" of public accommodation? Of anything else?

2. John Perry Barlow describes cyberspace as "a world that all may enter without privilege or prejudice accorded by race, economic power, military force, or station of birth." What about disabilities? Does the Internet efface offline differences, or exacerbate them?

3. Netflix provides DVD rentals by mail and offers streaming video on a subscription basis from its website. It does not have retail stores. Under *Target*, is Netflix obliged under the ADA to provide closed captioning on its streaming videos? On DVDs?

DEAD AIM PROBLEM

Dead Aim Hunting owns a 100-acre plot in central Texas, which it keeps well-stocked with game. It also operates a website at http://www.dead-aim-hunting.com. Users must pay monthly membership dues of $14.95 and a deposit of $1,000 to participate in what Dead Aim calls "drone hunting." Dead Aim has attached cameras and Remington .30-06 rifles to remote-control drones. Users who have reserved a time block can take control of one of the drones. By clicking on appropriate buttons in their web browser, they send a signal to Dead Aim's computer, which in turn sends signals to the drone to position itself and aim the attached rifle. By clicking on a "fire" button, they can move an actuator that pulls the trigger on the rifle. A hunter a thousand or more miles away can thus shoot at a deer, antelope, or other animal. If they succeed in killing one, Dead Aim bills them for its cost, then ships them the carcass for skinning, butchering, and/or mounting, as appropriate. In the words of Dead Aim's owner, "Hunter" Dan Lockwood, "Most hunters use blinds to conceal themselves. What's the difference between that and clicking a mouse? Nothing. That is the same exact motion, and it takes the same amount of time."

Lurleen Lumpkin, a resident of Illinois, used Dead Aim to kill a six-point buck on November 20. Cletus Spuckler, a resident of West Virginia, used Dead Aim to shoot at a rabbit on December 4, but missed. Texas has enacted a statute stating:

> A person may not attach a firearm to an aerial vehicle or operate an aerial vehicle to which a firearm has been attached if the aerial vehicle is located in Texas.

Illinois has enacted a statute stating:

> A person shall not operate, provide, sell, use, or offer to operate, provide, sell, or use any computer software or service that allows a person not physically present at the hunt site to remotely control a weapon that could be used to take wildlife by remote operation, including, but not limited to, weapons or devices set up to fire through the use of the Internet or through a remote control device.

Can either Texas or Illinois prosecute Dead Aim or any of its users? Are these laws a good idea?

B. Territoriality

The argument discussed in the previous section – that the Internet is *somewhere else* – has not fared well with the courts. Instead, they have grappled with more practical questions of when governments should and should not apply their law to activities taking place at least partially online. If Ava in Austria sends an email to Barry in Bolivia, which passes through a network operated by Comcast in Connecticut, and the email defames Darius in Djibouti, it is not immediately obvious which of these countries' courts can hear the case, or which law should apply.

We start the detailed discussion with choice of law, because the question of which jurisdictions have the power to make laws for the Internet is fundamental. As you read the rest of this chapter, ask yourself whether any of the following simple rules would be workable and just – and if not, why not?

- The law of the place where the relevant computer is located applies, and the plaintiff must sue there.
- The law of the plaintiff's home jurisdiction applies, and the plaintiff can sue there.
- The plaintiff can sue in any court with jurisdiction over the defendant, and the court will apply its local law.

But first, some terminology. It is common to distinguish between "territorial" and "extraterritorial" regulation. Territorial laws apply to conduct taking place within a jurisdiction's physical boundaries; extraterritorial laws apply to conduct taking place beyond them.

One might ask why a jurisdiction would ever seek to apply its laws extraterritorially. One reason is that certain acts are considered especially heinous: under the international-law principle of "universal jurisdiction," any sovereign state may prosecute genocide, piracy, and war crimes. Another is that jurisdictions can and do regulate their own nationals both at home and abroad. The United States prohibits its citizens from sexually abusing children, wherever they may be in the world. And finally, actions taken in one place can have consequences in another. "The principle that a man who outside of a country willfully puts in motion a force to take effect in it is answerable at the place where the evil is done, is recognized in the criminal jurisprudence of all countries." *Ford v. United States*, 273 U.S. 593, 623 (1927). In *Ford*, the defendants were arrested on the high seas, twenty-five miles west of San Francisco, while on a ship carrying 12,000 cases of liquor. The Supreme Court upheld their convictions for conspiracy to smuggle liquor into the United States in violation of the Prohibition laws.

International law has traditionally allowed countries nearly unlimited power to make law territorially, subject only to some specific prohibitions like the human rights norms against genocide and torture. The power to regulate extraterritorially, while broad, is not unlimited: a state may make law governing "conduct outside its territory that has or is intended to have substantial effect within its territory." RESTATEMENT (THIRD) OF FOREIGN RELATIONS LAW § 402(1)(c). So there is a lot of room in international law for sovereign states to regulate extraterritorially. There is also a practical reason why many states do: who is going to stop them?

Enter the Internet. From Djibouti's point of view, Ava, Barry, and Comcast are all acting in a way that "has ... substantial effect within its territory." So why not subject them to Djibouti defamation law?

DOW JONES & CO. V. GUTNICK
High Court of Australia
[2002] HCA 56

Gleeson, Chief Justice:

The appellant, Dow Jones & Company Inc ("Dow Jones"), prints and publishes the Wall Street Journal newspaper and Barron's magazine. Since 1996, Dow Jones has operated WSJ.com, a subscription news site on the World Wide Web. Those who pay an annual fee (set, at the times relevant to these proceedings, at $US59, or $US29 if they are subscribers to the printed editions of either the Wall Street Journal or Barron's) may have access to the information to be found at WSJ.com. Those who have not paid a subscription may also have access if they register, giving a user name and a password. The information at WSJ.com includes Barron's Online in which the text and pictures published in the current printed edition of Barron's magazine are reproduced.

The edition of Barron's Online for 28 October 2000 (and the equivalent edition of the magazine which bore the date 30 October 2000) contained an article entitled "Unholy Gains" in which several references were made to the respondent, Mr Joseph Gutnick. Mr Gutnick contends that part of the article defamed him. [As Justice Callinan's opinion explained, "The article associates the respondent with Mr. Nachum Goldberg who is apparently a convicted tax evader and another person awaiting trial for stock manipulation in New York." Gutnick "pleaded that the article meant, and was understood to mean that he:

> was a customer of Nachum Goldberg who had recently been imprisoned for tax evasion and money laundering; and
>
> was Nachum Goldberg's biggest customer; and

was masquerading as a reputable citizen when he was, in fact, a tax evader who had laundered large amounts of money through Nachum Goldberg; and

had bought Nachum Goldberg's silence so as to conceal his identity as one of Goldberg's customers."]

He has brought an action in the Supreme Court of Victoria against Dow Jones claiming damages for defamation. Mr Gutnick lives in Victoria. He has his business headquarters there. Although he conducts business outside Australia, including in the United States of America, and has made significant contributions to charities in the United States and Israel, much of his social and business life could be said to be focused in Victoria.

The originating process in the action which Mr. Gutnick brought against Dow Jones was served on it outside Australia. ...

Argument of the appeal proceeded from an acceptance, by both parties, of certain principles. First, it is now established that an Australian court will decline, on the ground of *forum non conveniens*, to exercise jurisdiction which has been regularly invoked by a plaintiff, whether by personal service or under relevant long-arm jurisdiction provisions, only when it is shown that the forum whose jurisdiction is invoked by the plaintiff is clearly inappropriate. Secondly, it is now established that in trying an action for tort in which the parties or the events have some connection with a jurisdiction outside Australia, the choice of law rule to be applied is that matters of substance are governed by the law of the place of commission of the tort. Neither party sought to challenge either proposition. Rather, argument focused upon where was the place of publication of the statements of which Mr Gutnick complained. Dow Jones contended that the statements were published in New Jersey and that it was, therefore, the law of that jurisdiction which would govern all questions of substance in the proceeding. ...

Dow Jones has its editorial offices for Barron's, Barron's Online and WSJ.com in the city of New York. Material for publication in Barron's or Barron's Online, once prepared by its author, is transferred to a computer located in the editorial offices in New York City. From there it is transferred either directly to computers at Dow Jones's premises at South Brunswick, New Jersey, or via an intermediate site operated by Dow Jones at Harborside, New Jersey. It is then loaded onto six servers maintained by Dow Jones at its South Brunswick premises. ...

The principal burden of the argument advanced by Dow Jones on the hearing of the appeal in this Court was that articles published on Barron's Online were published in South Brunswick, New Jersey, when they became available on the servers which it maintained at that place.

In the courts below, much weight appears to have been placed by Dow Jones on the contention that a relevant distinction was to be drawn between the apparently passive role played by a person placing material on a web server from which the would-be reader had actively to seek the material by use of a web browser and the (comparatively) active role played by a publisher of a widely circulated newspaper or a widely disseminated radio or television broadcast. In this Court, these arguments, though not abandoned, were given less prominence than policy arguments based on what was said to be the desirability of there being but a single law governing the conduct of a person who chooses to make material available on the World Wide Web.

Dow Jones submitted that it was preferable that the publisher of material on the World Wide Web be able to govern its conduct according only to the law of the place where it maintained its web servers, unless that place was merely adventitious or opportunistic. Those who, by leave, intervened in support of Dow Jones generally supported this contention. The alternative, so the argument went, was that a publisher would be bound to take account of the law of every country on earth, for there were no boundaries which a publisher could effectively draw to prevent anyone, anywhere, downloading the information it put on its web server. ...

It is necessary to begin by making the obvious point that the law of defamation seeks to strike a balance between, on the one hand, society's interest in freedom of speech and the free exchange of information and ideas (whether or not that information and those ideas find favour with any particular part of society) and, on the other hand, an individual's interest in maintaining his or her reputation in society free from unwarranted slur or damage. The way in which those interests are balanced differs from society to society. In some cases, for example as between the States in Australia, the differences in substantive law might be said to be differences of detail rather than substance, although even then it may be doubted that this is an accurate characterisation of the effect of the differences in the defamation laws of the Australian States. Whether or not that is so, comparing the law of defamation in different countries can reveal differences going well beyond matters of detail lying at the edge of debate. ...

The tort of defamation, at least as understood in Australia, focuses upon publications causing damage to reputation. It is a tort of strict liability, in the sense that a defendant may be liable even though no injury to reputation was intended and the defendant acted with reasonable care. Yet a publication made in the ordinary course of a business such as that of bookseller or news vendor, which the defendant shows to have been made in circumstances where the defendant did not know or suspect and, using reasonable diligence, would not have known or suspected was defamatory, will be held not to amount to publication of a libel. There is, nonetheless, obvious force in pointing to the need for the publisher to be able to identify, in advance, by what law of defamation the publication may be judged. But it is a tort concerned with damage to reputation and it is that damage which founds the cause of action. ...

Harm to reputation is done when a defamatory publication is comprehended by the reader, the listener, or the observer. Until then, no harm is done by it. This being so it would be wrong to treat publication as if it were a unilateral act on the part of the publisher alone. It is not. It is a bilateral act – in which the publisher makes it available and a third party has it available for his or her comprehension. ...

In the course of argument much emphasis was given to the fact that the advent of the World Wide Web is a considerable technological advance. So it is. But the problem of widely disseminated communications is much older than the Internet and the World Wide Web. The law has had to grapple with such cases ever since newspapers and magazines came to be distributed to large numbers of people over wide geographic areas. Radio and television presented the same kind of problem as was presented by widespread dissemination of printed material, although international transmission of material was made easier by the advent of electronic means of communication.

It was suggested that the World Wide Web was different from radio and television because the radio or television broadcaster could decide how far the signal was to be broadcast. It must be recognised, however, that satellite broadcasting now permits very wide dissemination of radio and television and it may, therefore, be doubted that it is right to say that the World Wide Web has a uniquely broad reach. It is no more or less ubiquitous than some television services. In the end, pointing to the breadth or depth of reach of particular forms of communication may tend to obscure one basic fact. However broad may be the reach of any particular means of communication, those who make information accessible by a particular method do so knowing of the reach that their information may have. In particular, those who post information on the World Wide Web do so knowing that the information they make available is available to all and sundry without any geographic restriction.

Because publication is an act or event to which there are at least two parties, the publisher and a person to whom material is published, publication to numerous persons may have as many territorial connections as there are those to whom particular words are published. It is only if one starts from a premise that the publication of particular words is necessarily a singular event which is to be located by reference only to the conduct of the publisher that it would be right to attach no significance to the territorial connections provided by the several places in which the publication is available for comprehension. ...

In defamation, the same considerations that require rejection of locating the tort by reference only to the publisher's conduct, lead to the conclusion that, ordinarily, defamation is to be located at the place where the damage to reputation occurs. Ordinarily that will be where the material which is alleged to be defamatory is available in comprehensible form assuming, of course, that the person defamed has in that place a reputation which is thereby damaged. It is only when the material is in comprehensible form that the damage to reputation is done and it is damage to reputation which is the principal focus of defamation, not any quality of the defendant's conduct. In the case of material on the World Wide Web, it is not available in comprehensible form until downloaded on to the computer of a person who has used a web browser to pull the material from the web server. It is where that person downloads the material that the damage to reputation may be done. Ordinarily then, that will be the place where the tort of defamation is committed. ...

Three other matters should be mentioned. In considering what further development of the common law defences to defamation may be thought desirable, due weight must be given to the fact that a claim for damage to reputation will warrant an award of substantial damages only if the plaintiff has a reputation in the place where the publication is made. Further, plaintiffs are unlikely to sue for defamation published outside the forum unless a judgment obtained in the action would be of real value to the plaintiff. The value that a judgment would have may be much affected by whether it can be enforced in a place where the defendant has assets.

Finally, if the two considerations just mentioned are not thought to limit the scale of the problem confronting those who would make information available on the World Wide Web, the spectre which Dow Jones sought to conjure up in the present appeal, of a publisher forced to consider every article it publishes on the World Wide Web against the defamation laws of every country from Afghanistan to Zimbabwe is seen to be unreal when it is recalled that in all except the most unusual of cases, identifying the person about whom material is to be published will readily identify the defamation law to which that person may resort.

The appeal should be dismissed with costs.

Kirby, Justice: ...

The law in different jurisdictions, reflecting local legal and cultural norms, commonly strikes different balances between rights to information and expression and the protection of individual reputation, honour and privacy. These disparities suggest the need for a clear and single rule to govern the conduct in question according to pre-established norms. If it is to be effective, such a rule must be readily ascertainable. To tell a person uploading potentially defamatory material onto a website that such conduct will render that person potentially liable to proceedings in courts of every legal jurisdiction where the subject enjoys a reputation, may have undesirable consequences. Depending on the publisher and the place of its assets, it might freeze publication or censor it or try to restrict access to it in certain countries so as to comply with the most restrictive defamation laws that could apply. Or it could result in the adoption of locational stratagems in an attempt to avoid liability. ...

The dismissal of the appeal does not represent a wholly satisfactory outcome. Intuition suggests that the remarkable features of the Internet (which is still changing and expanding) makes it more than simply another medium of human communication. It is indeed a revolutionary leap in the distribution of information, including about the reputation of individuals. It is a medium that overwhelmingly benefits humanity, advancing as it does the human right of access to information and to free expression. But the human right to protection by law for the reputation and honour of individuals must also be defended to the extent that the law provides. ...

However, such results are still less than wholly satisfactory. They appear to warrant national legislative attention and to require international discussion in a forum as global as the Internet itself. ...

Callinan, Justice:

The question which this case raises is whether the development of the Internet calls for a radical shift in the law of defamation. ...

A publisher, particularly one carrying on the business of publishing, does not act to put matter on the Internet in order for it to reach a small target. It is its ubiquity which is one of the main attractions to users of it. And any person who gains access to the Internet does so by taking an initiative to gain access to it in a manner analogous to the purchase or other acquisition of a newspaper, in order to read it.

The appellant contends that the Internet is not "pushed" into any particular jurisdiction. The contention ignores the commercial and social realities that greater publication produces both greater profit and broader persuasion. Indeed, the appellant's arguments would suggest that all of its objectives were exclusively high-minded. Revenues from increased advertising and circulation, and the word "profit" never passed the appellant's advocate's lips. It may well be that "firewalls" to deny access to the unintended or non-subscribing reader are at present perhaps imperfect. So be it. Publishers are not obliged to publish on the Internet. If the potential reach is uncontrollable then the greater the need to exercise care in publication. ...

The most important event so far as defamation is concerned is the infliction of the damage, and that occurs at the place (or the places) where the defamation is comprehended. Statements made on the Internet are neither more nor less "localized" than statements made in any other media or by other processes. Newspapers have always been circulated in many places. The reach of radio and television is limited only by the capacity of the technology to transmit and hear or view them, which already, and for many years, has extended beyond any one country. In any event, a "publisher," whether on the Internet or otherwise, will be likely to sustain only nominal, or no damages at all for publication of defamatory matter in a jurisdiction in which a person defamed neither lives, has any interests, nor in which he or she has no reputation to vindicate. Furthermore, it may be that an action inadvisably brought in such a jurisdiction might be met by a finding that the jurisdiction is not a convenient or appropriate forum.

The appellant argued that the respondent, having set out to make money in the United States, must expect to be subjected to lawful scrutiny in that country. No doubt the fact of lawful scrutiny in that country, if such the publication was, would provide a defence to the appellant to defamation proceedings there. That fact does not however have anything to say about unlawful publication in this country. ...

The appellant invited the Court to prefer, in effect, a United States jurisdiction to an Australian one because the latter would deprive it of the Constitutional protection available in the former. ...

Australian defamation law, and, for that matter, English defamation law also, and the policy underlying them are different from those of the United States. There is no doubt that the latter leans heavily, some might say far too heavily, in favour of defendants. Nor has the metaphor for free speech developed by Holmes J in a series of cases and beginning with his dissenting judgment in *Abrams v United States*, a marketplace of ideas, escaped criticism in the United States. ...

Quite deliberately, and in my opinion rightly so, Australian law places real value on reputation, and views with scepticism claims that it unduly inhibits freedom of discourse. In my opinion the law with respect to privilege in this country, now and historically, provides an appropriate balance which does justice to both a publisher and the subject of a publication. ...

I agree with the respondent's submission that what the appellant seeks to do, is to impose upon Australian residents for the purposes of this and many other cases, an American legal hegemony in relation to Internet publications.

QUESTIONS

1. One way of looking at *Gutnick* is as a response to Johnson and Post. Why is Australia unwilling to defer to the Internet?

2. If Australia is able to impose its defamation law on the Internet, can Saudi Arabia also impose its anti-pornography law on the Internet? What about China's laws against political activism? What content will remain online if each country can impose its idiosyncratic local speech restrictions on the Internet?

3. On the other hand, if Australia can't control defamation online, does that mean that United States copyright law is also unenforceable? What content will remain online if any country can effectively extend its free speech protections to the Internet?

4. If forced to choose between total control and total freedom, which would you pick? Is there any possible middle ground?

MAHFOUZ V. EHRENFELD
High Court of Justice (U.K.), Queen's Bench Division
[2005] EWHC 1156 (QB)

Eady, Justice:

The first claimant is Khalid Bin Mahfouz (KBM) and the second claimant is his son, Abdul Rahman Bin Mahfouz (ARBM). The third claimant is also a son of the first claimaint, Sultan Bin Mahfouz (SBM).

Each of the claimants is a well-known Saudi businessman. They have extensive business and financial holdings in Saudi Arabia and elsewhere in the world. Their interests cover a wide variety of investments including in the field of energy, that of real estate, and also in financial institutions. ...

It is also important to note for the purposes of these proceedings that until recently ARBM and SBM were the ultimate owners of Nimir, an oil exploration production company with its headquarters in London at 1 Knightsbridge. They sold their interests in Nimir on 4 August 2004.

With that brief introduction to the claimants I turn now to the first defendant, Dr Rachel Ehrenfeld. She has claimed to be "the world's foremost authority on narcoterrorism . . . and a sought after commentator and consultant on the problems of international terrorism". She is the director of an organisation called the American Centre for Democracy.

The second defendant, Bonus Books Incorporated, is a United States publisher. The book which forms the subject matter of this libel litigation is 'Funding Evil, How Terrorism is Financed - And How to Stop it'. The first defendant is the author of that book and the second defendant its publisher.

In December 2003 it came to the claimants' attention that the book was being published in England and Wales containing defamatory allegations about them. The book was being sold through online retailers such as Amazon.co.uk, Blackwells.co.uk and Amazon.com.

The claimants also discovered that the first chapter of the book was separately available on the ABC News website. ...

I turn now to the nature of the allegations which were made in the book and which form the subject matter of this complaint. As Cherif Sedky [the claimants' legal advisor] points out, they are of the most serious and defamatory kind. The book alleges that the Bin Mahfouz family is one of the main sponsors of Al Qaeda and other terrorist organisations. It also alleges that NCB, [a bank] which was owned by the Bin Mahfouz family was used as a conduit for financing Al Qaeda. The book also claims that in 1999 the Saudi government audited both NCB and Khalid Bin Mahfouz and revealed that over a ten-year period NCB had channelled money to charities acting as fronts for Al Qaeda.

Cherif Sedky offers the view, not surprisingly, that the connection made in the book to the funding of terrorism would be regarded, by anybody who knew any background information about NCB, as referring to the three individual claimants because they were the main family members involved with the running of the bank as I have described.

The meanings which the claimants themselves attribute to the published allegations are to be found in the Particulars of Claim at paragraph 8 as follows: (1) that the claimants supported and assisted in terrorism; (2) that the claimants were amongst the principal funders of terrorism, contributing millions of dollars to Al Qaeda and other terrorist organisations; (3) that the first claimant deposited tens of millions of dollars in London and New York into accounts held by terrorists who were implicated in the 1998 bombings of the United States Embassies in Kenya and Tanzania in which 254 people were killed and more than 4,000 injured; (4) that the first claimant provided money for the sponsorship of Al Qaeda, Hamas and Hezbollah in their campaign of terrorist atrocities; (5) that the first claimant, as Chairman and General Manager of the National Commercial Bank, assisted in and/or organised the channelling of funds by the National Commercial Bank to fund and support terrorism, including to fund the expansion of Al Qaeda throughout the world; (6) that the second and third claimants as members of the board of directors of NCB assisted in and/or approved of NCB's funding of terrorism including its funding of the expansion of Al Qaeda throughout the world. ...

At one point solicitors were acting for the defendants, namely Morgan Lewis, but they were, in due course, disinstructed and the defendants have not acknowledged the proceedings in question.

The claimants therefore obtained a default judgment and an injunction against the defendants. That was achieved by means of an order made by me on 7 December of last year and the defendants were served with that order on 30 December and 17 December respectively. Again, there is evidence before the court of the service of that order in the form of affidavits from United States process servers.

It appears that since 1 July 2003 some 23 hard copies of the book have been sold within this jurisdiction. I should perhaps make it clear that excludes any copies obtained by the claimants' advisers for the purposes of this litigation. However, as I have already indicated, the first chapter was separately available on www.ABCnews.com. There is a printout from that website in evidence before me today.

It has not proved possible, despite their best efforts, for the claimants' solicitors to establish how many hits there have been on chapter 1 of the book by that means. A conversation took place with the Executive Counsel of ABC Inc on 28 June last year and she confirmed that ABCnews.com did not have the technology to provide the required information. Nevertheless it is apparently the case that the number of hits worldwide on ABCnews.com is over 14 million unique visitors per month and Cherif Sedky has been informed by Hill and Knowlton, the claimants' public relations representatives, that according to information provided by a company specialising in measuring internet audiences, called Nielsen Net Ratings, the total number of hits from the UK on ABCnews.com website in the month of March 2004 was 211,000 unique visitors. The inference is thus invited that a significant proportion of those 211,000 UK visitors would have accessed the relevant pages. ...

It is, of course, a complete defence to a libel action in this jurisdiction to prove, on the balance of probabilities, that the defamatory allegations were substantially true. ...

Cherif Sedky therefore submits the defendants have not raised any matter which would be capable of justifying in any way the allegations in the book and the claimants would be prepared to demonstrate the lack of merit in any plea of justification that the defendants cared to raise. They have, however, not had the opportunity to do so.

The order made on 7 December 2004 has had some mitigating effect in relation to the publications which have taken place. The claimants' solicitors wrote to various retailers and requested that they did not publish the book in this jurisdiction. It seems that, in the light of those letters, some UK retailers have removed the book from sale. However, the hard copy of the book can still be purchased in this jurisdiction through the United States online retailer, Amazon.com. ...

I turn, therefore, to the relief which is claimed. I propose to grant first of all the maximum level of damages, in favour of each claimant, which is permitted under the summary procedure of Sections 8 to 9 of the Defamation Act 1996. I do that for fairly obvious reasons. The allegations are very serious and nothing whatever has been done to mitigate the effect of the original publication. Of course it is not suggested that £10,000 would, at the end of a trial, represent the full measure of compensation to which the claimants would be entitled if they succeeded, but it is the top level of compensation permitted under this summary procedure of which the claimants have chosen to avail themselves in the light of the attitude taken by the defendants.

I propose to make a declaration of falsity and to confirm the injunction as being in existence. I will make an order for the costs of these proceedings to be assessed at a detailed assessment, if not agreed, and for there to be a payment on account of those costs within 28 days of £30,000.

QUESTIONS

1. In the United States, the First Amendment would have required the plaintiffs to show that Ehrenfeld's speech was false and that she knew it was false or acted with reckless disregard of its truth or falsity. Did they meet these burdens?

2. Why did Bin Mahfouz and his sons, all Saudis, sue Ehrenfeld, an American, in England?

3. *Mahfouz* seems to pit the United Kingdom against the Internet. But another way of looking at the case is as a conflict between two countries. If the court dismisses the case, has the United States effectively imposed its free-speech values on the United Kingdom? If the court allows the case to proceed, has the United Kingdom effectively imposed its strong protections for personal reputation on the United States?

4. The tension between different national laws isn't new. Indeed, it has existed as long as different countries have had different laws. But perhaps the Internet exacerbates those tensions. Could this case have been brought in a pre-Internet era?

NOTE ON THE DORMANT COMMERCE CLAUSE

Matters are a little different at the state level. The Dormant Commerce Clause puts sharp limits on states' ability to regulate conduct crossing state lines. Here is a typical statement of the relevant doctrines (with numbering inserted to show the three-part structure of the test):

> This Court has adopted what amounts to a two-tiered approach to analyzing state economic regulation under the Commerce Clause. When a state statute [1] directly regulates or discriminates against interstate commerce, or when its effect is [2] to favor in-state economic interests over out-of-state interests, we have generally struck down the statute without further inquiry. When, however, a statute has only indirect effects on interstate commerce and regulates evenhandedly, we have examined [3] whether the State's interest is legitimate and whether the burden on interstate commerce clearly exceeds the local benefits.

Brown-Forman Distillers Corp. v. New York State Liquor Authority, 476 U.S. 573, 578–79 (1986). Applying these rules can be tricky, because of the conceptual problem: where are a state's borders on the Internet?

In *State v. Heckel*, 24 P.3d 404 (Wash. 2001), the Washington Supreme Court upheld a state anti-spam law that prohibited sending emails to Washington residents with false subject lines or return addresses. First, the law did not directly regulate interstate commerce by applying extraterritorially. Second, the Washington law regulated in-state and out-of-state economic interests evenhandedly because "just as the statute applied to Heckel, an Oregon resident, it is enforceable against a Washington business engaging in the same practices." *Id.* at 409. Third, the court held that the law's benefits exceeded its burdens. On the benefit side, spam consumes bandwidth, storage space, and users' time. On the burden side, emailers were only required to label their messages truthfully.

The court distinguished an earlier case, *American Libraries Association v. Pataki*, 969 F. Supp. 160 (S.D.N.Y. 1997), which struck down "a New York statute that made it a crime to use a computer to distribute harmful, sexually explicit content to minors."

> The statute applied not just to initiation of e-mail messages but to all Internet activity, including the creation of websites. Thus, under the New York statute, a website creator in California could inadvertently violate the law simply because the site could be viewed in New York. ... In contrast to the New York statute, which could reach all content posted on the Internet and therefore subject individuals to liability based on unintended access, the Act reaches only those deceptive UCE messages directed to a Washington resident or initiated from a computer located in Washington; in other words, the Act does not impose liability for messages that are merely routed through Washington or that are read by a Washington resident who was not the actual addressee.

Heckel, 24 P.2d at 412–13. Are you persuaded?

QUESTIONS

1. The Washington statute upheld in *Heckel*, like many other state anti-spam laws, was pre-empted by the federal CAN-SPAM Act of 2003, which sets uniform national standards on deceptive and unwanted email.[*] Is it a coincidence that Congress chose to federalize this particular slice of online law?

2. *ACLU v. Johnson*, 194 F.3d 1149 (10th Cir. 1999), struck down a New Mexico statute that made it a crime to communicate with a minor by computer "when such communication in whole or in part depicts actual or simulated nudity, sexual intercourse or any other sexual conduct." The court held that the statute "contains no express limitation confining it to communications which occur wholly within [New Mexico's] borders." Is this reasoning consistent with *Heckel*?

3. If businesses can pick what law applies to them by choosing where to locate, where do you think they will set up shop? Is this a new problem, or an old one? Consider *Quik Payday, Inc. v. Stork*, 549 F.3d 1302 (10th Cir. 2008), in which an online lender located in Utah challenged a Kansas statute that

---

[*] The CAN-SPAM Act is discussed further in Section 5.C.

capped payday-loan interest rates at 36%. The lender argued that the loans were "made" in Utah, but the court disagreed. Where is a loan? In a pre-Internet age, how hard or easy would it have been for Quik Payday to make loans to Kansas residents from its offices in Utah?

4. The Dormant Commerce Clause limits states' authority over the Internet. Why is there no similar limit on countries' authority over the Internet?

OVERSTOCK.COM V. NEW YORK STATE DEPT. OF TAXATION AND FINANCE

20 N.Y.3d 586 (2013)

Lippman, Chief Judge:

Plaintiffs challenge Tax Law § 1101(b)(8)(vi) (the Internet tax), alleging that it is unconstitutional on its face because it violates the Commerce Clause by subjecting online retailers, without a physical presence in the state, to New York sales and compensating use taxes. ...

I.

Plaintiff Amazon.com, LLC is a limited liability company formed in Delaware; Amazon Services LLC is a limited liability company formed in Nevada (collectively Amazon). Its principal corporate offices are located in the State of Washington. Amazon is strictly an online retailer – selling its merchandise solely through the Internet – and represents that it does not maintain any offices or property in New York.

Amazon offers an "Associates Program" through which third parties agree to place links on their own websites that, when clicked, direct users to Amazon's website. The Associates are compensated on a commission basis. They receive a percentage of the revenue from sales generated when a customer clicks on the Associate's link and completes a purchase from the Amazon site. The operating agreement governing this arrangement states that the Associates are independent contractors and that there is no employment relationship between the parties. Thousands of entities enrolled in the Associates Program have provided a New York address in connection with their applications. ...

[Overstock's Affiliates program was similar, except that Overstock suspended it for New York residents shortly after the enactment of the tax.]

In April 2008, the legislature amended the Tax Law to include the subparagraph at issue here. In connection with the statutory definition of "vendor," the Internet tax provides that

> "a person making sales of tangible personal property or services taxable under this article ('seller') shall be presumed to be soliciting business through an independent contractor or other representative if the seller enters into an agreement with a resident of this state under which the resident, for a commission or other consideration, directly or indirectly refers potential customers, whether by a link on an internet website or otherwise, to the seller, if the cumulative gross receipts from sales by the seller to customers in the state who are referred to the seller by all residents with this type of an agreement with the seller is in excess of ten thousand dollars during the preceding four quarterly periods." N.Y. Tax L. § 1101(b)(8)(vi). ...

Amazon commenced this action on April 25, 2008, seeking a judgment declaring that the statute was unconstitutional both on its face and as applied. ...

II.

Having elected to forgo their as-applied challenges, plaintiffs now confront the substantial hurdle of demonstrating that the Internet tax is unconstitutional on its face. It is well settled that facial constitutional challenges are disfavored. Legislative enactments enjoy a strong presumption of constitutionality and parties challenging a duly enacted statute face the initial burden of demonstrating the statute's invalidity beyond a reasonable doubt. Moreover, courts must avoid, if possible, interpreting a presumptively valid statute in a way that will needlessly render it unconstitutional. ...

The dormant Commerce Clause has been interpreted to prohibit states from imposing an undue tax burden on interstate commerce, *see Matter of Orvis Co. v. Tax Appeals Trib. of State of N.Y.*, 86 N.Y.2d 165 (1995). However, in the absence of an improper burden, entities participating in interstate commerce will not be excused from the obligation to pay their fair share of state taxes. To that end, a state tax impacting the Commerce Clause will be upheld [1] when the tax is applied to an activity with a substantial nexus with the taxing State, [2] is fairly apportioned, [3] does not discriminate against interstate commerce, and [4] is fairly related to the services provided by the State." The parties agree that the only prong at issue here is whether the statute satisfies the "substantial nexus" test.

In *National Bellas Hess, Inc. v. Department of Revenue of Ill.*, 386 U.S. 753 (1967), the United States Supreme Court held that a use tax could not be imposed on an out-of-state mailorder business that did not have offices, property or sales representatives in Illinois. The Court noted that it had never permitted such a tax where the seller's sole connection with its customers in the forum state was by mail or common carrier. Rather, the Court observed that, if Illinois were permitted to impose that type of tax burden, every other taxing jurisdiction in the country could do the same, which would result in a morass of obligations to local governments.

The Supreme Court confronted a similar issue involving a mail-order business in *Quill Corp. v. North Dakota*, 504 U.S. 298, 314 (1992) and considered whether the emphasis in *Bellas Hess* on physical presence within the state had been rendered obsolete by the Court's shift toward "more flexible balancing analyses" under the Commerce Clause. While allowing that the result might have been different if the issue was being considered for the first time, the Court retained the bright-line presence requirement articulated in *Bellas Hess*, recognizing the benefits provided by a clear rule that established the limits of state taxing authority.

The world has changed dramatically in the last two decades, and it may be that the physical presence test is outdated. An entity may now have a profound impact upon a foreign jurisdiction solely through its virtual projection via the Internet. That question, however, would be for the United States Supreme Court to consider. We are bound, and adjudicate this controversy, under the binding precedents of that Court, the ultimate arbiter of the meaning of the Commerce Clause.

Subsequent to *Quill*, we further explained that, although an in-state physical presence is necessary, it need not be substantial. Rather, it must be demonstrably more than a "slightest presence." *Orvis*. The presence requirement will be satisfied if economic activities are performed in New York by the seller's employees or on its behalf.

There are clearly parallels between a mail-order business and an online retailer – both are able to conduct their operations without maintaining a physical presence in a particular state. Indeed, physical presence is not typically associated with the Internet in that many websites are designed to reach a national or even a global audience from a single server whose location is of minimal import. However, through this statute, the legislature has attached significance to the physical presence of a resident website owner. The decision to do so recognizes that, even in the Internet world, many websites are geared toward predominantly local audiences – including, for instance, radio stations, religious institutions and schools – such that the physical presence of the website owner becomes relevant to Commerce Clause analysis. Indeed, the Appellate Division record in this case contains examples of such websites urging their local constituents to support them by making purchases through their Amazon links. Essentially, through these types of affiliation agreements, a vendor is deemed to have established an in-state sales force.

Viewed in this manner the statute plainly satisfies the substantial nexus requirement. Active, in-state solicitation that produces a significant amount of revenue qualifies as "demonstrably more than a 'slightest presence'" under *Orvis*. Although it is not a dispositive factor, it also merits notice that vendors are not required to pay these taxes out-of-pocket. Rather, they are collecting taxes that are unquestionably due, which are exceedingly difficult to collect from the individual purchasers themselves, and as to which there is no risk of multiple taxation.

Clearly, the statutory language allows for a range of possible types of compensation ("commission or other consideration"), which would include flat fee arrangements. However, no one disputes that a substantial nexus would be lacking if New York residents were merely engaged to post passive advertisements on their websites. The bottom line is that if a vendor is paying New York residents to actively solicit business in this state, there is no reason why that vendor should not shoulder the appropriate tax burden. We will not strain to invalidate this statute where plaintiffs have not met their burden of establishing that it is facially invalid. ...

Smith, Judge, dissenting: ...

Our task here is to decide whether certain New York-based websites – Overstock's "Affiliates" and Amazon's "Associates" – are the equivalent of sales agents, soliciting business for Overstock and Amazon, or are only media in which Overstock and Amazon advertise their products. I think they are the latter.

The Overstock and Amazon links that appear on websites owned by New York proprietors serve essentially the same function as advertising that a more traditional out-of-state retailer might place in local newspapers. The websites are not soliciting customers for Overstock and Amazon in the fashion of a local sales agent. Of course the website owners solicit business for themselves; they encourage people to visit their websites, just as a newspaper owner would seek to boost circulation. But there is no basis for inferring that they are actively soliciting for the out-of-state retailers. ...

It was no doubt true before the Internet existed that advertising was usually sold for a flat fee, while sales agents usually worked on commission, but that has changed. When an advertisement takes the form of a link on a website, it is easy, as well as efficient, for the advertiser to compensate the website on the basis of results. But the link is still only an ad. It seems quite unlikely, and the record contains no evidence, that compensation "based on the volume of completed sales" is an unusual way of charging for web advertising, or that such compensation is primarily associated with active solicitation on the seller's behalf by the website owner. ...

I would therefore hold that the statute challenged in this litigation is invalid under the Commerce Clause.

QUESTIONS

1. Is it fair that having Associates in New York subjects Amazon to tax on all its sales to New York residents, not just sales initiated by clicking a link from an Associate's site? How fair would it be for Amazon *not* to pay New York taxes, given that bookstores in New York City must pay them? If unfairness to bricks-and-mortar businesses is the concern, though, why should having Associates make a difference? If Amazon suspends its Associates program, is it now off the hook? Does *Overstock* create precisely the wrong incentive for online merchants?

2. One argument for taxing Amazon is that it ships physical books into New York. But what if it were only selling ebooks?

3. Sales tax rules can be surprisingly intricate. There are nearly 10,000 taxing jurisdictions (states, counties, and cities) in the United States, with their own rates and definitions. In some states, for example, an item is taxable "candy" unless it contains wheat, in which case it is it is untaxed food – so a Snickers is taxable but a Kit-Kat isn't. New York, however, also considers "how the product is labeled, packaged, advertised, displayed, and sold," so that maple sugar in the shape of a maple leaf could be either candy or food, depending on how it is described to customers. Does this explain some of the hostility online merchants have towards collecting sales taxes? Is it justified? Are there ways to reduce the complexity of calculating and collecting sales taxes without impinging on states' ability to set their own tax policies?

4. The Dormant Commerce Clause is a default rule; Congress is free to alter it. In the summer of 2013, the Senate passed the Marketplace Fairness Act, which would explicitly authorize states to collect sales tax from online merchants with total sales of $1 million or more. Is this a good idea?

DIPLOMATIC MISSION PROBLEM

You are on the staff of the United States Diplomatic Mission to Spain. The Ambassador has called a meeting to discuss the Mission's response to a potential diplomatic incident. Earlier today, Rebecca Zuckerman, the chief privacy officer for MagnaVideo, a United States-based website for users to upload, share, and comment on videos, was arrested in Madrid. She had been on her way to give a speech when a group of Spanish police served her with charging papers for criminal defamation and invasion of privacy. An autistic boy had been taunted by his classmates in a Spanish elementary school, who filmed the abuse with a camera-phone and posted the video to MagnaVideo. The video remained on MagnaVideo for approximately two months; several other users posted comments beneath it expressing shock and disgust. Eventually, an advocacy group on behalf of sufferers of Down syndrome and other developmental disorders complained to Magna-Video, and the video was removed. The prosecutor's theory of the case is that MagnaVideo was negligent in not removing the video more quickly. It seeks to hold MagnaVideo corporate officers, including Zuckerman, criminally liable, with possible prison sentences of up to one year. Under Spanish law, first-time offenders sentenced to one year or less are given the equivalent of a suspended sentence, rather than serving any actual prison time.

In ninety minutes, the Ambassador wants to release a public statement on Zuckerman's arrest and the United States's reaction to it. Before then, she needs to call her counterpart inside the Spanish diplomatic service to discuss the matter. She'll also need to field questions from MagnaVideo, and send a diplomatic cable back to the State Department in the U.S. discussing the implications for United States foreign policy. In the Ambassador's personal view, Zuckerman is an upstanding United States citizen who has done absolutely nothing wrong. Give her your advice on what the United States's diplomatic position should be about the arrest.

C. Enforcement

The previous section considered the problem of conflicting local laws. But just because a court in country A is willing to declare something illegal doesn't mean it will be able to force a defendant in country B to stop. This section considers the legal and practical tools available to countries to coerce foreign Internet users into complying with their laws. We start with the recognition of judgments (in civil cases) and the extradition of defendants (in criminal cases), both of which require the cooperation of country B. Then we consider more unilateral measures open to country A even if country B objects, including worldwide injunctions and brute force.

SPEECH ACT
[SECURING THE PROTECTION OF OUR ENDURING AND ESTABLISHED CONSTITUTIONAL HERITAGE ACT, 2010]
Title 28, United States Code

§ 4102 – *Recognition of foreign defamation judgments*

  (a) *FIRST AMENDMENT CONSIDERATIONS*. –

    (1) *IN GENERAL*. – Notwithstanding any other provision of Federal or State law, a domestic court shall not recognize or enforce a foreign judgment for defamation unless the domestic court determines that –

      (A) the defamation law applied in the foreign court's adjudication provided at least as much protection for freedom of speech and press in that case as would be provided by the first amendment to the Constitution of the United States and by the constitution and law of the State in which the domestic court is located; or

      (B) even if the defamation law applied in the foreign court's adjudication did not provide as much protection for freedom of speech and press as the first amendment to the Constitution of the United States and the constitution and law of the State, the party opposing recognition or enforcement of that foreign judgment would have been found liable for defamation by a domestic court applying the first amendment to the Constitution of the United States and the constitution and law of the State in which the domestic court is located. ...

  (b) *JURISDICTIONAL CONSIDERATIONS* –

    (1) *IN GENERAL*. – Notwithstanding any other provision of Federal or State law, a domestic court shall not recognize or enforce a foreign

judgment for defamation unless the domestic court determines that the exercise of personal jurisdiction by the foreign court comported with the due process requirements that are imposed on domestic courts by the Constitution of the United States. ...

§ 4104 – *Declaratory judgments*

(a) *CAUSE OF ACTION.* –

(1) *IN GENERAL.* – Any United States person against whom a foreign judgment is entered on the basis of the content of any writing, utterance, or other speech by that person that has been published, may bring an action in district court, under section 2201(a), for a declaration that the foreign judgment is repugnant to the Constitution or laws of the United States. For the purposes of this paragraph, a judgment is repugnant to the Constitution or laws of the United States if it would not be enforceable under section 4102 ...

QUESTIONS

1. What are the consequences of the judgment in *Mahfouz* for Ehrenfeld in a world without the SPEECH Act? With it? Could the *Mahfouz* plaintiffs collect on their judgment in the United States? Would you advise Ehrenfeld to travel to London?

2. What result if the initial judgment had been rendered in a state court in Florida and the plaintiff now seeks to enforce it in a federal court in California?

3. In light of the SPEECH Act, is the United States imposing its policies on the world? Without it, would the United Kingdom be imposing its policies on the world? How does the Internet exacerbate the conflict between those policies?

4. How does adding enforcement of judgments into the conflict-of-laws picture change matters? Does the choice between universal censorship and universal permissiveness on the Internet seem as stark as it did after *Gutnick*? Do you think that case-by-case ad hoc decisions about whether countries' courts will enforce foreign judgments will strike an appropriate balance between different national and individual interests?

NOTE ON EXTRADITION

Extradition is a loose analogue to civil recognition: one state arrests a defendant and hands him over for trial in another state. Domestically, extradition is governed by the Extradition Clause:

A person charged in any state with treason, felony, or other crime, who shall flee from justice, and be found in another state, shall on demand of the executive authority of the state from which he fled, be delivered up, to be removed to the state having jurisdiction of the crime.

U.S. CONST. art. IV, § 2, cl. 2. Internationally, extradition is generally a matter for bilateral treaties between nations in which they set out which classes of defendants they will extradite to each other. The usual rule is *dual criminality*: a defendant may not be extradited unless his alleged conduct is a crime under the laws of both nations. Procedurally, the defendant receives a hearing in the extraditing nation, and a full trial in the state to which he is extradited.

The highest-profile extradition cases in Internet law have involved United States copyright laws. The typical defendant allegedly acts in his home country in ways that facilitate infringement by others inside the United States. For example, Kim Dotcom ran the file-storage website MegaUpload from New Zealand. In a coordinated raid in January 2012, the United States Department of Justice shut down MegaUpload's servers in the United States and New Zealand authorities arrested Mr. Dotcom in New Zealand. As of mid-2017, the extradition proceedings are still ongoing. Other notable targets of potential U.S. extradition attempts include Edward Snowden (of the NSA leak) and Julian Assange (of WikiLeaks).

QUESTION

Does the availability of extradition extend countries' legal reach? How does it affect the global nature of the Internet?

GOOGLE INC. V. EQUUSTEK SOLUTIONS INC.
Supreme Court of Canada
2017 SCC 34

Abella, Justice:

1. The issue in this appeal is whether Google can be ordered, pending a trial, to globally de-index the websites of a company which, in breach of several court orders, is using those websites to unlawfully sell the intellectual property of another company. ...

BACKGROUND

2. Equustek Solutions Inc. is a small technology company in British Columbia. It manufactures networking devices that allow complex industrial equipment made by one manufacturer to communicate with complex industrial equipment made by another manufacturer.

3. The underlying action between Equustek and the Datalink defendants (Morgan Jack, Datalink Technology Gateways Inc., and Datalink Technologies Gateways LLC – "Datalink") was launched by Equustek on April 12, 2011. It claimed that Datalink, while acting as a distributor of Equustek's products, began to re-label one of the products and pass it off as its own. Datalink also acquired confidential information and trade secrets belonging to Equustek, using them to design and manufacture a competing product, the GW1000. [The court granted an injunction requiring Equustek to return documentation, refrain from referring to Equustek on its website, and post a statement that it was no longer an Equustek distributor.] ...

7. Datalink abandoned the proceedings and left the jurisdiction without producing any documents or complying with any of the orders.

8. On July 26, 2012, Punnett J. granted a *Mareva* injunction freezing Datalink's worldwide assets, including its entire product inventory. He found that Datalink had incorporated "a myriad of shell corporations in different jurisdictions", continued to sell the impugned product, reduced prices to attract more customers, and was offering additional services that Equustek claimed disclosed more of its trade secrets. [Another and even broader injunction followed.] ...

10. On September 26, 2012, Equustek brought an application to have Datalink and its principal, Morgan Jack, found in contempt. No one appeared on be-

half of Datalink. Groves J. issued a warrant for Morgan Jack's arrest. It remains outstanding.

11.   Despite the court orders prohibiting the sale of inventory and the use of Equustek's intellectual property, Datalink continues to carry on its business from an unknown location, selling its impugned product on its websites to customers all over the world.

12.   Not knowing where Datalink or its suppliers were, and finding itself unable to have the websites removed by the websites' hosting companies, Equustek approached Google in September 2012 and requested that it de-index the Datalink websites. Google refused. Equustek then brought court proceedings seeking an order requiring Google to do so.

13.   When it was served with the application materials, Google asked Equustek to obtain a court order prohibiting Datalink from carrying on business on the Internet. Google told Equustek it would comply with such an order by removing specific webpages. Pursuant to its internal policy, Google only voluntarily de-indexes individual webpages, not entire websites. Equustek agreed to try this approach.

14.   On December 13, 2012, Equustek appeared in court with Google. An injunction was issued by Tindale J. ordering Datalink to "cease operating or carrying on business through any website". Between December 2012 and January 2013, Google advised Equustek that it had de-indexed 345 specific webpages associated with Datalink. It did not, however, de-index *all* of the Datalink websites.

15.   Equustek soon discovered that de-indexing webpages but not entire websites was ineffective since Datalink simply moved the objectionable content to new pages within its websites, circumventing the court orders.

16.   Google had limited the de-indexing to those searches that were conducted on google.ca. Google's search engine operates through dedicated websites all over the world. The Internet search services are free, but Google earns money by selling advertising space on the webpages that display search results. Internet users with Canadian Internet Protocol addresses are directed to "google.ca" when performing online searches. But users can also access different Google websites directed at other countries by using the specific Uniform Resource Locator, or URL, for those sites. That means that someone in Vancouver, for example, can access the Google search engine as though he or she were in another country simply by typing in that country's Google URL. Potential Canadian customers could, as a result, find Datalink's websites even if they were blocked on google.ca. Given that the majority of the sales of Datalink's GW1000 were to purchasers outside of Canada, Google's de-indexing did not have the necessary protective effect.

17.   Equustek therefore sought an interlocutory injunction to enjoin Google from displaying any part of the Datalink websites on any of its search results worldwide. Fenlon J. granted the order. The operative part states:

> Within 14 days of the date of this order, Google Inc. is to cease indexing or referencing in search results on its internet search engines the [Datalink] websites ..., including all of the subpages and subdirectories of the listed websites, *until the conclusion of*

> *the trial of this action or further order of this court.* [Emphasis added]

18. Fenlon J. noted that Google controls between 70-75 percent of the global searches on the Internet and that Datalink's ability to sell its counterfeit product is, in large part, contingent on customers being able to locate its websites through the use of Google's search engine. Only by preventing potential customers from accessing the Datalink websites, could Equustek be protected. Otherwise, Datalink would be able to continue selling its product online and the damages Equustek would suffer would not be recoverable at the end of the lawsuit.

19. Fenlon J. concluded that this irreparable harm was being facilitated through Google's search engine; that Equustek had no alternative but to require Google to de-index the websites; that Google would not be inconvenienced; and that, for the order to be effective, the Datalink websites had to be prevented from being displayed on all of Google's search results, not just google.ca. As she said:

    > On the record before me it appears that to be effective, even within Canada, Google must block search results on all of its websites. Furthermore, [Datalink's] sales originate primarily in other countries, so the Court's process cannot be protected unless the injunction ensures that searchers from any jurisdiction do not find [Datalink's] websites.

20. The Court of Appeal of British Columbia dismissed Google's appeal. Groberman J.A. accepted Fenlon J.'s conclusion that she had *in personam* jurisdiction over Google and could therefore make an order with extraterritorial effect. He also agreed that courts of inherent jurisdiction could grant equitable relief against non-parties. Since ordering an interlocutory injunction against Google was the only practical way to prevent Datalink from flouting the court's several orders, and since there were no identifiable countervailing comity or freedom of expression concerns that would prevent such an order from being granted, he upheld the interlocutory injunction.

21. For the following reasons, I agree with Fenlon J. and Groberman J.A. that the test for granting an interlocutory injunction against Google has been met in this case.

ANALYSIS ...

23. Injunctions are equitable remedies. The powers of courts with equitable jurisdiction to grant injunctions are, subject to any relevant statutory restrictions, unlimited Robert Sharpe notes that "[t]he injunction is a flexible and drastic remedy. Injunctions are not restricted to any area of substantive law and are readily enforceable through the court's contempt power." (*Injunctions and Specific Performance* (loose-leaf ed.), at para. 2.10) ...

25. *RJR—MacDonald Inc. v. Canada (Attorney General)*, [1994] 1 S.C.R. 311, sets out a three-part test for determining whether a court should exercise its discretion to grant an interlocutory injunction: is there a serious issue to be tried; would the person applying for the injunction suffer irreparable harm if the injunction were not granted; and is the balance of convenience in favour of granting the interlocutory injunction or denying it. The fundamental question is whether the granting of an injunction is just and equi-

table in all of the circumstances of the case. This will necessarily be context-specific.

26. Google does not dispute that there is a serious claim. Nor does it dispute that Equustek is suffering irreparable harm as a result of Datalink's ongoing sale of the GW1000 through the Internet. And it acknowledges, as Fenlon J. found, that it inadvertently facilitates the harm through its search engine which leads purchasers directly to the Datalink websites.

27. Google argues, however, that the injunction issued against it is not necessary to prevent that irreparable harm, and that it is not effective in so doing. ... As for the balance of convenience, it challenges the propriety and necessity of the extraterritorial reach of such an order, and raises freedom of expression concerns that it says should have tipped the balance against granting the order. These arguments go both to whether the Supreme Court of British Columbia had jurisdiction to grant the injunction and whether, if it did, it was just and equitable to do so in this case. ...

37. The British Columbia courts in these proceedings concluded that because Google carried on business in the province through its advertising and search operations, this was sufficient to establish the existence of *in personam* and territorial jurisdiction. Google does not challenge those findings. It challenges instead the global reach of the resulting order. Google suggests that if any injunction is to be granted, it should be limited to Canada (or google.ca) alone.

38. When a court has *in personam* jurisdiction, and where it is necessary to ensure the injunction's effectiveness, it can grant an injunction enjoining that person's conduct anywhere in the world. ...

40. Fenlon J. explained why Equustek's request that the order have worldwide effect was necessary as follows:

> The majority of GW1000 sales occur outside Canada. Thus, quite apart from the practical problem of endless website iterations, the option Google proposes is not equivalent to the order now sought which would compel Google to remove the [Datalink] websites from all search results generated by any of Google's websites worldwide. I therefore conclude that [Equustek does] not have an out-of-court remedy available to [it]. ... To be effective, even within Canada, Google must block search results on all of its websites.

As a result, to ensure that Google did not facilitate Datalink's breach of court orders whose purposes were to prevent irreparable harm to Equustek, she concluded that the injunction had to have worldwide effect.

41. I agree. The problem in this case is occurring online and globally. The Internet has no borders — its natural habitat is global. The only way to ensure that the interlocutory injunction attained its objective was to have it apply where Google operates — globally. As Fenlon J. found, the majority of Datalink's sales take place outside Canada. If the injunction were restricted to Canada alone or to google.ca, as Google suggests it should have been, the remedy would be deprived of its intended ability to prevent irreparable harm. Purchasers outside Canada could easily continue purchasing from Datalink's websites, and Canadian purchasers could easily find Datalink's

websites even if those websites were de-indexed on google.ca. Google would still be facilitating Datalink's breach of the court's order which had prohibited it from carrying on business on the Internet. There is no equity in ordering an interlocutory injunction which has no realistic prospect of preventing irreparable harm.

42.   The interlocutory injunction in this case is necessary to prevent the irreparable harm that flows from Datalink carrying on business on the Internet, a business which would be commercially impossible without Google's facilitation. The order targets Datalink's websites — the list of which has been updated as Datalink has sought to thwart the injunction — and prevents them from being displayed where they do the most harm: on Google's global search results.

43.   Nor does the injunction's worldwide effect tip the balance of convenience in Google's favour. The order does not require that Google take any steps around the world, it requires it to take steps only where its search engine is controlled. This is something Google has acknowledged it can do — and does — with relative ease. There is therefore no harm to Google which can be placed on its "inconvenience" scale arising from the global reach of the order.

44.   Google's argument that a global injunction violates international comity because it is possible that the order could not have been obtained in a foreign jurisdiction, or that to comply with it would result in Google violating the laws of that jurisdiction is, with respect, theoretical. As Fenlon J. noted, "Google acknowledges that most countries will likely recognize intellectual property rights and view the selling of pirated products as a legal wrong."

45.   And while it is always important to pay respectful attention to freedom of expression concerns, particularly when dealing with the core values of another country, I do not see freedom of expression issues being engaged in any way that tips the balance of convenience towards Google in this case. As Groberman J.A. concluded:

> In the case before us, there is no realistic assertion that the judge's order will offend the sensibilities of any other nation. It has not been suggested that the order prohibiting the defendants from advertising wares that violate the intellectual property rights of the plaintiffs offends the core values of any nation. The order made against Google is a very limited ancillary order designed to ensure that the plaintiffs' core rights are respected.
>
> ... the order in this case is an interlocutory one, and one that can be varied by the court. In the unlikely event that any jurisdiction finds the order offensive to its core values, an application could be made to the court to modify the order so as to avoid the problem.

46.   If Google has evidence that complying with such an injunction would require it to violate the laws of another jurisdiction, including interfering with freedom of expression, it is always free to apply to the British Columbia courts to vary the interlocutory order accordingly. To date, Google has made no such application.

47.   In the absence of an evidentiary foundation, and given Google's right to seek a rectifying order, it hardly seems equitable to deny Equustek the extraterri-

torial scope it needs to make the remedy effective, or even to put the onus on it to demonstrate, country by country, where such an order is legally permissible. We are dealing with the Internet after all, and the balance of convenience test has to take full account of its inevitable extraterritorial reach when injunctive relief is being sought against an entity like Google.

48. This is not an order to remove speech that, on its face, engages freedom of expression values, it is an order to de-index websites that are in violation of several court orders. We have not, to date, accepted that freedom of expression requires the facilitation of the unlawful sale of goods.

49. And I have trouble seeing how this interferes with what Google refers to as its content neutral character. The injunction does not require Google to monitor content on the Internet, nor is it a finding of any sort of liability against Google for facilitating access to the impugned websites. As for the balance of convenience, the only obligation the interlocutory injunction creates is for Google to de-index the Datalink websites. The order is, as Fenlon J. observed, "only a slight expansion on the removal of individual URLs, which Google agreed to do voluntarily." ...

50. Google did not suggest that it would be inconvenienced in any material way, or would incur any significant expense, in de-indexing the Datalink websites. It acknowledges, fairly, that it can, and often does, exactly what is being asked of it in this case, that is, alter search results. It does so to avoid generating links to child pornography and websites containing "hate speech". It also complies with notices it receives under the US *Digital Millennium Copyright Act*, Pub. L. No. 105-304, 112 Stat. 2680 (1998) to de-index content from its search results that allegedly infringes copyright, and removes websites that are subject to court orders. ...

52. Datalink and its representatives have ignored all previous court orders made against them, have left British Columbia, and continue to operate their business from unknown locations outside Canada. Equustek has made efforts to locate Datalink with limited success. Datalink is only able to survive — at the expense of Equustek's survival — on Google's search engine which directs potential customers to its websites. In other words, Google is how Datalink has been able to continue harming Equustek in defiance of several court orders.

53. This does not make Google liable for this harm. It does, however, make Google the determinative player in allowing the harm to occur. On balance, therefore, since the interlocutory injunction is the only effective way to mitigate the harm to Equustek pending the resolution of the underlying litigation, the only way, in fact, to preserve Equustek itself pending the resolution of the underlying litigation, and since any countervailing harm to Google is minimal to non-existent, the interlocutory injunction should be upheld.

QUESTIONS

1. Is this the same problem as in *Gutnick*, or has anything changed?

2. Does *Equustek* do an appropriate job of balancing domestic concerns with the interests of other countries and their residents?

3. *Equustek* shows how search engines are a potential point of control for enforcing laws online. Are there others? The Stop Online Piracy Act, introduced in the House in 2011, but dropped by its sponsors in the face of mas-

sive online and offline protests in early 2012, would have increased copyright enforcement by allowing injunctions against search engines, payment networks, advertising platforms, and domain-name servers, requiring them to cut off service to specific identified "foreign infringing sites." What could these entities do to reduce infringement? Are there risks to this kind of enforcement strategy? Why did online activists argue that SOPA would "break the Internet?"

4. Is Google likely to comply with the injunction in *Equustek*? Why or why not? Consider ...

JACK GOLDSMITH AND TIMOTHY WU
DIGITAL BORDERS
LEGAL AFFAIRS (Jan. 2006)

In the 1990s, many pundits and scholars believed that the Internet was eroding the authority of governments. The web's salient features – instant and universal communication, geographical anonymity, and decentralized routing – made it easy for computer users inside a nation to get illegal information from computers outside the nation. American college students could download copyrighted songs from servers in the South Pacific and bet on digital blackjack tables on computers in Antigua. Saudi Arabians could access porn sites in Holland, and Italians could read banned books on web pages hosted in Australia. Nations seemed unable to stop violations of local laws via the Internet.

This conception of the Internet began to crumble in April 2000, when two French antiracism organizations sued Yahoo!, the American Internet portal, in France. The groups charged Yahoo! with hosting Nazi auction sites that were accessible in France and that violated French laws against trafficking in Nazi goods.

At the time, Yahoo! was the entrance point for more Internet users than any other website. Jerry Yang, Yahoo!'s billionaire cofounder, was confident and brash – he and David Filo had chosen the company's name because, according to the company's official history, they "liked the general definition of a yahoo: 'rude, unsophisticated, uncouth.'" Obsessed with expanding the firm's market share, Yang thought governments dumb and speech restrictions dumber still. When Yahoo! received a summons from Judge Jean-Jacques Gomez of Le Tribunal de Grande Instance de Paris, a French trial court, Yang shrugged. Reflecting conventional wisdom, he believed French officials had no authority over a computer in the United States.

And if France could do nothing to stop Yahoo! in the U.S., it also seemed hard for French officials to block access to the Nazi auction sites in their country. Too many Internet communications crossed France's borders for the government to stop and screen each one. The Internet's decentralized routing system carries messages from point to point, even if some connections along the way are blocked, damaged, or destroyed. "The Net treats censorship as a defect, and routes around it," declared John Gilmore, the libertarian Internet activist who cofounded the Electronic Frontier Foundation. To keep out the Nazi pages, it appeared that France would have needed to shut down every single Internet access point within its borders – a seemingly impossible task.

Yahoo!'s arguments were premised on the 1990s vision of a borderless Internet. Half a decade later, this vision is fast being replaced by the reality of an Internet that is splitting apart and reflecting national borders. Far from flattening the world, the Internet is in many ways conforming to local conditions. The result is an Internet that is increasingly separated by walls of law, language, and filters. This bordered Internet reflects top-down pressures from governments like France that are imposing national laws on the Internet within their borders. But it also reflects bottom-up pressures from individuals in different places who demand an Internet that corresponds to their preferences, and from the web page operators and other content providers who shape their Internet experience to satisfy these demands. ...

Judge Gomez ruled preliminarily in May 2000 that Yahoo!'s U.S. websites violated French law, and he ordered the company "to take all necessary measures to dissuade and make impossible" visits by French web surfers to the illegal Yahoo! Nazi auction sites on yahoo.com. Jerry Yang was dismissive. "We are not going to change the content of our sites in the United States just because someone in France is asking us to do so," he said. "Asking us to filter access to our sites according to the nationality of web surfers is very naïve."

Yang's defiance reflected turn-of-the-century assumptions about the Internet's architecture. Internet protocol addresses (each computer's Internet ID), Internet domain names (such as mcdonalds.com or cnn.com), and e-mail addresses were not designed to indicate the geographical location of computers on the Net. These architectural "facts" meant that most users of 1990s Internet technology did not know where their e-mail messages and web pages were being viewed, and thus what laws in which nations they might be violating. Yahoo! said that it didn't know where its users were, and which laws it should comply with.

Worse, if France could govern Yahoo! in America, every other nation could as well. And this raised the worrying possibility that Internet firms and users, confronted with a bevy of conflicting national laws, might begin to comply with the strictest among them in order to avoid legal jeopardy. "We now risk a race to the bottom," predicted Alan Davidson of the Center for Democracy and Technology, in which "the most restrictive rules about Internet content – influenced by any country – could have an impact on people around the world."

The specter of conflicting national laws applying to every Internet transaction might have given Yahoo! the edge at trial, had it not been for the unlikely intervention of Cyril Houri, a Frenchman then working in New York's Silicon Alley. On a trip home to Paris in 1999, Houri made a discovery that upended his career as a software engineer, not to mention conventional thinking about the Internet. Staying in his parents' apartment, he turned on his laptop after dinner to check his e-mail. As the computer came on, Houri saw the portal he was used to seeing in New York. Blinking cheerfully at the top of his screen was a banner advertisement for an American flower delivery service, accompanied by a 1-800-flowers number usable only in the U.S.

In that moment, Houri realized that the Internet did not point inexorably toward the flattening of frontiers. He saw that, to the contrary, a borderless flower-delivery service made no sense at all. And he grasped that people would pay for software that took the boundaries of the real world and re-created them on the Internet, so that flower deliverers and a thousand other e-tailers would know where their customers were. There would be big money, he thought, in a technology that prevented people outside America's borders from seeing the American ad, and that substituted a French ad for a French audience and a German ad for a German one. The same technology would allow news and entertainment sites to segment their content according to the whereabouts of their audiences. All it would take was a program to pinpoint the physical location of users. So Houri founded a dot-com, Infosplit, devoted to doing just that.

Ever since the Net became commercialized in the mid-1990s, Internet firms had tried, with varying degrees of success, to discover the geographical identity of their customers. The web's omnipresent "choose a country" links are one way. Another is to ask users to type in an area code or send geographical identification (such as a driver's license) by fax or mail before allowing access to a page. Yet another is to check the address associated with a credit card as proof of geographical identification. But these techniques are sometimes unreliable and, worse, they're time-consuming. "The entire point of the Web is to bring you information simply and quickly," thought Sanjay Parekh, the founder of the geo-ID firm Digital Envoy, during an "a-ha!" experience similar to Houri's. "Why do I have to scroll through dozens of countries before accessing the site? Surely there has to be a way for [the site] to recognize where I am."

In the past decade, Infosplit, Digital Envoy, and half a dozen other firms set out to make geographical identification on the Net easy, reliable, and invisible. Instead of requiring Net users to take steps to reveal or prove their location, they devised a way to identify a user's location using the very features of Internet architecture that supposedly defied geography.

IP addresses (like "192.168.0.55") don't readily reveal a computer user's physical location. But a savvy user can determine that location by sending "tracing" packets over the Internet. These packets report a list of computers through which they travel, much as a car driving along a network of highways collects a receipt at each toll. Just as a car's origin can be determined by looking at these receipts, computers can examine the path of these packets to figure out the computers closest to the originator and recipient of any communication of the Net. This information can then be cross-checked against other IP databases that offer different clues about the geographical location of almost every computer connected to the Internet. When the databases are cross-referenced and analyzed, the location of Internet users can be determined with over 99 percent accuracy at the country level.

Internet geo-identification services are still nascent, but they are starting to have effects on e-commerce. Online identity theft in the U.S. causes firms and consumers to lose billions of dollars each year. Geo-ID is helping to solve this problem by identifying when stolen credit card numbers are used on the Net from locations like Russia, the home of many such scams. It is also improving Internet advertising, as Houri and Parekh envisioned, by making it easier to display ads geared to local conditions. And it is speeding the delivery of electronic data, allowing firms to deliver content from the closest "cache" website without having to ask the consumer where he is.

Finally, and potentially most important, these technologies are starting to enable the geographical zoning of entertainment. An important hurdle to the distribution of entertainment on the Net has been that certain material cannot lawfully be viewed in certain places. Geo-ID technologies can help to solve this problem by ensuring that online movies, web gambling sites, software programs, and other digital products do not enter countries where they are illegal. In other words, the software designed to respond to the local demands of consumers can also be used to help ensure compliance with different laws in different places.

Following Judge Gomez's May 2000 preliminary ruling, Cyril Houri contacted the plaintiff's lawyer, Stephane Lilti, and told him that his software could identify and screen Internet content on the basis of its geographical source. Houri was invited to Paris where he showed Lilti how his software worked. When the plaintiff's legal team saw what it reported, they were astonished. Yahoo!'s servers, which the firm had claimed were protected by the First Amendment to the U.S. Constitution, were actually located on a website in Stockholm. Yahoo! had placed a constantly updated "mirror" copy of its U.S. site in Sweden to speed access to the site in Europe.

When the trial resumed in July 2000, Yahoo!'s lawyers reiterated that it was impossible to identify and filter out French visitors to the firm's U.S.-based websites. Lilti responded by explaining how Houri's geo-location technology showed that Yahoo! auctions in France were not coming from servers in the U.S. Suddenly, the assumption that every web page was equally accessible to every computer user everywhere in the world seemed wrong. If Yahoo! could direct content to French users from Swedish servers, it could potentially identify users by geography and, if it liked, it could screen them out.

After receiving additional expert testimony about the feasibility of geographical screening, Gomez issued a final decision in November 2000, reaffirming that Yahoo! had violated French law by allowing Nazi goods to appear for sale on web pages in France. Gomez determined that the French court had power over Yahoo! and its servers because the company had taken conscious steps to direct the prohibited Nazi auction pages into France. He pointed out that Yahoo! greeted French visitors to its U.S. website with French-language advertisements. This showed that Yahoo! was tailoring content for France and that, to some extent, it could identify and screen users by geography. Acknowledging that 100 percent blocking was impossible, the court ordered Yahoo! to make a reasonable "best effort" to block French users.

At first, Yahoo! threatened to ignore Gomez's decision. But the company had a problem: its assets in France, including income from its French subsidiary, were at risk of seizure. In January 2001, Yahoo! abruptly surrendered. It pulled all Nazi materials from its auction sites, announcing that it would "no longer allow items that are associated with groups which promote or glorify hatred and violence to be listed on any of Yahoo!'s commerce properties." The company claimed that it was motivated by bad publicity from the Nazi auctions and not the French ruling. "Society as a whole has rejected such groups," said a Yahoo! spokesperson. But the timing and threat of French sanctions suggested that Yahoo!'s will had been broken.

QUESTIONS

1. Initially, the *Yahoo!* litigation sounds familiar, pitting United States free-speech values versus French hate-speech laws. Why is it culturally important to France to prohibit trafficking in Nazi memorabilia? Can you think of any material that would be clearly offensive in the United States but considered innocuous in other countries?

2. When Cyril Houri enters the picture and starts talking about geolocation, the story takes a surprising turn. What is geolocation and why does it work? Why did it help persuade Judge Gomez to rule against Yahoo!? What other uses does it have?

3. Why did Yahoo! reverse course and comply with the French orders?

4. How important is the location of Yahoo!'s servers in this story? How important is the location of Yahoo!'s various offices?

5. Goldsmith and Wu argue that the Internet is becoming "bordered" rather than "borderless." What does that mean? How will the Internet in the United States differ from the Internet in France? Have you personally seen examples of the bordered Internet?

6. Does the possibility of geolocation change how you think about the injunction in *Equustek*? Should the injunction there have been limited to searches from Canadian IP addresses? Searches on google.ca?

SEAHAVEN PROBLEM

During the Second World War, Britain constructed a number of anti-aircraft platforms off its coast to provide an additional line of defense against German bombers. One of these platforms, Root Sands, is seven miles from the nearest coastline, which puts it in international waters. It consists of a 120'x50' steel deck, resting on two circular concrete legs, each 24' in diameter. The legs contain seven stories each, and the superstructure on the platform itself contains a living room, kitchen, two bedrooms, and two bathrooms. At the end of the war, the British government abandoned the platform.

In 1967, Douglas Shaftoe, an ex-major in the British army, occupied the Rough Sands tower with his family and declared it an independent country, the Sultanate of Shoreland (with himself as Sultan). The next year, his 14-year-old daughter, Amy, used her father's handgun to fire three shots across the bow of a boat from nearby Harwich harbor that was repairing buoys marking the shipping channel near Shoreland. The next time that Douglas and Amy went ashore to purchase groceries, they were arrested and tried on charges of possessing and using unlicensed firearms. They raised a jurisdictional objection, and the judge dismissed the charges, saying, "Parliament, I think, has not intended the Firearms Act to operate outside of the ordinary territorial limits [i.e. on English land and within three miles of its coast]."

The Shaftoes have been there ever since. Over the years, they have made the place, if not quite opulent, then at least livable, with a diesel generator, furniture, television sets, modern kitchen appliances, and so on. They don't pay taxes, and the British government has given up on trying to collect. In 1978, a group of Germans came to the platform while Douglas was away on business. They convinced Amy to hoist them on-board, saying they had a message from Douglas. It was a trick; they locked Amy in a cabin and seized control of Shoreland. When Douglas found out, he rented a helicopter and successfully retook the platform at shotgun-point. In 1995, Douglas retired and named Amy the new Sultana.

Two programmers, Randall Waterhouse and Avi Halaby, have befriended Amy Shaftoe, and they propose to set up a "data haven" on Shoreland, to be named SeaHaven. The idea is that material that other countries make illegal can safely be stored on computers on Shoreland, which will provide them with a legal umbrella. That is, Shoreland will redraft its legal code to make almost any use of the Internet legal. Some examples of possible customers:

• A company that wants to keep its corporate records subpoena-proof can simply store them on Shoreland using SeaHaven.

- Companies offering cheap downloads of music and movies can set up shop with SeaHaven, even if those downloads would be illegal under the copyright law of other countries.
- Many Islamic countries have strict laws against pornography. SeaHaven will host it.
- Falun Gong sites and the government-in-exile of Tibet are deeply unpopular with Chinese authorities. SeaHaven will give them an online home.
- Online gambling!

The only three no-nos under SeaHaven's planned terms of service will be child pornography, spam, and hacking. Physical security is also a serious concern. To forestall the possibility that an annoyed country will try to cut off SeaHaven with self-help, the business plan calls for redundant network links: satellite, line-of-sight microwave to Britain, and, eventually, undersea cables. Two on-site security professionals will be on duty at all times, carrying shotguns, tasers, and .50-caliber machine guns. The server rooms in the tower legs will be filled with pure nitrogen gas to reduce the risk of fire and keep unwanted intruders out. In the event that the guards can't fight off any attackers, SeaHaven plans to promise its customers that it will destroy their servers and refund their fees before allowing the machines to be physically seized. Meanwhile, Shoreland plans to apply for United Nations membership and defend its sovereignty in court if necessary.

You represent the Epiphyte Fund, a venture capital firm. Epiphyte's CEO, Hubert Kepler, has asked you to advise whether a proposed $5 million investment in SeaHaven is a good idea. He wants to know, based on your knowledge of Internet law and national jurisdiction, whether the data-haven plan is likely to work. Will it be able to attract customers? Will it be able to deliver on its promises of legal freedom to them? What other risks does SeaHaven face? Should Epiphyte invest?

GAMBLING TREATY PROBLEM

You have been appointed as the rapporteur for an international meeting to discuss the possibility of an international treaty on online gambling. Your job is to facilitate dialogue, identify points of possible consensus, and report on the discussion. You have identified the following countries as key players whose views in the meeting are likely to have significant weight:

- The Cardassian Union, a large and cosmopolitan Western nation with a culture that prizes tradition and order. It allows several forms of gambling, but subjects them to strict regulations to protect players. Gambling in person can take place only in casinos in a few designated cities; casino ownership is carefully supervised to guard against organized-crime influences; casinos must comply with extensive safeguards to prevent gambling addiction. Sports gaming is technically illegal but the government is content to look the other way as long as the wagering is among acquaintances rather than with professional bookmakers. Slot machines are strictly forbidden because of their potentially addictive qualities. Online, the Cardassian Union allows casino operators to offer virtual equivalents to the offline games they offer, with similar regulations. It has not thought much about the international issues involved.
- Ferenginar, an island nation in the Mediterranean, is a small and until recently underdeveloped country. In the 1980s it made a significant move to become a banking and tourism center, with significant success, resulting in

strong IT infrastructure and permissive morals laws. It allows most forms of private gambling, prohibiting only fraud and other conduct directly threatening the integrity of a game. It has slot machines in the airport, video poker machines in most bars, and extensive sports betting networks. Cardassian tourists who enjoy gambling speak of Ferenginar as a good place to visit. It has supported its local companies as they have started offering gambling services worldwide on the Internet.

- Bajor, an East Asian country with a rich but specific history of gambling. Sports betting, particularly on horse and other animal racing, is close to a national obsession. A few table games, like Tongo and Dabo, have devoted followings, but most Western games, like poker and blackjack, are not widely played. A few years ago, a conservative government took office on a national-pride and moral-rectitude platform. It was willing to tolerate existing forms of gambling but draw a hard line against expansion into new media and especially against "foreign" influences. It passed a law forbidding online gambling and requiring domestic financial intermediaries (banks, credit card companies, etc.) to cut off all business with gambling companies.

- The Hadar Dominion, a Middle Eastern country, regards gambling as un-Islamic and strictly prohibits it. Some underground social gambling takes place, but the Dominion police and judiciary are not shy about using long prison terms to punish people who are caught wagering. The government uses the country's Internet filtering infrastructure to block foreign sites that offer gambling and pornography, among other content considered sinful.

Looking over these positions, you doubt that it is possible to achieve substantive harmonization: Ferenginar and the Hadar Dominion are never going to agree on whether gambling should be permissible. But perhaps it's possible to make progress on reducing some of the sources of friction in the system. Can you identify rules under which countries would sometimes enforce or defer to each others' gambling regulations? How much consensus could you get on those rules? How promising are internationally treaties as a solution to the problems of online gambling? As a solution to the problems of online conflicts in general?

D. Personal Jurisdiction and Venue

So far, we have been dealing with what international lawyers would call "legislative" or "prescriptive" jurisdiction: a state's power to make law that binds people doing certain things. But that is only half the story, because the question of what *law* applies in a given case is distinct from the question of what *court* can hear the case. This is the question of "judicial" or "adjudicative" jurisdiction. The two questions are related: the choice of forum can influence the choice of law, and a forum that lacks prescriptive jurisdiction over a party will typically also lack adjudicative jurisdiction. But even when there is no dispute about what law applies, the parties still often care where it will be heard.

In a civil case, there are two conditions for a court to have personal jurisdiction over a party. First, there is the Constitutional Due Process requirement that the party must have sufficient "minimum contacts" with the forum. *Burdick v. Superior Court* is a modern Internet minimum contacts case. Some of the permissible bases of jurisdiction look much the same on the Internet, some do not:

- *General jurisdiction* over any cause of action is available in the state where a person is domiciled or where a corporation is incorporated or has its principal place of business. Everyone still lives somewhere, the Internet notwithstanding.

- *Transient jurisdiction* is available whenever the defendant is properly served with process while physically present in the forum. At most, the Internet makes it easier to dodge local service of process by doing business online.

- *Attachment jurisdiction* over property in the forum raises a few conceptual issues about where precisely intangible online assets like Bitcoins are located, but comparatively few actual cases.

- *Jurisdiction by consent* may be more common if people are more likely to accept a forum's jurisdiction over their online dealings. How many jurisdictions have you consented to be sued in in the last week? How many times have you waived your right to sue in a different jurisdiction?

- *Specific jurisdiction* based on out-of-forum activities that have consequences within the forum is where the rubber meets the road, because the Internet makes these scenarios far more common. *Young* is a specific-jurisdiction case.

Second, the forum must actually have authorized its courts to hear the case. This is the province of state long-arm statutes. Some confer jurisdiction to the full extent of the Due Process Clause; others, like the New York statute discussed in *Penguin Group (USA) Inc. v. American Buddha*, restrict jurisdiction to specific categories of cases.

In a criminal case, the geographical rules are slightly different. The most basic prerequisite is a (very loose) analogue of civil service of process. Because states do not enforce each others' criminal laws, to prosecute someone a state needs to get its hands on him. Sometimes, this is easy. Defendants can be arrested while passing through, or tricked into coming to the jurisdiction and then arrested. In *United States v. Gorshkov*, No. CR00-550C, 2001 WL 1024026 (W.D. Wash. May 23, 2001), for example, the FBI set up a fake company that offered to "hire" the defendant, a hacker based in Russia who had been extorting U.S. companies. He came to Seattle for a meeting, used an FBI-supplied laptop to log in to his home server, and was then immediately arrested. Unwilling defendants can be arrested by another jurisdiction and then extradited (see the Note on Extradition). Defendants can even be kidnapped. In *United States v. Alvarez-Machain*, 504 U.S. 655 (1992), the defendant was wanted for participating in the murder of a DEA agent. The DEA let it be known that it would pay a "pay a reward and expenses in return for the delivery of respondent to the United States." Armed men burst into his medical office in Guadalajara, put a gun to his head, and forced him to board a private plane with them to El Paso. The Supreme Court allowed his prosecution to go forward. More than anything else in law, criminal jurisdiction still turns on raw physical power over a person.

But this is not the only geographic constraint on criminal trials. At the federal level, there are two signifiant Constitutional limits. Article III restricts *venue* (where the trial takes place) in criminal trials to "the state where the said crimes shall have been committed; but when not committed within any state, the trial shall be at such place or places as the Congress may by law have directed." *Auernheimer* explores the problem of determining where an online crime "shall have been committed." The Sixth Amendment also restricts *vicinage* (where the jury pool is drawn from) to "the State and district wherein the crime shall have been committed." Vicinage is less often an issue once proper venue is established. At the state level, the rule that states will not enforce each others' penal laws means that a crime can only be prosecuted in the courts of the state whose legislature created that crime. Many states have their own venue rules, much like the federal ones but with lower geographical stakes.

BURDICK V. SUPERIOR COURT
233 Cal. App. 4th (Ct. App. 2015)

Fybel, Justice:

INTRODUCTION

In this writ proceeding, we address whether, in a lawsuit for defamation, a nonresident defendant is subject to personal jurisdiction in California on the ground that, while in his or her state of residence, the defendant posted (and removed) allegedly defamatory statements about the plaintiff on the defendant's publicly available Facebook page.

We hold that posting defamatory statements about a person on a Facebook page, while knowing that person resides in the forum state, is insufficient in itself to create the minimum contacts necessary to support specific personal jurisdiction in a lawsuit arising out of that posting. Instead, it is necessary that the nonresident defendant not only intentionally post the statements on the Facebook page, but that the defendant expressly aim or specifically direct his or her intentional conduct at the forum, rather than at a plaintiff who lives there. We emphasize the exercise of personal jurisdiction must be based upon forum-related acts that were personally committed by the nonresident defendant, not upon the plaintiff's contacts with the forum or acts committed by codefendants or third parties.

The plaintiffs in this case – John Sanderson and George Taylor (together, Plaintiffs) – sued Douglas Burdick, an Illinois resident, for defamation and other intentional torts, based on an allegedly defamatory posting made by Burdick on his personal Facebook page while he was in Illinois. The respondent court denied Burdick's motion to quash service of summons for lack of personal jurisdiction, and Burdick has challenged that ruling by petition for writ of mandate or prohibition. ...

ALLEGATIONS, JURISDICTIONAL FACTS, AND PROCEDURAL HISTORY
I. Allegations of the Complaint

Plaintiffs filed a verified complaint and a verified first amended complaint (the Complaint), naming as defendants Nerium International, LLC, Nerium Biotechnology, Inc., Nerium SkinCare, Inc., Jeff Olson, and Burdick. The Complaint asserted six causes of action against Burdick: (1) libel per se; (2) slander per se; (3) defamation; (4) intentional infliction of emotional distress; (5) negligent infliction of emotional distress; and (6) invasion of privacy.

The Complaint alleged the following:

Nerium International and Nerium SkinCare are incorporated in Texas, and Nerium Biotechnology is incorporated in Canada. The Nerium Entities are involved in the research, development, advertising, marketing, and sale of a skin care product called NeriumAD, the active ingredient of which is an extract of the nerium oleander plant. The primary purpose of Nerium International is to market and coordinate the sales of NeriumAD through "multi-level marketing," a marketing strategy in which salespersons are compensated not only for the sales they generate, but also for sales generated by other salespersons whom they had recruited.

Olson is the chief executive officer of Nerium International, and Burdick is "another high-level and highly compensated representative of Nerium International and is the company's Corporate Consultant." Plaintiffs are physician-scientists and entrepreneurs. They have, since November 2011, maintained a non-commercial Internet blog Web site known as BareFacedTruth.com, which "discusses science and skin care" and "is dedicated to providing educational material, including information and research, relating to medical-scientific matters that are in the public interest, including skin care science."

In June 2012, Plaintiffs began to question the science behind NeriumAD and published blog entries questioning its safety and efficacy and criticizing Nerium International's multilevel marketing organization. "In response to Plaintiffs' questioning of the science behind NeriumAD and criticisms of the Nerium organization, Defendants engaged in a campaign of harassment and defamation against Plaintiffs to destroy their reputations using false and misleading information." As a precursor to this campaign, Olson conducted a recorded teleconference aired to salespeople (called "Brand Partners"), in which he referred to Plaintiffs as "blatant, jerk liars" and stated, "wait till you see what we have heading your way. It's – actually, I hate to say this, but I'm going to really enjoy the day we put it out there, quite honestly."

In November 2012, Olson recorded and published on Nerium International's Web site a video recording in which he stated that an investigation had "uncovered the fact that the blogger has had 'multiple domestic violence issues.'"

Burdick, as his part of the campaign of harassment, in November 2012, posted on his Facebook page an announcement that "more scandalous information would be revealed regarding the 'Blogging Scorpions.'" The Facebook posting announcement stated that within a short period of time, new information would be posted on "'[w]hy he uses multiple social security numbers' and 'how many times he has been charged with domestic violence.' " Burdick posted those statements on Facebook "in his capacity as Corporate Consultant for Nerium International" and a person reading those statements would reasonably understand they referred to Sanderson or Taylor.

II. Motion to Quash Service of Summons

Burdick filed a motion to quash service of summons (the motion to quash), based on lack of personal jurisdiction. With the motion to quash, Burdick submitted his own declaration stating he is an independent contractor for Paradiselife, Inc., an Illinois corporation with its principal place of business in Illinois, through which he provides consulting services to Nerium International. Burdick declared he has been a resident of Illinois since 1971. He has never lived in California; maintained an office or been employed in California; had a bank account, safe deposit box, or mailing address in California; owned or leased real property in California; had employees in California; been a party to a contract with a person or entity in California; or held any licenses or certifications issued by any governmental agency or unit in California. Burdick declared he posted and later removed the allegedly defamatory Facebook posting from his personal Facebook page while he was in the State of Illinois.

Plaintiffs filed opposition to the motion to quash, which included a declaration (with exhibits) from Sanderson and a declaration from Plaintiffs' counsel. Sanderson declared that Burdick posted defamatory material on his "publicly-available Facebook wall." Among the exhibits attached to Sanderson's declaration was a print copy of the allegedly defamatory Facebook posting made by Burdick. That posting did not mention Sanderson or Taylor by name, but referred to a "Blogging scorpion, liar, terrorist, pretencer, amateur, wanna-be, con artist." The posting then stated:

> BOY DOES THIS 'BLOGGING SCORPION' HAVE A LOT TO HIDE! More to come shortly about the Truth and Facts about this 'Blogging Scorpion', things like:
>
> > Why he lost his medical license (yes we have the documents directly from the Medical Board of California)
> >
> > Why he personally uses multiple social security numbers
> >
> > How many times has he been charged with domestic violence
> >
> > Why he makes medical claims about his product that is not FDA approved (yes we have the video of him making these medical claims publically)
> >
> > And much much more!
>
> Stay tuned as we reveal the 'REAL' truth behind this 'Blogging Scorpion'.

The respondent court issued a minute order denying the motion to quash. After finding that all of Plaintiffs' claims against Burdick arose out of the Facebook posting, the respondent court concluded he was subject to personal jurisdiction under the "effects" test of *Calder v. Jones*, 465 U.S. 783 (1984), and *Pavlovich v. Superior Court*, 29 Cal. 4th 262 (2002).

III. Writ Proceedings

Burdick filed a petition for peremptory writ of mandate/prohibition to challenge the respondent court's order denying his motion to quash service of summons. We summarily denied the writ petition. The California Supreme Court granted Burdick's petition for review and transferred the matter to this court with directions to vacate the order denying mandate and to issue an order to show cause why the relief sought in Burdick's writ petition should not be granted in light of *Walden v. Fiore*, 134 S. Ct. 1115 (2014), which was decided after we denied Burdick's writ petition. This court issued an order to show cause with a briefing schedule. ...

DISCUSSION

I. General Principles of Personal Jurisdiction

California courts may exercise jurisdiction over nonresidents "on any basis not inconsistent with the Constitution of this state or of the United States." (Code Civ. Proc., § 410.10.) The United States Constitution permits a state to exercise jurisdiction over a nonresident defendant if the defendant has sufficient "minimum contacts" with the forum such that "maintenance of the suit does not offend 'traditional notions of fair play and substantial justice.'" *Internat. Shoe Co. v. Washington*, 326 U.S. 310 (1945). Personal jurisdiction may be either general or specific. A nonresident defendant is subject to the forum's general jurisdiction if the defendant's contacts are substantial, continuous and systematic. Plaintiffs have conceded Burdick is not subject to California's general jurisdiction.

The inquiry whether a forum State may assert specific jurisdiction over a nonresident defendant 'focuses on the relationship among the defendant, the forum, and the litigation. A nonresident defendant may be subject to specific jurisdiction if three requirements are met: (1) the defendant has purposefully availed itself of forum benefits with respect to the matter in controversy; (2) the controversy is related to or arises out of the defendant's contacts with the forum; and (3) the exercise of jurisdiction would comport with fair play and substantial justice.

II. May California Exercise Specific Personal Jurisdiction over Burdick?

May specific jurisdiction be exercised over Burdick, an Illinois resident, based on his conduct related to the lawsuit, that is, his posting of the allegedly defamatory statements on his personal Facebook page? When, as in this case, intentional torts are alleged, "[a] forum State's exercise of jurisdiction over an out-of-state intentional tortfeasor must be based on intentional conduct by the defendant that creates the necessary contacts with the forum." *Walden*, 134 S. Ct. at 1123.

A. The Effects Test

1. Calder

The respondent court concluded, and Plaintiffs argue, that Burdick is subject to specific jurisdiction under the effects test. The starting point for understanding the effects test is the United States Supreme Court decision in *Calder*. In that case, Shirley Jones, a well-known actress living in California, brought a libel suit in California against a reporter and an editor for an allegedly defamatory article published in the National Enquirer, a national weekly publication with a circulation of about 600,000 in California. Both the reporter and the editor worked for the National Enquirer at its headquarters in Florida. The reporter and the editor moved to quash service of process on the ground neither had sufficient minimum contacts with California.

The United States Supreme Court held that jurisdiction over the reporter and the editor in California was proper based on the effects of their Florida conduct in California. Those effects were felt in California because, the court explained, "[t]he allegedly libelous story concerned the California activities of a California resident. It impugned the professionalism of an entertainer whose television career was centered in California. The article was drawn from California sources, and the brunt of the harm, in terms both of respondent's emotional distress and the injury to her professional reputation, was suffered in California." *Id.* at 788–89. "In sum," the court concluded, "California is the focal point both of the story and of the harm suffered." *Id.* at 789. The court noted too the intentional acts of the reporter and the editor "were expressly aimed at California" in that they wrote or edited an article "they knew would have a potentially devastating impact upon respondent" and "knew that the brunt of that injury would be felt by respondent in the State in which she lives and works and in which the National Enquirer has its largest circulation." *Id.* at 788–89.

2. "Express Aiming" and *Pavlovich*

Courts have struggled with the import of *Calder* and have not applied the effects test uniformly. Most courts have agreed, nonetheless, that merely asserting that a defendant knew or should have known that his intentional acts would cause harm in the forum state is not enough to establish jurisdiction under the effects test.

To narrow the potentially broad scope of *Calder*, courts have interpreted the effects test as having an express aiming requirement and requiring the plaintiff to show (1) the defendant committed an intentional tort; (2) the plaintiff felt the brunt of the harm caused by that tort in the forum state such that the forum state was the focal point of the plaintiff's injury; and (3) the defendant expressly aimed the tortious conduct at the forum state such that the forum state was the focal point of the tortious activity. To satisfy the third prong, the plaintiff must show the defendant knew that the plaintiff would suffer the brunt of the harm caused by the tortious conduct in the forum, and point to specific activity indicating that the defendant expressly aimed its tortious conduct at the forum.

In *Pavlovich*, the California Supreme Court addressed the meaning of the *Calder* effects test and concluded the test requires "evidence of express aiming or intentional targeting," *Pavlovich*, 29 Cal. 4th at 273, in addition to "the defendant's knowledge that his intentional conduct would cause harm in the forum," *id.* at 271. The plaintiff in *Pavlovich* alleged the defendant had misappropriated trade secrets by posting on a Web site the source code of a program that would allow users to circumvent a system used to encrypt and protect copyrighted materials on DVD's and to enable users to place decrypted materials from DVD's onto computer hard drives or other storage media. The California Supreme Court concluded the defendant, an Indiana resident with no California contacts, was not subject to personal jurisdiction in California because the only evidence in the record suggesting express aiming was the defendant's knowledge his conduct could harm industries centered in California.

3. Effects Test and the Internet-based Defamation

Although *Pavlovich* made "express aiming or intentional targeting" part of California personal jurisdiction law, it was not a defamation case. Courts in other jurisdictions, which have considered *Calder* and the effects test in defamation actions arising out of Internet posts and advertising, have held the mere posting of information or advertisements on an Internet website does not confer nationwide personal jurisdiction. In *Young v. New Haven Advocate*, 315 F.3d 256 (4th Cir. 2002) [a suit against Connecticut newspapers for allegedly defamatory articles about a Virginia prison warden], the court explained:

> When the Internet activity is, as here, the posting of news articles on a website, we ask whether the newspapers manifested an intent to direct their website content – which included certain articles discussing conditions in a Virginia prison – to a Virginia audience. As we recognized in *ALS Scan Inc. v. Digital Service Consultants 293 F.3d 707* (4th Cir. 2002), "a person's act of placing information on the Internet" is not sufficient by itself to "subject that person to personal jurisdiction in each State in which the information is accessed." Otherwise, a "person placing information on the Internet would be subject to personal jurisdiction in every State," and the traditional due process principles governing a State's jurisdiction over persons outside of its borders would be subverted. Thus, the fact that the newspapers' websites could be accessed anywhere, including Virginia, does not by itself demonstrate that the newspapers were intentionally directing their website content to a Virginia audience. Something more than posting and accessibility is needed to "indicate that the newspapers purposefully (albeit electronically) directed their activity in a substantial way to the forum state." The newspapers must, through the Internet postings, manifest an intent to target and focus on Virginia readers.

Other courts have reached the same or a similar conclusion. ...

As summed up in *Gorman v. Jacobs*, 597 F. Supp. 2d 541, 548 (E.D. Pa. 2009): "Exercise of personal jurisdiction would also be proper over defendants who made allegedly defamatory statements on the Internet if the content of the statements themselves are directed into the forum. Simply (a) knowing that the plaintiff is in the forum state, (b) posting negative statements about the plaintiff's forum-related activities, and (c) referring to the forum in one's writing will not suffice to satisfy the *Calder* effects test."

4. *Walden*

Recently, in *Walden*, the United States Supreme Court readdressed the personal jurisdiction analysis for intentional torts. In that case, the plaintiffs, who were residents of California and Nevada, sued a Georgia police officer in federal court in Nevada for an intentional tort based on actions undertaken by the police officer while serving as a deputized Drug Enforcement Administration agent in Georgia. At the Atlanta airport, the police officer had seized cash carried by the plaintiffs while they were in transit from Puerto Rico to Las Vegas. The police officer moved the cash to a secured location, and, at some point, helped to draft an affidavit, which the plaintiffs claimed was false, to show probable cause for forfeiture of the funds and forwarded that affidavit to the United States Attorney's Office in Georgia. All of the police officer's actions took place in Georgia, none took place in Nevada, where the plaintiffs filed suit, yet the Ninth Circuit Court of Appeals upheld personal jurisdiction on the ground the police officer "expressly aimed his submission of the false affidavit at Nevada, knowing that doing so would affect persons with a significant connection" with that state.

The United States Supreme Court held that due process did not permit the court in Nevada to exercise personal jurisdiction over the police officer. The court confirmed that "[f]or a State to exercise jurisdiction consistent with due process, the defendant's suit-related conduct must create a substantial connection with the forum State." *Walden*, 134 S. Ct. at 1121. The court emphasized two concepts related to this principle. "First, the relationship must arise out of contacts that the defendant *himself* creates with the forum State." *Id.* at 1121–22. The plaintiff's contacts with the forum "cannot be decisive." *Id.* at 1122. "Second, our minimum contacts analysis looks to the defendant's contacts with the forum State itself, not the defendant's contacts with persons who reside there." *Id.* The defendant's conduct "must form the necessary connection with the forum State that is the basis for its jurisdiction over him." *Id.*

The *Walden* court explained those principles apply when intentional torts are involved and used *Calder* as an illustration of such application. After reviewing the nature of the contacts in *Calder,* the Supreme Court concluded:

> The crux of *Calder* was that the reputation-based "effects" of the alleged libel connected the defendants to California, not just to the plaintiff. The strength of that connection was largely a function of the nature of the libel tort. However scandalous a newspaper article might be, it can lead to a loss of reputation only if communicated to (and read and understood by) third persons. Accordingly, the reputational injury caused by the defendants' story would not have occurred but for the fact that the defendants wrote an article for publication in California that was read by a large number of California citizens. Indeed, because publication to third persons is a necessary element of libel, the defendants' intentional tort actually occurred *in* California. In this way, the "effects" caused by the defendants' article – *i.e.*, the injury to the plaintiff's reputation in the estimation of the California

> public – connected the defendants' conduct to *California*, not just to a
> plaintiff who lived there. That connection, combined with the various
> facts that gave the article a California focus, sufficed to authorize the
> California court's exercise of jurisdiction."

Id. at 1123. The defendants in *Calder* "expressly aimed" their intentional conduct
at California because they knew the National Enquirer had its largest circulation
in California and the article would "have a potentially devastating impact there."
Id. at 1124.

The Supreme Court in *Walden* applied those principles to conclude the police
officer lacked the minimal contacts with Nevada to support personal jurisdiction.
It was undisputed that no part of the defendant's course of conduct occurred in
Nevada; the defendant "never traveled to, conducted activities within, contacted
anyone in, or sent anything or anyone to Nevada." *Id.* at 1124. "In short, when
viewed through the proper lens – whether the *defendant's* actions connect him to
the *forum* – petitioner formed no jurisdictionally relevant contacts with Nevada."
Id.

B. Application of the Effects Test of Calder, Pavlovich, and Walden

Walden is not a defamation case, and the Supreme Court made clear that commission of intentional torts via the Internet presented some "very different questions"
which it left "for another day." *Id.* at 1125 n.9. Nonetheless, *Walden* 's essential
teachings and its interpretation of *Calder* directly apply to this case. *Walden*
teaches that the correct jurisdictional analysis focuses on (1) the defendant's contacts with the forum, not with the plaintiff, and (2) whether those contacts create
the relationship among the defendant, the forum, and the litigation necessary to
satisfy due process. And, "the proper question is not where the plaintiff experienced a particular injury or effect but whether the defendant's conduct connects
him to the forum in a meaningful way." *Id.* at 1125.

It is undisputed Burdick has no direct contacts with California. He is an Illinois
resident, has never resided or worked in California, has never owned or leased
property in the state, and, by all accounts, has been in the state only twice. He is a
consultant for Nerium International, a Texas corporation which markets products
throughout the country. The only conduct which might connect Burdick in a
meaningful way with California was the allegedly defamatory posting on his Facebook page. As the trial court found, all of Plaintiffs' claims arise out of that posting.

Plaintiffs assert the facts supporting jurisdiction are not limited to the Facebook posting because "[t]here was ample evidence that Burdick's conduct was part
of a far broader and more concerted scheme" and Burdick was "a principal participant in this plan to injure Californians." But in determining personal jurisdiction,
each defendant's contacts with the forum state must be assessed individually and
where conspiracy is alleged, an exercise of personal jurisdiction must be based on
forum-related acts that were personally committed by each nonresident defendant. Thus, we consider only acts committed by Burdick personally in determining
whether he is subject to jurisdiction in California.

The question under *Walden* is whether Burdick's "suit-related conduct" – the
posting and removal of the allegedly defamatory Facebook post – created a "substantial connection" between Burdick and California. It is undisputed Burdick
posted and removed that Facebook posting while he was in his home state of Illinois. Although it can be inferred from the posting itself that Burdick knew Plaintiffs resided in California and understood they would suffer any injury here, his

knowledge that the posting could harm California residents is not enough in itself to support jurisdiction. The substantial connection required by *Walden* is not created by Plaintiffs having suffered injury in California: "The crux of *Calder* was that the reputation-based 'effects' of the alleged libel connected the defendants to California, not just to the plaintiff." *Walden*, 134 S.Ct. at 1123–1124.

We agree with those cases holding that merely posting on the Internet negative comments about the plaintiff and knowing the plaintiff is in the forum state are insufficient to create minimum contacts. *Calder, Pavlovich,* and *Walden* emphasize the difference between conduct directed at the plaintiff and conduct directed at the forum state itself: Those cases require, in addition to intentional conduct causing harm to a forum resident, evidence the nonresident defendant expressly aimed or intentionally targeted his or her intentional conduct at the forum state. Plaintiffs did not produce evidence to show Burdick's personal Facebook page or the allegedly defamatory posting was expressly aimed or intentionally targeted at California, that either the Facebook page or the posting had a California audience, that any significant number of Facebook "friends," who might see the posting, lived in California, or that the Facebook page had advertisements targeting Californians. Sanderson declared that Burdick's Facebook page was "publicy-available," but that fact would mean it would have been less likely Burdick had intentionally targeted California as opposed to any other jurisdiction.

Plaintiffs argue *Calder* remains controlling law and, although it was decided before the advent of the Internet, is dispositive. *Walden* did not overrule *Calder*; however, as the *Walden* court explained, key to understanding *Calder* is the defamatory article had a "California focus" in that it was specifically about an actress living in California with a California-based movie and television career, and that the reporter and editor knew the article would be published in a magazine having its largest circulation in California. The *Walden* court explained that, based on those facts, the *Calder* court concluded the reporter and the editor " 'expressly aimed' " their intentional conduct at, and knew the article would have a potentially devastating impact in, California.

Such facts are absent here. Burdick declared he made the allegedly defamatory posting on his personal Facebook page while he was in Illinois. Neither Burdick's Facebook page nor the allegedly defamatory posting had a California focus like the defamatory article in *Calder*. The posting was about NeriumAD – a product sold throughout the country – and its critics. No evidence was presented that Burdick's Facebook page had its widest circulation, i.e., the greatest number of Facebook friends, in California, that Burdick expressly aimed his intentional conduct at California, or that Burdick knew the posting would cause harm connecting his conduct to California and not only to Plaintiffs. ...

III. Discovery

Plaintiffs argue that if we grant Burdick's writ petition, we should allow them to conduct discovery related to the issue of personal jurisdiction. [The court remanded to the Superior Court to rule on the request.]

QUESTIONS

1. *Burdick*-style "intentional targeting" tests are common in the United States, especially after *Walden*. *Calder*-style "effects" tests are more common internationally. (For example, Section 421(2)(j) of the Restatement (Third) of Foreign Relations allows a state to exercise personal jurisdiction over someone who "has carried on outside the state an activity having a substantial,

direct, and foreseeable effect within the state.") How sharp is the distinction between the two kinds of tests?

2. A third alternative for assessing personal jurisdiction online is an "interactivity" test, which focuses on the technical characteristics of a website. Active websites that interact with users are more likely to be subject to personal jurisdiction than passive websites that merely make information available to users. An active website is like a storefront; a passive website like a billboard. Here is how the early and influential case of *Zippo Mfg. Co. v. Zippo Dot Com*, 952 F. Supp. 1119 (W.D. Pa. 1997), phrased one such test:

> [T]he likelihood that personal jurisdiction can be constitutionally exercised is directly proportionate to the nature and quality of commercial activity that an entity conducts over the Internet. This sliding scale is consistent with well developed personal jurisdiction principles. At one end of the spectrum are situations where a defendant clearly does business over the Internet. If the defendant enters into contracts with residents of a foreign jurisdiction that involve the knowing and repeated transmission of computer files over the Internet, personal jurisdiction is proper. At the opposite end are situations where a defendant has simply posted information on an Internet Web site which is accessible to users in foreign jurisdictions. A passive Web site that does little more than make information available to those who are interested in it is not grounds for the exercise personal jurisdiction. The middle ground is occupied by interactive Web sites where a user can exchange information with the host computer. In these cases, the exercise of jurisdiction is determined by examining the level of interactivity and commercial nature of the exchange of information that occurs on the Web site.

  Id. at 1124. Although it has been cited hundreds of times by courts, the *Zippo* sliding scale has been subjected to ferocious scholarly criticism. Does it reach sensible results? How interactive is Facebook?

3. Would the result in *Burdick* have been the same if Burdick's post about the plaintiffs had appeared as an editorial on the website of the *New York Times*, which covers national and international news and has roughly 30 million unique visitors per month?

4. Look back at *Gutnick* and *Mahfouz*. How would they come out under an intent-to-direct test? An effects test? An interactivity test? What kinds of tests did they actually use?

PENGUIN GROUP (USA) INC. V. AMERICAN BUDDHA
16 N.Y. 3d 295 (2011)

Graffeo, Judge:

The United States Court of Appeals for the Second Circuit has asked us a question regarding the scope of long-arm jurisdiction under CPLR 302(a)(3)(ii) in the context of a federal copyright infringement action.

Plaintiff Penguin Group (USA) is a large trade book publisher with its principal place of business in New York City. Defendant American Buddha is an Oregon not-for-profit corporation whose principal place of business is in Arizona. It operates two Web sites – the American Buddha Online Library and the Ralph Nader Library[1] that are hosted on servers located in Oregon and Arizona.

Penguin commenced this copyright infringement action against American Buddha in the United States District Court for the Southern District of New York, alleging that American Buddha infringed on Penguin's copyrights to four books: "Oil!" by Upton Sinclair; "It Can't Happen Here" by Sinclair Lewis; "The Golden Ass" by Apuleius, as translated by E.J. Kenney; and "On the Nature of the Universe" by Lucretius, as translated by R.E. Latham. The complaint alleges that American Buddha published complete copies of these works on its two Web sites, making them available free of charge to its 50,000 members and anyone with an Internet connection. The electronic copying and uploading of the works was apparently undertaken in Oregon or Arizona. ...

American Buddha moved to dismiss the complaint for lack of personal jurisdiction, arguing that its ties to New York were too insubstantial. In response, Penguin asserted that it had secured long-arm jurisdiction over American Buddha by virtue of CPLR 302(a)(3)(ii), which provides jurisdiction over nondomiciliaries who commit tortious acts outside the state that result in injuries within New York. American Buddha countered that CPLR 302(a)(3)(ii) was inapplicable because Penguin did not suffer an in-state injury.

[The District Court granted the motion to dismiss. The plaintiff appealed, and the Second Circuit certified the question of the application of the long-arm statute to the New York Court of Appeals.]

Because the Internet plays a significant role in this case, we narrow and reformulate the certified question to read:

> In copyright infringement cases involving the uploading of a copyrighted printed literary work onto the Internet, is the situs of injury for purposes of determining long-arm jurisdiction under N.Y. C.P.L.R. § 302(a)(3)(ii) the location of the infringing action or the residence or location of the principal place of business of the copyright holder?

In answer to this reformulated question and under the circumstances of this case, we conclude it is the location of the copyright holder.

CPLR 302(a)(3)(ii) allows a court in New York to exercise personal jurisdiction over an out-of-state defendant when the nondomiciliary:

> 3. commits a tortious act without the state causing injury to person or property within the state, except as to a cause of action for defamation of character arising from the act, if he ...
>
>> (ii) expects or should reasonably expect the act to have consequences in the state and derives substantial revenue from interstate or international commerce.

Consequently, a plaintiff relying on this statute must show that (1) the defendant committed a tortious act outside New York; (2) the cause of action arose from that act; (3) the tortious act caused an injury to a person or property in New York; (4) the defendant expected or should reasonably have expected the act to have consequences in New York; and (5) the defendant derived substantial revenue from interstate or international commerce. If these five elements are met, a court must then assess whether a finding of personal jurisdiction satisfies federal due process.

---

1 The Ralph Nader Library is not affiliated with Ralph Nader.

The only issue before us concerns the third requirement – whether an out-of-state act of copyright infringement has caused injury in New York. ...

Our analysis begins with *Fantis Foods Fantis v. Standard Importing*, 49 N.Y.2d 317 (1980), where we found personal jurisdiction to be lacking in the absence of a "direct injury" within New York. In that case, Standard, a New York wholesaler of feta cheese, asserted a claim for conversion against a Greek entity that had diverted a cheese shipment – meant to be shipped to Standard in Chicago – to a competitor while the shipment was in Greece or on the high seas. We concluded that personal jurisdiction over the Greek defendant did not lie under CPLR 302(a)(3)(ii) because:

> "In final analysis the only possible connection between the claimed conversion and any injury or foreseeable consequence in New York is the fact that Standard is incorporated and maintains offices there. It has, however, long been held that the residence or domicile of the injured party within a State is not a sufficient predicate for jurisdiction, which must be based upon a more direct injury within the State and a closer expectation of consequences within the State than the indirect financial loss resulting from the fact that the injured person resides or is domiciled there."

In a different commercial tort context, in *Sybron Corp. v Wetzel*, 46 N.Y.2d 197 (1978), we held that an injury had occurred in New York under CPLR 302(a)(3)(ii). The defendant in *Sybron,* a nondomiciliary corporation, hired a former employee of Sybron – a competitor engaged in manufacturing in New York – allegedly to obtain Sybron's protected trade secrets. Recognizing that the locus of injury in commercial cases "is not as readily identifiable as it is in torts causing physical harm," we determined that Sybron sustained a sufficiently direct injury in New York to support jurisdiction under CPLR 302(a)(3)(ii) since its claim was based on more than just its in-state domicile. Rather, Sybron had alleged that it acquired the trade secrets at issue in New York and, further, that the defendant's unfair competition threatened to pilfer Sybron's significant New York customers.

Fantis Foods and *Sybron* both cited favorably to *American Eutectic Welding Alloys Sales Co. v Dytron Alloys Corp.,* 439 F.2d 428 (2d Cir. 1971). There, the plaintiffs, two related New York corporations, brought an action against an out-of-state competitor alleging that it induced their employees to work for the competitor and to use confidential information to lure away plaintiffs' customers in Kentucky and Pennsylvania. The Second Circuit identified three options for determining the situs of injury under CPLR 302(a)(3)(ii) in a commercial tort case: "(1) any place where plaintiff does business; (2) the principal place of business of the plaintiff; and (3) the place where plaintiff lost business." The court determined that the third choice "seemed most apt," observing that "the place where the plaintiff lost business would normally be a forum reasonably foreseeable by a tortfeasor." Because plaintiffs alleged a loss of business only in Kentucky and Pennsylvania, the claim against the competitor was dismissed for lack of personal jurisdiction in New York. The court rejected plaintiffs' reliance on their New York domicile, reasoning that any "derivative commercial injury" predicated on a loss of sales in other states was too remote to establish an in-state injury within the meaning of the statute.

The injury in the case before us is more difficult to identify and quantify because the alleged infringement involves the Internet, which by its nature is intangible and ubiquitous. But the convergence of two factors persuades us that a New

York copyright owner alleging infringement sustains an in-state injury pursuant to CPLR 302(a)(3)(ii) when its printed literary work is uploaded without permission onto the Internet for public access. First, it is clear that the Internet itself plays an important role in the jurisdictional analysis in the specific context of this case. It is widely recognized that "the digital environment poses a unique threat to the rights of copyright owners" and that "digital technology enables pirates to reproduce and distribute perfect copies of works – at virtually no cost at all to the pirate," House Commerce Comm. Rep. on Digital Millennium Copyright Act of 1998, H.R. Rep. 551, 105th Cong., 2d Sess, at 25. Indeed, the rate of e-book piracy has risen in conjunction with the increasing popularity of electronic book devices.

The crux of Penguin's copyright infringement claim is not merely the unlawful electronic copying or uploading of the four copyrighted books. Rather, it is the intended consequence of those activities – the instantaneous availability of those copyrighted works on American Buddha's Web sites for anyone, in New York or elsewhere, with an Internet connection to read and download the books free of charge. Unlike *American Eutectic,* where the locus of injury was clearly circumscribed to two other states, the alleged injury in this case involves online infringement that is dispersed throughout the country and perhaps the world. In cases of this nature, identifying the situs of injury is not as simple as turning to the place where plaintiff lost business, because there is no singular location that fits that description.

As a result, although it may make sense in traditional commercial tort cases to equate a plaintiff's injury with the place where its business is lost or threatened, it is illogical to extend that concept to online copyright infringement cases where the place of uploading is inconsequential and it is difficult, if not impossible, to correlate lost sales to a particular geographic area. In short, the out-of-state location of the infringing conduct carries less weight in the jurisdictional inquiry in circumstances alleging digital piracy and is therefore not dispositive. ...

Moreover, the absence of any evidence of the actual downloading of Penguin's four works by users in New York is not fatal to a finding that the alleged injury occurred in New York. In *Sybron,* we made clear that a tort committed outside the state that was likely to cause harm through the loss of business inside the state was sufficient to establish personal jurisdiction regardless of whether damages were likely recoverable or even ascertainable. ... In any event, it is undisputed that American Buddha's Web sites are accessible by any New Yorker with an Internet connection and, as discussed, an injury allegedly inflicted by digital piracy is felt throughout the United States, which necessarily includes New York.

In sum, the role of the Internet in cases alleging the uploading of copyrighted books distinguishes them from traditional commercial tort cases where courts have generally linked the injury to the place where sales or customers are lost. The location of the infringement in online cases is of little import inasmuch as the primary aim of the infringer is to make the works available to anyone with access to an Internet connection, including computer users in New York. In addition, the injury to a New York copyright holder, while difficult to quantify, is not as remote as a purely indirect financial loss due to the broad spectrum of rights accorded by copyright law. The concurrence of these two elements – the function and nature of the Internet and the diverse ownership rights enjoyed by copyright holders situated in New York – leads us to view this case as closer to *Sybron* than *Fantis Foods.*

Thus, we conclude that the alleged injury in this case occurred in New York for purposes of CPLR 302(a)(3)(ii).[5]

Finally, contrary to American Buddha's assertion, our decision today does not open a Pandora's box allowing any nondomiciliary accused of digital copyright infringement to be haled into a New York court when the plaintiff is a New York copyright owner of a printed literary work. Rather, CPLR 302(a)(3)(ii) incorporates built-in safeguards against such exposure by requiring a plaintiff to show that the nondomiciliary both "expects or should reasonably expect the act to have consequences in the state" and, importantly, "derives substantial revenue from interstate or international commerce." There must also be proof that the out-of-state defendant has the requisite "minimum contacts" with the forum state and that the prospect of defending a suit here comports with "traditional notions of fair play and substantial justice," as required by the Federal Due Process Clause, *International Shoe Co. v Washington*, 326 U.S. 310, 316 (1945). These issues are beyond the scope of this certified question and their resolution awaits further briefing before the federal courts. ...

QUESTIONS

1. Can *Burdick* and *American Buddha* exist together in the same legal system?

2. Why might it be a hard problem to identify the location of the "effects" of conduct involving information? Why might the Internet be making those problems more prominent?

3. What would David Johnson and David Post have to say about this case?

UNITED STATES V. AUERNHEIMER
748 F.3d 525 (3rd Cir. 2014)

Chagares, Circuit Judge:

This case calls upon us to determine whether venue for Andrew Auernheimer's prosecution for conspiracy to violate the Computer Fraud and Abuse Act ("CFAA"), 18 U.S.C. § 1030, and identity fraud under 18 U.S.C. § 1028(a)(7) was proper in the District of New Jersey. Venue in criminal cases is more than a technicality; it involves "matters that touch closely the fair administration of criminal justice and public confidence in it." *United States v. Johnson*, 323 U.S. 273, 276 (1944). This is especially true of computer crimes in the era of mass interconnectivity. Because we conclude that venue did not lie in New Jersey, we will reverse the District Court's venue determination and vacate Auernheimer's conviction.

---

5 We do not find it necessary to address whether a New York copyright holder sustains an in-state injury pursuant to CPLR 302(a)(3)(ii) in a copyright infringement case that does not allege digital piracy and, therefore, express no opinion on that question (compare *McGraw-Hill Cos. Inc. v Ingenium Tech. Corp.*, 375 F. Supp. 2d 252, 256 [S.D.N.Y. 2005] ["The torts of copyright and trademark infringement cause injury in the state where the allegedly infringed intellectual property is held"] with *Freeplay Music, Inc. v Cox Radio, Inc.*, 2005 WL 1500896, 2005 US Dist. LEXIS 12397 [S.D.N.Y. 2005] [holding that personal jurisdiction over a nondomiciliary in a copyright infringement case did not exist because the injury occurred where the alleged out-of-state infringement took place]).

I.

A.

[AT&T's website for iPad owners had a security flaw. In order to make logging in easier, if a user accessed the website from her iPad, it would automatically detect her iPad's unique identifier (or "ICC-ID") and take her to a login page with her email address already filled in. Daniel Spitler discovered that if he had his computer pretend to be an iPad and transmit a random ICC-IDs to AT&T's website, he would frequently be able to see iPad owners' email addresses. Spitler wrote a program he called an "account slurper" to automate the process of collecting email addresses.]

Spitler shared this discovery with Auernheimer, whom he knew through Internet-based chat rooms but had never met in person. Auernheimer helped him to refine his account slurper program, and the program ultimately collected 114,000 email addresses between June 5 and June 8, 2010. ...

While Spitler's program was still collecting email addresses, Auernheimer emailed various members of the media in order to publicize the pair's exploits. Some of those media members emailed AT&T, which immediately fixed the breach. One of the media members contacted by Auernheimer was Ryan Tate, a reporter at Gawker, a news website. Tate expressed interest in publishing Auernheimer's story. To lend credibility to it, Auernheimer shared the list of email addresses with him. Tate published a story on June 9, 2010 describing AT&T's security flaw, entitled "Apple's Worst Security Breach: 114,000 iPad Owners Exposed." The article mentioned some of the names of those whose email addresses were obtained, but published only redacted images of a few email addresses and ICC–IDs.

Evidence at trial showed that at all times relevant to this case, Spitler was in San Francisco, California and Auernheimer was in Fayetteville, Arkansas. The servers that they accessed were physically located in Dallas, Texas and Atlanta, Georgia. Although no evidence was presented regarding the location of the Gawker reporter, it is undisputed that he was not in New Jersey.

B.

Despite the absence of any apparent connection to New Jersey, a grand jury sitting in Newark returned a two-count superseding indictment charging Auernheimer with conspiracy to violate the CFAA, 18 U.S.C. § 1030(a)(2)(C) and (c)(2)(B)(ii), in violation of 18 U.S.C. § 371 (count one), and fraud in connection with personal information in violation of 18 U.S.C. § 1028(a)(7) (count two, commonly referred to as "identity fraud"). To enhance the potential punishment from a misdemeanor to a felony, the Government alleged that Auernheimer's CFAA violation occurred in furtherance of a violation of New Jersey's computer crime statute, N.J. Stat. Ann. § 2C:20–31(a). *See* 18 U.S.C. § 1030(c)(2)(B)(ii).

Auernheimer moved to dismiss the superseding indictment shortly after it was returned by the grand jury. In addition to asserting several challenges concerning the CFAA violation, he argued that venue was not proper in the District of New Jersey. The District Court acknowledged that neither he nor Spitler was ever in New Jersey while allegedly committing the crime, and that the servers accessed were not in New Jersey, but denied his motion nonetheless. It held that venue was proper for the CFAA conspiracy charge because Auernheimer's disclosure of the email addresses of about 4,500 New Jersey residents affected them in New Jersey and violated New Jersey law. It further held that because venue was proper for the

CFAA count, it was also proper for the identity fraud count because proving the CFAA violation was a necessary predicate to proving the identity fraud violation.

Auernheimer's trial lasted five days and resulted in a guilty verdict on both counts. ... After denying Auernheimer's post-trial motions, the District Court sentenced him to forty-one months of imprisonment. Auernheimer timely appealed.

III.

Although this appeal raises a number of complex and novel issues that are of great public importance in our increasingly interconnected age, we find it necessary to reach only one that has been fundamental since our country's founding: venue. The proper place of colonial trials was so important to the founding generation that it was listed as a grievance in the Declaration of Independence. *See* The Declaration of Independence para. 21 (U.S. 1776) (objecting to "transporting us beyond seas to be tried for pretended offences"). It was of such concern that the Constitution of the United States "twice safeguards the defendant's venue right." *United States v. Cabrales*, 524 U.S. 1, 6, (1998). Article III requires that "the Trial of all Crimes ... shall be held in the State where the said Crimes shall have been committed." U.S. Const. art. III, § 2, cl. 3. The Sixth Amendment further provides that "[i]n all criminal prosecutions, the accused shall enjoy the right to a speedy and public trial, by an impartial jury of the State and district wherein the crime shall have been committed." *Id.* amend VI. This guarantee is codified in the Federal Rules of Criminal Procedure, which require that "the [G]overnment must prosecute an offense in a district where the offense was committed." Fed. R. Crim. P. 18.

Congress may prescribe specific venue requirements for particular crimes. Where it has not, as is the case here, we must determine the crime's *locus delicti*. [*See*] Black's Law Dictionary 1025 (9th ed.2009) (defining *locus delicti* as the "place where an offense was committed"). "[T]he locus delicti must be determined from the nature of the crime alleged and the location of the act or acts constituting it." *United States v. Anderson*, 328 U.S. 699, 703 (1946); *accord United States v. Rodriguez–Moreno*, 526 U.S. 275, 279 (1999). To perform this inquiry, we "must [1] initially identify the conduct constituting the offense ... and then [2] discern the location of the commission of the criminal acts." *Rodriguez–Moreno*, 526 U.S. at 279. Venue should be narrowly construed. *Johnson*, 323 U.S. at 276.

Continuing offenses, such as conspiracy, that are "begun in one district and completed in another, or committed in more than one district, may be inquired of and prosecuted in any district in which such offense was begun, continued, or completed." 18 U.S.C. § 3237(a). In the context of a conspiracy charge, venue can be established wherever a co-conspirator has committed an act in furtherance of the conspiracy. The Government must prove venue by a preponderance of the evidence. ...

A.

Count one charged Auernheimer with conspiracy to violate CFAA § 1030(a)(2)(C) and (c)(2)(B)(ii). In the indictment and at trial, the Government identified the nature of the conduct constituting the offense as the agreement to commit a violation of the CFAA in furtherance of a violation of New Jersey's computer crime statute, N.J. Stat. Ann. § 2C:20–31(a). Venue would be proper in any district where the CFAA violation occurred, or wherever any of the acts in furtherance of the conspiracy took place.

The charged portion of the CFAA provides that "[w]hoever ... intentionally accesses a computer without authorization or exceeds authorized access, and thereby obtains ... information from any protected computer ... shall be punished as provided in subsection (c) of this section." 18 U.S.C. § 1030(a)(2)(C). To be found guilty, the Government must prove that the defendant (1) intentionally (2) accessed without authorization (or exceeded authorized access to a (3) protected computer and (4) thereby obtained information. The statute's plain language reveals two essential conduct elements: accessing without authorization and obtaining information.

New Jersey was not the site of either essential conduct element. The evidence at trial demonstrated that the accessed AT&T servers were located in Dallas, Texas, and Atlanta, Georgia. In addition, during the time that the conspiracy began, continued, and ended, Spitler was obtaining information in San Francisco, California and Auernheimer was assisting him from Fayetteville, Arkansas. No protected computer was accessed and no data was obtained in New Jersey.

This is not the end of our analysis, however, because the Government did not just charge Auernheimer with conspiracy to commit an ordinary violation of the CFAA, but also with conspiring to violate the CFAA in furtherance of a state crime. ...

The New Jersey statute allows for criminal liability "if the person purposely or knowingly and without authorization, or in excess of authorization, accesses any ... computer [or] computer system and knowingly or recklessly discloses, or causes to be disclosed any data ... or personal identifying information." N.J. Stat. Ann. § 2C: 20–31(a). Its essential conduct elements are accessing without authorization (or in excess of authorization) and disclosing data or personal identifying information.

Here, none of the essential conduct elements of a violation of the New Jersey statute occurred in New Jersey. As discussed, neither Auernheimer nor Spitler accessed a computer in New Jersey. The disclosure did not occur there either. The sole disclosure of the data obtained was to the Gawker reporter. There was no allegation or evidence that the Gawker reporter was in New Jersey. Further, there was no evidence that any email addresses of any New Jersey residents were ever disclosed publicly in the Gawker article. The alleged violation of the New Jersey statute thus cannot confer venue for count one.

Just as none of the conduct constituting the CFAA violation or its enhancement occurred in New Jersey, none of the overt acts that the Government alleged in the superseding indictment occurred in New Jersey either. The indictment listed four overt acts: writing the account slurper program, deploying the account slurper program against AT&T's servers, emailing victims to inform them of the breach, and disclosing the emails addresses obtained to Gawker. The co-conspirators collaborated on the account slurper program from California and Arkansas and deployed it against servers located in Texas and Georgia. The Government offered no evidence whatsoever that any of the victims that Auernheimer emailed were located in New Jersey, or that the Gawker reporter to whom the list of email addresses was disclosed was in the Garden State.

Because neither Auernheimer nor his co-conspirator Spitler performed any "essential conduct element" of the underlying CFAA violation or any overt act in furtherance of the conspiracy in New Jersey, venue was improper on count one. [The court concluded that venue was improper on count two for similar reasons.] ...

IV.

The Government does not dispute the locations of Auernheimer, Spitler, and AT&T's servers during the period of time that Auernheimer was committing the alleged crimes. Instead, it advances a series of other reasons why there was no defect in venue that warrants vacating his conviction. None of them are availing. ...

C.

Finally, the Government argues that even if venue were improper, we should apply harmless error analysis and disregard the error because it did "not affect substantial rights." Fed. R. Crim. P. 52(a). ...

The Supreme Court has repeatedly made clear that the constitutional limitations on venue are extraordinarily important. "[Q]uestions of venue are more than matters of mere procedure. They raise deep issues of public policy in the light of which legislation must be construed." *Travis v. United States*, 364 U.S. 631, 634 (1961). "The provision for trial in the vicinity of the crime is a safeguard against the unfairness and hardship involved when an accused is prosecuted in a remote place." *United States v. Cores*, 356 U.S. 405, 407 (1958); accord *United States v. Passodelis*, 615 F.2d 975, 977 (3d Cir. 1980). The founders were so concerned with the location of a criminal trial that they placed the venue requirement, which is "principally a protection for the defendant," *Cabrales*, 524 U.S. at 9, in the Constitution in two places.

They did so for good reason. A defendant who has been convicted "in a distant, remote, or unfriendly forum solely at the prosecutor's whim," *United States v. Salinas*, 373 F.3d 161, 164 (1st Cir. 2004), has had his substantial rights compromised. Auernheimer was hauled over a thousand miles from Fayetteville, Arkansas to New Jersey. Certainly if he had directed his criminal activity toward New Jersey to the extent that either he or his co-conspirator committed an act in furtherance of their conspiracy there, or performed one of the essential conduct elements of the charged offenses there, he would have no grounds to complain about his uprooting. But that was not what was alleged or what happened. While we are not prepared today to hold that an error of venue never could be harmless, we do not need to because the improper venue here – far from where he performed any of his allegedly criminal acts – denied Auernheimer's substantial right to be tried in the place where his alleged crime was committed.

V.

Venue issues are animated in part by the danger of allowing the Government to choose its forum free from any external constraints. The ever-increasing ubiquity of the Internet only amplifies this concern. As we progress technologically, we must remain mindful that cybercrimes do not happen in some metaphysical location that justifies disregarding constitutional limits on venue. People and computers still exist in identifiable places in the physical world. When people commit crimes, we have the ability and obligation to ensure that they do not stand to account for those crimes in forums in which they performed no essential conduct element of the crimes charged.

"Though our nation has changed in ways which it is difficult to imagine that the Framers of the Constitution could have foreseen, the rights of criminal defendants which they sought to protect in the venue provisions of the Constitution are neither outdated nor outmoded." *Passodelis*, 615 F.2d at 977. Just as this was true when we decided *Passodelis* in 1980 – after the advent of railroad, express mail, the telegraph, the telephone, the automobile, air travel, and satellite communications – it remains true in today's Internet age. For the forgoing reasons, we will reverse the District Court's venue determination and vacate Auernheimer's conviction.

QUESTIONS

1. Orin Kerr represented Auernheimer on appeal. Did he convince the court to adopt an internal or an external perspective on Spitler's conduct? Was this the right result?

2. Would venue have been proper in Texas? California?

3. Compare *Auernheimer* with *American Buddha*. Which provides a more coherent answer to the question of "where" online activity takes place? Which is more predictable? Which provides better notice to potential defendants?

TOO DAMN HIGH PROBLEM

McMillan Holdings is the owner of a federally registered trademark on THE RENT IS TOO DAMN HIGH, a hit musical about local politics in an inner-city neighborhood, which has been running on Broadway in New York, New York for the past five years. It has filed a trademark infringement lawsuit in federal court in the District of New Jersey against Damn High Inc., the San Bernadino, California, publisher of *Damn High* magazine. *Damn High* is a monthly publication focused on drug and skateboard culture in the Los Angeles area. *Damn High* has registered the domain name toodamnhigh.com for its website, which features selected stories from the printed magazine. The website is hosted on a server operated by the New Jersey company InfoBaud, and the server is physically located in the state of New Jersey. It provides about 10,000 page views per month and includes a link to send an email to the editors of the magazine. McMillan claims that Damn High's newspaper and website are confusing consumers into falsely believing that there is a connection between the musical and the newspaper, thereby harming the reputation of the THE RENT IS TOO DAMN HIGH trademark.

You have been retained by Damn High to advise it on the lawsuit. If Damn High moves to dismiss under F.R.C.P. 12(b)(2) for lack of personal jurisdiction, will the motion succeed? What should Damn High do?

FLOODZONE PROBLEM

Two residents of New Jersey and a resident of New York are suing FloodZone, an on-demand streaming-video movie service. They have filed a complaint in New Jersey state court for fraud and breach of contract, alleging that FloodZone illegally converted their memberships to more expensive plans without notice or consent. They are seeking to have the court certify a nationwide class of approximately 200,000 similarly situated FloodZone users.

FloodZone's corporate headquarters and main offices are located in Bellvue, Washington. It has advertising sales offices in four states: Washington, California, Texas, and New York. It does approximately $50 million of business annually. It has moved to dismiss the complaint for lack of jurisdiction and improper venue, citing a forum-selection clause in its membership agreement. The clause reads:

> You consent to the exclusive jurisdiction and venue of courts in King County, Washington, in all disputes arising out of or relating to your use of FloodZone or your FloodZone membership.

The parties have stipulated to the following statement of facts about FloodZone's signup process:

> Before becoming a FloodZone member, a prospective subscriber is prompted by FloodZone software to view multiple computer screens

of information, including a membership agreement which contains the above clause. FloodZone's membership agreement appears on the computer screen in a scrollable window next to blocks providing the choices "I Agree" and "I Don't Agree." Prospective members assent to the terms of the agreement by clicking on "I Agree" using a computer mouse. Prospective members have the option to click "I Agree or "I Don't Agree" at any point while scrolling through the agreement. Registration may proceed only after the potential subscriber has had the opportunity to view and has assented to the membership agreement, including FloodZone's forum selection clause. No charges are incurred until after the membership agreement review is completed and a subscriber has clicked on "I Agree."

How should the court rule on FloodZone's motion to dismiss?

CHAPTER 3: SPEECH

This chapter considers how the Internet affects the balances struck by free speech law. By changing the facts of how people communicate, software can unsettle existing legal doctrines. In particular, some have argued that new computer technologies undermine law by making it harder to enforce laws restricting speech, while others celebrate the open and uninhibited quality of online debates.

A. Defining "Speech"

At first glance, one might think that there is nothing new here: speech is speech, regardless of the medium that conveys it. But the novelty of online media can call this assumption into question. Courts have struggled to understand how online speech works; indeed, in some cases, it is far from clear what even counts as "speech." *Bland* and *Bernstein* concern the reach of the First Amendment's protection for speech on the Internet; they both turn on the threshold question of whether the challenged behavior contains protected "speech." *Too Much Media* is a little different. There, the speech itself is not directly at issue. Instead, an online speaker is claiming that she is entitled to a state statutory right enjoyed by newspaper and television journalists: the privilege not to name her sources in court. All three cases raise difficult questions about the differences between offline and online activities.

UNITED STATES CONSTITUTION, AMENDMENT I

Congress shall make no law respecting an establishment of religion, or prohibiting the free exercise thereof; or abridging the freedom of speech, or of the press; or the right of the people peaceably to assemble, and to petition the Government for a redress of grievances.

QUESTION

What is "speech"?

TEXAS V. JOHNSON
491 U.S. 397 (1989)

Justice Brennan delivered the opinion of the Court:

After publicly burning an American flag as a means of political protest, Gregory Lee Johnson was convicted of desecrating a flag in violation of Texas law. This case presents the question whether his conviction is consistent with the First Amendment. We hold that it is not. ...

In deciding whether particular conduct possesses sufficient communicative elements to bring the First Amendment into play, we have asked whether "[a]n intent to convey a particularized message was present, and [whether] the likelihood was great that the message would be understood by those who viewed it." *Spence v. Washington*, 418 U. S. 405, 410-411 (1974).

BLAND V. ROBERTS
857 F. Supp. 2d 599 (E.D. Va. 2012)

Jackson, District Judge: ...

I. FACTUAL & PROCEDURAL HISTORY

Plaintiffs ... were employed in the Hampton Sheriff's Office ("the Office"). ... The Sheriff of the Office, B.J. Roberts ("the Sheriff"), was slated for re-election in November 2009. The Plaintiffs claim that during his tenure the Sheriff used his authority to bolster his reelection efforts, including using employees to manage his political activities, using prisoners to set up campaign events and forcing his employees to sell and buy tickets to campaign fundraisers. Plaintiffs contend that in late 2009, the Sheriff learned that a number of his employees were actively supporting Jim Adams, one of the Sheriff's opponents in the election. ...

The Plaintiffs further allege that the Sheriff learned that each of them affirmatively expressed their support for Adams by informing other individuals of their support, attending a cookout which Adams also attended and "liking" Adams' Facebook page. According to the Plaintiffs, after learning of their support of his opponent, the Sheriff called a meeting in which he informed his employees that they should get on the "long train" with him rather than riding the "short train" with his opponent.

The Sheriff won the November 2009 election, and he decided not to retain the six Plaintiffs as well as six other employees. The Sheriff claims he did not reappoint three civilian employees (including Plaintiffs Bland and Woodward) based on a reduction in the number of sworn deputies which the Compensation Board allocated to him. He contends that he wanted to replace the civilian employees with sworn deputies. The Sheriff also declined to retain the remaining four deputy Plaintiffs and five other deputies for unsatisfactory work performance or for his belief that their actions "hindered the harmony and efficiency of the Office." ...

III. DISCUSSION

A. Freedom of Speech Retaliation Claim

Plaintiffs first allege that the Sheriff failed to reappoint them in retaliation for their exercise of their right to freedom of speech when they choose to support the Sheriff's opponent in the election. In order to prove that an adverse employment action violated their First Amendment right to freedom of speech, the Plaintiffs must satisfy the three-prong test the United States Court of Appeals for the Fourth Circuit ("the Fourth Circuit") laid out in *McVey v. Stacy*, 157 F.3d 271 (4th Cir. 1998):

> Thus, to determine whether a public employee has stated a claim under the First Amendment for retaliatory discharge, we must determine (1) whether the public employee was speaking as a citizen upon a matter of public concern or as an employee about a personal matter of personal interest; (2) whether the employee's interest in speaking upon the matter of public concern outweighed the government's interest in providing effective and efficient services to the public; and (3) whether the employee's speech was a substantial factor in the employee's termination decision.

Id. at 277–78.

The first prong of the *McVey* test necessarily requires that speech exists before an evaluation of the remaining prongs can occur. Plaintiffs Carter, McCoy, and

Woodward have not sufficiently alleged that they engaged in expressive speech ... .
Therefore, these Plaintiffs' claims fail as a matter of law.

a. Daniel Ray Carter, Jr. & Robert McCoy

Carter and McCoy each allege that they engaged in constitutionally protected speech when they "made statements" on Adams' Facebook page. McCoy's Facebook activity is more nebulous than Carter's. McCoy claims that he posted a message on Adams' Facebook page which he later took down. The Court, however, is unaware of the content of this message. McCoy's barebones assertion that he made some statement at some time is insufficient evidence for the Court to adequately evaluate his claim. Without more, the Court will not speculate as to what McCoy's actual statement might have been. McCoy has not sufficiently alleged any constitutionally protected speech.

Carter alleged that he sent a statement of support and attached the statement as an exhibit to his declaration in this case. However, after reviewing the record, the Court has not found any evidence of the "statement of support" Carter allegedly made. In fact, the only evidence regarding Carter's activity on Adams' Facebook page is that he "liked" Adams' page.

It is clear, based on the Sheriff's own admissions, that at some point he became aware of McCoy and Carter's presence on Adams' Facebook page. However, the Sheriff's knowledge of the posts only becomes relevant if the Court finds the activity of liking a Facebook page to be constitutionally protected. It is the Court's conclusion that merely "liking" a Facebook page is insufficient speech to merit constitutional protection. In cases where courts have found that constitutional speech protections extended to Facebook posts, actual statements existed within the record. For example, in *Mattingly v. Milligan,* Mattingly posted on her Facebook wall referring directly to the firing of various employees. No. 4:11CV00215, 2011 WL 5184283, at *2–*3 (E.D. Ark. Nov. 1, 2011) ("Two minutes after this post, Mattingly posted another comment: 'I am trying [sic] my heart goes out to the ladies in my office that were told by letter they were no longer needed ... It's sad.'"). There, the court held that Mattingly's specific post was an expression of constitutionally protected speech. *Id.* at *3–*4. Similarly, in *Gresham v. City of Atlanta,* the. plaintiff posted: "Who would like to hear the story of how I arrested a forgery perp at Best Buy online to find out later at the precinct that he was the nephew of an Atlanta Police Investigator ... ?" No. 1:10–CV–1301–RWS–ECS, 2011 WL 4601022, at *2 (N.D. Ga. Aug. 29, 2011), *report and recommendation adopted in part, rejected in part on other grounds by,* No. 1:10–CV–1301 RWS, 2011 WL 4601020 (N.D. Ga. Sep. 30, 2011). In *Gresham,* the district court adopted the Magistrate Judge's recommendation that although the statement was a close question, it constituted enough speech to be considered speaking out as a matter of public concern.

These illustrative cases differ markedly from the case at hand in one crucial way: Both *Gresham* and *Mattingly* involved actual statements. No such statements exist in this case. Simply liking a Facebook page is insufficient. It is not the kind of substantive statement that has previously warranted constitutional protection. The Court will not attempt to infer the actual content of Carter's posts from one click of a button on Adams' Facebook page. For the Court to assume that the Plaintiffs made some specific statement without evidence of such statements is improper. Facebook posts *can* be considered matters of public concern; however, the Court does not believe Plaintiffs Carter and McCoy have alleged sufficient speech to garner First Amendment protection.

BLAND V. ROBERTS
730 F.3d 368 (4th Cir. 2013)

Traxler, Chief Judge: ...

Here, Carter visited the Jim Adams's campaign Facebook page (the "Campaign Page"), which was named "Jim Adams for Hampton Sheriff," and he clicked the "like" button on the Campaign Page. When he did so, the Campaign Page's name and a photo of Adams – which an Adams campaign representative had selected as the Page's icon – were added to Carter's profile, which all Facebook users could view. On Carter's profile, the Campaign Page name served as a link to the Campaign Page. Carter's clicking on the "like" button also caused an announcement that Carter liked the Campaign Page to appear in the news feeds of Carter's friends. And it caused Carter's name and his profile photo to be added to the Campaign Page's "People [Who] Like This" list.

Once one understands the nature of what Carter did by liking the Campaign Page, it becomes apparent that his conduct qualifies as speech. On the most basic level, clicking on the "like" button literally causes to be published the statement that the User "likes" something, which is itself a substantive statement. In the context of a political campaign's Facebook page, the meaning that the user approves of the candidacy whose page is being liked is unmistakable. That a user may use a single mouse click to produce that message that he likes the page instead of typing the same message with several individual key strokes is of no constitutional significance.

Aside from the fact that liking the Campaign Page constituted pure speech, it also was symbolic expression. The distribution of the universally understood "thumbs up" symbol in association with Adams's campaign page, like the actual text that liking the page produced, conveyed that Carter supported Adams's candidacy. *See Spence v. Washington*, 418 U.S. 405, 410-11 (1974) (per curiam) (holding that person engaged in expressive conduct when there was "[a]n intent to convey a particularized message ... , and in the surrounding circumstances the likelihood was great that the message would be understood by those who viewed it").

In sum, liking a political candidate's campaign page communicates the user's approval of the candidate and supports the campaign by associating the user with it. In this way, it is the Internet equivalent of displaying a political sign in one's front yard, which the Supreme Court has held is substantive speech. *See City of Ladue v. Gilleo*, 512 U.S. 43, 54-56 (1994). Just as Carter's placing an "Adams for Sheriff" sign in his front yard would have conveyed to those passing his home that he supported Adams's campaign, Carter's liking Adams's Campaign Page conveyed that message to those viewing his profile or the Campaign Page. In fact, it is hardly surprising that the record reflects that this is exactly how Carter's action was understood. *See* J.A. 160 (McCoy's testimony that in light of Carter's liking Adams's Campaign Page, "everybody was saying that ... Carter is out of there because he supported Adams openly"); *see also* J.A. 793 (Sheriff's Office employee stating that Roberts had said that "certain employees were on the Facebook page of his opponent, Jim Adams, indicating their support of Adams for Sheriff").

QUESTIONS

1. What does a "like" mean?
2. McCoy and Carter's continued employment hinges on whether Facebook likes are speech. How else might the question of First Amendment coverage for Facebook likes come up?

3. The National Labor Relations Act protects employees' right "to engage in ... concerted activities for the purpose of collective bargaining or other mutual aid or protection." 29 U.S.C. § 157. A bartender at a sports bar posts to her Facebook page, "Maybe someone should do the owners of Triple Play a favor and buy it from them. They can't even do the tax paperwork correctly!!! Now I OWE money . . . Wtf!!!!" A cook responds by clicking "Like" on the post. Are these protected "concerted activities" or can the two be fired? Does it matter whether employees have been complaining to each other at work about the Triple Play's tax withholding?

NOTE ON FIRST AMENDMENT TIERS OF SCRUTINY

Different types of restrictions on speech are judged by different standards. The most stringent and exacting judicial test is used for restrictions on speech that are *viewpoint-based*, i.e., when "the government has singled out a subset of messages for disfavor based on the views expressed." *Matal v. Tam*, — U.S. — (2017) (Kennedy, J, concurring in part and concurring in the judgment). Such restrictions are presumptively unconstitutional.

Whenever the government tries to restrict access to speech because of its message, rather than how it's communicated, the restriction is said to be **content-based.**. A content-based restriction on speech must satisfy a three-pronged "strict scrutiny" test:

1. There must be a "compelling interest" in restricting access to the speech to be restricted. In practice, this usually means the speech must be actively harmful in some way and without any offsetting benefits.

2. The restriction must be "narrowly tailored" to the speech it prohibits.

3. There must be no "less restrictive alternatives" for preventing that speech.

In contrast, **content-neutral** restrictions on speech, such as "reasonable time, place, and manner" regulations, are allowed if they are "narrowly tailored to serve a significant governmental interest, and ... leave open ample alternative channels for communication of the information." *Ward v. Rock Against Racism*, 491 U.S. 781, 791 (1989). (Read the test closely; do you see why it is less strict than strict scrutiny?) Prohibiting "loud" speeches in the park is content-neutral; prohibiting "political" speeches in the park is content-based; prohibiting "liberal" speeches in the park is viewpoint-based.

And finally, there is a special test for **commercial speech** (such as advertising) which proposes a commercial transaction Commercial speech is protected if it concerns lawful activity and is not misleading. If so, then it may only be restricted if (1) there is a substantial government interest, (2) the regulation directly advances the governmental interest, and (3) the regulation is not more extensive than necessary. (Read this test closely, too; do you see how it too is less strict than strict scrutiny?)

All of these tests, despite their differences, are substantially more rigorous than the "rational basis review" applied to government regulations where no individual right protected by the Constitution is implicated. There, a law is valid if it is rationally related to a legitimate governmental interest.

PACKINGHAM V. NORTH CAROLINA
— U.S. — (June 19, 2017)

Justice Kennedy delivered the opinion of the Court.

In 2008, North Carolina enacted a statute making it a felony for a registered sex offender to gain access to a number of websites, including commonplace social media websites like Facebook and Twitter. The question presented is whether that law is permissible under the First Amendment's Free Speech Clause, applicable to the States under the Due Process Clause of the Fourteenth Amendment.

I

A

North Carolina law makes it a felony for a registered sex offender "to access a commercial social networking Web site where the sex offender knows that the site permits minor children to become members or to create or maintain personal Web pages." N.C. Gen. Stat. Ann. §§ 14–202.5(a), (e) (2015). A "commercial social networking Web site" is defined as a website that meets four criteria. First, it "[i]s operated by a person who derives revenue from membership fees, advertising, or other sources related to the operation of the Web site." § 14–202.5(b). Second, it "facilitates the social introduction between two or more persons for the purposes of friendship, meeting other persons, or information exchanges." Third, it "allows users to create Web pages or personal profiles that contain information such as the name or nickname of the user, photographs placed on the personal Web page by the user, other personal information about the user, and links to other personal Web pages on the commercial social networking Web site of friends or associates of the user that may be accessed by other users or visitors to the Web site." And fourth, it "provides users or visitors ... mechanisms to communicate with other users, such as a message board, chat room, electronic mail, or instant messenger."

The statute includes two express exemptions. The statutory bar does not extend to websites that "provide only one of the following discrete services: photo-sharing, electronic mail, instant messenger, or chat room or message board platform." § 14–202.5(c)(1). The law also does not encompass websites that have as their "primary purpose the facilitation of commercial transactions involving goods or services between [their] members or visitors." § 14–202.5(c)(2).

According to sources cited to the Court, § 14–202.5 applies to about 20,000 people in North Carolina and the State has prosecuted over 1,000 people for violating it.

B

In 2002, petitioner Lester Gerard Packingham—then a 21–year–old college student—had sex with a 13–year–old girl. He pleaded guilty to taking indecent liberties with a child. Because this crime qualifies as "an offense against a minor," petitioner was required to register as a sex offender—a status that can endure for 30 years or more. As a registered sex offender, petitioner was barred under § 14–202.5 from gaining access to commercial social networking sites.

In 2010, a state court dismissed a traffic ticket against petitioner. In response, he logged on to Facebook.com and posted the following statement on his personal profile:

> "Man God is Good! How about I got so much favor they dismissed the ticket before court even started? No fine, no court cost, no nothing spent...... Praise be to GOD, WOW! Thanks JESUS!"

At the time, a member of the Durham Police Department was investigating regis-tered sex offenders who were thought to be violating § 14–202.5. The officer no-ticed that a " 'J.R. Gerrard' " had posted the statement quoted above. By checking court records, the officer discovered that a traffic citation for petitioner had been dismissed around the time of the post. Evidence obtained by search warrant con-firmed the officer's suspicions that petitioner was J.R. Gerrard.

Petitioner was indicted by a grand jury for violating § 14–202.5. The trial court denied his motion to dismiss the indictment on the grounds that the charge against him violated the First Amendment. Petitioner was ultimately convicted and given a suspended prison sentence. At no point during trial or sentencing did the State allege that petitioner contacted a minor—or committed any other illicit act—on the Internet.

II

A fundamental principle of the First Amendment is that all persons have access to places where they can speak and listen, and then, after reflection, speak and listen once more. The Court has sought to protect the right to speak in this spatial con-text. A basic rule, for example, is that a street or a park is a quintessential forum for the exercise of First Amendment rights. Even in the modern era, these places are still essential venues for public gatherings to celebrate some views, to protest others, or simply to learn and inquire.

While in the past there may have been difficulty in identifying the most impor-tant places (in a spatial sense) for the exchange of views, today the answer is clear. It is cyberspace—the "vast democratic forums of the Internet" in general, *Reno v. American Civil Liberties Union*, 521 U.S. 844, 868 (1997), and social media in particular. Seven in ten American adults use at least one Internet social network-ing service. One of the most popular of these sites is Facebook, the site used by petitioner leading to his conviction in this case. According to sources cited to the Court in this case, Facebook has 1.79 billion active users. This is about three times the population of North America.

Social media offers relatively unlimited, low-cost capacity for communication of all kinds. On Facebook, for example, users can debate religion and politics with their friends and neighbors or share vacation photos. On LinkedIn, users can look for work, advertise for employees, or review tips on entrepreneurship. And on Twitter, users can petition their elected representatives and otherwise engage with them in a direct manner. Indeed, Governors in all 50 States and almost every Member of Congress have set up accounts for this purpose. In short, social media users employ these websites to engage in a wide array of protected First Amend-ment activity on topics as diverse as human thought.

The nature of a revolution in thought can be that, in its early stages, even its participants may be unaware of it. And when awareness comes, they still may be unable to know or foresee where its changes lead, So too here. While we now may be coming to the realization that the Cyber Age is a revolution of historic propor-tions, we cannot appreciate yet its full dimensions and vast potential to alter how we think, express ourselves, and define who we want to be. The forces and direc-tions of the Internet are so new, so protean, and so far reaching that courts must be conscious that what they say today might be obsolete tomorrow.

This case is one of the first this Court has taken to address the relationship be-tween the First Amendment and the modern Internet. As a result, the Court must exercise extreme caution before suggesting that the First Amendment provides scant protection for access to vast networks in that medium.

III

This background informs the analysis of the North Carolina statute at issue. Even making the assumption that the statute is content neutral and thus subject to intermediate scrutiny, the provision cannot stand. In order to survive intermediate scrutiny, a law must be narrowly tailored to serve a significant governmental interest. In other words, the law must not burden substantially more speech than is necessary to further the government's legitimate interests..

For centuries now, inventions heralded as advances in human progress have been exploited by the criminal mind. New technologies, all too soon, can become instruments used to commit serious crimes. The railroad is one example, and the telephone another. So it will be with the Internet and social media.

There is also no doubt that, as this Court has recognized, the sexual abuse of a child is a most serious crime and an act repugnant to the moral instincts of a decent people. And it is clear that a legislature may pass valid laws to protect children and other victims of sexual assault from abuse. The government, of course, need not simply stand by and allow these evils to occur. But the assertion of a valid governmental interest cannot, in every context, be insulated from all constitutional protections.

It is necessary to make two assumptions to resolve this case. First, given the broad wording of the North Carolina statute at issue, it might well bar access not only to commonplace social media websites but also to websites as varied as Amazon.com, Washingtonpost.com, and Webmd.com. The Court need not decide the precise scope of the statute. It is enough to assume that the law applies (as the State concedes it does) to social networking sites as commonly understood—that is, websites like Facebook, LinkedIn, and Twitter.

Second, this opinion should not be interpreted as barring a State from enacting more specific laws than the one at issue. Specific criminal acts are not protected speech even if speech is the means for their commission. Though the issue is not before the Court, it can be assumed that the First Amendment permits a State to enact specific, narrowly tailored laws that prohibit a sex offender from engaging in conduct that often presages a sexual crime, like contacting a minor or using a website to gather information about a minor. Specific laws of that type must be the State's first resort to ward off the serious harm that sexual crimes inflict. (Of importance, the troubling fact that the law imposes severe restrictions on persons who already have served their sentence and are no longer subject to the supervision of the criminal justice system is also not an issue before the Court.)

Even with these assumptions about the scope of the law and the State's interest, the statute here enacts a prohibition unprecedented in the scope of First Amendment speech it burdens. Social media allows users to gain access to information and communicate with one another about it on any subject that might come to mind. By prohibiting sex offenders from using those websites, North Carolina with one broad stroke bars access to what for many are the principal sources for knowing current events, checking ads for employment, speaking and listening in the modern public square, and otherwise exploring the vast realms of human thought and knowledge. These websites can provide perhaps the most powerful mechanisms available to a private citizen to make his or her voice heard. They allow a person with an Internet connection to "become a town crier with a voice that resonates farther than it could from any soapbox." *Reno,* 521 U.S., at 870.

In sum, to foreclose access to social media altogether is to prevent the user from engaging in the legitimate exercise of First Amendment rights. It is unsettling to suggest that only a limited set of websites can be used even by persons who have completed their sentences. Even convicted criminals—and in some instances especially convicted criminals—might receive legitimate benefits from these means for access to the world of ideas, in particular if they seek to reform and to pursue lawful and rewarding lives.

IV

The primary response from the State is that the law must be this broad to serve its preventative purpose of keeping convicted sex offenders away from vulnerable victims. The State has not, however, met its burden to show that this sweeping law is necessary or legitimate to serve that purpose.

It is instructive that no case or holding of this Court has approved of a statute as broad in its reach. The closest analogy that the State has cited is *Burson v. Freeman*, 504 U.S. 191 (1992). There, the Court upheld a prohibition on campaigning within 100 feet of a polling place. That case gives little or no support to the State. The law in *Burson* was a limited restriction that, in a context consistent with constitutional tradition, was enacted to protect another fundamental right—the right to vote. The restrictions there were far less onerous than those the State seeks to impose here. The law in *Burson* meant only that the last few seconds before voters entered a polling place were "their own, as free from interference as possible." *Id.*, at 210. And the Court noted that, were the buffer zone larger than 100 feet, it "could effectively become an impermissible burden" under the First Amendment. *Ibid.*

The better analogy to this case is *Board of Airport Comm'rs of Los Angeles v. Jews for Jesus, Inc.*, 482 U.S. 569 (1987), where the Court struck down an ordinance prohibiting any "First Amendment activities" at Los Angeles International Airport because the ordinance covered all manner of protected, nondisruptive behavior including "talking and reading, or the wearing of campaign buttons or symbolic clothing," *id.*, at 571, 575. If a law prohibiting all protected expression at a single airport is not constitutional, it follows with even greater force that the State may not enact this complete bar to the exercise of First Amendment rights on websites integral to the fabric of our modern society and culture.

* * *

It is well established that, as a general rule, the Government may not suppress lawful speech as the means to suppress unlawful speech. That is what North Carolina has done here. Its law must be held invalid.

Justice Alito, concurring in the judgment.

The North Carolina statute at issue in this case was enacted to serve an interest of surpassing importance—but it has a staggering reach. It makes it a felony for a registered sex offender simply to visit a vast array of websites, including many that appear to provide no realistic opportunity for communications that could facilitate the abuse of children. Because of the law's extraordinary breadth, I agree with the Court that it violates the Free Speech Clause of the First Amendment.

I cannot join the opinion of the Court, however, because of its undisciplined dicta. The Court is unable to resist musings that seem to equate the entirety of the internet with public streets and parks. And this language is bound to be interpreted by some to mean that the States are largely powerless to restrict even the most dangerous sexual predators from visiting any internet sites, including, for example, teenage dating sites and sites designed to permit minors to discuss personal problems with their peers. I am troubled by the implications of the Court's unnecessary rhetoric.

I ...

B

A content-neutral time, place, or manner restriction must serve a legitimate government interest, and the North Carolina law easily satisfies this requirement. As we have frequently noted, the prevention of sexual exploitation and abuse of children constitutes a government objective of surpassing importance. ...

The State's interest in protecting children from recidivist sex offenders plainly applies to internet use. Several factors make the internet a powerful tool for the would-be child abuser. First, children often use the internet in a way that gives offenders easy access to their personal information—by, for example, communicating with strangers and allowing sites to disclose their location. Second, the internet provides previously unavailable ways of communicating with, stalking, and ultimately abusing children. An abuser can create a false profile that misrepresents the abuser's age and gender. The abuser can lure the minor into engaging in sexual conversations, sending explicit photos, or even meeting in person. And an abuser can use a child's location posts on the internet to determine the pattern of the child's day-to-day activities—and even the child's location at a given moment. Such uses of the internet are already well documented, both in research and in reported decisions.

Because protecting children from abuse is a compelling state interest and sex offenders can (and do) use the internet to engage in such abuse, it is legitimate and entirely reasonable for States to try to stop abuse from occurring before it happens.

C

1

It is not enough, however, that the law before us is designed to serve a compelling state interest; it also must not burden substantially more speech than is necessary to further the government's legitimate interests. The North Carolina law fails this requirement.

A straightforward reading of the text of § 14–202.5 compels the conclusion that it prohibits sex offenders from accessing an enormous number of websites. ... The fatal problem for § 14–202.5 is that its wide sweep precludes access to a large number of websites that are most unlikely to facilitate the commission of a sex crime against a child. A handful of examples illustrates this point.

Take, for example, the popular retail website Amazon.com, which allows minors to use its services and meets all four requirements of § 14–202.5's definition of a commercial social networking website. First, as a seller of products, Amazon unquestionably derives revenue from the operation of its website. Second, the Amazon site facilitates the social introduction of people for the purpose of information exchanges. When someone purchases a product on Amazon, the purchaser can review the product and upload photographs, and other buyers can then respond to the review. This information exchange about products that Amazon sells undoubtedly fits within the definition in § 14–202.5. It is the equivalent of passengers on a bus comparing notes about products they have purchased. Third, Amazon allows a user to create a personal profile, which is then associated with the product reviews that the user uploads. Such a profile can contain an assortment of information, including the user's name, e-mail address, and picture. And fourth, given its back-and-forth comment function, Amazon satisfies the final statutory requirement. [Justice Alito also argued that that the Washington Post and Web-MD were covered by § 14–202.5.]

As these examples illustrate, the North Carolina law has a very broad reach and covers websites that are ill suited for use in stalking or abusing children. The focus of the discussion on these sites—shopping, news, health—does not provide a convenient jumping off point for conversations that may lead to abuse. In addition, the social exchanges facilitated by these websites occur in the open, and this reduces the possibility of a child being secretly lured into an abusive situation. These websites also give sex offenders little opportunity to gather personal details about a child; the information that can be listed in a profile is limited, and the profiles are brief. What is more, none of these websites make it easy to determine a child's precise location at a given moment. For example, they do not permit photo streams (at most, a child could upload a single profile photograph), and they do not include up-to-the minute location services. Such websites would provide essentially no aid to a would-be child abuser.

Placing this set of websites categorically off limits from registered sex offenders prohibits them from receiving or engaging in speech that the First Amendment protects and does not appreciably advance the State's goal of protecting children from recidivist sex offenders. I am therefore compelled to conclude that, while the law before us addresses a critical problem, it sweeps far too broadly to satisfy the demands of the Free Speech Clause.

II

While I thus agree with the Court that the particular law at issue in this case violates the First Amendment, I am troubled by the Court's loose rhetoric. After noting that "a street or a park is a quintessential forum for the exercise of First Amendment rights," the Court states that "cyberspace" and "social media in particular" are now "the most important places (in a spatial sense) for the exchange of views." The Court declines to explain what this means with respect to free speech law, and the Court holds no more than that the North Carolina law fails the test for content-neutral "time, place, and manner" restrictions. But if the entirety of the internet or even just "social media" sites are the 21st century equivalent of public streets and parks, then States may have little ability to restrict the sites that may be visited by even the most dangerous sex offenders. May a State preclude an adult previously convicted of molesting children from visiting a dating site for teenagers? Or a site where minors communicate with each other about personal problems? The Court should be more attentive to the implications of its rhetoric for, contrary to the Court's suggestion, there are important differences between cyberspace and the physical world.

I will mention a few that are relevant to internet use by sex offenders. First, it is easier for parents to monitor the physical locations that their children visit and the individuals with whom they speak in person than it is to monitor their internet use. Second, if a sex offender is seen approaching children or loitering in a place frequented by children, this conduct may be observed by parents, teachers, or others. Third, the internet offers an unprecedented degree of anonymity and easily permits a would-be molester to assume a false identity.

The Court is correct that we should be cautious in applying our free speech precedents to the internet. Cyberspace is different from the physical world, and if it is true, as the Court believes, that "we cannot appreciate yet" the "full dimensions and vast potential" of "the Cyber Age," we should proceed circumspectly, taking one step at a time. It is regrettable that the Court has not heeded its own admonition of caution.

QUESTIONS

1. How would § 14–202.5 fare under rational basis review?

2. If you were trying to draft a narrower version of § 14–202.5 that would survive Supreme Court review, what would you do differently? If you were trying to define "social media" sites for a privacy statute, how would you do it?

NOTE ON CRYPTOGRAPHY

Cryptography is the science of secret communications. As a starting point, consider the problem facing Alice, who would like to send a message to Bob. So far, so good, but Alice is also worried about Eve, who may be able to intercept the letter in transit (perhaps by sneaking into the post office, or taking it from Bob's mailbox before he can open it). So Alice would like a way to *encrypt* her message so that Bob can read (or *decrypt*) it but Eve cannot.

Traditional Cryptography

Here is an extremely simple form of encryption: rot13. In this code every letter is replaced by the letter thirteen letters later in the alphabet (the name is short for "rotate by 13"). Thus A becomes N, B becomes O, C becomes P, and so on. The full table is:

```
ABCDEFGHIJKLMNOPQRSTUVWXYZ

NOPQRSTUVWXYZABCDEFGHIJKLM
```

Thus, suppose Alice wishes to encode the message (or *plaintext*) THIS CODE SUCKS. She turns T into G, H into U, and so on. When she is done, she has the coded message (or *ciphertext*) GUVF PBQR FHPXF. Eve stares at this gibberish, mystified. But Bob, who knows the secret, simply rotates every letter back by 13 places. G becomes T, U becomes H, and so on, until he has THIS CODE SUCKS again. Bingo! Secret secure.

The only problem is that rot13 is a terrible code, because it is so widely known. Any lengthy English text encoded using rot-13 will have many words starting with GU in the ciphertext (e.g. THIS becomes GUVF and THE becomes GUR). This is a dead giveaway that Alice and Bob are using rot13. Better codes reduce these predictable patterns.

Inventing a new code from scratch for every use would be a lot of work. Instead, cryptographers achieve better security by creating families of codes that use the same encryption algorithm but can have many different possible *secret keys*. Metaphorically, Alice puts the message in a box and seals the box with a lock that only the secret key can open. Bob, who has the key, can open the lock and read the message; Eve, who doesn't have the key, is out of luck. If Bob wants to reply to Alice, he can use the secret key to lock the lock again; again, Alice can open the lock but Eve cannot. Even if Eve recognizes the general type of lock, it tells her nothing about which particular key opens it.

For example, a slightly more secure version of rot13 is rotN ("rotate by N"). Alice and Bob pick a number between 1 and 26 to serve as the secret key. To encrypt, Alice rotates each letter in the plaintext forward that many places in the alphabet; to decrypt, Bob rotates each letter back by the same number. rot13 is rotN with the secret key 13.

Unfortunately, rotN is still a terrible secret code. For one thing, it is vulnerable to a *brute force* attack. Eve can simply try rotating an encrypted message by one letter, then by two, then three, etc. With the aid of a computer, she can try each of the 26 possible secret keys in a small faction of a second. Better codes have more possible keys, so that brute force attacks take much longer. Fortunately, just as the number of possible values a computer can store grows exponentially with the number of bits, so too the number of possible keys grows exponentially with the number of bits in a key. A code using 256-bit keys is not twice as hard to brute-force as a code using 128-bit keys; it is 2^{128} times harder.

Brute force can be surprisingly effective, particularly when it comes to that most familiar of keys, the password. There are 208,827,064,576 eight-letter all-caps passwords. If a would-be hacker types in each possible password, one after the other, at a rate of one password every five seconds, it will take about 33,000 *years* of nonstop work to try them all. But if the hacker runs a program that can try a million passwords per second, it will take only about two and a half days. Basically, password guessing is futile, but a determined brute-force attack will succeed against many short or simple passwords.

Another problem with rotN is that it is vulnerable to *cryptanalysis*. Because it is a simple substitution cipher, in which each letter in the plaintext is consistently replaced by the same letter in the ciphertext, encrypted messages replicate all of the patterns of English, e.g. some letters are much more frequent than others. If Eve has a sample of Alice's messages and notices that the letter G appears more often than any other, she may guess that it represents E, so that Alice and Bob are using the secret key 2. Better codes disguise these patterns, so that even small changes to the plaintext or the secret key create large and unpredictable differences in the ciphertext, and so that encrypted messages are close to indistinguishable from completely random gibberish.

One well-known state-of-the-art algorithm is the Advanced Encryption Standard, or AES. It encrypts messages 128 bits at a time, using a secret key of up to 256 bits. It mixes the bytes of the plaintext by repeatedly scrambling bytes, adding them together, and rearranging them. Although the process is long, and requires dozens of steps, every step is easy to reverse – for someone like Bob who has the secret key. Cryptographers currently believe that it is infeasible for someone like Eve who lacks the secret key and must guess at it to decrypt encoded messages. Cryptographers have thought that about other algorithms before, and been wrong; they may yet discover that AES is also vulnerable.

Even a stronger encryption algorithm like AES doesn't solve all of Alice's and Bob's problems. Eve could find a way to steal the secret key from Bob. Or Alice might leave a copy of the plaintext lying around. Or Eve could kidnap Bob and force him to turn over the key. No cryptographic algorithm can guard perfectly against these other attacks. Cryptography is just one component of the larger project of computer security.

Public-Key Cryptography

This is essentially where the state of the art in cryptography stood as of 1970: Alice and Bob needed to share a single secret key, used for both encryption and decryption. In the next decade, though, two teams of researchers turned the world of cryptography on its head.* In 1976, Whitfield Diffie and Martin Hellman published the idea of *public-key* cryptography. Their crucial idea was that only the decryption key held by Bob really needs to be secret; if the encryption and decryption keys can be separated, then the encryption key can be public, and anyone from Alice to Zelda can use it to encrypt messages to Bob. As long as Bob keeps his *private key* secret, he can publish the *public key* to the world, including Eve. In the metaphor, the public key is like a lock blueprint: anyone can use it to manufacture locks that only Bob can open. Whenever Alice needs to send Bob a message, she manufactures a Bob-only lock.

As described, the Diffie-Hellman scheme was only an idea, not a workable system. But the next year, in 1977, Ron Rivest, Adi Shamir, and Leonard Adelman published an actual algorithm (now known as RSA after its inventors) that made public-key cryptography a reality. The insight behind the RSA algorithm is that as far as we know it is much easier to multiply numbers than to factor them. To simplify slightly, to create a secret key, Bob picks a pair of very large prime numbers p and q at random. He then uses their product, $n = p \times q$, as his public key. To encrypt a message, anyone can write out the plaintext as a number, raise that number to a high power, and take the remainder after dividing by the public key n. Thanks to some elegant mathematics, it is easy to undo the process but only if you know what the factors of n are. Bob knows that $n = p \times q$, but anyone else cannot decrypt the message without factoring n, which mathematicians believe to be impractically hard. Since the RSA breakthrough, numerous other cryptographic algorithms have been built up from the same algebraic building blocks: multiplication, powers, and remainders.

The asymmetry of public-key encryption opens up all kinds of new and interesting possibilities beyond simply keeping messages secret. For example, in many systems, Bob can use his private key to "sign" messages: only someone with the private key can generate this *digital signature*, but anyone with the public key can check that whoever signed it really did know the private key. Metaphorically, the digital signature lets Bob use his private key as a stamp, leaving an unforgeable imprint on the documents he signs. Bob could even combine a signature with encryption: signing a message with his private key and encrypting it with Alice's public key. Now Alice knows that the message is genuine and she is the only person who can read it.

Digital signatures and related technologies have many, many applications:

- If Bob is careful about guarding his private key, he can use his digital signature as a source of *authentication*: anyone receiving a signed document knows that it was generated by Bob. He could tell his correspondents not to trust anything purporting to come from him unless it is digitally signed. Banks and other financial institutions use signatures in this way to prove the authenticity of transactions.

- Digital signatures can also be used to certify the *integrity* of a document. If anyone unauthorized tries to alter the document, the signature will no longer correspond to the altered document. Almost anything can be signed

---

* A third team, working inside the United Kingdom's Government Communications Headquarters (GCHQ), hit upon many of the same ideas independently and earlier, but since spy agencies don't publish, their work remained unknown to the world for decades.

this way; some states now use digital signatures to establish the authenticity and integrity of their judicial opinions.

- Sometimes bits can be scrambled during the transmission of a message by cosmic rays, power surges, or bugs. A receiver who checks the signature against the message can use it as a form of *error detection* and see that something has gone wrong and ask the sender to transmit it again. Hard drives and other storage systems use error-detection algorithms to guard against accidental data loss. If data in storage is corrupted, the error can be spotted before it spreads, and the bad data can be replaced with a clean copy known to be good.

- It is often convenient to use short digests of documents as a shorthand for talking about them. So, for example, a two-megabyte image could be converted to a 256-bit *hash value*.* Two images with different hash values are definitely different; two images with the same hash value are extremely, extremely likely to be identical. The hash values provide a fast way to check whether two images are the same – very useful if you run a site where users upload images and you don't want to store the same image again and again. Some hashing algorithms are designed to be secure: even an adversary who is determined to find two documents with the same hash value is highly unlikely to succeed.

- A *watermark* embeds one message in another with the goal of making it possible to tell where a given file came from. Stock photograph websites watermark their sample images; movie studios watermark the promotional copies they distribute to media outlets. Watermarks need not be visible to humans; ideally they should be hard to remove. In 2000, the Recording Industry Association of America threatened a lawsuit against a team of academic researchers who showed it was easy to remove the watermarks in a proposed scheme for watermarking audio files.

- In *steganography*, the goal is to hide one message undetectably inside another. A crude steganography scheme might use one space after a period to indicate a 0 and two spaces to indicate 1, hiding a short coded message inside an email. More sophisticated forms of steganography tweak small bits in an image or video: tiny variations in color or sound levels are completely imperceptible to humans.

One hard problem in any encryption system is *key distribution*: how do Alice and Bob learn each others' keys? There is a chicken-and-egg problem here: unless Alice and Bob already have a secure way to communicate, Alice cannot be sure she is talking to Bob rather than to Eve pretending to be Bob. One common solution is for some trusted third party to certify Alice and Bob's identities (using its own digital signature, of course): either a major hard-to-imitate institution like Google, or a mutual friend. So, for example, *certificate authorities* like Symantec or Comodo issue *certificates* using the X.509 standard: these certificates contain the public key for some entity and are signed with the certificate authority's own secret key. Of course, certificate authorities have their own key-distribution problem: how do you know what the authority's public key is? For this reason, browser makers fre-

---

* Not to be confused with a Twitter hash *tag*.

quently include certificates; anyone using Firefox already has a copy, supplied by Firefox, of Comodo's public key.*

An Example

Real-world computer systems frequently combine many cryptographic techniques together into more complicated protocols. For example, Transport Layer Security, or TLS, is a widely used protocol for clients and servers to communicate securely. Here is a simplified version of the process:

1. Well in advance, the server obtains an X.509 certificate that lists its domain name and RSA public key.

2. The client sends a simple "hello" message to the server indicating that it wishes to communicate securely.

3. The server responds with its own "hello" message that includes the server's X.509 certificate.

4. The client checks the validity of the X.509 certificate. Among other things, it verifies:

    - That the signature is issued by a certificate authority the client trusts.

    - That the signature on the certificate is valid.

    - That the domain name listed on the certificate matches the domain name the client thinks it is contacting.

    - That the certificate has not expired or been revoked by the certification authority.†

5. The client now knows the server's RSA public key. It sends the server an RSA-encrypted message containing a random number.

6. The server uses its private RSA key to decrypt the random number. Both the client and the server now know the random number, but no one else does. They can therefore use it as a shared AES key.

7. The client encrypts its first substantive message to the server using their shared AES key and sends the encrypted message to the server.

8. The server decrypts the message using the AES key, dettermines its response, encrypts that response using the AES key, and sends the encrypted response to the client.

9. If desired, the client and server can continue the process using the same AES key as long as the connection stays open.

Among other things, TLS is the basis for HTTPS, the encrypted version of HTTP. When your browser shows you a lock in the address bar (or another visual indicator of a secure connection), it means that your HTTP messages to and from the server are encrypted using TLS, keeping the contents safe from eavesdroppers. The easiest way to request an HTTPS connection is to replace `http://` with `https://` when typing in a URL – although not all servers honor clients' requests to use HTTPS. Regular HTTP connections are unencrypted, so that anyone in a

---

* If it occurred to you to ask how you know that you received a properly authenticated copy of Firefox when you downloaded it, rather than a modified version that includes a forged public key for an impostor pretending to be Comodo, congratulations, you are starting to think like an Internet security expert.

† Test yourself. What could go wrong if the client omits any of these checks?

position to observe your messages (e.g. your ISP) can see what URLs you are browsing to and what those web pages contain.

Observe that in this example, TLS employs certificates (X.509), public-key encryption (RSA), and shared-key encryption (AES). This combination of smaller pieces is common in modern cryptography and enables some remarkable feats of security engineering. Unfortunately it also means that when one piece proves to be vulnerable, whole edifices are at risk. The infamous Heartbleed bug of 2014 was a coding mistake in the most common server implementation of TLS: by sending a particular kind of malformatted message, a client could cause a server to send back the contents of its memory. Since a common use of TLS is logging into websites, that part of memory often contained users' passwords. Ironically, until the bug was fixed, changing one's password actually made things worse, because a user would typically then log in using the new password, exposing it to attackers using Heartbleed. Despite striking advances in cryptography, Internet security remains a hard problem.

BERNSTEIN V. U.S. DEPT. OF JUSTICE
176 F.3d 1132 (9th Cir.),
withdrawn and reh'g en banc granted, 192 F.3d 1308 (9th Cir. 1999)

Fletcher, Circuit Judge: ...

BACKGROUND

A. Facts and Procedural History

Bernstein is currently a professor in the Department of Mathematics, Statistics, and Computer Science at the University of Illinois at Chicago. As a doctoral candidate at the University of California, Berkeley, he developed an encryption method – "a zero-delay private-key stream encryptor based upon a one-way hash function" that he dubbed "Snuffle." Bernstein described his method in two ways: in a paper containing analysis and mathematical equations (the "Paper") and in two computer programs written in "C," a high-level computer programming language ("Source Code"). Bernstein later wrote a set of instructions in English (the "Instructions") explaining how to program a computer to encrypt and decrypt data utilizing a one-way hash function, essentially translating verbatim his Source Code into prose form.

Seeking to present his work on Snuffle within the academic and scientific communities, Bernstein asked the State Department whether he needed a license to publish Snuffle in any of its various forms. The State Department responded that Snuffle was a munition under the [Export Administration Regulations ("EAR") administered by the Bureau of Export Administration ("BXA")], and that Bernstein would need a license to "export" the Paper, the Source Code, or the Instructions.

There followed a protracted and unproductive series of letter communications between Bernstein and the government, wherein Bernstein unsuccessfully attempted to determine the scope and application of the export regulations to Snuffle. [Bernstein sued, and the District Court held that the EAR constituted a constitutionally impermissible prior restraint on speech.]

B. Overview of Cryptography

Cryptography is the science of secret writing, a science that has roots stretching back hundreds, and perhaps thousands, of years. For much of its history, cryptography has been the jealously guarded province of governments and militaries. In the past twenty years, however, the science has blossomed in the civilian sphere, driven on the one hand by dramatic theoretical innovations within the field, and on the other by the needs of modern communication and information technologies. As a result, cryptography has become a dynamic academic discipline within applied mathematics. It is the cryptographer's primary task to find secure methods to encrypt messages, making them unintelligible to all except the intended recipients:

> Encryption basically involves running a readable message known as "plaintext" through a computer program that translates the message according to an equation or algorithm into unreadable "ciphertext." Decryption is the translation back to plaintext when the message is received by someone with an appropriate "key."

Bernstein v. U.S. Department of State, 974 F. Supp. 1288, 1292 (N.D. Cal. 1997)] The applications of encryption, however, are not limited to ensuring secrecy; encryption can also be employed to ensure data integrity, authenticate users, and facilitate nonrepudiation (e.g., linking a specific message to a specific sender).

It is, of course, encryption's secrecy applications that concern the government. The interception and deciphering of foreign communications has long played an important part in our nation's national security efforts. In the words of a high-ranking State Department official:

> Policies concerning the export control of cryptographic products are based on the fact that the proliferation of such products will make it easier for foreign intelligence targets to deny the United States Government access to information vital to national security interests. Cryptographic products and software have military and intelligence applications. As demonstrated throughout history, encryption has been used to conceal foreign military communications, on the battlefield, aboard ships and submarines, or in other military settings. Encryption is also used to conceal other foreign communications that have foreign policy and national security significance for the United States. For example, encryption can be used to conceal communications of terrorists, drug smugglers, or others intent on taking hostile action against U.S. facilities, personnel, or security interests.

Lowell Decl. at 4. As increasingly sophisticated and secure encryption methods are developed, the government's interest in halting or slowing the proliferation of such methods has grown keen. The EAR regulations at issue in this appeal evidence this interest.

C. The EAR regulations

The EAR contain specific regulations to control the export of encryption software, expressly including computer source code. [The "export" of encryption software was defined] to preclude the use of the internet and other global mediums if such publication would allow passive or active access by a foreign national within the United States or anyone outside the United States. 15 C.F.R. § 734.2(b)(9)(B)(ii). ...

If encryption software falls within the ambit of the relevant EAR provisions, the "export" of such software requires a prepublication license. When a prepublication license is requested, the relevant agencies undertake a "case-by-case" analysis to determine if the export is "consistent with U.S. national security and foreign policy interests." 15 C.F.R. § 742.15(b). ...

DISCUSSION

I. Prior Restraint

The parties and *amici* urge a number of theories on us. We limit our attention here, for the most part, to only one: whether the EAR restrictions on the export of encryption software in source code form constitute a prior restraint in violation of the First Amendment. We review *de novo* the district court's affirmative answer to this question.

It is axiomatic that "prior restraints on speech and publication are the most serious and least tolerable infringement on First Amendment rights." *Nebraska Press Ass'n v. Stuart*, 427 U.S. 539, 559 (1976). Indeed, the Supreme Court has opined that "it is the chief purpose of the [First Amendment] guaranty to prevent previous restraints upon publication." *Near v. Minnesota*, 283 U.S. 697, 713 (1931). Accordingly, "[a]ny prior restraint on expression comes . . . with a 'heavy presumption' against its constitutional validity." *Organization for a Better Austin v. Keefe*, 402 U.S. 415, 419 (1971). ...

A. Is Bernstein entitled to bring a facial attack?

A licensing regime is always subject to facial challenge as a prior restraint where it "gives a government official or agency substantial power to discriminate based on the content or viewpoint of speech by suppressing disfavored speech or disliked speakers," and has "a close enough nexus to expression, or to conduct commonly associated with expression, to pose a real and substantial threat of . . . censorship risks." *Id.* at 759.

The EAR regulations at issue plainly satisfy the first requirement – "the determination of who may speak and who may not is left to the unbridled discretion of a government official." *Id.* at 763. BXA administrators are empowered to deny licenses whenever export might be inconsistent with "U.S. national security and foreign policy interests." 15 C.F.R. § 742.15(b). No more specific guidance is provided. Obviously, this constraint on official discretion is little better than no constraint at all. ...

The more difficult issue arises in relation to the second requirement – that the challenged regulations exhibit "a close enough nexus to expression." We are called on to determine whether encryption source code is expression for First Amendment purposes.

We begin by explaining what source code is. "Source code," at least as currently understood by computer programmers, refers to the text of a program written in a "high-level" programming language, such as "PASCAL" or "C." The distinguishing feature of source code is that it is meant to be read and understood by humans and that it can be used to express an idea or a method. A computer, in fact, can make no direct use of source code until it has been translated ("compiled") into a "low-level" or "machine" language, resulting in computer-executable "object code." That source code is meant for human eyes and understanding, however, does not mean that an untutored lay-person can understand it. Because source code is destined for the maw of an automated, ruthlessly literal translator – the compiler – a programmer must follow stringent grammatical, syntactical, formatting, and punctuation conventions. As a result, only those trained in programming can easily understand source code.[11]

Also important for our purposes is an understanding of how source code is used in the field of cryptography. Bernstein has submitted numerous declarations from cryptographers and computer programmers explaining that cryptographic ideas and algorithms are conveniently expressed in source code.[12]

That this should be so is, on reflection, not surprising. As noted earlier, the chief task for cryptographers is the development of secure methods of encryption.

---

11   It must be emphasized, however, that source code is merely text, albeit text that conforms to stringent formatting and punctuation requirements. For example, the following is an excerpt from Bernstein's Snuffle source code:

```
for (; ;)
  (
  uch = gtchr( );
  if (!(n & 31))
    (
    for (i = 0; i<64; i + +)
    l[ctr[i]] = k[i] + h[n − 64 + i]
    Hash512 (wm, wl, level, 8);
    )
```

As source code goes, Snuffle is quite compact; the entirety of the Snuffle source code occupies fewer than four printed pages.

12   Source code's power to convey algorithmic information is illustrated by the declaration of MIT Professor Harold Abelson:

The square root of a number X is the number Y such that Y times Y equals X. This is declarative knowledge. It tells us something about square roots. But it doesn't tell us how to find a square root. In contrast, consider the following ancient algorithm, attributed to Heron of Alexandria, for approximating square roots:

To approximate the square root of a positive number X,

- Make a guess for the square root of X.
- Compute an improved guess as the average of the guess and X divided by the guess.
- Keep improving the guess until it is good enough.

Heron's method doesn't say anything about what square roots are, but it does say how to approximate them. This is a piece of imperative "how to" knowledge.

Computer science is in the business of formalizing imperative knowledge – developing formal notations and ways to reason and talk about methodology. Here is Heron's method formalized as a procedure in the notation of the Lisp computer language:

```
(define (sqrtx)
  (define (good-enough? guess)
    (<(abs ( − (square guess) x)) tolerance))
  (define (improve guess)
    (average guess (/ × guess)))
  (define (try guess)
    (if (good-enough? guess)
    guess
    (try (improve guess))))
  (try 1))
```

While the articulation of such a system in layman's English or in general mathematical terms may be useful, the devil is, at least for cryptographers, often in the algorithmic details. By utilizing source code, a cryptographer can express algorithmic ideas with precision and methodological rigor that is otherwise difficult to achieve. This has the added benefit of facilitating peer review – by compiling the source code, a cryptographer can create a working model subject to rigorous security tests. The need for precisely articulated hypotheses and formal empirical testing, of course, is not unique to the science of cryptography; it appears, however, that in this field, source code is the preferred means to these ends.

Thus, cryptographers use source code to express their scientific ideas in much the same way that mathematicians use equations or economists use graphs. Of course, both mathematical equations and graphs are used in other fields for many purposes, not all of which are expressive. But mathematicians and economists have adopted these modes of expression in order to facilitate the precise and rigorous expression of complex scientific ideas. Similarly, the undisputed record here makes it clear that cryptographers utilize source code in the same fashion.

In light of these considerations, we conclude that encryption software, in its source code form[15] and as employed by those in the field of cryptography, must be viewed as expressive for First Amendment purposes, and thus is entitled to the protections of the prior restraint doctrine. If the government required that mathematicians obtain a prepublication license prior to publishing material that included mathematical equations, we have no doubt that such a regime would be subject to scrutiny as a prior restraint. The availability of alternate means of expression, moreover, does not diminish the censorial power of such a restraint – that Adam Smith wrote *Wealth of Nations* without resorting to equations or graphs surely would not justify governmental prepublication review of economics literature that contain these modes of expression.

The government, in fact, does not seriously dispute that source code is used by cryptographers for expressive purposes. Rather, the government maintains that source code is different from other forms of expression (such as blueprints, recipes, and "how-to" manuals) because it can be used to control directly the operation of a computer without conveying information to the user. In the government's view, by targeting this unique functional aspect of source code, rather than the content of the ideas that may be expressed therein, the export regulations manage to skirt entirely the concerns of the First Amendment. This argument is flawed for at least two reasons.

First, it is not at all obvious that the government's view reflects a proper understanding of source code. As noted earlier, the distinguishing feature of source code is that it is meant to be read and understood by humans, and that it *cannot* be used to control directly the functioning of a computer. While source code, when properly prepared, can be easily compiled into object code by a user, ignoring the distinction between source and object code obscures the important fact that source code is not meant solely for the computer, but is rather written in a language intended also for human analysis and understanding.

---

15 We express no opinion regarding whether object code manifests a "close enough nexus to expression" to warrant application of the prior restraint doctrine. Bernstein's Snuffle did not involve object code, nor does the record contain any information regarding expressive uses of object code in the field of cryptography.

Second, and more importantly, the government's argument, distilled to its essence, suggests that even one drop of "direct functionality" overwhelms any constitutional protections that expression might otherwise enjoy. This cannot be so. The distinction urged on us by the government would prove too much in this era of rapidly evolving computer capabilities. The fact that computers will soon be able to respond directly to spoken commands, for example, should not confer on the government the unfettered power to impose prior restraints on speech in an effort to control its "functional" aspects. The First Amendment is concerned with expression, and we reject the notion that the admixture of functionality necessarily puts expression beyond the protections of the Constitution. ...

[The court held that the export restrictions were a constitutionally impermissible prior restraint on speech.]

Nelson, Circuit Judge, Dissenting: ...

The basic error which sets the majority and the district court adrift is the failure to fully recognize that the basic function of encryption source code is to act as a method of controlling computers. As defined in the EAR regulations, encryption source code is "[a] precise set of operating instructions to a computer, that when compiled, allows for the execution of an encryption function on a computer." 15 C.F.R. pt. 722. Software engineers generally do not create software in object code-the series of binary digits (1's and 0's) – which tells a computer what to do because it would be enormously difficult, cumbersome and time-consuming. Instead, software engineers use high-level computer programming languages such as "C" or "Basic" to create source code as a shorthand method for telling the computer to perform a desired function. In this respect, lines of source code are the building blocks or the tools used to create an encryption machine. Encryption source code, once compiled, works to make computer communication and transactions secret; it creates a lockbox of sorts around a message that can only be unlocked by someone with a key. It is the function or task that encryption source code performs which creates its value in most cases. This functional aspect of encryption source code contains no expression; it is merely the tool used to build the encryption machine. ...

This is not to say that this very same source code is not used expressively in some cases. Academics, such as Bernstein, seek to convey and discuss their ideas concerning computer encryption. As noted by the majority, Bernstein must actually use his source code textually in order to discuss or teach cryptology. In such circumstances, source code serves to express Bernstein's scientific methods and ideas.

While it is conceptually difficult to categorize encryption source code under our First Amendment framework, I am still inevitably led to conclude that encryption source code is more like conduct than speech. Encryption source code is a building tool. Academics and computer programmers can convey this source code to each other in order to reveal the encryption machine they have built. But, the ultimate purpose of encryption code is, as its name suggests, to perform the function of encrypting messages. Thus, while encryption source code may occasionally be used in an expressive manner, it is inherently a functional device. ...

The activity or conduct at issue here is the export of encryption source code. As I noted above, the basic nature of encryption source code lies in its functional capacity as a method to build an encryption device. Export of encryption source code is not conduct commonly associated with expression. Rather, it is conduct that is normally associated with providing other persons with the means to make their computer messages secret. The overwhelming majority of people do not want to talk about the source code and are not interested in any recondite message that may be contained in encryption source code. Only a few people can actually understand what a line of source code would direct a computer to do. Most people simply want to *use* the encryption source code to protect their computer communications. Export of encryption source code simply does not fall within the bounds of conduct commonly associated with expression such as picketing or handbilling. ...

[Following this decision, the Ninth Circuit granted rehearing *en banc*. While the rehearing was pending, the government exempted "publicly available encryption source code" from most of the EAR's restrictions, *see* 15 C.F.R. § 740.13(e), mooting the case. The export control laws continue to be enforced against other computer products: the Xbox.com website terms of service, for example, require users to agree to comply with export controls.]

QUESTIONS

1. How did computer software end up on the export control list along with surface-to-air missiles? How does the Internet make this a harder case?

2. How does the the First Amendment apply to object code?

3. Programs can be used not just to protect secrets but to discover them. There is a thriving grey market in "exploits": short programs that take advantage of security vulnerabilities in commonly-used software to let an attacker take control of a computer. Secrecy is key, because once an exploit is known, the company whose software it targets can fix the vulnerability. Some of the biggest exploit buyers are governments – including the United States government – looking to spy on each other, or on their own citizens. Some critics think that the sale of exploits should be criminalized. But others argue that they are protected by the First Amendment. Who is right? Would it make a difference if the defendant sold only a plain-English description of a security vulnerability, but did not include the code to exploit it? The Second Amendment protects "the right of the people to keep and bear Arms." Does it also protect the right to keep and bear exploits?

4. *Bernstein* deals with software exports; what about software imports? Consider the following not-entirely-hypothetical:

   > The International Trade Commission has the power to prohibit "the importation into the United States ... of articles that ... infringe a ... United States patent." 19 U.S.C. § 1337 (a)(1)(B). The Scrivello Corporation holds a patent on a particular style of dental braces that are customized to the wearer's mouth. A competitor, Szell Dental, creates digital models of the braces in Pakistan, then transmits the models over the Internet to a factory in the United States, where it manufactures the braces using a 3D printer.

   Has Szell "imported" infringing "articles?"

NOTE ON THE PRESS

The First Amendment protects both "the freedom of speech" and "of the press." Lawyers and scholars are divided on whether this second clause adds anything to the first. Some believe that the Constitution enshrines special protections for the media – especially the news media – because of their central role in democracy.

Others believe that the Constitution values all speakers equally, amateurs as well as professionals, as long as they are engaged in protected "speech." The Supreme Court has not settled the question, although it has been resistant to extending special rights to the press not available to individual citizens. *See, e.g., Branzburg v. Hayes*, 408 U.S. 665 (1972) (holding that the First Amendment does not require that reporters receive an evidentiary privilege against being compelled to testify).

The question has a special urgency online. Increasingly, bloggers and independent activists are invoking laws originally written for the benefit of reporters and institutional media. For example, "media shield" laws protect reporters from being required to identify their confidential sources or turn over their unpublished files. Although forty-nine states have some kind of media shield protections, the details of who and what are covered, and when, vary significantly.* As a concrete example, here is California's:

> A publisher, editor, reporter, or other person connected with or employed upon a newspaper, magazine, or other periodical publication, or by a press association or wire service ... cannot be adjudged in contempt by a judicial, legislative, administrative body, or any other body having the power to issue subpoenas, for refusing to disclose ... the source of any information procured while so connected or employed for publication in a newspaper, magazine or other periodical publication, or for refusing to disclose any unpublished information obtained or prepared in gathering, receiving or processing of information for communication to the public.

CAL. EVID. CODE § 1070(a). A similar provision applies to "a radio or television news reporter." *Id.* § 1070(b). Do those statutory terms include Apple Insider, a website devoted to rumors and leaks about forthcoming Apple products? Yes, said a California court in *O'Grady v. Superior Court*, 44 Cal. Rptr. 3d 72, 99 (2006), writing that "the open and deliberate publication on a news-oriented Web site of news gathered for that purpose by the site's operators" was "conceptually indistinguishable from publishing a newspaper." Compare *Too Much Media, LLC, v. Hale*, 20 A.3d 364, 367 (N.J. 2011), which refused to apply New Jersey's shield law to "a self- described journalist who posted comments on an Internet message board." It compared her posts to "a pamphlet full of unfiltered, unscreened letters to the editor submitted for publication." *Id.* at 379.

Similarly, courts have been willing to allow news media to publish stories even when some of the information in those stories was obtained illegally. *New York Times Co. v. United States*, 403 U.S. 713 (1971) held that an order forbidding the New York Times from publishing the "Pentagon Papers" (a secret Defense Department study documenting the United States's military involvement in Vietnam) violated the First Amendment as an unconstitutional prior restraint. *Bartnicki v. Vopper*, 532 U.S. 514 (2001) held that a radio commentator who was given a tape recording of two union officials discussing potentially violent negotiating tactics could play it on the air, because he "played no part in the illegal interception" and

---

* The Reporters Committee for Freedom of the Press has a detailed state-by-state survey of press shield laws and caselaw at http://www.rcfp.org/reporters-privilege. *See also U.S. v. Sterling*, 724 F.3d 482 (4th Cir. 2013) (holding 2–1 that there is no federal privilege against naming confidential sources and compelling *New York Times* reporter James Risen to say who told him about a classified C.I.A. operation to slow down Iran's nuclear weapons program).

because "the subject matter of the conversation was a matter of public concern.." *Id.* at 525.

Other laws more clearly protect speakers in general. So-called "anti-SLAPP statutes" give defendants a chance to obtain early dismissal of lawsuits designed to chill free speech. ("SLAPP" is an acronym for Strategic Lawsuit Against Public Participation). Indiana, for example, allows defendants to file a motion to dismiss on the basis that "the act upon which the claim [against them] is based is a lawful act in furtherance of the person's right of petition or free speech." IND. CODE § 34-7-7-9(d). All other discovery is stayed, *id.* § 34-7-7-6, and the court must act on the motion expeditiously, *id* § 34-7-7-9(a)(2). In essence, the statute changes the usual sequence of civil case management so that the defendant can litigate her First Amendment arguments first without the expense and hassle of discovery. If she prevails, she is entitled to her reasonable attorneys' fees. *Id.* § 34-7-7-7. (Why?) For example, in *Gilbert v. Skyes*, 147 Cal. App. 4th 13 (2007), the court dismissed a plastic surgeon's defamation claim against a former patient. It held that a "slight discrepancy" in before-and-after photos at her website, my-surgerynightmare.com, did not make them false, and that her statement "I didn't need procedures and I had no idea what I was really getting myself into" was not injuriously false.

QUESTIONS

1. If you were drafting a press shield law for the digital age, what would it say? What facts would you want to know about a self-described "citizen journalist" to decide whether to let him or her refuse to name a source?

2. Should media shield laws have a carve-out for national-security information, like the NSA surveillance documents leaked by Edward Snowden? Or is the rationale for such laws even stronger with government secrets? Should the answer depend on whether the leaks are to established journalists like Glenn Greenwald at *The Guardian* and Barton Gellman at the *Washington Post* (to whom Snowden released thousands of NSA documents) or to non-mainstream outlets like WikiLeaks (to whom Chelsea Manning released 250,000 classified State Department cables)? Should the answer depend on how the law treats leakers and whistleblowers themselves?

3. Does the *Bartnicki* rationale also apply to a blogger who comes into possession of a video, shot by a trespasser, showing conditions inside a poultry processing plant? Or is there something about the institutional press that makes it more likely to use this privilege for the broader social good?

4. Are anti-SLAPP statutes a sensible protection for free speech, or an unnecessary piece of First Amendment exceptionalism? If the anti-SLAPP procedures are so good, why not make them available in all cases?

5. More and more Americans get their news online, frequently through aggregator sites that link to stories elsewhere do little of their own reporting, like the Huffington Post. Newspaper advertising and circulation are down significantly. What will happen to news reporting if traditional offline news outlets disappear entirely? Is the Internet the source of this problem, or the solution?

B. Harmful Speech

Concluding that something is "speech" does not end the First Amendment inquiry. Some restrictions of speech are permissible; many of those restrictions are related to the harm that the speech causes. The materials in this section consider four kinds of harm that speech could cause: to the victim's reputation, sense of safety, privacy, and emotions. An early generation of theorists believed that these restrictions were either unenforceable or unnecessary on the Internet. They argued that online speech could and should be utterly uninhibited. As you read the following materials, ask what this view gets right and what it gets wrong.

DANAH BOYD*
IT'S COMPLICATED
THE SOCIAL LIVES OF NETWORKED TEENS
10–13 (Yale University Press 2014)

To understand what is new and what is not, it's important to understand how technology introduces new social possibilities and how these challenge assumptions people have about everyday interactions. The design and architecture of environments enable certain types of interaction to occur. Round tables with chairs make chatting with someone easier than classroom-style seating. Even though students can twist around and talk to the person behind them, a typical classroom is designed to encourage everyone to face the teacher. The particular properties or characteristics of an environment can be understood as *affordances* because they make possible – and, in some cases, are used to encourage – certain types of practices, even if they do not determine what practices will unfold. Understanding the affordances of a particular technology or space is important because it sheds light on what people can leverage or resist in achieving their goals. For example, the affordances of a thick window allow people to see each other without being able to hear each other. To communicate in spite of the window, they may pantomime, hold up signs with written messages, or break the glass. The window's affordances don't predict how people will communicate, but they do shape the situation nonetheless.

Because technology is involved, networked publics have different characteristics than traditional physical public spaces. Four affordances, in particular, shape many of the mediated environments that are created by social media. Although these affordances are not in and of themselves new, their relation to one another because of networked publics creates new opportunities and challenges. They are:

- persistence: the durability of online expressions and content;
- visibility: the potential audience who can bear witness;
- spreadability: the ease with which content can be shared;
- and searchability: the ability to find content.

Content shared through social media often sticks around because technologies are designed to enable *persistence*. The fact that content often persists has significant implications. Such content enables interactions to take place over time in an asynchronous fashion. Alice may write to Bob at midnight while Bob is sound asleep; but when Bob wakes up in the morning or comes back from summer camp three

---

* [Ed: The preferred way to write "danah boyd" is in lowercase letters.]

weeks later, that message will still be there waiting for him, even if Alice had forgotten about it. Persistence means that conversations conducted through social media are far from ephemeral; they endure. Persistence enables different kinds of interactions than the ephemerality of a park. Alice's message doesn't expire when Bob reads it, and Bob can keep that message for decades. What persistence also means, then, is that those using social media are often "on the record" to an unprecedented degree.

Through social media, people can easily share with broad audiences and access content from greater distances, which increases the potential *visibility* of any particular message. More often than not, what people put up online using social media is widely accessible because most systems are designed such that sharing with broader or more public audiences is the default. Many popular systems require users to take active steps to limit the visibility of any particular piece of shared content. This is quite different from physical spaces, where people must make a concerted effort to make content visible to sizable audiences. In networked publics, interactions are often public by default, private through effort.

Social media is often designed to help people spread information, whether by explicitly or implicitly encouraging the sharing of links, providing reblogging or favoriting tools that repost images or texts, or by making it easy to copy and paste content from one place to another. Thus, much of what people post online is easily *spreadable* with the click of a few keystrokes. Some systems provide simple buttons to "forward," "repost," or "share" content to articulated or curated lists. Even when these tools aren't built into the system, content can often be easily downloaded or duplicated and then forwarded along. The ease with which everyday people can share media online is unrivaled, which can be both powerful and problematic. Spreadability can be leveraged to rally people for a political cause or to spread rumors.

Last, since the rise of search engines, people's communications are also often *searchable*. My mother would have loved to scream, "Find!" and see where my friends and I were hanging out and what we were talking about. Now, any inquisitive onlooker can query databases and uncover countless messages written by and about others. Even messages that were crafted to be publicly accessible were not necessarily posted with the thought that they would reappear through a search engine. Search engines make it easy to surface esoteric interactions. These tools are often designed to eliminate contextual cues, increasing the likelihood that searchers will take what they find out of context.

None of the capabilities enabled by social media are new. The letters my grandparents wrote during their courtship were persistent. Messages printed in the school newspaper or written on bathroom walls have long been visible. Gossip and rumors have historically spread like wildfire through word of mouth. And although search engines certainly make inquiries more efficient, the practice of asking after others is not new, even if search engines mean that no one else knows. What is new is the way in which social media alters and amplifies social situations by offering technical features that people can use to engage in these well-established practices.

As people use these different tools, they help create new social dynamics. For example, teens "stalk" one another by searching for highly visible, persistent data about people they find interesting. "Drama" starts when teens increase the visibility of gossip by spreading it as fast as possible through networked publics. And teens seek attention by exploiting searchability, spreadability, and persistence to maximize the visibility of their garage band's YouTube video. The particular practices that emerge as teens use the tools around them create the impression that teen sociality is radically different even though the underlying motivations and social processes have not changed that much.

QUESTIONS

1. Is a handwritten letter persistent? Visible? Spreadable? Searchable? What about an email? A blog post?

2. How do these four affordances change the ways in which speech can inflict harms on listeners? On speakers? On third parties?

3. John Perry Barlow argues that online speech is different because the Internet is *all speech*. How does this play into his argument that governments should keep their hands off the Internet? Do boyd's claims support his argument, or undercut it?

BLU-RAY PROBLEM

Blu-Ray discs and players use a copy protection technology known as AACS. Each Blu-Ray disc is encrypted, so that it appears to contain only a large sequence of random bits. An authorized Blu-Ray player, however, can use a secret "processing key" to decrypt the sequence of bits into a viewable movie. The AACS Licensing Administrator ("AACS LA"), the organization that controls the AACS standard, gives out processing keys to Blu-Ray player manufacturers and requires them to sign licensing agreements that (a) restrict what their players will do (e.g. no burning unencrypted copies of Blu-Ray discs) and (b) promise to keep the processing key secret.

It now appears that a processing key has leaked. An unknown user by the username of BluRazor has managed to extract the processing key from a Magnavox Blu-Ray player. He posted the key, the thirty-two-digit hexadecimal number 09-F9-11-02-9D-74-E3-5B-D8-41-56-C5-63-56-88-C0, to the DVD Technical Forum, a web discussion board for digital video programmers. Three days later, AACS LA sued the DVD Technical Forum and BluRazor for breach of trade secrecy and violation of Section 1201 of the Copyright Act, which prohibits "trafficking" in "devices" designed to facilitate copyright infringement by disabling "technological protection measures."[*] The Forum and BluRazor immediately agreed to the entry of an injunction preventing them from distributing the processing key. The Forum replaced the post with a brief note that read, "This post has been deleted at the request of the AACS LA."

Hundreds of DVD Technical Forum users, however, had already seen the post and were furious at what they saw as censorship of their community. Some of them had copied down the number. Dozens of users reposted the number in threads all across the DVD Technical Forum. In addition, a user with the Forum username DVD Monkey considered it ridiculous that anyone could try to "own" a number. He created and posted this image.[*] Here's a partial explanation of the symbolism:

---

[*] For more on this provision, see *infra* Chapter 7.

[*] The image is *Mnemonic MonKey Pirate* by ApeLad, posted to Flickr at http://www.flickr.com/photos/apelad/487654055/ and is available under a Creative Commons Attribution Noncommercial 2.0 license. The full license details are available at http://creativecommons.org/licenses/by-nc/2.0/deed.en.

Beginning at the top, with the goose egg on the right, then proceeding clockwise we see a roman numeral. Next up is a function key. Then there's salt (I wonder what the atomic weight of sodium is?) followed by another goose egg. The monkey's holding up a couple of  fingers, and his tail is making a funny shape too! What's that on the flag? Down from there we see a tungsten bulb (again, what's the atomic weight of tungsten?). ...

If you were advising the AACS LA, what actions would you suggest?

NOTE ON TRUE THREATS

Our survey of harmful categories of speech begins with one of the most dramatic: threats of violence. The basic rule here is that "true threats," i.e. "unequivocal, unconditional and specific expressions of intention immediately to inflict injury," *United States v. Kelner*, 534 F.2d 1020, 1027 (2d Cir. 1976), are unprotected speech. As the Supreme Court explained in *Virginia v. Black*, 538 U.S. 343, 359–60 (2003):

> "True threats" encompass those statements where the speaker means to communicate a serious expression of an intent to commit an act of unlawful violence to a particular individual or group of individuals. The speaker need not actually intend to carry out the threat. Rather, a prohibition on true threats protects individuals from the fear of violence and from the disruption that fear engenders in addition to protecting people from the possibility that the threatened violence will occur.

But even though the speaker need not have any mens rea to *carry out* the threat, the speaker must still have some mens rea to *make* the threat. *In Elonis v. United States*, 135 S.Ct. 2001 (2015), the Court reversed the conviction of Anthony Elonis, whose ex-wife obtained a restraining order based on the tone of some of his Facebook posts. Elonis responded with another post:

> Fold up your [protection-from-abuse order] and put it in your pocket
> Is it thick enough to stop a bullet?

Two FBI agents visited Elonis, after which he posted:

> Little Agent lady stood so close
> Took all the strength I had not to turn the b**** ghost
> Pull my knife, flick my wrist, and slit her throat
> Leave her bleedin' from her jugular in the arms of her partner

Elonis was charged under 18 U.S.C. § 875(c), which prohibits transmitting "any communication containing any threat ... to injure the person of another." Elonis argued that he did not intend to threaten anyone, that the posts were rap lyrics in the style of Eminem, some of whose raps are violent murder-revenge fantasies. The jury was instructed that it could convict him if "a reasonable person would foresee that the statement would be interpreted by those to whom the maker communicates the statement as a serious expression of an intention to inflict bodily injury or take the life of an individual."

This "negligence standard," the Supreme Court held, was too low a mental state. It added that the statute would allow for a conviction if the government showed that the defendant subjectively *intended* to communicate a threat, or *knew* that the statement would be perceived as a threat. It left open the question of whether a showing that the defendant acted *recklessly* would suffice. Because the Court resolved the case as a matter of statutory interpretation, it also left open the question of whether the First Amendment required the same result.

QUESTIONS

1. After *Elonis*, are the following sufficient to support a conviction under the federal threat statute?

- A private email by a college student to an unknown Internet pen pal, describing the student's fantasy of abducting, raping, and murdering another student in his dorm:

    > As I said before, my room is right across from the girl's bathroom. Wiat until late at night. grab her when she goes to unlock the dorr. Knock her unconscious. and put her into one of those portable lockers (forget the word for it). or even a duffle bag. Then hurry her out to the car and take her away ... What do you think?

- A Facebook post complaining about the Drug Enforcement Agency:

    > I'll kill whoever I deem to be in the way of harmony to the human reace ... Policeman all deserve to be tortured to death and videos made n sent to their families ... BE WARNED IF U PULL LE OVER!! IM LIKE JASON VOORHEES WITH A BLOODLUST FOR PIG BLOOD.

- A tweet responding to the closure of an airport due to bad weather:

> Crap! LAX airport is closed. You've got a week and a bit to get your shit together otherwise I'm blowing the airport sky high!!

- An anti-abortion website that features the names of doctors who perform abortions, along with their home addresses and photographs. Beneath each picture, in an Old West-style font, is the logo "WANTED." A legend at the top of the page explains, "Black font (working); Greyed-out Name (wounded); Strikethrough (fatality)."

2. A related but narrow category of speech that can be restricted under the First Amendment consists of fighting words: "those which by their very utterance ... tend to incite an immediate breach of the peace." *Chaplinsky v. New Hampshire*, 315 U.S. 568 (1942). Another consists of incitement: "advocacy ... directed to inciting or producing imminent lawless action [that] is likely to incite or produce such action." *Brandenburg v. Ohio*, 319 U.S. 444 (1969). In person, "Come at me, bro!" might be fighting words, and "Kick him before he can get up!" might be incitement. Will the fighting words and incitement exceptions *ever* apply online?

RESTATEMENT (SECOND) OF TORTS [DEFAMATION]

§ 558 – *Elements [of Defamation] Stated*

To create liability for defamation there must be:

(a) a false and defamatory statement concerning another;[*]

(b) an unprivileged publication to a third party;

(c) fault amounting at least to negligence on the part of the publisher;[†] and

(d) [harm].

§ 559 – *Defamatory Communication Defined*

A communication is defamatory if it tends so to harm the reputation of another as to lower him in the estimation of the community or to deter third persons from associating or dealing with him.

§ 568 – *Libel and Slander Distinguished*

---

* [Ed: The First Amendment requires the plaintiff in a defamation action involving speech on a matter of public concern to bear the burden of showing that the speech in question is false. *See Philadelphia Newspapers v. Hepps*, 475 U.S. 767, 776 (1986).]

† [Ed: The First Amendment requires a higher threshold of fault where the plaintiff is a public figure – i.e., someone who has "pervasive fame or notoriety" or who "voluntarily injects himself or is drawn into a particular public controversy." *Gertz v. Robert Welch, Inc.*, 418 U.S. 323, 351 (1974). In such cases, he or she has the burden of showing not just negligence but actual malice, i.e., that the defendant knew the speech was false or acted with reckless disregard of its possible falsity. *See Hustler Magazine, Inc. v. Falwell*, 485 U.S. 46, 56–57 (1988). A plurality of the Supreme Court has held that the actual-malice standard does not apply to "speech on matters of purely private concern." *Dun & Bradstreet, Inc. v. Greenmoss Builders, Inc.*, 472 U.S. 749, 759 (1985). The decision, however, indicated that cases on matters of purely private concern would be rare. In the same case, six Justices in three separate opinions rejected a proposed distinction in the standard of fault applicable to the institutional media versus other defendants, but since the case was decided on other grounds, the issue technically remains open.]

(1) Libel consists of the publication of defamatory matter by written or printed words, by its embodiment in physical form or by any other form of communication that has the potentially harmful qualities characteristic of written or printed words.

(2) Slander consists of the publication of defamatory matter by spoken words, transitory gestures or by any form of communication other than those stated in Subsection (1).

(3) The area of dissemination, the deliberate and premeditated character of its publication and the persistence of the defamation are factors to be considered in determining whether a publication is a libel rather than a slander.

§ 623A – *Liability for Publication of Injurious Falsehood—General Principle*

One who publishes a false statement harmful to the interests of another is subject to liability for pecuniary loss resulting to the other if

(a) he intends for publication of the statement to result in harm to interests of the other having a pecuniary value, or either recognizes or should recognize that it is likely to do so, and

(b) he knows that the statement is false or acts in reckless disregard of its truth or falsity.

§ 566 – *Expressions of Opinion*

A defamatory communication may consist of a statement in the form of an opinion, but a statement of this nature is actionable only if it implies the allegation of undisclosed defamatory facts as the basis for the opinion.

QUESTIONS

1. On May 12, 2009, Amanda Bonnen used Twitter to tweet:

   > @JessB123 You should just come anyway. Who said sleeping in a moldy apartment was bad for you? Horizon realty thinks it's okay.

   Horizon Group Management, her former landlord, sued for defamation. Is Bonnen's 127-character tweet legally actionable? If Bonnen had talked to her friends in person, rather than using Twitter, could there have been a lawsuit?

2. The owners of the Kebapi Cafe have been frustrated by a series of bad Yelp reviews, which they suspect were written by the owners of the competing Cafe Ćevapi across the street. They are considering having all their customers sign an agreement stating, "By dining here, you agree not to post online reviews of this restaurant without permission of management." Is this a good idea? Congress thought not: the Consumer Review Fairness Act of 2016, 15 U.S.C. § 45b, voids provisions in form contracts that purport to restrict consumers' rights to publish reviews. How else should businesses deal with negative (often anonymous) online reviews?

3. Some commentators have argued that the tort of defamation is outdated in the digital world and should be abolished. They claim that victims can now take to the Internet to tell their side of the story, so they don't need legal remedies. Do you agree?

RESTATEMENT (SECOND) OF TORTS [EMOTIONAL DISTRESS]
§ 46 – *Outrageous Conduct Causing Severe Emotional Distress*

(1) One who by extreme and outrageous conduct intentionally or recklessly causes severe emotional distress to another is subject to liability for such emotional distress, and if bodily harm to the other results from it, for such bodily harm. ...

SNYDER V. PHELPS
131 S. Ct. 1207 (2011)

Chief Justice Roberts delivered the opinion of the Court. ...

I ...

Fred Phelps founded the Westboro Baptist Church in Topeka, Kansas, in 1955. The church's congregation believes that God hates and punishes the United States for its tolerance of homosexuality, particularly in America's military. [The church picketed the funeral of Marine Lance Corporal Matthew Snyder, who was killed in Iraq. The picketing took place on public land between 1,000 feet from the funeral service and 200 to 300 feet from the funeral procession; the picketers "complied with police instructions, ... did not yell or use profanity, and there was no violence associated with the picketing."] Although Snyder testified that he could see the tops of the picket signs as he drove to the funeral, he did not see what was written on the signs until later that night, while watching a news broadcast covering the event.

[Snyder sued Phelps and Westboro in federal court for state-law tort claims including intentional infliction of emotional distress, and obtained a jury verdict for $2.9 in compensatory damages and $8 million in punitive damages. The District Court reduced the punitive damage award to $2.1 million; the Court of Appeals granted Westboro judgment as a matter of law on First Amendment grounds.]

II

To succeed on a claim for intentional infliction of emotional distress in Maryland, a plaintiff must demonstrate that the defendant intentionally or recklessly engaged in extreme and outrageous conduct that caused the plaintiff to suffer severe emotional distress. The Free Speech Clause of the First Amendment – "Congress shall make no law ... abridging the freedom of speech" – can serve as a defense in state tort suits, including suits for intentional infliction of emotional distress. See, *e.g., Hustler Magazine, Inc. v. Falwell*, 485 U.S. 46 (1988).

Whether the First Amendment prohibits holding Westboro liable for its speech in this case turns largely on whether that speech is of public or private concern, as determined by all the circumstances of the case. ... The First Amendment reflects a profound national commitment to the principle that debate on public issues should be uninhibited, robust, and wide-open. ... Accordingly, speech on public issues occupies the highest rung of the hierarchy of First Amendment values, and is entitled to special protection.

Not all speech is of equal First Amendment importance, however, and where matters of purely private significance are at issue, First Amendment protections are often less rigorous. That is because restricting speech on purely private matters does not implicate the same constitutional concerns as limiting speech on matters of public interest: "There is no threat to the free and robust debate of public issues; there is no potential interference with a meaningful dialogue of ideas"; and the "threat of liability" does not pose the risk of "a reaction of self-censorship" on matters of public import. *Dun & Bradstreet, Inc. v. Greenmoss Builders, Inc.*, 472 U.S. 749, 760 (1985). ...

Speech deals with matters of public concern when it can be fairly considered as relating to any matter of political, social, or other concern to the community, or when it is a subject of legitimate news interest; that is, a subject of general interest and of value and concern to the public. ...

The content of Westboro's signs plainly relates to broad issues of interest to society at large, rather than matters of"purely private concern. The placards read "God Hates the USA/Thank God for 9/11," "America is Doomed," "Don't Pray for the USA," "Thank God for IEDs," "Fag Troops," "Semper Fi Fags," "God Hates Fags," "Maryland Taliban," "Fags Doom Nations," "Not Blessed Just Cursed," "Thank God for Dead Soldiers," "Pope in Hell," "Priests Rape Boys," "You're Going to Hell," and "God Hates You." While these messages may fall short of refined social or political commentary, the issues they highlight – the political and moral conduct of the United States and its citizens, the fate of our Nation, homosexuality in the military, and scandals involving the Catholic clergy – are matters of public import. The signs certainly convey Westboro's position on those issues, in a manner designed, unlike the private speech in *Dun & Bradstreet* [involving a particular individual's credit report], to reach as broad a public audience as possible. And even if a few of the signs – such as "You're Going to Hell" and "God Hates You" – were viewed as containing messages related to Matthew Snyder or the Snyders specifically, that would not change the fact that the overall thrust and dominant theme of Westboro's demonstration spoke to broader public issues. ...

Westboro's choice to convey its views in conjunction with Matthew Snyder's funeral made the expression of those views particularly hurtful to many, especially to Matthew's father. The record makes clear that the applicable legal term – "emotional distress" – fails to capture fully the anguish Westboro's choice added to Mr. Snyder's already incalculable grief. But Westboro conducted its picketing peacefully on matters of public concern at a public place adjacent to a public street. Such space occupies a special position in terms of First Amendment protection. We have repeatedly referred to public streets as the archetype of a traditional public forum, noting that time out of mind public streets and sidewalks have been used for public assembly and debate. ... Simply put, the church members had the right to be where they were. ...

Given that Westboro's speech was at a public place on a matter of public concern, that speech is entitled to "special protection" under the First Amendment. Such speech cannot be restricted simply because it is upsetting or arouses contempt. If there is a bedrock principle underlying the First Amendment, it is that the government may not prohibit the expression of an idea simply because society finds the idea itself offensive or disagreeable. *Texas v. Johnson*, 491 U.S. 397, 414 (1989). Indeed, "the point of all speech protection ... is to shield just those choices of content that in someone's eyes are misguided, or even hurtful." *Hurley v. Irish-American Gay, Lesbian and Bisexual Group of Boston, Inc.*, 515 U.S. 557, 574 (1995).

The jury here was instructed that it could hold Westboro liable for intentional infliction of emotional distress based on a finding that Westboro's picketing was "outrageous." "Outrageousness," however, is a highly malleable standard with "an inherent subjectiveness about it which would allow a jury to impose liability on the basis of the jurors' tastes or views, or perhaps on the basis of their dislike of a particular expression." *Hustler, 485 U.S., at 55.* In a case such as this, a jury is unlikely to be neutral with respect to the content of the speech, posing a real danger of becoming an instrument for the suppression of vehement, caustic, and sometimes unpleasant expression. Such a risk is unacceptable; "in public debate [we] must tolerate insulting, and even outrageous, speech in order to provide adequate breathing space to the freedoms protected by the First Amendment." *Boos v. Barry*, 485 U.S. 312, 322 (1988). What Westboro said, in the whole context of how and where it chose to say it, is entitled to "special protection" under the First Amendment, and that protection cannot be overcome by a jury finding that the picketing was outrageous.

For all these reasons, the jury verdict imposing tort liability on Westboro for intentional infliction of emotional distress must be set aside. ...

Justice Alito, dissenting.

Our profound national commitment to free and open debate is not a license for the vicious verbal assault that occurred in this case. ...

QUESTIONS

1. After *Snyder*, is the IIED tort a dead letter?
2. What result if Westboro's "picketing" takes place online rather than on a public street?

RESTATEMENT (SECOND) OF TORTS [PRIVACY TORTS]

§ 652B – *Intrusion upon Seclusion*

One who intentionally intrudes, physically or otherwise, upon the solitude or seclusion of another or his private affairs or concerns, is subject to liability to the other for invasion of his privacy, if the intrusion would be highly offensive to a reasonable person.

Comments

b. The invasion may be by physical intrusion into a place in which the plaintiff has secluded himself, as when the defendant forces his way into the plaintiff's room in a hotel or insists over the plaintiff's objection in entering his home. It may also be by the use of the defendant's senses, with or without mechanical aids, to oversee or overhear the plaintiff's private affairs, as by looking into his upstairs windows with binoculars or tapping his telephone wires. It may be by some other form of investigation or examination into his private concerns, as by opening his private and personal mail, searching his safe or his wallet, examining his private bank account, or compelling him by a forged court order to permit an inspection of his personal documents. ...

c. The defendant is subject to liability under the rule stated in this Section only when he has intruded into a private place, or has otherwise invaded a private seclusion that the plaintiff has thrown about his person or affairs. Thus there is no liability for the examination of a public record concerning the plaintiff, or of documents that the plaintiff is required to keep and make available for public inspection. Nor is there liability for observing him or even taking his photograph while he is walking on the public highway, since he is not then in seclusion, and his appearance is public and open to the public eye. Even in a public place, however, there may be some matters about the plaintiff, such as his underwear or lack of it, that are not exhibited to the public gaze; and there may still be invasion of privacy when there is intrusion upon these matters.

§ 652D - *Publicity Given to Private Life*

One who gives publicity to a matter concerning the private life of another is subject to liability to the other for invasion of his privacy, if the matter publicized is of a kind that

(a) would be highly offensive to a reasonable person, and

(b) is not of legitimate concern to the public.

PENNSYLVANIA RIGHT OF PUBLICITY
Title 42, Pennsylvania Consolidated Statutes

§ 8316 – *Unauthorized use of name or likeness*

(a) *CAUSE OF ACTION ESTABLISHED.*–Any natural person whose name or likeness has commercial value and is used for any commercial or advertising purpose without the written consent of such natural person ... may bring an action to enjoin such unauthorized use and to recover damages for any loss or injury sustained by such use. ...

(c) *REPOSE.*–No action shall be commenced under this section more than 30 years after the death of such natural person. ...

(e) *DEFINITIONS.*–As used in this section, the following words and phrases shall have the meanings given to them in this subsection:

"Commercial or advertising purpose."

(1) Except as provided in paragraph (2), the term shall include the public use or holding out of a natural person's name or likeness:

(i) on or in connection with the offering for sale or sale of a product, merchandise, goods, services or businesses;

(ii) for the purpose of advertising or promoting products, merchandise, goods or services of a business; or

(iii) for the purpose of fundraising.

(2) The term shall not include the public use or holding out of a natural person's name or likeness in a communications medium when:

(i) the natural person appears as a member of the public and the natural person is not named or otherwise identified;

(ii) it is associated with a news report or news presentation having public interest;

(iii) it is an expressive work; ...

"Expressive work."

A literary, dramatic, fictional, historical, audiovisual or musical work regardless of the communications medium by which it is exhibited, displayed, performed or transmitted, other than when used or employed for a commercial or advertising purpose.

QUESTIONS

1. What does the intrusion on seclusion tort have to do with speech? Is there a First Amendment right to listen and observe as well as to speak? If so, what work are the concepts of "public place" and "private place" doing in defining the contours of the tort? Is it legal to videotape interactions with the police?

To take photographs up the skirts of women seated on the subway? To fly a drone outside a neighbor's window?

2. What is the difference between "publicity given to private life" and the "right of publicity?"

GAWKER MEDIA, LLC V. BOLLEA
129 So. 3d 1196 (Dist. Ct. App. Fla. 2014)

Black, Judge:

Terry Bollea sought to enjoin Gawker Media, LLC, from publishing and otherwise distributing the written report about his extramarital affair that includes video excerpts from the sexual encounter. The circuit court granted Mr. Bollea's motion for temporary injunction, though it did not articulate the reasons for doing so. ... Because the temporary injunction is an unconstitutional prior restraint under the First Amendment, we reverse.

I. BACKGROUND

In 2006, Mr. Bollea engaged in extramarital sexual relations with a woman in her home. Allegedly without Mr. Bollea's consent or knowledge, the sexual encounter was videotaped. On or about October 4, 2012, Gawker Media posted a written report about the extramarital affair on its website, including excerpts of the videotaped sexual encounter ("Sex Tape"). Mr. Bollea maintains that he never consented to the Sex Tape's release or publication. Gawker Media maintains that it was not responsible for creating the Sex Tape and that it received a copy of the Sex Tape from an anonymous source for no compensation.

On October 15, 2012, Mr. Bollea initiated an action in federal court by filing a multicount complaint against Gawker Media and others, asserting claims for invasion of privacy, publication of private facts, violation of the right of publicity, and infliction of emotional distress. [He voluntarily dismissed the suit on December 28, 2012, after the court denied his motion for a preliminary injunction.] That same day, Mr. Bollea filed an amended complaint in state circuit court, asserting essentially the same claims that he asserted in federal court. Thereafter and as he did in federal court, Mr. Bollea filed a motion for temporary injunction seeking to enjoin Gawker Media ... from publishing and otherwise distributing the video excerpts from the sexual encounter and complementary written report. Following a hearing, the circuit court issued an order on April 25, 2012, granting the motion for temporary injunction. The court did not make any findings at the hearing or in its written order to support its decision. On May 15, 2013, this court stayed the order granting the motion for temporary injunction pending the resolution of this appeal.

II. APPLICABLE STANDARDS

The primary purpose of a temporary injunction is to preserve the status quo while the merits of the underlying dispute are litigated. In the context of the media, the status quo is to publish news promptly that editors decide to publish. A restraining order disturbs the status quo and impinges on the exercise of editorial discretion. A temporary injunction is an extraordinary remedy that should be granted sparingly and only after the moving party has alleged and proved facts entitling him to relief.

A temporary injunction aimed at speech, as it is here, is a classic example of prior restraint on speech triggering First Amendment concerns, and as such, it is prohibited in all but the most exceptional cases. Since "prior restraints on speech and publication are the most serious and least tolerable infringement on First Amendment rights," the moving party bears the "heavy burden" of establishing that there are no less extreme measures available to "mitigate the effects of the unrestrained . . . public[ation]" and that the restraint will indeed effectively accomplish its purpose. *Neb. Press Ass'n v. Stuart*, 427 U.S. 539, 558–59, 562 (1976). Furthermore, "[w]here . . . a direct prior restraint is imposed upon the reporting of news by the media, each passing day may constitute a separate and cognizable infringement of the First Amendment." *Neb. Press Ass'n v. Stuart*, 423 U.S. 1327, 1329 (Blackmun, Circuit Justice, 1975). . . .

III. FIRST AMENDMENT

It is not clear from the hearing transcript, and certainly not from the order, why the circuit court granted the motion for temporary injunction. Based upon the few interjections the court made during the hearing, it appears that the court believed Mr. Bollea's right to privacy was insurmountable and that publishing the content at issue was otherwise impermissible because it was founded upon illegal actions.

A. Privacy

"[W]here matters of purely private significance are at issue, First Amendment protections are often less rigorous." *Snyder v. Phelps*, 131 S.Ct. 1207, 1215 (2011). On the other hand, "speech on matters of public concern . . . is at the heart of the First Amendment's protection." *Id.*

> Speech deals with matters of public concern when it can be fairly considered as relating to any matter of political, social, or other concern to the community, or when it is a subject of legitimate news interest; that is, a subject of general interest and of value and concern to the public. The arguably inappropriate or controversial character of a statement is irrelevant to the question whether it deals with a matter of public concern.

Id. at 1216. Mr. Bollea, better known by his ring name Hulk Hogan, enjoyed the spotlight as a professional wrestler, and he and his family were depicted in a reality television show detailing their personal lives. Mr. Bollea openly discussed an affair he had while married to Linda Bollea in his published autobiography and otherwise discussed his family, marriage, and sex life through various media outlets. Further, prior to the publication at issue in this appeal, there were numerous reports by various media outlets regarding the existence and dissemination of the Sex Tape, some including still shots therefrom. Despite Mr. Bollea's public persona, we do not suggest that every aspect of his private life is a subject of public concern. *See generally Post–Newsweek Stations Orlando, Inc. v. Guetzloe*, 968 So. 2d 608, 612 (Fla. 5th DCA 2007) (noting that appellant's status as a public figure does not mean that every aspect of his private life is of public concern but nonetheless holding that enjoining the broadcaster from publicly airing appellant's personal records and those of his family operated as an unconstitutional prior restraint under the First Amendment). However, the mere fact that the publication contains arguably inappropriate and otherwise sexually explicit content does not remove it from the realm of legitimate public interest. *See Fla. Star v. B.J.F.*, 491 U.S. 524, 525 (1989) (holding that a news article about a rape was a matter of public concern and that the newspaper was not liable for the publication of the victim's identity obtained from a police report released by law enforcement in violation of a Florida statute); *Cape Publ'ns, Inc. v. Hitchner*, 549 So. 2d 1374, 1377 (Fla. 1989) (holding that confidential information regarding a child abuse trial was a matter of legitimate public concern and that thus the newspaper's publication of such did not violate privacy interests). It is clear that as a result of the public controversy surrounding the affair and the Sex Tape, exacerbated in part by Mr. Bollea himself,[5] the report and the related video excerpts address matters of public concern. *See Michaels v. Internet Entm't Grp., Inc.*, No. CV 98–0583 DDP (CWx), 1998 WL 882848, at *10 (C.D.Cal. Sept. 11, 1998) (*Michaels II*) ("[T]he private facts depicted in the [publication] ha[d] a substantial nexus to a matter of legitimate public interest," namely, a dispute over the dissemination of the sex tape, and the depiction of the sexual relations was "clearly part of the story."); *see also Jones v. Turner*, No. 94 Civ. 8603(PKL), 1995 WL 106111, at *21 (S.D.N.Y. Feb. 7, 1995) (holding that the preliminary injunction was unjustifiable where nude pictures were related to the accompanying article and the article itself was a matter of public concern). *But see City of San Diego, Cal. v. Roe*, 543 U.S. 77, 84 (2004) (holding that the sexually explicit acts of the government employee, depicted in a video, did not address a matter of public concern where the acts "did nothing to inform the public about any aspect of the [employing agency's] functioning or operation"); *Toffoloni v. LFP Publ'g Grp., LLC*, 572 F.3d 1201, 1213 (11th Cir. 2009) (holding that the publication of nude photographs of a female professional wrestler taken twenty years prior was not protected speech because their publication was not related to the content of the reporting, namely, her murder).

In support of his contention that the report and video excerpts do not qualify as matters of public concern, Mr. Bollea relies on *Michaels v. Internet Entertainment Group, Inc.*, 5 F. Supp. 2d 823 (C.D.Cal. 1998) (*Michaels I*), in which the court enjoined the commercial distribution of an entire sex tape that infringed the plaintiffs' copyrights. However, the court in *Michaels I* found the use of the sex tape to be purely commercial in nature. Specifically, the copyrighted tape was sold via the internet to paying subscribers, and the internet company displayed short segments of the tape as a means of advertisement to increase the number of subscriptions. In contrast, Gawker Media has not attempted to sell the Sex Tape or any of the material creating the instant controversy, for that matter.[6] Rather, Gawker Media reported on Mr. Bollea's extramarital affair and complementary thereto posted excerpts from the video.

The court in *Michaels I* pointed out that although "[t]he plaintiffs are entitled to an injunction against uses of their names or likenesses to sell the [sex tape,] [t]he injunction may not reach the use of their names or likenesses to report or

---

5   We are hard-pressed to believe that Mr. Bollea truly desired the affair and Sex Tape to remain private or to otherwise be "swept under the rug." For example, in March 2012, Mr. Bollea called into TMZ Live, a celebrity and entertainment media outlet, and disclosed that he could not identify the woman in the Sex Tape because he had a number of "conquests" during the time it was filmed. Furthermore, in October 2012, Mr. Bollea appeared on The Howard Stern Show and professed that his good friend, Todd Alan Clem, known professionally as Bubba the Love Sponge, allowed Mr. Bollea to have sex with Mr. Clem's then-wife Heather Clem. Mr. Bollea was certainly not shy about disclosing the explicit details of another affair he had while married to Linda Bollea in his autobiography.

6   We are aware that Gawker Media is likely to profit indirectly from publishing the report with video excerpts to the extent that it increases traffic to Gawker Media's website. However, this is distinguishable from selling the Sex Tape purely for commercial purposes.

comment on matters of public interest." In accord with this conclusion, the court held in the companion case that the publication of a news report and brief excerpts of the sex tape was not an invasion of privacy and was protected speech. *Michaels II*, 1998 WL 882848, at *7, *10 (distinguishing the dissemination of an entire sex tape with the use of excerpts from the tape); *see also Bollea v. Gawker Media, LLC*, 913 F. Supp. 2d 1325, 1331 n. 6 (M.D. Fla. 2012) ("[Gawker Media] did not simply post the entire [Sex Tape] – or substantial portions thereof, but rather posted a carefully edited excerpt consisting of less than two minutes of the thirty[-]minute video of which less than ten seconds depicted explicit sexual activity."). Here, the written report and video excerpts are linked to a matter of public concern – Mr. Bollea's extramarital affair and the video evidence of such – as there was ongoing public discussion about the affair and the Sex Tape, including by Mr. Bollea himself. Therefore, Mr. Bollea failed to meet the heavy burden to overcome the presumption that the temporary injunction is invalid as an unconstitutional prior restraint under the First Amendment. As such, it was within Gawker Media's editorial discretion to publish the written report and video excerpts.

B. Unlawful Interception

It appears that the circuit court may have been convinced by Mr. Bollea's argument that the speech at issue is not entitled to First Amendment protection because the Sex Tape was created in violation of the law.[7] However, there is no dispute that Gawker Media was not responsible for the creation of the Sex Tape. Nor has Mr. Bollea alleged that Gawker Media otherwise obtained it unlawfully. The Supreme Court in *Bartnicki* held that if a publisher lawfully obtains the information in question, the speech is protected by the First Amendment provided it is a matter of public concern, even if the source recorded it unlawfully. *see also N.Y. Times Co. v. United States*, 403 U.S. 713, 91 S.Ct. 2140, 29 L.Ed.2d 822 (1971) (holding that notwithstanding the fact that a third party had stolen the information, the press had a constitutional right to publish the Pentagon Papers because they were of public concern). As the speech in question here is indeed a matter of legitimate public concern, the holding in *Bartnicki* applies.[8] As such, the temporary injunction acts as an unconstitutional prior restraint on Gawker Media's protected speech. ...

V. CONCLUSION

The circuit court's order granting Mr. Bollea's motion for temporary injunction is reversed because it acts as an unconstitutional prior restraint under the First Amendment.

QUESTIONS

1. On remand, the case proceeded to trial. A jury awarded Bollea $115 million in compensatory damages and $25 million in punitive damages. Gawker appealed, but also declared bankruptcy. Is the jury verdict consistent with the opinion in *Gawker Media v. Bollea* above, or should it have been thrown out on appeal? (Gawker went bankrupt, reached a settlement with Bollea, and dropped the appeal.)

---

7 Mr. Bollea cites to the offense of video voyeurism, section 810.145(2)(a), Florida Statutes (2006), and to the offense of interception and disclosure of electronic communications, section 934.03, Florida Statutes (2006), in support of his contention.

8 This opinion should not be construed as making a ruling regarding whether or not the information itself was intercepted unlawfully by Gawker Media's source.

2. In May 2016, it emerged that Bollea's lawsuit against Gawker had been secretly funded by the libertarian billionaire tech investor Peter Thiel. In 2007, Gawker's Valleywag blog had published an article outing Thiel as gay. Thiel responded by paying lawyers to find other "victims" of its coverage sue Gawker. As Thiel later explained in an interview with the *New York Times*, "It's less about revenge and more about specific deterrence. I saw Gawker pioneer a unique and incredibly damaging way of getting attention by bullying people even when there was no connection with the public interest." Does knowing this fact change how you think about the merits of *Gawker Media v. Bollea*?

PEOPLE V. MARQUAN M.
24 N.Y.3d 1 (2014)

Graffeo, Justice:

Defendant, a 16–year–old high school student, anonymously posted sexual information about fellow classmates on a publicly-accessible Internet website. He was criminally prosecuted for "cyberbullying" under a local law enacted by the Albany County Legislature. We are asked to decide whether this cyberbullying statute comports with the Free Speech Clause of the First Amendment.

I ...

Elected officials in Albany County decided to tackle the problem of cyberbullying. They determined there was a need to criminalize such conduct because the "State Legislature ha[d] failed to address th[e] problem" of "non-physical bullying behaviors transmitted by electronic means." Local Law No. 11 [2010] of County of Albany § 1. In 2010, the Albany County Legislature adopted a new crime – the offense of cyberbullying – which was defined as

> "any act of communicating or causing a communication to be sent by mechanical or electronic means, including posting statements on the internet or through a computer or email network, disseminating embarrassing or sexually explicit photographs; disseminating private, personal, false or sexual information, or sending hate mail, with no legitimate private, personal, or public purpose, with the intent to harass, annoy, threaten, abuse, taunt, intimidate, torment, humiliate, or otherwise inflict significant emotional harm on another person."

The provision outlawed cyberbullying against "any minor or person" situated in the county. Knowingly engaging in this activity was deemed to be a misdemeanor offense punishable by up to one year in jail and a $1,000 fine. The statute, which included a severability clause, became effective in November 2010.

II

A month later, defendant Marquan M., a student attending Cohoes High School in Albany County, used the social networking website "Facebook" to create a page bearing the pseudonym "Cohoes Flame." He anonymously posted photographs of high-school classmates and other adolescents, with detailed descriptions of their alleged sexual practices and predilections, sexual partners and other types of personal information. The descriptive captions, which were vulgar and offensive, prompted responsive electronic messages that threatened the creator of the website with physical harm.

A police investigation revealed that defendant was the author of the Cohoes Flame postings. He admitted his involvement and was charged with cyberbullying under Albany County's local law. Defendant moved to dismiss, arguing that the statute violated his right to free speech under the First Amendment. ...

III

Defendant contends that Albany County's cyberbullying law violates the Free Speech Clause of the First Amendment because it is overbroad in that it includes a wide array of protected expression, and is unlawfully vague since it does not give fair notice to the public of the proscribed conduct. The County concedes that certain aspects of the cyberbullying law are invalid but maintains that those portions are severable, rendering the remainder of the act constitutional if construed in accordance with the legislative purpose of the enactment. Interpreted in this restrictive manner, the County asserts that the cyberbullying law covers only particular types of electronic communications containing information of a sexual nature pertaining to minors and only if the sender intends to inflict emotional harm on a child or children.

Under the Free Speech Clause of the First Amendment, the government generally "has no power to restrict expression because of its message, its ideas, its subject matter, or its content." *United States v. Stevens*, 559 U.S. 460, 468 (2010). Consequently, it is well established that prohibitions of pure speech must be limited to communications that qualify as fighting words, true threats, incitement, obscenity, child pornography, fraud, defamation or statements integral to criminal conduct. Outside of such recognized categories, speech is presumptively protected and generally cannot be curtailed by the government.

Yet, the government unquestionably has a compelling interest in protecting children from harmful publications or materials. Cyberbullying is not conceptually immune from government regulation, so we may assume, for the purposes of this case, that the First Amendment permits the prohibition of cyberbullying directed at children, depending on how that activity is defined. Our task therefore is to determine whether the specific statutory language of the Albany County legislative enactment can comfortably coexist with the right to free speech.

Challenges to statutes under the Free Speech Clause are usually premised on the overbreadth and vagueness doctrines. A regulation of speech is overbroad if constitutionally-protected expression may be "chilled" by the provision because it facially prohibits a real and substantial amount of expression guarded by the First Amendment This type of facial challenge, which is restricted to cases implicating the First Amendment, requires a court to assess the wording of the statute – without reference to the defendant's conduct – to decide whether a substantial number of its applications are unconstitutional, judged in relation to the statute's plainly legitimate sweep. A law that is overbroad cannot be validly applied against any individual. In contrast, a statute is seen by the courts as vague if it fails to give a citizen adequate notice of the nature of proscribed conduct, and permits arbitrary and discriminatory enforcement. Hence, the government has the burden of demonstrating that a regulation of speech is constitutionally permissible. ...

Based on the text of the statute at issue, it is evident that Albany County created a criminal prohibition of alarming breadth. The language of the local law embraces a wide array of applications that prohibit types of protected speech far beyond the cyberbullying of children. As written, the Albany County law in its broadest sense criminalizes "any act of communicating . . . by mechanical or electronic means . . . with no legitimate . . . personal . . . purpose, with the intent to harass [or] annoy . . . another person." On its face, the law covers communications aimed at adults, and fictitious or corporate entities, even though the county legislature justified passage of the provision based on the detrimental effects that cyberbullying has on school-aged children. The county law also lists particular examples of covered communications, such as "posting statements on the internet or through a computer or email network, disseminating embarrassing or sexually explicit photographs; disseminating private, personal, false or sexual information, or sending hate mail." But such methods of expression are not limited to instances of cyberbullying – the law includes every conceivable form of electronic communication, such as telephone conversations, a ham radio transmission or even a telegram. In addition, the provision pertains to electronic communications that are meant to "harass, annoy . . . taunt . . . [or] humiliate" any person or entity, not just those that are intended to "threaten, abuse . . . intimidate, torment . . . or otherwise inflict significant emotional harm on" a child. In considering the facial implications, it appears that the provision would criminalize a broad spectrum of speech outside the popular understanding of cyberbullying, including, for example: an email disclosing private information about a corporation or a telephone conversation meant to annoy an adult.

The County admits that the text of the statute is too broad and that certain aspects of its contents encroach on recognized areas of protected free speech. Because the law imposes a restriction on the content of protected speech, it is invalid unless the County can demonstrate that it passes strict scrutiny – that is, unless it is justified by a compelling government interest and is narrowly drawn to serve that interest. For this reason, the County asks us to sever the offending portions and declare that the remainder of the law survives strict scrutiny. What remains, in the County's view, is a tightly circumscribed cyberbullying law that includes only three types of electronic communications sent with the intent to inflict emotional harm on a child: (1) sexually explicit photographs; (2) private or personal sexual information; and (3) false sexual information with no legitimate public, personal or private purpose.

It is true, as the County urges, that a court should strive to save a statute when confronted with a Free Speech challenge. But departure from a textual analysis is appropriate only if the statutory language is fairly susceptible to an interpretation that satisfies applicable First Amendment requirements. The doctrine of separation of governmental powers prevents a court from rewriting a legislative enactment through the creative use of a severability clause when the result is incompatible with the language of the statute. And special concerns arise in the First Amendment context – excessive judicial revision of an overbroad statute may lead to vagueness problems because the statutory language would signify one thing but, as a matter of judicial decision, would stand for something entirely different. Under those circumstances, persons of ordinary intelligence reading [the law] could not know what it actually meant.

We conclude that it is not a permissible use of judicial authority for us to employ the severance doctrine to the extent suggested by the County or the dissent. It is possible to sever the portion of the cyberbullying law that applies to adults and other entities because this would require a simple deletion of the phrase "or person" from the definition of the offense. But doing so would not cure all of the law's constitutional ills. As we have recently made clear, the First Amendment protects annoying and embarrassing speech, even if a child may be exposed to it, so those references would also need to be excised from the definitional section. And, the

First Amendment forbids the government from deciding whether protected speech qualifies as "legitimate," as Albany County has attempted to do.[4]

It is undisputed that the Albany County statute was motivated by the laudable public purpose of shielding children from cyberbullying. The text of the cyberbullying law, however, does not adequately reflect an intent to restrict its reach to the three discrete types of electronic bullying of a sexual nature designed to cause emotional harm to children. Hence, to accept the County's proposed interpretation, we would need to significantly modify the applications of the county law, resulting in the amended scope bearing little resemblance to the actual language of the law. Such a judicial rewrite encroaches on the authority of the legislative body that crafted the provision and enters the realm of vagueness because any person who reads it would lack fair notice of what is legal and what constitutes a crime. Even if the First Amendment allows a cyberbullying statute of the limited nature proposed by Albany County, the local law here was not drafted in that manner. Albany County therefore has not met its burden of proving that the restrictions on speech contained in its cyberbullying law survive strict scrutiny.

There is undoubtedly general consensus that defendant's Facebook communications were repulsive and harmful to the subjects of his rants, and potentially created a risk of physical or emotional injury based on the private nature of the comments. He identified specific adolescents with photographs, described their purported sexual practices and posted the information on a website accessible world-wide. Unlike traditional bullying, which usually takes place by a face-to-face encounter, defendant used the advantages of the Internet to attack his victims from a safe distance, 24 hours a day, while cloaked in anonymity. Although the First Amendment may not give defendant the right to engage in these activities, the text of Albany County's law envelops far more than acts of cyberbullying against children by criminalizing a variety of constitutionally-protected modes of expression. We therefore hold that Albany County's Local Law No. 11 of 2010 – as drafted – is overbroad and facially invalid under the Free Speech Clause of the First Amendment. ...

Smith, Justice, dissenting:

Albany County has conceded that certain provisions of its Cyber–Bullying law are invalid. It seems to me that those provisions can be readily severed from the rest of the legislation and that what remains can, without any strain on its language, be interpreted in a way that renders it constitutionally valid. ...

The County concedes that the words "embarrassing" and "hate mail" are vague and thus unenforceable. It argues, correctly I think, that these terms can be dealt with in the same way as the reference to "person" in the operative section: simply by crossing them out. Once these deletions are made, I see nothing in the law that renders it unconstitutional.

The majority, it seems, is troubled by two other aspects of the definition of "Cyber–Bullying": the requirement that the forbidden communications be made "with

---

4 Contrary to the dissent's position, *Shack* and *Stuart* are distinguishable because they addressed statutes that criminalized conduct – repeated telephone harassment and stalking – without regard to the content of any communication. Here, however, the Albany County law facially allows law enforcement officials to charge a crime based on the communicative message that the accused intends to convey, as evidenced by the fact that defendant was prosecuted because of the offensive words he wrote on Facebook.

no legitimate private, personal, or public purpose"; and the series of verbs – "harass, annoy, threaten, abuse, taunt, intimidate, torment, humiliate" – that precedes the words "or otherwise." Neither requires us to invalidate the law.

I grant that the words "no legitimate . . . purpose" are not remarkable for their precision. We have twice held, however, that they are clear enough to withstand a constitutional challenge for vagueness. *People v. Shack*, 86 N.Y.2d 529, 533 (1995) (holding valid a prohibition on the making of a telephone call "with intent to harass, annoy, threaten or alarm another person . . . with no purpose of legitimate communication"); *People v. Stuart*, 100 N.Y.2d 412, 428 (2003) (holding valid an anti-stalking statute prohibiting a described course of conduct when engaged in "for no legitimate purpose"). We said in *Shack:*

> the phrase 'no purpose of legitimate communication' . . . notwithstanding its subjective quality, would be understood to mean the absence of expression of ideas or thoughts other than threats and/or intimidating or coercive utterances.

Similarly here, the phrase "no legitimate purpose" should be understood to mean the absence of expression of ideas or thoughts other than the mere abuse that the law proscribes.

It is true, as the majority says, that the criminal conduct at issue in *Shack* and *Stuart* was different from the conduct at issue here – but that does not make the words "no legitimate purpose" any more or less vague. The majority is also correct in saying that "the First Amendment forbids the government from deciding whether protected speech qualifies as 'legitimate' "but this begs the central question of what speech is "protected" and what is not. The Cyber–Bullying law prohibits a narrow category of valueless and harmful speech when the government proves, among other things, that the speaker had no legitimate purpose for engaging in it. The speech so prohibited is not protected speech.

As for the list of verbs beginning with "annoy" and ending with "humiliate," it is fair to read them, as the County urges, as "a non-exhaustive list of ways that the wrongdoer may formulate his or her intent to inflict emotional harm on the victim" In other words, the acts within the scope of the Cyber–Bullying law – disseminating sexually explicit photographs or private, personal, false or sexual information – are prohibited only where they are intended to "inflict significant emotional harm" on the victim, and the verbs merely serve as examples of ways in which significant emotional harm may be inflicted. That is not the only possible way to read the text of the law, but it is a perfectly reasonable way – indeed, the word "otherwise" seems to signal that the verbs preceding it are only illustrative. So read, the law does not prohibit conduct intended to harass, annoy, threaten or the like unless the actor specifically intended "significant emotional harm." I do not find such a prohibition to be unconstitutionally vague or overbroad. ...

QUESTIONS

1. After *Marquan M*, would the following statute be constitutional?

    > A minor commits the offense of cyberbullying if the minor knowingly transmits or disseminates any electronic communication, including a visual depiction of himself or any other person in a state of nudity, to another minor with the knowledge or intent that the communication would coerce, intimidate, torment, harass or otherwise cause emotional distress to the other minor.

2. Schools may not discipline students for speech at school unless the speech "will materially and substantially disrupt the work and discipline of the school." *Tinker v. Des Moines Independent Community School Dist.*, 393 U.S. 503, 509 (1969). How should this test apply to speech on social media? Is Facebook "on campus" or "off campus," or is that distinction itself beside the point? Here are some examples:

- L.W., a student at Douglas High School, sends MySpace instant messages to a friend, who is concerned enough to forward them to a school administrator:

    its pretty simple / i have a sweet gun / my neighbor is giving me 500 rounds / dhs is gay / ive watched these kinds of movies so i know how NOT to go wrong / i just cant decide who will be on my hit list / and thats totally deminted and it scares even my self

- J.S. and K.L., both eighth graders, create a fake MySpace profile using their principal's official photograph from the school's website (although not his name or the school's name), and listing his interests as:

    detention, being a tight ass, riding the fraintrain, spending time with my child (who looks like a gorilla), baseball, my golden pen, fucking in my office, hitting on students and their parents.

- K.K., a twelfth grader, creates a MySpace group named S.A.S.H. for discussing a fellow student, Shay H. (The name allegedly stands either for "Students Against Sluts Herpes" or "Students Against Shay's Herpes.)" She invites approximately 100 MySpace friends, including numerous other students, to join the group. Another student, R.P., posts a photograph of Shay H., altered to make it appear as though she has red dots on her face. A caption near her pelvic region reads, "Warning: Enter at your own risk." After Shay H's father calls R.P. and expresses anger, K.K. attempts to delete the group but is unable to, and instead renames it "Students Against Angry People."

Which of these examples should lead to school discipline?

UNITED STATES V. PETROVIC*
701 F.3d 849 (8th Cir. 2012)

Riley, Chief Judge:

Jovica Petrovic was convicted of four counts of interstate stalking and two counts of interstate extortionate threat. The district court sentenced Petrovic to ninety-six months imprisonment. Petrovic appeals his convictions and sentence …. We affirm.

I. BACKGROUND …

Petrovic and the victim, M.B., began a relationship in 2006, married in 2009, and later divorced. During their relationship, Petrovic resided in Florida and M.B. resided in Missouri, where she and her ex-husband, R.B., shared custody of their two young children. Petrovic and M.B. often met in Florida or Missouri, and M.B.

---

* [Ed: This case involves allegations of online harassment and threats of violence.]

occasionally allowed Petrovic to take pictures of her in the nude or performing various sex acts. M.B. also confided in Petrovic, revealing private and intimate information in text messages, such as the sexual abuse M.B. suffered as a young girl, her suicidal thoughts and tendencies, family secrets, and self-doubts about her fitness as a mother. Petrovic saved thousands of these text messages.

During their relationship, Petrovic also accumulated other potentially embarrassing information about M.B. In July 2009, M.B. attempted suicide at Petrovic's home after finding evidence leading her to believe Petrovic was having an extramarital affair. After M.B. was taken to the hospital for treatment, Petrovic took pictures of the pool of blood that had formed on the floor. In December 2009, Petrovic took several trips to Missouri to see M.B. During these trips, Petrovic stayed at a local hotel and secretly filmed M.B. having sexual intercourse with him. Petrovic took steps to ensure that M.B. was identifiable in the videos. He refused to turn off the lights, removed the sheets from the bed, and directed M.B.'s face and exposed genitalia toward the concealed camera.

On December 28, 2009, M.B. informed Petrovic by text message that she was ending their relationship. In response, Petrovic sent M.B. text messages informing her that he had secretly recorded their recent sexual encounters and had saved all of the text messages M.B. previously sent him. Petrovic threatened to post this information on the internet so M.B.'s family could read the messages and see the videos, if M.B. did not continue their relationship. Petrovic stated he was not "blackmail[ing]" M.B. and was only saving the information for his own "protection," but told M.B. to "be smart." Petrovic informed M.B. she and her family could soon visit his new website, "www.[M.B.]slut. com." M.B. understood Petrovic intended to "ruin [her] life" if she did not "get back together with [Petrovic]," but M.B. nevertheless permanently ended the relationship.

Petrovic then began a campaign to carry out his threats. Over the course of the next few months, Petrovic mailed dozens of homemade postcards to addresses throughout M.B.'s community, including to M.B.'s workplace, M.B.'s family members, R.B.'s home, and local businesses like the neighborhood drugstore. The postcards typically portrayed a picture of a scantily clad M.B. along with abusive language (for example, "I am just a whore 4 sale") and directions to a website, "www.marriedto [M.B.].com." The postcards were viewed by M.B.'s children, other family members, and many acquaintances. News of the website spread throughout the community, and almost everyone M.B. knew became aware of the site.

The website was publicly accessible in March 2010. Petrovic reported his site was "huge," containing "20,000 or 30,000 pages" of material reflecting months of preparation by Petrovic, who began creating the site in August 2009. The site contained links to dozens of images of M.B. posing in the nude or engaging in sex acts with Petrovic, and included many from the tapes Petrovic secretly recorded. Visitors to the site could view scores of pictures of M.B.'s children and other family members by clicking on a link next to the pornographic material. Several photographs of M.B. performing a sex act with Petrovic were repeatedly and prominently displayed throughout the website, including on the site's home page. Petrovic also posted thousands of pages of the text messages M.B. had sent him. The messages were color-coded by speaker and organized chronologically, with the most private and embarrassing messages given special pages to increase readership. Petrovic posted the pictures of the blood from M.B.'s suicide attempt, further highlighting her suicidal thoughts and history. Private information about M.B. and her family was also revealed, including M.B.'s contact information and the social security numbers of her children. M.B. did not authorize Petrovic to release any of this information. After learning of the website, M.B. "had a breakdown" and "wanted to die."

Besides the website and postcards, Petrovic sent several packages containing enlarged photographs of M.B. engaging in various sex acts with Petrovic to M.B. at her work, to M.B.'s boss, to M.B.'s family members, and to R.B.'s home, where M.B.'s seven-year-old child viewed the pornographic material. Petrovic also repeatedly made harassing phone calls to M.B's workplace, and physically intimidated M.B. on several occasions – on one such occasion, pursuing M.B. in a rental van at a high rate of speed while M.B. was on her way home from work.

In June 2010, M.B.'s sister was able to have Petrovic's website shut down for a few days. On June 20, 2010, Petrovic relaunched the site and posted a message stating, "Nobody can stop me to publish this website" and offering to shut down the site if M.B. gave him his "furniture, what she stoled [sic] from me, the wedding and engagement ring, ... and $100,000." M.B. did not comply with Petrovic's demands, and the website remained operational. On July 19, 2010, Petrovic was arrested by United States Postal Inspectors.

On October 6, 2010, a grand jury indicted Petrovic with, among other charges, four counts of interstate stalking, in violation of 18 U.S.C. § 2261A(2)(A), and two counts of interstate extortionate threat, in violation of 18 U.S.C. § 875(d). Petrovic moved to dismiss the four stalking charges on the grounds the statute violated the First Amendment both facially and as applied to Petrovic. The district court denied this motion. ...

II. DISCUSSION ...

Petrovic first argues 18 U.S.C. § 2261A(2)(A),[2] the interstate stalking statute, violates his right to freedom of speech under the First Amendment to the United States Constitution. Petrovic contends the statute is unconstitutional both facially and as applied to him. We review First Amendment challenges de novo.

"[W]hen 'speech' and 'nonspeech' elements are combined in the same course of conduct, a sufficiently important governmental interest in regulating the nonspeech element can justify incidental limitations on First Amendment freedoms." *United States v. O'Brien*, 391 U.S. 367, 376 (1968). A governmental regulation satisfies this standard if (1) "it is within the constitutional power of the Government"; (2) "it furthers an important or substantial governmental interest"; (3) "the governmental interest is unrelated to the suppression of free expression"; and (4) "the incidental restriction on alleged First Amendment freedoms is no greater than is essential to the furtherance of that interest." *Id.* at 377.

Petrovic contends § 2261A(2)(A) fails *O'Brien*'s four-pronged test in his case. However, we need not reach the merits of the *O'Brien* test if, as a preliminary matter, we determine the communications for which Petrovic was convicted under the statute are not protected by the First Amendment. Because we hold Petrovic's

---

2 "Whoever ... with the intent ... to ... injure, harass, or place under surveillance with intent to ... injure, harass, or intimidate, or cause substantial emotional distress to a person in another State ... uses the mail, any interactive computer service, or any facility of interstate or foreign commerce to engage in a course of conduct that causes substantial emotional distress to that person or places that person in reasonable fear of ... serious bodily injury ... shall be punished as provided in section 2261(b) of this title."

communications fall outside the First Amendment's protection, we do not reach the merits of the *O'Brien* test.

The First Amendment provides "Congress shall make no law ... abridging the freedom of speech." While it generally "means that government has no power to restrict expression because of its message, its ideas, its subject matter, or its content," *Ashcroft v. A.C.L.U.*, 535 U.S. 564, 573 (2002), certain "well-defined and narrowly limited classes of speech" permit content-based restrictions on speech, *United States v. Stevens*, 559 U.S. ___ (2010). One such category is "speech integral to criminal conduct." *Id.*; *see also Giboney v. Empire Storage & Ice Co.*, 336 U.S. 490, 498 (1949).

The jury convicted Petrovic of two counts of interstate extortionate threat in violation of 18 U.S.C. § 875(d) for his December 28, 2009 and June 20, 2010 communications. The communications for which Petrovic was convicted under § 2261A(2)(A) were integral to this criminal conduct as they constituted the means of carrying out his extortionate threats. *See Giboney*, 336 U.S. at 498, 501-02 (enjoining otherwise lawful picketing activities did not offend the First Amendment when the purpose of the picketing was to compel a company to unlawfully enter into an agreement in restraint of trade). Petrovic threatened to destroy M.B.'s reputation if she terminated their sexual relationship. When M.B. ended the relationship, Petrovic carried out this threat. Petrovic also threatened to continue the humiliating communications unless M.B. paid him $100,000, and when M.B. did not comply, Petrovic carried out this threat for continuing harassment as well. Because Petrovic's harassing and distressing communications were integral to his criminal conduct of extortion under § 875(d), the communications were not protected by the First Amendment.

Furthermore, "where matters of purely private significance are at issue, First Amendment protections are often less rigorous ... because restricting speech on purely private matters does not implicate the same constitutional concerns as limiting speech on matters of public interest." *Snyder v. Phelps*, 562 U.S. ___ (2011). We previously have held that in "extreme case[s]" it is "constitutionally permissible for a governmental entity to regulate the public disclosure of facts about private individuals." *Coplin v. Fairfield Pub. Access Television Comm.*, 111 F.3d 1395, 1404 (8th Cir. 1997). "[A]bsent a compelling state interest," such speech

> can be regulated ... because of its constitutionally proscribable content only if: (1) any such regulation is viewpoint-neutral; (2) the facts revealed are not already in the public domain; (3) the facts revealed about the otherwise private individual are not a legitimate subject of public interest; and (4) the facts revealed are highly offensive.

Id. at 1405.

M.B. was a private individual, and Petrovic's communications revealed intensely private information about M.B. *See id.* at 1404-05. Applying the *Coplin* test, the interstate stalking statute is viewpoint neutral. It proscribes stalking and harassing conduct without making the further content discrimination of proscribing only certain forms of that conduct. *See R.A.V. v. City of St. Paul, Minn.*, 505 U.S. 377, 384 (1992). Second, the intimately private facts and photographs revealed by Petrovic were never in the public domain before Petrovic began his campaign to humiliate M.B. Third, the public has no legitimate interest in the private sexual activities of M.B. or in the embarrassing facts revealed about her life. Finally, the information Petrovic publicized to the community was highly offensive. The communications for which Petrovic was convicted under § 2261A(2)(A) may be proscribed consistent with the First Amendment. The statute is not unconstitutional as applied to Petrovic.

QUESTIONS

1. How would *Petrovic* have come out if Petrovic merely intended to harass M.B., rather than extort her?

2. Compare the *Coplin* test to the elements of the tort of public disclosure of private facts. Are privacy laws automatically constitutional, or do they raise serious First Amendment issues?

3. Petrovic is a man; he wrote insulting and demeaning messages about a woman. Is this a coincidence, or is it part of a larger pattern? Would society be better or worse off with less First Amendment protection for people like him?

REVENGE PORN PROBLEM

You represent Rebecca Levendowski. Between 2011 and 2013, she was in a long-distance relationship with Derek Franks. During that time, Levendowski took about fifty sexually suggestive photographs of herself using her iPhone and emailed them to Franks. The relationship ended badly, with screaming matches and mutual accusations of infidelity. Recently, Levendowski has learned that Franks has posted the photographs on InHerPlace.com, a website that describes itself as "a place to get back at lying exes who done you wrong." Does Levendowski have a case against Franks? Will the First Amendment stand in her way? What are her other options?

C. Pornography

This section considers the problem that defined the first generation of mass Internet activism. There were computer *causes célèbres* before, but this was the first real Internet-wide moment of political awakening. This is the stuff that got John Perry Barlow up in arms – government attempts to censor the Internet. The materials walk through the following decade and a half in Internet history.

PORNOGRAPHY LAW PRIMER

When it comes to pornographic material, the courts have recognized three categories of harmful speech:

- **Obscenity** is material that fails the three-part Miller test:

  "(a) whether the average person, applying contemporary community standards would find that the work, taken as a whole, appeals to the prurient interest; (b) whether the work depicts or describes, in a patently offensive way, sexual conduct specifically defined by the applicable state law; and (c) whether the work, taken as a whole, lacks serious literary, artistic, political, or scientific value." *Miller v. California*, 413 U.S. 15 (1973).

  Obscene material can constitutionally be regulated because it has no redeeming social value and its offensiveness provides a positive justification for banning it. The mere possession of obscenity cannot be criminalized, see Stanley v. Georgia, 394 U.S. 557 (1969), because doing do would intrude on the privacy of the home, but the government can constitutionally prohibit its distribution and sale.

- **Child pornography** is material that depicts children engaging in sexual acts. It can constitutionally be prohibited outright – it is contraband – and mere possession of it is criminal. Two rationales are usually given for this rule: "First, as a permanent record of a child's abuse, the continued circulation itself would harm the child who had participated. ... Second, because the traffic in child pornography was an economic motive for its production, the State had an interest in closing the distribution network." *Ashcroft v. Free Speech Coalition*, 535 U.S. 234 (2002). Many child pornography prosecutions, like many drug possession prosecutions, turn on highly factual questions of whether the defendant had sufficient knowledge of or control over the material to "possess" it.

- Some material that is legal for adults to possess is nonetheless **harmful to minors**. Thus, for example, the government can prohibit the use of George Carlin's "seven words you can't say on television" on the radio, *see Federal Communications Commission v. Pacifica Foundation*, 438 U.S. 726 (1978), and fine television stations over Janet Jackson's nationally televised, breast-baring "wardrobe malfunction," *see Complaints Against Various Television Licensees Concerning Their February 1, 2004 Broadcast*, 21 FCC Rcd. 2760 (2006). In both cases, though it is lawful for adults to receive and exchange such material, children might be watching, and the government can pass laws that restrict minors' access to it. The exact contours of this category are subject to debate – one person's "vital sex ed" is another's "vile pornography" – but one thing is clear: the government may not ban such material outright or prevent adults from obtaining it. It can only attempt to restrict minors' access. *Reno v. ACLU* discusses some of the difficulties in drawing these lines.

Note what *isn't* on this list: "pornography." It's not usually a meaningful category for First Amendment purposes. Instead, arguments typically need to work within one of the above three categories – that the pornography has no redeeming value, that it depicts children, or that it is being shown to minors.

QUESTIONS

1. Which community's "contemporary community standards" define whether material appeals to the prurient interest under the Miller test? Pre-Internet law was clear:

> There is no constitutional barrier under Miller to prohibiting communications that are obscene in some communities under local standards even though they are not obscene in others. If the speaker's audience is comprised of different communities with different local standards, the speaker ultimately bears the burden of complying with the prohibition on obscene messages.

Ashcroft v. American Civil Liberties Union, 535 U.S. 564, 581 (2002). Is this rule as viable for email as it is for postal mail? If local community standards are problematic, what should replace them? National community standards? And if local community standards are problematic, does that also call into question the rule that measuring a work against community standards is a question for the jury?

2. The Child Pornography Prevention Act of 1996 (CPPA) prohibited "any visual depiction, including any ... computer-generated image or picture" that "is, or appears to be, of a minor engaging in sexually explicit conduct." In *Ashcroft v. Free Speech Coalition*, 535 U.S. 234 (2002), the Supreme Court held that this portion of the CPPA was unconstitutional, because it could apply to "virtual child pornography," which was generated without the involvement of any actual child, and some such material might have serious redeeming value. Is this reasoning sound? What effects will it have on child pornography prosecutions if "real" and "virtual" child pornography are visually indistinguishable? How should *Free Speech Coalition* apply to images of adults whose facial features have been altered to make them look like children? Images of actual children's' faces Photoshopped onto images of adults' bodies?

CDA NEGOTIATION PROBLEM

The year is 1995, and the Internet has exploded into public consciousness. Businesses are starting to realize the enormous potential for online commerce and are looking for ways to go online and connect with their customers. Policymakers have also recognized the Internet's huge potential to distribute information; this could be the library and the classroom of the future. But in the halls of Congress, there is fear, fear that all of this potential could be squandered.

Why? Because of the threat of cyberporn. A study carried out at Carnegie-Mellon and published in the *Georgetown Law Journal* surveyed almost a million images, descriptions, stories, and animations. It concluded that over 80% of them were pornographic. *Time* ran a cover story on the study and online threats to children. Now, everyone is talking about the online pornography menace and what to do about it.

On Capitol Hill, key senators have quietly convened a series of conversations about a potential bill to make the Internet safe for average users – and their children. You will represent one of the following groups in an in-class negotiation to work out a legislative compromise.

- **Family Values Coalition**. Religious conservatives, parents' organizations, and anti-pornography liberals dislike pornography in all of its forms and are especially concerned about the harms it imposes on children. They would like to keep as much pornography as possible off the Internet and especially want to prevent it from reaching children. They're hopping mad about the Carnegie-Mellon study and want immediate action. They have immense influence but not enough to pass a bill on their own.

- **Pornographers**. The adult entertainment industry has little influence in Washington. Whenever they can, however, its lawyers remind Congressional types that the First Amendment protects some forms of pornography. The industry supports efforts to prevent its wares from reaching children but will strongly defend, in court if necessary, its right to sell ordinary pornography to willing adults.

- **Civil Libertarians**. The ACLU, American Library Association, and other speech-friendly civil rights groups may not much like pornography, but they will defend anyone's rights to free speech online. These groups will fight any legislation that criminalizes distributing legal materials to adults and are also concerned about anything that restricts people's practical ability to receive such information. They're frustrated about the Carnegie-Mellon study, which was based on faulty, possibly fraudulent data, but has been uncritically accepted by the media.

- **The Internet Industry**. Companies like AOL and CompuServe provide access to the Internet and forums for discussion and posting information. They aren't in favor of obscenity or child pornography, or in favor of kids seeing porn, and are willing to help out a bit in restricting access to these materials. But they're strongly opposed to anything that would make them liable for failing to block access to pornography; they already are handling so many messages a day that it would be economically infeasible for them to review each one individually. Some of these Internet-focused companies are relatively new at the lobbying table, but the telecommunications industry in general has been throwing a lot of money around as Congress prepares to pass a major overhaul of telecommunications laws.

- **Congress**. The senators sponsoring this effort are not going to go home without a bill. They would like to take a firm stance to protect children from the dangers of pornography and to pave the way for safe commerce on the Internet. They're sensitive to coalitions; they don't want anyone so upset at the legislative result that campaign donations start flowing to their challengers. Whatever passes should hold up in court, if possible.

Can you think of provisions and compromises that might satisfy all – or most – of these constituencies? What will your negotiating position be, and what should the final bill look like? Keep in mind that a perfect agreement on all issues may not be possible, and that legislation can sometimes defer tough issues for later resolution (how?). Remember also that the technological savviness of these groups varies enormously. And, of course, don't forget that the question of whether ISPs and other internet intermediaries should be liable for pornographic content on their systems is also on the table.

RENO V. AMERICAN CIVIL LIBERTIES UNION
521 US 844 (1997)

Justice Stevens delivered the opinion of the Court.

At issue is the constitutionality of two statutory provisions enacted to protect minors from "indecent" and "patently offensive" communications on the Internet.

Notwithstanding the legitimacy and importance of the congressional goal of protecting children from harmful materials, we agree with the three-judge District Court that the statute abridges "the freedom of speech" protected by the First Amendment. ...

II

The Telecommunications Act of 1996 was an unusually important legislative enactment. ... An amendment offered in the Senate was the source of the two statutory provisions challenged in this case. They are informally described as the "indecent transmission" provision and the "patently offensive display" provision ... The first, 47 U. S. C. § 223(a) (1994 ed., Supp. II), prohibits the knowing transmission of obscene or indecent messages to any recipient under 18 years of age. It provides in pertinent part:

(a) Whoever –

  (1) in interstate or foreign communications – ...

    (B) by means of a telecommunications device knowingly –

      (i) makes, creates, or solicits, and

      (ii) initiates the transmission of, "any comment, request, suggestion, proposal, image, or other communication which is obscene or indecent, knowing that the recipient of the communication is under 18 years of age, regardless of whether the maker of such communication placed the call or initiated the communication; ...

  (2) knowingly permits any telecommunications facility under his control to be used for any activity prohibited by paragraph (1) with the intent that it be used for such activity

shall be fined under Title 18, or imprisoned not more than two years, or both.

The second provision, § 223(d), prohibits the knowing sending or displaying of patently offensive messages in a manner that is available to a person under 18 years of age. It provides:

(d) Whoever –

  (1) in interstate or foreign communications knowingly –

    (A) uses an interactive computer service to send to a specific person or persons under 18 years of age, or

    (B) uses any interactive computer service to display in a manner available to a person under 18 years of age, "any comment, request, suggestion, proposal, image, or other communication that, in context, depicts or describes, in terms patently offensive as measured by contemporary community standards, sexual or excretory activities or organs, regardless of whether the user of such service placed the call or initiated the communication; or

  (2) knowingly permits any telecommunications facility under such person's control to be used for an activity prohibited by paragraph (1) with the intent that it be used for such activity,

shall be fined under Title 18, or imprisoned not more than two years, or both.

The breadth of these prohibitions is qualified by two affirmative defenses. See § 223(e)(5). One covers those who take "good faith, reasonable, effective, and appropriate actions" to restrict access by minors to the prohibited communications. § 223(e)(5)(A). The other covers those who restrict access to covered material by requiring certain designated forms of age proof, such as a verified credit card or an adult identification number or code. § 223(e)(5)(B). ...

VII

We are persuaded that the CDA lacks the precision that the First Amendment requires when a statute regulates the content of speech. In order to deny minors access to potentially harmful speech, the CDA effectively suppresses a large amount of speech that adults have a constitutional right to receive and to address to one another. That burden on adult speech is unacceptable if less restrictive alternatives would be at least as effective in achieving the legitimate purpose that the statute was enacted to serve.

In evaluating the free speech rights of adults, we have made it perfectly clear that "[s]exual expression which is indecent but not obscene is protected by the First Amendment." *Sable*, 492 U.S. at 126. See also *Carey v. Population Services Int'l*, 431 U.S. 678, 701 (1977) ("[W]here obscenity is not involved, we have consistently held that the fact that protected speech may be offensive to some does not justify its suppression"). Indeed, *Pacifica* itself admonished that "the fact that society may find speech offensive is not a sufficient reason for suppressing it." 438 U.S. at 745.

It is true that we have repeatedly recognized the governmental interest in protecting children from harmful materials. But that interest does not justify an unnecessarily broad suppression of speech addressed to adults. As we have explained, the Government may not "reduc[e] the adult population . . . to . . . only what is fit for children." *Denver*, 518 U.S. at 759 (internal quotation marks omitted) (quoting *Sable*, 492 U.S. at 128). "[R]egardless of the strength of the government's interest" in protecting children, "[t]he level of discourse reaching a mailbox simply cannot be limited to that which would be suitable for a sandbox." *Bolger v. Youngs Drug Products Corp.*, 463 U.S. 60, 74–75 (1983). ...

In arguing that the CDA does not so diminish adult communication, the Government relies on the incorrect factual premise that prohibiting a transmission whenever it is known that one of its recipients is a minor would not interfere with adult-to-adult communication. The findings of the District Court make clear that this premise is untenable. Given the size of the potential audience for most messages, in the absence of a viable age verification process, the sender must be charged with knowing that one or more minors will likely view it. Knowledge that, for instance, one or more members of a 100-person chat group will be a minor – and therefore that it would be a crime to send the group an indecent message – would surely burden communication among adults.

The District Court found that at the time of trial existing technology did not include any effective method for a sender to prevent minors from obtaining access to its communications on the Internet without also denying access to adults. The Court found no effective way to determine the age of a user who is accessing material through e-mail, mail exploders, newsgroups, or chat rooms. As a practical matter, the Court also found that it would be prohibitively expensive for noncommercial – as well as some commercial – speakers who have Web sites to verify that their users are adults. These limitations must inevitably curtail a significant amount of adult communication on the Internet. By contrast, the District Court found that "[d]espite its limitations, currently available *user-based* software suggests that a reasonably effective method by which *parents* can prevent their children from accessing sexually explicit and other material which *parents* may believe is inappropriate for their children will soon be widely available." *Id.* at 842 (emphases added).

The breadth of the CDA's coverage is wholly unprecedented. Unlike the regulations upheld in *Ginsberg* and *Pacifica*, the scope of the CDA is not limited to commercial speech or commercial entities. Its open-ended prohibitions embrace all nonprofit entities and individuals posting indecent messages or displaying them on their own computers in the presence of minors. The general, undefined terms "indecent" and "patently offensive" cover large amounts of nonpornographic material with serious educational or other value. Moreover, the "community standards" criterion as applied to the Internet means that any communication available to a nationwide audience will be judged by the standards of the community most likely to be offended by the message. The regulated subject matter includes any of the seven "dirty words" used in the *Pacifica* monologue, the use of which the Government's expert acknowledged could constitute a felony. ... It may also extend to discussions about prison rape or safe sexual practices, artistic images that include nude subjects, and arguably the card catalog of the Carnegie Library. ...

The breadth of this content-based restriction of speech imposes an especially heavy burden on the Government to explain why a less restrictive provision would not be as effective as the CDA. It has not done so. The arguments in this Court have referred to possible alternatives such as requiring that indecent material be "tagged" in a way that facilitates parental control of material coming into their homes, making exceptions for messages with artistic or educational value, providing some tolerance for parental choice, and regulating some portions of the Internet – such as commercial Web sites – differently from others, such as chat rooms. Particularly in the light of the absence of any detailed findings by the Congress, or even hearings addressing the special problems of the CDA, we are persuaded that the CDA is not narrowly tailored if that requirement has any meaning at all.

VIII ...

The Government also asserts that the "knowledge" requirement of both §§ 223(a) and (d), especially when coupled with the "specific child" element found in § 223(d), saves the CDA from overbreadth. Because both sections prohibit the dissemination of indecent messages only to persons known to be under 18, the Government argues, it does not require transmitters to "refrain from communicating indecent material to adults; they need only refrain from disseminating such materials to persons they know to be under 18." This argument ignores the fact that most Internet forums – including chat rooms, newsgroups, mail exploders, and the Web – are open to all comers. The Government's assertion that the knowledge requirement somehow protects the communications of adults is therefore untenable. Even the strongest reading of the "specific person" requirement of § 223(d) cannot save the statute. It would confer broad powers of censorship, in the form of a "heckler's veto," upon any opponent of indecent speech who might simply log on and inform the would-be discoursers that his 17-year-old child – a "specific person . . . under 18 years of age," 47 U.S.C. § 223(d)(1)(A) (1994 ed., Supp. II) – would be present. ...

IX

The Government's three remaining arguments focus on the defenses provided in § 223(e)(5). First, relying on the "good faith, reasonable, effective, and appropriate actions" provision, the Government suggests that "tagging" provides a defense that saves the constitutionality of the CDA. The suggestion assumes that transmitters may encode their indecent communications in a way that would indicate their contents, thus permitting recipients to block their reception with appropriate software. It is the requirement that the good-faith action must be "effective" that makes this defense illusory. The Government recognizes that its proposed screening software does not currently exist. Even if it did, there is no way to know whether a potential recipient will actually block the encoded material. Without the impossible knowledge that every guardian in America is screening for the "tag," the transmitter could not reasonably rely on its action to be "effective."

For its second and third arguments concerning defenses – which we can consider together – the Government relies on the latter half of § 223(e)(5), which applies when the transmitter has restricted access by requiring use of a verified credit card or adult identification. Such verification is not only technologically available but actually is used by commercial providers of sexually explicit material. These providers, therefore, would be protected by the defense. Under the findings of the District Court, however, it is not economically feasible for most noncommercial speakers to employ such verification. Accordingly, this defense would not significantly narrow the statute's burden on noncommercial speech. Even with respect to the commercial pornographers that would be protected by the defense, the Government failed to adduce any evidence that these verification techniques actually preclude minors from posing as adults. Given that the risk of criminal sanctions "hovers over each content provider, like the proverbial sword of Damocles," the District Court correctly refused to rely on unproven future technology to save the statute. The Government thus failed to prove that the proffered defense would significantly reduce the heavy burden on adult speech produced by the prohibition on offensive displays.

We agree with the District Court's conclusion that the CDA places an unacceptably heavy burden on protected speech, and that the defenses do not constitute the sort of "narrow tailoring" that will save an otherwise patently invalid unconstitutional provision. In *Sable*, 492 U.S. at 127, we remarked that the speech restriction at issue there amounted to "'burn[ing] the house to roast the pig.'" The CDA, casting a far darker shadow over free speech, threatens to torch a large segment of the Internet community. ...

QUESTIONS

1. How much pornography is there on the Internet? How easy would it be for a ten-year-old to find it? How likely are they to stumble on it by accident? How effectively could parents prevent this from happening? How easy would it be for a child molester to find the ten-year-old?

2. How is it that a statute targeted at protecting *minors* could end up restricting the speech *adults* could receive?

3. If you wanted to post something online and be confident that only adults would see it, what would you do? How confident could you be that no minors were seeing it? How many adults would be wrongfully screened out? Is age-based targeting easier or harder than geographic targeting?

4. In a famous concurrence in part, Justice O'Connor described the CDA as an attempt to create a "zoning law" for the Internet, dividing it into child-safe and adults-only zones. Is it harder or easier to zone the Internet than to zone places? (Both?)

CPOEA PROBLEM

The federal Child Protection and Obscenity Enforcement Act of 1988 (CPOEA) requires those who create materials depicting "actual sexually explicit conduct" to maintain records of each performer or model's photo identification proving that they are not minors. This statute has survived various constitutional challenges, in part because its definition of "actual sexually explicit conduct" has been held to be both narrow and precise. A more recent amendment, the federal Prosecutorial Remedies and Other Tools to End the Exploitation of Children Today Act of 2003 (PROTECT Act), extends the records requirement to include digital and computer-manipulated images and videos. It also requires those who upload such materials onto websites to maintain the same records. The Free Speech Coalition, an adult entertainment industry trade association, challenges the amendment as imposing an insurmountable burden on website maintainers, who may be distributing many thousands of images or videos. What result, and why?

D. Filtering

As we have seen on multiple occasions, law is not the only force at work online. Because the Internet is made up of computers, those computers can potentially have their programming changed. If the code changes, so does the regulatory effect. This gives lawmakers an immensely powerful lever to pull: convince or compel companies that operate networks, websites, and other online applications to use their technical power in ways that make the lawmakers' regulatory goals easier to achieve. Thus, our second major theme – governmental power – is closely bound up with the first – code is law.

This section considers governmental attempts to regulate speech not by punishing speakers but instead by changing the programming of the Internet's technical architecture. Filtering has been popular around the world: studies suggest that a majority of countries require some form of Internet filtering. But the details vary widely. China's comprehensive system of filtering, which restricts access to politically sensitive materials on numerous topics, is the best-known. The section continues the chapter's emphasis on the United States legal free speech framework. As the cases illustrate, applying the First Amendment to these Internet filtering involves both conceptual and pragmatic difficulties. As the cases also illustrate, protecting children is far and away the most commonly proffered justification for filtering.

CENTER FOR DEMOCRACY AND TECHNOLOGY V. PAPPERT
337 F. Supp. 2d 606 (E.D. Pa. 2004)

DuBois, District Judge:

I. INTRODUCTION

In February of 2002, Pennsylvania enacted the Internet Child Pornography Act, 18 Pa. Cons. Stat. §§ 7621-7630, ("the Act"). The Act requires an Internet Service

Provider ("ISP") to remove or disable access to child pornography items "residing on or accessible through its service" after notification by the Pennsylvania Attorney General. It is the first attempt by a state to impose criminal liability on an ISP which merely provides access to child pornography through its network and has no direct relationship with the source of the content.

The plaintiffs are Center for Democracy and Technology ("CDT"), the American Civil Liberties Union of Pennsylvania ("ACLU"), and Plantagenet, Inc. CDT is a non-profit corporation incorporated for the purpose of educating the general public concerning public policy issues related to the Internet. The ACLU is a non-partisan organization of more than 13,000 members dedicated to defending the principles of liberty and equality embodied in the Bill of Rights. Plantagenet, Inc., is an ISP that provides a variety of services related to the Internet. Defendant is Gerald J. Pappert, Attorney General of the Commonwealth of Pennsylvania. ...

III. FINDINGS OF FACT ...

C. Internet Child Pornography Act ("The Act") ...

The Act permits defendant or a district attorney in Pennsylvania to seek a court order requiring an ISP to "remove or disable items residing on or accessible through" an ISP's service upon a showing of probable cause that the item constitutes child pornography. The application for a court order must contain the Uniform Resource Locator providing access to the item.

Child pornography is defined as images that display a child under the age of 18 engaged in a "prohibited sexual act." A prohibited sexual act is defined as "sexual intercourse . . . masturbation, sadism, masochism, bestiality, fellatio, cunnilingus, lewd exhibition of the genitals or nudity if such nudity is depicted for the purpose of sexual stimulation or gratification of any person who might view such depiction."

The court order may be obtained on an *ex parte* basis with no prior notice to the ISP or the web site owner and no post-hearing notice to the web site owner.

Under the Act, a judge may issue an order directing that the challenged content be removed or disabled from the ISP's service upon a showing that the items constitute probable cause evidence of child pornography. A judge does not make a final determination that the challenged content is child pornography.

Once a court order is issued, the Pennsylvania Attorney General notifies the ISP in question and provides the ISP with a copy of the court order. The ISP then has five days to block access to the specified content or face criminal liability, including fines of up to $30,000 and a prison term of up to seven years.

According to defendant, the purpose of the Act is: "To protect children from sexual exploitation and abuse. To serve this purpose by interfering with distribution of child pornography, particularly its distribution over the Internet."

Government law enforcement agencies have attempted to locate and criminally prosecute persons who produce or knowingly distribute child pornography. However, a state agency in the United States cannot easily prosecute producers and distributors of child pornography because they are rarely found in that particular state and often are not found in the United States. ...

E. ISP Compliance with Court Orders or Informal Notices ...

2. Methods of Implementation

According to the ISPs, on most occasions, they attempted to comply with the Informal Notices by implementing either IP filtering or DNS filtering. These methods were either used alone or together.

Use of IP filtering, DNS filtering, or URL filtering to block content accessible through the service of an ISP only affects Internet users who access the Internet through that ISP's service. Thus, Internet users that do not use the service of an ISP that blocked a web site would still have access to the blocked content.

a. DNS Filtering

To perform DNS filtering, an ISP makes entries in the DNS servers under its control that prevent requests to those servers for a specific web site's fully qualified domain name (found in the requested site's URL) from resolving to the web site's correct IP address. The entries cause the DNS servers to answer the requests for the IP addresses for such domain names with either incorrect addresses or error messages. Without the correct IP addresses of the requested sites, the requests either do not proceed at all or do not reach the desired sites.

b. IP Filtering ...

To implement IP filtering, an ISP first determines the IP address to which a specific URL resolves. It then makes entries in routing equipment that it controls that will stop all outgoing requests for the specific IP address.

c. URL Filtering

Mr. Stern testified that ISPs could comply with blocking orders using URL filtering. ... URL filtering involves the placement of an additional device, or in some cases the reconfiguration of an existing "router" or other device, in the ISP's network to (a) reassemble the packets for Internet traffic flowing through its network, (b) read each http web request, and (c) if the requested URL in the web request matches one of the URLs specified in a blocking order, discard or otherwise block the http request.

3. Comparison of Filtering Methods

a. Ease of Implementation and Cost ...

Most ISPs already have the hardware needed to implement IP filtering and IP filtering is a fairly routine aspect of the management of a network. IP filtering is used to respond to various types of attacks on a network, such as denial of service attacks and spam messages. ... For AOL, IP filtering is "in common use as a defensive mechanism against such activities as virus proliferation, spam, et cetera. It is a basic and common tool of the trade."...

Most ISPs that do not outsource Internet access would not be required to purchase new equipment to implement DNS filtering. If the ISP's staff is familiar with this method of filtering, the necessary entries in the DNS servers require no expenditure of money and little staff time. ...

No ISPs known to either plaintiffs' or defendant's experts utilize URL filtering to screen all World Wide Web traffic. ...

If an ISP did not purchase substantially more switches and routers, URL filtering would "significantly degrade" the performance of an ISP's network. Such degradation is caused by the fact that the technical process of comparing all of the URLs in the web traffic flowing through an ISP's network with a list of URLs to be blocked is "expensive" in the computational sense – it requires a significant amount of computing power. Performing these computations would slow down each switch and router substantially and decrease the overall capacity of the network. ...

The purchase and testing of the equipment necessary to perform URL filtering would require a significant investment by ISPs. ... It would cost Verizon "well into seven figures" to implement URL filtering across its entire network. "[M]oney aside, the current [URL filtering] technology ... would not be able to even operate in [WorldCom's] network" because the current URL filtering products (a) cannot support the speeds needed in WorldCom's network and (b) do not connect to the type of physical wiring (such as fiber optic and coaxial copper cable) that World-Com uses. ...

c. Overblocking

DNS filtering stops requests for all sub-pages under the blocked domain name. Thus, if the domain name included in the URL identified by an Informal Notice is of a Web Hosting Service that allows users to post their independent content as sub-pages on the service's site, the DNS server entries will stop requests for all of the independent pages on the service, not just the page that displays the targeted child pornography item. For example, DNS filtering results in overblocking when an online community such as the GeoCities web site, which allows many different users to have web sites on sub-pages of GeoCities.com, is targeted by an Informal Notice. ...

IP filtering leads to a significant amount of overblocking. As Mr. Stern stated, IP filtering "will block innocent sites to a great deal," and "IP address filtering is extremely likely to block untargeted sites due to the process known as virtual hosting," ...

IP filtering leads to blocking, of innocent web sites, because of the prevalence of shared IP addresses. ... If an ISP uses IP filtering to block access to a particular IP address, all web sites hosted at that IP address are blocked. As an example, in response to Informal Notice 2545, Epix.net blocked access to IP address 204.251.10.203, which in turn blocked access to two of Laura Blain's web sites and others hosted by directNIC.

URL filtering filters out URLs down to the specific subpage. It presents no risk of disabling access to untargeted sites.

Although URL filtering results in the least amount of overblocking, no ISPs are currently capable of implementing this method. Both DNS filtering and IP filtering result in overblocking. ...

8. Methods of Evasion

a. Anonymous Proxy Servers

Internet users who want to keep their identity secret can use anonymous proxy servers or anonymizers. In the context of visiting web sites, these services route all requests through the proxy server or anonymizer, which in turn sends the request to the desired web site. Requests using these services appear to the ISP routing the request as if they are requests directed to the proxy service, not to the underlying URL to which the user actually seeks access.

The use of anonymous proxy services or anonymizers completely circumvents both of the technical blocking methods – IP filtering and DNS filtering – used by the ISPs to comply with the Informal Notices and would circumvent URL filtering as well. For example, web sites blocked by AOL could be accessed through AOL's service using the anonymizer "Proxify.com."

If the child pornography seeker chooses to have all of his web requests run through a proxy or anonymizer, he faces obstacles and risks. First, he must learn how to configure his computer to do so. This requires a number of difficult entries.

Second, even if he successfully configures his computer, the seeker must then accept the risks of a reconfiguration that sends all requests through another computer that the user does not control – risks that the connection will not work or that the service will be slow. ...

b. The Ability of Child Pornographers to Evade Filters ...

IP filtering can be evaded by operators of child pornography sites by changing the IP address of the web site. In one instance, the OAG sent a second Informal Notice relating to one site because it had become available to AOL users at a different IP address after AOL blocked the original IP Address. AOL responded by blocking the second IP address as well.

Operators of child pornography sites can use a range of methods to evade DNS filtering, including: (1) using an IP address as a URL, i.e., a web site can use an IP address (or string of numbers) as the URL instead of a domain name like "www.example.com"; or (2) changing a portion of a domain name and promulgating the new domain name in hyperlinks to the web site in advertisements, search engines or newsgroups. ...

IV CONCLUSIONS OF LAW ...

B. Substantive First Amendment Issuses ...

1. Burden on Speech

Defendant proposes that the "only reasonable means" test should be used to determine whether the Act burdens speech. Under defendant's test, the Act is constitutional unless the only reasonable means of compliance requires blocking protected speech. Plaintiffs argue that if the effect of the Act has been to block protected speech, the Act is subject to First Amendment scrutiny.

This case is unusual in that the Act, on its face, does not burden protected speech. Facially, the Act only suppresses child pornography, which can be completely banned from the Internet. However, the action taken by private actors to comply with the Act has blocked a significant amount of speech protected by the First Amendment. *United States v. Playboy Entertainment Group*, 529 U.S. 803 (2000), relied upon by both parties, is the case that comes closest to addressing how this type of burden on protected speech should be addressed.

The federal statute at issue in *Playboy* required cable operators which provided sexually oriented programing to either fully scramble or block the channels that provided this programming, or limit the transmission of such programming to the hours between 10:00 P.M., and 6:00 A.M., referred to as "time channeling." The Supreme Court determined that the statute was unconstitutional because the government failed to establish that the two methods for compliance identified in the challenged section were the least restrictive means for achieving the government's goal. ...

The analysis of the *Playboy* Court is particularly instructive in this case. That is so because the majority of cable operators involved in that case chose to comply with the section of the statute at issue by using time channeling notwithstanding the fact that it silenced a significant amount of protected speech, whereas the other stated method of compliance, scrambling, did not. On that issue, the Court ruled that a reasonable cable operator could choose not to use the scrambling alternative provided by the statute because the available scrambling technology was "imprecise" and portions of the scrambled programs could be heard or seen by viewers, a phenomenon known as "signal bleed." Thus, "[a] rational cable operator, faced with the possibility of sanctions for intermittent bleeding, could well choose to time channel even if the bleeding is too momentary to pose any concern to most households." *Id.* at 821. The Court also noted that digital technology would have solved the signal bleed problem, but it was "not in wide-spread use."

The basis for the *Playboy* Court's determination that the statute was not the least restrictive means for achieving the government's goal was the fact that time channeling, deemed to be a reasonable method of compliance for cable operators, silenced "protected speech for two-thirds of the day in every home in a cable service area, regardless of the presence or likely presence of children or of the wishes of viewers." *Id.* In making this statement, the Court determined that "targeted blocking" at the request of a customer was a "less restrictive" and feasible means of furthering the government's compelling interest in the case. *Id.* at 816, 827. Targeted blocking required cable operators to block sexually-oriented channels at individual households. It was deemed to be less restrictive in that it enabled parents who did not want their child exposed to the program to block the offending channels without depriving willing viewers of the opportunity to watch a particular program.

The Act in this case has resulted in the blocking of in excess of 1,190,000 web sites that were not targeted by the Informal Notices. Defendant argues that this overblocking does not violate the First Amendment because it resulted from decisions made by ISPs, not state actors. According to defendant, ISPs have "options for disabling access that would and will not block any, or as many, sites as Plaintiffs claim were blocked in the past" and the choice of which filtering method to use was "completely the decision of the ISPs."

The Court rejects this argument. Like the statute analyzed in *Playboy*, the Act in this case provides ISPs with discretion to choose a method of compliance although such methods are not incorporated in the Act itself. Like the time channeling in *Playboy*, the court concludes that ISPs could reasonably choose IP filtering and DNS filtering in order to comply with Act. And, like Playboy, the alternatives reasonably available to the ISPs block protected speech to a significant degree.

The two filtering methods used by the ISPs to comply with the Informal Notices and the court order – IP filtering and DNS filtering – both resulted in overblocking. IP filtering blocks all web sites at an IP address and, given the prevalence of shared IP addresses, the implementation of this method results in blocking of a significant number of sites not related to the alleged child pornography. As an example, access to Ms. Blain's web sites and over 15,000 other sites was blocked to Epix users as a result of the IP Filtering Epix implemented to comply with Informal Notice 2545. Filtering also results in overblocking when the method is used to block a web site on an online community or a Web Hosting Service, or a web host that hosts web sites as sub-pages under a single domain name. Specifically, Verizon blocked hundreds of thousands of web sites unrelated to the targeted child pornography when it used DNS filtering to block access to a sub-page of the Terra.es web site, a large online community, in response to Informal Notice 5924. One of the web sites blocked was for a Spanish geological survey, and defendant acknowledged that this web site did not contain child pornography. Although a small subset of web hosts, Web Hosting Services host a large number of web sites and the OAG admitted that they are not always identifiable based on the URL. In fact, the OAG continued to issue notices to Web Hosting Services after it was aware of the overblocking problem and had implemented a new procedure to deal with these services.

Moreover, contacting the web host is not a legitimate alternative to use of technical filtering methods. ISPs will not always be able to contact the host within the time period provided by the Act. Even if they can contact a host, the host may not be willing to remove the offending content. In either event, the ISP would be forced to use IP filtering or DNS filtering to disable access. In addition, an ISP using this method of compliance risks criminal prosecution if the host decides to place the offending content back on the Internet. Thus, it is rational for an ISP to implement a method of compliance that is not based on the actions of a third party.

The Court will evaluate the constitutionality of the Act with respect to the technology that is currently available. The *Playboy* Court did not consider digital technology a feasible alternative because it was not "economical" for cable operators to use this technology. Similarly, in *Reno v. ACLU*, 521 U.S. 844 (1997), the Supreme Court rejected an argument that Internet content providers could rely on "tagging" or credit card verification technology because the proposed screening software did not exist at that time. ...

The URL filtering technology recommended by the OAG at trial was not available to any ISPs that received Informal Notices or a court order, with the exception of AOL. AOL's use of URL filtering was limited; it could not use URL filtering on its entire network. The evidence establishes that it would not be economical for ISPs to develop and implement URL filtering technology. Even if the ISPs invested in the development of this technology, it would take a significant amount of research and testing to implement this filtering method and none of the experts or engineers who testified were able to give a timetable for the completion of this research. Moreover, if the ISPs were able to develop the devices and software necessary to perform URL filtering, they would be required to purchase "substantially more" switches and routers to avoid "significantly" degrading the performance of their networks. Given the uncertain nature of the research, it is difficult to predict the cost of developing this technology. However, one expert estimated that it would cost the ISP that employs him, Verizon, "well into seven figures" to implement URL filtering across its entire network. Thus, URL filtering is not a feasible alternative to DNS filtering and IP filtering.

As this Court reads *Playboy*, if a statute regulating speech provides distributors of speech with alternatives for compliance and the majority of distributors reasonably choose an alternative that has the effect of burdening protected speech, the statute is subject to scrutiny as a burden on speech. Both of the filtering methods used by the ISPs in response to Informal Notices and the court order issued in this case resulted in the blocking of innocent speech. The method of filtering recommended by defendant at trial – URL filtering – was rejected by the ISPs as infeasible. As a result, the Court concludes that the Act burdens speech and is subject to First Amendment scrutiny.

2. Level of Scrutiny

[The court considered two possible standards of review. The plaintiffs argued for strict scrutiny, because the Act was a content-based restriction on speech. The defendants argued for intermediate scrutiny because the Act was targeted at unprotected speech but had incidental effects on protected speech.]

Although there are strong arguments for the application of strict and intermediate scrutiny, the Court need not choose between the two because, even under the less demanding standard – intermediate scrutiny – the Act does not pass Constitutional muster. Under *O'Brien*, a regulation must further an important government interest unrelated to the suppression of free expression and the incidental restriction on First Amendment freedoms must be no greater than is essential to the furtherance of that interest. The government has the burden of proving that the "regulation will in fact alleviate [the] harms [addressed by the regulation] in a direct and material way," *Turner* [*Broad. Sys. v. FCC*], 512 U.S. at 664, and it has not met that burden in this case. In addition, the Act suppresses substantially more protected material than is essential to the furtherance of the government's interest in reducing child sexual abuse.

Although the prevention of child exploitation and abuse is an state interest unrelated to the suppression of free expression, defendant has not produced any evidence that the implementation of the Act has reduced child exploitation or abuse. The Act does block some users' access to child pornography; however, the material is still available to Internet users accessing the material through ISPs other than the one that blocked the web site. In addition, there are a number of methods that users and producers of child pornography can implement to avoid the filtering methods. For example, both IP filtering and DNS filtering can be avoided by a person using an anonymous proxy server or an anonymizer. A child pornographer can evade an IP filter by moving his web site to another IP address without having to change the content or the URL identifying the site. A user attempting to evade a DNS filter can manually enter the IP address for a DNS server not controlled by his ISP to avoid the block. Moreover, there is no evidence that any child pornographers have been prosecuted as a result of defendant's enforcement of the Act. In fact, the OAG did not investigate the entities that produce, publish, and distribute the child pornography. Although the inference could be drawn that making it more difficult to access child pornography reduces the incentive to produce and distribute child pornography, this burden on the child pornography business is not sufficient to overcome the significant suppression of expression that resulted from the implementation of the Act.

More than 1,190,000 innocent web sites were blocked in an effort to block less than 400 child pornography web sites, and there is no evidence that the government made an effort to avoid this impact on protected expression. As discussed in the previous section of this Memorandum, all the currently available technical methods of disabling access to a web site accessible through an ISP's service result in significant overblocking. The Act fails to specify any means of compliance, let alone provide guidance as to which method will minimize or avoid suppression of protected speech. This burden on protected expression is substantial whereas there is no evidence that the Act has impacted child sexual abuse. Thus, the Act cannot survive intermediate scrutiny. ...

C. Procedural First Amendment Issues

1. Prior Restraint

The Act and Informal Notice process are not prior restraints in the traditional sense. They do not prevent speech from reaching the market place but remove material already available on the Internet from circulation. *Alexander v. United States*, 509 U.S. 544 (1993) ("The term 'prior restraint' describes orders forbidding certain communications that are issued before the communications occur.") However, they are administrative prior restraints as that term has been interpreted by the Supreme Court. According to the Court, "only a judicial determination in an adversary proceeding ensures the necessary sensitivity to freedom of expression, only a procedure requiring a judicial determination suffices to impose a valid final restraint." *Freedman v. Maryland*, 380 U.S. 51, 58 (1965). Thus, if material protected by the First Amendment is removed from circulation without these procedural protections, the seizure is invalid as a prior restraint. The Court used the term to describe a Rhode Island Commission's practice of sending letters to book distributors that asked the distributors to remove books from circulation in *Bantam Books v. Sullivan*, 372 U.S. 58 (1963) and a procedure that allowed courts to order pre-trial seizure of films alleged to be obscene in *Fort Wayne Books, Inc. v. Indiana*, 489 U.S. 46, 51-52, 109 S.Ct. 916, 103 L.Ed.2d 34 (1989). ...

Based on the decision in *Bantam Books* and *Fort Wayne Books*, this Court concludes the procedural protections provided by the Act are inadequate. These cases require a court to make a final determination that material is child pornography after an adversary hearing before the material is completely removed from circulation. Under the Act, a judge is only required to make a finding of probable cause, he can make this determination *ex parte*, and there is no requirement that the publisher or distributor receive notice or an opportunity to be heard.

Additionally, as argued by plaintiffs, the Act allows for an unconstitutional prior restraint because it prevents future content from being displayed at a URL based on the fact that the URL contained illegal content in the past. Plaintiffs compare this burden to the permanent ban on the publication of a newspaper with a certain title, *Near v. Minnesota*, 283 U.S. 697 (1931), or a permanent injunction against showing films at a movie theater, *Vance v. Universal Amusement Co.*, 445 U.S. 308 (1980). In *Near*, the Court examined a statute that provided for a permanent injunction against a "malicious, scandalous, and defamatory newspaper, magazine or other periodical." *Near*, 283 U.S. at 701-702, *Near* involved a county attorney who obtained an injunction against the publishers of a newspaper called "The Saturday Press" under a statute preventing them from "publishing, circulating, or having in their possession any future editions of said The Saturday Press." *Id*. at 705. The statute at issue in Near was held to be unconstitutional because it permitted censorship of future publications based on material published in the past.

There are some similarities between a newspaper and a web site. Just as the content of a newspaper changes without changing the title of the publication, the content identified by a URL can change without the URL itself changing. In fact, it is possible that the owner or publisher of material on a web site identified by a URL can change without the URL changing. Plaintiffs demonstrated this by purchasing the http://www.littleangels.tv/tr URL and converting the alleged child pornography web site into a web site dedicated to a description of this case. ... Despite the fact that the content at a URL can change frequently, the Act does not provide for any review of the material at a URL and, other than a verification that the site was still blocked thirty days after the initial Informal Notice, the OAG did not review the content at any blocked URLs. Moreover, other than the instances in which complaints were made about blocked innocent content, ISPs have continued to maintain their blocking action. Specifically, WorldCom, Comcast, AOL, and Verizon all testified that they routinely maintain the blocks implemented in response to Informal Notices or, with respect to World Com, the court order. ...

The fact that an ISP can challenge a judge's child pornography determination in a criminal prosecution does not save the Act. Only one ISP, WorldCom, challenged an Informal Notice and then promptly complied with a court order obtained by the OAG. An ISP has little incentive to challenge the suppression of a web site with which it has no business relationship. As stated by the Supreme Court, a statute that suppresses speech "must be tested by its operation and effect."

Near v. Minnesota, 283 U.S. 697, 708 (1931). The operation and effect of this Act is that speech will be suppressed when a court order is issued, and the procedural protections provided by the Act before the order can issue are insufficient to avoid constitutional infirmity. ...

QUESTIONS

1. How is the filtering problem faced by ISPs dealing with Pennsylvania like the filtering problem faced by Yahoo! dealing with France? How is it different?

2. Why is filtering hard? Would it be possible to create a filter that never let a child pornography website through? One that never blocked an innocent site? Would you want to subscribe to an ISP that used one of these filters?

3. Will ISPs subject to the Act err on the site of blocking too many websites, or too few?

4. Would the result in *Pappert* have been different if Pennsylvania had ordered ISPs to filter out some other category of websites, such as websites criticizing the governor, or websites offering illegal prostitution services?

5. It has become cheaper and easier for ISPs to detect, in real time, which URLs their subscribers are visiting. Indeed, some ISPs have used this technology to identify subscribers' interests to show them targeted ads. Would the Act be constitutional if all ISPs could use URL filtering at low cost?

6. Does the Act have any other legal problems? Some of the ISPs were only able to add filters to their entire network, not just the portions serving Pennsylvania. Does the statute violate the Dormant Commerce Clause? Keep the statute in mind as you read the materials on Section 230 in the next section.

7. Would the Act be constitutional if it applied only to public libraries? If it were phrased as a condition of state funding for local libraries rather than as a command? Would it matter whether the filters could be disabled at the request of a patron?

UNITED STATES V. KEITH
80 F. Supp. 2d 33 (D. Mass. 2013)

O'Toole, District Judge: ...

To prevent its communications network from serving as a conduit for illicit activity, AOL systematically attempts to identify suspected child pornography that may be sent through its facilities. It uses an Image Detection and Filtering Process ("IDFP") of its own devise which compares files embedded in or attached to transmitted emails against a database containing what is essentially a catalog of files that have previously been identified as containing child pornography.

Commonly, AOL may be alerted that an image or video file being transmitted through its facilities likely contains child pornography by a complaint from a customer. When AOL receives such a complaint, an employee called a "graphic review analyst" opens and looks at the image or video file and forms an opinion whether what is depicted likely meets the federal criminal definition of child pornography. If the employee concludes that the file contains child pornography, a hash value of the file is generated automatically by operation of an algorithm designed for that purpose. A hash value is an alphanumeric sequence that is unique to a specific digital file. Any identical copy of the file will have exactly the same hash value as the original, but any alteration of the file, including even a change of one or two pixels, would result in a different hash value. Consequently, once a file has been "hashed," a suspected copy can be determined to be identical to the original file if it has the same hash value as the original, and not to be identical if it has a different hash value.

AOL maintains a "flat file" database of hash values of files that AOL has at some time concluded contain child pornography. It does not maintain the actual files themselves; once a file is determined to contain child pornography, it is deleted from AOL's system. When AOL detects a file passing through its network that has the same hash value as one in the flat file database, AOL reports that fact to [he National Center for Missing and Exploited Children (NCMEC)] via the latter's CyberTipline. By statute, an ... ISP such as AOL has a duty to report to NCMEC any apparent child pornography it discovers "as soon as reasonably possible." 18 U.S.C. § 2258A(a)(1). The CyperTipline report transmits the intercepted file to NCMEC, but no AOL employee opens or views the file. AOL's decision to report a file to NCMEC is made solely on the basis of the match of the hash value of the file to a stored hash value.

... After a report is received, a NCMEC analyst opens and views the file to determine whether its content meets the federal criminal definition of child pornography.

QUESTIONS

1. Suppose that Pennsylvania rewrote its ICPA to require filtering by ISPs based on hash values as described in *Keith*. Would this revised ICPA be constitutional under the tests used in *Pappert*?

2. Keep *Keith* in mind when you get to the Fourth Amendment and Wiretap sections. Do you see any other legal issues here?

E. Section 230

Although the anti-indecency portions of the Communications Decency Act were held unconstitutional by the Supreme Court in *Reno*, another provision of the CDA has had a much more successful run. Telecommunications companies, concerned about their potential liability for offensive material posted by users, successfully lobbied Congress for statutory immunity. It was codified at 47 U.S.C. § 230 and is frequently referred to simply as "Section 230." It is, bar none, the single most important piece of law discussed in this book.

The basic idea of Section 230 is simple: if I post a defamatory video to YouTube, I'm the one who should be held liable for it, not YouTube. But, as we will see, the exact scope of this immunity was up for grabs in the late 1990s. The courts have chosen to interpret Section 230 broadly – creating a kind of immunity with no offline parallel. The first case in this section – *Zeran* – illustrates the crucial early decisions by the courts to read Section 230's immunities broadly. Although the subsequent cases will point out some of the factors that have made *Zeran* controversial, that controversy is not reflected in the trend of judicial decisions, which overwhelmingly agree with its holding.

The cases in this section heavily explore the book's third major theme: intermediary power. Intermediary immunity is a policy choice, one that increases the effective flexibility and power of the intermediaries it protects. As you read these materials, ask yourself what goals that immunity is meant to serve, and who else benefits (or loses) when intermediaries are empowered in this way. These cases also raise the book's fourth major theme: innovation on the Internet. Some scholars have argued that Section 230 has played a substantial role in encouraging the development of the Internet as a commercial and social resource. As you read, ask yourself how an intermediary immunity could be considered a kind of subsidy for entrepreneurialism online.

RESTATEMENT (SECOND) OF TORTS [DEFAMATION]

§ 577 – *What Constitutes Publication*

(1) Publication of defamatory matter is its communication intentionally or by a negligent act to one other than the person defamed.

(2) One who intentionally and unreasonably fails to remove defamatory matter that he knows to be exhibited on land or chattels in his possession or under his control is subject to liability for its continued publication.

§ 578 – *Liability of Republisher*

Except as to those who only deliver or transmit defamation published by a third person, one who repeats or otherwise republishes defamatory matter is subject to liability as if he had originally published it.

§ 581 – *Transmission of Defamation Published by Third Person*

(1) Except as stated in subsection (2), one who only delivers or transmits defamatory matter published by a third person is subject to liability if, but only if, he knows or has reason to know of its defamatory character.

(2) One who broadcasts defamatory matter by means of radio or television is subject to the same liability as an original publisher.

QUESTIONS

1. The Internet is famously capable of behaving like all sorts of different media: you can get movies, television, radio, newspapers, magazines, party invitations, and personal letters online. In media circles, this phenomenon is known as *convergence*. Does Twitter seem more like a letter, a telephone conversation, a newspaper, a public speech, or a television broadcast? What about email? The Web?

2. A reporter, Clark Kent, writes a false and injurious article accusing businessman Lex Luthor of involvement in criminal activity. The *Daily Planet* newspaper prints the article on its front page. Olsen Newsstands sells the papers to the public. Slow Lane Coffee has several copies set out for its patrons. At common law, which of them are liable to Luthor for defamation? What if Luthor notifies them of the article's falsity?

COMMUNICATIONS DECENCY ACT § 230
Title 47, United States Code

§ 230 -*Protection for private blocking and screening of offensive material ...*

(c) PROTECTION FOR "GOOD SAMARITAN" BLOCKING AND SCREENING OF OFFENSIVE MATERIAL

(1) TREATMENT OF PUBLISHER OR SPEAKER. – No provider or user of an interactive computer service shall be treated as the publisher or

speaker of any information provided by another information content provider.

(2) *CIVIL LIABILITY*. – No provider or user of an interactive computer service shall be held liable on account of –

    (A) any action voluntarily taken in good faith to restrict access to or availability of material that the provider or user considers to be obscene, lewd, lascivious, filthy, excessively violent, harassing, or otherwise objectionable, whether or not such material is constitutionally protected; or

    (B) any action taken to enable or make available to information content providers or others the technical means to restrict access to material described in paragraph (1). ...

(e) *EFFECT ON OTHER LAWS*

    (1) *NO EFFECT ON CRIMINAL LAW*. – Nothing in this section shall be construed to impair the enforcement of section 223 or 231 of this title, chapter 71 (relating to obscenity) or 110 (relating to sexual exploitation of children) of title 18, or any other Federal criminal statute.

    (2) *NO EFFECT ON INTELLECTUAL PROPERTY LAW*. – Nothing in this section shall be construed to limit or expand any law pertaining to intellectual property. ...

(f) *DEFINITIONS*. – As used in this section: ...

    (2) *INTERACTIVE COMPUTER SERVICE*. – The term "interactive computer service" means any information service, system, or access software provider that provides or enables computer access by multiple users to a computer server, including specifically a service or system that provides access to the Internet and such systems operated or services offered by libraries or educational institutions.

    (3) *INFORMATION CONTENT PROVIDER*. – The term "information content provider" means any person or entity that is responsible, in whole or in part, for the creation or development of information provided through the Internet or any other interactive computer service. ...

QUESTION

1. *Before* you read further, what do you think Section 230 means? What kinds of entities qualify for the immunity, from what kinds of liability, and under what circumstances? Does it adopt the Restatement's rules, or change them? Now read on.

ZERAN V. AMERICA ONLINE, INC.
129 F.3d 327 (4th Cir. 1997)

Wilkinson, Chief Judge:

    Kenneth Zeran brought this action against America Online, Inc. ("AOL"), arguing that AOL unreasonably delayed in removing defamatory messages posted by an unidentified third party, refused to post retractions of those messages, and failed to screen for similar postings thereafter. The district court granted judgment for AOL on the grounds that the Communications Decency Act of 1996 ("CDA") – 47 U.S.C. § 230 – bars Zeran's claims. Zeran appeals, arguing that § 230 leaves intact liability for interactive computer service providers who possess notice of defamatory material posted through their services. He also contends that § 230 does not apply here because his claims arise from AOL's alleged negligence prior to the CDA's enactment. Section 230, however, plainly immunizes computer service providers like AOL from liability for information that originates with third parties. Furthermore, Congress clearly expressed its intent that § 230 apply to lawsuits, like Zeran's, instituted after the CDA's enactment. Accordingly, we affirm the judgment of the district court.

I.

"The Internet is an international network of interconnected computers," currently used by approximately 40 million people worldwide. *Reno v. ACLU*, 521 U.S. 844, 849, (1997). One of the many means by which individuals access the Internet is through an interactive computer service. These services offer not only a connection to the Internet as a whole, but also allow their subscribers to access information communicated and stored only on each computer service's individual proprietary network. *Id.* AOL is just such an interactive computer service. Much of the information transmitted over its network originates with the company's millions of subscribers. They may transmit information privately via electronic mail, or they may communicate publicly by posting messages on AOL bulletin boards, where the messages may be read by any AOL subscriber.

The instant case comes before us on a motion for judgment on the pleadings, so we accept the facts alleged in the complaint as true. On April 25, 1995, an unidentified person posted a message on an AOL bulletin board advertising "Naughty Oklahoma T-Shirts." The posting described the sale of shirts featuring offensive and tasteless slogans related to the April 19, 1995, bombing of the Alfred P. Murrah Federal Building in Oklahoma City. Those interested in purchasing the shirts were instructed to call "Ken" at Zeran's home phone number in Seattle, Washington. As a result of this anonymously perpetrated prank, Zeran received a high volume of calls, comprised primarily of angry and derogatory messages, but also including death threats. Zeran could not change his phone number because he relied on its availability to the public in running his business out of his home. Later that day, Zeran called AOL and informed a company representative of his predicament. The employee assured Zeran that the posting would be removed from AOL's bulletin board but explained that as a matter of policy AOL would not post a retraction. The parties dispute the date that AOL removed this original posting from its bulletin board.

On April 26, the next day, an unknown person posted another message advertising additional shirts with new tasteless slogans related to the Oklahoma City bombing. Again, interested buyers were told to call Zeran's phone number, to ask for "Ken," and to "please call back if busy" due to high demand. The angry, threatening phone calls intensified. Over the next four days, an unidentified party continued to post messages on AOL's bulletin board, advertising additional items including bumper stickers and key chains with still more offensive slogans. During this time period, Zeran called AOL repeatedly and was told by company representatives that the individual account from which the messages were posted would soon be closed. Zeran also reported his case to Seattle FBI agents. By April 30, Zeran was receiving an abusive phone call approximately every two minutes.

Meanwhile, an announcer for Oklahoma City radio station KRXO received a copy of the first AOL posting. On May 1, the announcer related the message's contents on the air, attributed them to "Ken" at Zeran's phone number, and urged the listening audience to call the number. After this radio broadcast, Zeran was inundated with death threats and other violent calls from Oklahoma City residents. Over the next few days, Zeran talked to both KRXO and AOL representatives. He also spoke to his local police, who subsequently surveilled his home to protect his safety. By May 14, after an Oklahoma City newspaper published a story exposing the shirt advertisements as a hoax and after KRXO made an on-air apology, the number of calls to Zeran's residence finally subsided to fifteen per day.

Zeran first filed suit on January 4, 1996, against radio station KRXO in the United States District Court for the Western District of Oklahoma. On April 23, 1996, he filed this separate suit against AOL in the same court. Zeran did not bring any action against the party who posted the offensive messages.[1] After Zeran's suit against AOL was transferred to the Eastern District of Virginia pursuant to 28 U.S.C. § 1404(a), AOL answered Zeran's complaint and interposed 47 U.S.C. § 230 as an affirmative defense. AOL then moved for judgment on the pleadings pursuant to Fed.R.Civ.P. 12(c). The district court granted AOL's motion, and Zeran filed this appeal.

II.

A.

Because § 230 was successfully advanced by AOL in the district court as a defense to Zeran's claims, we shall briefly examine its operation here. Zeran seeks to hold AOL liable for defamatory speech initiated by a third party. He argued to the district court that once he notified AOL of the unidentified third party's hoax, AOL had a duty to remove the defamatory posting promptly, to notify its subscribers of the message's false nature, and to effectively screen future defamatory material. Section 230 entered this litigation as an affirmative defense pled by AOL. The company claimed that Congress immunized interactive computer service providers from claims based on information posted by a third party.

The relevant portion of § 230 states: "No provider or user of an interactive computer service shall be treated as the publisher or speaker of any information provided by another information content provider." 47 U.S.C. § 230(c)(1). By its plain language, § 230 creates a federal immunity to any cause of action that would make service providers liable for information originating with a third-party user of the service. Specifically, § 230 precludes courts from entertaining claims that would place a computer service provider in a publisher's role. Thus, lawsuits seeking to hold a service provider liable for its exercise of a publisher's traditional editorial functions – such as deciding whether to publish, withdraw, postpone or alter content – are barred.

The purpose of this statutory immunity is not difficult to discern. Congress recognized the threat that tort-based lawsuits pose to freedom of speech in the new and burgeoning Internet medium. The imposition of tort liability on service providers for the communications of others represented, for Congress, simply another form of intrusive government regulation of speech. Section 230 was enacted, in part, to maintain the robust nature of Internet communication and, accordingly, to keep government interference in the medium to a minimum. In specific statutory findings, Congress recognized the Internet and interactive computer services as offering "a forum for a true diversity of political discourse, unique opportunities for cultural development, and myriad avenues for intellectual activity." *Id.*

---

1 Zeran maintains that AOL made it impossible to identify the original party by failing to maintain adequate records of its users. The issue of AOL's record keeping practices, however, is not presented by this appeal.

§ 230(a)(3). It also found that the Internet and interactive computer services "have flourished, to the benefit of all Americans, *with a minimum of government regulation.*" *Id.* § 230(a)(4) (emphasis added). Congress further stated that it is "the policy of the United States . . . to preserve the vibrant and competitive free market that presently exists for the Internet and other interactive computer services, *unfettered by Federal or State regulation.*" *Id.* § 230(b)(2) (emphasis added).

None of this means, of course, that the original culpable party who posts defamatory messages would escape accountability. While Congress acted to keep government regulation of the Internet to a minimum, it also found it to be the policy of the United States "to ensure vigorous enforcement of Federal criminal laws to deter and punish trafficking in obscenity, stalking, and harassment by means of computer." *Id.* § 230(b)(5). Congress made a policy choice, however, not to deter harmful online speech through the separate route of imposing tort liability on companies that serve as intermediaries for other parties' potentially injurious messages.

Congress' purpose in providing the § 230 immunity was thus evident. Interactive computer services have millions of users. See Reno v. ACLU, 521 U.S. at 849 (noting that at time of district court trial, "commercial online services had almost 12 million individual subscribers"). The amount of information communicated via interactive computer services is therefore staggering. The specter of tort liability in an area of such prolific speech would have an obvious chilling effect. It would be impossible for service providers to screen each of their millions of postings for possible problems. Faced with potential liability for each message republished by their services, interactive computer service providers might choose to severely restrict the number and type of messages posted. Congress considered the weight of the speech interests implicated and chose to immunize service providers to avoid any such restrictive effect.

Another important purpose of § 230 was to encourage service providers to self-regulate the dissemination of offensive material over their services. In this respect, § 230 responded to a New York state court decision, *Stratton Oakmont, Inc. v. Prodigy Servs. Co.*, 1995 WL 323710 (N.Y. Sup .Ct. May 24, 1995). There, the plaintiffs sued Prodigy – an interactive computer service like AOL – for defamatory comments made by an unidentified party on one of Prodigy's bulletin boards. The court held Prodigy to the strict liability standard normally applied to original publishers of defamatory statements, rejecting Prodigy's claims that it should be held only to the lower "knowledge" standard usually reserved for distributors. The court reasoned that Prodigy acted more like an original publisher than a distributor both because it advertised its practice of controlling content on its service and because it actively screened and edited messages posted on its bulletin boards.

Congress enacted § 230 to remove the disincentives to self-regulation created by the *Stratton Oakmont* decision. Under that court's holding, computer service providers who regulated the dissemination of offensive material on their services risked subjecting themselves to liability, because such regulation cast the service provider in the role of a publisher. Fearing that the specter of liability would therefore deter service providers from blocking and screening offensive material, Congress enacted § 230's broad immunity "to remove disincentives for the development and utilization of blocking and filtering technologies that empower parents to restrict their children's access to objectionable or inappropriate online material." 47 U.S.C. § 230(b)(4). In line with this purpose, § 230 forbids the imposition of publisher liability on a service provider for the exercise of its editorial and self-regulatory functions.

B.

Zeran argues, however, that the § 230 immunity eliminates only publisher liability, leaving distributor liability intact. Publishers can be held liable for defamatory statements contained in their works even absent proof that they had specific knowledge of the statement's inclusion. W. Page Keeton et al., Prosser and Keeton on the Law of Torts § 113, at 810 (5th ed. 1984). According to Zeran, interactive computer service providers like AOL are normally considered instead to be distributors, like traditional news vendors or book sellers. Distributors cannot be held liable for defamatory statements contained in the materials they distribute unless it is proven at a minimum that they have actual knowledge of the defamatory statements upon which liability is predicated. Id. at 811 (explaining that distributors are not liable "in the absence of proof that they knew or had reason to know of the existence of defamatory matter contained in matter published"). Zeran contends that he provided AOL with sufficient notice of the defamatory statements appearing on the company's bulletin board. This notice is significant, says Zeran, because AOL could be held liable as a distributor only if it acquired knowledge of the defamatory statements' existence.

Because of the difference between these two forms of liability, Zeran contends that the term "distributor" carries a legally distinct meaning from the term "publisher." Accordingly, he asserts that Congress' use of only the term "publisher" in § 230 indicates a purpose to immunize service providers only from publisher liability. He argues that distributors are left unprotected by § 230 and, therefore, his suit should be permitted to proceed against AOL. We disagree. Assuming *arguendo* that Zeran has satisfied the requirements for imposition of distributor liability, this theory of liability is merely a subset, or a species, of publisher liability, and is therefore also foreclosed by § 230.

The terms "publisher" and "distributor" derive their legal significance from the context of defamation law. Although Zeran attempts to artfully plead his claims as ones of negligence, they are indistinguishable from a garden variety defamation action. Because the publication of a statement is a necessary element in a defamation action, only one who publishes can be subject to this form of tort liability. RESTATEMENT (SECOND) OF TORTS § 558(b) (1977); Keeton et al., *supra*, § 113, at 802. Publication does not only describe the choice by an author to include certain information. In addition, both the negligent communication of a defamatory statement and the failure to remove such a statement when first communicated by another party – each alleged by Zeran here under a negligence label – constitute publication. RESTATEMENT (SECOND) OF TORTS § 577. In fact, every repetition of a defamatory statement is considered a publication. Keeton et al., *supra*, § 113, at 799.

In this case, AOL is legally considered to be a publisher. "[E]very one who takes part in the publication . . . is charged with publication." *Id.* Even distributors are considered to be publishers for purposes of defamation law:

> Those who are in the business of making their facilities available to disseminate the writings composed, the speeches made, and the information gathered by others may also be regarded as participating to such an extent in making the books, newspapers, magazines, and information available to others as to be regarded as publishers. They are intentionally making the contents available to others, sometimes

> without knowing all of the contents – including the defamatory con-
> tent – and sometimes without any opportunity to ascertain, in ad-
> vance, that any defamatory matter was to be included in the matter
> published.

Id. at 803. AOL falls squarely within this traditional definition of a publisher and, therefore, is clearly protected by § 230's immunity.

Zeran contends that decisions like *Stratton Oakmont* and *Cubby, Inc. v. CompuServe Inc.*, 776 F. Supp.. 135 (S.D.N.Y. 1991), recognize a legal distinction between publishers and distributors. He misapprehends, however, the significance of that distinction for the legal issue we consider here. It is undoubtedly true that mere conduits, or distributors, are subject to a different standard of liability. As explained above, distributors must at a minimum have knowledge of the existence of a defamatory statement as a prerequisite to liability. But this distinction signifies only that different standards of liability may be applied *within* the larger publisher category, depending on the specific type of publisher concerned. To the extent that decisions like *Stratton* and *Cubby* utilize the terms "publisher" and "distributor" separately, the decisions correctly describe two different standards of liability. *Stratton* and *Cubby* do not, however, suggest that distributors are not also a type of publisher for purposes of defamation law.

Zeran simply attaches too much importance to the presence of the distinct notice element in distributor liability. The simple fact of notice surely cannot transform one from an original publisher to a distributor in the eyes of the law. To the contrary, once a computer service provider receives notice of a potentially defamatory posting, it is thrust into the role of a traditional publisher. The computer service provider must decide whether to publish, edit, or withdraw the posting. In this respect, Zeran seeks to impose liability on AOL for assuming the role for which § 230 specifically proscribes liability – the publisher role.

Our view that Zeran's complaint treats AOL as a publisher is reinforced because AOL is cast in the same position as the party who originally posted the offensive messages. According to Zeran's logic, AOL is legally at fault because it communicated to third parties an allegedly defamatory statement. This is precisely the theory under which the original poster of the offensive messages would be found liable. If the original party is considered a publisher of the offensive messages, Zeran certainly cannot attach liability to AOL under the same theory without conceding that AOL too must be treated as a publisher of the statements.

Zeran next contends that interpreting § 230 to impose liability on service providers with knowledge of defamatory content on their services is consistent with the statutory purposes outlined in Part IIA. Zeran fails, however, to understand the practical implications of notice liability in the interactive computer service context. Liability upon notice would defeat the dual purposes advanced by § 230 of the CDA. Like the strict liability imposed by the *Stratton Oakmont* court, liability upon notice reinforces service providers' incentives to restrict speech and abstain from self-regulation.

If computer service providers were subject to distributor liability, they would face potential liability each time they receive notice of a potentially defamatory statement – from any party, concerning any message. Each notification would require a careful yet rapid investigation of the circumstances surrounding the posted information, a legal judgment concerning the information's defamatory character, and an on-the-spot editorial decision whether to risk liability by allowing the continued publication of that information. Although this might be feasible for the traditional print publisher, the sheer number of postings on interactive computer services would create an impossible burden in the Internet context. *Cf. Auvil v. CBS 60 Minutes*, 800 F. Supp.. 928, 931 (E.D.Wash. 1992) (recognizing that it is unrealistic for network affiliates to "monitor incoming transmissions and exercise on-the-spot discretionary calls"). Because service providers would be subject to liability only for the publication of information, and not for its removal, they would have a natural incentive simply to remove messages upon notification, whether the contents were defamatory or not. *See Philadelphia Newspapers, Inc. v. Hepps*, 475 U.S. 767, 777 (1986) (recognizing that fears of unjustified liability produce a chilling effect antithetical to First Amendment's protection of speech). Thus, like strict liability, liability upon notice has a chilling effect on the freedom of Internet speech.

Similarly, notice-based liability would deter service providers from regulating the dissemination of offensive material over their own services. Any efforts by a service provider to investigate and screen material posted on its service would only lead to notice of potentially defamatory material more frequently and thereby create a stronger basis for liability. Instead of subjecting themselves to further possible lawsuits, service providers would likely eschew any attempts at self-regulation.

More generally, notice-based liability for interactive computer service providers would provide third parties with a no-cost means to create the basis for future lawsuits. Whenever one was displeased with the speech of another party conducted over an interactive computer service, the offended party could simply "notify" the relevant service provider, claiming the information to be legally defamatory. In light of the vast amount of speech communicated through interactive computer services, these notices could produce an impossible burden for service providers, who would be faced with ceaseless choices of suppressing controversial speech or sustaining prohibitive liability. Because the probable effects of distributor liability on the vigor of Internet speech and on service provider self-regulation are directly contrary to § 230's statutory purposes, we will not assume that Congress intended to leave liability upon notice intact.

QUESTIONS

1. *Zeran* is one of the most important texts in all of Internet law. It rewards careful reading. State the post-*Zeran* rule of Section 230 in your own words, in one sentence.

2. Explain the distinction between "publisher" and "distributor" liability at common law. Then explain *Zeran's* holding in terms of these categories. Now explain it again, slowly. Now test yourself: After *Zeran*, if you find a defamatory post about you on AOL, can you sue AOL? What if you pick up the phone and call AOL and tell them, "There's a defamatory post about me!" Your answers should be "no" and "no." Explain why.

3. Why did Ken Zeran need to sue AOL? Couldn't he have sued the user who posted the fake ads?

4. How would AOL have to change the way it does business if it were treated as a distributor? If it were treated as a publisher? What about YouTube, to which users upload hundreds of thousands of videos daily?

5. Is *Zeran* an extension of offline principles to Internet activity, or does it create a new, Internet-only legal regime?

JONES V. DIRTY WORLD ENTERTAINMENT RECORDINGS LLC
755 F.3d 398 (6th Cir. 2014)

Gibbons, Circuit Judge:

This case presents the issue of whether the Communications Decency Act of 1996 (CDA), 47 U.S.C. § 230, bars the state-law defamation claims of plaintiff-appellee Sarah Jones. Jones was the unwelcome subject of several posts anonymously uploaded to www.TheDirty.com, a popular website operated by defendants-appellants Nik Lamas–Richie and DIRTY WORLD, LLC ("Dirty World"), and of remarks Richie posted on the site. The website enables users to anonymously upload comments, photographs, and video, which Richie then selects and publishes along with his own distinct, editorial comments. In short, the website is a user-generated tabloid primarily targeting nonpublic figures.

In response to the posts appearing on www.TheDirty.com, Jones brought an action in federal district court alleging state tort claims of defamation, libel *per se,* false light, and intentional inflection of emotional distress. Richie and Dirty World claimed that § 230(c)(1) barred these claims. The district court rejected this argument and denied defendants-appellants' motion to dismiss, motion for summary judgment, motion to revise judgment, and motion for judgment as a matter of law. The district court also denied Richie's and Dirty World's motion for leave to file an interlocutory appeal. The case was submitted to a jury, twice. The first trial ended in a mistrial upon a joint motion. The second trial resulted in a verdict in favor of Jones for $38,000 in compensatory damages and $300,000 in punitive damages. On appeal, Richie and Dirty World maintain that § 230(c)(1) barred Jones's claims. ...

I.

Richie is currently employed as the manager of DIRTY WORLD, LLC ("Dirty World"), which owns and operates the website www.TheDirty.com. ... The website receives approximately six hundred thousand visits each day and eighteen million visits each month.

As the website grew, its focus and format changed. In the beginning, Richie created nearly all the content on the site, and users could not directly upload content. This is no longer true. For the past several years and currently, users of the site, who colloquially refer to themselves as "The Dirty Army," may submit "dirt" – *i.e.,* content that may include text, photographs, or video about any subject. Users may also post comments about the content submitted by others. The vast majority of the content appearing on www.TheDirty.com is comprised of submissions uploaded directly by third-party users.

The content submission form instructs users to "Tell us what's happening. Remember to tell us who, what, when, where, why." The content submission form requires users to submit a title and category for their submission as well as their city or college for indexing. Submissions appear on the website as though they were authored by a single, anonymous author – "THE DIRTY ARMY." This eponymous introduction is automatically added to every post that Richie receives from a third-party user. Many, but not all, of the submissions and commentaries appearing on the website relate to stories, news, and gossip about local individuals who are not public figures. The site receives thousands of new submissions each day. Richie or his staff selects and edits approximately 150 to 200 submissions for publication each day. The editing done to published submissions only consists of deletion. Richie or his staff briefly reviews each submission selected for publication to ensure that nudity, obscenity, threats of violence, profanity, and racial slurs are removed. Richie typically adds a short, one-line comment about the post with "some sort of humorous or satirical observation." Richie, however, does not materially change, create, or modify any part of the user-generated submission, nor does he fact-check submissions for accuracy. Apart from his clearly denoted comments appended at the end of each submission, which appear in bold-face text and are signed "-nik," Richie does not create any of the posts that appear on www.TheDirty.com. The bold-face text and signature are designed to distinguish editorial remarks from third-party submissions. Comments that appear in bold face and are signed "-nik" are only written and published by Richie.

Sarah Jones is a resident of northern Kentucky. Jones was a teacher at Dixie Heights High School in Edgewood, Kentucky, and a member of the Cincinnati BenGals, the cheerleading squad for the Cincinnati Bengals professional football team. From October 2009 to January 2010, Jones was the subject of several submissions posted by anonymous users on www.TheDirty.com and of editorial remarks posted by Richie.

First, on October 27, 2009, a visitor to www.TheDirty.com submitted two photographs of Jones and a male companion and the following post:

> THE DIRTY ARMY: Nik, this is Sara J, Cincinnati Bengal Cheerleader. She's been spotted around town lately with the infamous Shayne Graham. She has also slept with every other Bengal Football player. This girl is a teacher too!! You would think with Graham's paycheck he could attract something a little easier on the eyes Nik!

Appearing directly beneath this post, Richie added:

> Everyone in Cincinnati knows this kicker is a Sex Addict. It is no secret ... he can't even keep relationships because his Red Rocket has freckles that need to be touched constantly. – nik

Jones requested that the post be removed. Richie informed Jones that the post would not be removed.

Second, on December 7, 2009, a visitor submitted a photograph of Jones and the following post:

> THE DIRTY ARMY: Nik, here we have Sarah J, captain cheerleader of the playoff bound cinci bengals.. Most ppl see Sarah has [sic] a gorgeous cheerleader AND highschool teacher.. yes she's also a teacher.. but what most of you don't know is.. Her ex Nate.. cheated on her with over 50 girls in 4 yrs.. in that time he tested positive for Chlamydia Infection and Gonorrhea.. so im sure Sarah also has both.. whats worse is he brags about doing sarah in the gym .. football field.. her class room at the school she teaches at DIXIE Heights.

Appearing directly after this post, Richie remarked: "Why are all high school teachers freaks in the sack?nik"

Third, on December 9, 2009, a visitor submitted another photograph of Jones and a male companion and the following post:

> THE DIRTY ARMY: Nik, ok you all seen the past posting of the dirty Bengals cheerleader/teacher ... well here is her main man Nate. Posted a few pics of the infected couple. Oh an for everyone saying sarah is so gorgeous check her out in these non photoshopped pics.

Appearing directly after this post, Richie added:

> Cool tribal tat man. For a second yesterday I was jealous of those high
> school kids for having a cheerleader teacher, but not anymore. – nik

Jones sent Richie over twenty-seven emails, pleading for Richie to remove these posts from the website, to no avail. Jones's father similarly wrote to Richie, also to no avail. She then sought legal help, and her attorney informed Richie that if the posts were not removed by December 14, 2009, Jones would file suit. The posts were not removed. Jones, *qua* Jane Doe, filed in federal district court this action on December 23, 2009, against Dirty World Entertainment Recordings, LLC, which operated a website called www.thedirt.com. Apparently, Jones sued the wrong party, as neither Richie nor Dirty World has or ever had any relationship with either Dirty World Entertainment Recordings, LLC, or www.thedirt.com. Nevertheless, the lawsuit sparked national media attention, which precipitated further postings on www.TheDirty.com regarding Jones.

For instance, on December 29, a visitor submitted a photograph and the following post:

> THE DIRTY ARMY: Nik, i just saw the Huffington Post and I just [sic] the latest post on beat Bang–GALS cheer squad and back in May I was out clubbing in Cinci and those cheer chicks were hosting the club and i could not believe how ugly they were, here is some pics of them from that night.

Richie added:

> I think they all need to be kicked off and the Cincinnati Bengals should start over. Note to self: Never try to battle the DIRTY ARMY. – nik ...

... After the litigation commenced, Richie posted a public letter to Jones:

> If you know the truth then why do you care? With all the media attention this is only going to get worse for you. Your lawyer is trying to make a name for himself using you as his pawn. If anything me just seeing your face on the news right now will get you fired from your job. All you had to do is read the FAQ section like every other normal person to get stuff removed. You dug your own grave here Sarah. I am a very reasonable person ... hope it was worth it.nik.

He also removed the first three posts regarding Jones. The posts on www.TheDirty.com humiliated Jones, allegedly undermining her position as an educator, her membership in the Cincinnati BenGals, and her personal life.

Jones amended her action to proceed against [the proper defendants], alleging claims of defamation, libel *per se*, false light, and intentional inflection of emotional distress. [The case proceeded as summarized above.]

II.

A.

We review a district court's denial of a motion for judgment as a matter of law or a renewed motion for judgment as a matter of law *de novo*. ...

B.

[The court summarized the extensive caselaw according with *Zeran*'s interpretation of § 230.]

By barring publisher-liability and notice-liability defamation claims lodged against interactive computer service providers, § 230 serves three main purposes.

First, it "maintain[s] the robust nature of Internet communication and, accordingly, ... keep[s] government interference in the medium to a minimum." [*Zeran*, 129 F.3d] at 330. Second, the immunity provided by § 230 protects against the "heckler's veto" that would chill free speech. Without § 230, persons who perceive themselves as the objects of unwelcome speech on the internet could threaten litigation against interactive computer service providers, who would then face a choice: remove the content or face litigation costs and potential liability. Third, § 230 encourages interactive computer service providers to self-regulate. ...

The protection provided by § 230 has been understood to merit expansion. Congress has extended the protection of § 230 into new areas. *See* 28 U.S.C. § 4102(c)(1) (providing that U.S. courts "shall not recognize or enforce" foreign defamation judgments that are inconsistent with § 230). And courts have construed the immunity provisions in § 230 broadly. Moreover, "close cases ... must be resolved in favor of immunity, lest we cut the heart out of section 230 by forcing websites to face death by ten thousand duck-bites, fighting off claims that they promoted or encouraged – or at least tacitly assented to – the illegality of third parties." *Fair Hous. Council of San Fernando Valley v. Roommates. Com, LLC*, 521 F.3d 1157, 1174 (9th Cir. 2008) (en banc).

Section 230(c)(1)'s grant of immunity is not without limits, however. It applies only to the extent that an interactive computer service provider is not also the information content provider of the content at issue. An "information content provider" is defined as "any person or entity that is responsible, in whole or in part, for the creation or development of information provided through the Internet or any other interactive computer service." 47 U.S.C. § 230(f)(3). A website operator can simultaneously act as both a service provider and a content provider. If a website displays content that is created entirely by third parties, then it is only a service provider with respect to that content – and thus is immune from claims predicated on that content. But if a website operator is in part responsible for the creation or development of content, then it is an information content provider as to that content – and is not immune from claims predicated on it. Thus, a website may be immune from liability for some of the third-party content it publishes but be subject to liability for the content that it is responsible for as a creator or developer. In short, immunity under the CDA depends on the pedigree of the content at issue. ...

C.

This case turns on how narrowly or capaciously the statutory term "development" in § 230(f)(3) is read. ...

... Decisions from our sister circuits ... provide a workable measure of "development" that not only preserves the broad immunity the CDA provides for website operators' exercise of traditional publisher functions but also highlights the limited circumstances under which exercises of those functions are not protected. The leading case is *Roommates*. There, the Ninth Circuit sitting *en banc* discussed the meaning of "development" at length. In *Roommates,* as a condition for using an online roommate-finding service, a website required each user seeking to offer living space to create a profile describing his desired roommate and, in so doing, required that user "to disclose his sex, sexual orientation and whether he would bring children to a household." *Id.* at 1161. The website also encouraged its users to provide additional comments describing themselves and their desired roommate. The fair housing councils of San Fernando Valley and San Diego sued, alleging that the website violated the Fair Housing Act and state housing discrimination laws. The court held that a website operator was not entitled to immunity with respect to allegedly unlawful content that it *required* its users to submit and with respect to the search engine that was built on that content. But the court also held that the website was immune as to claims based on the website's encouragement that users provide additional comments, some of which were alleged to be discriminatory. To arrive at these divergent holdings, the court applied a specific measure of development:

> [W]e interpret the term "development" as referring not merely to augmenting the content generally, but *to materially contributing to its alleged unlawfulness.* In other words, a website helps to develop unlawful content, and thus falls within the exception to section 230, *if it contributes materially to the alleged illegality of the conduct.*

521 F.3d at 1167–68 (emphasis added). A material contribution to the alleged illegality of the content does not mean merely taking action that is necessary to the display of allegedly illegal content. Rather, it means being responsible for what makes the displayed content allegedly unlawful. *Cf.* [*Chicago Lawyers' Comm. for Civil Rights Under Law, Inc. v. Craigslist, Inc.,* 519 F.3d 666, 671 (7th Cir. 2008)] ("Causation ... must refer to causing a particular statement to be made, or perhaps the discriminatory content of a statement. That's the sense in which a nonpublisher can cause a discriminatory ad, while one who causes the forbidden content may not be a publisher."). "In an abundance of caution," the *Roommates* court gave several examples of applications of the "material contribution" test. For example:

> If an individual uses an ordinary search engine to query for a "white roommate," the search engine has not contributed to any alleged unlawfulness in the individual's conduct; providing *neutral* tools to carry out what may be unlawful or illicit searches does not amount to "development" for purposes of the immunity exception. A dating website that requires users to enter their sex, race, religion and marital status through drop-down menus, and that provides means for users to search along the same lines, retains its CDA immunity insofar as it does not contribute to any alleged illegality.

521 F.3d at 1169. In contrast to this example, the court observed that Roommates required subscribers to disclose information about protected characteristics as a condition of accessing its service and "designed its search and email systems to limit the listings available to subscribers based on sex, sexual orientation and presence of children." *Id. at* 1166, 1169. Because Roommates required information about protected characteristics and engineered its search and email systems to limit access to housing listings based on those protected characteristics, the court held that the website materially contributed to the alleged illegality of hiding certain listings.

The court also gave specific examples of the application of the material contribution test for a website that solicits, edits, and displays content originating from third parties (*i.e.,* a website akin to www.TheDirty.com). For example:

> A website operator who edits user-created content – such as by correcting spelling, removing obscenity or trimming for length – retains his immunity for any illegality in the user-created content, provided that the edits are unrelated to the illegality. However, a website operator who edits in a manner that contributes to the alleged illegality –

such as by removing the word "not" from a user's message reading "[Name] did *not* steal the artwork" in order to transform an innocent message into a libelous one – is directly involved in the alleged illegality and thus not immune.

Id. at 1169; *see also Batzel v. Smith*, 333 F.3d 1018, 1035 (9th Cir. 2003) (holding that an editor of an email newsletter who received and published allegedly actionable information, adding a short headnote, was immune under § 230 because an editor's changes to the length and spelling of third-party content do not contribute to the libelousness of the message). The *Roommates* court further explained:

> And any activity that can be boiled down to deciding whether to exclude material that third parties seek to post online is perforce immune under section 230. But if the editor publishes material that he does not believe was tendered to him for posting online, then he is the one making the affirmative decision to publish, and so he contributes materially to its allegedly unlawful dissemination. He is thus properly deemed a developer and not entitled to CDA immunity.

521 F.3d at 1170–71.

Accordingly, the *Roommates* court held that § 230 barred the fair housing councils' claims grounded on the allegedly discriminatory statements displayed through Roommate's operation of the "additional comments" section of its website. The court explained:

> Roommate publishes these comments as written. It does not provide any specific guidance as to what the essay should contain, nor does it urge subscribers to input discriminatory preferences. Roommate is not responsible, in whole or in part, for the development of this content, which comes entirely from subscribers and is passively displayed by Roommate. Without reviewing every essay, Roommate would have no way to distinguish unlawful discriminatory preferences from perfectly legitimate statements. Nor can there be any doubt that this information was tendered to Roommate for publication online. This is precisely the kind of situation for which section 230 was designed to provide immunity.

Id. at 1173–74. Furthermore, the court rejected the argument made by the fair housing councils that the website developed the allegedly illegal content displayed in the additional comments section because the website encouraged the submission of discriminatory preferences. The court reasoned that "[t]he fact that Roommate encourages subscribers to provide *something* in response to the prompt is not enough to make it a 'develop[er]' of the information." *Id.* Because "Roommate does not tell subscribers what kind of information they should or must include as 'Additional Comments,' and certainly does not encourage or enhance any discriminatory content created by users," the court held that the operation of the additional comments section did not materially contribute to the alleged unlawfulness of the content displayed on the website's comments section. *Id.*

The material contribution test has been adopted and applied by other circuits, with instructive effect. *Compare Nemet Chevrolet, Ltd. v. Consumeraffairs.com, Inc.*, 591 F.3d 250, 254 (4th Cir. 2009)(holding that a website *did not* contribute to alleged illegality), *with FTC v. Accusearch Inc.*, 570 F.3d 1187 (10th Cir. 2009) (holding that a website *did* contribute to alleged illegality). In *Nemet*, Nemet, the owner of a Chevrolet dealership, sued Consumeraffairs.com, a website allowing users to comment on the quality of goods and services, after various allegedly tortious, third-party posts appeared on the website relating to automobiles sold or serviced by him. The website claimed immunity under the CDA. Nemet responded that the website was, in fact, an information content provider under § 230(f)(3), and was thus liable as a co-developer, because of the "structure and design of its website" and because "Consumeraffiars.com solicited its customers' complaints and steered them into specific categories]" *Id.* at 256. The panel affirmed the district court's grant of the website's motion to dismiss because "even accepting as true all of the facts Nemet pled as to Consumeraffairs.com's liability for the structure and design of its website, the amended complaint does not show, or even intimate, that Consumeraffairs.com contributed to the allegedly fraudulent nature of the comments at issue." *Id. at 257.*

In *Accusearch,* Accusearch operated a website that sold the confidential information of individuals, including their telephone records, which the website paid researchers to obtain. The Federal Trade Commission brought suit against the website operator to curtail its sale of confidential information and to disgorge its profits from the sale of information in telephone records. Accusearch claimed immunity under the CDA, arguing that it merely displayed the allegedly illegal conduct that originated from its third-party researchers. The panel rejected this argument and held that the website operator developed the confidential telephone records within the meaning of the CDA. The panel cited *Roommates's* material contribution test and found "that language applies to Accusearch's role in this case." *Id.* at 1200. The *Accusearch* panel reasoned that "by paying its researchers to acquire telephone records, knowing that the confidentiality of the records was protected by law, it contributed mightily to the unlawful conduct of its researchers." *Id.* The panel noted that "the offensive postings were Accusearch's *raison d'etre* and it affirmatively solicited them." *Id.* It thus found that "Accusearch's actions were not 'neutral' with respect to generating offensive content; on the contrary, its actions were intended to generate such content." *Id.* at 1201. Accordingly, the panel held that "Accusearch is not entitled to immunity under the CDA." *Id.* ...

D.

Consistent with our sister circuits, we adopt the material contribution test to determine whether a website operator is "responsible, in whole or in part, for the creation or development of [allegedly tortious] information." 47 U.S.C. § 230(f)(3). And we expressly decline to adopt the definition of "development" set forth by the district court.

The district court read the foregoing decisions, identified *Roommates* as the guiding precedent, but derived a different rule. In its memorandum opinion explaining the denial of Dirty World's and Richie's Rule 50 motion, the district court gave two formulations of a rule providing when the CDA does not bar a plaintiff's claim. First, the district court said that a "website owner who intentionally encourages illegal or actionable third-party postings to which he adds his own comments ratifying or adopting the posts becomes a 'creator' or 'developer' of that content and is not entitled to immunity." Second, in a different formulation, the district court said that "if ... [website] owners, as in the instant case, invite invidious postings, elaborate on them with comments of their own, and call upon others to respond in kind, the immunity does not apply." ...

We do not adopt the district court's encouragement test of immunity under the CDA. The district court misapprehended how other circuits, particularly the

Ninth Circuit in *Roommates*, have separated what constitutes "development" in § 230(f)(3) from what does not. The district court elided the crucial distinction between, on the one hand, taking actions (traditional to publishers) that are necessary to the display of unwelcome and actionable content and, on the other hand, responsibility for what makes the displayed content illegal or actionable. This is the distinction that divides the holdings in *Roommates* and *Accusearch*, which stripped the respective defendants of the CDA's protection, from the holdings in *Roommates, Chicago Lawyers' Committee, Johnson, Batzel, Nemet,* and *Zeran,* which barred the respective plaintiffs' claims. In *Roommates*, the website was responsible for the alleged discrimination by requiring users to submit protected characteristics and hiding listings based on those submissions. In *Accusearch*, the website was responsible for the illegal purchase and resale of confidential telephone records. But in *Chicago Lawyers' Committee* and *Nemet*, for example, the website operators provided a forum for user posts, did not require users to violate the law as a condition of posting, did not compensate for the posting of actionable speech, did not post actionable content themselves, and therefore were not responsible for the actionable speech that was displayed on their websites. The district court's rule does not neatly divide these cases. An encouragement theory of "development" does not obviously capture what was allegedly unlawful about the design of Roommate's website, particularly its search engine, or Accusearch's payment for unlawful conduct. And it does not obviously leave out the neutral fora created by the commercially oriented websites targeted by the claims in *Chicago Lawyers' Committee* and *Nemet* (craigslist.com and www.consumeraffairs.com, respectively).

More importantly, an encouragement test would inflate the meaning of "development" to the point of eclipsing the immunity from publisher-liability that Congress established. Many websites not only allow but also actively invite and encourage users to post particular types of content. Some of this content will be unwelcome to others – *e.g.*, unfavorable reviews of consumer products and services, allegations of price gouging, complaints of fraud on consumers, reports of bed bugs, collections of cease-and-desist notices relating to online speech. And much of this content is commented upon by the website operators who make the forum available. Indeed, much of it is "adopted" by website operators, gathered into reports, and republished online. Under an encouragement test of development, these websites would lose the immunity under the CDA and be subject to hecklers' suits aimed at the publisher. Moreover, under the district court's rule, courts would then have to decide what constitutes "encouragement" in order to determine immunity under the CDA – a concept that is certainly more difficult to define and apply than the Ninth Circuit's material contribution test. Congress envisioned an uninhibited, robust, and wide-open internet, but the muddiness of an encouragement rule would cloud that vision. Accordingly, other courts have declined to hold that websites were not entitled to the immunity furnished by the CDA because they selected and edited content for display, thereby encouraging the posting of similar content. We do the same.

The district court also suggested that when an interactive computer service provider adds commentary to third-party content that "ratifies or adopts" that content, then the provider becomes a "creator" or "developer" of that content and is not entitled to the CDA's protection. An adoption or ratification theory, however, is not only inconsistent with the material contribution standard of "development" but also abuses the concept of responsibility. A website operator cannot be responsible for what makes another party's statement actionable by commenting on that statement *post hoc*. To be sure, a website operator's previous comments on prior postings could encourage subsequent invidious postings, but that loose understanding of responsibility collapses into the encouragement measure of "development," which we reject. As other courts have recognized, the adoption theory of "development" would undermine the CDA for the same reasons as an encouragement theory.

III.

We now apply the material contribution measure of "development" to the facts of this case. Jones's defamation claims target the statements that were posted by a third party on October 27 and December 7, 2009. Because Dirty World and Richie did not materially contribute to the illegality of those statements, the CDA bars Jones's claims.

Dirty World and Richie did not author the statements at issue; however, they did select the statements for publication. But Richie and Dirty World cannot be found to have materially contributed to the defamatory content of the statements posted on October 27 and December 7, 2009, simply because those posts were selected for publication. Nor can they be found to have materially contributed to the defamatory content through the decision not to remove the posts. The CDA expressly bars "lawsuits seeking to hold a service provider liable for its exercise of a publisher's traditional editorial functions – such as deciding whether to publish, withdraw, postpone or alter content." [*Zeran*, 129 F.3d at 330.]

Unlike in *Roommates*, the website that Richie operated did not require users to post illegal or actionable content as a condition of use. Nor does the name of the website, www.TheDirty.com, suggest that only illegal or actionable content will be published. Unlike in *Accusearch*, Richie or Dirty World did not compensate users for the submission of unlawful content. The website's content submission form simply instructs users to "[t]ell us what's happening. Remember to tell us who, what, when, where, why." The form additionally provides labels by which to categorize the submission. These tools, neutral (both in orientation and design) as to what third parties submit, do not constitute a material contribution to any defamatory speech that is uploaded.

Further, Richie's comment on the December 7 post – *viz.*, "Why are all high school teachers freaks in the sack?" – although absurd, did not materially contribute to the defamatory content of the statements uploaded on October 27 and December 7, 2009. Richie's remark was made after each of the defamatory postings had already been displayed. It would break the concepts of responsibility and material contribution to hold Richie responsible for the defamatory content of speech because he later commented on that speech. Although ludicrous, Richie's remarks did not materially contribute to the defamatory content of the posts appearing on the website. More importantly, the CDA bars claims lodged against website operators for their editorial functions, such as the posting of comments concerning third-party posts, so long as those comments are not themselves actionable.

To be sure, Richie was an information content provider as to his comment on the December 7 post. But Jones did not allege that *Richie's* comments were defamatory. And the district court did not hold that Richie's comments were themselves tortious. Rather, the court concluded that those comments "effectively ratified and adopted the defamatory third-party post" and thereby developed the defamatory statements, thus ruling that the CDA did not bar Jones's claims. The district court's adoption or ratification test, however, is inconsistent with the material contribution standard of "development" and, if established, would undermine the CDA. Therefore, Dirty World and Richie did not develop the statements forming the basis of Jones's tort claims and accordingly are not information content providers as to them.

Because (1) the defendants are interactive service providers, (2) the statements at issue were provided by another information content provider, and (3) Jones's claim seeks to treat the defendants as a publisher or speaker of those statements, the CDA bars Jones's claims. Given the role that the CDA plays in an open and robust internet by preventing the speech-chilling threat of the heckler's veto, we point out that determinations of immunity under the CDA should be resolved at an earlier stage of litigation.[4] *See Nemet*, 591 F.3d at 254 ("[I]mmunity is an *immunity from suit* rather than a mere defense to liability [and] is effectively lost if a case is erroneously permitted to go to trial.").

IV.

We note that the broad immunity furnished by the CDA does not necessarily leave persons who are the objects of anonymously posted, online, defamatory content without a remedy. In this case, Jones conceded that she did not attempt to recover from the person(s) whose comments Richie elected to publish. She conceded that she did not attempt to subpoena Richie or Dirty World to discover who authored the defamatory posts. Instead, she sued Dirty World and Richie. But, under the CDA, Jones cannot seek her recovery from the online publisher where that publisher did not materially contribute to the tortious content. Congress envisioned a free and open internet, and the immunity provision of § 230(c)(1), which subverts common-law publisher-liability, serves that purpose. While some exercises of the considerable freedom that Congress allowed online publishers are regrettable, freedom and its uses are distinct. Congress enacted § 230(c)(1) to preserve a free internet, and that enactment resolves this case.

For the foregoing reasons, we vacate the judgment in favor of Jones and reverse the district court's denial of Dirty World's and Richie's motion for judgment as a matter of law with instructions to enter judgment as a matter of law in their favor.

QUESTIONS

1. *Dirty World* argues that Section 230 "encourages interactive computer service providers to self-regulate." How effectively was Dirty World self-regulating? Should Section 230 only apply to services that act in good faith?

2. After *Dirty World*, can a website pay its contributors while retaining the protection of Section 230? Can it refuse to delete defamatory posts unless the victim pays a $250 "arbitration filing fee?" Can it delete users' posts praising a person while leaving up posts attacking that person? Can it be dedicated entirely to user-submitted content attacking a specific person (e.g. DefameMonica.com)?

3. In *Enigma Software Group USA, LLC v. Bleeping Computer LLC*, No. 16 Civ. 57 (PAE), 2016 WL 3773394 (S.D.N.Y. July 8, 2016), Enigma objected to allegedly defamatory posts by Quietman7 on forums operated by Bleeping. In its complaint, Enigma alleged that:

---

4 Certification of the interlocutory appeal sought by Dirty World and Richie could have obviated the need for the second trial. An even earlier interlocutory appeal would have resolved the case prior to trial.

- Bleeping designated Quietman7 as an "Advisor" and "Global Moderator." Advisors are described as users who "can be trusted to give correct and understandable answers to questions." Global Moderators have the power to close discussion threads, edit users' posts, and ban users who violate forum rules.

- Bleeping receives commissions whenever users click on links from "Affiliate" advertisers and buy their products. Bleeping directs Advisors to promote Affiliates' products. Enigma was not an Affiliate, but a competitor was.

- Quietman7 signed his posts "Bleepin' Janitor" and "The BC Staff"

Are these sufficient to defeat Bleeping's Section 230 motion to dismiss?

4. Popular blogger Harlan Reynoso, who has tens of thousands of daily readers, creates a post which reads, in its entirety, "Yes <u>indeedy</u>." The word "indeedy" is a hyperlink to a webpage maintained by Jeff Albertson accusing Flancrest Enterprises of making its hand-hooked rugs with child labor. The claims are false and Albertson knows it. Flancrest sues Albertson and Reynoso for defamation. What result?

5. Xcentric Ventures operates the Ripoff Report website, which actively solicits negative comments on businesses. Unsurprisingly, it is a frequent Section 230 litigant. As one court described it:

> The business practices of Xcentric, as presented by the evidence before this Court, are appalling. Xcentric appears to pride itself on having created a forum for defamation. ... Even when, as here, a user regrets what she has posted and takes every effort to retract it, Xcentric refuses to allow it. Moreover, Xcentric insists in its brief that its policy is never to remove a post. It will not entertain any scenario in which, despite the clear damage that a defamatory or illegal post would continue to cause so long as it remains on the website, Xcentric would remove an offending post.

Giordano v. Romeo, 76 So.3d 1100, 1102 (Fla. App. Ct. 2011) Is this an ethical business model? Is it good for society to have websites like this one? Should the law protect them?

6. Was Richie's message to Jones that "seeing your face on the news right now will get you fired from your job" a threat? The phenomenon that lawsuits to keep secrets or protect privacy can cause the information to be even more widely publicized on the Internet is often known as the "Streisand effect." The singer (in)famously sued a photographer who took photographs of her home from a plane. Before the suit, the photographs had been viewed six times, twice by Streisand's lawyer. But the high-profile lawsuit by a celebrity, together with extensive criticism by Internet commenters, brought them to the attention of hundreds of thousands of people. Is the Streisand effect a positive or a negative development in media culture? Does it change how you would proceed if you were representing Jones?

DOE V. MYSPACE, INC.
474 F. Supp. 2d 843 (W.D. Tex. 2007)
aff'd 528 F.3d 413 (5th Cir. 2008)

Sparks, District Judge:

Be it remembered on the 1st day of February 2007, the Court held a hearing in the above-styled cause, to consider Defendants MySpace, Inc. and News Corporation's ("MySpace") Motion to Dismiss, Plaintiffs' responses thereto, and Defendants' reply thereto. Having considered the motion, the responses, the replies, the arguments of counsel at the hearing, the relevant case law, and the case file as a whole, the Court now enters the following opinion and orders.

BACKGROUND

MySpace.com is the most visited web site in the United States, and it is owned by Defendant MySpace, Inc.[2] MySpace.com is a "social networking web site" that allows its members to create online "profiles," which are individual web pages on which members post photographs, videos, and information about their lives and interests. The idea of online social networking is that members will use their online profiles to become part of an online community of people with common interests. Once a member has created a profile, she can extend "friend invitations" to other members and communicate with her friends over the MySpace.com platform via e-mail, instant messaging, or blogs.

MySpace.com is free to users who agree to the MySpace Terms of Use Agreement. Every new member of MySpace.com, including Julie Doe, agrees to be bound by the MySpace.com Terms of Service, by clicking a check box on the website. MySpace's Terms of Service provide that MySpace cannot verify the age or identity of MySpace.com members and cautions members not to provide "telephone numbers, street addresses, last names, URLs or email addresses" to other members.

According to Plaintiffs' Verified Complaint, Julie Doe created a MySpace profile when she was 13 years old. At the hearing, Plaintiffs' counsel admitted that Julie Doe lied about her age and represented that she was 18 years old when she joined MySpace.com.[3] Plaintiffs allege Pete Solis, a nineteen-year-old, initiated contact with Julie Doe, then fourteen years old, through MySpace.com on April 6, 2006. Subsequently, Julie Doe provided Pete Solis with her telephone number and the two communicated over the phone for several weeks. At some point, Julie Doe and Pete Solis arranged to meet for a date on May 12, 2006. Plaintiffs allege that during that meeting Pete Solis sexually assaulted Julie Doe. On May 13, 2006, Jane Doe, Julie's mother, called the Austin Police Department to report the sexual assault of her daughter. Pete Solis was subsequently arrested and indicted by the Travis County District Attorney's Office for Sexual Assault, a second degree felony.

... Plaintiffs' Verified Complaint ... asserts the following causes of action against Defendants: negligence, gross negligence, fraud, and negligent misrepresentation.

I. DEFENDANTS' MOTION TO DISMISS

MySpace moves to dismiss this case with prejudice pursuant to Federal Rule of Civil Procedure 12(b)(6) and 9(b). Defendants assert they are immune from this suit under the Communications Decency Act of 1996. ...

---

2 Defendant MySpace, Inc. is wholly owned by Fox Interactive Media, Inc., a subsidiary of Defendant News Corporation.

3 MySpace.com requires that a user be at least fourteen years old to use their services.

A. Communications Decency Act of 1996 ...

Despite Plaintiffs' arguments to the contrary, the Court finds *Zeran* and its rationale to be applicable to the case at hand. Here, Plaintiffs seek to impose tort liability on MySpace, a company that functions as an intermediary by providing a forum for the exchange of information between third party users. Plaintiffs' allegations that MySpace knew sexual predators were using the service to communicate with minors and failed to react appropriately can be analogized to Zeran's claims that AOL failed to act quickly enough to remove the ads and to prevent the posting of additional ads after AOL was on notice that the content was false.

Plaintiffs contend the CDA is inapplicable to their claims, so Defendants should not be granted immunity under the CDA. Plaintiffs assert Section 230(c)(1) is inapplicable here because Plaintiffs have not sued MySpace for the publication of third-party content but rather for failing to implement basic safety measures to prevent sexual predators from communicating with minors on MySpace. Plaintiffs attempt to distinguis [*Zeran* and other cases following it] from the case at hand, by pointing out that each of these cases was based on the listing of third-party content without taking into account its defamatory or inaccurate nature. Plaintiffs assert their case is not based on MySpace's posting of third-party content, but rather on MySpace's failure to institute safety measures to protect minors.

Plaintiffs seek to limit CDA immunity to cases involving defamation or related actions and assert that their claims against MySpace have nothing to do with the content of the information provided. Plaintiffs contend that neither the plain language of the CDA nor the cases interpreting it contemplate the extension of the CDA's immunity provision to MySpace in this case.

Nothing on the face of the statute supports Plaintiffs' narrow interpretation that the CDA's immunity applies only to cases involving defamation and defamation-related claims. 47 U.S.C. § 230. The Eastern District of Texas recently addressed the application of CDA immunity in a case involving claims of negligence, negligence per se, intentional infliction of emotional distress, invasion of privacy, civil conspiracy, and distribution of child pornography. *Doe v. Bates*, No. 5:05- CV-91-DF-CMC, 2006 WL 3813758 (E.D. Tex. Dec. 27, 2006). This case dealt with a lawsuit against Yahoo! Inc., which arose from an e-group hosted by Yahoo! on which illegal child pornography pictures were posted by a third party. Among the photos were sexually explicit photos of Johnny Doe, a minor. The district court determined that Section 230(c)(1) applied to immunize Yahoo! because Plaintiffs' claims sought to treat Defendant as the "publisher or speaker" of the third-party content (the photos). *Id.* at * 2-4. It is important to note that in *Bates*, as here, the Plaintiffs did not allege that there was anything defamatory or inaccurate about the posted content, but the court still applied the CDA to immunize Yahoo! from suit.

Defendants have presented numerous cases in which the CDA has been applied to bar non-defamation claims. *See, e.g., Ben Ezra, Weinstein & Co. v. America Online, Inc.*, 206 F.3d 980, 986 (10th Cir. 2000) (negligence claim); *Zeran*, 129 F.3d at 330 (negligence claims); *Bates*, 2006 WL 3813758 at *5 (negligence, negligence per se, intentional infliction of emotional distress, invasion of privacy, civil conspiracy and distribution of child pornography); *Beyond Sys., Inc. v. Keynetics, Inc.*, 422 F. Supp. 2d 523, 536 (D. Md. 2006) (claim under Maryland Commercial Electronic Mail Act); *Barnes v. Yahoo!, Inc.*, No. Civ. 05-926-AA, 2005 WL 3005602, at *4 (D. Or. Nov. 8, 2005) (negligence claim resulting in personal injury). All of these cases involved attempts to hold an interactive computer service liable for its publication of third-party content or harms flowing from the dissemination of that content.

Plaintiffs argue the CDA does not bar their claims against MySpace because their claims are not directed toward MySpace in its capacity as a publisher. Plaintiffs argue this suit is based on MySpace's negligent failure to take reasonable safety measures to keep young children off of its site and not based, on MySpace's editorial acts. The Court, however, finds this artful pleading to be disingenuous. It is quite obvious the underlying basis of Plaintiffs' claims is that, through postings on MySpace, Pete Solis and Julie Doe met and exchanged personal information which eventually led to an in-person meeting and the sexual assault of Julie Doe. If MySpace had not published communications between Julie Doe and Solis, including personal contact information, Plaintiffs assert they never would have met and the sexual assault never would have occurred. No matter how artfully Plaintiffs seek to plead their claims, the Court views Plaintiffs' claims as directed toward MySpace in its publishing, editorial, and/or screening capacities. Therefore, in accordance with the cases cited above, Defendants are entitled to immunity under the CDA, and the Court dismisses Plaintiffs' negligence and gross negligence claims with prejudice under rule 12(c) of the Federal Rules of Civil Procedure.

i. Self-Regulation

In addition to the protection afforded to interactive computer services in their publishing capacity, the CDA also immunizes such services from liability based on efforts to self-regulate material. Specifically, "[n]o provider or user of an interactive computer service shall be held liable on account of – (A) any action voluntarily taken in good fath to restrict access to or availability of material that the provider or user-considers to be obscene, lewd, lascivious, filthy, excessively violent, harassing, or otherwise objectionable. . . ." 47 U.S.C. § 230(c)(2)(A). This section reflects Congress's recognition that the potential for liability attendant to implementing safety features and policies created a disincentive for interactive computer services to implement any safety features or policies at all. To the extent Plaintiffs seek to hold MySpace liable for ineffective security measures and/or policies relating to age verification,[6] the Court alternately finds such claims are barred under § 230(c)(2)(A). ...

QUESTIONS

1. Explain what the following sentence from *MySpace* means: "Plaintiffs argue the CDA does not bar their claims against MySpace because their claims are not directed toward MySpace in its capacity as a publisher." Why does the court disagree? Does *Zeran* compel this result? What other causes of action are now preempted?

2. Note that *MySpace* draws on 230(c)(2) as well as on 230(c)(1). What does this add to the analysis? How do the two of them fit together? How is it that 230(c)(2), which on its face protects intermediaries for decisions to *remove* harmful content, ends up helping to protect MySpace when it *failed* to remove harmful content?

---

6 The Court finds Plaintiffs' claims particularly unwarranted here given that Julie Doe lied about her actual age to bypass the age requirement and then violated MySpace's express rules by giving out her personal information.

DOE NO. 14 V. INTERNET BRANDS, INC.
824 F. 3d 846 (9th Cir. May 2016)

Clifton, Circuit Judge:

Model Mayhem is a networking website, found at modelmayhem.com, for people in the modeling industry. ...

Unbeknownst to Jane Doe, two persons, Lavont Flanders and Emerson Callum, were using Model Mayhem to identify targets for a rape scheme, allegedly as early as 2006. Flanders and Callum are not alleged to have posted their own profiles on the website. Instead, they browsed profiles on Model Mayhem posted by models, contacted potential victims with fake identities posing as talent scouts, and lured the victims to south Florida for modeling auditions. Once a victim arrived, Flanders and Callum used a date rape drug to put her in a semi-catatonic state, raped her, and recorded the activity on videotape for sale and distribution as pornography.

... It is not alleged precisely how Internet Brands obtained that information, but it is alleged that the company "as early as August, 2010, knew that two individuals, Lavont Flanders and Emerson Callum, had been criminally charged in this scheme, and further knew from the criminal charges, the particular details of the scheme, including how MODELMAYHEM.COM had been used in the scheme and its members victimized." ...

In February 2011, several months after Internet Brands had learned about the criminal activity, Flanders, pretending to be a talent scout and using a false identity, contacted Jane Doe, in the words of the Complaint, "through" the Model Mayhem website. [The court noted in a footnote that its analysis did not turn on whether the contact was through Model Mayhem or outside the site] Jane Doe went to south Florida for a purported audition, where Flanders and Callum drugged, raped, and recorded her. ...

Jane Doe's claim is different, however. She does not seek to hold Internet Brands liable as a "publisher or speaker" of content someone posted on the Model Mayhem website, or for Internet Brands' failure to remove content posted on the website. Jane Doe herself posted her profile, but she does not seek to hold Internet Brands liable for its content. Nor does she allege that Flanders and Callum posted anything to the website. The Complaint alleges only that "JANE DOE was contacted by Lavont Flanders through MODELMAYHEM.COM using a fake identity." Jane Doe does not claim to have been lured by any posting that Internet Brands failed to remove. Internet Brands is also not alleged to have learned of the predators' activity from any monitoring of postings on the website, nor is its failure to monitor postings at issue.

Instead, Jane Doe attempts to hold Internet Brands liable for failing to warn her about information it obtained from an outside source about how third parties targeted and lured victims through Model Mayhem. The duty to warn allegedly imposed by California law would not require Internet Brands to remove any user content or otherwise affect how it publishes or monitors such content.

Any alleged obligation to warn could have been satisfied without changes to the content posted by the website's users and without conducting a detailed investigation. Internet Brands could have given a warning to Model Mayhem users, perhaps by posting a notice on the website or by informing users by email what it knew about the activities of Flanders and Callum. Posting or emailing such a warning could be deemed an act of publishing information, but section 230(c)(1) bars only liability that treats a website as a publisher or speaker of content provided by somebody else: in the words of the statute, "information provided by another information content provider." 47 U.S.C. § 230(c)(1). A post or email warning that Internet Brands generated would involve only content that Internet Brands itself produced. ...

The core policy of section 230(c)(1) supports this conclusion. As the heading to section 230(c) indicates, the purpose of that section is to provide "[p]rotection for 'Good Samaritan' blocking and screening of offensive material." That means a website should be able to act as a "Good Samaritan" to self-regulate offensive third party content without fear of liability. ...

Jane Doe's failure to warn claim has nothing to do with Internet Brands' efforts, or lack thereof, to edit, monitor, or remove user generated content. Plaintiff's theory is that Internet Brands should be held liable, based on its knowledge of the rape scheme and its "special relationship" with users like Jane Doe, for failing to generate its own warning. Thus, liability would not discourage the core policy of section 230(c), "Good Samaritan" filtering of third party content.

Another policy of section 230 is to avoid the chilling effect upon Internet free speech that would be occasioned by the imposition of tort liability upon companies that do not create potentially harmful messages but are simply intermediaries for their delivery. ... Jane Doe's cause of action does not seek to impose "intermediary" liability. Although Internet Brands may have been an "intermediary" between Jane Doe and the rapists in a broad sense, there is no allegation that Model Mayhem transmitted any potentially harmful messages between Jane Doe and Flanders or Callum. There is also no allegation that Flanders or Callum posted their own profiles on the website. That Internet Brands was in some sense an "intermediary" between Jane Doe and the rapists simply does not mean that the failure to warn claim treats Internet Brands as the publisher or speaker of user content.

It may be true that imposing any tort liability on Internet Brands for its role as an interactive computer service could be said to have a "chilling effect" on the internet, if only because such liability would make operating an internet business marginally more expensive. But such a broad policy argument does not persuade us that the CDA should bar the failure to warn claim. ... Congress has not provided an all purpose get-out-of-jail-free card for businesses that publish user content on the internet, though any claims might have a marginal chilling effect on internet publishing businesses. Moreover, the argument that our holding will have a chilling effect presupposes that Jane Doe has alleged a viable failure to warn claim under California law. That question is not before us and remains to be answered. ...

The tort duty asserted here does not arise from an alleged failure to adequately regulate access to user content or to monitor internal communications that might send up red flags about sexual predators. *Doe II v. MySpace, Inc.*, 175 Cal. App. 4th 561, 573 (Ct. App. 2009) (holding that the CDA bars tort claims based on a duty to restrict access to minors' MySpace profiles); *Doe v. MySpace, Inc.*, 528 F.3d 413 (5th Cir. 2008) (holding that CDA bars claims for negligence and gross negligence in not preventing a 13 year old girl from lying about her age to create a personal profile that led to contact by a sexual predator). Jane Doe alleges actual knowledge by Internet Brands from an outside source of information about criminal activity.

QUESTIONS

1. *Doe No. 14 v. Internet Brands* claims to be consistent with *Doe v. MySpace*, but is it?

2. Without Section 230, would Facebook be viable? Wikipedia? Google? Is Section 230 a recognition of the difficult job Internet intermediaries face? A subsidy to encourage the development of the Internet? Do your answers to these questions affect your opinion about whether *Doe No. 14 v. Internet Brands* and *Doe v. MySpace* are correctly decided?

3. As these cases show, plaintiffs who try to plead around Section 230 usually lose, but not always. In *Barnes v. Yahoo!, Inc.*, 570 F.3d 1096 (9th Cir. 2009), the plaintiff alleged that her ex-boyfriend posted nude photographs of her to Yahoo!, that Yahoo!'s Director of Communications promised to "personally walk the statements over to the division responsible for stopping unauthorized profiles and they would take care of it," and that the photographs remained on Yahoo! for two months after the promise. The Ninth Circuit held that Barnes's claim for promissory estoppel survived Section 230, writing, "Contract liability here would come not from Yahoo's publishing conduct, but from Yahoo's manifest intention to be legally obligated to do something, which happens to be removal of material from publication." Is this distinction persuasive? Is it a good idea? Should Ken Zeran have pleaded promissory estoppel?

4. San Francisco has a local ordinance that prohibits the short-term rental of residential properties unless they are registered with the city. But when the city checked on compliance with the ordinance in 2016, it found 7,046 short-term rental listings on Airbnb in San Francisco, even though only 1,647 properties had been registered with the city in total. In response, it passed a follow-up ordinance which allows a "reservation and/or payment service" to collect a fee in connection with the short-term rental of a residential property only when the property is registered with the city. Airbnb sues, arguing that the ordinance is preempted by Section 230. Who is right? Is there a way to satisfy all concerned?

PEOPLE'S FRONT OF JUDEA PROBLEM

Federal law makes it a crime to "knowingly provide[] material support or resources to a foreign terrorist organization." 18 U.S.C. § 2339B(a)(1). One need not intend to support the organization's terroristic activities; it is enough to "have knowledge that the organization is a designated terrorist organization" on a list maintained by the Secretary of State. *Id.* And "material support or resources" is defined as

> any property, tangible or intangible, or service, including currency or monetary instruments or financial securities, financial services, lodging, training, expert advice or assistance, safehouses, false documentation or identification, communications equipment, facilities, weapons, lethal substances, explosives, personnel ... and transportation, except medicine or religious materials.

Id. § 2239A(b)(1). Violations are punishable by prison terms of up to 20 years – or up to life in prison "if the death of any person results." *Id.* Federal law also provides a civil cause of action:

> Any national of the United States injured in his or her person, property, or business by reason of an act of international terrorism, or his or her estate, survivors, or heirs, may sue therefor in any appropriate district court of the United States and shall recover threefold the

damages he or she sustains and the cost of the suit, including attorney's fees.

Id. § 2333(a).

The People's Front of Judea (PFJ), a millenarian group responsible for numerous suicide bombings in Nazareth, has been designated as a terrorist organization since 2002. The PFJ, or someone claiming to act on its behalf, has an account on Brightside, a social network incorporated in and with headquarters in California that has 600 million active users worldwide. Many of its leaders also have Brightside accounts under their own names, which they also use to post statements about the PFJ's activities and praising others who carry out violent attacks on Westerners. Numerous people post comments on these various accounts. expressing sympathy for the PFJ and solidarity with its goals. Posts by the PFJ and its leaders have received millions of views and thousands of "smiles" (the Brightside equivalent to Facebook "likes"). Brightside's terms of service state, among others thing, that "You may use Brightside only if you are not barred from receiving services under the laws of the United States" and "You agree not to post content that is hate speech, makes threats, or incites or promotes violence."

On April 5, 2015, a PFJ member carried out a suicide bombing that killed Brian Cohen, an American tourist. His mother, Mandy Cohen, has sued Brightside under § 2333(a). She alleges that in March 2015, a series of Brightside posts by PFJ leaders called for "acts of righteous revenge" and that the suicide bomber who killed Cohen posted long comments on the PFJ's Brightside page pledging his loyalty to the PFJ and promising "to carry out the PFJ's divinely ordained mission of violent retribution." She further alleges that in 2013 and 2014, activists repeatedly wrote to Brightside identifying PFJ accounts and posts and asking it to delete them as violations of its terms of service.

Does Section 230 bar Mandy Cohen's suit against Brightside or can it go forward?

SECTION 230 REFORM PROBLEM

You are on the staff of the Senate Judiciary Committee. Senator Aykroyd (R-NE), who is upset at the level of "filth and abuse" on the Internet, has introduced a bill that would replace paragraph (c)(1) of Section 230 with the sentence, "A provider of an interactive computer service shall be treated as a publisher of any information transmitted by means of the service." Senator Radner (D-NJ), who believes that free speech needs to be balanced with protections from harassment, has introduced a competing bill that would amend paragraph (c)(1) by adding to the end an additional clause that would read, "except where the provider or user has encouraged the creation of the information."

You work for Senator Curtin (R-VA), who would like your opinion on whether these measures to limit Section 230 are a good idea. He would like to encourage vibrant free speech online, encouraging online innovation and commerce, to give the victims of online attacks meaningful legal recourse, and as far as possible to improve the quality of online discourse by limiting the spread of truly noxious and harmful content. But he freely admits that he has not followed the state of Section 230 caselaw or the policy debates over it, so he is unsure what reforms, if any, would make sense.

Senator Curtin would like to know what effect, the Aykroyd and Radner bills would have on the state of the law. Are there any precedents under Section 230 that would come out differently under the proposed bills? Should Senator Curtin support the Ackroyd bill? The Radner bill? Should he oppose them both? Or should he introduce a bill of his own to amend Section 230? If you recommend the latter, provide him with draft text.

CHAPTER 4: PRIVACY

This chapter explores the vexed problem of online privacy. On the one hand, the Internet seems to offer new and unprecedented opportunities for interacting discreetly. As a dog in a *New Yorker* cartoon famously put it, "On the Internet, nobody knows you're a dog."* On the other hand, online activities leave behind a trail of data in the hands of websites, ISPs, and others. That trail can be used to identify individual users, and in some cases to build detailed profiles of what they have been doing.

The first half of the chapter focuses on criminal investigations, examining constitutional and statutory restrictions on how law enforcement can gain access to individuals' data. Governmental control provides the thematic backbone. The second half then shifts to the problem of what private parties know and can learn abut Internet users. Here, intermediary power comes to the fore: if knowledge is power, then these intermediaries have quite a lot, indeed.

A. The Fourth and Fifth Amendments

We begin with criminal procedure: the body of law that regulates investigation, prosecution, and criminal trials. The overriding concern here is evidentiary. The police are looking to gather evidence that can be used against a defendant at trial; the defendant is looking either to keep the police from getting access to the evidence, or to keep the prosecutors from presenting it to the jury. The Fourth Amendment exclusionary rule provides the legal backdrop for this struggle: police must respect the defendant's privacy rights during the investigation, or the resulting evidence will be inadmissible. It fits together with the Fifth Amendment, which prevents the police from shortcutting their own investigation by compelling the defendant to tell the complete story of what happened.

This section considers how the Fourth and Fifth Amendments apply when there are computers involved. *Riley v. California* introduces the ways in which computers may be meaningfully different from other objects the police search; *United States v. Warshak* brings third parties into the picture and asks what happens to information as it travels on the Internet. *United States v. Doe* asks how the Fifth Amendment applies to encrypted data protected by a password.

FOURTH AND FIFTH AMENDMENT OVERVIEW

The Fourth Amendment reads:

> The right of the people to be secure in their persons, houses, papers, and effects, against unreasonable searches and seizures, shall not be violated, and no warrants shall issue, but upon probable cause, supported by oath or affirmation, and particularly describing the place to be searched, and the persons or things to be seized.

At the outset, two threshold issues are particularly important. First, only searches by the government implicate the Fourth Amendment; it does not apply to "a

---

* The cartoon, by Peter Steiner, appeared on page 61 of the July 5, 1993 issue.

search or seizure, even an unreasonable one, effected by a private individual not acting as an agent of the Government or with the participation or knowledge of any governmental official." *United States v. Jacobsen*, 466 U.S. 109, 114 (1984). If a FedEx clerk opens your wrapped package and drugs tumble out, this is a "private search" and the Fourth Amendment is uninterested. Indeed, the clerk can take the package to the police to show them what he found. Second, unless the governmental action violates your "reasonable expectation of privacy," no "search" has taken place. If a police officer sees you run out of a bank wearing a ski mask and waving a gun, the officer's act of looking at you is not a "search" for Fourth Amendment purposes, and the officer is free to testify at trial that she saw you leaving the bank – or to arrest you.

The "reasonable expectation of privacy" test comes from *Katz v. United States*, 389 U.S. 347 (1967). There, the police bugged a phone booth they knew the defendant regularly used; the Supreme Court held that this constituted a search. *Katz* was a watershed in criminal procedure; it repudiated older cases holding that there was no search without an "actual physical invasion" of a defendant's property. *Olmstead v. United States*, 277 U. S. 438, 466 (1928). *Katz* shifted the focus of the Fourth Amendment from spaces and objects protected against trespassers to "expectation[s] of privacy ... that society is prepared to recognize as reasonable." *Katz*, 389 U.S. at 361 (Harlan, J., concurring).

Drawing the line that defines a "reasonable expectation of privacy" is extremely hard, but a few examples are relatively clear. You have a reasonable expectation of privacy in your home and in sealed containers, such as locked suitcases within your control. By contrast, you have no reasonable expectation of privacy in anything you have voluntarily exposed to public view.

Complicating the issue, the Fourth Amendment prohibits only "unreasonable" searches and seizures. A search is automatically reasonable if it is carried out pursuant to a search warrant: a judicial order that gives the police permission to carry out the search. A court can issue a warrant after the police provide "probable cause," i.e., "a fair probability that contraband or evidence of a crime will be found in a particular place." *Illinois v. Gates*, 462 U.S. 213, 238 (1983). It must also specify which particular places are to be searched or which items are to be seized; a search or seizure that goes beyond those limits is invalid.

Some warrantless searches can still be "reasonable" and thus permissible. Some of these exceptions (each of which has its own tests) would take us well outside the scope of this course – at the U.S. border, in government workplaces, in schools and prisons, and as part of a lawful stop or arrest. The police may also conduct warrantless searches and seizures when "exigent circumstances" make obtaining a warrant infeasible – most commonly, when there is a risk that evidence will be destroyed if they do not act. An unreasonable search is illegal, and the "exclusionary rule" governs any evidence the police obtain as a result: it may not be introduced at trial.

Two other exceptions are important for our purposes. First, there's the "consent" exception: if the owner or someone else with authority over the property consents, the police may search it. If you invite the police into your basement meth lab, you may not later argue that it was a private space they needed a warrant to enter. The same goes if your housemate invites them into the shared meth lab. The second is the "plain view" rule. If the police are executing a valid search warrant, they may also search and seize evidence whose incriminating nature is "immediately apparent." If the police are searching the basement meth lab pursuant to a valid warrant, they can also follow the trail of blood up the stairs. These two exceptions have a lot in common with the basic reasonable expectation of privacy test. Can you articulate a general principle that unites them?

The Fourth Amendment also applies to "seizures." A seizure of your person is an arrest or other involuntary restriction of your liberty to leave. A seizure of your property takes place when there is "some meaningful interference with [your] possessory interest." *United States v. Jacobsen*, 466 U.S. 109, 113 (1984). Again, a search warrant, issued by a judge, with a probable-cause standard of evidence, and particularly describing who or what is to be seized, is ordinarily required.

The Fifth Amendment provides:

> *No person shall* be held to answer for a capital, or otherwise infamous crime, unless on a presentment or indictment of a Grand Jury, except in cases arising in the land or naval forces, or in the Militia, when in actual service in time of War or public danger; nor shall any person be subject for the same offence to be twice put in jeopardy of life or limb; nor shall *be compelled in any criminal case to be a witness against himself*, nor be deprived of life, liberty, or property, without due process of law; nor shall private property be taken for public use, without just compensation. (emphasis added)

This is the familiar "right to remain silent": a criminal defendant has an absolute privilege to refuse to testify. She is also free to refuse to answer questions from police, grand juries, even Congress – anything that might potentially incriminate her. The government can compel her testimony only by offering the defendant immunity: a promise that neither the testimony, nor anything discovered using the testimony, will be used against the defendant at trial. Some of the hard questions, as *United States v. Doe* illustrates, depend on the question of what actions count as "testimony."

NOTE ON WARRANT JURISDICTION

Another important limit on search warrants is that they are only valid where the issuing court has territorial authority. In a world where most crimes are planned and committed locally and where most search warrants describe houses and other buildings, this last constraint is rarely likely to pose an obstacle. But modern technologies create difficulties. For example, cars drive around. In *United States v. Jones* (discussed below), investigators obtained a warrant to install a GPS tracker on the defendant's car from a federal court in the District of Columbia but actually installed the tracker in Maryland. Whoops. (This is why the case reached the Supreme Court as a case on whether a warrant was necessary at all.)

Computers pose even more vexing issues. In one notable case, the FBI took over a child pornography website and used it to install tracking software on the computers of users who visited it so they could be identified and prosecuted. It obtained a warrant from a magistrate judge in the Eastern District of Virginia allowing a search of the "computers … of any user or administrator who logs into the TARGET WEBSITE by entering a username and password." But those computers were located all over the United States. Judges in the resulting prosecutions split over whether the warrant was valid under the current version of the Federal Rules of Criminal Procedure, which allowed only a "magistrate judge *with authority in the district*" to issue a warrant. Fed. R. Crim. Proc. 41(b)(1) (emphasis added). But within the U.S. federal judicial system, where Congress controls the jurisdictional rules and can change them, such problems (if they really are problems) are solvable. An amendment to Rule 41 that explicitly authorized nationwide warrants in such cases wen into effect on December 1, 2016.

Internationally, the jurisdictional overlaps can be messy. If Microsoft, a U.S. company with subsidiaries and operations around the world, stores a user's emails on a server in Ireland, can United States authorities compel Microsoft to turn over the emails? What about Irish authorities? Does it matter whether the user is American or Irish? In *In the Matter of a Warrant to Search a Certain E-Mail Account Controlled and Maintained by Microsoft Corporation*, 829 F.3d 197 (2d Cir. 2016), the court held that a warrant issued by a federal court under the Stored Communications Act could not reach emails stored in Ireland. In June 2017, the government asked he Supreme Court to review the case — so perhaps this is not the last word.

NOTE ON UNITED STATES V. JONES

The Supreme Court's decision *United States v. Jones*, 132 S. Ct. 945 (2012), complicates this picture; although the judgment itself was unanimous, the court's three separate opinions took wildly different approaches to the Fourth Amendment. In brief, government agents police installed a GPS tracking device on Antoine Jones's car and recorded thousands of pages of data about its movements over a 28-day period. The GPS data connected him to a stash house containing 97 kilograms of cocaine; he was convicted of conspiracy to distribute illegal drugs and sentenced to life imprisonment.

The starting point for the legal analysis was that there is generally no expectation of privacy in one's movements in public. The police can tail you and take photographs as you go into a stash house. Two previous Supreme Court cases – *United States v. Knotts*, 460 U.S. 276 (1983), and *United States v. Karo*, 468 U.S. 705 (1984) – had upheld police of use of more primitive tracking devices: radio transmitters, called "beepers," that actively signaled their location to help police with the appropriate receiving equipment follow a suspect.

Justice Scalia's majority opinion in *Jones* sidestepped the question of how the *Katz* reasonable expectation test would apply to long-term GPS tracking by holding that the agents had *trespassed* on Jones's car by installing the GPS device. (In both *Knotts* and *Karo*, the beeper was installed in an object before it came into the defendant's possession.) For the majority, *Katz* left intact the older, property-based cases:

> It is important to be clear about what occurred in this case: The Government physically occupied private property for the purpose of obtaining information. We have no doubt that such a physical intrusion would have been considered a "search" within the meaning of the Fourth Amendment when it was adopted.

Jones, 132 S. Ct. at 949.

Justice Alito, concurring in the judgment for four justices, read *Katz* to have replaced "18th-century tort law" with the reasonable expectations test. Applying that test, Alito's opinion drew a distinction based on the scale of the surveillance:

> Under this approach, relatively short-term monitoring of a person's movements on public streets accords with expectations of privacy that our society has recognized as reasonable. But the use of longer term GPS monitoring in investigations of most offenses impinges on expectations of privacy. For such offenses, society's expectation has been

that law enforcement agents and others would not – and indeed, in the main, simply could not –secretly monitor and catalogue every single movement of an individual's car for a very long period. In this case, for four weeks, law enforcement agents tracked every movement that respondent made in the vehicle he was driving. We need not identify with precision the point at which the tracking of this vehicle became a search, for the line was surely crossed before the 4-week mark.

Id. at 964 (Alito, J., concurring in the judgment). This approach has become known as the "mosaic" theory of the Fourth Amendment: the individual tiles are trivial and uninteresting, but when assembled they become highly revealing.

But is the mosaic theory law? At the Supreme Court, not as such. Justice Sotomayor's concurrence expressed great sympathy for the mosaic theory but concluded that it was unnecessary to resolve the "difficult questions" adopting it would raise "because the Government's physical intrusion on Jones' Jeep supplies a narrower basis for decision." *Id.* at 957 (Sotomayor, J., concurring). This split puts lower courts in an awkward position in electronic surveillance cases that lack the easy out of a physical intrusion. Five Justices have praised the mosaic theory, but only four have endorsed it as law in the case before them.

Here is an example of the kind of controversies now raging through the lower courts. Under *Smith v. Maryland*, 442 U.S. 735 (1979) (discussed in *Warshak* and the NSA cases below), the telephone numbers a defendant dials are not protected by the Fourth Amendment under the "third party doctrine": he voluntarily surrendered his privacy in them by revealing them to the phone company. But cell phone towers also necessarily track a caller's location so they can hand off a phone call from one tower to the next as the phone moves around. Suppose the police are interested in finding out *where* a defendant was when he made calls from his cell phone. Do they need a warrant to obtain this "cell site location information" (CSLI) from the defendant's cell phone carrier? So far, the federal Courts of Appeals have agreed that no warrant is needed. *See, e.g., In re U.S. for Historical Cell Site Data*, 724 F.3d 600, 613 (5th Cir. 2013) ("Cell phone users, therefore, understand that their service providers record their location information when they use their phones at least to the same extent that the landline users in *Smith* understood that the phone company recorded the numbers they dialed.") Despite the absence of a circuit split, the Supreme Court agreed to hear a CSLI case, *Carpenter v. United States*, during its 2017–18 term. Stay tuned.

RILEY V. CALIFORNIA
134 S. Ct. 2473 (2014)

Chief Justice Roberts delivered the opinion of the Court.

These two cases raise a common question: whether the police may, without a warrant, search digital information on a cell phone seized from an individual who has been arrested.

I

A

In the first case, petitioner David Riley was stopped by a police officer for driving with expired registration tags. In the course of the stop, the officer also learned that Riley's license had been suspended. The officer impounded Riley's car, pursuant to department policy, and another officer conducted an inventory search of the car. Riley was arrested for possession of concealed and loaded firearms when that search turned up two handguns under the car's hood.

An officer searched Riley incident to the arrest and found items associated with the "Bloods" street gang. He also seized a cell phone from Riley's pants pocket. According to Riley's uncontradicted assertion, the phone was a "smart phone," a cell phone with a broad range of other functions based on advanced computing capability, large storage capacity, and Internet connectivity. The officer accessed information on the phone and noticed that some words (presumably in text messages or a contacts list) were preceded by the letters "CK"-a label that, he believed, stood for "Crip Killers," a slang term for members of the Bloods gang.

At the police station about two hours after the arrest, a detective specializing in gangs further examined the contents of the phone. The detective testified that he "went through" Riley's phone "looking for evidence, because . . . gang members will often video themselves with guns or take pictures of themselves with the guns." Although there was "a lot of stuff" on the phone, particular files that "caught [the detective's] eye" included videos of young men sparring while someone yelled encouragement using the moniker "Blood." The police also found photographs of Riley standing in front of a car they suspected had been involved in a shooting a few weeks earlier.

Riley was ultimately charged, in connection with that earlier shooting, with firing at an occupied vehicle, assault with a semiautomatic firearm, and attempted murder. The State alleged that Riley had committed those crimes for the benefit of a criminal street gang, an aggravating factor that carries an enhanced sentence. Prior to trial, Riley moved to suppress all evidence that the police had obtained from his cell phone. He contended that the searches of his phone violated the Fourth Amendment, because they had been performed without a warrant and were not otherwise justified by exigent circumstances. The trial court rejected that argument. At Riley's trial, police officers testified about the photographs and videos found on the phone, and some of the photographs were admitted into evidence. Riley was convicted on all three counts and received an enhanced sentence of 15 years to life in prison.

The California Court of Appeal affirmed. ...

The California Supreme Court denied Riley's petition for review and we granted certiorari.

B

In the second case, a police officer performing routine surveillance observed respondent Brima Wurie make an apparent drug sale from a car. Officers subsequently arrested Wurie and took him to the police station. At the station, the officers seized two cell phones from Wurie's person. The one at issue here was a "flip phone," a kind of phone that is flipped open for use and that generally has a smaller range of features than a smart phone. Five to ten minutes after arriving at the station, the officers noticed that the phone was repeatedly receiving calls from a source identified as "my house" on the phone's external screen. A few minutes later, they opened the phone and saw a photograph of a woman and a baby set as the phone's wallpaper. They pressed one button on the phone to access its call log, then another button to determine the phone number associated with the "my house" label. They next used an online phone directory to trace that phone number to an apartment building.

When the officers went to the building, they saw Wurie's name on a mailbox and observed through a window a woman who resembled the woman in the photograph on Wurie's phone. They secured the apartment while obtaining a search warrant and, upon later executing the warrant, found and seized 215 grams of crack cocaine, marijuana, drug paraphernalia, a firearm and ammunition, and cash.

Wurie was charged with distributing crack cocaine, possessing crack cocaine with intent to distribute, and being a felon in possession of a firearm and ammunition. He moved to suppress the evidence obtained from the search of the apartment, arguing that it was the fruit of an unconstitutional search of his cell phone. The District Court denied the motion. Wurie was convicted on all three counts and sentenced to 262 months in prison.

A divided panel of the First Circuit reversed ...

We granted certiorari.

II

The Fourth Amendment provides:

> The right of the people to be secure in their persons, houses, papers, and effects, against unreasonable searches and seizures, shall not be violated, and no Warrants shall issue, but upon probable cause, supported by Oath or affirmation, and particularly describing the place to be searched, and the persons or things to be seized.

As the text makes clear, the ultimate touchstone of the Fourth Amendment is reasonableness. Our cases have determined that where a search is undertaken by law enforcement officials to discover evidence of criminal wrongdoing, reasonableness generally requires the obtaining of a judicial warrant. Such a warrant ensures that the inferences to support a search are drawn by a neutral and detached magistrate instead of being judged by the officer engaged in the often competitive enterprise of ferreting out crime. In the absence of a warrant, a search is reasonable only if it falls within a specific exception to the warrant requirement.

The two cases before us concern the reasonableness of a warrantless search incident to a lawful arrest. In 1914, this Court first acknowledged in dictum "the right on the part of the Government, always recognized under English and American law, to search the person of the accused when legally arrested to discover and seize the fruits or evidences of crime." *Weeks v. United States*, 232 U.S. 383, 392 (1914). Since that time, it has been well accepted that such a search constitutes an exception to the warrant requirement. ...

Although the existence of the exception for such searches has been recognized for a century, its scope has been debated for nearly as long. ... That debate has focused on the extent to which officers may search property found on or near the arrestee. Three related precedents set forth the rules governing such searches:

The first, *Chimel v. California*, 395 U.S. 752 (1969), laid the groundwork for most of the existing search incident to arrest doctrine. Police officers in that case arrested Chimel inside his home and proceeded to search his entire three-bedroom house, including the attic and garage. In particular rooms, they also looked through the contents of drawers.

The Court crafted the following rule for assessing the reasonableness of a search incident to arrest:

> When an arrest is made, it is reasonable for the arresting officer to search the person arrested in order to remove any weapons that the latter might seek to use in order to resist arrest or effect his escape. Otherwise, the officer's safety might well be endangered, and the ar-

rest itself frustrated. In addition, it is entirely reasonable for the arresting officer to search for and seize any evidence on the arrestee's person in order to prevent its concealment or destruction. . . . There is ample justification, therefore, for a search of the arrestee's person and the area 'within his immediate control'-construing that phrase to mean the area from within which he might gain possession of a weapon or destructible evidence.

Id., at 762-763. The extensive warrantless search of Chimel's home did not fit within this exception, because it was not needed to protect officer safety or to preserve evidence.

Four years later, in *United States v. Robinson*, 414 U.S. 218 (1973), the Court applied the *Chimel* analysis in the context of a search of the arrestee's person. A police officer had arrested Robinson for driving with a revoked license. The officer conducted a patdown search and felt an object that he could not identify in Robinson's coat pocket. He removed the object, which turned out to be a crumpled cigarette package, and opened it. Inside were 14 capsules of heroin. ...

This Court ... reject[ed] the notion that "case-by-case adjudication" was required to determine "whether or not there was present one of the reasons supporting the authority for a search of the person incident to a lawful arrest." ...

The Court thus concluded that the search of Robinson was reasonable even though there was no concern about the loss of evidence, and the arresting officer had no specific concern that Robinson might be armed.

The search incident to arrest trilogy concludes with *Arizona v. Gant*, 556 U.S. 332 (2009), which analyzed searches of an arrestee's vehicle. *Gant*, like *Robinson*, recognized that the *Chimel* concerns for officer safety and evidence preservation underlie the search incident to arrest exception. As a result, the Court concluded that *Chimel* could authorize police to search a vehicle "only when the arrestee is unsecured and within reaching distance of the passenger compartment at the time of the search." 556 U.S., at 343. *Gant* added, however, an independent exception for a warrantless search of a vehicle's passenger compartment "when it is 'reasonable to believe evidence relevant to the crime of arrest might be found in the vehicle." *Ibid.* That exception stems not from *Chimel*, the Court explained, but from "circumstances unique to the vehicle context." 556 U.S., at 343.

III

These cases require us to decide how the search incident to arrest doctrine applies to modern cell phones, which are now such a pervasive and insistent part of daily life that the proverbial visitor from Mars might conclude they were an important feature of human anatomy. A smart phone of the sort taken from Riley was unheard of ten years ago; a significant majority of American adults now own such phones. Even less sophisticated phones like Wurie's, which have already faded in popularity since Wurie was arrested in 2007, have been around for less than 15 years. Both phones are based on technology nearly inconceivable just a few decades ago, when *Chimel* and *Robinson* were decided.

Absent more precise guidance from the founding era, we generally determine whether to exempt a given type of search from the warrant requirement by assessing, on the one hand, the degree to which it intrudes upon an individual's privacy and, on the other, the degree to which it is needed for the promotion of legitimate governmental interests. Such a balancing of interests supported the search incident to arrest exception in *Robinson*, and a mechanical application of *Robinson* might well support the warrantless searches at issue here.

But while *Robinson's* categorical rule strikes the appropriate balance in the context of physical objects, neither of its rationales has much force with respect to digital content on cell phones. On the government interest side, *Robinson* concluded that the two risks identified in *Chimel* – harm to officers and destruction of evidence-are present in all custodial arrests. There are no comparable risks when the search is of digital data. In addition, *Robinson* regarded any privacy interests retained by an individual after arrest as significantly diminished by the fact of the arrest itself. Cell phones, however, place vast quantities of personal information literally in the hands of individuals. A search of the information on a cell phone bears little resemblance to the type of brief physical search considered in *Robinson*.

We therefore decline to extend *Robinson* to searches of data on cell phones, and hold instead that officers must generally secure a warrant before conducting such a search.

A

We first consider each *Chimel* concern in turn. ...

1

Digital data stored on a cell phone cannot itself be used as a weapon to harm an arresting officer or to effectuate the arrestee's escape. Law enforcement officers remain free to examine the physical aspects of a phone to ensure that it will not be used as a weapon-say, to determine whether there is a razor blade hidden between the phone and its case. Once an officer has secured a phone and eliminated any potential physical threats, however, data on the phone can endanger no one.

Perhaps the same might have been said of the cigarette pack seized from Robinson's pocket. Once an officer gained control of the pack, it was unlikely that Robinson could have accessed the pack's contents. But unknown physical objects may always pose risks, no matter how slight, during the tense atmosphere of a custodial arrest. The officer in *Robinson* testified that he could not identify the objects in the cigarette pack but knew they were not cigarettes. Given that, a further search was a reasonable protective measure. No such unknowns exist with respect to digital data. As the First Circuit explained, the officers who searched Wurie's cell phone "knew exactly what they would find therein: data. They also knew that the data could not harm them." ...

2

The United States and California focus primarily on the second *Chimel* rationale: preventing the destruction of evidence.

Both Riley and Wurie concede that officers could have seized and secured their cell phones to prevent destruction of evidence while seeking a warrant. That is a sensible concession. And once law enforcement officers have secured a cell phone, there is no longer any risk that the arrestee himself will be able to delete incriminating data from the phone.

The United States and California argue that information on a cell phone may nevertheless be vulnerable to two types of evidence destruction unique to digital data-remote wiping and data encryption. Remote wiping occurs when a phone, connected to a wireless network, receives a signal that erases stored data. This can happen when a third party sends a remote signal or when a phone is preprogrammed to delete data upon entering or leaving certain geographic areas (socalled "geofencing"). Encryption is a security feature that some modern cell phones use in addition to password protection. When such phones lock, data becomes protected by sophisticated encryption that renders a phone all but "unbreakable" unless police know the password. ...

We have also been given little reason to believe that either problem is prevalent. The briefing reveals only a couple of anecdotal examples of remote wiping triggered by an arrest. Similarly, the opportunities for officers to search a password-protected phone before data becomes encrypted are quite limited. Law enforcement officers are very unlikely to come upon such a phone in an unlocked state because most phones lock at the touch of a button or, as a default, after some very short period of inactivity. See, *e.g.*, iPhone User Guide for iOS 7.1 Software 10 (2014) (default lock after about one minute). ...

Moreover, in situations in which an arrest might trigger a remote-wipe attempt or an officer discovers an unlocked phone, it is not clear that the ability to conduct a warrantless search would make much of a difference. The need to effect the arrest, secure the scene, and tend to other pressing matters means that law enforcement officers may well not be able to turn their attention to a cell phone right away. Cell phone data would be vulnerable to remote wiping from the time an individual anticipates arrest to the time any eventual search of the phone is completed, which might be at the station house hours later. Likewise, an officer who seizes a phone in an unlocked state might not be able to begin his search in the short time remaining before the phone locks and data becomes encrypted.

In any event, as to remote wiping, law enforcement is not without specific means to address the threat. Remote wiping can be fully prevented by disconnecting a phone from the network. There are at least two simple ways to do this: First, law enforcement officers can turn the phone off or remove its battery. Second, if they are concerned about encryption or other potential problems, they can leave a phone powered on and place it in an enclosure that isolates the phone from radio waves. Such devices are commonly called "Faraday bags," after the English scientist Michael Faraday. They are essentially sandwich bags made of aluminum foil: cheap, lightweight, and easy to use. They may not be a complete answer to the problem, but at least for now they provide a reasonable response. In fact, a number of law enforcement agencies around the country already encourage the use of Faraday bags.

To the extent that law enforcement still has specific concerns about the potential loss of evidence in a particular case, there remain more targeted ways to address those concerns. If the police are truly confronted with a now or never situation – for example, circumstances suggesting that a defendant's phone will be the target of an imminent remote-wipe attempt – they may be able to rely on exigent circumstances to search the phone immediately. Or, if officers happen to seize a phone in an unlocked state, they may be able to disable a phone's automatic-lock feature in order to prevent the phone from locking and encrypting data. Such a preventive measure could be analyzed under the principles set forth in our decision in *McArthur*, 531 U.S. 326, 331–33 (2001), which approved officers' reasonable steps to secure a scene to preserve evidence while they awaited a warrant.

B

The search incident to arrest exception rests not only on the heightened government interests at stake in a volatile arrest situation, but also on an arrestee's reduced privacy interests upon being taken into police custody. ...

The fact that an arrestee has diminished privacy interests does not mean that the Fourth Amendment falls out of the picture entirely. ...

Robinson is the only decision from this Court applying *Chimel* to a search of the contents of an item found on an arrestee's person. ... Lower courts applying *Robinson* and *Chimel*, however, have approved searches of a variety of personal items carried by an arrestee. See, e.g., *United States v. Carrion*, 809 F. 2d 1120, 1123, 1128 (5th Cir. 1987) (billfold and address book); *United States v. Watson*, 669 F. 2d 1374, 1383–1384 (11th Cir. 1982) (wallet); *United States v. Lee*, 501 F. 2d 89 , 892 (D.C. Cir. 1974) (purse).

The United States asserts that a search of all data stored on a cell phone is "materially indistinguishable" from searches of these sorts of physical items. That is like saying a ride on horseback is materially indistinguishable from a flight to the moon. Both are ways of getting from point A to point B, but little else justifies lumping them together. Modern cell phones, as a category, implicate privacy concerns far beyond those implicated by the search of a cigarette pack, a wallet, or a purse. A conclusion that inspecting the contents of an arrestee's pockets works no substantial additional intrusion on privacy beyond the arrest itself may make sense as applied to physical items, but any extension of that reasoning to digital data has to rest on its own bottom.

1

Cell phones differ in both a quantitative and a qualitative sense from other objects that might be kept on an arrestee's person. The term "cell phone" is itself misleading shorthand; many of these devices are in fact minicomputers that also happen to have the capacity to be used as a telephone. They could just as easily be called cameras, video players, rolodexes, calendars, tape recorders, libraries, diaries, albums, televisions, maps, or newspapers.

One of the most notable distinguishing features of modern cell phones is their immense storage capacity. Before cell phones, a search of a person was limited by physical realities and tended as a general matter to constitute only a narrow intrusion on privacy. Most people cannot lug around every piece of mail they have received for the past several months, every picture they have taken, or every book or article they have read-nor would they have any reason to attempt to do so. ...

But the possible intrusion on privacy is not physically limited in the same way when it comes to cell phones. The current top-selling smart phone has a standard capacity of 16 gigabytes (and is available with up to 64 gigabytes). Sixteen gigabytes translates to millions of pages of text, thousands of pictures, or hundreds of videos. Cell phones couple that capacity with the ability to store many different types of information: Even the most basic phones that sell for less than $20 might hold photographs, picture messages, text messages, Internet browsing history, a calendar, a thousand-entry phone book, and so on. We expect that the gulf between physical practicability and digital capacity will only continue to widen in the future.

The storage capacity of cell phones has several interrelated consequences for privacy. First, a cell phone collects in one place many distinct types of information – an address, a note, a prescription, a bank statement, a video – that reveal much more in combination than any isolated record. Second, a cell phone's capacity allows even just one type of information to convey far more than previously possible. The sum of an individual's private life can be reconstructed through a thousand photographs labeled with dates, locations, and descriptions; the same cannot be said of a photograph or two of loved ones tucked into a wallet. Third, the data on a phone can date back to the purchase of the phone, or even earlier. A person might carry in his pocket a slip of paper reminding him to call Mr. Jones; he would not carry a record of all his communications with Mr. Jones for the past several months, as would routinely be kept on a phone. [1]

Finally, there is an element of pervasiveness that characterizes cell phones but not physical records. Prior to the digital age, people did not typically carry a cache of sensitive personal information with them as they went about their day. Now it is the person who is not carrying a cell phone, with all that it contains, who is the exception. According to one poll, nearly three-quarters of smart phone users report being within five feet of their phones most of the time, with 12% admitting that they even use their phones in the shower. A decade ago police officers searching an arrestee might have occasionally stumbled across a highly personal item such as a diary. But those discoveries were likely to be few and far between. Today, by contrast, it is no exaggeration to say that many of the more than 90% of American adults who own a cell phone keep on their person a digital record of nearly every aspect of their lives-from the mundane to the intimate. Allowing the police to scrutinize such records on a routine basis is quite different from allowing them to search a personal item or two in the occasional case.

Although the data stored on a cell phone is distinguished from physical records by quantity alone, certain types of data are also qualitatively different. An Internet search and browsing history, for example, can be found on an Internet-enabled phone and could reveal an individual's private interests or concerns-perhaps a search for certain symptoms of disease, coupled with frequent visits to WebMD. Data on a cell phone can also reveal where a person has been. Historic location information is a standard feature on many smart phones and can reconstruct someone's specific movements down to the minute, not only around town but also within a particular building. See *United States v. Jones*, 565 U.S. ___, ___ (2012) (Sotomayor, J., concurring) (slip op., at 3) ("GPS monitoring generates a precise, comprehensive record of a person's public movements that reflects a wealth of detail about her familial, political, professional, religious, and sexual associations.").

Mobile application software on a cell phone, or "apps," offer a range of tools for managing detailed information about all aspects of a person's life. There are apps for Democratic Party news and Republican Party news; apps for alcohol, drug, and gambling addictions; apps for sharing prayer requests; apps for tracking pregnancy symptoms; apps for planning your budget; apps for every conceivable hobby or pastime; apps for improving your romantic life. There are popular apps for buying or selling just about anything, and the records of such transactions may be accessible on the phone indefinitely. There are over a million apps available in each of the two major app stores; the phrase "there's an app for that" is now part of the popular lexicon. The average smart phone user has installed 33 apps, which together can form a revealing montage of the user's life.

In 1926, Learned Hand observed ... that it is "a totally different thing to search a man's pockets and use against him what they contain, from ransacking his house for everything which may incriminate him." *United States v. Kirschenblatt*, 16 F. 2d 202, 203 (2nd Cir. 1926). If his pockets contain a cell phone, however, that is no longer true. Indeed, a cell phone search would typically expose to the government far *more* than the most exhaustive search of a house: A phone not only contains in

---

1   Because the United States and California agree that these cases involve *searches* incident to arrest, these cases do not implicate the question whether the collection or inspection of aggregated digital information amounts to a search under other circumstances.

digital form many sensitive records previously found in the home; it also contains a broad array of private information never found in a home in any form – unless the phone is.

2

To further complicate the scope of the privacy interests at stake, the data a user views on many modern cell phones may not in fact be stored on the device itself. Treating a cell phone as a container whose contents may be searched incident to an arrest is a bit strained as an initial matter. See *New York v. Belton*, 453 U.S. 454, 460, n.4 (1981) (describing a "container" as "any object capable of holding another object"). But the analogy crumbles entirely when a cell phone is used to access data located elsewhere, at the tap of a screen. That is what cell phones, with increasing frequency, are designed to do by taking advantage of "cloud computing." Cloud computing is the capacity of Internet-connected devices to display data stored on remote servers rather than on the device itself. Cell phone users often may not know whether particular information is stored on the device or in the cloud, and it generally makes little difference. Moreover, the same type of data may be stored locally on the device for one user and in the cloud for another.

The United States concedes that the search incident to arrest exception may not be stretched to cover a search of files accessed remotely – that is, a search of files stored in the cloud. Such a search would be like finding a key in a suspect's pocket and arguing that it allowed law enforcement to unlock and search a house. But officers searching a phone's data would not typically know whether the information they are viewing was stored locally at the time of the arrest or has been pulled from the cloud.

Although the Government recognizes the problem, its proposed solutions are unclear. It suggests that officers could disconnect a phone from the network before searching the device – the very solution whose feasibility it contested with respect to the threat of remote wiping. Alternatively, the Government proposes that law enforcement agencies "develop protocols to address" concerns raised by cloud computing. Probably a good idea, but the Founders did not fight a revolution to gain the right to government agency protocols. The possibility that a search might extend well beyond papers and effects in the physical proximity of an arrestee is yet another reason that the privacy interests here dwarf those in *Robinson*.

C

Apart from their arguments for a direct extension of *Robinson*, the United States and California offer various fallback options for permitting warrantless cell phone searches under certain circumstances. Each of the proposals is flawed and contravenes our general preference to provide clear guidance to law enforcement through categorical rules. ...

The United States first proposes that the *Gant* standard be imported from the vehicle context, allowing a warrantless search of an arrestee's cell phone whenever it is reasonable to believe that the phone contains evidence of the crime of arrest. ...

At any rate, a *Gant* standard would prove no practical limit at all when it comes to cell phone searches. In the vehicle context, *Gant* generally protects against searches for evidence of past crimes. In the cell phone context, however, it is reasonable to expect that incriminating information will be found on a phone regardless of when the crime occurred. Similarly, in the vehicle context *Gant* restricts broad searches resulting from minor crimes such as traffic violations. That would not necessarily be true for cell phones. It would be a particularly inexperienced or unimaginative law enforcement officer who could not come up with several reasons to suppose evidence of just about any crime could be found on a cell phone. Even an individual pulled over for something as basic as speeding might well have locational data dispositive of guilt on his phone. An individual pulled over for reckless driving might have evidence on the phone that shows whether he was texting while driving. The sources of potential pertinent information are virtually unlimited, so applying the *Gant* standard to cell phones would in effect give "police officers unbridled discretion to rummage at will among a person's private effects." 556 U.S., at 345 .

The United States also proposes a rule that would restrict the scope of a cell phone search to those areas of the phone where an officer reasonably believes that information relevant to the crime, the arrestee's identity, or officer safety will be discovered. This approach would again impose few meaningful constraints on officers. The proposed categories would sweep in a great deal of information, and officers would not always be able to discern in advance what information would be found where.

We also reject the United States' final suggestion that officers should always be able to search a phone's call log, as they did in Wurie's case. The Government relies on *Smith v. Maryland*, 442 U.S. 735 (1979), which held that no warrant was required to use a pen register at telephone company premises to identify numbers dialed by a particular caller. The Court in that case, however, concluded that the use of a pen register was not a "search" at all under the Fourth Amendment. There is no dispute here that the officers engaged in a search of Wurie's cell phone. Moreover, call logs typically contain more than just phone numbers; they include any identifying information that an individual might add, such as the label "my house" in Wurie's case.

Finally, at oral argument California suggested a different limiting principle, under which officers could search cell phone data if they could have obtained the same information from a pre-digital counterpart. But the fact that a search in the pre-digital era could have turned up a photograph or two in a wallet does not justify a search of thousands of photos in a digital gallery. The fact that someone could have tucked a paper bank statement in a pocket does not justify a search of every bank statement from the last five years. And to make matters worse, such an analogue test would allow law enforcement to search a range of items contained on a phone, even though people would be unlikely to carry such a variety of information in physical form. In Riley's case, for example, it is implausible that he would have strolled around with video tapes, photo albums, and an address book all crammed into his pockets. But because each of those items has a pre-digital analogue, police under California's proposal would be able to search a phone for all of those items-a significant diminution of privacy.

In addition, an analogue test would launch courts on a difficult line-drawing expedition to determine which digital files are comparable to physical records. Is an e-mail equivalent to a letter? Is a voicemail equivalent to a phone message slip? It is not clear how officers could make these kinds of decisions before conducting a search, or how courts would apply the proposed rule after the fact. An analogue test would keep defendants and judges guessing for years to come.

IV

We cannot deny that our decision today will have an impact on the ability of law enforcement to combat crime. Cell phones have become important tools in facilitating coordination and communication among members of criminal enterprises, and can provide valuable incriminating information about dangerous criminals. Privacy comes at a cost.

Our holding, of course, is not that the information on a cell phone is immune from search; it is instead that a warrant is generally required before such a search, even when a cell phone is seized incident to arrest. Our cases have historically recognized that the warrant requirement is an important working part of our machinery of government, not merely an inconvenience to be somehow 'weighed' against the claims of police efficiency. Recent technological advances similar to those discussed here have, in addition, made the process of obtaining a warrant itself more efficient.

Moreover, even though the search incident to arrest exception does not apply to cell phones, other case-specific exceptions may still justify a warrantless search of a particular phone. One well-recognized exception applies when the exigencies of the situation make the needs of law enforcement so compelling that a warrantless search is objectively reasonable under the Fourth Amendment. Such exigencies could include the need to prevent the imminent destruction of evidence in individual cases, to pursue a fleeing suspect, and to assist persons who are seriously injured or are threatened with imminent injury. In *United States v. Chadwick*, 433 U.S. 1, 15 (1977), for example, the Court held that the exception for searches incident to arrest did not justify a search of [a 200-pound footlocker], but noted that "if officers have reason to believe that luggage contains some immediately dangerous instrumentality, such as explosives, it would be foolhardy to transport it to the station house without opening the luggage." 433 U.S., at 15 n.9.

In light of the availability of the exigent circumstances exception, there is no reason to believe that law enforcement officers will not be able to address some of the more extreme hypotheticals that have been suggested: a suspect texting an accomplice who, it is feared, is preparing to detonate a bomb, or a child abductor who may have information about the child's location on his cell phone. The defendants here recognize – indeed, they stress – that such fact-specific threats may justify a warrantless search of cell phone data. The critical point is that, unlike the search incident to arrest exception, the exigent circumstances exception requires a court to examine whether an emergency justified a warrantless search in each particular case.

*   *   *

Our cases have recognized that the Fourth Amendment was the founding generation's response to the reviled "general warrants" and "writs of assistance" of the colonial era, which allowed British officers to rummage through homes in an unrestrained search for evidence of criminal activity. Opposition to such searches was in fact one of the driving forces behind the Revolution itself. In 1761, the patriot James Otis delivered a speech in Boston denouncing the use of writs of assistance. A young John Adams was there, and he would later write that "[e]very man of a crowded audience appeared to me to go away, as I did, ready to take arms against writs of assistance." 10 Works of John Adams 247-248 (C. Adams ed. 1856). According to Adams, Otis's speech was "the first scene of the first act of opposition to the arbitrary claims of Great Britain. Then and there the child Independence was born." *Id.*, at 248.

Modern cell phones are not just another technological convenience. With all they contain and all they may reveal, they hold for many Americans the privacies of life. The fact that technology now allows an individual to carry such information in his hand does not make the information any less worthy of the protection for which the Founders fought. Our answer to the question of what police must do before searching a cell phone seized incident to an arrest is accordingly simple – get a warrant. ...

QUESTIONS

1. Does *Riley* translate familiar Fourth Amendment principles from the physical world to the digital one? Or does it create new, distinctive principles for computers?

2. A police officer arrests Wiley and finds a phone in his pocket. Just then, a text message from one of Wiley's co-conspirators arrives, listing the location for a drug buy. The police drive to the location and arrest the co-conspirator. Legal? (Does it matter whether Wiley is using a flip phone or a smartphone that displays incoming texts on the lock screen?) What if the co-conspirator calls Wiley instead, and the police officer picks up the phone and successfully impersonates Wiley long enough to arrange the drug buy?

3. What counts as a "search" of an electronic device? The answer is not always obvious, given that one can interact with it digitally as well as physically. Suppose the police dial what they think is the defendant's phone number to see whether the phone in his pocket rings. Search? Or what if they use a cell-site simulator (sometimes called a "stingray"): a device that pretends to be a cell tower and records the identifying information and location of cell phones that attempt to connect to it?

4. Dom Toretto was involved in an automobile collision and his badly-damages car was impounded while he was in the hospital receiving treatment for his injuries. The police suspect that the crash occurred during an illegal high-speed drift-racing competition. They would like to inspect the car's electronic data recorder, a/k/a "black box," a small onboard computer which automatically records the car's speed, engine RPM, steering wheel position, brake status, and other data. Obtaining the data will require inserting a cable into the car's dashboard, and decoding it will require specialized software available only to mechacnics certified by the car's manufacturer. Do the police need a warrant?

5. Computer searches raise difficult pragmatic questions. The police arrest Bill Maplewood for possession of child pornography. Having read *Riley*, they plan to obtain a warrant to seize his laptop computer and search it for evidence. The laptop's hard drive also contains his tax records, his emails, and patient records from his psychiatric practice. Which of these can the police examine? How should they carry out the examination? Can they also look for evidence of tax evasion? How long can they retain the laptop? Which of these limits should be detailed in the warrant itself?

UNITED STATES V. WARSHAK
631 F.3d 266 (6th Cir. 2010)

Boggs, Circuit Judge: ...

I. STATEMENT OF THE FACTS

A. Factual Background

In 2001, Steven Warshak ("Warshak") owned and operated a number of small businesses in the Cincinnati area [including Berkeley Premium Neutraceuticals, Inc. ("Berkeley")]. ...

In the latter half of 2001, Berkeley launched Enzyte, its flagship product. At the time of its launch, Enzyte was purported to increase the size of a man's erection. The product proved tremendously popular, and business rose sharply. By 2004, demand for Berkeley's products had grown so dramatically that the company employed 1500 people, and the call center remained open throughout the night, taking orders at breakneck speed. Berkeley's line of supplements also expanded, ballooning from approximately four products to around thirteen. By year's end, Berkeley's annual sales topped out at around $250 million, largely on the strength of Enzyte.

1. Advertising

The popularity of Enzyte appears to have been due in large part to Berkeley's aggressive advertising campaigns. The vast majority of the advertising – approximately 98% – was conducted through television spots. Around 2004, network television was saturated with Enzyte advertisements featuring a character called "Smilin' Bob," whose trademark exaggerated smile was presumably the result of Enzyte's efficacy. The "Smilin' Bob" commercials were rife with innuendo and implied that users of Enzyte would become the envy of the neighborhood.

... [Print and radio commercials] cited a 2001 independent customer study, which purported to show that, over a three-month period, 100 English-speaking men who took Enzyte experienced a 12 to 31% increase in the size of their penises. The 2001 study was also referenced in radio advertisements and appeared on the company's website, as well as in brochures and sales calls. James Teegarden later testified that the survey was bogus. He stated that, prior to the appearance of the advertisements, Warshak instructed him to create a spreadsheet and to fill it with fabricated data. Teegarden testified that he plucked the numbers out of the air and generated the spreadsheet over a twenty-four hour period. ...

2. The Auto-Ship Program

The "life blood" of the business was its auto-ship program, which was instituted in 2001, shortly before Enzyte hit the market. The auto-ship program was a continuity or negative-option program, in which a customer would order a free trial of a product and then continue to receive additional shipments of that product until he opted out. Before each new continuity shipment arrived on the customer's doorstep, a corresponding charge would appear on his credit-card statement. The shipments and charges would continue until the customer decided to withdraw from the program, which required the customer to notify the company.

In the early days of the auto-ship program, customers who ordered products over the phone were not told that they were being enrolled. From August 2001 to at least the end of December 2002, customers were simply added to the program at the time of the initial sale without any indication that they would be on the hook for additional charges. Apparently, products were shipped with literature explaining the program, but no authorization was sought in advance of the shipment. According to Teegarden, Warshak explained that the auto-ship program was never mentioned because "nobody would sign up." If nobody signed up, "you couldn't make revenue."

This policy resulted in a substantial volume of complaints, both to Berkeley and to outside organizations. In October 2002, the Better Business Bureau ("BBB") contacted Berkeley and indicated that more than 1,500 customers had called to voice their consternation. Because of the complaints, Berkeley's sales scripts and website began to include some language disclosing the auto-ship program. ...

However, as a number of Berkeley insiders testified, the compulsory disclosure language was not always read, and it was designed not to work. Shelley Kinmon testified that the disclosure of the continuity shipments was only made after the customer had placed his order. In other words, the sales representative had already taken the customer's credit-card information when auto-ship was mentioned. Also, the disclosures were deliberately made with haste, and they were placed after unrelated language that was intended to divert or deaden the customer's attention. In the case of Enzyte, sales reps were instructed to lead into the disclosure language by stating that "the product is not a contraceptive nor will it prevent or treat any sexually transmitted disease." According to Teegarden, the thinking was that, "if we started off with a statement about a contraceptive, something other than what it was, that people wouldn't really listen to what we were disclosing to them."

Moreover, disclosure of the auto-ship program was sometimes irrelevant. For example, in November 2003, Berkeley hired a company called West to handle "sales calls that were from . . . Avlimil or Enzyte advertisements." During the calls, West's representatives asked customers if they wanted to be enrolled in the auto-ship program, and over 80% of customers declined. When Warshak learned what was happening, he issued instructions to "take those customers, even if they decline[d], even if they said no to the Auto-Ship program, go ahead and put them on the Auto-Ship program." A subsequent email between Berkeley employees indicated that "all [West] customers, whether they know it or not, are going on [auto-ship]." As a result, numerous telephone orders resulted in unauthorized continuity shipments. ...

[Warshak and Berkeley also systematically misled the banks who processed Berkeley's credit-card payments. Many customers would dispute Berkeley charges with their credit card companies, resulting in "chargebacks" in which Berkeley was required to issue them refunds. Since many banks and credit-card processors will not do business with merchants who have too many chargebacks, Berkeley lied to banks about its chargeback history and engaged in fake transactions solely to lower its chargeback ratio.]

B. Procedural History

In September 2006, a grand jury sitting in the Southern District of Ohio returned a 112-count indictment charging Warshak ... and several others with various crimes related to Berkeley's business. Warshak was charged with conspiracy to commit mail, wire, and bank fraud (Count 1); mail fraud (Counts 2-13); making false statements to banks (Counts 14, 16–22, 24–26, 28); bank fraud (Counts 15, 23, 27); conspiracy to commit and attempt to commit access-device fraud (Count 29); conspiracy to commit money laundering (Count 34); money laundering (Counts 32–98, 102–106, 108); conspiracy to commit misbranding (Count 109); misbranding (Count 110); and, lastly, conspiracy to obstruct a Federal Trade Commission ("FTC") proceeding (Count 112). ...

Before trial, numerous motions were filed. First, Warshak moved to exclude thousands of emails that the government obtained from his Internet Service Providers. That motion was denied. ...

Over fifteen months later, in January 2008, the case proceeded to trial. Approximately six weeks later, the trial ended and the defendants were convicted of the majority of the charges. ...

On August 27, 2008, the defendants were sentenced. Warshak received a sentence of 25 years of imprisonment. He was also ordered to pay a fine of $93,000 and a special assessment of $9,300. In addition, he was ordered to surrender $459,540,000 in proceeds-money-judgment forfeiture and $44,876,781.68 in money-laundering-judgment forfeiture. ...

II. ANALYSIS

A. The Search & Seizure of Warshak's Emails

Warshak argues that the government's warrantless, ex parte seizure of approximately 27,000 of his private emails constituted a violation of the Fourth Amendment's prohibition on unreasonable searches and seizures. The government counters that, even if government agents violated the Fourth Amendment in obtaining the emails, they relied in good faith on the Stored Communications Act ("SCA"), 18 U.S.C. §§ 2701 et seq., a statute that allows the government to obtain certain electronic communications without procuring a warrant. The government also argues that any hypothetical Fourth Amendment violation was harmless. We find that the government did violate Warshak's Fourth Amendment rights by compelling his Internet Service Provider ("ISP") to turn over the contents of his emails. ...

1. The Stored Communications Act

The Stored Communications Act ("SCA"), 18 U.S.C. §§ 2701 et seq., "permits a 'governmental entity' to compel a service provider to disclose the contents of [electronic] communications in certain circumstances." *Warshak II*, 532 F.3d at 523. ...

2. Factual Background

Email was a critical form of communication among Berkeley personnel. As a consequence, Warshak had a number of email accounts with various ISPs, including an account with NuVox Communications. In October 2004, the government formally requested that NuVox prospectively preserve the contents of any emails to or from Warshak's email account. ... NuVox acceded to the government's request and began preserving copies of Warshak's incoming and outgoing emails – copies that would not have existed absent the prospective preservation request. Per the government's instructions, Warshak was not informed that his messages were being archived.

In January 2005, the government obtained a subpoena under § 2703(b) and compelled NuVox to turn over the emails that it had begun preserving the previous year. In May 2005, the government served NuVox with an ex parte court order under § 2703(d) that required NuVox to surrender any additional email messages in Warshak's account. In all, the government compelled NuVox to reveal the contents of approximately 27,000 emails. Warshak did not receive notice of either the subpoena or the order until May 2006.

3. The Fourth Amendment

The Fourth Amendment provides that "[t]he right of the people to be secure in their persons, houses, papers, and effects, against unreasonable searches and seizures, shall not be violated, and no Warrants shall issue, but upon probable cause. . . ." U.S. Const. amend. IV. The fundamental purpose of the Fourth Amendment "is to safeguard the privacy and security of individuals against arbitrary invasions by government officials." *Camara v. Mun. Ct.*, 387 U.S. 523, 528 (1967)...

Not all government actions are invasive enough to implicate the Fourth Amendment. "The Fourth Amendment's protections hinge on the occurrence of a 'search,' a legal term of art whose history is riddled with complexity." *Widgren v. Maple Grove Twp.*, 429 F.3d 575, 578 (6th Cir. 2005). A "search" occurs when the government infringes upon "an expectation of privacy that society is prepared to consider reasonable." *United States v. Jacobsen*, 466 U.S. 109, 113 (1984). This standard breaks down into two discrete inquiries: "first, has the [target of the investigation] manifested a subjective expectation of privacy in the object of the challenged search? Second, is society willing to recognize that expectation as reasonable?" *California v. Ciraolo*, 476 U.S. 207 (1986).

Turning first to the subjective component of the test, we find that Warshak plainly manifested an expectation that his emails would be shielded from outside scrutiny. As he notes in his brief, his "entire business and personal life was contained within the . . . emails seized." Appellant's Br. at 39–40. Given the often sensitive and sometimes damning substance of his emails, we think it highly unlikely that Warshak expected them to be made public, for people seldom unfurl their dirty laundry in plain view. Therefore, we conclude that Warshak had a subjective expectation of privacy in the contents of his emails.

The next question is whether society is prepared to recognize that expectation as reasonable. This question is one of grave import and enduring consequence, given the prominent role that email has assumed in modern communication. Since the advent of email, the telephone call and the letter have waned in importance, and an explosion of Internet-based communication has taken place. People are now able to send sensitive and intimate information, instantaneously, to friends, family, and colleagues half a world away. Lovers exchange sweet nothings, and businessmen swap ambitious plans, all with the click of a mouse button. Commerce has also taken hold in email. Online purchases are often documented in email accounts, and email is frequently used to remind patients and clients of imminent appointments. In short, "account" is an apt word for the conglomeration of stored messages that comprises an email account, as it provides an account of its owner's life. By obtaining access to someone's email, government agents gain the ability to peer deeply into his activities. Much hinges, therefore, on whether the government is permitted to request that a commercial ISP turn over the contents of a subscriber's emails without triggering the machinery of the Fourth Amendment.

In confronting this question, we take note of two bedrock principles. First, the very fact that information is being passed through a communications network is a paramount Fourth Amendment consideration. Second, the Fourth Amendment must keep pace with the inexorable march of technological progress, or its guarantees will wither and perish.

With those principles in mind, we begin our analysis by considering the manner in which the Fourth Amendment protects traditional forms of communication. In *Katz*, the Supreme Court was asked to determine how the Fourth Amendment applied in the context of the telephone. There, government agents had affixed an electronic listening device to the exterior of a public phone booth, and had used the device to intercept and record several phone conversations. The Supreme

Court held that this constituted a search under the Fourth Amendment, not-withstanding the fact that the telephone company had the capacity to monitor and record the calls, In the eyes of the Court, the caller was "surely entitled to assume that the words he utter[ed] into the mouthpiece w[ould] not be broadcast to the world." *Katz*, 389 U.S. at 352. The Court's holding in Katz has since come to stand for the broad proposition that, in many contexts, the government infringes a rea-sonable expectation of privacy when it surreptitiously intercepts a telephone call through electronic means.

Letters receive similar protection. While a letter is in the mail, the police may not intercept it and examine its contents unless they first obtain a warrant based on probable cause. This is true despite the fact that sealed letters are handed over to perhaps dozens of mail carriers, any one of whom could tear open the thin pa-per envelopes that separate the private words from the world outside. Put another way, trusting a letter to an intermediary does not necessarily defeat a reasonable expectation that the letter will remain private. *See Katz*, 389 U.S. at 351 ("[W]hat [a person] seeks to preserve as private, even in an area accessible to the public, may be constitutionally protected.").

Given the fundamental similarities between email and traditional forms of communication, it would defy common sense to afford emails lesser Fourth Amendment protection. ... Email is the technological scion of tangible mail, and it plays an indispensable part in the Information Age. Over the last decade, email has become "so pervasive that some persons may consider [it] to be [an] essential means or necessary instrument[] for self-expression, even self-identification." [*City of Ontario v.*] *Quon*, 130 S. Ct. at 2630. It follows that email requires strong protection under the Fourth Amendment; otherwise, the Fourth Amendment would prove an ineffective guardian of private communication, an essential purpose it has long been recognized to serve. ... As some forms of com-munication begin to diminish, the Fourth Amendment must recognize and protect nascent ones that arise. *See Warshak I*, 490 F.3d at 473 ("It goes without saying that like the telephone earlier in our history, e-mail is an ever-increasing mode of private communication, and protecting shared communications through this medium is as important to Fourth Amendment principles today as protecting telephone conversations has been in the past.").

If we accept that an email is analogous to a letter or a phone call, it is manifest that agents of the government cannot compel a commercial ISP to turn over the contents of an email without triggering the Fourth Amendment. An ISP is the in-termediary that makes email communication possible. Emails must pass through an ISP's servers to reach their intended recipient. Thus, the ISP is the functional equivalent of a post office or a telephone company. As we have discussed above, the police may not storm the post office and intercept a letter, and they are like-wise forbidden from using the phone system to make a clandestine recording of a telephone call – unless they get a warrant, that is. It only stands to reason that, if government agents compel an ISP to surrender the contents of a subscriber's emails, those agents have thereby conducted a Fourth Amendment search, which necessitates compliance with the warrant requirement absent some exception.

In *Warshak I*, the government argued that this conclusion was improper, point-ing to the fact that NuVox contractually reserved the right to access Warshak's emails for certain purposes. While we acknowledge that a subscriber agreement might, in some cases, be sweeping enough to defeat a reasonable expectation of privacy in the contents of an email account, ... we doubt that will be the case in most situations, and it is certainly not the case here.

As an initial matter, it must be observed that the mere ability of a third-party intermediary to access the contents of a communication cannot be sufficient to extinguish a reasonable expectation of privacy. In *Katz*, the Supreme Court found it reasonable to expect privacy during a telephone call despite the ability of an operator to listen in. *See Smith*, 442 U.S. at 746-47 (Stewart, J., dissenting). Similarly, the ability of a rogue mail handler to rip open a letter does not make it unreasonable to assume that sealed mail will remain private on its journey across the country. Therefore, the threat or possibility of access is not decisive when it comes to the reasonableness of an expectation of privacy.

Nor is the *right* of access. As the Electronic Frontier Foundation points out in its *amicus* brief, at the time *Katz* was decided, telephone companies had a right to monitor calls in certain situations. Specifically, telephone companies could listen in when reasonably necessary to "protect themselves and their properties against the improper and illegal use of their facilities." *Bubis v. United States*, 384 F.2d 643, 648 (9th Cir. 1967). In this case, the NuVox subscriber agreement tracks that language, indicating that "NuVox *may* access and use individual Subscriber information in the operation of the Service and as necessary to protect the Service." Acceptable Use Policy, available at http://business.windstream.com/Legal/acceptableUse.htm (last visited Aug. 12, 2010). Thus, under *Katz*, the degree of access granted to NuVox does not diminish the reasonableness of Warshak's trust in the privacy of his emails.[16]

Our conclusion finds additional support in the application of Fourth Amendment doctrine to rented space. Hotel guests, for example, have a reasonable expectation of privacy in their rooms. *See United States v. Allen*, 106 F.3d 695, 699 (6th Cir. 1997). This is so even though maids routinely enter hotel rooms to replace the towels and tidy the furniture. Similarly, tenants have a legitimate expectation of privacy in their apartments. *See United States v. Washington*, 573 F.3d 279, 284 (6th Cir. 2009). That expectation persists, regardless of the incursions of handymen to fix leaky faucets. Consequently, we are convinced that some degree of routine access is hardly dispositive with respect to the privacy question.

Again, however, we are unwilling to hold that a subscriber agreement will never be broad enough to snuff out a reasonable expectation of privacy. As the panel noted in *Warshak I*, if the ISP expresses an intention to "audit, inspect, and monitor" its subscriber's emails, that might be enough to render an expectation of privacy unreasonable. *See* 490 F.3d at 472-73 (quoting *United States v. Simons*, 206 F.3d 392, 398 (4th Cir. 2000)). But where, as here, there is no such statement, the ISP's "control over the [emails] and ability to access them under certain limited circumstances will not be enough to overcome an expectation of privacy." *Id.* at 473.

We recognize that our conclusion may be attacked in light of the Supreme Court's decision in *United States v. Miller*, 425 U.S. 435 (1976). In *Miller*, the Supreme Court held that a bank depositor does not have a reasonable expectation of privacy in the contents of bank records, checks, and deposit slips. *Id.* at 442. The Court's holding in *Miller* was based on the fact that bank documents, "includ-

---

16 We note that the access granted to NuVox was also temporally limited, as Warshak's email account was configured to delete his emails from NuVox's servers as soon as he opened them on his personal computer.

ing financial statements and deposit slips, contain only information voluntarily conveyed to the banks and exposed to their employees in the ordinary course of business." *Ibid.* The Court noted,

> The depositor takes the risk, in revealing his affairs to another, that the information will be conveyed by that person to the Government. . . . [T]he Fourth Amendment does not prohibit the obtaining of information revealed to a third party and conveyed by him to Government authorities, even if the information is revealed on the assumption that it will be used only for a limited purpose and the confidence placed in the third party will not be betrayed.

Id. at 443 (citations omitted).

But *Miller* is distinguishable. First, *Miller* involved simple business records, as opposed to the potentially unlimited variety of "confidential communications" at issue here. *See ibid.* Second, the bank depositor in *Miller* conveyed information to the bank so that the bank could put the information to use "in the ordinary course of business." *Ibid.* By contrast, Warshak received his emails through NuVox. NuVox was an intermediary, not the intended recipient of the emails. *See* Bellia & Freiwald, *Stored E-Mail*, 2008 U. Chi. Legal F. at 165 ("[W]e view the best analogy for this scenario as the cases in which a third party carries, transports, or stores property for another. In these cases, as in the stored e-mail case, the customer grants access to the ISP because it is essential to the customer's interests."). Thus, *Miller* is not controlling.

Accordingly, we hold that a subscriber enjoys a reasonable expectation of privacy in the contents of emails "that are stored with, or sent or received through, a commercial ISP." *Warshak I*, 490 F.3d at 473. ... The government may not compel a commercial ISP to turn over the contents of a subscriber's emails without first obtaining a warrant based on probable cause. Therefore, because they did not obtain a warrant, the government agents violated the Fourth Amendment when they obtained the contents of Warshak's emails. Moreover, to the extent that the SCA purports to permit the government to obtain such emails warrantlessly, the SCA is unconstitutional.

QUESTIONS

1. Presumably, Warshak's computer also contained copies of his emails. Why didn't the government simply seize the computer and search through the emails on it?

2. In the actual case, the government obtained a subpoena under § 2703 of the Stored Communications Act (SCA). The SCA is discussed in more detail in the Wiretapping section, but the relevant standard is that the government must present the court with "specific and articulable facts showing that there are reasonable grounds to believe that the contents of a wire or electronic communication, or the records or other information sought, are relevant and material to an ongoing criminal investigation." Is this an easier standard to meet than probable cause, or harder? Why doesn't the government's compliance with the terms of the SCA dispose of this case? (*Hint*: these two questions are related.)

3. If you send an email to a friend describing your plans to assassinate the mayor of Metropolis, does the Fourth Amendment prohibit your friend from turning over the email to the Metropolis Police Department? If you send sexually explicit instant messages to "WetRiffs13," who turns out to be a 35-

year-old FBI agent, have your Fourth Amendment rights been violated? Are these hypotheticals on point with *Warshak*? Or consider *United States v. Morel*, 2017 DNH 072, 2017 WL 1376363 (D.N.H. Apr. 14, 2017), in which the defendant uploaded several images containing child pornography to the file-sharing site Imgur, where anyone with the URL could view them. This, the court held, was inconsistent with "taking affirmative steps to protect the information" — even without further proof that the defendant had actually shared the URL with anyone. Is this result consistent with *Warshak*?

4. *Warshak* explains that an email is more like a letter or a phone call (*Katz*) than a bank record (*Miller*). Is the argument persuasive? How effective is the process of reasoning by analogy when it comes to new technologies? Consider another hypothetical. Google's Chrome web browser has a "sync" feature that will transfer your bookmarks from one computer to another. To make it work, your copy of Chrome on the first computer needs to transmit the list of bookmarks to Google's servers, from which your second computer can then download it. After *Warshak*, would the government need a search warrant to get the list of your bookmarks from Google?

5. If you were reading the quoted language from NuVox'x subscriber agreement, when, if ever, would you expect a human employee of NuVox to read your emails? Until 2017, Gmail used computers to automatically scan the contents of users' emails and display ads based on the topics they're discussing. After *Warshak*, did Gmail users have an expectation of privacy in their emails? What about people who sent email *to* Gmail users?

6. Other courts have been more willing to hold that terms of service can destroy an expectation of privacy. For example, in *Holmes v. Petrovich Development Co.*, 191 Cal. App. 4th 1047 (Ct. App. 2011), the court held that a company's acceptable use policy (which stated that work computers were not to be used for personal purposes and that all computer use could be monitored) meant that an employee waived the attorney-client privilege by using her work computer to email her lawyer. Can *Holmes* be reconciled with *Warshak*?

UNITED STATES V. APPLE MACPRO COMPUTER
851 F.3d 238 (3d Cir. 2017)

Vanaskie, Circuit Judge: ...

The District Court found Appellant John Doe in civil contempt for refusing to comply with an order issued pursuant to the All Writs Act, 28 U.S.C. § 1651, which required him to produce several seized devices in a fully unencrypted state. Doe contends that ... the order itself violates his Fifth Amendment privilege against self-incrimination.

I.

During an investigation into Doe's access to child pornography over the internet, the Delaware County Criminal Investigations Unit executed a valid search warrant at Doe's residence. During the search, officers seized an Apple iPhone 5S and an Apple Mac Pro Computer with two attached Western Digital External Hard Drives, all of which had been protected with encryption software. Police subsequently seized a password-protected Apple iPhone 6 Plus as well.

Agents from the Department of Homeland Security then applied for a federal search warrant to examine the seized devices. Doe voluntarily provided the password for the Apple iPhone 5S, but refused to provide the passwords to decrypt the Apple Mac Pro computer or the external hard drives. Despite Doe's refusal, forensic analysts discovered the password to decrypt the Mac Pro Computer, but could not decrypt the external hard drives. Forensic examination of the Mac Pro revealed an image of a pubescent girl in a sexually provocative position and logs showing that the Mac Pro had been used to visit sites with titles common in child exploitation, such as "toddler_cp," "lolicam," "tor-childporn," and "pthc." he Forensic examination also disclosed that Doe had downloaded thousands of files known by their "hash" values to be child pornography. The files, however, were not on the Mac Pro, but instead had been stored on the encrypted external hard drives. Accordingly, the files themselves could not be accessed.

As part of their investigation, the Delaware County law enforcement officers also interviewed Doe's sister, who had lived with Doe during 2015. She related that Doe had shown her hundreds of images of child pornography on the encrypted external hard drives. She told the investigators that the external hard drives included "videos of children who were nude and engaged in sex acts with other children." Doe provided the password to access the iPhone 6 Plus, but did not grant access to an application on the phone which contained additional encrypted information. Forensic analysts concluded that the phone's encrypted database contained approximately 2,015 image and video files.

On August 3, 2015, upon application of the Government, a Magistrate Judge issued an order pursuant to the All Writs Act requiring Doe to produce his iPhone 6 Plus, his Mac Pro computer, and his two attached external hard drives in a fully unencrypted state (the "Decryption Order"). ...

Doe produced the Apple iPhone 6 Plus, including the files on the secret application, in a fully unencrypted state by entering three separate passwords on the device. The phone contained adult pornography, a video of Doe's four-year-old niece in which she was wearing only her underwear, and approximately twenty photographs which focused on the genitals of Doe's six-year-old niece. Doe, however, stated that he could not remember the passwords necessary to decrypt the hard drives and entered several incorrect passwords during the forensic examination. The Government remains unable to view the decrypted content of the hard drives without his assistance.

Following the forensic examination, the Magistrate Judge granted the Government's Motion for Order to Show Cause Why Doe Should Not Be Held in Contempt, finding that Doe willfully disobeyed and resisted the Decryption Order. Based on the evidence presented at the hearing, the Magistrate Judge found that Doe remembered the passwords needed to decrypt the hard drives but chose not to reveal them because of the devices' contents. ...

III. ...

B. ...

Doe also contends that the Decryption Order violates his Fifth Amendment privilege against self-incrimination ...

The Fifth Amendment states that "[n]o person ... shall be compelled in any criminal case to be a witness against himself." U.S. Const. amend. V. The Fifth Amendment, however, "does not independently proscribe the compelled production of every sort of incriminating evidence but applies only when the accused is compelled to make a Testimonial Communication that is incriminating." *Fisher v. United States*, 425 U.S. 391, 408 (1976). To be testimonial, a communication must either "explicitly or implicitly ... relate a factual assertion or disclose information." *Doe v. United States*, 487 U.S. 201, 210 (1988).

The Supreme Court has recognized that in some instances, the production of evidence can implicate the Fifth Amendment. In *Fisher*, the Court stated that "[t]he act of producing evidence in response to a subpoena ... has communicative aspects of its own, wholly aside from the contents of the papers produced." 425 U.S. at 410. The Court reasoned that compliance with a request for evidence may "tacitly concede[ ] the existence of the documents demanded and their possession and control by the [defendant]." *Id.* By "producing documents, one acknowledges that the documents exist, admits that the documents are in one's custody, and concedes that the documents are those that the [Government] requests." *United States v. Chabot*, 793 F.3d 338, 342 (3d Cir.). When the production of evidence does concede the existence, custody, and authenticity of that evidence, the Fifth Amendment privilege against self-incrimination applies because that production constitutes compelled testimony.

In *Fisher*, however, the Court also articulated the "foregone conclusion" rule, which acts as an exception to the otherwise applicable act-of-production doctrine. Under this rule, the Fifth Amendment does not protect an act of production when any potentially testimonial component of the act of production—such as the existence, custody, and authenticity of evidence—is a "foregone conclusion" that "adds little or nothing to the sum total of the Government's information." For the rule to apply, the Government must be able to "describe with reasonable particularity" the documents or evidence it seeks to compel. *U.S. v. Hubbell*, 530 U.S. 27, 30 (2000).

Although we have not confronted the Fifth Amendment implications of compelled decryption, the Eleventh Circuit has addressed the issue and found that the privilege against self-incrimination should apply. In that case, a suspect appealed a judgment of contempt entered after he refused to produce the unencrypted contents of his laptop and hard drives. *In re Grand Jury Subpoena Duces Tecum Dated Mar. 25, 2011*, 670 F.3d 1335, 1337 (11th Cir. 2012). The court found that "(1) [the suspect's] decryption and production of the contents of the drives would be testimonial, not merely a physical act; and (2) the explicit and implicit factual communications associated with the decryption and production are not foregone conclusions." *Id.* at 1346. The court reached this decision after noting that the Government did not show whether any files existed on the hard drives and could not show with any reasonable particularity that the suspect could access the encrypted portions of the drives. Although the court did not require the Government to identify exactly the documents it sought, it did require that, at the very least, the Government be able to demonstrate some knowledge that files do exist on the encrypted devices.

Despite Doe's argument to the contrary, the Eleventh Circuit's reasoning in *In re Grand Jury Subpoena* does not compel a similar result here. The Magistrate Judge found that, though the Fifth Amendment may be implicated by Doe's decryption of the devices, any testimonial aspects of that production were a foregone conclusion. According to the Magistrate Judge, the affidavit supporting the application for the search warrant established that (1) the Government had custody of the devices; (2) prior to the seizure, Doe possessed, accessed, and owned all devices; and (3) there are images on the electronic devices that constitute child pornography. ...

Unlike *In re Grand Jury Subpoena*, the Government has provided evidence to show both that files exist on the encrypted portions of the devices and that Doe can access them. The affidavit supporting the search warrant states that an investigation led to the identification of Doe as a user of an internet file sharing network that was used to access child pornography. When executing a search of Doe's residence, forensic analysts found the encrypted devices, and Doe does not dispute their existence or his ownership of them. Once the analysts accessed Doe's Mac Pro Computer, they found one image depicting a pubescent girl in a sexually suggestive position and logs that suggested the user had visited groups with titles common in child exploitation. Doe's sister then reported that she had witnessed Doe unlock his Mac Pro while connected to the hard drives to show her hundreds of pictures and videos of child pornography. Forensic analysts also found an additional 2,015 videos and photographs in an encrypted application on Doe's phone, which Doe had opened for the police by entering a password. Based on these facts, the Magistrate Judge found that, for the purposes of the Fifth Amendment, any testimonial component of the production of decrypted devices added little or nothing to the information already obtained by the Government. The Magistrate Judge determined that any testimonial component would be a foregone conclusion. The Magistrate Judge did not commit a clear or obvious error in his application of the foregone conclusion doctrine. In this regard, the Magistrate Judge rested his decision rejecting the Fifth Amendment challenge on factual findings that are amply supported by the record.[*] Accordingly, Doe's challenges to the Decryption Order and Quashal Denial fail.

So, too, does Doe's challenge to the contempt order. At the hearing on the contempt motion, Doe maintained that he could not remember the passwords to decrypt the hard drives. In a civil contempt proceeding, when a defendant raises a challenge of impossibility of compliance, the defendant bears the burden of production. At the contempt hearing, the Government presented several witnesses to support its prima facie case of contempt. Doe's sister testified to the fact that, while in her presence, Doe accessed child pornography files on his Mac Pro computer by means of entering passwords from memory. Further, a detective who executed the original search warrant stated that Doe did not provide his password at the time because he wanted to prevent the police from accessing his computer. Doe never asserted an inability to remember the passwords at that time. Doe presented no evidence to explain his failure to comply or to challenge the evidence brought by the Government. The District Court thus found Doe in contempt and ordered he be held in custody until he complies with the Decryption Order. The

---

7. It is important to note that we are not concluding that the Government's knowledge of the content of the devices is necessarily the correct focus of the "foregone conclusion" inquiry in the context of a compelled decryption order. Instead, a very sound argument can be made that the foregone conclusion doctrine properly focuses on whether the Government already knows the testimony that is implicit in the act of production. In this case, the fact known to the government that is implicit in the act of providing the password for the devices is "I, John Doe, know the password for these devices." Based upon the testimony presented at the contempt proceeding, that fact is a foregone conclusion. However, because our review is limited to plain error, and no plain error was committed by the District Court in finding that the Government established that the contents of the encrypted hard drives are known to it, we need not decide here that the inquiry can be limited to the question of whether Doe's knowledge of the password itself is sufficient to support application of the foregone conclusion doctrine.

District Court did not abuse its discretion in finding Doe to be in contempt of the Decryption Order.

QUESTIONS

1. Is the password to a computer like the key to a locked box? The combination to a safe? Would it be "testimonial" to require the production of a key or a combination?

2. Do you see how something can be testimonial and still also be a foregone conclusion?

3. When Al Bertillon is arrested for conspiracy to distribute a controlled substance, the police seize an iPhone from his backpack, which is secured not with a passcode but with a fingerprint lock. Can the police compel him to put his thumb on the phone's fingerprint sensor?

4. The government can also try to obtain passwords surreptitiously. This works surprisingly often. In *United States v. Scarfo*, 180 F. Supp. 2d 572 (D.N.J. 2001), the FBI broke into the defendant's office and installed a "key logger" on his computer keyboard that recorded his keystrokes. The FBI thereby obtained the password he used to encrypt his files, which contained evidence of gambling and loansharking. Do you see any Fourth Amendment issues with this procedure? If so, how would you carry it out so that the resulting evidence would be admissible in court?

COFFEESHOP PROBLEM

Officer Augusta Zenobia from the King County Sheriff's Office is ordering an americano at a Tully's Coffee Shop in Seattle when she notices that one of the other patrons has left an unattended laptop sitting on a table. It has shifted over into the screensaver, which appears to be pulling random pictures from the computer's hard drive. Some of them show people who appear to be naked and underage.

A few seconds later, a man emerges from the men's room and walks towards the table with the laptop. He makes brief eye contact with Officer Zenobia, then looks back to the laptop, which has just flashed up another photo of someone without clothes on. He runs for the computer and slams it shut. Officer Zenobia is a few steps behind; she orders him away from the computer and places him under arrest. He turns out to be one Lucius Aurelian; he has a clean criminal record. The computer, along with the other items he had on his person (a wallet, keys, a laptop bag, some papers for work), are currently sitting in the evidence locker at the police station.

You work in the King County Prosecuting Attorney's office, and you have been assigned the case. Officer Zenobia is willing to testify that the images she saw were clearly child pornography. How good a case will you be able to build? What should the next steps in the investigation be?

B. Wiretapping

The Constitution is hardly the only source of communications privacy law. A variety of federal and state statutes also regulate the use and disclosure of information stored in computers or transmitted on networks. This section examines three principal federal statutes on point: the Wiretap Act (codified at 18 U.S.C. §§ 2510–

2522), the Stored Communications Act (the SCA, codified at 18 U.S.C. §§ 2701–2712) and the Pen Register and Trap and Trace statute (codified at 18 U.S.C. §§ 3121–27). All three were heavily amended by the Electronic Communications Privacy Act of 1986, or ECPA, which is sometimes used to refer to the field as a whole and sometimes used as a synonym for the SCA. These statutes have two interlocking roles:

- To protect individuals from having their private communications seen by other private parties.

- To regulate the process by which the government acquires private communications during investigations.

Unfortunately for statutory clarity, these two roles are utterly intermingled in the federal communications privacy statutes. All three take the form of a general prohibition on unauthorized access, together with exceptions for private and governmental access under certain circumstances. Figuring out what law applies to a given situation is often a matter of extensive back-and-forth cross-referencing. As you read through the statutes, keep in mind the private/governmental distinction and, also, whether the communications are being intercepted while in transit ("prospectively"), or retrieved after the fact ("retrospectively"). A third crucial distinction, familiar from the Fourth Amendment materials, is between the "contents" of a communication and other "non-content" information about it.

WIRETAP ACT
Title 18, United States Code

§ 2510 – *Definitions*

(1) "wire communication" means any aural transfer made in whole or in part through the use of facilities for the transmission of communications by the aid of wire, cable, or other like connection between the point of origin and the point of reception (including the use of such connection in a switching station) furnished or operated by any person engaged in providing or operating such facilities for the transmission of interstate or foreign communications or communications affecting interstate or foreign commerce;

(2) "oral communication" means any oral communication uttered by a person exhibiting an expectation that such communication is not subject to interception under circumstances justifying such expectation, but such term does not include any electronic communication; ...

(4) "intercept" means the aural or other acquisition of the contents of any wire, electronic, or oral communication through the use of any electronic, mechanical, or other device. ...

(8) "contents", when used with respect to any wire, oral, or electronic communication, includes any information concerning the substance, purport, or meaning of that communication; ...

(12) "electronic communication" means any transfer of signs, signals, writing, images, sounds, data, or intelligence of any nature transmitted in whole or in part by a wire, radio, electromagnetic, photoelectronic or photooptical system that affects interstate or foreign commerce, but does not include –

  (A) any wire or oral communication;

  (B) any communication made through a tone-only paging device;

(C) any communication from a tracking device (as defined in section 3117 of this title); or

(D) electronic funds transfer information stored by a financial institution in a communications system used for the electronic storage and transfer of funds; ...

(14) "electronic communications system" means any wire, radio, electromagnetic, photooptical or photoelectronic facilities for the transmission of wire or electronic communications, and any computer facilities or related electronic equipment for the electronic storage of such communications; ...

(15) "electronic communication service" means any service which provides to users thereof the ability to send or receive wire or electronic communications; ...

(17) "electronic storage" means –

(A) any temporary, intermediate storage of a wire or electronic communication incidental to the electronic transmission thereof; and

(B) any storage of such communication by an electronic communication service for purposes of backup protection of such communication; ...

§ 2511 – *Interception and disclosure of wire, oral, or electronic communications prohibited*

(1) Except as otherwise specifically provided in this chapter any person who –

(a) intentionally intercepts, endeavors to intercept, or procures any other person to intercept or endeavor to intercept, any wire, oral, or electronic communication; ...

shall be punished as provided in subsection (4). ...

(2)

(a)

(i) It shall not be unlawful under this chapter for an operator of a switchboard, or an officer, employee, or agent of a provider of wire or electronic communication service, whose facilities are used in the transmission of a wire or electronic communication, to intercept, disclose, or use that communication in the normal course of his employment while engaged in any activity which is a necessary incident to the rendition of his service or to the protection of the rights or property of the provider of that service, except that a provider of wire communication service to the public shall not utilize service observing or random monitoring except for mechanical or service quality control checks. ...

(c) It shall not be unlawful under this chapter for a person acting under color of law to intercept a wire, oral, or electronic communication, where such person is a party to the communication or one of the parties to the communication has given prior consent to such interception.

(d) It shall not be unlawful under this chapter for a person not acting under color of law to intercept a wire, oral, or electronic communication where such person is a party to the communication or where one of the parties to the communication has given prior consent to such interception unless such communication is intercepted for the purpose of committing any criminal or tortious act in violation of the Constitution or laws of the United States or of any State. ...

(g) It shall not be unlawful under this chapter or chapter 121 of this title for any person –

(i) to intercept or access an electronic communication made through an electronic communication system that is configured so that such electronic communication is readily accessible to the general public ...

§ 2515 – *Prohibition of use as evidence of intercepted wire or oral communications*

Whenever any wire or oral communication has been intercepted, no part of the contents of such communication and no evidence derived therefrom may be received in evidence in any trial, hearing, or other proceeding in or before any court, grand jury, department, officer, agency, regulatory body, legislative committee, or other authority of the United States, a State, or a political subdivision thereof if the disclosure of that information would be in violation of this chapter.

§ 2518 – *Procedure for interception of wire, oral, or electronic communications*

(1) Each application for an order authorizing or approving the interception of a wire, oral, or electronic communication under this chapter shall be made in writing upon oath or affirmation to a judge of competent jurisdiction and shall state the applicant's authority to make such application. Each application shall include the following information:

(a) the identity of the investigative or law enforcement officer making the application, and the officer authorizing the application;

(b) a full and complete statement of the facts and circumstances relied upon by the applicant, to justify his belief that an order should be issued ...

(c) a full and complete statement as to whether or not other investigative procedures have been tried and failed or why they reasonably appear to be unlikely to succeed if tried or to be too dangerous; ...

(3) Upon such application the judge may enter an ex parte order, as requested or as modified, authorizing or approving interception of wire, oral, or electronic communications ... if the judge determines on the basis of the facts submitted by the applicant that –

(a) there is probable cause for belief that an individual is committing, has committed, or is about to commit a particular offense enumerated in section 2516 of this chapter;

(b) there is probable cause for belief that particular communications concerning that offense will be obtained through such interception;

(c) normal investigative procedures have been tried and have failed or reasonably appear to be unlikely to succeed if tried or to be too dangerous;

(d) except as provided in subsection (11), there is probable cause for belief that the facilities from which, or the place where, the wire, oral, or electronic communications are to be intercepted are being used, or are about to be used, in connection with the commission of such offense, or are leased to, listed in the name of, or commonly used by such person. ...

QUESTIONS

1. The core prohibition of the Wiretap Act is in § 2511(1), which must be read together with the relevant definitions in § 2510. Which of the following are illegal under the Wiretap Act?

   • Planting a hidden digital voice recorder in a meeting room used by corporate executives?

   • Standing on a toilet seat to overhear a conversation between two other people in the bathroom without being noticed?

   • Setting up the laptop computers issued to middle-school students to take a picture using the built-in camera every thirty seconds?

   • Using a radio receiver to listen in on cordless phone conversations from nearby houses (but not saving a copy of the audio).

2. The Wiretap Act contains many exceptions. The most important of these is set forth in § 2518, which outlines a procedure for submitting an application to a court to install a wiretap. Who is allowed to make the application? What evidence do they need to provide? Is it easier to obtain a search warrant or a wiretap order? Can private parties obtain judicial authorization for one?

3. The "provider exception" in § 2511(2)(a) is also important. To whom does it apply, and how broad is it? Is it a Wiretap Act violation for Gmail to deliver email to users? To display ads next to the emails based on their contents? For Google employees to randomly inspect a sample of emails to see whether the ad displays are working?

4. States have their own wiretapping laws. New York, for example, prohibits "recording of a telephonic ... communication by a person other than a sender or a receiver thereof." N.Y. Penal L. §§ 250.00, 250.05. In California, it is illegal to record a "confidential communication" without the "consent of all parties." Cal. Pen. Code § 632(a). If Linda, in California, tape-records her phone calls with Monica, in New York, and Monica doesn't know about it, is this a violation of New York Law? California Law?

O'BRIEN V. O'BRIEN
899 So. 2d 1133 (Fla. Dist. Ct. App. 5th 2005)

Sawaya, Chief Judge:

Emanating from a rather contentious divorce proceeding is an issue we must resolve regarding application of certain provisions of the Security of Communications Act (the Act) found in Chapter 934, Florida Statutes (2003). Specifically, we must determine whether the trial court properly concluded that pursuant to section 934.03(1), Florida Statutes (2003), certain communications were inadmissible because they were illegally intercepted by the Wife who, unbeknownst to the Husband, had installed a spyware program on a computer used by the Husband that copied and stored electronic communications between the Husband and another woman.

When marital discord erupted between the Husband and the Wife, the Wife secretly installed a spyware program called Spector on the Husband's computer. It is undisputed that the Husband engaged in private on-line chats with another woman while playing Yahoo Dominoes on his computer. The Spector spyware secretly took snapshots of what appeared on the computer screen, and the frequency of these snapshots allowed Spector to capture and record all chat conversations, instant messages, e-mails sent and received, and the websites visited by the user of the computer. When the Husband discovered the Wife's clandestine attempt to monitor and record his conversations with his Dominoes partner, the Husband uninstalled the Spector software and filed a Motion for Temporary Injunction, which was subsequently granted, to prevent the Wife from disclosing the communications. ...

... The Wife argues that the electronic communications do not fall under the umbra [sic] of the Act because these communications were retrieved from storage and, therefore, are not "intercepted communications" as defined by the Act. In opposition, the Husband contends that the Spector spyware installed on the computer acquired his electronic communications real-time as they were in transmission and, therefore, are intercepts illegally obtained under the Act.

The trial court found that the electronic communications were illegally obtained in violation of section 934.03(1)(a)(e), and so we begin our analysis with the pertinent provisions of that statute, which subjects any person to criminal penalties who engages in the following activities:

> (a) Intentionally intercepts, endeavors to intercept, or procures any other person to intercept or endeavor to intercept any wire, oral, or electronic communication; ...

§ 934.03(1)(a)-(e), Fla. Stat. (2003).

... It is beyond doubt that what the trial court excluded from evidence are "electronic communications." The core of the issue lies in whether the electronic communications were intercepted. The term "intercept" is defined by the Act as "the aural or other acquisition of the contents of any wire, electronic, or oral communication through the use of any electronic, mechanical, or other device." § 934.02(3), Fla. Stat. (2003). We discern that there is a rather fine distinction between what is transmitted as an electronic communication subject to interception and the storage of what has been previously communicated. It is here that we tread upon new ground. Because we have found no precedent rendered by the Florida courts that considers this distinction, and in light of the fact that the Act was modeled after the Federal Wiretap Act, we advert to decisions by the federal courts that have addressed this issue for guidance.

The federal courts have consistently held that electronic communications, in order to be intercepted, must be acquired contemporaneously with transmission and that electronic communications are not intercepted within the meaning of the Federal Wiretap Act if they are retrieved from storage. United States v. Steiger, 318 F.3d 1039 (11th Cir.), ... [T]he particular facts and circumstances of the instant case reveal that the electronic communications were intercepted contemporaneously with transmission.

The Spector spyware program that the Wife surreptitiously installed on the computer used by the Husband intercepted and copied the electronic communications as they were transmitted. We believe that particular method constitutes interception within the meaning of the Florida Act, and the decision in *Steiger* supports this conclusion. In *Steiger*, an individual was able to hack into the defendant's computer via a Trojan horse virus that allowed the hacker access to pornographic materials stored on the hard drive. The hacker was successful in transferring the pornographic material from that computer to the hacker's computer. The court held that because the Trojan horse virus simply copied information that had previously been stored on the computer's hard drive, the capture of the electronic communication was not an interception within the meaning of the Federal Wiretap Act. The court did indicate, however, that interception could occur if the virus or software intercepted the communication as it was being transmitted and copied it. The court stated:

> [T]here is only a narrow window during which an E-mail interception may occur – the seconds or mili-seconds before which a newly composed message is saved to any temporary location following a send command. Therefore, unless some type of automatic routing software is used (for example, a duplicate of all of an employee's messages are automatically sent to the employee's boss), interception of E-mail within the prohibition of [the Wiretap Act] is virtually impossible.

Steiger, 318 F.3d at 1050 (quoting Jarrod J. White, *E-Mail@Work.com: Employer Monitoring of Employee E-Mail*, 48 Ala. L.Rev. 1079, 1083 (1997)). Hence, a valid distinction exists between a spyware program similar to that in *Steiger*, which simply breaks into a computer and retrieves information already stored on the hard drive, and a spyware program similar to the one installed by the Wife in the instant case, which copies the communication as it is transmitted and routes the copy to a storage file in the computer.

The Wife argues that the communications were in fact stored before acquisition because once the text image became visible on the screen, the communication was no longer in transit and, therefore, not subject to intercept. We disagree. We do not believe that this evanescent time period is sufficient to transform acquisition of the communications from a contemporaneous interception to retrieval from electronic storage. We conclude that because the spyware installed by the Wife intercepted the electronic communication contemporaneously with transmission, copied it, and routed the copy to a file in the computer's hard drive, the electronic communications were intercepted in violation of the Florida Act.

We must next determine whether the improperly intercepted electronic communications may be excluded from evidence under the Act. The exclusionary provisions of the Act are found in section 934.06, Florida Statutes (2003), which provides that "[w]henever any wire or oral communication has been intercepted, no part of the contents of such communication and no evidence derived therefrom may be received in evidence. . . ." Conspicuously absent from the provisions of this statute is any reference to electronic communications. The federal courts, which interpreted an identical statute contained in the Federal Wiretap Act, have held that because provision is not made for exclusion of intercepted electronic communications, Congress intended that such communications not be excluded under the Federal Wiretap Act. *See Steiger.* We agree with this reasoning and conclude that the intercepted electronic communications in the instant case are not excludable under the Act. But this does not end the inquiry.

Although not specifically excludable under the Act, it is illegal and punishable as a crime under the Act to intercept electronic communications. § 934.03, Fla. Stat. (2003). The trial court found that the electronic communications were illegally intercepted in violation of the Act and ordered that they not be admitted in evidence. Generally, the admission of evidence is a matter within the sound discretion of the trial court. Because the evidence was illegally obtained, we conclude that the trial court did not abuse its discretion in refusing to admit it.

QUESTIONS

1. *O'Brien* is a civil suit between two private parties. How does the Florida criminal wiretapping statute enter into it?

2. The Wiretap Act includes a prohibition on the manufacture or sale in interstate commerce of "any electronic, mechanical, or other device ... primarily useful for the purpose of the surreptitious interception of wire, oral, or electronic communications." 18 U.S.C. § 2512(1)(a). What does this prohibition add to the prohibition on wiretapping itself? Is Spector such a device?

3. Email works by successively copying the entire message from one computer to another until it reaches its destination. Once it has been copied to the final computer, a program called a "mail delivery agent" (MDA) makes one last copy, adding the email to a particular user's inbox file, which her own email program can then read. Consider:

    > Umberto Causabon, a rare-book dealer, runs a small email service that gives accounts to other rare book dealers. He configures the MDA on his server to scan each incoming email. If the email contains the word "book, " the MDA saves a copy of the email in Causabon's account as well as copying it to the user's inbox file. Neither Causabon nor any other person has ever examined the copies made this way.

    Has Causabon violated the Wiretap Act?

STORED COMMUNICATIONS ACT
Title 18, United States Code

§ 2701 – *Unlawful access to stored communications*

(a) *OFFENSE.* – Except as provided in subsection (c) of this section whoever –

    (1) intentionally accesses without authorization a facility through which an electronic communication service is provided; or

    (2) intentionally exceeds an authorization to access that facility;

and thereby obtains, alters, or prevents authorized access to a wire or electronic communication while it is in electronic storage in such system shall be punished as provided in subsection (b) of this section. ...

(c) *EXCEPTIONS.* – Subsection (a) of this section does not apply with respect to conduct authorized –

    (1) by the person or entity providing a wire or electronic communications service;

    (2) by a user of that service with respect to a communication of or intended for that user; or

    (3) in section 2703, 2704 or 2518 of this title.

§ 2702 – *Voluntary disclosure of customer communications or records*

(a) *PROHIBITIONS.* – Except as provided in subsection (b) or (c) –

    (1) a person or entity providing an electronic communication service to the public shall not knowingly divulge to any person or entity the contents of a communication while in electronic storage by that service;

    ...

(3) a provider of ... electronic communication service to the public shall not knowingly divulge a record or other information pertaining to a subscriber to or customer of such service (not including the contents of communications covered by paragraph (1) ...) to any governmental entity.

(b) *EXCEPTIONS FOR DISCLOSURE OF COMMUNICATIONS.* – A provider described in subsection (a) may divulge the contents of a communication –

(1) to an addressee or intended recipient of such communication or an agent of such addressee or intended recipient;

(2) as otherwise authorized in section 2517, 2511 (2)(a), or 2703 of this title;

(3) with the lawful consent of the originator or an addressee or intended recipient of such communication ... ;

(4) to a person employed or authorized or whose facilities are used to forward such communication to its destination;

(5) as may be necessarily incident to the rendition of the service or to the protection of the rights or property of the provider of that service; ...

(7) to a law enforcement agency –

(A) if the contents –

(i) were inadvertently obtained by the service provider; and

(ii) appear to pertain to the commission of a crime; or

(8) to a governmental entity, if the provider, in good faith, believes that an emergency involving danger of death or serious physical injury to any person requires disclosure without delay of communications relating to the emergency.

(c) *EXCEPTIONS FOR DISCLOSURE OF CUSTOMER RECORDS.* – A provider described in subsection (a) may divulge a record or other information pertaining to a subscriber to or customer of such service... –

(1) as otherwise authorized in section 2703;

(2) with the lawful consent of the customer or subscriber;

(3) as may be necessarily incident to the rendition of the service or to the protection of the rights or property of the provider of that service;

(4) to a governmental entity, if the provider, in good faith, believes that an emergency involving danger of death or serious physical injury to any person requires disclosure without delay of information relating to the emergency; ... or

(6) to any person other than a governmental entity.

§ 2703 – *Required disclosure of customer communications or records*

(a) *CONTENTS OF WIRE OR ELECTRONIC COMMUNICATIONS IN ELECTRONIC STORAGE.* – A governmental entity may require the disclosure by a provider of electronic communication service of the contents of a wire or electronic communication, that is in electronic storage in an electronic communications system for one hundred and eighty days or less, only pursuant to a warrant issued using the procedures described in the Federal Rules of Criminal Procedure by a court with jurisdiction over the offense under investigation or equivalent State warrant. A governmental entity may require the disclosure by a provider of electronic communications services of the contents of a wire or electronic communication that has been in electronic storage in an electronic communications system for more than one hundred and eighty days by the means available under subsection (b) of this section.

(b) *CONTENTS OF WIRE OR ELECTRONIC COMMUNICATIONS* [stored with an electronic communication service]. –

    (1) A governmental entity may require a provider of [electronic communication service] to disclose the contents of any wire or electronic communication [held in electronic storage for more than 180 days] –

        (A) without required notice to the subscriber or customer, if the governmental entity obtains a warrant issued using the procedures described in the Federal Rules of Criminal Procedure by a court with jurisdiction over the offense under investigation or equivalent State warrant; or

        (B) with prior notice from the governmental entity to the subscriber or customer if the governmental entity –

            (i) uses an administrative subpoena authorized by a Federal or State statute or a Federal or State grand jury or trial subpoena; or

            (ii) obtains a court order for such disclosure under subsection (d) of this section;

        except that delayed notice may be given pursuant to section 2705 of this title. ...

(c) *RECORDS CONCERNING ELECTRONIC COMMUNICATION SERVICE*. –

    (1) A governmental entity may require a provider of electronic communication service ... to disclose a record or other information pertaining to a subscriber to or customer of such service (not including the contents of communications) only when the governmental entity –

        (A) obtains a warrant issued using the procedures described in the Federal Rules of Criminal Procedure by a court with jurisdiction over the offense under investigation or equivalent State warrant;

        (B) obtains a court order for such disclosure under subsection (d) of this section;

        (C) has the consent of the subscriber or customer to such disclosure; ... or

        (E) seeks information under paragraph (2).

    (2) A provider of electronic communication service ... shall disclose to a governmental entity the –

        (A) name;

        (B) address;

        (C) local and long distance telephone connection records, or records of session times and durations;

        (D) length of service (including start date) and types of service utilized;

(E) telephone or instrument number or other subscriber number or identity, including any temporarily assigned network address; and

(F) means and source of payment for such service (including any credit card or bank account number)

of a subscriber to or customer of such service when the governmental entity uses an administrative subpoena authorized by a Federal or State statute or a Federal or State grand jury or trial subpoena or any means available under paragraph (1).

(3) A governmental entity receiving records or information under this subsection is not required to provide notice to a subscriber or customer.

(d) *REQUIREMENTS FOR COURT ORDER.* – A court order for disclosure under subsection (b) or (c) may be issued by any court that is a court of competent jurisdiction and shall issue only if the governmental entity offers specific and articulable facts showing that there are reasonable grounds to believe that the contents of a wire or electronic communication, or the records or other information sought, are relevant and material to an ongoing criminal investigation. In the case of a State governmental authority, such a court order shall not issue if prohibited by the law of such State. A court issuing an order pursuant to this section, on a motion made promptly by the service provider, may quash or modify such order, if the information or records requested are unusually voluminous in nature or compliance with such order otherwise would cause an undue burden on such provider.

(e) *NO CAUSE OF ACTION AGAINST A PROVIDER DISCLOSING INFORMATION UNDER THIS CHAPTER.* – No cause of action shall lie in any court against any provider of wire or electronic communication service, its officers, employees, agents, or other specified persons for providing information, facilities, or assistance in accordance with the terms of a court order, warrant, subpoena, statutory authorization, or certification under this chapter. ...

QUESTIONS

1. What is the difference between the SCA and the Wiretap Act? They have a similar structure – prohibition with exceptions – but different coverage. Explain.

2. Start with the portions of the SCA that govern access to communications themselves. (The provisions that govern access to "subscriber information" are discussed in the next section.) There are actually two of them, in §§ 2701(a) and 2702(a)(1). What is the difference between them? Do these sections prohibit actions by private parties, by the government, or by both? And do these sections make Gmail illegal? After all, doesn't it "access" stored emails all the time?

3. The SCA's strong protections for stored communications are subject to a great many exceptions. Read the exceptions in §§ 2701(c) and 2702(b). Which situations do they apply to? For whose benefit were they drafted? Which ones do you think are the most important and most frequently used in practice? Are they broader or narrower than the exceptions under the Wiretap Act?

4. The SCA also includes provisions that allow the police to require the disclosure of stored communications under certain circumstances. Where are they? What showing must the police make? Under what circumstances can the government gain access to stored electronic communications with less than a full search warrant? Can private parties avail themselves of this required disclosure procedure?

5. Refer back to *United States v. Warshak, supra.* After *Warshak*, which portions of § 2703 are unconstitutional? What must the government do if it seeks email content held by Yahoo! Mail? How much of a difference is this likely to make in a typical investigation?

6. The SCA does not have a suppression remedy: evidence obtained in violation of it can still be used in court. Would a suppression remedy be a good idea?

7. The SCA's implications for criminal prosecutions are obvious. What does it do to the discovery process in civil litigation? Suppose you represent the defendant in a personal-injury suit and you suspect that the plaintiff's emails to a friend discussing a recent vacation will demonstrate that her injuries are less severe than she claims. What will happen if you send a subpoena to her email provider?

EHLING V. MONMOUTH-OCEAN HOSPITAL SERVICE CORP.

872 F. Supp. 2d 369 (D.N.J. 2012)

Martini, District Judge:

Plaintiff Deborah Ehling filed this action against Monmouth–Ocean Hospital Service Corp. ("MONOC"), Vincent Robbins, and Stacy Quagliana (collectively "Defendants"). This matter comes before the Court on Defendants' motion for summary judgment ...

I. BACKGROUND

Plaintiff Deborah Ehling is a registered nurse and paramedic. Defendant MONOC is a non-profit hospital service corporation dedicated to providing emergency medical services to the citizens of the State of New Jersey. Defendant Vincent Robbins is the President and CEO of MONOC. Defendant Stacy Quagliana is the Executive Director of Administration at MONOC.

Plaintiff was hired by MONOC in 2004 as a registered nurse and paramedic. ...

A. The Facebook Incident ...

During the 2008–2009 timeframe, Plaintiff maintained a Facebook account and had approximately 300 Facebook friends. Plaintiff selected privacy settings for her account that limited access to her Facebook wall to only her Facebook friends. Plaintiff did not add any MONOC managers as Facebook friends. However, Plaintiff added many of her MONOC coworkers as friends, including a paramedic named Tim Ronco. Plaintiff posted on Ronco's Facebook wall, and Ronco had access to Plaintiff's Facebook wall. Unbeknownst to Plaintiff, Ronco was taking screenshots of Plaintiff's Facebook wall and printing them or emailing them to MONOC manager Andrew Caruso. Ronco and Caruso became friends while working together at a previous job, but Ronco never worked in Caruso's division at MONOC. The evidence reflects that Ronco independently came up with the idea to provide Plaintiff's Facebook posts to Caruso. Caruso never asked Ronco for any information about Plaintiff, and never requested that Ronco keep him apprised of

Plaintiff's Facebook activity. In fact, Caruso was surprised that Ronco showed him Plaintiff's Facebook posts. Caruso never had the password to Ronco's Facebook account, Plaintiff's Facebook account, or any other employee's Facebook account. Once Caruso received copies of Plaintiff's Facebook posts, he passed them on to Quagliana, MONOC's Executive Director of Administration.

On June 8, 2009, Plaintiff posted the following statement to her Facebook wall:

> An 88 yr old sociopath white supremacist opened fire in the Wash D.C. Holocaust Museum this morning and killed an innocent guard (leaving children). Other guards opened fire. The 88 yr old was shot. He survived. I blame the DC paramedics. I want to say 2 things to the DC medics. 1. WHAT WERE YOU THINKING? and 2. This was your opportunity to really make a difference! WTF!!!! And to the other guards .... go to target practice.

After MONOC management was alerted to the post, Plaintiff was temporarily suspended *with* pay, and received a memo stating that MONOC management was concerned that Plaintiff's comment reflected a "deliberate disregard for patient safety." ...

[Ehling accumulated numerous warning notices and disciplinary points for "unauthorized late swipe-outs, excessive call-outs, failing to have sufficient paid time off to cover hours not worked, refusing 9–1–1 calls, and failing to submit the proper documentation for her ambulance shifts." She was issued a notice of termination on July 22, 2011, but it was never enforced. Instead, Ehling's employment was terminated on February 7, 2012, following a dispute about her eligibility for a medical leave of absence. She filed a nine-count complaint, and the defendants moved for summary judgment.]

III. DISCUSSION

A. Count 1: Federal Stored Communications Act

In Count 1, Plaintiff asserts a claim for violation of the Federal Stored Communications Act (or "SCA"), 18 U.S.C. § § 2701–11. Plaintiff argues that Defendants violated the SCA by improperly accessing her Facebook wall post about the museum shooting. Plaintiff argues that her Facebook wall posts are covered by the SCA because she selected privacy settings limiting access to her Facebook page to her Facebook friends. Defendants disagree and argue that, even if the SCA applies, the facts in this case fall under one of the SCA's statutory exceptions. For the reasons set forth below, the Court finds that non-public Facebook wall posts are covered by the SCA, and that one of the exceptions to the SCA applies. The Court will address each issue in turn.

i. The SCA Covers Non–Public Facebook Wall Posts

The first issue before the Court is whether the SCA applies to Facebook wall posts. ...

Because the SCA was passed in 1986, the statute "is best understood by considering its operation and purpose in light of the technology that existed in 1986." William Jeremy Robison, *Free at What Cost?: Cloud Computing Privacy Under the Stored Communications Act,* 98 GEO. L.J. 1195, 1204 (2010). Computer networking was in its infancy in 1986. In the mid–1980s, "personal users [had just begun] subscribing to self-contained networks, such as Prodigy, CompuServe, and America Online." *Id.* After connecting to a network via a modem, users could download or send e-mail to other users, access a closed universe of content, and post messages on electronic bulletin board systems ("BBS's"). A BBS was "a computer program that simulate[d] an actual bulletin board by allowing computer users who access[ed] a particular computer to post messages" for a community of people. *United States v. Riggs*, 739 F. Supp. 414, 417 n.4 (N.D. Ill. 1990). Notably, the SCA was enacted before the advent of the World Wide Web in 1990 and before the introduction of the web browser in 1994. "Despite the rapid evolution of computer and networking technology since the SCA's adoption, its language has remained surprisingly static." *Id.* at 1196. Thus, the "task of adapting the Act's language to modern technology has fallen largely upon the courts." *Id.*

The SCA provides that whoever "(1) intentionally accesses without authorization a facility through which an electronic communication service is provided; or (2) intentionally exceeds an authorization to access that facility; and thereby obtains, alters or prevents the authorized access to a wire or electronic communication while in electronic storage in such a system" shall be liable for damages. 18 U.S.C. § 2701(a); 18 U.S.C. § 2707 (providing for civil liability under the statute). The statute further provides that "[i]t shall not be unlawful ... [to] access an electronic communication made through an electronic communication system that is configured so that such electronic communication is readily accessible to the general public." 18 U.S.C. § 2511(2)(g)(i). In other words, the SCA covers: (1) electronic communications, (2) that were transmitted via an electronic communication service, (3) that are in electronic storage, and (4) that are not public. Facebook wall posts that are configured to be private meet all four criteria.

First, Facebook wall posts are electronic communications. The SCA defines "electronic communication" as "any transfer of signs, signals, writing, images, sounds, data, or intelligence of any nature transmitted in whole or in part by a wire, radio, electromagnetic, photoelectronic or photooptical system." 18 U.S.C. § 2510(12). To create Facebook wall posts, Facebook users transmit writing, images, or other data via the Internet from their computers or mobile devices to Facebook's servers. Thus, Facebook wall posts are electronic communications.

Second, Facebook wall posts are transmitted via an electronic communication service. The SCA defines "electronic communication service" as "any service which provides to users thereof the ability to send or receive wire or electronic communications." 18 U.S.C. § 2510(15). Facebook provides its users with the ability to send and receive electronic communications, including private messages and Facebook wall posts.

Third, Facebook wall posts are in electronic storage. The SCA distinguishes between two different types of electronic storage. The first is defined as "any temporary, intermediate storage of a wire or electronic communication incidental to the electronic transmission thereof." 18 U.S.C. § 2510(17)(A). The second type of storage is defined as "any storage of such communication by an electronic communication service for purposes of backup protection of such communication." 18 U.S.C. § 2510(17)(B). Unlike email, Facebook wall posts are not held somewhere temporarily before they are delivered. Rather, the website itself is the final destination for the information. Thus, Facebook wall posts are not held in temporary, intermediate storage.

However, Facebook does store electronic communications for backup purposes. When Facebook users post information, the information is immediately saved to a Facebook server. When new posts are added, Facebook archives older posts on separate pages that are accessible, but not displayed. Because Facebook saves and archives wall posts indefinitely, the Court finds that wall posts are stored for back-up purposes. Accordingly, Facebook wall posts are in electronic storage.

Fourth, Facebook wall posts that are configured to be private are, by definition, not accessible to the general public. The touchstone of the Electronic Communications Privacy Act is that it protects private information. The language of the statute makes clear that the statute's purpose is to protect information that the communicator took steps to keep private. *See* 18 U.S.C. § 2511(2)(g)(i) (there is no protection for information that is "configured [to be] readily accessible to the general public"). Cases interpreting the SCA confirm that information is protectable as long as the communicator actively restricts the public from accessing the information. *See Viacom Int'l Inc. v. Youtube Inc.,* 253 F.R.D. 256, 265 (S.D.N.Y. 2008) (holding that SCA prevented Viacom from accessing YouTube "videos that [users] have designated as private and chosen to share only with specified recipients"); [*Crispin v. Christian Audigier Inc.,* 717 F. Supp. 2d at 965, 991 (C.D. Cal. 2010)] (finding that SCA protection for Facebook wall posts depends on plaintiff's use of privacy settings); *cf. Snow v. DirecTV, Inc.,* 450 F.3d 1314, 1321 (11th Cir. 2006) ("an express warning, on an otherwise publicly accessible webpage" is insufficient to give rise to SCA protection).

Facebook allows users to select privacy settings for their Facebook walls. Access can be limited to the user's Facebook friends, to particular groups or individuals, or to just the user. The Court finds that, when users make their Facebook wall posts inaccessible to the general public, the wall posts are "configured to be private" for purposes of the SCA. The Court notes that when it comes to privacy protection, the critical inquiry is whether Facebook users took steps to limit access to the information on their Facebook walls. Privacy protection provided by the SCA does not depend on the number of Facebook friends that a user has. "Indeed, basing a rule on the number of users who can access information would result in arbitrary line-drawing" and would be legally unworkable. *Crispin,* 717 F. Supp. 2d at 990.

At least one other court has determined that non-public Facebook wall posts are covered by the SCA, albeit in a slightly different context. In *Crispin,* the District Court for the Central District of California was asked to decide whether a third-party subpoena should be quashed under the SCA. The defendants in *Crispin* subpoenaed information located on the plaintiff's MySpace and Facebook pages, including the plaintiff's Facebook wall posts and MySpace comments. The plaintiff sought to quash the subpoena, arguing that the SCA prohibited Facebook and MySpace from disclosing the information. To determine whether the SCA applied to these communications, the court analogized a Facebook wall post to technology that existed in 1986: a posting on a BBS. A BBS could be configured to be public or private. If a BBS was configured to be private, access to the BBS was restricted to a particular community of users, and the messages posted to the BBS were only viewable by those users. The *Crispin* court recognized that there was a long line of cases finding that the SCA was intended to reach private BBS's. *Id.* at 981 (collecting cases). The court then found that there was "no basis for distinguishing between a restricted-access BBS and a user's Facebook wall or MySpace comments": both technologies allowed users to post content to a restricted group of people, but not the public at large. *Id.* at 981. The court therefore concluded that, if the plaintiff's Facebook page was configured to be private, then his wall posts were covered by the SCA. This Court agrees in all respects with the reasoning of *Crispin.*

Accordingly, the Court finds that non-public Facebook wall posts are covered by the SCA. Because Plaintiff in this case chose privacy settings that limited access to her Facebook wall to only her Facebook friends, the Court finds that Plaintiff's Facebook wall posts are covered by the SCA.

ii. The SCA's Authorized User Exception Applies in this Case

Having concluded that the SCA applies to the type of communication at issue in this case, the Court next evaluates whether either of the SCA's statutory exceptions apply. The SCA "does not apply with respect to conduct authorized (1) by the person or entity providing a wire or electronic communications service; [or] (2) by a user of that service with respect to a communication of or intended for that user." 18 U.S.C. § 2701(c); *see also Pietrylo v. Hillstone Rest. Grp.*, No. 06–5754, 2009 WL 3128420, at *2 (D.N.J. Sept. 25, 2009) ("According to the SCA, if access to [a restricted website] was authorized by a user of that service with respect to a communication of or intended for that user, there is no statutory violation"). For the reasons set forth below, the Court finds that the authorized user exception (the second exception) applies in this case.

The authorized user exception applies where (1) access to the communication was "authorized," (2) "by a user of that service," (3) "with respect to a communication ... intended for that user." 18 U.S.C. § 2701(c)(2). Access is not authorized if the "purported 'authorization' was coerced or provided under pressure." *Pietrylo*, 2009 WL 3128420, at *3. In this case, all three elements of the authorized user exception are present.

First, access to Plaintiff's Facebook wall post was "authorized." 18 U.S.C. § 2701(c)(2). The undisputed evidence establishes that Ronco voluntarily provided Plaintiff's Facebook posts to MONOC management without any coercion or pressure. Caruso testified at his deposition that Plaintiff's Facebook friend Ronco voluntarily took screenshots of Plaintiff's Facebook page and either emailed those screenshots to Caruso or printed them out for him. This information was completely unsolicited. Caruso never asked Ronco for any information about Plaintiff and never requested that Ronco keep him apprised of Plaintiff's Facebook activity; in fact, Caruso was surprised that Ronco showed him Plaintiff's Facebook postings. Caruso never had the password to Ronco's Facebook account, Plaintiff's Facebook account, or any other employee's Facebook account. ...

Second, access to Plaintiff's Facebook wall post was authorized "by a user of that service." 18 U.S.C. § 2701(c)(2). A "user" is "any person or entity who (A) uses an electronic communications service; and (B) is duly authorized by the provider of such service to engage in such use." 18 U.S.C. § 2510(13). It is undisputed that Ronco was a Facebook user: Plaintiff acknowledged that she added Ronco as a Facebook friend and posted on Ronco's Facebook wall.

Third, Plaintiff's Facebook wall post was "intended for that user." 18 U.S.C. § 2701(c)(2). Based on the privacy settings that Plaintiff selected for her Facebook page, Plaintiff's wall posts were visible to, and intended to be viewed by, Plaintiff's Facebook friends. On June 8, 2009, when Plaintiff posted the comment about the museum shooting, Ronco was one of Plaintiff's Facebook friends. Thus, the post was intended for Ronco.

In conclusion, access to Plaintiff's Facebook wall post was authorized by a Facebook user with respect to a communication intended for that user. Therefore, the authorized user exception applies and Defendants are not liable under the SCA. Accordingly, the motion for summary judgment on Count 1 is GRANTED. ...

QUESTIONS

1. *Ehling* provides a clear explanation of the SCA's ambit. But is the court's holding on the first crucial question – whether Wall posts are "in electronic storage" – convincing?

2. Does the SCA protect emails? Text messages? Skype calls taped and saved by one of the participants? Shared spreadsheets on Google Docs?

3. How much work are Facebook's privacy controls doing in this opinion? The court points to them to show both that Ehling's posts were not "readily accessible to the general public" and that access to them was "authorized." Are these holdings consistent?

4. Would the result change if Ehling testified that she misunderstood Facebook's privacy controls and had not meant to share the post in question with Ronco? What if she made the post visible only to a few family members, but Facebook's privacy settings subsequently changed so that it became visible to Ronco and her other co-workers?

PEN REGISTERS AND TRAP AND TRACE DEVICES
Title 18, United States Code

§ 3121 – *General prohibition on pen register and trap and trace device use; exception*

(a) *IN GENERAL*. – Except as provided in this section, no person may install or use a pen register or a trap and trace device without first obtaining a court order under section 3123 of this title or under the Foreign Intelligence Surveillance Act of 1978.

(b) *EXCEPTION*. – The prohibition of subsection (a) does not apply with respect to the use of a pen register or a trap and trace device by a provider of electronic or wire communication service –

    (1) relating to the operation, maintenance, and testing of a wire or electronic communication service or to the protection of the rights or property of such provider, or to the protection of users of that service from abuse of service or unlawful use of service; or

    (2) to record the fact that a wire or electronic communication was initiated or completed in order to protect such provider, another provider furnishing service toward the completion of the wire communication, or a user of that service, from fraudulent, unlawful or abusive use of service; or

    (3) where the consent of the user of that service has been obtained.

(c) *LIMITATION*. – A government agency authorized to install and use a pen register or trap and trace device under this chapter or under State law shall use technology reasonably available to it that restricts the recording or decoding of electronic or other impulses to the dialing, routing, addressing, and signaling information utilized in the processing and transmitting of wire or electronic communications so as not to include the contents of any wire or electronic communications.

(d) Penalty. – Whoever knowingly violates subsection (a) shall be fined under this title or imprisoned not more than one year, or both.

§ 3122 – *Application for an order for a pen register or a trap and trace device*

(a) *APPLICATION.* –

    (1) An attorney for the Government may make application for an order or an extension of an order under section 3123 of this title authorizing or approving the installation and use of a pen register or a trap and trace device under this chapter, in writing under oath or equivalent affirmation, to a court of competent jurisdiction.

    (2) Unless prohibited by State law, a State investigative or law enforcement officer may make application for an order or an extension of an order under section 3123 of this title authorizing or approving the installation and use of a pen register or a trap and trace device under this chapter, in writing under oath or equivalent affirmation, to a court of competent jurisdiction of such State.

(b) *CONTENTS OF APPLICATION.* – An application under subsection (a) of this section shall include –

    (1) the identity of the attorney for the Government or the State law enforcement or investigative officer making the application and the identity of the law enforcement agency conducting the investigation; and

    (2) a certification by the applicant that the information likely to be obtained is relevant to an ongoing criminal investigation being conducted by that agency.

§ 3127 - Definitions for chapter

As used in this chapter – ...

    (3) the term "pen register" means a device or process which records or decodes dialing, routing, addressing, or signaling information transmitted by an instrument or facility from which a wire or electronic communication is transmitted, provided, however, that such information shall not include the contents of any communication, but such term does not include any device or process used by a provider or customer of a wire or electronic communication service for billing, or recording as an incident to billing, for communications services provided by such provider or any device or process used by a provider or customer of a wire communication service for cost accounting or other like purposes in the ordinary course of its business;

    (4) the term "trap and trace device" means a device or process which captures the incoming electronic or other impulses which identify the originating number or other dialing, routing, addressing, and signaling information reasonably likely to identify the source of a wire or electronic communication, provided, however, that such information shall not include the contents of any communication; ...

QUESTIONS

1.   What is a pen register? A trap and trace device? How significant is the difference, if any, between the two? The statute refers to "dialing, routing, addressing, or signaling information"; what are these for a telephone? For a home Internet connection? For a VoIP service like Skype?

2. What legal standard must the government satisfy to obtain a pen register order? How does this compare to the standard for a wiretap order? Does this standard satisfy the Fourth Amendment?

NOTE ON TECHNICAL ASSISTANCE

Sometimes the government needs help to install a wiretap, a pen register, or other surveillance device. The best way to tap a phone line, for example, is at the phone company's facilities, using its equipment. Thus, surveillance statutes generally contain provisions requiring that specified private parties provide "technical assistance" to the government. Consider, for example, the technical assistance provision of the Wiretap Act, 18 U.S.C. § 2518(4):

> An order authorizing the interception of a wire, oral, or electronic communication under this chapter shall, upon request of the applicant, direct that a provider of wire or electronic communication service, landlord, custodian or other person shall furnish the applicant forthwith all information, facilities, and technical assistance necessary to accomplish the interception unobtrusively and with a minimum of interference with the services that such service provider, landlord, custodian, or person is according the person whose communications are to be intercepted.

In *The Company v. United States*, 349 F.3d 1132 (9th Cir. 2003), the appellant operated a network for on-board navigation systems in luxury cars. The FBI obtained a § 2518 order compelling the appellant to activate the system in a particular car, turn on the microphone, and allow the FBI to listen in. The court held (over a dissent) that although § 2518 could apply to the appellant, this particular order required more than "a minimum of interference with the services" because it would disable the other functions of the navigation system.

There is a similar provision in the pen register statute, 18 U.S.C. § 3124, and you have already seen that the Stored Communications Act requires providers simply to turn over the target's communications on receipt of a proper court order. The Communications Assistance to Law Enforcement Act (CALEA) goes even further: it requires that a "telecommunications carrier" (i.e. someone who provides "the transmission or switching of wire or electronic communications as a common carrier for hire") be capable of complying with interception orders. 47 U.S.C. § 1002 So the phone company must design and operate its network so that it can provide the necessary technical assistance under Wiretap Act and pen register orders. CALEA provides, however, that it does not apply to "information services" (i.e., "generating, acquiring, storing, transforming, processing, retrieving, utilizing, or making available information via telecommunications"), so as a result only providers of physical infrastructure tend to be subject to CALEA. It also provides that "A telecommunications carrier shall not be responsible for decrypting, or ensuring the government's ability to decrypt, any communication encrypted by a subscriber or customer, unless the encryption was provided by the carrier and the carrier possesses the information necessary to decrypt the communication."

Finally, there is the All Writs Act, initially enacted as part of the Judiciary Act of 1789, gives the federal courts the power to issue "all writs necessary or appropriate in aid of their respective jurisdictions and agreeable to the usages and principles of law." 28 U.S.C. § 1651. In *United States v. New York Telephone Co.*, 434 U.S. 159 (1977), the FBI wanted to install pen registers on two suspects' telephone lines, but could only do so unobtrusively if the telephone company provided some additional wiring. The Supreme Court held that the FBI could obtain an order under the All Writs Act directing the company to do so. The Court appeared to balance three factors: the closeness of the relationship of the company to the matter being investigated, the necessity of the order, and the burden on the company.

Most recently, the technical assistance debate has come to a head in fights over smartphone encryption. The FBI attempted to compel Apple to assist in unlocking an iPhone used by Syed Farook, who killed 14 people in San Bernadino on December 2, 2015. That case was mooted when the FBI paid more than $1.3 million to a third party for software that unlocked the phone. In another case, a magistrate judge rejected an All Writs Act demand for Apple's assistance because between CALEA and the SCA (neither of which imposed such a duty on device manufacturers) there was no legislatively unforseen gap for the court to fill with the All Writs Act. *In re Apple, Inc.*, 149 F. Supp. 3d 341 (E.D.N.Y. 2016).

QUESTIONS

1. In court and in the press, Apple has made broader arguments against compelled technical assistance: that the Apple is an uninvolved party and the burden on it is excessive, that requiring it to bypass the encryption on its devices creates a "backdoor" that makes everyone's devices less secure, that requiring it to write software it disagrees with is a form of compelled speech prohibited by the First Amendment, and that compelling its engineers to write software for the government takes property without due process of law. How persuasive are these objections? If Apple has a constitutional right not to write encryption-cracking software, does Tesla have a constitutional right not to write software that makes left-turn signals?

2. How much can and should companies say when they receive surveillance orders? Many of the authorizing statutes allow the government to obtain nondisclosure orders prohibiting the company from disclosing the contents of the surveillance order? Are these orders unconstitutional restrictions on freedom of speech? Can a company subject to one publish an aggregate report listing the number and type of orders it has received for customer data in the past year? How about a so-called "warrant canary" stating, "We have not received any court orders for customer data. Watch closely for the removal of this notice."?

C. National Security

Alongside the system of law enforcement surveillance discussed above there is a vast parallel system of national-security surveillance. Although the work is carried out by a variety of intelligence agencies and their international counterparts, it centered on, and has come to be identified with, the National Security Agency (NSA). This section sketches the legal framework governing national security surveillance, and some of the ways the NSA's bulk surveillance programs complicate the story told above.

The discussion here will necessarily be incomplete, and not just because of space restrictions. The NSA is legendarily secretive. Its unofficial nickname for many years was "No Such Agency," and though it is now forthcoming about its own existence, both its activities and the legal authority it purports to act under are often highly classified. Some of the following came to light as a result of investigative journalism during the 2000s. Other information was revealed through the actions of whisteblowers, or under pressure from members of Congress concerned about the NSA's actions, particularly Oregon senator Ron Wyden.

But the real catalyst for public discussion of the NSA's surveillance programs was the extraordinary series of leaks by former NSA contractor Edward Snowden in the summer of 2013. While working as a technician on NSA information systems, he systematically downloaded thousands of documents. Snowden then reached out to investigative journalist Glenn Greenwald (then working with the British newspaper The Guardian) and began supplying Greenwald and other reporters with highly revealing slide decks, internal memoranda, legal opinions, and court orders describing the NSA's programs. Other reporters working with or inspired by Snowden have also dug into the secretive world of NSA surveillance, and further information has been released by the government in response to their efforts – but much still remains unknown. This section draws heavily from the December 2013 report of a five-member committee appointed by President Obama to review the NSA's surveillance programs, and from opinions issued by the Foreign Intelligence Surveillance Court in response to applications from the NSA and other law-enforcement and security agencies. But keep in mind that even these documents tell only part of the story.

The NSA is officially charged with "signals intelligence" – collecting information about the communications of the enemies of the United States, while safeguarding the United States's own communications. Following World War II, military codebreaking operations were ultimately centralized in the NSA by President Truman in 1952. As electronic communications have grown in importance, so has the NSA's role in intercepting them.

Modern oversight of the NSA dates to 1975, when the Senate formed a committee to study United States intelligence operations. The committee, known as the "Church Committee" after its chairman, Frank Church, produced a series of fourteen reports on widespread abuses by the intelligence agencies. In a project codenamed MINARET, the NSA intercepted and monitored the contents of the communications of Americans, including Martin Luther King. Jr. and critics of the Vietnam war, without judicial oversight. And in a project codenamed SHAMROCK, the NSA collected all telegrams entering and leaving the United States, passing many of them along to other agencies. Congressional concern about these and other programs resulted in the passage of the Foreign Intelligence Surveillance Act of 1978, or FISA.

PRESIDENT'S REVIEW GROUP ON INTELLIGENCE
AND COMMUNICATIONS TECHNOLOGIES
LIBERTY AND SECURITY IN A CHANGING WORLD
Report and Recommendations (2013)

CHAPTER II: LESSONS OF HISTORY ...

B. The Legal Framework as of September 11, 2001 ...

FISA attempted to safeguard the nation against the kinds of abuses that had been documented by the Church Committee, while at the same time preserving the nation's ability to protect itself against external threats. FISA was a carefully designed compromise between those who wanted to preserve maximum flexibility for the intelligence agencies and those who wanted to place foreign intelligence surveillance under essentially the same restrictions as ordinary surveillance activities (at least insofar as the rights of Americans were concerned).

To that end, FISA brought foreign intelligence surveillance within a legal regime involving strict rules and structured oversight by all three branches of the government, but also granted the government greater freedom in the realm of foreign intelligence surveillance than it had in the context of others types of surveillance.

FISA restricted the government's authority to use electronic surveillance *inside the United States* to obtain foreign intelligence from "foreign powers." The term "foreign powers" was defined to include not only foreign nations, but also the agents of foreign nations and any "group engaged in international terrorism." FISA established the Foreign Intelligence Surveillance Court (FISC), consisting of seven (now eleven) federal judges appointed by the Chief Justice of the United States to serve staggered terms on the FISC. FISA provided that any government agency seeking to use electronic surveillance for foreign intelligence purposes inside the United States had to obtain a warrant from the FISC. For such a warrant to be issued, the government had to show "probable cause to believe that the target of the electronic surveillance" is an agent of a foreign power.

It is important to note several significant elements to this approach. First, by requiring the government to obtain a warrant from the FISC, FISA denied the President the previously assumed authority to engage in foreign intelligence surveillance inside the United States without judicial supervision. This was a major innovation.

Second, Congress created the FISC so it could deal with classified information and programs involved in foreign intelligence surveillance. Ordinary federal courts lacked the facilities and clearances to deal with such matters. A special court was therefore necessary if such classified matters were to be brought under the rule of law.

Third, FISA did not deal with the President's authority to engage in foreign intelligence activities *outside the United States*. FISA did not require the government to obtain a FISA warrant from the FISC before it could legally wiretap a telephone conversation between two Russians in Moscow or between a US citizen in France and a US citizen in England. In such circumstances, FISA left the issue, as in the past, to the Executive Branch, operating under the National Security Act of 1947, the National Security Agency Act of 1959, and the US Constitution.

Fourth, FISA did not limit the government's use of electronic surveillance in the foreign intelligence context to those situations in which the government has probable cause to believe that criminal activity is afoot. Rather, FISA permitted the government to engage in electronic surveillance in the United States to obtain foreign intelligence information as long as the government can establish to the satisfaction of the FISC that it has probable cause to believe that the "target" of the surveillance is an "agent of a foreign power."

These features of the system established by FISA reflect Congress' understanding at the time of the central differences between electronic surveillance for foreign intelligence purposes and electronic surveillance for traditional criminal investigation purposes. But in light of past abuses, the possibility of politicization, and the decision to authorize foreign intelligence surveillance of individuals, including American citizens, for whom there is no probable cause to suspect criminal conduct, FISA instituted a broad range of safeguards to prevent misuse of this authority.

For example, FISA requires the Attorney General to approve all applications for FISA warrants; it requires the Attorney General to report to the House and Senate

Intelligence Committees every six months on the FISA process and the results of FISA-authorized surveillance; it requires the Attorney General to make an annual report to Congress and the public about the total number of applications made for FISA warrants and the total number of applications granted, modified, or denied; and it expressly provides that no United States citizen or legal resident of the United States may be targeted for surveillance under FISA "solely upon the basis of activities protected by the first amendment to the Constitution of the United States." Finally, FISA requires the use of "minimization" procedures to protect the privacy rights of individuals who are not themselves "targets" of FISA surveillance but whose conversations or personal information are *incidentally* picked up in the course of electronic surveillance of legitimate targets under the Act.

FISA changed only modestly from 1978 until the events of September 11, 2001. Although FISA originally applied only to electronic surveillance, Congress gradually widened its scope to other methods of investigation. In 1995, it was extended to physical searches; in 1998, it was extended to pen register and trap-and-trace orders (which enable the government to obtain lists of the telephone numbers and e-mails contacted by an individual after the issuance of the order); and in that same year it was extended to permit access to limited forms of business records, including documents kept by common carriers, public accommodation facilities, storage facilities, and vehicle rental facilities. ...

FISA is not the only legal authority governing foreign intelligence activities. Other statutes and Executive Orders address other facets of the operations of the Intelligence Community. The National Security Act and other laws relating to specific agencies, such as the Central Intelligence Agency Act and the National Security Agency Act, regulate what agencies can do, and the Intelligence Community is also governed by laws such as the Privacy Act and the Electronic Communications Privacy Act.

Executive Order 12333 is the principal Executive Branch authority for foreign intelligence activities *not governed by FISA*. Executive Order 12333 specifies the missions and authorities of each element of the Intelligence Community; sets forth the principles designed to strike an appropriate balance between the acquisition of information and the protection of personal privacy; and governs the collection, retention, and dissemination of information about United States Persons (American citizens and non-citizens who are legal residents of the United States).

Executive Order 12333 authorizes the Attorney General to promulgate guidelines requiring each element of the Intelligence Community to have in place procedures prescribing how it can collect, retain, and disseminate information about US persons. The guidelines define each agency's authorities and responsibilities. With respect to National Security Agency (NSA), for example, Executive Order 12333 designates NSA as the manager for Signals Intelligence (SIGINT) for the Intelligence Community, and the Attorney General's Guidelines define how SIGINT may be conducted for collection activities not governed by FISA.

Section 2.4 of Executive Order 12333 prohibits specific elements of the Intelligence Community from engaging in certain types of activities inside the United States. The CIA, for example, is generally prohibited from engaging in electronic surveillance, and members of the Intelligence Community other than the FBI are generally prohibited from conducting non-consensual physical searches inside the United States. ...

CHAPTER IV: REFORMING FOREIGN INTELLIGENCE SURVEILLANCE
DIRECTED AT NON- UNITED STATES PERSONS ...

B. Foreign Intelligence Surveillance and Section 702

In general, the federal government is prohibited from intercepting the contents of private telephone calls and e-mails of *any* person, except in three circumstances. First, in the context of criminal investigations, Title III of the Electronic Communications Privacy Act authorizes the government to intercept such communications if a federal judge issues a warrant based on a finding that there is probable cause to believe that an individual is committing, has committed, or is about to commit a federal crime and that communications concerning that crime will be seized as a result of the proposed interception.

Second, as enacted in 1978, FISA authorized the federal government to intercept electronic communications if a judge of the FISC issues a warrant based on a finding that the purpose of the surveillance is to obtain *foreign intelligence information*, the interception takes place *inside the United States*, and there is probable cause to believe that the target of the surveillance is an agent of a foreign power (which includes, among other things, individuals engaged in international terrorism, the international proliferation of weapons of mass destruction, and clandestine intelligence activities).

Third, there is foreign intelligence surveillance that takes place *outside the United States*. At the time FISA was enacted, Congress expressly decided not to address the issue of electronic surveillance of persons located outside the United States, including American citizens, noting that the "standards and procedures for overseas surveillance may have to be different than those provided in this bill for electronic surveillance within the United States." It was apparently assumed that intelligence collection activities outside the United States would be conducted under the Executive Branch's inherent constitutional authority and the statutory authorizations granted to each Intelligence Community agency by Congress, and that it would be governed by presidential Executive Orders and by procedures approved by the Attorney General. To that end, in 1981 President Ronald Reagan issued Executive Order 12333, discussed above, which (as amended) specifies the circumstances in which the nation's intelligence agencies can engage in foreign intelligence surveillance outside the United States.

Although Congress did not take up this issue in the immediate aftermath of the terrorist attacks of September 11, 2001, several developments brought the question to the fore. First, technological advances between 1978 and the early 21st century complicated the implementation of the original FISA rules. The distinction FISA drew between electronic surveillance conducted inside the United States and electronic surveillance conducted outside the United States worked reasonably well in 1978, because then-existing methods of communication and collection made that distinction meaningful. But the development of a global Internet communications grid with linchpins located within the United States undermined the distinction.

By the early twenty-first century, a large percentage of the world's electronic communications passed through the United States, and foreign intelligence collection against persons located outside the United States was therefore increasingly conducted with the assistance of service providers inside the United States. Unless the legislation was amended, this new state of affairs meant that the government would have to go to the FISC to obtain orders authorizing electronic surveillance for foreign intelligence purposes even of individuals who were in fact outside the

United States, a state of affairs Congress had not anticipated at the time it enacted FISA in 1978.

Second, in late 2005 it came to light that, shortly after the attacks of September 11, President George W. Bush had secretly authorized NSA to conduct foreign intelligence surveillance of individuals who were *inside* the United States without complying with FISA. Specifically, the President authorized NSA to monitor electronic communications (e.g., telephone calls and e-mails) between people inside the United States and people outside the United States whenever NSA had "a reasonable basis to conclude that one party to the communication" was affiliated with or working in support of al-Qa'ida.

Because this secret program did not require the government either to obtain a warrant from the FISC or to demonstrate that it had probable cause that the target of the surveillance was an agent of a foreign power – even when the target was inside the United States – it clearly exceeded the bounds of what Congress had authorized in FISA. The Bush administration maintained that this program was nonetheless lawful, invoking both Congress' 2001 Authorization to Use Military Force and the President's inherent constitutional authority as commander-in-chief.

In light of these developments, Congress decided to revisit FISA. In 2007, Congress amended FISA in the Protect America Act (PAA), which provided, among other things, that FISA was inapplicable to any electronic surveillance that was "directed at a person reasonably believed to be located outside the United States." In effect, the PAA excluded from the protections of FISA warrantless monitoring of international communications if the target of the surveillance was outside the United States, even if the target was an American citizen. The PAA was sharply criticized on the ground that it gave the government too much authority to target the international communications of American citizens.

The following year, Congress revised the law again in the FISA Amendments Act of 2008 (FAA). The FAA adopted different rules for international communications depending on whether the target of the surveillance was a "*United States person*" (a category that was defined to include both American citizens and non-citizens who are legal permanent residents of the United States) or a "*non-United States person*." The FAA provides that if the government targets a United States person who is outside the United States, the surveillance must satisfy the traditional requirements of FISA. That is, the surveillance is permissible only if it is intended to acquire foreign intelligence information and the FISC issues a warrant based on a finding that there is probable cause to believe that the United States person is an agent of a foreign power, within the meaning of FISA. Thus, if the target of the surveillance is a United States person, the same FISA procedures apply – without regard to whether the target is inside or outside the United States.

On the other hand, the FAA provided in section 702 that if the target of foreign intelligence surveillance is a *non-United States person* who is "reasonably believed to be located outside the United States," the government need not have probable cause to believe that the target is an agent of a foreign power and need not obtain an individual warrant from the FISC, even if the interception takes place *inside* the United States. Rather, section 702 authorized the FISC to approve annual certifications submitted by the Attorney General and the Director of National Intelligence (DNI) that identify certain *categories* of foreign intelligence targets whose communications may be collected, subject to FISC-approved targeting and minimization procedures. The categories of targets specified by these certifications typically consist of, for example, international terrorists and individuals involved in the proliferation of weapons of mass destruction.

Under section 702, the determination of which *individuals* to target pursuant to these FISC-approved certifications is made by NSA without any additional FISC approval. In implementing this authority, NSA identifies specific "identifiers" (for example, e-mail addresses or telephone numbers) that it reasonably believes are being used by non-United States persons located outside of the United States to communicate foreign intelligence information within the scope of the approved categories (e.g., international terrorism, nuclear proliferation, and hostile cyber activities). NSA then acquires the content of telephone calls, e-mails, text messages, photographs, and other Internet traffic using those identifiers from service providers in the United States.

Illustrative identifiers might be an e-mail account used by a suspected terrorist abroad or other means used by by high-level terrorist leaders in two separate countries to pass messages. The number of identifiers for which NSA collects information under section 702 has gradually increased over time.

Section 702 requires that NSA's certifications attest that a "significant purpose" of any acquisition is to obtain foreign intelligence information (i.e. directed at international terrorism, nuclear proliferation, or hostile cyber activities), that it does not intentionally target a United States person, that it does not intentionally target any person known at the time of acquisition to be in the United States, that it does not target any person outside the United States for the purpose of targeting a person inside the United States, and that it meets the requirements of the Fourth Amendment. The annual certification provided to the FISC must attest that the Attorney General and the Director of National Intelligence have adopted guidelines to ensure compliance with these and other requirements under section 702, including that the government does not intentionally use section 702 authority to target United States persons, inside or outside the United States.135 The FISC annually reviews the targeting and minimization procedures to ensure that they satisfy all statutory and constitutional requirements.

Other significant restrictions govern the use of section 702:

- If a section 702 acquisition inadvertently obtains a communication of or concerning a United States person, section 702's minimization procedures require that any information about such a United States person must be destroyed unless there are compelling reasons to retain it, for example, if the information reveals a communications security vulnerability or an imminent threat of serious harm to life or property.

- If a target reasonably believed to be a non-United States person located outside the United States either enters the United States or is discovered to be a United States person, acquisition must immediately be terminated.

- Any information collected after a non-United States person target enters the United States must promptly be destroyed, unless it constitutes evidence of criminal conduct or has significant foreign intelligence value.

- Any information collected prior to the discovery that a target believed to be a non-United States person is in fact a United States person must be promptly destroyed, unless it constitutes evidence of criminal conduct or has significant foreign intelligence value.

- The dissemination of any information about a United States person collected during the course of a section 702 acquisition is prohibited, unless it is necessary to understand foreign intelligence or assess its importance, is evidence of criminal conduct, or indicates an imminent threat of death or serious bodily injury.

Section 702 imposes substantial reporting requirements on the government in order to enable both judicial and congressional oversight, in addition to the oversight conducted within the Executive Branch ...

Although compliance issues under section 702 have been infrequent, they have been vexing when they arise. In one instance, the FISC held that, for technical reasons concerning the manner in which the collection occurred, the minimization procedures that applied to NSA's upstream collection of electronic communications did not satisfy the requirements of either FISA or the Fourth Amendment. This was so because NSA's use of upstream collection often involves the inadvertent acquisition of multi-communication transactions (MCTs), many of which do not fall within the parameters of section 702. Judge John Bates of the FISC noted that the "government's revelations regarding the scope of NSA's upstream collection implicate 50 U.S.C. § 1809(a), which makes it a crime (1) to 'engage[] in electronic surveillance under color of law except as authorized' by statute. . . ."

Judge Bates observed that "NSA acquires more than two hundred fifty million Internet communications each year pursuant to Section 702" and that the vast majority of those communications are "not at issue here." But, he added, the upstream collection represents "approximately 9 percent of the total Internet communications being acquired by NSA under Section 702," and those acquisitions inadvertently sweep in "tens of thousands of wholly domestic communications" because they happen to be contained within an MCT that includes a targeted selector.

In such circumstances, Judge Bates noted that the "fact that NSA's technical measures cannot prevent NSA from acquiring transactions containing wholly domestic communications . . . does not render NSA's acquisition of those transactions 'unintentional.'" Judge Bates concluded that "NSA's minimization procedures, as applied to MCTs," did not meet the requirements of either FISA or the Fourth Amendment. He therefore refused to approve NSA's continuing acquisition of MCTs. Thereafter, the government substantially revised its procedures for handling MCTs, and in November 2011 Judge Bates approved the future acquisition of such communications subject to the new minimization standards. In addition, NSA took the additional step of deleting all previously acquired upstream communications.

According to NSA, section 702 "is the most significant tool in NSA collection arsenal for the detection, identification, and disruption of terrorist threats to the US and around the world." To cite just one example, collection under section 702 "was critical to the discovery and disruption" of a planned bomb attack in 2009 against the New York City subway system" and led to the arrest and conviction of Najibullah Zazi and several of his co-conspirators. ...

OTHER SURVEILLANCE PROGRAMS

Tracing the government's surveillance programs – and their legal status – is a challenging task. Any given surveillance *program* could be *collected* using multiple different techniques (e.g. secret overseas wiretaps or court orders to telecommunications companies), could be justified under multiple different legal *authorities* (e..g, Executive Order 12333 or FISA's pen-register provisions), and could be *carried out* by multiple different agencies (e.g., the NSA, the CIA, or the FBI). The details have come to light only in fragments, and existing programs have frequently been modified or placed on different legal foundations. In addition, even when some facts about a program have leaked, the government often refuses to confirm their authenticity and does its best to keep further details out of court. Here are a few of the many programs that have come to light:

- The PRISM program targets Internet communications as they pass through the United States. The NSA collects emails, videos, photos, chats, stored files, and other data from major Internet companies including Microsoft, Google, Yahoo!, Facebook, and Apple. Following the passage of the FISA Amendments Act, PRISM collection now takes place under Section 702 pursuant to directives approved by the FISC. As summarized by the Privacy and Civil Liberties Oversight Board:

  > [A]n example using a fake United States company ("USA-ISP Company") may clarify how PRISM collection works in practice: The NSA learns that John Target, a non-U.S. person located outside the United States, uses the email address "johntarget@usa-ISP.com" to communicate with associates about his efforts to engage in international terrorism. The NSA ... "tasks" johntarget@usa-ISP.com to Section 702 acquisition for the purpose of acquiring information about John Target's involvement in international terrorism. The FBI would then contact USA-ISP Company (a company that has previously been sent a Section 702 directive) and instruct USA-ISP Company to provide to the government all communications to or from email address johntarget@usa-ISP.com. The acquisition continues until the government "detasks" johntarget@usa-ISP.com.

  PRIVACY AND CIVIL LIBERTIES OVERSIGHT BOARD, REPORT ON THE SURVEILLANCE PROGRAM OPERATED PURSUANT TO SECTION 702 OF THE FOREIGN INTELLIGENCE SURVEILLANCE ACT 34 (2014).

- A variety of "upstream collection" programs collect data as it passes through telecommunications networks. Upstream collection of telephone calls are essentially wiretaps carried out in the middle of the phone network rather than at the target's phone; upstream collection of Internet traffic involves installing specialized interception devices in the facilities of Internet backbone providers. Both are carried out under Section 702 directives approved by the FISC. The information collected on Internet communications is in some ways broader:

  > Upstream collection acquires Internet transactions that are "to," "from," or "about" a tasked selector. With respect to "to" and "from" communications, the sender or a recipient is a user of a Section 702–tasked selector. This is not, however, necessarily true for an "about" communication. An "about" communication is one in which the tasked selector is referenced within the acquired Internet transaction, but the target is not necessarily a participant in the communication. If the NSA therefore applied its targeting procedures to task email address "JohnTarget@example.com," to Section 702 upstream collection, the NSA would potentially acquire communications routed through the Internet backbone that were sent from email

address JohnTarget@example.com, that were sent to JohnTar-
get@example.com, and communications that mentioned John-
Target@example.com in the body of the message. The NSA
would not, however, acquire communications simply because
they contained the name "John Target."

Id. at 37. Although upstream collection is primarily based on the compelled
assistance of United States telecommunications companies, the government
has in place several ways of carrying it out abroad, including through
partnerships between domestic and foreign telecommunications providers
and under other legal authorities.

- The MUSCULAR program intercepted communications inside Google and
  Yahoo! networks. It was conducted in collaboration with the United Kingdom intelligence agency GCHQ and involved interceptions outside of the
  United States. It took advantage of the fact that while data was encrypted
  while being sent to and from users, it was unencrypted while being sent
  from one data center to another. In response, Google and Yahoo! began encrypting their internal traffic. It is not known whether the NSA has found a
  way to continue tis surveillance.

- The NSA's Tailored Access Operations unit specializes in installing surveillance software directly on targets' networks and computers using exploits and other vulnerabilities. One of its programs, QUANTUM, allows the
  NSA to impersonate websites, delivering malware to selected users who attempt to visit those sites.

- The MYSTIC program records every telephone call to and from an unspecified foreign nation and stores them for thirty days.

- Various programs attempt to extract information from smartphone apps
  such as Angry Birds and Google Maps. NOSEY SMURF is the codename for a
  tool that turns on a phone's microphone to listen in to communications.

- All of these collection efforts feed into massive databases. Searching and
  analyzing these databases to extract patterns of interest is itself a major
  challenge. The NSA has abandoned some projects – such as an earlier program to collect Internet metadata – because of an inability to extract information with intelligence value from the masses of collected data. Programs
  like XKEYSCORE attempt to give intelligence analysts the tools to sift through
  the volumes of collected data and then to drill down and examine the communications of targets of interest in detail.

LEGAL CHALLENGES TO NSA SURVEILLANCE

The litigation over the surveillance programs is equally complex. In 2005, after
the *New York Times* revealed the existence of telephone and Internet surveillance
programs under the name of the "Terrorist Surveillance Program" (TSP), a former
AT&T technician, Mark Klein, went public with the existence of Room 641A at
AT&T's Folsom Street building in in San Francisco, where NSA upstream collection took place. Based on Klein's claims, the Electronic Frontier Foundation filed a
class-action, alleging that AT&T violated the Constitution, the Wiretap Act, the
Stored Communications Act, and other laws. The government resisted the suit,
asserting the state secrets doctrine, which applies when "the evidence will expose
military matters which, in the interest of national security, should not be divulged."
United States v. Reynolds, 345 U.S. 1, 10 (1953). The District Court allowed the

suit to proceed, *Hepting v. AT&T Corp.*, 439 F. Supp. 2d 97 (N.D. Cak. 2006), and the decision was on appeal to the Ninth Circuit when the FISA Amendments Act passed in 2008.

With more than 40 cases pending against telecommunications companies for their role in TSP, the debate in Congress over what to do with it took on a special urgency. The FISA Amendments Act as passed included a blanket retroactive immunity, effectively terminating the litigation against the companies. The *Hepting* Plaintiffs challenged Congress's authority to confer retroactive immunity, but without success. *In re National Security Agency Telecommunications Records Litigation*, 671 F.3d 881 (9th Cir. 2011).

Now, challenges were brought against the government itself. Most notably, the same day that the FISA Amendments Act created Section 702, a coalition of human-rights and media groups sued to block it, claiming it violated the First and Fourth Amendments. But the Supreme Court held they lacked standing to sue. *Clapper v. Amnesty Int'l USA*, 113 S. Ct. 1138 (2013). Section 702 and other legal authorities merely provided a framework for surveillance. Their existence did not show that any surveillance was taking place. What was publicly known about the government's actual surveillance programs was too vague and fragmentary to establish that those programs reached any particular people or communications. Thus, the plaintiffs had "no actual knowledge of the Government's ... targeting practices" but could "merely speculate and make assumptions about whether their communications with their foreign contacts will be acquired." *Id.* at 1148.

Clapper was decided in February of 2013, and seemed to sound a death knell for m anti-NSA litigation. But only a few months later, Edward Snowden upended all of that. The first stories based on the internal NSA documents he leaked were published on June 6, 2013, simultaneously by the *Guardian* and the *Washington Post*. And the first story was a blockbuster: the FISC had issued an order to Verizon Business Network Services to produce all of its call records for the period from April 25, 2013 to July 19, 2013. That was a game-changer, because it established the factual predicate of likely surveillance that had been missing in *Clapper*. Lawsuits followed, and some plaintiffs now had standing. *See Wikimedia Foundation v. NSA*, 857 F.3d 193 (4th Cir. 2017); *Schuchardt v. President of the United States*, 839 F.3d 336 (3d Cir. 2016). But in *United States v. Mohamud*, 843 F.3d 420 (9th Cir. 2016), the Ninth Circuit held that section 702 surveillance was constitutional, and so was the use of evidence thereby obtained in the criminal prosecution of the defendant. There, the government's section 702 surveillance targeted a non-U.S. person located outside the United States, and Mohamud's emails with that person were collected incident to that surveillance. The court was unconcerned with the greater scope of section 702 surveillance as compared with more traditional methods. Litigation over NSA surveillance programs continues.

QUESTIONS

1. Which of the following should the NSA attempt to wiretap:

    *   Ayman al-Zawahiri, the leader of al Qaeda?
    *   Vladimir Putin, the president of Russia?
    *   Angela Merkel, the chancellor of Germany?
    *   Rand Paul, senator from Kentucky and potential presidential candidate?
    *   Drug gang leaders in the United States?

- Drug gang leaders in Mexico?
- Executives of major Chinese electronics firms?

2. Intelligence acquisition is a complicated business. Some wiretaps require the cooperation of companies in the United States and abroad. Others are carried out surreptitiously (and sometimes illegally according to other countries' laws) by breaking into facilities or through wireless surveillance. (For example, the NSA has tapped the internal networks of major Internet companies like Google.) Still others require creating software to break into the computers of intelligence targets. What kind of rules should govern *how* the NSA intercepts communications?

3. In addition to its offensive mission of conducting surveillance on foreign targets, the NSA has a defensive mission of protecting American targets from foreign surveillance. It advises other agencies on network security, and it provides input into private-sector cryptographic standard-setting. Some have alleged that this dual mission creates a conflict of interest and that the two missions should be separated into different agencies. Do you agree?

4. If the NSA has detailed records stored anyway, should the FBI, DEA, and other law-enforcement agencies be able to use them in criminal investigations? Should criminal defendants be able to obtain them in discovery – for example, to establish an alibi at the time of the crime?

ZIPPER PROBLEM

Senator Bernard Abbott (R-TX) has become concerned about the balance of power in the cryptography world. He is afraid that criminals, terrorists, and foreign powers can too easily spy on Americans' communications – and that they're also using encryption to keep their own nefarious plans hidden. Accordingly, he is preparing legislation to standardize American cryptography. His bill would:

1. Require all telephones (land-line and cellular) and Internet connections in the U.S. to be built with a new, standard encryption technology called Zipper. Devices using Zipper would have unique ID numbers; whenever two Zipper devices establish a connection, they will use their unique IDs to negotiate a secret key to encrypt their communications. The two Zipper devices will be able to turn the encrypted message back into intelligible sounds, images, text or whatever, but anyone eavesdropping on the connection will see only random 1s and 0s.[*]

2. Well, *almost* anyone. The U.S. government will manage a "key escrow database" that contains a second secret key for each unique Zipper ID number. Zipper will be designed in such a way that the government, using the second secret key, can *also* decrypt the communications. This database will be kept secure; a court order will be needed to allow law enforcement to look up the secret key for any given Zipper device.

3. In order to keep the system from breaking down, it will also be necessary to restrict the use of non-Zipper cryptography. Accordingly, after the imple-

---

[*] Yes, this actually works! The basic idea is a technique by the name of "Diffie-Hellman key exchange"; the math behind it is simple but a little mind-blowing. Its inventors, as the name suggests, are the same guys who invented public-key cryptography. An accessible video explanation of the technique is available at https://www.youtube.com/watch?v=3QnD2c4Xovk.

mentation of Zipper, it will be illegal to encrypt communications using any other method.

You are on the legal staff of SETEC, a non-profit advocacy group whose mission is to "keep the Internet open, free, and safe." You have just learned about Senator Abbott's proposal. You are flying to Washington for a meeting with the Senator's staff tomorrow. Is the bill a good idea? Should you support it, oppose it, or push for modifications? What arguments will you make to the Senator's staff, and how do you expect them to respond?

D. Anonymity

Our next topic has to do not with the *contents* of online communications, but rather with the *identity* of individuals using the Internet. The materials in this section consider what legal tests apply when one Internet user seeks to learn the real-life identity of another.

A short review of some of the technical aspects of Internet identity may be helpful. To communicate on the Internet, you need at the very least an IP address – and that address can then be used as a crucial link in identifying you. IP addresses are assigned to ISPs in blocks; ISPs generally keep records of which IP addresses they assigned to which subscribers and when.

To be sure, it is often possible to forge your IP address when sending messages. But then anyone trying to respond to your message will send their response to the wrong address. Thus, forged IP addresses are nearly useless for any interactive protocol – including, for example, HTTP for web browsing. The biggest use of forged IP addresses is in committing denial of service attacks: if your only goal is to overload a target computer, you don't particularly care what it has to say in response.

There are other, more robust ways to communicate while obscuring your IP address from the computer you are trying to reach. They all require giving your IP address to an intermediary – here called a *proxy* – that forwards your packets on to the destination, listing its own IP address as the place to send responses. The proxy stands between the two endpoints; each talks only to the proxy, rather than directly to the other. Particularly if your traffic is encrypted on its way to the proxy (as it is on a "virtual private network" or "VPN"), this is good enough for many purposes. The BBC, for example, makes its shows available online, but only to viewers inside the United Kingdom, so American fans of the BBC have been known to use proxies that make it appear they are inside the U.K.

Proxies, however, require that the user trust the proxy at least with her IP address. For some, this is too much trust. More sophisticated systems will bounce messages through multiple proxies, so that anyone trying to track down a user must work through all of the proxies. At the highest level of security, *onion routing* systems like Tor separately encrypt each layer of the communication: each proxy except the last knows only that it is somewhere in the middle of a chain, and has no idea of the contents of the message. But even these systems don't guarantee anonymity. In December 2013, Harvard University received a bomb threat during final exams; the threat was emailed by a Tor user. Rather than trying to trace him back one hop at a time (through many potentially uncooperative nodes), Harvard checked its own network records and found that exactly one student had been us-

ing Tor at the relevant time. When questioned by an FBI agent, the student con-
fessed.

IP addresses are hardly the only digital identifiers at work online. Email addresses are an obvious example; so are usernames. Cookies (discussed below in the
next section) identify a web user's browser uniquely over time; it is also possible to
use other details, such as the list of fonts a user has installed, to uniquely finger
print a particular web user's browser. Cell phones and other mobile devices have
unique hardware identifiers, as do the SIM cards they use to connect to a cellular
network. And any device communicating on an Ethernet or Wi-Fi network has a
unique "media access control" address, commonly known as a MAC address. But
because these are local rather than global networks, it is technically easy to change
one's MAC address with few untoward consequences.

STORED COMMUNICATIONS ACT

[Refer back to the SCA excerpts, *supra*.]

QUESTIONS

1. The basic rule on voluntarily disclosing the identity of a user is set forth in
   18 U.S.C. § 2702(a)(3). Suppose that you work for Hotmail. You have just
   received a letter from the NYPD requesting the real name, address, and any
   other relevant contact information of the user with the email address
   "ThinBlueLiar@hotmail.com." How should you respond? Why? What if the
   letter came from the Whole Foods Market corporation instead?

2. A second rule in § 2703 deals with *required* disclosures. If you work for the
   NYPD and you want to compel Hotmail to disclose the subscriber informa-
   tion for ThinBlueLiar, can you, and if so, how? What if you work for Whole
   Foods Market?

JUKT MICRONICS PROBLEM

You are an Assistant U.S. Attorney assigned to help the FBI investigate a computer
intrusion at Jukt Micronics, which designs and manufactures circuit boards for
high-performance scientific computing in physics and chemistry labs. Recently,
someone has managed to gain access to – and overwrite – a file containing the pro-
totype design for the JK-478, the company's next big project. The file was replaced
with a pornographic picture which was captioned, "THE BIG BAD BIONIC BOY
HAS BEEN HERE BABY."

This morning, the firm's CEO received an email from eatmyjukt@hiert.com.
Hiert.com is an ad-supported web email system: users don't need to supply anything more than a desired username and password to create an account. The
email's author, "Ian," claimed to be responsible for the computer intrusion and to
have the original file in his possession. He demanded $250 million for its return.
The number is obviously outrageous – Jukt's entire annual revenues are only about
$40 million. You and your FBI contact are starting to suspect you're dealing with a
talented (and possibly underage) amateur.

Leaving aside other possible investigative avenues, how should you attempt to
turn "eatmyjukt" into an actual name and address so that the FBI can ask "Ian"
some questions? How likely is this process to succeed? What could go wrong? Your
strategy should consider both the technical and legal aspects of the problem.
(*Hint*: The technical part will take more than one step. The legal part is straight-

forward, if you do things right. Refer back to the Stored Communications Act, *supra*, as needed.)

DOE I V. INDIVIDUALS, WHOSE TRUE NAMES ARE UNKNOWN*
561 F. Supp. 2d 249 (D. Conn. 2008)

Droney, District Judge:

On February 1, 2008, the plaintiffs, Jane Doe I and Jane Doe II (the "Does") issued a subpoena *duces tecum*† to SBC Internet Services, Inc., now known as AT&T Internet Services ("AT&T"), the internet service provider, for information relating to the identity of the person assigned to the Internet Protocol ("IP") address from which an individual using the pseudonym "AK47" posted comments on a website. The individual whose internet account is associated with the IP address at issue, referring to himself as John Doe 21,[1] has moved to quash that subpoena. John Doe 21 has also moved for permission to proceed anonymously in this matter.

I. BACKGROUND

This action was brought by Doe I and Doe II, both female students at Yale Law School, against unknown individuals using thirty-nine different pseudonymous names to post on a law school admissions website named AutoAdmit.com ("Auto-Admit"). The plaintiffs allege that they were the targets of defamatory, threatening, and harassing statements posted on AutoAdmit from 2005 to 2007.

AutoAdmit is an internet discussion board on which participants post and review comments and information about undergraduate colleges, graduate schools, and law schools. It draws between 800,000 and one million visitors per month. Anyone who can access the internet can access AutoAdmit and view the messages posted on its discussion boards. Individuals who register with AutoAdmit, which can be done under real or assumed names, may post new messages and respond to the messages of other registered users. When a participant posts a new message, any further comments or responses to that message are collected as a "thread." Messages and threads containing certain words or subject matter can be found by searching for those words using an internet search engine.

The first message about Doe II that appeared on AutoAdmit was posted on January 31, 2007, by an anonymous poster. The message linked to a photograph of Doe II and encouraged others to "Rate this HUGE breasted cheerful big tit girl from YLS." After this message was posted, dozens of additional messages about Doe II appeared in the thread. These messages contained comments on Doe II's breasts and the posters' desire to engage in sexual relations with her. Certain of the posters appeared to be Doe II's classmates at Yale Law School because of personal information they revealed. The posts regarding Doe II continued throughout the

---

* [Ed: This case involves allegations of online harassment and threats of violence.]

† [Ed: A subpoena is a court order demanding that the recipient appear or produce specified documents. Subpoenas aren't subject to judicial oversight before they issue. *See* Fed. R. Civ. Proc. 45(a)(3) ("The clerk must issue a subpoena, signed but otherwise in blank, to a party who requests it. That party must complete it before service.") Instead, the proper response from the recipient of an improper subpoena is a motion to *quash* (not "squash") it.]

1 Because John Doe 21 chose a male pseudonymous name to proceed under, the Court will refer to John Doe 21 using male pronouns. This does not reflect a finding by the Court that John Doe 21 is indeed male.

winter and spring of 2007, and included statements, for example, that she fanta-
sized about being raped by her father, that she enjoyed having sex while family
members watched, that she encouraged others to punch her in the stomach while
seven months pregnant, that she had a sexually transmitted disease, that she had
abused heroin, and that a poster "hope[s] she gets raped and dies." On March 9,
2007, a poster sent an email directly to Doe II and at least one member of the Yale
Law School faculty describing the alleged criminal history of Doe II's father. This
message was also posted on AutoAdmit.

By March, nearly two hundred threads had been posted about Doe II on Auto-
Admit. It is in this context that an anonymous poster under the moniker "AK47,"
known on AutoAdmit for posting threatening and derogatory comments about
minority groups, posted a message falsely stating "Alex Atkind, Stephen Reynolds,
[Doe II], and me: GAY LOVERS."

The posting of comments regarding Doe II continued into April and May of
2007, including one message which the poster claimed had also been sent to Doe
II's future employer which recounted some of the claims made about Doe II on
AutoAdmit. On June 8, 2007, Doe II, along with Doe I, filed the complaint in the
instant action, alleging libel, invasion of privacy, negligent and intentional infliction of emotional distress, and copyright violations. Doe II's complaint described
the harm and results she experienced because of the comments about her on AutoAdmit, including treatment for severe emotional distress, interference with her
educational progress, reputational harm, and pecuniary harm.

The news of the filing of the Does' complaint quickly became a subject of discussion on AutoAdmit. AK47, for example, wrote a post concerning his opinion on
the merits of the plaintiffs' case, and wondered whether posters were "allowed to
use [Doe II's] name in thread's anymore." Subsequently, on June 17, 2007, AK47
posted the statement "Women named Jill and Doe II should be raped." On June
24, 2007, AK47 started a thread entitled "Inflicting emotional distress on cheerful
girls named [Doe II]."

On February 1, 2008, the plaintiffs issued a subpoena *duces tecum* to AT&T for
information relating to the identity of the person assigned to the IP address from
which an individual using the pseudonym "AK47" posted comments on AutoAdmit about Doe II. This subpoena was issued in accordance with this Court's order
of January 29, 2008, which granted the Does' motion to engage in limited, expedited discovery to uncover the identities of the defendants in this case. On February 7, 2008, AT&T sent a letter to the person whose internet account corre-
sponded with the IP address at issue, John Doe 21 ("Doe 21"), notifying Doe 21
that it had received a subpoena ordering it to produce certain information relating
to Doe 21's internet account. The letter stated that Doe 21 could file a motion to
quash or for a protective order before the date of production, which was February
25, 2008, and that AT&T must receive a copy of such a motion prior to that date.
Doe 21 filed the instant motion to quash on February 25, 2008, and on February
26, 2008, AT&T complied with the subpoena. On March 12, 2008, Doe 21 filed his
motion to proceed anonymously.

Because Doe 21 does not have counsel and his true identity is yet unknown to
the Court, the Court appointed pro bono counsel to represent the interests of Doe
21 at oral argument on the instant motions, which took place on May 5, 2008.

II. MOTION TO QUASH

A. Threshold Issues ...

2. Mootness

Doe II argues that the motion to quash is moot because the information sought has already been turned over to the plaintiffs by AT&T. However, the Court rejects this argument because the plaintiffs can be ordered to return the information and be prohibited from using it. *See Sony Music Entertainment Inc. v. Does 1-40*, 326 F. Supp. 2d 556, 561 (S.D.N.Y. 2004).

B. Merits of the Motion to Quash

A subpoena shall be quashed if it "requires disclosure of privileged or other protected matter and no exception or waiver applies." Fed.R.Civ.P. 45(c)(3)(A)(iii). Doe 21 moves to quash the subpoena because he claims disclosure of his identity would be a violation of his First Amendment right to engage in anonymous speech.

The First Amendment generally protects anonymous speech. ... The United States Supreme Court has also made clear that the First Amendment's protection extends to speech on the internet. ... Courts also recognize that anonymity is a particularly important component of Internet speech. "Internet anonymity facilitates the rich, diverse, and far ranging exchange of ideas[;] . . . the constitutional rights of Internet users, including the First Amendment right to speak anonymously, must be carefully safeguarded." *Doe v. 2TheMart.com Inc.*, 140 F. Supp. 2d 1088, 1092, 1097 (W.D. Wash. 2001). However, the right to speak anonymously, on the internet or otherwise, is not absolute and does not protect speech that otherwise would be unprotected. *See, e.g.,* ... *In re Subpoena Duces Tecum to America Online, Inc.*, No. 40570, 2000 WL 1210372, at *6 (Va. Cir. Ct. 2000) ("Those who suffer damages as a result of tortious or other actionable communications on the Internet should be able to seek appropriate redress by preventing the wrongdoers from hiding behind an illusory shield of purported First Amendment rights."). ...

The forgoing principles and decisions make clear that Doe 21 has a First Amendment right to anonymous Internet speech, but that the right is not absolute and must be weighed against Doe II's need for discovery to redress alleged wrongs. Courts have considered a number of factors in balancing these two competing interests. This balancing analysis ensures that the First Amendment rights of anonymous Internet speakers are not lost unnecessarily, and that plaintiffs do not use discovery to "harass, intimidate or silence critics in the public forum opportunities presented by the Internet." *Dendrite Intern. Inc. v. Doe No. 3*, 775 A.2d 756, 771 (2001). The Court will address each factor in turn.

First, the Court should consider whether the plaintiff has undertaken efforts to notify the anonymous posters that they are the subject of a subpoena and withheld action to afford the fictitiously named defendants a reasonable opportunity to file and serve opposition to the application. ... In this case, the plaintiffs have satisfied this factor by posting notice regarding the subpoenas on AutoAdmit in January of 2008, which allowed the posters ample time to respond, as evidenced by Doe 21's activity in this action.

Second, the Court should consider whether the plaintiff has identified and set forth the exact statements purportedly made by each anonymous poster that the plaintiff alleges constitutes actionable speech. ... Doe II has identified the allegedly actionable statements by AK47/Doe 21: the first such statement is "Alex Atkind, Stephen Reynolds, 255 [Doe II], and me: GAY LOVERS;" and the second such statement is "Women named Jill and Doe II should be raped." The potential liability for at least the first statement is more fully discussed below.

The Court should also consider the specificity of the discovery request and whether there is an alternative means of obtaining the information called for in the subpoena. ... Here, the subpoena sought, and AT&T provided, only the name, address, telephone number, and email address of the person believed to have posted defamatory or otherwise tortious content about Doe II on AutoAdmit, and is thus sufficiently specific. Furthermore, there are no other adequate means of obtaining the information because AT&T's subscriber data is the plaintiffs' only source regarding the identity of AK47.

Similarly, the Court should consider whether there is a central need for the subpoenaed information to advance the plaintiffs' claims. ... Here, clearly the defendant's identity is central to Doe II's pursuit of her claims against him.

Next, the Court should consider the subpoenaed party's expectation of privacy at the time the online material was posted. ... Doe 21's expectation of privacy here was minimal because AT&T's Internet Services Privacy Policy states, in pertinent part: "We may, where permitted or required by law, provide personal identifying information to third parties . . . without your consent . . . To comply with court orders, subpoenas, or other legal or regulatory requirements." Thus, Doe 21 has little expectation of privacy in using AT&T's service to engage in tortious conduct that would subject him to discovery under the federal rules.

Finally, and most importantly, the Court must consider whether the plaintiffs have made an adequate showing as to their claims against the anonymous defendant. Courts have differed on what constitutes such an adequate showing. Several courts have employed standards fairly deferential to the plaintiff, requiring that the plaintiff show a "good faith basis" to contend it may be the victim of conduct actionable in the jurisdiction where the suit was filed; ... ; or to show that there is probable cause for a claim against the anonymous defendant. ... The Court finds these standards set the threshold for disclosure too low to adequately protect the First Amendment rights of anonymous defendants, and thus declines to follow these approaches.

Other courts have required that a plaintiff show its claims can withstand a motion to dismiss. ... However, other courts have rejected this procedural label as potentially confusing because of the variations in the motion to dismiss standard in different jurisdictions. ... Similarly, but more burdensome, some courts have used a standard which required plaintiffs to show their claims could withstand a motion for summary judgment. ... The Court finds this standard to be both potentially confusing and also difficult for a plaintiff to satisfy when she has been unable to conduct any discovery at this juncture. Indeed, it would be impossible to meet this standard for any cause of action which required evidence within the control of the defendant.

Several courts have required that a plaintiff make a concrete showing as to each element of a prima facie case against the defendant. ... Under such a standard, "[w]hen there is a factual and legal basis for believing [actionable speech] has occurred, the writer's message will not be protected by the First Amendment." ... The Court finds such a standard strikes the most appropriate balance between the First Amendment rights of the defendant and the interest in the plaintiffs of pursuing their claims, ensuring that the plaintiff "is not merely seeking to harass or embarrass the speaker or stifle legitimate criticism." ...

Doe II has presented evidence constituting a concrete showing as to each element of a prima facie case of libel against Doe 21. Libel is written defamation. To establish a prima facie case of defamation under Connecticut law, the Doe II must demonstrate that: (1) Doe 21 published a defamatory statement; (2) the defamatory statement identified the plaintiff to a third person; (3) the defamatory statement was published to a third person; and (4) the plaintiffs reputation suffered injury as a result of the statement. ...

A defamatory statement is defined as a communication that tends to "harm the reputation of another as to lower him in the reputation of the community or to deter third persons from associating or dealing with him . . ." ... Doe II alleges, and has presented evidence tending to show that, AK47's statement, "Alex Atkind, Stephen Reynolds, [Doe II], and me: GAY LOVERS," is defamatory, because any discussion of Doe II's sexual behavior on the internet tends to lower her reputation in the community, particular in the case of any potential employers who might search for her name online.[7] In fact, in the similar context of slander (spoken defamation), any statement that imputes "serious sexual misconduct" to a person subjects the publisher to liability, without any need to prove the special harms required for other slanderous speech. *See* 3 RESTATEMENT (SECOND), TORTS § 574, at 195–96.

Doe II has also alleged and presented evidence that Doe 21's statement clearly identified Doe II by name and was available to a large number of third persons (peers, colleagues, potential employers), whether they were on Autoadmit for their own purposes, or searched for Doe II via a search engine. Finally, Doe II has alleged and provided evidence that her reputation did suffer injury because of this comment. In her interviews with potential employers in the Fall of 2007, Doe II felt she needed to disclose that existence of this and other such comments on AutoAdmit and explain that she had been targeted by pseudonymous online posters. In addition, this statement has contributed to difficulties in Doe II's relationships with her family, friends, and classmates at Yale Law School.

Thus, the plaintiff has shown sufficient evidence supporting a prima facie case for libel, and thus the balancing test of the plaintiff's interest in pursuing discovery in this case outweighs the defendant's First Amendment right to speak anonymously. The defendant's motion to quash is denied.

QUESTIONS

1. Note the case caption: *Doe v. Individuals.* The plaintiffs are attempting to proceed anonymously, while asking the court to reveal publicly the identities of the defendants. Is this fair? Why does each side seek to remain anonymous?

2. Doe 21 has filed a motion to quash but the subpoena was actually issued to AT&T. Why didn't AT&T move to quash? Could it have? How did Doe 21 find out about the subpoena?

---

7 Context is relevant in determining the meaning of a statement. *See* 3 RESTATEMENT (SECOND), TORTS 563, at 163. Doe 21 suggests that the context in which the statements were made also shows that they were not defamatory, because AutoAdmit is well-known as a place for inane discussion and meaningless derogatory postings, such that one would not take such a statement seriously. However, not everyone who searched for Doe II's name on the internet, or who came across the postings on AutoAdmit, would be aware of the site's alleged reputation. Thus, Doe II has put forth sufficient evidence for a prima facie case of defamation.

3. The critical question of law in *Doe v. Individuals* is the standard the court should use in deciding whether the plaintiffs have made an "adequate showing as to their claims against the anonymous defendant." Civil procedure gives us plenty of familiar standards. For example, the court could use a motion to dismiss standard, asking whether the plaintiff has pleaded all the elements of a valid cause of action. Or the court could use a summary judgment standard: the plaintiff must introduce sufficient uncontroverted evidence to prove every element of her claim. What are the advantages and disadvantages of these different tests? What standard does the court settle on?

4. Courts are usually good at fact-finding, but courts in unmasking cases are often visibly uncomfortable. Why? What's missing in a John Doe case that makes the judicial task significantly more difficult?

5. You have been retained by Liskula Cohen, a fashion model who lives in New York. Someone created a blog named "Skanks of NYC" on Google's Blogspot blog hosting service. It consists entirely of posts about Cohen, such as:

> I would have to say that the first place award for "Skankiest in NYC" would have to go to Liskula Gentile Cohen. How old is this skank? 40 something? She's a psychotic, lying, whoring, still going to clubs at her age, skank. ...
>
> Yeah she may have been hot 10 years ago, but is it really attractive to watch this old hag straddle dudes in a nightclub or lounge? Desperation seeps from her soul, if she even has one.

Your client strongly suspects that the author of the blog is someone she knows. She is not interested in litigating a full case, but she would like to find out who is responsible for this "disgusting, scurrilous trash," as she calls it. A friend of hers suggested filing a John Doe suit for defamation against the anonymous author, serving a subpoena for the author's identity on Google, and then dropping the lawsuit once the poster's identity has been revealed. Is this a good idea?

E. Consumer Privacy

Our next topic is the personal privacy issues that arise out of ordinary web use. What do websites know about you, what can they do with that information, and what information do you expose about yourself to the world?

IN RE DOUBLECLICK INC. PRIVACY LITIG.
154 F. Supp. 2d 497 (S.D.N.Y. 2001)

Buchwald, District Judge:

Plaintiffs bring this class action on behalf of themselves and all others similarly situated against defendant DoubleClick, Inc. ("defendant" or "DoubleClick") seeking injunctive and monetary relief for injuries they have suffered as a result of DoubleClick's purported illegal conduct. ...

PROCEDURAL HISTORY

This case is a multidistrict consolidated class action. The initial complaint was filed in this Court on January 31, 2000. On May 10, 2000, this Court consolidated the set of related federal class actions against DoubleClick in the Southern and

Eastern Districts of New York pursuant to Rule 42(a) of the Fed.R.Civ.P. and Local Rule 1.6 of the Southern and Eastern Districts of New York. ...

BACKGROUND

DoubleClick, a Delaware corporation, is the largest provider of Internet advertising products and services in the world. Its Internet-based advertising network of over 11,000 Web publishers has enabled DoubleClick to become the market leader in delivering online advertising. DoubleClick specializes in collecting, compiling and analyzing information about Internet users through proprietary technologies and techniques, and using it to target online advertising. DoubleClick has placed billions of advertisements on its clients' behalf and its services reach the majority of Internet users in the United States. ...

DOUBLECLICK'S TECHNOLOGY AND SERVICES

DoubleClick provides the Internet's largest advertising service. Commercial Web sites often rent-out online advertising "space" to other Web sites. In the simplest type of arrangement, the host Web site (e.g., Lycos.com) rents space on its webpages to another Web site (e.g., The-Globe.com) to place a "hotlink" banner advertisement ("banner advertisement"). When a user on the host Web site "clicks" on the banner advertisement, he is automatically connected to the advertiser's designated Web site.

DoubleClick acts as an intermediary between host Web sites and Web sites seeking to place banner advertisements. It promises client Web sites that it will place their banner advertisements in front of viewers who match their demographic target. For example, DoubleClick might try to place banner advertisements for a Web site that sells golfclubs in front of high-income people who follow golf and have a track record of making expensive online purchases. DoubleClick creates value for its customers in large part by building detailed profiles of Internet users and using them to target clients' advertisements. ...

When users visit any of these DoubleClick-affiliated Web sites, a "cookie" is placed on their hard drives. Cookies are computer programs commonly used by Web sites to store useful information such as usernames, passwords, and preferences, making it easier for users to access Web pages in an efficient manner. However, Plaintiffs allege that DoubleClick's cookies collect "information that Web users, including plaintiffs and the Class, consider to be personal and private, such as names, e-mail addresses, home and business addresses, telephone numbers, searches performed on the Internet, Web pages or sites visited on the Internet and other communications and information that users would not ordinarily expect advertisers to be able to collect." DoubleClick's cookies store this personal information on users' hard drives until DoubleClick electronically accesses the cookies and uploads the data.

How DoubleClick targets banner advertisements and utilizes cookies to collect user information is crucial to our analysis under the three statutes. Therefore, we examine both processes in greater detail.

A. Targeting Banner Advertisements

DoubleClick's advertising targeting process involves three participants and four steps. The three participants are: (1) the user; (2) the DoubleClick-affiliated Web site; (3) the DoubleClick server. For the purposes of this discussion, we assume that a DoubleClick cookie already sits on the user's computer with the identification number "# 0001."

In Step One, a user seeks to access a DoubleClick-affiliated Web site such as Lycos.com. The user's browser sends a communication to Lycos.com (technically, to Lycos.com's server) saying, in essence, "Send me your homepage." This communication may contain data submitted as part of the request, such as a query string or field information.

In Step Two, Lycos.com receives the request, processes it, and returns a communication to the user saying "Here is the Web page you requested." The communication has two parts. The first part is a copy of the Lycos.com homepage, essentially the collection article summaries, pictures and hotlinks a user sees on his screen when Lycos.com appears. The only objects missing are the banner advertisements; in their places lie blank spaces. The second part of the communication is an IP-address link to the DoubleClick server. This link instructs the user's computer to send a communication automatically to DoubleClick's server.

In Step Three, as per the IP-address instruction, the user's computer sends a communication to the DoubleClick server saying "I am cookie # 0001, send me banner advertisements to fill the blank spaces in the Lycos.com Web page." This communication contains information including the cookie identification number, the name of the DoubleClick-affiliated Web site the user requested, and the user's browsertype.

Finally, in Step Four, the DoubleClick server identifies the user's profile by the cookie identification number and runs a complex set of algorithms based, in part, on the user's profile, to determine which advertisements it will present to the user. It then sends a communication to the user with banner advertisements saying "Here are the targeted banner advertisements for the Lycos.com homepage." Meanwhile, it also updates the user's profile with the information from the request.

DoubleClick's targeted advertising process is invisible to the user. His experience consists simply of requesting the Lycos.com homepage and, several moments later, receiving it complete with banner advertisements.

B. Cookie Information Collection

DoubleClick's cookies only collect information from one step of the above process: Step One. The cookies capture certain parts of the communications that users send to DoubleClick-affiliated Web sites. They collect this information in three ways: (1) "GET" submissions, (2) "POST" submissions, and (3) "GIF" submissions.

GET information is submitted as part of a Web site's address or "URL," in what is known as a "query string." For example, a request for a hypothetical online record store's selection of Bon Jovi albums might read: http://recordstore.hypothetical.com/search?terms=bonjovi. The URL query string begins with the "?" character meaning the cookie would record that the user requested information about Bon Jovi.

Users submit POST information when they fill-in multiple blank fields on a web-page. For example, if a user signed-up for an online discussion group, he might have to fill-in fields with his name, address, email address, phone number and discussion group alias. The cookie would capture this submitted POST information.

Finally, DoubleClick places GIF tags on its affiliated Web sites. GIF tags are the size of a single pixel and are invisible to users. Unseen, they record the users' movements throughout the affiliated Web site, enabling DoubleClick to learn what information the user sought and viewed.

Although the information collected by DoubleClick's cookies is allegedly voluminous and detailed, it is important to note three clearly defined parameters. First, DoubleClick's cookies only collect information concerning users' activities on DoubleClick-affiliated Web sites. Thus, if a user visits an unaffiliated Web site, the DoubleClick cookie captures no information. Second, plaintiff does not allege that DoubleClick ever attempted to collect any information other than the GET, POST, and GIF information submitted by users. DoubleClick is never alleged to have accessed files, programs or other information on users' hard drives. Third, Double-Click will not collect information from any user who takes simple steps to prevent DoubleClick's tracking. As plaintiffs' counsel demonstrated at oral argument, users can easily and at no cost prevent DoubleClick from collecting information from them. They may do this in two ways: (1) visiting the DoubleClick Web site and requesting an "opt-out" cookie; and (2) configuring their browsers to block any cookies from being deposited.

Once DoubleClick collects information from the cookies on users' hard drives, it aggregates and compiles the information to build demographic profiles of users. Plaintiffs allege that DoubleClick has more than 100 million user profiles in its database. Exploiting its proprietary Dynamic Advertising Reporting & Targeting ("DART") technology, DoubleClick and its licensees target banner advertisements using these demographic profiles. ...

DISCUSSION ...

CLAIM I. TITLE II OF THE ECPA

Title II ("Title II") of the Electronic Communications Privacy Act ("ECPA"), 18 U.S.C. §2701 et seq. ("§ 2701"), aims to prevent hackers from obtaining, altering or destroying certain stored electronic communications. It creates both criminal sanctions and a civil right of action against persons who gain unauthorized access to communications facilities and thereby access electronic communications stored incident to their transmission. Title II specifically defines the relevant prohibited conduct as follows:

(a) *OFFENSE.* – Except as provided in subsection (c) of this section whoever(1) intentionally accesses without authorization a facility through which an electronic information service is provided; or (2) intentionally exceeds an authorization to access that facility; and thereby obtains ... access to a wire or electronic communication while it is in electronic storage in such system shall be punished. . . .

Plaintiffs contend that DoubleClick's placement of cookies on plaintiffs' hard drives constitutes unauthorized access and, as a result, DoubleClick's collection of information from the cookies violates Title II. However, Title II contains an exception to its general prohibition.

(c) *EXCEPTIONS.* – Subsection (a) of this section does not apply with respect to conduct authorized... (2) by a user of that [wire or electronic communications] service with respect to a communication of or intended for that user;

DoubleClick argues that its conduct falls under this exception. It contends that the DoubleClick-affiliated Web sites are "users" of the Internet and that all of plaintiffs' communications accessed by DoubleClick's cookies have been "of or intended for" these Web sites. Therefore, it asserts, the Web sites' authorization excepts DoubleClick's access from § 2701(a)'s general prohibition. ...

C. All of the communications DoubleClick has accessed through its cookies have been authorized or have fallen outside of Title II's scope.

Because plaintiffs only allege that DoubleClick accessed communications from plaintiffs to DoubleClick-affiliated Web sites, the issue becomes whether the Web sites gave DoubleClick adequate authorization under § 2701(c)(2) to access those communications. This issue, in turn, has two parts: (1) have the DoubleClick-affiliated Web sites authorized DoubleClick to access plaintiffs' communications to them?; and (2) is that authorization sufficient under § 2701(c)(2)?

1. The DoubleClick-affiliated Web sites have consented to DoubleClick's interception of plaintiffs' communications. ...

Examining DoubleClick's technological and commercial relationships with its affiliated Web sites, we find it implausible to infer that the Web sites have not authorized DoubleClick's access. In a practical sense, the very reason clients hire DoubleClick is to target advertisements based on users' demographic profiles. DoubleClick has trumpeted this fact in its advertising, patents and Securities and Exchange filings. True, officers of certain Web sites might not understand precisely how DoubleClick collects demographic information through cookies and records plaintiffs' travels across the Web. However, that knowledge is irrelevant to the authorization at issue – Title II in no way outlaws collecting personally identifiable information or placing cookies, qua such. All that the Web sites must authorize is that DoubleClick access plaintiffs' communications to them. As described in the earlier section "Targeting Banner Advertisements," the DoubleClick-affiliated Web sites actively notify DoubleClick each time a plaintiff sends them an electronic communication (whether through a page request, search, or GIF tag). The data in these notifications (such as the name of the Web site requested) often play an important role in determining which advertisements are presented to users. Plaintiffs have offered no explanation as to how, in anything other than a purely theoretical sense, the DoubleClick-affiliated Web sites could have played such a central role in the information collection and not have authorized DoubleClick's access. This purely theoretical possibility that a DoubleClick-affiliated Web site might have been so ignorant as to have been unaware of the defining characteristic of DoubleClick's advertising service – the service the Web site knowingly and purposely purchased – and its own role in facilitating that service, is too remote to be the basis for extensive and costly discovery of DoubleClick and its affiliates. Therefore, we find that the DoubleClick-affiliated Web sites consented to DoubleClick's access of plaintiffs' communications to them.

2. DoubleClick is authorized to access plaintiffs' GET, POST and GIF submissions to the DoubleClick-affiliated Web sites.

Plaintiffs' GET, POST and GIF submissions to DoubleClick-affiliated Web sites are all "intended for" those Web sites. In the case of the GET and POST submissions, users voluntarily type-in information they wish to submit to the Web sites, information such as queries, commercial orders, and personal information. GIF information is generated and collected when users use their computer "mouse" or other instruments to navigate through Web pages and access information. Although the users' requests for data come through clicks, not keystrokes, they nonetheless are voluntary and purposeful. Therefore, because plaintiffs' GET, POST and GIF submissions to DoubleClick-affiliated Web sites are all "intended for" those Web sites, the Web sites' authorization is sufficient to except DoubleClick's access under § 2701(c)(2)....

3. To the extent that the DoubleClick cookies' identification numbers are electronic communications, (1) they fall outside of Title II's scope, and (2) DoubleClick's access to them is otherwise authorized. ...

(b) If the DoubleClick cookies' identification numbers are considered stored electronic communications, they are "of or intended for" DoubleClick and DoubleClick's acquisition of them does not violate Title II.

Even if we were to assume that cookies and their identification numbers were "electronic communication[s] . . . in electronic storage," DoubleClick's access is still authorized. Section 2701(c)(2) excepts from Title II's prohibition access, authorized by a "user," to communications (1) "of" (2) "or intended for" that user. In every practical sense, the cookies' identification numbers are internal DoubleClick communications – " both "of" and "intended for" DoubleClick. DoubleClick creates the cookies, assigns them identification numbers, and places them on plaintiffs' hard drives. The cookies and their identification numbers are vital to DoubleClick and meaningless to anyone else. In contrast, virtually all plaintiffs are unaware that the cookies exist, that these cookies have identification numbers, that DoubleClick accesses these identification numbers and that these numbers are critical to DoubleClick's operations.

In this sense, cookie identification numbers are much akin to computer bar-codes or identification numbers placed on "business reply cards" found in magazines. These bar-codes and identification numbers are meaningless to consumers, but are valuable to companies in compiling data on consumer responses (e.g. from which magazine did the consumer get the card?). Although consumers fill-out business reply cards and return them to companies by mail, the bar-codes and identification numbers that appear on the cards are purely internal administrative data for the companies. The cookie identification numbers are every bit as internal to DoubleClick as the bar-codes and identification numbers are to business reply mailers. Therefore, it seems both sensible to consider the identification numbers to be "of or intended for" DoubleClick and bizarre to describe them as "of or intended for" plaintiffs. Accordingly, because the identification numbers are "of or intended for" DoubleClick, it does not violate Title II for DoubleClick to obtain them from plaintiffs' electronic storage.

To summarize, plaintiffs' GET, POST and GIF submissions are excepted from § 2701(c)(2) because they are "intended for" the DoubleClick-affiliated Web sites who have authorized DoubleClick's access. The cookie identification numbers sent to DoubleClick from plaintiffs' computers fall outside of Title II's protection because they are not in "electronic storage" and, even if they were, DoubleClick is authorized to access its own communications.

In light of the above findings, we rule that all of plaintiffs' communications accessed by DoubleClick fall under § 2701(c)(2)'s exception or outside Title II and, accordingly, are not actionable. Therefore, plaintiffs' claim under the Title II (Claim I) is dismissed.

CLAIM II. WIRETAP ACT

[The court rejected the plaintiffs' Wiretap Act claim because it held that the affiliated websites were "parties" to the communication and consented to DoubleClick's actions.]

QUESTIONS

1. Cookies were originally designed to allow users to log in to web sites and have the sites remember them later. The web site "sets a cookie" when you log in; later, it "retrieves" the cookie and recognizes you. Companies like DoubleClick figured out how to use this technology to serve personalized ads. The court's discussion of how cookies work is a bit dry. Can you do better? Draw a picture: what information is transmitted to whom, and when?

2. *DoubleClick* holds that DoubleClick's use of cookies violated neither the SCA nor the Wiretap Act. Why? Are you convinced by the court's reading of the statutes? Once you draw the pictures, do cookies seem more or less like a form of worrisome surveillance? Is the harm here a harm of the sort these laws were intended to prevent?

3. Or is it not a harm at all? Ad networks like DoubleClick have always said that they offer consumers a useful service. What service is that? How useful do you find it? How would the Web change if DoubleClick-style tracking cookies were banned tomorrow? Which forms of web advertising do you find most annoying? Creepiest? Which, if any, would you prohibit?

4. DoubleClick (now owned by Google) offers an opt-out from its cookie tracking at http://www.google.com/privacy/ads/. The fraction of Internet users who have opted out it is infinitesimal. Why might that be? Does the fact that most users haven't opted out indicate that they don't care about personal privacy of this sort? Would an opt-in system be better?

IN RE GOOGLE, INC. PRIVACY POLICY LITIG.
No. C-12-01382-PSG12/03/2013, 2013 WL 6248499 (N.D. Cal. Dec. 2, 2013)

Grewal, Magistrate Judge:

After this court's order dismissing their consolidated complaint on standing grounds with leave to amend, Plaintiffs Robert Demars, Pedro Marti, David Nisenbaum, Lorena Barrios, Nicholas Anderson, Matthew Villani and Scott McCullough ("Plaintiffs") filed an amended complaint. In their amended complaint, Plaintiffs again challenge the introduction of a new, unified privacy policy by Defendant Google, Inc. ("Google") permitting the commingling of user data across different Google products. Plaintiffs also challenge Google's disclosure of this data to third parties, including developers of applications for the Google Play market and advertising partners. Google again moves to dismiss, arguing that Plaintiffs still lack standing because they have not sufficiently alleged any injury-in-fact traceable to Google. Google also argues that Plaintiffs have failed to state any claim upon which relief may be granted. As detailed below, the court agrees with Google that the amended complaint is defective and therefore must be dismissed, but only in part and with further leave to amend.

I. BACKGROUND

By now, most people know who Google is and what Google does. Google serves billions of online users in this country and around the world. What started as simply a search engine has expanded to many other products such as YouTube and Gmail. Google offers these products and most others without charge. With little or no revenue from its users, Google still manages to turn a healthy profit by selling advertisements within its products that rely in substantial part on users' personal identification information ("PII"). As some before have observed, in this model, the users are the real product.

Before March 1, 2012, Google maintained separate privacy policies for each of its products, each of which confirmed that Google used a user's PII to provide that particular product.[3] These policies also confirmed that Google would not use the PII for any other purpose without the user's explicit consent. As Google put it, "[w]hen you sign up for a particular service that requires registration, we ask you to provide personal information. If we use this information in a manner different than the purpose for which it was collected, then we will ask for your consent prior to such use."

On March 1, 2012, Google announced a new policy. The majority of its separate privacy policies were eliminated in favor of a single, universal privacy policy that spells out that Google may combine a user's PII across multiple Google products. Google explained the basis for the change in policy as follows:

> Our new Privacy Policy makes clear that, if you're signed in, we may combine information that you've provided from one service with information from other services. In short, we'll treat you as a single user across all our products, which will mean simpler, more intuitive Google experience.

In other words, through the new policy, Google is explicit that it may combine PII collected from a user's Gmail or YouTube account, including the content of that account, with PII collected from that user's Google search queries, along with the user's activities on other Google products, such as Picasa, Maps, Docs, and Reader. This PII includes:

- first and last name;
- home or other physical address (including street name and city);
- current, physical location, a user's email address, and other online contact information (such as the identifier or screen name);
- IP address;
- telephone number (both home and mobile numbers);
- list of contacts;
- search history from Google's search engine;
- web surfing history from cookies placed on the computer; and
- posts on Google+.

Plaintiffs contend that Google's new policy violates its prior policies because the new policy no longer allows users to keep information gathered from one Google product separate from information gathered from other Google products. Plaintiffs further contend that Google's new policy violates users' privacy rights by allowing Google to take information from a user's Gmail account, for which users may have one expectation of privacy, for use in a different context, such as to personalize Google search engine results, or to personalize advertisements shown while a user is surfing the internet, products for which a user may have an entirely different expectation of privacy. In addition to commingling Plaintiffs' PII across

---

3   For example, in a legal notice issued to Gmail users in 2011, Google stated, "We will not use any of your content [defined to include 'text, data, information, images, photographs, music, sound, video, or other material'] for any purpose except to provide you with the service." Google has also pledged that "Gmail stores processes, and maintains your messages, contact lists, and other data related to your account in order to provide the service to you."

the various Google products, Plaintiff contend Google has shared Plaintiffs' PII with third-party entities who have partnered with Google in order to develop applications for the Google Play app store to help it place targeted advertisements.

Plaintiffs bring this nationwide class action against Google on behalf of all persons and entities in the United States who acquired a Google account between August 19, 2004, and February 29, 2012, and maintained such an account until, on, or after March 1, 2012. Plaintiffs also bring this action on behalf of [two subclasses of purchasers of Android phones].

Plaintiffs allege that they each acquired a Gmail account before the March 1, 2012 announcement of the new policy and continued to use it after the new policy took effect. They each further allege they purchased an Android phone before March 1 and that after implementing the new policy Google aggregated their personal information without consent or compensation. Mr. Marti further alleges Google used his likeness in display advertisements without authorization. Mr. Nisenbaum further alleges that after March 1, for privacy reasons, he replaced his Android phone for privacy reasons with an iPhone. The other plaintiffs allege use of various Android-powered phones and that they downloaded various Android Applications ("apps") from the Google Play store. Based on these allegations, Plaintiffs bring claims against Google for statutory and common law misappropriation of likeness, violation of California's Unfair Competition Law ("UCL"), breach of contract, common law intrusion upon seclusion, violation of California's User Legal Remedies Act ("CLRA"), violation of the Wiretap Act, and violation of the Stored Communications Act ("SCA").

II. Legal Standards

To satisfy Article III, a plaintiff "must show that (1) it has suffered an 'injury in fact' that is (a) concrete and particularized and (b) actual or imminent, not conjectural or hypothetical; (2) the injury is fairly traceable to the challenged action of the defendant; and (3) it is likely, as opposed to merely speculative, that the injury will be redressed by a favorable decision." *See Friends of the Earth, Inc. v. Laidlaw Envtl. Sys. (TOC), Inc.*, 528 U.S. 167, 180–181 (2000). A suit brought by a plaintiff without Article III standing is not a "case or controversy," and an Article III court therefore lacks subject matter jurisdiction over the suit. In that event, the suit should be dismissed under Fed. R. Civ. Pro. 12(b)(1). ...

[The court recited the usual pleading standards to survive a Rule 12(b)(6) motion to dismiss for failure to state a claim – a "short plain statement of the claim showing that the pleader is entitled to relief" – and the heightened pleading standards of Rule 9(b) for claims sounding in fraud or mistake – "pleading with particularity the circumstances surrounding the fraud or mistake."]

Dismissal with prejudice and without leave to amend is not appropriate unless it is clear that the complaint could not be saved by amendment. A dismissal with prejudice, except one for lack of jurisdiction, improper venue, or failure to join a party operates as an adjudication on the merits. Dismissal without leave to amend, however, may be granted for reasons of undue delay, bad faith, repeated failure to cure deficiencies by previous amendments, futility of the amendment, and prejudice.

III. Discussion

A. Article III Standing ...

Plaintiffs aim to establish their standing with six theories of injury that can fairly be grouped into three categories: (1) commingling of Plaintiffs' PII, (2) direct economic injury, and (3) violations of statutorily created rights. The court considers each category in turn.

1. Personal Identification Information

Plaintiffs claim that when Google combined information that Plaintiffs provided to discrete Google products, without Plaintiffs' consent, Google injured them in two different ways. First, Google did not compensate them for the substantial economic value of the combined information. Second, Google's unauthorized commingling of their information, especially their likeness, was a breach of contract. Neither alleged harm, however, is sufficient to establish an injury-in-fact.

As the court previously explained, injury-in-fact in this context requires more than an allegation that a defendant profited from a plaintiff's personal identification information. Rather, a plaintiff must allege how the defendant's use of the information deprived the plaintiff of the information's economic value. Put another way, a plaintiff must do more than point to the dollars in a defendant's pocket; he must sufficient allege that in the process he lost dollars of his own. Plaintiffs' allegations certainly plead that Google made money using information about them for which they were provided no compensation beyond free access to Google's services. But an allegation that Google profited is not enough equivalent to an allegation that such profiteering deprived Plaintiffs' of economic value from that same information.

As before, the court finds the reasoning in *LaCourt v. Specific Media*, No. SACV 10–1256–GW (JCGX), 2011 WL 1661532 (C.D. Cal. Apr. 28, 2011), instructive. There the plaintiffs alleged that the defendant installed cookies to track users' internet browsing to build behavior profiles to better target advertisements. The court found the tracked users lacked standing because, among other reasons, they did not "explain how they were 'deprived' of the economic value of their personal information simply because their unspecified personal information was purportedly collected by a third party." ...

Finally, although Plaintiffs assert that the breach of contract arising from Google's unauthorized commingling activities offers a separate basis for injury-in-fact, they still fail to articulate a sufficient contract injury. Nominal damages are not available in California for breach of contract, and the amended complaint does not allege any other injury based on the breach. ... This is insufficient.

2. Direct Economic Injuries

The court next considers whether Plaintiffs have alleged direct economic injuries sufficient to establish injury-in-fact. As the Supreme Court has noted, palpable economic injuries have long been recognized as sufficient to lay the basis for standing. Plaintiffs each allege that they were injured when their Android devices sent their respective names, email addresses, and locations to the developer of each app they purchased or downloaded because they had to pay for the battery and bandwidth consumed by the unauthorized transmissions. Mr. Nisenbaum, representing the Android Device Switch Subclass, claims further injury in that he overpaid for his Android phone in 2010 because he would not have bought the phone had Google disclosed its intention to use his information as alleged in the complaint. Mr. Nisenbaum also claims that he replaced his Android phone with an iPhone in 2012 as a result of Google's policy change, causing him further economic injury.

The Court will consider each of these direct economic injury theories in turn to determine if they articulate "something more" than pure economic harm to support subject-matter jurisdiction under Rule 12(b)(1).

With respect to Plaintiffs' injury claims based on battery and bandwidth consumption, courts have found that the unauthorized use of system resources can suffice to establish a cognizable injury. For example, in *Goodman v. HTC America, Inc.*, No. C11–1793MJP, 2012 WL 2412070 (W.D. Wash. June 26, 2012), the court found standing based upon battery discharge where the application at issue sent fine location data every three hours or whenever the device's screen was refreshed. Similarly, in *In re iPhone Application Litigation*, No. 5:11–md–02250–LHK, 2011 WL 4403963 (N.D. Cal. Sept. 20, 2011), the court found standing where the device systematically collected and transmitted location information. In *In re Google Android User Privacy Litig.*, No. 5:11–md–02264–JSW, 2013 WL 1283236 (N.D. Cal. Mar. 26, 2013), the plaintiffs did not clearly allege how frequently Google collected geolocation data from a phone, but did allege that collecting relocation data was particularly battery intensive, that "their batteries discharged more quickly[,] and that their services were interrupted." This latter allegation was deemed sufficient to establish standing. At the same time, in *Hernandez v. Path, Inc.*, No. 12–CV–01515 YGR, 2012 WL 5194120 (N.D. Cal. Oct. 19, 2012), the court found that any harm from the use of phone resources in an app's uploading a user's address book a single time upon first running the app was *de minimis* and thus insufficient to establish injury.

Plaintiffs' allegations here are closer to *Goodman, iPhone I* and *Android* than *Hernandez*. Like *Hernandez*, Plaintiffs' alleged unauthorized battery consumption only happened infrequently, when a plaintiff first downloaded an app. But in *Hernandez* the allegedly unauthorized upload only happened once, when a plaintiff downloaded the Path app. Here, it happens each time a user downloads any app. The plaintiff who downloaded the most apps, according to the amended complaint, did so at least 27 times. In addition, like the plaintiffs in *Goodman* and *Android,* Plaintiffs here specifically allege a greater discharge of battery power as a result of unauthorized conduct and as in *iPhone I* the discharge is systemic rather than episodic. This is sufficient to establish more than a *de minimis* injury.

With respect to Mr. Nisenbaum's further allegations of injury, they, too, support standing for purposes of Article III.

First, the allegation that Mr. Nisenbaum bought a new phone after the policy change and that his motivation for choosing an iPhone over the Android device was substantially for privacy reasons, establishes that he was injured by making the purchase. To be sure, users frequently replace old phones for all kinds of reasons beyond privacy. For example, from the complaint, it appears Mr. Nisenbaum had his Android device for approximately two years, the length of most phone contracts that often include a discount for bundled phones, before purchasing a new phone. But Mr. Nisenbaum specifically alleges that but for the policy switch he would not have otherwise have bought a new phone. The alleged injury is fairly traceable to Google based on Mr. Nisenbaum's allegation that he relied on Google's previous policies in purchasing the Android phone in the first place.

Second, Mr. Nisembaum's allegations regarding overpayment establish injury. ...

3. Violation of Statutory Rights

The final category of Plaintiffs' injury-in-fact theories concerns statutory rights. The Ninth Circuit has made it clear that Article III standing can also be established by virtue of "statutes creating legal rights, the invasion of which creates standing. *Edwards v. First Am. Corp.*, 610 F.3d 514, 517 (9th Cir. 2010). ... To decide if a statute created such a legal right, a court must determine whether the "standing provision on which the claim rests properly can be understood as granting persons in the plaintiff's position a right to judicial relief." *Id.* ... Although Article III always requires an injury, the alleged violation of a statutory right that does not otherwise require a showing of damages is an injury sufficient to establish Article III standing. For example, in a case where a credit card company failed to make required disclosures and the Truth in Lending Act created a private right of action for such failures without a showing of damages, the Ninth Circuit held that the plaintiff "suffered the loss of a statutory right to disclosure and has therefore suffered injury in fact for purposes of Article III standing." *DeMando v. Morris*, 206 F.3d 1300, 1303 (9th Cir. 2000). ...

Plaiintiffs have alleged unauthorized access and wrongful disclosure of communications, including disclosure to third parties. Plaintiffs also have alleged the interception of communications. Courts have recognized that such alleged violations of the Wiretap Act or the Stored Communications Act are sufficient to establish Article III injury. These statutes grant persons in Plaintiffs' position a right to relief and thus Plaintiffs have standing for these claims.

The complaint also alleges that Mr. Marti was injured when Google used his name or likeness in connection with its "+1" function without authorization. California Civil Code Section 3344 prohibits the commercial use another's name or likeness. The statute thus creates a right of action for "persons injured as a result thereof." ...

Google disputes any injury-in-fact from the +1 feature because Plaintiffs have not alleged an unauthorized use. However, the amended complaint states that Google did not compensate Mr. Marti for the commercial use of his personal endorsement and that he "did not authorize Google's use of that endorsement." As explained above, whatever the merits of the parties' competing views of consent, a merits analysis is not appropriate when considering standing. ...

B. [Wiretap Act] ...

The Wiretap Act, as amended by the Electronic Communication Privacy Act ("ECPA"), generally prohibits the intentional interception of "wire, oral, or electronic communications." 18 U.S.C. § 2511(1). The purpose of the Wiretap Act is to protect the privacy of communications. ... The Act defines "intercept" as "the aural or other acquisition of the contents of any wire, electronic, or oral communication through the use of any electronic, mechanical, or other device." *Id.* § 2510(4). However, the definition of "electronic, mechanical, or other device" excludes [any instrument "being used by a provider of wire or electronic communication service in the ordinary course of its business." *Id.* § 2510(5)(a)(ii)].

The amended complaint fails to allege any interception by Google that falls outside the scope of this broad immunity. While Plaintiffs point to their allegations that Google's use of the accused devices to intercept Gmail communications and co-mingle the contents and distribute those contents without consent was not necessary to the delivery of Gmail, this narrow read of the exemption, as being limited to only action taken to deliver the electronic communication, does not square with the plain meaning of the statutory text at issue. The text exempts from the definition of "intercept" any use of a device by a provider "in the ordinary course of its business." Rather than narrowing the exemption to only the provision of electronic communications services itself, or some such narrower scope, Congress specifically chose the broader term "business" that covers more far-ranging activity. For good measure, Congress also teamed the term "business" with the terms "ordinary course," suggesting an interest in protecting a provider's customary and routine business practices. ...

Although the Ninth Circuit has yet to rule on the subject, other appellate courts that have agreed that the "ordinary course of business" exception is not limited to actions necessary to providing the electronic communication services ("ECS") at issue. ... In *Kirch v. Embarq Management Co.*, 702 F.3d 1245, 1250 (10th Cir. 2012), the Tenth Circuit held that the defendant was protected by the exception when it conducted a test using third-party advertising technology and its customers' communications, because the defendant had "no more of its users' electronic communications than it had in the ordinary course of its business as an ISP." The trial court's decision affirmed by *Kirch* noted that the "ordinary course of its business" defense "appears to have merit, as plaintiffs have admitted that Embarq conducted the NebuAd test to further legitimate business purposes and that behavioral advertising is a widespread business and is commonplace on the Internet." *Kirch*, No. 10–2047–JAR, 2011 WL 3651359, at *9 n.42 (D. Kan. Aug. 19, 2011). *Kirch* thus supports the application of Section 2510(5)(a)(ii) where the provider is furthering its "legitimate business purposes" – including advertising – and is not limited to only those acts that are technically necessary to processing email.

The more fundamental problem with Plaintiffs' narrow construction of Section 2510(5)(a)(ii) is that in defining "ordinary course of business" as "necessary" it begs the question of what exactly its means for a given action to be "necessary" to the delivery of Gmail. For example, in delivering Gmail is it really "necessary" do more than just the comply with email protocols such as POP, IMAP and MAPI? What about spam-filtering or indexing? None of these activities have anything specifically to do with transmitting email. And yet not even Plaintiffs suggest that these activities are unnecessary and thus lie outside of the "ordinary course business." ...

C. Stored Communications Act

The SCA was enacted because the advent of the Internet presented a host of potential privacy breaches that the Fourth Amendment does not address. Despite this purpose, the SCA has a narrow scope: the SCA is not a catch-all statute designed to protect the privacy of stored Internet communications.

Plaintiffs claim that Google violated the SCA in two ways. First, they claim that in aggregating users' information between Google services without their consent, Google exceeded the scope of Google's authorized access in violation of 18 U.S.C. § 2701(a). This claim borders on frivolous, considering the plain language of subsection (c) of Section 2701(a) that exempts conduct authorized "by the person or entity providing a wire or electronic communications service." Whatever the propriety of Google's actions, it plainly authorized actions that it took itself.

Second, Plaintiffs claim that Google shared stored communications with third parties in violation of Section 2702(a). Section 2702(a) prohibits providers of electronic communication services from "knowingly divulg[ing] to any person or entity the contents of a communication...." Plaintiffs' only allegation supporting its second theory is that:

> insofar as Google engages independent, unidentified third-party entities to process and distribute user information across its product platforms, including the contents of Plaintiffs' Gmail communications,

Google intentionally discloses the contents of those communications outside of Google.

But "insofar" is not a concrete allegation; it is theoretical and does not support a claim. Even if this were a concrete allegation, it is too conclusory to support a claim. Plaintiffs simply fail to state any claim under the SCA.

D. Misappropriation of Likeness

California Civil Code Section 3344 prohibits the use of another's name or likeness ["to defendant's advantage, commercially or otherwise"] without the person's consent. ... Here, Plaintiffs fail to adequately allege lack of consent. ...

Plaintiffs in this case only make a threadbare allegation that Google did not obtain their consent to use their name or likeness in advertisements associated with its "+1" feature, and the claim is not supported by other allegations. To the contrary, the complaint alleges that Ms. Marti voluntarily clicked on the "+1" feature, that Google clearly disclosed how the feature worked as part of the feature's launch, and that the feature worked as Google said it would when Marti used it. In particular, the amended complaint quotes Google as: describing the "+1" feature as "the digital shorthand for 'this is pretty cool' " and a way "to share recommendations with the world;" explaining that to "[t]o recommend something, all you have to do is click +1 on a webpage or ad you find useful;" and giving the example of a person planning a winter trip to Tahoe, California who, when doing a search, "may now see a +1 from [his] slalom-skiing aunt next to the result for a lodge in the area."

Without some contradictory allegations,[113] this is a clear disclosure of how the feature worked such that the voluntary use of it constituted consent. Plaintiffs therefore have not stated any claim for statutory or common law misappropriation of likeness.

E. Breach of Contract ...

Google argues that it has not breached its contact with Plaintiffs because the original contract included provisions for it to make the types of very changes that Plaintiffs allege breached the contract. ...

The policy plainly includes a provision for the commingling of PII across Google products. That provision states: "We may combine the information you submit under your account with information from other services." In light of this express provision, it is not plausible to say that Google could be considered to have breached the contract. Plaintiffs again have failed to state a claim.

F. California's Unfair Competition Law ("UCL")

California's UCL provides a private cause of action for users who are harmed by unfair, unlawful, or fraudulent business practices. Plaintiffs here plead their UCL claim under all three prongs. To sustain a claim under the unlawful prong, Plaintiffs must allege facts that, if proven, would demonstrate that Defendant's conduct violated another, underlying law. ... Under the fraudulent prong, Plaintiffs must allege specific facts to show that the members of the public are likely to be deceived by the actions of the defendant. The Ninth Circuit has established that this

---

113   For example, Plaintiffs might have a claim if they could allege that the feature did not work as Google explained, that Google did not adequately disclose how the feature worked, a theory of how clicking on the "+1" feature did not demonstrate consent, or an allegation that his name or likeness was associated with brands, products, or websites he did not "+1."

prong is subject to Fed. Rule Civ. P. 9(b)'s heightened pleading requirements. With respect to Plaintiffs' final claim under the UCL's unfair prong, the standard for determining what business acts or practices are "unfair" in user actions under the UCL is currently unsettled. Generally speaking, an unfair business practice under the UCL is "one that either offends an established public policy or is immoral, unethical, oppressive, unscrupulous, or substantially injurious to users." *McDonald v. Coldwell Banker*, 543 F.3d 498, 506 (9th Cir. 2008). To determine whether a business practice is unfair, a court should consider "the impact of the practice or act on its victim, balanced against the reasons, justifications and motives of the alleged wrongdoer;" this prong of the UCL should be used to enjoin deceptive or sharp practices." *Wilson v. Hynek*, 207 Cal. App. 4th 999, 1008 (Cal. Ct. App. 2012).

To support their claim under the UCL's unlawful prong, Plaintiffs allege that Google's conduct violates [the laws discussed above]. As discussed in other sections, Plaintiffs have failed to set forth sufficient factual allegations to support these underlying charges, and without having plead any underlying unlawful conduct, Plaintiffs unlawful conduct claim under the UCL must be dismissed.

With respect to their claim under the fraudulent prong, Plaintiffs allege that when Google collected their PII before March 1, 2012, it assured them that it would not use the information for any purpose other than delivering the service for which the users provided it. [But] the documents submitted for judicial notice undermine any notion that Google failed to disclose its data commingling practices before March 1, 2012.

Finally, Plaintiffs seek to support their claim of unfair conduct by alleging that Google lead them to believe that they could opt out of endorsements, profiting from the use of the plaintiff's information, and "encouraging Plaintiffs and the Class to make Google products indispensable to their lives," before making it incredibly difficult for them to effectively "opt out" of programs making use of their data. These facts, as alleged, do not rise to the level of "unscrupulous" or "unethical." Even if its earlier policies were not transparent, Google provided notice to its users when it changed its privacy policy, which undercuts any unethical or immoral allegations; this was not a change made in the dark, but rather one broadcast to all those affected. In addition, the overall benefit to users in receiving free, "indispensable" services offsets much of the harm they may suffer through the change. As it stands, Plaintiffs have not set forth sufficient allegations to support an unfairness prong claim.

G. Common Law Intrusion Upon Seclusion

In order to put forth a claim for intrusion upon seclusion, a plaintiff must plead facts to support two elements: 1) intrusion into a private place, conversation or matter, and 2) in a manner highly offensive to a reasonable person. To show intrusion, a plaintiff must have an objectively reasonable expectation of seclusion or solitude in the place, conversation or data source, and the defendant must have 'penetrated some zone of physical or sensory privacy surrounding, or obtained unwanted access to data about, the plaintiff. ... In this context, the concept of 'seclusion' is relative. The mere fact that a person or their information can be seen by someone does not automatically mean that he or she can legally be forced to be subject to being seen by everyone. Courts have recognized facts sufficient to support these elements in the context of repeated phone calls, eavesdropping on workplace conversations, and unauthorized review of email.

Plaintiffs here allege that Google's PII commingling intruded upon their email, contact lists, web histories, and other secluded and private spaces. According to Plaintiffs, this expectation was reasonable in light of the previous privacy policies, which assured Plaintiffs of the isolated use of their data. But once again, the court does not find any expectation to be plausible in light of Google's earlier disclosure that it would commingle PII across products to support its advertising model. Without a plausible expectation, Plaintiffs seclusion on intrusion claim cannot stand.

H. California's User Legal Remedies Act ("CLRA")

Plaintiffs' sixth cause of action seeks recovery under Sections (a)(9), (14), and (16) of the CLRA, which ban advertising goods with intent not to sell them in the manner advertised, representing that a transaction conveys rights which it does not, and representing that the subject of a transaction has been conveyed in accordance with terms of a previous transaction, when it has not. In order to recover, Plaintiffs must also allege facts to establish that they relied on the misrepresentations in question, and that in so relying, they suffered damage. These allegations are subject to Rule 9(b)'s heightened pleading standards.

Plaintiffs' claims are insufficiently plead because they fail to allege that Google intended to use the PII in a manner other was advertised at the time that the plaintiffs purchased the goods and registered for the services in question. Under the CLRA, the intent to deceive or misuse information must be present at the time of sale in order for a plaintiff to recover. Yet even if its commingling practices were not disclosed in 2010, Plaintiffs offer no factual allegations indicating that Google planned to change its policies as far back as 2010, such that the existing policies were aimed to deceive at the time the business relationship began. They have not put forth any allegations suggesting that Google did not intend to honor its existing privacy policies, at the time they became customers. They certainly do not provide the requisite level of detail under Rule 9(b) to support allegations of intent to deceive.

IV. Conclusion

Google's motion to dismiss is GRANTED. Plaintiffs must file any further amended complaint by January 16, 2014. Having dismissed two complaints already, Plaintiffs are on notice that any further dismissal will likely be with prejudice.

QUESTIONS

1. Why is it so hard for the plaintiffs to plead injury? Is their problem that they haven't actually been injured, or that the legal system doesn't care about privacy harms?

2. Loss of battery life? Seriously?

3. Suppose that the defendant suffers a data breach that exposes plaintiffs' names, addresses, phone numbers, email addresses, and dates of birth. Plaintiffs sue, alleging increased likelihood of identity theft. Have they suffered an injury in fact for standing purchases? What if they have had unauthorized purchases made using their credit cards, but are not financially responsible for those purchases under their credit-card agreements? Can they claim injury-in-fact based on the time and hassle involved in reversing the unauthorized charges?

4. Is the court right that Google's earlier statements put plaintiffs on notice that it might commingle their data? If so, how much are privacy promises really worth?

IN RE SNAPCHAT, INC.
2015-1 Trade Cas. (CCH) ¶ 17,115, 2014 WL 7495798 (F.T.C. 2014)

COMPLAINT

The Federal Trade Commission, having reason to believe that Snapchat, Inc. ("respondent") has violated the provisions of the Federal Trade Commission Act, and it appearing to the Commission that this proceeding is in the public interest, alleges: ...

Respondent's Business Practices

3. Snapchat provides a mobile application that allows consumers to send and receive photo and video messages known as "snaps." Before sending a snap, the application requires the sender to designate a period of time that the recipient will be allowed to view the snap. Snapchat markets the application as an "ephemeral" messaging application, having claimed that once the timer expires, the snap "disappears forever."

4. Snapchat launched its mobile application on Apple Inc.'s iOS operating system in September 2011 and on Google Inc.'s Android operating system in October 2012. Snapchat added video messaging to the iOS version of its application in December 2012 and to the Android version of its application in February 2013.

5. Both the iTunes App Store and the Google Play store list Snapchat among the top 15 free applications. As of September 2013, users transmit more than 350 million snaps daily.

Snapchat's "Disappearing" Messages (Counts 1 and 2)

6. Snapchat marketed its application as a service for sending "disappearing" photo and video messages, declaring that the message sender "control[s] how long your friends can view your message." Before sending a snap, the application requires the sender to designate a period of time - with the default set to a maximum of 10 seconds - that the recipient will be allowed to view the snap ...

7. Since the application's launch on iOS until May 2013, and since the application's launch on Android until June 2013, Snapchat disseminated, or caused to be disseminated, to consumers the following statements on its product description page on the iTunes App Store and Google Play:

8. From October 2012 to October 2013, Snapchat disseminated, or caused to be disseminated, to consumers the following statement on the "FAQ" page on its website:

> **Is there any way to view an image after the time has expired?**
> No, snaps disappear after the timer runs out ....

9. Despite these claims, several methods exist by which a recipient can use tools outside of the application to save both photo and video messages, allowing the recipient to access and view the photos or videos indefinitely.

10. For example, when a recipient receives a video message, the application stores the video file in a location outside of the application's "sandbox" (*i.e.*, the application's private storage area on the device that other applications cannot access). Because the file is stored in this unrestricted area, until October 2013, a recipient could connect his or her mobile device to a computer and use simple file browsing tools to locate and save the video file. This method for saving video files sent through the application was widely publicized as early as December 2012. Snapchat did not mitigate this flaw until October 2013, when it began encrypting video files sent through the application.

11. Furthermore, third-party developers have built applications that can connect to Snapchat's application programming interface ("API"), thereby allowing recipients to log into the Snapchat service without using the official Snapchat application. Because the timer and related "deletion" functionality is dependent on the recipient's use of the official Snapchat application, recipients can instead simply use a third-party application to download and save both photo and video messages. As early as June 2012, a security researcher warned Snapchat that it would be "pretty easy to write a tool to download and save the images a user receives" due to the way the API functions. Indeed, beginning in spring 2013, third-party developers released several applications on the iTunes App Store and Google Play that recipients can use to save and view photo or video messages indefinitely. On Google Play alone, ten of these applications have been downloaded as many as 1.7 million times.

12. The file browsing tools and third-party applications described in paragraphs 10 and 11 are free or low cost and publicly available on the Internet. In order to download, install, and use these tools, a recipient need not make any modifications to the iOS or Android operating systems and would need little technical knowledge.

13.   In addition to the methods described in paragraphs 10-12, a recipient can use the mobile device's screenshot capability to capture an image of a snap while it appears on the device screen.

14.   Snapchat claimed that if a recipient took a screenshot of a snap, the sender would be notified. On its product description pages, as described in paragraph 7, Snapchat stated: "We'll let you know if [recipients] take a screenshot!" In addition, from October 2012 to February 2013, Snapchat disseminated, or caused to be disseminated, to consumers the following statement on the "FAQ" page on its website:

> **What if I take a screenshot?**
> Screenshots can be captured if you're quick. The sender will be notified immediately.

15.   However, recipients can easily circumvent Snapchat's screenshot detection mechanism. For example, on versions of iOS prior to iOS 7, the recipient need only double press the device's Home button in rapid succession to evade the detection mechanism and take a screenshot of any snap without the sender being notified. This method was widely publicized.

Count 1

16.   As described in Paragraphs 6, 7, and 8, Snapchat has represented, expressly or by implication, that when sending a message through its application, the message will disappear forever after the user-set time period expires.

17.   In truth and in fact, as described in Paragraph 9-12, when sending a message through its application, the message may not disappear forever after the user-set time period expires. Therefore, the representation set forth in Paragraph 16 is false or misleading.

Count 2

18.   As described in Paragraphs 7 and 14, Snapchat has represented, expressly or by implication, that the sender will be notified if the recipient takes a screenshot of a snap.

19.   In truth and in fact, as described in Paragraph 15, the sender may not be notified if the recipient takes a screenshot of a snap. Therefore, the representation set forth in Paragraph 18 is false or misleading.

Snapchat's Collection of Geolocation Information (Count 3)

20.   From June 2011 to February 2013, Snapchat disseminated or caused to be disseminated to consumers the following statements in its privacy policy:

> We do not ask for, track, or access any location-specific information from your device at any time while you are using the Snapchat application.

21.   In October 2012, Snapchat integrated an analytics tracking service in the Android version of its application that acted as its service provider. While the Android operating system provided notice to consumers that the application may access location information, Snapchat did not disclose that it would, in fact, access location information, and continued to represent that Snapchat did "not ask for, track, or access any location-specific information ..."

22.   Contrary to the representation in Snapchat's privacy policy, from October 2012 to February 2013, the Snapchat application on Android transmitted

Wi-Fi-based and cell-based location information from users' mobile devices to its analytics tracking service provider.

Count 3

23. As described in Paragraph 21, Snapchat has represented, expressly or by implication, that it does not collect users' location information.

24. In truth and in fact, as described in Paragraph 22, Snapchat did collect users' location information. Therefore, the representation set forth in Paragraph 23 is false or misleading. ...

Snapchat's Collection of Contacts Information (Counts 4 and 5) ...

25. Snapchat provides its users with a feature to find friends on the service. During registration, the application prompts the user to "Enter your mobile number to find your friends on Snapchat!," implying - prior to September 2012 - through its user interface that the mobile phone number was the only information Snapchat collected to find the user's friends, as depicted below:
    ...

26. However, when the user chooses to Find Friends, Snapchat collects not only the phone number a user enters, but also, without informing the user, the names and phone numbers of all the contacts in the user's mobile device address book.

[The FTC alleged that the failure to notify users was false or misleading. and that Snapchat made deceptive statements in its privacy policy about the feature.]

Snapchat's Failure to Secure Its Find Friends Feature (Count 6) ...

35. From September 2011 to December 2012, Snapchat failed to verify that the phone number that an iOS user entered into the application did, in fact, belong to the mobile device being used by that individual. Due to this failure, an individual could create an account using a phone number that belonged to another consumer, enabling the individual to send and receive snaps associated with another consumer's phone number.

36. Numerous consumers complained to Snapchat that individuals had created Snapchat accounts with phone numbers belonging to other consumers, leading to the misuse and unintentional disclosure of consumers' personal information. For example, consumers complained that they had sent snaps to accounts under the belief that they were communicating with a friend, when in fact they were not, resulting in the unintentional disclosure of photos containing personal information. In addition, consumers

complained that accounts associated with their phone numbers had been used to send inappropriate or offensive snaps.

37. Snapchat could have prevented the misuse and unintentional disclosure of consumers' personal information by verifying phone numbers using common and readily available methods.

38. Indeed, in December 2012, Snapchat began performing short-message-service ("SMS") verification to confirm that the entered phone number did in fact belong to the mobile device being used by that individual.

39. In addition, from September 2011 to December 2013, Snapchat failed to implement effective restrictions on the number of Find Friend requests that any one account could make to its API. Furthermore, Snapchat failed to implement any restrictions on serial and automated account creation. As a result of these failures, in December 2013, attackers were able to use multiple accounts to send millions of Find Friend requests using randomly generated phone numbers. The attackers were able to compile a database of 4.6 million Snapchat usernames and the associated mobile phone numbers. The exposure of usernames and mobile phone numbers could lead to costly spam, phishing, and other unsolicited communications. ...

40. ... Snapchat disseminated or caused to be disseminated to consumers the following statement in its privacy policy:

> Snapchat takes reasonable steps to help protect your personal information in an effort to prevent loss, misuse, and unauthorized access, disclosure, alteration, and destruction. ...

Count 6

43. As described in Paragraphs 40-42, Snapchat has represented, expressly or by implication, that it employs reasonable security measures to protect personal information from misuse and unauthorized disclosure.

44. In truth and in fact, as described in Paragraphs 34-39, in many instances, Snapchat did not employ reasonable security measures to protect personal information from misuse and unauthorized disclosure. Therefore, the representation set forth in Paragraph 43 is false or misleading.

45. The acts and practices of respondent as alleged in this complaint constitute deceptive acts or practices in or affecting commerce in violation of Section 5(a) of the Federal Trade Commission Act, 15 U.S.C. § 45(a).

THEREFORE, the Federal Trade Commission this twenty-third day of December, 2014, has issued this complaint against respondent.

DECISION AND ORDER ...

[Snapchat entered into a consent order under which it neither admitted nor denied the allegations in the complaint but agreed to certain changes in its business practices.]

Definitions

For purposes of this Order, the following definitions shall apply: ...

3. "Covered information" shall mean information from or about an individual consumer, including but not limited to (a) a first and last name; (b) a home or other physical address, including street name and name of city or town; (c) an email address or other online contact information, such as an instant messaging user identifier or a screen name; (d) a telephone number; (e) a

persistent identifier, such as a customer number held in a "cookie," a static Internet Protocol ("IP") address, a mobile device ID, or processor serial number; (f) precise geo-location data of an individual or mobile device, including GPS-based, Wi-Fi-based, or cell-based location information; (g) an authentication credential, such as a username or password; or (h) any communications or content that is transmitted or stored through respondent's products or services.

I.

IT IS ORDERED that respondent and its officers, agents, representatives, and employees, directly or indirectly, shall not misrepresent in any manner, expressly or by implication, in or affecting commerce, the extent to which respondent or its products or services maintain and protect the privacy, security, or confidentiality of any covered information, including but not limited to: (1) the extent to which a message is deleted after being viewed by the recipient; (2) the extent to which respondent or its products or services are capable of detecting or notifying the sender when a recipient has captured a screenshot of, or otherwise saved, a message; (3) the categories of covered information collected; or (4) the steps taken to protect against misuse or unauthorized disclosure of covered information.

II.

IT IS FURTHER ORDERED that respondent, in or affecting commerce, shall, no later than the date of service of this order, establish and implement, and thereafter maintain, a comprehensive privacy program that is reasonably designed to: (1) address privacy risks related to the development and management of new and existing products and services for consumers, and (2) protect the privacy and confidentiality of covered information, whether collected by respondent or input into, stored on, captured with, or accessed through a computer using respondent's products or services. Such program, the content and implementation of which must be fully documented in writing, shall contain privacy controls and procedures appropriate to respondent's size and complexity, the nature and scope of respondent's activities, and the sensitivity of the covered information, including [designation of employees responsible for the privacy program, identification of forseeable privacy risks, implementation of reasonable privacy controls to address those risks, appropriate security practices, and ongoing adjustment of the program in light of changing circumstances].

III.

IT IS FURTHER ORDERED that, in connection with its compliance with Part II of this order, respondent shall obtain initial and biennial assessments and reports ("Assessments") from a qualified, objective, independent third-party professional ...

VIII.

This order will terminate twenty (20) years from the date of its issuance ...

QUESTIONS

1. The FTC has the power to investigate and prohibit "unfair or deceptive acts or practices in or affecting commerce." Compare the FTC's civil enforcement action to the private consumer lawsuit in *DoubleClick*. Does the FTC have any advantages? Disadvantages?

2. Was there anything wrong with Snapchat's features, or just with how they were described?

3. No statute or regulation specifically tells companies that "reasonable" security measures include "two-factor-authentication" techniques like sending SMS messages to confirm a user's phone number. But the FTC dinged Snapchat anyway for failing to use two-factor-authentication. Did Snapchat have reasonable notice of its legal obligations? What about future companies deciding what security measures to employ in light of *Snapchat*?

4. People send each other all kinds of things on Snapchat, and post all kinds of things on Facebook and other social media services. Does this mean that people no longer care about privacy, and the FTC should get out of the way?

5. The consent decree's remedies are all forward-looking: they are attempts to reform Snapchat's privacy practices in the future, rather than to penalize it for its past conduct. How effective will they be? If Snapchat already has a duty not to commit "unfair or deceptive acts," is the consent decree redundant?

6. One recent survey found that six out of ten Americans surveyed responded "true" to the question, "If a website has a privacy policy, it means that the site cannot share information about you with other companies, unless you give the website your permission." Are they correct? After reading *In re Snapchat*, are you inclined to change your online behavior?

7. California has a "data breach law" requiring companies to inform consumers whose personal information (such as social security number, driver's license number, or credit card number) is acquired by unauthorized persons. What is the purpose of this kind of notification law? How effective do you think it will be in limiting security breaches?

COOKIE MONSTER PROBLEM

Cookie Monster is a browser extension that eats cookies. Users install it by downloading it from the Cookie Monster website. After that, every fifteen minutes. it deletes all third-party cookies of the sort used by DoubleClick and other advertising networks. Consumers can turn off Cookie Monster for a particular website by clicking a button in the top left corner of the browser window.

Ozalytics is a "website analytics" service used by websites to keep track of how many visitors they have and what those visitors are doing on the site. It works very much like advertising networks (and Twitter "tweet this" buttons, for that matter): by embedding a small image hosted at ozalytics.com into every page on a website that uses it service. That image can then set a cookie in the user's browser to track the user's engagement with the website.

Unfortunately for Ozalytics, Cookie Monster deletes its cookies, making the information it returns to websites much less useful. Ozalytics has responded by asking host websites to include a "Cookie Monster workaround," consisting of little bit of Ozalytics JavaScript code on each webpage, in addition to the Ozalyitics image. That code instructs the user's browser to simulate a mouse click on the corner of the window where the button to disable Cookie Monster for that website is located.

You represent SometimeSnack.com, a website devoted to healthy cooking tips for parents. You have been asked to consider whether to implement Ozalytics' proposed Cookie Monster workaround, and if so, how to do it. What is your advice?

F. An International Perspective

In the European Union (E.U.), privacy is considered a fundamental right; privacy laws are both stronger and more general than in the United States. Article 8 of the Charter of Fundamental Rights of the European Union gives all people "the right to the protection of personal data concerning him or her." The Data Protection Directive of 1995 (DPD) implements these rights in more detail by requiring each country in the EU to have strong privacy legislation. This section sets out the key passages from the DPD, along with some recent decisions from the European Court of Justice (CJEU) – a loose European parallel to the United States Supreme Court – that show some of the recent controversies raised by the DPD and Europe's increasingly strong commitments to privacy. Note that DPD will be updated with a new General Data Protection Regulation which will take effect in May 2018.

DATA PROTECTION DIRECTIVE

Directive 95/46/EC of the European Parliament and of the Council of 24 October 1995
on the protection of individuals with regard to the processing of personal data
and on the free movement of such data
1995 O.J. (L 281) 31

Art. 1 – *Object of the Directive*

1. In accordance with this Directive, Member States shall protect the fundamental rights and freedoms of natural persons, and in particular their right to privacy with respect to the processing of personal data. ...

Art. 2 – *Definitions*

For the purposes of this Directive:

(a) 'personal data' shall mean any information relating to an identified or identifiable natural person ('data subject'); an identifiable person is one who can be identified, directly or indirectly, in particular by reference to an identification number or to one or more factors specific to his physical, physiological, mental, economic, cultural or social identity;

(b) 'processing of personal data' ('processing') shall mean any operation or set of operations which is performed upon personal data, whether or not by automatic means, such as collection, recording, organization, storage, adaptation or alteration, retrieval, consultation, use, disclosure by transmission, dissemination or otherwise making available, alignment or combination, blocking, erasure or destruction; ...

(d) 'controller' shall mean the natural or legal person, public authority, agency or any other body which alone or jointly with others determines the purposes and means of the processing of personal data; where the purposes and means of processing are determined by national or Community laws or regulations, the controller or the specific criteria for his nomination may be designated by national or Community law; ...

Art. 6

1. Member States shall provide that personal data must be:

(a) processed fairly and lawfully;

(b) collected for specified, explicit and legitimate purposes and not further processed in a way incompatible with those purposes. Further processing of data for historical, statistical or scientific purposes shall not be considered as incompatible provided that Member States provide appropriate safeguards;

(c) adequate, relevant and not excessive in relation to the purposes for which they are collected and/or further processed;

(d) accurate and, where necessary, kept up to date; every reasonable step must be taken to ensure that data which are inaccurate or incomplete, having regard to the purposes for which they were collected or for which they are further processed, are erased or rectified;

(e) kept in a form which permits identification of data subjects for no longer than is necessary for the purposes for which the data were collected or for which they are further processed....

2. It shall be for the controller to ensure that paragraph 1 is complied with.

Art. 7

Member States shall provide that personal data may be processed only if:

(a) the data subject has unambiguously given his consent; or

(b) processing is necessary for the performance of a contract to which the data subject is party or in order to take steps at the request of the data subject prior to entering into a contract; or

(c) processing is necessary for compliance with a legal obligation to which the controller is subject; or

(d) processing is necessary in order to protect the vital interests of the data subject; or

(e) processing is necessary for the performance of a task carried out in the public interest or in the exercise of official authority vested in the controller or in a third party to whom the data are disclosed; or

(f) processing is necessary for the purposes of the legitimate interests pursued by the controller or by the third party or parties to whom the data are disclosed, except where such interests are overridden by the interests for fundamental rights and freedoms of the data subject ...

Art. 12 – *Right of access*

Member States shall guarantee every data subject the right to obtain from the controller:

(a) without constraint at reasonable intervals and without excessive delay or expense:

- confirmation as to whether or not data relating to him are being processed and information at least as to the purposes of the processing, the categories of data concerned, and the recipients or categories of recipients to whom the data are disclosed,

- communication to him in an intelligible form of the data undergoing processing and of any available information as to their source,

- knowledge of the logic involved in any automatic processing of data concerning him at least in the case of the automated decisions referred to in Article 15 (1);

(b) as appropriate the rectification, erasure or blocking of data the processing of which does not comply with the provisions of this Directive, in particular because of the incomplete or inaccurate nature of the data; ...

Art. 13 – *Exemptions and restrictions*

1. Member States may adopt legislative measures to restrict the scope of the obligations and rights provided for in Articles 6 (1), 10, 11 (1), 12 and 21 when such a restriction constitutes a necessary measures to safeguard:

    (a) national security;

    (b) defence;

    (c) public security;

    (d) the prevention, investigation, detection and prosecution of criminal offences, or of breaches of ethics for regulated professions;

    (e) an important economic or financial interest of a Member State or of the European Union, including monetary, budgetary and taxation matters;

    (f) a monitoring, inspection or regulatory function connected, even occasionally, with the exercise of official authority in cases referred to in (c), (d) and (e);

    (g) the protection of the data subject or of the rights and freedoms of others.

2. Subject to adequate legal safeguards, in particular that the data are not used for taking measures or decisions regarding any particular individual, Member States may, where there is clearly no risk of breaching the privacy of the data subject, restrict by a legislative measure the rights provided for in Article 12 when data are processed solely for purposes of scientific research or are kept in personal form for a period which does not exceed the period necessary for the sole purpose of creating statistics.

Art. 14 – *The data subject's right to object*

Member States shall grant the data subject the right:

(a) at least in the cases referred to in Article 7 (e) and (f), to object at any time on compelling legitimate grounds relating to his particular situation to the processing of data relating to him ... . Where there is a justified objection, the processing instigated by the controller may no longer involve those data;

(b) to object, on request and free of charge, to the processing of personal data relating to him which the controller anticipates being processed for the purposes of direct marketing ...

Art. 15 – *Automated individual decisions*

1. Member States shall grant the right to every person not to be subject to a decision which produces legal effects concerning him or significantly affects him and which is based solely on automated processing of data intended to evaluate certain personal aspects relating to him, such as his performance at work, creditworthiness, reliability, conduct, etc. ...

Art. 17 – *Security of processing*

1. Member States shall provide that the controller must implement appropriate technical and organizational measures to protect personal data against accidental or unlawful destruction or accidental loss, alteration, unautho-

rized disclosure or access, in particular where the processing involves the transmission of data over a network, and against all other unlawful forms of processing. ...

Art. 25 – *Principles*

1. The Member States shall provide that the transfer to a third country of personal data which are undergoing processing or are intended for processing after transfer may take place only if, without prejudice to compliance with the national provisions adopted pursuant to the other provisions of this Directive, the third country in question ensures an adequate level of protection.

2. The adequacy of the level of protection afforded by a third country shall be assessed in the light of all the circumstances surrounding a data transfer operation or set of data transfer operations; particular consideration shall be given to the nature of the data, the purpose and duration of the proposed processing operation or operations, the country of origin and country of final destination, the rules of law, both general and sectoral, in force in the third country in question and the professional rules and security measures which are complied with in that country. ...

Art. 28 – *Supervisory authority*

1. Each Member State shall provide that one or more public authorities are responsible for monitoring the application within its territory of the provisions adopted by the Member States pursuant to this Directive. ...

QUESTIONS

1. How does the European approach to the privacy of personal data compare with the American approach discussed above?

2. United States privacy law is usually referred to as "sectoral" because it applies to specific types of information. For example, the Children's Online Privacy Protection Act (COPPA) prohibits collecting private information from children under 13 without parental consent, and the Video Privacy Protection Act prohibits the disclosure of any "personally identifiable information" about consumers who rent or buy "prerecorded video cassette tapes or similar audio visual materials." The most rigorous such law is probably the Health Insurance Portability and Accountability Act, which imposes quite rigorous confidentiality and security obligations on medical professionals and those working with health records. Should the United States switch to the European approach, or are tailored privacy protections better?

3. What do you make of Article 15's prohibition on decision-making "solely on automated processing of [personal] data?" Credit checks are ubiquitous in the United States, not just when applying for loans but also in applying for jobs and leases. How would they fare under the Data Protection Directive?

EUROPEAN UNION: ECJ INVALIDATES DATA RETENTION DIRECTIVE
Law Library of Congress (2014)
https://www.loc.gov/law/help/eu-data-retention-directive/eu-data-retention-directive.pdf

On April 8, 2014, the Grand Chamber of the Court of Justice of the European Union (ECJ) delivered a much-anticipated judgment concerning the legality of

Directive No. 2006/24/EC, commonly referred to as the Data Retention Directive. The Directive was challenged on the grounds of infringement of the right to private life, and the right to the protection of personal data of individuals, as guaranteed in articles 7 and 8, respectively, of the Charter of Fundamental Rights of the European Union.

The Data Retention Directive required the providers of publicly available electronic communications services or public communications networks to retain traffic and location data belonging to individuals or legal entities. Such data included the calling telephone number and name and address of the subscriber or register user, user IDs (a unique identifier assigned to each person who signs with an electronic communications service), Internet protocol addresses, the numbers dialed, and call forwarding or call transfer records. The retention period was to last for a minimum period of six months and up to two years, and the sole purpose of processing and storing the data was to prevent, investigate, detect, and prosecute serious crimes, such as organized crime and terrorism. The content of the communications of individuals was not retained. ...

In considering the broad category of data to be retained, the ECJ observed that such data

> may allow very precise conclusions to be drawn concerning the private lives of the persons whose data has been retained, such as the habits of everyday life, permanent or temporary places of residence, daily or other movements, the activities carried out, the social relationships of those persons and the social environment.

The Court observed that under such circumstances, even though it is not permissible to retain the content of communications, it is possible that the freedom of expression of subscribers or registered users might be in jeopardy.

The ECJ stated that the retention of data in order to allow access by the competent national authorities constitutes processing of data and therefore affects two basic rights of the Charter of Fundamental Rights: (a) the right to private life guaranteed by article 7, and (b) the protection of personal data guaranteed by article 8. ...

Article 52(1) of the Charter requires that any limitation on the exercise of rights guaranteed by the Charter must be provided by law and must respect the essence of such rights. Any limitations are subject to a proportionality test and can be imposed only if they are necessary and meet the objectives of general interest as recognized by the EU or the need to protect the rights and freedoms of others. ...

The Court reasoned that ... the Directive does not establish clear and precise rules that regulate the "extent of interference with the fundamental rights of Art. 7 and 8 of the Charter." Therefore, it concluded that the Directive "entails a wide-ranging and particularly serious interference with those fundamental rights in the legal order of the EU, without such an interference being precisely circumscribed by provisions to ensure that it is actually limited to what is strictly necessary." ...

The Data Retention Directive becomes invalid *ab initio*, that is from the time it became effective in 2006, since the ECJ did not specify otherwise. The EU Members that have transposed the Directive into their national legal systems are required to take steps to ensure compliance with the judgment.

GOOGLE SPAIN SP V. AGENCIA ESPAÑOLA DE PROTECCIÓN DE DATOS

European Court of Justice
ECLI:EU:C:2014:616

... THE DISPUTE IN THE MAIN PROCEEDINGS AND THE QUESTIONS REFERRED FOR A PRELIMINARY RULING

14. On 5 March 2010, Mr Costeja González, a Spanish national resident in Spain, lodged with the [Agencia Española de Protección de Datos (Spanish Data Protection Agency) (AEPD)] a complaint against La Vanguardia Ediciones SL, which publishes a daily newspaper with a large circulation, in particular in Catalonia (Spain) ('La Vanguardia'), and against Google Spain and Google Inc. The complaint was based on the fact that, when an internet user entered Mr Costeja González's name in the search engine of the Google group ('Google Search'), he would obtain links to two pages of La Vanguardia's newspaper, of 19 January and 9 March 1998 respectively, on which an announcement mentioning Mr Costeja González's name appeared for a real-estate auction connected with attachment proceedings for the recovery of social security debts.

15. By that complaint, Mr Costeja González requested, first, that La Vanguardia be required either to remove or alter those pages so that the personal data relating to him no longer appeared or to use certain tools made available by search engines in order to protect the data. Second, he requested that Google Spain or Google Inc. be required to remove or conceal the personal data relating to him so that they ceased to be included in the search results and no longer appeared in the links to La Vanguardia. Mr Costeja González stated in this context that the attachment proceedings concerning him had been fully resolved for a number of years and that reference to them was now entirely irrelevant.

16. By decision of 30 July 2010, the AEPD rejected the complaint in so far as it related to La Vanguardia, taking the view that the publication by it of the information in question was legally justified as it took place upon order of the Ministry of Labour and Social Affairs and was intended to give maximum publicity to the auction in order to secure as many bidders as possible.

17. On the other hand, the complaint was upheld in so far as it was directed against Google Spain and Google Inc. The AEPD considered in this regard that operators of search engines are subject to data protection legislation given that they carry out data processing for which they are responsible and act as intermediaries in the information society. The AEPD took the view that it has the power to require the withdrawal of data and the prohibition of access to certain data by the operators of search engines when it considers that the locating and dissemination of the data are liable to compromise the fundamental right to data protection and the dignity of persons in the broad sense, and this would also encompass the mere wish of the person concerned that such data not be known to third parties. The AEPD considered that that obligation may be owed directly by operators of search engines, without it being necessary to erase the data or information from the website where they appear, including when retention of the information on that site is justified by a statutory provision.

18. Google Spain and Google Inc. brought separate actions against that decision before the Audiencia Nacional (National High Court). ...

19. That court states in the order for reference that the actions raise the question of what obligations are owed by operators of search engines to protect personal data of persons concerned who do not wish that certain information, which is published on third parties' websites and contains personal data relating to them that enable that information to be linked to them, be located, indexed and made available to internet users indefinitely. The answer to that question depends on the way in which Directive 95/46 must be interpreted in the context of these technologies, which appeared after the directive's publication.

20. In those circumstances, the Audiencia Nacional decided to stay the proceedings and to refer the following questions to the Court for a preliminary ruling ...

CONSIDERATION OF THE QUESTIONS REFERRED

Question 2(a) and (b), concerning the material scope of Directive 95/46

21. By Question 2(a) and (b), which it is appropriate to examine first, the referring court asks, in essence, whether Article 2(b) of Directive 95/46 is to be interpreted as meaning that the activity of a search engine as a provider of content which consists in finding information published or placed on the internet by third parties, indexing it automatically, storing it temporarily and, finally, making it available to internet users according to a particular order of preference must be classified as 'processing of personal data' within the meaning of that provision when that information contains personal data. If the answer is in the affirmative, the referring court seeks to ascertain furthermore whether Article 2(d) of Directive 95/46 is to be interpreted as meaning that the operator of a search engine must be regarded as the 'controller' in respect of that processing of the personal data, within the meaning of that provision.

22. According to Google Spain and Google Inc., the activity of search engines cannot be regarded as processing of the data which appear on third parties' web pages displayed in the list of search results, given that search engines process all the information available on the internet without effecting a selection between personal data and other information. Furthermore, even if that activity must be classified as 'data processing', the operator of a search engine cannot be regarded as a 'controller' in respect of that processing since it has no knowledge of those data and does not exercise control over the data. ...

25. Article 2(b) of Directive 95/46 defines 'processing of personal data' as 'any operation or set of operations which is performed upon personal data, whether or not by automatic means, such as collection, recording, organisation, storage, adaptation or alteration, retrieval, consultation, use, disclosure by transmission, dissemination or otherwise making available, alignment or combination, blocking, erasure or destruction'. ...

27. So far as concerns the activity at issue in the main proceedings, it is not contested that the data found, indexed and stored by search engines and made available to their users include information relating to identified or identifiable natural persons and thus 'personal data' within the meaning of Article 2(a) of that directive.

28. Therefore, it must be found that, in exploring the internet automatically, constantly and systematically in search of the information which is published there, the operator of a search engine 'collects' such data which it subsequently 'retrieves', 'records' and 'organises' within the framework of its indexing programmes, 'stores' on its servers and, as the case may be, 'discloses' and 'makes available' to its users in the form of lists of search results. As those operations are referred to expressly and unconditionally in Article 2(b) of Directive 95/46, they must be classified as 'processing' within the meaning of that provision, regardless of the fact that the operator of the search engine also carries out the same operations in respect of other types of information and does not distinguish between the latter and the personal data.

29. Nor is the foregoing finding affected by the fact that those data have already been published on the internet and are not altered by the search engine. ...

[The court then found that Google was the "controller" of the processing of personal data by its search engine because "the search engine operator which determines the purposes and means of that activity and thus of the processing of personal data that it itself carries out."]

Question 1(a) to (d), concerning the territorial scope of Directive 95/46 ...

60   ... Article 4(1)(a) of Directive 95/46 is to be interpreted as meaning that processing of personal data is carried out in the context of the activities of an establishment of the controller on the territory of a Member State, within the meaning of that provision, when the operator of a search engine sets up in a Member State a branch or subsidiary which is intended to promote and sell advertising space offered by that engine and which orientates its activity towards the inhabitants of that Member State. ...

Question 2(c) and (d), concerning the extent of the responsibility of the operator of a search engine under Directive 95/46

62. By Question 2(c) and (d), the referring court asks, in essence, whether Article 12(b) and subparagraph (a) of the first paragraph of Article 14 of Directive 95/46 are to be interpreted as meaning that, in order to comply with the rights laid down in those provisions, the operator of a search engine is obliged to remove from the list of results displayed following a search made on the basis of a person's name links to web pages, published by third parties and containing information relating to that person, also in a case where that name or information is not erased beforehand or simultaneously from those web pages, and even, as the case may be, when its publication in itself on those pages is lawful.

63. Google Spain and Google Inc. submit that, by virtue of the principle of proportionality, any request seeking the removal of information must be addressed to the publisher of the website concerned because it is he who takes the responsibility for making the information public, who is in a position to appraise the lawfulness of that publication and who has available to him the most effective and least restrictive means of making the information inaccessible. Furthermore, to require the operator of a search engine to withdraw information published on the internet from its indexes would take insufficient account of the fundamental rights of publishers of websites, of other internet users and of that operator itself. ...

66. First of all, it should be remembered that, as is apparent from Article 1 and recital 10 in the preamble, Directive 95/46 seeks to ensure a high level of protection of the fundamental rights and freedoms of natural persons, in particular their right to privacy, with respect to the processing of personal data. ...

72. Under Article 6 of Directive 95/46 and without prejudice to specific provisions that the Member States may lay down in respect of processing for historical, statistical or scientific purposes, the controller has the task of ensuring that personal data are processed 'fairly and lawfully', that they are 'collected for specified, explicit and legitimate purposes and not further processed in a way incompatible with those purposes', that they are 'adequate, relevant and not excessive in relation to the purposes for which they are collected and/or further processed', that they are 'accurate and, where necessary, kept up to date' and, finally, that they are 'kept in a form which permits identification of data subjects for no longer than is necessary for the purposes for which the data were collected or for which they are further processed'. In this context, the controller must take every reasonable step to ensure that data which do not meet the requirements of that provision are erased or rectified. ...

74. This provision permits the processing of personal data where it is necessary for the purposes of the legitimate interests pursued by the controller or by the third party or parties to whom the data are disclosed, except where such interests are overridden by the interests or fundamental rights and freedoms of the data subject – in particular his right to privacy with respect to the processing of personal data ...

76. Under subparagraph (a) of the first paragraph of Article 14 of Directive 95/46, Member States are to grant the data subject the right ... to object at any time on compelling legitimate grounds relating to his particular situation to the processing of data relating to him, save where otherwise provided by national legislation. ...

77. Requests under Article 12(b) and subparagraph (a) of the first paragraph of Article 14 of Directive 95/46 may be addressed by the data subject directly to the controller who must then duly examine their merits and, as the case may be, end processing of the data in question. Where the controller does not grant the request, the data subject may bring the matter before the supervisory authority or the judicial authority so that it carries out the necessary checks and orders the controller to take specific measures accordingly.

78. In this connection ... each supervisory authority is to hear claims lodged by any person concerning the protection of his rights and freedoms in regard to the processing of personal data and ... has investigative powers and effective powers of intervention enabling it to order in particular the blocking, erasure or destruction of data or to impose a temporary or definitive ban on such processing.

79. It is in the light of those considerations that it is necessary to interpret and apply the provisions of Directive 95/46 governing the data subject's rights when he lodges with the supervisory authority or judicial authority a request such as that at issue in the main proceedings.

80. It must be pointed out at the outset that, as has been found in paragraphs 36 to 38 of the present judgment, processing of personal data, such as that

at issue in the main proceedings, carried out by the operator of a search engine is liable to affect significantly the fundamental rights to privacy and to the protection of personal data when the search by means of that engine is carried out on the basis of an individual's name, since that processing enables any internet user to obtain through the list of results a structured overview of the information relating to that individual that can be found on the internet – information which potentially concerns a vast number of aspects of his private life and which, without the search engine, could not have been interconnected or could have been only with great difficulty – and thereby to establish a more or less detailed profile of him. Furthermore, the effect of the interference with those rights of the data subject is heightened on account of the important role played by the internet and search engines in modern society, which render the information contained in such a list of results ubiquitous.

81. In the light of the potential seriousness of that interference, it is clear that it cannot be justified by merely the economic interest which the operator of such an engine has in that processing. However, inasmuch as the removal of links from the list of results could, depending on the information at issue, have effects upon the legitimate interest of internet users potentially interested in having access to that information, in situations such as that at issue in the main proceedings a fair balance should be sought in particular between that interest and the data subject's fundamental rights under Articles 7 and 8 of the Charter. Whilst it is true that the data subject's rights protected by those articles also override, as a general rule, that interest of internet users, that balance may however depend, in specific cases, on the nature of the information in question and its sensitivity for the data subject's private life and on the interest of the public in having that information, an interest which may vary, in particular, according to the role played by the data subject in public life.

82. ... when a request such as that at issue in the main proceedings is lodged with it, the supervisory authority or judicial authority may order the operator of the search engine to remove from the list of results displayed following a search made on the basis of a person's name links to web pages published by third parties containing information relating to that person, without an order to that effect presupposing the previous or simultaneous removal of that name and information – from the web page on which they were published. ...

84. Given the ease with which information published on a website can be replicated on other sites and the fact that the persons responsible for its publication are not always subject to European Union legislation, effective and complete protection of data users could not be achieved if the latter had to obtain first or in parallel the erasure of the information relating to them from the publishers of websites. ...

87. Indeed, since the inclusion in the list of results, displayed following a search made on the basis of a person's name, of a web page and of the information contained on it relating to that person makes access to that information appreciably easier for any internet user making a search in respect of the person concerned and may play a decisive role in the dissemination of that information, it is liable to constitute a more significant interference with the

data subject's fundamental right to privacy than the publication on the web page.

88. In the light of all the foregoing considerations ... the operator of a search engine is obliged to remove from the list of results displayed following a search made on the basis of a person's name links to web pages ... even, as the case may be, when its publication in itself on those pages is lawful.

Question 3, concerning the scope of the data subject's rights guaranteed by Directive 95/46

89. By Question 3, the referring court asks, in essence, whether Article 12(b) and subparagraph (a) of the first paragraph of Article 14 of Directive 95/46 are to be interpreted as enabling the data subject to require the operator of a search engine to remove [links] on the ground that that information may be prejudicial to him or that he wishes it to be 'forgotten' after a certain time. ...

93. ... even initially lawful processing of accurate data may, in the course of time, become incompatible with the directive where those data are no longer necessary in the light of the purposes for which they were collected or processed. That is so in particular where they appear to be inadequate, irrelevant or no longer relevant, or excessive in relation to those purposes and in the light of the time that has elapsed.

94. Therefore, if it is found, following a request by the data subject pursuant to Article 12(b) of Directive 95/46, that the inclusion in the list of results displayed following a search made on the basis of his name of the links to web pages published lawfully by third parties and containing true information relating to him personally is, at this point in time, incompatible with Article 6(1)(c) to (e) of the directive because that information appears, having regard to all the circumstances of the case, to be inadequate, irrelevant or no longer relevant, or excessive in relation to the purposes of the processing at issue carried out by the operator of the search engine, the information and links concerned in the list of results must be erased. ...

97. [The rights of the data subject] override, as a rule, not only the economic interest of the operator of the search engine but also the interest of the general public in finding that information upon a search relating to the data subject's name. However, that would not be the case if it appeared, for particular reasons, such as the role played by the data subject in public life, that the interference with his fundamental rights is justified by the preponderant interest of the general public in having, on account of inclusion in the list of results, access to the information in question.

98. As regards [Mr. González], it should be held that, having regard to the sensitivity for the data subject's private life of the information contained in those announcements and to the fact that its initial publication had taken place 16 years earlier, the data subject establishes a right that that information should no longer be linked to his name by means of such a list. Accordingly, since in the case in point there do not appear to be particular reasons substantiating a preponderant interest of the public in having, in the context of such a search, access to that information, a matter which is, however, for the referring court to establish, the data subject may, ... require those links to be removed from the list of results. ...

QUESTIONS

1. Some observers have referred to this decision as creating a "right to be forgotten" in the EU. Does it?

2. After *Google Spain*, what process does someone in the EU need to follow to have unflattering search results removed from search engines? Who will make the ultimate decision on whether the results will be removed, and what evidence will they consider?

3. What result under United States law? Why?

4. What does Google need to do to comply with this and similar requests? What do you find when you search for [Costeja González] on google.com and on google.es?

SCHREMS V. DATA PROTECTION COMMISSIONER
European Court of Justice
ECLI:EU:C:2015:650

1. This request for a preliminary ruling relates to the interpretation, in the light of Articles 7, 8 and 47 of the Charter of Fundamental Rights of the European Union ('the Charter'), of Articles 25(6) and 28 of Directive 95/46/EC of the European Parliament and of the Council of 24 October 1995 on the protection of individuals with regard to the processing of personal data and on the free movement of such data (OJ 1995 L 281, p. 31) ... and, in essence, to the validity of Commission Decision 2000/520/EC of 26 July 2000 pursuant to Directive 95/46 on the adequacy of the protection provided by the safe harbour privacy principles and related frequently asked questions issued by the US Department of Commerce (OJ 2000 L 215, p. 7).

2. The request has been made in proceedings between Mr Schrems and the Data Protection Commissioner ('the Commissioner') concerning the latter's refusal to investigate a complaint made by Mr Schrems regarding the fact that Facebook Ireland Ltd ('Facebook Ireland') transfers the personal data of its users to the United States of America and keeps it on servers located in that country. ...

LEGAL CONTEXT ...

Decision 2000/520 ...

[The preamble to Decision 2000/520 states:

(5) The adequate level of protection for the transfer of data from the Community to the United States recognised by this Decision, should be attained if organisations comply with the safe harbour privacy principles for the protection of personal data transferred from a Member State to the United States ... issued by the Government of the United States on 21 July 2000. Furthermore the organisations should publicly disclose their privacy policies and be subject to the jurisdiction of the Federal Trade Commission (FTC) under Section 5 of the Federal Trade Commission Act which prohibits unfair or deceptive acts or practices in or affecting commerce, or that of another statutory body that will effectively ensure compliance with the Principles implemented in accordance with the FAQs. ...

Article 1 of Decision 2000/520 states:

2. In relation to each transfer of data the following conditions shall be met:

(a) the organisation receiving the data has unambiguously and publicly disclosed its commitment to comply with the Principles implemented in accordance with the FAQs; and

(b) the organisation is subject to the statutory powers of a government body in the United States listed in Annex VII to this Decision which is empowered to investigate complaints and to obtain relief against unfair or deceptive practices as well as redress for individuals, irrespective of their country of residence or nationality, in case of non-compliance with the Principles ...

The safe harbor principles state:

NOTICE: An organization must inform individuals about the purposes for which it collects and uses information about them, how to contact the organization with any inquiries or complaints, the types of third parties to which it discloses the information, and the choices and means the organization offers individuals for limiting its use and disclosure. This notice must be provided in clear and conspicuous language when individuals are first asked to provide personal information to the organization or as soon thereafter as is practicable, but in any event before the organization uses such information for a purpose other than that for which it was originally collected or processed by the transferring organization or discloses it for the first time to a third party.

CHOICE: An organization must offer individuals the opportunity to choose (opt out) whether their personal information is (a) to be disclosed to a third party or (b) to be used for a purpose that is incompatible with the purpose(s) for which it was originally collected or subsequently authorized by the individual. Individuals must be provided with clear and conspicuous, readily available, and affordable mechanisms to exercise choice.

For sensitive information (i.e. personal information specifying medical or health conditions, racial or ethnic origin, political opinions, religious or philosophical beliefs, trade union membership or information specifying the sex life of the individual), they must be given affirmative or explicit (opt in) choice if the information is to be disclosed to a third party or used for a purpose other than those for which it was originally collected or subsequently authorized by the individual through the exercise of opt in choice. In any case, an organization should treat as sensitive any information received from a third party where the third party treats and identifies it as sensitive.

ONWARD TRANSFER: To disclose information to a third party, organizations must apply the Notice and Choice Principles. ...

SECURITY: Organizations creating, maintaining, using or disseminating personal information must take reasonable precautions to protect it from loss, misuse and unauthorized access, disclosure, alteration and destruction.

DATA INTEGRITY: Consistent with the Principles, personal information must be relevant for the purposes for which it is to be used. An organization may not process personal information in a way that is incompatible with the purposes for which it has been collected or subsequently authorized by the individual. To the extent necessary for those purposes, an organization should take reasonable steps to ensure that data is reliable for its intended use, accurate, complete, and current.

ACCESS: Individuals must have access to personal information about them that an organization holds and be able to correct, amend, or delete that information where it is inaccurate, except where the burden or expense of providing access would be disproportionate to the risks to the individual's privacy in the case in question, or where the rights of persons other than the individual would be violated.

ENFORCEMENT: Effective privacy protection must include mechanisms for assuring compliance with the Principles, recourse for individuals to whom the data relate affected by non-compliance with the Principles, and consequences for the organization when the Principles are not followed. At a minimum, such mechanisms must include (a) readily available and affordable independent recourse mechanisms by which each individual's complaints and disputes are investigated and resolved by reference to the Principles and damages awarded where the applicable law or private sector initiatives so provide; (b) follow up procedures for verifying that the attestations and assertions businesses make about their privacy practices are true and that privacy practices have been implemented as presented; and (c) obligations to remedy problems arising out of failure to comply with the Principles by organizations announcing their adherence to them and consequences for such organizations. Sanctions must be sufficiently rigorous to ensure compliance by organizations.]

[The court reviewed two communications adopted by the European Commission on November 27, 2013 based on reports from an ad hoc EU-US working group. *Rebuilding Trust in EU-US Data Flows* (COM(2013) 846 final) stated in part that '[t]he personal data of [Union] citizens sent to the [United States] under the Safe Harbour may be accessed and further processed by US authorities in a way incompatible with the grounds on which the data was originally collected in the [European Union] and the purposes for which it was transferred to the [United States]" and that "[a] majority of the US internet companies that appear to be more directly concerned by [the surveillance] programmes are certified under the Safe Harbour scheme." *The Functioning of the Safe Harbour from the Perspective of EU Citizens and Companies Established in the EU* (COM(2013) 847 final) observed that 246 companies were self-certified under the safe harbor but, "in practice, a significant number of certified companies did not comply, or did not comply fully, with the safe harbour principles." Moreover, "safeguards that are provided under US law are mostly available to US citizens or legal residents" and "there are no opportunities for either EU or US data subjects to obtain access, rectification or erasure of data, or administrative or judicial redress with regard to collection and further processing of their personal data taking place under the US surveillance programmes."]

THE DISPUTE IN THE MAIN PROCEEDINGS AND THE QUESTIONS REFERRED FOR A PRELIMINARY RULING

26. Mr Schrems, an Austrian national residing in Austria, has been a user of the Facebook social network ('Facebook') since 2008.

27. Any person residing in the European Union who wishes to use Facebook is required to conclude, at the time of his registration, a contract with Facebook Ireland, a subsidiary of Facebook Inc. which is itself established in the United States. Some or all of the personal data of Facebook Ireland's users who reside in the European Union is transferred to servers belonging to

Facebook Inc. that are located in the United States, where it undergoes processing.

28. On 25 June 2013 Mr Schrems made a complaint to the Commissioner by which he in essence asked the latter to exercise his statutory powers by prohibiting Facebook Ireland from transferring his personal data to the United States. He contended in his complaint that the law and practice in force in that country did not ensure adequate protection of the personal data held in its territory against the surveillance activities that were engaged in there by the public authorities. Mr Schrems referred in this regard to the revelations made by Edward Snowden concerning the activities of the United States intelligence services, in particular those of the National Security Agency ('the NSA').

29. Since the Commissioner took the view that he was not required to investigate the matters raised by Mr Schrems in the complaint, he rejected it as unfounded. The Commissioner considered that there was no evidence that Mr Schrems' personal data had been accessed by the NSA. He added that the allegations raised by Mr Schrems in his complaint could not be profitably put forward since any question of the adequacy of data protection in the United States had to be determined in accordance with Decision 2000/520 and the Commission had found in that decision that the United States ensured an adequate level of protection.

30. Mr Schrems brought an action before the High Court challenging the decision at issue in the main proceedings. After considering the evidence adduced by the parties to the main proceedings, the High Court found that the electronic surveillance and interception of personal data transferred from the European Union to the United States serve necessary and indispensable objectives in the public interest. However, it added that the revelations made by Edward Snowden had demonstrated a 'significant over-reach' on the part of the NSA and other federal agencies.

31. According to the High Court, Union citizens have no effective right to be heard. Oversight of the intelligence services' actions is carried out within the framework of an *ex parte* and secret procedure. Once the personal data has been transferred to the United States, it is capable of being accessed by the NSA and other federal agencies, such as the Federal Bureau of Investigation (FBI), in the course of the indiscriminate surveillance and interception carried out by them on a large scale. ...

35. The High Court further observes that in his action Mr Schrems in reality raises the legality of the safe harbour regime which was established by Decision 2000/520 and gives rise to the decision at issue in the main proceedings. Thus, even though Mr Schrems has not formally contested the validity of either Directive 95/46 or Decision 2000/520, the question is raised, according to the High Court, as to whether, on account of Article 25(6) of Directive 95/46, the Commissioner was bound by the Commission's finding in Decision 2000/520 that the United States ensures an adequate level of protection or whether Article 8 of the Charter authorised the Commissioner to break free, if appropriate, from such a finding.

36. In those circumstances the High Court decided to stay the proceedings and to refer the following questions to the Court of Justice for a preliminary ruling:

(1) Whether in the course of determining a complaint which has been made to an independent office holder who has been vested by statute with the functions of administering and enforcing data protection legislation that personal data is being transferred to another third country (in this case, the United States of America) the laws and practices of which, it is claimed, do not contain adequate protections for the data subject, that office holder is absolutely bound by the Community finding to the contrary contained in [Decision 2000/520] having regard to Article 7, Article 8 and Article 47 of [the Charter], the provisions of Article 25(6) of Directive [95/46] notwithstanding?

(2) Or, alternatively, may and/or must the office holder conduct his or her own investigation of the matter in the light of factual developments in the meantime since that Commission decision was first published?

CONSIDERATION OF THE QUESTIONS REFERRED ...

The powers of the national supervisory authorities, within the meaning of Article 28 of Directive 95/46, when the Commission has adopted a decision pursuant to Article 25(6) of that directive ...

66   Having regard to the foregoing considerations, the answer to the questions referred is that Article 25(6) of Directive 95/46, read in the light of Articles 7, 8 and 47 of the Charter, must be interpreted as meaning that a decision adopted pursuant to that provision, such as Decision 2000/520, by which the Commission finds that a third country ensures an adequate level of protection, does not prevent a supervisory authority of a Member State, within the meaning of Article 28 of that directive, from examining the claim of a person concerning the protection of his rights and freedoms in regard to the processing of personal data relating to him which has been transferred from a Member State to that third country when that person contends that the law and practices in force in the third country do not ensure an adequate level of protection.

The validity of Decision 2000/520

67   As is apparent from the referring court's explanations relating to the questions submitted, Mr Schrems contends in the main proceedings that United States law and practice do not ensure an adequate level of protection within the meaning of Article 25 of Directive 95/46. ... Mr Schrems expresses doubts, which the referring court indeed seems essentially to share, concerning the validity of Decision 2000/520. In such circumstances ... it should be examined whether that decision complies with the requirements stemming from Directive 95/46 read in the light of the Charter. ...

Article 1 of Decision 2000/520 ...

81.   Whilst recourse by a third country to a system of self-certification is not in itself contrary to the requirement laid down in Article 25(6) of Directive 95/46 that the third country concerned must ensure an adequate level of protection 'by reason of its domestic law or ... international commitments', the reliability of such a system, in the light of that requirement, is founded essentially on the establishment of effective detection and supervision mechanisms enabling any infringements of the rules ensuring the protection of fundamental rights, in particular the right to respect for private life and

the right to protection of personal data, to be identified and punished in practice.

82. In the present instance, by virtue of the second paragraph of Annex I to Decision 2000/520, the safe harbour principles are 'intended for use solely by US organisations receiving personal data from the European Union for the purpose of qualifying for the safe harbour and the presumption of "adequacy" it creates'. Those principles are therefore applicable solely to self-certified United States organisations receiving personal data from the European Union, and United States public authorities are not required to comply with them. ...

84. In addition, under the fourth paragraph of Annex I to Decision 2000/520, the applicability of the safe harbour principles may be limited, in particular, 'to the extent necessary to meet national security, public interest, or law enforcement requirements' and 'by statute, government regulation, or case-law that create conflicting obligations or explicit authorisations, provided that, in exercising any such authorisation, an organisation can demonstrate that its non-compliance with the Principles is limited to the extent necessary to meet the overriding legitimate interests furthered by such authorisation'.

85. In this connection, Decision 2000/520 states in Part B of Annex IV, with regard to the limits to which the safe harbour principles' applicability is subject, that, '[c]learly, where US law imposes a conflicting obligation, US organisations whether in the safe harbour or not must comply with the law'.

86. Thus, Decision 2000/520 lays down that 'national security, public interest, or law enforcement requirements' have primacy over the safe harbour principles, primacy pursuant to which self-certified United States organisations receiving personal data from the European Union are bound to disregard those principles without limitation where they conflict with those requirements and therefore prove incompatible with them. ...

88. In addition, Decision 2000/520 does not contain any finding regarding the existence, in the United States, of rules adopted by the State intended to limit any interference with the fundamental rights of the persons whose data is transferred from the European Union to the United States, interference which the State entities of that country would be authorised to engage in when they pursue legitimate objectives, such as national security.

89. Nor does Decision 2000/520 refer to the existence of effective legal protection against interference of that kind. ... [P]rocedures before the Federal Trade Commission — the powers of which ... are limited to commercial disputes — and the private dispute resolution mechanisms concern compliance by the United States undertakings with the safe harbour principles and cannot be applied in disputes relating to the legality of interference with fundamental rights that results from measures originating from the State.

90. Moreover, the foregoing analysis of Decision 2000/520 is borne out by the Commission's own assessment of the situation resulting from the implementation of that decision. Particularly in points 2 and 3.2 of Communication COM(2013) 846 final and in points 7.1, 7.2 and 8 of Communication COM(2013) 847 final ... the Commission found that the United States authorities were able to access the personal data transferred from the Member States to the United States and process it in a way incompatible, in particular, with the purposes for which it was transferred, beyond what was strictly

necessary and proportionate to the protection of national security. Also, the Commission noted that the data subjects had no administrative or judicial means of redress enabling, in particular, the data relating to them to be accessed and, as the case may be, rectified or erased. ...

92. Furthermore and above all, protection of the fundamental right to respect for private life at EU level requires derogations and limitations in relation to the protection of personal data to apply only in so far as is strictly necessary.

93. Legislation is not limited to what is strictly necessary where it authorises, on a generalised basis, storage of all the personal data of all the persons whose data has been transferred from the European Union to the United States without any differentiation, limitation or exception being made in the light of the objective pursued and without an objective criterion being laid down by which to determine the limits of the access of the public authorities to the data, and of its subsequent use, for purposes which are specific, strictly restricted and capable of justifying the interference which both access to that data and its use entail.

94. In particular, legislation permitting the public authorities to have access on a generalised basis to the content of electronic communications must be regarded as compromising the essence of the fundamental right to respect for private life, as guaranteed by Article 7 of the Charter.

95. Likewise, legislation not providing for any possibility for an individual to pursue legal remedies in order to have access to personal data relating to him, or to obtain the rectification or erasure of such data, does not respect the essence of the fundamental right to effective judicial protection, as enshrined in Article 47 of the Charter. ...

96. [I]n order for the Commission to adopt a decision pursuant to Article 25(6) of Directive 95/46, it must find, duly stating reasons, that the third country concerned in fact ensures, by reason of its domestic law or its international commitments, a level of protection of fundamental rights essentially equivalent to that guaranteed in the EU legal order, a level that is apparent in particular from the preceding paragraphs of the present judgment.

97. However, the Commission did not state, in Decision 2000/520, that the United States in fact 'ensures' an adequate level of protection by reason of its domestic law or its international commitments.

98. Consequently, without there being any need to examine the content of the safe harbour principles, it is to be concluded that Article 1 of Decision 2000/520 fails to comply with the requirements laid down in Article 25(6) of Directive 95/46, read in the light of the Charter, and that it is accordingly invalid. ...

QUESTIONS

1. What is wrong with the safe harbor framework? Could it be fixed if the European Commission made the appropriate statements in reenacting the safe harbor? Could it be fixed with more detailed voluntary commitments by U.S. companies? With realistically feasible changes to U.S. law? Or is the divide between U.S. and E.U. approaches to privacy so fundamental that no cross-border data transfers will be feasible going forward?

2. One of the most notable revelations in the Snowden leaks was the extent to which the NSA collaborated with foreign intelligence agencies on mass

surveillance projects. Is it hypocritical of the CJEU to invalidate the safe harbor on the basis of privacy violations of the sort European intelligence agencies are themselves deeply implicated in?

3. Does the rule against transfers of data to non-E.U. countries depend on an outdated concept of data having a physical location?

CHAPTER 5: ACCESS TO COMPUTERS

This chapter describes the various legal theories that owners and operators of servers can use to control how users are allowed to access those systems. A user who does what the server owner disapproves of might be breaching a contract, committing a crime, or committing a tort. Each of these three bodies of law has confronted the problem of access to computer systems by drawing on its own traditional categories, and evolved according to its own logic. It is not clear that the results are logical or consistent: what is legal behavior under one may be a serious wrong under another. Complicating matters even further, the categories draw on each other. The scope of "authorized" access under the Computer Fraud and Abuse Act, for example, may depend on the enforceability of a contract between the server owner and the user. As you read the following materials, be alert to the ways in which clever lawyers take advantage of this doctrinal ambiguity by seeking ways to frame a dispute using the legal categories that most favor their clients.

A. Contracts

Our first source of potential legal control over servers is contract law. The mechanics of contract formation should be familiar to you from your first-year course in contract law. Rules on offer and acceptance, parol evidence, and modifications were created long before electronic computers and the Internet. *Smoking Everywhere* illustrates some of the issues involved in translating them to a new factual context.

The issues posed by standardized form contracts have been well known for decades. But on the Internet, such issues are almost inescapable. Because the Internet enables near-strangers to meet and interact, it makes sense that one of the things they will do is enter into commercial relationships. Cheap and instant mass-market contracts would appear to be an obvious complement to cheap and instant communications. But for precisely the same reason, perhaps offerors will be tempted to overreach in claiming that a contract has been formed by virtue of online interactions.

CX DIGITAL MEDIA, INC. V. SMOKING EVERYWHERE, INC.
No. 09-62020-CIV (S.D. Fla. Mar. 23, 2011)
2011 U.S. Dist. LEXIS 29999, 2011 WL 1102782

Altonaga, District Judge: ...

I. FINDINGS OF FACT

Defendant, Smoking Everywhere Inc. ("Smoking Everywhere"), sold through its website an alternative to regular cigarettes called "electronic cigarettes," "E-Cigarettes," or "E-Cigs." To generate web traffic to its site and increase sales of E-Cigs, Smoking Everywhere approached Plaintiff, CX Digital Media, Inc. ("CX Digital"), about a free-trial offer that Smoking Everywhere wanted to promote.

CX Digital provides "advertising solutions" through "affiliate marketing." More simply put, CX Digital acts as a middleman between its network of affiliates or "third-party publishers," who purchase or provide advertising on the internet ("CX [Affiliates]"), and businesses that want to advertise online ("CX Client[s]"). How this works in practice is a bit technical.

CX Digital has relationships with approximately 10,000 independent affiliates. These affiliates are typically small entrepreneurs who purchase advertising space on web sites, social media sites, or who do direct emailing. When CX Digital enters an agreement called an "insertion order" with a new Client, CX Digital may work with the Client to design a campaign and to design appropriate web pages for the campaign.

CX Digital makes the Client's campaign available to CX Affiliates, who place advertisements for the CX Client's campaign. Each of the advertisements is clickable. When a consumer sees the ad, becomes interested in the product or service, and clicks on the advertisement [the consumer's browser loads a webpage from CX Digital's server, while also setting a cookie on the user's computer to track which CX Affiliate's ad the consumer clicked on].

Upon arriving at the CX Digital server, CX Digital records which affiliate's advertisement was clicked on by the consumer. The consumer is then redirected to the Client's "landing page," which contains the campaign offer details and a link to purchase the Client's product or service. ... The completion of a Sale triggers two obligations. First, the Client owes CX Digital the unit price for a Sale, and second, CX Digital owes its referring affiliate a payment for a completed Sale. CX Digital pays its affiliates, usually on a weekly basis, even if it has not received payment from the Client.

On August 4, 2009, Nick Touris, the vice-president of advertising for Smoking Everywhere, entered an agreement, entitled Insertion Order #6921, with CX Digital on behalf of Smoking Everywhere. In the Insertion Order, Smoking Everywhere promised to pay $45.00 to CX Digital for each completed Sale of the "Gold E-Cigarette Kit Free-Trial." The term "Sale" is defined by the Insertion Order as "a consumer who accesses the content via a CX Digital link and completes a one-page registration consisting of: filling in the appropriate field of information and successful credit card submi[ssion] . . . . No further action will be required from the consumer for the [cost per action] to be payable."

During the month of August, CX Digital provided 670 Sales pursuant to the Insertion Order. CX Digital never provided more than 200 Sales on any given day in August; from August 13, 2009 until August 31, 2009, the average number of Sales per day was about 39. ...

On September 2, 2011 [sic], Touris and Pedram Soltani, an account manager at CX Digital, engaged in a day-long instant-message conversation covering a number of topics ... After [discussing other topics] Soltani began a conversation about increasing the number of Sales CX Digital was sending Smoking Everywhere:

> pedramcx (2:49:45 PM): A few of our big guys are really excited about the new page and they're ready to run it
>
> pedramcx (2:50:08 PM): We can do 2000 orders/day by Friday if I have your blessing
>
> pedramcx (2:50:39 PM): You also have to find some way to get the Sub IDs working
>
> pedramcx (2:52:13 PM): those 2000 leads are going to be generated by our best affiliate and he's legit

nicktouris is available (3:42:42 PM): I am away from my computer right now.

pedramcx (4:07:57 PM): And I want the AOR when we make your offer #1 on the network

nicktouris (4:43:09 PM): NO LIMIT

pedramcx (4:43:21 PM): awesome!

The same day as this conversation, the number of Sales per day that CX Digital sent to Smoking Everywhere began to increase substantially. Between September 2, 2009 and September 23, 2009, CX Digital sent an average of 1,244 Sales per day, with a peak of 2,896 Sales on September 22, 2009. ...

At the end of September, CX Digital sent a second invoice for both August and September 2009. That invoice demanded that Smoking Everywhere pay a balance of $1,339,419.00 upon receipt. That figure included a price increase from $45.00 to $51.00 per Sale for 17,294 Sales between September 14 and 23, 2009.[7] CX Digital acknowledges that Smoking Everywhere paid a $5,000.00 deposit when it entered the Insertion Order. Accordingly, CX Digital asserts Smoking Everywhere owes it $1,260,805.00, which Smoking Everywhere has not yet paid. The Complaint contains one count alleging breach of contract, and in addition to compensatory damages, seeks attorney's fees pursuant to the Insertion Order.

II. CONCLUSIONS OF LAW

A. The Insertion Order

Smoking Everywhere does not dispute it signed the Insertion Order and that the Insertion Order constitutes a valid contract between CX Digital and Smoking Everywhere. ...

Smoking Everywhere also contends that, beginning in early September, CX Digital breached the Insertion Order by sending more than 200 Sales per day ... CX Digital does not dispute it engaged in this conduct, but it argues it was performing in accordance with the modified Insertion Order. Because Smoking Everywhere's allegations of breach by CX Digital turn on whether there was an enforceable modification to the Insertion Order, these arguments are addressed below in the discussion of the alleged changes.

B. Modification of the Insertion Order

The central dispute in this case is whether the Insertion Order was modified to permit an unlimited number of leads ... This raises two questions: (1) did Touris and Soltani agree to modify the Insertion Order during their September 2, 2009 instant-message conversation; and if so, (2) is their agreement to modify the contract enforceable?

1. Agreement to Modify Insertion Order

CX Digital contends the September 2, 2009 instant-message conversation between Touris and Soltani ... eliminated the 200-Sale-per-day limit. "The manifestation of assent may be made wholly or partly by written or spoken words or by other acts or by failure to act." RESTATEMENT (SECOND) CONTRACTS § 19 (1981). Under Delaware law, "overt manifestation of assent – not subjective intent – controls the formation of a contract; [and] the 'only intent of the parties to a contract which is essential is an intent to say the words or do the acts which constitute their

---

7 CX Digital is not seeking to recover the additional $6.00 per Sale in this litigation.

manifestation of assent'; . . . 'the intention to accept is unimportant except as manifested.'" *Indus. Am., Inc. v. Fulton Indus., Inc.*, 285 A.2d 412, 415 (Del. 1971) (quoting RESTATEMENT § 20). ...

In the "Campaign Details" section on the first page of the Insertion Order, the term "VOLUME:" appears in bold type followed by "200 leads/day." CX Digital contends Touris and Soltani agreed to remove the limit on the number of leads or Sales per day during their September 2, 2009 instant-message conversation.

After the discussion between Touris and Soltani about switching the URLs, Soltani sends an offer to Touris: "We can do 2000 orders/day by Friday if I have your blessing . . . . [a]nd I want the AOR when we make your offer number one on the network." Touris responds, "NO LIMIT." CX Digital argues that Touris accepted Soltani's offer by saying "NO LIMIT." The Court agrees a contract was formed but clarifies that Touris's response acted as a rejection and counter-offer that Soltani accepted by then replying "awesome!"

"In order to constitute an 'acceptance,' a response to an offer must be on identical terms as the offer and must be unconditional." *PAMI-LEMB I Inc. v. EMB-NHC, L.L.C.*, 857 A.2d 998, 1015 (Del. Ch. 2004). "A reply to an offer which purports to accept it but is conditional on the offeror's assent to terms additional to or different from those offered is not an acceptance but is a counter-offer." RESTATEMENT § 59; see also *PAMI-LEMB I*, 857 A.2d at 1015 n.80. "The words and conduct of the response are to be interpreted in light of all the circumstances." *PAMI-LEMB I*, 857 A.2d at 1015 n.81.

Here, Touris's response of "NO LIMIT" varies from the two specific terms Soltani offered and so acts as a counter-offer. Soltani proposed CX Digital provide 2,000 Sales per day and that CX Digital be the AOR or agent of record, a term of art meaning the exclusive provider of affiliate advertising on the advertising campaign. Touris makes a simple counter-offer that there be no limit on the number of Sales per day that CX Digital's affiliates may generate and makes no mention of the AOR term. Soltani enthusiastically accepts the counter-offer by writing, "awesome!" and by beginning to perform immediately by increasing the volume of Sales.

Touris testified he could have been responding to something other than Soltani's offer of 2,000 Sales per day when he said "NO LIMIT." Touris acknowledged that he had engaged in contract negotiations about "changing the number of leads, changing URLs, deposits, that type of thing" although he added, "we mainly spoke on the phone. A little bit of email but I had trouble receiving his emails so I mean we used Instant Messaging but you know there was a lot more than what was presented here, last court appearance." The implication of this testimony was that Touris could have been responding to something else he and Soltani had discussed by phone. But when pressed on just what else he could have been referring to when he said "NO LIMIT," Touris's memory failed him. In particular, he denied that "NO LIMIT" was some kind of personal motto.[15]

Indeed, neither Touris nor [Smoking Everywhere president Elicko] Taieb ever suggested any plausible alternative interpretation for why Touris wrote "NO LIM-

---

15 It is clear from Soltani's "awesome!" reply that Soltani interpreted Touris's statement as a direct response to the offer to increase the number of Sales. Moreover, Touris does not react to or correct Soltani's exclamation of "awesome!" in any way that would indicate confusion about the subject matter of their discussion. Indeed, the conversation reads most naturally when understood as two people negotiating and reaching a modification of an existing agreement.

IT" to Soltani, nor did they explain the content of the alleged additional negotiations that took place outside of the September 2, 2009 instant messages or what effect those would have had on the apparent agreement the parties reached on September 2nd. Considering Touris's admission that he was engaged in instant-message negotiations with Soltani about changing the number of leads along with the September 2nd instant-message transcript, directs the conclusion that those negotiations, wherever and however they occurred, culminated with a modification of the Insertion Order when Touris and Soltani agreed to "NO LIMIT."

Smoking Everywhere also observes that a significant amount of time – almost two hours – passed between Soltani's offer of 2,000 Sales per day and Touris's counter-offer of "NO LIMIT," which it suggests adds uncertainty to the meaning of the conversation. However, more than an hour passes before Soltani added that he would like CX Digital to be the AOR; yet this is clearly part of Soltani's offer. It is then only thirty-four minutes later that Touris responds "NO LIMIT." Given that Touris testified he would not have approved such an increase without first discussing it with Taieb, one explanation for the time delay, if one is needed, is that Touris was doing just that – asking Taieb for approval.[16]

2. Enforceability of the Modifications

Smoking Everywhere contends that even if it and CX Digital agreed to modify the Insertion Order, the modification is not enforceable for several reasons. First, an oral modification of a contract must be proven with "specificity and directness." Second, the language of the Insertion Order provides that it "may be changed only by a subsequent writing signed by both parties," and Smoking Everywhere did not waive this provision. Third, "the Defendant did not give the required consideration for any modifications to the initial insertion order, thus the alleged changes to the insertion order are not enforceable." Fourth, Touris lacked the authority to bind Smoking Everywhere. Lastly, Smoking Everywhere also raises the defenses of commercial frustration, violation of the implied covenant of good faith and fair dealing, and mutual mistake. These defenses are addressed in turn.

a. Specificity and Directness

Drawing from Delaware case law, Smoking Everywhere contends "[a] party asserting an oral modification must prove the intended change with 'specificity and directness as to leave no doubt of the intention of the parties to change what they previously solemnized by formal document.'" *Cont'l Ins. Co. v. Rutledge & Co.*, 750 A.2d 1219, 1230 (Del. Ch. 2000). In particular, Smoking Everywhere relies on *Reserves Dev. LLC v. Severn Sav. Bank, FSB*, No. 2502-VCP, 2007 WL 4054231, at *10 (Del. Ch. Nov. 9, 2007). The court in that case found a series of emails in the "record [was] not sufficiently 'specific and direct' to support a conclusion that the parties orally modified an existing written contract." *Id.* Smoking Everywhere contends that in this case, the instant messages between Touris and Soltani are not specific and direct enough evidence that it agreed with CX Digital to modify the Insertion Order. ...

The agreement to modify the Insertion Order to remove the limit is also supported by specific and direct evidence. As discussed, during the September 2nd instant messages, Touris made a counter-offer of "NO LIMIT" in response to Soltani's offer of 2,000 leads per day with AOR status for CX Digital. Soltani ac-

---

16 Moreover, anyone who has used an instant-message application in an office setting will recognize these time lags between responses as typical of the medium.

cepted the counter-offer. This modification clearly changed the "VOLUME" term in the details contract of the Insertion Order from 200 per day to unlimited. The language in the instant messages and the increase in the volume of leads that immediately follows provide specific and direct support that the change was intended.

Moreover, the *Severn Savings* case is easily distinguished from this case. ... First, the scope and complexity of the modifications alleged in *Severn Savings* far exceed the narrow and straightforward changes here. The emails in *Severn Savings* showed the parties discussing potential payment arrangements on two letters of credit, but evidence of an agreement "to change the party responsible for effectuating construction of the infrastructure" was only "sketchy" and "muddled." Id. at *9–10. Reading the emails excerpted in Severn Savings, one has the impression that the parties had discussed different options orally, but never reached any agreement. The emails were a continuation of the oral negotiations that tried to pin down the details of the parties' obligations. In this case, although there may have been conversations by phone, ... once the limit was removed on the number of Sales per day, CX Digital began to send more – no further negotiation was needed. The instant messages therefore, rather than showing continued debate like the emails in *Severn Savings*, show the parties had come to an agreement.

Second, the emails in *Severn Savings* were provided as evidence of an oral modification that had specific terms, not as a record of those specific terms. Here, the instant messages operate collectively as an unsigned writing containing the terms of the agreement to modify the Insertion Order. CX Digital is not alleging there are additional oral terms to the modification that are not evident from the instant messages. In fact, unlike in *Severn Savings*, Smoking Everywhere and CX Digital do not argue about what the specific terms of the alleged modification are, but about whether the modification actually occurred. As already discussed, the instant-message conversation and the parties' conduct surrounding it provide specific and direct evidence the parties agreed to modify the Insertion Order.

b. The Signed-Writing Clause

The Insertion Order provides it "may be changed only by a subsequent writing signed by both parties." Delaware follows the common law rule with respect to "no oral-modification clauses" or signed-writing clauses.[19] The common law rule is that "an oral agreement is sufficient to modify or rescind a written contract, notwithstanding a provision in the written contract purporting to require that subsequent modifications be evidenced by writing." WILLISTON ON CONTRACTS § 29.42 (4th ed. 1999). On this point, the Supreme Court of Delaware has held:

> We think, therefore, that a written agreement between contracting parties, despite its terms, is not necessarily only to be amended by formal written agreement. We agree with [*Bartlett v. Stanchfield*, 148 Mass. 394 (1889),] that a written agreement does not necessarily govern all conduct between contracting parties until it is renounced in so many words. The reason for this is that the parties have a right to renounce or amend the agreement in any way they see fit and by any mode of expression they see fit. They may, by their conduct, substitute

19 The common-law rule applies because this a contract for the sale of services, not goods. Therefore, Delaware Code § 2-209, derived from the Uniform Commercial Code and permitting a signed- writing requirement, does not apply.

a new oral contract without a formal abrogation of the written agreement. We think the existence of Paragraphs 16 in the plaintiffs' appointments does not prohibit the modification of making of a new agreement by conduct of the parties, despite a prohibition of Paragraphs 18 against any change except by written bilateral agreement.

Pepsi-Cola Bottling Co. of Asbury Park v. Pepsico, Inc., 297 A.2d 28, 33 (Del. 1972). In this case, the modification was not oral, but appeared in writing in an instant-message conversation. Nevertheless, the same principle applies to this informal, unsigned writing as to an oral modification. Therefore, the instant-message conversation, as an unsigned writing, suffices under Delaware law to modify the Insertion Order despite the signed-writing clause and notwithstanding the Court's preliminary observation stated during the trial.

Nevertheless, even if the instant-message conversation did not qualify as an enforceable modification under Delaware law and the signed-writing clause of the Insertion Order were enforceable, Smoking Everywhere would have waived the provision because, following the instant messages, CX Digital materially changed its position in reliance on Touris's statements. "[W]here, following the oral modification, one of the parties materially changes position in reliance on the oral modification, the courts are in general agreement that the other party will be held to have waived or be estopped from asserting the no oral modification clause." WILLISTON § 29:42.

There is no dispute that after the September 2nd instant-message conversation between Touris and Soltani, CX Digital began to send an increased number of Sales to two new URLs. CX Digital did this because it believed Touris had agreed with Soltani to modify the Insertion Order; that is, CX Digital relied on the instant messages to change the course of its performance. As discussed, Smoking Everywhere was aware of both changes and did not complain. Accordingly, Smoking Everywhere is estopped from asserting the signed- writing provision of the Insertion Order as a defense.

III. DAMAGES

CX Digital is entitled to damages pursuant to the Insertion Order as modified by the September 2nd instant messages. This includes payment for up to 600 Sales per day prior to September 2, 2009, and to an unlimited number of Sales per day after September 2, 2009. CX Digital through its affiliates, completed or caused to be completed 670 Sales before September 2, 2009, and 27,459 Sales during the remainder of September 2009. CX Digital is entitled to $45.00 for each of those Sales. This totals $30,150.00 for the 670 Sales completed prior to the modification and $1,235,655.00 for the 27,459 Sales completed after the modification. Smoking Everywhere paid a $5,000 deposit toward the balance. Therefore, Smoking Everywhere owes CX Digital $1,260,805.00.

Pursuant to the Insertion Order, CX Digital is entitled to 1.5% interest per month on the $25,150.00 August 31, 2009 invoice accruing from September 15, 2009. CX Digital is also entitled to 1.5% interest per month on the balance of $1,240,655.00 accruing from October 15, 2009. (See Insertion Order ¶ 3). CX Digital is also entitled to all attorney's fees and costs related to the enforcement of the Insertion Order. (See id. ¶ 3).

QUESTIONS

1. Smoking Everywhere ends up owing $1,260,805.00, plus interest, attorneys' fees, and court costs – all based on the instant message "NO LIMIT". How

much is that per character? Is this the most expensive instant message ever sent?

2. The court treats Touris's instant messages as "unsigned writings." Is that correct? Could you make an argument that they are oral communications, not writings? Could you make an argument that they are signed?*

3. What would have been the result if Touris and Soltani had exchanged letters? Talked on the phone? Which of these does an instant-message conversation most closely resemble? What result if they had exchanged emails or SMS text messages instead? How much should the enforceability of contracts turn on the details of the particular medium the parties use?

4. How did CX Digital prove the contents of the conversation? What if Smoking Everywhere alleged that the whole thing was a forgery by CX Digital?

5. *CX Digital* provides a window onto the world of affiliate marketing. What is the relationship among Smoking Everywhere, CX Digital, CX Affiliates, and the websites where the ads appear? Who pays whom? Why would Smoking Everywhere use this kind of decentralized advertising, rather than renting billboards or buying banner ads itself?

NGUYEN V. BARNES & NOBLE, INC.
763 F.3d 1171 (9th Cir. 2014)

Noonan, Circuit Judge:

Barnes & Noble, Inc. ("Barnes & Noble") appeals the district court's denial of its motion to compel arbitration against Kevin Khoa Nguyen ("Nguyen") pursuant to the arbitration agreement contained in its website's Terms of Use. In order to resolve the issue of arbitrability, we must address whether Nguyen, by merely using Barnes & Noble's website, agreed to be bound by the Terms of Use, even though Nguyen was never prompted to assent to the Terms of Use and never in fact read them. ...

I. BACKGROUND

A.

The underlying facts are not in dispute. Barnes & Noble is a national bookseller that owns and operates hundreds of bookstores as well as the website . In August 2011, Barnes & Noble, along with other retailers across the country, liquidated its inventory of discontinued Hewlett-Packard Touchpads ("Touchpads"), an unsuccessful competitor to Apple's iPad, by advertising a "fire sale" of Touchpads at a heavily discounted price. Acting quickly on the nationwide liquidation of Touchpads, Nguyen purchased two units on Barnes & Noble's website on August 21, 2011, and received an email confirming the transaction. The following day, Nguyen received another email informing him that his order had been cancelled due to unexpectedly high demand. Nguyen alleges that, as a result of "Barnes & Noble's representations, as well as the delay in informing him it would not honor the sale," he was "unable to obtain an HP Tablet during the liquidation period for the dis-

---

* If you really want to get into the weeds of electronic records and signatures, see the federal Electronic Signatures in Global and National Commerce Act (E-SIGN) and the Uniform Electronic Transactions Act (UETA), which has been enacted by forty-seven states as of 2014. Be careful to distinguish *electronic* signatures (which can be as simple as clicking to agree) from *digital* signatures (which generally mean only cryptographically authenticated signatures).

counted price," and was "forced to rely on substitute tablet technology, which he subsequently purchased ... [at] considerable expense."

B.

In April 2012, Nguyen filed this lawsuit in California Superior Court on behalf of himself and a putative class of consumers whose Touchpad orders had been cancelled, alleging that Barnes & Noble had engaged in deceptive business practices and false advertising in violation of both California and New York law. Barnes & Noble removed the action to federal court and moved to compel arbitration under the Federal Arbitration Act ("FAA"), arguing that Nguyen was bound by the arbitration agreement in the website's Terms of Use.

The website's Terms of Use are available via a "Terms of Use" hyperlink located in the bottom left-hand corner of every page on the Barnes & Noble website, which appears alongside other hyperlinks labeled "NOOK Store Terms," "Copyright," and "Privacy Policy." These hyperlinks also appear underlined and set in green typeface in the lower lefthand corner of every page in the online checkout process.

Nguyen neither clicked on the "Terms of Use" hyperlink nor actually read the Terms of Use. Had he clicked on the hyperlink, he would have been taken to a page containing the full text of Barnes & Noble's Terms of Use, which state, in relevant part: "By visiting any area in the Barnes & Noble.com Site, creating an account, [or] making a purchase via the Barnes & Noble.com Site ... a User is deemed to have accepted the Terms of Use." Nguyen also would have come across an arbitration provision, which states:

> XVIII. DISPUTE RESOLUTION
>
> Any claim or controversy at law or equity that arises out of the Terms of Use, the Barnes & Noble.com Site or any Barnes & Noble.com Service (each a "Claim"), shall be resolved through binding arbitration conducted by telephone, online or based solely upon written submissions where no in-person appearance is required. In such cases, arbitration shall be administered by the American Arbitration Association under its Commercial Arbitration Rules (including without limitation the Supplementary Procedures for Consumer-Related Disputes, if applicable), and judgment on the award rendered by the arbitrator(s) may be entered in any court having jurisdiction thereof. . . . .
>
> Any claim shall be arbitrated or litigated, as the case may be, on an individual basis and shall not be consolidated with any Claim of any other party whether through class action proceedings, class arbitration proceedings or otherwise. . . . .
>
> [The arbitration clause also waived the parties' rights to jury trial.]

Nguyen contends that he cannot be bound to the arbitration provision because he neither had notice of nor assented to the website's Terms of Use. Barnes & Noble, for its part, asserts that the placement of the "Terms of Use" hyperlink on its website put Nguyen on constructive notice of the arbitration agreement. Barnes & Noble contends that this notice, combined with Nguyen's subsequent use of the website, was enough to bind him to the Terms of Use. The district court disagreed, and Barnes & Noble now appeals. ...

III. DISCUSSION

A.

The FAA, 9 U.S.C. § 1 *et seq.*, requires federal district courts to stay judicial proceedings and compel arbitration of claims covered by a written and enforceable arbitration agreement. *Id.* § 3. The FAA limits the district court's role to determining whether a valid arbitration agreement exists, and whether the agreement encompasses the disputes at issue. The parties do not quarrel that Barnes & Noble's arbitration agreement, should it be found enforceable, encompasses Nguyen's claims. The only issue is whether a valid arbitration agreement exists. ...

B.

"While new commerce on the Internet has exposed courts to many new situations, it has not fundamentally changed the principles of contract." *Register.com, Inc. v. Verio, Inc.*, 356 F.3d 393, 403 (2d Cir. 2004). One such principle is the requirement that "[m]utual manifestation of assent, whether by written or spoken word or by conduct, is the touchstone of contract." *Specht v. Netscape Commc'ns Corp.*, 306 F.3d 17, 29 (2d Cir. 2002).

Contracts formed on the Internet come primarily in two flavors: "clickwrap" (or "click-through") agreements, in which website users are required to click on an "I agree" box after being presented with a list of terms and conditions of use; and "browsewrap" agreements, where a website's terms and conditions of use are generally posted on the website via a hyperlink at the bottom of the screen. Barnes & Noble's Terms of Use fall in the latter category.

"Unlike a clickwrap agreement, a browsewrap agreement does not require the user to manifest assent to the terms and conditions expressly ... [a] party instead gives his assent simply by using the website." *Hines v. Overstock.com, Inc.*, 668 F. Supp. 2d 362, 366-67 (E.D.N.Y. 2009). Indeed, "in a pure — form browsewrap agreement, the website will contain a notice that — by merely using the services of, obtaining information from, or initiating applications within the website — the user is agreeing to and is bound by the site's terms of service." *Fteja v. Facebook, Inc.*, 841 F. Supp. 2d 829, 837 (S.D.N.Y. 2012). Thus, "by visiting the website — something that the user has already done — the user agrees to the Terms of Use not listed on the site itself but available only by clicking a hyperlink." *Id.* "The defining feature of browsewrap agreements is that the user can continue to use the website or its services without visiting the page hosting the browsewrap agreement or even knowing that such a webpage exists." *Be In, Inc. v. Google Inc.*, No. 12-CV-03373-LHK, 2013 WL 5568706, at *6 (N.D.Cal. Oct. 9, 2013). "Because no affirmative action is required by the website user to agree to the terms of a contract other than his or her use of the website, the determination of the validity of the browsewrap contract depends on whether the user has actual or constructive knowledge of a website's terms and conditions." *Van Tassell v. United Mktg. Grp., LLC*, 795 F. Supp. 2d 770, 790 (N.D.Ill. 2011) (citing *Sw. Airlines Co. v. Board-First, LLC*, No. 06-CV-0891-B, 2007 WL 4823761, at *4 (N.D.Tex. Sept. 12, 2007)); *see also* Mark A. Lemley, *Terms of Use*, 91 MINN. L.REV. 459, 477 (2006) ("Courts may be willing to overlook the utter absence of assent only when there are reasons to believe that the [website user] is aware of the [website owner's] terms.").

Were there any evidence in the record that Nguyen had actual notice of the Terms of Use or was required to affirmatively acknowledge the Terms of Use before completing his online purchase, the outcome of this case might be different. Indeed, courts have consistently enforced browsewrap agreements where the user had actual notice of the agreement. *See, e.g., Register.com*, 356 F.3d at 401-04 (finding likelihood of success on the merits in a breach of browsewrap claim where the defendant "admitted that ... it was fully aware of the terms" of the offer); *Sw. Airlines Co.*, 2007 WL 4823761, at *4-6 (finding proper contract formation where defendant continued its breach after being notified of the terms in a cease and desist letter); *Ticketmaster Corp. v. Tickets.Com, Inc.*, No. CV-997654, 2003 WL 21406289, at *2C (C.D. Cal. Mar. 7, 2003) (denying defendants' summary judgment motion on browsewrap contract claim where defendants continued breaching contract after receiving letter quoting the browsewrap contract terms). Courts have also been more willing to find the requisite notice for constructive assent where the browsewrap agreement resembles a clickwrap agreement — that is, where the user is required to affirmatively acknowledge the agreement before proceeding with use of the website. *See, e.g., Zaltz v. JDATE*, 952 F. Supp. 2d 439, 451-52 (E.D.N.Y. 2013) (enforcing forum selection clause where prospective members had to check box confirming that they both read and agreed to the website's Terms and Conditions of Service to obtain account); *Fteja*, 841 F. Supp. 2d at 838-40 (enforcing forum selection clause in website's terms of service where a notice below the "Sign Up" button stated, "By clicking Sign Up, you are indicating that you have read and agree to the Terms of Service," and user had clicked "Sign Up").

But where, as here, there is no evidence that the website user had actual knowledge of the agreement, the validity of the browsewrap agreement turns on whether the website puts a reasonably prudent user on inquiry notice of the terms of the contract. Whether a user has inquiry notice of a browsewrap agreement, in turn, depends on the design and content of the website and the agreement's webpage. Where the link to a website's terms of use is buried at the bottom of the page or tucked away in obscure corners of the website where users are unlikely to see it, courts have refused to enforce the browsewrap agreement. *See, e.g., Specht, 306 F. 3d at 23* (refusing to enforce terms of use that "would have become visible to plaintiffs only if they had scrolled down to the next screen"); *In re Zappos.com, Inc. Customer Data Sec. Breach Litig.*, 893 F. Supp. 2d 1058, 1064 (D. Nev. 2012) ("The Terms of Use is inconspicuous, buried in the middle to bottom of every Zappos.com webpage among many other links, and the website never directs a user to the Terms of Use."); *Van Tassell*, 795 F. Supp. 2d at 792-93 (refusing to enforce arbitration clause in browsewrap agreement that was only noticeable after a "multistep process" of clicking through non-obvious links); *Hines*, 668 F. Supp. 2d at 367 (plaintiff "could not even see the link to [the terms and conditions] without scrolling down to the bottom of the screen — an action that was not required to effectuate her purchase"). On the other hand, where the website contains an explicit textual notice that continued use will act as a manifestation of the user's intent to be bound, courts have been more amenable to enforcing browsewrap agreements. *See, e.g., Cairo, Inc. v. Crossmedia Servs., Inc.*, No. 04-04825, 2005 WL 756610, at *2, *4-5 (N.D. Cal. Apr. 1, 2005) (enforcing forum selection clause in website's terms of use where every page on the website had a textual notice that read: "By continuing past this page and/or using this site, you agree to abide by the Terms of Use for this site, which prohibit commercial use of any information on this site"). *But see Pollstar v. Gigmania, Ltd.*, 170 F. Supp. 2d 974, 981 (E.D.Cal. 2000) (refusing to enforce browsewrap agreement where textual notice appeared in small gray print against a gray background). In short, the conspicuousness and placement of the "Terms of Use" hyperlink, other notices given to users of the terms of use, and the website's general design all contribute to whether a reasonably prudent user would have inquiry notice of a browsewrap agreement.

Barnes & Noble argues that the placement of the "Terms of Use" hyperlink in the bottom left-hand corner of every page on the Barnes & Noble website, and its close proximity to the buttons a user must click on to complete an online purchase, is enough to place a reasonably prudent user on constructive notice. It is true that the location of the hyperlink on Barnes & Noble's website distinguishes this case from *Specht,* the leading authority on the enforceability of browsewrap terms under New York law. There, the Second Circuit refused to enforce an arbitration provision in a website's licensing terms where the hyperlink to the terms was located at the bottom of the page, hidden below the "Download" button that users had to click to initiate the software download. Then-Second Circuit Judge Sotomayor, writing for the panel, held that "a reference to the existence of license terms on a submerged screen is not sufficient to place consumers on inquiry or constructive notice of those terms." *Specht,* 306 F.3d at 32. By contrast, here the "Terms of Use" link appears either directly below the relevant button a user must click on to proceed in the checkout process or just a few inches away. On some pages, the content of the webpage is compact enough that a user can view the link without scrolling. On the remaining pages, the hyperlink is close enough to the "Proceed with Checkout" button that a user would have to bring the link within his field of vision in order to complete his order.

But the proximity or conspicuousness of the hyperlink alone is not enough to give rise to constructive notice, and Barnes & Noble directs us to no case law that supports this proposition.[1] The most analogous case the court was able to locate is *PDC Labs., Inc. v. Hach Co.,* an unpublished district court order cited by neither party. No. 09-1110, 2009 WL 2605270 (C.D. Ill. Aug. 25, 2009). There, the "Terms [and Conditions of Sale] were hyperlinked on three separate pages of the online ... order process in underlined, blue, contrasting text." *Id.* at *3. The court held that "[t]his contrasting text is sufficient to be considered conspicuous," thereby placing a reasonable user on notice that the terms applied. *Id.* It also observed, however, that the terms' conspicuousness was reinforced by the language of the final checkout screen, which read, "`STEP 4 of 4: *Review terms,* add any comments, and submit order,'" and was followed by a hyperlink to the Terms. *Id.* (emphasis added).

As in *PDC,* the checkout screens here contained "Terms of Use" hyperlinks in underlined, color-contrasting text. But *PDC* is dissimilar in that the final screen on that website contained the phrase "Review terms." This admonition makes *PDC* distinguishable, despite the court's explanation that the blue contrasting hyperlinks were sufficiently conspicuous on their own. That the *PDC* decision couched

---

1 Indeed, in cases where courts have relied on the proximity of the hyperlink to enforce a browsewrap agreement, the websites at issue have also included something more to capture the user's attention and secure her assent. *See, e.g., 5381 Partners LLC v. Sharesale.com, Inc.,* No. 12-CV-4263 JFB AKT, 2013 WL 5328324, at *7 (E.D.N.Y. Sept. 23, 2013) (in addition to hyperlink that appeared adjacent to the activation button users had to click on, website also contained a text warning near the button that stated "By clicking and making a request to Activate, you agree to the terms and conditions in the [agreement]"); *Zaltz,* 952 F. Supp. 2d at 451-52 (users required to check box confirming that they had reviewed and agreed to website's Terms and Conditions, even though hyperlink to Terms and Conditions was located on the same screen as the button users had to click on to complete registration).

its holding in terms of procedural unconscionability rather than contract formation further distinguishes it from our case.

In light of the lack of controlling authority on point, and in keeping with courts' traditional reluctance to enforce browsewrap agreements against individual consumers, we therefore hold that where a website makes its terms of use available via a conspicuous hyperlink on every page of the website but otherwise provides no notice to users nor prompts them to take any affirmative action to demonstrate assent, even close proximity of the hyperlink to relevant buttons users must click on — without more — is insufficient to give rise to constructive notice. While failure to read a contract before agreeing to its terms does not relieve a party of its obligations under the contract, the onus must be on website owners to put users on notice of the terms to which they wish to bind consumers. Given the breadth of the range of technological savvy of online purchasers, consumers cannot be expected to ferret out hyperlinks to terms and conditions to which they have no reason to suspect they will be bound.

Barnes & Noble's argument that Nguyen's familiarity with other websites governed by similar browsewrap terms, including his personal website, gives rise to an inference of constructive notice is also of no moment. Whether Nguyen has experience with the browsewrap agreements found on other websites such as Facebook, LinkedIn, MySpace, or Twitter, has no bearing on whether he had constructive notice of Barnes & Noble's Terms of Use. There is nothing in the record to suggest that those browsewrap terms are enforceable by or against Nguyen, much less why they should give rise to constructive notice of Barnes & Noble's browsewrap terms. ...

We hold that Nguyen had insufficient notice of Barnes & Noble's Terms of Use, and thus did not enter into an agreement with Barnes & Noble to arbitrate his claims.

QUESTIONS

1. Reconsider the FloodZone problem in the Jurisdiction chapter. Based on *Nguyen*, are contracts like FloodZone's enforceable?

2. How useful is the distinction between "clickwrap" and "browsewrap?"

3. Why isn't *Nguyen* controlled by the usual rule that the offeror is "master of his offer" and may define what conduct counts as acceptance? As James J. White puts it in *Contracting Under Amended 2-207*, 2004 WIS. L. REV. 723:

   > Suppose that your form asserts that my intentional tying my shoelaces tomorrow will be assent to all of your terms. Since I cannot tie my shoelaces unintentionally and since I have no valet, I'm stuck, not so?

   How would you respond?

4. Look at the Central Pacific Railroad Photographic History Museum website at http://cprr.org, including its User Agreement at http://cprr.org/Museum/legal.html. Are these terms enforceable? All of them? Against whom? What's going on here?

SMURFBERRY PROBLEM

Stewart Griffin is 8 years old and loves the game Smurfs Village (made by Capcom) which he plays on his mother Lois's iPad (made by Apple). He asked his mother if he could buy some Smurfberries so he could expand his village. Thinking that this would be a $2 or $5 in-game purchase like some of the other items she'd bought Stewart in the past, Lois told Stewart her iTunes Store password ("stewie123"). But a wagon of smurfberries (the largest amount one can buy at once) costs $100, and in the next twelve days, Stewart bought $2700 worth of Smurfberries. Then Lois's credit card bill came, and she took away the iPad and changed her password. It is undisputed that when Lois activated her account she tapped "I agree" to the iTunes Store terms and conditions, which include the statement:

> You are solely responsible for maintaining the confidentiality and se-curity of your Account, and for all activities that occur on or through your Account, and you agree to immediately notify Apple of any secu-rity breach of your Account. Apple shall not be responsible for any losses arising out of the unauthorized use of your Account.

Lois and Stewart have sued Apple and Capcom, seeking to void the Smurfberry sale. What result?

PROCD, INC. V. ZEIDENBERG
86 F.3d 1447 (7th Cir. 1996)

[ProCD sold telephone directories on CD-ROM.

> Every box containing [ProCD's] consumer product declares that the software comes with restrictions stated in an enclosed license. This license, which is encoded on the CD-ROM disks as well as printed in the manual, and which appears on a user's screen every time the soft-ware runs, limits use of the application program and listings to non-commercial purposes.

Zeidenberg resold the information online; ProCD sued for breach of contract. The Seventh Circuit, per Judge Easterbrook, upheld the contract:

> Notice on the outside, terms on the inside, and a right to return the software for a refund if the terms are unacceptable (a right that the license expressly extends), may be a means of doing business valuable to buyers and sellers alike.]

QUESTIONS

1. What would be wrong with a purported "contract" in which one of these three elements was missing? Were they all present in *Specht*? Contrariwise, would a "reasonably prudent offeree" in Zeidenberg's shoes have been aware of the existence of the terms?

2. Telephone directory listings are uncopyrightable facts. *Feist Publ'ns, Inc. v. Rural Tel. Serv. Co.*, 499 U.S. 430 (1991), so it could not have sued Zeiden-berg for copyright infringement. Should contract law limit Zeidenberg's use of the listings where copyright law would allow it?

3. ProCD created its CD-ROM telephone directory by shipping physical tele-phone books to China, where it paid workers $3.50 per day to type out the listings manually. Could the telephone companies have stopped it by putting a sticker on each telephone book reading, "BY OPENING THIS BOOK, YOU AGREE NOT TO USE ITS CONTENTS FOR COMMERCIAL PUR-POSES"?

KRUSTILU PROBLEM

Your client, Bartholomew Calvin, was seriously injured when the bowl of Chocolate Frosted Sugar Bombs (CFSBs) he was eating turned out to contain a jagged piece of metal, which perforated his esophagus, requiring hospitalization and surgery. It appears that one of the machines used to make CFSBs suffered a shattered fan blade; pieces of the blade ended up in boxes of CFSBs sold to hundreds of consumers in six states over a period of several weeks in October 2013. You have filed a personal injury products liability action against the Krustilu Corporation, the maker of CFSBs. The suit is styled as a class action on behalf of all purchasers of the contaminated CFBSs, with Mr. Calvin and three other consumers as representative plaintiffs.

Krustilu has moved to dismiss the class action complaint and compel arbitration. Krustilu avers that between August 1, 2013 and January 31, 2014, a banner at the top of every page on its website read, in 14-point type, "Please note we also have new legal terms which require all disputes related to the purchase or use of any Krustilu product or service to be resolved through binding arbitration." The underlined words were a hyperlink to its terms of service page at krustilu.com/legal. Krustilu also avers that from August 1, 2013 through the present date, those terms of service have read, in relevant part:

> These terms are a binding legal agreement ("Agreement") between you and Krustilu. In exchange for the benefits, discounts, content, features, services, or other offerings that you receive or have access to by using our websites, subscribing to our email newsletters, downloading or printing a digital coupon, entering a sweepstakes or contest, redeeming a promotional offer, using entertainment content supplied by Krustilu through Facebook, Twitter, or another social media service, or otherwise participating in any other Krustilu offering, you are agreeing to these terms. ...
>
> Any dispute or claim (hereinafter, a "Dispute") made by you against Krustilu arising out of or relating to your purchase or use of any Krustilu product (including Krustilu products purchased at online or physical stores for personal or household use) regardless of the legal theory upon which said claim is based will be resolved through binding arbitration. ...

How will you respond to Krustilu's motion?

SEASELLS PROBLEM

You are counsel to SeaSells.com, an e-commerce startup that is creating an online marketplace for seashell collectors to show off their favorite shells and trade with each other. User accounts are free, and are required to post, but not to view the site. SeaSells takes a 10% commission plus a $1.00 listing fee on any sale. What are the essential substantive terms you will need to put in your terms of service? Draw up a checklist of issues the terms should address.

In addition, as SeaSells adds new site features, such as new payment options, new forums, and new technology partnerships, you expect to revise your terms and conditions to take into account these new features. You also expect that you will want to revise the terms and conditions to respond to shifts in the legal landscape. Design a process – both technical and legal – to ensure that any future changes to the terms will be enforceable. Your proposal will need to be approved by the CEO, and you will need to be prepared to respond to any objections from Marketing and Operations that your process makes the site harder to use.

B. Computer Misuse Statutes

Although computer intrusions were initially prosecuted under existing common-law or statutory theft laws, the field is now primarily defined by special-purpose computer misuse statutes. The federal Computer Fraud and Abuse Act (CFAA) has been the leading model here, but every state has its own statute, most of which parallel the CFAA in their essentials.

The details of these statutes and their interpretation vary enormously, and the CFAA itself has been frequently amended, so the materials in this section don't focus on the exact structure of any particular statute. Instead, they consider a number of common interpretive questions that arise under any of this family of statutes. The general scheme of the CFAA and related statutes is that they prohibit "access" to a computer "without authorization." In many such statutes additional elements, such as causing "damage or loss" above a certain threshold, increase the gravity of the offense. The materials in this section consider some of the ambiguities those phrases create.

COMPUTER FRAUD AND ABUSE ACT
Title 18, United States Code

§ 1030 – *Fraud and related activity in connections with computers*

(a) Whoever – ...

    (2) intentionally accesses a computer without authorization or exceeds authorized access, and thereby obtains – ...

        (C) information from any protected computer; ...

    (4) knowingly and with intent to defraud, accesses a protected computer without authorization, or exceeds authorized access, and by means of such conduct furthers the intended fraud and obtains anything of value, unless the object of the fraud and the thing obtained consists only of the use of the computer and the value of such use is not more than $5,000 in any 1-year period;

    (5)

        (A) knowingly causes the transmission of a program, information, code, or command, and as a result of such conduct, intentionally causes damage without authorization, to a protected computer;

        (B) intentionally accesses a protected computer without authorization, and as a result of such conduct, recklessly causes damage; or

        (C) intentionally accesses a protected computer without authorization, and as a result of such conduct, causes damage and loss. ...

    shall be punished as provided in subsection (c) of this section. ...

(e) As used in this section –

(1) the term "computer" means an electronic, magnetic, optical, electrochemical, or other high speed data processing device performing logical, arithmetic, or storage functions, and includes any data storage facility or communications facility directly related to or operating in conjunction with such device, but such term does not include an automated typewriter or typesetter, a portable hand held calculator, or other similar device;

(2) the term "protected computer" means a computer – ...

    (B) which is used in or affecting interstate or foreign commerce or communication, including a computer located outside the United States that is used in a manner that affects interstate or foreign commerce or communication of the United States; ...

(6) the term "exceeds authorized access" means to access a computer with authorization and to use such access to obtain or alter information in the computer that the accesser is not entitled so to obtain or alter; ...

(8) the term "damage" means any impairment to the integrity or availability of data, a program, a system, or information; ...

(11) the term "loss" means any reasonable cost to any victim, including the cost of responding to an offense, conducting a damage assessment, and restoring the data, program, system, or information to its condition prior to the offense, and any revenue lost, cost incurred, or other consequential damages incurred because of interruption of service; ...

(g) Any person who suffers damage or loss by reason of a violation of this section may maintain a civil action against the violator to obtain compensatory damages and injunctive relief or other equitable relief. A civil action for a violation of this section may be brought only if the conduct involves [loss aggregating at least $5,000 in value, physical injury, or one of three other specialized factors]. ...

QUESTION

1. Fred Felon steals Violet Victim's purse. In it, he finds her HTB online banking password on a piece of paper. He logs in as her and makes an electronic transfer of $10,000 to his own HTB account. Which subsections of the CFAA has he violated?

2. Is Mr. Felon guilty of any ordinary theft crimes? If so, what purpose do special-purpose computer-misuse statutes like the CFAA serve?

3. What does it mean to "access" a computer? Does a thief who steals an unattended cell phone "access" it when he picks it up? What if he goes to the lock screen and tries several passcodes, all unsuccessfully? What if he correctly guesses and inputs "1234" but is caught before using any of the apps? Are these access or only failed attempts at access?

4. How about "damage" and "loss?" A hacker calling herself "Acid Burn" finds a vulnerability in to the Ellingson County Fire Department's email system and leaks some embarrassing emails to a local newspaper. The department's IT administrators spend 25 hours investigating the intrusion, at the end of which they report that she also deleted six stored emails that are now unrecoverable. They spend another 5 hours writing a "patch": a modification to

the email software to prevent future intrusions of this sort. Has the department suffered "damage" and/or "loss" within the meaning of the CFAA?

UNITED STATES V. MORRIS
928 F. 2d 504 (2d Cir. 1991)

Newman, Circuit Judge:

In the fall of 1988, [Robert Tappan] Morris was a first-year graduate student in Cornell University's computer science Ph.D. program. Through undergraduate work at Harvard and in various jobs he had acquired significant computer experience and expertise. When Morris entered Cornell, he was given an account on the computer at the Computer Science Division. This account gave him explicit authorization to use computers at Cornell. ...

In October 1988, Morris began work on a computer program, later known as the INTERNET "worm" or "virus." The goal of this program was to demonstrate the inadequacies of current security measures on computer networks by exploiting the security defects that Morris had discovered. ... Morris designed the program to spread across a national network of computers after being inserted at one computer location connected to the network. Morris released the worm into INTERNET, which is a group of national networks that connect university, governmental, and military computers around the country. The network permits communication and transfer of information between computers on the network.

Morris sought to program the INTERNET worm to spread widely without drawing attention to itself. The worm was supposed to occupy little computer operation time, and thus not interfere with normal use of the computers. Morris programmed the worm to make it difficult to detect and read, so that other programmers would not be able to "kill" the worm easily.

Morris also wanted to ensure that the worm did not copy itself onto a computer that already had a copy. [Due to programming and mathematical mistakes, Morris's safeguard failed, leading the worm to install thousands of copies of itself on each computer it reached.]

Morris identified four ways in which the worm could break into computers on the network:

(1) through a "hole" or "bug" (an error) in SENDMAIL, a computer program that transfers and receives electronic mail on a computer;

(2) through a bug in the "finger demon" program, a program that permits a person to obtain limited information about the users of another computer;

(3) through the "trusted hosts" feature, which permits a user with certain privileges on one computer to have equivalent privileges on another computer without using a password; and

(4) through a program of password guessing, whereby various combinations of letters are tried out in rapid sequence in the hope that one will be an authorized user's password, which is entered to permit whatever level of activity that user is authorized to perform.

On November 2, 1988, Morris released the worm from a computer at the Massachusetts Institute of Technology. MIT was selected to disguise the fact that the worm came from Morris at Cornell. Morris soon discovered that the worm was replicating and reinfecting machines at a much faster rate than he had anticipated. Ultimately, many machines at locations around the country either crashed or became "catatonic." When Morris realized what was happening, he contacted a friend at Harvard to discuss a solution. Eventually, they sent an anonymous message from Harvard over the network, instructing programmers how to kill the worm and prevent reinfection. However, because the network route was clogged, this message did not get through until it was too late. Computers were affected at numerous installations, including leading universities, military sites, and medical research facilities. The estimated cost of dealing with the worm at each installation ranged from $200 to more than $53,000.

Morris was found guilty, following a jury trial, of violating 18 U.S.C. § 1030(a)(5)(A). He was sentenced to three years of probation, 400 hours of community service, a fine of $10,050, and the costs of his supervision.

DISCUSSION ...

II. THE UNAUTHORIZED ACCESS REQUIREMENT IN SECTION 1030(A)(5)(A)

Section 1030(a)(5)(A) penalizes the conduct of an individual who "intentionally accesses a Federal interest computer without authorization." ... Morris argues that there was insufficient evidence to convict him of "unauthorized access," ...

We assess the sufficiency of the evidence under the traditional standard. Morris was authorized to use computers at Cornell, Harvard, and Berkeley, all of which were on INTERNET. As a result, Morris was authorized to communicate with other computers on the network to send electronic mail (SENDMAIL), and to find out certain information about the users of other computers (finger demon). The question is whether Morris's transmission of his worm constituted ... accessing without authorization. ...

The evidence permitted the jury to conclude that Morris's use of the SENDMAIL and finger demon features constituted access without authorization. ... Morris did not use either of those features in any way related to their intended function. He did not send or read mail nor discover information about other users; instead he found holes in both programs that permitted him a special and unauthorized access route into other computers.

Moreover, the jury verdict need not be upheld solely on Morris's use of SENDMAIL and finger demon. As the District Court noted, in denying Morris' motion for acquittal,

> Although the evidence may have shown that defendant's initial insertion of the worm simply exceeded his authorized access, the evidence also demonstrated that the worm was designed to spread to other computers at which he had no account and no authority, express or implied, to unleash the worm program. Moreover, there was also evidence that the worm was designed to gain access to computers at which he had no account by guessing their passwords. Accordingly, the evidence did support the jury's conclusion that defendant accessed without authority as opposed to merely exceeding the scope of his authority.

In light of the reasonable conclusions that the jury could draw from Morris's use of SENDMAIL and finger demon, and from his use of the trusted hosts feature and password guessing, his challenge to the sufficiency of the evidence fails.

QUESTIONS

1. *Morris* confronts the most vexing issue in the CFAA caselaw: the the nature of "unauthorized" access. The court's first theory of authorization has to do with the "intended function" of the programs Morris used. How does a user (or a court) determine what the "intended function" of a computer program is? Did Fred Felon use the HTB computer for its "intended function?" Is sending spam an "intended function" of an email program?

2. The court's second theory of authorization has to do with Morris's lack of an account on various systems. Under this test, was Fred Felon's use of the HTB computer "authorized?" Do you always need an account to use a computer with permission?

3. The *Daily Planet*'s website uses a paywall: users are allowed to read ten articles a month for free, but must buy a subscription at $9.99 a month to read more. The paywall is enforced using cookies[*]: the website sets a cookie on a user's computer that keeps track of the number of articles she has read. Alexander Luthor realizes that if he deletes the cookies from his computer after reading ten articles, the *Daily Planet* website will think he is a new reader, and let him read another ten articles before the paywall kicks in. By repeatedly deleting the *Daily Planet* cookie, Luthor is able to read hundreds of articles for free. Has he accessed the *Daily Planet* website without authorization?

UNITED STATES V. NOSAL [I]
676 F.3d 854 (9th Cir. 2012) (en banc)

Kozinski, Chief Judge:

Computers have become an indispensable part of our daily lives. We use them for work; we use them for play. Sometimes we use them for play at work. Many employers have adopted policies prohibiting the use of work computers for non-business purposes. Does an employee who violates such a policy commit a federal crime? How about someone who violates the terms of service of a social networking website? This depends on how broadly we read the Computer Fraud and Abuse Act (CFAA), 18 U.S.C. § 1030.

FACTS

David Nosal used to work for Korn/Ferry, an executive search firm. Shortly after he left the company, he convinced some of his former colleagues who were still working for Korn/Ferry [Becky Christian and Mark Jacobson] to help him start a competing business. The employees used their log-in credentials to download source lists, names and contact information from a confidential database on the company's computer, and then transferred that information to Nosal. The employees were authorized to access the database, but Korn/Ferry had a policy that forbade disclosing confidential information.[1]

The government indicted Nosal on twenty counts, including trade secret theft, mail fraud, conspiracy and violations of the CFAA. The CFAA counts charged Nosal with violations of 18 U.S.C. § 1030(a)(4), for aiding and abetting the Korn/Ferry employees in "exceed[ing their] authorized access" with intent to defraud. ...

----

[*] For a technical overview of how cookies work, see *In re Doubleclick, supra.*

1 The opening screen of the database also included the warning: "This product is intended to be used by Korn/Ferry employees for work on Korn/Ferry business only."

DISCUSSION

The CFAA defines "exceeds authorized access" as "to access a computer with authorization and to use such access to obtain or alter information in the computer that the accesser is not entitled so to obtain or alter." 18 U.S.C. § 1030(e)(6). This language can be read either of two ways: First, as Nosal suggests and the district court held, it could refer to someone who's authorized to access only certain data or files but accesses unauthorized data or files – what is colloquially known as "hacking." For example, assume an employee is permitted to access only product information on the company's computer but accesses customer data: He would "exceed [ ] authorized access" if he looks at the customer lists. Second, as the government proposes, the language could refer to someone who has unrestricted physical access to a computer, but is limited in the use to which he can put the information. For example, an employee may be authorized to access customer lists in order to do his job but not to send them to a competitor.

The government argues that the statutory text can support only the latter interpretation of "exceeds authorized access." In its opening brief, it focuses on the word "entitled" in the phrase an "accesser is not *entitled* so to obtain or alter." *Id.* § 1030(e)(6) (emphasis added). Pointing to one dictionary definition of "entitle" as "to furnish with a right," *Webster's New Riverside University Dictionary* 435, the government argues that Korn/Ferry's computer use policy gives employees certain rights, and when the employees violated that policy, they "exceed[ed] authorized access." But "entitled" in the statutory text refers to how an accesser "obtain[s] or alter[s]" the information, whereas the computer use policy uses "entitled" to limit how the information is used after it is obtained. This is a poor fit with the statutory language. An equally or more sensible reading of "entitled" is as a synonym for "authorized." So read, "exceeds authorized access" would refer to data or files on a computer that one is not authorized to access. ...

While the CFAA is susceptible to the government's broad interpretation, we find Nosal's narrower one more plausible. Congress enacted the CFAA in 1984 primarily to address the growing problem of computer hacking, recognizing that, "[i]n intentionally trespassing into someone else's computer files, the offender obtains at the very least information as to how to break into that computer system." S. Rep. No. 99–432, at 9 (1986), 1986 U.S.C.C.A.N. 2479, 2487 (Conf. Rep.). The government agrees that the CFAA was concerned with hacking, which is why it also prohibits accessing a computer "without authorization." According to the government, *that* prohibition applies to hackers, so the "exceeds authorized access" prohibition must apply to people who are authorized to use the computer, but do so for an unauthorized purpose. But it is possible to read both prohibitions as applying to hackers: "[W]ithout authorization" would apply to *outside* hackers (individuals who have no authorized access to the computer at all) and "exceeds authorized access" would apply to *inside* hackers (individuals whose initial access to a computer is authorized but who access unauthorized information or files). This is a perfectly plausible construction of the statutory language that maintains the CFAA's focus on hacking rather than turning it into a sweeping Internet-policing mandate.

The government's construction of the statute would expand its scope far beyond computer hacking to criminalize any unauthorized use of information obtained from a computer. This would make criminals of large groups of people who would have little reason to suspect they are committing a federal crime. While ignorance of the law is no excuse, we can properly be skeptical as to whether Congress, in 1984, meant to criminalize conduct beyond that which is inherently wrongful, such as breaking into a computer.

The government argues that defendants here did have notice that their conduct was wrongful by the fraud and materiality requirements in subsection 1030(a)(4), which punishes whoever:

> knowingly and with intent to defraud, accesses a protected computer without authorization, or exceeds authorized access, and by means of such conduct furthers the intended fraud and obtains anything of value, unless the object of the fraud and the thing obtained consists only of the use of the computer and the value of such use is not more than $5,000 in any 1–year period.

18 U.S.C. § 1030(a)(4). But "exceeds authorized access" is used elsewhere in the CFAA as a basis for criminal culpability without intent to defraud. Subsection 1030(a)(2)(C) requires only that the person who "exceeds authorized access" have "obtain[ed] ... information from any protected computer." Because "protected computer" is defined as a computer affected by or involved in interstate commerce – effectively all computers with Internet access – the government's interpretation of "exceeds authorized access" makes every violation of a private computer use policy a federal crime. *See id.* § 1030(e)(2)(B). ...

In the case of the CFAA, the broadest provision is subsection 1030(a)(2)(C), which makes it a crime to exceed authorized access of a computer connected to the Internet *without* any culpable intent. Were we to adopt the government's proposed interpretation, millions of unsuspecting individuals would find that they are engaging in criminal conduct.

Minds have wandered since the beginning of time and the computer gives employees new ways to procrastinate, by g-chatting with friends, playing games, shopping or watching sports highlights. Such activities are routinely prohibited by many computer-use policies, although employees are seldom disciplined for occasional use of work computers for personal purposes. Nevertheless, under the broad interpretation of the CFAA, such minor dalliances would become federal crimes. While it's unlikely that you'll be prosecuted for watching Reason.TV on your work computer, you *could* be. Employers wanting to rid themselves of troublesome employees without following proper procedures could threaten to report them to the FBI unless they quit. Ubiquitous, seldom-prosecuted crimes invite arbitrary and discriminatory enforcement.[7]

Employer-employee and company-consumer relationships are traditionally governed by tort and contract law; the government's proposed interpretation of the CFAA allows private parties to manipulate their computer-use and personnel policies so as to turn these relationships into ones policed by the criminal law. Sig-

---

7 This concern persists even if intent to defraud is required. Suppose an employee spends six hours tending his FarmVille stable on his work computer. The employee has full access to his computer and the Internet, but the company has a policy that work computers may be used only for business purposes. The employer should be able to fire the employee, but that's quite different from having him arrested as a federal criminal. Yet, under the government's construction of the statute, the employee "exceeds authorized access" by using the computer for non-work activities. Given that the employee deprives his company of six hours of work a day, an aggressive prosecutor might claim that he's defrauding the company, and thereby violating section 1030(a)(4)

nificant notice problems arise if we allow criminal liability to turn on the vagaries of private polices that are lengthy, opaque, subject to change and seldom read. Consider the typical corporate policy that computers can be used only for business purposes. What exactly is a "nonbusiness purpose"? If you use the computer to check the weather report for a business trip? For the company softball game? For your vacation to Hawaii? And if minor personal uses are tolerated, how can an employee be on notice of what constitutes a violation sufficient to trigger criminal liability?

Basing criminal liability on violations of private computer use polices can transform whole categories of otherwise innocuous behavior into federal crimes simply because a computer is involved. Employees who call family members from their work phones will become criminals if they send an email instead. Employees can sneak in the sports section of the *New York Times* to read at work, but they'd better not visit ESPN.com. And sudoku enthusiasts should stick to the printed puzzles, because visiting www.dailysudoku.com from their work computers might give them more than enough time to hone their sudoku skills behind bars.

The effect this broad construction of the CFAA has on workplace conduct pales by comparison with its effect on everyone else who uses a computer, smart-phone, iPad, Kindle, Nook, X-box, Blu-Ray player or any other Internet-enabled device. The Internet is a means for communicating via computers: Whenever we access a web page, commence a download, post a message on somebody's Facebook wall, shop on Amazon, bid on eBay, publish a blog, rate a movie on IMDb, read www.NYT.com, watch YouTube and do the thousands of other things we routinely do online, we are using one computer to send commands to other computers at remote locations. Our access to those remote computers is governed by a series of private agreements and policies that most people are only dimly aware of and virtually no one reads or understands.

For example, it's not widely known that, up until very recently, Google forbade minors from using its services. *See* Google Terms of Service, effective April 16, 2007 – March 1, 2012, § 2.3, http://www.google.com/intl/en/policies/terms/archive/20070416 ("You may not use the Services and may not accept the Terms if . . . you are not of legal age to form a binding contract with Google. . . .") (last visited Mar. 4, 2012). Adopting the government's interpretation would turn vast numbers of teens and pre-teens into juvenile delinquents – and their parents and teachers into delinquency contributors. Similarly, Facebook makes it a violation of the terms of service to let anyone log into your account. *See* Facebook Statement of Rights and Responsibilities § 4.8 http://www.facebook.com/legal/terms ("You will not share your password, . . . let anyone else access your account, or do anything else that might jeopardize the security of your account.") (last visited Mar. 4, 2012). Yet it's very common for people to let close friends and relatives check their email or access their online accounts. Some may be aware that, if discovered, they may suffer a rebuke from the ISP or a loss of access, but few imagine they might be marched off to federal prison for doing so.

Or consider the numerous dating websites whose terms of use prohibit inaccurate or misleading information. *See, e.g.*, eHarmony Terms of Service § 2(I), http://www. eharmony.com/about/terms ("You will not provide inaccurate, misleading or false information to eHarmony or to any other user.") (last visited Mar. 4, 2012). Or eBay and Craigslist, where it's a violation of the terms of use to post items in an inappropriate category. *See, e.g.*, eBay User Agreement, http://pages.ebay.com/help/policies/user- agreement.html ("While using eBay sites, services and tools, you will not: post content or items in an inappropriate category or areas on our sites and services . . . .") (last visited Mar. 4, 2012). Under the government's proposed interpretation of the CFAA, posting for sale an item prohibited by Craigslist's policy, or describing yourself as "tall, dark and handsome," when you're actually short and homely, will earn you a handsome orange jumpsuit.

Not only are the terms of service vague and generally unknown – unless you look real hard at the small print at the bottom of a webpage – but website owners retain the right to change the terms at any time and without notice. *See, e.g.,* YouTube Terms of Service § 1.B, http://www.youtube.com/t/terms ("YouTube may, in its sole discretion, modify or revise these Terms of Service and policies at any time, and you agree to be bound by such modifications or revisions.") (last visited Mar. 4, 2012). Accordingly, behavior that wasn't criminal yesterday can become criminal today without an act of Congress, and without any notice whatsoever.

The government assures us that, whatever the scope of the CFAA, it won't prosecute minor violations. But we shouldn't have to live at the mercy of our local prosecutor. And it's not clear we *can* trust the government when a tempting target comes along. Take the case of the mom who posed as a 17–year–old boy and cyberbullied her daughter's classmate. The Justice Department prosecuted her under 18 U.S.C. § 1030(a)(2)(C) for violating MySpace's terms of service, which prohibited lying about identifying information, including age. *See United States v. Drew*, 259 F.R.D. 449 (C.D. Cal. 2009). Lying on social media websites is common: People shave years off their age, add inches to their height and drop pounds from their weight. The difference between puffery and prosecution may depend on whether you happen to be someone an AUSA has reason to go after. ...

CONCLUSION

We need not decide today whether Congress *could* base criminal liability on violations of a company or website's computer use restrictions. Instead, we hold that the phrase "exceeds authorized access" in the CFAA does not extend to violations of use restrictions. If Congress wants to incorporate misappropriation liability into the CFAA, it must speak more clearly. ...

The rule of lenity not only ensures that citizens will have fair notice of the criminal laws, but also that Congress will have fair notice of what conduct its laws criminalize. We construe criminal statutes narrowly so that Congress will not unintentionally turn ordinary citizens into criminals. "[B]ecause of the seriousness of criminal penalties, and because criminal punishment usually represents the moral condemnation of the community, legislatures and not courts should define criminal activity." *United States v. Bass*, 404 U.S. 336, 348 (1971). "If there is any doubt about whether Congress intended [the CFAA] to prohibit the conduct in which [Nosal] engaged, then 'we must choose the interpretation least likely to impose penalties unintended by Congress.'" *United States v. Cabaccang*, 332 F.3d 622, 635 n. 22 (9th Cir.2003).

This narrower interpretation is also a more sensible reading of the text and legislative history of a statute whose general purpose is to punish hacking – the circumvention of technological access barriers – not misappropriation of trade secrets – a subject Congress has dealt with elsewhere. Therefore, we hold that "exceeds authorized access" in the CFAA is limited to violations of restrictions on *access* to information, and not restrictions on its *use*.

Because Nosal's accomplices had permission to access the company database and obtain the information contained within, the government's charges fail to meet the element of "without authorization, or exceeds authorized access" under

18 U.S.C. § 1030(a)(4). Accordingly, we affirm the judgment of the district court dismissing counts 2 and 4–7 for failure to state an offense. The government may, of course, prosecute Nosal on the remaining counts of the indictment. ...

Silverman, Circuit Judge, with whom Tallman, Circuit Judge concurs, dissenting:

This case has nothing to do with playing sudoku, checking email, fibbing on dating sites, or any of the other activities that the majority rightly values. It has everything to do with stealing an employer's valuable information to set up a competing business with the purloined data, siphoned away from the victim, knowing such access and use were prohibited in the defendants' employment contracts. The indictment here charged that Nosal and his co-conspirators knowingly exceeded the access to a protected company computer they were given by an executive search firm that employed them; that they did so with the intent to defraud; and further, that they stole the victim's valuable proprietary information by means of that fraudulent conduct in order to profit from using it. In ridiculing scenarios not remotely presented by *this* case, the majority does a good job of knocking down straw men – far-fetched hypotheticals involving neither theft nor intentional fraudulent conduct, but innocuous violations of office policy.

The majority also takes a plainly written statute and parses it in a hyper-complicated way that distorts the obvious intent of Congress. No other circuit that has considered this statute finds the problems that the majority does.

18 U.S.C. § 1030(a)(4) is quite clear. It states, in relevant part:

> (a) Whoever –
>
>> (4) knowingly and with intent to defraud, accesses a protected computer without authorization, or exceeds authorized access, and by means of such conduct furthers the intended fraud and obtains anything of value . . .
>
> shall be punished . . . .

Thus, it is perfectly clear that a person with *both* the requisite mens rea *and* the specific intent to defraud – but *only* such persons – can violate this subsection in one of two ways: first, by accessing a computer without authorization, or second, by exceeding authorized access. 18 U.S.C. § 1030(e)(6) defines "exceeds authorized access" as "to access a computer with authorization and to use such access to obtain or alter information in the computer that the accesser is not entitled so to obtain or alter."

"As this definition makes clear, an individual who is authorized to use a computer for certain purposes but goes beyond those limitations is considered by the CFAA as someone who has 'exceed[ed] authorized access.'" *LVRC Holdings LLC v. Brekka*, 581 F.3d 1127, 1133 (9th Cir.2009).

"[T]he definition of the term 'exceeds authorized access' from § 1030(e)(6) implies that an employee can violate employer-placed limits on accessing information stored on the computer and still have authorization to access that computer. The plain language of the statute therefore indicates that 'authorization' depends on actions taken by the employer." *Id.* at 1135. In *Brekka*, we explained that a person "exceeds authorized access" when that person has permission to access a computer but accesses information on the computer that the person is not entitled to access. In that case, an employee allegedly emailed an employer's proprietary documents to his personal computer to use in a competing business. We held that one does not exceed authorized access simply by "breach[ing] a state law duty of loyalty to an employer" and that, because the employee did not breach a contract with his employer, he could not be liable under the Computer Fraud and Abuse Act.

This is not an esoteric concept. A bank teller is entitled to access a bank's money for legitimate banking purposes, but not to take the bank's money for himself. A new car buyer may be entitled to take a vehicle around the block on a test drive. But the buyer would not be entitled – he would "exceed his authority" – to take the vehicle to Mexico on a drug run. A person of ordinary intelligence understands that he may be totally prohibited from doing something *altogether,* or authorized to do something but prohibited from going *beyond* what is authorized. This is no doubt why the statute covers not only "unauthorized access," but also "exceed[ing] authorized access." The statute contemplates both means of committing the theft.

The majority holds that a person "exceeds authorized access" only when that person has permission to access a computer generally, but is *completely* prohibited from accessing a different portion of the computer (or different information on the computer). The majority's interpretation conflicts with the plain language of the statute. Furthermore, none of the circuits that have analyzed the meaning of "exceeds authorized access" as used in the Computer Fraud and Abuse Act read the statute the way the majority does. Both the Fifth and Eleventh Circuits have explicitly held that employees who knowingly violate clear company computer restrictions agreements "exceed authorized access" under the CFAA. [The dissent describes cases from the First, Fifth, Eighth, and Eleventh Circuits.]

The indictment here alleges that Nosal and his coconspirators knowingly exceeded the authority that they had to access their employer's computer, and that they did so with the intent to defraud and to steal trade secrets and proprietary information from the company's database for Nosal's competing business. It is alleged that at the time the employee coconspirators accessed the database they *knew* they only were allowed to use the database for a legitimate business purpose because the co-conspirators allegedly signed an agreement which restricted the use and disclosure of information on the database except for legitimate Korn/Ferry business. Moreover, it is alleged that before using a unique username and password to log on to the Korn/Ferry computer and database, the employees were notified that the information stored on those computers were the property of Korn/Ferry and that to access the information without relevant authority could lead to disciplinary action and criminal prosecution. Therefore, it is alleged, that when Nosal's co-conspirators accessed the database to obtain Korn/Ferry's secret source lists, names, and contact information with the intent to defraud Korn/Ferry by setting up a competing company to take business away using the stolen data, they "exceed[ed their] authorized access" to a computer with an intent to defraud Korn/Ferry and therefore violated 18 U.S.C. § 1030(a)(4). If true, these allegations adequately state a crime under a commonsense reading of this particular subsection.

Furthermore, it does not advance the ball to consider, as the majority does, the parade of horribles that might occur under *different* subsections of the CFAA, such as subsection (a)(2)(C), which does not have the scienter or specific intent to defraud requirements that subsection (a)(4) has. Other sections of the CFAA may or may not be unconstitutionally vague or pose other problems. We need to wait for an actual case or controversy to frame these issues, rather than posit a laundry list of wacky hypotheticals. I express no opinion on the validity or application of other subsections of 18 U.S.C. § 1030, other than § 1030(a)(4), and with all due respect, neither should the majority.

The majority's opinion is driven out of a well meaning but ultimately misguided concern that if employment agreements or internet terms of service violations could subject someone to criminal liability, all internet users will suddenly become criminals overnight. I fail to see how anyone can seriously conclude that reading ESPN.com in contravention of office policy could come within the ambit of 18 U.S.C. § 1030(a)(4), a statute explicitly requiring an intent to defraud, the obtaining of something of value by means of that fraud, while doing so "knowingly." And even if an imaginative judge can conjure up far-fetched hypotheticals producing federal prison terms for accessing word puzzles, jokes, and sports scores while at work, well, ... that is what an as-applied challenge is for. Meantime, back to this case, 18 U.S.C. § 1030(a)(4) clearly is aimed at, and limited to, knowing and intentional fraud. Because the indictment adequately states the elements of a valid crime, the district court erred in dismissing the charges.

I respectfully dissent.

UNITED STATES V. NOSAL [II]
— F.3d — (9th Cir. 2016)

McKeown, Circuit Judge:

... Before leaving Korn/Ferry [Nosal, Christian and Jacobs] used their own usernames and passwords, compiling proprietary Korn/Ferry data in violation of Korn/Ferry's computer use policy. Those efforts were encompassed in the CFAA accounts appealed in *Nosal I.*

After Nosal became a contractor and Christian and Jacobson left Korn/Ferry, Korn/Ferry revoked each of their credentials to access Korn/Ferry's computer system. Not to be deterred, on three occasions Christian and Jacobson borrowed access credentials from [Nosal's former executive assistant, Jacqueline Froehlich–L'Heureaux ("FH")], who stayed on at Korn/Ferry at Nosal's request. In April 2005, Nosal instructed Christian to obtain some source lists from Searcher to expedite their work for a new client. Thinking it would be difficult to explain the request to FH, Christian asked to borrow FH's access credentials, which Christian then used to log in to Korn/Ferry's computer system and run queries in Searcher. Christian sent the results of her searches to Nosal. In July 2005, Christian again logged in as FH to generate a custom report and search for information on three individuals. Later in July, Jacobson also logged in as FH, to download information on 2,400 executives. None of these searches related to any open searches that fell under Nosal's independent contractor agreement. ...

In *Nosal I,* authorization was not in doubt. The employees who accessed the Korn/Ferry computers unquestionably had authorization from the company to access the system; the question was whether they exceeded it. What *Nosal I* did not address was whether Nosal's access to Korn/Ferry computers after both Nosal and his co-conspirators had terminated their employment and Korn/Ferry revoked their permission to access the computers was "without authorization." *Brekka* is squarely on point on that issue: Nosal and his co-conspirators acted "without authorization" when they continued to access Searcher by other means after Korn/Ferry rescinded permission to access its computer system. As *Nosal I* made clear, the CFAA was not intended to cover unauthorized use of information. Such *use* is not at issue here. Rather, under § 1030(a)(4), Nosal is charged with unauthorized access—getting into the computer after categorically being barred from entry. ...

Implicit in the definition of authorization is the notion that someone, including an entity, can grant or revoke that permission. Here, that entity was Korn/Ferry and FH had no mantle or authority to override Korn/Ferry's authority to control access to its computers and confidential information by giving permission to former employees whose access had been categorically revoked by the company. Korn/Ferry owned and controlled access to its computers, including the Searcher database, and it retained exclusive discretion to issue or revoke access to the database. By revoking Nosal's login credentials on December 8, 2004, Korn/Ferry unequivocally conveyed to Nosal that he was an "outsider" who was no longer authorized to access Korn/Ferry computers and confidential information, including Searcher.Korn/Ferry also rescinded Christian and Jacobson's credentials after they left, at which point the three former employees were no longer "insiders" accessing company information. Rather, they had become "outsiders" with no authorization to access Korn/Ferry's computer system. One can certainly pose hypotheticals in which a less stark revocation is followed by more sympathetic access through an authorized third party. But the facts before us — in which Nosal received particularized notice of his revoked access following a prolonged negotiation — present no such difficulties, which can be reserved for another day. ...

In the face of multiple circuits that agree with our plain meaning construction of the statute, the dissent would have us ignore common sense and turn the statute inside out. Indeed, the dissent frames the question upside down in assuming that permission from FH is at issue. Under this approach, ignoring reality and practice, an employee could willy nilly give out passwords to anyone outside the company—former employees whose access had been revoked, competitors, industrious hackers, or bank robbers who find it less risky and more convenient to access accounts via the Internet rather than through armed robbery. ...

Reinhardt, Circuit Judge, dissenting:

This case is about password sharing. People frequently share their passwords, notwithstanding the fact that websites and employers have policies prohibiting it. In my view, the Computer Fraud and Abuse Act ("CFAA") does not make the millions of people who engage in this ubiquitous, useful, and generally harmless conduct into unwitting federal criminals. Whatever other liability, criminal or civil, Nosal may have incurred in his improper attempt to compete with his former employer, he has not violated the CFAA. ...of

The majority is wrong to conclude that a person necessarily accesses a computer account "without authorization" if he does so without the permission of the system owner. Take the case of an office worker asking a friend to log onto his email in order to print a boarding pass, in violation of the system owner's access policy; or the case of one spouse asking the other to log into a bank website to pay a bill, in violation of the bank's password sharing prohibition. There are other examples that readily come to mind, such as logging onto a computer on behalf of a colleague who is out of the office, in violation of a corporate computer access policy, to send him a document he needs right away. "Facebook makes it a violation of the terms of service to let anyone log into your account," we noted in *Nosal I*, but "it's very common for people to let close friends and relatives check their email or access their online accounts."

Was access in these examples authorized? Most people would say "yes." Although the system owners' policies prohibit password sharing, a legitimate account holder "authorized" the access. Thus, the best reading of "without authorization" in the CFAA is a narrow one: a person accesses an account "without authorization" if he does so without having the permission of *either* the system owner *or* a legitimate account holder. ...

It is impossible to discern from the majority opinion what principle distinguishes authorization in Nosal's case from one in which a bank has clearly told customers that no one but the customer may access the customer's account, but a husband nevertheless shares his password with his wife to allow her to pay a bill. So long as the wife knows that the bank does not give her permission to access its servers in any manner, she is in the same position as Nosal and his associates. It is not "advisory" to ask why the majority's opinion does not criminalize this under § 1030(a)(2)(C); yet, the majority suggests no answer to why it does not. ...

QUESTIONS

1. How would Fred Felon's use of the HTB computer come out under *Nosal I*? *Nosal II*? Under the dissents? What about Morris's worm program?

2. Is it now a federal crime to use a friend's Netflix password? To let a friend use yours?

3. One court has gone further than *Nosal I* in limiting the CFAA. In *United States v. Drew*, 259 F.R.D. 449 (C.D. Cal. 2009), the defendant, Lori Drew, participated in a scheme to create a MySpace profile under the name of "Josh Evans," a fictitious 16-year-old boy. This was a violation of the MySpace terms of service, which prohibited using false "registration information." "Josh" flirted online with Megan Meier, a 13-year-old neighbor of Drew's, then told Megan that he was moving away and "the world would be a better place without her in it." Megan killed herself. Drew was convicted under the CFAA, but court held that the CFAA was unconstitutionally vague because it delegated to website owners the power to define a federal crime- and failed to put website users on fair notice of the criminal law. Is this really a vagueness problem, or something else?

4. Other courts go further in the other direction. They would hold that Christan and Jacobsen's access would have been unauthorized even if Korn/Ferry had not had explicit terms of use. Under this "agency" theory, if a company provides an employee with a work laptop and the employee uses the laptop disloyally to harm the employer, that "terminate[s] his agency relationship ... and with it his authority to access the laptop, because the only basis of his authority had been that relationship." *International Airport Centers, LLC v. Citrin*, 440 F. 3d 418 (7th Cir. 2006). Is that better or worse?

5. Dora is a travel site that provides information on family tour packages. No usernames or passwords are required to use the site. Swiper, a competing travel site, repeatedly has employees view the prices on Dora's website, even after Dora sends Swiper a cease-and-desist letter stating that "all further use of the Dora.com website is unauthorized." Is this a violation of the CFAA?

6. Could Korn/Ferry bring a civil suit against Nosal?

C. Trespass to Chattels

Our final source of law for control over servers comes from the borderline between property law and tort law. If I use your computer without permission and cause it to burst into flames, it's generally accepted that you will have a valid lawsuit against me for trespass to chattels. The harder, more controversial questions arise when your use of the computer doesn't cause physical damage, but only some form of intangible trouble: deleted data, a slowed-down computer, or, perhaps, no visible harm at all.

RESTATEMENT (SECOND) OF TORTS [TRESPASS]

§ 158 – *Liability for Intentional Intrusions on Land*

One is subject to liability to another for trespass, irrespective of whether he thereby causes harm to any legally protected interest of the other, if he intentionally

(a) enters land in the possession of the other, or causes a thing or a third person to do so, or

(b) remains on the land, or

(c) fails to remove from the land a thing which he is under a duty to remove.

§ 218 – *Liability to Person in Possession*

One who commits a trespass to a chattel is subject to liability to the possessor of the chattel if, but only if,

(a) he dispossesses the other of the chattel, or

(b) the chattel is impaired as to its condition, quality, or value, or

(c) the possessor is deprived of the use of the chattel for a substantial time, or

(d) bodily harm is caused to the possessor, or harm is caused to some person or thing in which the possessor has a legally protected interest.

QUESTION

In 2007, a group of Harvard students created a website named CrimsonReading.org, which allowed students to comparison-shop for textbooks. In order to make a list of the books for the upcoming semester, they visited the Coop, a local bookstore where most professors place their book orders, to copy down courses, book names, and ISBNs.* The Coop, which has a policy against copying down ISBNs, objected and asked the students to leave, eventually calling the police. It is undisputed that the ISBNs themselves are not copyrightable and that the Coop has no rights over the numbers themselves. Can the Coop use tort law to keep CrimsonReading at bay?

INTEL V. HAMIDI
71 P. 3d 296 (Cal. 2003)

Werdegar, Justice: ...

[Kourosh Kenneth] Hamidi, a former Intel engineer, together with others, formed an organization named Former and Current Employees of Intel (FACE-Intel) to disseminate information and views critical of Intel's employment and personnel policies and practices. FACE-Intel maintained a Web site (which identified Hamidi as Webmaster and as the organization's spokesperson) containing such material. In addition, over a 21-month period Hamidi, on behalf of FACE-Intel, sent six mass e-mails to employee addresses on Intel's electronic mail system. The messages criticized Intel's employment practices, warned employees of the dangers those practices posed to their careers, suggested employees consider moving to other companies, solicited employees' participation in FACE-Intel, and urged employees to inform themselves further by visiting FACE-Intel's Web site.

---

* Short for International Standard Book Number, a 10- or 13-digit number that uniquely identifies an edition of a book.

The messages stated that recipients could, by notifying the sender of their wishes, be removed from FACE-Intel's mailing list; Hamidi did not subsequently send messages to anyone who requested removal.

Each message was sent to thousands of addresses (as many as 35,000 according to FACE-Intel's Web site), though some messages were blocked by Intel before reaching employees. Intel's attempt to block internal transmission of the messages succeeded only in part; Hamidi later admitted he evaded blocking efforts by using different sending computers. When Intel, in March 1998, demanded in writing that Hamidi and FACE-Intel stop sending e-mails to Intel's computer system, Hamidi asserted the organization had a right to communicate with willing Intel employees; he sent a new mass mailing in September 1998.

The summary judgment record contains no evidence Hamidi breached Intel's computer security in order to obtain the recipient addresses for his messages; indeed, internal Intel memoranda show the company's management concluded no security breach had occurred. Hamidi stated he created the recipient address list using an Intel directory on a floppy disk anonymously sent to him. Nor is there any evidence that the receipt or internal distribution of Hamidi's electronic messages damaged Intel's computer system or slowed or impaired its functioning. Intel did present uncontradicted evidence, however, that many employee recipients asked a company official to stop the messages and that staff time was consumed in attempts to block further messages from FACE-Intel. According to the FAC-Intel Web site, moreover, the messages had prompted discussions between "[e]xcited and nervous managers" and the company's human resources department.

Intel sued Hamidi and FACE-Intel [for trespass to chattels] and seeking both actual damages and an injunction against further e-mail messages. [The trial court granted Intel's motion for summary judgment and enjoined Hamidi from any further mailings. A divided Court of Appeal affirmed.]

I. CURRENT CALIFORNIA TORT LAW

Dubbed by Prosser the "little brother of conversion," the tort of trespass to chattels allows recovery for interferences with possession of personal property "not sufficiently important to be classed as conversion, and so to compel the defendant to pay the full value of the thing with which he has interfered." PROSSER & KEETON, TORTS § 14 (5th ed. 1984).

Though not amounting to conversion, the defendant's interference must, to be actionable, have caused some injury to the chattel or to the plaintiff's rights in it. ...

The Restatement, too, makes clear that some actual injury must have occurred in order for a trespass to chattels to be actionable. Under section 218 of the Restatement Second of Torts, dispossession alone, without further damages, is actionable, but other forms of interference require some additional harm to the personal property or the possessor's interests in it.

> The interest of a possessor of a chattel in its inviolability, unlike the similar interest of a possessor of land, is not given legal protection by an action for nominal damages for harmless intermeddlings with the chattel. In order that an actor who interferes with another's chattel may be liable, his conduct must affect some other and more important interest of the possessor. Therefore, one who intentionally intermeddles with another's chattel is subject to liability only if his intermeddling is harmful to the possessor's materially valuable interest in the physical condition, quality, or value of the chattel, or if the possessor is deprived of the use of the chattel for a substantial time, or some other

legally protected interest of the possessor is affected as stated in Clause (c). Sufficient legal protection of the possessor's interest in the mere inviolability of his chattel is afforded by his privilege to use reasonable force to protect his possession against even harmless interference.

Intel suggests that the requirement of actual harm does not apply here because it sought only injunctive relief, as protection from future injuries. But as Justice Kolkey, dissenting below, observed, "[t]he fact the relief sought is injunctive does not excuse a showing of injury, whether actual or threatened." Indeed, in order to obtain injunctive relief the plaintiff must ordinarily show that the defendant's wrongful acts threaten to cause irreparable injuries, ones that cannot be adequately compensated in damages. ...

The dispositive issue in this case, therefore, is whether the undisputed facts demonstrate Hamidi's actions caused or threatened to cause damage to Intel's computer system, or injury to its rights in that personal property, such as to entitle Intel to judgment as a matter of law. To review, the undisputed evidence revealed no actual or threatened damage to Intel's computer hardware or software and no interference with its ordinary and intended operation. Intel was not dispossessed of its computers, nor did Hamidi's messages prevent Intel from using its computers for any measurable length of time. Intel presented no evidence its system was slowed or otherwise impaired by the burden of delivering Hamidi's electronic messages. Nor was there any evidence transmission of the messages imposed any marginal cost on the operation of Intel's computers. In sum, no evidence suggested that in sending messages through Intel's Internet connections and internal computer system Hamidi used the system in any manner in which it was not intended to function or impaired the system in any way. Nor does the evidence show the request of any employee to be removed from FACE-Intel's mailing list was not honored. The evidence did show, however, that some employees who found the messages unwelcome asked management to stop them and that Intel technical staff spent time and effort attempting to block the messages. A statement on the FACE-Intel Web site, moreover, could be taken as an admission that the messages had caused "[e]xcited and nervous managers" to discuss the matter with Intel's human resources department.

Relying on a line of decisions, most from federal district courts, applying the tort of trespass to chattels to various types of unwanted electronic contact between computers, Intel contends that, while its computers were not damaged by receiving Hamidi's messages, its interest in the "physical condition, quality or value," RESTATEMENT (SECOND) OF TORTS § 218 cmt. e, of the computers was harmed. We disagree. The cited line of decisions does not persuade us that the mere sending of electronic communications that assertedly cause injury only because of their contents constitutes an actionable trespass to a computer system through which the messages are transmitted. Rather, the decisions finding electronic contact to be a trespass to computer systems have generally involved some actual or threatened interference with the computers' functioning.

In *Thrifty-Tel, Inc. v. Bezenek*, 46 Cal. App. 4th 1559 (1996), the California Court of Appeal held that evidence of automated searching of a telephone carrier's system for authorization codes supported a cause of action for trespass to chattels. The defendant's automated dialing program "overburdened the [plaintiffs] system, denying some subscribers access to phone lines," showing the requisite injury.

Following *Thrifty-Tel*, a series of federal district court decisions held that sending UCE through an ISP's equipment may constitute trespass to the ISP's computer system. The lead case, *CompuServe, Inc. v. Cyber Promotions, Inc.*, 962 F. Supp. 1015 (S.D. Ohio 1997), was followed by *Hotmail Corp. v. Van$ Money Pie, Inc.*, No. C 98-20064 JW, 1998 WL 388389 (N.D. Cal., Apr. 16, 1998), *America Online, Inc. v. IMS*, 24 F. Supp. 2d 548, (E.D. Va. 1998), and *America Online, Inc. v. LCGM, Inc.*, 46 F. Supp. 2d 444 (E.D. Va. 1998).

In each of these spamming cases, the plaintiff showed, or was prepared to show, some interference with the efficient functioning of its computer system. In *CompuServe*, the plaintiff ISP's mail equipment monitor stated that mass UCE mailings, especially from nonexistent addresses such as those used by the defendant, placed "a tremendous burden" on the ISP's equipment, using "disk space and draining] the processing power," making those resources unavailable to serve subscribers. Similarly, in *Hotmail Corp. v. Van$ Money Pie, Inc.*, the court found the evidence supported a finding that the defendant's mailings "fill[ed] up Hotmail's computer storage space and threatened to damage Hotmail's ability to service its legitimate customers." ...

In the leading case, *eBay, Inc. v. Bidder's Edge, Inc.*, 100 F. Supp. 2d 1058 (N.D. Cal. 2000), the defendant Bidder's Edge (BE), operating an auction aggregation site, accessed the eBay Web site about 100,000 times per day, accounting for between 1 and 2 percent of the information requests received by eBay and a slightly smaller percentage of the data transferred by eBay. The district court rejected eBay's claim that it was entitled to injunctive relief because of the defendant's unauthorized presence alone, or because of the incremental cost the defendant had imposed on operation of the eBay site, but found sufficient proof of *threatened* harm in the potential for others to imitate the defendant's activity: "If BE's activity is allowed to continue unchecked, it would encourage other auction aggregators to engage in similar recursive searching of the eBay system such that eBay would suffer irreparable harm from reduced system performance, system unavailability, or data losses." *Id.* at 1066. Again, in addressing the likelihood of eBay's success on its trespass to chattels cause of action, the court held the evidence of injury to eBay's computer system sufficient to support a preliminary injunction: "If the court were to hold otherwise, it would likely encourage other auction aggregators to crawl the eBay site, potentially to the point of denying effective access to eBay's customers. If preliminary injunctive relief were denied, and other aggregators began to crawl the eBay site, there appears to be little doubt that the load on eBay's computer system would qualify as a substantial impairment of condition or value." *Id.* at 1071-1072. ...

That Intel does not claim the type of functional impact that spammers and robots have been alleged to cause is not surprising in light of the differences between Hamidi's activities and those of a commercial enterprise that uses sheer quantity of messages as its communications strategy. Though Hamidi sent thousands of copies of the same message on six occasions over 21 months, that number is minuscule compared to the amounts of mail sent by commercial operations. The individual advertisers sued in *America Online, Inc. v. IMS* and *America Online, Inc. v. LCGM, Inc.* were alleged to have sent more than 60 million messages over 10 months and more than 92 million messages over seven months, respectively. Collectively, UCE has reportedly come to constitute about 45 percent of all e-mail. The functional burden on Intel's computers, or the cost in time to individual recipients, of receiving Hamidi's occasional advocacy messages cannot be compared to the burdens and costs caused ISP's and their customers by the ever-rising deluge of commercial e-mail.

Intel relies on language in the eBay decision suggesting that unauthorized use of another's chattel is actionable even without any showing of injury: "Even if, as [defendant] BE argues, its searches use only a small amount of eBay's computer system capacity, BE has nonetheless deprived eBay of the ability to use that portion of its personal property for its own purposes. The law recognizes no such right to use another's personal property." *eBay*, 100 F. Supp. 2d at 1071. But as the *eBay* court went on immediately to find that the defendant's conduct, if widely replicated, would likely impair the functioning of the plaintiffs system, we do not read the quoted remarks as expressing the court's complete view of the issue. In isolation, moreover, they would not be a correct statement of California or general American law on this point. While one may have no right temporarily to use another's personal property, such use is actionable as a trespass only if it "has proximately caused injury." *Thrifty-Tel*, 46 Cal. App. 4th at 1566. ... That Hamidi's messages temporarily used some portion of the Intel computers' processors or storage is, therefore, not enough; Intel must, but does not, demonstrate some measurable loss from the use of its computer system. ...

This theory of "impairment by content," Burk, *The Trouble with Trespass*, 4 J. SMALL & EMERGING BUS. L. 1 (1999), threatens to stretch trespass law to cover injuries far afield from the harms to possession the tort evolved to protect. Intel's theory would expand the tort of trespass to chattels to cover virtually any unconsented-to communication that, solely because of its content, is unwelcome to the recipient or intermediate transmitter. As the dissenting justice below explained

> "Damage" of this nature – the distraction of reading or listening to an unsolicited communication – is not within the scope of the injury against which the trespass-to-chattel tort protects, and indeed trivializes it. After all, "[t]he property interest protected by the old action of trespass was that of possession; and this has continued to affect the character of the action." PROSSER & KEETON § 14. Reading an e-mail transmitted to equipment designed to receive it, in and of itself, does not affect the possessory interest in the equipment. Indeed, if a chattel's receipt of an electronic communication constitutes a trespass to that chattel, then not only are unsolicited telephone calls and faxes trespasses to chattel, but unwelcome radio waves and television signals also constitute a trespass to chattel every time the viewer inadvertently sees or hears the unwanted program.

We agree. While unwelcome communications, electronic or otherwise, can cause a variety of injuries to economic relations, reputation and emotions, those interests are protected by other branches of tort law; in order to address them, we need not create a fiction of injury to the communication system.

Nor may Intel appropriately assert a property interest in its employees' time. "The Restatement test clearly speaks in the first instance to the impairment of the chattel.... But employees are not chattels (at least not in the legal sense of the term)." Burk, *The Trouble with Trespass*, at 36. Whatever interest Intel may have in preventing its employees from receiving disruptive communications, it is not an interest in personal property, and trespass to chattels is therefore not an action that will lie to protect it. Nor, finally, can the fact Intel staff spent time attempting to block Hamidi's messages be bootstrapped into an injury to Intel's possessory interest in its computers. To quote, again, from the dissenting opinion in the Court of Appeal: "[I]t is circular to premise the damage element of a tort solely upon the steps taken to prevent the damage. Injury can only be established by the completed tort's consequences, not by the cost of the steps taken to avoid the injury and prevent the tort; otherwise, we can create injury for every supposed tort."

Intel connected its e-mail system to the Internet and permitted its employees to make use of this connection both for business and, to a reasonable extent, for their own purposes. In doing so, the company necessarily contemplated the employees' receipt of unsolicited as well as solicited communications from other companies and individuals. That some communications would, because of their contents, be unwelcome to Intel management was virtually inevitable. Hamidi did nothing but use the e-mail system for its intended purpose – to communicate with employees. The system worked as designed, delivering the messages without any physical or functional harm or disruption. These occasional transmissions cannot reasonably be viewed as impairing the quality or value of Intel's computer system. We conclude, therefore, that Intel has not presented undisputed facts demonstrating an injury to its personal property, or to its legal interest in that property, that support, under California tort law, an action for trespass to chattels. ...

Kennard, Justice, concurring: ...

Intel has my sympathy. Unsolicited and unwanted bulk e-mail, most of it commercial, is a serious annoyance and inconvenience for persons who communicate electronically through the Internet, and bulk e-mail that distracts employees in the workplace can adversely affect overall productivity. But, as the majority persuasively explains, to establish the tort of trespass to chattels in California, the plaintiff must prove either damage to the plaintiff's personal property or actual or threatened impairment of the plaintiff's ability to use that property. Because plaintiff Intel has not shown that defendant Hamidi's occasional bulk e-mail messages to Intel's employees have damaged Intel's computer system or impaired its functioning in any significant way, Intel has not established the tort of trespass to chattels.

This is not to say that Intel is helpless either practically or legally. As a practical matter, Intel need only instruct its employees to delete messages from Hamidi without reading them and to notify Hamidi to remove their workplace e-mail addresses from his mailing lists. Hamidi's messages promised to remove recipients from the mailing list on request, and there is no evidence that Hamidi has ever failed to do so. From a legal perspective, a tort theory other than trespass to chattels may provide Intel with an effective remedy if Hamidi's messages are defamatory or wrongfully interfere with Intel's economic interests. Additionally, the Legislature continues to study the problems caused by bulk e-mails and other dubious uses of modern communication technologies and may craft legislation that accommodates the competing concerns in these sensitive and highly complex areas.

Accordingly, I join the majority in reversing the Court of Appeal's judgment.

Brown, Justice, dissenting:

Candidate A finds the vehicles that candidate B has provided for his campaign workers, and A spray paints the water soluble message, "Fight corruption, vote for A" on the bumpers. The majority's reasoning would find that notwithstanding the time it takes the workers to remove the paint and the expense they incur in altering the bumpers to prevent further unwanted messages, candidate B does not deserve an injunction unless the paint is so heavy that it reduces the cars' gas mileage or otherwise depreciates the cars' market value. Furthermore, candidate B has an obligation to permit the paint's display, because the cars are driven by workers and not B personally, because B allows his workers to use the cars to pick up their lunch or retrieve their children from school, or because the bumpers display B's own slogans. I disagree.

Intel has invested millions of dollars to develop and maintain a computer system. It did this not to act as a public forum but to enhance the productivity of its employees. Kourosh Kenneth Hamidi sent as many as 200,000 e-mail messages to Intel employees. The time required to review and delete Hamidi's messages diverted employees from productive tasks and undermined the utility of the computer system. "There may . . . be situations in which the value to the owner of a particular type of chattel may be impaired by dealing with it in a manner that does not affect its physical condition." RESTATEMENT (SECOND) OF TORTS § 218 cmt. h. This is such a case.

The majority repeatedly asserts that Intel objected to the hundreds of thousands of messages solely due to their content, and proposes that Intel seek relief by pleading content-based speech torts. This proposal misses the point that Intel's objection is directed not toward Hamidi's message but his use of Intel's property to display his message. Intel has not sought to prevent Hamidi from expressing his ideas on his Web site, through private mail (paper or electronic) to employees' homes, or through any other means like picketing or billboards. But as counsel for Intel explained during oral argument, the company objects to Hamidi's using Intel's property to advance his message.

Of course, Intel deserves an injunction even if its objections are based entirely on the e-mail's content. Intel is entitled, for example, to allow employees use of the Internet to check stock market tables or weather forecasts without incurring any concomitant obligation to allow access to pornographic Web sites. A private property owner may choose to exclude unwanted mail for any reason, including its content. ...

Mosk, Justice, dissenting: ...

The majority fail to distinguish open communication in the public "commons" of the Internet from unauthorized intermeddling on a private, proprietary intranet. Hamidi is not communicating in the equivalent of a town square or of an unsolicited "junk" mailing through the United States Postal Service. His action, in crossing from the public Internet into a private intranet, is more like intruding into a private office mailroom, commandeering the mail cart, and dropping off unwanted broadsides on 30,000 desks. Because Intel's security measures have been circumvented by Hamidi, the majority leave Intel, which has exercised all reasonable self-help efforts, with no recourse unless he causes a malfunction or systems "crash." Hamidi's repeated intrusions did more than merely "prompt[] discussions between '[e]xcited and nervous managers' and the company's human resource department" (maj. opn., ante); they also constituted a misappropriation of Intel's private computer system contrary to its intended use and against Intel's wishes.

QUESTIONS

1. What harms did Hamidi cause to Intel, if any? Which of these is trespass to chattels intended to defend against? Which of them "count" in deciding whether Hamdi committed an actionable tort? Are *Hamidi* and the caselaw it discusses (especially *eBay v. Bidder's Edge*) consistent?

2. Intel tried to block Hamidi's emails by discarding emails sent from his IP address. Hamidi evaded the block by sending emails from different computers. Does this cat-and-mouse game affect your opinion of who ought to win?

3. How persuasive are Justice Brown's campaign-cars analogy and Justice Mosk's mail-cart analogy.?

4. After *Hamidi*, is a trespass to chattels a viable way to claim misuse of a computer server in California? Elsewhere in the United States? Does a contract claim or a Computer Fraud and Abuse Act civil claim provide computer owners with an effective substitute? Is *Hamidi* a landmark in Internet law or an irrelevancy?

NOTE ON SPAM

As *Hamidi* and the cases it cites illustrate, one of the principal uses of the trespass to chattels tort was to combat unwanted email. The usual term for such email is "spam,"*and although its precise definition is controversial, the most common definition is *bulk unsolicited commercial email.*

In the 1990s, some email providers, like CompuServe and AOL, obtained large judgments (often default judgments) against spammers. But some of the difficulties of the tort (as seen in *Hamidi*) along with frustrations at other common tactics used by spammers, led to a wave of state anti-spam statutes in the late 1990s and early 2000s. The wave crested with the passage of the federal Controlling the Assault of Non-Solicited Pornography and Marketing Act of 2003, 15 U.S.C. §§ 7701–7713, better known by its acronym, CAN-SPAM. It does not attempt to prohibit bulk unsolicited commercial email as such, only to restrict some particularly unjustifiable practices.

First, CAN-SPAM prohibits the use of false or misleading "header information," 15 U.S.C. § 7704(a)(1), which is defined in part as "source, destination, and routing information attached to an electronic mail message, including the originating domain name and originating electronic mail address," *id.* § 7702(8). An email purporting to be from accounts@colossusbank.com but which is actually from a Bulgarian con artist would violate this provision. So would an email that uses a fictitious IP address or domain name to avoid spam filters. This part of CAN-SPAM also prohibits deceptive "subject headings," like a subject line that says "Warning: Your ColossusBank account has been suspended" on an email that actually advertises cut-rate Lorex watches. *Id.* § 7704(a)(2). Immaterial inaccuracies don't give rise to CAN-SPAM liability. *See, e.g., Omega World Travel Inc. v. Mummagraphics Inc.*, 469 F.3d 348 (4th Cir. 2006).

Second, CAN-SPAM allows recipients to opt out of future emails. Commercial emails must "contain a functioning return electronic mail address or other Inter-

---

* The name comes from a Monty Python sketch:

MAN: Well, what've you got?

WAITRESS: Well, there's egg and bacon; egg sausage and bacon; egg and spam; egg bacon and spam; egg bacon sausage and spam; spam bacon sausage and spam; spam egg spam spam bacon and spam; spam sausage spam spam bacon spam tomato and spam; … spam spam spam egg and spam; spam spam spam spam spam spam baked beans spam spam spam …

Monty Python: Spam (BBC television broadcast Dec. 15, 1970).

net-based mechanism, clearly and conspicuously displayed," *id.* § 7704(a)(3)(A), that the recipient can use to request "not to receive future commercial electronic mail messages from that sender," *id.* § 7704(a)(3)(A)(i). It is illegal for a sender to transmit further commercial emails more than ten business days after receiving such an opt-out request. *Id.* § 7704(a)(4).

The Federal Trade Commission received primary authority to punish violations of these rules. It was also instructed to study the feasibility of a Do-Not-Email registry along the lines of the Do-Not-Call list, and reported back that such a registry would probably backfire, because "spammers would most likely use a Registry as a mechanism for verifying the validity of email addresses and, without authentication, the Commission would be largely powerless to identify those responsible for misusing the Registry." FEDERAL TRADE COMMISSION, NATIONAL DO NOT EMAIL REGISTRY: A REPORT TO CONGRESS i (2004). States and other federal agencies were also given enforcement powers. Private causes of action, though, were limited. While ISPs "adversely affected" by violations of the Act were allowed to seek injunctions and recover damages and attorneys fees, users were given no private right of action. 15 U.S.C. § 7706(g). State laws are generally to the same effect. As a result, a regular question in spam litigation is whether an ISP is bona fide. *See, e.g., Beyond Sys., Inc. v. Kraft Foods, Inc.,* 777 F.3d 712, 718 (4th Cir. 2015) (plaintiff who "created fake e-mail addresses, solely for the purpose of gathering spam" consented to any resulting injury).

Another significant limitation on CAN-SPAM's reach was its restrictive definition of "commercial electronic mail message." *See* 15 U.S.C. § 7702(2) (definition); 16 C.F.R. § 316.3 (implementing regulations). It exempts "transactional or relationship message[s]," so Amazon can email customers that the packages they ordered have shipped, and ColossusBank can email its customers every month to let them know their account statements are ready. 15 U.S.C. § 7702(2)(B), (17). Noncommercial messages are exempted entirely. Moreover, CAN-SPAM broadly preempts related state laws. *See id.* § 7707(b). The only laws that survive are those that are "not specific to electronic mail," *id.* § 7707(b)(2)(A) or "prohibit[] falsity or deception," *id.* § 7707(b)(1). *See, e.g., Hypertouch, Inc. v. Valueclick, Inc.,* 192 Cal. App. 4th 805 (2011) (surveying CAN-SPAM preemption caselaw).

Broadly speaking, anti-spam laws did two things. First, they established a clear set of safe harbors and best practices for legitimate marketing. Unsubscribe links in advertising emails from major companies are ubiquitous, and they usually work. Second, spam laws cleared the field for hucksters, con artists, criminals, and others uninterested in complying with any spam laws at all. These senders are frequently unidentifiable, and not amenable to United States jurisdiction even when they are.

Thus, the other major front line in the spam wars involves self-help. One group of frustrated recipients tried to persuade ISPs to cut off service to spammers; another tried to develop filtering software that could identify spam email and either delete it outright or automatically route it to junk folders. The two efforts were complementary: as more and more "reputable" ISPs took aggressive stances against spam, it became easier to flag certain ISPs as being likely sources of spam, and the threat of having emails from legitimate customers blocked was a powerful weapon in persuading ISPs to kick off spammers. They also gave rise to some high-profile controversies: for example, some victims of filtering claimed that the filters illegally interfered with their speech and their business.* These technical efforts have made spam a manageable problem for most users: your email provider typically does a decent job keeping spam out of your inbox. But the other manifestations of the underground spam economy – from blog comment spam to drive-by malware downloads – are much uglier, and unfortunately likely to be with us for a long time.

WIRELESS ROUTER PROBLEM

You are associate general counsel for the FixPoint Corporation, which makes consumer and enterprise networking equipment. You have recently become aware of an issue with your company's WX11N series of home wireless routers. Once daily, each router connects to a "time server" to reset its internal clock. Each router ships with a list of roughly 100 different time servers. Each time they check what time it is, they pick a random server from the list. The goal is to spread the burden of checking what time it is across a large number of servers, so that none of them bears an excessive burden.

Unfortunately, due to a bug in the WX11N's software, the random-number generator always returns "16" when it picks which time server to consult. That means that the roughly three million WX11Ns in consumers' homes are all querying the same time server at the University of Helsinki. Worse, due to another bug, they all do it at 2:00 AM local time. This leads to a flood of hundreds of thousands of queries to the time server at the University of Helsinki, which has caused it to crash on multiple occasions. The University is threatening to file suit and possibly also to deactivate its time server entirely.

Evaluate the legal risk the FixPoint Corporation faces. You have a meeting scheduled with the engineering team later today. Are there any questions you would want to ask them, either to evaluate the legal risks or to consider possible mitigation strategies?

LINEJUMP PROBLEM

National Airlines has an egalitarian boarding policy. It has no first-class or business-class seats, and boarding passes do not come with assigned seats. Instead, it has a "cattle call" at boarding; passengers pick their own seats on a first-come, first-served basis.

The only differentiation among passengers is that each boarding pass is printed with the letter "A," "B," or "C." Passengers in the A group board first, followed by the Bs, and the the Cs. The letters are assigned based on when the passengers checked in on National's website. The earlier passengers receive A passes, the middle passengers receive B passes, and the last passengers to check in receive C passes. To check in online, a passenger must go to nationalair.com and click on a tab marked "Check in." A window then opens in which the customer inputs his or her name and flight number. National's computers then retrieve the reservation and display s an image of the boarding pass for printing. Online checkin opens 24 hours before each flight.

LineJump's only line of business is assisting National passengers to secure A boarding passes so they can be among the first on the plane. Passengers holding National tickets log on to the linejump.com website and supply their names, flight numbers, and credit card information, and authorize LineJump to act as their

---

* For one such example, see the SpamPosse problem in Section 9.A.

agents. Once a passenger's boarding pass becomes available for checkin, a Line-Jump employee manually uses the "Check in" feature on National's website, then emails the passenger an image of the boardingpass to print. LineJump charges $5 per pass, and serves about 100 National passengers per day. It typically succeeds in obtaining A passes for 95 or more of them; it gives a full refund to any passenger for whom it is unable to obtain an A pass.

National believes that LineJump's use of its website violates its terms and conditions. The National homepage states in small black print at the bottom of each page that "use of the National website constitutes acceptance of our Terms and Conditions." The words "Terms and Conditions" are in blue; they are a hyperlink which takes the user to the Terms and Conditions page on nationalair.com. In relevant part, the terms read:

> National's websites and any Company Information is available to you only to learn about, evaluate, or purchase National services and products. Unless you are an approved National travel agent, you may use the National website only for personal, non-commercial purposes. For example, third parties may not use the National web sites for the purpose of checking Customers in online or attempting to obtain for them a boarding pass in any certain boarding group.
>
> As a condition of your use of the National website, you promise that you will not use the National website for any purpose that is unlawful or prohibited by these terms and conditions.

On December 20, 2010, National sent a cease-and-desist letter to LineJump stating that National's terms and conditions prohibited the use of nationalair.com for commercial purposes and that LineJump's activities breached the Terms. When LineJump's use did not stop, National filed suit on May 17, 2011. Its complaint includes claims for breach of contract, trespass to chattels, and violation of the Computer Fraud and Abuse Act. National and LineJump have filed cross motions for summary judgment. How should the court rule?

CHAPTER 6: TRADEMARKS & DOMAIN NAMES

This chapter discusses the application of trademark law to the Internet. Although the focus is primarily on private disputes and on the power of intermediaries to shape those disputes, there is also a public-law dimension to trademark policy on the Internet. Our examination of trademarks will take us inside the domain-name system, where a private non-governmental body wields a surprising power over trademark rights.

This chapter and the next offer a sustained discussion of how the law deals with intermediaries like ISPs, web hosts, and email providers. In particular, they discuss the extent to which these intermediaries can be held liable for the actions of their users. These laws reflect a balance between the desire to use the intermediary's power to police user behavior, and a concern that doing so could stifle user speech and activity. They also reflect a balance between the desire to encourage the development of intermediaries and a desire to keep them from abusing their power. We have already seen similar concerns in the material on Section 230. As you consider the variations on this theme in the next two chapters, ask yourself what is new and what has changed.

A. Trademark Basics

A trademark is a word, phrase, or other symbol that identifies to consumers the source of a product or service. Thus, the trademark COCA-COLA* tells you that the cola beverage you're considering buying is made and distributed under the authority of the Coca-Cola Company. Why does this matter? Scholars usually give three reasons:

1. The mark is a signal helping me find a product. If I'm in the supermarket looking for a soda rather than a bottle of carrot juice, the COCA-COLA mark tells me where to look.

2. The mark is a promise of quality. If I liked the taste of the soda the last time I drank it, then I know that by buying one in a similar package with the COCA-COLA trademark, I'll get something similar.

3. The mark protects brand value against competitors. If Nola Cola starts putting the COCA-COLA trademark on its bottles, I might be misled into buying Nola Cola by mistake. That hurts me (it doesn't taste the same) and it hurts the Coca-Cola Company (which invested in creating good products and in a recognizable trademark).

The core rule of trademark law is that the owner of a trademark can sue for infringement anyone else who "uses" its trademark in a manner "likely to cause consumer confusion." The relevant form of confusion is confusion over *source*: that is, confusion about who supplied the goods.

---

* By convention, trademarks are written in ALL CAPS.

An important limitation on trademark rights and on infringement liability is inherent in this rule. There are no trademark rights over non-source-identifying uses. If I describe my liquid beverage as WATER, I have no trademark rights over the word WATER. A consumer picking up the bottle will think that WATER describes the product, rather than being a trademark. This rule also has consequences on the infringement side. A variety of doctrines provide that it's not infringement to use a trademark to describe your own product truthfully. This could be because you need to use the word (e.g. "water" to describe a beverage) or because you need to use the trademark itself to explain what your product or service is (e.g. "We repair Ford trucks.").

Trademark rights are in theory defined geographically. If one restaurant uses the trademark BILGEWATER BILL's in Portland, Maine, and another uses the trademark BILGEWATER BILL's in Portland, Oregon, each of them has trademark rights in its respective region, and neither can oust the other. This makes intuitive sense: the groups of consumers in the two Portlands don't overlap, so no one in either city is likely to be confused about which restaurant is which. Federal registration of a trademark gives the registrant nationwide rights, subject to any existing rights of other users. If the Maine restaurant registers its trademark, it now has "priority" everywhere but around Portland, Oregon. So, for example, if both restaurants open branches in Chicago, the Maine-based chain can sue the Portland-based one for infringement, but not vice-versa. There is also a system of federal registration for trademarks, which gives nationwide — but not worldwide — rights.

Unsurprisingly, this geographic logic starts to break down when the Internet is involved. The question can arise in two ways. First, can a business's web presence create consumer confusion in areas beyond the locality where it has a physical presence? (Recall the *Too Damn High* problem from the Jurisdiction chapter.) Second, can a business's web presence give it priority in areas beyond the locality where it has a physical presence? The answer to both questions is almost certainly "yes," particularly now that many businesses connect with their customers almost exclusively online. But courts remain reluctant to collapse the entire country – or worse, the entire world – into a single market for trademark purposes.

MULTI TIME MACHINE, INC. V. AMAZON. COM, INC.
804 F. 3d 930 (9th Cir. 2015)

Silverman, Circuit Judge:

In the present appeal, we must decide whether the following scenario constitutes trademark infringement: A customer goes online to Amazon.com looking for a certain military-style wristwatch — specifically the "MTM Special Ops" — marketed and manufactured by Plaintiff Multi Time Machine, Inc. The customer types "mtm special ops" in the search box and presses "enter." Because Amazon does not sell the MTM Special Ops watch, what the search produces is a list, with photographs, of several other brands of military style watches that Amazon does carry, specifically identified by their brand names — Luminox, Chase-Durer, TAWATEC, and Modus.

MTM brought suit alleging that Amazon's response to a search for the MTM Special Ops watch on its website is trademark infringement in violation of the Lanham Act. MTM contends that Amazon's search results page creates a likelihood of confusion, even though there is no evidence of any actual confusion and even though the other brands are clearly identified by name. The district court granted summary judgment in favor of Amazon, and MTM now appeals.

We affirm. The core element of trademark infringement is whether the defendant's conduct "is likely to confuse customers about the source of the products. Because Amazon's search results page clearly labels the name and manufacturer of each product offered for sale and even includes photographs of the items, no reasonably prudent consumer accustomed to shopping online would likely be confused as to the source of the products. ....

I. Factual and Procedural Background

MTM manufactures and markets watches under various brand names including MTM, MTM Special Ops, and MTM Military Ops. MTM holds the federally registered trademark "MTM Special Ops" for timepieces. MTM sells its watches directly to its customers and through various retailers. To cultivate and maintain an image as a high-end, exclusive brand, MTM does not sell its watches through Amazon.com. Further, MTM does not authorize its distributors, whose agreements require them to seek MTM's permission to sell MTM's products anywhere but their own retail sites, to sell MTM watches on Amazon.com. Therefore, MTM watches have never been available for sale on Amazon.com.

Amazon is an online retailer that purports to offer "Earth's Biggest Selection of products." Amazon has designed its website to enable millions of unique products to be sold by both Amazon and third party sellers across dozens of product categories.

Consumers who wish to shop for products on Amazon's website can utilize Amazon's search function. ... In order to provide search results in which the consumer is most likely to be interested, Amazon's search function does not simply match the words in the user's query to words in a document, such as a product description in Amazon.com's catalog. Rather, Amazon's search function — like general purpose web search engines such as Google or Bing — employs a variety of techniques, including some that rely on user behavior, to produce relevant results. By going beyond exactly matching a user's query to text describing a product, Amazon's search function can provide consumers with relevant results that would otherwise be overlooked.

Consumers who go onto Amazon.com and search for the term "mtm special ops" are directed to a search results page. On the search results page, the search query used — here, "mtm special ops" — is displayed twice: in the search query box and directly below the search query box in what is termed a "breadcrumb." The breadcrumb displays the original query, "mtm special ops," in quotation marks to provide a trail for the consumer to follow back to the original search. Directly below the breadcrumb, is a "Related Searches" field, which provides the consumer with alternative search queries in case the consumer is dissatisfied with the results of the original search. Here, the Related Search that is suggested to the consumer is: "mtm special ops watch." Directly below the "Related Searches" field is a gray bar containing the text "Showing 10 Results." Then, directly below the gray bar is Amazon's product listings. The gray bar separates the product listings from the breadcrumb and the "Related Searches" field. The particular search results page at issue is displayed below:

MTM watches are not listed on the page for the simple reason that neither Amazon nor MTM sells MTM watches on Amazon.

MTM filed a complaint against Amazon, alleging that Amazon's search results page infringes MTM's trademarks in violation of the Lanham Act. Amazon filed a

motion for summary judgment, arguing that (1) it is not using MTM's mark in commerce and (2) there is no likelihood of consumer confusion. In ruling on Amazon's motion for summary judgment, the district court declined to resolve the issue of whether Amazon is using MTM's mark in commerce, and, instead, addressed the issue of likelihood of confusion. In evaluating likelihood of confusion, the district court utilized the eight-factor test set forth in *AMF Inc. v. Sleekcraft Boats*,

599 F.2d 341 (9th Cir.1979).* Relying on our recent decision in *Network Automation, Inc. v. Advanced Systems Concepts*, 638 F.3d 1137 (9th Cir. 2011), the district court focused in particular on the following factors: (1) the strength of MTM's mark; (2) the evidence of actual confusion and the evidence of no confusion; (3) the type of goods and degree of care likely to be exercised by the purchaser; and (4) the appearance of the product listings and the surrounding context on the screen displaying the results page. Upon reviewing the factors, the district court concluded that the relevant *Sleekcraft* factors established "that there is no likelihood of confusion in Amazon's use of MTM's trademarks in its search engine or display of search results." Therefore, the district court granted Amazon's motion for summary judgment. ...

III. DISCUSSION

To prevail on a claim of trademark infringement under the Lanham Act, a trademark holder must show that the defendant's use of its trademark is likely to cause confusion, or to cause mistake, or to deceive. The test for likelihood of confusion is whether a reasonably prudent consumer in the marketplace is likely to be confused as to the origin of the good or service bearing one of the marks. The confusion must be probable, not simply a possibility.

Here, the district court was correct in ruling that there is no likelihood of confusion. Amazon is responding to a customer's inquiry about a brand it does not carry by doing no more than stating clearly (and showing pictures of) what brands it does carry. To whatever extent the *Sleekcraft* factors apply in a case such as this — a merchant responding to a request for a particular brand it does not sell by offering other brands clearly identified as such — the undisputed evidence shows that confusion on the part of the inquiring buyer is not at all likely. Not only are the other brands clearly labeled and accompanied by photographs, there is no evidence of actual confusion by anyone.

To analyze likelihood of confusion, we utilize the eight-factor test set forth in *Sleekcraft*. However, we have long cautioned that applying the *Sleekcraft* test is not like counting beans. "Some factors are much more important than others, and the relative importance of each individual factor will be case-specific." *Brookfield Commc'ns v. West Coast Entm't Corp.*, 174 F.3d 1036, 1054 (9th Cir.1999). Moreover, the *Sleekcraft* factors are not exhaustive and other variables may come into play depending on the particular facts presented. This is particularly true in the Internet context. Indeed, in evaluating claims of trademark infringement in cases involving Internet search engines, we have found particularly important an additional factor that is out-side of the eight-factor *Sleekcraft* test: "the labeling and appearance of the advertisements and the surrounding context on the screen displaying the results page." *Network Automation*, 638 F.3d at 1154.

In the present case, the eight-factor *Sleekcraft* test is not particularly apt. This is not surprising as the *Sleekcraft* test was developed for a different problem — i.e., for analyzing whether two competing brands' marks are sufficiently similar to cause consumer confusion. Although the present case involves brands that compete with MTM, such as Luminox, Chase-Durer, TAWATEC, and Modus, MTM

---

1   The eight factors enumerated in *Sleekcraft* are as follows: "1. strength of the mark; 2. proximity of the goods; 3. similarity of the marks; 4. evidence of actual confusion; 5. marketing channels used; 6. type of goods and the degree of care likely to be exercised by the purchaser; 7. defendant's intent in selecting the mark; and 8. likelihood of expansion of the product lines." 599 F.2d at 348-49.

does not contend that the marks for these competing brands are similar to its trademarks. Rather, MTM argues that the design of Amazon's search results page creates a likelihood of initial interest confusion[*]

[2] because when a customer searches for MTM Special Ops watches on Amazon.com, the search results page displays the search term used — here, "mtm special ops" — followed by a display of numerous watches manufactured by MTM's competitors and offered for sale by Amazon, without explicitly informing the customer that Amazon does not carry MTM watches.

Thus, the present case focuses on a different type of confusion than was at issue in *Sleekcraft*. Here, the confusion is not caused by the design of the competitor's mark, but by the design of the web page that is displaying the competing mark and offering the competing products for sale. *Sleekcraft* aside, the ultimate test for determining likelihood of confusion is whether a reasonably prudent consumer in the marketplace is likely to be confused as to the origin of the goods. Our case can be resolved simply by a evaluation of the web page at issue and the relevant consumer. In other words, the case will turn on the answers to the following two questions: (1) Who is the relevant reasonable consumer?; and (2) What would he reasonably believe based on what he saw on the screen? ...

The goods in the present case are expensive. It is undisputed that the watches at issue sell for several hundred dollars. Therefore, the relevant consumer in the present case is a reasonably prudent consumer accustomed to shopping online.

Turning to the second question, as MTM itself asserts, the labeling and appearance of the products for sale on Amazon's web page is the most important factor in this case. This is because we have previously noted that clear labeling can eliminate the likelihood of initial interest confusion in cases involving Internet search terms. Thus, MTM agrees that summary judgment of its trademark claims is appropriate if there is clear labeling that avoids likely confusion.

Here, the products at issue are clearly labeled by Amazon to avoid any likelihood of initial interest confusion by a reasonably prudent consumer accustomed to online shopping. When a shopper goes to Amazon's website and searches for a product using MTM's trademark "mtm special ops," the resulting page displays several products, all of which are clearly labeled with the product's name and manufacturer in large, bright, bold letters and includes a photograph of the item. In fact, the manufacturer's name is listed twice. For example, the first result is "Luminox Men's 8401 Black Ops Watch by Luminox." The second result is "Chase-Durer Men's 246.4BB7-XL-BR Special Forces 1000XL Black Ionic-Plated Underwater Demolition Team Watch by Chase-Durer." Because Amazon clearly labels each of the products for sale by brand name and model number accompanied by a photograph of the item, it is unreasonable to suppose that the reasonably prudent

---

2 "Initial interest confusion is customer confusion that creates initial interest in a competitor's product. Although dispelled before an actual sale occurs, initial interest confusion impermissibly capitalizes on the goodwill associated with a mark and is therefore actionable trademark infringement." *Playboy Enters. v. Netscape Commc'ns Corp.*, 354 F.3d 1020, 1025 (9th Cir. 2004).

   Following the issuance of the original opinion in this action, several amici filed briefs questioning the validity of the doctrine of initial interest confusion in the context of the Internet. However, in the present appeal, the parties did not dispute the application of the doctrine of initial interest confusion, and we as a three-judge panel are bound by the precedent of our court.

consumer accustomed to shopping online would be confused about the source of the goods.

MTM argues that initial interest confusion might occur because Amazon lists the search term used — here the trademarked phrase "mtm special ops" — three times at the top of the search page. MTM argues that because Amazon lists the search term "mtm special ops" at the top of the page, a consumer might conclude that the products displayed are types of MTM watches. But, merely looking at Amazon's search results page shows that such consumer confusion is highly unlikely. None of these watches is labeled with the word "MTM" or the phrase "Special Ops," let alone the specific phrase "MTM Special Ops." Further, some of the products listed are not even watches. The sixth result is a book entitled "Survive!: The Disaster, Crisis and Emergency Handbook by Jerry Ahem." The tenth result is a book entitled "The Moses Expedition: A Novel by Juan Gomez-Jurado." No reasonably prudent consumer, accustomed to shopping online or not, would assume that a book entitled "The Moses Expedition" is a type of MTM watch or is in any way affiliated with MTM watches. Likewise, no reasonably prudent consumer accustomed to shopping online would view Amazon's search results page and conclude that the products offered are MTM watches. It is possible that someone, somewhere might be confused by the search results page. But, unreasonable, imprudent and inexperienced web-shoppers are not relevant. To establish likelihood of confusion, MTM must show that confusion is likely, not just possible.

MTM argues that in order to eliminate the likelihood of confusion, Amazon must change its search results page so that it explains to customers that it does not offer MTM watches for sale before suggesting alternative watches to the customer. We disagree. The search results page makes clear to anyone who can read English that Amazon carries only the brands that are clearly and explicitly listed on the web page. The search results page is unambiguous — not unlike when someone walks into a diner, asks for a Coke, and is told "No Coke. Pepsi."

In light of the clear labeling Amazon uses on its search results page, no reasonable trier of fact could conclude that Amazon's search results page would likely confuse a reasonably prudent consumer accustomed to shopping online as to the source of the goods being offered. As Judge Berzon put it, "I do not think it is reasonable to find initial interest confusion when a consumer is never confused as to source or affiliation, but instead knows, or should know, from the outset that a product or web link is not related to that of the trademark holder because the list produced by the search engine so informs him." *Playboy*, 354 F.3d at 1034-35 (9th Cir. 2004) (Berzon, J., concurring). ...

Further, we are able to conclude that summary judgment is appropriate in the present case without delving into any factors other than: (1) the type of goods and the degree of care likely to be exercised by the purchaser; and (2) the labeling and appearance of the products for sale and the surrounding context on the screen displaying the results page. However, if we were to evaluate each of the remaining Sleekcraft factors, those factors would not change our conclusion, here, because those factors are either neutral or unimportant.

"Actual confusion" — We have held that "[a] showing of actual confusion among significant numbers of consumers provides strong support for the likelihood of confusion." *Playboy*, 354 F.3d at 1026. However, here, there is no evidence of actual confusion. The only "evidence" MTM presented to the district court of actual confusion is the deposition testimony of MTM's president stating that someone named Eric told him, in reference to Amazon's web page, "it's confusing."

Hearsay problems aside, this testimony is too speculative to show actual confusion because there is no evidence showing that Eric was a potential consumer. ...

"Defendant's Intent" — We have also held that "[a] defendant's intent to confuse constitutes probative evidence of likely confusion: Courts assume that the defendant's intentions were carried out successfully." *Playboy*, 354 F.3d at 1028. MTM argues that the design of Amazon's search results page is evidence of its intent to cause confusion. The design, however, indisputably produces results that are clearly labeled as to the type of product and brand. Amazon has designed its results page to alleviate any possible confusion about the source of the products by clearly labeling each of its products with the product's name and manufacturer. Therefore, this factor also does not weigh in MTM's favor.

"Strength of the Mark" — MTM argues that it has presented sufficient evidence below from which a jury could properly conclude that its trademark is both conceptually strong and commercially strong. However, we find that this factor is unimportant under the circumstances of this case. Even assuming MTM's mark is one of the strongest in the world — on the same level as Apple, Coke, Disney, or McDonald's — there is still no likelihood of confusion because Amazon clearly labels the source of the products it offers for sale.

Further, as we previously found in *Network Automation*, the remaining *Sleekcraft* factors are unimportant in a case, such as this, involving Internet search terms where the competing products are clearly labeled and the relevant consumer would exercise a high degree of care. *See Network Automation*, 638 F.3d at 1150-53 (finding "proximity of goods," "similarity of marks," "marketing channels," and "likelihood of expansion" to be unimportant in a trademark case involving Internet search terms where the advertisements are clearly labeled and the relevant consumers would exercise a high degree of care).

IV. CONCLUSION

In light of Amazon's clear labeling of the products it carries, by brand name and model, accompanied by a photograph of the item, no rational trier of fact could find that a reasonably prudent consumer accustomed to shopping online would likely be confused by the Amazon search results. Accordingly, we affirm the district court's grant of summary judgment in favor of Amazon.

Bea, Circuit Judge, dissenting: ...

Because I believe that an Amazon shopper seeking an MTM watch might well initially think that the watches Amazon offers for sale when he searches "MTM Special Ops" are affiliated with MTM, I must dissent.

If her brother mentioned MTM Special Ops watches, a frequent internet shopper might try to purchase one for him through her usual internet retail sites, perhaps Overstock.com, Buy.com, and Amazon.com. At Overstock's site, if she typed "MTM special ops," the site would respond "Sorry, your search: 'mtm special ops' returned no results." Similarly, at Buy.com, she would be informed "0 results found. Sorry. Your search for mtm special ops did not return an exact match. Please try your search again."

Things are a little different over at "Earth's most customer-centric company," as Amazon styles itself. There, if she were to enter "MTM Special Ops" as her search request on the Amazon website, Amazon would respond with its page showing (1) MTM Special Ops in the search field (2) "MTM Specials Ops" again — in quotation marks — immediately below the search field and (3) yet again in the phrase "Related Searches: MTM special ops watch," (emphasis in original) all before stating "Showing 10 Results." What the website's response will not state is the truth recognized by its competitors: that Amazon does not carry MTM products any more than do Overstock.com or Buy.com. Rather, below the search field, and below the second and third mentions of "MTM Special Ops" noted above, the site will display aesthetically similar, multi-function watches manufactured by MTM's competitors. The shopper will see that Luminox and Chase-Durer watches are offered for sale, in response to her MTM query.

MTM asserts the shopper might be confused into thinking a relationship exists between Luminox and MTM; she may think that MTM was acquired by Luminox, or that MTM manufactures component parts of Luminox watches, for instance. As a result of this initial confusion, MTM asserts, she might look into buying a Luminox watch, rather than junk the quest altogether and seek to buy an MTM watch elsewhere. MTM asserts that Amazon's use of MTM's trademarked name is likely to confuse buyers, who may ultimately buy a competitor's goods.

MTM may be mistaken. But whether MTM is mistaken is a question that requires a factual determination, one this court does not have authority to make.

By usurping the jury function, the majority today makes new trademark law. ... Capturing initial consumer attention has been recognized by our court to be a grounds for finding of infringement of the Lanham Act since 1997. *Dr. Seuss Enterprises, L.P. v. Penguin Books USA, Inc.*, 109 F.3d 1394, 1405 (9th Cir. 1997) (identifying "initial consumer attention" as a basis for infringement). In 1999, citing *Dr. Seuss*, we expressly adopted the initial interest confusion doctrine in the internet context, and never repudiated it. *Brookfield Communications, Inc. v. West Coast Entertainment Corp.*, 174 F.3d 1036, 1062 (9th Cir. 1999). It may not apply where the competing goods or services are "clearly labeled" such that they cause only mere diversion, but whether such goods or services are clearly labeled so as to prevent a prudent internet shopper's initial confusion depends on the overall function and presentation of the web page. The issue is whether a prudent internet shopper who made the search request and saw the Amazon result — top to bottom — would more likely than not be affected by that "initial interest confusion." That is, an impression — when first shown the results of the requested MTM Special Ops search — that Amazon carries watches that have some connection to MTM, and that those watches are sold under the name Luminox or Chase-Durer. Whether there is likelihood of such initial interest confusion, I submit, is a jury question. Intimations in our case law that initial interest confusion is bad doctrine notwithstanding, it is the law of our circuit, and, I submit, the most fair reading of the Lanham Act. ...

In *Network Automation*, the "diversionary" goods were clearly labeled on the response page as "Sponsored Links," showing that the producers of those products were the ones advertising for themselves, not for the firm named in the search request. *Network Automation*, 638 F.3d at 1144. Unlike the sponsored links at issue in Network Automation, and unlike its competitors Buy.com and Overstock.com, Amazon does not forestall any confusion by informing customers who are searching "MTM Special Ops" that Amazon does not carry any such products. Amazon does just the opposite. It responds by twice naming MTM, and once specifically naming watches. ...

In any event, even as to expensive goods — for instance, pianos sold under a mark very similar to the famous Steinway and Sons brand's mark — the issue is not that a buyer might buy a piano manufactured by someone other than Steinway thinking that it was a Steinway. The issue is that the defendant's use of the mark would cause initial interest confusion by attracting potential customers' attention to buy the infringing goods because of the trademark holder's hard-won reputation. ...

Similarly, the majority finds that Amazon's intent weighs in favor of Amazon. A defendant's intent is relevant because a "defendant's intent to confuse constitutes probative evidence of likely confusion." *Playboy*, 354 F.3d at 1029. MTM submitted evidence that Amazon vendors and customers had complained to Amazon because they did not understand why they received certain non-responsive search results when they searched for products that are not carried by Amazon. The evidence showed that Amazon employees did not take action to address the complaints by explaining to the public how its search function works. ...

From evidence that "Earth's most customer-centric company" took no action on these complaints, a jury could infer that Amazon intended to confuse its customers.

QUESTIONS

1. *Brookfield* (discussed in *MTM*) gave the following analogy to explain initial interest confusion:

   > [It] is much like posting a sign with another's trademark in front of one's store. Suppose West Coast's competitor (let's call it "Blockbuster") puts up a billboard on a highway reading – "West Coast Video: 2 miles ahead at Exit 7" – where West Coast is really located at Exit 8 but Blockbuster is located at Exit 7. Customers looking for West Coast's store will pull off at Exit 7 and drive around looking for it. Unable to locate West Coast, but seeing the Blockbuster store right by the highway entrance, they may simply rent there. Even consumers who prefer West Coast may find it not worth the trouble to continue searching for West Coast since there is a Blockbuster right there. Customers are not confused in the narrow sense: they are fully aware that they are purchasing from Blockbuster and they have no reason to believe that Blockbuster is related to, or in any way sponsored by, West Coast. Nevertheless, the fact that there is only initial consumer confusion does not alter the fact that Blockbuster would be misappropriating West Coast's acquired goodwill.

   Is this a persuasive theory of trademark harm in the offline context? Does it strike you as a persuasive analogy to what Amazon is doing?

2. What do Amazon users want when they search for "mtm special ops"? Will the majority or the dissent do a better job of giving it to them?

3. Suppose that the toy company Hasbro wants to show that the TRANS-FORMERS mark has strong secondary meaning with consumers by introducing into evidence the first ten pages of Google results in a search for "transformers," the vast majority of which refer to the toys, cartoons and movies. Should it be allowed to?

TIFFANY (NJ) INC. V. EBAY, INC.
576 F. Supp. 2d 463 (S.D.N.Y. 2008)
aff'd in part, 600 F.3d 93 (2nd Cir. 2010)

Sullivan, District Judge:

Tiffany, the famous jeweler with the coveted blue boxes, brings this action against eBay, the prominent online marketplace, for the sale of counterfeit Tiffany silver jewelry on its website. ...

II. FINDINGS OF FACT

Over its 170-year history, Tiffany has achieved great renown as a purveyor of high-quality and luxury goods under the TIFFANY Marks (defined below), including jewelry, watches, and home items such as china, crystal, and clocks. ...

In order to maintain its reputation for high-quality jewelry, Tiffany quality control personnel inspect Tiffany merchandise before it is released for distribution. Before a silver jewelry item can be released to Tiffany's channels of trade, the item must satisfy Tiffany's exacting standards for, inter alia, composition, quality, shape, and polish of the metal, as well as the quality and integrity of the TIFFANY Marks appearing on the item. To determine if an item is authentic Tiffany silver jewelry, Tiffany quality inspectors must be able to physically inspect each item. Tiffany closely protects its quality standards and does not make them available to the public or to other jewelry manufacturers. ...

C. eBay and Its Business

1. eBay's Listings, Buyers, and Sellers

eBay is a well-known online marketplace, located at www.ebay.com, that allows eBay sellers to sell goods directly to eBay buyers. The listings are created and posted by third-party users, who register with eBay and agree to abide by a User Agreement.While users often go by descriptive user names instead of their real names, users are required to supply identifying information to eBay when registering. Sellers can also use multiple user names. ...

2. eBay's Business Model and Support to Sellers

eBay's business model is based on two components: first, the creation of listings, and second, the successful completion of sales between the seller and the buyer. For each posted listing, sellers pay an initial insertion fee, ranging from $0.20 to $4.80 depending on the starting price. If the item is successfully sold, sellers pay a final value fee based upon the final price for the item. Final value fees range from 5.25% to 10% of the final price of the item. In addition, sellers who opt for various additional features to differentiate their listings, such as a border or bold-faced type, are charged additional fees. ...

3. eBay's Control Over Sales Made On Its Website

eBay is an electronic marketplace, not a retailer. Thus, eBay itself never takes physical possession of the goods sold through its website; instead, it facilitates a transaction between two independent parties. Nevertheless, eBay exercises some limited control over those who trade its website by requiring all users to register with eBay and sign eBay's User Agreement. The User Agreement requires users to refrain from violating any laws, third party rights, including intellectual property rights, and eBay policies. If a user violates the terms or conditions of the User Agreement, eBay may take disciplinary action against the seller, including removing the seller's listings, issuing a warning, and/or suspending the user.

In addition to exercising some control over users, eBay also restricts the types of items which can be listed on its website. For example, eBay maintains a list of prohibited items, e.g., drugs, firearms, and alcohol, for which it routinely screens in order to prevent such items from being offered for sale on eBay.

4. eBay's Anti-Fraud Efforts

a. Trust and Safety Department

eBay has made substantial investments in anti-counterfeiting initiatives. eBay has invested as much as $20 million each year on tools to promote trust and safety on its website. One quarter of eBay's workforce of roughly 16,000 employees is devoted to trust and safety. Of these 4,000 individuals, approximately 2,000 serve as eBay Customer Service Representatives ("CSRs"). More than 200 of these individuals focus exclusively on combating infringement, at a significant cost to eBay. eBay also employs 70 persons who work exclusively with law enforcement. In several instances, information that eBay has provided to law enforcement agencies has led to the arrest of counterfeiters.

b. Fraud Engine

Between December 2000 and May 2002, eBay manually searched for keywords in listings in an effort to identify blatant instances of potentially infringing or otherwise problematic activity. In May 2002, eBay began using technology to perform that function. These technological tools are known as the eBay fraud engine. The fraud engine uses rules and complex models that automatically search for activity that violates eBay policies. eBay spends over $5 million per year in maintaining and enhancing its fraud engine, which is principally dedicated to ferreting out illegal listings, including counterfeit listings.

The fraud engine currently uses more than 13,000 different search rules, and was designed in part to capture listings that contain indicia of counterfeiting apparent on the face of the listings without requiring expertise in rights owners' brands or products. ... For example, at all times relevant to this litigation, eBay monitored its website for and removed listings expressly offered "knock-off," "counterfeit," "replica," or "pirated" merchandise, and listings in which the seller stated he "cannot guarantee the authenticity" of the items being offered. For obvious reasons, the fraud engine could not determine whether a listed item was actually counterfeit. However, the fraud engine also contained numerous other data elements designed to evaluate listings based on, for example, the seller's Internet protocol address, any issues associated with the seller's account on eBay, and the feedback the seller has received from other eBay users. Between 2003 and the close of discovery in 2006, eBay modified and updated its fraud engine at least weekly.

At all times relevant to this case, eBay's fraud engine flagged thousands of listings on a daily basis that contained obvious indicia of infringing or otherwise fraudulent activity. Listings flagged by the fraud engine were sent to eBay's CSRs for review and possible further action. ...

Upon reviewing a potentially infringing, fraudulent, or problematic listing, the CSR would: (1) remove the listing from eBay; (2) send a warning to the seller; (3) place restrictions on the seller's account, such as a selling restriction, temporary suspension, or indefinite suspension; and/or (4) refer the matter to law enforcement. eBay removed thousands of listings per month based on CSR reviews of listings captured by the fraud engine. ...

c. The VeRO Program

In addition to the fraud engine, eBay has, for nearly a decade, maintained a set of procedures, known as the Verified Rights Owner ("VeRO") Program, to address listings offering potentially infringing items posted on the eBay website. At all times relevant to this litigation, the VeRO Program was a "notice-and-takedown" system, whereby rights owners could report to eBay any listing offering potentially infringing items, so that eBay could remove such reported listings. At the present time, more than 14,000 rights owners, including Tiffany, participate in the VeRO Program.

At all times, eBay's VeRO Program rested on the responsibility of rights owners to police their own trademarks. Under the VeRO Program, a rights owner who saw a potentially infringing item listed on eBay could report the listing directly to eBay, by submitting a Notice of Claimed Infringement form or "NOCI." A NOCI attested that the rights owner possessed a "good-faith belief" that the item infringed on a copyright or a trademark. NOCIs could be faxed to eBay, emailed to eBay, or reported to eBay via a software tool called the VeRO Reporting Tool. As part of the VeRO Program, eBay offered rights owners tools to assist in efficiently identifying potentially infringing listings. These included the VeRO Reporting Tool as well as an automated search tool called "My Favorite Searches." These tools allowed rights owners to search automatically for particular listings every day, to save their favorite searches, and to email the search results directly to the rights owner for review on a daily basis.

Upon receipt of such a notice, CSRs first verified that the NOCI contained all of the required information and had indicia of accuracy. Thereafter, eBay promptly removed the challenged listing. Indeed, at all times relevant to this litigation, the Court finds that eBay's practice was to remove reported listings within 24 hours of receiving a NOCI. Seventy to 80 percent of reported listings were removed within 12 hours of notification during the time period at issue in this litigation. At present, three quarters of the listings are removed within four hours. eBay typically removed thousands of listings per week based on the submission of NOCIs by rights holders. ...

D. The Sale of Tiffany Goods on eBay ...

3. eBay Generated Revenue From The Sale of Tiffany Items

During the relevant time period, eBay generated substantial revenue from the sale of "Tiffany" silver jewelry on its website. Indeed, between April 2000 and August 2005, there were 456,551 sales of Tiffany jewelry in the Jewelry & Watches category. eBay's Jewelry & Watches category manager estimated that, between April 2000 and June 2004, eBay earned $4.1 million in revenue from completed listings with "Tiffany" in the listing title in the Jewelry & Watches category. ...

G. Tiffany Participated in the VeRO Program

1. Tiffany Filed Increasing Numbers of NOCIs ...

From the time of eBay's June 2003 letter through May 2004, Tiffany reported 46,252 listings for which Tiffany claimed a good-faith belief that the items being sold were counterfeit. In August 2003, Tiffany was the second-highest reporter of NOCIs in the VeRO Program. ...

2. Tiffany's Staffing

Notwithstanding the significance of the online counterfeiting problem, it is clear that Tiffany invested relatively modest resources to combat the problem. In fiscal year 2003, Tiffany budgeted approximately $763,000 to the issue, representing less than 0.05 percent of its net sales for that year. Tiffany's CEO, Michael Kowalski, testified that over the past five years, Tiffany has budgeted $14 million to anti-counterfeiting efforts – of which approximately $3–5 million was spent in litigating the instant action.

More specifically, Tiffany's time dedicated to monitoring the eBay website and preparing NOCIs was limited. Beginning in the summer of 2003, Ewa Zalewska, then a paralegal in Tiffany's legal department, devoted two days a week to reviewing the eBay website and answering emails from buyers and sellers involving removed listings. John Pollard, then Tiffany's security manager, also devoted one day a week to monitoring and reporting on the eBay website. ...

III. Conclusions of Law ...

D. Contributory Infringement under Federal and Common Law ...

1. Elements of Contributory Infringement

Contributory trademark infringement is a judicially constructed doctrine articulated by the Supreme Court in *Inwood Laboratories, Inc. v. Ives Laboratories, Inc.,* 456 U.S. 844, 850 n.10 (1982). In that opinion, the Supreme Court held that:

> [I]f a manufacturer or distributor intentionally induces another to infringe a trademark, or if it continues to supply its product to one whom it knows or has reason to know is engaging in trademark infringement, the manufacturer or distributor is contributorily responsible for any harm done as a result of the deceit.

456 U.S. at 854. ...

3. Knowledge Or Reason To Know

Under the *Inwood* test, Tiffany must prove that eBay continued to supply its services "to one whom it knows or has reason to know is engaging in trademark infringement." *Inwood,* 456 U.S. at 854. The evidence produced at trial demonstrated that eBay had *generalized* notice that some portion of the Tiffany goods sold on its website might be counterfeit. First, Tiffany sent eBay demand letters in 2003 and 2004, articulating its belief that large quantities of counterfeit Tiffany merchandise were being sold through the eBay website, and that any seller of a significant lot – *e.g.,* of five or more pieces of purported Tiffany jewelry – was "almost certainly" selling counterfeit merchandise. Second, Tiffany apprised eBay of [a Tiffany survey which found that]73.1% of the Tiffany items it purchased in [that survey] were counterfeit. Third, Tiffany filed thousands of NOCIs alleging a good faith belief that certain listings were counterfeit or otherwise infringing on Tiffany's marks, and eBay received numerous complaints from buyers stating that they had purchased what they believed to be fake Tiffany jewelry through the eBay website.

Tiffany argues that this generalized knowledge required eBay to preemptively remedy the problem at the very moment that it knew or had reason to know that the infringing conduct was generally occurring, even without specific knowledge as to individual instances of infringing listings or sellers. By contrast, eBay asserts that such generalized knowledge is insufficient, and that the law demands more specific knowledge of individual instances of infringement and infringing sellers before imposing a burden upon eBay to remedy the problem. ...

a. Legal Standard

The Second Circuit has not defined how much knowledge or what type of knowledge a defendant must have to satisfy the "know or reason to know" standard set forth in *Inwood*. ...

[C]ourts have been reluctant to extend contributory trademark liability to defendants where there is some uncertainty as to the extent or the nature of the infringement. In *Inwood*, Justice White emphasized in his concurring opinion that a defendant is not "require[d] . . . to refuse to sell to dealers who merely *might* pass off its goods." *Inwood*, 456 U.S. at 861 (White, J., concurring). In *Coca-Cola Co. v. Snow Crest Beverages*, 64 F. Supp. 980 (D. Mass. 1946), *aff'd*, 162 F.2d 280 (1st. Cir. 1947), an early and important contributory infringement case cited in *Inwood*, Coca-Cola asserted that Snow Crest had contributorily infringed its mark by selling "Polar Cola" to bartenders who sometimes mixed the soda into customers' "rum and Coke" drinks. Coca-Cola argued that Snow Crest should have known about the infringement because attorneys for Coca-Cola had informed Snow Crest's president of the bartending practice and indicated that their investigation revealed that the practice had occurred in 82 bars. The district court found that such "lawyer's argumentative talk" was inadequate to establish that a reasonable businessperson in Snow Crest's position should have known that its products were being used to infringe, particularly because "plaintiff's counsel . . . did not give the names or the numbers of any offending bars," "did not inform defendant of the details of the investigation of the 82 bars," and "did not ask defendant to take any specific step to notify or caution bars against passing off." The court reasoned that if it imputed knowledge to the defendant based on Coca-Cola's blanket demand, the court would be expanding Coca-Cola's property right in its trademark, allowing Coca-Cola to secure a monopoly over the entire mixed drink trade. Such generalized notice, the court reasoned, was simply inadequate to impute knowledge to the defendants. ...

By contrast, those courts that have determined that defendants had "reason to know" of infringement have relied on far more specific notice from plaintiffs to defendants. For example, in *Habeeba's Dance of the Arts, Ltd. v. Knoblauch*, 430 F. Supp. 2d 709, 714 (S.D. Ohio 2006), the court determined that advance written notice of a specific infringing event, providing the date, the event, and the location of the event, would be sufficient to meet the knowledge requirement for contributory trademark infringement.

Significantly, Tiffany has not alleged, nor does the evidence support a conclusion, that all of the Tiffany merchandise sold through eBay is counterfeit. Rather, a substantial number of authentic Tiffany goods are sold on eBay, including both new and vintage silver jewelry, sometimes in lots of five or more. ...

b. Analysis

The evidence adduced at trial demonstrates eBay had *general knowledge* of infringement by sellers using its website. Such general knowledge, however, does not require eBay to take action to discontinue supplying its service to all those who *might* be engaged in counterfeiting. ...

5. Continues To Supply

The Court has concluded that the generalized allegations of trademark infringement described above are insufficient to impute either knowledge or a reason to know of trademark infringement to eBay. However, the situation is distinct with respect to the individual sellers against whom Tiffany filed NOCIs. Tiffany argues that the filing of a NOCI provided eBay with actual or constructive knowledge of Tiffany's good-faith belief that an item was counterfeit or otherwise infringing.[38] Nevertheless, even assuming *arguendo* that the filing of a NOCI provided eBay with knowledge or reason to know of infringement by particular sellers on its website, the test under *Inwood* is not merely that eBay had knowledge, but instead whether eBay "continue[d] to supply" its product to known infringers. The *Inwood* test thus directs the Court to consider what action eBay took upon receiving such notice of infringement through Tiffany's NOCIs.

When Tiffany filed a NOCI, eBay's practice was to promptly remove the challenged listing from its website. In addition to removing the listing, eBay also warned sellers and buyers, cancelled all fees associated with the listing, and directed buyers not to consummate the sale of the listed item. Accordingly, the Court concludes that Tiffany has failed to prove that eBay continued to supply its services in instances where it knew or had reason to know of infringement. ...

Tiffany's own evidence supports the Court's conclusion that eBay's policy was an "appropriate step" in cutting off the supply of its services to infringers. *AT&T v. Winback*, 42 F.3d 1421, 1433 n.14 (3rd Circuit, 1994). While Tiffany identified close to 200 "repeat offenders," Tiffany does not contest that once Tiffany sent in a NOCI for these users, eBay pulled the listing. Furthermore, with only a few exceptions, the users who reappeared on the eBay website appeared three or fewer times, frequently within a very short time span (*e.g.*, within one week or even one day). Accordingly, Tiffany has failed to establish by a preponderance of the evidence that eBay failed to take appropriate action against these sellers upon receiving notice of infringing activity. ...

Second, while the Court is sympathetic to Tiffany's frustrations in this regard, the fact remains that rights holders bear the principal responsibility to police their trademarks. See *MDT Corp. v. New York Stock Exch.*, 858 F. Supp. 1028, 1034 (C.D. Cal. 1994) ("The owner of a trade name must do its own police work."); *see also Hard Rock Cafe*, 955 F.2d at 1149 (defendants are not required "to be more dutiful guardians of [trademark plaintiffs'] commercial interests). In effect, Tiffany's contributory trademark infringement argument rests on the notion that because eBay was able to screen out potentially counterfeit Tiffany listings more cheaply, quickly, and effectively than Tiffany, the burden to police the Tiffany trademark should have shifted to eBay. Certainly, the evidence adduced at trial failed to prove that eBay was a cheaper cost avoider than Tiffany with respect to policing its marks. But more importantly, even if it were true that eBay is best situated to staunch the tide of trademark infringement to which Tiffany and countless other rights owners are subjected, that is not the law. ...

Under these circumstances, the Court concludes that Tiffany has failed to prove that eBay continued to supply its service to those whom it knew or had reason to know were engaging in infringement, and that eBay took appropriate steps to cease making its website available in those instances where Tiffany brought objectionable conduct to its attention.

QUESTIONS

1. Holly owns a Tiffany pocketwatch. Is she liable for trademark infringement if she puts it up for sale on eBay and describes it as a "Tiffany watch?" What result if she puts a Casio watch up for sale on eBay and describes it as a

---

38 Of course, a NOCI was not a notice of actual infringement, but instead, was a notice of Tiffany's good-faith belief that a particular item or listing was infringing.

"Tiffany watch?" What if she puts up a Casio and describes it as a "Casio watch" but it shows up in eBay search results for "tiffany watch?" And what if she puts up an inexpensive modern replica of a classic Tiffany watch and describes it as a "Tiffany-style watch?"

2. But *Tiffany* isn't about the liability of the sellers; it's about the liability of eBay. Why would eBay ever be held liable for someone else's acts of trademark infringement?

3. Explain the court's distinction between generalized and specific knowledge. Which does eBay have? What is the legal significance of the distinction?

4. What does eBay do to screen out counterfeit listings? Which of these steps are legally required, in the sense that eBay might become liable for contributory trademark infringement if it stopped doing them? All in all, what is the relative distribution of costs between eBay and Tiffany?

5. If eBay were held liable here, what more could it do to prevent the sale of counterfeit Tiffany merchandise? What would it be likely to do in practice? How would Tiffany feel about that outcome?

HAPPY FUN BALL PROBLEM

When a user types a query into a general search engine, like Google or Bing, the search engine responds in two ways. First, it displays a list of websites that the search engine thinks will be relevant to the user, with the most relevant ones first. Second, it displays ads, typically labeled as "advertisements" or "sponsored links." Each ad consists of a few lines of text, plus a link to a page chosen by the advertiser. The ads are also designed to be relevant to the user's query, but in a different way.

Google's AdWords system, for example, lets advertisers "purchase" terms in search queries (also called "keywords") in an auction. The advertisers' bids on search terms indicate the amount they're willing to pay Google for each user who sees the ad and clicks on the link. Google then displays the ads from the advertisers who made the highest bids, after adjusting for a number of factors, one being how likely users have been to click on similar ads in the past. Google also offers a Keyword Suggestion Tool, which helps advertisers choose which keywords to purchase by making recommendations. The recommendations use Google's data from past searches and advertisements to suggest keywords that are likely to have high click-through rates (i.e. many users who will click on the ad after searching on the keyword). Advertising is responsible for the vast majority of search engines' revenue.

The SHFB Corporation, maker of the Happy Fun Ball and owner of the trademark HAPPY FUN BALL, is upset at its treatment by Google. SHFB has sued Google, alleging that the following activities by Google constitute trademark infringement:

1. Displaying any search results other than links to happyfunball.com when a user types "happy fun ball" into the Google search box;

2. Displaying any advertisements other than ads placed by SHFB when a user types "happy fun ball" into the Google search box;

3. Displaying search results that take users to competitors' web sites that make infringing uses of the words "happy fun ball" trademark;

4. Displaying advertisements placed by SHFB competitors that include the words "happy fun ball" in text visible to users;

5. Selling the words "happy fun ball" as an advertising keyword using the AdWords program; and

6. Using the Keyword Suggestion Tool to advise SHFB competitors that they purchase ads triggered by the words "happy fun ball" trademark.

The District Court granted Google's motion to dismiss for failure to state a claim, finding no infringement under any of the six theories. SHFB has appealed. How should the Court of Appeals rule?

B. Domain Names

Domain names pose special problems for trademark law. Their navigational function has vexed courts; a domain name plays a role *like* that of a trademark on a product package or in an advertisement, but in a different context. Courts have struggled to understand what is different and what is the same about a trademark in an address bar rather than on a webpage.

One source of difficulty is that while trademark rights flow from using the trademark and from federal registration, domain names are handed out on a first-come first-serve basis to whoever registers a domain name first. Large established companies with existing trademarks were not always among the first to realize the importance of the Internet — so they were not always the first to pounce on the corresponding domain names. (Today, a company or entrepreneur contemplating a new potential trademark or business name would be well-advised to register an appropriate domain name as soon as possible, just to have it available.)

Consider *Panavision International, L.P. v. Toeppen*, 141 F.3d 1316 (9th Cir. 1998). The plaintiff was Panavision – a reasonably well-known Hollywood camera company. The defendant was Dennis Toeppen, an entrepreneur who registered panavision.com. He didn't sell cameras, or anything else for that matter. Instead, his business plan, as found by the court, was to sell the domain name to the one and only party who could legitimately extract value from it: Panavision. It's not easy to describe the problem here in terms of consumer confusion. Nobody who went to panavision.com was confused about the source of goods. Even an initial-interest confusion story is a stretch, since Toeppen wasn't selling anything at all: his site at panavision.com displayed pictures of Pana, Illinois. Indeed, Toeppen had a plausible argument that he had never even "used" the PANAVISION trademark in the first place.

Panavision won its lawsuit against Toeppen, and several other courts also found infringement on similar facts, but trademark owners feared that they lacked the tools to deal effectively with squatters like Toeppen. Congress eventually stepped in with a number of domain-name specific statutes, most notably the Anticybersquatting Consumer Protection Act (ACPA).

15 U.S.C. § 1125 [Lanham Act § 43] - *False designations of origin, false descriptions, and dilution forbidden [Anticybersquatting Consumer Protection Act]*

(d) *CYBERPIRACY PREVENTION*

   (1)

      (A) A person shall be liable in a civil action by the owner of a mark, including a personal name which is protected as a mark under this section, if, without regard to the goods or services of the parties, that person –

         (i) has a bad faith intent to profit from that mark, including a personal name which is protected as a mark under this section; and

         (ii) registers, traffics in, or uses a domain name [that is confusingly similar to a registered trademark]

      (B)

         (i) In determining whether a person has a bad faith intent described under subparagraph (A), a court may consider factors such as, but not limited to –

            (I) the trademark or other intellectual property rights of the person, if any, in the domain name;

            (II) the extent to which the domain name consists of the legal name of the person or a name that is otherwise commonly used to identify that person;

            (III) the person's prior use, if any, of the domain name in connection with the bona fide offering of any goods or services;

            (IV) the person's bona fide noncommercial or fair use of the mark in a site accessible under the domain name;

            (V) the person's intent to divert consumers from the mark owner's online location to a site accessible under the domain name that could harm the goodwill represented by the mark, either for commercial gain or with the intent to tarnish or disparage the mark, by creating a likelihood of confusion as to the source, sponsorship, affiliation, or endorsement of the site;

            (VI) the person's offer to transfer, sell, or otherwise assign the domain name to the mark owner or any third party for financial gain without having used, or having an intent to use, the domain name in the bona fide offering of any goods or services, or the person's prior conduct indicating a pattern of such conduct;

            (VII) the person's provision of material and misleading false contact information when applying for the

registration of the domain name, the person's intentional failure to maintain accurate contact information, or the person's prior conduct indicating
a pattern of such conduct;

(VIII) the person's registration or acquisition of multiple
domain names which the person knows are identical or confusingly similar to marks of others that
are distinctive at the time of registration of such
domain names, or dilutive of famous marks of others that are famous at the time of registration of
such domain names, without regard to the goods or
services of the parties; and

(IX) the extent to which the mark incorporated in the
person's domain name registration is or is not distinctive and famous within the meaning of subsection (c).

(ii) Bad faith intent described under subparagraph (A) shall
not be found in any case in which the court determines
that the person believed and had reasonable grounds to
believe that the use of the domain name was a fair use or
otherwise lawful.

(C) In any civil action involving the registration, trafficking, or use
of a domain name under this paragraph, a court may order the
forfeiture or cancellation of the domain name or the transfer of
the domain name to the owner of the mark. ...

15 U.S.C. § 8131 [formerly 15 U.S.C. § 1129] – *Cyberpiracy protections for individuals*

(1) *IN GENERAL*

(A) *CIVIL LIABILITY*. – Any person who registers a domain name that
consists of the name of another living person, or a name substantially
and confusingly similar thereto, without that person's consent, with
the specific intent to profit from such name by selling the domain
name for financial gain to that person or any third party, shall be liable in a civil action by such person. ...

(2) *REMEDIES*. – In any civil action brought under paragraph (1), a court may
award injunctive relief, including the forfeiture or cancellation of the domain name or the transfer of the domain name to the plaintiff. The court
may also, in its discretion, award costs and attorneys fees to the prevailing
party.

QUESTIONS

1. Summarize the cybersquatting provision of the ACPA codified in 15 U.S.C.
    § 1125(d)? How is "bad faith intent" defined? What defenses are available?

2. Congress responded to trademark owners' fear of a flood of domain-name
    squatters with the ACPA. How would *Toeppen* have come out under it? Is it
    an appropriate legislative response? Did Congress go far enough? Too far?

3. In 2002, Indiana resident Kerry Edwards created a website to advertise his
    bail bond business: kerryedwards.com. Two years later, Democratic presi-

dential candidate John Kerry picked John Edwards as his running mate. The Kerry campaign asked Kerry Edwards to donate the domain to the campaign, but he declined, saying he had received offers of up to $30,000 for it. Would John Kerry or his campaign have had a valid ACPA cause of action against Kerry Edwards?

TAUBMAN CO. V. WEBFEATS
319 F.3d 770 (6th Cir. 2003)

Suhrheinrich, Circuit Judge:

Defendant-Appellant Henry Mishkoff, d/b/a Webfeats, appeals from two preliminary injunctions, respectively entered on October 11, 2001, and December 7, 2001, in the United States District Court for the Eastern District of Michigan, together granting Plaintiff-Appellee the Taubman Company's (Taubman) request to prevent Mishkoff from using six internet domain names because they likely violate Taubman's trademarks in the terms "Taubman," and "The Shops at Willow Bend."
...

I. FACTS

Mishkoff is a resident of Carrollton, Texas, and a web designer by trade. Upon hearing the news that Taubman, a Delaware corporation with its principal place of business in Michigan, was building a shopping mall called "The Shops at Willow Bend," in Plano, Texas, Mishkoff registered the domain name, "shopsatwillowbend.com," and created an internet website with that address. Mishkoff had no connection to the mall except for the fact that it was being built near his home.

Mishkoff's website featured information about the mall, with a map and links to individual websites of the tenant stores. The site also contained a prominent disclaimer, indicating that Mishkoff's site was unofficial, and a link to Taubman's official site for the mall, found at the addresses "theshopsatwillowbend.com," and "shopwillowbend.com."

Mishkoff describes his site as a "fan site," with no commercial purpose. The site did, however, contain a link to the website of a company run by Mishkoff's girlfriend, Donna Hartley, where she sold custom-made shirts under the name "shirtbiz.com;" and to Mishkoff's site for his web design business, "Webfeats."

When Taubman discovered that Mishkoff had created this site, it demanded he remove it from the internet. Taubman claimed that Mishkoff's use of the domain name "shopsatwillowbend.com" infringed on its registered mark, "The Shops at Willow Bend." Taubman filed a complaint on August 7, 2001, claiming, *inter alia*, trademark infringement under the Lanham Act, 15 U.S.C. § 1114, asking for a preliminary injunction, and demanding surrender of Mishkoff's domain name.

Mishkoff responsively registered five more domain names: 1) taubmansucks.com; 2) shopsatwillowbendsucks.com; 3) theshopsatwillowbendsucks.com; 4) willowbendmallsucks.com; and 5) willowbendsucks.com. All five of these web names link to the same site, which is a running editorial on Mishkoff's battle with Taubman and its lawyers, and exhaustively documents his proceedings in both the district court and this Court, both through visual scans of filed motions, as well as a first person narrative from Mishkoff. In internet parlance, a web name with a "sucks.com" moniker attached to it is known as a "complaint name," and the process of registering and using such names is known as "cybergriping."

On October 11, 2001, the district court granted Taubman's motion for a preliminary injunction, enjoining Mishkoff from using the first host name, "shopsatwillowbend.com." On October 15, 2001, Taubman filed a motion to amend the preliminary injunction to include the five "complaint names" used by Mishkoff. On December 7, 2001, the district court allowed the amendment and enjoined Mishkoff from using the complaint names. ...

III. ANALYSIS

Mishkoff claims the injunctions preventing his use of the domain name "shopsatwillowbend.com" and the five "complaint names" are inappropriate because Taubman has not demonstrated a likelihood of success on the merits and because the orders represent a prior restraint on his First Amendment right to speak.

A. Standard of Review

We review the district court's grant of a motion for a preliminary injunction for abuse of discretion. "A district court abuses its discretion when it relies on clearly erroneous findings of fact . . . or when it improperly applies the law or uses an erroneous legal standard. Under this standard, this court must review the district court's legal conclusions de novo and its factual findings for clear error."

We have held that an injunction is proper in trademark cases where:

1) There is a likelihood of success on the merits;

2) There is the potential for irreparable harm;

3) There is the potential of adverse public impact;

4) Potential harm to the plaintiff outweighs the potential harm to the defendant.

None of these factors, standing alone, is a prerequisite to relief; rather, they must be balanced.

B. Propriety of the Injunctions

1. Likelihood of Success on the Merits

The likelihood of success of Taubman's claim rests with the language of the Lanham Act, 15 U.S.C. § 1114(1), which imposes liability for infringement of trademarks on:

> Any person who shall, without the consent of the registrant
>
> > (a) use in commerce any reproduction, counterfeit, copy, or colorable imitation of a registered mark in connection with the sale, offering for sale, distribution, or advertising of any goods or services on or in connection with which such use is likely to cause confusion, or to cause mistake, or to deceive. . . .

Mishkoff proposes that, regardless of whether his use of Taubman's marks violates the Lanham Act, any injunction prohibiting his use violates the Constitution as a prior restraint on his First Amendment right of Free Speech. Since Mishkoff has raised Free Speech concerns, we will first explain the interrelation between the First Amendment and the Lanham Act. First, this Court has held that the Lanham Act is constitutional. ... The Lanham Act is constitutional because it only regulates commercial speech, which is entitled to reduced protections under the First Amendment. ... Thus, we must first determine if Mishkoff's use is commercial and therefore within the jurisdiction of the Lanham Act, worthy of lesser First Amendment protections.

If Mishkoff's use is commercial, then, and only then, do we analyze his use for a likelihood of confusion. If Mishkoff's use is also confusing, then it is misleading commercial speech, and outside the First Amendment.

Hence, as per the language of the Lanham Act, any expression embodying the use of a mark not "in connection with the sale . . . or advertising of any goods or services," and not likely to cause confusion, is outside the jurisdiction of the Lanham Act and necessarily protected by the First Amendment. Accordingly, we need not analyze Mishkoff's constitutional defenses independent of our Lanham Act analysis. With this backdrop in mind, we proceed to analyze the nature of the two websites.

a. November 9 Injunction[*] – The "shopsatwillowbend" Website

In regard to the first website, "shopsatwillowbend.com," Mishkoff argues that his use is completely non-commercial and not confusing, and therefore speech entitled to the full protections of the First Amendment. Taubman offers three arguments that Mishkoff is using its name commercially to sell or advertise goods or services. First, Mishkoff had a link to a site owned by Hartley's blouse company, "shirtbiz.com." Second, he had a link to his own site for his web design company, Webfeats. Third, Mishkoff had accepted a $1000 offer to relinquish the name to Taubman.

Although Mishkoff claims his intention in creating his website was non-commercial, the proper inquiry is not one of intent. In that sense, the Lanham Act is a strict liability statute. If consumers are confused by an infringing mark, the offender's motives are largely irrelevant. We believe the advertisements on Mishkoff's site, though extremely minimal, constituted his use of Taubman's mark "in connection with the advertising" of the goods sold by the advertisers. This is precisely what the Lanham Act prohibits.

However, Mishkoff had at least removed the shirtbiz.com link prior to the injunction. A preliminary injunction is proper only to prevent an on-going violation. As long as Mishkoff has no commercial links on either of his websites, including links to shirtbiz.com, Webfeats, or any other business, we find no use "in connection with the advertising" of goods and services to enjoin, and the Lanham Act cannot be properly invoked.[3]

Taubman's assertion that its offer to buy the domain name "shopsatwillowbend.com" from Mishkoff qualifies Mishkoff's use of the mark as "in connection with the sale of goods" is meritless. Although other courts have held that a so-called cybersquatter, who registers domain names with the intent to sell the name to the trademark holder, uses the mark "in connection with the sale of goods," they have also limited their holdings to such instances where the defendant had made a habit and a business of such practices. *See, e.g., E & J Gallo Winery v. Spider Webs Ltd.*, 286 F.3d 270, 270 (5th Cir. 2002) (noting that defendant had made a business practice of selling domain names on eBay for no less than $10,000); *Panavision Int'l, L.P. v. Toeppen*, 141 F.3d 1316 (9th Cir. 1998).

In *Panavision*, the defendant, Toeppen, purchased and offered to sell the name "panavision.com" to Panavision for $13,000. *Id.* at 1318. Evidence showed that Toeppen had attempted similar deals with a myriad of other companies, ranging

---

* [Ed: This should presumably read "October 11."]

3 Mishkoff sent a letter to Taubaman's attorneys on August 10, 2001, referencing the removal of the shirtbiz.com link, and declaring that Mishkoff "will not place any advertising of any kind on the site in the future." It is unclear whether Mishkoff also removed the Webfeats link at this time. To be clear, we also find the Webfeats link to be "use in connection with the advertising of goods and services" which likewise must remain removed to avoid a finding of commerciality.

from Delta Airlines to Eddie Bauer. *Id.* at 1319. The Ninth Circuit found Toeppen's intent to sell the domain name relevant in determining that his creation of the site was a commercial use of Panavision's mark. *Id.* at 1325. In contrast, not only has Mishkoff not made a practice of registering and selling domain names, but he did not even initiate the bargaining process here. Although Taubman's counsel intimated at oral argument that Mishkoff had in fact initiated the negotiation process, correspondence in the record supports the opposite conclusion, and shows that Taubman first offered Mishkoff $1000 to relinquish the site on August 16, 2001, and Mishkoff initially accepted it under threat of litigation. Hence, this case is distinguishable from *Panavision*. There is no evidence that Mishkoff's initial motive in selecting Taubman's mark was to re-sell the name. Therefore, we hold his use of the name "shopsatwillowbend.com" is not "in connection with the sale of goods."

Even if Mishkoff's use is commercial speech, i.e., "in connection with the sale . . . or advertising of any goods or services," and within the jurisdiction of the Lanham Act, there is a violation only if his use also creates a likelihood of confusion among customers. 15 U.S.C. § 1114(1). Moreover, the only important question is whether there is a likelihood of confusion *between the parties' goods or services*. Under Lanham Act jurisprudence, it is irrelevant whether customers would be confused as to the origin of the websites, unless there is confusion as to the origin of the respective products.

Since its inception, Mishkoff had always maintained a disclaimer on the website, indicating that his was not the official website. In *Holiday Inns, Inc. v. 800 Reservation, Inc.*, 86 F.3d 619 (6th Cir. 1996), we found the existence of a disclaimer very informative, and held that there was no likelihood of confusion, partly on that basis.

In *Holiday Inns*, the plaintiff hotel chain used the phone number 1-800-HOLIDAY for its guest room reservation hotline. Holiday Inns claimed a Lanham Act violation when the defendant company, a business that profited by taking reservations for several hotel chains, used the phone number 1-800-H0LIDAY (with a zero instead of an "O") in order to take advantage of any calls misdialed by customers seeking Holiday Inns' hotline. We found no Lanham Act violation, partly because the defendant played an unmistakable disclaimer upon answering each call, explaining that it was unaffiliated with Holiday Inns, and providing customers with Holiday Inns' correct phone number. We found that the defendant was, in fact, directing business to Holiday Inns that otherwise would have been lost, and although some callers chose to do business with the defendant, others hung up and called Holiday Inns. Had it not been for defendants' service, Holiday Inns would likely never have recovered many customers who had misdialed.

We find the analysis here indistinguishable from the disclaimer analysis in *Holiday Inns*. Mishkoff has placed a conspicuous disclaimer informing customers that they had not reached Taubman's official mall site. Furthermore, Mishkoff placed a hyperlink to Taubman's site within the disclaimer. We find this measure goes beyond even what was done by the defendant in *Holiday Inns*. There, a customer who reached the defendant's hotline in error had to hang up and redial the correct Holiday Inns number. Here, a misplaced customer simply has to click his mouse to be redirected to Taubman's site. Moreover, like *Holiday Inns*, the customers who stumble upon Mishkoff's site would otherwise have reached a dead address. They would have received an error message upon typing "shopsatwillowbend.com," simply stating that the name was not a proper domain name, with no message relating how to arrive at the official site. Hence, Mishkoff's website and its disclaimer actually serve to re-direct lost customers to Taubman's site that might otherwise be lost. Accordingly, we find no likelihood that a customer would be confused as to the source of Taubman's and Mishkoff's respective goods.

b. December 7 Injunction – The "sucks" Site

In regard to Mishkoff's "complaint site," Taubman claims that Mishkoff's use is necessarily "in connection with the sale of goods" because his intent behind the use of the names "taubmansucks.com," *et al.*, is to harm Taubman economically.

In *Planned Parenthood Fed'n of Amer., Inc. v. Bucci*, No. 97 Civ. 0629, 1997 WL 133313 (S.D.N.Y. March 24, 1997), *aff'd*, No. 97-7492, 1998 WL 336163 (2d Cir. Feb. 9, 1998), the defendant usurped the domain name "plannedparenthood.com" and created a website displaying anti-abortion pictures and pro-life messages in clear contradiction of the plaintiff's stated mission. The court there found that, although not selling or advertising any goods, the defendant's use of Planned Parenthood's mark was commercial because he had used plaintiff's mark and attempted to cause economic harm. *Id.* at *4. (noting that Lanham Act is applicable because "defendant's action in appropriating plaintiff's mark has a connection to plaintiff's distribution of its services").

Following *Planned Parenthood*, Taubman argues that all cybergriping sites are per se commercial and "in connection with the sale of goods." However, *Planned Parenthood*, as an unpublished district court opinion, is not binding on this Court, and is nonetheless distinguishable. Even if Mishkoff's use is commercial, it must still lead to a likelihood of confusion to be violative of the Lanham Act. 15 U.S.C. § 1114(1). In *Planned Parenthood*, the defendant used the plaintiff's trade name as a domain name, without the qualifying moniker "sucks," or any other such addendum to indicate that the plaintiff was not the proprietor of the website. In contrast, "taubmansucks.com" removes any confusion as to source. We find no possibility of confusion and no Lanham Act violation.

We find that Mishkoff's use of Taubman's mark in the domain name "taubmansucks.com" is purely an exhibition of Free Speech, and the Lanham Act is not invoked. And although economic damage might be an intended effect of Mishkoff's expression, the First Amendment protects critical commentary when there is no confusion as to source, even when it involves the criticism of a business. Such use is not subject to scrutiny under the Lanham Act. In fact, Taubman concedes that Mishkoff is "free to shout 'Taubman Sucks!' from the rooftops. . . ." Essentially, this is what he has done in his domain name. The rooftops of our past have evolved into the internet domain names of our present. We find that the domain name is a type of public expression, no different in scope than a billboard or a pulpit, and Mishkoff has a First Amendment right to express his opinion about Taubman, and as long as his speech is not commercially misleading, the Lanham Act cannot be summoned to prevent it. ...

QUESTIONS

1. What was Mishkoff's motivation for registering the various domain names? Was it personal? Ideological? Commercial? A combination?

2. What is a "commercial" use of a domain name? Every blog on Google's Blogger service contains a link at the bottom that reads "Powered by Blogger," which links to the Blogger homepage. Is that enough to make a blog on Blogspot commercial? What about a site which includes text ads from Google's AdSense program? A link to the site owner's book for sale on Amazon?

3. Is the court's analogy between a domain name and a custom phone number convincing?

4. Eric Corley, who goes by the name Emmanuel Goldstein, registered the domain fuckgeneralmotors.com. Instead of creating a website of his own, however, he set up the domain name to point to Ford's homepage at ford.com. If General Motors sues Corley/Goldstein for trademark infringement and violation of ACPA, how should the court rule? What result if Ford sues him?

DRUNK KIDS PROBLEM

Robert Duff, a web developer from Ames, Iowa, created a website named Drunk-Kids.com. It features user-submitted videos of minors saying and doing silly things while drunk. The site achieved Internet fame with a video of an 8-year-old in an untucked dress shirt who had been sipping wine from glasses left on tables at his cousin's wedding, trying to dance and repeatedly falling down. Other popular videos include a 14-year-old trying to explain to his father that the beer bottle he is holding is not a beer bottle and two 12-year-old girls shouting "ponies!" at each other and giggling uncontrollably for seven minutes. The site now has over 500,000 visits per month and makes approximately $15,000 a month from banner ads and merchandise.

Emily Szyslak has registered the domain names drunkids.com, drunkkid.com, drunkkids.net, and kidsdrunk.com. Visitors were shown a page with dozens of banner ads and a list of links to Wikipedia pages on childhood, alcohol addiction, and several others. Duff sent Szyslak a cease-and-desist letter, claiming trademark infringement. Szyslak did not respond. Instead, she changed her four websites to pages claiming that they were a "political protest":

> This is a page of POLITICAL PROTEST
> – Against the web site drunkkids.com –
> drunkkids is a web site that depicts illegal behavior and alcohol abuse. many children are inticed to the website, not knowing what is really there, and then lured into sinful debaucherous behavior through the use of the offensive videos being presented there.
> As the owner of this domain name, I am being sued by drunkkids for $10,000,000 so he can use this domain to direct more kids to a web site that not only desensitizes children to the dangers of drinking, but makes it seem like great fun and games.
> I will under no circumstances hand this domain name over to him so he can do that.
> – Thank You –

Duff has sued for trademark infringement and violation of ACPA. The parties have agreed to a bench trial on the facts as stipulated above. Who should prevail?

ICANN AND THE DOMAIN-NAME SYSTEM

The technical introduction in Chapter 2 discussed how the domain-name system works. It might be good to review its description of the different servers that cooperate to translate domain names into IP addresses. Now, let's look at who runs these different servers.

The root name servers (there are actually thirteen of them, which are supposed to work identically) are operated under contract from the Internet Corporation for Assigned Names and Numbers (ICANN), a non-profit entity whose job is to oversee the domain-name and IP address systems. ICANN sets the policies for which top-level domains can exist. Currently, there are about two dozen "generic TLDs": (e.g. .com, .net, .edu, and .org,) plus about two hundred "country code TLDs," one for each country (e.g. .fr, .ru, .de, .cn, and .tv). (They are called "gTLDs" and "ccTLDs" for short.)

Each top-level domain and corresponding top-level domain name server is operated by a "registry" – an organization which keeps track of which second-level domains within that top-level domain exist, and updates the name server accordingly. The registries for the generic TLDs are operated by contract with ICANN, which picks operators on the basis of their technological ability to keep the name server running reliably. For example, the registry for .edu is operated by EDU-CAUSE, a nonprofit "whose mission is to advance higher education by promoting the intelligent use of information technology." The country-code TLDs are delegated to entities in the relevant countries (with varying relationships to the countries' governments). Each registry sets basic policies for who can register a second-level domain: for example, anyone can register a domain in .com, only accredited colleges and universities can register a domain in .edu, and only Dutch citizens can register a domain in .nl.

The entities that actually take domain-name registrations from the public are called "registrars" (that's regis-*trars*, not regis-*tries*). The registrars keep track of who owns a domain, where its name servers are located, and so on. Then they communicate the necessary technical information to the appropriate registries for inclusion on the top-level domain name servers. Registrars you may have heard of include GoDaddy, Tucows, Register.com, and Dotster.

Registrants themselves are responsible for handling second-level name-serving if they need it. For example, Google's IT department (in coordination with external vendors and service providers) manages the name server for google.com. It decides which "subdomains" to allow: thus, there is a voice.google.com but no monsterravingloony.google.com. This job can easily be outsourced; plenty of commercial web hosting companies will take care of it for you while helping you register a domain for your web site.

The entire system is overseen by an entity called the Internet Corporation for Assigned Names and Numbers (ICANN). To understand its complicated role and ambiguous status, a little history is helpful. What we now know as the "Internet" grew by accretion and agglomeration as new computers were added to existing networks and existing networks were linked together. Some of these networks were owned by the United States government, others at universities and research labs were privately owned but supported with government funding, first from the Department of Defense and later the National Science Foundation. The government also gave grants and contracts to support the work necessary to provide the addresses and names the networked computers used to communicate with each other. But actual authority over the naming system was unclear. The institutions that maintained the necessary computers were paid by the government to do so, but many of the policy decisions – such as how the DNS protocols would work, what generic TLDs to recognize, and who would administer the ccTLDs – were made by researchers either unilaterally or through a collaborative process of "rough consensus and running code."

This informal constitution worked while the Internet was a smaller network funded by the government and used primarily by academics, but it came under severe strain as the Internet took off commercially in the 1990s. The government wanted to privatize ownership and control of the Internet as much as possible; it contracted with a private company, Network Solutions Inc. (NSI, now Verisign), to administer the system. In effect, it was both registrar and registry. NSI was allowed to charge $100 per two-year registration and rode the Internet boom – it went from 7,500 domain names total in 1991 to 30,000 new domain names *per month* in 1995 – to corporate wealth and power, but also found itself embroiled in unwelcome policy controversies, like what to do about conflicting demands to the same name. Technologists and representatives from civil society, resentful of NSI's monopoly and worried about its power over the Internet, wanted to introduce competition and tried to take control over the policy-making aspects. The government's response was firm: it was not about to give up control of these governance functions without a strong baseline of accountability.

The result – following some political details too complex to relate here – was a compromise that split NSI's work into three parts. NSI kept control over .com, .net., and (for a time) .org as the official registry for these three gTLDs. The market for registrar services was opened up to competition, which has driven the cost of registering a domain down from $50/year to roughly $10-$15/year. And the policy functions were handed over to a newly created entity: a California nonprofit organization named ICANN. It uses a web of contracts with registrars and registries to specify the technical standards and operating procedures they must follow. Whether ICANN would go further and impose substantive policies was fiercely contested. The World Intellectual Property Organization (WIPO) proposed that ICANN should require mandatory arbitration of any online intellectual property disputes. There was a backlash from civil society; in the end, ICANN required mandatory arbitration only for trademark disputes involving domain names themselves, in the form of the Uniform Domain-Name Dispute Resolution Policy (UDRP). ICANN's contracts with the registrars for gTLDs require that registrants must agree to the terms of the UDRP when they register a domain name.

Where did ICANN itself get the authority to do all of this? The answer was unclear. ICANN signed a Memorandum of Understanding with the Department of Commerce in late 1998. That's all well and good, but it begs the question, because it doesn't explain where the Department of Commerce got its authority over the domain name system in the first place. One answer would be to say that all that was transferred was control over a few computers – the root name servers – and everyone on the Internet has voluntarily agreed to look to those servers in resolving domain names.

ICANN's status has remained ambiguous in the years since. It has grown with the Internet: its budget now shows more than $150 million a year in revenues. It remains a nonprofit: its governing board contains members appointed by an alphabet soup of "supporting organizations" who are supposed to represent the interests of its various constituencies. The U.S. government has gradually taken its hands off the reins; in 2014, it announced an intention to "transition key Internet domain name functions to the global multistakeholder community." That process completed in 2016, when ICANN's contract with the Department of Commerce expired.

ICANN's biggest – and most controversial – recent move has been its introduction of new gTLDs. After a long planning process, it opened up applications in 2012: it received 1,930 applications for domains such as .xbox, .mormon, .sexy, and 公益. One reason for expanding the list is to add diversity, including gTLDs for particular communities and in a variety of scripts, such as Arabic and Chinese.

Another is to experiment with different registration policies. Consider a few examples:

- .mba is operated by Google. Registration is limited to "verified MBA-awarding institutions and MBA-related product and service providers."

- .cars is operated by the domain-name company Uniregistry. Its goal is "to provide information about cars and the driving experience"; registration is open to the public and is first-come first-served.

- .montblanc is operated by the corporate parent of the French pen company. It will provide authorized retailers with "a space that sets them apart from counterfeiters and provides them with the direct relation to Montblanc in the minds of the public."

- .paris is a "geographic" gTLD operated by the municipal government of Paris, France. Registration is restricted to people and legal entities with a presence in the Paris area and their use of the domain must be "conducive to the welfare of the Paris area."

- .islam is a proposed "community" gTLD, operated by the Turkish company AGITSys. Its application explained:

  > As a part of this, since the .ISLAM gTLD is community based and designed to serve those of Muslim faith, as well as to protect its good name, AGITSys intends to limit second-level domain registrations to those of Muslim faith, or those with a clear interest in serving the Muslim community and faith beneficially. Such a designation is almost impossible to police, because faith is a highly personal thing requiring no proof beyond belief, and to restrict, for example, registrations to those geographically located in predominantly Muslim nations would alienate the myriad Muslims in other nations. Thus, these limitations will mostly be self-imposed, with registrants agreeing themselves that they are of Muslim faith. Equally, AGITSys will not tolerate radical content, nor will it tolerate content that criticizes Islam and the Muslim faith. Immediate and severe action will be taken against registrants promulgating either, and a black list will be created in an attempt to pre-empt any such attempts. Once content is registered, the community will be to an extent self-policing, with facilities to report abusive, irrelevant or anti-Muslim registrations available on the Registry website.

Applicants pay a nonrefundable $185,000 processing fee and undergo an intensive screening process, which includes things like resolving competing applications for the same name, making sure that the applicant has the technical and operational capacity to provide reliable naming services, evaluating registration policies (e.g. accepting registrations only from a particular geographic community or industry), ensuring policies to prevent abusive registrations, and much, much more.

QUESTIONS

1. Look at the examples of new gTLDs given above. Do their benefits strike you as justifying the various costs that creating new gTLDs impose on the domain-name system and on Internet users? Do any of them need new TLDs, or could they be accomplished using second-level domains within existing

TLDs (e.g., mba.google, paris.fr, or islamic.org)? Or should the burden fall on those who favor the status quo to explain why proposed new gTLDs would be harmful?

2. The .sucks gTLD charges $2,499 for a registration. Why? Who would pay that much for a domain name? Trademark owners have accused its operator of extortion. Is this something that ICANN should try to stop?

3. If the United States government objects to an ICANN action – say, approving a new .xxx gTLD for pornography – what influence will it have? How can the government (or any government) make sure that ICANN acts in the best interests of the Internet and its users?

4. Does anyone *make* you use the domain-name system? If you type an IP address into your browser, rather than a domain name, what happens? (Try 74.125.228.224 and see what happens.) Would it be possible to abandon the domain-name system and use just IP addresses? How about using an "alternate root" domain server: one operated by someone other than ICANN? Several companies have tried to create their own alternate root name servers. OpenNIC, for example, offers .geek and .indy TLDs. Why haven't these alternate domain-name systems caught on more widely? Are there advantages to having everyone use the same DNS? Disadvantages?

UNIFORM DOMAIN NAME DISPUTE RESOLUTION POLICY

... 4. *MANDATORY ADMINISTRATIVE PROCEEDING*. – This Paragraph sets forth the type of disputes for which you are required to submit to a mandatory administrative proceeding. These proceedings will be conducted before one of the administrative-dispute-resolution service providers listed at www.i-cann.org/udrp/approved-providers.htm (each, a "Provider").

   a. *APPLICABLE DISPUTES*. – You are required to submit to a mandatory administrative proceeding in the event that a third party (a "complainant") asserts to the applicable Provider, in compliance with the Rules of Procedure, that

      (i) your domain name is identical or confusingly similar to a trademark or service mark in which the complainant has rights; and

      (ii) you have no rights or legitimate interests in respect of the domain name; and

      (iii) your domain name has been registered and is being used in bad faith.

   In the administrative proceeding, the complainant must prove that each of these three elements are present.

   b. *EVIDENCE OF REGISTRATION AND USE IN BAD FAITH*. - For the purposes of Paragraph 4(a)(iii), the following circumstances, in particular but without limitation, if found by the Panel to be present, shall be evidence of the registration and use of a domain name in bad faith:

      (i) circumstances indicating that you have registered or you have acquired the domain name primarily for the purpose of selling, renting, or otherwise transferring the domain name registration to the complainant who is the owner of the trademark or service mark or to a competitor of that complainant, for valuable consideration in excess of your documented out-of-pocket costs directly related to the domain name; or

(ii) you have registered the domain name in order to prevent the owner of the trademark or service mark from reflecting the mark in a corresponding domain name, provided that you have engaged in a pattern of such conduct; or

(iii) you have registered the domain name primarily for the purpose of disrupting the business of a competitor; or

(iv) by using the domain name, you have intentionally attempted to attract, for commercial gain, Internet users to your web site or other on-line location, by creating a likelihood of confusion with the complainant's mark as to the source, sponsorship, affiliation, or endorsement of your web site or location or of a product or service on your web site or location.

c. *HOW TO DEMONSTRATE YOUR RIGHTS TO AND LEGITIMATE INTERESTS IN THE DOMAIN NAME IN RESPONDING TO A COMPLAINT.* - When you receive a complaint, you should refer to Paragraph 5 of the Rules of Procedure in determining how your response should be prepared. Any of the following circumstances, in particular but without limitation, if found by the Panel to be proved based on its evaluation of all evidence presented, shall demonstrate your rights or legitimate interests to the domain name for purposes of Paragraph 4(a)(ii):

(i) before any notice to you of the dispute, your use of, or demonstrable preparations to use, the domain name or a name corresponding to the domain name in connection with a bona fide offering of goods or services; or

(ii) you (as an individual, business, or other organization) have been commonly known by the domain name, even if you have acquired no trademark or service mark rights; or

(iii) you are making a legitimate noncommercial or fair use of the domain name, without intent for commercial gain to misleadingly divert consumers or to tarnish the trademark or service mark at issue.

d. *SELECTION OF PROVIDER.* - The complainant shall select the Provider from among those approved by ICANN by submitting the complaint to that Provider. The selected Provider will administer the proceeding, except in cases of consolidation as described in Paragraph 4(f). ...

e. *INITIATION OF PROCEEDING AND PROCESS AND APPOINTMENT OF ADMINISTRATIVE PANEL.* - The Rules of Procedure state the process for initiating and conducting a proceeding and for appointing the panel that will decide the dispute (the "Administrative Panel"). ...

g. *FEES.* - All fees charged by a Provider in connection with any dispute before an Administrative Panel pursuant to this Policy shall be paid by the complainant, except in cases where you elect to expand the Administrative Panel from one to three panelists as provided in Paragraph 5(b)(iv) of the Rules of Procedure, in which case all fees will be split evenly by you and the complainant.

h. *OUR INVOLVEMENT IN ADMINISTRATIVE PROCEEDINGS.* - We do not, and will not, participate in the administration or conduct of any proceeding before an Administrative Panel. In addition, we will not be liable as a result of any decisions rendered by the Administrative Panel.

i. *REMEDIES.* - The remedies available to a complainant pursuant to any proceeding before an Administrative Panel shall be limited to requiring the cancellation of your domain name or the transfer of your domain name registration to the complainant. ...

k. *AVAILABILITY OF COURT PROCEEDINGS.* - The mandatory administrative proceeding requirements set forth in Paragraph 4 shall not prevent either you or the complainant from submitting the dispute to a court of competent jurisdiction for independent resolution before such mandatory administrative proceeding is commenced or after such proceeding is concluded. If an Administrative Panel decides that your domain name registration should be canceled or transferred, we will wait ten (10) business days (as observed in the location of our principal office) after we are informed by the applicable Provider of the Administrative Panel's decision before implementing that decision. We will then implement the decision unless we have received from you during that ten (10) business day period official documentation (such as a copy of a complaint, file-stamped by the clerk of the court) that you have commenced a lawsuit against the complainant in a jurisdiction to which the complainant has submitted under Paragraph 3(b)(xiii) of the Rules of Procedure. (In general, that jurisdiction is either the location of our principal office or of your address as shown in our Whois database. See Paragraphs 1 and 3(b)(xiii) of the Rules of Procedure for details.) If we receive such documentation within the ten (10) business day period, we will not implement the Administrative Panel's decision, and we will take no further action, until we receive (i) evidence satisfactory to us of a resolution between the parties; (ii) evidence satisfactory to us that your lawsuit has been dismissed or withdrawn; or (iii) a copy of an order from such court dismissing your lawsuit or ordering that you do not have the right to continue to use your domain name.

QUESTIONS

1. How are the results of UDRP arbitrations enforced?

2. What legal standard must the arbitrator hearing a UDRP complaint use to decide the case? How does it resemble United States law? How is it different? Is it appropriate to describe the UDRP process as a kind of common law for the Internet?

3. Is it an appropriate use of ICANN's authority to impose this system for the protection of trademark owners?

FLEXEGRITY PROBLEM

You have been retained by Flexegrity, LLC to advise on a trademark matter. Flexegrity operates a chain of yoga studios with a strong emphasis on sustainability, ethical development, and social justice. It uses the FLEXEGRITY trademark and a website at flexegrity.net. It has recently learned of a website at flexegritty.com; the site contains nothing but links to fitness-themed websites and a large number of ads (mostly, but not exclusively, for fitness-related products). Flexegrity's CEO has asked you to advise on the relative merits of filing an ACPA lawsuit and a UDRP complaint. Explain to her the mechanics of each. Which will cost more? What is the likelihood of prevailing under each? Are they mutually exclusive? What are the advantages and disadvantages of each course of action? What do you recommend that Flexegrity do, and why?

CURT MFG., INC. V. SABIN

No. FA0808001220025 (National Arbitration Forum Sept. 20, 2008)
available at http://www.citizen.org/documents/decision1.pdf

PARTIES

Complainant is Curt Manufacturing, Inc. ("Complainant"), represented by Jeffrey D. Shewchuk, of Shewchuk IP Services, LLC, Minnesota, USA. Respondent is George Sabin ("Respondent"), California, USA.

REGISTRAR AND DISPUTED DOMAIN NAME

The domain name at issue is <curt-mfg.com>, registered with Godaddy.com, Inc.

PANEL

The undersigned certifies that he or she has acted independently and impartially and to the best of his or her knowledge has no known conflict in serving as Panelist in this proceeding.

Joel M. Grossman, Esq., as Panelist.

PROCEDURAL HISTORY

Complainant submitted a Complaint to the National Arbitration Forum electronically on August 12, 2008; the National Arbitration Forum received a hard copy of the Complaint on August 13, 2008.

On August 12, 2008, Godaddy.com, Inc. confirmed by e-mail to the National Arbitration Forum that the <curt-mfg.com> domain name is registered with Godaddy.com, Inc. and that the Respondent is the current registrant of the name. Godaddy.com, Inc. has verified that Respondent is bound by the Godaddy.com, Inc. registration agreement and has thereby agreed to resolve domain-name disputes brought by third parties in accordance with ICANN's Uniform Domain Name Dispute Resolution Policy (the "Policy").

On August 15, 2008, a Notification of Complaint and Commencement of Administrative Proceeding (the "Commencement Notification"), setting a deadline of September 4, 2008 by which Respondent could file a Response to the Complaint, was transmitted to Respondent via e-mail, post and fax, to all entities and persons listed on Respondent's registration as technical, administrative and billing contacts, and to postmaster@curt-mfg.com by e-mail.

A timely Response was received and determined to be complete on September 2, 2008.

An Additional Submission was received from Complainant on September 5, 2008, and was determined to be timely and complete pursuant to Supplemental Rule 7.

An Additional Submission was received from Respondent on September 9, 2008, and was determined to be timely and complete pursuant to Supplemental Rule 7.

On September 4, pursuant to Complainant's request to have the dispute decided by a single-member Panel, the National Arbitration Forum appointed Joel M. Grossman, Esq. as Panelist.

RELIEF SOUGHT

Complainant requests that the domain name be transferred from Respondent to Complainant.

PARTIES' CONTENTIONS

A. Complainant

Complainant first asserts that the domain name is identical or confusingly similar to a mark in which it has rights. Complainant's "Curt" mark is wholly incorporated in the domain name, and Complainant's website, <curtmfg.com> is virtually identical to the name, the sole exception being a hyphen, which must be ignored for this purpose. Complainant asserts rights in the mark since at least 1993. The "CURT" mark has received a federal trademark. Complainant next contends that Respondent has no rights or legitimate interests in the name. Specifically, Complainant asserts that Respondent's domain name, which is virtually identical to that of Complainant, is being used to confuse Internet users and deceive them concerning the origin or source of the content of the website, which is extremely critical of Complainant's products. Complainant contends that the name is not being used for any *bona fide* offering of goods and services, and its sole purpose is to harm Complainant's products and create confusion among Internet users. Additionally Complainant asserts that the name is not being used for a noncommercial use since it appears to invite others who might be injured by Complainant's products to contact a lawyer for purposes of filing a lawsuit. Finally, Complainant contends that the name was registered and is being used in bad faith, because Respondent is intentionally using the name to attract, possibly for commercial gain, Internet users to Respondent's website by creating a likelihood of confusion with Complainant's mark and website. As stated above, Complainant notes that because of the manner in which Respondent's website criticizes Complainant's products, it may be that Respondent is hoping to solicit one or more users for an individual or class action lawsuit against Complainant.

B. Respondent

Respondent contends that the domain name is a parody, and the parody is fully protected by the First Amendment. More specifically, Respondent claims that one of Complainant's hitch products failed, and nearly caused a fatal accident on a congested freeway. The purpose of the website, according to Respondent, is noncommercial and educational, namely advising interested persons about the problems with Complainant's products. While not specifically engaging in an analysis of whether the name is identical or confusingly similar to Complainant's mark, Respondent contends that the name does not cause confusion, because anyone who visits Respondent's website will clearly see that the content was not created by Complainant. Respondent also points out that a disclaimer has been placed on the website advising visitors that it is not affiliated with Complainant. Respondent also challenges the jurisdiction of the National Arbitration Forum in this proceeding, as well as the ability of Complainant's counsel to appear in Wisconsin. Finally, Respondent purports to assert a counterclaim for damages against Complainant, asserting that Complainant's case should never have been submitted.

C. Additional Submissions

In its Additional Submission Complainant asserts that Respondent has not presented any facts to support its position. Complainant also notes that on Respondent's website there is a note to send an e-mail to what appears to be a law firm website, <oklaw.us>. This suggests that visitors to Respondent's website who might have potential legal claims against Complainant could contact that law firm. Complainant asserts further that the name is not a parody or so-called gripe site such as <walmartsucks.com>. Citing *Dykema Gosett PLLC v. DefaultData.com and Brian Wick*, FA 97031 (Nat. Arb. Forum May 29, 2001). Complainant states that while parody and criticism are certainly permitted as part of the content of a website, the domain name itself must be identifiable as parody, such as <walmartsucks.com," not <walmart.com>. In the *Dykema* case, the respondent registered as a domain name <dykemagossett.com>. *Id.* The complainant in that case was a law firm called Dykema Gossett. *Id.* The respondent in that case argued that the website was a parody of law firms, but the domain name was held to be registered in bad faith because it appropriated the complainant law firm's name and confused the public. *Id.* Complainant thus contends that as in the *Dykema* case, in the instant case, regardless of the content of Respondent's website, which may well be protected by the First Amendment, the domain name is not in any manner a parody or criticism to let the public know its purpose; instead it confuses the public because it appears to be Complainant's own site.

In its Additional Submission Respondent asserts that only the "CURT" mark has been trademarked, not "curtmfg" so that the domain name is not confusingly similar to the mark. Respondent reiterates that the website is a parody, as well as educational news, protected by the First Amendment.

FINDINGS

The Panel finds that: the domain name is identical to, or confusingly similar to a mark in which Complainant has rights; that Respondent has no rights or legitimate interests in the name; and that the name was registered and is being used in bad faith.

DISCUSSION

Paragraph 15(a) of the Rules for Uniform Domain Name Dispute Resolution Policy (the "Rules") instructs this Panel to "decide a complaint on the basis of the statements and documents submitted in accordance with the Policy, these Rules and any rules and principles of law that it deems applicable."

Paragraph 4(a) of the Policy requires that the Complainant must prove each of the following three elements to obtain an order that a domain name should be cancelled or transferred:

1. the domain name registered by the Respondent is identical or confusingly similar to a trademark or service mark in which the Complainant has rights;

2. the Respondent has no rights or legitimate interests in respect of the domain name; and

3. the domain name has been registered and is being used in bad faith.

Identical and/or Confusingly Similar

The domain name is clearly identical to or confusingly similar to the mark. The mark is wholly incorporated in the name. The addition of the generic "mfg" does not in any manner erase the confusion. So too, hyphens are ignored for this purpose. See *Trip Network Inc. v. Alviera*, FA 914943 (Nat. Arb. Forum Mar. 27,

2007). Additionally, the registered trademark "Curt" is clearly sufficient to provide rights in the mark for Complainant. The Panel therefore finds that the name is identical to or confusingly similar to a mark in which Complainant has rights.

Rights or Legitimate Interests

Respondent is not commonly known by the name, and Respondent has not shown that it is using the name for the bona fide offering of goods or services. Respondent contends that it has an absolute right under the First Amendment to parody or criticize Complainant's products, and of course that is true. However, prior panels have recognized that there is a difference between placing critical or satiric content on a website, which is clearly permissible, and identifying oneself as the Complainant in the domain name, which is not. As the panel explained in *Monty & Pat Roberts, Inc. v. Keith* D2000-0299 (WIPO June 9, 2000): "The Panel does not dispute Respondent's right to establish and maintain a website critical of Complainant . . . However, the panel does not consider that this gives Respondent the right to identify itself as Complainant." The same applies here. As noted in summarizing Complainant's contentions, the panel in the *Dykema* case, which is quite similar to this one, reached the same conclusion. In that case the respondent used the name of a law firm as its domain name, without adding an additional phrase such as "sucks." The panel determined there that even if the purpose of the website was to criticize or parody lawyers, the respondent could not identify itself as the law firm in the domain name. Additionally the Panel finds that the invitation to contact a law firm reveals a commercial purpose for the use of the domain name. Thus, the name is being used, for commercial gain, to divert Internet users from Complainant's site to Respondent's site through use of an extremely confusing and virtually (save the hypen) identical domain name. For these reasons the Panel determines that Respondent has no rights or legitimate interests in the name.

Registration and Use in Bad Faith

As noted above, the Panel determines that Respondent is attempting to cause likely confusion among Interest users as to the source of the domain name and Complainant's website. It is using the name to divert Internet users, possibly for gain from lawsuits filed against Complainant, by confusing Internet users who may be searching for Complainant's website. For this reason the Panel holds that the name was registered and is being used in bad faith. *See Allianz of Am. Corp. v. Bond* FA 680624 (Nat. Arb. Forum June 2, 2006). While Respondent contends that there is no bad faith in that its sole intent is to criticize Complainant's products, activity which is protected by the First Amendment, the Panel determines that this freedom of speech applies to the content of the website, not to the domain name. As the panel stated in *Diners Club Int'l Ltd. v. Infotechnics Ltd.* FA 169085 (Nat. Arb. Forum Aug. 20, 2003): "Respondent may have the right to post criticism of Complainant on the Internet, however, Respondent does not have the right to completely appropriate Complainant's registered trademark in a domain name in a way that will mislead Internet users as to the source or affiliation of the attached website." This would be a different case if Respondent's domain name were <curtmfgsucks.com> or something similar. But it is not. For these reasons the Panel determines that the name was registered and is being used in bad faith.

DECISION

Having established all three elements required under the ICANN Policy, the Panel concludes that relief shall be GRANTED.

Accordingly, it is Ordered that the <curt-mfg.com> domain name be TRANS-FERRED from Respondent to Complainant.

Joel M. Grossman, Panelist

QUESTIONS

1. Who is Joel Grossman? What is his authority to decide this dispute? How was he selected?

2. Compare and contrast the format of this arbitration with a typical judicial decision. What is the same? What is different? Which is faster? Cheaper? Are there any jurisdictional distinctions?

3. On what basis did the arbitrator rule in favor of Curt? Is the reasoning consistent with the trademark cases, *supra*? Some commentators argue that UDRP arbitrations reach inconsistent and unpredictable results. Why might that be? Others think that UDRP arbitrators tend to favor complainants. Why might that be?

4. Now that the arbitrator has ruled in favor of Curt, what will happen? What are Sabin's options? What would Curt's options have been if Sabin had won? Did Curt have any other options besides filing for a UDRP arbitration in the first place? Did Sabin have any options besides participating in the arbitration?

5. If you are a trademark owner and you discover a gripe site, how should you respond? If you run a gripe site, what should you do when contacted by a trademark owner's lawyers?

6. Facebook allows users to "claim their names" and associate a URL with their profile pages. If Arnaud du Tilh claims http://www.facebook.com/martinguerre, does Guerre have any recourse?

ARISTA RECORDS, LLC V. TKACH
122 F. Supp. 3d 32 (S.D.N.Y. 2015)

Nathan, District Judge: ...

I. BACKGROUND

On May 5, 2015, the Court entered a Stipulation, Consent Judgment, and Permanent Injunction against Escape Media Group, Inc. ("Escape"), which operated the website www.grooveshark.com ("Grooveshark"). Similarly, on May 1, 2015, in a separate action, Judge Griesa entered a Stipulation, Consent Judgment, and Permanent Injunction against Escape and its founders. As part of this latter settlement, among other things, Escape conveyed to Plaintiff UMG Recordings, Inc. ownership of its federally registered trademarks relating to the Grooveshark service.

A. The Temporary Restraining Order

Shortly after the consent judgments were entered, a "copycat" version of Grooveshark appeared on the internet, which led Plaintiffs to file the present action on May 12, 2015 against Defendants Vita Tkach and Does 1-10 who are allegedly operating the copycat version of Grooveshark. That same day, Plaintiffs obtained from the Part 1 Judge of this Court a TRO against Defendants "and any persons acting in concert or participation with them or third parties providing services used in connection with Defendants' operations" from, among other things, "[u]sing, linking to, transferring, selling, exercising control over, or otherwise owning the domain names grooveshark.io or grooveshark.pw or any other domain name that incorporates, in whole or in part, any of Grooveshark Marks" and from "[d]irectly or secondarily infringing Plaintiffs' copyrighted sound recordings via the [Defendants' service] or any variations thereof."

Plaintiffs explain that they were then drawn into what they describe as a technological globetrotting game of "whack-a-mole" in an effort to enforce the TRO. On May 13, 2015, Plaintiffs served the TRO on Defendants and Namecheap, Inc., a California-based domain name registrar through which Defendants had registered "grooveshark.io" (.io is the country-code domain reserved for the British Indian Ocean Territory) and "grooveshark.pw" (.pw is the country-code domain reserved for the Republic of Palau). Namecheap, Inc. complied with the TRO, which effectively disabled the ".io" and ".pw" Grooveshark domain names. Defendants then registered "grooveshark.vc" (.vc is the country-code domain reserved for Saint Vincent and the Grenadines) through Dynadot, which was subsequently served with the TRO. After Dynadot complied with the TRO, the "grooveshark.vc" domain name was disabled. Defendants then registered a "grooveshark.li" domain name (.li is the country-code domain reserved for the principality of Liechtenstein). The domain name registrar through which Defendants registered the .li domain is located in Switzerland. At roughly this point, Plaintiffs opted for a different tactic and served the TRO on CloudFlare.

B. CloudFlare, Inc.'s Services

CloudFlare is an internet service provider that provides authoritative domain name system servers for its customers as a means of providing content delivery network and reverse-proxy services. CloudFlare explained that an "authoritative domain name server" is a "computer on the Internet that is designated by the domain name owner to report the correct IP address for that domain, which information is then propagated to other DNS servers worldwide as it is needed." In laymen's terms, this appears to mean that when someone types a domain name such as "grooveshark.li" into a web browser, the Defendants have engaged CloudFlare to convert the domain name into the IP address for the website associated with that domain name so that the user can connect to the website they are trying to reach. Without CloudFlare, a user could still get to "grooveshark.li" if the user had the actual IP address for the website associated with that domain name; alternatively, Defendants could obtain CloudFlare's authoritative domain name system server from another third-party service provider comparable to CloudFlare or Defendants could provide that same service on their own. CloudFlare also "optimizes the delivery of customers' websites from the customers' origin server to visitors' browsers. This gives visitors to a customer's website faster page load times and better performance, while blocking threats and abusive bots and crawlers from attacking the websites."

On May 2, 2015, a user opened a free account at CloudFlare and configured the domain names grooveshark.pw and grooveshark.io to use CloudFlare's services. On May 13, 2015, an anonymous user using a different email address and server address opened a new free account and configured the domain name grooveshark.vc to use CloudFlare's services.

On May 14, 2015, Plaintiffs served a copy of the TRO on CloudFlare and requested that it cease providing support to the Grooveshark sites. CloudFlare confirmed receipt of the TRO, but stated that it did not construe the TRO as applying to it, insisting that Plaintiffs seek an order from this Court requiring CloudFlare's compliance. Then, on May 15, 2015, an anonymous user opened yet another free account at CloudFlare and configured the domain name grooveshark.li to use CloudFlare's services; this anonymous user used another email address and server IP address that were not the same as either of the ones used earlier..

C. The Motion for Contempt/Clarification

As explained in the Court's May 27, 2015 Order, on May 22, 2015, Plaintiffs filed an *ex parte* "Proposed Supplemental Order to Show Cause" requesting a court order requiring third-party CloudFlare, Inc. to comply with the existing TRO. After a conference was held on May 26, 2015, the Court clarified that it would construe Plaintiffs' request as an expedited contempt motion for violation of the existing TRO or, alternatively, an expedited motion for clarification of the existing TRO. The Court set a briefing schedule and provided the parties with an opportunity to request an evidentiary hearing, which they declined. Therefore, factual findings contained herein are based on the parties' written submissions, which were fully submitted today – June 3, 2015. Both sides requested an expedited process and this Court is issuing this Order on an expedited basis.

II. DISCUSSION

Plaintiffs contend that CloudFlare is in active concert or participation with (i.e., aiding and abetting) the Defendants because it (1) owns and operates the authoritative name server for grooveshark.li (and the other Grooveshark sites) and (2) optimizes the performance of grooveshark.li (and the other Grooveshark sites), making them faster and more resistant to malicious attack. Although there is no genuine factual dispute regarding the services CloudFlare provides to the Grooveshark sites, CloudFlare contends that it should not be bound by the injunction because its service is "passive" and not necessary for the operation of the Grooveshark sites.

CloudFlare rests its legal argument on the longstanding principal that a court "cannot lawfully enjoin the world at large, no matter how broadly it words its decree." *Alemite Mfg. Corp. v. Staff*, 42 F.2d 832, 832 (2d Cir. 1930) (Hand, J.). The problem for CloudFlare is the equally venerable proposition that "a person who knowingly assists a defendant in violating an injunction subjects himself to civil as well as criminal proceedings for contempt." *Id.* ; *see also* 11A *Charles A. Wright, et al.*, Federal Practice and Procedure § 2956 at 394 (3d ed. 2013) (explaining that *Alemite* "clearly does not grant immunity to someone who knowingly aids, abets, assists, or acts in concert with a person who has been enjoined from violating the injunction"). Federal Rule of Civil Procedure 65 expressly incorporates this countervailing "other persons who are in active concert or participation with them." Fed. R. Civ. P. 65(d)(2) .

CloudFlare makes two primary arguments in opposition. First, it takes the position that it is not in such "active concert or participation" with Defendants because its "systems have passively and automatically served the domain names at issue." It further argues that it need not comply with the TRO because, even if it complies, the Plaintiffs will not accomplish their ultimate goal: "Even if CloudFlare – and *every company in the world that provides similar services* – took proactive steps to identify and block the Defendants, the website would remain up and running at its current domain name." The Court finds neither argument persuasive.

A. CloudFlare's Passivity Argument

Turning to CloudFlare's passivity argument first, the Court notes that there is a surprising dearth of authority addressing the meaning of Rule 65 's "active concert or participation" language in the context of internet service providers such as CloudFlare. ... Therefore, the Court must rely on more general applications of Rule 65 , which have noted that "active concert or participation" exists if the third party "aided and abetted" the party subject to the injunction. This requires "show[ing] that the non-party had actual knowledge of the judicial decree and violated it, and that the challenged action was taken for the benefit of, or to assist, a party subject to the decree." *Adcor Indus. v. Bevcorp, LLC*, 411 F. Supp. 2d 778, 794 (N.D. Ohio 2005); *see also Lindland v. U.S. Wrestling Ass'n*, 227 F.3d 1000, 1006 (7th Cir. 2000) ("The 'active concert or participation' clause is designed to prevent what may well have happened here: the addressee of an injunction, eager to avoid its obligations, persuades a friendly third party to take steps that frustrate the injunction's effectiveness.").

There is no real dispute that CloudFlare had knowledge of the TRO at least as of May 14, 2015 and that it subsequently permitted an anonymous user to establish a free account that configured the domain name grooveshark.li to use CloudFlare's services. CloudFlare's authoritative domain name server translates grooveshark.li as entered in a search browser into the correct IP address associated with that site, thus allowing the user to connect to the site. Connecting internet users to grooveshark.li in this manner benefits Defendants and quite fundamentally assists them in violating the injunction because, without it, users would not be able to connect to Defendants' site unless they knew the specific IP address for the site. Beyond the authoritative domain name server, CloudFlare also provides additional services that it describes as improving the performance of the grooveshark.li site.

As noted, there is limited authority addressing services such as CloudFlare's, but the few courts that have addressed comparable technological services have similarly held that they fall within an injunction's reach if those services are knowingly used to facilitate injunction violations. *See, e.g.*, The North Face Apparel Corp. v. Fujian Sharing Imp. & Exp. Ltd Co., No. 10 Civ. 1630 (AKH), slip op. 4-6 (S.D.N.Y. June 24, 2011) ("Public Interest Registry, for example, cannot continue to make the connections that enable customers attracted to defendants' websites to access those websites."); *South Cent. Bell Tel. Co. Constant, Inc.*, 304 F. Supp. 732, 736 (D.La. 1969) ("As soon as South Central Bell was apprised of the fact that the subscriber, Constant, was, by use of South Central Bell's equipment, violating the injunction imposed by this Court, it had a duty not to act in any way in concert with Constant to effectuate or perpetuate the violation. South Central Bell had the means to prevent its equipment from being used to violate the injunction, and its failure to do so would, at the very least, have amounted to a passive participation in the violation."). Indeed, at least one district court has included CloudFlare within the reach of an injunction aimed at an infringing website: "[A]ll website hosting, website optimization, and any other company or person that provides website services for the MFN domains, including without limitation, CloudFlare, Inc., shall within 24 hours of receipt of this Order, cease all website services made in connection with the MFN domains." *Dish Network LLC v. Dillion*, No. 12cv157 BTM (NLS), 2012 U.S. Dist. LEXIS 13277 (S.D. Cal. Feb. 3, 2012).

In opposition, CloudFlare relies heavily on *Blockowicz v. Williams*, 630 F.3d 563 (7th Cir. 2010), which involved a third-party website that refused to removed allegedly defamatory content posted by enjoined defendants. But that case, which applied an abuse of discretion standard of review to a district court's refusal to enforce an injunction against third parties, is distinguishable from the facts here. To begin with, the *Blockowicz* court emphasized that the only act of the third-party service provider, "entering into a contract with the defendants, occurred long before the injunction was issued." *Id.* But CloudFlare acknowledges that it permitted an anonymous user to register a "grooveshark" domain name to use its services *after* it had received notice of the TRO. The *Blockowicz* court also highlighted the fact that the third-party service provider merely continued to host the defamatory content on its website as it had done prior to the issuance of the injunction. In contrast, CloudFlare's authoritative domain name server connects users to the new Grooveshark site by translating a user's browser entry into the IP address for the site, and it also ensures faster load times and optimal performance for the site, both of which are far from the passive hosting of content at issue in *Blockowicz*.

CloudFlare's passivity argument also implies that it should not be bound by the injunction because it is not motivated by a desire to help Defendants violate the injunction; rather, CloudFlare contends it is merely providing the same service to Defendants that it would provide to anyone else. But the Second Circuit has "held that a court's inquiry into the fact of aiding and abetting is 'directed to the actuality of concert or participation, without regard to the motives that prompt the concert or participation.'" *Eli Lilly & Co. v. Gottstein*, 617 F.3d 186, 193 (2d Cir. 2010). Thus, CloudFlare's motivations are not at issue.

B. CloudFlare's Futility Argument

CloudFlare's second, or "futility," argument is equally unpersuasive. In essence, CloudFlare contends that Plaintiffs will obtain a short-lived victory if it complies with the temporary restraining order because another third-party service provider could provide the same service or Defendants could provide that service on their own. In other words, even if CloudFlare complied with the injunction, this would not "necessarily" shut down grooveshark.li or other various incarnations of Grooveshark that Defendants might set up. But just because another third party could aid and abet the Defendants in violating the injunction does not mean that CloudFlare is not doing so. Similarly, the Court is unaware of any principle requiring Plaintiffs to show that Defendants' site would be inaccessible but for Cloud-Flare's services; they need only show that CloudFlare is in active concert or participation with Defendants.

CloudFlare also suggests that it would not be able to comply with the injunction because it "has no way of identifying accounts opened by the Defendants, *other than* their alleged use of domains containing the name 'grooveshark.'" But as Plaintiffs note, "[t]he word 'grooveshark' is a highly-distinctive registered trademark, owned by Plaintiff UMG, and preventing CloudFlare from 'linking to' any domain name that includes the 'grooveshark' word mark is precisely what the TRO requires (among other things), regardless of which top-level domain (e.g., .li, .io, .pw, .vc., etc.) is used." Thus, far from being unable to comply, Cloud-Flare acknowledges that it can identify customers using domain names containing the name "grooveshark."

Finally, CloudFlare suggests that the TRO could potentially enjoin any service provider that is remotely connected to the new Grooveshark site(s). The Court does not share this concern in light of the wording of the TRO, which is sufficiently narrow in scope that "the party enjoined [is] able to ascertain from the four corners of the order precisely what acts" are forbidden, *Sanders v. Air Line Pilots Association*, 473 F.2d 244, 247 (2d Cir. 1972). While there may be more attenuated services that indirectly support Defendants' sites, the Court is addressing the facts before it, which involve a service that is directly engaged in facilitating access to Defendants' sites with knowledge of the specific infringing names of those sites.

In this respect, CloudFlare seems quite similar to a domain name registrar, which both parties appear to agree is covered by the injunction. ...The Court thus hereby concludes and clarifies that CloudFlare was bound by the TRO and is now bound by the existing preliminary injunction.

QUESTIONS

1. What role does CloudFlare play in the domain-name system? Is it an appropriate target for this use of the court's authority?

2. Does the injunction pose risks to innocent third parties, or has the court appropriately limited its scope?

CHAPTER 7: COPYRIGHT

Out of all the topics in a typical Internet Law course, online copyright is the one that could most easily be a course unto itself. Almost every facet of copyright doctrine (which was complicated to begin with) has been challenged by the Internet. This chapter couldn't possibly cover all of these twists and turns. Instead, its tour of digital copyright will focus on providing a basic framework and introducing the defining issues of the last decade.

COPYRIGHT OVERVIEW

The following is a brief and necessarily simplified overview of copyright law. There are plenty of complications and exceptions – some of which are explored in the materials that follow. The goal here is just to provide an overview, so that the remaining materials make sense in context.

Copyright starts from the axiom that *original works of authorship* are copyrightable. 17 U.S.C. § 102. A course on copyright law will help unpack what "original" or "authorship" means. For present purposes, the key distinction is between significantly creative "works" – like novels, songs, and sculptures – and facts that no one creates, like the temperature in Times Square at 5:30 PM on March 15, 1994. The former are copyrightable, the latter aren't.

The author of an original work is its initial copyright owner; she can then assign the copyright to someone else if she wants, like a publisher. Paying attention to ownership is important because only a copyright owner can sue for infringement. For example, the copyright in a movie is typically owned by the production company. When the producer Mark Basseley Youssef, who had hired Cindy Lee Garcia to act in what he said would be a historical epic, recut the footage of her performance into the offensive anti-Islamic video *Innocence of Muslims*, she had potential claims against him for fraud but not copyright claims against the websites where the video was hosted. *Garcia v. Google, Inc.*, 786 F.3d 733 (9th Cir. 2015).

Once a work is copyrighted, the copyright owner has six exclusive rights detailed in 17 U.S.C. § 106. "Use" is not one of them; it has never been copyright infringement to read a book. Instead, an infringer is one who violates one or more of the six exclusive rights. The first and easiest-to-understand is the *reproduction* right: to "reproduce the copyrighted work in copies." 17 U.S.C. § 106(1). We'll also be concerned with the *public distribution*, *public display*, and *public performance* rights. 17 U.S.C. § 106(3)–(5). Note that the statutory language of these three rights includes the words "to the public" or "publicly." Purely private distributions, displays, and performances are not infringements. Here's how the Copyright Act explains the difference:

> To perform or display a work "publicly" means –
>
> (1) to perform or display it at a place open to the public or at any place where a substantial number of persons outside of a normal circle of a family and its social acquaintances is gathered; or
>
> (2) to transmit or otherwise communicate a performance or display of the work to a place specified by clause (1) or to the public, by means of any device or process ...

17 U.S.C. § 101.

To analyze an infringement case, start by asking whether you can find a *direct infringer*, i.e., someone who personally does something prohibited by one of the exclusive rights. The prototypical direct infringer is the pirate publisher: someone who prints and sells thousands of unauthorized copies of a book. The printing is an infringement of the reproduction right, regardless of whether the copies are sold; the sales are an infringement of the distribution right.

At this stage, you should also check whether the alleged direct infringer has any valid defenses. Obviously, permission of the copyright holder is a complete defense. In copyright terms, the copyright owner's permission is a *license* to engage in acts that would otherwise constitute infringement. Licenses can be express or implied.

Another common defense is *fair use*, a complex and very case-specific defense that requires the court to balance four statutory factors. 17 U.S.C. § 107. These factors tend to favor certain types of defendants, such as reviewers who quote from the book they're discussing in their reviews.

A third defense to consider is *first sale*: once the copyright owner has legitimately sold a copy of a work, she has no further right to restrict the distribution of *that copy*. Thus, the owner of the copy is free to sell it, give it away, lend it, etc.

If there is a direct infringer, next you need to consider whether anyone else is a *secondary infringer*. Three doctrines make these secondary infringers jointly and severally liable with the primary infringers:

- *Vicarious Infringement.* A *vicarious* infringer (a) has the *right and ability to control* the infringing acts and (b) stands to gain a *direct financial benefit* from the infringement. This doctrine is an extension of *respondeat superior*, but it can cover cases in which there is no employment relationship. The classic cases here are the "dance hall cases," in which a nightclub hires a band that includes infringing songs in its set. The band is an independent contractor under agency law, but the nightclub is still liable. The nightclub could have supervised the band more closely, and the nightclub profited because people came to see the band play.

- *Contributory Infringement.* A *contributory* infringer (a) *materially contributes* to the infringement and (b) had *knowledge* of the infringement. A classic example of a contributory infringer is a store that rents high-speed audio cassette duplicating machines and sells large numbers of blank cassettes pre-timed to be the same length as specific major-label albums. The store is directly helping its customers make unauthorized copies, and clearly knows that is what the customers are up to.

- *Inducement.* An *inducing* infringer (a) *distributes a device* (b) with the *object of promoting infringement* (c) as shown by *clear expression or other affirmative steps* taken to foster infringement. This is a souped-up version of contributory infringement (some courts and commentators treat it as a subset of contributory infringement). This is the most recent of the secondary infringement doctrines, and the least developed.

As these doctrines have developed, contributory infringement – but not vicarious or inducement infringement – has been subject to the *substantial non-infringing uses* (or "*Sony*") defense. One who merely supplies a device is not liable for the resulting infringements, so long as the device is capable of substantial non-infringing uses. To understand this defense, think about the cassette store, mentioned above. The high-speed tape duplicators have substantial non-infringing uses (e.g.

a motivational speaker trying to self-distribute her talks). The pre-cut cassette tapes don't: they're designed to be useful for copying popular albums, and nothing else.

Copyright is notable for its strong remedies. The Copyright Act provides for statutory damages of between $200 and $150,000 per work infringed, which the copyright owner may elect in lieu of actual damage (provided she registered the work with the Copyright Office in a timely fashion). The court may also award attorney's fees to a "prevailing party" (which can be either plaintiff of defendant). In addition, injunctions against future infringement are common in copyright cases. Taken together, these remedies mean that the threat of a copyright lawsuit can pose substantial risks for defendants.

A final word of warning. The Copyright Act is studded with surprising definitions, exceptions, and complicated licensing schemes. Musical copyright, in particular, is far more intricate than one would expect – or believe. Internet radio, ringtones, and digital downloads all raise difficult statutory and licensing problems. This chapter could only scratch the surface of these issues, so other than warning you about them, it will not try.

A. The Exclusive Rights

This section explores the most fundamental issue that arises in applying copyright law to computers and the Internet: determining when copyright law is triggered at all. While the Copyright Act was drafted to be technology neutral, it has not always been obvious how some of its terms apply when works are stored and transmitted digitally, rather than in paper books or on vinyl records. *Cartoon Network* considers the scope of the reproduction and public performance rights where digital technologies are concerned; *London-Sire* addresses the distribution right; *Perfect 10* discusses the display right.

There is a further twist. Whichever of the exclusive rights is at stake, the mere fact that a reproduction or a performance has taken place doesn't necessarily tell us who is responsible for it. *Cartoon Network* and *Perfect 10* also take up the question of determining *who* is a direct infringer.

COPYRIGHT ACT [EXCLUSIVE RIGHTS AND FIRST SALE]
Title 17, United States Code

§ 106 – *Exclusive rights in copyrighted works*

Subject to sections 107 through 122, the owner of copyright under this title has the exclusive rights to do and to authorize any of the following:

(1) to reproduce the copyrighted work in copies or phonorecords;

(2) to prepare derivative works based upon the copyrighted work;

(3) to distribute copies or phonorecords of the copyrighted work to the public by sale or other transfer of ownership, or by rental, lease, or lending;

(4) in the case of literary, musical, dramatic, and choreographic works, pantomimes, and motion pictures and other audiovisual works, to perform the copyrighted work publicly;

(5) in the case of literary, musical, dramatic, and choreographic works, pantomimes, and pictorial, graphic, or sculptural works, including the individ-

ual images of a motion picture or other audiovisual work, to display the copyrighted work publicly;

(6) in the case of sound recordings, to perform the copyrighted work publicly by means of a digital audio transmission.

§ 109 – *Limitations on exclusive rights: Effect of transfer of particular copy or phonorecord*

(a) Notwithstanding the provisions of section 106(3), the owner of a particular copy or phonorecord lawfully made under this title, or any person authorized by such owner, is entitled, without the authority of the copyright owner, to sell or otherwise dispose of the possession of that copy or phonorecord. ...

(d) The privileges prescribed by subsections (a) and (c) do not, unless authorized by the copyright owner, extend to any person who has acquired possession of the copy or phonorecord from the copyright owner, by rental, lease, loan, or otherwise, without acquiring ownership of it.

CAPITOL RECORDS, LLC V. REDIGI, INC.
934 F. Supp. 2d 640 (S.D.N.Y. 2013)

Sullivan, District Judge:

Capitol Records, LLC ("Capitol"), the recording label for such classic vinyls as *Frank Sinatra's "Come Fly With Me" and The Beatles' "Yellow Submarine," brings this action against ReDigi Inc. ("ReDigi"), a twenty-first century technology company that touts itself as a "virtual" marketplace for "pre-owned" digital music. What has ensued in a fundamental clash over culture, policy, and copyright law, with Capitol alleging that ReDigi's web-based service amounts to copyright infringement in violation of the Copyright Act of 1976, 17 U.S.C. § 101 et seq. Now before the Court are Capitol's motion for partial summary judgment and ReDigi's motion for summary judgment, both filed pursuant to Federal Rule of Civil Procedure 56. Because this is a court of law and not a congressional subcommittee or technology blog, the issues are narrow, technical, and purely legal. Thus, for the reasons that follow, Capitol's motion is granted and ReDigi's motion is denied.

I. BACKGROUND

A. Facts

ReDigi markets itself as "the world's first and only online marketplace for digital used music." Launched on October 13, 2011, ReDigi's website invites users to "sell their legally acquired digital music files, and buy used digital music from others at a fraction of the price currently available on iTunes." Thus, much like used record stores, ReDigi permits its users to recoup value on their unwanted music. Unlike used record stores, however, ReDigi's sales take place entirely in the digital domain.

To sell music on ReDigi's website, a user must first download ReDigi's "Media Manager" to his computer. Once installed, Media Manager analyzes the user's computer to build a list of digital music files eligible for sale. A file is eligible only if it was purchased on iTunes or from another ReDigi user; music downloaded from a CD or other file-sharing website is ineligible for sale. After this validation process, Media Manager continually runs on the user's computer and attached devices to ensure that the user has not retained music that has been sold or uploaded for sale. However, Media Manager cannot detect copies stored in other locations. If a copy is detected, Media Manager prompts the user to delete the file. The file is not deleted automatically or involuntarily, though ReDigi's policy is to suspend the accounts of users who refuse to comply.

After the list is built, a user may upload any of his eligible files to ReDigi's "Cloud Locker," an ethereal moniker for what is, in fact, merely a remote server in Arizona. ReDigi's upload process is a source of contention between the parties. ReDigi asserts that the process involves "migrating" a user's file, packet by packet – "analogous to a train" – from the user's computer to the Cloud Locker so that data does not exist in two places at any one time.[2]

Capitol asserts that, semantics aside, ReDigi's upload process "necessarily involves copying" a file from the user's computer to the Cloud Locker. Regardless, at the end of the process, the digital music file is located in the Cloud Locker and not on the user's computer. Moreover, Media Manager deletes any additional copies of the file on the user's computer and connected devices.

Once uploaded, a digital music file undergoes a second analysis to verify eligibility. If ReDigi determines that the file has not been tampered with or offered for sale by another user, the file is stored in the Cloud Locker, and the user is given the option of simply storing and streaming the file for personal use or offering it for sale in ReDigi's marketplace. If a user chooses to sell his digital music file, his access to the file is terminated and transferred to the new owner at the time of purchase. Thereafter, the new owner can store the file in the Cloud Locker, stream it, sell it, or download it to her computer and other devices. No money changes hands in these transactions. (Instead, users buy music with credits they either purchased from ReDigi or acquired from other sales. ReDigi credits, once acquired, cannot be exchanged for money. Instead, they can only be used to purchase additional music.

...

Finally, ReDigi earns a fee for every transaction. ReDigi's website prices digital music files at fifty-nine to seventy-nine cents each. When users purchase a file, with credits, 20% of the sale price is allocated to the seller, 20% goes to an "escrow" fund for the artist, and 60% is retained by ReDigi. ...

III. DISCUSSION

Section 106 of the Copyright Act grants "the owner of copyright under this title" certain "exclusive rights," including the right "to reproduce the copyrighted work in copies or phonorecords," "to distribute copies or phonorecords of the copyrighted work to the public by sale or other transfer of ownership," and to publicly perform and display certain copyrighted works. ...

A. Infringement of Capitol's Copyrights

To state a claim for copyright infringement, a plaintiff must establish that it owns a valid copyright in the work at issue and that the defendant violated one of the exclusive rights the plaintiff holds in the work. It is undisputed that Capitol owns copyrights in a number of the recordings sold on ReDigi's website. It is also undisputed that Capitol did not approve the reproduction or distribution of its copyrighted recordings on ReDigi's website. Thus, if digital music files are "reproduce[d]" and "distribute[d]" on ReDigi's website within the meaning of the Copyright Act, Capitol's copyrights have been infringed.

---

2. A train was only one of many analogies used to describe ReDigi's service. At oral argument, the device was likened to the Star Trek transporter – "Beam me up, Scotty" – and Willy Wonka's teleportation device, Wonkavision.

1. Reproduction Rights

Courts have consistently held that the unauthorized duplication of digital music files over the Internet infringes a copyright owner's exclusive right to reproduce. *See, e.g., A & M Records, Inc. v. Napster, Inc.*, 239 F.3d 1004, 1014 (9th Cir. 2001). However, courts have not previously addressed whether the unauthorized transfer of a digital music file over the Internet – where only one file exists before and after the transfer – constitutes reproduction within the meaning of the Copyright Act. The Court holds that it does.

The Copyright Act provides that a copyright owner has the exclusive right "to reproduce the copyrighted work in ... phonorecords." 17 U.S.C. § 106(1). Copyrighted works are defined to include, *inter alia*, "sound recordings," which are "works that result from the fixation of a series of musical, spoken, or other sounds." *Id.* § 101. Such works are distinguished from their material embodiments. These include phonorecords, which are the "*material objects* in which sounds ... are fixed by any method now known or later developed, and from which the sounds can be perceived, reproduced, or otherwise communicated, either directly or with the aid of a machine or device." *Id.* § 101 (emphasis added). Thus, the plain text of the Copyright Act makes clear that reproduction occurs when a copyrighted work is fixed in a new *material object*.

Courts that have dealt with infringement on peer-to-peer ("P2P") file-sharing systems provide valuable guidance on the application of this right in the digital domain. For instance, in *London–Sire Records, Inc. v. John Doe 1*, the court addressed whether users of P2P software violated copyright owners' distribution rights. 542 F. Supp. 2d 153, 166 & n.16 (D. Mass. 2008). Citing the "material object" requirement, the court expressly differentiated between the copyrighted work – or digital music file – and the phonorecord – or "appropriate segment of the hard disk" that the file would be embodied in following its transfer. Specifically,

> [w]hen a user on a [P2P] network downloads a song from another user, he receives into his computer a digital sequence representing the sound recording. That sequence is magnetically encoded on a segment of his hard disk (or likewise written on other media). With the right hardware and software, the downloader can use the magnetic sequence to *reproduce* the sound recording. The electronic file (or, perhaps more accurately, the appropriate segment of the hard disk) is therefore a "phonorecord" within the meaning of the statute.

Id. (emphasis added). Accordingly, when a user downloads a digital music file or "digital sequence" to his "hard disk," the file is "reproduce[d]" on a new phonorecord within the meaning of the Copyright Act.

This understanding is, of course, confirmed by the laws of physics. It is simply impossible that the same "material object" can be transferred over the Internet. Thus, logically, the court in *London–Sire* noted that the Internet transfer of a file results in a material object being "created elsewhere at its finish." *Id.* at 173. Because the reproduction right is necessarily implicated when a copyrighted work is embodied in a new material object, and because digital music files must be embodied in a new material object following their transfer over the Internet, the Court determines that the embodiment of a digital music file on a new hard disk is a reproduction within the meaning of the Copyright Act.

This finding holds regardless of whether one or multiple copies of the file exist. *London–Sire*, like all of the P2P cases, obviously concerned multiple copies of one digital music file. But that distinction is immaterial under the plain language of the Copyright Act. Simply put, it is the creation of a *new* material object and not an *additional* material object that defines the reproduction right. The dictionary defines "reproduction" to mean, *inter alia*, "to produce again" or "to cause to exist again *or* anew." *See Merriam-Webster Collegiate Edition* 994 (10th ed. 1998) (emphasis added). Significantly, it is not defined as "to produce again while the original exists." Thus, the right "to reproduce the copyrighted work in ... phonorecords" is implicated whenever a sound recording is fixed in a new material object, regardless of whether the sound recording remains fixed in the original material object.

Given this finding, the Court concludes that ReDigi's service infringes Capitol's reproduction rights under any description of the technology. ReDigi stresses that it "migrates" a file from a user's computer to its Cloud Locker, so that the same file is transferred to the ReDigi server and no copying occurs. However, even if that were the case, the fact that a file has moved from one material object – the user's computer – to another – the ReDigi server – means that a reproduction has occurred. Similarly, when a ReDigi user downloads a new purchase from the ReDigi website to her computer, yet another reproduction is created. It is beside the point that the original phonorecord no longer exists. It matters only that a new phonorecord has been created.

ReDigi struggles to avoid this conclusion by pointing to *C.M. Paula Co. v. Logan,* a 1973 case from the Northern District of Texas where the defendant used chemicals to lift images off of greeting cards and place them on plaques for resale. 355 F. Supp. 189, 190 (N.D. Tex. 1973). The court determined that infringement did not occur because "should defendant desire to make one hundred ceramic plaques ... , defendant would be required to purchase one hundred separate ... prints." *C.M. Paula,* 355 F. Supp. at 191. ReDigi argues that, like the defendant in *C.M. Paula,* its users must purchase a song on iTunes in order to sell a song on ReDigi. Therefore, no "duplication" occurs. ReDigi's argument is unavailing. Ignoring the questionable merits of the court's holding in *C.M. Paula,* ReDigi's service is distinguishable from the process in that case. There, the copyrighted print, or material object, was lifted from the greeting card and transferred in toto to the ceramic tile; no new material object was created. By contrast, ReDigi's service by necessity creates a new material object when a digital music file is either uploaded to or downloaded from the Cloud Locker.

ReDigi also argues that the Court's conclusion would lead to "irrational" outcomes, as it would render illegal any movement of copyrighted files on a hard drive, including relocating files between directories and defragmenting. However, this argument is nothing more than a red herring. As Capitol has conceded, such reproduction is almost certainly protected under other doctrines or defenses, and is not relevant to the instant motion.

Accordingly, the Court finds that, absent the existence of an affirmative defense, the sale of digital music files on ReDigi's website infringes Capitol's exclusive right of reproduction.

2. Distribution Rights

In addition to the reproduction right, a copyright owner also has the exclusive right "to distribute copies or phonorecords of the copyrighted work to the public by sale or other transfer of ownership." 17 U.S.C. § 106(3). Like the court in *London-Sire,* the Court agrees that "[a]n electronic file transfer is plainly within the sort of transaction that § 106(3) was intended to reach [and] ... fit[s] within the definition of 'distribution' of a phonorecord." *London-Sire,* 542 F. Supp. 2d at 173–74. For that reason, "courts have not hesitated to find copyright infringement by distribution in cases of file-sharing or electronic transmission of copyrighted works." *Arista Records LLC v. Greubel*, 453 F. Supp. 2d 961, 968 (N.D. Tex. 2006) (collecting cases); Indeed, in *New York Times Co., Inc. v. Tasini*, the Supreme Court stated it was "clear" that an online news database violated authors' distribution rights by selling electronic copies of their articles for download. 533 U.S. 483, 498 (2001).

There is no dispute that sales occurred on ReDigi's website. Capitol has established that it was able to buy more than one-hundred of its own recordings on ReDigi's webite, and ReDigi itself compiled a list of its completed sales of Capitol's recordings. ReDigi, in fact, does not contest that distribution occurs on its website – it only asserts that the distribution is protected by the fair use and first sale defenses.

Accordingly, the Court concludes that, absent the existence of an affirmative defense, the sale of digital music files on ReDigi's website infringes Capitol's exclusive right of distribution.[6] ...

B. Affirmative Defenses

Having concluded that sales on ReDigi's website infringe Capitol's exclusive rights of reproduction and distribution, the Court turns to whether the fair use or first sale defenses excuse that infringement. For the reasons set forth below, the Court determines that they do not.

2. First Sale

The first sale defense, a common law principle recognized in *Bobbs–Merrill Co. v. Straus*, 210 U.S. 339, 350 (1908) and now codified at Section 109(a) of the Copyright Act, provides that:

> Notwithstanding the provisions of section 106(3), the owner of a particular copy or phonorecord lawfully made under this title, or any person authorized by such owner, is entitled, without the authority of the copyright owner, to sell or otherwise dispose of the possession of that copy or phonorecord.

17 U.S.C. § 109. Under the first sale defense, "once the copyright owner places a copyrighted item [here, a phonorecord] in the stream of commerce by selling it, he has exhausted his exclusive statutory right to control its distribution." *Quality King Distribs., Inc. v. L'anza Research Int'l, Inc.*, 523 U.S. 135, 152 (1998); *see Kirtsaeng v. John Wiley & Sons, Inc.*, 133 S.Ct. 1351, 1354–55 (2013). ...

As an initial matter, it should be noted that the fair use [*Ed*: presumably "first sale"] defense is, by its own terms, limited to assertions of the *distribution right*. Because the Court has concluded that ReDigi's service violates Capitol's reproduc-

---

6   Capitol argues that ReDigi also violated its distribution rights simply by making Capitol's recordings available for sale to the public, regardless of whether a sale occurred. However, a number of courts, including one in this district, have cast significant doubt on this "make available" theory of distribution. *See, e.g., Elektra Entm't Grp., Inc. v. Barker*, 551 F. Supp. 2d 234, 243 (S.D.N.Y. 2008) ("[T]he support in the case law for the "make available" theory of liability is quite limited."); *London–Sire*, 542 F. Supp. 2d at 169 ("[T]he defendants cannot be liable for violating the plaintiffs' distribution right unless a 'distribution' actually occurred."). In any event, because the Court concludes that actual sales on ReDigi's website infringed Capitol's distribution right, it does not reach this additional theory of liability.

tion right, the first sale defense does not apply to ReDigi's infringement of those rights.

In addition, the first sale doctrine does not protect ReDigi's distribution of Capitol's copyrighted works. This is because, as an unlawful reproduction, a digital music file sold on ReDigi is not "lawfully made under this title." Moreover, the statute protects only distribution by "the owner of a *particular* copy or phonorecord ... of *that* copy or phonorecord." Here, a ReDigi user owns the phonorecord that was created when she purchased and downloaded a song from iTunes to her hard disk. But to sell that song on ReDigi, she must produce a new phonorecord on the ReDigi server. Because it is therefore impossible for the user to sell her "particular" phonorecord on ReDigi, the first sale statute cannot provide a defense. Put another way, the first sale defense is limited to material items, like records, that the copyright owner put into the stream of commerce. Here, ReDigi is not distributing such material items; rather, it is distributing *reproductions* of the copyrighted code embedded in new material objects, namely, the ReDigi server in Arizona and its users' hard drives. The first sale defense does not cover this any more than it covered the sale of cassette recordings of vinyl records in a bygone era.

Rejecting such a conclusion, ReDigi argues that, because "technological change has rendered its literal terms ambiguous, the Copyright Act must be construed in light of [its] basic purpose," namely, to incentivize creative work for the "ultimate[ ] ... cause of promoting broad public availability of literature, music, and the other arts." *Sony Corp. of America v. Universal City Studios, Inc*, 464 U.S. 417, 432 (1984). Thus, ReDigi asserts that refusal to apply the first sale doctrine to its service would grant Capitol "a Court sanctioned extension of rights under the [C]opyright [A]ct ... which is against policy, and should not be endorsed by this Court."

The Court disagrees. ReDigi effectively requests that the Court amend the statute to achieve ReDigi's broader policy goals – goals that happen to advance ReDigi's economic interests. However, ReDigi's argument fails for two reasons. First, while technological change may have rendered Section 109(a) unsatisfactory to many contemporary observers and consumers, it has not rendered it ambiguous. The statute plainly applies to the lawful owner's "particular" phonorecord, a phonorecord that by definition cannot be uploaded and sold on ReDigi's website. Second, amendment of the Copyright Act in line with ReDigi's proposal is a legislative prerogative that courts are unauthorized and ill suited to attempt.

Nor are the policy arguments as straightforward or uncontested as ReDigi suggests. For instance, the United States Copyright Office stated that "the impact of the [first sale] doctrine on copyright owners [is] limited in the off-line world by a number of factors, including geography and the gradual degradation of books and analog works." USCO, Library of Cong., DMCA Section 104 Report at xi (2001). Specifically,

> [p]hysical copies of works degrade with time and use, making used copies less desirable than new ones. Digital information does not degrade, and can be reproduced perfectly on a recipient's computer. The "used" copy is just as desirable as (in fact, is indistinguishable from) a new copy of the same work. Time, space, effort and cost no longer act as barriers to the movement of copies, since digital copies can be transmitted nearly instantaneously anywhere in the world with minimal effort and negligible cost. The need to transport physical copies of

works, which acts as a natural brake on the effect of resales on the copyright owner's market, no longer exists in the realm of digital transmissions. The ability of such "used" copies to compete for market share with new copies is thus far greater in the digital world.

Id. at 82–83 (footnotes omitted). Thus, while ReDigi mounts attractive policy arguments, they are not as one-sided as it contends.

Finally, ReDigi feebly argues that the Court's reading of Section 109(a) would in effect exclude digital works from the meaning of the statute. That is not the case. Section 109(a) still protects a lawful owner's sale of her "particular" phonorecord, be it a computer hard disk, iPod, or other memory device onto which the file was originally downloaded. While this limitation clearly presents obstacles to resale that are different from, and perhaps even more onerous than, those involved in the resale of CDs and cassettes, the limitation is hardly absurd – the first sale doctrine was enacted in a world where the ease and speed of data transfer could not have been imagined. There are many reasons, some discussed herein, for why such physical limitations may be desirable. It is left to Congress, and not this Court, to deem them outmoded.

Accordingly, the Court concludes that the first sale defense does not permit sales of digital music files on ReDigi's website. ...

QUESTIONS

1. Kirk uses a starship's replicator to make an identical copy of a book. Is this a reproduction, a distribution, or both? Spock uses a starship's transporter to move a book from the ship to a nearby planet, where Uhura picks it up. Is this a reproduction, a distribution, or both? (If you like your metaphors more low-tech, substitute "photocopier" for "replicator" and "FedEx" for "transporter.") In light of these answers, how can a sale on ReDigi be *both* a reproduction and a distribution? Shouldn't it be one or other? Is ReDigi some kind of crazy transporticator, or have our offline metaphors simply broken down in the digital world?

2. What do you think of the RIAA's "making available" theory (see footnote 6)? It was unnecessary here, but are there cases where copyright owners could prove that the defendant offered a work for download but might have trouble showing that anyone downloaded it?

3. What does *ReDigi* do to first sale in a world where people buy media as downloads rather than on dead trees and shiny plastic discs? What might first sale even look like for iTunes downloads? Should first sale apply to streaming services like Spotify and Netflix?

NOTE ON RAM COPIES

An influential early case, *MAI Systems v. Peak Computer Inc.*, 991 F.2d 511 (9th Cir. 1993), held that running a computer program without the copyright owner's permission infringed the reproduction right. The act of loading the program into the computer's memory created a new "copy" by fixing the program in a "material object[ ] ... from which the work can be perceived, reproduced, or otherwise communicated" (in the language of the Copyright Act). This result has become known as the "RAM copy doctrine": copies in a computer's memory count for copyright purposes, even if they vanish when the computer is turned off. *MAI* is unpopular with academic commentators, but it has been consistently followed by the courts.

A more recent case, *Cartoon Network LP, LLLP v. CSC Holdings, Inc.*, 536 F.3d 121 (2nd Cir. 2008), distinguished *MAI* on the grounds that it said nothing about how *long* a work must be present in a medium. *Cartoon Network* involved a "buffer" used as part of a process for copying streaming video from a cable television signal to individual hard drives. Every 1.2 seconds, the buffer was erased and filled with the next portion of the video. *Held*, no infringing "copies":

> And unlike the data in cases like *MAI Systems*, which remained embodied in the computer's RAM memory until the user turned the computer off, each bit of data here is rapidly and automatically overwritten as soon as it is processed. ... Given that the data reside in no buffer for more than 1.2 seconds before being automatically overwritten ... we believe that the copyrighted works here are not "embodied" in the buffers for a period of more than transitory duration, and are therefore not "fixed" in the buffers.

QUESTIONS

1. In light of *ReDigi*, *MAI*, and *Cartoon Network*, which of the following could be an infringing "reproduction?" (*Hint*: identify the "material object" in from which the work can be communicated, or explain why there is none, and then consider whether any copies could be be described as transitory under *Cartoon Network*.)

   - Reading a book?
   - Photocopying a chapter from a textbook?
   - Singing a song in the shower?
   - Running a computer program like Microsoft Word?
   - Burning a set of MP3s to a CD?
   - Ripping a CD to a computer?
   - Downloading (using right-click "save as") a video file?
   - Browsing to a web page that contains pictures?
   - Watching a YouTube video on a cell phone?

2. If copies on computers are "reproductions" subject to copyright law, how does that affect the relative importance of copyright law in the online world as opposed to the offline one? If more activities are subject to copyright law, will copyright doctrines need to be adjusted to reflect the law's wider reach?

PERFECT 10, INC. V. AMAZON.COM, INC.
508 F.3d 1146 (9th Cir. 2007)

Ikuta, Circuit Judge:

In this appeal, we consider a copyright owner's efforts to stop an Internet search engine from facilitating access to infringing images. Perfect 10, Inc. sued Google Inc., for infringing Perfect 10's copyrighted photographs of nude models, among other claims. ... The district court preliminarily enjoined Google from creating and publicly displaying thumbnail versions of Perfect 10's images, but did not enjoin Google from linking to third-party websites that display infringing full-size versions of Perfect 10's images. ... Perfect 10 and Google both appeal the district court's order. ...

I. BACKGROUND ...

Google operates a search engine, a software program that automatically accesses thousands of websites (collections of webpages) and indexes them within a database stored on Google's computers. When a Google user accesses the Google website and types in a search query, Google's software searches its database for websites responsive to that search query. Google then sends relevant information from its index of websites to the user's computer. Google's search engines can provide results in the form of text, images, or videos.

The Google search engine that provides responses in the form of images is called "Google Image Search." In response to a search query, Google Image Search identifies text in its database responsive to the query and then communicates to users the images associated with the relevant text. Google's software cannot recognize and index the images themselves. Google Image Search provides search results as a webpage of small images called "thumbnails," which are stored in Google's servers. The thumbnail images are reduced, lower-resolution versions of full-sized images stored on third-party computers.

When a user clicks on a thumbnail image, the user's browser program interprets HTML instructions on Google's webpage. These HTML instructions direct the user's browser to cause a rectangular area (a "window") to appear on the user's computer screen. The window has two separate areas of information. The browser fills the top section of the screen with information from the Google webpage, including the thumbnail image and text. The HTML instructions also give the user's browser the address of the website publisher's computer that stores the full-size version of the thumbnail. By following the HTML instructions to access the third-party webpage, the user's browser connects to the website publisher's computer, downloads the full-size image, and makes the image appear at the bottom of the window on the user's screen. Google does not store the images that fill this lower part of the window and does not communicate the images to the user; Google simply provides HTML instructions directing a user's browser to access a third-party website. However, the top part of the window (containing the information from the Google webpage) appears to frame and comment on the bottom part of the window. Thus, the user's window appears to be filled with a single integrated presentation of the full-size image, but it is actually an image from a third-party website framed by information from Google's website. The process by which the webpage directs a user's browser to incorporate content from different computers into a single window is referred to as "in-line linking." The term "framing" refers to the process by which information from one computer appears to frame and annotate the in-line linked content from another computer. ...

Perfect 10 markets and sells copyrighted images of nude models. Among other enterprises, it operates a subscription website on the Internet. Subscribers pay a monthly fee to view Perfect10 images in a "members' area" of the site. Subscribers must use a password to log into the members' area. Google does not include these password-protected images from the members' area in Google's index or database. Perfect 10 has also licensed Fonestarz Media Limited to sell and distribute Perfect 10's reduced-size copyrighted images for download and use on cell phones.

Some website publishers republish Perfect 10's images on the Internet without authorization. Once this occurs, Google's search engine may automatically index the webpages containing these images and provide thumbnail versions of images in response to user inquiries. When a user clicks on the thumbnail image returned by Google's search engine, the user's browser accesses the third-party webpage and in-line links to the full-sized infringing image stored on the website publisher's computer. This image appears, in its original context, on the lower portion of the window on the user's computer screen framed by information from Google's webpage. ...

III. DIRECT INFRINGEMENT

Perfect 10 claims that Google's search engine program directly infringes two exclusive rights granted to copyright holders: its display rights and its distribution rights. Plaintiffs must satisfy two requirements to present a prima facie case of direct infringement: (1) they must show ownership of the allegedly infringed material and (2) they must demonstrate that the alleged infringers violate at least one exclusive right granted to copyright holders under 17 U.S.C. § 106. Even if a plaintiff satisfies these two requirements and makes a prima facie case of direct infringement, the defendant may avoid liability if it can establish that its use of the images is a "fair use" as set forth in 17 U.S.C. § 107.

Perfect 10's ownership of at least some of the images at issue is not disputed.

The district court held that Perfect 10 was likely to prevail in its claim that Google violated Perfect 10's display right with respect to the infringing thumbnails. However, the district court concluded that Perfect 10 was not likely to prevail on its claim that Google violated either Perfect 10's display or distribution right with respect to its full-size infringing images. We review these rulings for an abuse of discretion.

A. Display Right ...

We have not previously addressed the question when a computer displays a copyrighted work for purposes of section 106(5). Section 106(5) states that a copyright owner has the exclusive right "to display the copyrighted work publicly." The Copyright Act explains that "display" means "to show a copy of it, either directly or by means of a film, slide, television image, or any other device or process. . . ." 17 U.S.C. § 101. Section 101 defines "copies" as "material objects, other than phonorecords, in which a work is fixed by any method now known or later developed, and from which the work can be perceived, reproduced, or otherwise communicated, either directly or with the aid of a machine or device." *Id.* Finally, the Copyright Act provides that "[a] work is 'fixed' in a tangible medium of expression when its embodiment in a copy or phonorecord, by or under the authority of the author, is sufficiently permanent or stable to permit it to be perceived, reproduced, or otherwise communicated for a period of more than transitory duration." *Id.*

We must now apply these definitions to the facts of this case. A photographic image is a work that is "'fixed' in a tangible medium of expression," for purposes of the Copyright Act, when embodied (i.e., stored) in a computer's server (or hard disk, or other storage device). The image stored in the computer is the "copy" of the work for purposes of copyright law. *See MAI Sys. Corp. v. Peak Computer, Inc.,* 991 F.2d 511, 517–18 (9th Cir.1993) ... The computer owner shows a copy "by means of a . . . device or process" when the owner uses the computer to fill the computer screen with the photographic image stored on that computer, or by communicating the stored image electronically to another person's computer. 17 U.S.C. § 101. In sum, based on the plain language of the statute, a person displays a photographic image by using a computer to fill a computer screen with a copy of the photographic image fixed in the computer's memory. There is no dispute that Google's computers store thumbnail versions of Perfect 10's copyrighted images and communicate copies of those thumbnails to Google's users. Therefore, Perfect10 has made a prima facie case that Google's communication of its stored thumbnail images directly infringes Perfect 10's display right.

[The court's analysis of Google's fair use defense to infringement of the thumbnail images is excerpted in Section III *infra.*]

Google does not, however, display a copy of full-size infringing photographic images for purposes of the Copyright Act when Google frames in-line linked images that appear on a user's computer screen. Because Google's computers do not store the photographic images, Google does not have a copy of the images for purposes of the Copyright Act. In other words, Google does not have any "material objects . . . in which a work is fixed . . . and from which the work can be perceived, reproduced, or otherwise communicated" and thus cannot communicate a copy. 17 U.S.C. § 101.

Instead of communicating a copy of the image, Google provides HTML instructions that direct a user's browser to a website publisher's computer that stores the full-size photographic image. Providing these HTML instructions is not equivalent to showing a copy. First, the HTML instructions are lines of text, not a photographic image. Second, HTML instructions do not themselves cause infringing images to appear on the user's computer screen. The HTML merely gives the address of the image to the user's browser. The browser then interacts with the computer that stores the infringing image. It is this interaction that causes an infringing image to appear on the user's computer screen. Google may facilitate the user's access to infringing images. However, such assistance raises only contributory liability issues and does not constitute direct infringement of the copyright owner's display rights.

Perfect 10 argues that Google displays a copy of the full-size images by framing the full-size images, which gives the impression that Google is showing the image within a single Google webpage. While in-line linking and framing may cause some computer users to believe they are viewing a single Google webpage, the Copyright Act, unlike the Trademark Act, does not protect a copyright holder against acts that cause consumer confusion. ...

B. Distribution Right

The district court also concluded that Perfect 10 would not likely prevail on its claim that Google directly infringed Perfect 10's right to distribute its full-size images. The district court reasoned that distribution requires an "actual dissemination" of a copy. Because Google did not communicate the full-size images to the user's computer, Google did not distribute these images.

Again, the district court's conclusion on this point is consistent with the language of the Copyright Act. Section 106(3) provides that the copyright owner has the exclusive right "to distribute copies or phonorecords of the copyrighted work to the public by sale or other transfer of ownership, or by rental, lease, or lending." 17 U.S.C. § 106(3). As noted, "copies" means "material objects . . . in which a work is fixed." 17 U.S.C. § 101. The Supreme Court has indicated that in the electronic context, copies may be distributed electronically. *See N.Y. Times Co. v. Tasini*, 533 U.S. 483, 498 (2001) ... Google's search engine communicates HTML instructions that tell a user's browser where to find full-size images on a website publisher's computer, but Google does not itself distribute copies of the infringing photographs. It is the website publisher's computer that distributes copies of the images by transmitting the photographic image electronically to the user's computer. ...

Accordingly, the district court correctly concluded that Perfect 10 does not have a likelihood of success in proving that Google violates Perfect 10's distribution rights with respect to full-size images.

QUESTIONS

1. The works here are pornographic images copyrighted by Perfect 10. Note that Google found these images not on Perfect 10's website, but on the websites of companies allegedly using those images without permission (call them the "Bootleg Websites"). Draw a picture of the relationship between Google, the Bootleg Websites, and Google users. Illustrate where the thumbnails and the full-size images come from when a user sees one of them on Google Image Search.

2. Visit a few of your favorite blogs and figure out where their images are coming from. Try right-clicking on an image; try also using the "view source" command from your browser's pull-down menu. How did the blog's creator decide whether to host her own images, or to link to images hosted elsewhere?

3. Who is a direct infringer of the thumbnails: the Bootleg Websites, Google, or the users? More than one of the above?

4. What is Perfect 10's theory of Google's liability for direct infringement of the full-size images, and why does the court reject it? Are the Bootleg Websites direct infringers? What about the users?

5. Is *Perfect 10* right to place so much emphasis on the underlying technical details and so little emphasis on user experience? When you're browsing the web, do you ordinarily pay attention to which server particular images come from?

6. *Perfect 10* illustrates the overlap of the exclusive rights. It discusses the display and distribution rights. Is the reproduction right also implicated by Google's actions? The derivative works right? The performance right?

AMERICAN BROADCASTING CO. V. AEREO, INC.
134 S. Ct. 2498 (2014)

Justice Breyer delivered the opinion of the Court.

The Copyright Act of 1976 gives a copyright owner the "exclusive righ[t]" to "perform the copyrighted work publicly." 17 U.S.C. § 106(4). The Act's Transmit Clause defines that exclusive right as including the right to

> transmit or otherwise communicate a performance ... of the [copyrighted] work ... to the public, by means of any device or process, whether the members of the public capable of receiving the performance ... receive it in the same place or in separate places and at the same time or at different times.

§ 101. We must decide whether respondent Aereo, Inc., infringes this exclusive right by selling its subscribers a technologically complex service that allows them to watch television programs over the Internet at about the same time as the programs are broadcast over the air. We conclude that it does.

I.

A.

For a monthly fee, Aereo offers subscribers broadcast television programming over the Internet, virtually as the programming is being broadcast. Much of this programming is made up of copyrighted works. Aereo neither owns the copyright in those works nor holds a license from the copyright owners to perform those works publicly.

Aereo's system is made up of servers, transcoders, and thousands of dime-sized antennas housed in a central warehouse. It works roughly as follows: First, when a subscriber wants to watch a show that is currently being broadcast, he visits Aereo's website and selects, from a list of the local programming, the show he wishes to see.

Second, one of Aereo's servers selects an antenna, which it dedicates to the use of that subscriber (and that subscriber alone) for the duration of the selected show. A server then tunes the antenna to the over-the-air broadcast carrying the show. The antenna begins to receive the broadcast, and an Aereo transcoder translates the signals received into data that can be transmitted over the Internet.

Third, rather than directly send the data to the subscriber, a server saves the data in a subscriber-specific folder on Aereo's hard drive. In other words, Aereo's system creates a subscriber-specific copy – that is, a "personal" copy – of the subscriber's program of choice.

Fourth, once several seconds of programming have been saved, Aereo's server begins to stream the saved copy of the show to the subscriber over the Internet. (The subscriber may instead direct Aereo to stream the program at a later time, but that aspect of Aereo's service is not before us.) The subscriber can watch the streamed program on the screen of his personal computer, tablet, smart phone, Internet-connected television, or other Internet-connected device. The streaming continues, a mere few seconds behind the over-the-air broadcast, until the subscriber has received the entire show.

Aereo emphasizes that the data that its system streams to each subscriber are the data from his own personal copy, made from the broadcast signals received by the particular antenna allotted to him. Its system does not transmit data saved in one subscriber's folder to any other subscriber. When two subscribers wish to watch the same program, Aereo's system activates two separate antennas and saves two separate copies of the program in two separate folders. It then streams the show to the subscribers through two separate transmissions — each from the subscriber's personal copy.

B.

Petitioners are television producers, marketers, distributors, and broadcasters who own the copyrights in many of the programs that Aereo's system streams to its subscribers. They brought suit against Aereo for copyright infringement in Federal District Court. They sought a preliminary injunction, arguing that Aereo was infringing their right to "perform" their works "publicly," as the Transmit Clause defines those terms.

The District Court denied the preliminary injunction. Relying on prior Circuit precedent, a divided panel of the Second Circuit affirmed. In the Second Circuit's view, Aereo does not perform publicly within the meaning of the Transmit Clause because it does not transmit "to the public." Rather, each time Aereo streams a program to a subscriber, it sends a *private* transmission that is available only to that subscriber. The Second Circuit denied rehearing en banc, over the dissent of two judges. We granted certiorari.

II.

[The core of Justice Breyer's opinion for the Court relates to the history of cable regulation, and would not be informative to reproduce at length here. The Court summarized its conclusion thus:]

> This history makes clear that Aereo is not simply an equipment provider. Rather, Aereo, and not just its subscribers, "perform[s]" (or "transmit[s]"). Aereo's activities are substantially similar to those of the [cable] companies that Congress amended the [Copyright] Act to reach. Aereo sells a service that allows subscribers to watch television programs, many of which are copyrighted, almost as they are being broadcast. In providing this service, Aereo uses its own equipment, housed in a centralized warehouse, outside of its users' homes.

[In a later portion of the opinion, the Court gave some guidance on the interpretation of "perform" and "publicly," and some thoughts about the implications of the holding for other technologies.]

> Aereo and many of its supporting amici argue that to apply the Transmit Clause to Aereo's conduct will impose copyright liability on other technologies, including new technologies, that Congress could not possibly have wanted to reach. We agree that Congress, while intending the Transmit Clause to apply broadly to cable companies and their equivalents, did not intend to discourage or to control the emergence or use of different kinds of technologies. But we do not believe that our limited holding today will have that effect. ...
>
> For one thing, the history of cable broadcast transmissions that led to the enactment of the Transmit Clause informs our conclusion that Aereo "perform [s]," but it does not determine whether different kinds of providers in different contexts also "perform." For another, an entity only transmits a performance when it communicates contemporaneously perceptible images and sounds of a work. See Brief for Respondent 31 ("If a distributor sells multiple copies of a digital video disc by mail to consumers, its distribution of the DVDs merely makes it possible for the recipients to perform the work themselves – it is not a device or process by which the *distributor* publicly performs the work).
>
> Further, we have interpreted the term "the public" to apply to a group of individuals acting as ordinary members of the public who pay primarily to watch broadcast television programs, many of which are copyrighted. We have said that it does not extend to those who act as owners or possessors of the relevant product. And we have not considered whether the public performance right is infringed when the user of a service pays primarily for something other than the transmission of copyrighted works, such as the remote storage of content. See Brief for United States as Amicus Curiae 31 (distinguishing cloud-based storage services because they "offer consumers more numerous and convenient means of playing back copies that the consumers have already lawfully acquired"). In addition, an entity does not transmit to the public if it does not

transmit to a substantial number of people outside of a family and its social circle. ...

We cannot now answer more precisely how the Transmit Clause or other provisions of the Copyright Act will apply to technologies not before us. We agree with the Solicitor General that "[q]uestions involving cloud computing, [remote storage] DVRs, and other novel issues not before the Court, as to which Congress has not plainly marked the course," should await a case in which they are squarely presented." And we note that, to the extent commercial actors or other interested entities may be concerned with the relationship between the development and use of such technologies and the Copyright Act, they are of course free to seek action from Congress.

MUSIC LOCKER PROBLEM

Tune.ly, Thunderhead, and Bleeper are three cloud-based "music locker" services. All three of them promise to let music fans enjoy their music from any computer. Behind the scenes, however, the three work somewhat differently:

- Tune.ly is a music file locker. Users can upload tracks to their Tune.ly accounts that then be downloaded from Tune.ly's servers to any device from which the user signs in with her username and password. The tracks are not available to other users; each user's account is only available to her, and Tune.ly stores a separate copy of each track for each user.

- Thunderhead is a music-matching streaming service. A feature called Thunderhead Match automatically scans the user's hard drive, looking for tracks that Thunderhead hasn't already seen. If it finds a new track, it uploads a copy of that track to Thunderhead's servers. Now the user can stream the track to any device from which she logs in with her Thunderhead username and password. If Thunderhead Match finds a track that is already on Thunderhead's servers, it does not re-upload it. Instead, it flags the track as being available to the user; she can then stream it to any device from which she logs in.

- Bleeper markets itself as a way for users to listen to family-friendly "bleeped" versions of music, even when it has not been released by the copyright owner in a "clean" version. Bleeper buys a CD for each customer who wants access to an album and stores the CDs in a huge array. Each customer also has a dedicated CD player. When a customer wants to listen to a track, Bleeper's robots retrieve that customer's CD containing the track, put it in her dedicated CD player, and stream the audio to her over the Internet — automatically bleeping out the bad words.

You work for the Recording Industry Association of America. The RIAA is concerned about Tune.ly, Thunderhead, and Bleeper. Prepare a report that explains which of the exclusive rights are implicated by these services, and how.

B. Licenses

Licensing is a major part of the copyright system. Consider the contract an author signs with a publisher. In exchange for an advance and royalties, the author gives a license to the publisher to print and sell the book. The publisher, in turn, hires a printer to physically print the books, and commissions an artist to design the cover. Both of these transactions also involve copyright licenses. Translations, paperback editions, and audiobooks require licenses of their own, and so on.

The legal rules governing licenses – like almost everything else in copyright – are being adapted to apply online. This section considers three common issues in digital licensing law. *Field v. Google* explores when a copyright owner will be deemed to have implicitly licensed particular uses of her work by putting it online. *Vernor v. Autodesk* shows how a license can be used to limit, as well as grant, user rights. And *Jacobsen v. Katzer* gives a window on "open-source" or "free software" licensing: copyright licenses designed with goals other than profit in mind.

FIELD V. GOOGLE INC.
412 F. Supp. 2d 1106 (D. Nev. 2006)

Jones, District Judge:

This is an action for copyright infringement brought by plaintiff Blake Field ("Field") against Google Inc. ("Google"). Field contends that by allowing Internet users to access copies of 51 of his copyrighted works stored by Google in an online repository, Google violated Field's exclusive rights to reproduce copies and distribute copies of those works. ...

STATEMENT OF PROCEDURAL HISTORY AND UNDISPUTED FACTS

Procedural History

On April 6, 2004, Plaintiff Field, an author and an attorney who is a member of the State Bar of Nevada, filed a complaint against Google asserting a single claim for copyright infringement based on Google's alleged copying and distribution of his copyrighted work entitled Good Tea. Field himself had previously published this work on his personal Web site, www.blakeswritings.com.

On May 25, 2004, Field filed an Amended Complaint, alleging that Google infringed the copyrights to an additional fifty of Field's works, which likewise had been published on his personal website. Field did not seek actual damages, but instead requested $2,550,000 in statutory damages ($50,000 for each of fifty-one registered copyrighted works) along with injunctive relief.

On September 27, 2005, Field filed a motion for summary judgment that Google infringed the copyrighted works at issue and that Google's defenses based on fair use, implied license, estoppel and the Digital Millennium Copyright Act ("DMCA") should be dismissed as a matter of law. Google filed a motion for summary judgment based on non-infringement, implied license, estoppel and fair use ...

Undisputed Facts

Google, the Google Cache, and "Cached" Links.

Google maintains one of the world's largest and most popular Internet search engines, accessible, among other places, on the World Wide Web at www.google.com. Internet search engines like Google's allow Internet users to sift through the massive amount of information available on the Internet to find specific information that is of particular interest to them.

There are billions of Web pages accessible on the Internet. It would be impossible for Google to locate and index or catalog them manually. Accordingly, Google, like other search engines, uses an automated program (called the "Googlebot") to continuously crawl across the Internet, to locate and analyze available Web pages, and to catalog those Web pages into Google's searchable Web index.

As part of this process, Google makes and analyzes a copy of each Web page that it finds, and stores the HTML code from those pages in a temporary repository called a cache. Once Google indexes and stores a Web page in the cache, it can include that page, as appropriate, in the search results it displays to users in response to their queries.

When Google displays Web pages in its search results, the first item appearing in each result is the title of a Web page which, if clicked by the user, will take the user to the online location of that page. The title is followed by a short "snippet" from the Web page in smaller font. Following the snippet, Google typically provides the full URL for the page. Then, in the same smaller font, Google often displays another link labeled "Cached."

When clicked, the "Cached" link directs an Internet user to the archival copy of a Web page stored in Google's system cache, rather than to the original Web site for that page. By clicking on the "Cached" link for a page, a user can view the "snapshot" of that page, as it appeared the last time the site was visited and analyzed by the Googlebot.

The page a user retrieves from Google after clicking on a "Cached" link contains a conspicuous disclaimer at the top explaining that it is only a snapshot of the page from Google's cache, not the original page, and that the page from the cache may not be current. The disclaimer also includes two separate hyperlinks to the original, current page.

Google has provided "Cached" links with its search results since 1998. Until this action, Google had never before been sued for providing "Cached" links. The "Cached" link, and the consequences that flow when a user clicks on it, is the subject of Field's lawsuit.

The Purposes Served By Google's "Cached" Links

Google enables users to access its copy of Web pages through "Cached" links for several reasons.

Archival Copies. Google's "Cached" links allow users to view pages that the user cannot, for whatever reason, access directly. A Web page can become inaccessible to Internet users because of transmission problems, because nations or service providers seek to censor certain information, because too many users are trying to access the same page at the same time, or because the page has been removed from its original location. In each case, users who request access to the material from the inaccessible site are still able to access an archival copy of the page via the "Cached" link in Google's search results. Google's users, including those in academia, describe this functionality as highly valuable. This feature also benefits Web site publishers because it allows users to access their sites when the sites are otherwise unavailable and has allowed Web site owners to recover copies of their own sites that might otherwise have been lost due to computer problems.

Web Page Comparisons. Google's archival functionality is also of considerable importance to those who wish to determine how a particular Web page has been altered over time. By examining Google's copy of the page, people can identify subtle but potentially significant differences between the current version of a page, and the page as it existed when last visited by the Googlebot.

Identification of Search Query Terms. Google's "Cached" links also allow users to immediately determine why a particular page was deemed responsive to their search query, by highlighting the terms from the user's query as they appear on the page. In some cases, if a user clicks on Google's link to an original Web page, he may be unable to determine how the page relates to his inquiry. That is particularly true for text intensive pages where the user's search term may be very difficult to find. In some cases it may be impossible for a user to find the information on a page that is responsive to a given search where a site owner has altered the text on the original page and removed the relevant language. By allowing access to copies of Web pages through "Cached" links, Google enables users to more quickly determine whether and where a user's search query appears, and thus whether the page is germane to their inquiry.

Given the breadth of the Internet, it is not possible for Google (or other search engines) to personally contact every Web site owner to determine whether the owner wants the pages in its site listed in search results or accessible through "Cached" links.

The Internet industry has developed a set of widely recognized and well-publicized industry standard protocols by which Web site owners can automatically communicate their preferences to search engines such as Google. Google provides instructions for Web site owners to communicate their preferences to Google at http://www.google.com/remove.html.

A principal way for Web site owners to communicate with Google's robot is by placing specific instructions in "metatags" within the computer code (called HTML) that comprises a given page. When the Googlebot visits a page, it reads through this code. If it encounters metatags, it follows the instructions provided. Thus, for example, a site owner can place the following meta-tag within a page to tell Google's robot not to analyze the page or include it in Google's Web index and search results: "<META NAME=' ROBOTS' CONTENT='NOINDEX, NOFOLLOW'>"

Using meta-tags, a Web site owner can also tell Google's robot that it can include a given page in Google's index, but that it should not provide a "Cached" link to that page in Google's search results. To do so, the Web site owner uses a "no-archive" meta-tag "<META NAME='ROBOTS' CONTENT='NOARCHIVE'>" The "no-archive" meta-tag has been a widely recognized industry standard for years.

If a Web site owner includes the "no-archive" meta-tag on a page, then Google does not provide a "Cached" link when it lists that page in its search results.

Web site owners can also communicate with search engines' robots by placing a "robots.txt" file on their Web site. For example, if the Web site owner does not want robots to crawl the owner's Web site, the owner can create a robots.txt file with the following text: "User-agent: * Disallow: /". The above text tells the robots that they should not crawl the owner's Web site. If Google's robot encounters a robots.txt file with the above text, then it will not crawl the Web site, and there will be no entry for that Web page in Google's search results and no cached link. The Internet industry has widely recognized the robots.txt file as a standard for controlling automated access to Web pages since 1994.

Plaintiff Blake Field and His Copyright Claim

Plaintiff Blake Field has regularly used Google's search engine over the past several years and was familiar with the manner in which it operates.

Field has long been aware that Google automatically provides "Cached" links for pages that are included in its index and search results unless instructed otherwise. Field decided to manufacture a claim for copyright infringement against Google in the hopes of making money from Google's standard practice.

Field admits he knew that any Web site owner could instruct Google not to provide a "Cached" link to a given Web page by using the "no-archive" meta-tag (as discussed above). Field also knew that Google provided a process to allow Web site owners to remove pages from Google's system cache. With this knowledge, Field set out to get his copyrighted works included in Google's index, and to have Google provide "Cached" links to Web pages containing those works.

Over a three-day period in January 2004, Field created the 51 works at issue in this lawsuit.

Field registered copyrights for each of these works separately on January 16, 2004. Field then created a Web site at www.blakeswritings.com and published his works on pages where they were accessible, for free, to the world starting in late January 2004.

Field created a robots.txt file for his site and set the permissions within this file to *allow* all robots to visit and index all of the pages on the site. Field created the robots.txt file because he wanted search engines to visit his site and include the site within their search results.

Field knew that if he used the "no-archive" meta-tag on the pages of his site, Google would not provide "Cached" links for the pages containing his works. Field consciously chose not to use the "no-archive" meta-tag on his Web site.

As Field expected, the Googlebot visited his site and indexed its pages, making the pages available in Google search results. When the pages containing Field's copyrighted works were displayed in Google's search results, they were automatically displayed with "Cached" links, as Field intended they would be.

According to Google's records, an individual or individuals clicked on the "Cached" links for each of the pages containing Field's works, and retrieved copies of each of the those pages from Google's system cache.

When Google learned that Field had filed (but not served) his complaint, Google promptly removed the "Cached" links to all of the pages of his site. Google also wrote to Field explaining that Google had no desire to provide "Cached" links to Field's pages if Field did not want them to appear.

CONCLUSIONS OF LAW ...

II. GOOGLE'S DEFENSES ...

A. Implied License

A license is a defense to a claim of copyright infringement. A copyright owner may grant a nonexclusive license expressly or impliedly through conduct. An implied license can be found where the copyright holder engages in conduct "from which [the] other [party] may properly infer that the owner consents to his use." Consent to use the copyrighted work need not be manifested verbally and may be inferred based on silence where the copyright holder knows of the use and encourages it. *See Keane Dealer Servs., Inc. v. Harts*, 968 F. Supp. 944, 947 (S.D.N.Y. 1997) ("consent given in the form of mere permission or lack of objection is also equivalent to a nonexclusive license").

According to the undisputed testimony of Google's Internet expert, Dr. John Levine, Web site publishers typically communicate their permissions to Internet search engines (such as Google) using "metatags." A Web site publisher can instruct a search engine not to cache the publisher's Web site by using a "no-archive" meta-tag. According to Dr. Levine, the "no-archive" meta-tag is a highly publicized and well-known industry standard. Field concedes he was aware of these industry standard mechanisms, and knew that the presence of a "no archive" meta-tag on the pages of his Web site would have informed Google not to display "Cached" links to his pages. Despite this knowledge, Field chose not to include the no-archive meta-tag on the pages of his site. He did so, knowing that Google would interpret the absence of the metatag as permission to allow access to the pages via "Cached" links. Thus, with knowledge of how Google would use the copyrighted works he placed on those pages, and with knowledge that he could prevent such use, Field instead made a conscious decision to permit it. His conduct is reasonably interpreted as the grant of a license to Google for that use. *See, e.g., Keane*, 968 F. Supp. at 947 (copyright owner's knowledge of defendant's use coupled with owner's silence constituted an implied license)... Accordingly, the Court grants Google's motion that it is entitled to the defense of implied license, and denies Field's cross-motion that the defense is inapplicable.

QUESTIONS

1. Find and examine Google's cached copy of a webpage. Can you find any differences between the cached copy and the original? As a web user, were you at all surprised by the court's description of how the cache works?

2. This is pretty much the definition of a "test case," isn't it? Would the result have been any different if Field had learned about the Google cache only *after* he put his writings online and Google started caching them?

3. If you post a webpage on the Internet, then under the logic of *MAI v. Peak*, any user who views the page in his browser has "reproduced" it. Have you granted him an implied license to do so?

4. Can Google rely on *Field's* implied license theory if the creator of the webpage used someone else's copyrighted work without permission?

5. Google's is not the only web cache available on the Internet. Visit the Wayback Machine at http://waybackmachine.org/. Play around with typing a few URLs and exploring. How is the Wayback Machine different from the Google cache? Does *Field* mean that the Wayback Machine also has an implied license from webpage authors?

6. In 2004, Google began scanning books borrowed from major research libraries, and creating a search index based on their contents. When users run a search at books.google.com, Google shows them a short "snippet" of text around the search term where it occurs in the book. After some controversy, Google agreed that it would not scan or show snippets from any book whose copyright owner objected, and created a webpage where copyright owners could make such a request. Does Google have an implied license to scan, index, and show snippets from those books whose copyright owners do not opt out?

7. Photographer Daniel Morel uploaded photographs of the devastation in Haiti following the January 2010 earthquake to Twitpic. Agence France-Presse (AFP), a news agency, distributed copies of the photographs to CBS, CNN, and other news outlets. Morel claims copyright infringement; AFP's defense is that Morel's act of uploading the photographs resulted in a license that authorized AFP's uses. Twitpic's terms of service read, in part:

> By [uploading content], you grant us a worldwide, non-exclusive, royalty-free license (with the right to sublicense) to use, copy reproduce, process, adapt, modify, publish, transmit, dis-

play and distribute such content in any and all media or distribution methods ...

Should the court rule for Morel or for AFP?

8. As seen in *Field*, nonexclusive licenses can arise without any particular formalities. The Copyright Act, however, requires a "writing ... signed by the owner" to transfer ownership of the copyright itself. 17 U.S.C. § 204. What does this even mean online? Could Craigslist use its terms of service to obtain ownership of the copyright in user-uploaded ads? Why might it want to? Why might it not?

VERNOR V. AUTODESK, INC.
621 F.3d 1102 (9th Cir. 2010)

Callahan, Circuit Judge: ...

A. Autodesk's Release 14 software and licensing practices

The material facts are not in dispute. Autodesk makes computer-aided design software used by architects, engineers, and manufacturers. It has more than nine million customers. It first released its AutoCAD software in 1982. It holds registered copyrights in all versions of the software including the discontinued Release 14 version, which is at issue in this case. It provided Release 14 to customers on CD-ROMs.

Since at least 1986, Autodesk has offered AutoCAD to customers pursuant to an accompanying software license agreement ("SLA"), which customers must accept before installing the software. A customer who does not accept the SLA can return the software for a full refund. Autodesk offers SLAs with different terms for commercial, educational institution, and student users. The commercial license, which is the most expensive, imposes the fewest restrictions on users and allows them software upgrades at discounted prices.

The SLA for Release 14 first recites that Autodesk retains title to all copies. Second, it states that the customer has a nonexclusive and nontransferable license to use Release 14. Third, it imposes transfer restrictions, prohibiting customers from renting, leasing, or transferring the software without Autodesk's prior consent and from electronically or physically transferring the software out of the Western Hemisphere. Fourth, it imposes significant use restrictions:

> YOU MAY NOT: (1) modify, translate, reverse-engineer, decompile, or disassemble the Software . . . (3) remove any proprietary notices, labels, or marks from the Software or Documentation; (4) use . . . the Software outside of the Western Hemisphere; (5) utilize any computer software or hardware designed to defeat any hardware copy-protection device, should the software you have licensed be equipped with such protection; or (6) use the Software for commercial or other revenue-generating purposes if the Software has been licensed or labeled for educational use only.

Fifth, the SLA provides for license termination if the user copies the software without authorization or does not comply with the SLA's restrictions. Finally, the SLA provides that if the software is an upgrade of a previous version:

> [Y]ou must destroy the software previously licensed to you, including any copies resident on your hard disk drive . . . within sixty (60) days of the purchase of the license to use the upgrade or update. . . . Au-

todesk   reserves the right to require you to show satisfactory proof that previous copies of the software have been destroyed.

Autodesk takes measures to enforce these license requirements. It assigns a serial number to each copy of AutoCAD and tracks registered licensees. It requires customers to input "activation codes" within one month after installation to continue using the software.1 The customer obtains the code by providing the product's serial number to Autodesk. Autodesk issues the activation code after confirming that the serial number is authentic, the copy is not registered to a different customer, and the product has not been upgraded. Once a customer has an activation code, he or she may use it to activate the software on additional computers without notifying Autodesk. ...

C. Vernor's eBay business and sales of Release 14

Vernor has sold more than 10,000 items on eBay. In May 2005, he purchased an authentic used copy of Release 14 at a garage sale from an unspecified seller. He never agreed to the SLA's terms, opened a sealed software packet, or installed the Release 14 software. Though he was aware of the SLA's existence, he believed that he was not bound by its terms. He posted the software copy for sale on eBay.

Autodesk filed a Digital Millennium Copyright Act ("DMCA") take-down notice with eBay claiming that Vernor's sale infringed its copyright, and eBay terminated Vernor's auction. [The DMCA notice-and-takedown procedure is discussed *infra*.]

[Vernor then purchased four copies of Release 14 from Cardwell/Thomas & Associates ("CTA"). As the court explained, in an earlier part of the opinion, CTA had "upgraded to the newer, fifteenth version of the AutoCAD program, AutoCAD 2000. It paid $495 per upgrade license, compared to $3,750 for each new license. The SLA for AutoCAD 2000, like the SLA for Release 14, required destruction of copies of previous versions of the software, with proof to be furnished to Autodesk on request. However, rather than destroying its Release 14 copies, CTA sold them to Vernor at an office sale with the handwritten activation codes necessary to use the software."]

[Autodesk submitted more DMCA notices, and Vernor filed a declaratory judgment action against Autodesk, claiming that his resales were protected by the first sale doctrine.]

III.

Copyright is a federal law protection provided to the authors of "original works of authorship," including software programs. 17 U.S.C. §§ 101–103. The Copyright Act confers several exclusive rights on copyright owners, including the exclusive rights to reproduce their works and to distribute their works by sale or rental. *Id.* § 106(1), (3). The exclusive distribution right is limited by the first sale doctrine, an affirmative defense to copyright infringement that allows owners of copies of copyrighted works to resell those copies. ...

This case requires us to decide whether Autodesk sold Release 14 copies to its customers or licensed the copies to its customers. If CTA owned its copies of Release 14, then both its sales to Vernor and Vernor's subsequent sales were non-

---

1 Prior to using activation codes, Autodesk required users to return one disc of an earlier version of the software to upgrade to a later version. Autodesk has abandoned this return policy, deeming it slow and unworkable.

infringing under the first sale doctrine.[6] However, if Autodesk only licensed CTA to use copies of Release 14, then CTA's and Vernor's sales of those copies are not protected by the first sale doctrine and would therefore infringe Autodesk's exclusive distribution right.

A. The first sale doctrine

The Supreme Court articulated the first sale doctrine in 1908, holding that a copyright owner's exclusive distribution right is exhausted after the owner's first sale of a particular copy of the copyrighted work. *See Bobbs-Merrill Co. v. Straus*, 210 U.S. 339, 350–51 (1908). In *Bobbs-Merrill*, the plaintiff-copyright owner sold its book with a printed notice announcing that any retailer who sold the book for less than one dollar was responsible for copyright infringement. Plaintiff sought injunctive relief against defendants-booksellers who failed to comply with the price restriction. The Supreme Court rejected the plaintiff's claim, holding that its exclusive distribution right applied only to first sales of copies of the work. The distribution right did not permit plaintiff to dictate that subsequent sales of the work below a particular price were infringing. The Court noted that its decision solely applied to the rights of a copyright owner that distributed its work without a license agreement. *Id.* at 350 ("There is no claim in this case of contract limitation, nor license agreement controlling the subsequent sales of the book.").

Congress codified the first sale doctrine the following year. *See* 17 U.S.C. § 41 (1909). In its current form, it allows the "owner of a particular copy" of a copyrighted work to sell or dispose of his copy without the copyright owner's authorization. *Id.* § 109(a) (enacted 1976). The first sale doctrine does not apply to a person who possesses a copy of the copyrighted work without owning it, such as a licensee. *See id.* § 109(d); *cf. Quality King Distribs., Inc. v. L'Anza Research Int'l Inc.*, 523 U.S. 135, 146–47 (1998) ("[T]he first sale doctrine would not provide a defense to . . . any non-owner such as a bailee, a licensee, a consignee, or one whose possession of the copy was unlawful.").

B. Owners vs. licensees

We turn to our precedents governing whether a transferee of a copy of a copyrighted work is an owner or licensee of that copy. We then apply those precedents to CTA's and Vernor's possession of Release 14 copies.

[In *United States v. Wise*, 550 F.2d 1180 (9th Cir. 1977)], a criminal copyright infringement case, we considered whether copyright owners who transferred copies of their motion pictures pursuant to written distribution agreements had executed first sales. The defendant was found guilty of copyright infringement based on his for-profit sales of motion picture prints. The copyright owners distributed their films to third parties pursuant to written agreements that restricted their use and transfer. On appeal, the defendant argued that the government failed to prove the absence of a first sale for each film. If the copyright owners' initial transfers of the films were first sales, then the defendant's resales were protected by the first sale doctrine and thus were not copyright infringement.

---

6 If Autodesk's transfer of Release 14 copies to CTA was a first sale, then CTA's resale of the software in violation of the SLA's terms would be a breach of contract, but would not result in copyright liability. See *United States v. Wise*, 550 F.2d 1180, 1187 (9th Cir. 1977) ("[T]he exclusive right to vend the transferred copy rests with the vendee, who is not restricted by statute from further transfers of that copy, even though in breach of an agreement restricting its sale.").

To determine whether a first sale occurred, we considered multiple factors pertaining to each film distribution agreement. Specifically, we considered whether the agreement (a) was labeled a license, (b) provided that the copyright owner retained title to the prints, (c) required the return or destruction of the prints, (d) forbade duplication of prints, or (e) required the transferee to maintain possession of the prints for the agreement's duration. Our use of these several considerations, none dispositive, may be seen in our treatment of each film print.

For example, we reversed the defendant's conviction with respect to *Camelot*. It was unclear whether the Camelot print sold by the defendant had been subject to a first sale. Copyright owner Warner Brothers distributed Camelot prints pursuant to multiple agreements, and the government did not prove the absence of a first sale with respect to each agreement. We noted that, in one agreement, Warner Brothers had retained title to the prints, required possessor National Broadcasting Company ("NBC") to return the prints if the parties could select a mutual agreeable price, and if not, required NBC's certification that the prints were destroyed. We held that these factors created a license rather than a first sale.

We further noted, however, that Warner Brothers had also furnished another Camelot print to actress Vanessa Redgrave. The print was provided to Redgrave at cost, and her use of the print was subject to several restrictions. She had to retain possession of the print and was not allowed to sell, license, reproduce, or publicly exhibit the print. She had no obligation to return the print to Warner Brothers. We concluded, "While the provision for payment for the cost of the film, standing alone, does not establish a sale, when taken with the rest of the language of the agreement, it reveals a transaction strongly resembling a sale with restrictions on the use of the print." *Id.* There was no evidence of the print's whereabouts, and we held that "[i]n the absence of such proof," the government failed to prove the absence of a first sale with respect to this Redgrave print. Since it was unclear which copy the defendant had obtained and resold, his conviction for sale of Camelot had to be reversed.

Thus, under *Wise*, where a transferee receives a particular copy of a copyrighted work pursuant to a written agreement, we consider all of the provisions of the agreement to determine whether the transferee became an owner of the copy or received a license. ...

IV. ...

B. Analysis

We hold today that a software user is a licensee rather than an owner of a copy where the copyright owner (1) specifies that the user is granted a license; (2) significantly restricts the user's ability to transfer the software; and (3) imposes notable use restrictions. Applying our holding to Autodesk's SLA, we conclude that CTA was a licensee rather than an owner of copies of Release 14 and thus was not entitled to invoke the first sale doctrine.

Autodesk retained title to the software and imposed significant transfer restrictions: it stated that the license is nontransferable, the software could not be transferred or leased without Autodesk's written consent, and the software could not be transferred outside the Western Hemisphere. The SLA also imposed use restrictions against the use of the software outside the Western Hemisphere and against modifying, translating, or reverse-engineering the software, removing any proprietary marks from the software or documentation, or defeating any copy protection device. Furthermore, the SLA provided for termination of the license upon the licensee's unauthorized copying or failure to comply with other license restrictions. Thus, because Autodesk   reserved title to Release 14 copies and imposed significant transfer and use restrictions, we conclude that its customers are licensees of their copies of Release 14 rather than owners.

CTA was a licensee rather than an "owner of a particular copy" of Release 14, and it was not entitled to resell its Release 14 copies to Vernor under the first sale doctrine. 17 U.S.C. § 109(a). Therefore, Vernor did not receive title to the copies from CTA and accordingly could not pass ownership on to others. Both CTA's and Vernor's sales infringed Autodesk's exclusive right to distribute copies of its work. *Id.*

Because Vernor was not an owner, his customers are also not owners of Release 14 copies. Therefore, when they install Release 14 on their computers, the copies of the software that they make during installation infringe Autodesk's exclusive reproduction right ...

3. The Supreme Court's holding in Bobbs-Merrill

Vernor contends that *Bobbs-Merrill* establishes his entitlement to a first sale defense. However, *Bobbs-Merrill* stands only for the proposition that a copyright owner's exclusive distribution right does not allow it to control sales of copies of its work after the first sale. Decided in 1908, *Bobbs-Merrill* did not and could not address the question of whether the right to use software is distinct from the ownership of copies of software. Moreover, the Supreme Court in *Bobbs-Merrill* made explicit that its decision did not address the use of restrictions to create a license. *Id.* ("There is no claim in this case of contract limitation, nor license agreement controlling the subsequent sales of the book.")

4. Economic realities of the transaction

Finally, Vernor contends   that "economic realities" demonstrate that Autodesk makes "first sales" to its customers, because Autodesk allows its customers to possess their copies of the software indefinitely and does not require recurring license payments. We held supra that neither of these factors is dispositive. Vernor cites no first sale doctrine case in support of this proposition. ...

QUESTIONS

1. It is helpful to start by thinking about the Software License "Agreement" which sets forth the Autocad license. Why are its terms enforceable against CTA?

2. There is no argument, however, that Vernor "agreed" to the SLA. Why not? How, then, could he possibly be held to its terms? Explain how the distribution right, the first sale defense, and the SLA interact to produce the result in *Vernor*.

3. Vernor asks the court to focus on the "economic realities" of the transaction. Why? Is this really his best argument? How did CTA end up with copies of Release 14 that it was willing to sell?

4. The same panel that decided *Vernor* also that when record companies mailed promotional CDs to radio stations, the CDs had been given away rather than licensed, so that first sale applied. *See UMG Recordings Inc. v. Augusto*, 628 F.3d 1175 (2011). The CDs bore labels such as "Promotional Use Only – Not for Sale." Is this result reconcilable with *Vernor*?

5. In 2012, the British tabloid *The Sun* (falsely) reported that actor Bruce Willis was planning to sue to establish his right to give his MP3 collection to his daughters in his will. If Bruce Willis buys a CD from Amazon, can he

give it to his daughter Rumer? What if he rips the CD to MP3s on his computer first? If he buys the same album as a download from Amazon's MP3 store, can he email a copy of the MP3s to Rumer? What if he deletes the MP3s from his computer after he sends her the email? Can he give Rumer his computer? Can he give her the password to his Amazon account so she can download a copy? (It may help to refer to Amazon's music download terms and conditions, which are available at http://www.amazon.com/gp/help/customer/display.html?nodeId=200154280.)

6. *Vernor* also dealt with the "essential step" defense in 17 U.S.C. § 117:

> [I]t is not an infringement for the owner of a copy of a computer program to make or authorize the making of another copy or adaptation of that computer program provided:
>
> > (1) that such a new copy or adaptation is created as an essential step in the utilization of the computer program in conjunction with a machine and that it is used in no other manner, or
> >
> > (2) that such new copy or adaptation is for archival purposes only and that all archival copies are destroyed in the event that continued possession of the computer program should cease to be rightful.

What is the purpose of this defense? After *Vernor*, is there anything left of it?

7. Suppose that instead of buying a CD containing copyrighted software subject to a license agreement, Vernor had bought a tractor containing copyrighted software subject to a license agreement. What result?

MIT LICENSE

Copyright (c) <year> <copyright holders>

Permission is hereby granted, free of charge, to any person obtaining a copy of this software and associated documentation files (the "Software"), to deal in the Software without restriction, including without limitation the rights to use, copy, modify, merge, publish, distribute, sublicense, and/or sell copies of the Software, and to permit persons to whom the Software is furnished to do so, subject to the following conditions:

The above copyright notice and this permission notice shall be included in all copies or substantial portions of the Software.

THE SOFTWARE IS PROVIDED "AS IS", WITHOUT WARRANTY OF ANY KIND, EXPRESS OR IMPLIED, INCLUDING BUT NOT LIMITED TO THE WARRANTIES OF MERCHANTABILITY, FITNESS FOR A PARTICULAR PURPOSE AND NONINFRINGEMENT. IN NO EVENT SHALL THE AUTHORS OR COPYRIGHT HOLDERS BE LIABLE FOR ANY CLAIM, DAMAGES OR OTHER LIABILITY, WHETHER IN AN ACTION OF CONTRACT, TORT OR OTHERWISE, ARISING FROM, OUT OF OR IN CONNECTION WITH THE SOFTWARE OR THE USE OR OTHER DEALINGS IN THE SOFTWARE.

QUESTIONS

1. Why would a programmer choose to give away her software, voluntarily and for free?

2. How will a larger project that requires hundreds of programmers to collaborate – like the Linux operating system or the Firefox web browser – ever get written if the program is available to anyone for free?

3. Simple as it is, the MIT license does impose two conditions on the licensee. What are they? Why would a programmer who is otherwise letting people do absolutely whatever they want insist on these conditions?

4. If Jessamyn uses the MIT license on an accounting program, and gives Matt a copy of it, is Matt allowed to sell that copy to Josh? Is Matt allowed to add a new invoicing feature to the software, then sell a copy of the modified software to Josh?

5. The Hacktivismo Enhanced-Source Software License Agreement states that a licensee may not use the software "to violate or infringe any human rights or to deprive any person of human rights, including, without limitation, rights of privacy, security, collective action, expression, political freedom, due process of law, and individual conscience." How does this license trade off one kind of freedom against another? How effective will it be? How should an ethical programmer choose between a more permissive license like the MIT license or a more restrictive license like the Hacktivismo license? Are there other substantive values you could use a copyright license to promote?

GNU GENERAL PUBLIC LICENSE (GPL)
Version 2

PREAMBLE

The licenses for most software are designed to take away your freedom to share and change it. By contrast, the GNU General Public License is intended to guarantee your freedom to share and change free software – to make sure the software is free for all its users. This General Public License applies to most of the Free Software Foundation's software and to any other program whose authors commit to using it. (Some other Free Software Foundation software is covered by the GNU Lesser General Public License instead.) You can apply it to your programs, too.

When we speak of free software, we are referring to freedom, not price. Our General Public Licenses are designed to make sure that you have the freedom to distribute copies of free software (and charge for this service if you wish), that you receive source code or can get it if you want it, that you can change the software or use pieces of it in new free programs; and that you know you can do these things.

To protect your rights, we need to make restrictions that forbid anyone to deny you these rights or to ask you to surrender the rights. These restrictions translate to certain responsibilities for you if you distribute copies of the software, or if you modify it.

For example, if you distribute copies of such a program, whether gratis or for a fee, you must give the recipients all the rights that you have. You must make sure that they, too, receive or can get the source code. And you must show them these terms so they know their rights.

We protect your rights with two steps: (1) copyright the software, and (2) offer you this license which gives you legal permission to copy, distribute and/or modify the software. ...

The precise terms and conditions for copying, distribution and modification follow.

GNU GENERAL PUBLIC LICENSE TERMS AND CONDITIONS FOR COPYING, DISTRIBUTION AND MODIFICATION

0. This License applies to any program or other work which contains a notice placed by the copyright holder saying it may be distributed under the terms of this General Public License. The "Program", below, refers to any such program or work, and a "work based on the Program" means either the Program or any derivative work under copyright law: that is to say, a work containing the Program or a portion of it, either verbatim or with modifications and/or translated into another language. (Hereinafter, translation is included without limitation in the term "modification".) Each licensee is addressed as "you". ...

1. You may copy and distribute verbatim copies of the Program's source code as you receive it, in any medium, provided that you conspicuously and appropriately publish on each copy an appropriate copyright notice and disclaimer of warranty; keep intact all the notices that refer to this License and to the absence of any warranty; and give any other recipients of the Program a copy of this License along with the Program.

   You may charge a fee for the physical act of transferring a copy, and you may at your option offer warranty protection in exchange for a fee.

2. You may modify your copy or copies of the Program or any portion of it, thus forming a work based on the Program, and copy and distribute such modifications or work under the terms of Section 1 above, provided that you also meet all of these conditions:

   a) You must cause the modified files to carry prominent notices stating that you changed the files and the date of any change.

   b) You must cause any work that you distribute or publish, that in whole or in part contains or is derived from the Program or any part thereof, to be licensed as a whole at no charge to all third parties under the terms of this License.

   c) If the modified program normally reads commands interactively when run, you must cause it, when started running for such interactive use in the most ordinary way, to print or display an announcement including an appropriate copyright notice and a notice that there is no warranty (or else, saying that you provide a warranty) and that users may redistribute the program under these conditions, and telling the user how to view a copy of this License. (Exception: if the Program itself is interactive but does not normally print such an announcement, your work based on the Program is not required to print an announcement.) ...

   Thus, it is not the intent of this section to claim rights or contest your rights to work written entirely by you; rather, the intent is to exercise the right to control the distribution of derivative or collective works based on the Program.

In addition, mere aggregation of another work not based on the Program with the Program (or with a work based on the Program) on a volume of a storage or distribution medium does not bring the other work under the scope of this License.

3. You may copy and distribute the Program (or a work based on it, under Section 2) in object code or executable form under the terms of Sections 1 and 2 above provided that you also do one of the following:

   a) Accompany it with the complete corresponding machine-readable source code, which must be distributed under the terms of Sections 1 and 2 above on a medium customarily used for software interchange; or,

   b) Accompany it with a written offer, valid for at least three years, to give any third party, for a charge no more than your cost of physically performing source distribution, a complete machine-readable copy of the corresponding source code, to be distributed under the terms of Sections 1 and 2 above on a medium customarily used for software interchange; or,

   c) Accompany it with the information you received as to the offer to distribute corresponding source code. (This alternative is allowed only for noncommercial distribution and only if you received the program in object code or executable form with such an offer, in accord with Subsection b above.)

The source code for a work means the preferred form of the work for making modifications to it. For an executable work, complete source code means all the source code for all modules it contains, plus any associated interface definition files, plus the scripts used to control compilation and installation of the executable. ...

6. Each time you redistribute the Program (or any work based on the Program), the recipient automatically receives a license from the original licensor to copy, distribute or modify the Program subject to these terms and conditions. You may not impose any further restrictions on the recipients' exercise of the rights granted herein. You are not responsible for enforcing compliance by third parties to this License. ...

NO WARRANTY

11. BECAUSE THE PROGRAM IS LICENSED FREE OF CHARGE, THERE IS NO WARRANTY FOR THE PROGRAM, TO THE EXTENT PERMITTED BY APPLICABLE LAW. EXCEPT WHEN OTHERWISE STATED IN WRITING THE COPYRIGHT HOLDERS AND/OR OTHER PARTIES PROVIDE THE PROGRAM "AS IS" WITHOUT WARRANTY OF ANY KIND, EITHER EXPRESSED OR IMPLIED, INCLUDING, BUT NOT LIMITED TO, THE IMPLIED WARRANTIES OF MERCHANTABILITY AND FITNESS FOR A PARTICULAR PURPOSE. THE ENTIRE RISK AS TO THE QUALITY AND PERFORMANCE OF THE PROGRAM IS WITH YOU. SHOULD THE PROGRAM PROVE DEFECTIVE, YOU ASSUME THE COST OF ALL NECESSARY SERVICING, REPAIR OR CORRECTION.

12. IN NO EVENT UNLESS REQUIRED BY APPLICABLE LAW OR AGREED TO IN WRITING WILL ANY COPYRIGHT HOLDER, OR ANY

OTHER PARTY WHO MAY MODIFY AND/OR REDISTRIBUTE THE PROGRAM AS PERMITTED ABOVE, BE LIABLE TO YOU FOR DAMAGES, INCLUDING ANY GENERAL, SPECIAL, INCIDENTAL OR CONSEQUENTIAL DAMAGES ARISING OUT OF THE USE OR INABILITY TO USE THE PROGRAM (INCLUDING BUT NOT LIMITED TO LOSS OF DATA OR DATA BEING RENDERED INACCURATE OR LOSSES SUSTAINED BY YOU OR THIRD PARTIES OR A FAILURE OF THE PROGRAM TO OPERATE WITH ANY OTHER PROGRAMS), EVEN IF SUCH HOLDER OR OTHER PARTY HAS BEEN ADVISED OF THE POSSIBILITY OF SUCH DAMAGES.

QUESTIONS

1. The GPL is more elaborate than the MIT license, but they have much in common. First, find the clause that gives the recipient the same basic rights as the MIT license does. Revisit question (4) from above, involving Jessamyn, Matt, and Josh. Has anything changed?

2. The first characteristic feature of the GPL is in clause 2(b). Read it closely. What does it do? Consider Jessamyn, Matt, and Josh again. Matt has just added an invoicing feature to the accounting program. If he wishes to give Josh a copy of his modified version, what must she do? What rights does this give Josh? And if Josh then modifies his copy of Matt's version of the program to add a time-tracking feature ... ?

3. The second characteristic feature of the GPL is in clause 3. What is source code, and why does it matter to programmers? Software whose source code is made publicly available is often referred to as "open source" software. How does clause 3 ensure that GPL-licensed software will always remain open-source? Why did the authors of the GPL consider this condition as an essential companion of the self-perpetuating condition in clause 2?

4. The creators of the GPL refer to it as a "free software" license, with the slogan "Free as in 'free speech,' not as in 'free beer.'" What do they mean by that? How do the GPL's features attempt to promote free speech? People – most often critics – sometimes also refer to it as a "viral" license. Is there a sense in which GPL-licensed software can propagate itself by "infecting" other software it is combined with?

5. The MIT license is an especially simple example of a group of licenses generally known as "BSD-style" licenses. BSD-style licenses allow licensees to modify the software and apply a more restrictive copyright license to their modifications; the GPL and licenses like it do not. What factors might lead a programmer to choose a BSD-style license or a GPL-like one?

6. The Microsoft XBox 360 will not run software unless it has been digitally signed by Microsoft. Microsoft can reject software at its sole discretion and can require the software developer to pay a license fee. Is it possible to modify a GPL-licensed game and distribute it to XBox users without violating the GPL? Without violating its spirit? If your answers to these questions are different, how would you modify the GPL to fix the problem?

7. Both the MIT license and the GPL include clauses disclaiming any and all warranties. Why might open source and free software programmers be especially worried about being held liable for any defects in the software they

write? How common do you think warranty disclaimers are in commercial software?

JACOBSEN V. KATZER
535 F.3d 1373 (Fed. Cir. 2008)

Hochberg, District Judge:

We consider here the ability of a copyright holder to dedicate certain work to free public use and yet enforce an "open source" copyright license to control the future distribution and modification of that work. Appellant Robert Jacobsen ("Jacobsen") appeals from an order denying a motion for preliminary injunction. Jacobsen holds a copyright to computer programming code. He makes that code available for public download from a website without a financial fee pursuant to the Artistic License, an "open source" or public license. Appellees Matthew Katzer and Kamind Associates, Inc. (collectively "Katzer/Kamind") develop commercial software products for the model train industry and hobbyists. Jacobsen accused Katzer/Kamind of copying certain materials from Jacobsen's website and incorporating them into one of Katzer/Kamind's software packages without following the terms of the Artistic License. Jacobsen brought an action for copyright infringement and moved for a preliminary injunction.

The District Court held that the open source Artistic License created an "intentionally broad" nonexclusive license which was unlimited in scope and thus did not create liability for copyright infringement. The District Court reasoned:

> The plaintiff claimed that by modifying the software the defendant had exceeded the scope of the license and therefore infringed the copyright. Here, however, the JMRI Project license provides that a user may copy the files verbatim or may otherwise modify the material in any way, including as part of a larger, possibly commercial software distribution. The license explicitly gives the users of the material, any member of the public, "the right to use and distribute the [material] in a more-or-less customary fashion, plus the right to make reasonable accommodations." The scope of the nonexclusive license is, therefore, intentionally broad. The condition that the user insert a prominent notice of attribution does not limit the scope of the license. Rather, Defendants' alleged violation of the conditions of the license may have constituted a breach of the nonexclusive license, but does not create liability for copyright infringement where it would not otherwise exist.

On this basis, the District Court denied the motion for a preliminary injunction. We vacate and remand.

I.

Jacobsen manages an open source software group called Java Model Railroad Interface ("JMRI"). Through the collective work of many participants, JMRI created a computer programming application called DecoderPro, which allows model railroad enthusiasts to use their computers to program the decoder chips that control model trains. DecoderPro files are available for download and use by the public free of charge from an open source incubator website called SourceForge; Jacobsen maintains the JMRI site on SourceForge. The downloadable files contain copyright notices and refer the user to a "COPYING" file, which clearly sets forth the terms of the Artistic License.

Katzer/Kamind offers a competing software product, Decoder Commander, which is also used to program decoder chips. During development of Decoder Commander, one of Katzer/Kamind's predecessors or employees is alleged to have downloaded the decoder definition files from DecoderPro and used portions of these files as part of the Decoder Command – er software. The Decoder Commander software files that used DecoderPro definition files did not comply with the terms of the Artistic License. Specifically, the Decoder Commander software did not include (1) the author' names, (2) JMRI copyright notices, (3) references to the COPYING file, (4) an identification of SourceForge or JMRI as the original source of the definition files, and (5) a description of how the files or computer code had been changed from the original source code. The Decoder Commander software also changed various computer file names of Decoder-Pro files without providing a reference to the original JMRI files or information on where to get the Standard Version.

Jacobsen moved for a preliminary injunction, arguing that the violation of the terms of the Artistic License constituted copyright infringement and that, under Ninth Circuit law, irreparable harm could be presumed in a copyright infringement case. The District Court reviewed the Artistic License and determined that "Defendants' alleged violation of the conditions of the license may have constituted a breach of the nonexclusive license, but does not create liability for copyright infringement where it would not otherwise exist." The District Court found that Jacobsen had a cause of action only for breach of contract, rather than an action for copyright infringement based on a breach of the conditions of the Artistic License. Because a breach of contract creates no presumption of irreparable harm, the District Court denied the motion for a preliminary injunction. ...

II. ...

... [A]n order granting or denying a preliminary injunction will be reversed only if the district court relied on an erroneous legal premise or abused its discretion. ... A district court's order denying a preliminary injunction is reversible for factual error only when the district court rests its conclusions on clearly erroneous findings of fact. ...

... Thus, for a preliminary injunction to issue, Jacobsen must either show (1) a likelihood of success on the merits of his copyright infringement claim from which irreparable harm is presumed; or (2) a fair chance of success on the merits and a clear disparity in the relative hardships that tips sharply in his favor.

A.

Public licenses, often referred to as "open source" licenses, are used by artists, authors, educators, software developers, and scientists who wish to create collaborative projects and to dedicate certain works to the public. Several types of public licenses have been designed to provide creators of copyrighted materials a means to protect and control their copyrights. Creative Commons, one of the amici curiae, provides free copyright licenses to allow parties to dedicate their works to the public or to license certain uses of their works while keeping some rights reserved.

Open source licensing has become a widely used method of creative collaboration that serves to advance the arts and sciences in a manner and at a pace that few could have imagined just a few decades ago. For example, the Massachusetts Institute of Technology ("MIT") uses a Creative Commons public license for an OpenCourseWare project that licenses all 1800 MIT courses. Other public licenses support the GNU/Linux operating system, the Perl programming language, the

Apache web server programs, the Firefox web browser, and a collaborative web-based encyclopedia called Wikipedia. Creative Commons notes that, by some estimates, there are close to 100,000,000 works licensed under various Creative Commons licenses. The Wikimedia Foundation, another of the amici curiae, estimates that the Wikipedia website has more than 75,000 active contributors working on some 9,000,000 articles in more than 250 languages.

Open Source software projects invite computer programmers from around the world to view software code and make changes and improvements to it. Through such collaboration, software programs can often be written and debugged faster and at lower cost than if the copyright holder were required to do all of the work independently. In exchange and in consideration for this collaborative work, the copyright holder permits users to copy, modify and distribute the software code subject to conditions that serve to protect downstream users and to keep the code accessible. By requiring that users copy and restate the license and attribution information, a copyright holder can ensure that recipients of the redistributed computer code know the identity of the owner as well as the scope of the license granted by the original owner. The Artistic License in this case also requires that changes to the computer code be tracked so that downstream users know what part of the computer code is the original code created by the copyright holder and what part has been newly added or altered by another collaborator.

Traditionally, copyright owners sold their copyrighted material in exchange for money. The lack of money changing hands in open source licensing should not be presumed to mean that there is no economic consideration, however. There are substantial benefits, including economic benefits, to the creation and distribution of copyrighted works under public licenses that range far beyond traditional license royalties. For example, program creators may generate market share for their programs by providing certain components free of charge. Similarly, a programmer or company may increase its national or international reputation by incubating open source projects. Improvement to a product can come rapidly and free of charge from an expert not even known to the copyright holder. ...

B.

The parties do not dispute that Jacobsen is the holder of a copyright for certain materials distributed through his website. Katzer/Kamind also admits that portions of the DecoderPro software were copied, modified, and distributed as part of the Decoder Commander software. Accordingly, Jacobsen has made out a prima facie case of copyright infringement. Katzer/Kamind argues that they cannot be liable for copyright infringement because they had a license to use the material. Thus, the Court must evaluate whether the use by Katzer/Kamind was outside the scope of the license. The copyrighted materials in this case are downloadable by any user and are labeled to include a copyright notification and a COPYING file that includes the text of the Artistic License. The Artistic License grants users the right to copy, modify, and distribute the software:

> provided that [the user] insert a prominent notice in each changed file stating how and when [the user] changed that file, and provided that [the user] do at least ONE of the following:
>
>> a) place [the user's] modifications in the Public Domain or otherwise make them Freely Available, such as by posting said modifications to Usenet or an equivalent medium, or placing the modifications on a major archive site such as ftp.uu.net, or by allowing the Copyright

Holder to include [the user's] modifications in the Standard Version of the Package.

b) use the modified Package only within [the user's] corporation or organization.

c) rename any non-standard executables so the names do not conflict with the standard executables, which must also be provided, and provide a separate manual page for each nonstandard executable that clearly documents how it differs from the Standard Version, or

d) make other distribution arrangements with the Copyright Holder.

The heart of the argument on appeal concerns whether the terms of the Artistic License are conditions of, or merely covenants to, the copyright license. Generally, a copyright owner who grants a nonexclusive license to use his copyrighted material waives his right to sue the licensee for copyright infringement and can sue only for breach of contract. If, however, a license is limited in scope and the licensee acts outside the scope, the licensor can bring an action for copyright infringement.

Thus, if the terms of the Artistic License allegedly violated are both covenants and conditions, they may serve to limit the scope of the license and are governed by copyright law. If they are merely covenants, by contrast, they are governed by contract law. The District Court did not expressly state whether the limitations in the Artistic License are independent covenants or, rather, conditions to the scope; its analysis, however, clearly treated the license limitations as contractual covenants rather than conditions of the copyright license.

Jacobsen argues that the terms of the Artistic License define the scope of the license and that any use outside of these restrictions is copyright infringement. Katzer/Kamind argues that these terms do not limit the scope of the license and are merely covenants providing contractual terms for the use of the materials, and that his violation of them is neither compensable in damages nor subject to injunctive relief. ...

III.

The Artistic License states on its face that the document creates conditions: "The intent of this document is to state the *conditions* under which a Package may be copied." (Emphasis added.) The Artistic License also uses the traditional language of conditions by noting that the rights to copy, modify, and distribute are granted *"provided that"* the conditions are met. Under California contract law, "provided that" typically denotes a condition.

The conditions set forth in the Artistic License are vital to enable the copyright holder to retain the ability to benefit from the work of downstream users. By requiring that users who modify or distribute the copyrighted material retain the reference to the original source files, downstream users are directed to Jacobsen's website. Thus, downstream users know about the collaborative effort to improve and expand the SourceForge project once they learn of the "upstream" project from a "downstream" distribution, and they may join in that effort.

The District Court interpreted the Artistic License to permit a user to "modify the material in any way" and did not find that any of the "provided that" limitations in the Artistic License served to limit this grant. The District Court's interpretation of the conditions of the Artistic License does not credit the explicit restrictions in the license that govern a downloader's right to modify and distribute the copyrighted work. The copyright holder here expressly stated the terms upon which the right to modify and distribute the material depended and invited direct contact if a downloader wished to negotiate other terms. These restrictions were both clear and necessary to accomplish the objectives of the open source licensing collaboration, including economic benefit. ...

Copyright holders who engage in open source licensing have the right to control the modification and distribution of copyrighted material. ... Copyright licenses are designed to support the right to exclude; money damages alone do not support or enforce that right. The choice to exact consideration in the form of compliance with the open source requirements of disclosure and explanation of changes, rather than as a dollar-denominated fee, is entitled to no less legal recognition. Indeed, because a calculation of damages is inherently speculative, these types of license restrictions might well be rendered meaningless absent the ability to enforce through injunctive relief.

In this case, a user who downloads the JMRI copyrighted materials is authorized to make modifications and to distribute the materials "provided that" the user follows the restrictive terms of the Artistic License. A copyright holder can grant the right to make certain modifications, yet retain his right to prevent other modifications. Indeed, such a goal is exactly the purpose of adding conditions to a license grant. The Artistic License, like many other common copyright licenses, requires that any copies that are distributed contain the copyright notices and the COPYING file.

It is outside the scope of the Artistic License to modify and distribute the copyrighted materials without copyright notices and a tracking of modifications from the original computer files. If a down loader does not assent to these conditions stated in the COPYING file, he is instructed to "make other arrangements with the Copyright Holder." Katzer/Kamind did not make any such "other arrangements." The clear language of the Artistic License creates conditions to protect the economic rights at issue in the granting of a public license. These conditions govern the rights to modify and distribute the computer programs and files included in the downloadable software package. The attribution and modification transparency requirements directly serve to drive traffic to the open source incubation page and to inform downstream users of the project, which is a significant economic goal of the copyright holder that the law will enforce. Through this controlled spread of information, the copyright holder gains creative collaborators to the open source project; by requiring that changes made by downstream users be visible to the copyright holder and others, the copyright holder learns about the uses for his software and gains others' knowledge that can be used to advance future software releases.

IV.

For the aforementioned reasons, we vacate and remand. While Katzer/Kamind appears to have conceded that they did not comply with the aforedescribed conditions of the Artistic License, the District Court did not make factual findings on the likelihood of success on the merits in proving that Katzer/Kamind violated the conditions of the Artistic License. Having determined that the terms of the Artistic License are enforceable copyright conditions, we remand to enable the District Court to determine whether Jacobsen has demonstrated (1) a likelihood of success on the merits and either a presumption of irreparable harm or a demonstration of irreparable harm; or (2) a fair chance of success on the merits and a clear disparity in the relative hardships and tipping in his favor.

QUESTIONS

1. Of course, all of this licensing machinery is useless if you can't get a court to enforce your license conditions. Why are open-source developers particularly concerned about the enforceability of license terms? Why might they have more to worry about?

2. Is the Artistic License more like the MIT license or like the GPL?

3. *Jacobsen* is about a narrow and seemingly technical distinction: whether terms are contractual covenants or conditions that limit the scope of a copyright license. Why does this matter? What would the remedies be for breach of a contractual covenant? How about for copying the software beyond the scope of the license?

4. How does *Jacobsen* answer the "covenant or condition" question? What sources of evidence does it look to? Is the result it reaches consistent with what the creators of JMRI would have wanted? With what they intended? With what users of JMRI would have expected?

5. How do you think open source programmers would feel about this decision? How do you think commercial developers would feel about it? Consider, for example, Autodesk, from *Vernor v. Autodesk*. Does the question of whether license terms are contracts or covenants affect Autodesk's litigation position?

6. MIT's Open Course Ware and Wikipedia (discussed in *Jacobsen*) both use the Creative Commons Attribution ShareAlike 3.0 license, the United States version of which is available at http://creativecommons.org/licenses/by-nc-sa/3.0/us/. What kind of projects are these? What kind of license is this? How is it like the open source licenses discussed above? How is it different? Why are they using it?

C. Fair Use

The fair use doctrine provides a complete defense to copyright infringement. Unfortunately, because it is equitable and fact-specific, it is impossible to give a definitive test for what kinds of uses are fair. Instead, the statute specifies four nonexclusive factors that courts must consider. Over time, courts have asked certain standard questions about each factor, and have tended to allow fair use defenses for certain patterns of use, but not for others. The best way to understand the likely scope of fair use is reading substantial numbers of fair use cases.

The materials in this section focus on two common patterns of claimed fair uses. The first has to do with personal uses made by individual consumers, and is explored in the note on *Sony* and in *Napster*. The second is a new idea of what a "transformative" use of a copyrighted work might look like online, and is explored in *Katz* and in *Perfect 10*.

COPYRIGHT ACT [FAIR USE]
Title 17, United States Code

§ 107 – *Limitations on exclusive rights: Fair use*

Notwithstanding the provisions of sections 106 and 106A, the fair use of a copyrighted work, including such use by reproduction in copies or phonorecords or by any other means specified by that section, for purposes such as criticism, comment, news reporting, teaching (including multiple copies for classroom use), scholarship, or research, is not an infringement of copyright. In determining whether the use made of a work in any particular case is a fair use the factors to be considered shall include –

(1) the purpose and character of the use, including whether such use is of a commercial nature or is for nonprofit educational purposes;

(2) the nature of the copyrighted work;

(3) the amount and substantiality of the portion used in relation to the copyrighted work as a whole; and

(4) the effect of the use upon the potential market for or value of the copyrighted work.

The fact that a work is unpublished shall not itself bar a finding of fair use if such finding is made upon consideration of all the above factors.

NOTE ON SONY V. UNIVERSAL (FAIR USE)

The Supreme Court's 1984 decision in *Sony Corp. of Am. v. Universal City Studios, Inc.*, 464 U.S. 417 (1984) is a landmark in copyright. Unfortunately, the way that it framed the issues has not held up well. While both of its core holdings are (probably) good law, the Supreme Court has since repudiated much of *Sony*'s language of "presumptions" about future harm to copyright owners based on whether a use is commercial or not. This note surveys what you need to know about *Sony*'s fair use discussion to understand subsequent developments.

The lawsuit was brought by copyright owners in movies and television shows against Sony, which manufactured the Betamax video-tape recorder (what we would today call a VCR). The copyright owners objected to Betamax owners' use of their VCRs to record over-the-air television. This theory obviously raises the question whether it is copyright infringement to use a VCR to record TV programs.

For reasons discussed in the second note on *Sony*, *infra*, the Supreme Court only faced this issue for some home taping, not all. The Court first held that some copyright owners authorized home taping. Fred Rogers – i.e. Mister Rogers from *Mister Rogers' Neighborhood* – testified that he encouraged parents to tape his show so they could watch it later with their children. The copyright owners in various religious, educational, and sporting programs similarly authorized home tapings. All of these uses were clearly legal, because a use made with the copyright owner's permission is not an infringement.

The Court then turned to *unauthorized* home taping, specifically the practice of "time-shifting": using a VCR "to record a program [the owner] cannot view as it is being televised and then to watch it once at a later time." The Court held that the plaintiffs hadn't shown that time-shifting was likely to harm the markets for their works. Time-shifting was private and noncommercial – VCR owners were keeping the tapes for personal viewing, not selling or renting them. Nor was it likely that the overall audience size would decrease if some VCR owners watched programs later, rather than live; if anything, the opposite was true. And since time-shifting expanded "public access to freely broadcast television programs," it would benefit society overall.

Sony left open more questions than it answered. The fair use holding seems to turn on a few salient facts: consumers were making private copies for themselves, of works to which they already lawfully had access, in a way that had not been linked to any demonstrated harm to the copyright owners' sales. But the precise holding is elusive. Would the result have been different for cable television, which is not "freely broadcast?" Would it matter if copyright owners could show that VCR owners were keeping the tapes ("librarying") rather than deleting them after one viewing? Would it affect the reasoning if, as the dissent suggested, there were strong evidence that many VCR users skipped over the commercials?

Caselaw on these questions is surprisingly sparse. One court stated that copying music from a CD to a computer's hard drive for use on an MP3 player was "paradigmatic noncommercial personal use" and tossed in a *cf.* citation to *Sony*'s fair use holding, perhaps suggesting in passing that "space-shifting" from a CD to one's iPod was also fair use. *Recording Indu. Assoc. of Am. v. Diamond Multimedia Sys.*, 180 F.3d 1072 (9th Cir. 1999). Other courts rejected fair use claims by companies making internal copies for their employees, *see, e.g., Am. Geophysical Union v. Texaco, Inc.*, 60 F.3d 913 (2d Cir. 1994), and by copy shops making photocopies on behalf of students – even where the students might have a fair use defense if they made the copies themselves, *see, e.g. Princeton Univ. Press v. Mich. Document Services*, 99 F.3d 1381 (6th Cir. 1996).

Most recently, *Fox Broadcasting Co., Inc. v. Dish Network L.L.C.*, 747 F.3d 1060 (9th Cir. 2013), considered the Dish Hopper, a home digital video recorder (DVR) for use with the company's subscription satellite TV service. The Hopper is notable for two features. First, it is capable of recording "any and all primetime programming on the four major broadcast networks (including Fox) every night of the week," at the touch of a button. *Id.* at 1064. Second, it automatically skips over commercials, also at the touch of a button. According to the Ninth Circuit, both features were fair use. The automatic recordings were made to enable private noncommercial time-shifting, and hence they were fair use under *Sony*. As for the commercial skipping, it

> does not implicate Fox's copyright interest because Fox owns the copy-
> rights to the television programs, not to the ads aired in the commer-
> cial breaks. If recording an entire copyrighted program is a fair use,
> the fact that viewers do not watch the ads not copyrighted by Fox
> cannot transform the recording into a copyright violation. ...

Id. at 1068–69. Are you persuaded?

A & M RECORDS, INC. V. NAPSTER, INC.
239 F.3d 1004 (9th Cir. 2001)

Beezer, Circuit Judge:

I. ...

In 1987, the Moving Picture Experts Group set a standard file format for the storage of audio recordings in a digital format called MPEG-3, abbreviated as "MP3." Digital MP3 files are created through a process colloquially called "ripping." Ripping software allows a computer owner to copy an audio compact disk ("audio CD") directly onto a computer's hard drive by compressing the audio information on the CD into the MP3 format. The MP3's compressed format allows for rapid transmission of digital audio files from one computer ...

[In the terminology of *Columbia Pictures v. Fung, supra* Section 2.A, Napster was a "centralized" P2P system. A few important technical details were:

If a registered user wants to list available files stored in his computer's hard drive on Napster for others to access, he must first create a "user library" directory on his computer's hard drive. The user then saves his MP3 files in the library directory, using self-designated file names. He next must log into the Napster system using his user name and password. His MusicShare software then searches his user library and verifies that the available files are properly formatted. If in the correct MP3 format, the names of the MP3 files will be uploaded from the user's computer to the Napster servers. The content of the MP3 files remains stored in the user's computer. ...

Software located on the Napster servers maintains a "search index" of Napster's collective directory. To search the files available from Napster users currently connected to the network servers, the individual user accesses a form in the MusicShare software stored in his computer and enters either the name of a song or an artist as the object of the search. The form is then transmitted to a Napster server and automatically compared to the MP3 file names listed in the server's search index. Napster's server compiles a list of all MP3 file names pulled from the search index which include the same search terms entered on the search form and transmits the list to the searching user. The Napster server does not search the contents of any MP3 file; rather, the search is limited to a text search of the file names indexed in a particular cluster. Those file names may contain typographical errors or otherwise inaccurate descriptions of the content of the files since they are designated by other users.]

III. ...

B. Fair Use

Napster contends that its users do not directly infringe plaintiffs' copyrights because the users are engaged in fair use of the material. *See* 17 U.S.C. § 107 ("[T]he fair use of a copyrighted work . . . is not an infringement of copyright."). Napster identifies three specific alleged fair uses: sampling, where users make temporary copies of a work before purchasing; space-shifting, where users access a sound recording through the Napster system that they already own in audio CD format; and permissive distribution of recordings by both new and established artists.

The district court considered factors listed in 17 U.S.C. § 107, which guide a court's fair use determination. These factors are: (1) the purpose and character of the use; (2) the nature of the copyrighted work; (3) the "amount and substantiality of the portion used" in relation to the work as a whole; and (4) the effect of the use upon the potential market for the work or the value of the work. *See* 17 U.S.C. § 107. The district court first conducted a general analysis of Napster system uses under § 107, and then applied its reasoning to the alleged fair uses identified by Napster. The district court concluded that Napster users are not fair users. We agree. We first address the court's overall fair use analysis.

1. Purpose and Character of the Use

This factor focuses on whether the new work merely replaces the object of the original creation or instead adds a further purpose or different character. In other words, this factor asks "whether and to what extent the new work is 'transformative.'" *See Campbell v. Acuff-Rose Music, Inc.*, 510 U.S. 569, 579 (1994).

... Courts have been reluctant to find fair use when an original work is merely retransmitted in a different medium. *See, e.g., Infinity Broadcast Corp. v. Kirkwood*, 150 F.3d 104, 108 (2d Cir. 1998) (concluding that retransmission of radio broadcast over telephone lines is not transformative); *UMG Recordings, Inc. v. MP3.com, Inc.*, 92 F. Supp. 2d 349, 351 (S.D.N.Y.) (finding that reproduction of audio CD into MP3 format does not "transform" the work), *certification denied*, 2000 WL 710056 (S.D.N.Y. June 1, 2000) ("Defendant's copyright infringement was clear, and the mere fact that it was clothed in the exotic webbing of the Internet does not disguise its illegality.").

This "purpose and character" element also requires the district court to determine whether the allegedly infringing use is commercial or noncommercial. *See Campbell*, 510 U.S. at 584–85. A commercial use weighs against a finding of fair use but is not conclusive on the issue. *Id.* The district court determined that Napster users engage in commercial use of the copyrighted materials largely because (1) "a host user sending a file cannot be said to engage in a personal use when distributing that file to an anonymous requester" and (2) "Napster users get for free something they would ordinarily have to buy." The district court's findings are not clearly erroneous. ...

2. The Nature of the Use

Works that are creative in nature are closer to the core of intended copyright protection" than are more fact-based works. *See Campbell*, 510 U.S. at 586. The district court determined that plaintiffs' "copyrighted musical compositions and sound recordings are creative in nature . . . which cuts against a finding of fair use under the second factor." We find no error in the district court's conclusion.

3. The Portion Used

"While 'wholesale copying does not preclude fair use per se,' copying an entire work 'militates against a finding of fair use.'" *Worldwide Church [of God v. Philadelphia Church of God, Inc.* 227 F.3d 1110, 1118] (quoting *Hustler Magazine, Inc. v. Moral Majority, Inc.*, 796 F.2d 1148, 1155 (9th Cir. 1986)). The district court determined that Napster users engage in "wholesale copying" of copyrighted work because file transfer necessarily "involves copying the entirety of the copyrighted work." We agree. ...

4. Effect of Use on Market

"Fair use, when properly applied, is limited to copying by others which does not materially impair the marketability of the work which is copied." *Harper & Row Publishers, Inc. v. Nation Enters.*, 471 U.S. 539, 566–67 (1985). "[T]he importance of this [fourth] factor will vary, not only with the amount of harm, but also with the relative strength of the showing on the other factors." *Campbell*, 510 U.S. at 591 n. 21. ...

Addressing this factor, the district court concluded that Napster harms the market in "at least" two ways: it reduces audio CD sales among college students and it "raises barriers to plaintiffs' entry into the market for the digital downloading of music." ...

5. Identified Uses

Napster maintains that its identified uses of sampling and space-shifting were wrongly excluded as fair uses by the district court.

a. Sampling

Napster contends that its users download MP3 files to "sample" the music in order to decide whether to purchase the recording. ...

... Plaintiffs have established that they are likely to succeed in proving that even authorized temporary downloading of individual songs for sampling purposes is commercial in nature. The record supports a finding that free promotional downloads are highly regulated by the record company plaintiffs and that the companies collect royalties for song samples available on retail Internet sites. Evidence relied on by the district court demonstrates that the free downloads provided by the record companies consist of thirty-to-sixty second samples or are full songs programmed to "time out," that is, exist only for a short time on the downloader's computer. In comparison, Napster users download a full, free and permanent copy of the recording. ...

[O]verall, Napster has an adverse impact on the audio CD and digital download markets. Contrary to Napster's assertion that the district court failed to specifically address the market impact of sampling, the district court determined that "[e]ven if the type of sampling supposedly done on Napster were a non-commercial use, plaintiffs have demonstrated a substantial likelihood that it would adversely affect the potential market for their copyrighted works if it became widespread." The record supports the district court's preliminary determinations that: (1) the more music that sampling users download, the less likely they are to eventually purchase the recordings on audio CD; and (2) even if the audio CD market is not harmed, Napster has adverse effects on the developing digital download market.

Napster further argues that the district court erred in rejecting its evidence that the users' downloading of "samples" increases or tends to increase audio CD sales. The district court, however, correctly noted that "any potential enhancement of plaintiffs' sales . . . would not tip the fair use analysis conclusively in favor of defendant." We agree that increased sales of copyrighted material attributable to unauthorized use should not deprive the copyright holder of the right to license the material. Nor does positive impact in one market, here the audio CD market, deprive the copyright holder of the right to develop identified alternative markets, here the digital download market.

We find no error in the district court's factual findings or abuse of discretion in the court's conclusion that plaintiffs will likely prevail in establishing that sampling does not constitute a fair use.

b. Space-Shifting

Napster also maintains that space-shifting is a fair use. Space-shifting occurs when a Napster user downloads MP3 music files in order to listen to music he already owns on audio CD. Napster asserts that we have already held that space-shifting of musical compositions and sound recordings is a fair use. *See Recording Indus. Ass'n of Am. v. Diamond Multimedia Sys., Inc.*, 180 F.3d 1072, 1079 (9th Cir. 1999) ("Rio [a portable MP3 player] merely makes copies in order to render portable, or 'space-shift,' those files that already reside on a user's hard drive. . . . Such copying is a paradigmatic noncommercial personal use."). *See also generally Sony*, 464 U.S. at 423 (holding that "time-shifting," where a video tape recorder owner records a television show for later viewing, is a fair use).

... Both *Diamond* and *Sony* are inapposite because the methods of shifting in these cases did not also simultaneously involve distribution of the copyrighted material to the general public; the time or space-shifting of copyrighted material exposed the material only to the original user. In *Diamond*, for example, the copyrighted music was transferred from the user's computer hard drive to the user's portable MP3 player. So too *Sony*, where the majority of VCR purchasers did not distribute taped television broadcasts, but merely enjoyed them at home. Conversely, it is obvious that once a user lists a copy of music he already owns on the Napster system in order to access the music from another location, the song becomes available to millions of other individuals, not just the original CD owner.

...

... We find no error in the district court's determination that plaintiffs will likely succeed in establishing that Napster users do not have a fair use defense.

QUESTIONS

1. The liability of Napster itself for its users' activities is discussed in the next section. But do you see why the argument that its users were making fair uses helps Napster's defense?

2. Did you need to read this opinion to know that downloading complete songs on the original Napster was not a fair use?

3. The market-harm question is surprisingly tricky. It was the subject of dueling expert reports in the *Napster* case and continues to rage in the scholarly literature. Why is it incorrect to assume that each download on Napster is a lost sale for the record companies? How would you establish that file-sharing does or does not affect music sales?

4. Why did the court reject Napster's argument that sampling is a fair use? Would it have been simpler to hold that most Napster users, in fact, were keeping the downloaded MP3s they liked, rather than buying the CDs?

5. MP3.com was a Napster contemporary. It created a library of tens of thousands of MP3s copied from CDs. A subscriber was required to "prove" he or she owned a CD by inserting it into a computer that then connected to MP3.com's servers. After that, MP3.com would let the subscriber stream the music on that CD to any computer. When sued, MP3.com argued that it was helping its subscribers engage in fair-use space-shifting. Was it right?

KATZ V. GOOGLE INC.
802 F.3d 1178 (11th Cir. 2015)

Per Curiam:

Raanan Katz holds the copyright to a candid photograph (the Photo) of himself in which his tongue protrudes askew from his mouth. Katz considers the Photo unflattering and embarrassing. Irina Chevaldina copied the Photo into several scathing blog posts she wrote about Katz and his business practices. ... Katz argues the district court erred in finding Chevaldina was entitled to summary judgment based on her affirmative defense that her use of the Photo constituted fair use under 17 U.S.C. § 107. Upon review, we affirm.

I. BACKGROUND

Katz is a minority investor in the Miami Heat basketball team and a commercial real estate tycoon who owns and operates shopping centers through corporate entities collectively known as RK Centers. In February 2011, Seffi Magriso, a professional photographer, took a photograph of Katz while Katz was standing courtside at a basketball practice in Jerusalem. The Photo is a candid headshot of Katz in which his eyebrows are arched sharply upwards and his tongue is sticking out of his mouth. In Katz's opinion, the Photo is "ugly," "embarrassing," and "compromising." *Haaretz,* an Israeli newspaper, published the Photo online in an article about Katz's interest in buying the Hapoel Jerusalem basketball team.

Chevaldina is a disgruntled former tenant in one of Katz's shopping centers. She found the Photo through a Google image search. Chevaldina created a blog devoted to sharply criticizing Katz and the business practices of RK Centers. From May 3, 2011, to September 24, 2012, Chevaldina published 25 blog posts that reproduced the Photo and criticized Katz. Chevaldina reproduced the Photo in her blog posts in three ways: (1) copied in its unaltered, original state; (2) accompanied by sharply worded captions; or (3) cropped and pasted into mocking cartoons. For example, in a September 18, 2011 blog post where the Photo was copied in its unaltered, original state, Chevaldina lambasted Katz for allegedly ripping off a "young American Jewish single mother of [a] special needs child," calling him "the most immoral human-being in the world." In a September 12, 2012, blog post, Chevaldina criticized Katz's litigation strategies as frivolous and copied the Photo with a caption across Katz's chest that says, "HE RIPPED–OFF SPECIAL NEEDS LITTLE JEWISH GIRL." In a February 19, 2012, post about Katz's preparation for a deposition, Chevaldina cropped Katz's face and superimposed it against a cartoon dunce hat.

On June 3, 2012, Magriso assigned all of his rights in the Photo to Katz. Katz then filed a complaint against Chevaldina alleging direct copyright infringement. ...

III. DISCUSSION

The only issue in this appeal is whether Chevaldina's use of the Photo in her blog posts constitutes fair use ... .

A. Purpose and Character of the Work

The first factor—the purpose and character of the allegedly infringing work—requires consideration of (1) whether the use serves a nonprofit educational purpose, as opposed to a commercial purpose; and (2) the degree to which the work is a

transformative use, as opposed to a merely superseding use, of the copyrighted work. The district court did not err in concluding Chevaldina's use of the work was both noncommercial and transformative.

Every use of the Photo on the blog was of a primarily educational, rather than commercial, character. Chevaldina unabashedly criticized and commented on the dealings of Katz, his businesses, and his lawyers. Chevaldina's blog posts sought to warn and educate others about the alleged nefariousness of Katz, and she made no money from her use of the photo. *See* 17 U.S.C. § 107 (designating "criticism" and "comment" as fair use).

Katz argues the Photo served a primarily commercial purpose because, in a March 4, 2012, blog post, Chevaldina said she was "in the process of writing a book 'Why RK Centers Was The Wrong Choice.'" Thus, Katz argues, Chevaldina used the Photo to advertise for commercial book sales. Chevaldina's reference to her intention to write a book about her experiences with Katz does not alone, however, transform the blog post into a commercial venture. Overall, the blog post retains her educational purpose of lambasting Katz and deterring others from conducting business with him. *See* March 4, 2012 Blog Post ("I hope my book will help ambitious people in their dream to be successful without selling the[ir] soul to the [d]evil."). Moreover, the link between Chevaldina's commercial gain and her copying of the Photo was attenuated given that Chevaldina never wrote a book nor made any profits whatsoever. *See Swatch Grp. Mgmt. Servs. Ltd. v. Bloomberg L.P.*, 756 F.3d 73, 83 (2d Cir.2014) (discounting commercial nature of use where "the link between the defendant's commercial gain and its copying is attenuated such that it would be misleading to characterize the use as commercial exploitation").

Chevaldina's use of the Photo was also transformative. A use is transformative when it "adds something new, with a further purpose or different character, altering the first with new expression, meaning, or message." *See Campbell v. Acuff-Rose Music, Inc.*, 510 U.S. 569, 579 (1994). Chevaldina's use of the Photo was transformative because, in the context of the blog post's surrounding commentary, she used Katz's purportedly "ugly" and "compromising" appearance to ridicule and satirize his character. *See Swatch*, 756 F.3d at 84 ("Courts often find such uses [of faithfully reproduced works] transformative by emphasizing the altered purpose or context of the work, as evidenced by the surrounding commentary or criticism.").

Chevaldina's use of the Photo was noncommercial and transformative. Accordingly, the first factor weighs in favor of fair use.

B. Nature of the Copyrighted Work

The second fair use factor—the nature of the copyrighted work – recognizes that there is a hierarchy of copyright protection in which original, creative works are afforded greater protections than derivative works or factual compilations. In evaluating this factor, courts consider (1) whether the work was previously published and (2) whether the work is primarily creative or factual. *See Harper & Row Publishers, Inc. v. Nation Enters.*, 471 U.S. 539, 563–64 (1985).

There is no dispute that the Photo was published prior to Chevaldina's use. As such, the time of publication weighs in favor of fair use. *See Kelly v. Arriba Soft Corp.*, 336 F.3d 811, 820 (9th Cir. 2003) (holding publication of images on internet before defendant's copying favored fair use).

The district court did not err in finding the Photo was primarily a factual work. The law generally recognizes a greater need to disseminate factual works than works of fiction or fantasy. Photography is an art form that may require the photographer to make many important creative decisions. *See Leibovitz v. Paramount*

Pictures Corp., 137 F.3d 109, 116 (2d Cir. 1998) (stating a photographer "is entitled to protection for such artistic elements as the particular lighting, the resulting skin tone on the subject, and the camera angle that she selected"). The Photo, however, is merely a candid shot in a public setting, and there is no evidence in the record that Magriso, the photographer, attempted to convey ideas, emotions, or in any way influence Katz's pose, expression, or clothing. *See Fitzgerald v. CBS Broad., Inc.*, 491 F.Supp. 2d 177, 188 (D. Mass. 2007) (concluding candid photograph of mobster leaving police station was a primarily factual work). While Magriso's photojournalistic timing was fortuitous (at least from Chevaldina's perspective), this alone was not enough to make the creative gilt of the Photo predominate over its plainly factual elements.

The Photo was previously published and primarily factual. The second factor therefore weighs in favor of fair use.

C. Amount of the Work Used

The third factor is "the amount and substantiality of the portion used in relation to the copyrighted work as a whole." 17 U.S.C. § 107(3). A court must ask whether the defendant has "helped herself overmuch to the copyrighted work in light of the purpose and character of the use." *Peter Letterese & Assocs., Inc. v. World Inst. of Scientology Enters.*, 533 F.3d 1287, 1314 (11th Cir. 2008). This factor "weighs less when considering a photograph—where all or most of the work often must be used in order to preserve any meaning at all—than a work such as a text or musical composition, where bits and pieces can be excerpted without losing all value." *Fitzgerald*, 491 F. Supp. 2d at 188.

The district court did not err in finding the third factor was neutral as applied to the blog posts incorporating the Photo. Though ten blog posts reproduced the Photo in its entirety and without alteration, to copy any less of the image "would have made the picture useless to [Chevaldina's] story" that Katz is a predatory commercial landlord. As such, the third factor neither weighs for nor against a finding of fair use.

D. Effect of the Use on the Potential Market for the Work

The fourth factor is "the effect of the use upon the potential market for or value of the copyrighted work." 17 U.S.C. 107(4). The "central question" is whether, assuming that everyone engaged in the conduct of the defendant, the use would cause *substantial* economic harm such that allowing the conduct would frustrate the purposes of copyright by materially impairing the defendant's incentive to publish the work.

The district court did not err in finding Chevaldina's use of the Photo would not materially impair Katz's incentive to publish the work. Katz took the highly unusual step of obtaining the copyright to the Photo and initiating this lawsuit specifically to *prevent* its publication. Katz profoundly distastes the Photo and seeks to extinguish, for all time, the dissemination of his "embarrassing" countenance. Due to Katz's attempt to utilize copyright as an instrument of censorship against unwanted criticism, there is no potential market for his work. While we recognize that even an author who disavows any intention to publish his work "has the right to change his mind," *see Monge v. Maya Magazines, Inc.*, 688 F.3d 1164, 1181 (9th Cir.2012), the likelihood of Katz changing his mind about the Photo is, based on the undisputed evidence in the record, incredibly remote. Since there is no evidence Chevaldina's use of the Photo had or would have any impact upon any actual or potential market, the fourth factor weighs in favor of fair use.

IV. CONCLUSION

Three factors in our fair use inquiry—the purpose and character of the work, the nature of the work, and the effect of the use on the potential market—weigh in favor of Chevaldina. The amount and substantiality of the work is neutral. After weighing all four factors, our analysis tilts strongly in favor of fair use. The district court did not err in granting summary judgment to Chevaldina because every reasonable factfinder would conclude the inclusion of the Photo in her blog posts constituted fair use. ...

QUESTIONS

1. *Campbell* involved 2 Live Crew's foul-mouthed rap version of Roy Orbison's pop hit "Oh, Pretty Woman." The Supreme Court held that 2 Live Crew was engaged in a parody of the Orbison song, that it had "add[ed] something new, with a further purpose or different character, altering the first with new expression, meaning, or message." Why does copyright law favor transformative uses like this?

2. Chevaldina didn't crop, retouch, or modify the Photo in any way. Is the idea of "transformative" use really helpful in explaining why her use of the Photo should be considered fair use?

3. How much is the court's opinion in *Katz* influenced by the fact that Katz is trying to suppress criticism of himself? Based on other cases you have seen, how consistent are the courts in their treatment of such plaintiffs?

PERFECT 10, INC. V. AMAZON.COM, INC.

508 F.3d 1146 (9th Cir. 2007)

[The facts of the case are given *supra* in Section A.]

C. Fair Use Defense

Because Perfect 10 has succeeded in showing it would prevail in its prima facie case that Google's thumbnail images infringe Perfect 10's display rights, the burden shifts to Google to show that it will likely succeed in establishing an affirmative defense. Google contends that its use of thumbnails is a fair use of the images and therefore does not constitute an infringement of Perfect 10's copyright. *See* 17 U.S.C. § 107.

The fair use defense permits the use of copyrighted works without the copyright owner's consent under certain situations. The defense encourages and allows the development of new ideas that build on earlier ones, thus providing a necessary counterbalance to the copyright law's goal of protecting creators' work product. "From the infancy of copyright protection, some opportunity for fair use of copyrighted materials has been thought necessary to fulfill copyright's very purpose. . . ." *Campbell v. Acuff-Rose Music, Inc.* 510 U.S. 569, 575 (1994). "The fair use doctrine thus permits and requires courts to avoid rigid application of the copyright statute when, on occasion, it would stifle the very creativity which that law is designed to foster." *Id.* at 577. ...

In applying the fair use analysis in this case, we are guided by *Kelly v. Arriba Soft Corp.*, 336 F.3d 811 (9th Cir. 2003), which considered substantially the same use of copyrighted photographic images as is at issue here. In *Kelly*, a photographer brought a direct infringement claim against Arriba, the operator of an Internet search engine. The search engine provided thumbnail versions of the photographer's images in response to search queries. We held that Arriba's use of thumbnail images was a fair use primarily based on the transformative nature of a search engine and its benefit to the public. We also concluded that Arriba's use of the thumbnail images did not harm the photographer's market for his image.

In this case, the district court determined that Google's use of thumbnails was not a fair use and distinguished *Kelly*. We consider these distinctions in the context of the four-factor fair use analysis.

Purpose and character of the use. The first factor, 17 U.S.C. § 107(1), requires a court to consider "the purpose and character of the use, including whether such use is of a commercial nature or is for nonprofit educational purposes." The central purpose of this inquiry is to determine whether and to what extent the new work is "transformative." *Campbell*, 510 U.S. at 579. A work is "transformative" when the new work does not "merely supersede the objects of the original creation" but rather "adds something new, with a further purpose or different character, altering the first with new expression, meaning, or message." *Id.* Conversely, if the new work supersedes the use of the original, the use is likely not a fair use.

As noted in *Campbell*, a "transformative work" is one that alters the original work "with new expression, meaning, or message." "A use is considered transformative only where a defendant changes a plaintiff's copyrighted work or uses the plaintiff's copyrighted work in a different context such that the plaintiff's work is transformed into a new creation." *Wall Data [Inc. v. Los Angeles County Sheriff's Dep't*, 447 F.3d 769, 778 (9th Cir. 2006)].

Google's use of thumbnails is highly transformative. In *Kelly*, we concluded that Arriba's use of thumbnails was transformative because "Arriba's use of the images serve[d] a different function than Kelly's use – improving access to information on the [I]nternet versus artistic expression." *Kelly*, 336 F.3d at 819. Although an image may have been created originally to serve an entertainment, aesthetic, or informative function, a search engine transforms the image into a pointer directing a user to a source of information. Just as a "parody has an obvious claim to transformative value" because "it can provide social benefit, by shedding light on an earlier work, and, in the process, creating a new one," *Campbell*, 510 U.S. at 579, a search engine provides social benefit by incorporating an original work into a new work, namely, an electronic reference tool. Indeed, a search engine may be more transformative than a parody because a search engine provides an entirely new use for the original work, while a parody typically has the same entertainment purpose as the original work. In other words, a search engine puts images "in a different context" so that they are "transformed into a new creation." *Wall Data*, 447 F.3d at 778.

The fact that Google incorporates the entire Perfect 10 image into the search engine results does not diminish the transformative nature of Google's use. As the district court correctly noted, we determined in *Kelly* that even making an exact copy of a work may be transformative so long as the copy serves a different function than the original work. ...

We conclude that the significantly transformative nature of Google's search engine, particularly in light of its public benefit, outweighs Google's superseding and commercial uses of the thumbnails in this case. ...

The nature of the copyrighted work. With respect to the second factor, "the nature of the copyrighted work," 17 U.S.C. § 107(2), our decision in *Kelly* is directly on point. There we held that the photographer's images were "creative in nature" and thus "closer to the core of intended copyright protection than are more fact-based works." *Kelly*, 336 F.3d at 820 (internal quotation omitted). However, because the photos appeared on the Internet before Arriba used thumbnail versions in its search engine results, this factor weighed only slightly in favor of the photographer. *Id.*

Here, the district court found that Perfect 10's images were creative but also previously published. ... Once Perfect 10 has exploited this commercially valuable right of first publication by putting its images on the Internet for paid subscribers, Perfect 10 is no longer entitled to the enhanced protection available for an unpublished work. Accordingly the district court did not err in holding that this factor weighed only slightly in favor of Perfect 10.

The amount and substantiality of the portion used. "The third factor asks whether the amount and substantiality of the portion used in relation to the copyrighted work as a whole . . . are reasonable in relation to the purpose of the copying." *Campbell*, 510 U.S. at 586 (internal quotation omitted); *see also* 17 U.S.C. § 107(3). In *Kelly*, we held Arriba's use of the entire photographic image was reasonable in light of the purpose of a search engine. Specifically, we noted, "[i]t was necessary for Arriba to copy the entire image to allow users to recognize the image and decide whether to pursue more information about the image or the originating [website]. If Arriba only copied part of the image, it would be more difficult to identify it, thereby reducing the usefulness of the visual search engine." *Id.* Accordingly, we concluded that this factor did not weigh in favor of either party. Because the same analysis applies to Google's use of Perfect 10's image, the district court did not err in finding that this factor favored neither party.

Effect of use on the market. The fourth factor is "the effect of the use upon the potential market for or value of the copyrighted work." 17 U.S.C. § 107(4). In Kelly, we concluded that Arriba's use of the thumbnail images did not harm the market for the photographer's full-size images. We reasoned that because thumbnails were not a substitute for the full-sized images, they did not harm the photographer's ability to sell or license his full-sized images. The district court here followed Kelly's reasoning, holding that Google's use of thumbnails did not hurt Perfect 10's market for full-size images. We agree.

Perfect 10 argues that the district court erred because the likelihood of market harm may be presumed if the intended use of an image is for commercial gain. However, this presumption does not arise when a work is transformative because "market substitution is at least less certain, and market harm may not be so readily inferred." *Campbell*, 510 U.S. at 591. ...

Perfect 10 also has a market for reduced-size images, an issue not considered in *Kelly*. The district court held that "Google's use of thumbnails likely does harm the potential market for the downloading of [Perfect 10's] reduced-size images onto cell phones." *Perfect 10*, 416 F. Supp. 2d at 851 (emphasis omitted). The district court reasoned that persons who can obtain Perfect 10 images free of charge from Google are less likely to pay for a download, and the availability of Google's thumbnail images would harm Perfect 10's market for cell phone downloads. As we discussed above, the district court did not make a finding that Google users have downloaded thumbnail images for cell phone use. This potential harm to Perfect 10's market remains hypothetical. We conclude that this factor favors neither party.

Having undertaken a case-specific analysis of all four factors, we now weigh these factors together "in light of the purposes of copyright." *Campbell*, 510 U.S. at 578; *see also Kelly*, 336 F.3d at 818 ("We must balance [the section 107] factors in light of the objectives of copyright law, rather than view them as definitive or determinative tests."). In this case, Google has put Perfect 10's thumbnail images (along with millions of other thumbnail images) to a use fundamentally different than the use intended by Perfect 10. In doing so, Google has provided a significant benefit to the public. Weighing this significant transformative use against the unproven use of Google's thumbnails for cell phone downloads, and considering the other fair use factors, all in light of the purpose of copyright, we conclude that Google's use of Perfect 10's thumbnails is a fair use.

QUESTIONS

1. What distinguishes the thumbnails from the full-sized images they stand in for? After *Perfect 10*, is it always a fair use to make a postage-stamp-sized copy of a larger image?

2. Didn't *Napster* just reject previewing music before buying it as a basis for a fair use claim? And doesn't *Perfect 10* now hold that thumbnail images are a fair use because they help users preview the full-sized image they're looking for? How can these two decisions – by the same court, no less – be reconciled?

3. Compare *Perfect 10* with *Field*. What would be the consequences for Google Image Search if Perfect 10 were to prevail on its infringement claim with respect to the thumbnails? Does this help explain the result?

4. In 2004, Google began scanning tens of millions of books (loaned to it by academic libraries) to construct a search engine for books. It showed "snippets" of up to an eighth of a page in response to queries. Authors and publisher sued, claiming copyright infringement. Does *Perfect 10* control, or is the case distinguishable?

BUBONIC PLAGIARISM PROBLEM

Your cousin Denny is a high-school junior; his school has recently started using a service called The Bubonic Plagiarism Detector. The school requires students to submit all their papers in Microsoft Word; the school then uploads the papers to Bubonic. The papers are analyzed using a series of what Bubonic describes as "sophisticated proprietary algorithms to detect similarities between submitted essays and the hundreds of thousands of essays in our databases." If it finds similarities over a predefined threshold, Bubonic emails the teacher several paragraphs from the portion of the essay that the student's paper matched with. The teacher can then look to see whether the similarities result from coincidence, quoting common sources, or possible plagiarism. Each time an essay is submitted, Bubonic also keeps a copy, so that it can compare future students' submissions to see whether they have been plagiarized from it.

Denny is annoyed by the process. He thinks it's a sign of disrespect and distrust by his school; as an honest honor-roll student, he's bothered by the insult to his integrity. He also doesn't like the fact that Bubonic is a for-profit company, so that it's making money off of his work. He's approached you about the possibility of filing a copyright infringement lawsuit against Bubonic. How strong a case might Denny have? Are there ways you could make it stronger? Are there factual issues you'd want to research before giving Denny an answer?

D. Direct and Secondary Liability

Copyright is confusingly divided into direct and secondary infringement. The division itself is familiar, but copyright's system is unusually complicated. This section starts with a threshold condition for direct infringement (the so-called "volitional conduct" test), and then considers four doctrines of secondary liability: vicarious infringement, contributory infringement, the *Sony* defense to contributory infringement, and inducement infringement.

PERFECT 10, INC. V. GIGANEWS, INC.
No. CV11–07098 AHM (SHx), 2013 WL 2109963 (C.D. Cal. Mar. 8, 2013)

Matz, District Judge: ...

I. FACTS

Plaintiff is an adult entertainment company that produces and sells adult photographs, video productions, and other media. Plaintiff derives its main source of revenue from selling access to adult images displayed on its website perfect10.com. Due to the rampant infringement of its products, Plaintiff alleges, it has been forced to close down its previously well-known magazine *Perfect 10* and it no longer earns revenue from merchandise featuring its images. ...

Defendants provide access to an online network called USENET. USENET is a global system of online bulletin boards that allow users to post materials related to a particular topic. Each bulletin board is commonly referred to as a "newsgroup." When a user posts something in a newsgroup, that post is called an "article." Plaintiff alleges that in one category of newsgroups, called the "alt.binaries.* " newsgroups, users post almost exclusively pirated materials.

Although Plaintiff obscures these facts in the Complaint, the Court takes judicial notice of the following two generally known aspects about USENET. First, many other commercial providers besides Defendants provide access to USENET. *See Religious Technology Center v. Netcom On–Line Communication Services, Inc.,* 907 F. Supp. 1361, 1366, n.4 (N.D. Cal. 1995) (*"Netcom"*) ("There is no specific network that is the Usenet. Usenet traffic flows over a wide range of networks, including the Internet and dial-up phone links."); *Arista Records LLC v. Usenet.com, Inc.,* 633 F. Supp. 2d 124, 129–130 (S.D.N.Y. 2009) (*"Usenet"*) ("To obtain access to the USENET, a user must gain access through a commercial USENET provider ... or an internet service provider."). Second, the content on USENET is primarily user-driven – that is, the content that is stored on a USENET provider's server is generally uploaded by USENET users or subscribers.

Defendants own and operate websites that sell USENET access for a monthly fee, starting at $4.99 per month. The content posted by Defendants' subscribers and other USENET users, including infringing content, is stored on Defendants' servers. Visitors to Defendants' websites can display the USENET content from the Defendants' servers or they may download that content directly onto their own computer. Defendants' service permits their subscribers to search USENET content for specific files. For example, a user interested in finding Perfect 10 works on Defendants' USENET servers might search for the term "Perfect 10." ...

Plaintiff alleges that Defendants program their servers to distribute and download infringing content. Plaintiff also alleges that Defendants control which materials are distributed to and copied from other third party servers. Plaintiff contends that Defendants have infringed on more than 165,000 Perfect 10 copyrighted images and that Defendants are aware that they are illegally copying, distributing, and selling infringing materials. According to Plaintiff, Defendants' ability to generate revenue is based almost exclusively on demand for the pirated works contained in the alt.binaries* newsgroups. ...

III. DISCUSSION

A. Copyright Infringement

Plaintiff proceeds on its copyright infringement claim under theories of direct, contributory, and vicarious liability. The analysis of the sufficiency of these claims is complicated by two factors. First, as the Supreme Court has recognized, the "lines between direct infringement, contributory infringement, and vicarious liability are not clearly drawn." *A & M Records, Inc. v. Napster, Inc.*, 239 F.3d 1004, 1022 (9th Cir. 2001) (*"Napster II"*) (quoting *Sony Corp. of America v. Universal City Studios, Inc.*, 464 U.S. 417, 435, n.17 (1984)). Courts have struggled in particular with the question of whether a defendant who offers technology that enables third parties to exchange infringing content should be held *directly* liable. As discussed *infra*, courts have reached different results on this issue. ...

1. Direct Copyright Infringement

To allege a prima facie case of direct copyright infringement, Plaintiff must satisfy two requirements: (1) it must show ownership of the allegedly infringed material, and (2) it must demonstrate that Defendants committed an act of "copying" this material. The word "copying" is shorthand for the infringing of any of the copyright owner's five exclusive rights under 17 U.S.C. § 106. ... Plaintiff alleges that Defendants have copied, reproduced, distributed, adapted, and/or publicly displayed works copyrighted by Perfect 10, thereby directly violating its exclusive rights.

The parties do not dispute that Plaintiff has sufficiently alleged ownership of the allegedly infringed material. Indeed, Plaintiff has pleaded that it owns the copyrights to more than 165,000 images that Defendants have sold and distributed through their service. Plaintiff has also attached as Exhibit 1 to the Complaint a list of the copyright registration numbers of some of its photographs.The Court therefore concludes that Plaintiff's allegations satisfy the first element (ownership) of a direct infringement claim.

Whether Plaintiff has alleged an act of "copying" is a closer question. Based on the facts alleged by Plaintiff, it is clear that USENET users who upload copyrighted Perfect 10 images to the newsgroup infringe Perfect 10's copyrights. Moreover, it is clear that copyright infringement is a strict liability tort, making Defendants' mental state irrelevant. But it is less clear whether by merely creating and operating programs that automatically copy copyrighted images in response to the commands of its users, Defendants can be said to have engaged in "copying" themselves. Courts have struggled with the question of when and whether ownership of an apparatus or system that automatically creates copies when prompted by third party users can lead to direct infringement liability. A leading case in the field, involving claims of direct infringement against another USENET access provider, provides a helpful analogy: does the "owner of a copy machine who lets the public make copies with it" commit direct copyright infringement if individuals use his machine to make unauthorized copies of copyrighted works? *Netcom*, 907 F. Supp. at 1369.

In *Netcom*, Judge Whyte answered that question in the negative, and his ruling has become a seminal opinion in the field. He reasoned that direct copyright infringement requires "some element of volition or causation which is lacking where a defendant's system is merely used to create a copy by a third party." *Id.* at 1370. Because Netcom's servers were programmed to *automatically* copy all content that was posted on Netcom's servers – including infringing content – without any volitional act by Netcom, Judge Whyte held that it could not be said to have "caused the copying," and thus could not be held liable for direct infringement. *Id.* at 1369.

Although the Ninth Circuit has not spoken on the issue, the *Netcom* principle that "volitional" conduct is required for direct liability has been widely adopted, including by the Second and Fourth Circuits. *See, e.g., Cartoon Network LP, LLLP v. CSC Holdings, Inc.,* 536 F.3d 121, 131 (2nd Cir. 2008) ("[A] significant difference exists between making a request to a human employee, who then volitionally operates the copying system, and issuing a command directly to a system, which automatically obeys commands and engages in no volitional conduct."); *CoStar Group, Inc. v. LoopNet, Inc.,* 373 F.3d 544, 551 (4th Cir. 2004) ("[W]e conclude that *Netcom* made a particularly rational interpretation of § 106 when it concluded that a person had to engage in volitional conduct – specifically, the act constituting infringement – to become a direct infringer.").

Notwithstanding these sound decisions, the concept of "volition" can be confusing. "Volitional" is sometimes understood to mean "intentional," and yet no showing of intent is required for direct infringement liability. In this Court's view, the key to understanding the so-called "volitional conduct" requirement is to equate it with the requirement of causation, not intent. "Just who caused the copyrighted material to be infringed?" The Second Circuit's opinion in *Cartoon Network* is particularly helpful in this regard. In the words of that court, "the question is *who* made this copy." 536 F.3d at 130. The Second Circuit further clarified that the goal of the inquiry is to "identify the actor (or actors) whose conduct has been so significant and important a cause that [he or she] should be legally responsible." *Id.* at 132. Other district courts have astutely described this element of direct liability as requiring that plaintiffs show that the defendants must "actively engage" in or "directly cause" the infringing activity in order to be held liable for direct infringement. [citing cases] ...

Turning to the allegations in Plaintiff's Complaint, the Court finds that Plaintiff has not alleged that Defendants were the direct cause of, or actively engaged in, direct infringement. Plaintiff does allege that Defendants copy all of the material on their servers from content uploaded onto USENET. Plaintiff claims Defendants store these materials, most of which are infringing, on their servers and "program their servers" to distribute and download the infringing content. In addition, Plaintiff alleges Defendants "control which materials are distributed to and copied from other third party servers." These facts do not indicate that it was Defendants themselves that committed the act of copying, displaying or distributing Plaintiff's copyrighted content. Instead, these allegations are like the similar facts alleged in *Netcom:* that Defendants simply programmed their servers to automatically copy, distribute, and display content, including infringing content, uploaded by USENET users. To use *Netcom's* analogy, Defendants here created virtual copy machines that some USENET users have used to create illegal copies. Defendants merely engaged in the act of "designing or implementing a system that automatically and uniformly creates temporary copies of all data sent through it," whether that data contains infringing content or not. *See Netcom,* 907 F. Supp. at 1369. Such conduct does not constitute any volitional act.

Plaintiff's allegations regarding Defendants' knowledge of the pirated content on its servers do not salvage Plaintiff's direct infringement claim. As the *Netcom* court pointed out, "knowledge" is not a required element of direct infringement (although it is a required element for contributory infringement). A participant in the chain of events that ultimately allows viewers to obtain infringed material does not become the "direct cause" of the copying merely because he learns of it. Nor is it enough, as Plaintiff alleges, that Defendants "control which materials are distributed to and copied from other third party servers." An allegation that Defendants control the content on their servers, without a good-faith allegation specifying how Defendants exercised that control to directly create copies, cannot alone create an inference that Defendants engaged in a volitional act directly causing infringement. All owners of internet servers presumably can determine the content on their servers. To hold that such control gives rise to a direct infringement claim would create "unreasonable liability." *See Netcom*, 907 F. Supp. at 1368 (finding no direct infringement despite Netcom's ability to suspend accounts of subscribers and reprogram its system to block certain content); *CoStar*, 373 F.3d at 556 (holding that defendant's procedure of screening and blocking photos that violated its terms of service did not constitute a volitional act of infringement).

Plaintiff relies heavily on *Arista Records LLC v. Usenet.com, Inc.*, 633 F. Supp. 2d 124 (S.D.N.Y. 2009) (*"Usenet"*) to support its argument that knowledge of infringement does satisfy the "volitional conduct" inquiry. The defendants in *Usenet* were USENET providers who were found to have acted volitionally because, among other things, they were aware that copyrighted music files were the most popular items on their servers, they actively created servers dedicated to storing music files, and they increased the file retention time of newsgroups that shared music. In addition, the defendants determined which newsgroups their servers accepted and which they rejected, "routinely exercis[ing] that control" through "both automated filtering and human review." Given these facts, the court concluded that the defendants were liable for direct infringement, finding that "their service [was] not merely a 'passive conduit' that facilitate[d] the exchange of content between users who upload[ed] infringing content and users who download [ed] such content; rather, Defendants actively engaged in the process so as to satisfy the 'volitional-conduct' requirement for direct infringement."

Like the *Usenet* court, several other district courts have taken into account a defendant's knowledge in determining whether that defendant engaged in volitional conduct. *See Perfect 10, Inc. v. Mega Upload*, CV 11–0191, Doc. 16 at *7 (S.D. Cal. July 26, 2011) (finding Plaintiff had fulfilled volitional conduct requirement by alleging that the defendant created different websites to allow users to easily find different types of infringing media and encouraged and paid users to upload vast amounts of popular media); *Capitol Records, Inc. v. MP3tunes, LLC*, 2009 WL 3364036 at *3 (S.D.N.Y. 2009) (finding that plaintiffs' allegation that defendant's program collected and organized links to infringing music files fulfilled volitional conduct requirement); *Playboy Enterprises, Inc. v. Russ Hardenburgh, Inc.*, 982 F. Supp. 503, 513 (N.D.Ohio 1997) (finding defendants acted volitionally by encouraging subscribers to upload files, including adult photographs, onto the system).

The Court disagrees with the application of the volitional act requirement in *Usenet, Mega Upload, Capitol Records,* and *Playboy Enterprises.* By focusing on the defendant's awareness or state of mind – rather than on *who* actually caused the infringement – these cases effectively hold defendants liable for copyright infringement committed by third parties without requiring a full assessment of the additional elements of secondary copyright infringement claims. ... Accordingly, the Court holds that Plaintiff has not alleged that Defendants actively engage in or directly cause the infringement allegedly committed by their users. As such, the Court dismisses Plaintiff's claims for direct copyright infringement. ...

QUESTIONS

1. Why should a defendant who admittedly created a system used for massive infringement escape liability simply because she didn't intend any particular act of infringement? Or is this the wrong way of phrasing the question? "[T]he fact that the copy shop does not choose the content simply means that its culpability will be assessed using secondary-liability rules rather than direct-liability rules." *ABC v. Aereo*, 134 S. Ct. 2498, 2514 (2014) (Scalia, J., dissenting). Does this help?

2. Is the court's discussion of cases like *Arista v. Usenet.com* persuasive? Is the volitional conduct doctrine determinate enough to be useful?

NOTE ON SONY V. UNIVERSAL (CONTRIBUTORY INFRINGEMENT)

[The first portion of this note, *supra* in Section III, discusses the Supreme Court's fair use analysis.]

The Supreme Court did not hold that all uses of VCRs were lawful, only that some were. Other consumers might well use their VCRs to infringe. The Court therefore focused on the nature of the secondary liability claim that would tie Sony to VCR owners' conduct:

> If ... liability is to be imposed on Sony in this case, it must rest on the fact that it has sold equipment with constructive knowledge of the fact that its customers may use that equipment to make unauthorized copies of copyrighted material.

This is a contributory infringement theory: it bases liability on knowingly doing something that meaningfully assists in someone else's act of infringement. Make sure you understand why a vicarious infringement theory was a bad fit for the facts. Once Sony sold a VCR to a retailer, it had no further "right and ability control" what happened with that VCR. Sony was not in a position to knock on a consumer's doors and seize a VCR that was being used to infringe.

Notice also that this contributory infringement theory rests on constructive knowledge. Things might be very different if Sony had actual knowledge of a customer's planned acts of infringement at the time it sold a VCR. While Sony might know in a general, perhaps statistical, sense that some of its customers would do blatantly infringing things with their VCRs, it couldn't know in advance which customers would, or how, or when. The only way Sony could have prevented the infringement would have been to stop selling VCRs altogether (or at least to stop selling VCRs with a "record" button).

The problem, from the Court's perspective, was thus that the VCR had both infringing and noninfringing uses. A finding of contributory infringement against Sony would have the effect of taking VCRs off the market for non-infringing uses, as well: no more taping *Mister Rogers' Neighborhood* to watch with your kids later. Thus was born the "*Sony* defense." The Court held that so-called dual-use technologies – those with both infringing and noninfringing uses – were legal:

> Accordingly, the sale of copying equipment, like the sale of other arti-
> cles of commerce, does not constitute contributory infringement if the
> product is widely used for legitimate, unobjectionable purposes. In-
> deed, it need merely be capable of substantial noninfringing uses.

This seems straightforward enough. The Court created a defense specifically to contributory infringement. It applies when one sells a product "capable of substantial noninfringing uses." Direct and vicarious infringement are unaffected.

But interpretive issues wait in the wings. First, how many noninfringing uses are required to count as "substantial?" The Court gives some guidance in its discussion of fair-use time-shifting and authorized home taping: presumably those uses qualify. But then notice the phrase "merely be capable of" – does this now mean that uses which are not yet taking place, but could, would also qualify?

The second issue lurking in this passage is precisely which activities it shields. The sale of physical devices that users carry off and use on their own seems clearly protected. But computer technologies raised difficult new issues in the two decades after *Sony*. What about the sale of software? Is that a "product" that ought to qualify? What about a company that uses software to supply a service to users, rather than giving them standalone software they can use on their own? Once again, the increasing unimportance of physical things creates problems for copyright law.

And finally, there is the basic point of incredulity. Did the Court really mean what it appeared to say? Will a product that is "capable" of "substantial" lawful use really be shielded, even if they are dwarfed by the product's infringing uses? Was *Sony* really meant to offer an absolute safe harbor, as long as one's product could theoretically be used in a noninfringing way?

All of these questions would be aired, if not necessarily answered, in the file-sharing wars.

A & M RECORDS, INC. V. NAPSTER, INC.
239 F.3d 1004 (9th Cir. 2001)

[The facts of this case and its discussion of Napster's users' fair use defense are set forth *supra* in Section III.]

IV.

We first address plaintiffs' claim that Napster is liable for contributory copyright infringement. Traditionally, "one who, with knowledge of the infringing activity, induces, causes or materially contributes to the infringing conduct of another, may be held liable as a 'contributory' infringer." *Gershwin Publ'g Corp. v. Columbia Artists Mgmt., Inc.*, 443 F.2d 1159, 1162 (2d Cir. 1971); *see also Fonovisa, Inc. v. Cherry Auction, Inc.*, 76 F.3d 259, 264 (9th Cir. 1996). Put differently, liability exists if the defendant engages in "personal conduct that encourages or assists the infringement." *Matthew Bender & Co. v. West Publ'g Co.*, 158 F.3d 693, 706 (2d Cir. 1998).

The district court determined that plaintiffs in all likelihood would establish Napster's liability as a contributory infringer. The district court did not err; Napster, by its conduct, knowingly encourages and assists the infringement of plaintiffs' copyrights.

A. Knowledge

Contributory liability requires that the secondary infringer "know or have reason to know" of direct infringement. The district court found that Napster had both actual and constructive knowledge that its users exchanged copyrighted music. The district court also concluded that the law does not require knowledge of "specific acts of infringement" and rejected Napster's contention that because the company cannot distinguish infringing from noninfringing files, it does not "know" of the direct infringement.

It is apparent from the record that Napster has knowledge, both actual and constructive,[5] of direct infringement. Napster claims that it is nevertheless protected from contributory liability by the teaching of *Sony Corp. v. Universal City Studios, Inc.*, 464 U.S. 417 (1984). We disagree. We observe that Napster's actual, specific knowledge of direct infringement renders *Sony's* holding of limited assistance to Napster. We are compelled to make a clear distinction between the architecture of the Napster system and Napster's conduct in relation to the operational capacity of the system.

The *Sony* Court refused to hold the manufacturer and retailers of video tape recorders liable for contributory infringement despite evidence that such machines could be and were used to infringe plaintiffs' copyrighted television shows. *Sony* stated that if liability "is to be imposed on petitioners in this case, it must rest on the fact *that they have sold equipment with constructive knowledge of the fact that their customers may use that equipment to make unauthorized copies of copyrighted material."* *Id.* at 439 (emphasis added). The *Sony* Court declined to impute the requisite level of knowledge where the defendants made and sold equipment capable of both infringing and "substantial noninfringing uses." *Id.* at 442 (adopting a modified "staple article of commerce" doctrine from patent law).

We are bound to follow *Sony*, and will not impute the requisite level of knowledge to Napster merely because peer-to-peer file sharing technology may be used to infringe plaintiffs' copyrights. ... Regardless of the number of Napster's infringing versus noninfringing uses, the evidentiary record here supported the district court's finding that plaintiffs would likely prevail in establishing that Napster knew or had reason to know of its users' infringement of plaintiffs' copyrights.

This analysis is similar to that of *Religious Technology Center v. Netcom On-Line Communication Services, Inc.* [907 F. Supp. 1361 (N.D. Cal. 1995)], which suggests that in an online context, evidence of actual knowledge of specific acts of infringement is required to hold a computer system operator liable for contributory copyright infringement. *Netcom* considered the potential contributory copyright liability of a computer bulletin board operator whose system supported the posting of infringing material. The court, in denying Netcom's motion for summary judgment of noninfringement and plaintiff's motion for judgment on the pleadings, found that a disputed issue of fact existed as to whether the operator had sufficient knowledge of infringing activity.

The court determined that for the operator to have sufficient knowledge, the copyright holder must "provide the necessary documentation to show there is like-

---

5 The district court found actual knowledge because: (1) a document authored by Napster co-founder Sean Parker mentioned "the need to remain ignorant of users' real names and IP addresses 'since they are exchanging pirated music' "; and (2) the Recording Industry Association of America ("RIAA") informed Napster of more than 12,000 infringing files, some of which are still available. The district court found constructive knowledge because: (a) Napster executives have recording industry experience; (b) they have enforced intellectual property rights in other instances; (c) Napster executives have downloaded copyrighted songs from the system; and (d) they have promoted the site with "screen shots listing infringing files."

ly infringement." 907 F. Supp. at 1374. If such documentation was provided, the court reasoned that Netcom would be liable for contributory infringement because its failure to remove the material "and thereby stop an infringing copy from being distributed worldwide constitutes substantial participation" in distribution of copyrighted material. *Id.*

We agree that if a computer system operator learns of specific infringing material available on his system and fails to purge such material from the system, the operator knows of and contributes to direct infringement. Conversely, absent any specific information which identifies infringing activity, a computer system operator cannot be liable for contributory infringement merely because the structure of the system allows for the exchange of copyrighted material. To enjoin simply because a computer network allows for infringing use would, in our opinion, violate *Sony* and potentially restrict activity unrelated to infringing use.

We nevertheless conclude that sufficient knowledge exists to impose contributory liability when linked to demonstrated infringing use of the Napster system. The record supports the district court's finding that Napster has actual knowledge that specific infringing material is available using its system, that it could block access to the system by suppliers of the infringing material, and that it failed to remove the material.

B. Material Contribution

Under the facts as found by the district court, Napster materially contributes to the infringing activity. Relying on *Fonovisa*, the district court concluded that "[w]ithout the support services defendant provides, Napster users could not find and download the music they want with the ease of which defendant boasts." *Napster*, 114 F. Supp. 2d at 919–20. We agree that Napster provides "the site and facilities" for direct infringement. *See Fonovisa*, 76 F.3d at 264; *cf. Netcom*, 907 F. Supp. at 1372 ("Netcom will be liable for contributory infringement since its failure to cancel [a user's] infringing message and thereby stop an infringing copy from being distributed worldwide constitutes substantial participation."). The district court correctly applied the reasoning in *Fonovisa*, and properly found that Napster materially contributes to direct infringement. ...

V.

We turn to the question whether Napster engages in vicarious copyright infringement. Vicarious copyright liability is an "outgrowth" of respondeat superior. *Fonovisa*, 76 F.3d at 262. In the context of copyright law, vicarious liability extends beyond an employer/employee relationship to cases in which a defendant "has the right and ability to supervise the infringing activity and also has a direct financial interest in such activities." *Id.* (quoting *Gershwin*, 443 F.2d at 1162.

Before moving into this discussion, we note that *Sony*'s "staple article of commerce" analysis has no application to Napster's potential liability for vicarious copyright infringement. ...

A. Financial Benefit

The district court determined that plaintiffs had demonstrated they would likely succeed in establishing that Napster has a direct financial interest in the infringing activity. We agree. Financial benefit exists where the availability of infringing material "acts as a 'draw' for customers." *Fonovisa*, 76 F.3d at 263–64 (stating that financial benefit may be shown "where infringing performances enhance the attractiveness of a venue"). Ample evidence supports the district court's finding that Napster's future revenue is directly dependent upon "increases in userbase." More users register with the Napster system as the "quality and quantity of available music increases." 114 F. Supp. 2d at 902. We conclude that the district court did not err in determining that Napster financially benefits from the availability of protected works on its system.

B. Supervision

The district court determined that Napster has the right and ability to supervise its users' conduct. *Napster*, 114 F. Supp. 2d at 920–21 (finding that Napster's representations to the court regarding "its improved methods of blocking users about whom rights holders complain . . . is tantamount to an admission that defendant can, and sometimes does, police its service"). We agree in part.

The ability to block infringers' access to a particular environment for any reason whatsoever is evidence of the right and ability to supervise. *See Fonovisa*, 76 F. 3d at 262 ("Cherry Auction had the right to terminate vendors for any reason whatsoever and through that right had the ability to control the activities of vendors on the premises."); *cf. Netcom*, 907 F. Supp.. at 1375–76 (indicating that plaintiff raised a genuine issue of fact regarding ability to supervise by presenting evidence that an electronic bulletin board service can suspend subscriber's accounts). Here, plaintiffs have demonstrated that Napster retains the right to control access to its system. Napster has an express reservation of rights policy, stating on its website that it expressly reserves the "right to refuse service and terminate accounts in [its] discretion, including, but not limited to, if Napster believes that user conduct violates applicable law . . . or for any reason in Napster's sole discretion, with or without cause."

To escape imposition of vicarious liability, the reserved right to police must be exercised to its fullest extent. Turning a blind eye to detectable acts of infringement for the sake of profit gives rise to liability. *See, e.g., Fonovisa*, 76 F.3d at 261 ("There is no dispute for the purposes of this appeal that Cherry Auction and its operators were aware that vendors in their swap meets were selling counterfeit recordings."); *see also Gershwin*, 443 F.2d at 1161–62 (citing *Shapiro, Bernstein & Co. v. H.L. Green Co.*, 316 F.2d 304 (2d Cir.1963)), for the proposition that "failure to police the conduct of the primary infringer" leads to imposition of vicarious liability for copyright infringement).

The district court correctly determined that Napster had the right and ability to police its system and failed to exercise that right to prevent the exchange of copyrighted material. The district court, however, failed to recognize that the boundaries of the premises that Napster "controls and patrols" are limited. *See, e.g., Fonovisa*, 76 F.3d at 262–63 (in addition to having the right to exclude vendors, defendant "controlled and patrolled" the premises); *see also Polygram*, 855 F. Supp.. at 1328–29 (in addition to having the contractual right to remove exhibitors, trade show operator reserved the right to police during the show and had its "employees walk the aisles to ensure 'rules compliance'"). Put differently, Napster's reserved "right and ability" to police is cabined by the system's current architecture. As shown by the record, the Napster system does not "read" the content of indexed files, other than to check that they are in the proper MP3 format.

Napster, however, has the ability to locate infringing material listed on its search indices, and the right to terminate users' access to the system. The file name indices, therefore, are within the "premises" that Napster has the ability to police. We recognize that the files are user-named and may not match copyrighted material exactly (for example, the artist or song could be spelled wrong). For Napster to function effectively, however, file names must reasonably or roughly correspond to the material contained in the files, otherwise no user could ever locate any desired music. As a practical matter, Napster, its users and the record company plaintiffs have equal access to infringing material by employing Napster's "search function."

Our review of the record requires us to accept the district court's conclusion that plaintiffs have demonstrated a likelihood of success on the merits of the vicarious copyright infringement claim. Napster's failure to police the system's "premises," combined with a showing that Napster financially benefits from the continuing availability of infringing files on its system, leads to the imposition of vicarious liability.

QUESTIONS

1. Start with the contributory infringement analysis in Part IV. Material contribution is easy to establish. Why? Knowledge is also not hard to show, but requires some precision. Does Napster have specific (or "actual") knowledge of its users' infringements? Does it have general (or "constructive") knowledge?

2. Was Napster capable of substantial noninfringing uses? If so, why doesn't *Sony* shield if from liability? What is the new rule of *Sony*, post-*Napster*?

3. Next, take up the vicarious infringement liability analysis in Part V. How is it that a company with no revenue to speak of could have a "direct financial interest" in anything? Similarly, walk through the court's reasoning on the "right and ability to control." Note that Napster users aren't employees. How is it that Napster could still have the "right and ability" to control what they do? Would Sony, back in the 1980s, have had the "right and ability" to control VCR users? What accounts for the difference?

METRO-GOLDWYN-MAYER STUDIOS INC. V. GROKSTER, LTD.
545 U.S. 913 (2005)

Justice Souter delivered the opinion of the Court.

The question is under what circumstances the distributor of a product capable of both lawful and unlawful use is liable for acts of copyright infringement by third parties using the product. We hold that one who distributes a device with the object of promoting its use to infringe copyright, as shown by clear expression or other affirmative steps taken to foster infringement, is liable for the resulting acts of infringement.

I.

A.

Respondents, Grokster, Ltd., and StreamCast Networks, Inc., defendants in the trial court, distribute free software products that allow computer users to share electronic files through peer-to-peer networks ... . [In the language of *Columbia Pictures v. Fung, supra* Section 2.A, both systems were "hybrid" P2P systems using supernodes. The defendants distributed the necessary client software, but did not operate centralized index servers, the way that Napster did.]

Other users of peer-to-peer networks include individual recipients of Grokster's and StreamCast's software, and although the networks that they enjoy through using the software can be used to share any type of digital file, they have prominently employed those networks in sharing copyrighted music and video files without authorization. A group of copyright holders (MGM for short, but including motion picture studios, recording companies, songwriters, and music publishers) sued Grokster and StreamCast for their users' copyright infringements, alleging that they knowingly and intentionally distributed their software to enable users to reproduce and distribute the copyrighted works in violation of the Copyright Act. MGM sought damages and an injunction. ...

Although Grokster and StreamCast do not therefore know when particular files are copied, a few searches using their software would show what is available on the networks the software reaches. MGM commissioned a statistician to conduct a systematic search, and his study showed that nearly 90% of the files available for download on the FastTrack system were copyrighted works. Grokster and Stream-Cast dispute this figure, raising methodological problems and arguing that free copying even of copyrighted works may be authorized by the rightholders. They also argue that potential noninfringing uses of their software are significant in kind, even if infrequent in practice. Some musical performers, for example, have gained new audiences by distributing their copyrighted works for free across peer-to-peer networks, and some distributors of unprotected content have used peer-to-peer networks to disseminate files, Shakespeare being an example. Indeed, StreamCast has given Morpheus users the opportunity to download the briefs in this very case, though their popularity has not been quantified.

As for quantification, the parties' anecdotal and statistical evidence entered thus far to show the content available on the FastTrack and Gnutella networks does not say much about which files are actually downloaded by users, and no one can say how often the software is used to obtain copies of unprotected material. But MGM's evidence gives reason to think that the vast majority of users' downloads are acts of infringement, and because well over 100 million copies of the software in question are known to have been downloaded, and billions of files are shared across the FastTrack and Gnutella networks each month, the probable scope of copyright infringement is staggering. ...

B.

After discovery, the parties on each side of the case crossmoved for summary judgment. [The District Court ruled in favor of Grokster and StreamCast].

The Court of Appeals affirmed. In the court's analysis, a defendant was liable as a contributory infringer when it had knowledge of direct infringement and materially contributed to the infringement. But the court read *Sony Corp. of America v. Universal City Studios, Inc.*, 464 U. S. 417 (1984), as holding that distribution of a commercial product capable of substantial noninfringing uses could not give rise to contributory liability for infringement unless the distributor had actual knowledge of specific instances of infringement and failed to act on that knowledge. The fact that the software was capable of substantial noninfringing uses in the Ninth Circuit's view meant that Grokster and StreamCast were not liable, because they had no such actual knowledge, owing to the decentralized architecture of their software. ...

The Ninth Circuit also considered whether Grokster and StreamCast could be liable under a theory of vicarious infringement. The court held against liability because the defendants did not monitor or control the use of the software, had no agreed-upon right or current ability to supervise its use, and had no independent duty to police infringement. We granted certiorari.

II. ...

B.

Despite the currency of these principles of secondary liability, this Court has dealt with secondary copyright infringement in only one recent case, and because MGM has tailored its principal claim to our opinion there, a look at our earlier holding is in order. In *Sony Corp. v. Universal City Studios, supra*, this Court addressed a claim that secondary liability for infringement can arise from the very distribution of a commercial product. There, the product, novel at the time, was what we know today as the videocassette recorder or VCR. ...

On those facts, with no evidence of stated or indicated intent to promote infringing uses, the only conceivable basis for imposing liability was on a theory of contributory infringement arising from its sale of VCRs to consumers with knowledge that some would use them to infringe. But because the VCR was "capable of commercially significant noninfringing uses," we held the manufacturer could not be faulted solely on the basis of its distribution. ...

In sum, where an article is good for nothing else but infringement, there is no legitimate public interest in its unlicensed availability, and there is no injustice in presuming or imputing an intent to infringe. Conversely, the doctrine absolves the equivocal conduct of selling an item with substantial lawful as well as unlawful uses, and limits liability to instances of more acute fault than the mere understanding that some of one's products will be misused. It leaves breathing room for innovation and a vigorous commerce.

The parties and many of the *amici* in this case think the key to resolving it is the *Sony* rule and, in particular, what it means for a product to be "capable of commercially significant noninfringing uses." *Sony Corp. v. Universal City Studios, supra*, at 442. MGM advances the argument that granting summary judgment to Grokster and StreamCast as to their current activities gave too much weight to the value of innovative technology, and too little to the copyrights infringed by users of their software, given that 90% of works available on one of the networks was shown to be copyrighted. Assuming the remaining 10% to be its noninfringing use, MGM says this should not qualify as "substantial," and the Court should quantify *Sony* to the extent of holding that a product used "principally" for infringement does not qualify. As mentioned before, Grokster and StreamCast reply by citing evidence that their software can be used to reproduce public domain works, and they point to copyright holders who actually encourage copying. Even if infringement is the principal practice with their software today, they argue, the noninfringing uses are significant and will grow. ...

... Because *Sony* did not displace other theories of secondary liability, and because we find below that it was error to grant summary judgment to the companies on MGM's inducement claim, we do not revisit *Sony* further, as MGM requests, to add a more quantified description of the point of balance between protection and commerce when liability rests solely on distribution with knowledge that unlawful use will occur. It is enough to note that the Ninth Circuit's judgment rested on an erroneous understanding of *Sony* and to leave further consideration of the *Sony* rule for a day when that may be required.

C.

Sony's rule limits imputing culpable intent as a matter of law from the characteristics or uses of a distributed product. But nothing in *Sony* requires courts to ignore evidence of intent if there is such evidence, and the case was never meant to foreclose rules of fault-based liability derived from the common law. Thus, where evidence goes beyond a product's characteristics or the knowledge that it may be put to infringing uses, and shows statements or actions directed to promoting infringement, *Sony*'s staple-article rule will not preclude liability. ...

For the same reasons that *Sony* took the staple-article doctrine of patent law as a model for its copyright safe-harbor rule, the inducement rule, too, is a sensible one for copyright. We adopt it here, holding that one who distributes a device with the object of promoting its use to infringe copyright, as shown by clear expression or other affirmative steps taken to foster infringement, is liable for the resulting acts of infringement by third parties. We are, of course, mindful of the need to keep from trenching on regular commerce or discouraging the development of technologies with lawful and unlawful potential. Accordingly, just as *Sony* did not find intentional inducement despite the knowledge of the VCR manufacturer that its device could be used to infringe, mere knowledge of infringing potential or of actual infringing uses would not be enough here to subject a distributor to liability. Nor would ordinary acts incident to product distribution, such as offering customers technical support or product updates, support liability in themselves. The inducement rule, instead, premises liability on purposeful, culpable expression and conduct, and thus does nothing to compromise legitimate commerce or discourage innovation having a lawful promise.

III.

A.

The only apparent question about treating MGM's evidence as sufficient to withstand summary judgment under the theory of inducement goes to the need on MGM's part to adduce evidence that StreamCast and Grokster communicated an inducing message to their software users. The classic instance of inducement is by advertisement or solicitation that broadcasts a message designed to stimulate others to commit violations. MGM claims that such a message is shown here. It is undisputed that StreamCast beamed onto the computer screens of users of Napster-compatible programs ads urging the adoption of its OpenNap program, which was designed, as its name implied, to invite the custom of patrons of Napster, then under attack in the courts for facilitating massive infringement. Those who accepted StreamCast's OpenNap program were offered software to perform the same services, which a factfinder could conclude would readily have been understood in the Napster market as the ability to download copyrighted music files. Grokster distributed an electronic newsletter containing links to articles promoting its software's ability to access popular copyrighted music. And anyone whose Napster or free file-sharing searches turned up a link to Grokster would have understood Grokster to be offering the same file-sharing ability as Napster, and to the same people who probably used Napster for infringing downloads; that would also have been the understanding of anyone offered Grokster's suggestively named Swaptor software, its version of OpenNap. And both companies communicated a clear message by responding affirmatively to requests for help in locating and playing copyrighted materials.

In StreamCast's case, of course, the evidence just described was supplemented by other unequivocal indications of unlawful purpose in the internal communications and advertising designs aimed at Napster users ("When the lights went off at Napster . . . where did the users go?"). Whether the messages were communicated is not to the point on this record. The function of the message in the theory of inducement is to prove by a defendant's own statements that his unlawful purpose disqualifies him from claiming protection (and incidentally to point to actual violators likely to be found among those who hear or read the message). Proving that a message was sent out, then, is the preeminent but not exclusive way of showing that active steps were taken with the purpose of bringing about infringing acts, and of showing that infringing acts took place by using the device distributed. Here, the summary judgment record is replete with other evidence that Grokster and StreamCast, unlike the manufacturer and distributor in *Sony*, acted with a purpose to cause copyright violations by use of software suitable for illegal use.

Three features of this evidence of intent are particularly notable. First, each company showed itself to be aiming to satisfy a known source of demand for copyright infringement, the market comprising former Napster users. StreamCast's internal documents made constant reference to Napster, it initially distributed its Morpheus software through an OpenNap program compatible with Napster, it advertised its OpenNap program to Napster users, and its Morpheus software functions as Napster did except that it could be used to distribute more kinds of files, including copyrighted movies and software programs. Grokster's name is apparently derived from Napster, it too initially offered an OpenNap program, its software's function is likewise comparable to Napster's, and it attempted to divert queries for Napster onto its own Web site. Grokster and StreamCast's efforts to supply services to former Napster users, deprived of a mechanism to copy and distribute what were overwhelmingly infringing files, indicate a principal, if not exclusive, intent on the part of each to bring about infringement.

Second, this evidence of unlawful objective is given added significance by MGM's showing that neither company attempted to develop filtering tools or other mechanisms to diminish the infringing activity using their software. While the Ninth Circuit treated the defendants' failure to develop such tools as irrelevant because they lacked an independent duty to monitor their users' activity, we think this evidence underscores Grokster's and StreamCast's intentional facilitation of their users' infringement.

Third, there is a further complement to the direct evidence of unlawful objective. It is useful to recall that StreamCast and Grokster make money by selling advertising space, by directing ads to the screens of computers employing their software. As the record shows, the more the software is used, the more ads are sent out and the greater the advertising revenue becomes. Since the extent of the software's use determines the gain to the distributors, the commercial sense of their enterprise turns on high-volume use, which the record shows is infringing. This evidence alone would not justify an inference of unlawful intent, but viewed in the context of the entire record its import is clear.

The unlawful objective is unmistakable.

B.

In addition to intent to bring about infringement and distribution of a device suitable for infringing use, the inducement theory of course requires evidence of actual infringement by recipients of the device, the software in this case. As the account of the facts indicates, there is evidence of infringement on a gigantic scale, and there is no serious issue of the adequacy of MGM's showing on this point in order to survive the companies' summary judgment requests. Although an exact calculation of infringing use, as a basis for a claim of damages, is subject to dispute, there is no question that the summary judgment evidence is at least adequate to entitle MGM to go forward with claims for damages and equitable relief.

* * *

In sum, this case is significantly different from *Sony* and reliance on that case to rule in favor of StreamCast and Grokster was error. *Sony* dealt with a claim of liability based solely on distributing a product with alternative lawful and unlawful uses, with knowledge that some users would follow the unlawful course. The case struck a balance between the interests of protection and innovation by holding that the product's capability of substantial lawful employment should bar the imputation of fault and consequent secondary liability for the unlawful acts of others.

MGM's evidence in this case most obviously addresses a different basis of liability for distributing a product open to alternative uses. Here, evidence of the distributors' words and deeds going beyond distribution as such shows a purpose to cause and profit from third-party acts of copyright infringement. If liability for inducing infringement is ultimately found, it will not be on the basis of presuming or imputing fault, but from inferring a patently illegal objective from statements and actions showing what that objective was.

There is substantial evidence in MGM's favor on all elements of inducement, and summary judgment in favor of Grokster and StreamCast was error. On remand, reconsideration of MGM's motion for summary judgment will be in order.

...

QUESTIONS

1. The Supreme Court doesn't discuss it, but could Morpheus and StreamCast have been held liable on a vicarious liability theory?

2. Given the unavailability of a vicarious infringement theory, the copyright-owner plaintiffs pushed hard on the contributory infringement theory. Does StreamCast have the right kind of knowledge of infringement to be held liable? Can it raise a *Sony* defense? Why doesn't *Napster* control this case?

3. When the Supreme Court granted certiorari in *Grokster*, the Courts of Appeals were split on how to apply *Sony*. The Ninth Circuit held that *Sony* would shield decentralized file-sharing networks because they had or could have noninfringing uses that were "substantial." In contrast, the Seventh Circuit held that *Sony* did not apply to a network whose current uses were overwhelmingly infringing, regardless of how it could be used, because "some estimate of the respective magnitudes" of infringing and noninfringing uses was required. Which of these two approaches would lead to more sensible copyright policy?

4. Each side convinced three Supreme Court justices of its position (in separate concurrences not reproduced here). The Court as a whole, however, side-stepped the issue. How is the "inducement" standard something of a cop-out?

5. What did Morpheus and StreamCast do wrong? Do you agree that it was wrong? How reliable a test does inducement provide to distinguish good actors from bad?

6. Is inducement infringement a new theory of secondary liability, or is it a form of contributory infringement? Was the Supreme Court clear on this point? Does it matter?

CACHET PROBLEM

CACHET is a network of financial institutions that collectively issue and process transactions made with Cachet-branded credit cards. Some of CACHET's members are banks, which issue credit cards to consumers. Others are payment processors, who take consumers' card information from merchants and charge the payments through to the consumers' accounts. The card issuers charge various fees to consumers (such as for cash advances) and interest on late payments. The payment processors charge merchants a small fee (25 to 50 cents) on each transaction, plus a percentage (2% to 3%) of the total amount.

You are associate general counsel to CACHET International, the umbrella group that manages the CACHET trademarks, enforces member agreements with individual CACHET members, coordinates overall CACHET strategy, and provides legal advice to CACHET members. You have received a letter from Perfect Tan, an adult entertainment company.

The letter states that Perfect Tan sells pornography in magazines and through its website. It claims that numerous websites, based in over a dozen countries including the United States, have used its copyrighted images and videos without permission, offering them for sale online. It further claims that many of these websites accept CACHET cards as payment from users, and process those payments through CACHET members. Perfect Tan has sent repeated notices to individual payment processors informing them of the websites' infringement, identifying specific websites by URL, and demanding that they stop supplying service to the websites. Most of the recipients of these notices have taken no action in response to them

You have been asked to prepare a legal briefing for CACHET members on their potential copyright liability. What will you tell them?

RIP-MIX-BURN PROBLEM

Apple's Mac computers have CD drives which can read and write CDs. Apple's iTunes software, which ships pre-installed on every Mac, has features that can "rip" a CD into MP3 files stored on a user's hard drive and can "burn" a playlist of MP3s to a CD. You are Associate General Counsel at Apple, with responsibility for approving any marketing materials released by the company. Your outside advertising agency has proposed the following print ad to run in large-circulation magazines throughout the U.S. What's your call on it?

E. Section 512

Technically, "section 512" is the Online Copyright Infringement Liability Limitation Act, which was Title II of the Digital Millennium Copyright Act, which added Section 512 to Title 17 of the U.S. Code. But people will make fun of you if you insist on these details, and with good reason. So "section 512" it is. In basic form, Section 512 provides protection for various online intermediaries from copyright liability.

The motivation for such a statute should be fairly clear at this point. Suppose that Irene Infringer uploads a copyrighted MP3 to her personal web site on a server operated by Epitome Hosting, and that Doug Downloader downloads it via his Ultraband cable Internet service. *Sony* will presumably supply a defense to the manufacturers of the server, the cable modem, and the various network cables. They all supply products which fit within *Sony*'s rule.

But what about Epitome and Ultraband, who provide services? Epitome's servers made a reproduction and publicly distributed the MP3, and Ultraband used its cables and routers to transmit the MP3, which is arguably a reproduction, a distribution, and/or a performance.

Congress responded in 1998 by enacting section 512. It gives Epitome, Ultraband, and other "service providers" immunity from copyright liability provided they comply with various threshold conditions. The basic structure is that Congress provided four independent immunities in clauses (a) through (d), each of which covers a different aspect of a service provider's operations. It is possible for a defendant to be immune under one for certain activities (e.g. hosting content at YouTube.com) and under another for different activities (e.g. providing a search engine at Google.com).

Each immunity comes with its own laundry list of conditions. Most notably, the immunity applicable to Epitome – the "hosting" immunity under 512(c) – includes an obligation known as "notice and takedown." The immunity vanishes if the copyright owner sends a specially formatted notice of infringement to the service provider, unless the service provider takes the allegedly infringing material down. As discussed in the cases, the scope of this immunity is intensely controversial. This section concludes by considering Content ID, a kind of private alternative to the DMCA takedown process.

COPYRIGHT ACT [SECTION 512]

Title 17, United States Cde

§ 512 – *Limitations on liability relating to material online*

(a) *TRANSITORY DIGITAL NETWORK COMMUNICATIONS.* – A service provider shall not be liable ... for infringement of copyright by reason of the provider's transmitting, routing, or providing connections for, material through a system or network controlled or operated by or for the service provider, or by reason of the intermediate and transient storage of that material in the course of such transmitting, routing, or providing connections, if [the transmission is initiated by a user, automatic, sent to recipients selected by the user, made accessible only to recipients and deleted promptly from the provider's system, and unmodified]. ...

(c) *INFORMATION RESIDING ON SYSTEMS OR NETWORKS AT DIRECTION OF USERS.* –

(1) *IN GENERAL*. – A service provider shall not be liable ... for infringement of copyright by reason of the storage at the direction of a user of material that resides on a system or network controlled or operated by or for the service provider, if the service provider –

(A)

(i) does not have actual knowledge that the material or an activity using the material on the system or network is infringing;

(ii) in the absence of such actual knowledge, is not aware of facts or circumstances from which infringing activity is apparent; or

(iii) upon obtaining such knowledge or awareness, acts expeditiously to remove, or disable access to, the material;

(B) does not receive a financial benefit directly attributable to the infringing activity, in a case in which the service provider has the right and ability to control such activity; and

(C) upon notification of claimed infringement as described in paragraph (3), responds expeditiously to remove, or disable access to, the material that is claimed to be infringing or to be the subject of infringing activity.

(2) *DESIGNATED AGENT*. – The limitations on liability established in this subsection apply to a service provider only if the service provider has designated an agent to receive notifications of claimed infringement described in paragraph (3), by making available through its service, including on its website in a location accessible to the public, and by providing to the Copyright Office, substantially the following information:

(A) the name, address, phone number, and electronic mail address of the agent.

(B) other contact information which the Register of Copyrights may deem appropriate.

(3) *ELEMENTS OF NOTIFICATION*. –

(A) To be effective under this subsection, a notification of claimed infringement must be a written communication provided to the designated agent of a service provider that includes substantially the following:

(i) A physical or electronic signature of a person authorized to act on behalf of the owner of an exclusive right that is allegedly infringed.

(ii) Identification of the copyrighted work claimed to have been infringed, or, if multiple copyrighted works at a single online site are covered by a single notification, a representative list of such works at that site.

(iii) Identification of the material that is claimed to be infringing or to be the subject of infringing activity and that is to be removed or access to which is to be disabled, and information reasonably sufficient to permit the service provider to locate the material.

(iv) Information reasonably sufficient to permit the service provider to contact the complaining party, such as an address, telephone number, and, if available, an electronic mail address at which the complaining party may be contacted.

(v) A statement that the complaining party has a good faith belief that use of the material in the manner complained of is not authorized by the copyright owner, its agent, or the law.

(vi) A statement that the information in the notification is accurate, and under penalty of perjury, that the complaining party is authorized to act on behalf of the owner of an exclusive right that is allegedly infringed. ...

(d) *INFORMATION LOCATION TOOLS.* – A service provider shall not be liable for monetary relief, or, except as provided in subsection (j), for injunctive or other equitable relief, for infringement of copyright by reason of the provider referring or linking users to an online location containing infringing material or infringing activity, by using information location tools, including a directory, index, reference, pointer, or hypertext link, if the service provider [compiles with the procedures given in subsection (c), above]. ...

(f) *MISREPRESENTATIONS.* – Any person who knowingly materially misrepresents under this section –

(1) that material or activity is infringing, or

(2) that material or activity was removed or disabled by mistake or misidentification,

shall be liable for any damages, including costs and attorneys' fees, incurred by the alleged infringer, by any copyright owner or copyright owner's authorized licensee, or by a service provider, who is injured by such misrepresentation, as the result of the service provider relying upon such misrepresentation in removing or disabling access to the material or activity claimed to be infringing, or in replacing the removed material or ceasing to disable access to it.

(g) *REPLACEMENT OF REMOVED OR DISABLED MATERIAL AND LIMITATION ON OTHER LIABILITY.* –

(1) *NO LIABILITY FOR TAKING DOWN GENERALLY.* – Subject to paragraph (2), a service provider shall not be liable to any person for any claim based on the service provider's good faith disabling of access to, or removal of, material or activity claimed to be infringing or based on facts or circumstances from which infringing activity is apparent, regardless of whether the material or activity is ultimately determined to be infringing.

(2) *EXCEPTION.* – Paragraph (1) shall not apply with respect to material residing at the direction of a subscriber of the service provider on a system or network controlled or operated by or for the service provider that is removed, or to which access is disabled by the service

provider, pursuant to a notice provided under subsection (c)(1)(C), unless the service provider –

    (A) takes reasonable steps promptly to notify the subscriber that it has removed or disabled access to the material;

    (B) upon receipt of a counter notification described in paragraph (3), promptly provides the person who provided the notification under subsection (c)(1)(C) with a copy of the counter notification, and informs that person that it will replace the removed material or cease disabling access to it in 10 business days; and

    (C) replaces the removed material and ceases disabling access to it not less than 10, nor more than 14, business days following receipt of the counter notice, unless its designated agent first receives notice from the person who submitted the notification under subsection (c)(1)(C) that such person has filed an action seeking a court order to restrain the subscriber from engaging in infringing activity relating to the material on the service provider's system or network.

(3) *CONTENTS OF COUNTER NOTIFICATION.* – To be effective under this subsection, a counter notification must be a written communication provided to the service provider's designated agent that includes substantially the following:

    (A) A physical or electronic signature of the subscriber.

    (B) Identification of the material that has been removed or to which access has been disabled and the location at which the material appeared before it was removed or access to it was disabled.

    (C) A statement under penalty of perjury that the subscriber has a good faith belief that the material was removed or disabled as a result of mistake or misidentification of the material to be removed or disabled.

    (D) The subscriber's name, address, and telephone number, and a statement that the subscriber consents to the jurisdiction of Federal District Court for the judicial district in which the address is located, or if the subscriber's address is outside of the United States, for any judicial district in which the service provider may be found, and that the subscriber will accept service of process from the person who provided notification under subsection (c)(1)(C) or an agent of such person.

(4) *LIMITATION ON OTHER LIABILITY.* – A service provider's compliance with paragraph (2) shall not subject the service provider to liability for copyright infringement with respect to the material identified in the notice provided under subsection (c)(1)(C). ...

(i) *CONDITIONS FOR ELIGIBILITY.* –

    (1) *ACCOMMODATION OF TECHNOLOGY.* – The limitations on liability established by this section shall apply to a service provider only if the service provider –

        (A) has adopted and reasonably implemented, and informs subscribers and account holders of the service provider's system or network of, a policy that provides for the termination in appropriate circumstances of subscribers and account holders of the service provider's system or network who are repeat infringers;

...

(k) **DEFINITIONS.** –

    (1) **SERVICE PROVIDER.** –

        (A) As used in subsection (a), the term "service provider" means an entity offering the transmission, routing, or providing of connections for digital online communications, between or among points specified by a user, of material of the user's choosing, without modification to the content of the material as sent or received.

        (B) As used in this section, other than subsection (a), the term "service provider" means a provider of online services or network access, or the operator of facilities therefor, and includes an entity described in subparagraph (A). ...

(l) **OTHER DEFENSES NOT AFFECTED.** – The failure of a service provider's conduct to qualify for limitation of liability under this section shall not bear adversely upon the consideration of a defense by the service provider that the service provider's conduct is not infringing under this title or any other defense.

(m) **PROTECTION OF PRIVACY.** – Nothing in this section shall be construed to condition the applicability of subsections (a) through (d) on –

    (1) a service provider monitoring its service or affirmatively seeking facts indicating infringing activity ... or

    (2) a service provider gaining access to, removing, or disabling access to material in cases in which such conduct is prohibited by law.

QUESTIONS

1. Continuing the example from above, consider first Ultraband. Read through § 512(a). How closely does it fit what Ultraband does? Also read through § 512(k), to make sure that Ultraband is a "service provider" in the first place. Are there any further conditions on what Ultraband must do in order to remain eligible for its § 512(a) immunity?

2. Epitome, by way of comparison, depends on the 512(c) immunity for "storage [of infringing material] at the direction of a user." But notice that 512(c)(1)(C) conditions that immunity on taking prompt action when it receives a notice of claimed infringement. What's the statutory language that tells us what Epitome must do? Compare this legal regime to Section 230 and to the common-law trademark doctrines applied in *Tiffany v. eBay*.

3. Section 512(c) imposes two important threshold tests for a hosting provider to qualify for the safe harbor. The first is codified in § 512(c)(1)(A). Read it closely. Does it remind you of any other doctrines? The second is codified in § 512(c)(1)(B). Does it remind you of any other doctrines?

4. Congress responded to the risk of overly aggressive DMCA notices with two provisions, One, codified in § 512(g), is generally called "counter-notice and

putback." Why is it called that? How does it work? (The other is § 512(f), discussed in *Lenz, infra*.)

5. Note that § 512(d) uses a similar notice-and-takedown regime, but § 512(a) doesn't.* Why not? What explains the difference in treatment of these different intermediaries?

6. Given the volitional conduct doctrine, was Section 512 even necessary? Conversely, is there any work for the the volitional conduct doctrine now that Section 512 is on the books?

7. The Copyright Office has adopted a rule under which designations of agents to receive notifications expire every three years and must be renewed. *See* 37 C.F.R. § 201.38(c)(4) What are the likely effects of this rule for small websites? For major sites?

FRIDAY PROBLEM

Rebecca Black's music video for "Friday" has been viewed over 100 million times on YouTube. But in June 2011, the official version of the video was removed from YouTube. Fans promptly rushed in to fill the gap. One of them, with a username of PinkDressGirl, uploaded a copy to YouTube, describing it as "Friday (Totally Unauthorized)."

1. Suppose you work for ARK Music (Black's record label) and you would like to have this unauthorized version removed from YouTube. What is the process you will need to go through to submit a takedown notice? What will the notice need to contain, and what will you need to do with it?

2. Now suppose you work for YouTube. You have just received the notice from ARK Music. What will happen if you ignore it? What will happen if you disable access to the video? What will you do?

3. Now suppose you are PinkDressGirl. YouTube has just informed you that the video has been disabled due to a copyright complaint from ARK Music. What are your options? What are their advantages and disadvantages?

4. Now, suppose you work for YouTube and you have just received PinkDress-Girl's counter-notice. What are your options and obligations? How quickly must you act? What will you do?

5. Finally, suppose you work for ARK Music again, and YouTube has just informed you of PinkDressGirl's counter-notice. What are your options? Is the video online or offline while you deliberate? What will you do?

LENZ V. UNIVERSAL MUSIC CORP.

815 F.3d 1145 (9th Cir. 2016)

Tallman, Circuit Judge:

Stephanie Lenz filed suit under 17 U.S.C. § 512(f) – part of the Digital Millennium Copyright Act ("DMCA") – against Universal Music Corp., Universal Music Publishing, Inc., and Universal Music Publishing Group (collectively "Universal"). She alleges Universal misrepresented in a takedown notification that her 29–second home video (the "video") constituted an infringing use of a portion of a composition by the Artist known as Prince, which Universal insists was unauthorized

---

* You may be wondering what happened to § 512(b). This immunity, for "system caching," is far and away the most complex, and has almost never been litigated.

by the law. Her claim boils down to a question of whether copyright holders have been abusing the extrajudicial takedown procedures provided for in the DMCA by declining to first evaluate whether the content qualifies as fair use. We hold that the statute requires copyright holders to consider fair use before sending a takedown notification, and that in this case, there is a triable issue as to whether the copyright holder formed a subjective good faith belief that the use was not authorized by law. ...

I

Founded in May 2005, YouTube (now owned by Google) operates a website that hosts user-generated content. Users upload videos directly to the website. On February 7, 2007, Lenz uploaded to YouTube a 29–second home video of her two young children in the family kitchen dancing to the song *Let's Go Crazy* by Prince. Available at https://www.youtube.com/watch?v=N1KfJHFWlhQ (last visited September 4, 2015). She titled the video " 'Let's Go Crazy' # 1." About four seconds into the video, Lenz asks her thirteen month-old son "what do you think of the music?" after which he bobs up and down while holding a push toy.

At the time Lenz posted the video, Universal was Prince's publishing administrator responsible for enforcing his copyrights. To accomplish this objective with respect to YouTube, Robert Allen, Universal's head of business affairs, assigned Sean Johnson, an assistant in the legal department, to monitor YouTube on a daily basis. Johnson searched YouTube for Prince's songs and reviewed the video postings returned by his online search query. When reviewing such videos, he evaluated whether they "embodied a Prince composition" by making "significant use of ... the composition, specifically if the song was recognizable, was in a significant portion of the video or was the focus of the video." According to Allen, "[t]he general guidelines are that ... we review the video to ensure that the composition was the focus and if it was we then notify YouTube that the video should be removed."

Johnson contrasted videos that met this criteria to those "that may have had a second or less of a Prince song, literally a one line, half line of Prince song" or "were shot in incredibly noisy environments, such as bars, where there could be a Prince song playing deep in the background ... to the point where if there was any Prince composition embodied ... in those videos that it was distorted beyond reasonable recognition." None of the video evaluation guidelines explicitly include consideration of the fair use doctrine.

When Johnson reviewed Lenz's video, he recognized *Let's Go Crazy* immediately. He noted that it played loudly in the background throughout the entire video. Based on these details, the video's title, and Lenz's query during the video asking if her son liked the song, he concluded that Prince's song "was very much the focus of the video." As a result, Johnson decided the video should be included in a takedown notification sent to YouTube that listed more than 200 YouTube videos Universal believed to be making unauthorized use of Prince's songs. The notice included a "good faith belief" statement as required by 17 U.S.C. § 512(c)(3) (A)(v): "We have a good faith belief that the above-described activity is not authorized by the copyright owner, its agent, or the law."

After receiving the takedown notification, YouTube removed the video and sent Lenz an email on June 5, 2007, notifying her of the removal. On June 7, 2007, Lenz attempted to restore the video by sending a [defective] counter-notification to YouTube pursuant to § 512(g)(3). ... After obtaining *pro bono* counsel, Lenz sent a second counter-notification on June 27, 2007, which resulted in YouTube's reinstatement of the video in mid-July.

II

Lenz filed the instant action on July 24, 2007, and her Amended Complaint on August 15, 2007. ...

On February 25, 2010, the district court granted Lenz's partial motion for summary judgment on Universal's six affirmative defenses, including the third affirmative defense that Lenz suffered no damages. Both parties subsequently moved for summary judgment on Lenz's § 512(f) misrepresentation claim. On January 24, 2013, the district court denied both motions in an order that is now before us. ...

IV ...

B

We must first determine whether 17 U.S.C. § 512(c)(3)(A)(v) requires copyright holders to consider whether the potentially infringing material is a fair use of a copyright under 17 U.S.C. § 107 before issuing a takedown notification. Section 512(c)(3)(A)(v) requires a takedown notification to include a "statement that the complaining party has a good faith belief that the use of the material in the manner complained of is not authorized by the copyright owner, its agent, or the law." The parties dispute whether fair use is an authorization under the law as contemplated by the statute ...

Fair use is not just excused by the law, it is wholly authorized by the law. ...

Even if, as Universal urges, fair use is classified as an "*affirmative* defense," we hold – for the purposes of the DMCA – fair use is uniquely situated in copyright law so as to be treated differently than traditional affirmative defenses. We conclude that because 17 U.S.C. § 107 created a type of non-infringing use, fair use is "authorized by the law" and a copyright holder must consider the existence of fair use before sending a takedown notification under § 512(c).

C

We must next determine if a genuine issue of material fact exists as to whether Universal knowingly misrepresented that it had formed a good faith belief the video did not constitute fair use. This inquiry lies not in whether a court would adjudge the video as a fair use, but whether Universal formed a good faith belief that it was not. Contrary to the district court's holding, Lenz may proceed under an actual knowledge theory, but not under a willful blindness theory.

1

Though Lenz argues Universal should have known the video qualifies for fair use as a matter of law, we have already decided a copyright holder need only form a subjective good faith belief that a use is not authorized. *Rossi v. Motion Picture Ass'n of Am. Inc.*, 391 F.3d 1000 (9th Cir. 2004). In *Rossi*, we explicitly held that "the 'good faith belief' requirement in § 512(c)(3)(A)(v) encompasses a subjective, rather than objective standard," and we observed that "Congress understands this distinction." *Id.* at 1004. We further held:

> When enacting the DMCA, Congress could have easily incorporated an objective standard of reasonableness. The fact that it did not do so indicates an intent to adhere to the subjective standard traditionally associated with a good faith requirement....
>
> In § 512(f), Congress included an expressly limited cause of action for improper infringement notifications, imposing liability only if the copyright owner's notification is a knowing misrepresentation. A

> copyright owner cannot be liable simply because an unknowing mistake is made, even if the copyright owner acted unreasonably in making the mistake. Rather, there must be a demonstration of some actual knowledge of misrepresentation on the part of the copyright owner.

Id. at 1004–05. Neither of these holdings are dictum. We therefore judge Universal's actions by the subjective beliefs it formed about the video.

2

Universal faces liability if it knowingly misrepresented in the takedown notification that it had formed a good faith belief the video was not authorized by the law, i.e., did not constitute fair use. Here, Lenz presented evidence that Universal did not form any subjective belief about the video's fair use – one way or another – because it failed to consider fair use at all, and knew that it failed to do so. Universal nevertheless contends that its procedures, while not formally labeled consideration of fair use, were tantamount to such consideration. Because the DMCA requires consideration of fair use prior to sending a takedown notification, a jury must determine whether Universal's actions were sufficient to form a subjective good faith belief about the video's fair use or lack thereof.

To be clear, if a copyright holder ignores or neglects our unequivocal holding that it must consider fair use before sending a takedown notification, it is liable for damages under § 512(f). If, however, a copyright holder forms a subjective *good faith* belief the allegedly infringing material does not constitute fair use, we are in no position to dispute the copyright holder's belief even if we would have reached the opposite conclusion. A copyright holder who pays lip service to the consideration of fair use by claiming it formed a good faith belief when there is evidence to the contrary is still subject to § 512(f) liability. *Cf. Disney Enters., Inc. v. Hotfile Corp.*, No. 11–cv–20427, 2013 WL 6336286, at *48 (S.D. Fla. Sept. 20, 2013) (denying summary judgment of § 512(f) counterclaim due to "sufficient evidence in the record to suggest that [Plaintiff] Warner intentionally targeted files it knew it had no right to remove"); *Rosen v. Hosting Servs., Inc.*, 771 F. Supp. 2d 1219, 1223 (C.D. Cal. 2010) (denying summary judgment of § 512(f) counterclaim where the takedown notification listed four URL links that did not contain content matching the description of the purportedly infringed material); *Online Policy Grp. v. Diebold, Inc.*, 337 F. Supp. 2d 1195, 1204–05 (N.D. Cal. 2004) ("[T]here is no genuine issue of fact that Diebold knew – and indeed that it specifically intended – that its letters to OPG and Swarthmore would result in prevention of publication of that content.... The fact that Diebold never actually brought suit against any alleged infringer suggests strongly that Diebold sought to use the DMCA's safe harbor provisions – which were designed to protect ISPs, not copyright holders – as a sword to suppress publication of embarrassing content rather than as a shield to protect its intellectual property.").

3

We hold the willful blindness doctrine may be used to determine whether a copyright holder "knowingly materially misrepresent[ed]" that it held a "good faith belief" the offending activity was not a fair use. ... But, based on the specific facts presented during summary judgment, we reject the district court's conclusion that Lenz may proceed to trial under a willful blindness theory.

To demonstrate willful blindness a plaintiff must establish two factors: "(1) the defendant must subjectively believe that there is a high probability that a fact exists and (2) the defendant must take deliberate actions to avoid learning of that fact." *Global–Tech Appliances, Inc. v. SEB S.A.*, 563 U.S. 754 (2011). "Under this formulation, a willfully blind defendant is one who takes deliberate actions to avoid confirming a high probability of wrongdoing and who can almost be said to have actually known the critical facts." *Id.* To meet the *Global–Tech* test, Lenz must demonstrate a genuine issue as to whether – before sending the takedown notification – Universal (1) subjectively believed there was a high probability that the video constituted fair use, and (2) took deliberate actions to avoid learning of this fair use.

On summary judgment Lenz failed to meet a threshold showing of the first factor. To make such a showing, Lenz must provide evidence from which a juror could infer that Universal was aware of a high probability the video constituted fair use. But she failed to provide any such evidence. ... Lenz may not therefore proceed to trial on a willful blindness theory.

V

Section 512(f) provides for the recovery of "any damages, including costs and attorneys['] fees, incurred by the alleged infringer ... who is injured by such misrepresentation, as the result of the service provider relying upon such misrepresentation in removing or disabling access to the material or activity claimed to be infringing...." 17 U.S.C. § 512(f). We hold a plaintiff may seek recovery of nominal damages for an injury incurred as a result of a § 512(f) misrepresentation.

Universal incorrectly asserts that Lenz must demonstrate she incurred "actual monetary loss." Section 512(k) provides a definition for "monetary relief" as "damages, costs, attorneys['] fees, and any other form of monetary payment." The term "monetary relief" appears in § 512(a), (b)(1), (c)(1), and (d), but is notably absent from § 512(f). As a result, the damages an alleged infringer may recover under § 512(f) from "any person" are broader than monetary relief. Because Congress specified the recovery of "any damages," we reject Universal's contention that Congress did not indicate its intent to depart from the common law presumption that a misrepresentation plaintiff must have suffered a monetary loss. ...

Lenz may seek recovery of nominal damages due to an unquantifiable harm suffered as a result of Universal's actions. The DMCA is akin to a statutorily created intentional tort whereby an individual may recover nominal damages for a "knowingly material misrepresent[ation] under this section [512]." 17 U.S.C. § 512(f). ...

We agree that Lenz may vindicate her statutorily created rights by seeking nominal damages. Because a jury has not yet determined whether Lenz will prevail at trial, we need not decide the scope of recoverable damages, i.e., whether she may recover expenses following the initiation of her § 512(f) suit or *pro bono* costs and attorneys' fees, both of which arose as a result of the injury incurred.

VI

Copyright holders cannot shirk their duty to consider – in good faith and prior to sending a takedown notification – whether allegedly infringing material constitutes fair use, a use which the DMCA plainly contemplates as authorized by the law. That this step imposes responsibility on copyright holders is not a reason for us to reject it.

M. Smith, Circuit Judge, concurring in part and dissenting in part:
I concur in all but Part IV.C of the majority opinion. However, I disagree with the majority's conclusion that "whether Universal's actions were sufficient to form

a subjective good faith belief about the video's fair use or lack thereof" presents a triable issue of fact. Universal admittedly did not consider fair use before notifying YouTube to take down Lenz's video. It therefore could not have formed a good faith belief that Lenz's video was infringing, and its notification to the contrary was a knowing material misrepresentation. Accordingly, I would hold that Lenz is entitled to summary judgment. ...

However, I part ways with the majority on two issues. First, I would clarify that § 512(f)'s requirement that a misrepresentation be "knowing [ ]" is satisfied when the party knows that it is ignorant of the truth or falsity of its representation. Second, I would hold that Universal's actions were insufficient as a matter of law to form a subjective good-faith belief that Lenz's video was not a fair use.

QUESTIONS

1. Was "Let's Go Crazy # 1" a fair use?

2. Why are the parties litigating over a single takedown notice, given that Lenz sent a counter-notice and the video was made available again?

3. How much of an investigation must a copyright owner undertake before sending a takedown notice? In an earlier version of its opinion, the majority originally wrote:

> In order to comply with the strictures of § 512(c)(3)(A)(v), a copyright holder's consideration of fair use need not be searching or intensive. ... We are mindful of the pressing crush of voluminous infringing content that copyright holders face in a digital age. But that does not excuse a failure to comply with the procedures outlined by Congress.
>
> We note, without passing judgment, that the implementation of computer algorithms appears to be a valid and good faith middle ground for processing a plethora of content while still meeting the DMCA's requirements to somehow consider fair use. For example, consideration of fair use may be sufficient if copyright holders utilize computer programs that automatically identify for takedown notifications content where: (1) the video track matches the video track of a copyrighted work submitted by a content owner; (2) the audio track matches the audio track of that same copyrighted work; and (3) nearly the entirety is comprised of a single copyrighted work.
>
> Copyright holders could then employ individuals like Johnson to review the minimal remaining content a computer program does not cull.

   Lenz v. Universal Music Corp., 801 F.3d 1126, 1135–36 (9th Cir. 2015) Is that right? Or was the panel right to withdraw this portion of its opinion? Would such a process be better or worse than the one Universal actually used?

4. Michael Crook posted a fake ad on Craigslist pretending to be a 19-year-old female college student seeking a casual sexual encounter, and asking men to send pictures. When men responded, he published their names and pictures to his web site. Blogger Jeffery Diehl wrote a post about Crook, which he illustrated with a photograph of Crook appearing on FOX News. Crook sent a DMCA takedown notice to Diehl's web host, which insisted that Diehl re-

move the photograph. Diehl sued Crook under § 512(f). Did Diehl have a case?

PERFECT 10, INC. V. CCBILL LLC
488 F.3d 1102 (9th Cir. 2007)

Smith, Circuit Judge:

Perfect 10, the publisher of an adult entertainment magazine and the owner of the subscription website perfect10.com, alleges that CCBill and CWIE violated copyright, trademark, and state unfair competition, false advertising and right of publicity laws by providing services to websites that posted images stolen from Perfect 10's magazine and website. Perfect 10 appeals the district court's finding that CCBill and CWIE qualified for certain statutory safe harbors from copyright infringement liability under the Digital Millennium Copyright Act ("DMCA"), 17 U.S.C. § 512 ...

BACKGROUND

Perfect 10 is the publisher of the eponymous adult entertainment magazine and the owner of the website, perfect10.com. Perfect10.com is a subscription site where consumers pay a membership fee in order to gain access to content on the website. Perfect 10 has created approximately 5,000 images of models for display in its website and magazine. Many of the models in these images have signed releases assigning their rights of publicity to Perfect 10. Perfect 10 also holds registered U.S. copyrights for these images and owns several related, registered trademark and service marks.

CWIE provides webhosting and related Internet connectivity services to the owners of various websites. For a fee, CWIE provides "ping, power, and pipe," services to their clients by ensuring the "box" or server is on, ensuring power is provided to the server and connecting the client's service or website to the Internet via a data center connection. CCBill allows consumers to use credit cards or checks to pay for subscriptions or memberships to e-commerce venues.

Beginning August 10, 2001, Perfect 10 sent letters and emails to CCBill and CWIE stating that CCBill and CWIE clients were infringing Perfect 10 copyrights. Perfect 10 directed these communications to Thomas A. Fisher, the designated agent to receive notices of infringement. Fisher is also the Executive Vice-President of both CCBill and CWIE. Representatives of celebrities who are not parties to this lawsuit also sent notices of infringement to CCBill and CWIE. On September 30, 2002, Perfect 10 filed the present action alleging copyright and trademark violations, state law claims of violation of right of publicity, unfair competition, false and misleading advertising, as well as RICO claims. ...

DISCUSSION

I. SECTION 512 SAFE HARBORS

The DMCA established certain safe harbors to "provide protection from liability for: (1) transitory digital network communications; (2) system caching; (3) information residing on systems or networks at the direction of users; and (4) information location tools." [*Ellison v Robertson*, 357 F.3d 1072, 1076–77 (9th Cir. 2004)] (citing 17 U.S.C. §§ 512(a)–(d)) (footnotes omitted). These safe harbors limit liability but "do not affect the question of ultimate liability under the various doctrines of direct, vicarious, and contributory liability," *Perfect 10, Inc. v. Cybernet Ventures, Inc.*, 213 F. Supp. 2d 1146, 1174 (C.D. Cal. 2002) (citing H.R. Rep. 105-551 (II), at 50 (1998) ("H.R. Rep."), and "nothing in the language of *§ 512* indicates that the limitation on liability described therein is exclusive." *CoStar Group, Inc. v. LoopNet, Inc.*, 373 F.3d 544, 552 (4th Cir. 2004).

A. Reasonably Implemented Policy: § 512(i)(1)(A)

To be eligible for any of the four safe harbors at §§ 512(a)–(d), a service provider must first meet the threshold conditions set out in § 512(i), including the requirement that the service provider:

> [H]as adopted and reasonably implemented, and informs subscribers and account holders of the service provider's system or network of, a policy that provides for the termination in appropriate circumstances of subscribers and account holders of the service provider's system or network who are repeat infringers.

Section 512(i)(1)(A); *Ellison*, 357 F.3d at 1080. The statute does not define "reasonably implemented." We hold that a service provider "implements" a policy if it has a working notification system, a procedure for dealing with DMCA-compliant notifications, and if it does not actively prevent copyright owners from collecting information needed to issue such notifications. The statute permits service providers to implement a variety of procedures, but an implementation is reasonable if, under "appropriate circumstances," the service provider terminates users who repeatedly or blatantly infringe copyright.

1. *"Implementation"*

Perfect 10 argues that there is a genuine issue of material fact whether CCBill and CWIE prevented the implementation of their policies by failing to keep track of repeatedly infringing webmasters. The district court found that there was not, and we agree.

In *Ellison*, Stephen Robertson posted copies of Harlan Ellison's copyrighted short stories on Internet newsgroups available through USENET servers. 357 F.3d at 1075. Ellison asserted that America Online, Inc. ("AOL") had infringed his copyright by providing access to the USENET servers. *Id.* Based on evidence that AOL changed its contact email address for copyright infringement notices from copyright@aol.com to aolcopyright@aol.com in the fall of 1999, but neglected to register the change with the U.S. Copyright Office until April 2000, we held that the district court erred in concluding on summary judgment that AOL satisfied the requirements of § 512(i). Even though Ellison did not learn of the infringing activity until after AOL had notified the U.S. Copyright Office of the correct email address, we found that "AOL allowed notices of potential copyright infringement to fall into a vacuum and go unheeded; that fact is sufficient for a reasonable jury to conclude that AOL had not reasonably implemented its policy against repeat infringers." *Id.* at 1080.

Similarly, the *Aimster* cases hold that a repeat infringer policy is not implemented under § 512(i)(1)(A) if the service provider prevents copyright holders from providing DMCA-compliant notifications. In *Aimster*, the district court held that Aimster did not reasonably implement its stated repeat infringer policy because "the encryption on Aimster renders it impossible to ascertain which users are transferring which files." [*In re Aimster Copyright Litig.*, 252 F. Supp. 634, 659 (N.D. Ill. 2002).] The court found that "[a]dopting a repeat infringer policy and then purposely eviscerating any hope that such a policy could ever be carried out is not an 'implementation' as required by § 512(i)." *Id.* The Seventh Circuit affirmed, finding that Aimster did not meet the requirement of § 512(i)(1)(A) because, in part, "by teaching its users how to encrypt their unlawful distribution of copyrighted materials [Aimster] disabled itself from doing anything to prevent infringement." *In re Aimster Copyright Litig.*, 334 F.3d 643, 655 (7th Cir. 2003).

Based on *Ellison* and the *Aimster* cases, a substantial failure to record webmasters associated with allegedly infringing websites may raise a genuine issue of material fact as to the implementation of the service provider's repeat infringer policy. In this case, however, the record does not reflect such a failure. Perfect 10 references a single page from CCBill and CWIE's "DMCA Log." Although this page shows some empty fields in the spreadsheet column labeled "Webmasters [sic] Name," Perfect 10's conclusion that the DMCA Log thus "does not reflect any effort to track notices of infringements received by webmaster identity" is not supported by evidence in the record. The remainder of the DMCA Log indicates that the email address and/or name of the webmaster is routinely recorded in CCBill and CWIE's DMCA Log. CCBill's interrogatory responses dated December 11, 2003 also contain a chart indicating that CCBill and CWIE largely kept track of the webmaster for each website.

Unlike *Ellison* and *Aimster*, where the changed email address and the encryption system ensured that *no* information about the repeat infringer was collected, it is undisputed that CCBill and CWIE recorded most webmasters. The district court properly concluded that the DMCA Log does not raise a triable issue of fact that CCBill and CWIE did not implement a repeat infringer policy.

2. Reasonableness

A service provider reasonably implements its repeat infringer policy if it terminates users when "appropriate." *See* [*Corbis Corp. v. Amazon.com, Inc.* 351 F. Supp. 2d 1090, 1104 (W.D. Wash. 2004)]. Section 512(i) itself does not clarify when it is "appropriate" for service providers to act. It only requires that a service provider terminate users who are "repeat infringers."

To identify and terminate repeat infringers, a service provider need not affirmatively police its users for evidence of repeat infringement. Section 512(c) states that "[a] service provider shall not be liable for monetary relief" if it does not know of infringement. A service provider is also not liable under § 512(c) if it acts "expeditiously to remove, or disable access to, the material" when it (1) has actual knowledge, (2) is aware of facts or circumstances from which infringing activity is apparent, or (3) has received notification of claimed infringement meeting the requirements of § 512(c)(3). Were we to require service providers to terminate users under circumstances other than those specified in § 512(c), § 512(c)'s grant of immunity would be meaningless. This interpretation of the statute is supported by legislative history. *See* H.R. Rep., at 61 (Section 512(i) is not intended "to undermine the . . . knowledge standard of [§ 512](c).").

Perfect 10 claims that CCBill and CWIE unreasonably implemented their repeat infringer policies by tolerating flagrant and blatant copyright infringement by its users despite notice of infringement from Perfect 10, notice of infringement from copyright holders not a party to this litigation and "red flags" of copyright infringement.

a. Perfect 10's Claimed Notice of Infringement

Perfect 10 argues that CCBill and CWIE implemented their repeat infringer policy in an unreasonable manner because CCBill and CWIE received notices of infringement from Perfect 10, and yet the infringement identified in these notices continued. The district court found that Perfect 10 did not provide notice that substantially complied with the requirements of § 512(c)(3), and thus did not raise a genuine issue of material fact as to whether CCBill and CWIE reasonably implemented their repeat infringer policy. We agree.

Compliance is not "substantial" if the notice provided complies with only some of the requirements of § 512(c)(3)(A). Section 512(c)(3)(B)(ii) explains that a service provider will not be deemed to have notice of infringement when "the notification that is provided to the service provider's designated agent fails to comply substantially with all the provisions of subparagraph (A) but substantially complies with clauses (ii), (iii), and (iv) of subparagraph (A)" so long as the service provider responds to the inadequate notice and explains the requirements for substantial compliance. The statute thus signals that substantial compliance means substantial compliance with *all* of *§ 512(c)(3)'s* clauses, not just some of them. *See* H.R. Rep., at 56 (A communication substantially complies even if it contains technical errors such as misspellings or outdated information.). *See also Recording Indus. Ass'n of Am., Inc. v. Verizon Internet Servs., Inc.,* 351 F.3d 1229, 1236 (D.C. Cir. 2003).

Perfect 10 claims that it met the requirements of § 512(c)(3) through a combination of three sets of documents. The first set of documents is a 22,185 page bates-stamped production on October 16, 2002 that includes pictures with URLs of Perfect 10 models allegedly posted on CCBill or CWIE client websites. The October 16, 2002 production did not contain a statement under penalty of perjury that the complaining party was authorized to act, as required by § 512(c)(3)(A)(vi). The second set of documents was also not sworn to, and consisted of a spreadsheet emailed to Fisher on July 14, 2003 identifying the Perfect 10 models in the October 16, 2002 production by bates number. On December 2, 2003, Perfect 10 completed interrogatory responses which were signed under penalty of perjury. These responses incorporated the July 14, 2003 spreadsheet by reference.

Taken individually, Perfect 10's communications do not substantially comply with the requirements of § 512(c)(3). Each communication contains more than mere technical errors; often one or more of the required elements are entirely absent. *See Perfect 10, Inc. v. CCBill, LLC,* 340 F. Supp. 2d 1077, 1100–01 (C.D. Cal. 2004) ("Order"). In order to substantially comply with § 512(c)(3)'s requirements, a notification must do more than identify infringing files. The DMCA requires a complainant to declare, under penalty of perjury, that he is authorized to represent the copyright holder, and that he has a good-faith belief that the use is infringing. This requirement is not superfluous. Accusations of alleged infringement have drastic consequences: A user could have content removed, or may have his access terminated entirely. If the content infringes, justice has been done. But if it does not, speech protected under the First Amendment could be removed. We therefore do not require a service provider to start potentially invasive proceedings if the complainant is unwilling to state under penalty of perjury that he is an authorized representative of the copyright owner, and that he has a good-faith belief that the material is unlicensed.

Permitting a copyright holder to cobble together adequate notice from separately defective notices also unduly burdens service providers. Indeed, the text of § 512(c)(3) requires that the notice be "*a* written communication." (Emphasis added). Again, this requirement is not a mere technicality. It would have taken Fisher substantial time to piece together the relevant information for each instance of claimed infringement. To do so, Fisher would have to first find the relevant line in the spreadsheet indicating ownership information, then comb the 22,185 pages provided by Perfect 10 in order to find the appropriate image, and finally copy into a browser the location printed at the top of the page – a location which was, in some instances, truncated. The DMCA notification procedures place the burden of policing copyright infringement – identifying the potentially infringing material and adequately documenting infringement – squarely on the owners of the copyright. We decline to shift a substantial burden from the copyright owner to the provider; Perfect 10's separate communications are inadequate.

Since Perfect 10 did not provide effective notice, knowledge of infringement may not be imputed to CCBill or CWIE based on Perfect 10's communications. Perfect 10's attempted notice does not raise a genuine issue of material fact that CCBill and CWIE failed to reasonably implement a repeat infringer policy within the meaning of § 512(i)(1)(A).

b. Non-Party Notices

Perfect 10 also cites to notices of infringement by other copyright holders, and argues that CCBill and CWIE did not reasonably implement their repeat infringer policies because they continued to provide services for websites that infringed non-party copyrights. The district court expressly declined to consider evidence of notices provided by any party other than Perfect 10 on the basis that these notices were irrelevant to Perfect 10's claims. We disagree.

CCBill and CWIE's actions towards copyright holders who are not a party to the litigation are relevant in determining whether CCBill and CWIE reasonably implemented their repeat infringer policy. Section 512(i)(1)(A) requires an assessment of the service provider's "policy," not how the service provider treated a particular copyright holder. *See Ellison*, 357 F.3d at 1080 (AOL's repeat infringer policy was not reasonably implemented because copyright holders other than Ellison could have attempted to notify AOL during the time that AOL's email address was incorrectly listed.). Thus, CCBill and CWIE's response to adequate non-party notifications is relevant in determining whether they reasonably implemented their policy against repeat infringers.

A policy is unreasonable only if the service provider failed to respond when it had knowledge of the infringement. The district court in this case did not consider any evidence relating to copyright holders other than Perfect 10. We remand for determination of whether CCBill and/or CWIE implemented its repeat infringer policy in an unreasonable manner with respect to any copyright holder other than Perfect 10. ...

QUESTION

1. If CCBill receives a compliant DMCA takedown notice from Perfect 10, what are the consequences? If CCBill receives an email from Perfect 10 with a URL and the words, "this is infringing." what are the consequences? What if CCBill receives the email not from Perfect 10 but from an unrelated third party?

2. What was Perfect 10's likely goal in bringing this lawsuit? What could it have gained from a broader win?

SECTION 512 COMPLIANCE QUESTIONS

As *CCBill* indicates, the contours of Section 512 compliance can be subtle. Consider the following hypotheticals. In each case, identify the relevant text from Section 512 and do your best to apply it.

1. Rubber Band is a website for users to upload and share music; it offers extensive features for users to annotate uploaded songs and to embed short (ten-second or less) clips in other webpages. In the space of two hours, Rubber Band receives 315 separate takedown notices relating to songs uploaded by the user FreakFlag99. All of the notices were sent by Cacophony Records and they all relate to songs by its recording artists.

2. Rubber Band's CEO sends an email to one of its employees: "Hey, Doug, we need more ambient dub to improve our demographics for the advertisers. You've got a good collection of Wispher's B-sides and other good stuff. Can you upload some of that today?"

3. Rubber Band user MusicMatt uploads the the isolated vocal part from the song "Minimum Working Pressure" by the band Chill Sitch. He uses Rubber Band's annotation features to mark all of the different vocal techniques used by the lead singer, and assigns it to his high school vocal performance students. Chill Sitch sends a takedown notice.

4. Observation Deck is a website that allows users to livestream video. The National Football League sends a takedown notice that identifies a stream that consists of a rebroadcast of an ongoing football game. The notice demands that ObservationDeck take down the stream immediately, while the game is still ongoing.

5. Mugshot is a website that allows users to upload images and have them printed on coffee mugs for $9.99 each (plus shipping). Once a user has ordered a mug, the design remains online for others to buy. Photographer Errol Sontag sues Mugshot for copyright infringement without previously sending a takedown notice, claiming the Section 512 safe harbors do not apply to physical goods.

6. Red Handed, a celebrity gossip blog, accepts user-submitted photos. Frequently, users submit professional paparazzi photos copied from other websites rather than photographs they have taken themselves. It receives a takedown notice from movie actor Ranier Wolfcastle, who claims that a photograph of him infringes on his right of publicly.

7. Errol Sontag also sues Red Handed without previously sending a takedown notice. This time, he argues that Red Handed should have known his photos were copyrighted because paparazzi photos in general are, and because some of them bear the watermark "ErrolSontag.com."

8. Sontag further argues that Red Handed's policy of having its employees review user-submitted photos before posting them means that Section 512 does not apply.

MATERIALS ON CONTENT ID

WHAT IS YOUTUBE'S CONTENT ID TOOL?
YOUTUBE (last visited June 26, 2012)
http://support.google.com/youtube/bin/answer.py?hl=en&topic=13656&answer=83766

What is the Content ID tool?

The Content ID tool is the latest way YouTube offers copyright holders to easily identify and manage their content on YouTube. The tool creates ID files which are then run against user uploads and, if a match occurs, the copyright holders policy preferences are then applied to that video. Rights owners can choose to block, track or monetize their content.

What are "ID files?"

The digital content identification file which corresponds to a reference file (a piece of content like a movie, music or other audiovisual material). This file is generated using Google software and is also known as a "fingerprint."

Where does the reference library come from?

The reference library is generated from copies of content or from ID files that are submitted by content owners.

How accurate is Content ID?

The solution is very accurate in finding uploads that look similar to reference files that are of sufficient length and quality to generate an effective ID File. The system is tuned to offer the best possible automated matches while eliminating most false positive matches. We are constantly tuning the system to deal with attempts to circumvent it, therefore exact rates are not available. ...

What happens when Content ID identifies a match?

If Content ID identifies a match between a user upload and material in the reference library, it applies the usage policy designated by the content owner. The usage policy tells the system what to do with the video. Matches can be to only the audio portion of an upload, the video portion only, or both.

What kinds of usage policies are there?

There are three usage policies -- Block, Track or Monetize. If a rights owner specifies a Block policy, the video will not be viewable on YouTube. If the rights owner specifies a Track policy, the video will continue to be made available on YouTube and the rights owner will receive information about the video, such as how many views it receives. For a Monetize policy, the video will continue to be available on YouTube and ads will appear in conjunction with the video. The policies can be region-specific, so a content owner can allow a particular piece of material in one country and block the material in another. ...

What happens if Content ID identifies multiple matches for an upload?

To the extent possible, Content ID applies all usage policies for all of the matches.

What if a video is blocked in the uploader's region?

The uploader will be unable to view the video. Users in other regions may still be able to view and interact with the video as usual. The uploader will still be able to view, moderate, and respond to comments on the video from the "all comments" page. ...

How do I know if one of my videos has been matched?

A note will appear next to the video on the "My Videos" page, and the video will be listed on the "Content ID Matches" page. ...

DAVID KING
CONTENT ID TURNS THREE
Broadcasting Ourselves: The Official YouTube Blog (Dec. 2, 2010)
http://youtube-global.blogspot.com/2010/12/content-id-turns-three.html

Fast forward to 2010. We've just passed a significant milestone: more than 100 million videos have been claimed with Content ID. Nearly every major media company and music label in the world uses our tools. The number of reference files provided to us by rights holders now stands at more than four million, or over 300,000 hours of content - we think it's the most comprehensive database of its kind in the world.

Rights holders who claim their content with Content ID generally more than double the number of views against which we can run ads, doubling their potential revenue. And we're seeing media companies make the most of this revenue opportunity - in the last quarter alone, claims to make money from videos increased 200%. Content ID contributes more than a third of YouTube's monetized views each week, and overall, the revenue generated by Content ID is financing the ongoing creation of culture, both by established artists and new ones,

When we developed Content ID, we were hopeful that we'd gone some way toward helping solve a really tough problem -- how to manage rights issues, across platforms and countries, in a quickly evolving technology world. We've already invested tens of millions of dollars in this technology, and we'll keep investigating new ways to give rights holders ever better tools, while supporting new forms of creative expression.

SHENAZ ZACK
CONTENTID AND FAIR USE
GOOGLE PUBLIC POLICY BLOG (Apr. 23, 2010)
http://googlepublicpolicy.blogspot.com/2010/04/content-id-and-fair-use.html

Over the past decade, the evolution of the Internet has altered the landscape for both traditional media companies and the doctrine of fair use, and the media industry has tried to keep up. The new ways that consumers create and distribute content are not a niche phenomenon. Hundreds of millions of people around the world now use the Web to connect and interact with content online, and a huge percentage of them go even further: they express themselves via parodies, celebrate their favorite videos with mashups, and use music in educational presentations. The people that upload these videos are typically the biggest fans, and are exactly the kinds of consumers rights holders should be embracing.

We listen closely to our partners and we're constantly improving our content identification and management tools ("Content ID") to make sure they have choices in dealing with these different uses of their content on YouTube. Over 1,000 content owners use Content ID, and we've built it in a way that lets them account for fair uses of their content: they can easily create policies depending on the proportion of a claimed video that contains their work, or the absolute length of the clip used. For example, a record label might decide to block videos that contain over one minute of a given song, but leave up videos that contain less than one minute.

Since Content ID can't identify context (like "educational use" or "parody"), we give partners the tools to use length and match proportion as a proxy. Of course, it's not a perfect system. That's why two videos -- one of a baby dancing to one minute of a pop song, and another using the exact same audio clip in a videotaped University lecture about copyright law -- might be treated identically by Content ID and taken down by the rights holder, even though one may be fair use and the other may not. Rights holders are the only ones in a position to know what is and is not an authorized use of their content, and we require them to enforce their policies in a manner that complies with the law.

Still, to make sure that users also have choices when dealing with the content they upload to YouTube, Content ID makes it easy for users to dispute inappropriate claims.

- When you receive a notice in your account via Content ID, we tell you who claimed the content, and direct you to a form that lets you dispute the claim if you so choose.

- If you believe your video is fair use, check the box that reads "This video uses copyrighted material in a manner that does not require approval of the copyright holder." If you're not sure if your video qualifies, you can learn more about fair use here.

- Once you've filed your dispute, your video immediately goes back up on YouTube.

- From this point, the claimant then makes a decision about whether to file a formal DMCA notification, and remove the content from the site according to the process set forth in the DMCA.

DAVID KRAVETS
ROGUES FALSELY CLAIM COPYRIGHT ON YOUTUBE VIDEOS TO HIJACK AD DOLLARS
THREAT LEVEL BLOG, WIRED NEWS (Nov. 21, 2011)
http://www.wired.com/threatlevel/2011/11/youtube-filter-profiting

Cat videos are all the rage on YouTube, so much so that a Russian company hijacked a recent cute clip of a feline named "Pepper" in order to steal the ad revenue.

Kidnapping YouTube videos, which anecdotal evidence suggests has happened thousands of times, is as easy as it gets.

A Russian company called Netcom Partners and others are taking advantage of YouTube's copyright-control filters, known as Content ID. It's not clear how much money the scammers are stealing from YouTube videomakers. But if you judge by the volume of complaints about the hijacking on Google's forums, it's likely Netcom and others are doing pretty well making money for nothing. ...

When Content ID finds a match between videos, the uploaders receive an e-mail from YouTube informing them only of the name of the company claiming a copyright breach. Unless the uploader files a counter-notice disputing the copyright violation charge, the claimer gets control of the video. The scammers seem to be hoping that a copyright claim from an official-sounding company sounds scary enough that users won't protest.

In most every case, when a victim files a counter-notice, Netcom and others abandon their claims, and the original video maker wins back complete control of their work.

PATRICK MCKAY
YOUTUBE COPYFRAUD & ABUSE OF THE CONTENT ID SYSTEM
FairUseTube.org (Nov. 23, 2011)
http://fairusetube.org/youtube-copyfraud

A. Introduction: Three Fundamental Flaws with the Content ID System

In order to understand the problem of copyright fraud enabled by YouTube's Content ID system, it is first necessary to understand the three fundamental flaws in its design which enable this abuse.

1. The Content ID program apparently requires no proof of copyright ownership

YouTube's Content ID system works by allowing copyright owners to upload digital copies of video or audio works, which YouTube's servers use to create a digital "fingerprint," against which all other videos on the site are scanned. If even a portion of another video matches the sample in either its visual or audio content, the video is flagged as containing that copyrighted content. From there, the copyright claimant can choose to either block, allow, or "monetize" matched videos. Monetization is done by allowing YouTube to run ads next to the a video, from which the copyright claimant receives a cut of the ad revenue.

While it seems obvious that a system which allows alleged copyright owners to upload any audio/visual work and claim copyright ownership over that work should at minimum require that person to provide some documentation or proof that they own the copyright to each work they claim, anecdotal evidence suggests that no such proof is in fact required. The sheer number of Content ID claims involving content which the claimant could not possibly have any copyright interest in, indicates that either no proof of copyright ownership is required at all, or at least that YouTube does very little to verify this and copyright ownership is easily faked.

The impact of this flaw is that anyone who manages to gain admission to the Content ID program can upload any content they want into the system, which it then flags as belonging to them. They can then block or monetize any video they want, regardless of whether they really own any copyright interest in it. As a result, there is nothing to prevent any Content ID partner from uploading a copy of the latest popular viral video and claiming it as there own, allowing them to hijack the ad revenue from that video, which can be substantial.

2. Content ID identifications are notoriously inaccurate

While YouTube claims the Content ID system results in very few false positives, experience suggests these matches are highly inaccurate and incapable of considering the context of the material in question. Many works are outright misidentified. In other cases, the specific work is correctly identified, but matched incorrectly. For example, if a Content ID partner makes video game reviews which include cutscenes from a popular videogame, Content ID might attribute all other videos using cutscenes from that game to the other reviewer. Likewise if a song by one artist uses royalty free music loops from something like GarageBand or Final Cut, and another song by a different artist uses those same loops, Content ID may identify the second song as matching the first--even though the only elements those songs have in common are in the public domain.

3. The Content ID dispute process is ineffective and gives copyright claimants the ability to unilaterally "confirm" their claim with no further recourse for the uploader

The Content ID system includes a supposed "dispute" process, wherein a user who believes his video has been incorrectly flagged by Content ID can use a simple webform to dispute the Content ID match for one of three reasons (1) misidentification, (2) license to use the material in question, and (3) fair use. YouTube describes this dispute process as being a sort of front-end buffer to the notice and counter-notice process established by the Digital Millennium Copyright Act (17 USC § 512). According to YouTube, once the user files a dispute, the video is automatically restored. If the copyright claimant wishes to have the video blocked again, they must file a DMCA takedown notice. If the user still disagrees, they can then file a DMCA counter-notice and get the video restored. At that point, if the copyright claimant still objects to the video, they must file a lawsuit seeking an injunction.

If this was the way the dispute process actually worked, the impact of the first two problems would be minimal, as false identifications could be easily corrected by filling out a simple online form. As it is however, this is not the way the dispute process works in practice. In reality, after the original uploader files a dipsute, YouTube allows the Content ID claimant to simply "confirm" their claim to the video, allowing them to either permanently block or monetize the video with no further recourse for the uploader. The user is then met with a message saying "All content owners have reviewed your video and confirmed their claims to some or all of its content." After that, there is nothing the uploader can do to fight the copyright claim on their video. Further Content ID disputes are not allowed, and neither can they file a DMCA counter-notice because no DMCA takedown notice has been filed. ...

The upshot of this is that Content ID allows claimants to unilaterally reject any dispute filed against their own copyright claim, essentially making them the judge of their own case. Many, if not most, entities that use the Content ID system make it their policy to blanketly confirm their claims against all disputes that are filed, and don't even bother to evaluate whether individual disputes have merit or not. As a result, the Content ID dispute process as it exists now is simply a joke, and provides no effective means to appeal false copyright claims against a user's videos. This leaves the system wide-open for abuse, with little to no accountability for those who seek to use the Content ID system for nefarious purposes.

DISPUTE A CONTENT ID CLAIM
YOUTUBE HELP (last visited July 27, 2016)
https://support.google.com/youtube/answer/2797454?p=dispute_appeal&rd=2

If you get a Content ID claim on your video that you believe is invalid, you can choose to dispute that claim. When you dispute a Content ID claim the copyright owner will be notified and they'll have 30 days to respond. ...

You can dispute a Content ID claim if you believe the system misidentified your video, or if you have all the rights to use that copyright-protected content. ...

What happens after I dispute?

After you submit your dispute, the copyright owner has 30 days to respond. During this time, the claim will be temporarily released. If they don't respond within 30 days, their claim on your video will expire, and you don't need to do anything.

There are a few things that the copyright owner can do after you dispute:

Release the claim: If they agree with your dispute, they can choose to release their claim. If you were previously monetizing the video, your monetization settings will be restored automatically when all claims on your video are released.

Uphold the claim: If they believe their claim is still valid, they can choose to uphold it. If you feel it was mistakenly upheld, you may be able to appeal their decision.

Take down your video: They can submit a copyright takedown request to remove your video from YouTube, which means you'll get a copyright strike on your account.

How to appeal rejected disputes

If you've already disputed a Content ID claim and feel it was mistakenly upheld by the copyright owner, you may be able to appeal their decision. In the same place in your Video Manager where you disputed the claim, you may now see the option to appeal.

There might be restrictions that affect your ability to appeal, such as the date of your appeal. You'll also need to verify your account if you haven't already done so.

What happens after I appeal?

After you appeal a rejected dispute, the copyright owner has 30 days to respond.

There are a few things the copyright owner can do after you appeal:

Do nothing, let the claim expire: If they don't respond within 30 days, their claim on your video will expire, and you don't need to do anything.

Release the claim: If the copyright owner agrees with your dispute, they can release their claim, and you don't need to do anything.

Request immediate removal of your video: They may issue a copyright takedown request against your video if they believe their claim is still valid. This means you'll get a copyright strike on your account, which will put your account into bad copyright standing. If you still believe that you have the rights to the content, you can submit a counter notification at this point.

Schedule a takedown request for your video: If the copyright owner issues a delayed copyright takedown request, you can cancel your appeal within 7 days, which prevents the takedown and keeps the claim active on your video.

If you change your mind, you can take back your appeal after you've submitted it. Click cancel appeal on the page where you disputed the claim. Keep in mind, once you cancel, you won't be able to appeal the claim again.

QUESTIONS

1. What is the relationship between Section 512 and Conent ID? Why would a site like YouTube implement something like Content ID? Compare the rights and remedies available with a DMCA takedown notice to those available with a Content ID claim. Which would a video uploader rather receive? Which would a copyright owner rather send?

2. Content ID detects videos that match particular fingerprints when they're uploaded, rather than requiring copyright owners to find infringing videos. How does this affect its effectiveness?

3. The media company Viacom claimed that YouTube refused to make its Content ID tools available to Viacom until Viacom entered into a licensing and revenue-sharing arrangement with YouTube. Did YouTube have an obligation to start making Content ID available once it existed? Did it have an obligation to develop Content ID in the first place? Now that it exists, do other websites have an obligation to deploy their own similar tools?

4. Are McKay's criticisms fair? Does the appeals process (created after McKay's initial post) help?

5. Doesn't YouTube, as a privately owned and operated website, have the freedom to decide which videos to allow? If it wants to let some users veto other users' videos, isn't that its prerogative?

6. Another "voluntary" private enforcement initiative is the Copyright Alert System, under which several major ISPs have agreed to accept notices of infringement by their subscribers. As a subscriber accumulates more notices, she is subject to a series of escalating sanctions, starting with warnings and going up to reductions in her connection speed. Why would ISPs agree to do more than the DMCA requires of them, and why would copyright owners send these notices rather than filing suits against infringing subscribers? Several other countries have experimented with similar "graduated response" systems. France's, called HADOPI, was required by law from 2009 to 2013, and required ISPs to cut off service to subscribers who accumulated three infringing "strikes." Is this an appropriate sanction for copyright infringement? Would you rather be sued for thousands of dollars or have your Internet service cut off? What kinds of procedural safeguards would a well-designed graduated response system have?

MANGLE PROBLEM

You have been retained by Mary DeNooy, the creator of Mangle.com, a successful but under-the-radar lolcat-generator site. Lolcats are one of the Internet's native art forms: pictures of cats with humorous captions superimposed on them. Users of the anonymous image-sharing and discussion site 4chan posted pictures of cats and jokes about "Caturday" until some unknown genius posted this picture of a smiling grey cat with the caption, "I CAN HAS CHEEZBURGER?" Other users followed with their own pictures of cats "speaking" in mangled English, the phenomenon spread to other sites, and the cat was out of the bag.

Mangle.com is a lolcat-generator: it offers tools for users to create their own lolcats. They can upload their own images or choose from images contributed by other users and add their own captions. The site also has extensive tools for users to post comments and annotations on other users' lolcats, to make lolcat galleries and comic strips, and even to make lolcats out of animated gifs. You've played around with it for a bit, and Mangle is really, really easy to use. It's also free; users can register for accounts but don't need to. It supports itself with banner ads.

DeNooy isn't a copyright expert, and she can't afford to hire a lawyer to do anything other than get the site off the ground. (You asked whether she has employees, and she replied that her only assistant is her cat Cuddles.) She wants your help in putting together a DMCA policy. She's heard that there's some kind of copyright protection for user-generated content sites, and wants to know what she needs to do to avoid getting in any legal trouble. Ideally, whatever she does to comply should take as little of her time and mental effort as possible, not get in the way of the site's smooth operation, and not disrupt users' experience any more than necessary.

Advise DeNooy on what she should do to make the best use of the DMCA safe harbor.

F. Digital Rights Management

"Section 1201" was enacted as part of the Digital Millennium Copyright Act, in 1998. It is a kind of paracopyright statute: its purpose is not directly to prohibit infringing acts, but rather to protect the copyright owner's interests by making it harder to infringe in the first place. To understand how, it is necessary first to understand a bit about digital rights management (DRM) technologies (sometimes also called "technological protection measures" or TPMs).

NOTE ON DIGITAL RIGHTS MANAGEMENT

It is the best of times for copyright owners; it is the worst of times. Computers and the Internet let them distribute their works worldwide, saving enormously on the fixed costs of printing books, pressing CDs, and so on. But computers and the Internet also let *other people* distribute copyrighted works worldwide, making infringement much easier. We have seen this at length in the discussion of the file-sharing wars.

DRM responds to this dilemma by trying to enable authorized digital distribution while preventing consumers from making copies of the work except on the copyright owner's terms. Consider, for example, the FairPlay DRM that protects iTunes movie rentals. If you want to view *Inception,* you pay Apple and your computer downloads a file containing the movie from Apple's servers. That file is encrypted; in its raw form, it will not be viewable, or even comprehensible.

Instead, your computer also needs a key from Apple. The key is much shorter than the file. Apple will only send the key to an "authorized" computer that has been linked to your iTunes account (and Apple only allows up to five computers to be authorized at a time). Your copy of iTunes (or your iPhone, iPad, etc.) uses the key to decrypt *Inception* into a regular video file, which you can then watch. When the rental expires, however (either 30 days from when you downloaded it, or 24 hours from when you started watching), your copy of iTunes throws away the key, and Apple will not send you a fresh copy. The encrypted file is now once again unintelligible to you.

Do you see how this scheme is intended to enable authorized distributions while preventing unauthorized ones? It is easy to copy the encrypted file and give it to a friend – but the file is useless to your friend without a key. By controlling access to the keys, Apple controls who can view the movie.

QUESTIONS

1. What business models does DRM enable? Time-limited rentals of media are one; are there others? Think about iTunes, Netflix, Rhapsody, and DVDs, then keep going.

2. What other advantages does DRM have for copyright owners? For example, *Inception* might cost $9.99 to buy, and $3.99 to rent. Why the difference? Would it be possible without DRM?

3. Does the widespread use of DRM change the balance of copyright law between copyright owners and users? Look back at *Vernor v. Autodesk*. Are there significant differences between a consumer who buys a DVD of *Inception* at Best Buy and a consumer who downloads *Inception* from Amazon? What about fair uses, such as clipping short sections from movies for reviews?

4. How effective would the following schemes be at escaping the limitations in the FairPlay DRM on *Inception*?

   - Turning your computer's clock back so that you stay within the "24-hour" viewing period forever?

   - Pointing a camcorder at your computer screen and recording the movie as it plays?

   - Copying the key downloaded to your computer and keeping your copy after the rental ends?

   - Copying the key downloaded to your computer, using it to decrypt *Inception* on your own, and saving the decrypted version?

   - Trying to guess a key?

5. Some consumer-rights advocates are fiercely critical of DRM. Why? How much does Apple know about iTunes viewers, compared with how much Best Buy knows about DVD buyers? How usable is a device that uses DRM, compared with one that doesn't? Does DRM have other downsides?

NOTE ON THE MOTIVATION FOR ANTI-CIRCUMVENTION LAW

Now that you have worked through the questions above, you may be wondering whether DRM on its own is a complete solution to the worries of the copyright owners who allow Apple to distribute their music and movies through iTunes. Even with FairPlay in place, there are still some ways that technically sophisticated users might be able to escape iTunes's limitations and extract unencrypted versions of *Inception*. Worse still, these skilled users might develop tools to automate the process and share those tools with less skilled users, making the DRM futile for everyone.

Thus, if FairPlay is a kind of code protecting law, i.e. software that helps enforce copyright, then § 1201 is law protecting code, i.e. it makes "breaking" the DRM around a work into a violation of federal law. Section 1201 has a two-pronged approach. First, it directly prohibits "circumvent[ing]" DRM that "effectively controls access" to copyrighted works. *See* 17 U.S.C. § 1201(a)(1). Second, it prohibits trafficking in technologies designed to circumvent DRM. *See id.* §§ 1201(a)(2), 1201(b).[*]

---

* The difference between subsections (a) and (b) is technical, controversial, and unsettled. This casebook will discuss only subsection (a).

COPYRIGHT ACT [ANTI-CIRCUMVENTION]
Title 17, United States Code

§ 1201 – *Circumvention of copyright protection systems*

(a) *VIOLATIONS REGARDING CIRCUMVENTION OF TECHNOLOGICAL MEASURES. –*

(1)

(A) No person shall circumvent a technological measure that effectively controls access to a work protected under this title. The prohibition contained in the preceding sentence shall take effect at the end of the 2-year period beginning on the date of the enactment of this chapter.

(B) The prohibition contained in subparagraph (A) shall not apply to persons who are users of a copyrighted work which is in a particular class of works, if such persons are, or are likely to be in the succeeding 3-year period, adversely affected by virtue of such prohibition in their ability to make noninfringing uses of that particular class of works under this title, as determined [by the Librarian of Congress in a triennial rulemaking] under subparagraph (C)....

(2) No person shall manufacture, import, offer to the public, provide, or otherwise traffic in any technology, product, service, device, component, or part thereof, that –

(A) is primarily designed or produced for the purpose of circumventing a technological measure that effectively controls access to a work protected under this title;

(B) has only limited commercially significant purpose or use other than to circumvent a technological measure that effectively controls access to a work protected under this title; or

(C) is marketed by that person or another acting in concert with that person with that person's knowledge for use in circumventing a technological measure that effectively controls access to a work protected under this title.

(3) As used in this subsection –

(A) to "circumvent a technological measure" means to descramble a scrambled work, to decrypt an encrypted work, or otherwise to avoid, bypass, remove, deactivate, or impair a technological measure, without the authority of the copyright owner; and

(B) a technological measure "effectively controls access to a work" if the measure, in the ordinary course of its operation, requires the application of information, or a process or a treatment, with the authority of the copyright owner, to gain access to the work.

QUESTION

Why does the DMCA both prohibit circumvention and restrict the circulation of circumvention tools? Who are the anti-circumvention provisions of (a)(1) aimed at? Who are the trafficking prohibitions in (a)(2) aimed at?

UNIVERSAL CITY STUDIOS, INC. V. CORLEY
273 F.3d 429 (2d Cir. 2001)

Newman, Circuit Judge:

BACKGROUND

For decades, motion picture studios have made movies available for viewing at home in what is called "analog" format. Movies in this format are placed on video-tapes, which can be played on a video cassette recorder ("VCR"). In the early 1990s, the studios began to consider the possibility of distributing movies in digital form as well. Movies in digital form are placed on discs, known as DVDs, which can be played on a DVD player (either a stand-alone device or a component of a computer). DVDs offer advantages over analog tapes, such as improved visual and audio quality, larger data capacity, and greater durability. However, the improved quality of a movie in a digital format brings with it the risk that a virtually perfect copy, i.e., one that will not lose perceptible quality in the copying process, can be readily made at the click of a computer control and instantly distributed to count-less recipients throughout the world over the Internet. This case arises out of the movie industry's efforts to respond to this risk by invoking the anti-trafficking pro-visions of the DMCA.

I. CSS

The movie studios were reluctant to release movies in digital form until they were confident they had in place adequate safeguards against piracy of their copyright-ed movies. The studios took several steps to minimize the piracy threat. First, they settled on the DVD as the standard digital medium for home distribution of movies. The studios then sought an encryption scheme to protect movies on DVDs. They enlisted the help of members of the consumer electronics and com-puter industries, who in mid-1996 developed the Content Scramble System ("CSS"). CSS is an encryption scheme that employs an algorithm configured by a set of "keys" to encrypt a DVD's contents. The algorithm is a type of mathematical formula for transforming the contents of the movie file into gibberish; the "keys" are in actuality strings of 0's and 1's that serve as values for the mathematical for-mula.

Decryption in the case of CSS requires a set of "player keys" contained in com-pliant DVD players, as well as an understanding of the CSS encryption algorithm. Without the player keys and the algorithm, a DVD player cannot access the con-tents of a DVD. With the player keys and the algorithm, a DVD player can display the movie on a television or a computer screen, but does not give a viewer the abil-ity to use the copy function of the computer to copy the movie or to manipulate the digital content of the DVD.

The studios developed a licensing scheme for distributing the technology to manufacturers of DVD players. Player keys and other information necessary to the CSS scheme were given to manufacturers of DVD players for an administrative fee. In exchange for the licenses, manufacturers were obliged to keep the player keys confidential. Manufacturers were also required in the licensing agreement to prevent the transmission of "CSS data" (a term undefined in the licensing agree-ment) from a DVD drive to any "internal recording device," including, presumably, a computer hard drive.

With encryption technology and licensing agreements in hand, the studios be-gan releasing movies on DVDs in 1997, and DVDs quickly gained in popularity, becoming a significant source of studio revenue. In 1998, the studios secured added protection against DVD piracy when Congress passed the DMCA, which prohibits the development or use of technology designed to circumvent a technological protection measure, such as CSS. The pertinent provisions of the DMCA are examined in greater detail below.

II. DeCSS

In September 1999, Jon Johansen, a Norwegian teenager, collaborating with two unidentified individuals he met on the Internet, reverse-engineered a licensed DVD player designed to operate on the Microsoft operating system, and culled from it the player keys and other information necessary to decrypt CSS. The record suggests that Johansen was trying to develop a DVD player operable on Linux, an alternative operating system that did not support any licensed DVD players at that time. In order to accomplish this task, Johansen wrote a decryption program executable on Microsoft's operating system. That program was called, appropriately enough, "DeCSS."

If a user runs the DeCSS program (for example, by clicking on the DeCSS icon on a Microsoft operating system platform) with a DVD in the computer's disk drive, DeCSS will decrypt the DVD's CSS protection, allowing the user to copy the DVD's files and place the copy on the user's hard drive. The result is a very large computer file that can be played on a non-CSS-compliant player and copied, manipulated, and transferred just like any other computer file. DeCSS comes complete with a fairly user-friendly interface that helps the user select from among the DVD's files and assign the decrypted file a location on the user's hard drive. The quality of the resulting decrypted movie is "virtually identical" to that of the encrypted movie on the DVD. And the file produced by DeCSS, while large, can be compressed to a manageable size by a compression software called "DivX," available at no cost on the Internet. This compressed file can be copied onto a DVD, or transferred over the Internet (with some patience).

Johansen posted the executable object code, but not the source code, for DeCSS on his web site. The distinction between source code and object code is relevant to this case, so a brief explanation is warranted. A computer responds to electrical charges, the presence or absence of which is represented by strings of 1's and 0's. Strictly speaking, "object code" consists of those 1's and 0's. While some people can read and program in object code, it would be inconvenient, inefficient and, for most people, probably impossible to do so. Computer languages have been written to facilitate program writing and reading. A program in such a computer language – BASIC, C, and Java are examples – is said to be written in "source code." Source code has the benefit of being much easier to read (by people) than object code, but as a general matter, it must be translated back to object code before it can be read by a computer. This task is usually performed by a program called a compiler. Since computer languages range in complexity, object code can be placed on one end of a spectrum, and different kinds of source code can be arrayed across the spectrum according to the ease with which they are read and understood by humans. Within months of its appearance in executable form on Johansen's web site, DeCSS was widely available on the Internet, in both object code and various forms of source code.

In November 1999, [defendant Eric] Corley wrote and placed on his web site, 2600.com, an article about the DeCSS phenomenon. His web site is an auxiliary to the print magazine, 2600: The Hacker Quarterly, which Corley has been publishing since 1984. As the name suggests, the magazine is designed for "hackers," as is the web site. While the magazine and the web site cover some issues of general interest to computer users – such as threats to online privacy – the focus of the publications is on the vulnerability of computer security systems, and more specifically, how to exploit that vulnerability in order to circumvent the security systems. Representative articles explain how to steal an Internet domain name and how to break into the computer systems at Federal Express.

Corley's article about DeCSS detailed how CSS was cracked, and described the movie industry's efforts to shut down web sites posting DeCSS. It also explained that DeCSS could be used to copy DVDs. At the end of the article, the Defendants posted copies of the object and source code of DeCSS. In Corley's words, he added the code to the story because "in a journalistic world, . . . [y]ou have to show your evidence . . . and particularly in the magazine that I work for, people want to see specifically what it is that we are referring to," including "what evidence . . . we have" that there is in fact technology that circumvents CSS. Writing about DeCSS without including the DeCSS code would have been, to Corley, "analogous to printing a story about a picture and not printing the picture." Corley also added to the article links that he explained would take the reader to other web sites where DeCSS could be found.

2600.com was only one of hundreds of web sites that began posting DeCSS near the end of 1999. The movie industry tried to stem the tide by sending cease-and-desist letters to many of these sites. These efforts met with only partial success; a number of sites refused to remove DeCSS. In January 2000, the studios filed this lawsuit.

QUESTIONS

1. Why was there no licensed DVD player available for Linux? (It may help to keep in mind that Linux is an open-source operating system, distributed under the GPL.) Why might copyright owners have been unwilling to license a software DVD player for Linux? What distinguishes Windows from Linux in this respect?

2. What does it say about CSS that it was broken by a teenager? Was the problem that the designers of CSS did a bad job, or is this a sign of something deeper about DRM?

3. The "DeCSS case," as it was called, was a *cause célèbre* for user-rights advocates. Why? Note that Eric Corley a/k/a Emmanuel Goldstein is a defendant here, rather than Jon Johannsen. Why?

4. Consider the Gallery of DeCSS Descramblers (available at http://www.cs.c-mu.edu/~dst/DeCSS/Gallery/). What is the point of putting DeCSS on a T-shirt, or performing it as a square dance, or encoding it in a game of Minesweeper? Is this still about watching DVDs, or is something else going on?

UNIVERSAL CITY STUDIOS, INC. V. REIMERDES
111 F. Supp. 2d 294 (S.D.N.Y. 2000)

Kaplan, District Judge:

[*Corley, supra,* and *Reimerdes* are the same case; it received a new caption on appeal. I have chosen to give you the facts from *Corley* (the decision of the appellate court) and the legal discussion from *Remeirdes* (the decision of the trial court) for purely pedagogical reasons.]

II. THE DIGITAL MILLENNIUM COPYRIGHT ACT

A. Background and Structure of the Statute

In December 1996, the World Intellectual Property Organization ("WIPO"), held a diplomatic conference in Geneva that led to the adoption of two treaties. Article 11 of the relevant treaty, the WIPO Copyright Treaty, provides in relevant part that contracting states "shall provide adequate legal protection and effective legal remedies against the circumvention of effective technological measures that are used by authors in connection with the exercise of their rights under this Treaty or the Berne Convention and that restrict acts, in respect of their works, which are not authorized by the authors concerned or permitted by law."

The adoption of the WIPO Copyright Treaty spurred continued Congressional attention to the adaptation of the law of copyright to the digital age. Lengthy hearings involving a broad range of interested parties both preceded and succeeded the Copyright Treaty. As noted above, a critical focus of Congressional consideration of the legislation was the conflict between those who opposed anti-circumvention measures as inappropriate extensions of copyright and impediments to fair use and those who supported them as essential to proper protection of copyrighted materials in the digital age. The DMCA was enacted in October 1998 as the culmination of this process.

The DMCA contains two principal anti-circumvention provisions. The first, Section 1201(a)(1), governs "[t]he act of circumventing a technological protection measure put in place by a copyright owner to control access to a copyrighted work," an act described by Congress as "the electronic equivalent of breaking into a locked room in order to obtain a copy of a book." The second, Section 1201(a)(2), which is the focus of this case, "supplements the prohibition against the act of circumvention in paragraph (a)(1) with prohibitions on creating and making available certain technologies ... developed or advertised to defeat technological protections against unauthorized access to a work." As defendants are accused here only of posting and linking to other sites posting DeCSS, and not of using it themselves to bypass plaintiffs' access controls, it is principally the second of the anticircumvention provisions that is at issue in this case.

B. Posting of DeCSS

1. Violation of Anti-Trafficking Provision

Section 1201(a)(2) of the Copyright Act, part of the DMCA, provides that:

> "No person shall . . . offer to the public, provide or otherwise traffic in any technology . . . that –
>
> (A)   is primarily designed or produced for the purpose of circumventing a technological measure that effectively controls access to a work protected under [the Copyright Act];
>
> (B)   has only limited commercially significant purpose or use other than to circumvent a technological measure that effectively controls access to a work protected under [the Copyright Act]; or
>
> (C)   is marketed by that person or another acting in concert with that person with that person's knowledge for use in circumventing a technological measure that effectively controls access to a work protected under [the Copyright Act]."

In this case, defendants concededly offered and provided and, absent a court order, would continue to offer and provide DeCSS to the public by making it available for download on the 2600.com web site. DeCSS, a computer program, unquestionably is "technology" within the meaning of the statute. "[C]ircumvent a technological measure" is defined to mean descrambling a scrambled work, decrypting an encrypted work, or "otherwise to avoid, bypass, remove, deactivate, or impair a technological measure, without the authority of the copyright owner," so DeCSS clearly is a means of circumventing a technological access control measure. In consequence, if CSS otherwise falls within paragraphs (A), (B) or (C) of Section 1201(a)(2), and if none of the statutory exceptions applies to their actions, defendants have violated and, unless enjoined, will continue to violate the DMCA by posting DeCSS.

a. Section 1201(a)(2)(A)

(1) CSS Effectively Controls Access to Copyrighted Works

During pretrial proceedings and at trial, defendants attacked plaintiffs' Section 1201(a)(2)(A) claim, arguing that CSS, which is based on a 40-bit encryption key, is a weak cipher that does not "effectively control" access to plaintiffs' copyrighted works. They reasoned from this premise that CSS is not protected under this branch of the statute at all. Their post-trial memorandum appears to have abandoned this argument. In any case, however, the contention is indefensible as a matter of law.

First, the statute expressly provides that "a technological measure 'effectively controls access to a work' if the measure, in the ordinary course of its operation, requires the application of information or a process or a treatment, with the authority of the copyright owner, to gain access to a work." One cannot gain access to a CSS-protected work on a DVD without application of the three keys that are required by the software. One cannot lawfully gain access to the keys except by entering into a license with the DVD CCA under authority granted by the copyright owners or by purchasing a DVD player or drive containing the keys pursuant to such a license. In consequence, under the express terms of the statute, CSS "effectively controls access" to copyrighted DVD movies. It does so, within the meaning of the statute, whether or not it is a strong means of protection.

This view is confirmed by the legislative history, which deals with precisely this point. The House Judiciary Committee section-by-section analysis of the House bill, which in this respect was enacted into law, makes clear that a technological measure "effectively controls access" to a copyrighted work if its function is to control access:

> "The bill does define the functions of the technological measures that are covered – that is, what it means for a technological measure to 'effectively control access to a work' ... and to 'effectively protect a right of a copyright owner under this title' .... The practical, common-sense approach taken by H.R.2281 is that if, in the ordinary course of its operation, a technology actually works in the defined ways to control access to a work ... then the 'effectiveness' test is met, and the prohibitions of the statute are applicable. This test, which focuses on the function performed by the technology, provides a sufficient basis for clear interpretation."

Further, the House Commerce Committee made clear that measures based on encryption or scrambling "effectively control" access to copyrighted works, although it is well known that what may be encrypted or scrambled often may be decrypted or unscrambled. As CSS, in the ordinary course of its operation – that is, when

DeCSS or some other decryption program is not employed – "actually works" to prevent access to the protected work, it "effectively controls access" within the contemplation of the statute.

Finally, the interpretation of the phrase "effectively controls access" offered by defendants at trial – viz., that the use of the word "effectively" means that the statute protects only successful or efficacious technological means of controlling access – would gut the statute if it were adopted. If a technological means of access control is circumvented, it is, in common parlance, ineffective. Yet defendants' construction, if adopted, would limit the application of the statute to access control measures that thwart circumvention, but withhold protection for those measures that can be circumvented. In other words, defendants would have the Court construe the statute to offer protection where none is needed but to withhold protection precisely where protection is essential. The Court declines to do so. Accordingly, the Court holds that CSS effectively controls access to plaintiffs' copyrighted works.

(2) DeCSS Was Designed Primarily to Circumvent CSS

As CSS effectively controls access to plaintiffs' copyrighted works, the only remaining question under Section 1201(a)(2)(A) is whether DeCSS was designed primarily to circumvent CSS. The answer is perfectly obvious. By the admission of both Jon Johansen, the programmer who principally wrote DeCSS, and defendant Corley, DeCSS was created solely for the purpose of decrypting CSS – that is all it does. Hence, absent satisfaction of a statutory exception, defendants clearly violated Section 1201(a)(2)(A) by posting DeCSS to their web site.

b. Section 1201(a)(2)(B)

As the only purpose or use of DeCSS is to circumvent CSS, the foregoing is sufficient to establish a prima facie violation of Section 1201(a)(2)(B) as well.

c. The Linux Argument

Perhaps the centerpiece of defendants' statutory position is the contention that DeCSS was not created for the purpose of pirating copyrighted motion pictures. Rather, they argue, it was written to further the development of a DVD player that would run under the Linux operating system, as there allegedly were no Linux compatible players on the market at the time. The argument plays itself out in various ways as different elements of the DMCA come into focus. But it perhaps is useful to address the point at its most general level in order to place the preceding discussion in its fullest context.

As noted, Section 1201(a) of the DMCA contains two distinct prohibitions. Section 1201(a)(1), the so-called basic provision, "aims against those who engage in unauthorized circumvention of technological measures. . . . [It] focuses directly on wrongful conduct, rather than on those who facilitate wrongful conduct. . . ." Section 1201(a)(2), the anti-trafficking provision at issue in this case, on the other hand, separately bans offering or providing technology that may be used to circumvent technological means of controlling access to copyrighted works. If the means in question meets any of the three prongs of the standard set out in Section 1201(a)(2)(A), (B), or (C), it may not be offered or disseminated.

As the earlier discussion demonstrates, the question whether the development of a Linux DVD player motivated those who wrote DeCSS is immaterial to the question whether the defendants now before the Court violated the anti-trafficking provision of the DMCA. The inescapable facts are that (1) CSS is a technological means that effectively controls access to plaintiffs' copyrighted works, (2) the one and only function of DeCSS is to circumvent CSS, and (3) defendants offered and provided DeCSS by posting it on their web site. Whether defendants did so in order to infringe, or to permit or encourage others to infringe, copyrighted works in violation of other provisions of the Copyright Act simply does not matter for purposes of Section 1201(a)(2). The offering or provision of the program is the prohibited conduct – and it is prohibited irrespective of why the program was written, except to whatever extent motive may be germane to determining whether their conduct falls within one of the statutory exceptions. ...

2. Statutory Exceptions ...

d. Fair use

Finally, defendants rely on the doctrine of fair use. Stated in its most general terms, the doctrine, now codified in Section 107 of the Copyright Act, limits the exclusive rights of a copyright holder by permitting others to make limited use of portions of the copyrighted work, for appropriate purposes, free of liability for copyright infringement. For example, it is permissible for one other than the copyright owner to reprint or quote a suitable part of a copyrighted book or article in certain circumstances. The doctrine traditionally has facilitated literary and artistic criticism, teaching and scholarship, and other socially useful forms of expression. It has been viewed by courts as a safety valve that accommodates the exclusive rights conferred by copyright with the freedom of expression guaranteed by the First Amendment.

The use of technological means of controlling access to a copyrighted work may affect the ability to make fair uses of the work. Focusing specifically on the facts of this case, the application of CSS to encrypt a copyrighted motion picture requires the use of a compliant DVD player to view or listen to the movie. Perhaps more significantly, it prevents exact copying of either the video or the audio portion of all or any part of the film. This latter point means that certain uses that might qualify as "fair" for purposes of copyright infringement – for example, the preparation by a film studies professor of a single CD-ROM or tape containing two scenes from different movies in order to illustrate a point in a lecture on cinematography, as opposed to showing relevant parts of two different DVDs – would be difficult or impossible absent circumvention of the CSS encryption. Defendants therefore argue that the DMCA cannot properly be construed to make it difficult or impossible to make any fair use of plaintiffs' copyrighted works and that the statute therefore does not reach their activities, which are simply a means to enable users of DeCSS to make such fair uses.

Defendants have focused on a significant point. Access control measures such as CSS do involve some risk of preventing lawful as well as unlawful uses of copyrighted material. Congress, however, clearly faced up to and dealt with this question in enacting the DMCA.

The Court begins its statutory analysis, as it must, with the language of the statute. Section 107 of the Copyright Act provides in critical part that certain uses of copyrighted works that otherwise would be wrongful are "not . . . infringement[s] of copyright." Defendants, however, are not here sued for copyright infringement. They are sued for offering and providing technology designed to circumvent technological measures that control access to copyrighted works and otherwise violating Section 1201(a)(2) of the Act. If Congress had meant the fair use defense to apply to such actions, it would have said so. Indeed, as the legislative history demonstrates, the decision not to make fair use a defense to a claim under Section 1201(a) was quite deliberate.

Congress was well aware during the consideration of the DMCA of the traditional role of the fair use defense in accommodating the exclusive rights of copyright owners with the legitimate interests of noninfringing users of portions of copyrighted works. It recognized the contention, voiced by a range of constituencies concerned with the legislation, that technological controls on access to copyrighted works might erode fair use by preventing access even for uses that would be deemed "fair" if only access might be gained. And it struck a balance among the competing interests.

The first element of the balance was the careful limitation of Section 1201(a) (1)'s prohibition of the act of circumvention to the act itself so as not to "apply to subsequent actions of a person once he or she has obtained authorized access to a copy of a [copyrighted] work. . . ." By doing so, it left "the traditional defenses to copyright infringement, including fair use, . . . fully applicable" provided "the access is authorized." ...

Third, it created a series of exceptions to aspects of Section 1201(a) for certain uses that Congress thought "fair," including reverse engineering, security testing, good faith encryption research, and certain uses by nonprofit libraries, archives and educational institutions. ...

Defendants claim also that the possibility that DeCSS might be used for the purpose of gaining access to copyrighted works in order to make fair use of those works saves them under *Sony Corp. v. Universal City Studios, Inc.* But they are mistaken. *Sony* does not apply to the activities with which defendants here are charged. ...

When *Sony* was decided, the only question was whether the manufacturers could be held liable for infringement by those who purchased equipment from them in circumstances in which there were many noninfringing uses for their equipment. But that is not the question now before this Court. The question here is whether the possibility of noninfringing fair use by someone who gains access to a protected copyrighted work through a circumvention technology distributed by the defendants saves the defendants from liability under Section 1201. But nothing in Section 1201 so suggests. By prohibiting the provision of circumvention technology, the DMCA fundamentally altered the landscape. A given device or piece of technology might have a substantial noninfringing use, and hence be immune from attack under *Sony*'s construction of the Copyright Act – but nonetheless still be subject to suppression under Section 1201. Indeed, Congress explicitly noted that Section 1201 does not incorporate *Sony*.

The policy concerns raised by defendants were considered by Congress. Having considered them, Congress crafted a statute that, so far as the applicability of the fair use defense to Section 1201(a) claims is concerned, is crystal clear. In such circumstances, courts may not undo what Congress so plainly has done by "construing" the words of a statute to accomplish a result that Congress rejected. The fact that Congress elected to leave technologically unsophisticated persons who wish to make fair use of encrypted copyrighted works without the technical means of doing so is a matter for Congress unless Congress' decision contravenes the Constitution, a matter to which the Court turns below. Defendants' statutory fair use argument therefore is entirely without merit.

[The court also concluded that Section 1201 does not unconstitutionally abridge free speech rights.]

QUESTIONS

1. Explain why using or trafficking in DeCSS violates § 1201(a). What is the "technological protection measure"? How does it "control access?" How does DeCSS "circumvent" it? And how does DeCSS fit within the categories of § 1201(a)(2)?

2. The argument that CSS is not "effective" is clever. Can you imagine a technological protection measure that is too weak to be "effective?" What about a system that protects a copyrighted novel by translating it into Pig Latin?

3. Is it copyright infringement to watch a DVD on your computer? What if your computer runs Linux and uses an unauthorized DVD player? Why would Congress prohibit acts of circumvention that are not tied to an underlying act of infringement? Why would Congress prohibit circumvention devices that have significant other uses?

4. Recall that *Bernstein v. U.S. Dep't of Justice* held that computer source code is expressive speech protected by the First Amendment. If the DMCA is interpreted so that source code can be considered a "technology" that violates § 1201(a)(2), then doesn't the DMCA have a First Amendment problem? Or is there a way to distinguish *Bernstein*?

SECTION 1201 PROBLEMS

Apply § 1201(a) to the following facts. Has anyone committed a § 1201(a) violation? Is it a violation of § 1201(a)(1), of § 1201(a)(2), or both?

1. The Decay-Disc, manufactured and sold by Contour Systems with appropriate licenses from copyright owners, is similar to a DVD, but is coated with a chemical that breaks down in the presence of oxygen. It is viewable in an ordinary DVD player for about 72 hours after being first exposed to air, after which the decay makes the disc unwatchable. A chemist, Eileen Boyle, discovers that immediately washing a Decay-Disc in rubbing alcohol after opening the vacuum package in which it is shipped prevents the chemical breakdown from occurring at all, making the Decay-Disc viewable forever. After testing the procedure on several discs, she posts the details to her blog, and starts selling rubbing alcohol.

2. Cauchy Systems writes research reports on the healthcare industry, which are posted to a password-protected website; clients pay $1,000 or more for access to particular reports. Cauchy has sued a competitor, Riemann Incorporated, claiming that Riemann obtained (through unknown means) the password of a Cauchy subscriber, then used it to access Cauchy's website and download research reports.

3. Ali Baba Appliances makes garage door openers. Each opener contains a small computer chip that contains a short (~500-word) computer program. When the user pushes the button on the wireless remote control, it sends a signal to the opener, which runs the program on the chip to confirm that the signal comes from the matching remote control. If it does, the door opens. Sesame Industries manufactures and sells to the public generic remote controls, which work with any brand of garage door opener, including Ali Baba's.

4. The Videlectrix video game console only runs games that have been digitally signed by its manufacturer. Game developers must pay a license fee and

submit their games for certification for them to be signed. It is well known in the gaming community that it is possible to "mod" a Videlectrix console to disable the digital-signature check by opening it up and carefully soldering twenty-nine pairs of wires to one of its circuit boards. Modded consoles will run any games, whether or not they have been signed. Enthusiasts like having modded consoles for several reasons: because they will run unauthorized copies of games duplicated using home DVD burners, because they will run obscure games created by independent game developers who cannot afford the expensive licensing fees, and because they will run custom software like a user's own screen saver. A hacker who calls himself Trogdor mods other people's Videlectrix consoles for $50 each.

NOTE ON DMCA EXEMPTIONS

Congress built a small safety valve into Section 1201 by requiring the Librarian of Congress to conduct a rulemaking every three years to identify cases in which users would be "adversely affected ... in their ability to make noninfringing uses ... of a particular class of copyrighted works." 17 U.S.C. § 1201(a)(1)(C). Applicants for exemptions submit detailed petitions describing cases in which they believe the prohibition on circumvention in § 1201(a) inhibits lawful conduct. For example, the 2006 rulemaking granted an exemption for

> Audiovisual works included in the educational library of a college or university's film or media studies department, when circumvention is accomplished for the purpose of making compilations of portions of those works for educational use in the classroom by media studies or film professors.

There are a few interesting things to notice about this exemption.

- First, the underlying conduct – showing excerpts from works in a classroom to make a pedagogical point – is typically fair use. Hence the need for an exemption: a professor who would like to show her students a clp from *Top Gun* to illustrate popular conceptions of the military in the 1980s could do so legally if she already had the clip, but might not be able to obtain such a clip from a DVD without circumventing CSS.

- Second, the exemption's terms are narrow: a high-school teacher is out of luck, and so is a professor who works with a copy from her university's central library rather than his departmental library.

- Third, the exemption only applies to the anti-circumvention rules in section 1201(a)(1). It does *not* apply to the prohibitions on trafficking in circumvention technology in section 1201(a)(2). So the professor can legally use DeCSS, but it remains illegal for anyone to "provide" it to her.

- Fourth, the exemption didn't just happen on its own. Three professors at the University of Pennsylvania proposed it as part of a 39-page request. The triennial rulemakings involve multiple rounds of public comments and multi-day hearings conducted by the Copyright Office.

- Fifth, because the rulemaking is triennial, this particular exemption only applied from November 27, 2006 through October 27, 2009. It was re-upped and broadened in the 2009 and 2012 rulemakings, but each time, proponents had to come forward with a new proposal and a fresh factual record showing the need for an exemption.

The number of requests for exemptions has increased over time, as has the number of exemptions granted. The 2012 rulemaking, for example, granted five proposed exemptions: to facilitate reading by the blind, to "jailbreak" cell phones (i.e., to disable the software controls that prevent installing unauthorized apps), to "unlock" cell phones (i.e., enable them to work on other carriers' networks), to engage in critical or educational uses of movies, and to develop closed-captioning technology. It denied another four: to access public-domain books, to jailbreak video game consoles, to jailbreak personal computers, and to rip DVDs onto computers so they could be played on devices without DVD drives. In the 2015 rulemaking, the Copyright Office identified twenty-seven distinct classes of proposed exemptions and granted ten, some with multiple subclasses

QUESTIONS

1. Are there any common themes among the proposed exemptions? What criteria ought to be used in deciding whether to grant them?

2. Does the design of the exemption system – an administrative rulemaking, three-year exemptions that do not automatically renew, and exemptions from section 1201(a)(1) but not from 1201(a)(2) – make sense?

3. Does the expansion over time of proposed exemptions show that Section 1201 is working as designed, or that it is failing?

CHAPTER 8: PATENT

A patent is a government-granted right to prevent others from making and selling particular technologies. Unlike copyright law, which protects creative expression, and trademark law, which protects consumer associations with a brand, patent law protects "any new and useful process, machine, manufacture, or composition of matter, or any new and useful improvement thereof." 35 U.S.C. § 101. The focus is squarely on usefulness and squarely on economic value.

To obtain a patent, an inventor must demonstrate to the United States Patent and Trademark Office (USPTO) that she has developed an invention that is *novel*. *Id.* § 102. If someone has previously sold a thing or described it publicly, no one else can subsequently obtain a patent on it. We say that the previous uses are part of the "prior art": if the prior art includes a roast beef sandwich, then no one can patent a roast beef sandwich. Indeed, even if no one else has done exactly the same thing, our hypothetical inventor still may not receive a patent if her idea would have been "obvious" in light of the prior art to a person with "ordinary skill" in her field. *Id.* § 103. If someone else has already invented the roast beef sandwich, the ham sandwich is also obvious. In addition, the inventor must submit a detailed application to the USPTO which *discloses* the details of the invention in sufficient detail for others to be able to use it. *Id.* § 112. The inventor's actual rights are set out in a series of *claims* which describe (in highly technical language) precisely which other products and processes she seeks to prevent others from using. If the USPTO is satisfied that she has met these requirements, it will issue a patent good for twenty years from the date the application was filed. A threatened infringer can defend either on the ground that its product does not actually fall within the terms of the patent's claims ("noninfringement"), or that the patent should never have been granted in the first place ("invalidity).

Software patents are big business. Both the number of computer-related patents and the number of computer-related patent lawsuits have skyrocketed. Major technology companies have spent billions of dollars to build patent portfolios. Some observers see software patents as a crucial source of high-tech innovation: they protect technology companies from having their ideas stolen and provide a financial incentive to invest in research and development. Other observers see software patents as weapons used to keep new entrants out of established industries, effectively a tax on innovation.

This section explores a few basic issues in patent law: what types of technologies are patentable at all (*CLS Bank*), how the obviousness inquiry functions for software (*Soverain*), the nature of claims and infringement (*Function Media*), and a bit about remedies and "standards-essential" patents (*Apple v. Motorola*).

ALICE CORP. V. CLS BANK INT'L
134 S. Ct. 2347 (2014)

Justice Thomas delivered the opinion of the Court.

The patents at issue in this case disclose a computer-implemented scheme for mitigating "settlement risk" (*i.e.*, the risk that only one party to a financial transaction will pay what it owes) by using a third-party intermediary. The question presented is whether these claims are patent eligible under 35 U.S.C. § 101, or are instead drawn to a patent-ineligible abstract idea. We hold that the claims at issue are drawn to the abstract idea of intermediated settlement, and that merely requiring generic computer implementation fails to transform that abstract idea into a patent-eligible invention. ...

I

A

Petitioner Alice Corporation is the assignee of several patents that disclose schemes to manage certain forms of financial risk.[1] According to the specification largely shared by the patents, the invention "enabl[es] the management of risk relating to specified, yet unknown, future events." The specification further explains that the "invention relates to methods and apparatus, including electrical computers and data processing systems applied to financial matters and risk management."

The claims at issue relate to a computerized scheme for mitigating "settlement risk" – *i.e.*, the risk that only one party to an agreed-upon financial exchange will satisfy its obligation. In particular, the claims are designed to facilitate the exchange of financial obligations between two parties by using a computer system as a third-party intermediary. *Id.*, at 383–384.[2] The intermediary creates "shadow" credit and debit records (*i.e.*, account ledgers) that mirror the balances in the parties' real-world accounts at "exchange institutions" (*e.g.*, banks). The intermediary updates the shadow records in real time as transactions are entered, allowing only those transactions for which the parties' updated shadow records indicate sufficient resources to satisfy their mutual obligations. At the end of the day, the intermediary instructs the relevant financial institutions to carry out the "permitted" transactions in accordance with the updated shadow records, thus mitigating the risk that only one party will perform the agreed-upon exchange.

---

1 The patents at issue are United States Patent Nos. 5,970,479 (the '479 patent), 6,912,510, 7,149,720, and 7,725,375.

2 The parties agree that claim 33 of the '479 patent is representative of the method claims. Claim 33 recites:

> A method of exchanging obligations as between parties, each party holding a credit record and a debit record with an exchange institution, the credit records and debit records for exchange of predetermined obligations, the method comprising the steps of:
>
> (a) creating a shadow credit record and a shadow debit record for each stakeholder party to be held independently by a supervisory institution from the exchange institutions;
>
> (b) obtaining from each exchange institution a start-of-day balance for each shadow credit record and shadow debit record;
>
> (c) for every transaction resulting in an exchange obligation, the supervisory institution adjusting each respective party's shadow credit record or shadow debit record, allowing only these transactions that do not result in the value of the shadow debit record being less than the value of the shadow credit record at any time, each said adjustment taking place in chronological order, and
>
> (d) at the end-of-day, the supervisory institution instructing on[e] of the exchange institutions to exchange credits or debits to the credit record and debit record of the respective parties in accordance with the adjustments of the said permitted transactions, the credits and debits being irrevocable, time invariant obligations placed on the exchange institutions.

In sum, the patents in suit claim (1) the foregoing method for exchanging obligations (the method claims), (2) a computer system configured to carry out the method for exchanging obligations (the system claims), and (3) a computer-readable medium containing program code for performing the method of exchanging obligations (the media claims). All of the claims are implemented using a computer; the system and media claims expressly recite a computer, and the parties have stipulated that the method claims require a computer as well.

B

Respondents CLS Bank International and CLS Services Ltd. (together, CLS Bank) operate a global network that facilitates currency transactions. In 2007, CLS Bank filed suit against petitioner, seeking a declaratory judgment that the claims at issue are invalid, unenforceable, or not infringed. Petitioner counterclaimed, alleging infringement. Following this Court's decision in *Bilski* v. *Kappos*, 561 U. S. 593 (2010), the parties filed cross-motions for summary judgment on whether the asserted claims are eligible for patent protection under 35 U.S.C. § 101. The District Court held that all of the claims are patent ineligible because they are directed to the abstract idea of "employing a neutral intermediary to facilitate simultaneous exchange of obligations in order to minimize risk."

A divided panel of the United States Court of Appeals for the Federal Circuit reversed, holding that it was not "manifestly evident" that petitioner's claims are directed to an abstract idea. The Federal Circuit granted rehearing en banc, vacated the panel opinion, and affirmed the judgment of the District Court in a one-paragraph *per curiam* opinion. Seven of the ten participating judges agreed that petitioner's method and media claims are patent ineligible. With respect to petitioner's system claims, the en banc Federal Circuit affirmed the District Court's judgment by an equally divided vote. ...

We granted certiorari, and now affirm.

II

Section 101 of the Patent Act defines the subject matter eligible for patent protection. It provides:

> Whoever invents or discovers any new and useful process, machine, manufacture, or composition of matter, or any new and useful improvement thereof, may obtain a patent therefor, subject to the conditions and requirements of this title."

"We have long held that this provision contains an important implicit exception: Laws of nature, natural phenomena, and abstract ideas are not patentable." *Association for Molecular Pathology* v. *Myriad Genetics, Inc.*, 569 U. S. ___ (2013) (slip op., at 11). We have interpreted § 101 and its predecessors in light of this exception for more than 150 years.

We have described the concern that drives this exclusionary principle as one of pre-emption. See, *e.g., Bilski, supra,* at 611–612 (upholding the patent "would pre-empt use of this approach in all fields, and would effectively grant a monopoly over an abstract idea"). Laws of nature, natural phenomena, and abstract ideas are "the basic tools of scientific and technological work." *Myriad, supra,* at ___ (slip op., at 11). "[M]onopolization of those tools through the grant of a patent might tend to impede innovation more than it would tend to promote it," thereby thwarting the primary object of the patent laws. *Mayo, supra,* at ___ (slip op., at 2); see U. S. Const., Art. I, §8, cl. 8 (Congress "shall have Power . . . To promote the Progress of Science and useful Arts"). We have "repeatedly emphasized this . . . concern that patent law not inhibit further discovery by improperly tying up the future use of" these building blocks of human ingenuity. *Mayo, supra,* at ___ (slip op., at 16) (citing *Morse, supra,* at 113).

At the same time, we tread carefully in construing this exclusionary principle lest it swallow all of patent law. *Mayo,* 566 U. S., at ___ (slip op., at 2). At some level, "all inventions . . . embody, use, reflect, rest upon, or apply laws of nature, natural phenomena, or abstract ideas." *Id.,* at ___ (slip op., at 2). Thus, an invention is not rendered ineligible for patent simply because it involves an abstract concept. See *Diamond* v. *Diehr,* 450 U. S. 175, 187 (1981). "[A]pplication[s]" of such concepts " 'to a new and useful end,' " we have said, remain eligible for patent protection. *Gottschalk* v. *Benson,* 409 U. S. 63, 67 (1972).

Accordingly, in applying the § 101 exception, we must distinguish between patents that claim the building blocks of human ingenuity and those that integrate the building blocks into something more, thereby transforming them into a patent-eligible invention, The former would risk disproportionately tying up the use of the underlying ideas, and are therefore ineligible for patent protection. The latter pose no comparable risk of pre-emption, and therefore remain eligible for the monopoly granted under our patent laws.

III

In *Mayo Collaborative Services* v. *Prometheus Laboratories, Inc.,* 566 U. S. ___ (2012), we set forth a framework for distinguishing patents that claim laws of nature, natural phenomena, and abstract ideas from those that claim patent-eligible applications of those concepts. First, we determine whether the claims at issue are directed to one of those patent-ineligible concepts. If so, we then ask, what else is there in the claims before us? To answer that question, we consider the elements of each claim both individually and as an ordered combination to determine whether the additional elements "transform the nature of the claim" into a patent-eligible application. We have described step two of this analysis as a search for an "inventive concept" – *i.e.,* an element or combination of elements that is "sufficient to ensure that the patent in practice amounts to significantly more than a patent upon the [ineligible concept] itself." *Id.,* at ___ (slip op., at 3).

A

We must first determine whether the claims at issue are directed to a patent-ineligible concept. We conclude that they are: These claims are drawn to the abstract idea of intermediated settlement.

The "abstract ideas" category embodies "the longstanding rule that "[a]n idea of itself is not patentable." *Benson, supra,* at 67. In *Benson,* for example, this Court rejected as ineligible patent claims involving an algorithm for converting binary-coded decimal numerals into pure binary form, holding that the claimed patent was "in practical effect . . . a patent on the algorithm itself." 409 U. S., at 71–72. And in *Parker* v. *Flook,* 437 U. S. 584, 594–595 (1978), we held that a mathematical formula for computing "alarm limits" in a catalytic conversion process was also a patent-ineligible abstract idea.

We most recently addressed the category of abstract ideas in *Bilski* v. *Kappos,* 561 U. S. 593 (2010). The claims at issue in *Bilski* described a method for hedging against the financial risk of price fluctuations. Claim 1 recited a series of steps for hedging risk, including: (1) initiating a series of financial transactions between providers and consumers of a commodity; (2) identifying market participants that have a counterrisk for the same commodity; and (3) initiating a series of transactions between those market participants and the commodity provider to balance the risk position of the first series of consumer transactions. Claim 4 put the concept articulated in claim 1 into a simple mathematical formula. The remaining claims were drawn to examples of hedging in commodities and energy markets.

All members of the Court agreed that the patent at issue in *Bilski* claimed an abstract idea. Specifically, the claims described the basic concept of hedging, or protecting against risk. The Court explained that "[h]edging is a fundamental economic practice long prevalent in our system of commerce and taught in any introductory finance class." *Ibid.* The concept of hedging as recited by the claims in suit was therefore a patent-ineligible abstract idea, just like the algorithms at issue in *Benson* and *Flook*.

It follows from our prior cases, and *Bilski* in particular, that the claims at issue here are directed to an abstract idea. Petitioner's claims involve a method of exchanging financial obligations between two parties using a third-party intermediary to mitigate settlement risk. The intermediary creates and updates "shadow" records to reflect the value of each party's actual accounts held at "exchange institutions," thereby permitting only those transactions for which the parties have sufficient resources. At the end of each day, the intermediary issues irrevocable instructions to the exchange institutions to carry out the permitted transactions.

On their face, the claims before us are drawn to the concept of intermediated settlement, *i.e.*, the use of a third party to mitigate settlement risk. Like the risk hedging in *Bilski*, the concept of intermediated settlement is "a fundamental economic practice long prevalent in our system of commerce." *Ibid.*; see, *e.g.*, Emery, Speculation on the Stock and Produce Exchanges of the United States, in 7 Studies in History, Economics and Public Law 283, 346–356 (1896) (discussing the use of a "clearing-house" as an intermediary to reduce settlement risk). The use of a third-party intermediary (or "clearing house") is also a building block of the modern economy. Thus, intermediated settlement, like hedging, is an "abstract idea" beyond the scope of § 101.

Petitioner acknowledges that its claims describe intermediated settlement, but rejects the conclusion that its claims recite an "abstract idea." Drawing on the presence of mathematical formulas in some of our abstract-ideas precedents, petitioner contends that the abstract-ideas category is confined to "preexisting, fundamental truth[s]" that " 'exis[t] in principle apart from any human action."

Bilski belies petitioner's assertion. The concept of risk hedging we identified as an abstract idea in that case cannot be described as a "preexisting, fundamental truth." The patent in *Bilski* simply involved a "series of steps instructing how to hedge risk." 561 U. S., at 599. Although hedging is a longstanding commercial practice, it is a method of organizing human activity, not a truth about the natural world that has always existed. One of the claims in *Bilski* reduced hedging to a mathematical formula, but the Court did not assign any special significance to that fact, much less the sort of talismanic significance petitioner claims. Instead, the Court grounded its conclusion that all of the claims at issue were abstract ideas in the understanding that risk hedging was a "fundamental economic practice." ...

B

Because the claims at issue are directed to the abstract idea of intermediated settlement, we turn to the second step in *Mayo*'s framework. We conclude that the method claims, which merely require generic computer implementation, fail to transform that abstract idea into a patent-eligible invention.

1

At *Mayo* step two, we must examine the elements of the claim to determine whether it contains an "inventive concept" sufficient to "transform" the claimed abstract idea into a patent-eligible application. A claim that recites an abstract idea must include "additional features" to ensure "that the [claim] is more than a drafting effort designed to monopolize the [abstract idea]." *Id.*, at ___ (slip op., at 8–9). *Mayo* made clear that transformation into a patent-eligible application requires "more than simply stat[ing] the [abstract idea] while adding the words 'apply it.'" *Id.*, at ___ (slip op., at 3).

Mayo itself is instructive. The patents at issue in *Mayo* claimed a method for measuring metabolites in the bloodstream in order to calibrate the appropriate dosage of thiopurine drugs in the treatment of autoimmune diseases. The respondent in that case contended that the claimed method was a patent-eligible application of natural laws that describe the relationship between the concentration of certain metabolites and the likelihood that the drug dosage will be harmful or ineffective. But methods for determining metabolite levels were already well known in the art, and the process at issue amounted to nothing significantly more than an instruction to doctors to apply the applicable laws when treating their patients. Simply appending conventional steps, specified at a high level of generality, was not enough to supply an inventive concept.

The introduction of a computer into the claims does not alter the analysis at *Mayo* step two. In *Benson*, for example, we considered a patent that claimed an algorithm implemented on a general-purpose digital computer. Because the algorithm was an abstract idea, the claim had to supply a new and useful application of the idea in order to be patent eligible. But the computer implementation did not supply the necessary inventive concept; the process could be carried out in existing computers long in use. We accordingly held that simply implementing a mathematical principle on a physical machine, namely a computer, is not a patentable application of that principle.

Flook is to the same effect. There, we examined a computerized method for using a mathematical formula to adjust alarm limits for certain operating conditions (*e.g.*, temperature and pressure) that could signal inefficiency or danger in a catalytic conversion process. Once again, the formula itself was an abstract idea and the computer implementation was purely conventional. In holding that the process was patent ineligible, we rejected the argument that implementing a principle in some specific fashion will automatically fall within the patentable subject matter of § 101. Thus, *Flook* stands for the proposition that the prohibition against patenting abstract ideas cannot be circumvented by attempting to limit the use of the idea to a particular technological environment.

In *Diehr*, by contrast, we held that a computer-implemented process for curing rubber was patent eligible, but not because it involved a computer. The claim employed a well-known mathematical equation, but it used that equation in a process designed to solve a technological problem in conventional industry practice. The invention in *Diehr* used a thermocouple to record constant temperature measurements inside the rubber mold – something the industry had not been able to obtain. The temperature measurements were then fed into a computer, which repeatedly recalculated the remaining cure time by using the mathematical equation. These additional steps, we recently explained, "transformed the process into an inventive application of the formula." *Mayo, supra,* at ___ (slip op., at 12). In other words, the claims in *Diehr* were patent eligible because they improved an existing technological process, not because they were implemented on a computer.

These cases demonstrate that the mere recitation of a generic computer cannot transform a patent-ineligible abstract idea into a patent-eligible invention. Stating an abstract idea "while adding the words 'apply it'" is not enough for patent eligibility. *Mayo, supra,* at ___ (slip op., at 3). Nor is limiting the use of an abstract idea "'to a particular technological environment.'" *Bilski, supra,* at 610–611. Stating an abstract idea while adding the words "apply it with a computer" simply combines those two steps, with the same deficient result. Thus, if a patent's recitation of a computer amounts to a mere instruction to implement an abstract idea on a computer, that addition cannot impart patent eligibility. ...

The fact that a computer necessarily exists in the physical, rather than purely conceptual, realm, is beside the point. There is no dispute that a computer is a tangible system (in § 101 terms, a "machine"), or that many computer-implemented claims are formally addressed to patent-eligible subject matter. But if that were the end of the § 101 inquiry, an applicant could claim any principle of the physical or social sciences by reciting a computer system configured to implement the relevant concept. Such a result would make the determination of patent eligibility "depend simply on the draftsman's art," *Flook, supra,* at 593, thereby eviscerating the rule that laws of nature, natural phenomena, and abstract ideas are not patentable.

2

The representative method claim in this case recites the following steps: (1) "creating" shadow records for each counterparty to a transaction; (2) "obtaining" start-of-day balances based on the parties' real-world accounts at exchange institutions; (3) "adjusting" the shadow records as transactions are entered, allowing only those transactions for which the parties have sufficient resources; and (4) issuing irrevocable end-of-day instructions to the exchange institutions to carry out the permitted transactions. Petitioner principally contends that the claims are patent eligible because these steps "require a substantial and meaningful role for the computer." As stipulated, the claimed method requires the use of a computer to create electronic records, track multiple transactions, and issue simultaneous instructions; in other words, the computer is itself the intermediary.

In light of the foregoing, the relevant question is whether the claims here do more than simply instruct the practitioner to implement the abstract idea of intermediated settlement on a generic computer. They do not.

Taking the claim elements separately, the function performed by the computer at each step of the process is purely conventional. Using a computer to create and maintain "shadow" accounts amounts to electronic recordkeeping – one of the most basic functions of a computer. The same is true with respect to the use of a computer to obtain data, adjust account balances, and issue automated instructions; all of these computer functions are well-understood, routine, conventional activities previously known to the industry. In short, each step does no more than require a generic computer to perform generic computer functions.

Considered as an ordered combination, the computer components of petitioner's method add nothing . . . that is not already present when the steps are considered separately. Viewed as a whole, petitioner's method claims simply recite the concept of intermediated settlement as performed by a generic computer. The method claims do not, for example, purport to improve the functioning of the computer itself. Nor do they effect an improvement in any other technology or technical field. Instead, the claims at issue amount to "nothing significantly more" than an instruction to apply the abstract idea of intermediated settlement using some unspecified, generic computer. Under our precedents, that is not enough to transform an abstract idea into a patent-eligible invention.

C

Petitioner's claims to a computer system and a computer-readable medium fail for substantially the same reasons. Petitioner conceded below that its media claims rise or fall with its method claimsAs to its system claims, petitioner emphasizes that those claims recite "specific hardware" configured to perform "specific computerized functions." But what petitioner characterizes as specific hardware – a "data processing system" with a "communications controller" and "data storage unit," for example – is purely functional and generic. Nearly every computer will include a "communications controller" and "data storage unit" capable of performing the basic calculation, storage, and transmission functions required by the method claims. As a result, none of the hardware recited by the system claims offers a meaningful limitation beyond generally linking the use of the method to a particular technological environment, that is, implementation via computers.

Put another way, the system claims are no different from the method claims in substance. The method claims recite the abstract idea implemented on a generic computer; the system claims recite a handful of generic computer components configured to implement the same idea. This Court has long "warn[ed] . . . against" interpreting § 101 "in ways that make patent eligibility depend simply on the draftsman's art." *Mayo, supra,* at ____ (slip op., at 3) Holding that the system claims are patent eligible would have exactly that result.

Because petitioner's system and media claims add nothing of substance to the underlying abstract idea, we hold that they too are patent ineligible under § 101. ...

QUESTIONS

1. The Supreme Court's leading opinion on software patents never uses the word "software." How much guidance does it provide as to which computer-related inventions are and are not patentable?

2. Some critics of software patents argue that all computer software is simply the implementation of mathematical principles. (Recall the discussion of how computers and programming languages work, and also the *Bernstein* case on encryption source code). As such, they argue, all software consists of unpatentable abstract ideas: 2+2=4 with more detail. Do you find this argument persuasive? Does *CLS Bank* adopt this view?

3. Other critics of software patents think the problems have principally to do with low-quality patents and that § 101 is the wrong tool for weeding them out. What other tools are available? Does *CLS Bank* adopt this view?

4. On the other hand, it cannot be the case that every invention involving a computer is for that reason an unpatentable abstract idea. What about inventions like the rubber-curing process in *Diehr,* where a computer carried out the calculations to determine how long to leave rubber in a high-temperature press? Is it even possible to draw a line between patents that do and don't involve a computer?

5. How would the Court's test in *CLS Bank* apply to the following inventions:
   - A video camera that detects when the lens has moved slightly and manually moves the lens back to compensate for the motion?

- A video camera that detects when the lens has moved slightly and digitally modifies the resulting images to compensate for the motion?

- Offering videos for sale over the Internet using a computer system that requires consumers to watch an advertisement before the video begins playback?

- A technique for data compression that encodes music using 10% fewer bytes than existing techniques with no perceptible loss of audio quality?

SOVERAIN SOFTWARE LLC V. NEWEGG INC.
705 F.3d 1333 (Fed. Cir. 2013)

Newman, Circuit Judge:

Soverain Software LLC brought this patent infringement suit against Newegg Inc. for infringement of specified claims of United States Patent No. 5,715,314 ("the '314 patent"), its continuation Patent No. 5,909,492 ("the '492 patent"), and Patent No. 7,272,639 ("the '639 patent"). The patents relate to electronic commerce, wherein a merchant's products are offered and purchased online, through computers interconnected by a network. The patents arise from a software system called "Transact" that was developed in 1996 by a company named Open Market, Inc. ...

In 2001 Open Market was sold, with the Transact software and patents, to a company named Divine, Inc. Former Divine employee and current Soverain President Katharine Wolanyk testified that the Transact software was "a very complex product" that required constant support services and engineering development, that Divine was unable to provide the necessary support and development, and that Divine declared bankruptcy after fifteen months. Soverain acquired the Transact software and patents. Soverain then sued seven online retailers, including Newegg, for patent infringement. The record states that all of the defendants except Newegg took paid-up licenses to the patents.

Newegg declined to pay for a license, stating that its system is materially different from that described and claimed in the patents, and that the patents are invalid if given the scope asserted by Soverain. Newegg pointed out that similar electronic commerce systems were known before the patented system, that the Transact software was generally abandoned, and that Newegg's system, which is based on the different principle of using "cookies" on the buyer's computer to collect shopping data, is outside of the claims.

Suit against Newegg proceeded in the United States District Court for the Eastern District of Texas. The jury found Newegg liable for infringement of the '314 and '492 patents, and awarded Soverain damages of $2.5 million. The jury found that Newegg did not infringe the '639 patent, but the district court granted Soverain's motion for JMOL of infringement of the '639 patent, and ordered a new trial to assess damages for the '639 patent, to be tried after the completion of appeals. The district court awarded Soverain post-verdict damages and an ongoing royalty.

After the close of evidence the district court removed the question of obviousness from the jury, the court stating: "I don't think there's sufficient testimony to present an obviousness case to the jury. I think it would be very confusing to them." The district court then held that the claims are not invalid on the ground of obviousness. Newegg's motions for JMOL or a new trial were denied.

OBVIOUSNESS

Obviousness is a question of law based on underlying facts, as set forth in *Graham v. John Deere Co.*, 383 U.S. 1 (1966). The *Graham* factors are (1) the scope and content of the prior art, (2) the difference between the prior art and the claimed invention, (3) the level of ordinary skill in the field of the invention, and (4) any relevant objective considerations. The *Graham* Court explained that "the ultimate question of patent validity is one of law." *Id.* at 17. Thus on appellate review, the question of obviousness is decided *de novo.* ...

On these premises, we determine the question of obviousness. Newegg relied primarily on a prior electronic commerce system called "CompuServe Mall." The district court, sustaining validity of all claims in suit, did not discuss the claims or the prior art; the court stated that Newegg's expert had not presented a prima facie case of obviousness, and criticized Newegg for not presenting "some articulated reasoning with some rational underpinning to support the legal conclusion of obviousness."

The parties divided the claims in suit into three groups, and presented evidence and argument, including expert and other witness testimony, for the claims as grouped. We retain the parties' groupings, as follows:

A. The '314 and '492 patents – the "shopping cart" claims

Soverain asserted claims 34 and 51 of the '314 patent and claim 17 of the '492 patent as a group called the "shopping cart" claims. These claims are directed to the overall system wherein products are offered online by a merchant, a buyer designates products for purchase, and payment for the designated products is initiated upon the buyer's request for checkout, all operating through a computer network. The parties agreed that claim 34 of the '314 patent is representative of this group. Claim 34 follows (with bracketed numbers added):

> 34. A network-based sales system, comprising:
>
>   [1] at least one buyer computer for operation by a user desiring to buy products;
>
>   [2] at least one shopping cart computer; and
>
>   [3] a shopping cart database connected to said shopping cart computer;
>
>   [4] said buyer computer and said shopping cart computer being interconnected by a computer network;
>
>   [5] said buyer computer being programmed to receive a plurality of requests from a user to add a plurality of respective products to a shopping cart in said shopping cart database, and, in response to said requests to add said products, to send a plurality of respective shopping cart messages to said shopping cart computer each of which comprises a product identifier identifying one of said plurality of products;
>
>   [6] said shopping cart computer being programmed to receive said plurality of shopping cart messages, to modify said shopping cart in said shopping cart database to reflect said plurality of requests to add said plurality of products to said shopping cart, and to cause a payment message associated with said shopping cart to be created; and

[7] said buyer computer being programmed to receive a request from said user to purchase said plurality of products added to said shopping cart and to cause said payment message to be activated to initiate a payment transaction for said plurality of products added to said shopping cart;

[8] said shopping cart database being a database of stored representations of collections of products, and said shopping cart computer being a computer that modifies said stored representations of collections of products in said database.

At the trial the CompuServe Mall system was the primary reference against the shopping cart claims, including two books describing the system: Bowen & Peyton, *How to Get the Most Out of CompuServe* (4th ed. 1989) and Ellsworth & Ellsworth, *Using CompuServe* (1994). Newegg presented testimony of CompuServe's former Chief Technology Officer Alexander Trevor, Newegg's expert witness Mr. Edward Tittel, and Newegg's Chief Technology Officer James Wu, who designed the Newegg system.

Mr. Tittel compared claim 34 with the prior art system, element by element. Mr. Tittel testified that the CompuServe Mall was a "network-based sales system" (claim preamble) in which the buyer computer (clause [1]) interacted with a CompuServe server computer (clause [2]) that stored buyers' product selections in "shopping carts" called personal holding files (clause [3]), all via a computer network (clause [4]). Mr. Tittel explained that products were added to the personal holding files when the buyer computer sent an order command "O" to the CompuServe server, at which time the server would "update" the personal holding file for each such selection (clauses [5], [6] and [8]). When the buyer was ready for checkout, the buyer typed "checkout" and was presented with a screen to review the designated items, and with a request to initiate payment (clause [7]). Mr. Tittel concluded that all of the elements and limitations of Soverain's shopping cart claims were "shown or apparent" in the prior art CompuServe Mall.

Mr. Trevor testified as to the CompuServe Mall system, for which he had been the Chief Technology Officer. According to Mr. Trevor, the CompuServe Mall provided the buyer with access to over a hundred online stores. Within each store, products were presented in menus. When a buyer found a product of interest, the buyer selected the product from the store menu and a detailed description would be displayed, in some cases with a photograph. If the buyer wanted to purchase the product, the buyer would type the order command "O" and CompuServe would store the product in the buyer's personal holding file on the server. The buyer could designate up to forty items for placement in the personal holding file. By typing "checkout," the buyer could review selections and modify or delete items in the personal holding file, or proceed to purchase.

Soverain's expert witness Dr. Michael Shamos stated that the Newegg witnesses' description of the CompuServe Mall was "consistent with my understanding," but presented the argument that the CompuServe Mall lacked two elements of the shopping cart claims: first, that the CompuServe system lacked the "shopping cart message [that] comprises a product identifier" of claim clause [5]; and second, that CompuServe lacked the "shopping cart database" of clause [3]. Dr. Shamos did not dispute that the other elements of claim 34 were embodied in the CompuServe Mall. We have given particular attention to the two aspects on which the witnesses stated divergent views.

1. the product identifier message, clause [5]

Dr. Shamos did not disagree with Mr. Tittel that the CompuServe Mall's "order command" was a "shopping cart message" as in clause [5], and agreed that when a CompuServe Mall buyer entered the order command, the CompuServe server computer would identify the product and place it in a personal holding file for that buyer. However, Dr. Shamos argued that the CompuServe Mall was different because the "product identifier" in the CompuServe Mall was not "in the message." Dr. Shamos stated that the CompuServe Mall system of product identification was based not on the order command itself, but on what the server "knew" based on "previously sent" messages "It was just an indication that the order key had been – had been hit at that time." Thus Dr. Shamos argued that the CompuServe order command was not a "message ... which comprises a product identifier" as required by claim clause [5].

The distinction proposed by Dr. Shamos and advanced by Soverain is not embodied in the claims and not reflected in the claim construction. It was not disputed that the CompuServe Mall order command designated a specific product for placement in the buyer's personal holding file, or shopping cart, as recited in claim clause [3]. Nor was it disputed that, regardless of how the order command was structured, it conveyed the requisite information to the CompuServe server computer. The message set forth in the claims is not distinguished from the message in the CompuServe Mall. The term "product identifier" was not given a special meaning in the specification or through claim construction, and contains no designated format requirements.

Soverain also argues that its system is superior to the CompuServe "order command" because the system of the patents in suit is adapted to the Internet, whereas the CompuServe Mall operated on a pre-Internet network. In *Muniauction* [*v. Thomson Corp.*, 532 F.3d 1318 (Fed. Cir. 2008)], this court held that "conducting previously known methods through an Internet web browser was obvious because it amounted to no more than applying the use of the Internet to existing electronic processes at a time when doing so was commonplace." 532 F.3d at 1327. Precedent agrees with Newegg that a person of ordinary skill could have adapted the CompuServe order command to known browser capabilities when these capabilities became commonplace, and that it was obvious to do so. The product identifier message term does not distinguish the shopping cart claims from the prior art CompuServe Mall.

2. the shopping cart database, clause [3]

Dr. Shamos also stated his opinion that the CompuServe Mall did not have a "shopping cart database" as in the claims in suit. Dr. Shamos agreed with Newegg's expert Mr. Tittel that the CompuServe Mall system included "personal holding files," and Dr. Shamos agreed that a shopping cart database "might have been a reasonable design choice," but he opined that such database "wasn't required" by the CompuServe Mall and that the prior art did not "necessarily disclose a database."

The agreed claim construction for "shopping cart database" was "a database of stored representations of collections of products," where "database means a collection of logically related data stored together by one or more computerized files." The use of personal holding files in the CompuServe Mall is easily within this definition. ...

The Ellsworth & Ellsworth book describes the storage of customer product selections in the CompuServe personal holding files. *Using CompuServe* 376 ("When you find a product that you want to buy, press O for order. Your order will be stored in a personal holding file until you leave that merchant's store."). The book further describes that items placed in the personal holding file are not yet purchased, and are held until the buyer types the "checkout" command. *Id.* ("When you are finished shopping in that store, type **checkout.** An electronic order form appears.").

When Dr. Shamos was asked how a person of skill in the art would have implemented the CompuServe online shopping system other than through a database, he suggested that CompuServe could have used a "fulfillment house," which would "fill your order and send it to you without ever recording it in a database." Whether that alternative was feasible, it is not stated to be what CompuServe did. The Ellsworth & Ellsworth book states that the buyer's product selections are "stored" – not sent "without ever recording it in a database." The "fulfillment house" alternative proposed by Dr. Shamos does not relate to a personal holding file, and appears to have no relation to either the prior art or the patents. ...

We conclude that the prior art CompuServe Mall system, by clear and convincing evidence, rendered obvious the "shopping cart" claims: claims 34 and 51 of the '314 patent and claim 17 of the '492 patent. These claims are invalid; the district court's contrary ruling is reversed. ...

D. Secondary Considerations

Before reaching our conclusions regarding obviousness referred to above, we have also considered the matter of secondary considerations. Soverain argues that obviousness of all of the claims in suit is negated by the favorable market response that was achieved by Open Market's Transact product, which Soverain states received "widespread recognition in the general media," "an excellence award from the industry," and was "widely licensed." Newegg responds with evidence that the Transact system was abandoned by its developers and almost all of its original users. Newegg points out that licenses were taken to avoid the costs of litigation, and not to use the flawed Transact system embodied in its software.

The record does not establish a nexus between use of the Transact software and the patents. At trial, former Open Market employee and inventor Alexander Treese testified that Open Market had attempted to license its patents apart from the software, but without success. The record shows that the software was abandoned by almost all of its initial licensees, and is not used by those who bought litigation peace. The assertions of commercial success as here presented do not support nonobviousness.

SUMMARY

The claims in suit of the '314 and '492 patents are invalid for obviousness over the CompuServe Mall system. ...

QUESTIONS

1. Would claim 34 have been obvious if the only relevant prior art were physical shopping carts in offline stores?

2. It does not seem to be substantially disputed that Open Market used electronic shopping carts before Newegg did. Why, then, can Newegg raise a defense that someone else (CompuServe) had something like an electronic shopping even earlier?

3. Soverain does not make or sell shopping cart software. Instead, it is in the patent licensing business, making it a "patent assertion entity" (or to its

enemies, a "patent troll"). Should this fact affect how a court treats its patents?

FUNCTION MEDIA, L.L.C. V. GOOGLE
708 F.3d 1310 (Fed. Cir. 2013)

Reyna, Circuit Judge:

In this patent case, Function Media, L.L.C. ("FM") appeals ... the jury's verdict that two ... FM patents are ... not infringed. ... For the reasons explained below, we affirm.

BACKGROUND

FM sued Google, Inc. ("Google") in the United States District Court for the Eastern District of Texas for infringing U.S. Patent Nos. 6,446,045 (the "'045 Patent"), 7,240,025 (the "'025 Patent"), and 7,249,059 (the "'059 Patent"). The purpose of the invention disclosed in all three patents is to facilitate advertising on multiple advertising outlets such as newspapers and websites. The specification characterizes the prior art as inefficient because, among other reasons, it requires advertisers to manually ensure that their ads conform to the differing requirements of each advertising venue. For example, if one website required square ads with red borders, while another required rectangular ads with blue borders, the prior art systems required the advertiser to manually create both ads. The invention is designed to eliminate this inefficiency by automatically formatting the ads to fit each publisher's requirements and sending them out for publication.

In each of the patents, a "central computer" coordinates interactions between sellers, media venues, and buyers. A "seller" is an entity that wishes to place ads, and is sometimes referred to as an "advertiser." "Media venues" are locations where ads can be placed, sometimes called "publishers"; in this case, the publishers are websites. "Buyers" are the targets of the ads, i.e., the people viewing the websites. The central computer hosts a number of databases and software processes, including the presentation rules database and the Presentation Generating Program ("PGP").

Claim 1 of the '025 Patent is representative of the asserted claims:

1. A computer system for creating and publishing customized electronic advertisements, for a seller, to internet media venues owned or controlled by other than the seller, comprising:

> a first interface to the computer system through which each of the internet media venues is prompted to input presentation rules for the internet media venue for displaying electronic advertisements on the internet media venue;

> a first database storing the presentation rules input by the internet media venues through the first interface;

> a second interface to the computer system through which a seller is prompted to input information *to select one or more of the internet media venues* and prompted to input information *to create an electronic advertisement* for publication to the selected internet media venues;

> a second database storing the information input by the seller through the second interface; and

a computer controller of the computer system *processing and publishing the electronic advertisement to one or more of the selected internet media venues* in compliance with the presentation rules of the internet media venue, whereby the electronic advertisement is displayed on each of the one or more of the selected internet media venues in compliance with the presentation rules of the internet media venue.

(emphases added) Thus, the invention requires: rule setting by the media venues to inform the system how the ads must be formatted; storage of the rules; inputting information to select media venues where the ads will be displayed; inputting information to create an ad; storing the ad information; processing the ad; and publishing the ad to the internet media venue. The disputed elements are the "creation and processing," "selection," and "publishing" elements.

FM asserted that Google's AdSense for Content and AdSense for Mobile products infringed when used in conjunction with Google's AdWords interface. AdSense for Content is a system that selects relevant ads to display to buyers viewing web pages containing certain embedded Google code. Every time a buyer visits a site, the embedded code prompts Google's system to run an auction. Which ads are displayed is determined by a proprietary Google algorithm that considers the amount of money the seller (advertiser) is willing to spend per click when weighed against the relevancy, or "quality," of the ad. Generally, to get a less relevant ad displayed, an advertiser must bid more money than another advertiser supplying a more relevant ad. Once the ad is chosen it is sent directly to the buyer's browser – not to the website publisher – and is displayed in such a way that it appears to be part of that webpage.

AdWords Front End is a site where sellers input the content of an ad, how much they are willing to pay, keywords with which the ad should be associated, and requests for the ad to be placed on specific sites. Sellers cannot customize the "look" of the ads, so all ads look the same except for the actual text displayed. Sellers can request placement on specific sites but they have no way to guarantee they will be placed on those sites – they still have to win the auction (even after requesting placement on specific sites), be relevant, and be allowed to advertise on the site by the publisher. ...

The case was tried to a jury on claims 1, 20, 37, 52, 63, 90, 179, and 231 of the '025 Patent and claim 1 of the '059 Patent, and the jury found these claims to be both invalid and not infringed.

After trial, FM filed for a motion for judgment as a matter of law ("JMOL") on validity and also moved for a new trial on the grounds that the verdict was against the great weight of the evidence and otherwise irreconcilable. The district court granted JMOL for claims 52, 63, 90, and 231 of the '025 Patent, finding that Google had not submitted sufficient evidence for the jury to find that those claims were invalid. Thus, of the asserted claims, only these four remained valid, but none of them were found to be infringed.

FM appeals, and Google does not cross-appeal the district court's JMOL regarding those four claims.

STANDARD OF REVIEW

[The standard of review announced in the case has been superseded by *Teva Pharmaceuticals USA, Inc. v. Sandoz, Inc.*, 135 S. Ct. 831 (2015). Accrding to *Teva*, "when the district court reviews only evidence intrinsic to the patent (the patent claims and specifications, along with the patent's prosecution history), the judge's determination will amount solely to a determination of law, and the Court of Appeals will review that construction *de novo.*" *Id.* at 841. But factual findings on subsidiary issues, such as "the background science or the meaning of a term in the relevant art during the relevant time period ... must be reviewed for clear error on appeal." *Id.*]

DISCUSSION ...

With regard to the claims that went to the jury, FM contends that the district court's claim constructions were incorrect, and that the district court improperly allowed claim construction disputes to be decided by the jury. FM also argues that the jury's verdict was against the great weight of the evidence, was based upon an incorrect statement of the law, and was irreconcilable. Google responds that FM's arguments are really factual questions disguised as claim construction arguments, that the district court did construe all of the disputed terms, and that FM has waived many of its arguments. ...

II. CLAIM CONSTRUCTION

FM contends that the district court erred in construing [various terms] and that these errors require a new trial. We address each of these arguments in turn. ...

C. "Publishing"

Lastly, claim 1 requires "publishing the electronic advertisement to one or more of the selected internet media venues." '025 Patent col. 65 ll. 10–17. The district court construed this term to mean "placing or making available the customized electronic advertisement within the framework of *and at* each internet media venue so that it is accessible by the end users, consumers, viewers, or buyers." (emphasis added). FM argues that the district court erred by including the "and at" language requested by Google, which it believes improperly removes from the scope of the claim any system (including Google's systems here) which sends ads directly to the buyer's computers. Without those two words, FM argues, the claim would encompass the publishing of ads directly to buyers so long as the displayed ads look like they are "within the framework" of the website.

We see no error in the district court's construction. Claim 1 requires "publishing the electronic advertisement *to* one or more of the selected internet media venues ... whereby the electronic advertisement is *displayed on* each of the one or more of the selected internet media venues." (emphases added). Thus, the terms of the claim require the ads to be sent to the internet media venue, not simply made to look like they are on the internet media venue on the buyer's computer as in Google's system. And the claim language makes it clear that internet media venues are different than the buyers' web browsers. Claim 1 requires an interface for specifying different presentation rules for each internet media venue, not for each buyer or each web browser. Furthermore, the parties agreed that internet media venues are "internet locations where presentations are placed or made available" such that they may be "accessible by the end users, consumers, viewers, or [b]uyers." The claim terms thus require ads to be published to internet media venues, where they are accessible to buyers using web browsers.

Although FM identifies various portions of the specification that it claims show that the patent contemplates delivering ads directly to buyers, we are not persuaded. For example, FM relies on a sentence in the specification stating that the PGP "creates presentations that can be accessed by the buying public ... through ... the Buyers Interface." But the fact that ads may be accessed in browsers does not remove the requirement that they must be published to internet media venues. FM also argues that figure 1b shows the option of sending the ad directly to the buyer:

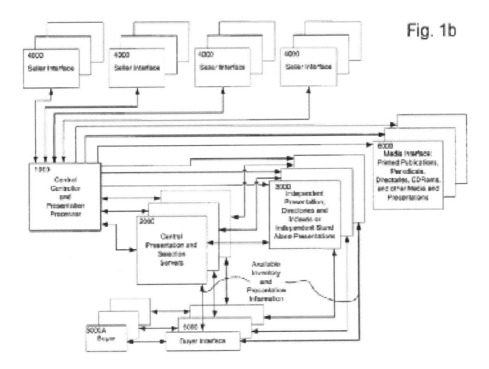

Fig. 1b

Figure 1b does not show ads going directly to the buyer. Instead, ads are made available through the "Independent Presentation[s], Directories and Indexes or Independent Standalone Presentations," shown in box 3000. Indeed, FM acknowledges this – as it must – in its argument. Appellant's Br. 39 (arguing that the path "from block 1000 to block 3000 and corresponding line extending from block 5000 to block 3000" supported its theory that ads could be sent directly to the web browser). But box 3000 does not include the buyer's web browser or computer. *See id.* col. 10 ll. 8–15 (limiting the definition of "Internet Browser" to "[c]lientside program[s] that reside[ ] on the [b]uyer [i]nterface 5000"). The specifications reinforce the district court's construction, not FM's.

We affirm the district court's construction of the "publishing" element because the addition of the word "at" to the definition correctly indicates that the ads must be sent to the internet media venues, not to buyers. ...

V. MOTION FOR NEW TRIAL

FM argues that it is entitled to a new trial because the jury's non-infringement verdict was against the great weight of the evidence under either its construction or the court's. The district court's decision to deny FM's motion is reviewed for abuse of discretion and will be affirmed unless there is a clear showing of an absolute absence of evidence to support the jury's verdict.

The record contains evidence to support the noninfringement verdict. To prove infringement, the patentee must show that the accused device contains each limitation of the asserted claim, or an equivalent of each limitation. We have affirmed the court's construction of the term "publishing," which excludes publishing ads directly to the buyer. But it is undisputed that Google's systems sends ads directly to the buyer, and the jury could properly find that Google does not infringe on that basis.[7] ...

CONCLUSION

As FM has not shown that reversible error occurred, the decision of the district court is AFFIRMED

QUESTIONS

1. In theory, claim construction establishes the meaning of terms in a patent's claims as a matter of law. Only in a subsequent step is the fact-finder asked to compare the claims (as construed) to the defendant's product. But frequently, a court's claim construction decisions will be dispositive of an infringement case. Why might that be?

2. What is the significance of the disputed two words "and at" in the court's construction of the term "publishing?" Why did each side argue for the construction it did?

3. The standard justification for having inventors' rights defined by the language of the claims they draft is that it provides certainty about their rights and fair notice to potential infringers. How effectively does the claim language here serve that goal?

4. Google's advertising programs have made it one of the most valuable companies on the planet. Few people had even heard of Function Media before it obtained its patents and filed this lawsuit. Is this a sign that the patent system is open to abuse by losers in the marketplace who hope to strike it rich extracting money from the companies who actually create successful products? Or is this precisely why we have a patent system: to protect little-guy inventors against corporate giants who use their ideas without paying?

APPLE V. MOTOROLA
869 F. Supp. 2d 901 (N.D. Ill 2012)

Posner, Circuit Judge[*] ...

The remaining patent for which damages are sought is Motorola's '898, part of a portfolio of patents for enabling communication between cell phones and cell towers (called "cellular base stations" in the patent). The '898 and '559 (a Motorola patent for which I granted Apple's motion for summary judgment of noninfringement) have both been declared by Motorola to be "standards essential" patents. These are patents that cell phone makers must use to communicate over specified telecommunications networks and therefore that the patentee (Motorola) has committed to licensing to anyone on fair, reasonable, and nondiscriminatory (acronym "FRAND," or sometimes "RAND" – the word "fair" adds nothing to "rea-

---

7   This is true for Ad Sense for Content and Ad Sense for Mobile, except for certain types of older phones, which do publish ads directly to internet media venues. Google argues that FM never presented actual evidence of infringement for the older phones so there can be no infringement. FM does not contradict this claim in its Reply Brief. Infringement requires specific instances of direct infringement or a finding that every accused device necessarily infringes. FM has not carried that burden with respect to the older phones so we affirm the district court's denial of new trial with respect to them as well.

*   [Ed: sitting by designation.]

sonable" and "nondiscriminatory") terms, as required by the standards-setting organizations as a condition of the patented technology's being deemed essential to compliance with the standard. ...

There is another decisive objection to Motorola's damages claim. The proper method of computing a FRAND royalty starts with what the cost to the licensee would have been of obtaining, just before the patented invention was declared essential to compliance with the industry standard, a license for the function performed by the patent. That cost would be a measure of the value of the patent qua patent. But once a patent becomes essential to a standard, the patentee's bargaining power surges because a prospective licensee has no alternative to licensing the patent; he is at the patentee's mercy. The purpose of the FRAND requirements, the validity of which Motorola doesn't question, is to confine the patentee's royalty demand to the value conferred by the patent itself as distinct from the additional value – the hold-up value – conferred by the patent's being designated as standard-essential. *Broadcom Corp. v. Qualcomm Inc.*, 501 F.3d 297, 313–14 (3d Cir. 2007); Daniel G. Swanson & William J. Baumol, *Reasonable and Nondiscriminatory (RAND) Royalties, Standards Selection, and Control of Market Power*, 73 ANTITRUST L.J. 1, 7–11 (2005). Motorola has provided no evidence for calculating a reasonable royalty that would be consistent with this point.

So damages are out for both parties. But a patentee can also seek injunctive relief for infringement, and both parties seek such relief ...

Injunctive Relief. To begin with Motorola's injunctive claim, I don't see how, given FRAND, I would be justified in enjoining Apple from infringing the '898 unless Apple refuses to pay a royalty that meets the FRAND requirement. By committing to license its patents on FRAND terms, Motorola committed to license the '898 to anyone willing to pay a FRAND royalty and thus implicitly acknowledged that a royalty is adequate compensation for a license to use that patent. How could it do otherwise? How could it be permitted to enjoin Apple from using an invention that it contends Apple *must* use if it wants to make a cell phone with UMTS telecommunications capability – without which it would not be a cell *phone.*

The Federal Trade Commission recently issued a policy statement which implies that injunctive relief is indeed unavailable for infringement of a patent governed by FRAND. "Third Party United States Federal Trade Commission's Statement on the Public Interest," filed on June 6, 2012, in *In re Certain Wireless Communication Devices, Portable Music & Data Processing Devices, Computers & Components Thereof, Inv. No. 337–TA–745*, www.ftc.gov/os/2012/06/1206ftcwirelesscom.pdf (visited June 22, 2012). This was said in the context of an exclusion order by the International Trade Commission, but its logic embraces any claim to enjoin the sale of an infringing product. For the FTC says it's "explaining the potential economic and competitive impact of injunctive relief on disputes involving SEPs [standard-essential patents]." *Id.* at 2. It goes on to note that

> a royalty negotiation that occurs under threat of an exclusion order may be weighted heavily in favor of the patentee in a way that is in tension with the RAND commitment. High switching costs combined with the threat of an exclusion order could allow a patentee to obtain unreasonable licensing terms despite its RAND commitment, not because its invention is valuable, but because implementers are locked in to practicing the standard. The resulting imbalance between the value of patented technology and the rewards for innovation may be

especially acute where the exclusion order is based on a patent covering a small component of a complex multicomponent product. In
these ways, the threat of an exclusion order may allow the holder of a
RAND-encumbered SEP to realize royalty rates that reflect patent
hold-up, rather than the value of the patent relative to alternatives.

Id. at 3–4; see also (besides the *Broadcom* case and the Swanson & Baumol article)
Douglas Lichtman, *Understanding the RAND Commitment*, 47 HOUS. L. REV.
1023, 1039–43 (2010); Mark A. Lemley, *Intellectual Property Rights and Standard-Setting Organizations*, 90 CAL. L. REV. 1889, 1916 (2002).

Motorola counters that Apple's refusal to negotiate with it after rejecting its
initial offer of a 2.25 percent royalty warrants injunctive relief; by opting not to
take a license ex ante, it argues, Apple should lose the FRAND safe harbor. But
Apple's refusal to negotiate for a license (if it did refuse – the parties offer competing accounts, unnecessary for me to resolve, of why negotiations broke down) was
not a defense to a claim by Motorola for a FRAND royalty. If Apple said no to 2.25
percent, it ran the risk of being ordered by a court to pay an equal or even higher
royalty rate, but that is not the same thing as Motorola's being excused from no
longer having to comply with its FRAND obligations. Motorola agreed to license
its standards-essential patents on FRAND terms as a *quid pro quo* for their being
declared essential to the standard. It does not claim to have conditioned agreement on prospective licensees' making counteroffers in license negotiations.

Motorola argues further that deprived of the possibility of injunctive relief, it
will not be able to extract a reasonable royalty from Apple. Suppose, hypothetical-
ly, that the maximum reasonable FRAND royalty would be $10 million. If Motoro-
la therefore demanded such a royalty, Apple, knowing that litigation is costly,
would refuse, and Motorola would accept a lesser amount. Of course litigation
would also be costly for Apple, and this might induce it to pay the $10 million
rather than fight. But the deeper objection to Motorola's argument is that the
"American rule," which with immaterial exceptions makes the winning party in a
litigation bear his litigation costs rather than being able to shift them to the loser,
does not deem damages an inadequate remedy just because, unless backed by a
threat of injunction, it may induce a settlement for less than the damages rightly
sought by the plaintiff. You can't obtain an injunction for a simple breach of contract on the ground that you need the injunction to pressure the defendant to settle your damages claim on terms more advantageous to you than if there were no
such pressure.

APPLE V. MOTOROLA
757 F.3d 1286 (Fed. Cir. 2014)

Reyna, Circuit Judge: ...

To the extent that the district court applied a *per se* rule that injunctions are
unavailable for SEPs, it erred. While Motorola's FRAND commitments are certainly criteria relevant to its entitlement to an injunction, we see no reason to create, as some *amici* urge, a separate rule or analytical framework for addressing
injunctions for FRAND-committed patents. The framework laid out by the
Supreme Court in *eBay* [*Inc. v. MercExchange, L.L.C.*, 547 U.S. 388 (2006)], as
interpreted by subsequent decisions of this court, provides ample strength and
flexibility for addressing the unique aspects of FRAND committed patents and
industry standards in general. A patentee subject to FRAND commitments may
have difficulty establishing irreparable harm. On the other hand, an injunction

may be justified where an infringer unilaterally refuses a FRAND royalty or unreasonably delays negotiations to the same effect. *See, e.g.*, U.S. Dep't of Justice and U.S. Patent and Trademark Office, *Policy Statement on Remedies for Standard-Essential Patents Subject to Voluntary F/RAND Commitments*, at 7–8 (Jan. 8, 2013). To be clear, this does not mean that an alleged infringer's refusal to accept any license offer necessarily justifies issuing an injunction. For example, the license offered may not be on FRAND terms. In addition, the public has an interest in encouraging participation in standard-setting organizations but also in ensuring that SEPs are not overvalued. While these are important concerns, the district courts are more than capable of considering these factual issues when deciding whether to issue an injunction under the principles in *eBay*.

Applying those principles here, we agree with the district court that Motorola is not entitled to an injunction for infringement of the '898 patent. Motorola's FRAND commitments, which have yielded many license agreements encompassing the '898 patent, strongly suggest that money damages are adequate to fully compensate Motorola for any infringement. Similarly, Motorola has not demonstrated that Apple's infringement has caused it irreparable harm. Considering the large number of industry participants that are already using the system claimed in the '898 patent, including competitors, Motorola has not provided any evidence that adding one more user would create such harm. Again, Motorola has agreed to add as many market participants as are willing to pay a FRAND royalty. Motorola argues that Apple has refused to accept its initial licensing offer and stalled negotiations. However, the record reflects that negotiations have been ongoing, and there is no evidence that Apple has been, for example, unilaterally refusing to agree to a deal. Consequently, we affirm the district court's grant of summary judgment that Motorola is not entitled to an injunction for infringement of the '898 patent.

Rader, Chief Judge, dissenting-in-part:

I join the court's opinion in its entirety, except for the affirmance of the district court's denial of Motorola's request for an injunction. To my eyes, the record contains sufficient evidence to create a genuine dispute of material fact on Apple's posture as an unwilling licensee whose continued infringement of the '898 patent caused irreparable harm. Because of the unique and intensely factual circumstances surrounding patents adopted as industry standards, I believe the district court improperly granted summary judgment. ...

At the outset, a patent adopted as a standard undoubtedly gains value by virtue of that adoption. This enhancement complicates the evaluation of the technology independent of the standardization. By the same token, the standardization decision may also simply reflect and validate the inherent value of the technology advance accomplished by the patent. Untangling these value components (at the heart of deciding whether a putative licensee was "unwilling" to license, and thus irreparable harm and other injunction factors) requires intense economic analysis of complex facts. In sum, right from the theoretical outset, this question is not likely to be susceptible to summary adjudication. ...

Market analysts will no doubt observe that a "hold out" (i.e., an unwilling licensee of an SEP seeking to avoid a license based on the value that the technological advance contributed to the prior art) is equally as likely and disruptive as a "hold up" (i.e., an SEP owner demanding unjustified royalties based solely on value contributed by the standardization). These same complex factual questions regarding "hold up" and "hold out" are highly relevant to an injunction request. In sum, differentiating "hold up" from "hold out" requires some factual analysis of the sources of value – the inventive advance or the standardization.

The record in this case shows evidence that Apple may have been a hold out. This evidence alone would create a dispute of material fact. ...

In my opinion, the court should have allowed Motorola to prove that Apple was an unwilling licensee, which would strongly support its injunction request. ... Motorola should have had the opportunity to prove its case that Apple's alleged unwillingness to license or even negotiate supports a showing that money damages are inadequate and that it suffered irreparable harm. The district court refused to develop the facts necessary to apply *eBay* as it should have. Consequently, the case should be remanded to develop that record. ...

QUESTIONS

1. What is the difference to Apple between a damage award and an injunction? The difference to Motorola?

2. Why are standard-essential patents different from all other patents? (Or are they?)

3. What does a company stand to gain by tying its hands when it makes a FRAND commitment?

CHAPTER 9: PRIVATE POWER

The early chapters of this book were heavily concerned with the issue of government power. The last two chapters, however, have shown in many cases the most important decisions are made by private intermediaries, such as ISPs, web hosts, and search engines. This chapter brings these two themes together, by asking what the limits on intermediary power might be. If an ISP abuses its position, what can its users, or the government, do about it? Part I discusses common-law and constitutional doctrines, along with some problems that illustrate the complexity of the challenges faced by intermediaries and those who would question their judgments. Part II considers one statutory response to these challenges, in the form of antitrust law. And Part III provides a brief excursion into telecommunications law, by considering the highly controversial issue now known as "network neutrality."

Threaded through of the chapter is another theme: generativity. One common fear about intermediaries is that they will suppress both user creativity and any innovations that threaten their business models. Proposals to rein in intermediary power frequently do so in the name of promoting innovation by others. At the same time, one of the most common responses to such proposals is that they will suppress valuable innovations coming from intermediaries themselves.

A. First Amendment Limits

CYBER PROMOTIONS, INC. V. AMERICAN ONLINE, INC.
948 F. Supp. 436 (E.D. Pa. 1996)

Weiner, District Judge:

The cases have their genesis in a letter dated January 26, 1996, in which American Online, Inc. ("AOL") advised Cyber Promotions, Inc. ("Cyber") that AOL was upset with Cyber's dissemination of unsolicited e-mail to AOL members over the Internet. ...

AOL has vehemently argued throughout the brief history of these suits that Cyber has no right to send literally millions of e-mail messages each day to AOL's Internet servers free of charge and resulting in the overload of the e-mail servers. Indeed, the court has received a plethora of letters from disgruntled AOL members who object to having to receive Cyber's unsolicited e-mail whenever they sign on to AOL despite repeated attempts to be removed from Cyber's lists. Cyber, on the other hand, has contended that without the right to send unsolicited e-mail to AOL members, it will go out of business.

Recognizing that Cyber's contention that it has the right to send unsolicited e-mail to AOL members over the Internet implicates the First Amendment and therefore is a threshold issue, the Court directed the parties to brief the following issue: Whether Cyber has a right under the First Amendment of the United States Constitution to send unsolicited e-mail to AOL members via the Internet and concomitantly whether AOL has the right under the First Amendment to block the e-mail sent by Cyber from reaching AOL members over the Internet. ...

The Court also directed the parties to enter into a Stipulation of Facts solely for the purpose of resolving the First Amendment issue. Pursuant to the Court's directive, the parties have stipulated to the following facts:

1. Cyber is a corporation organized and existing under the laws of the Commonwealth of Pennsylvania, having a place of business at 1255 Passmore Street, 1st Floor, Philadelphia, Pennsylvania 19111.

2. AOL is a corporation organized and existing under the laws of the State of Delaware with its principal place of business at 22000 AOL Way, Dulles, Virginia 20166.

3. AOL was and is a private online company that has invested substantial sums of its own money in equipment, name, software and reputation. AOL is not owned in whole or in part by the government.

4. AOL is owned by shareholders, and its stock trades on the New York Stock Exchange.

5. AOL is not a government entity or political subdivision.

6. AOL's members or subscribers pay prescribed fees for use of AOL resources, access to AOL and access and use of AOL's e-mail system and its connection to the Internet.

7. AOL's e-mail system operates through dedicated computers known as servers, which consist of computer hardware and software purchased, maintained and owned by AOL. AOL's computer servers have a finite, though expandable, capacity to handle e-mail. All Internet e-mail from non-AOL members to AOL customers or members and from AOL customers or members to non-AOL members requires the use of AOL's computer hardware and software in combination with the hardware and software of the Internet and the hardware and software of the non-AOL members.

8. Private companies compete with AOL in the online business.

9. There has been no government involvement in AOL's business decision to institute or reinstitute a block directed to Internet e-mail sent by Cyber to AOL members or subscribers.

10. Although the Internet is accessible to all persons with just a computer, a modem and a service provider, the constituent parts of the Internet (namely the computer hardware and software, servers, service providers and related items) are owned and managed by private entities and persons, corporations, educational institutions and government entities, who cooperate to allow their constituent parts to be interconnected by a vast network of phone lines.

11. In order for non-AOL members to send Internet e-mail to AOL members, non-AOL members must utilize a combination of their own hardware and software, the Internet and AOL's network.

12. To obtain its initial access to the Internet, AOL obtained an Internet address and domain name from IANA, a clearinghouse that routinely and ministerially assigns Internet addresses and domain names.

13. Cyber, an advertising agency incorporated in 1996, provides advertising services for companies and individuals wishing to advertise their products and services via e-mail.

14. Cyber sends its e-mail via the Internet to members of AOL, members of other commercial online services and other individuals with an Internet e-mail address.

15. AOL provides its subscribing members with one or more e-mail addresses so that members can exchange e-mail with one another and exchange e-mail (both sending and receiving) over the Internet with non-AOL members.

16. AOL has attached to its Memorandum of Law in Support of its Motion for Partial Summary Judgment on First Amendment Issues three sets of examples of e-mail messages sent by Cyber to AOL members. The first set (Tab 1) consists of a multi-page set of advertisements; the second set (Tab 2) consists of an exclusive or single-advertiser e-mail; and the third set (Tab 3) consists of a document called by Cyber an "e-mag." Under each tab are two examples, the first selected by AOL and the second selected by Cyber. The Court has reviewed all of the examples and notes that many of the ads include get-rich-quick ads, weight loss ads, health aid promises and even phone sex services.

17. To attract membership, AOL offers a variety of services, options, resources and support, including content-based services, access to stock quotes, children's entertainment, news, and the ability to send and receive Internet e-mail to and from non-AOL members. ...

The First Amendment to the United States Constitution states that "Congress shall make no law respecting an establishment of religion, or prohibiting the free exercise thereof; or abridging the freedom of speech, or of the press." The United States Supreme Court has recognized that "the constitutional guarantee of free speech is a guarantee only against abridgement by government, federal or state." *Hudgens v. NLRB*, 424 U.S. 507, 513 (1976). Only recently, the Supreme Court has stated that "the guarantees of free speech . . . guard only against encroachment by the government and 'erec[t] no shield against merely private conduct.'" *Hurley v. Irish-American Gay Group of Boston*, 515 U.S. 557, 566 (1995).

In the case *sub judice*, the parties have stipulated that AOL is a *private* online company that is not owned in whole or part by the government. The parties have further stipulated that "AOL is not a government entity or political subdivision." They have also stipulated that there has been no government involvement in AOL's business decision to institute or reinstitute a block directed to Internet e-mail sent by Cyber to AOL members or subscribers.

Despite these stipulations, Cyber argues that AOL's conduct has the character of state action. As a general matter, private action can only be considered state action when "there is a sufficiently close nexus between the State and the challenged action of [the private entity] so that the action of the latter may be fairly treated as that of the State itself." *Blum v. Yaretsky*, 457 U.S. 991, 1004 (1982). Recently, our Court of Appeals observed that the Supreme Court appears to utilize three distinct tests in determining whether there has been state action. *Mark v. Borough of Hatboro*, 51 F.3d 1137, 1142 (3rd Cir. 1995). First, we must consider whether "'the private entity has exercised powers that are traditionally the *exclusive* prerogative of the state.'" *Id*. This test is known as the exclusive public function test. If the private entity does not exercise such powers, we must consider whether "'the private entity has acted with the help of or in concert with state officials.'" *Mark*, 51 F.3d at 1142. The final test is whether "'[t]he State has so far insinuated itself into a position of interdependence with . . . [the acting party] that it must be recognized as a joint participant in the challenged activity.'" *Mark*, 51 F.3d at 1142.

With regard to the first test, AOL exercises absolutely no powers which are in any way the prerogative, let alone the *exclusive* prerogative, of the State. In *ACLU*, *supra,* this Court previously found that no single entity, including the State, administers the Internet. *ACLU,* 929 F. Supp. at 832. Rather, the Court found that the Internet is a "global Web of linked networks and computers" which exists and functions as the result of the desire of hundreds of thousands of computer operators and networks to use common data transfer data protocol to exchange communications and information. *Id.* In addition, "the constituent parts of the Internet . . . are owned and managed by private entities and persons, corporations, educational institutions and government entities, who cooperate to allow their constituent parts to be interconnected by a vast network of phone lines." As a result, tens of millions of people with access to the Internet can exchange information. AOL is merely one of many private online companies which allow its members access to the Internet through its e-mail system where they can exchange information with the general public. The State has absolutely no interest in, and does not regulate, this exchange of information between people, institutions, corporations and governments around the world.

Cyber argues, however, that "by providing Internet e-mail and acting as the sole conduit to its members' Internet e-mail boxes, AOL has opened up that part of its network and as such, has sufficiently devoted this domain for public use. This dedication of AOL's Internet e-mail accessway performs a public function in that it is open to the public, free of charge to any user, where public discourse, conversations and commercial transactions can and do take place." Cyber therefore contends that AOL's Internet e-mail accessway is similar to the company town in *Marsh v. Alabama,* 326 U.S. 501 (1946), which the Supreme Court found performed a public function and therefore was a state actor.

In *Marsh,* a Jehovah's Witness was convicted of criminal trespass for distributing literature without a license on a sidewalk in a town [Chickasaw, Alabama] owned by a private company [the Gulf Shipbuilding Corporation]. The Supreme Court found that since the private company owned the streets, sidewalks, and business block, paid the sheriff, privately owned and managed the sewage system, and owned the building where the United States post office was located, the company, in effect, operated as the municipal government of the town. *Marsh,* 326 U.S. at 502-03. "[T]he owner of the company town was performing the full spectrum of municipal powers and stood in the shoes of the State." *Lloyd Corp. v. Tanner,* 407 U.S. 551, 569 (1972). The Court observed that "[t]he more an owner, for his advantage, opens up his property for use by the public in general, the more do his rights become circumscribed by the statutory and constitutional rights of those who use it." *Marsh,* 326 U.S. at 506. As a result, the Court found state action in "the State['s] . . . attempt[] to impose criminal punishment on appellant for undertaking to distribute religious literature in a company town . . ." *Marsh,* 326 U.S. at 509. Our Court of Appeals has noted that "*Marsh* has been construed narrowly." *Cable Investments, Inc. v. Woolley,* 867 F.2d 151, 162 (3d Cir.1989).

By providing its members with access to the Internet through its e-mail system so that its members can exchange information with those members of the public who are also connected to the Internet, AOL is not exercising *any* of the municipal powers or public services traditionally exercised by the State as did the private company in *Marsh.* Although AOL has technically opened its e-mail system to the public by connecting with the Internet, AOL has not opened its property to the public by performing any municipal power or essential public service and, therefore, does not stand in the shoes of the State. *Marsh* is simply inapposite to the facts of the case*s sub judice.*

Cyber also argues that AOL's Internet e-mail connection constitutes an exclusive public function because there are no alternative avenues of communication for Cyber to send its e-mail to AOL members. ...

Cyber has numerous alternative avenues of sending its advertising to AOL members. An example of another avenue Cyber has of sending its advertising to AOL members over the Internet is the World Wide Web which would allow access by Internet users, including AOL customers, who *want* to receive Cyber's e-mail. Examples of non-Internet avenues include the United States mail, telemarketing, television, cable, newspapers, magazines and even passing out leaflets. Of course, AOL's decision to block Cyber's e-mail from reaching AOL's members does not prevent Cyber from sending its e-mail advertisements to the members of competing commercial online services, including CompuServe, the Microsoft Network and Prodigy. ...

[The court held that AOL had not acted in concert with State officials, nor had the State insinuated itself into a position of interdependence with AOL.]

QUESTIONS

1. The starting point for *Cyber Promotions* is the "state action" rule: the First Amendment only restricts the actions of the government, not of private parties. What is it about streets and sidewalks that led the Supreme Court in *Marsh* to make an exception and treat the Gulf Shipbuilding Corporation as a state actor for First Amendment purposes? Does the same rationale apply to AOL?

2. Does the widespread availability of speech from around the world on the Internet eliminate the need for doctrines preserving access to physical streets for free-speech purposes?

3. Why is AOL blocking Cyber Promotions' emails? Won't its customers object?

ZHANG V. BAIDU.COM INC
10 F. Supp. 3d 433 (S.D.N.Y. 2014)

Furman, District Judge:

In this suit, a group of New York residents who advocate for increased democracy in China sue one of China's largest companies, Baidu, Inc. Plaintiffs contend that Baidu, which operates an Internet search engine akin to Google, unlawfully blocks from its search results here in the United States articles and other information concerning "the Democracy movement in China" and related topics. The case raises the question of whether the First Amendment protects as speech the results produced by an Internet search engine. The Court concludes that, at least in the circumstances presented here, it does. Accordingly, allowing Plaintiffs to sue Baidu for what are in essence editorial judgments about which political ideas to promote would run afoul of the First Amendment. Baidu's motion for judgment on the pleadings pursuant to Rule 12(c) of the Federal Rules of Civil Procedure is therefore GRANTED, and the Complaint is dismissed.

BACKGROUND

The following facts, which are taken from the Complaint unless otherwise noted, are assumed to be true for purposes of this motion. Baidu operates a Chinese search engine service called Baidu.com, through which it offers multiple services to locate information, products and services using Chinese-language search terms, such as, search by Chinese phonetics, advanced search, snapshots, spell checker, stock quotes, news, images, video, weather, train and flight schedules and other local information. As of 2010, Baidu purported to be the third largest search engine service provider in the world and the largest in China, with an estimated more than 70% share of the Chinese-language market.

Plaintiffs, self-described "promoters of democracy in China through their writings, publications and reporting of pro-democracy events," allege that Baidu conspires to prevent "pro-democracy political speech" from appearing in its search-engine results here in the United States. Specifically, Plaintiffs claim that Baidu

> censor[s] and block[s] from search engine results any article, publication, video, audio and any information in whatever format if its content deals with the Democracy movement in China or any of the following topics that are related to the Chinese Democracy movement: The June 4th Movement, The Jasmine Revolution, The Jasmine Movement; The China Democracy Party National Committee and the Tiananmen Square Incident or movement.

Plaintiffs claim that Baidu engages in this "censorship" at the behest of the People's Republic of China ("China"), which was named as a defendant in the Complaint but was never served and is no longer a party to the case.

Each Plaintiff has published – on the Internet – articles, video recordings, audio recordings, or other publications regarding the democracy movement in China. Although such publications appear in results returned by other search engines, such as Google and Bing, they do not appear in Baidu's search results because Baidu deliberately blocks them. On these bases, Plaintiffs bring eight claims: (1) conspiracy to violate their civil rights, pursuant to 42 U.S.C. § 1985; (2) violation of their civil rights on the basis of race, pursuant to 42 U.S.C. § 1981; (3) violation of their civil rights under color of state law, pursuant to 42 U.S.C. § 1983; (4-7) denial of their right to equal public accommodations, in violation of New York Civil Rights Law §§ 40 and 40-c, New York Executive Law § 296(2), and New York City Administrative Code § 8-107(4)(a); and (8) denial of the equal protection of the laws guaranteed by New York Constitution Article 1, § 11. Plaintiffs seek $16,000,000 in damages, plus attorney's fees and costs.

LEGAL STANDARD

The standard of review for a motion for judgment on the pleadings under Rule 12(c) of the Federal Rules of Civil Procedure is the same as that governing motions to dismiss under Rule 12(b)(6). A plaintiff must plead facts sufficient to state a claim to relief that is plausible on its face. In applying this standard, a court must assume all of the plaintiff's factual allegations to be true and draw all reasonable inferences in the plaintiff's favor.

DISCUSSION

The question of whether search-engine results constitute speech protected by the First Amendment has been the subject of vigorous academic debate. *See, e.g.,* James Grimmelmann, *Speech Engines,* 98 MINN. L.REV. 868 (2014); Stuart Minor Benjamin, *Algorithms and Speech,* 161 U. PA. L .REV. 1445 (2013); Tim Wu, *Machine Speech,* 161 U. PA. L. REV. 1495 (2013); Michael J. Ballanco, Comment, *Searching for the First Amendment: An Inquisitive Free Speech Approach to Search Engine Rankings,* 24 GEO. MASON U. C.R.L.J. 89 (2013); Eugene Volokh & Donald M. Falk, *Google First Amendment Protection for Search Engine Search Results,* 8 J.L. ECON. & POL'Y 883 (2012); Oren Bracha & Frank Pasquale, *Federal Search Commission? Access, Fairness, and Accountability in the Law of Search,* 93 COR-

NELL L. REV. 1149 (2008); Josh Blackman, *What Happens if Data Is Speech?*, 16 U. PA. J. CONST. L. ONLINE 25 (2014). By contrast, it has garnered relatively little attention from courts. To date, only two courts appear to have addressed the question, both concluding (albeit with somewhat sparse analysis) that search engine results are indeed protected by the First Amendment. *See Langdon v. Google, Inc.*, 474 F. Supp. 2d 622 (D. Del. 2007); *Search King, Inc. v. Google Tech., Inc.*, No. CIV-02-1457-M, 2003 WL 21464568 (W.D. Okla. May 27, 2003). It is therefore a question of first impression in this Circuit.

Although the Supreme Court has not addressed the precise question at issue, its First Amendment jurisprudence all but compels the conclusion that Plaintiffs' suit must be dismissed. The starting point for analysis is *Miami Herald Publishing Co. v. Tornillo*, 418 U.S. 241 (1974), in which the Court held that a Florida statute requiring newspapers to provide political candidates with a right of reply to editorials critical of them violated the First Amendment. "Although the statute did not censor speech in the traditional sense – it only required newspapers to grant access to the messages of others," the Court "found that it imposed an impermissible content-based burden on newspaper speech." *Turner Broad. Sys., Inc. v. FCC*, 512 U.S. 622, 653 (1994). The Court noted that, "in practical effect, Florida's right-of-reply statute would deter newspapers from speaking in unfavorable terms about political candidates" and that it also "induced the newspaper to respond to the candidates' replies when it might have preferred to remain silent." *Id.* at 654. In both respects, the statute impermissibly infringed the newspaper's First Amendment right to exercise editorial control and judgment.

The Court later reinforced that principle, and extended it well beyond the newspaper context, in *Hurley v. Irish-American Gay, Lesbian, & Bisexual Group of Boston*, 515 U.S. 557 (1995). The question in *Hurley* was whether Massachusetts could "require private citizens who organize a parade to include among the marchers a group imparting a message the organizers do not wish to convey." *Id.* at 559. The Court held that allowing the state to do so would "violate[] the fundamental rule of protection under the First Amendment, that a speaker has the autonomy to choose the content of his own message." *Id.* at 573. "Since all speech inherently involves choices of what to say and what to leave unsaid," the Court explained, "one important manifestation of the principle of free speech is that one who chooses to speak may also decide what not to say." *Id.* at 573. Notably, the Court found that principle applied even though the parade organizers did not themselves create the floats and other displays that formed the parade and were "rather lenient in admitting participants." *Id.* at 569. "[A] private speaker," the Court stated, "does not forfeit constitutional protection simply by combining multifarious voices, or by failing to edit their themes to isolate an exact message as the exclusive subject matter of the speech. Nor . . . does First Amendment protection require a speaker to generate, as an original matter, each item featured in the communication." *Id.* at 569-70.

Taken together, those decisions establish several principles relevant to this case. First, as a general matter, the Government may not interfere with the editorial judgments of private speakers on issues of public concern – that is, it may not tell a private speaker what to include or not to include in speech about matters of public concern. Second, that rule is not "restricted to the press, being enjoyed by business corporations generally and by ordinary people engaged in unsophisticated expression as well as by professional publishers." *Hurley*, 515 U.S. at 574. Third, the First Amendment's protections apply whether or not a speaker articulates, or even has, a coherent or precise message, and whether or not the speaker generated the underlying content in the first place. And finally, it does not matter if the Government's intentions are noble – for example, to promote press responsibility, or to prevent expression that is misguided, or even hurtful. Put simply, "[d]isapproval of a private speaker's statement" – no matter how justified disapproval may be – "does not legitimize use of the [Government's] power to compel the speaker to alter the message by including one more acceptable to others." *Hurley*, 515 U.S. at 581.

In light of those principles, there is a strong argument to be made that the First Amendment fully immunizes search-engine results from most, if not all, kinds of civil liability and government regulation. The central purpose of a search engine is to retrieve relevant information from the vast universe of data on the Internet and to organize it in a way that would be most helpful to the searcher. In doing so, search engines inevitably make editorial judgments about what information (or kinds of information) to include in the results and how and where to display that information (for example, on the first page of the search results or later). In these respects, a "search engine's editorial judgment is much like many other familiar editorial judgments," such as the newspaper editor's judgment of which wire-service stories to run and where to place them in the newspaper, the guidebook writer's judgments about which attractions to mention and how to display them, and Matt Drudge's judgments about which stories to link and how prominently to feature them. Volokh & Falk, *supra*, at 884.

On that theory of the First Amendment's protection of search-engine results, the fact that search engines often collect and communicate facts, as opposed to opinions, does not alter the analysis. As the Supreme Court has held, "the creation and dissemination of information are speech within the meaning of the First Amendment. Facts, after all, are the beginning point for much of the speech that is most essential to advance human knowledge and to conduct human affairs." *Sorrell v. IMS Health Inc.*, 131 S.Ct. 2653, 2667, (2011); *see also* Volokh & Falk, *supra*, at 889-90 (noting that the First Amendment "protects the collection and communication of facts as much as it protects opinions, including facts that are not ideologically laden – such as names of crime victims in three-sentence crime reports, names of accused juvenile offenders, lists of bestselling books, lists of tenants who had been evicted by local landlords, information in a mushroom encyclopedia, recipes in a cookbook, and computer program source code"). Nor does the fact that search-engine results may be produced algorithmically matter for the analysis. After all, the algorithms themselves were written by human beings, and they "inherently incorporate the search engine company engineers' judgments about what material users are most likely to find responsive to their queries." Volokh & Falk, *supra*, at 884. In short, one could forcefully argue that "what is true for parades and newspaper op-ed pages is at least as true for search engine output. When search engines select and arrange others' materials, and add the all-important ordering that causes some materials to be displayed first and others last, they are engaging in fully protected First Amendment expression – the presentation of an edited compilation of speech generated by other persons." Volokh & Falk, *supra*, at 891.

In contrast to that robust theory of the First Amendment in this context, some scholars have relied on the Supreme Court's decision in *Turner* – which Plaintiffs here do not cite – to advocate for a lower level of protection of search-engine results. *See, e.g.*, Bracha & Pasquale, *supra*, at 1191-94. In *Turner*, the Court reviewed regulations requiring cable operators to carry the signals of a specified number of local broadcast television stations, and applied only intermediate scrutiny. Significantly, the Court began its analysis by stating that "[t]here can be no disagreement on an initial premise": that cable operators, "by exercising editorial discretion over which stations or programs to include in its repertoire" – that is, by exercising editorial discretion over speech created by others – themselves "engage in and transmit speech" protected by the First Amendment. *Id.* at 636. Nevertheless, the Court held that an intermediate level of scrutiny was appropriate for several reasons: first, because cable operators were mere "conduit[s] for the speech of others, transmitting it on a continuous and unedited basis to subscribers," *id.* at 629; second, because cable operators had the ability to shut out some speakers, "giv[ing] rise to the Government's interest in limiting monopolistic autonomy in order to allow for the survival of broadcasters who might otherwise be silenced and consequently destroyed," *Hurley*, 515 U.S. at 577; and third, because the regulations at issue were content-neutral, as they did not "impose[] a restriction, penalty, or burden by reason of the views, programs, or stations the cable operator has selected or will select," *Turner*, 512 U.S. at 644. That is, although acknowledging that the cable operators were engaged in speech, the Court granted lesser protection to that speech because of its less expressive nature, the technological quasi-monopoly in the marketplace of ideas enjoyed by the cable companies, and the fact that the regulations did not discriminate on the basis of content. Taking these rationales as lodestars, some scholars argue that search-engine results should also be afforded lesser protection under the First Amendment.

This Court, however, need not resolve the scholarly debate in order to decide the present motion because, whether or not the First Amendment shields all search engines from lawsuits based on the content of their search results, it plainly shields Baidu from Plaintiffs' claims in this lawsuit.[4] Here, the very theory of Plaintiffs' claims is that Baidu exercises editorial control over its search results on certain political topics – namely, by disfavoring expression concerning "the Democracy movement in China" and related subjects. In other words, Plaintiffs do not – and, in light of their own allegations, cannot – make any argument that Baidu is merely an "infrastructure or platform that delivers content" in a neutral way. Bracha & Pasquale, *supra*, at 1192-97 (arguing that because "search engines do not function as publishers or editors of the content to which they channel users," their results should not be treated as speech covered by the First Amendment). Instead, they seek to hold Baidu liable for, and thus punish Baidu for, a conscious decision to design its search-engine algorithms to favor certain expression on core political subjects over other expression on those same political subjects. To allow such a suit to proceed would plainly "violate[] the fundamental rule

---

4   Given the allegations in this case, there is also no need to address whether laws of general applicability, such as antitrust laws, can be applied to search engines without implicating the First Amendment. Nor is there any need to address whether a search engine could be held liable for false statements concerning its methodology or search results. *Cf., e.g., Connecticut v. Moody's Corp.*, No. X04HHDCV106008836S, 2012 WL 2149408, at *9 (Conn. Super. Ct. May 10, 2012) (holding that a state civil-enforcement action against a bond-rating agency for false statements about the manner in which the agency operated its business was not barred by the First Amendment even if the underlying ratings themselves enjoyed First Amendment protection).

of protection under the First Amendment, that a speaker has the autonomy to choose the content of his own message." *Hurley*, 515 U.S. at 573.

That conclusion is compelled as much by *Turner* as it is by *Tornillo* and *Hurley*. First, in light of *Turner*, "[t]here can be no disagreement" that Baidu is "engage[d] in and transmit[s] speech" and is thus "entitled to the protection of the speech and press provisions of the First Amendment" because Plaintiffs' own theory is that the company "exercise[s] editorial discretion" over its search results and thereby "seek[s] to communicate messages on a wide variety of topics and in a wide variety of formats." 512 U.S. at 636. Second, *Turner's* three principal rationales for applying a lower level of scrutiny to the must-carry cable regulations – namely, that cable companies were mere conduits for the speech of others, that they had the physical ability to silence other speakers, and that the regulations at issue were content-neutral – are inapplicable here. With respect to the first rationale, it is debatable whether any search engine is a mere "conduit" given the judgments involved in designing algorithms to choose, rank, and sort search results. But whether or not that proposition is true as a general matter, it is plainly "not apt here," as Plaintiffs' own allegations of censorship make clear that Baidu is "more than a passive receptacle or conduit for news, comment, and advertising." *Hurley*, 515 U.S. at 575. As Plaintiffs themselves allege, for example, Baidu "purposely designs its search engine algorithms to exclude any pro-democracy topics, articles, publications, and multimedia coverage."

The second rationale, too, has no application here, as search engine operators (at least in the United States and given today's technology) lack the physical power to silence anyone's voices, no matter what their alleged market shares may be. As Plaintiffs' own publications make clear, Baidu does not have the ability to block "pro-democracy" writings from appearing on the Internet in this country altogether; it can only control whether it will help users find them. And if a user is dissatisfied with Baidu's search results, he or she "has access, with just a click of the mouse, to Google, Microsoft's Bing, Yahoo! Search, and other general-purpose search engines, as well as to almost limitless other means of finding content on the Internet, including specialized search engines, social networks, and mobile apps." Volokh & Falk, *supra*, at 898. In fact, Plaintiffs themselves acknowledge that their pro-democracy works are widely available to the public on the Internet "via any of the well known [sic] search engines such as Google, Yahoo[,] and Bing."

It is, however, *Turner's* third rationale for applying intermediate scrutiny that puts the final nail in the coffin for Plaintiffs' claims in this case. In *Turner*, the Court concluded that the regulations at issue were content-neutral, as they did not "impose[] a restriction, penalty, or burden by reason of the views, programs, or stations the cable operator has selected or will select." 512 U.S. at 644. By contrast, although the present case does not involve government regulation *per se*, Plaintiffs call upon the Court to impose a penalty on Baidu precisely because of what it does and does not choose to say. As the *Turner* Court made clear, however, "the First Amendment, subject only to narrow and well-understood exceptions" – inapplicable here – "does not countenance governmental control over the content of messages expressed by private individuals." *Id.* at 641. Accordingly, to allow Plaintiffs' suit to proceed, let alone to hold Baidu liable for its editorial judgments, would contravene the principle upon which "[o]ur political system and cultural life rest": "that each person should decide for himself or herself the ideas and beliefs deserving of expression, consideration, and adherence." *Id.* at 641.

Plaintiffs' arguments to the contrary are wholly unpersuasive. First, Plaintiffs assert – without citation to any legal authority – that "Baidu is not speaking," but rather "engaging in discriminatory conduct" for which it can be held liable under federal civil rights laws and New York State's public accommodations law. That assertion, however, is belied by Plaintiffs' own theory of the case, which is that by exercising editorial discretion, Baidu favors some "political speech" over other "political speech." *See also, e.g., Hurley*, 515 U.S. at 569 ("[A] narrow, succinctly articulable message is not a condition of constitutional protection, which if confined to expressions conveying a particularized message would never reach the unquestionably shielded painting of Jackson Pollock, music of Arnold Schoenberg, or Jabberwocky verse of Lewis Carroll."). Further, Plaintiffs' argument is indistinguishable from the argument rejected in *Hurley*, that the parade at issue was a public accommodation subject to Massachusetts' own public accommodations law. That is, "once the expressive character" of Baidu's search results "is understood, it becomes apparent" that allowing Plaintiffs to sue Baidu based on the content of those results would have "the effect of declaring [Baidu's] speech itself to be the public accommodation." 515 U.S. at 572-73.

Second, Plaintiffs argue that, even if Baidu's search results are a form of speech, the First Amendment is not implicated because this is a private suit and thus does not involve direct government regulation. But that argument is also flatly inconsistent with *Hurley*, which was likewise a private suit in which the plaintiffs relied on a state public accommodations law. Moreover, the Supreme Court has long made clear that the First Amendment's protections extend to private suits for money damages based on the content of speech. ... *See also Langdon*, 474 F. Supp.. 2d at 629-30 (dismissing First Amendment, fraud, and deceptive business practices claims against a search engine as barred by the First Amendment); *Search King*, 2003 WL 21464568, at *4 (same with respect to a tortious-interference claim).

Third, Plaintiffs contend that Baidu's search results, if speech, are a form of commercial speech subject to "relaxed" scrutiny under the First Amendment. "The search engine," Plaintiffs reason, "is both Baidu's product and advertisement. There are no membership requirements and no usage fees because Baidu makes money selling advertisements and sponsorships. Thus, Baidu has a profit motive to retrieve and disseminate information on its search engine, for example, by drawing traffic to its site to sell advertisement [sic]." Commercial speech, however, is defined as "expression related *solely* to the economic interests of the speaker and its audience." *Cent. Hudson Gas & Elec. Corp. v. Pub. Serv. Comm'n of N.Y.*, 447 U.S. 557, 561 (1980) (emphasis added); *see also United States v. United Foods, Inc.*, 533 U.S. 405, 409 (2001) (stating that commercial speech is "usually defined as speech that does no more than propose a commercial transaction"). That definition would presumably apply to advertisements displayed by a search engine, and might even apply to "search results shown to purposefully advance an internal commercial interest of the search provider." Ballanco, *supra*, at 90 (arguing that such results "should be classified as commercial speech and, therefore, subject to less First Amendment protection"); *see also* Volokh & Falk, *supra*, at 885 (implicitly acknowledging that paid advertisements may be entitled to less protection under the First Amendment than "search results for which no payment has been made"). But that definition plainly does not apply to the search results at issue in this case, which relate to matters of public concern and do not themselves propose transactions. And, of course, the fact that Baidu has a "profit motive" does not deprive it of the right to free speech any more than the profit motives of the newspapers in *Tornillo* and *New York Times* did.

In short, Plaintiffs' efforts to hold Baidu accountable in a court of law for its editorial judgments about what political ideas to promote cannot be squared with the First Amendment. There is no irony in holding that Baidu's alleged decision to disfavor speech concerning democracy is itself protected by the democratic ideal of free speech. As the Supreme Court has explained, "[t]he First Amendment does not guarantee that . . . concepts virtually sacred to our Nation as a whole . . . will go unquestioned in the marketplace of ideas." *Texas v. Johnson*, 491 U.S. 397, 418 (1989). For that reason, the First Amendment protects Baidu's right to advocate for systems of government other than democracy (in China or elsewhere) just as surely as it protects Plaintiffs' rights to advocate for democracy. Indeed, "[i]f there is a bedrock principle underlying the First Amendment, it is that the government may not prohibit the expression of an idea simply because society finds the idea itself offensive or disagreeable." *Id.* at 414. Thus, the Court's decision – that Baidu's choice not to feature "pro-democracy political speech" is protected by the First Amendment – is itself "a reaffirmation of the principles of freedom and inclusiveness that [democracy] best reflects, and of the conviction that our toleration of criticism . . . is a sign and source of our strength." *Id.* at 419.

QUESTIONS

1. What do you want when you use a search engine? Are Baidu's editorial policies good for users or bad for users? Or is that the wrong question?

2. What do you make of the court's suggestion in footnote 4 that the result might be different if Baidu lied about how it ranked websites? Does that undermine the entire basis of the decision? Or does it just encourage plaintiffs to engage in another round of futile pleading? *Search King*, cited in *Zhang*, dismissed a tortious interference with contract suit against Google because search results are "subjective opinions" rather than "objectively verifiable fact[s]." Is that right? Aren't search algorithms precise and objective?

3. Closely related to the question of how search engines rank websites is the question of whether they must disclose how they rank websites. What would be the advantages and disadvantages of requiring Baidu to disclose its algorithms? Would it raise any First Amendment issues?

WIKILEAKS PROBLEM

In November 2010, the website WikiLeaks began releasing an archive of roughly 250,000 classified diplomatic cables sent by various United States embassies. Sources inside the United States government with access to the cables made copies and gave them to WikiLeaks. The cables contain a mixture of routine, sensitive, and embarrassing diplomatic chatter – they show the unguarded thoughts of American diplomats. For example, one cable calls Russian President Dmitri Medvedev "Robin to [Vladimir] Putin's Batman." Another reports that North Korean officials asked their American counterparts to arrange an Eric Clapton concert in Pyongyang as a show of good will, as one of the sons of dictator Kim Jong-il is a "great fan." WikiLeaks works by giving the cables to newspapers; when the newspapers report on specific cables, WikiLeaks then posts the full text of those cables to its website.

The legal status of WikiLeaks under United States law is deeply unclear. The Espionage Act of 1917, 18 U.S.C. ch. 37, makes it a crime to "knowingly and willfully ... publish ... any classified information," or to communicate certain national defense information to anyone not authorized to possess it, but its constitutionality is uncertain in light of the First Amendment. No one who merely received classified information and distributed it has been successfully prosecuted under the Act. Cases have mostly been brought against agents of foreign governments or United States officials who gave those agents information. Members of the press have never been successfully prosecuted for publishing classified information leaked to them by government officials.

Nonetheless, members of the executive and legislative branches of the federal government are furious at WikiLeaks and its most prominent public face, cofounder Julian Assange. Attorney General Eric Holder has announced that the Justice Department is investigating possible violations of the Espionage Act; several members of Congress have called for new legislation in the event that the Espionage Act is not sufficient to prosecute Assange. Senator Joseph Lieberman has also suggested that newspapers, such as the *New York Times*, which have reported on WikiLeaks cables could perhaps face prosecution. He has also stated publicly that Americans and American companies should avoid any cooperation with WikiLeaks: "I call on any other company or organization that is hosting WikiLeaks to immediately terminate its relationship with them." Multiple companies did just that. For example:

- WikiLeaks had been hosted on servers supplied by Amazon's Elastic Compute Cloud service, which supplies as much storage and bandwidth as needed. Amazon explained that WikiLeaks violated its terms of service, which required customers to promise that they "own or otherwise control all of the rights to the content" they posted and that the content "will not cause injury to any person or entity."

- WikiLeaks's domain-name services were provided by EveryDNS, a free service that relies on donations. EveryDNS explained that WikiLeaks violated its terms of service, which required users not to "interfere with another Member's use and enjoyment of the Service." Specifically, EveryDNS claimed that WikiLeaks had become the target of massive denial-of-service attacks, which were threatening the stability of the EveryDNS servers and their ability to provide service to the other 500,000 websites served by WikiLeaks.

- PayPal froze the account used by WikiLeaks to receive donations, including funds currently in the account. PayPal explained that WikiLeaks violated its terms of service, which prohibited, in PayPal's summary, "any activities that encourage, promote, facilitate or instruct others to engage in illegal activity."[1]

WikiLeaks has moved its website to a new URL, wikileaks.ch, has found new hosting providers in Europe (including in a former nuclear bunker dug out of a mountainside), and has set up new channels for receiving donations.

Does WikiLeaks have any legal grounds to object to what Amazon, EveryDNS, and PayPal have done? What are its long-term prospects for remaining online?

---

1 PayPal's actual Acceptable Use Policy is slightly different. It prohibits "activities that violate any law, statute, ordinance, or regulation," and "activities that ... relate to sales of ... items that encourage, promote, facilitate or instruct others to engage in illegal activity." Does the difference matter?

CURRENC PROBLEM

You are General Counsel and Senior Vice President of Compliance and Regulatory Affairs at CurrenC, a citizen-journalism website. Users post raw video and photographs that they have taken of breaking events, along with written, audio, and visual news reports that they have created themselves. The site then offers extensive tools for other users to annotate, excerpt, and embed each others' reporting in creating customized news feeds. The site has seen explosive growth due to recent events worldwide, including the multiple revolutions in the the Middle East and natural disasters such as the Japanese earthquake of March 2011. You have have 25,000 active users, in 43 countries, and over two million unique daily visitors. They are uploading nearly 1,000 hours of video and 10,000 still images a day.

You also have a problem: the site's sudden popularity has made it a magnet for all kinds of chaos and abuse. Some users are taking advantage of the site's easy tools to upload and edit pornographic movies. Others are posting content that is illegal in one or more countries, such as anti-Semitic videos (illegal in many European countries) and videos of demonstrations in Arab countries (often banned by the local regimes). Users are complaining about low-quality images and about reports on subjects they consider offensive – everything from coming-out documentaries to anti-American sermons by Yemeni clerics to cartoon animations portraying the Thai royal family as roadkill. They have taken to posting negative comments about the content they dislike, complaining to local authorities and occasionally trying to launch denial-of-service attacks on the CurrenC website. You are now receiving upwards of three dozen complaints a day from law enforcement agencies in various countries, and the number appears to be spiking upward quickly.

The old compliance and review system, under which you and the two attorneys, who report to you personally, examined each complaint and law-enforcement request and made a case-by-case determination of what to do, is collapsing. The CEO has asked you to design a new system. She has indicated that she will authorize you to engage in significant hiring if you can present a convincing strategy for how CurrenC will monitor the content of users' uploads and respond to complaints.

Design a strategy to minimize the business and regulatory issues faced by CurrenC while maximizing user satisfaction and positive impact on the world. Be sure to consider:

- who you will employ, how they will respond to complaints;
- what authority they have;
- how much individual discretion they will have;
- how you will oversee their work; and
- how you will develop policies for various kinds of common cases.

SPAM POSSE PROBLEM

SpamPosse.org is a non-profit coalition of system administrators who are annoyed by spam – *really* annoyed. Email providers who discover that an ISP is consistently sending them large volumes of spam send a report to SpamPosse. When SpamPosse receives enough reports about an ISP, it puts the ISP on its "Wanted" list, together with some summary statistics (number of reports, total estimated volume of spam, etc.). Individual email providers can download the Wanted list; many of them have configured their servers so that all email coming from an ISP on the list is automatically rejected.

Being put on SpamPosse's Wanted list can be, for obvious reasons, incredibly damaging to an ISP. Not only will the spammers rapidly desert it for another ISP where they can send spam that is more likely to get through, but other customers will discover that their emails are bouncing. In many cases, they have no idea that their emails have been rejected at all; in others, they know that the emails aren't getting through, but can't easily find out why. If an ISP is put on the list, its business is likely to suffer severely. From the perspective of some of SpamPosse's members, this is the point: it gives ISPs a real incentive to clean up their act and kick spammers off. Others just rely on it as a way of knowing where the major sources of spam on the Internet are, so they can defend themselves appropriately.

One ISP, Manhattan On-Line, has recently found itself on the SpamPosse Wanted list. It doesn't know why, or which of its customers are allegedly engaged in spamming. Emails and phone messages to SpamPosse have gone unanswered. This happened 36 hours ago, and the situation is looking increasingly dire. One corporate customer has already cancelled its service, and others are very angry.

The CEO of Manhattan On-Line, Franklin Ressler, has asked you to consider representing it in a suit against SpamPosse. The immediate goal would be a TRO ordering SpamPosse to take Manhattan On-Line off the Wanted list, to be followed ultimately by a permanent injunction and damages. Possible causes of action batted around include trade libel and interference with contractual relations.[*] What is your advice to Ressler? Is this a case worth bringing?

B. Antitrust

Antitrust law is doctrinally complex and heavily informed by economic analysis. Accordingly, this section will not attempt to provide a full treatment of the subject. Even a brief survey would fill multiple chapters. Instead, it gives the flavor of the questions facing courts in antitrust cases by focusing on a single legal theory – maintaining a monopoly through anticompetitive means – in a single context – the design of a software product.

NOTE ON ANTITRUST LAW AND ECONOMICS

The dominant modern theory of antitrust law is economic: competitive markets are more efficient. (There are other theories – for example, that competition promotes freedom, or that concentrated power is bad for democracy – but even they are partly informed by economic analysis.) And the basic economic intuition is simple, even if the details rapidly become complex.

Suppose that Alice and Bob sell widgets, which cost $2 a piece to make. If Alice sells her widgets for $9 and Bob sells his for $10, everyone will buy Alice's widgets and Bob will go out of business. So Bob cuts his price to $8, and now Alice has to match him or do better, and so it goes until both Alice and Bob are both selling widgets very close to their "marginal cost" of $2. If Alice charged less, she'd go out of business, because she'd be taking a loss on each widget. (Making it up on volume only works in jokes.) But if Alice and Bob meet for dinner in a fancy restau-

---

* If you are unfamiliar with these torts, consider looking them up. The Restatement might be a good place to start.

rant and agree that they will *both* charge $10, everything changes. Consumers who don't like Bob's prices can't get a better deal from Alice, and vice versa. Now, everyone who wants a widget has to pay $10, not $2. Alice and Bob have colluded to raise prices above their marginal costs.

This deal has two effects. First, it causes a *wealth transfer* from consumers to Alice and Bob. Wally pays $10 instead of $2 for his widget, leaving him $8 poorer and making either Alice (or Bob) $8 richer. In economic terms, Wally has $8 less in "consumer surplus" and Alice has $8 more in "producer surplus." Multiplied by thousands or millions of consumers, these numbers can add up fast. Being a monopolist is profitable.

Second, the deal *reduces output*. Wanda wants a widget, but she's only willing to pay $5 for it. (Maybe she only has $5, or maybe once the price goes up to $10 she decides she'd rather have a bedistor instead if it's going to cost that much.) She would have bought and enjoyed a widget at $2, but at $10 she says "no thanks." So fewer widgets change hands, which means that fewer people who would value having a widget have one. This is a "deadweight loss." Wally's $8 goes into Alice or Bob's pocket, but Wanda's lost value isn't compensated for by anyone's gain. Antitrust economists are generally indifferent to wealth transfers: there is no good reason to prefer Wally to Alice or to Bob since society has the $8 either way. But they are worried about deadweight losses, and would prefer to avoid them if possible.

Enter antitrust law. Alice and Bob's agreement violates Section 1 of the Sherman Antitrust Act:

> Every contract, combination in the form of trust or otherwise, or conspiracy, in restraint of trade or commerce among the several States, or with foreign nations, is declared to be illegal. ...

15 U.S.C. § 1. Blatant price-fixing schemes like Alice and Bob's sometimes happen in high-tech markets. For example, the CEOs of the five major book publishers in the United States agreed among themselves to use the launch of Apple's ebook store as an occasion for simultaneously changing the terms of their deals with Amazon. *U.S. v. Apple Inc.*, 952 F. Supp. 2d 638 (S.D.N.Y. 2013). More common, however, are subtler cases, often involving questionable conduct by a single firm rather than collusion among multiple firms. Many such cases (including the excerpted portions of *Microsoft* and *LiveUniverse* below) are decided under Section 2 of the Sherman Act:

> Every person who shall monopolize, or attempt to monopolize, or combine or conspire with any other person or persons, to monopolize any part of the trade or commerce among the several States, or with foreign nations, shall be deemed guilty of a felony ...

While straightforward price-fixing like Alice and Bob's is generally treated as *per se* illegal, many other kinds of potentially anticompetitive conduct are analyzed under a more forgiving "rule of reason," in which the court must compare the procompetitive benefits of the conduct with its anti-competitive costs. Examples include exclusive dealing (in which a firm requires its customers not to buy from its competitors) and vertical price restraints (in which a manufacturer restricts the prices its distributors can charge to consumers).

This basic story gets complicated quickly, even in "simple" Section 1 cases. For one thing, once Alice and Bob start raking in the cash, other companies will be tempted to get into the lucrative widget business, restoring competitive pricing.

For another, Alice and Bob will be tempted to cheat on their price-fixing deal, selling widgets at $9 on the side to take some of each others' customers away. And even when a firm has a monopoly, it may be for entirely legitimate reasons. Maybe Alice has a patent on an improved widget design, so Bob can't sell that design without infringing. Or maybe Bob has invested in an improved process that allows him to make widgets for $1 rather than $2, so Alice can't match his prices and won't try. As a result of these complications, and many others, antitrust economic analysis is a specialized and technical field, dominated by experts with subtle and intricate models, and extensive empirical surveys. Each theory of antitrust injury and liability requires its own analysis and has its own controversies. Intuition is not a reliable guide in all but the simplest settings.

The enforcement mechanisms of antitrust law are as complicated as its substantive doctrine. The Department of Justice can bring civil enforcement actions and prosecute criminal violations of the antitrust laws. Competitors harmed by violations of the antitrust laws are able to bring private suits, and receive trebled damages if they win. In addition, state attorney generals often have the power to bring antitrust actions on behalf of their states' citizens, and the Federal Trade Commission and Department of Justice have the power to review and to bring suit to block mergers if they would have anticompetitive effects.

UNITED STATES V. MICROSOFT CORP.

253 F.3d 34 (D.C. Cir. 2001) (*en banc*)

Per Curiam:

Microsoft Corporation appeals from judgments of the District Court finding the company in violation of §§ 1 and 2 of the Sherman Act and ordering various remedies.

The action against Microsoft arose pursuant to a complaint filed by the United States and separate complaints filed by individual States. The District Court determined that Microsoft had maintained a monopoly in the market for Intel compatible PC operating systems in violation of § 2 ... and illegally tied two purportedly separate products, Windows and Internet Explorer ("IE") ...

II. MONOPOLIZATION

Section 2 of the Sherman Act makes it unlawful for a firm to "monopolize." 15 U.S.C. § 2. The offense of monopolization has two elements: "(1) the possession of monopoly power in the relevant market and (2) the willful acquisition or maintenance of that power as distinguished from growth or development as a consequence of a superior product, business acumen, or historic accident." *United States v. Grinnell Corp.*, 384 U.S. 563, 570–71 (1966). The District Court applied this test and found that Microsoft possesses monopoly power in the market for Intel-compatible PC operating systems. Focusing primarily on Microsoft's efforts to suppress Netscape Navigator's threat to its operating system monopoly, the court also found that Microsoft maintained its power not through competition on the merits, but through unlawful means. Microsoft challenges both conclusions. We defer to the District Court's findings of fact, setting them aside only if clearly erroneous.

We begin by considering whether Microsoft possesses monopoly power, *see infra* Section II.A, and finding that it does, we turn to the question whether it maintained this power through anticompetitive means. Agreeing with the District Court that the company behaved anticompetitively, and that these actions contributed to the maintenance of its monopoly power, we affirm the court's finding of liability for monopolization.

A. Monopoly Power

While merely possessing monopoly power is not itself an antitrust violation, it is a necessary element of a monopolization charge. The Supreme Court defines monopoly power as "the power to control prices or exclude competition." *United Statesv. E.I. du Pont de Nemours & Co.*, 351 U.S. 377, 391 (1956). More precisely, a firm is a monopolist if it can profitably raise prices substantially above the competitive level. Where evidence indicates that a firm has in fact profitably done so, the existence of monopoly power is clear. Because such direct proof is only rarely available, courts more typically examine market structure in search of circumstantial evidence of monopoly power. Under this structural approach, monopoly power may be inferred from a firm's possession of a dominant share of a relevant market that is protected by entry barriers. "Entry barriers" are factors (such as certain regulatory requirements) that prevent new rivals from timely responding to an increase in price above the competitive level.

The District Court considered these structural factors and concluded that Microsoft possesses monopoly power in a relevant market. Defining the market as Intel-compatible PC operating systems, the District Court found that Microsoft has a greater than 95% share. It also found the company's market position protected by a substantial entry barrier. ...

b. Market power ...

Instead, Microsoft claims that even a predominant market share does not by itself indicate monopoly power. Although the "existence of [monopoly] power ordinarily may be inferred from the predominant share of the market," *Grinnell*, 384 U.S. at 571, we agree with Microsoft that because of the possibility of competition from new entrants, *see Ball Mem'l Hosp., Inc.*, 784 F.2d at 1336, looking to current market share alone can be "misleading." *Hunt-Wesson Foods, Inc. v. Ragu Foods, Inc.*, 627 F.2d 919, 924 (9th Cir. 1980); *see also Ball Mem'l Hosp., Inc.*, 784 F.2d at 1336 ("Market share reflects current sales, but today's sales do not always indicate power over sales and price tomorrow.") In this case, however, the District Court was not misled. Considering the possibility of new rivals, the court focused not only on Microsoft's present market share, but also on the structural barrier that protects the company's future position. That barrier – the "applications barrier to entry" – stems from two characteristics of the software market: (1) most consumers prefer operating systems for which a large number of applications have already been written; and (2) most developers prefer to write for operating systems that already have a substantial consumer base. This "chicken-and-egg" situation ensures that applications will continue to be written for the already dominant Windows, which in turn ensures that consumers will continue to prefer it over other operating systems.

Challenging the existence of the applications barrier to entry, Microsoft observes that software developers do write applications for other operating systems, pointing out that at its peak IBM's OS/2 supported approximately 2,500 applications. This misses the point. That some developers write applications for other operating systems is not at all inconsistent with the finding that the applications barrier to entry discourages many from writing for these less popular platforms. Indeed, the District Court found that IBM's difficulty in attracting a larger number of software developers to write for its platform seriously impeded OS/2's success.

Microsoft does not dispute that Windows supports many more applications than any other operating system. It argues instead that "[i]t defies common sense" to suggest that an operating system must support as many applications as Windows does (more than 70,000, according to the District Court) to be competitive. Consumers, Microsoft points out, can only use a very small percentage of these applications. As the District Court explained, however, the applications barrier to entry gives consumers reason to prefer the dominant operating system even if they have no need to use all applications written for it:

> The consumer wants an operating system that runs not only types of applications that he knows he will want to use, but also those types in which he might develop an interest later. Also, the consumer knows that if he chooses an operating system with enough demand to support multiple applications in each product category, he will be less likely to find himself straitened later by having to use an application whose features disappoint him. Finally, the average user knows that, generally speaking, applications improve through successive versions. He thus wants an operating system for which successive generations of his favorite applications will be released – promptly at that. The fact that a vastly larger number of applications are written for Windows than for other PC operating systems attracts consumers to Windows, because it reassures them that their interests will be met as long as they use Microsoft's product.

Thus, despite the limited success of its rivals, Microsoft benefits from the applications barrier to entry. ...

Microsoft next argues that the applications barrier to entry is not an entry barrier at all, but a reflection of Windows' popularity. It is certainly true that Windows may have gained its initial dominance in the operating system market competitively – through superior foresight or quality. But this case is not about Microsoft's initial acquisition of monopoly power. It is about Microsoft's efforts to maintain this position through means other than competition on the merits. Because the applications barrier to entry protects a dominant operating system irrespective of quality, it gives Microsoft power to stave off even superior new rivals. The barrier is thus a characteristic of the operating system market, not of Microsoft's popularity, or, as asserted by a Microsoft witness, the company's efficiency. ...

B. Anticompetitive Conduct

As discussed above, having a monopoly does not by itself violate § 2. A firm violates § 2 only when it acquires or maintains, or attempts to acquire or maintain, a monopoly by engaging in exclusionary conduct "as distinguished from growth or development as a consequence of a superior product, business acumen, or historic accident." *Grinnell*, 384 U.S. at 571; *see also United States v. Aluminum Co. of Am.*, 148 F.2d 416, 430 (2d Cir. 1945) (Hand, J.) ("The successful competitor, having been urged to compete, must not be turned upon when he wins."). ...

Whether any particular act of a monopolist is exclusionary, rather than merely a form of vigorous competition, can be difficult to discern: the means of illicit exclusion, like the means of legitimate competition, are myriad. The challenge for an antitrust court lies in stating a general rule for distinguishing between exclusionary acts, which reduce social welfare, and competitive acts, which increase it.

From a century of case law on monopolization under § 2, however, several principles do emerge. First, to be condemned as exclusionary, a monopolist's act must have an "anticompetitive effect." That is, it must harm the competitive *process* and thereby harm consumers. In contrast, harm to one or more *competitors* will not suffice. "The [Sherman Act] directs itself not against conduct which is competitive, even severely so, but against conduct which unfairly tends to destroy competition itself." *Spectrum Sports, Inc. v. McQuillan*, 506 U.S. 447, 458 (1993); *see also Brooke Group Ltd. v. Brown & Williamson Tobacco Corp.*, 509 U.S. 209, 225 (1993) ("Even an act of pure malice by one business competitor against another does not, without more, state a claim under the federal antitrust laws. . . .").

Second, the plaintiff, on whom the burden of proof of course rests, must demonstrate that the monopolist's conduct indeed has the requisite anticompetitive effect. ...

Third, if a plaintiff successfully establishes a prima facie case under § 2 by demonstrating anticompetitive effect, then the monopolist may proffer a "procompetitive justification" for its conduct. If the monopolist asserts a procompetitive justification – a nonpretextual claim that its conduct is indeed a form of competition on the merits because it involves, for example, greater efficiency or enhanced consumer appeal – then the burden shifts back to the plaintiff to rebut that claim.

Fourth, if the monopolist's pro-competitive justification stands unrebutted, then the plaintiff must demonstrate that the anticompetitive harm of the conduct outweighs the procompetitive benefit. ...

Finally, in considering whether the monopolist's conduct on balance harms competition and is therefore condemned as exclusionary for purposes of § 2, our focus is upon the effect of that conduct, not upon the intent behind it. Evidence of the intent behind the conduct of a monopolist is relevant only to the extent it helps us understand the likely effect of the monopolist's conduct. ...

1. Licenses Issued to Original Equipment Manufacturers

The District Court condemned a number of provisions in Microsoft's agreements licensing Windows to OEMs, because it found that Microsoft's imposition of those provisions (like many of Microsoft's other actions at issue in this case) serves to reduce usage share of Netscape's browser and, hence, protect Microsoft's operating system monopoly. ...

If a consumer could have access to the applications he desired – regardless of the operating system he uses – simply by installing a particular browser on his computer, then he would no longer feel compelled to select Windows in order to have access to those applications; he could select an operating system other than Windows based solely upon its quality and price. In other words, the market for operating systems would be competitive.

Therefore, Microsoft's efforts to gain market share in one market (browsers) served to meet the threat to Microsoft's monopoly in another market (operating systems) by keeping rival browsers from gaining the critical mass of users necessary to attract developer attention away from Windows as the platform for software development. ...

a. Anticompetitive effect of the license restrictions

The restrictions Microsoft places upon Original Equipment Manufacturers are of particular importance in determining browser usage share because having an OEM pre-install a browser on a computer is one of the two most cost-effective methods by far of distributing browsing software. ... The District Court found that the restrictions Microsoft imposed in licensing Windows to OEMs prevented many OEMs from distributing browsers other than IE. In particular, the District

Court condemned the license provisions prohibiting the OEMs from: (1) removing any desktop icons, folders, or "Start" menu entries; (2) altering the initial boot sequence; and (3) otherwise altering the appearance of the Windows desktop.

The District Court concluded that the first license restriction – the prohibition upon the removal of desktop icons, folders, and Start menu entries – thwarts the distribution of a rival browser by preventing OEMs from removing visible means of user access to IE. The OEMs cannot practically install a second browser in addition to IE, the court found, in part because "[p]re-installing more than one product in a given category . . . can significantly increase an OEM's support costs, for the redundancy can lead to confusion among novice users." That is, a certain number of novice computer users, seeing two browser icons, will wonder which to use when and will call the OEM's support line. Support calls are extremely expensive and, in the highly competitive original equipment market, firms have a strong incentive to minimize costs....

The second license provision at issue prohibits OEMs from modifying the initial boot sequence – the process that occurs the first time a consumer turns on the computer. Prior to the imposition of that restriction, "among the programs that many OEMs inserted into the boot sequence were Internet sign-up procedures that encouraged users to choose from a list of IAPs [Internet Access Providers, such as AOL] assembled by the OEM." Microsoft's prohibition on any alteration of the boot sequence thus prevents OEMs from using that process to promote the services of IAPs, many of which – at least at the time Microsoft imposed the restriction – used Navigator rather than IE in their internet access software. (Upon learning of OEM practices including boot sequence modification, Microsoft's Chairman, Bill Gates, wrote: "Apparently a lot of OEMs are bundling non-Microsoft browsers and coming up with offerings together with [IAPs] that get displayed on their machines in a FAR more prominent way than MSN or our Internet browser.") Microsoft does not deny that the prohibition on modifying the boot sequence has the effect of decreasing competition against IE by preventing OEMs from promoting rivals' browsers. Because this prohibition has a substantial effect in protecting Microsoft's market power, and does so through a means other than competition on the merits, it is anticompetitive. Again the question whether the provision is nonetheless justified awaits later treatment.

Finally, Microsoft imposes several additional provisions that, like the prohibition on removal of icons, prevent OEMs from making various alterations to the desktop: Microsoft prohibits OEMs from causing any user interface other than the Windows desktop to launch automatically, from adding icons or folders different in size or shape from those supplied byMicrosoft, and from using the "Active Desktop" feature to promote third-party brands. These restrictions impose significant costs upon the OEMs; prior to Microsoft's prohibiting the practice, many OEMs would change the appearance of the desktop in ways they found beneficial. (March 1997 letter from Hewlett-Packard to Microsoft: "We are responsible for the cost of technical support of our customers, including the 33% of calls we get related to the lack of quality or confusion generated by your product. . . . We must have more ability to decide how our system is presented to our end users. If we had a choice of another supplier, based on your actions in this area, I assure you [that you] would not be our supplier of choice."). ...

b. Microsoft's justifications for the license restrictions

Microsoft argues that the license restrictions are legally justified because, in imposing them, Microsoft is simply "exercising its rights as the holder of valid copyrights." Microsoft also argues that the licenses "do not unduly restrict the opportunities of Netscape to distribute Navigator in any event."

Microsoft's primary copyright argument borders upon the frivolous. The company claims an absolute and unfettered right to use its intellectual property as it wishes: "[I]f intellectual property rights have been lawfully acquired," it says, then "their subsequent exercise cannot give rise to antitrust liability." That is no more correct than the proposition that use of one's personal property, such as a baseball bat, cannot give rise to tort liability. As the Federal Circuit succinctly stated: "Intellectual property rights do not confer a privilege to violate the antitrust laws." *In re Indep. Serv. Orgs. Antitrust Litig.*, 203 F.3d 1322, 1325 (Fed.Cir. 2000). ...

The only license restriction Microsoft seriously defends as necessary to prevent a "substantial alteration" of its copyrighted work is the prohibition on OEMs automatically launching a substitute user interface upon completion of the boot process. We agree that a shell that automatically prevents the Windows desktop from ever being seen by the user is a drastic alteration of Microsoft's copyrighted work, and outweighs the marginal anticompetitive effect of prohibiting the OEMs from substituting a different interface automatically upon completion of the initial boot process. We therefore hold that this particular restriction is not an exclusionary practice that violates § 2 of the Sherman Act. ...

Apart from copyright, Microsoft raises one other defense of the OEM license agreements: It argues that, despite the restrictions in the OEM license, Netscape is not completely blocked from distributing its product. That claim is insufficient to shield Microsoft from liability for those restrictions because, although Microsoft did not bar its rivals from all means of distribution, it did bar them from the cost-efficient ones. ...

2. Integration of IE and Windows

Although Microsoft's license restrictions have a significant effect in closing rival browsers out of one of the two primary channels of distribution, the District Court found that "Microsoft's executives believed . . . its contractual restrictions placed on OEMs would not be sufficient in themselves to reverse the direction of Navigator's usage share. Consequently, in late 1995 or early 1996, Microsoft set out to bind [IE] more tightly to Windows 95 as a technical matter."

Technologically binding IE to Windows, the District Court found, both prevented OEMs from pre-installing other browsers and deterred consumers from using them. In particular, having the IE software code as an irremovable part of Windows meant that pre-installing a second browser would "increase an OEM's product testing costs," because an OEM must test and train its support staff to answer calls related to every software product preinstalled on the machine; moreover, pre-installing a browser in addition to IE would to many OEMs be "a questionable use of the scarce and valuable space on a PC's hard drive." ...

As with the license restrictions, we consider first whether the suspect actions had an anticompetitive effect, and then whether Microsoft has provided a pro-competitive justification for them.

a. Anticompetitive effect of integration

As a general rule, courts are properly very skeptical about claims that competition has been harmed by a dominant firm's product design changes. *See, e.g., Foremost Pro Color, Inc. v. Eastman Kodak Co.*, 703 F.2d 534, 544–45 (9th Cir. 1983). In a competitive market, firms routinely innovate in the hope of appealing to consumers, sometimes in the process making their products incompatible with those of rivals; the imposition of liability when a monopolist does the same thing will inevitably deter a certain amount of innovation. This is all the more true in a market, such as this one, in which the product itself is rapidly changing. Judicial deference to product innovation, however, does not mean that a monopolist's product design decisions are per se lawful.

The District Court first condemned as anticompetitive Microsoft's decision to exclude IE from the "Add/Remove Programs" utility in Windows 98. Microsoft had included IE in the Add/Remove Programs utility in Windows 95, but when it modified Windows 95 to produce Windows 98, it took IE out of the Add/Remove Programs utility. This change reduces the usage share of rival browsers not by making Microsoft's own browser more attractive to consumers but, rather, by discouraging OEMs from distributing rival products. Because Microsoft's conduct, through something other than competition on the merits, has the effect of significantly reducing usage of rivals' products and hence protecting its own operating system monopoly, it is anticompetitive; we defer for the moment the question whether it is nonetheless justified. ...

Finally, the District Court condemned Microsoft's decision to bind IE to Windows 98 "by placing code specific to Web browsing in the same files as code that provided operating system functions." Putting code supplying browsing functionality into a file with code supplying operating system functionality "ensure[s] that the deletion of any file containing browsing-specific routines would also delete vital operating system routines and thus cripple Windows. . . ." As noted above, preventing an OEM from removing IE deters it from installing a second browser because doing so increases the OEM's product testing and support costs; by contrast, had OEMs been able to remove IE, they might have chosen to pre-install Navigator alone. ...

b. Microsoft's justifications for integration

Microsoft proffers no justification for two of the three challenged actions that it took in integrating IE into Windows – excluding IE from the Add/Remove Programs utility and commingling browser and operating system code. Although Microsoft does make some general claims regarding the benefits of integrating the browser and the operating system, it neither specifies nor substantiates those claims. Nor does it argue that either excluding IE from the Add/Remove Programs utility or commingling code achieves any integrative benefit. Plaintiffs plainly made out a prima facie case of harm to competition in the operating system market by demonstrating that Microsoft's actions increased its browser usage share and thus protected its operating system monopoly from a middleware threat and, for its part, Microsoft failed to meet its burden of showing that its conduct serves a purpose other than protecting its operating system monopoly. Accordingly, we hold that Microsoft's exclusion of IE from the Add/Remove Programs utility and its commingling of browser and operating system code constitute exclusionary conduct, in violation of § 2. ...

QUESTIONS

1. During the relevant period, both browsers – Netscape Navigator and Internet Explorer – were free to users. Why was Microsoft so insistent on promoting a product that was generating essentially no revenue?

2. What, precisely, was the threat to consumers posed by Microsoft's actions?

3. What did Microsoft do to pressure OEMs (computer manufacturers like Dell and HP) to install IE and not to install Navigator? What did Microsoft do to give IE a technical advantage over Navigator? Are you convinced by the court's analysis of whether these tactics had anticompetitive effects and legitimate justifications?

4. What operating systems do you and people you know use on a regular basis? What browsers do you use? Does antitrust law seem like it is doing a good job in these markets?

5. Antitrust doctrine requires courts to make complex technological findings of fact in computer and Internet antitrust cases. How confident are you that they'll get these findings right? Would the DoJ and FTC be better or worse at this task?

6. How accurate were Microsoft's fears of a world in which the browser matters more than the operating system? Has the rise of Internet-based email and document editing systems, like Hotmail and Google Docs, changed the nature of the competitive game? What about the rise of Internet-connected devices like the Playstation and the iPhone?

LIVEUNIVERSE, INC. V. MYSPACE, INC.
No. CV 06-6994-AHM (RZx),
2007 U.S. Dist LEXIS 43739, 2007 WL 6865852 (N.D. Cal. June 4, 2007),
aff'd, 304 Fed. Appx. 554 (9th Cir. 2008)

Matz, District Judge:

I. INTRODUCTION

Plaintiff LiveUniverse, Inc. ("LiveUniverse") and Defendant MySpace, Inc. ("MySpace") operate online "social networking" websites at www.vidilife.com and www.myspace.com, respectively. Social networking websites allow visitors to create personal profiles containing text, graphics, and videos, as well as to view profiles of their friends and other users with similar interests. LiveUniverse alleges that MySpace prevents users from watching vidiLife videos that they or other users previously loaded onto their MySpace webpage, deletes references to "vidilife.com" on MySpace, and prevents MySpace users from mentioning "vidilife.com."
...

On January 16, 2007, LiveUniverse filed a First Amended Complaint ("FAC") that again alleges that MySpace's conduct violates Section 2 of the Sherman Act and Cal. Bus. & Prof. Code § 17200. ...

II. GENERAL PRINCIPLES

On a motion to dismiss pursuant to Rule 12(b)(6) of the Federal Rules of Civil Procedure for failure to state a claim, the allegations of the complaint must be accepted as true and are to be construed in the light most favorable to the nonmoving party. ...

Section 2 of the Sherman Antitrust Act states: "Every person who shall monopolize, or attempt to monopolize, or combine or conspire with any other person or persons, to monopolize any part of the trade or commerce among the several States, or with foreign nations, shall be deemed guilty of a felony . . ." 15 U.S.C. § 2.
...

The elements of a monopolization claim are: (1) possession of monopoly power in the relevant market; (2) "the willful acquisition or maintenance of that power as distinguished from growth or development as a consequence of a superior product, business acumen, or historic accident;" and (3) causal antitrust injury. *Eastman Kodak Co. v. Image Technical Services, Inc.*, 504 U.S. 451, 481 (1992) (internal citations omitted); . ...

III. "MONOPOLIZATION" ALLEGATIONS IN MARKET CONSISTING OF "INTERNET-BASED SOCIAL NETWORKING SITES"

A. Relevant Market ...

The FAC defines the first relevant market as "Internet-based social networking in the geographic region of the United States." ...

The FAC also alleges that:

> Social networking websites offer a set of unique products and services that competing media cannot offer. The interactive, user-generated aspects of Internet-based social networking offer consumers an unprecedented degree of control over their experience, allowing them to collectively determine both the content and structure of networks of friends that they and others create. Passive internet media sites and other communication products such as e-mail do not possess these organic, interactive qualities. ...

LiveUniverse's allegation that the proposed market is unique is not conclusory; it alleges that the market has "unique products and services" and that the "interactive, user-generated aspects" give users "an unprecedented degree of control over their experience, allowing them to collectively determine both the content and structure of networks of friends that they and others create." The FAC also alleges that because other websites and means of communication, such as e-mail, do not contain these "organic, interactive qualities," they are not reasonably interchangeable substitutes for Internet-based social networking websites. MySpace nevertheless argues that even these allegations are insufficient, because they do not "distinguish online dating sites and Internet connectivity services like America Online." The Court disagrees. Internet connectivity services are not reasonable substitutes, because their primary function is simply to give users the ability to access the Internet. As to online dating sites, although they do have similar "organic, interactive qualities" to social networking websites, their dominant function and purpose is to enable users to meet potential dates. Online dating sites are not reasonable substitutes for social networking websites, because the latter websites have significantly more functions and appeal than do online dating sites. For example, social networking websites are used to get in touch with old friends and to keep current friends informed about what's new and exciting. Although social networking websites may also be used for dating, if MySpace suddenly were to shut down, its members would not fill the social void by turning to online dating sites. Instead, they would likely set up profiles on a different social networking website.

For the foregoing reasons, the Court finds that LiveUniverse sufficiently alleges a relevant antitrust market of Internet-based social networking websites.

B. Monopoly Power

"Monopoly power is the power to control prices or exclude competition." *du Pont*, 351 U.S. at 391. It may be demonstrated through either direct evidence or circumstantial evidence. LiveUniverse alleges that MySpace's market power may be inferred from its having a dominant share of the market (social networking websites) and from its being protected from competition by entry barriers. This requires that plaintiff: "(1) define the relevant market, (2) show that the defendant owns a dominant share of that market, and (3) show that there are significant barriers to entry and show that existing competitors lack the capacity to increase their output in the short run." *Id.* (internal citations omitted).

1. LiveUniverse Adequately Alleges That Myspace Owns The Dominant Share of the Market

The FAC alleges that "[a]ccording to comScore Media Metrix, a leading Internet traffic measurement service, approximately 55.8 million of the more than 62.7 million individuals who frequented social networking sites in the United States in September 2006 visited MySpace, equal to 89% of the market." "According to Hitwise, another leading Internet traffic measurement service, in September 2006, MySpace accounted for nearly '82% of visits to the leading social networking websites. . . .'"

Courts have consistently found that an 80 percent share of the market constitutes a dominant share, with the Supreme Court having found that even a two-thirds share of the market can be considered dominant. ...

2. Live Universe Adequately Alleges Barriers to Entry

"A mere showing of substantial or even dominant market share alone cannot establish market power sufficient [for an antitrust violation]. The plaintiff must show that new rivals are barred from entering the market and show that existing competitors lack the capacity to expand their output to challenge the [market leader's anticompetitive conduct]." *Rebel Oil*, 51 F.3d at 1439. LiveUniverse's allegations of barriers to entry are based on the concept of "network effects" in the market for Internet-based social networking websites.

In *Microsoft, supra*, the D.C. Circuit Court of Appeals characterized "network effects" as follows: "In markets characterized by network effects, one product or standard tends towards dominance, because the utility that a user derives from consumption of the good increases with the number of other agents consuming the good." For example, an individual consumer's demand for and benefit from a telephone network increases if there are more people using that network whom the consumer can call or from whom she can receive calls. *Id.* "Once a product or standard achieves wide acceptance, it becomes more or less entrenched. Competition in such industries is 'for the field' rather than 'within the field.'" *Id.*

The FAC alleges that in the market for Internet-based social networking websites, network effects occur largely due to the "user-generated nature" of the content on those websites. Quoting the Hitwise Report, the FAC alleges that "[t]he network effect in relation to social networking websites means that the more people use a website by adding profiles and content, the more valuable it becomes to each of its users. These users will be more likely to find content that interests them and connect with people they know. Thus more new people want to join it because they know they can be further assured of finding friends and interesting content." Based on these network effects, LiveUniverse alleges that it is "difficult for new entrants to acquire any more than a very small market share without an enormous capital investment." ...

MySpace does not dispute that the phenomenon of network effects applies to the proposed market of Internet-based social networking websites. Instead, it argues that LiveUniverse fails to allege how these network effects result in barriers to entry in the relevant market. It stresses that the *Microsoft* court cautioned that "[s]imply invoking the phrase 'network effects' without pointing to more evidence does not suffice to carry plaintiffs' burden in this respect."

The Court rejects MySpace's contention on this point; the allegations of barriers to entry in the FAC are adequate, ... in addition to alleging "network effects," LiveUniverse alleges other characteristics of the market that combine with network effects to create barriers to entry. Quoting the Hitwise Report, for example, the FAC alleges that social networking websites rely on users to create profiles and content that, in turn, attract new users and visitors. Just as the *Microsoft* court noted that an operating system requires developers to write applications for it, *Microsoft*, 253 F.3d at 55, social networking websites require a large number of profiles, content, and potential friends. Just as "most developers prefer to write for operating systems that already have a substantial consumer base," *Microsoft*, 253 F.3d at 55, users of social networking websites prefer to create their profiles and add content to a website where they are likely to be viewed by a greater number of users.

MySpace goes on to argue that notwithstanding "network effects," the dynamic nature of the market and the constant entry and exit of competitors undermine plaintiff's allegations about barriers to entry. It contends that "anyone with a computer and Internet access can start his or her own network and . . . there is no limit (other than time) to the number of websites a user can access." There is some merit to this argument. MySpace itself quickly overtook the former market leader, Friendster, despite the same alleged barriers to entry in the market. In addition, as the Hitwise Report points out, four social networking websites experienced market growth that outpaced the category between March and September 2006. Moreover, social networking websites with special niches have shown the capacity to compete with MySpace. For example, Facebook became the preferred network among college students, because it was closed to non-students and thus appeared safer than MySpace. (According to the Hitwise Report, Facebook has the second highest market share among social networking websites.). Furthermore, at the March 5, 2007 hearing, this Court mentioned a then-recent New York Times article stating that "[s]ocial networks are sprouting on the Internet these days like wild mushrooms." Brad Stone, *Social Networking's Next Phase*, N.Y. Times, March 3, 2007, at B 1, B9 [hereinafter "Social Networking's Next Phase"].

Although the fluidity that currently characterizes this industry does beg the question as to just how long MySpace can retain its market power, that there are many new entrants does not necessarily mean that LiveUniverse's allegations about barriers to entry are deficient. "The fact that entry has occurred does not necessarily preclude the existence of 'significant' entry barriers. If the output or capacity of the new entrant is insufficient to take significant business away from the [monopolist], they are unlikely to represent a challenge to the [monopolist's] market power." *Rebel Oil*, 51 F.3d at 1440 (internal citations omitted). The article "Social Networking's Next Phase" itself notes that although there are many new social networking websites entering the market, at least some of the new entrants are finding it difficult to attract users when there are only a relatively few other members at the outset. *Social Networking's Next Phase*, at 89. For example, Google helped Nike design a soccer community site, but the site "does not appear to have significantly attracted users." *Id.* at B9. If two companies having the size, power and reputation of Google and Nike are encountering such difficulties, it is likely that other new entrants would, too. ...

For the foregoing reasons, the Court finds, LiveUniverse sufficiently alleges that MySpace has monopoly power in the relevant market.

C. Exclusionary Conduct

To establish monopolization, plaintiff must allege and prove that MySpace acquired or maintains monopoly power by engaging in exclusionary conduct, "as distinguished from growth or development as a consequence of a superior product, business acumen, or historic accident." *United States v. Grinnell Corp.*, 384 U.S. 563, 571 (1966). "The [Sherman Act] directs itself not against conduct which is competitive, even severely so, but against conduct which unfairly tends to destroy competition itself." *Spectrum Sports, Inc. v. McQuillan*, 506 U.S. 447, 458 (1993). "[T]o be condemned as exclusionary, a monopolist's act must have an 'anticompetitive effect.' That is, it must harm the competitive process and thereby harm consumers. In contrast, harm to one or more competitors will not suffice." *Microsoft*, 253 F.3d at 58.

LiveUniverse alleges that MySpace committed three anticompetitive acts. First, MySpace destroyed users' ability to load and display their vidiLife videos on the MySpace system by redesigning its platform so that "all links to vidiLife video content embedded by MySpace users in their online profiles no longer function." Second, MySpace deleted all references to "vidilife.com." Third, MySpace has blocked users not only from mentioning "vidiLife.com" on the MySpace system, but also from embedding links to the vidiLife website in their personal profiles. MySpace also has allegedly blocked users from using social networking services offered by stickam.com, another Internet-based social networking service, and it deleted all references to yet another social networking site, revver.com. ...

MySpace proffers several arguments why its conduct is not anticompetitive as a matter of law. The Court will deal with the two that are appropriate for determination on a motion to dismiss: First, that MySpace has the right to refuse to deal with a rival in the promotion of its own products and services, and second, that it has the right to prevent plaintiff from "free riding" off its investment and innovation.

1. Refusal to Deal and "Free Riding"

A company generally has a right to deal, or refuse to deal, with whomever it likes. As the Supreme Court stated in *Verizon Communications Inc. v. Law Offices of Curtis V. Trinko, LLP*, 540 U.S. 398, 407–08 (2004):

> Firms may acquire monopoly power by establishing an infrastructure that renders them uniquely suited to serve their customers. Compelling such firms to share the source of their advantage is in some tension with the underlying purpose of antitrust law, since it may lessen the incentive for the monopolist, the rival, or both to invest in those economically beneficial facilities. Enforced sharing also requires antitrust courts to act as central planners, identifying the proper price, quantity, and other terms of dealing-a role for which they are ill suited. Moreover, compelling negotiation between competitors may facilitate the supreme evil of antitrust: collusion. Thus, as a general matter, the Sherman Act "does not restrict the long recognized right of [a] trader or manufacturer engaged in an entirely private business, freely to exercise his own independent discretion as to parties with whom he will deal." ...

... MySpace also argues that it has a right to prevent LiveUniverse from "free-riding" on MySpace's investment in its own website. In *Olympia Equipment Leasing Co. v. Western Union Telegraph Co.*, 797 F.2d 370 (7th Cir. 1986), the plaintiff won a judgment in district court that the defendant violated Section 2 by changing its policies so that its sales force no longer referred customers to the plaintiff. In an opinion authored by Judge Posner, the Seventh Circuit reversed. *Id.* at 383. The opinion ... concluded that the plaintiff had no right under antitrust law to benefit from its competitor's sales force: "Advertising a competitor's products free of charge is not a form of cooperation commonly found in competitive markets; it is the antithesis of competition." *Id.* at 377–378.

MySpace's allegedly anticompetitive conduct is somewhat similar to the conduct that the court found permissible in *Olympia*. Social networking websites derive the bulk of their income from advertising displayed on their sites, with revenue directly related to the number of visits to the site. Every time a user "travels" from the MySpace site to the vidiLife site by clicking on a link, vidiLife's advertising revenue stands to grow. Assuming that advertisers' budgets are not unlimited, that could lead to a diminution in MySpace's revenue. Looked at another way, by eliminating any references to vidiLife.com and by deleting links to that site, MySpace may be viewed as merely preventing LiveUniverse from advertising its website free of charge on the MySpace site.

In *Morris Communications Corp. v. PGA Tours, Inc.*, 364 F.3d 1288, 1290 (11th Cir. 2004), a media company challenged the PGA Tour, Inc.'s ("PGA") alleged monopolization of markets for publication of real-time golf scores on the Internet and the sale of these scores. The PGA had developed a Real-Time Scoring System that quickly recorded players' scores, which it would not allow the plaintiff to re-sell to other Internet website publishers without first buying a license to do so. Plaintiff claimed this constituted an unlawful refusal to deal. The Eleventh Circuit affirmed the District Court's grant of summary judgment to the PGA. *Id.* at 1290. It stated that a "refusal to deal that is designed to protect or further the legitimate business purposes of a defendant does not violate the antitrust laws even if that refusal injures competition." *Id.* at 1295. The Court found that the PGA's justification for its conduct was sufficient: it sought to prevent plaintiff from "free-riding" on its technology. *Id.* at 1295–98. The court stressed that unlike the cases plaintiff relied on, the PGA was not preventing plaintiff from selling a product that plaintiff created and owned. *Id.* at 1297. Here, too, MySpace has taken no action that prevents plaintiff from promoting and operating its own site, independently of MySpace.

For the foregoing reasons, LiveUniverse fails to state a refusal to deal claim.

2. Product Design Changes

In general, it is not inherently anticompetitive for even a monopolist to make changes to its product design. "A monopolist, no less than any other competitor, is permitted and indeed encouraged to compete aggressively on the merits, and any success it may achieve solely through 'the process of invention and innovation' is necessarily tolerated by the antitrust laws." *Foremost Pro Color, Inc. v. Eastman Kodak Co.*, 703 F.2d 534, 544–45 (9th Cir. 1983) (holding that plaintiff-photofinisher failed to state a Section 2 claim against defendant-manufacturer who allegedly developed new products that were incompatible with then-existing products and with photofinishing equipment); overruled on other grounds and on another claim by *Hasbrouck v. Texaco, Inc.*, 842 F.2d 1034 (9th Cir. 1987). As the Ninth Circuit noted, the defendant had no duty "to constrict[] product development so as to facilitate sales of rival products" or to help competitors "survive or expand." *Id.* at 545 (internal citations omitted).

Despite these principles, LiveUniverse nevertheless argues that MySpace modified its system so as to delete links to vidiLife.com from the MySpace site, to delete users' references to "vidilife.com" and to prevent users from making any future mention of or links to vidiLife.com. LiveUniverse alleges that these modifications constitute a change of product design that is actionable. ...[8]

Live Universe's allegations are not sufficient to establish anticompetitive conduct. MySpace's conduct is distinguishable from that of Microsoft, because it in no way prevents consumers from accessing the vidiLife site. It simply prevents them from using the MySpace site to do so. Unlike Microsoft's override of users' choice of default browsers, the destruction of links to vidiLife.com does not "override" users' preferences. Nor is the content of these links converted into MySpace content. Moreover, users are not restricted to MySpace content in the manner that the override restricted Windows users to Microsoft's browser, Internet Explorer. Users are only prevented from viewing and creating links to the vidiLife site directly through the MySpace site- they may still do so elsewhere. Thus, the only product design change by MySpace was an algorithm that enables it to compete in the relevant market without enabling LiveUniverse to take advantage of MySpace's success. Such behavior even a monopolist has the right to display. ...

QUESTIONS

1. What is the market in which MySpace competes? Is it the market for social-network users? For Internet users? For advertisers looking to advertise to social-network users? Why does the difference matter?

2. As of March 2011, Facebook, with over 500 million users, had almost ten times as many users as MySpace, with roughly 60 million. Vidilife's website was defunct. Do these facts shed any light on the court's analysis of MySpace's market power?

3. What are network effects? A group of users who are dissatisfied with Facebook's privacy policies developed a more privacy-friendly alternative, Disapora, at https://joindiaspora.com. Does the existence of network effects make it easier or harder for Disapora to convince Facebook users to switch?

4. Why did MySpace disable vidilife.com links? It appears that MySpace left other links posted by its users intact. Did MySpace's decision to disable links to vidilife.com benefit MySpace users, or harm them?

5. Does MySpace have a First Amendment right to block Vidilife links?

GOOGLE MAPS PROBLEM

If you go to google.com and search for "pizza," the results page is likely to have a small map showing the locations of pizzerias near where Google thinks you are. The same thing will happen if you search on an address – e.g. "1600 Pennsylvania Avenue, Washington DC." This feature – which integrates material from other Google services like Google Maps, YouTube, and Google Image Search – is called "Universal Search" and dates to 2007. Before that, Google was much more liberal in linking to other sites. Searches on addresses, for example, would return links to

---

8 This overstates what actually has occurred, evidently. As MySpace argues (without refutation), "Users - including MySpace users - can email, blog and chat with their friends about 'LiveUniverse' and 'vidiLife' to their heart's content. The only thing that has been eliminated - and the only conduct at issue - is the presence of separate active links (i.e., website addresses like 'www.vidiLife.com') on the MySpace.com website that take users directly from MySpace.com to vidiLife.com in a single mouse click."

other map services, such as MapQuest. Between 2007 and 2010, YouTube's market share grew from 40% to 80%, and Google Maps's market share from under 20% to over 50%. Meanwhile, previously market-leading MapQuest dropped from over 50% to a roughly 30% market share.

Is Google violating Section 2 of the Sherman Act with Universal Search?

C. Network Neutrality

"Network neutrality" rules require ISPs not to discriminate against legal uses of their networks. The Federal Communication Commission (FCC) has made three major tries at requiring network neutrality: an adjudication against Comcast in 2008, a set of "Open Internet" rules in 2011, and a second set of Open Internet rules in 2015. The first two were substantially struck down by the courts for administrative-law reasons; challenges to the third are pending. Under the most recent rules, ISPs cannot *block* service to websites, applications, content, or devices their users wish to use; cannot *throttle* service by deliberately slowing Internet traffic down; cannot *prioritize* some traffic over others by creating dedicated "fast lanes" open to those who pay; and cannot unreasonably *interfere* with particular traffic. The details are complicated, and this section offers only a brief survey of the issues.

The modern debates over network neutrality are rooted in three widely-shared beliefs about the Internet. The first is access: that as many people as possible ought to be able to use the Internet to connect, communicate, and do business with each other. The second is competition: that the Internet is better because different companies compete with each other to offer superior service. The third is innovation: that investments in technological improvements to and on the Internet benefit society. Sometimes these values reinforce each other; sometimes they conflict. As you read this section, pay attention to how advocates and opponents of network neutrality invoke these different values in support of their arguments.

Before pressing into the historical, technical, and administrative thicket, we begin with a high-level overview of the policy case for network neutrality, presented in an excerpt from one of the judicial opinions reviewing the FCC's actions. It is an approving paraphrase of the FCC's rationale, and also provides an introduction to some of the essential terminology. These are followed by a short background note on relevant principles of administrative law, extended notes on the history of network regulation, starting with Alexander Graham Bell and tracing the FCC's first two (failed) attempts to impose binding network neutrality rules. Next come excerpts from the FCC's third try and a popular essay criticizing both the rules and the entire project of network neutrality regulation. The section concludes with a problem asking you to think through how the FCC's rules might play out in practice.

VERIZON V. FCC
740 F.3d 623 (D.C. Cir. 2014)

Tatel, Circuit Judge: ...

Four major participants in the Internet marketplace are relevant to the issues before us: backbone networks, broadband providers, edge providers, and end users. Backbone networks are interconnected, long-haul fiber-optic links and

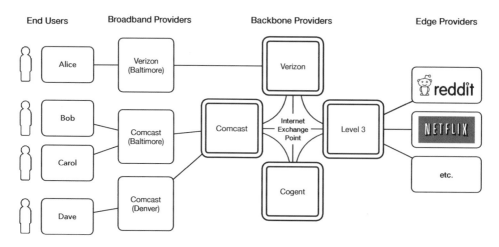

high-speed routers capable of transmitting vast amounts of data. Internet users generally connect to these networks – and, ultimately, to one another – through local access providers like petitioner Verizon, who operate the "last-mile" transmission lines. In the Internet's early days, most users connected to the Internet through dial-up connections over local telephone lines. Today, access is generally furnished through "broadband," i.e., high-speed communications technologies, such as cable modem service. Edge providers are those who, like Amazon or Google, provide content, services, and applications over the Internet, while end users are those who consume edge providers' content, services, and applications. To pull the whole picture together with a slightly oversimplified example: when an edge provider such as YouTube transmits some sort of content – say, a video of a cat – to an end user, that content is broken down into packets of information, which are carried by the edge provider's local access provider to the backbone network, which transmits these packets to the end user's local access provider, which, in turn, transmits the information to the end user, who then views and hopefully enjoys the cat.

These categories of entities are not necessarily mutually exclusive. For example, end users may often act as edge providers by creating and sharing content that is consumed by other end users, for instance by posting photos on Facebook. Similarly, broadband providers may offer content, applications, and services that compete with those furnished by edge providers.

Proponents of net neutrality – or, to use the Commission's preferred term, "Internet openness" – worry about the relationship between broadband providers and edge providers. They fear that broadband providers might prevent their end-user subscribers from accessing certain edge providers altogether, or might degrade the quality of their end-user subscribers' access to certain edge providers, either as a means of favoring their own competing content or services or to enable them to collect fees from certain edge providers. Thus, for example, a broadband provider like Comcast might limit its end-user subscribers' ability to access the New York Times website if it wanted to spike traffic to its own news website, or it might degrade the quality of the connection to a search website like Bing if a competitor like Google paid for prioritized access. ...

One set of rules applies to "fixed" broadband providers – i.e., those furnishing residential broadband service and, more generally, Internet access to end users "primarily at fixed end points using stationary equipment." The other set of requirements applies to "mobile" broadband providers – i.e., those "serv[ing] end users primarily using mobile stations," such as smart phones.

To begin with, the Commission has more than adequately supported and explained its conclusion that edge-provider innovation leads to the expansion and improvement of broadband infrastructure. The Internet, the Commission observed in the *Open Internet Order*, is, "[l]ike electricity and the computer," a "general purpose technology that enables new methods of production that have a major impact on the entire economy." Certain innovations – the lightbulb, for example – create a need for infrastructure investment, such as in power generation facilities and distribution lines, that complement and further drive the development of the initial innovation and ultimately the growth of the economy as a whole. The rise of streaming online video is perhaps the best and clearest example the Commission used to illustrate that the Internet constitutes one such technology: higher-speed residential Internet connections in the late 1990s "stimulated" the development of streaming video, a service that requires particularly high bandwidth, "which in turn encouraged broadband providers to increase network speeds." The Commission's emphasis on this connection between edge-provider innovation and infrastructure development is uncontroversial. ...

The Commission's finding that Internet openness fosters the edge-provider innovation that drives this "virtuous cycle" was likewise reasonable and grounded in substantial evidence. Continued innovation at the edge, the Commission explained, "depends upon low barriers to innovation and entry by edge providers," and thus restrictions on edge providers' "ability to reach end users ... reduce the rate of innovation." This conclusion finds ample support in the economic literature on which the Commission relied, as well as in history and the comments of several edge providers. For one prominent illustration of the relationship between openness and innovation, the Commission cited the invention of the World Wide Web itself by Sir Tim Berners-Lee, who, although not working for an entity that operated the underlying network, was able to create and disseminate this enormously successful innovation without needing to make any changes to previously developed Internet protocols or securing "any approval from network operators." It also highlighted the comments of Google and Vonage – both innovative edge providers – who emphasized the importance of the Internet's open design to permitting new content and services to develop at the edge. The record amassed by the Commission contains many similar examples ...

Equally important, the Commission has adequately supported and explained its conclusion that, absent rules such as those set forth in the *Open Internet Order*, broadband providers represent a threat to Internet openness and could act in ways that would ultimately inhibit the speed and extent of future broadband deployment. First, nothing in the record gives us any reason to doubt the Commission's determination that broadband providers may be motivated to discriminate against and among edge providers. The Commission observed that broadband providers – often the same entities that furnish end users with telephone and television services – "have incentives to interfere with the operation of third-party Internet-based services that compete with the providers' revenue-generating telephone and/or pay-television services." As the Commission noted, Voice-over-Internet-Protocol (VoIP) services such as Vonage increasingly serve as substitutes for traditional telephone services, and broadband providers like AT&T and Time Warner have acknowledged that online video aggregators such as Netflix and Hulu compete directly with their own core video subscription service. Broadband providers also have powerful incentives to accept fees from edge providers, either in return for excluding their competitors or for granting them prioritized access to end users. ... Although Verizon dismisses the Commission's assertions regarding broadband providers' incentives as "pure speculation," those assertions are, at the very least, speculation based firmly in common sense and economic reality.

Moreover, as the Commission found, broadband providers have the technical and economic ability to impose such restrictions. Verizon does not seriously contend otherwise. ... The Commission also convincingly detailed how broadband providers' position in the market gives them the economic power to restrict edge-provider traffic and charge for the services they furnish edge providers. Because all end users generally access the Internet through a single broadband provider, that provider functions as a "terminating monopolist," with power to act as a "gatekeeper" with respect to edge providers that might seek to reach its end-user subscribers. As the Commission reasonably explained, this ability to act as a "gatekeeper" distinguishes broadband providers from other participants in the Internet marketplace – including prominent and potentially powerful edge providers such as Google and Apple – who have no similar "control [over] access to the Internet for their subscribers and for anyone wishing to reach those subscribers."

To be sure, if end users could immediately respond to any given broadband provider's attempt to impose restrictions on edge providers by switching broadband providers, this gatekeeper power might well disappear. *Cf. Open Internet Order* (declining to impose similar rules on "dial-up Internet access service because telephone service has historically provided the easy ability to switch among competing dial-up Internet access services"). For example, a broadband provider like Comcast would be unable to threaten Netflix that it would slow Netflix traffic if all Comcast subscribers would then immediately switch to a competing broadband provider. But we see no basis for questioning the Commission's conclusion that end users are unlikely to react in this fashion. According to the Commission, "end users may not know whether charges or service levels their broadband provider is imposing on edge providers vary from those of alternative broadband providers, and even if they do have this information may find it costly to switch." As described by numerous commenters, and detailed more thoroughly in a Commission report compiling the results of an extensive consumer survey, the costs of switching include: "early termination fees; the inconvenience of ordering, installation, and set-up, and associated deposits or fees; possible difficulty returning the earlier broadband provider's equipment and the cost of replacing incompatible customer-owned equipment; the risk of temporarily losing service; the risk of problems learning how to use the new service; and the possible loss of a provider-specific email address or website." Moreover, the Commission emphasized, many end users may have no option to switch, or at least face very limited options: "[a]s of December 2009, nearly 70 percent of households lived in census tracts where only one or two wireline or fixed wireless firms provided" broadband service. As the Commission concluded, any market power that such broadband providers might have with respect to end users would only increase their power with respect to edge providers. ...

Furthermore, the Commission established that the threat that broadband providers would utilize their gatekeeper ability to restrict edge-provider traffic is not, as the Commission put it, "merely theoretical." In support of its conclusion that broadband providers could and would act to limit Internet openness, the Commission pointed to four prior instances in which they had done just that.

These involved a mobile broadband provider blocking online payment services after entering into a contract with a competing service; a mobile broadband provider restricting the availability of competing VoIP and streaming video services; a fixed broadband provider blocking VoIP applications; and, of course, Comcast's impairment of peer-to-peer file sharing that was the subject of the *Comcast Order*. ...

QUESTIONS

1. Is this a persuasive theory of the relationship between openness and innovation? Can greater control over a platform lead to more innovation on it? What about innovation in improving the network itself? And don't edge providers also innovate in exchanging illegal material, in launching hacking attacks, and in undermining the stability of the Internet?

2. Do the arguments for network neutrality also imply a need for search neutrality to keep Google from unfairly demoting its competitors like Yelp? What about payments neutrality for PayPal, app neutrality for the Apple iOS app store, social graph neutrality for Facebook, or or e-book neutrality for Amazon? What would these mean? Is there a reason to treat ISPs differently?

3. Is there even a problem here? Are neutrality violations common or rare? If there is a problem, is it a one that antitrust law and consumer protection law can't fix?

NOTE ON ADMINISTRATIVE LAW

If you are only interested in the substance of what network neutrality rules require and whether they are good policy, you can skip this note, which deals with whether the FCC's attempt to enact them is procedurally legal.

Agency Procedures: Agencies like the FCC are empowered by Congress to make legally binding regulations, but their power is also limited by Congress. Agencies' own specific "organic" statutes and general statutes like the Administrative Procedure Act (APA) regulate the substance of the regulations agencies can promulgate and the procedures they must follow to do so. Broadly speaking, agencies do three things. First, they engage in rulemaking to create binding rules of general applicability. The more common "informal" version of rulemaking starts with publishing a "Notice of Proposed Rulemaking" (NPRM) in the in which the agency describes the issues it is considering and outlines potential regulations. 5 U.S.C. § 553(b) The public is invited to comment, *id.* § 553(c), and the agency's final order is supposed to take those comments into account and respond to significant objections, *see Citizens to Preserve Overton Park, Inc. v. Volpe*, 401 U. S. 402 (1971). The final order is also published in the Federal Register at least 30 days before it takes effect, *see* 5 U.S.C. § 553(d), and the resulting rules are typically codified in the Code of Federal Regulations. The process of issuing an NPRM, taking comments, and responding to them produces a written record of the evidence the agency considered and the reasoning behind its decisions. Second, agencies engage in adjudication and enforcement actions involving individual cases, some of which are initiated by the agency itself and some by complaints from interested parties. Like notice-and-comment rulemaking, adjudication also typically produces a written record. Third, agencies issue a blizzard of less formal paperwork: guidance documents, advisory opinions, interpretations of their own regulations, policy statements, and so forth.

Judicial Review: When agencies step beyond their substantive and procedural limits, their actions typically are subject to judicial review and a court may set aside any illegal agency actions. Under the APA, any "person suffering legal wrong because of agency action, or adversely affected or aggrieved by agency action," *id.* § 702, may file a petition for judicial review. The standard jurisdiction and venue rules for these suits against federal agencies are spelled out in 28 U.S.C. ch. 158: they provide for direct review by the circuit Court of Appeals where the petitioner seeking review resides.[*] If more than one person petitions for review within ten days, the reviewing court is selected randomly among those eligible, and any subsequent petitions will be sent to that court. See *id.* § 2112. Since only "final agency action," *id.* § 704, is subject to review, there is often a characteristic flurry of activity immediately after new rules are made binding by being published in the Federal Register.

Questions of Law: The first question a reviewing court asks is whether the agency has acted within the scope of the authority delegated to it by Congress. Typically, the agency can point to an express authorization in one of its statutes that allows it to engage in rulemaking or to adjudicate individual cases. The harder question is usually whether the resulting rules or decisions are consistent with the text of the statute. Here, agencies enjoy an extra degree of latitude under Chevron USA Inc. v. Natural Resources Defense Council, Inc., 467 U.S. 837 (1984). An unambiguous statute controls according to its terms ("Chevron step one"), but the agency's construction of an ambiguous statute will be upheld as long as it is reasonable, even if the court might prefer a different construction ("Chevron step two"). Two important limits-on "Chevron deference" are that the agency must be interpreting its own statute and that more formal procedures (such as notice-and-comment rulemakings) receive greater deference than less formal ones (such as advisory opinions issued without public comment).

Questions of Fact and Policy: Courts also defer to agencies' factual findings and the conclusions agencies draw from those findings. Here, the basic test comes from the APA: a court will set aside any agency action that is "arbitrary, capricious, [or] an abuse of discretion." 5 U.S.C. § 706(2)(A). Another test, sometimes explicitly required by the APA and sometimes rolled into arbitrary-and-capricious review, is whether the agency's factual findings and conclusions were supported by "substantial evidence." *Id.* § 706(2)(E). Both tests examine whether the agency's decisions are supported by evidence in the record compiled by the agency at the time it acted: the agency cannot wait until it is sued to present new evidence or give new reasoning. The standard overall is deferential and procedural: it shifts the focus significantly away from the question of whether the agency is right and significantly toward the question of whether the agency has taken a "hard look" (in administrative-law jargon) at the problem.

Changes of Position: A consequence of the deference courts give to agencies on questions of law, fact, and policy is that agencies are free to change their positions, provided they justify the new one under the ordinary standards of review:

> [An agency] need not demonstrate to a court's satisfaction that the reasons for the new policy are *better* than the reasons for the old one; it suffices that the new policy is permissible under the statute, that there are good reasons for it, and that the agency *believes* it to be bet-

---

[*] Some FCC actions are subject to these rules, *see* 47 U.S.C. § 402(a); others are reviewable only in the District of Columbia Circuit, *see id.* § 402(b).

ter, which the conscious change of course adequately indicates. This means that the agency need not always provide a more detailed justification than what would suffice for a new policy created on a blank slate. Sometimes it must – when, for example, its new policy rests upon factual findings that contradict those which underlay its prior policy; or when its prior policy has engendered serious reliance interests that must be taken into account. It would be arbitrary or capricious to ignore such matters. In such cases it is not that further justification is demanded by the mere fact of policy change; but that a reasoned explanation is needed for disregarding facts and circumstances that underlay or were engendered by the prior policy.

FCC v. Fox Television Stations, Inc., 556 U.S. 502, 515 (2009).

NOTE ON TELEPHONE REGULATION

It impossible to understand the modern debates over network neutrality without some sense of the regulatory backdrop against which they take place. And it is impossible to understand the regulatory backdrop without a generous helping of history. We start with the history of telephone regulation, because for many observers it supplies the most closely analogous baseline.

AT&T and the Telephone System

For present purposes,[*] the story starts in 1877, when Alexander Graham Bell, the inventor of the first practical telephone,[†] founded the Bell Telephone Company. It combined a national headquarters, an equipment manufacturing division, and a set of local operation companies, each of which had an exclusive license from Bell for its territory. Initially, local service was the big draw of having a telephone. Businessmen wanted to talk to their customers and their suppliers; individuals wanted to talk to their friends. Bell affiliates built out networks in major cities, with long-distance lines to other cities as an expensive separate service. But in 1889, Bell placed a major bet on the future of the telephone, upgrading its local systems so local subscribers could also use its city-to-city links.

The last of Bell's patents on the telephone expired in 1894, opening the field to competition from a variety of companies who gradually became known as the "independents." Although they had difficulty maintaining competition in urban areas that Bell had already wired, they were frequently able to establish themselves in suburbs, towns, and rural areas. For the next two decades, local Bells and independents competed vigorously. A crucial area of controversy was whether or not their networks would "interconnect," allowing subscribers on one to talk to subscribers on the other. At first, Bell followed a policy of refusing to interconnect,

---

[*] Similar issues arose in regulating the telegraph, and even before that, postal service. And there are related issues in other networked industries, like railroads and electric power. But a line must be drawn somewhere, and ours is drawn at the telephone.

[†] Perhaps. Elisha Gray was also working on transmitting speech electrically, and the two of them filed paperwork with the Patent Office on the same day in 1876. Bell ultimately was awarded a patent, and Gray was not, but there is also strong circumstantial evidence that Bell's filing was plagiarized from Gray's. It may not be accurate to call either of them "the" inventor, especially given how many other people were active in developing the numerous technologies required to build a working telephone *system*: microphones, switchboards, speakers, etc.

trying to use its long-distance network as a weapon to convince telephone users to drop their independent subscription and jump ship to Bell.

But then, under the leadership of president Theodore Vail, who coined the slogan, "One System, One Policy, Universal Service," Bell (now known as American Telephone and Telegraph or AT&T for short) switched course. It started offering interconnection to the independents, effectively weaving them into its own network one-by-one rather than leaving them to band together to create their own competing long-distance network. It also started to buy up independents where it could, until a 1913 agreement with the Department of Justice, known as the Kingsbury Commitment, formalized the interconnection policy and required AT&T to obtain the government's consent for further acquisitions. As it knit its long-distance lines together into a truly coast-to-coast network, Bell was now the dominant provider of telephone service, with an effectively unassailable monopoly in long-distance service. (During World War I, the government briefly took control of the network by giving the Postmaster General authority over AT&T, then quickly gave up on the plan and handed control back to AT&T.)

The Communications Act of 1934 recognized this fact, establishing AT&T as a legally regulated monopoly under the jurisdiction of the newly-created Federal Communications Commission. For nearly the next fifty years, AT&T (or "Ma Bell," as it was often called), for most practical purposes, *was* the telephone system. Long-distance rates gradually dropped, but remained absurdly expensive by 21st-century standards. In 1950, a ten-minute call from New York to Los Angeles cost $65.78 (in 2015 dollars); in 1975, that same call cost $18.29 (again in 2015 dollars). The company's research arm, Bell Labs, became the country's preeminent industrial laboratory: it produced the first transistor and basic advances in physics, computing, and communications engineering.[*]

As a regulated monopoly, AT&T lived under a legal regime that both empowered and restricted it. Three legal concepts capture the nature of the regulations. First, AT&T was treated as a common carrier under Title II of the Communications Act, under a duty to provide service to all comers on even-handed terms. Second, it was regulated by the FCC as a public utility – that is, an operator of infrastructure used by the public – not unlike an electric company or a water district. The FCC regulated both the terms and the price of telephone service; AT&T was required to file a "tariff" with the FCC that spelled out the details of its service offerings. And third, AT&T was the holder of a public franchise: a government-granted right to carry on its line of business. Because of the need to string wires on poles or underground, or to place transmitters on towers, most telecommunica-

---

[*] A 1956 consent decree with the Department of Justice kept AT&T out of the computer business. Ironically, the consent decree helped IBM maintain its dominant position in the computer business, which became the subject of a thirteen-year antitrust case, ultimately dropped by the government in 1982. Another ironic consequence was that when Bell Labs engineers Ken Thompson and Dennis Ritchie developed a new computer operating system, UNIX, in the 1970s, AT&T licensed it broadly to companies and educational institutions, rather than directly commercializing it by selling it bundled with computers. These licenses came with the UNIX source code, which educated a generation of operating system programmers. As a result, the design of modern open-source operating systems like Linux derives directly from AT&T's UNIX, even though their actual code has long since been rewritten.

tions businesses require franchises, and negotiating with local zoning boards and state public utility commissions is a big part of their work.

The FCC and AT&T worked together to extend telephone service broadly throughout the country, following a policy under which AT&T charged businesses higher rates to subsidize cheaper service for individuals. Within the limits of the basic nondiscrimination rule and the FCC's rate regulation, AT&T had near-total control over its network. The company adopted an attitude of technocratic paternalism. For example, its equipment was rigidly standardized, even down to the telephones in people's houses – which AT&T insisted were leased from it, not owned by the subscriber. The company was paranoid about non-AT&T equipment connected to its network. In the words of one of its tariffs:

> No equipment, apparatus, circuit or device not furnished by the Telephone Company shall be attached to or connected with the facilities furnished by the Telephone Company, whether physically, by induction or otherwise, except as provided in this tariff.

In a move that would backfire badly, AT&T tried to prohibit use of the Hush-a-Phone, a cup-shaped object with no electric parts. The user would attach the Hush-a-Phone to the mouthpiece on his standard AT&T telephone, and *voilà*: no one else in the room could see his lips move or hear what he was saying into the telephone. AT&T convinced the FCC to declare that even though the Hush-a-Phone could not possibly harm the workings of the telephone network itself, it somehow was "deleterious to the telephone system and injure[d] the service rendered by it." A user who desired privacy should instead cup her hand around her mouth and the phone.

Hush-a-Phone took the case to the D.C. Circuit, which set aside the FCC's order in a brief and incredulous opinion, *Hush-a-Phone Corp. v. United States*, 238 F.2d 266 (D.C. Cir. 1956). The court held that, as applied to the Hush-a-Phone by the FCC, the tariff was an "unwarranted interference with the telephone subscriber's right reasonably to use his telephone in ways which are privately beneficial without being publicly detrimental."

A decade later, the FCC itself enshrined this principle in In Re *Carterfone*, 13 F.C.C. 420 (1968). The device there was essentially a way of connecting a telephone to a walkie-talkie – enabling a kind of primitive roaming cell phone. The FCC held that AT&T could not prohibit the use of this or other "interconnecting devices" as long as they did not "adversely affect the telephone system."

Meanwhile, AT&T started to face significant competition again. It still had a stranglehold on local service – for most Americans it was simply "the telephone company" – but for reasons including the FCC's rate regulation policies, long distance was the most lucrative part of the market. If you could figure out how to connect point A to point B on your own, then you could interconnect with AT&T's network at points A and B, and offer long-distance service for customers near A and B, using AT&T's network only as necessary for the local portions of the call.

This was the play made by a new company, Microwave Communications, Inc., better-known to history as MCI. After the FCC approved its application to offer long-distance service via microwave relay towers linking Chicago and St. Louis in 1969, numerous other would-be long-distance competitors rushed in. In a rulemaking in 1971, the FCC approved their entry in principle. Although AT&T agreed to work with these new competitors to set the terms on which they would interconnect, negotiations broke down over numerous technical and pricing issues. The fight quickly spilled over into court. MCI sued, alleging that AT&T was using its dominant position in local service and its tremendous resources to prevent the new long-distance companies from competing with it. The Department of Justice, which had been eyeing AT&T on and off for decades, filed its own antitrust lawsuit in 1974. The old compromise, which had long accepted AT&T as a benign and universalizing monopolist, was breaking down.

The trial began in 1981. It ran for almost a year, and the two sides presented over three hundred witnesses and tens of thousands of pages of documents. But on January 8, 1982, with only about a month to go, the parties returned to the judge with a remarkable announcement: AT&T had agreed to a consent decree under which it would agree to be broken up. The judge approved the decree later that year, *United States v. American Telelphone and Telegraph Co.*, 552 F. Supp. 131 (D.D.C. 1982), and the breakup took place on January 1, 1984.

The breakup fragmented AT&T into three major pieces. AT&T itself kept the long-distance business, which would now be entirely open to competition. AT&T Technologies (today known as Lucent) took Bell Labs and AT&T's equipment-manufacturing arm. The local service part of the company was split up into seven regional "Baby Bells." While each of the Baby Bells still had a dominant position in providing local service, they were prohibited from entering other lines of business – thereby, in theory, keeping them from being tempted to drive competitors out of any other market.

The decade between the breakup in 1984 and the mid-1990s was a time of vibrant long-distance competition. Rates tumbled, as Americans chose between AT&T, MCI, Sprint, and a host of smaller long-distance providers. Local service, however, changed much less; the Baby Bells retained their dominant positions.

When Congress reworked the telecommunications laws in the 1990s, it repudited treating the Baby Bells as regulated monopolies in favor of trying to create structural competition for them. The Telecommunications Act of 1996 relaxed the restrictions on the lines of business the Baby Bells could enter. In exchange, Baby Bells were required to "unbundle" many of their facilities and offer them for interconnection at specified prices to competitors. A competing regional phone company, for example, was supposed to be able to lease access to switches and cables from the incumbent Baby Bell. The FCC would set appropriate prices if necessary; the goal was vibrant competition in local service from a large number of providers.

It didn't work out that way. Perhaps the Act was wrong to assume that this kind of interconnection was workable; perhaps the FCC failed to implement the Act effectively; perhaps the Baby Bells were more efficient than their new competitors. For whatever reason, few local providers made substantial inroads against their Baby Bell. The Supreme Court also beat back an antitrust challenge to one Baby Bell's actions in allegedly shirking its obligations to assist its competitors. *Verizon Commc'ns Inc. v. Law Offices of Curtis v. Trinko, LLP*, 540 U.S. 398 (2004).

With their regulations relaxed, the Baby Bells entered into several waves of expansions and mergers. By now, they have all been reabsorbed into three phone empires: AT&T, Verizon, and CenturyLink. For most Americans, one of these three is their landline phone company. Note that two of the three are also cell phone providers, and that all three also offer television and Internet along with their phone service. Note also that the other communications wire running to many Americans' houses – the one carrying cable television – had always typically been a regulated monopoly, and that the cable companies have expanded into telephone and Internet service.

BROADBAND INTERNET REGULATION: A BRIEF HISTORY

In the 1990s, as Congress took up the project of telecommunications reform, complex and highly distinct regulatory regimes had grown up around the country's major networks: telephone, broadcast television, cable television, radio, and so on. The proponents of what would become the Telecommunications Act of 1996 were eager to replicate the competition they saw in the long-distance market throughout the system. They also could tell that data and computer services – which the FCC had been rather clumsily attempting to regulate in a series of *Computer Inquiries* (in 1971, 1980, and 1986) – were important enough that they needed to be included in the framework of the Act they were drafting.

The crucial statutory question for these new services was whether to treat them as common carriers under Title II of the Communications Act being updated. Common carriage is an old concept, rooted in the common-law regulation of certain particularly "public" forms of service. The basic duty of common carriage was to serve all comers:

> Also, when a man takes upon himself a public employment, he is bound to serve the public as far as his employment goes, or an action lies against him for refusing. Thus, if a farrier refuse to shoe a horse, an innkeeper to receive a guest, a carrier to carry, when they may do it, an action lies; their understanding is in proportion to their power and convenience.

Lane v. Cotton (1703) 91 Eng. Rep. 17 (K.B.). Over time, common carriage in the United States was used primarily in regulation transportation and telecommunications. Railroads and telegraphs were the archetypal nineteenth century common carriers. Today, the basic duties of common carriers in communications are spelled out in Title II of the Communications Act:

- First, there is the essential duty to serve all comers, that is, "to furnish such communication service upon reasonable request therefor." 47 U.S.C. § 201(a).

- Second, each common carrier must file with the FCC the details of its pricing, called a tariff, *id.* § 203(a), and may charge customers only in accordance with the filed tariff, *id.* § 203(c).

- Third, a common carrier's rates must be "just and reasonable." *Id.* § 201(b).

- Fourth, a common carrier may not engage in "unjust or unreasonable discrimination" between customers. *Id.* § 202(a). Note that not all discrimination is "unjust" or "unreasonable." Customers who make more calls have higher long-distance bills. And a company's tariff might define different classes of service: it can have a different billing structure for customers who are willing to buy service in bulk, and it can offer various service options for customers who are willing to pay for them. What a common carrier cannot do is strike different bargains for the same service with similarly situated customers.

- Fifth, and relatedly, common carriers must "establish physical connections with other carriers," *id.* § 201(a), when ordered to do so by the FCC. *See also id.* § 251(a). These interconnection agreements are the equivalent of two railroads bringing their tracks together at a common trainyard and agreeing on terms to move freight from one railroad's trains to the other's

- Sixth, common carriers require FCC permission to build new lines or to discontinue an existing service. *Id.* § 214.

- Last but not least, the FCC has broad authority to hold hearings on and accept or reject filed tariffs, *id.* § 204, to make general rules about permitted and prohibited practices, *id.* § 205, to investigate complaints about violations of common carriers' obligations, *id.* § 208, and to obtain information about common carriers' operations and business agreements, *id.* §§ 215, 218.

The drafters of the Act decided to draw a line between traditional "telecommunications" services, to which Title II common-carrier regulations would continue to apply, and new kinds of "information" services, which would be much less strictly regulated. The line itself wasn't new – the second *Computer Inquiry* had distinguished between "basic" and "enhanced" services in 1980 – but the Act gave it sweeping new applicability.

(24) *INFORMATION SERVICE*. – The term "information service" means the offering of a capability for generating, acquiring, storing, transforming, processing, retrieving, utilizing, or making available information via telecommunications ...

(50) *TELECOMMUNICATIONS*. – The term "telecommunications" means the transmission, between or among points specified by the user, of information of the user's choosing, without change in the form or content of the information as sent and received. ...

(51) *TELECOMMUNICATIONS CARRIER*. – The term "telecommunications carrier" means any provider of telecommunications services ... . A telecommunications carrier shall be treated as a common carrier under this chapter only to the extent that it is engaged in providing telecommunications services ... .

(53) *TELECOMMUNICATIONS SERVICE*. – The term "telecommunications service" means the offering of telecommunications for a fee directly to the public ...

47 U.S.C. § 153.

In hindsight, these definitions were unfortunate. Telephone service was clearly a type of telecommunications service, since it involved the transmission of unmodified information in the form of audio signals, and remained subject to Title II. Cable television service had its own regulatory regime. But what to make of the broadband Internet offered by telephone and cable companies using telephone and cable networks? Was this also a "telecommunications service" involving unmodified transmission of user information? Or was it an "information service" involving the "capability for ... making available information via telecommunications?"

The FCC, reflecting the competition-oriented spirit of the 1996 Act, took a deregulatory view. In a 1999 report to Congress, its chair, William Kennard, envisioned a future of "fully competitive domestic communications markets with minimal or no regulation." NEW FEDERAL COMMUNICATIONS COMMISSION FOR THE 21ST CENTURY (report attached to written testimony of William E. Kennard, Chairman, Federal Communications Commission, before the House Subcommittee on Telecommunications, Trade, and Consumer Protection, Mar. 17, 1999). The FCC's role would become minimal, focusing on universal service, consumer protection, and spectrum management. Accordingly, the FCC decided in 2000 that broadband Internet offered over a cable network was an "information service not subject to Title II common-carrier obligations." *In re Inquiry Concerning High-*

Speed Access to the Internet Over Cable and Other Facilities, 17 F.C.C. Rcd. 4798 (2000).* Lawsuits promptly followed, and in 2005, the Supreme Court held that the FCC's interpretation was a reasonable construction of the statute. *Nat'l Cable & Telecomm. Assn. v. Brand X Internet Services*, 545 U.S. 967 (2005). Also in 2005, the FCC classified the broadband Internet service offered by telephone companies as an unregulated information service. *In Re Matters of Appropriate Framework for Broadband Access to the Internet over Wireline Facilities*, 20 F.C.C. Rcd. 14853 (2005). The net result is that the home Internet service used by most Americans is not subject to rate regulation, to obligations to provide service to any and all sites on the Internet, or to the other traditional components of common carriage under Title II.

The Four Freedoms and the Madison River Case

The term "network neutrality" comes from an article by the legal scholar Tim Wu, *Network Neutrality, Broadband Discrimination*, 2 J. TELECOMM. & HIGH TECH. L. 141 (2003). He recommended rules that would obligate ISPS not to discriminate among applications, protocols, sites, or content. As Wu and others articulated it, network neutrality drew on the nondiscrimination principles of common carriage and the user-autonomy principles of *Carterfone*. At the same time, it stopped well short of full Title II common-carrier treatment of ISPs with filed tariffs and rate regulation.

Wu's article was published in 2003, at the height (or the nadir, depending on your perspective) of the FCC's deregulatory campaign. But the next step towards Wu's network neutrality principle came from a perhaps unlikely source: Michael K. Powell, the chairman of the FCC from 2001 to 2005 and a major advocate of industry self-regulation. In a 2004 speech, Chairman Powell outlined four "Internet Freedoms" he hoped that the broadband industry would preserve:

A. Freedom to Access Content

First, I believe consumers should have their choice of legal content. Consumers expect to be able to go where they want on high-speed connections, and those who have migrated from dial-up would presumably object to paying the premium asked for broadband if certain content were restricted. Thus, I challenge all facets of the industry to commit to allowing consumers to reach the content of their choice. I do recognize that operators have legitimate needs to manage their networks and ensure quality experiences, and reasonable limits sometimes must be placed in service contracts. But such restraints should be clearly spelled out and should be as minimal as necessary.

B. Freedom to Use Applications

Second, consumers should be able to run applications of their choice. As with access to content, consumers have come to expect that they can generally run whatever applications they choose or perhaps

---

* Note that cable *television* service remains regulated under Title VI, 47 U.S.C. §§ 521–573. For example, cable operators must provide community and educational access channels, *id.* § 531, must carry local broadcast television channels if the broadcaster insists, *id.* § 534, and are subject to local franchising, *id.* § 541. The FCC is currently considering the future of cable television regulations in a world in which video is increasingly provided "over the top" on the Internet rather than through dedicated video-only networks.

even develop. Again, these applications are crucial to continuing the Digital Broadband Migration because they can drive the demand that fuels infrastructure and content deployment. Applications developers must remain confident that their products will continue to work without interference from other companies. No one can know for sure what "killer applications" will emerge to drive deployment of next generation technologies. Again, it is important to challenge all facets of the industry to let the market work and allow consumers to run their applications provided they fall within service plans and will not disrupt the network.

C. Freedom to Attach Personal Devices

Third, consumers should be permitted to attach personal devices they choose to the connections that they pay for in their homes. Devices give consumers more choice, value, and personalization with respect to how they use their high-speed connections, and they are critical to the future of broadband. I challenge all facets of the industry to permit consumers to attach those devices they choose to their broadband connection, so long as the devices operate within their plans, and are not designed and used to enable theft of service.

D. Freedom to Obtain Service Plan Information

Finally, and most importantly, consumers must receive clear and meaningful information regarding their service plans and what the limits of those plans are. Simply put, information is absolutely necessary to ensure that the market is working. Consumers need to know whether and how their service plans protect them against spam, spyware, and other potential invasions of privacy. I challenge all facets of the industry to ensure that consumers can easily obtain this information.

Michael K. Powell, *Preserving Internet Freedom: Guiding Principles for the Industry*, 3 J. TELECOMM & HIGH TECH. L. 5 (2004).

Powell's speech was hortatory, but the FCC quickly acted on its principles. In 2005, the VoIP service Vonage complained to the FCC that a North Carolina ISP, Madison River, was blocking customers' Vonage calls. The allegations presented an especially stark stark violation of the network neutrality principle and of Powell's second freedom, the freedom for consumers "to run applications of their choice." And because Madison River was also a telephone company, it was easy to see how it might have a commercial interest in making it harder for its customers to make Vonage calls. The FCC opened an investigation and quickly reached a consent decree in which Madison River agreed to pay a $15,000 fine and promised that it would not "block ports used for VoIP applications or otherwise prevent customers from using VoIP applications." *In re Madison River Communications, LLC*, 20 F.C.C. Rcd. 4295 (2005). Because it ended in a consent decree, the *Madison River* case made no new law binding on other ISPs, nor did the FCC take the occasion to explain its legal reasoning in any detail. The FCC did, however, adopt a nonbinding Internet Policy Statement later in 2005 paraphrasing Powell's four freedoms and promising to "incorporate the above principles into its ongoing policymaking activities." *In re Appropriate Framework for Broadband Access to the Internet over Wireline Facilities*, 20 F.C.C. Rcd 14986 (2005). In a footnote, the FCC added that the "the principles we adopt are subject to reasonable network management."

Comcast and BitTorrent

The next major test of network neutrality came in 2008 under Powell's successor as chairman, Kevin J. Martin. Some Comcast subscribers noticed that they were having difficulty using BitTorrent to share files. A close investigation by networking experts discovered evidence that the difficulties were deliberate on Comcast's part. Specifically, BitTorrent uses TCP to connect a computer uploading a chunk of a file with a computer downloading that chunk. Ordinarily, when one of the computers in a TCP believes concludes that something has gone seriously wrong, it will send an "RST packet" – a packet with a particular bit set to 1 – to tell the other computer to stop sending data and give up on the connection. Analysis of Comcast subscribers' BitTorrent connections showed that they were receiving RST packets that *the other computer in the TCP connection had not sent.* In ordinary Internet use, this situation simply would not occur; it is the technical equivalent of receiving forged postcards that claim to be from a friend, bear the right postmark, and refer to events you and the friend have discussed with each other in previous postcards.

Following an investigation by the press, Comcast admitted that it inspected customers' Internet traffic to detect BitTorrent connections and that it injected RST packets to terminate those connections when it identified them. Comcast explained that it interrupted BitTorrent connections as a way of managing bandwidth. The advocacy group Free Press asked for a declaratory ruling "that an Internet service provider violates the FCC's Internet Policy Statement when it intentionally degrades a targeted Internet application." The FCC agreed. It concluded that the BitTorrent interference violated the principles allowing consumers to access content of their choice and using applications of their choice. Comcast argued that restricting BitTorrent qualified as "reasonable network management," but the FCC was unpersuaded:

> Next, Comcast asserts that even if its practice is discriminatory, it qualifies as reasonable network management. However, experts in the field generally disagree strongly with Comcast's assertion that its network management practices are reasonable. The Internet Engineering Task Force, a repository for the standards and protocols that underlie the functioning of the Internet, has promulgated universal definitions for how the TCP protocol is intended to work. ... Significantly, Comcast's practices contravene those standards. Comcast's method of sending RST packets to interrupt and terminate TCP connections thus contravene the established expectations of users and software developers for seamless and transparent communications across the Internet – this practice, known as RST Injection, "violate[s] the expectation that the contents of the envelopes are untouched inside and between Autonomous Systems" and "potentially disrupt[s] systems and applications that are designed assuming the expected behavior of the Internet." ...
>
> We next must ask whether Comcast's means are carefully tailored to its interest in easing network congestion, and it is apparent that no such fit exists. As an initial matter, Comcast's practice is overinclusive for at least three independent reasons. First, it can affect customers who are using little bandwidth simply because they are using a disfavored application. Second, it is not employed only during times of the day when congestion is prevalent: Comcast's current P2P

management is triggered ... regardless of the level of overall network congestion at that time, and regardless of the time of day. And third, its equipment does not appear to target only those neighborhoods that have congested nodes – evidence suggests that Comcast has deployed some of its network management equipment several routers (or hops) upstream from its customers, encompassing a broader geographic and system area. With some equipment deployed over a wider geographic or system area, Comcast's technique may impact numerous nodes within its network simultaneously, regardless of whether any particular node is experiencing congestion. Furthermore, Comcast's practice suffers from the flaw of being underinclusive. A customer may use an extraordinary amount of bandwidth during periods of network congestion and will be totally unaffected so long as he does not utilize a disfavored application.

Moreover, Comcast has several available options it could use to manage network traffic without discriminating as it does. Comcast could cap the average users' capacity and then charge the most aggressive users overage fees. Or Comcast could throttle back the connection speeds of high-capacity users (rather than any user who relies on peer-to-peer technology, no matter how infrequently). Or Comcast can work with the application vendors themselves. As Comcast has touted in this very dispute, negotiations with Pando and BitTorrent, Inc. and other peer-to-peer application companies have advanced the creation of the P4P protocol, which promises "backbone bandwidth optimization" and "improve[d] P2P download performance." Although we do not endorse any of these particular solutions today, they all appear far better tailored to Comcast's basic complaint that a "disproportionately large amount of the traffic currently on broadband networks originates from a relatively small number of users."

Comcast and several other commenters maintain a continual refrain that "all network providers must manage bandwidth in some manner" and that providers need "flexibility to engage in the reasonable network management practices." We do not disagree, which is precisely why we do not adopt here an inflexible framework micromanaging providers' network management practices. We also note that because "consumers are entitled to access the lawful Internet content of their choice," providers, consistent with federal policy, may block transmissions of illegal content (e.g., child pornography) or transmissions that violate copyright law. To the extent, however, that providers choose to utilize practices that are not application or content neutral, the risk to the open nature of the Internet is particularly acute and the danger of network management practices being used to further anticompetitive ends is strong. As a result, it is incumbent on the Commission to be vigilant and subject such practices to a searching inquiry, and here Comcast's practice falls well short of being carefully tailored to further the interest offered by the company. ...

In re [Complaint Against] Comcast Corp. for Secretly Degrading Peer-to-Peer Applications, 23 F.C.C. Rcd. 13028 (2008). By the time the ruling issued, Comcast had already pledged to discontinue its BitTorrent blocking and replace it with a more nuanced approach to managing congestion. As a result, the FCC's order was limited to requiring Comcast to provide the FCC with details of its congestion management practices to ensure compliance with the pledge. But that was enough to get Comcast into court; it sued the FCC to set aside the order.

As it turned out, the case turned less on the FCC's decision itself and more on its authority to act. The basic problem was that nothing in the Telecommunications Act purported to give the FCC general authority over the Internet. And by 2008, the FCC had spent most of a decade telling anyone who would listen that broadband Internet was an unregulated "information service" not subject to Title II common-carrier rules. The Internet Policy Statement from which the *Comcast* order derived its legal standards, recall, was the FCC's paraphrase of four voluntary principles originally suggested by a chairman who wanted to avoid governmental regulation in favor of industry self-regulation. The FCC's strategy, then, was to point to a variety of regulatory powers it did have, and to argue that the anti-blocking policy applied in *Comcast* was "ancillary" to those powers. *See generally* 47 U.S.C. § 154(i) (authorizing the FCC to "perform any and all acts, make such rules and regulations, and issue such orders, not inconsistent with this chapter, as may be necessary in the execution of its functions").

The D.C. Circuit was unimpressed. In an opinion by Judge David Tatel, it vacated the order. *See Comcast Corp. v. F.C.C.*, 600 F.3d 642 (D.C. Cir. 2010). In the court's view, none of the FCC's claimed sources of jurisdiction held up to scrutiny. Statements of Congressional policy "to promote the continued development of the Internet," 47 U.S.C. § 230(b)(1), and the like, for example, were "just that – statements of policy. They are not delegations of regulatory authority." Other sections explicitly denied that they provided regulatory authority, or gave the FCC only limited powers to write reports. And still others were waived because they were either not mentioned in the order or not mentioned on appeal. But the FCC did have one near-miss:

> We begin with section 706 of the Telecommunications Act of 1996, which provides that "[t]he Commission ... shall encourage the deployment on a reasonable and timely basis of advanced telecommunications capability to all Americans ... by utilizing ... price cap regulation, regulatory forbearance, measures that promote competition in the local telecommunications market, or other regulating methods that remove barriers to infrastructure investment." 47 U.S.C. § 1302(a). As the Commission points out, section 706 does contain a direct mandate – the Commission "shall encourage ... ." In an earlier, still-binding order, however, the Commission ruled that section 706 "does not constitute an independent grant of authority." *In re Deployment of Wireline Servs. Offering Advanced Telecomms. Capability*, 13 F.C.C.R. 24,012, 24,047, ¶ 77 (1998). Instead, the Commission explained, section 706 "directs the Commission to use the authority granted in other provisions ... to encourage the deployment of advanced services." *Id.* at 24,045, ¶ 69. ...

Comcast Corp., 600 F.3d at 658.

The *Preserving the Open Internet* Order

By the time the *Comcast Corp.* decision came down in April 2010, the FCC was on a new chairman, Julius Genachowski. Unlike Powell and Martin, he bad been appointed by a Democratic president, and he came into office as a strong proponent of network neutrality. Even before the decision, the FCC had started a rulemaking procecss, and the final rule was published in the *Federal Register* in 2011. The new rule explicitly rested on § 706, which the FCC now interpreted as a source of authority. Substantively, it added a nondiscrimination rule to the familiar rules against blocking. As the FCC explained:

> Today the Commission takes an important step to preserve the Internet as an open platform for innovation, investment, job creation, economic growth, competition, and free expression. To provide greater clarity and certainty regarding the continued freedom and openness of the Internet, we adopt three basic rules that are grounded in broadly accepted Internet norms, as well as our own prior decisions:
>
> i.   **Transparency**. Fixed and mobile broadband providers must disclose the network management practices, performance characteristics, and terms and conditions of their broadband services;
>
> ii. **No blocking.** Fixed broadband providers may not block lawful content, applications, services, or non-harmful devices; and
>
> iii. **No unreasonable discrimination**. Fixed broadband providers may not unreasonably discriminate in transmitting lawful network traffic.
>
> We believe these rules, applied with the complementary principle of reasonable network management, will empower and protect consumers and innovators while helping ensure that the Internet continues to flourish, with robust private investment and rapid innovation at both the core and the edge of the network. ...

Preserving the Open Internet, 76 Fed. Reg. 59,192 (2011). Again the FCC was sued, this time by Verizon. Again the case went before the D.C. Circuit. Again, Judge Tatel wrote the opinion. And again, he mostly struck down the FCC's rules on statutory authority grounds. *See Verizon v. F.C.C.*, 740 F.3d 623 (D.C. Cir. 2014). The reasons why the rules failed are subtle, and an understanding of them is crucial to understanding the FCC's next move. The court was untroubled by the FCC's decision to reverse its interpretation of § 706:

> But the Commission need not remain *forever* bound by the *Advanced Services Order*'s restrictive reading of section 706(a). An initial agency interpretation is not instantly carved in stone. The APA's requirement of reasoned decision-making ordinarily demands that an agency acknowledge and explain the reasons for a changed interpretation. But so long as an agency adequately explains the reasons for a reversal of policy, its new interpretation of a statute cannot be rejected simply because it is new. At the time we issued our *Comcast* opinion, the Commission failed to satisfy this requirement, as its assertion that section 706(a) gave it regulatory authority represented, at that point, an attempt to depart from a prior policy *sub silentio*.
>
> In the *Open Internet Order*, however, the Commission has offered a reasoned explanation for its changed understanding of section 706(a).
> ...
> The question, then, is this: Does the Commission's current understanding of section 706(a) as a grant of regulatory authority

represent a reasonable interpretation of an ambiguous statute? We believe it does.

Id. at 636–37. And the court agreed that "the Commission's prediction that the *Open Internet Order* regulations will encourage broadband deployment" was "both rational and supported by substantial evidence." *Id.* at 644.

Nonetheless, the *Open Internet* rulemaking still came to naught. The problem was the FCC's classification, still on the books, of fixed broadband Internet as an "information service" rather than as a "telecommunications service." Because the Act provided that a fixed ISP "shall be treated as a common carrier under this [Act] *only to the extent that it is engaged in providing telecommunications services,*" 47 U.S.C. § 153(51) (emphasis added), the court reasoned that the FCC was prohibited from treating it as a common carrier under any other source of authority. But that was precisely what the no-blocking and no-discrimination rules did:

> Significantly for our purposes, the Commission never argues that the *Open Internet Order*'s "no unreasonable discrimination" standard somehow differs from the nondiscrimination standard applied to common carriers generally ... . [T]he *Order* defines "reasonable network management" to include practices designed to protect the network itself by "addressing traffic that is harmful to the network" and "reducing or mitigating the effects of congestion." As Verizon correctly points out, however, this allowance "merely preserves a common carrier's traditional right to turn away business either because it is not of the type normally accepted or because the carrier's capacity has been exhausted." Railroads have no obligation to allow passengers to carry bombs on board, nor need they permit passengers to stand in the aisles if all seats are taken. It is for this reason that the Communications Act bars common carriers from engaging in "*unjust or unreasonable* discrimination," not *all* discrimination. 47 U.S.C. § 202 (emphasis added). ...
>
> Whether the *Open Internet Order*'s anti-blocking rules, applicable to both fixed and mobile broadband providers, likewise establish *per se* common carrier obligations is somewhat less clear. According to Verizon, they do because they deny "broadband providers discretion in deciding which traffic from ... edge providers to carry," and deny them "discretion over carriage terms by setting a uniform price of zero." This argument has some appeal. The anti-blocking rules establish a minimum level of service that broadband providers must furnish to all edge providers: edge providers' "content, applications [and] services" must be "effectively []usable." *Open Internet Order*, 25 F.C.C.R. at 17943 ¶ 66. The *Order* also expressly prohibits broadband providers from charging edge providers any fees for this minimum level of service. In requiring that all edge providers receive this minimum level of access for free, these rules would appear on their face to impose *per se* common carrier obligations with respect to that minimum level of service.

Verizon, 740 F.3d at 656–58. Only the transparency rules survived.

By the time the *Verizon v. FCC* decision came down in January 2014, chairman Genachowski had moved on. Now, network neutrality was in the hands of its fourth FCC chairman, Tom Wheeler. That the FCC would try again was not in much doubt. But the nature of the new rules was up in the air. At first, in its notice of proposed rulemaking, the agency offered to rely for the third time on § 706 but to write rules that fell slightly short of outright bans on blocking and discrimination so as not to fall afoul of the *de facto* common carriage doctrine. *Protecting and Promoting the Open Internet*, 79 Fed. Reg. 37,448 (proposed July 1, 2014).

Some network neutrality advocates were skeptical, arguing either that this middle course was unlikely to stand up in court, or that it would leave broadband ISPs with too much power over consumers' Internet connections. They argued instead that the FCC should bite the bullet and "reclassify" fixed broadband as a "telecommunications service" subject to Title II's common-carriage requirements. The administrative difficulty with that approach was that Title II classification would bring with it numerous common-carriage requirements in addition to the no-blocking and no-discrimination rules the FCC had promulgated in its first *Open Internet* order in 2011. For critics of network neutrality, the prospect of regulating ISPs' prices was a clear example of the kinds of intrusive regulations they had been warning against; the FCC's original decision to treat fixed broadband Internet service as an unregulated information service had been the right one. And most network neutrality advocates agreed that full-on Title II regulation was massive overkill – it was just such a concern that had led the FCC to rely on § 706 in the previous go-around. The workability of reclassification hinged, therefore, on the FCC's authority to "forbear" from applying some of the Title II rules to ISPs. Specifically, Congress had instructed the FCC to forbear when it determined that:

(1) enforcement of such regulation or provision is not necessary to ensure that the charges, practices, classifications, or regulations by, for, or in connection with that telecommunications carrier or telecommunications service are just and reasonable and are not unjustly or unreasonably discriminatory;

(2) enforcement of such regulation or provision is not necessary for the protection of consumers; and

(3) forbearance from applying such provision or regulation is consistent with the public interest.

47 U.S.C. § 160(a). Through 2014, a broad debate raged between advocates of strong neutrality rules under reclassification with forbearance, advocates of (possibly) weaker neutrality rules under § 706, and advocates of no neutrality rules at all. Everyone from HBO's John Oliver to President Obama weighed in, and the FCC received millions of public comments on the proposed rules. In the end – as detailed below – it chose reclassification with forbearance.

QUESTIONS

1. Why isn't the market for broadband Internet service more competitive? If consumers really have few good options for Internet service, why don't more companies get into the business?

2. Why did Madison River restrict VoIP use? Who won and who lost when it did? Why did Comcast restrict BitTorrent use? Who won and who lost?

3. In judging alleged network neutrality violations, how should regulators and the public think about arguments like the claim that sending RST packets conflicts with the technical standard defining TCP/IP? Who should get to decide what counts as a "right" or "wrong" way of using technologies like TCP/IP?

4. (If you have read the Note on Administrative Law) Did the D.C. Circuit get it right in *Comcast* and *Verizon*? If so, what was the FCC thinking when it twice tried - and twice failed – to rely on section 706 to justify network neutrality regulation? After *Verizon*, could the FCC have tried section 706 a third time by narrowing the rules? Or was Title II reclassification the only feasible option left for network neutrality rules?

5. Where is Congress in all of this? Congress could certainly clean up the mess it created in the 1996 Act if it wanted. Why hasn't it?

NOTE ON WIRELESS REGULATION

This note covers the barest basics of how the FCC regulates wireless communications, with an emphasis on how it differs from the regulation of "fixed" or "wireline" communications discussed above.

Since the Radio Act of 1927, the agency that became the FCC has strictly regulated use of "spectrum." That is, it restricts who can transmit electromagnetic signals, with what devices, at what frequencies, and at how much power. Until the last few years, the economically dominant use of spectrum encountered by ordinary consumers was for *broadcasting*: transmitting radio or television signals to everyone in a station's service area. Broadcast regulation is the subject of Title III of the Communications Act of 1934 (as extensively amended over the decades). The FCC divides the country into allotments, which consist of a location and a frequency, and then assigns licenses to local broadcasters, which allow them to broadcast in that location on that frequency, at specified power levels. For example, in the Boston area, channel 4 is assigned to WBZ, a CBS affiliate, which is allowed to broadcast from an antenna located at latitude 42°18'37" north and longitude 71°14'14" west at a power of 41.88 kilowatts and using the frequencies between 66 and 72 megahertz.

Broadcasters like WBZ enjoy near-complete freedom in choosing what programs to air, *see* 47 U.S.C. § 326, subject only to a few restrictions. For example, television stations may not air more than 10.5 minutes of commercials per hour during shows directed at children, *see id.* § 303a(b), and they may not broadcast hoax news reports they know will cause public harm, *see id.* § 325(a).

But broadcasting is hardly the only way to use spectrum; there is also a long history of using it for two-way communications. The simplest and oldest such systems involved nothing more complicated than radio users transmitting and listening on the same frequency. To this day, this is how CB radio and ham radio work: everyone in the same area using the same frequency can hear everyone else, and users take turns speaking. It took two crucial engineering advances to get from there to the mobile phones we enjoy today. First, because most phone users want private conversations rather than chat rooms, phones had to become sophisticated about picking unused bits of spectrum to keep different calls from interfering with each other. Second, because mobile phone users want to be mobile, phones had to become equally sophisticated about finding a nearby tower (or "base station") to take their calls and at switching from one tower to another. Thanks in large part to a series of breakthroughs by Bell Labs researchers from the 1940s through the 1970s, both problems were successfully solved. Major commercial buildouts of the necessary technical infrastructure followed, and in the 1990s and 2000s, mobile phone service went mainstream. Mass-market mobile data services – using the same engineering principles but carrying bits rather than voice signals – soon followed. Today, mobile telephone and data service are so immensely popular that the FCC is engaged in a massive effort to reallocate spectrum from broadcasting to mobile, using a series of "incentive auctions" to sell spectrum to mobile entrepreneurs and use the revenues to compensate broadcasters for giving up their licenses.

The regulatory treatment of mobile service has traditionally fallen somewhere between Title II and Title III. The major cellular carriers (currently AT&T, Verizon, Sprint, and T-Mobile) are licensed by the FCC to allow consumers' phones to transmit to and from their towers, and they use those back-and-forth transmissions to provide phone and data connections for their customers. The FCC has traditionally treated cellular telephone service as a "commercial mobile service," defined as "any mobile service ... that is provided for profit and makes interconnected service available ... to the public," 47 U.S.C. § 332(d)(1). The crucial term is "interconnected services," which is itself defined as "service that is interconnected with the public switched network," id. § 332(d)(2). The "public switched network," has traditionally referred to the telephone network; see, e.g., 47 C.F.R. § 20.3 (2014) (defining "public switched network" in terms of the "North American Numbering Plan," i.e., telephone numbers), but the FCC has the authority to redefine the term by regulation, see 47 U.S.C. § 332(d)(2).

Commercial mobile services are generally treated as common carriers, subject to the same forbearance authority the FCC enjoys with respect to Title II for telecommunications services. Id. § 332(c). Here, the FCC has exercised its forbearance authority liberally, exempting cellular voice from almost all common-carriage requirements beyond the most basic nondiscrimination rules. Thus, the cellular carriers are free to charge different customers different rates; if Verizon Wireless gives your next-door neighbor a discount to keep her as a customer but refuses to offer you the same deal, neither the FCC nor the courts will object. See, e.g., Orloff v. F.C.C., 352 F.3d 415 (D.C. Cir. 2003).

While there is little question that cellular *telephone* service is a commercial mobile service subject to common-carrier rules, it was not until 2007 that the FCC took a definitive position on cellular *data*. In a declaratory ruling, it held that cellular data is a "private mobile service" instead, *In re Appropriate Regulatory Treatment for Broadband Access to the Internet Over Wireless Networks*, 22 F.C.C. Rcd. 5901 (2007), and hence almost entirely exempt from regulation. See 47 U.S.C. § 332(c)(2) (stating that private mobile services "shall not be treated as a common carrier for any purpose").

Thus, cellular carriers generally had a free hand in operating their networks. There has never been a general equivalent to *Carterfone* for mobile phones. You can plug your own handset into the telephone jack in the wall, but you can only use an approved phone on a mobile carrier's network. The carriers have traditionally used this control to "lock down" phones, so that they work only on one carrier's network and run only applications approved by the carrier. Carriers also typically put strict limits on data usage, with high fees for going over your monthly quota. Some of this tight grip has been loosening recently: Apple, not the carriers, determines which apps are available for the iPhone.

The FCC's first serious foray into neutrality for cellular data came in 2008, only a year after the FCC had classified it as a private mobile service. By reassigning UHF television stations to lower-numbered channels, the FCC was able to free up channels 52 through 69, corresponding to frequencies between roughly 700 and 800 megahertz (and hence known as the "700 megahertz" auction). The FCC auctioned off this spectrum in several blocks. Google made a high-stakes play for the

C Block, offering to make a minimum bid of $4.6 billion in exchange for open-device and open-application rules. The FCC agreed, writing the rules into its regulations:

> Licensees offering service on spectrum subject to this section shall not deny, limit, or restrict the ability of their customers to use the devices and applications of their choice on the licensee's C Block network, except: (1) Insofar as such use would not be compliant with published technical standards reasonably necessary for the management or protection of the licensee's network, or (2) As required to comply with statute or applicable government regulation.

47 C.F.R. § 27.16(b). Verizon Wireless won the auctions for the C Block in the continental United States; as a result, it has been bound by a flavor of network neutrality ever since.

In its first *Open Internet* order in 2011, the FCC subjected mobile data services to weaker neutrality rules than their fixed counterparts. While fixed broadband services were prohibited from blocking "lawful content, applications, services, or non-harmful devices"; mobile broadband services were prohibited from blocking only "lawful websites" and "applications that compete with the provider's voice or video telephony services." The FCC declined entirely to apply the no-discrimination rule to mobile. But even this narrower no-blocking rule suffered the same fate as the broader rules for fixed broadband, again because of the FCC's own previous regulatory moves. Thanks to the FCC's classification of cellular data as private mobile service rather than as commercial mobile service in 2007, it was subject to section 332's prohibition on treating private mobile services as common carriers – and the no-blocking rule was, in the court's view, equivalent to common carriage.

Here, too, the FCC had the choice between doing nothing, trying to push through with neutrality rules narrow enough to avoid being treated as common carriage, and full-on reclassification. In the end, it accepted the analogy to Title II reclassification for fixed broadband and reclassified cellular data as a commercial mobile service.

NOTE ON INTERCONNECTION

Another emerging issue has to do with the terms on which ISPs connect their networks to each other. To understand the issue, a little technical background will be helpful. A broadband provider has a relationship with its customers, and it has relationships with the other networks its own network connects to. It has no direct relationship with websites (usually now called "edge providers"). To block or discriminate against an edge provider, it can detect that packets are headed to or from a particular IP address, or it can use deep packet inspection to discover that they are carrying a particular kind of data, such as VoIP calls or streaming video. Checking IP addresses is easy; ISPs do that all the time already as part of their work delivering packets. Deep packet inspection is harder; it requires specialized routing equipment.

But these are far from the only reasons that customers will experience different edge providers differently. To take a simple example, your home ISP will help you load a site hosted in the United States more quickly than one hosted in rural Sri Lanka. This isn't the result of a deliberate action to disfavor the Sri Lankan website; it reflects the fact that the signals must travel much further, through more computers along the way. The architecture of the Internet itself – the *interconnec-*

tion between different networks – affects the speed and reliability of transmissions.

So take another example slightly closer to the point. Twitch.tv lets videogame fans watch live streams of each other playing games: it broadcasts everything from major videogame tournaments to speedruns (in which players try to beat a level a fast as possible). All this video, combined with Twitch's booming popularity (more than 40 million viewers), make it a huge user of bandwidth. It now accounts for more than 1% of all home Internet bandwidth use in the United States. Twitch couldn't possibly hope to get that video to viewers without some serious bandwidth connecting its servers to the Internet. It pays its own ISP, and pays handsomely, to connect it to the Internet. No one thinks that it's a violation of any relevant neutrality principle that Twitch has to pay more than the all-text IsItChristmas.com does.

So: Twitch.tv pays its ISP and viewers pay their ISPs. This leaves open the question of how the video gets from the former to the latter. This is the province of interconnection: how, where, and on what terms different companies link their networks together and exchange packets. To interconnect, two companies must bring their networks to a single location (an "interconnection point") where they can hand off packets one to the other. Just like any buildout of a network, interconnection is costly: it requires purchasing and installing hardware, laying the cables to reach a shared interconnection point, and maintaining the whole apparatus.

The interconnection market is global, complicated, opaque, and almost entirely unregulated. Because the terms of many interconnection contracts are secret, the market is poorly understood. Interconnection agreements provide a mechanism for money to flow to the parts of the Internet – especially backbone networks – that have few or no end-user customers. The customers pay their own ISPs, who pay the backbone networks for *transit*: connectivity to the rest of the Internet. Sometimes, networks (often ones that are roughly comparable in size and/or type) will agree to *peer* with each other and carry each others' traffic for free.*

For a good example of the complexity that interconnection introduces, consider *content delivery networks* (or CDNs), such as Akamai and Amazon CloudFront. A CDN operates its own global network of servers. Instead of having a massive bank of servers all located at its headquarters in Bristol, Connecticut, an Akamai customer like ESPN will contract to have Akamai distribute its content using Akamai's network. ESPN continually supplies Akamai with webpages and videos, which Akamai then sends out to its servers around the world using its private network. Then, when an ESPN fan in San Francisco wants to check the latest basketball headlines, the request is routed to a nearby Akamai server, which responds far more quickly than a server in Connecticut could. Moreover, when a thousand fans in San Francisco check the latest basketball headlines, their requests all go to the same local Akamai server: the content had to be sent across the country only once, rather than a thousand times. (A CDN is, therefore, a clever form of geographic caching.)

But now for the twist. *How does content get from a CDN to a user?* The answer, obviously, is through the user's local ISP. But this requires interconnection – and the terms of the interconnection are subject to private negotiation between the CDN and the ISP. Compare a CDN that has access to interconnection with an ISP

---

* There are other differences between transit and peering, but this is not the place to get into them.

around the country with one that doesn't. The connected CDN will be perceptibly faster for users; its clients will get better connectivity to users. The ISP is therefore in a position to discriminate among websites, at least at the level of discriminating among CDNs. Or perhaps more lucratively, it is in a position to demand that the CDNs pay it handsomely for interconnection. The ISP isn't charging websites directly, but it is charging them indirectly.

Interconnection boiled over into public consciousness in a series of disputes involving Comcast and Netflix. Initially, Netflix had been using Akamai as a CDN; Akamai in turn paid Comcast to connect to the Comcast network. But in 2010, Netflix signed a deal with Level3 instead, which had peering and transit agreements with Comcast. Comcast objected, and threatened to terminate its relationship with Level3 unless the terms were renegotiated to send more money from Level3 (and thus, ultimately from Netflix) to Comcast. Level3 went public, angrily.

To Comcast, this was simply a standard interconnection dispute about the relative flows of traffic from Comcast to Level3 and from Level3 to Comcast. When the inbound traffic Level3 was sending Comcast went up sharply, Comcast demanded to be paid for it. But to Level3 and to Netflix, this was a network neutrality violation. Comcast was seeking to extract money by discriminating in the terms on which it provided service to Netflix. The argument bubbled for several years, during which Netflix's overall share of bandwidth on the Internet in the U.S. spiked dramatically to over 30%. Netflix bought transit from a variety of other networks, but its overall bandwidth usage was so high that it was simply unable to get the level of bandwidth to its customers on Comcast's network that it wanted without upgrades to the interconnection between those other networks and Comcast's – and Comcast held firm in demanding payment. Finally, in 2014, the still-complaining Netflix agreed to pay for direct interconnection with Comcast.

Legally, both Title II telecommunications carriers and commercial mobile services are required to interconnect when ordered to do so by the FCC. *See* 47 U.S.C. §§ 201(a) (general common-carrier duty to connect), § 251(a) (telecommunications carriers), 332(c)(1)(B) (commercial mobile services). Reclassification without forbearance would therefore have immediately regulated the currently unregulated market for interconnection. Instead, as discussed below, the FCC adopted a wait-and-see attitude toward interconnection, not applying its new open Internet rules but asserting authority to step in as needed on a case-by-case basis.

QUESTIONS

1. Is interconnection a network neutrality issue? If so, does this cut for or against regulation?

2. Now that Netflix interconnects directly with Comcast, streaming video traffic flows from Netflix to Comcast to consumers. How does the money flow? Suppose that Comcast starts billing Netflix an amount that works out to $5 per month for each Netflix customer on Comcast's network. What will that do to the subscription fees Netflix and Comcast charge their customers?

PROTECTING AND PROMOTING THE OPEN INTERNET
80 Fed. Reg. 19,738 (Apr. 13, 2015)

I. INTRODUCTION

The open Internet drives the American economy and serves, every day, as a critical tool for America's citizens to conduct commerce, communicate, educate, entertain, and engage in the world around them. The benefits of an open Internet are undisputed. But it must remain open: open for commerce, innovation, and speech; open for consumers and for the innovation created by applications developers and content companies; and open for expansion and investment by America's broadband providers. For over a decade, the Commission has been committed to protecting and promoting an open Internet. ...

II. EXECUTIVE SUMMARY

A. Strong Rules That Protect Consumers from Past and Future Tactics that Threaten the Open Internet

1. Clear, Bright-Line Rules

Because the record overwhelmingly supports adopting rules and demonstrates that three specific practices invariably harm the open Internet – Blocking, Throttling, and Paid Prioritization – this Order bans each of them, applying the same rules to both fixed and mobile broadband Internet access service.

No Blocking. Consumers who subscribe to a retail broadband Internet access service must get what they have paid for – access to all (lawful) destinations on the Internet. This essential and well-accepted principle has long been a tenet of Commission policy, stretching back to its landmark decision in *Carterfone*, which protected a customer's right to connect a telephone to the monopoly telephone network. Thus, this Order adopts a straightforward ban:

[47 C.F.R. § 8.5 – *No blocking*]

> A person engaged in the provision of broadband Internet access service, insofar as such person is so engaged, shall not block lawful content, applications, services, or non- harmful devices, subject to reasonable network management.

No Throttling. The 2010 open Internet rule against blocking contained an ancillary prohibition against the degradation of lawful content, applications, services, and devices, on the ground that such degradation would be tantamount to blocking. This Order creates a separate rule to guard against degradation targeted at specific uses of a customer's broadband connection:

[47 C.F.R. § 8.7 – *No throttling*]

> A person engaged in the provision of broadband Internet access service, insofar as such person is so engaged, shall not impair or degrade lawful Internet traffic on the basis of Internet content, application, or service, or use of a non-harmful device, subject to reasonable network management.

The ban on throttling is necessary both to fulfill the reasonable expectations of a customer who signs up for a broadband service that promises access to all of the lawful Internet, and to avoid gamesmanship designed to avoid the no-blocking rule by, for example, rendering an application effectively, but not technically, unusable. It prohibits the degrading of Internet traffic based on source, destination, or content. It also specifically prohibits conduct that singles out content competing with a broadband provider's business model.

No Paid Prioritization. Paid prioritization occurs when a broadband provider accepts payment (monetary or otherwise) to manage its network in a way that benefits particular content, applications, services, or devices. To protect against "fast lanes," this Order adopts a rule that establishes that:

[47 C.F.R. § 8.9 - *No paid prioritization*]

[(a)] A person engaged in the provision of broadband Internet access service, insofar as such person is so engaged, shall not engage in paid prioritization.

[(b)] "Paid prioritization" refers to the management of a broadband provider's network to directly or indirectly favor some traffic over other traffic, including through use of techniques such as traffic shaping, prioritization, resource reservation, or other forms of preferential traffic management, either (a) in exchange for consideration (monetary or otherwise) from a third party, or (b) to benefit an affiliated entity.[18]

[(c)] The Commission may waive the ban on paid prioritization only if the petitioner demonstrates that the practice would provide some significant public interest benefit and would not harm the open nature of the Internet.]

The record demonstrates the need for strong action. The Verizon court itself noted that broadband networks have "powerful incentives to accept fees from edge providers, either in return for excluding their competitors or for granting them prioritized access to end users." Mozilla, among many such commenters, explained that "[p]rioritization . . . inherently creates fast and slow lanes." Although there are arguments that some forms of paid prioritization could be beneficial, the practical difficulty is this: the threat of harm is overwhelming, case-by-case enforcement can be cumbersome for individual consumers or edge providers, and there is no practical means to measure the extent to which edge innovation and investment would be chilled. And, given the dangers, there is no room for a blanket exception for instances where consumer permission is buried in a service plan – the threats of consumer deception and confusion are simply too great.

2. No Unreasonable Interference or Unreasonable Disadvantage to Consumers or Edge Providers ...

The key insight of the virtuous cycle is that broadband providers have both the incentive and the ability to act as gatekeepers standing between edge providers and consumers. As gatekeepers, they can block access altogether; they can target competitors, including competitors to their own video services; and they can extract unfair tolls. Such conduct would, as the Commission concluded in 2010, "reduce the rate of innovation at the edge and, in turn, the likely rate of improvements to network infrastructure." In other words, when a broadband provider acts as a gatekeeper, it actually chokes consumer demand for the very broadband product it can supply.

The bright-line bans on blocking, throttling, and paid prioritization will go a long way to preserve the virtuous cycle. But not all the way. Gatekeeper power can be exercised through a variety of technical and economic means, and without a catch-all standard, it would be that, as Benjamin Franklin said, "a little neglect may breed great mischief." Thus, the Order adopts the following standard:

---

18 Unlike the no-blocking and no-throttling rules, there is no "reasonable network management" exception to the paid prioritization rule because paid prioritization is inherently a business practice rather than a network management practice.

[47 C.F.R. § 8.11 – *No unreasonable interference or unreasonable disadvantage standard for Internet conduct.*]

> Any person engaged in the provision of broadband Internet access service, insofar as such person is so engaged, shall not unreasonably interfere with or unreasonably disadvantage (i) end users' ability to select, access, and use broadband Internet access service or the lawful Internet content, applications, services, or devices of their choice, or (ii) edge providers' ability to make lawful content, applications, services, or devices available to end users. Reasonable network management shall not be considered a violation of this rule.

This "no unreasonable interference/disadvantage" standard protects free expression, thus fulfilling the congressional policy that "the Internet offer[s] a forum for a true diversity of political discourse, unique opportunities for cultural development, and myriad avenues for intellectual activity." And the standard will permit considerations of asserted benefits of innovation as well as threatened harm to end users and edge providers.

3. Enhanced Transparency

The Commission's 2010 transparency rule, upheld by the *Verizon* court, remains in full effect:

[47 C.F.R. § 8.3 – *Transparency.*]

> A person engaged in the provision of broadband Internet access service shall publicly disclose accurate information regarding the network management practices, performance, and commercial terms of its broadband Internet access services sufficient for consumers to make informed choices regarding use of such services and for content, application, service, and device providers to develop, market, and maintain Internet offerings.

Today's Order reaffirms the importance of ensuring transparency, so that consumers are fully informed about the Internet access they are purchasing and so that edge providers have the information they need to understand whether their services will work as advertised. To do that, the Order builds on the strong foundation established in 2010 and enhances the transparency rule for both end users and edge providers, including by adopting a requirement that broadband providers always must disclose promotional rates, all fees and/or surcharges, and all data caps or data allowances; adding packet loss as a measure of network performance that must be disclosed; and requiring specific notification to consumers that a "network practice" is likely to significantly affect their use of the service. Out of an abundance of caution and in response to a request by the American Cable Association, we also adopt a temporary exemption from these enhancements for small providers (defined for the purposes of the temporary exception as providers with 100,000 or fewer subscribers), and we direct our Consumer & Governmental Affairs Bureau to adopt an Order by December 15, 2015 concerning whether to make the exception permanent and, if so, the appropriate definition of "small." Lastly, we create for all providers a "safe harbor" process for the format and nature of the required disclosure to consumers, which we believe will result in more effective presentation of consumer-focused information by broadband providers.

4. Scope of the Rules

The open Internet rules described above apply to both fixed and mobile broadband Internet access service. Consistent with the 2010 Order, today's Order applies its rules to the consumer-facing service that broadband networks provide, which is known as "broadband Internet access service" (BIAS) and is defined to be:

[47 C.F.R. § 8.2 – *Definitions*.]

A mass-market retail service by wire or radio that provides the capability to transmit data to and receive data from all or substantially all Internet endpoints, including any capabilities that are incidental to and enable the operation of the communications service, but excluding dial-up Internet access service. This term also encompasses any service that the Commission finds to be providing a functional equivalent of the service described in the previous sentence, or that is used to evade the protections set forth in this Part.

As in 2010, BIAS does not include enterprise services, virtual private network services, hosting, or data storage services. Further, we decline to apply the open Internet rules to premises operators to the extent they may be offering broadband Internet access service as we define it today.

In defining this service we make clear that we are responding to the *Verizon* court's conclusion that broadband providers "furnish a service to edge providers" (and that this service was being treated as common carriage *per se*). As discussed further below, we make clear that broadband Internet access service encompasses this service to edge providers. Broadband providers sell retail customers the ability to go anywhere (lawful) on the Internet. Their representation that they will transport and deliver traffic to and from all or substantially all Internet endpoints includes the promise to transmit traffic to and from those Internet endpoints back to the user.

Interconnection. BIAS involves the exchange of traffic between a broadband Internet access provider and connecting networks. The representation to retail customers that they will be able to reach "all or substantially all Internet endpoints" necessarily includes the promise to make the interconnection arrangements necessary to allow that access.

As discussed below, we find that broadband Internet access service is a "telecommunications service" and subject to sections 201, 202, and 208 (along with key enforcement provisions). As a result, commercial arrangements for the exchange of traffic with a broadband Internet access provider are within the scope of Title II, and the Commission will be available to hear disputes raised under sections 201 and 202 on a case-by-case basis: an appropriate vehicle for enforcement where disputes are primarily over commercial terms and that involve some very large corporations, including companies like transit providers and Content Delivery Networks (CDNs), that act on behalf of smaller edge providers.

But this Order does not apply the open Internet rules to interconnection. Three factors are critical in informing this approach to interconnection. First, the nature of Internet traffic, driven by massive consumption of video, has challenged traditional arrangements – placing more emphasis on the use of CDNs or even direct connections between content providers (like Netflix or Google) and last-mile broadband providers. Second, it is clear that consumers have been subject to degradation resulting from commercial disagreements, perhaps most notably in a series of disputes between Netflix and large last- mile broadband providers. But, third, the causes of past disruption and – just as importantly – the potential for future degradation through interconnection disputes – are reflected in very different narratives in the record.

While we have more than a decade's worth of experience with last-mile practices, we lack a similar depth of background in the Internet traffic exchange context. Thus, we find that the best approach is to watch, learn, and act as required, but not intervene now, especially not with prescriptive rules. This Order – for the first time – provides authority to consider claims involving interconnection, a process that is sure to bring greater understanding to the Commission.

Reasonable Network Management. As with the 2010 rules, this Order contains an exception for reasonable network management, which applies to all but the paid prioritization rule (which, by definition, is not a means of managing a network):

[47 C.F.R § 8.2 – *Definitions*]

A network management practice is a practice that has a primarily technical network management justification, but does not include other business practices. A network management practice is reasonable if it is primarily used for and tailored to achieving a legitimate network management purpose, taking into account the particular network architecture and technology of the broadband Internet access service.

Recently, significant concern has arisen when mobile providers have attempted to justify certain practices as reasonable network management practices, such as applying speed reductions to customers using "unlimited data plans" in ways that effectively force them to switch to price plans with less generous data allowances. For example, in the summer of 2014, Verizon announced a change to its "unlimited" data plan for LTE customers, which would have limited the speeds of LTE customers using grandfathered "unlimited" plans once they reached a certain level of usage each month. Verizon briefly described this change as within the scope of "reasonable network management," before changing course and withdrawing the change.

With mobile broadband service now subject to the same rules as fixed broadband service, the Order expressly recognizes that evaluation of network management practices will take into account the additional challenges involved in the management of mobile networks, including the dynamic conditions under which they operate. It also recognizes the specific network management needs of other technologies, such as unlicensed Wi-Fi networks.

Non-Broadband Internet Access Service Data Services. The 2010 rules included an exception for "specialized services." This Order likewise recognizes that some data services – like facilities-based VoIP offerings, heart monitors, or energy consumption sensors – may be offered by a broadband provider but do not provide access to the Internet generally. The term "specialized services" can be confusing because the critical point is not whether the services are "specialized"; it is that they are not broadband Internet access service. IP services that do not travel over broadband Internet access service, like the facilities-based VoIP services used by many cable customers, are not within the scope of the open Internet rules, which protect access or use of broadband Internet access service. Nonetheless, these other non-broadband Internet access service data services could be provided in a manner that undermines the purpose of the open Internet rules and that will not be permitted. The Commission expressly reserves the authority to take action if a service is, in fact, providing the functional equivalent of broadband Internet access service or is being used to evade the open Internet rules. The Commission will vigilantly watch for such abuse, and its actions will be aided by the existing transparency requirement that non-broadband Internet access service data services be disclosed.

5. Enforcement

The Commission may enforce the open Internet rules through investigation and the processing of complaints (both formal and informal). In addition, the Commission may provide guidance through the use of enforcement advisories and advisory opinions, and it will appoint an ombudsperson. In order to provide the Commission with additional understanding, particularly of technical issues, the Order delegates to the Enforcement Bureau the authority to request a written opinion from an outside technical organization or otherwise to obtain objective advice from industry standard-setting bodies or similar organizations. ...

C. Sustainable Open Internet Rules

We ground our open Internet rules in multiple sources of legal authority – including both section 706 and Title II of the Communications Act. The *Verizon* court upheld the Commission's use of section 706 as a substantive source of legal authority to adopt open Internet protections. But it held that, "[g]iven the Commission's still-binding decision to classify broadband providers ... as providers of 'information services,'" open Internet protections that regulated broadband providers as common carriers would violate the Act. Rejecting the Commission's argument that broadband providers only served retail consumers, the *Verizon* court went on to explain that "broadband providers furnish a service to edge providers, thus undoubtedly functioning as edge providers' 'carriers,'" and held that the 2010 no blocking and no unreasonable discrimination rules impermissibly "obligated [broadband providers] to act as common carriers."

The *Verizon* decision thus made clear that section 706 affords the Commission substantive authority, and that open Internet protections are within the scope of that authority. And this Order relies on section 706 for the open Internet rules. But, in light of *Verizon*, absent a classification of broadband providers as providing a "telecommunications service," the Commission could only rely on section 706 to put in place open Internet protections that steered clear of regulating broadband providers as common carriers *per se*. Thus, in order to bring a decade of debate to a certain conclusion, we conclude that the best path is to rely on all available sources of legal authority – while applying them with a light touch consistent with further investment and broadband deployment. Taking the *Verizon* decision's implicit invitation, we revisit the Commission's classification of the retail broadband Internet access service as an information service and clarify that this service encompasses the so-called "edge service."

Exercising our delegated authority to interpret ambiguous terms in the Communications Act, as confirmed by the Supreme Court in *Brand X*, today's Order concludes that the facts in the market today are very different from the facts that supported the Commission's 2002 decision to treat cable broadband as an information service and its subsequent application to fixed and mobile broadband services. Those prior decisions were based largely on a factual record compiled over a decade ago, during an earlier time when, for example, many consumers would use homepages supplied by their broadband provider. In fact, the *Brand X* Court explicitly acknowledged that the Commission had previously classified the transmission service, which broadband providers offer, as a telecommunications service and that the Commission could return to that classification if it provided an adequate justification. Moreover, a number of parties who, in this proceeding, now oppose our reclassification of broadband Internet access service, previously argued that cable broadband should be deemed a telecommunications service. As the record reflects, times and usage patterns have changed and it is clear that broadband providers are offering both consumers and edge providers straightforward transmission capabilities that the Communications Act defines as a "telecommunications service."

The *Brand X* decision made famous the metaphor of pizza delivery. Justice Scalia, in dissent, concluded that the Commission had exceeded its legal authority by classifying cable-modem service as an "information service." To make his point, Justice Scalia described a pizzeria offering delivery services as well as selling pizzas and concluded that, similarly – broadband providers were offering "telecommunications services" even if that service was not offered on a "stand-alone basis."

To take Justice Scalia's metaphor a step further, suppose that in 2014, the pizzeria owners discovered that other nearby restaurants did not deliver their food and thus concluded that the pizza- delivery drivers could generate more revenue by delivering from any neighborhood restaurant (including their own pizza some of the time). Consumers would clearly understand that they are being offered a delivery service.

Today, broadband providers are offering stand-alone transmission capacity and that conclusion is not changed even if, as Justice Scalia recognized, other products may be offered at the same time. The trajectory of technology in the decade since the *Brand X* decision has been towards greater and greater modularity. For example, consumers have considerable power to combine their mobile broadband connections with the device, operating systems, applications, Internet services, and content of their choice. Today, broadband Internet access service is fundamentally understood by customers as a transmission platform through which consumers can access third-party content, applications, and services of their choosing.

Based on this updated record, this Order concludes that the retail broadband Internet access service available today is best viewed as separately identifiable offers of (1) a broadband Internet access service that is a telecommunications service (including assorted functions and capabilities used for the management and control of that telecommunication service) and (2) various "add-on" applications, content, and services that generally are information services. This finding more than reasonably interprets the ambiguous terms in the Communications Act, best reflects the factual record in this proceeding, and will most effectively permit the implementation of sound policy consistent with statutory objectives, including the adoption of effective open Internet protections.

This Order also revisits the Commission's prior classification of mobile broadband Internet access service as a private mobile service, which cannot be subject to common carrier regulation, and finds that it is best viewed as a commercial mobile service or, in the alternative, the functional equivalent of commercial mobile service. Under the statutory definition, commercial mobile services must be "interconnected with the public switched network (as such terms are defined by regulation by the Commission)." Consistent with that delegation of authority to define these terms, and with the Commission's previous recognition that the public switched network will grow and change over time, this Order updates the definition of public switched network to reflect current technology, by including services that use public IP addresses. Under this revised definition, the Order concludes that mobile broadband Internet access service is interconnected with the public switched network. In the alternative, the Order concludes that mobile broadband

Internet access service is the functional equivalent of commercial mobile service because, like commercial mobile service, it is a widely available, for profit mobile service that offers mobile subscribers the capability to send and receive communications, including voice, on their mobile device.

By classifying broadband Internet access service under Title II of the Act, in our view the Commission addresses any limitations that past classification decisions placed on the ability to adopt strong open Internet rules, as interpreted by the D.C. Circuit in the *Verizon* case.

Having classified broadband Internet access service as a telecommunications service, we respond to the *Verizon* court's holding, supporting our open Internet rules under the Commission's Title II authority and removing any common carriage limitation on the exercise of our section 706 authority. For mobile broadband services, we also ground the open Internet rules in our Title III authority to protect the public interest through the management of spectrum licensing.

D. Broad Forbearance

In finding that broadband Internet access service is subject to Title II, we simultaneously exercise the Commission's forbearance authority to forbear from 30 statutory provisions and render over 700 codified rules inapplicable, to establish a light-touch regulatory framework tailored to preserving those provisions that advance our goals of more, better, and open broadband. We thus forbear from the vast majority of rules adopted under Title II. [Most notably, the FCC forbore from applying:

- Sections 203 and 204, which required service providers to file tariffs and required FCC approval of their rates and practices, along with numerous other sections relating to the FCC's enforcement and investigatory powers in connection with tariffs;

- Section 214, which requires FCC approval before a carrier discontinues existing service;

- Sections 251, 252, and 256, which set out a detailed framework for the negotiation, arbitration, and approval of interconnection agreements, preferring to leave interconnection disputes for case-by-case resolution; and

- Numerous provisions whose applicability to Internet, rather than telephone, service is hard to discern, such as sections 227 (relating to the national Do Not Call list), and 228 (relating to the pay-per-call services popularly known as "1-900 numbers").

The FCC chose not to forbear from the basic service-to-all and non-discrimination rules of sections 201 and 202, along with its authority to investigate and act on complaints under section 208. Many of the details of the forbearance decisions, such as their interaction with the roaming rules for mobile services, are highly technical. All in all, the forbearance section of the order spans sixty-four pages.]

QUESTIONS

1. How is paid prioritization different from throttling, interference, or blocking? Is it a good thing or a bad thing?

2. Suppose that YouTube, in light of its overwhelming popularity with users, demands that ISPs start paying it. When Time Warner refuses, YouTube makes its HD videos unavailable to Time Warner customers by detecting Time Warner IP addresses; it delivers them lower-quality SD videos instead. Would this violate the *Open Internet* order? Should it?

3. The Wayne Foundation has proposed to give inexpensive free smartphones to every American living below 150% of the poverty line. These phones would come with 500 minutes a month of free voice calls and would have unlimited free data use for "basic services" provided at wayne.org, so that anyone can get online for essential resources like government services, maps, messaging, etc. Anyone who wants would be eligible to be issued a subdomain (e.g. google.wayne.org, fbi.gov.wayne.org, lolcats.wayne.org, etc.), but the sites must be coded in a restricted subset of HTML to ensure that they are low-bandwidth: they cannot use video, play music, download large images, etc. Users would be permitted to purchase additional phone time and data, but at their own expense. Is this plan legal under the *Open Internet* order? Should it be?

4. (If you have read the Note on Administrative Law) In *United States Telecom Association v. FCC*, 825 F.3d 674 (D.C. Cir. 2016), the D.C. Circuit upheld the *Open Internet* order against a battery of administrative-law challenges. Is that right? Are the FCC's interpretations of "telecommunications service" and "commercial mobile service" reasonable constructions of ambiguous statutory terms under *Chevron*? Is its decision to reverse course and engage in reclassification adequately justified under *Fox*? Are its views on the costs and benefits of neutrality rules supported by substantial evidence? And are the rules themselves arbitrary and capricious?

5. (If you have read the Note on Wireless Network Regulation) Why did the FCC adopt a more hands-off attitude towards mobile Internet service in its 2011 Open Internet order? Why did it change its mind in the 2015 order?

6. (If you have read the Note on Interconnection) Does the order have anything to say about the Comcast/Level 3 interconnection dispute?

DISSENTING STATEMENT OF COMMISSIONER AJIT PAI
PROTECTING AND PROMOTING THE OPEN INTERNET
GN Docket No. 14–28 (Feb. 26, 2015)

Americans love the free and open Internet. We relish our freedom to speak, to post, to rally, to learn, to listen, to watch, and to connect online. The Internet has become a powerful force for freedom, both at home and abroad. So it is sad to witness the FCC's unprecedented attempt to replace that freedom with government control.

It shouldn't be this way. For twenty years, there's been a bipartisan consensus in favor of a free and open Internet. A Republican Congress and a Democratic President enshrined in the Telecommunications Act of 1996 the principle that the Internet should be a "vibrant and competitive free market . . . unfettered by Federal or State regulation." And dating back to the Clinton Administration, every FCC Chairman—Republican and Democrat—has let the Internet grow free from utility-style regulation. The result? The Internet has been an amazing success story, changing our lives and the world in ways that would have been unimaginable when the 1996 Act was passed.

But today, the FCC abandons those policies. It reclassifies broadband Internet access service as a Title II telecommunications service. It seizes unilateral authority to regulate Internet conduct, to direct where Internet service providers put their investments, and to determine what service plans will be available to the American public. This is not only a radical departure from the bipartisan, market-oriented policies that have served us so well for the last two decades. It is also an about-face from the proposals the FCC made just last May. ...

The courts will ultimately decide this Order's fate. And I doubt they will countenance this unlawful power grab. Litigants are already lawyering up to seek judicial review of these new rules. Given the Order's many glaring legal flaws, they will have plenty of fodder.

But if this Order manages to survive judicial review, these will be the consequences: higher broadband prices, slower speeds, less broadband deployment, less innovation, and fewer options for American consumers. To paraphrase Ronald Reagan, President Obama's plan to regulate the Internet isn't the solution to a problem. His plan is the problem.

In short, because this Order imposes intrusive government regulations that won't work to solve a problem that doesn't exist using legal authority the FCC doesn't have, I dissent.

I.

The Commission's decision to adopt President Obama's plan marks a monumental shift toward government control of the Internet. It gives the FCC the power to micromanage virtually every aspect of how the Internet works. It's an overreach that will let a Washington bureaucracy, and not the American people, decide the future of the online world.

One facet of that control is rate regulation. For the first time, the FCC will regulate the rates that Internet service providers may charge and will set a price of zero for certain commercial agreements. And the Order goes out of its way to reject calls to forbear from section 201's authorization of rate regulation, thus making clear that the FCC will have the authority to determine the appropriate rates and charges for service. The Order also expressly invites parties to file such complaints with the Commission. A government agency deciding whether a rate is lawful is the very definition of rate regulation.

As a consequence, if the FCC decides that it does not like how broadband is being priced, Internet service providers may soon face admonishments, citations, notices of violation, notices of apparent liability, monetary forfeitures and refunds, cease and desist orders, revocations, and even referrals for criminal prosecution. The only limit on the FCC's discretion to regulate rates is its own determination of whether rates are "just and reasonable," which isn't much of a restriction at all.

Although the Order plainly regulates rates, the plan takes pains to claim that it is not imposing further "ex ante rate regulation." Of course, that concedes that the new regulatory regime will involve ex post rate regulation. But even the agency's suggestion that it today "cannot ... envision" ex ante rate regulations "in this context" says nothing of what a future Commission—perhaps this very Commission in a few months or years—could envision. Indeed, the FCC grants forbearance against ex ante rate regulation but then turns around and says there's no apparent "incremental benefit" to doing so since the Commission could just reverse that decision in any future rulemaking. ...

Just as pernicious is the FCC's new "Internet conduct" standard, a standard that gives the FCC a roving mandate to review business models and upend pricing plans that benefit consumers. Usage-based pricing plans and sponsored data plans are the current targets. So if a company doesn't want to offer an expensive, unlimited data plan, it could find itself in the FCC's cross hairs.

Consider that activists promoting this rule had previously targeted neither AT&T nor Verizon with their first net-neutrality complaint but MetroPCS—an upstart competitor with a single-digit market share and not an ounce of market power. Its crime? Unlimited YouTube. MetroPCS offered a $40-per-month plan with unlimited talk, text, Web browsing and YouTube streaming. The company's strategy was to entice customers to switch from the four national carriers or to upgrade to its newly built 4G Long Term Evolution network. Whatever the benefits of MetroPCS's approach, activists have said "there can be no compromise." ...

Affordable, prepaid plans are now also suspect. These plans have enabled millions of low-income households to have mobile service. And yet the Order plays up the "concern that such practices can potentially be used by broadband providers to disadvantage over-the-top providers." In other words, these plans aren't the all-you-can-eat plans endorsed by the FCC, and so they, too, may violate the Internet conduct standard.

Our standard should be simple: If you like your current service plan, you should be able to keep your current service plan. The FCC shouldn't take it away from you. Indeed, economists have long understood innovative business models like these are good for consumers because they give them more choices and lower prices. To apply outmoded economic thinking to the Internet marketplace would just hurt consumers, especially the middle-class and low-income Americans who are the biggest beneficiaries of these plans.

In all, the FCC will have almost unfettered discretion to decide what business practices clear the bureaucratic bar, so these won't be the last business models targeted by the agency. And though the FCC spends several paragraphs describing seven vaguely worded factors that it will consider when applying the Internet conduct standard—end-user control; competitive effects; consumer protection; effect on innovation, investment, or broadband deployment; free expression; application agnostic; and standard practices—these factors lead to more questions than they answer. ...

Net neutrality proponents are already bragging that it will turn the FCC into the "Department of the Internet"—and it's no wonder. The FCC's newfound control extends to the design of the Internet itself, from the last mile through the backbone. Section 201(a) of the Communications Act gives the FCC authority to order "physical connections" and "through routes," meaning the FCC can decide where the Internet should be built and how it should be interconnected. And with the broad Internet conduct standard, decisions about network architecture and design will no longer be in the hands of engineers but bureaucrats and lawyers.

So if one Internet service provider wants to follow in the footsteps of Google Fiber and enter the market incrementally, the FCC may say no. If another wants to upgrade the bandwidth of its routers at the cost of some latency, the FCC may block it. Every decision to invest in ports for interconnection may be second-guessed; every use of priority coding to enable latency-sensitive applications like Voice over LTE may be reviewed with a microscope. How will this all be resolved? No one knows. 81-year-old laws like this don't self-execute, and even in 317 pages, there's not enough room for the FCC to describe how it would decide whether this or that broadband business practice is just and reasonable. So businesses will have to decide for themselves—with newly-necessary counsel from high-priced attorneys and accountants—whether to take a risk. ...

And then there is the temporary forbearance. Did I forget to mention that? Although the Order crows that its forbearance from Title II's provisions and rules yields a "'light-touch' regulatory framework," in reality it isn't light at all, coming as it does with the provisos, limitations, and qualifications that the public has come to expect from Washington, DC. The plan is quite clear about the limited duration of its forbearance decisions, stating that the FCC will revisit them in the future and proceed in an incremental manner with respect to additional regulation. In discussing additional rate regulation, tariffs, last-mile unbundling, burdensome administrative filing requirements, accounting standards, and entry and exit regulation, the plan repeatedly states that it is only forbearing "at this time." For others, the FCC will not impose rules "for now."

A. ...

2. *Slower Broadband.*—These Internet regulations will work another serious harm on consumers. Their broadband speeds will be slower than they would have been without these regulations.

The record is replete with evidence that Title II regulations will slow investment and innovation in broadband networks. Remember: Broadband networks don't have to be built. Capital doesn't have to be invested here. Risks don't have to be taken. The more difficult the FCC makes the business case for deployment—and micromanaging everything from interconnection to service plans makes it difficult indeed—the less likely it is that broadband providers big and small will connect Americans with digital opportunities. And neither big nor small providers will bring rural and poor Americans online if it's economically irrational for them to do so. Utility-style regulation of the kind the FCC adopts here thus will simply broaden the digital divide.

The Old World offers a cautionary tale here. Compare the broadband market in the United States to that in Europe, where broadband is generally regulated as a public utility. Data show that 82% of Americans, and 48% of rural Americans, have access to 25 Mbps broadband speeds. In Europe, those figures are only 54% and 12%, respectively. Similarly, wireline broadband providers in the United States are investing more than twice as much as their European counterparts ($562 per household versus $244). The data for wireless broadband providers shows the same pattern ($110 per person versus $55). In the United States, broadband providers deploy fiber to the premises about twice as often (23% versus 12%). And with respect to mobile broadband, 30% of subscribers in the United States have the fastest technology in wide deployment, 4G LTE, but in Europe that figure is only 4%. Moreover, in the United States, average mobile speeds are about 30% faster than they are in Western Europe. ...

And these are just the intended results of reclassification! ...

C.

So while the FCC is abandoning a 20-year-old, bipartisan framework for keeping the Internet free and open in favor of Great Depression-era legislation designed to regulate Ma Bell, at least the American public is getting something in return, right? Wrong. The Internet is not broken. There is no problem for the government to solve.

That the Internet works—that Internet freedom works—should be obvious to anyone with a Dell laptop or an HP Desktop, an Apple iPhone or Microsoft Surface, a Samsung Smart TV or a Roku, a Nest Thermostat or a Fitbit. We live in a time where you can buy a movie from iTunes, watch a music video on YouTube, post a photo of your daughter on Facebook, listen to a personalized playlist on Pandora, watch your favorite Philip K. Dick novel come to life on Amazon Streaming Video, help someone make potato salad on KickStarter, check out the latest comic at XKCD, see what Seinfeld's been up to on Crackle, manage your fantasy football team on ESPN, get almost any question answered on Quora, navigate bad traffic with Waze, and do literally hundreds of other things all with an online connection. At the start of the millennium, we didn't have any of this Internet innovation.

And no, the federal government didn't build that. It didn't trench the fiber. It didn't erect the towers. It didn't string the cable from one pole to the next, and it didn't design the routers that direct terabits of data across the Internet each and every second. It didn't invest in startups at the angel or seed stage or Series A rounds. It didn't code the webpages, the software, the applications, or the databases that make the online world useful. And it didn't create the content that makes going online so worthwhile.

For all intents and purposes, the Internet didn't exist until the private sector took it over in the 1990s, and it's been the commercial Internet that has led to the innovation, the creativity, the engineering genius that we see today.

Nevertheless, the Order ominously claims that "[t]hreats to Internet openness remain today," that broadband providers "hold all the tools necessary to deceive consumers, degrade content or disfavor the content that they don't like," and that the FCC continues "to hear concerns about other broadband provider practices involving blocking or degrading third-party applications."

The evidence of these continuing threats? There is none; it's all anecdote, hypothesis, and hysteria. A small ISP in North Carolina allegedly blocked VoIP calls a decade ago. Comcast capped BitTorrent traffic to ease upload congestion eight years ago. Apple introduced FaceTime over Wi-Fi first, cellular networks later. Examples this picayune and stale aren't enough to tell a coherent story about net neutrality. The bogeyman never had it so easy.

But the Order trots out other horribles: "[B]roadband providers have both the incentive and the ability to act as gatekeepers," "the potential to cause a variety of other negative externalities that hurt the open nature of the Internet," and "the incentive and ability to engage in paid prioritization" or other "consumer harms." The common thread linking these and countless other exhibits is that they simply do not exist. One could read the entire document—and I did—without finding anything more than hypothesized harms. One would think that a broken Internet marketplace would be rife with anticompetitive examples. But the agency doesn't list them. And it's not for a lack of effort. ...

To put it another way, Title II is not just a solution in search of a problem—it's a government solution that creates a real-world problem. This is not what the Internet needs, and it's not what the American people want. ...

[Commissioner Pai criticized at length the FCC's rulemaking process, including the FCC's shift from relying on Section 706 to Title II reclassification, extensive substantive differences between the proposed rules described in the initial notice and the final rules, the secrecy of the drafting process, and undue influence from the White House. He also provided an extensive legal critique of reclassification and forbearance.]

QUESTIONS

1. Has the FCC just "regulated the Internet?" How far will the FCC go with its new-found powers?

2. How is it that people on both sides of the network neutrality debate can couch their arguments in terms of protecting "freedom" and in terms of not "breaking" the Internet?

3. What do you think of the market-discipline argument: that if an ISP's customers don't like its policies, they can buy Internet service elsewhere? How many reasonable choices do you personally have for getting online? Even if an ISP's customers don't have good alternatives, might it still have an incentive to give consumers what they want?

4. How does this *Open Internet* order affect ISPs' incentives to invest in its infrastructure and to innovate in developing in new network technologies?

5. Network neutrality critics also raise First Amendment arguments. Do the rules impermissibly interfere with ISPs' decisions about the speech they will allow on their network? Is *Zhang v. Baidu* on point? What about the cases it discusses, such as *Turner*?

DOUBLENET PROBLEM

You are Senior Counsel at DoubleNet, a major residential and commercial ISP that serves customers in twelve states. You report directly to the Vice President for Legal Affairs. You are the chief legal officer responsible for overseeing DoubleNet's operations, including intellectual property and regulatory compliance. (Your three peers are responsible, respectively, for the company's securities and corporate legal issues, for its labor and employment matters, and for its marketing and consumer relations.)

DoubleNet offers its residential customers their choice of telephone, television, and Internet service. In most of the metropolitan areas that it serves, DoubleNet reaches its customers along fiber-optic links installed in the early and mid-2000s. Unfortunately, many of its routers are a full generation behind the current state of the art, limiting the bandwidth available to DoubleNet's customers. The company is about to embark on an expensive (tens of billions of dollars in capital investment) upgrade of the routers, but most of that roll-out won't be complete for 18–24 months. In the meantime, the company's engineers have become concerned by the rising intensity of bandwidth usage among its residential customers. In essence, the problem is that DoubleNet's current network can only supply the full promised bandwidth to a small number of users at a time. As long as only a few users connected to a given router are downloading large files continually, each user experiences a fast, zippy Internet. But as more users download large files, watch videos online from sites like Hulu, engage in voice- and video-chats, and make other bandwidth-intensive uses, the overall effective bandwidth available to most users has been dropping. Meanwhile, the chief financial officer has become concerned that DoubleNet's revenue projections don't appear to be sufficient to convince shareholders of the value of spending tens of billions on greater bandwidth.

You have been summoned to a daylong strategic retreat at which various DoubleNet technical and business teams will pitch ideas for increasing value in the next few years. The following ideas are up for consideration:

*   DoubleNet could switch from its current billing system ($35 to $120 a month for all-you-can-eat Internet access at various speeds) to a "metered" system in which the user pays $1 per gigabyte downloaded.

*   DoubleNet could partner with a major sports cable network to offer a premium service for watching high-definition sports videos, live, at $25/month. A substantial portion of the revenues from this service would be used to deploy special-purpose devices that provide the necessary bandwidth *solely* for the sports network's videos. The goal would be to shift many of your video-

hungry customers to the sports network's programming, freeing up band-width for other uses.

- DoubleNet could start blocking all voice-over-IP traffic, such as Vonage, Skype, and FaceTime video chats.

- DoubleNet could institute a policy that when its routers have more traffic than they can handle, they will attempt to deliver web pages and emails first. Streaming video and peer-to-peer programs will be given lower priority, which may lead them to slow down or, in times of high congestion, fail entirely.

- DoubleNet could attempt to charge bandwidth-intensive web sites (such as YouTube, Hulu, and ChatRoulette) for preferential access to DoubleNet's customers. Those who paid would be given priority; those who didn't would be pushed to the end of the queue. The result is that DoubleNet's customers would see the paid-up sites as being speedier than the ones that refuse to pay.

- DoubleNet could raise its rates for Internet service by 50%.

As the head of legal affairs for operations, you will be asked for your views on the various proposals. The executives, of course, are interested in the tradeoff between reward and legal risk; they will want to know what you think of the business prospects of the proposals, as well as their likely legal implications. Prepare an opinion on the legality and advisability of the proposals.

THE PUNCHLINE?

In January 2017, President Trump named Commissioner Pai chairman of the FCC. The FCC announced its intention to conduct yet another rulemaking, this time to repeal the Open Internet Order. As of mid-2017, the Order remains good law, but its days may be numbered.

CHAPTER 10: BEYOND THE INTERNET

Recall Judge Easterbrook's claim that Internet law is the "law of the horse." In a famous reply, Lawrence Lessig wrote:

> My claim is to the contrary. I agree that our aim should be courses that "illuminate the entire law," but unlike Easterbrook, I believe that there is an important general point that comes from thinking in particular about how law and cyberspace connect. ...
>
> I do not argue that any specialized area of law would produce the same insight. I am not defending the law of the horse. My claim is specific to cyberspace. We see something when we think about the regulation of cyberspace that other areas would not show us.

Lawrence Lessig, *The Law of the Horse: What Cyberspace Might Teach*, 113 HARV. L. REV. 501, 502 (1999). Does our study of Internet law teach us anything useful about other parts of the law?

A. Virtual Property

It should be apparent by now that domain names are both valuable and contested. This suggests that the legal system might categorize them as "property." What other digital resources share those characteristics?

KREMEN V. COHEN
337 F.3d 1024 (9th Cir. 2000)

Kozinski, Circuit Judge:

We decide whether Network Solutions may be liable for giving away a registrant's domain name on the basis of a forged letter.

BACKGROUND

"Sex on the Internet?," they all said. "*That*'ll never make any money." But computer-geek-turned-entrepreneur Gary Kremen knew an opportunity when he saw it. The year was 1994; domain names were free for the asking, and it would be several years yet before Henry Blodget and hordes of eager NASDAQ day traders would turn the Internet into the Dutch tulip craze of our times. With a quick e-mail to the domain name registrar Network Solutions, Kremen became the proud owner of sex.com. He registered the name to his business, Online Classifieds, and listed himself as the contact.

Con man Stephen Cohen, meanwhile, was doing time for impersonating a bankruptcy lawyer. He, too, saw the potential of the domain name. Kremen had gotten it first, but that was only a minor impediment for a man of Cohen's boundless resource and bounded integrity. Once out of prison, he sent Network Solutions what purported to be a letter he had received from Online Classifieds. It claimed the company had been "forced to dismiss Mr. Kremen," but "never got around to changing our administrative contact with the internet registration [sic] and now our Board of directors has decided to abandon the domain name sex.com." Why

ONLINE CLASSIFIEDS, INC.
(FOR YOUR ONLINE AD'S)
949 COLE STREET
SAN FRANCISCO, CA 94117

October 15, 1995

Stephen Cohen
1251 North Lakeview Drive
Suite J-425
Anaheim, CA 92807

Re: SEX.COM

Dear Mr. Cohen:

Per our numerous conversations, we understand that you have been using sex.com on your French Connections BBS since 1979 and now you want to use sex.com as a domain name on the internet. Our corporation is the owner of sex.com as it relates to the internet.

At one time, we employed Gary Kremen who was hired for the express purpose of setting up our system. We allowed Mr. Kremen to be our administrative and technical contact with the internet, because of his vast experience with computers and their connections to the internet.

Subsequently, we were forced to dismiss Mr. Kremen. At no time, was Mr. Kremen ever a stockholder, officer, nor a director of our corporation and as such, Mr. Kremen has no rights, titles or interest in our domain name. Further, the internet shows that sex.com is listed in our corporation and not in Mr. Kremen's personal name. In fact, Mr. Kremen is the president of a different and unrelated corporation called Electric Classifieds, which is located at 340 Brandon Street in San Francisco, California. Further, Mr. Kremen's corporation owns eatcf.com which is listed with the internet registration.

We never got around to changing our administrative contact with the internet registration and now our Board of directors has decided to abandon the domain name sex.com.

Because we do not have a direct connection to the internet, we request that you notify the internet registration on our behalf, to delete our domain name sex.com. Further, we have no objections to your use of the domain name sex.com and this letter shall serve as our authorization to the internet registration to transfer sex.com to your corporation.

Sincerely,

Sharon Dimmick, President

N380102

was this unusual letter being sent via Cohen rather than to Network Solutions directly? It explained:

> Because we do not have a direct connection to the internet, we request that you notify the internet registration on our behalf, to delete our domain name sex.com. Further, we have no objections to your use of the domain name sex.com and this letter shall serve as our authoriza-

tion to the internet registration to transfer sex.com to your corpora-tion.[2]

Despite the letter's transparent claim that a company called *"Online* Classifieds" had no Internet connection, Network Solutions made no effort to contact Kremen. Instead, it accepted the letter at face value and transferred the domain name to Cohen. When Kremen contacted Network Solutions some time later, he was told it was too late to undo the transfer. Cohen went on to turn sex.com into a lucrative online porn empire.

And so began Kremen's quest to recover the domain name that was rightfully his. He sued Cohen and several affiliated companies in federal court, seeking re-turn of the domain name and disgorgement of Cohen's profits. The district court found that the letter was indeed a forgery and ordered the domain name returned to Kremen. It also told Cohen to hand over his profits, invoking the constructive trust doctrine and California's "unfair competition" statute, Cal. Bus. & Prof. Code § 17200 *et seq.* It awarded $40 million in compensatory damages and another $25 million in punitive damages.

Kremen, unfortunately, has not had much luck collecting his judgment. The district court froze Cohen's assets, but Cohen ignored the order and wired large sums of money to offshore accounts. His real estate property, under the protection of a federal receiver, was stripped of all its fixtures – even cabinet doors and toilets – in violation of another order. The court commanded Cohen to appear and show cause why he shouldn't be held in contempt, but he ignored that order, too. The district judge finally took off the gloves – he declared Cohen a fugitive from justice, signed an arrest warrant and sent the U.S. Marshals after him.

Then things started getting *really* bizarre. Kremen put up a "wanted" poster on the sex.com site with a mug shot of Cohen, offering a $50,000 reward to anyone who brought him to justice. Cohen's lawyers responded with a motion to vacate the arrest warrant. They reported that Cohen was under house arrest in Mexico and that gunfights between Mexican authorities and would-be bounty hunters seeking Kremen's reward money posed a threat to human life. The district court rejected this story as "implausible" and denied the motion. Cohen, so far as the record shows, remains at large.

Given his limited success with the bounty hunter approach, it should come as no surprise that Kremen seeks to hold someone else responsible for his losses. That someone is Network Solutions, the exclusive domain name registrar at the time of Cohen's antics. Kremen sued it for mishandling his domain name ...

BREACH OF CONTRACT

Kremen had no express contract with Network Solutions ...

CONVERSION

Kremen's conversion claim is another matter. To establish that tort, a plaintiff must show "ownership or right to possession of property, wrongful disposition of the property right and damages." *G.S. Rasmussen & Assoc., Inc. v. Kalitta Flying Service, Inc.*, 958 F.2d 896, 906 (9th Cir. 1992). The preliminary question, then, is whether registrants have property rights in their domain names. Network Solu-

---

2 The letter was signed "Sharon Dimmick," purported president of Online Classifieds. Dimmick was actually Kremen's housemate at the time; Cohen later claimed she sold him the domain name for $1000. This story might have worked a little better if Co-hen hadn't misspelled her signature.

tions all but concedes that they do. This is no surprise, given its positions in prior litigation. *See Network Solutions, Inc. v. Umbro Int'l, Inc.*, 259 Va. 759 (2000) ("[Network Solutions] acknowledged during oral argument before this Court that the right to use a domain name is a form of intangible personal property."); *Network Solutions, Inc. v. Clue Computing, Inc.*, 946 F. Supp. 858, 860 (D. Colo. 1996) (same). The district court agreed with the parties on this issue, as do we.

Property is a broad concept that includes "every intangible benefit and prerogative susceptible of possession or disposition." *Downing v. Mun. Court*, 88 Cal. App. 2d 345, 350, 198 P.2d 923 (1948) (internal quotation marks omitted). We apply a three-part test to determine whether a property right exists: "First, there must be an interest capable of precise definition; second, it must be capable of exclusive possession or control; and third, the putative owner must have established a legitimate claim to exclusivity." *G.S. Rasmussen*, 958 F.2d at 903 (footnote omitted). Domain names satisfy each criterion. Like a share of corporate stock or a plot of land, a domain name is a well-defined interest. Someone who registers a domain name decides where on the Internet those who invoke that particular name – whether by typing it into their web browsers, by following a hyperlink, or by other means – are sent. Ownership is exclusive in that the registrant alone makes that decision. Moreover, like other forms of property, domain names are valued, bought and sold, often for millions of dollars, and they are now even subject to in rem jurisdiction, *see* 15 U.S.C. § 1125(d)(2).

Finally, registrants have a legitimate claim to exclusivity. Registering a domain name is like staking a claim to a plot of land at the title office. It informs others that the domain name is the registrant's and no one else's. Many registrants also invest substantial time and money to develop and promote websites that depend on their domain names. Ensuring that they reap the benefits of their investments reduces uncertainty and thus encourages investment in the first place, promoting the growth of the Internet overall.

Kremen therefore had an intangible property right in his domain name, and a jury could find that Network Solutions "wrongfully disposed of" that right to his detriment by handing the domain name over to Cohen. *Id.* at 906. The district court nevertheless rejected Kremen's conversion claim. It held that domain names, although a form of property, are intangibles not subject to conversion. This rationale derives from a distinction tort law once drew between tangible and intangible property: Conversion was originally a remedy for the wrongful taking of another's lost goods, so it applied only to tangible property. *See Prosser and Keeton on the Law of Torts* § 15, at 89, 91 (W. Page Keeton ed., 5th ed. 1984). Virtually every jurisdiction, however, has discarded this rigid limitation to some degree. Many courts ignore or expressly reject it. Others reject it for some intangibles but not others. The Restatement, for example, recommends the following test:

(1) Where there is conversion of a document in which intangible rights are merged, the damages include the value of such rights.

(2) One who effectively prevents the exercise of intangible rights of the kind customarily *merged in a document* is subject to a liability similar to that for conversion, even though the document is not itself converted.

RESTATEMENT (SECOND) OF TORTS § 242 (1965) (emphasis added). An intangible is "merged" in a document when, "by the appropriate rule of law, the right to the immediate possession of a chattel and the power to acquire such possession is *represented by* [the] document," or when "an intangible obligation [is] *represented by*

[the] document, which is regarded as equivalent to the obligation." *Id.* cmt. a (emphasis added). ...

Kremen's domain name falls easily within this class of property. He argues that the relevant document is the Domain Name System, or "DNS" – the distributed electronic database that associates domain names like sex.com with particular computers connected to the Internet. We agree that the DNS is a document (or perhaps more accurately a collection of documents). That it is stored in electronic form rather than on ink and paper is immaterial. It would be a curious jurisprudence that turned on the existence of a paper document rather than an electronic one. Torching a company's file room would then be conversion while hacking into its mainframe and deleting its data would not. That is not the law, at least not in California. ...

The DNS also bears some relation to Kremen's domain name. We need not delve too far into the mechanics of the Internet to resolve this case. It is sufficient to observe that information correlating Kremen's domain name with a particular computer on the Internet must exist somewhere in some form in the DNS; if it did not, the database would not serve its intended purpose. Change the information in the DNS, and you change the website people see when they type "www.sex.com."

Network Solutions quibbles about the mechanics of the DNS. It points out that the data corresponding to Kremen's domain name is not stored in a single record, but is found in several different places: The components of the domain name ("sex" and "com") are stored in two different places, and each is copied and stored on several machines to create redundancy and speed up response times. Network Solutions's theory seems to be that intangibles are not subject to conversion unless they are associated only with a single document.

Even if Network Solutions were correct that there is no single record in the DNS architecture with which Kremen's intangible property right is associated, that is no impediment under California law. A share of stock, for example, may be evidenced by more than one document. *See Payne* [*v. Elliot*, 54 Cal. 339, 342 (1880)] ("The certificate is only evidence of the property; and it is not the only evidence, for a transfer on the books of the corporation, without the issuance of a certificate, vests title in the shareholder: the certificate is, therefore, but additional evidence of title. . . ."); ...

Network Solutions also argues that the DNS is not a document because it is refreshed every twelve hours when updated domain name information is broadcast across the Internet. This theory is even less persuasive. A document doesn't cease being a document merely because it is often updated. If that were the case, a share registry would fail whenever shareholders were periodically added or dropped, as would an address file whenever business cards were added or removed. Whether a document is updated by inserting and deleting particular records or by replacing an old file with an entirely new one is a technical detail with no legal significance.

Kremen's domain name is protected by California conversion law, even on the grudging reading we have given it. Exposing Network Solutions to liability when it gives away a registrant's domain name on the basis of a forged letter is no different from holding a corporation liable when it gives away someone's shares under the same circumstances. We have not "creat[ed] new tort duties" in reaching this result. We have only applied settled principles of conversion law to what the parties and the district court all agree is a species of property. ...

We must, of course, take the broader view, but there is nothing unfair about holding a company responsible for giving away someone else's property even if it was not at fault. Cohen is obviously the guilty party here, and the one who should in all fairness pay for his theft. But he's skipped the country, and his money is stashed in some offshore bank account. Unless Kremen's luck with his bounty hunters improves, Cohen is out of the picture. The question becomes whether Network Solutions should be open to liability for its decision to hand over Kremen's domain name. Negligent or not, it was Network Solutions that gave away Kremen's property. Kremen never did anything. It would not be unfair to hold Network Solutions responsible and force it to try to recoup its losses by chasing down Cohen. This, at any rate, is the logic of the common law, and we do not lightly discard it.

The district court was worried that "the threat of litigation threatens to stifle the registration system by requiring further regulations by [Network Solutions] and potential increases in fees." Given that Network Solutions's "regulations" evidently allowed it to hand over a registrant's domain name on the basis of a facially suspect letter without even contacting him, "further regulations" don't seem like such a bad idea. And the prospect of higher fees presents no issue here that it doesn't in any other context. A bank could lower its ATM fees if it didn't have to pay security guards, but we doubt most depositors would think that was a good idea.

The district court thought there were "methods better suited to regulate the vagaries of domain names" and left it "to the legislature to fashion an appropriate statutory scheme." The legislature, of course, is always free (within constitutional bounds) to refashion the system that courts come up with. But that doesn't mean we should throw up our hands and let private relations degenerate into a free-for-all in the meantime. We apply the common law until the legislature tells us otherwise. And the common law does not stand idle while people give away the property of others.

The evidence supported a claim for conversion, and the district court should not have rejected it.

QUESTIONS

1. *Kremen* holds that domain names are property. Why does it matter? Are there commercial transactions that will be easier or harder as a result of *Kremen*?

2. What else could be property under the *Kremen* test? A Twitter account? An email address? A Facebook 'Like'?

3. Another Internet resource whose status as property is disputed is IP addresses. A group of Regional Internet Registries manage the allocation of "blocks" (groups of 256 or more numerically consecutive addresses) of IP addresses. For many years, they simply gave out a fresh block to any organization that needed one; these organizations would then assign IP addresses to their members or their customers as needed. In 2011, however, the supply of unallocated IP addresses ran out. The RIRs have taken the position that IP addresses cannot be bought or sold, only reclaimed by the RIR for reallocation to someone else who needs them. If you represent a major university with a large block of IP addresses it isn't currently using, would you advise your client to give them back to the RIR?

4. There is a tension between *Kremen* and the ACPA. *Kremen* creates a system of *personal* property in domain names: the "owner" is the one with a valid registration. The ACPA creates a system of *intellectual* property in domain names: the "owner" is the first to use a trademark in commerce and establish goodwill with consumers. What should courts do when the two systems conflict?

5. *Kremem* holds that sex.com is property, but what about .com itself? In *Stern v. Islamic Republic of Iran*, 73 F. Supp. 3d 46, (D.D.C. 2014), *aff'd on other grounds sub nom. Weinstein v. Islamic Republic of Iran*, — F.3d — (D.C. Cir. Aug. 2, 2016), plaintiffs held substantial judgments against Iran arising out of its support for terrorist activities. The court denied their request to attach the .ir TLD, holding that Iran's rights were contractual, not property:

> The ccTLDs exist only as they are made operational by the ccTLD managers that administer the registries of second level domain names within them and by the parties that cause the ccTLDs to be listed on the root zone file. A ccTLD, like a domain name, cannot be conceptualized apart from the services provided by these parties. The Court cannot order plaintiffs' insertion into this arrangement.

Is this persuasive? Is it *too* persuasive? Is *Kremen* wrong? Or is there something different about ccTLDs?

UNITED STATES V. ALEYNIKOV
676 F.3d 71 (2nd Cir. 2012)

Jacobs, Chief Judge:

Sergey Aleynikov was convicted, following a jury trial in the United States District Court for the Southern District of New York of stealing and transferring some of the proprietary computer source code used in his employer's high frequency trading system, in violation of the National Stolen Property Act, 18 U.S.C. § 2314 (the "NSPA") and the Economic Espionage Act of 1996, 18 U.S.C. § 1832 (the "EEA"). On appeal, Aleynikov argues, inter alia, that his conduct did not constitute an offense under either statute. He argues that: [1] the source code was not a "stolen" "good" within the meaning of the NSPA, and [2] the source code was not "related to or included in a product that is produced for or placed in interstate or foreign commerce" within the meaning of the EEA. We agree, and reverse the judgment of the district court.

Background

Sergey Aleynikov, a computer programmer, was employed by Goldman Sachs & Co. ("Goldman") from May 2007 through June 2009, developing computer source code for the company's proprietary high-frequency trading ("HFT") system. An HFT system is a mechanism for making large volumes of trades in securities and commodities based on trading decisions effected in fractions of a second. Trades are executed on the basis of algorithms that incorporate rapid market developments and data from past trades. The computer programs used to operate Goldman's HFT system are of three kinds: [1] market connectivity programs that process real-time market data and execute trades; [2] programs that use algorithms to determine which trades to make; and [3] infrastructure programs that facilitate the flow of information throughout the trading system and monitor the system's performance. Aleynikov's work focused on developing code for this last category of infrastructure programs in Goldman's HFT system. High frequency trading is a competitive business that depends in large part on the speed with which information can be processed to seize fleeting market opportunities. Goldman closely guards the secrecy of each component of the system, and does not license the system to anyone. Goldman's confidentiality policies bound Aleynikov to keep in strict confidence all the firm's proprietary information, including any intellectual property created by Aleynikov. He was barred as well from taking it or using it when his employment ended.

By 2009, Aleynikov was earning $400,000, the highest-paid of the twenty-five programmers in his group. In April 2009, he accepted an offer to become an Executive Vice President at Teza Technologies LLC, a Chicago-based startup that was looking to develop its own HFT system. Aleynikov was hired, at over $1 million a year, to develop the market connectivity and infrastructure components of Teza's HFT system. Teza's founder (a former head of HFT at Chicago-based hedge fund Citadel Investment Group) emailed Aleynikov (and several other employees) in late May, conveying his expectation that they would develop a functional trading system within six months. It usually takes years for a team of programmers to develop an HFT system from scratch.

Aleynikov's last day at Goldman was June 5, 2009. At approximately 5:20 p.m., just before his going-away party, Aleynikov encrypted and uploaded to a server in Germany more than 500,000 lines of source code for Goldman's HFT system, including code for a substantial part of the infrastructure, and some of the algorithms and market data connectivity programs. Some of the code pertained to programs that could operate independently of the rest of the Goldman system and could be integrated into a competitor's system. After uploading the source code, Aleynikov deleted the encryption program as well as the history of his computer commands. When he returned to his home in New Jersey, Aleynikov downloaded the source code from the server in Germany to his home computer, and copied some of the files to other computer devices he owned.

On July 2, 2009, Aleynikov flew from New Jersey to Chicago to attend meetings at Teza. He brought with him a flash drive and a laptop containing portions of the Goldman source code. When Aleynikov flew back the following day, he was arrested by the FBI at Newark Liberty International Airport. ...

DISCUSSION

On appeal ... Aleynikov argues that the source code – as purely intangible property – is not a "good" that was "stolen" within the meaning of the NSPA. ...

I

The NSPA makes it a crime to "transport[ ], transmit[ ], or transfer[ ] in interstate or foreign commerce any goods, wares, merchandise, securities or money, of the value of $5,000 or more, knowing the same to have been stolen, converted or taken by fraud." 18 U.S.C. § 2314. The statute does not define the terms "goods," "wares," or "merchandise." We have held that they provide "a general and comprehensive designation of such personal property or chattels as are ordinarily a subject of commerce." *In re Vericker*, 446 F.2d 244, 248 (2d Cir. 1971) (Friendly, C.J.). The decisive question is whether the source code that Aleynikov uploaded to a server in Germany, then downloaded to his computer devices in New Jersey, and later transferred to Illinois, constituted stolen "goods," "wares," or "merchandise" within the meaning of the NSPA. Based on the substantial weight of the case law, as well as the ordinary meaning of the words, we conclude that it did not.

A.

We first considered the applicability of the NSPA to the theft of intellectual property in *United States v. Bottone*, 365 F.2d 389 (2d Cir. 1966) (Friendly, J.), in which photocopied documents outlining manufacturing procedures for certain pharmaceuticals were transported across state lines. Since the actual processes themselves (as opposed to photocopies) were never transported across state lines, the "serious question" (we explained) was whether "the papers showing [the] processes that were transported in interstate or foreign commerce were 'goods' which had been 'stolen, converted or taken by fraud' in view of the lack of proof that any of the physical materials so transported came from [the manufacturer's] possession." *Id.* at 393. We held that the NSPA was violated there, observing that what was "stolen and transported" was, ultimately, "tangible goods," notwithstanding the "clever intermediate transcription [and] use of a photocopy machine." *Id.* However, we suggested that a different result would obtain if there was no physical taking of tangible property whatsoever: "To be sure, where no tangible objects were ever taken or transported, a court would be hard pressed to conclude that 'goods' had been stolen and transported within the meaning of 2314." *Id.* Hence, we observed, "the statute would presumably not extend to the case where a carefully guarded secret formula was memorized, carried away in the recesses of a thievish mind and placed in writing only after a boundary had been crossed." *Id. Bottone* itself thus treats its holding as the furthest limit of a statute that is not endlessly elastic: Some tangible property must be taken from the owner for there to be deemed a "good" that is "stolen" for purposes of the NSPA.

Bottone's reading of the NSPA is confirmed by the Supreme Court's opinion in *Dowling v. United States*, 473 U.S. 207 (1985), which held that the NSPA did not apply to an interstate bootleg record operation. *Dowling* rejected the Government's argument that the unauthorized use of the musical compositions rendered them "stolen, converted or taken by fraud." Cases prosecuted under the NSPA "have always involved physical 'goods, wares, [or] merchandise' that have themselves been 'stolen, converted or taken by fraud'" – even if the stolen thing does not "remain in entirely unaltered form," and "owes a major portion of its value to an intangible component." *Id.* at 216.

"This basic element" – the taking of a physical thing – "comports with the common-sense meaning of the statutory language: by requiring that the 'goods, wares [or] merchandise' be 'the same' as those 'stolen, converted or taken by fraud,' the provision seems clearly to contemplate a physical identity between the items unlawfully obtained and those eventually transported, and hence some prior physical taking of the subject goods." *Id.*

We join other circuits in relying on *Dowling* for the proposition that the theft and subsequent interstate transmission of purely intangible property is beyond the scope of the NSPA.

In a close analog to the present case, the Tenth Circuit affirmed the dismissal of an indictment alleging that the defendant transported in interstate commerce a computer program containing source code that was taken from his employer. *United States v. Brown*, 925 F.2d 1301, 1305, 1309 (10th Cir. 1991). Citing *Dowling*, the court held that the NSPA "applies only to physical 'goods, wares or merchandise'" and that "[p]urely intellectual property is not within this category. It can be represented physically, such as through writing on a page, but the underlying, intellectual property itself, remains intangible." *Id.* at 1307. The Court concluded that "the computer program itself is an intangible intellectual property, and as such, it alone cannot constitute goods, wares, merchandise, securities or moneys which have been stolen, converted or taken" for purposes of the NSPA. *Id.* at 1308.

Similarly, the Seventh Circuit has held that numerical "Comdata codes" used by truckers to access money transfers at truck stops constitute intangible property the theft of which is not a violation of the NSPA. *United States v. Stafford*, 136 F.3d 1109 (7th Cir.1998). The court reasoned that the codes themselves were not "goods, wares, or merchandise," but rather "information"; that the defendant had not been charged with transporting pieces of paper containing the codes; and that the only conduct charged was "transferring the codes themselves, which are simply sequences of digits." *Id.* at 1114–15.

The First Circuit has also concluded that the NSPA does not criminalize the theft of intangible things: The NSPA "does not apply to purely 'intangible information,' the theft of which is punishable under copyright law and other intellectual property statutes" but " *does apply* when there has been 'some tangible item taken, however insignificant or valueless it may be, absent the intangible component.'" *United States v. Martin*, 228 F.3d 1, 14–15 (1st Cir. 2000).

The Government argues that a tangibility requirement ignores a 1988 amendment, which added the words "transmit[ ]" and "transfer[ ]" to the terms: "transport[ ], transmit[ ], or transfer[ ]." The Government contends that the added words reflect an intent to cover generally transfers and transmissions of non-physical forms of stolen property. The evident purpose of the amendment, however, was to clarify that the statute applied to non-physical electronic transfers of *money. See United States v. Piervinanzi*, 23 F.3d 670, 678 n.6 (2d Cir. 1994). Money, though it can be intangible, is specifically enumerated in § 2314 as a thing apart and distinct from "goods," "wares," or "merchandise." The addition to the possible means of transport does not bespeak an intent to alter or expand the ordinary meaning of "goods," "wares," or "merchandise" and therefore does not obviate the Government's need to identify a predicate good, ware, merchandise, security, or money that has been stolen.

B.

By uploading Goldman's proprietary source code to a computer server in Germany, Aleynikov stole purely intangible property embodied in a purely intangible format. There was no allegation that he physically seized anything tangible from Goldman, such as a compact disc or thumb drive containing source code, so we need not decide whether that would suffice as a physical theft. Aleynikov later transported portions of the source code to Chicago, on his laptop and flash drive. However, there is no violation of the statute unless the good is transported with knowledge that "the same" has been stolen; the statute therefore presupposes that the thing stolen was a good or ware, etc., *at the time of the theft*. The wording "contemplate[s] a physical identity between the items unlawfully obtained and those eventually transported." *Dowling*, 473 U.S. at 216. The later storage of intangible property on a tangible medium does not transform the intangible property into a stolen good.

The infringement of copyright in *Dowling* parallels Aleynikov's theft of computer code. Although "[t]he infringer invades a statutorily defined province guaranteed to the copyright holder alone[,] . . . he does not assume physical control over the copyright; nor does he wholly deprive its owner of its use." *Id. at 217.* Because Aleynikov did not "assume physical control" over anything when he took the source code, and because he did not thereby "deprive [Goldman] of its use," Aleynikov did not violate the NSPA.

As the district court observed, Goldman's source code is highly valuable, and there is no doubt that in virtually every case involving proprietary computer code worth stealing, the value of the intangible code will vastly exceed the value of any physical item on which it might be stored. But federal crimes are "solely creatures of statute." *Dowling*, 473 U.S. at 213. We decline to stretch or update statutory words of plain and ordinary meaning in order to better accommodate the digital age. ...

II

[The EEA is a federal trade secret statute. Trade secrets consist of information that is valuable to a business because it is kept confidential. Typical trade secrets include manufacturing processes, customer lists. and future business plans. All fifty states have civil trade secret statutes that prohibit the unauthorized disclosure or misuse of trade secrets. The federal EEA imposes criminal sanctions on anyone who "copies, duplicates, sketches, draws, photographs, downloads, uploads, alters, destroys, photocopies, replicates, transmits, delivers, sends, mails, communicates, or conveys" for the economic benefit of anyone other than the owner. 18 U.S.C. § 1832(a)(2). But the EEA also contains a jurisdictional hook: the version on the books at the time *Aleynikov* was decided required that the trade secret be "related to or included in a product that is produced for or placed in interstate or foreign commerce." *Id.* (2012)]

Goldman's HFT system was neither "produced for" nor "placed in" interstate or foreign commerce. Goldman had no intention of selling its HFT system or licensing it to anyone. It went to great lengths to maintain the secrecy of its system. The enormous profits the system yielded for Goldman depended on no one else having it. Because the HFT system was not designed to enter or pass in commerce, or to make something that does, Aleynikov's theft of source code relating to that system was not an offense under the EEA. ...

QUESTIONS

1. If Aleynikov takes $5,001 of Goldman Sachs coffee mugs to Germany, he violates the NSPA. But by transmitting the top-secret trading software, worth much more than $5,000, to a competitor, he doesn't. How does this result make sense?

2. *Kremen* holds that intangibles can be "property" capable of conversion; *Aleynikov* holds that intangibles can't be "goods" capable of theft. Can these two results be reconciled?

3. Samarth Agrawal also took his employer's HFT source code to a competitor. But unlike Aleynikov, Agrawal printed out the code and took the printouts home in a backpack. The Second Circuit upheld his conviction under the NSPA, writing, "Agrawal stole computer code in the tangible form of thousands of sheets of paper ... . This makes all the difference." *United States v. Agrawal*, 726 F.3d 235 (2nd Cir. 2014). Is this right? Should it really matter whether the defendant hits "print" before (Agrawal) or after (Aleynikov) he gets home? Or should the NSPA treat them both as criminals, as many states' theft laws do?

4. Congress responded to *Aleynikov* by leaving the NSPA alone and amending the EEA so that it applies to "a product or service used in or intended for use

in interstate or foreign commerce." Does this change catch future Aleynikovs? Why might Congress have chosen to revise the EEA but not the NSPA?

BRAGG V. LINDEN RESEARCH, INC
No. 06-08711 (Pa. Ct. Com. Pl)
No. 06-4925 (E.D. Pa.)*

COMPLAINT
(filed Oct. 9, 2006)

AND NOW COMES, the Plaintiff, Marc Bragg, Esq., by and through his attorneys, Jason A. Archinaco, Esq. and the law firm of WHITE AND WILLIAMS, LLP, and avers as follows:

THE PARTIES

1. Plaintiff, Marc Bragg (hereinafter "Bragg"), is an adult individual resident of the County of Chester, Commonwealth of Pennsylvania.

2. Defendant Linden Research, Inc. (hereinafter "Linden"), is a Delaware corporation, with a primary business address and at all relevant times, providing its services out of the State of California at 1100 Sansome Street, San Francisco, CA. Linden uses the name "Linden Labs" on the internet to conduct business.

3. Defendant, Phillip Rosedale, (hereinafter "Rosedale") is an adult individual and a resident of the State of California with an address of 2717 Pacific Avenue, San Francisco, CA 94115-1129.

BACKGROUND

4. Linden operates a massively multiplayer role-playing game ("MMORPG") known as "Second Life" and hosted at http://secondlife.com.

5. To participate in Second Life, a participant must download Linden's client software and install it on the user's computer. A participant may participate for free, or upgrade to a premium membership.

6. In Second Life, participants from around the world interact together in a huge "virtual" world / environment.

7. The virtual world environment contains many of the real world goods and items from cars to homes to slot machines. Linden represents that it promotes the creation and trade of such goods and items by its participants and refers to such items as "virtual property."

8. Defendants' computer code was designed and intended to act like real world property that requires the payment of U.S. Dollars to buy, own, and sell that property and to allow for the conveyance of title and ownership rights in that property separate and apart from the code itself, and as such, Plaintiff's rights in the virtual property should be regulated and protected like real world property.

---

* [Ed: This excerpt and the following one are drawn from the pleadings in a case that settled before reaching the substantive legal issues. They present the plaintiff's and defendant's dueling views of the facts. In case you are wondering about the multiple jurisdictions, the case was removed from state to federal court – hence the complaint was filed in a Pennsylvania state court but the answer in a federal district court.]

9. Participants in Second Life create characters called "avatars," develop their own unique reputation and/or buy and sell unique software, encoded and scripted "objects," design numerous creative and unique buildings, clothes, equipment, furnishings, etc., run businesses, and purchase uniquely located and described pieces of "virtual land" from the Defendants.

10. Although referred to as a "game," Second Life is a business operated to generate a profit for Linden and, upon information and belief, Second Life generates a substantial profit for Linden and Rosedale. ...

VIRTUAL WORLDS

11. Linden is not the only company that operates a virtual world for a profit and, indeed, the industry has become saturated with such games ranging from Blizzard's Worlds of Warcraft, to Sony's Everquest and Star Wars Galaxies. However, unlike the industry leaders, Linden is the only MMORPG that represents that its participants retain / obtain ownership rights to the land they purchase from Linden and retain all intellectual property rights for any virtual items or content created by the participant and, indeed, Linden does not even restrict or disclaim such ownership interests in their "Terms of Service" agreement (hereinafter "TOS"). ...

16. In many respects, these virtual Worlds exist similar to theme parks such as Disney World. Thus, although the park itself is an "attraction" in some respects, like Disney World, shops selling merchandise exist and a variety of transactions occur inside the virtual World just like such shops and transactions occur inside Disney World, and independent of entrance to the park itself. Unlike Disney World where Disney chooses to operate many of the shops and control many of the transactions inside of Disney World, nearly every sale of virtual goods and/or virtual "shops" are operated by the third party individual participants of Second Life, as opposed to Linden itself. Moreover, just like the transactions that occur inside Disney World are subject to the laws of the United States of America, so too are the transactions that occur inside and in connection with Second Life.

17. Unlike Disney World, however, Linden has been in the business of selling the land inside the "theme park". Thus, Linden no longer owns the very world they created, instead choosing to sell the world / land to consumers. Rosedale has referred generally to Second Life as a "country." ...

VIRTUAL ITEM AND PROPERTY OWNERSHIP

21. Typically, in such virtual worlds, the operators of the Worlds claim to not permit the participants to hold any rights to "virtual items" (houses, buildings, cars and other virtual objects) or "virtual land" that exist inside the game world. Both are referred to generally by participants in such Worlds as "virtual property."

22. Indeed, several of such companies who have not provided any rights to the participants have threatened lawsuits to prevent the trade and sale of virtual items, land, money and accounts and have attempted to prevent the sale and trade of virtual items, land, money, goods and even the accounts that contain such virtual items, lands, money and goods. ...

25. Despite such denials of ownership by participants, the trade of virtual items, land, money and goods is believed, by some estimates, to have approached

nearly $1 billion annually and is, in any event, a market and industry in excess of $100 million a year. ...

SECOND LIFE'S PLACE IN THE CROWDED MMORPG MARKET

28. When Second Life was first "opened" by Linden in 2003, the competition in the industry for participants in virtual worlds was fierce and the industry was dominated by well known players.

29. Upon information and belief, Linden had difficulty differentiating itself from other, higher profile games and turning a profit for Linden.

30. Initially, Linden chose the familiar route of refusing to recognize the participants' rights to the virtual property in-game.

31. Second Life, unlike other virtual worlds, was devoid of any fancy graphics or exciting game-play. As such, Second Life generally languished and trailed its peers in terms of participants.

32. As such, desperate for a participant base to generate profits, Linden made a calculated business decision to depart from the industry standard of denying that participants had any rights to virtual items, land and/or goods. Linden decided that it could maximize its own profits if it, instead, represented to the participants in its world that their rights to the virtual items, land and goods held in the participants' accounts would be preserved and recognized for the participant and that participants' intellectual property rights are preserved.

33. Linden announced its new business model at the "State of Play" conference in or about November, 2003 and followed with a press release shortly thereafter.

34. Linden and Rosedale made oral representations at the "State of Play," and then reduced those representations to writing.

35. In the November 14, 2003 press release, Linden touted its modifications to Second Life's Terms of Service, stating that "the revised TOS allows subscribers to retain full intellectual property protection for the digital content they create."

36. In the same press release, Linden, by and through Rosedale, stated: "Until now, any content created by users for persistent state worlds, such as Ever-Quest or Star Wars Galaxies, has essentially become the property of the company developing and hosting the world," said Rosedale. "We believe our new policy recognizes the fact that persistent world users are making significant contributions to building these Worlds and should be able to both own the content they create and share in the value that is created. The preservation of users' property rights is a necessary step toward the emergence of genuinely real online worlds." ...

46. Defendants published their representations on the Second Life website, including a section called "Own Virtual Land" which discusses "owning land" in Second Life. Defendants also published on the Second Life website a section entitled "IP Rights" which stated that "Linden Lab's Terms of Service agreement recognizes Residents' right to retain full intellectual property protection for the digital content they create in Second Life . . . . This right is enforceable and applicable both in-world and offline . . . You create it, you own it – and it's yours to do with as you please." ...

VIRTUAL PROPERTY IN SECOND LIFE

65. As set forth above and herein, Linden represented that it recognized rights of in game participants to their virtual items, land, money and goods. Moreover, Linden represented that it recognized the intellectual property rights of the participants in their creations.

66. The virtual items created by participants as well as the land owned by the participants-is retained, preserved and stored by Linden on its servers.

67. In other Words, a participant's account and valuables of Second Life are stored as electromagnetic records on the Linden's servers. Defendants are simply paid for that storage and to hold the land and objects in trust for the owners of the virtual items and property.

68. The owner of the account is entitled to control the account and valuables' electromagnetic record and may freely sell or transfer it. Although a participant's account and valuables are "virtual," they are valuable property in the real world. The participants can auction them, sell them, license them or transfer them online and through other third independent parties, like eBay.com, slexchangecom, and others. ...

71. A participant's accounts and valuables are the same as the property in the real world.

72. A participant's interests in these virtual items, objects and properties persist regardless of the system currently connected to it, separate from the intellectual property that exists in Defendants' underlying code, much similar to a document or book simply created with a program such as Microsoft Word. ...

73. A participant can invite people into his virtual property, hold meetings in it, invest in it, and sell it to other people who might want to do the same independent of and regardless of the intellectual property that exists in Defendants' code.

74. Accordingly, Plaintiff's virtual property rights are divisible and severable from the rights of other participants in the game and the owner of the server upon which Defendants' code resides.

75. These properties, both the virtual land and the virtual objects, have value in real U.S. Dollars across the globe measuring in the billions of dollars and millions of participants. ...

78. Along with Defendants' promise of the transfer of title to Plaintiff of the title to their land and the ownership rights to their copyright and intellectual property creations, Defendants' virtual world possesses all of the real world features of exclusive ownership; persistence of rights, transfer under conditions of agreement and duress, free alienability of title, and a currency system to support trade in these property-based assets, including the buying and selling of these assets with U.S. currency. Private property is the default in Defendants' service, providing its customers with a bundle of rights, including the fundamental rights to use, exclude and transfer property interests.

VIRTUAL PROPERTY IN SECOND LIFE – PROPERTY OWNERSHIP

79. For a participant to purchase and own land in Second Life, the participant must upgrade to a premium membership and pay a monthly "tier," or tax

which varies in amount depending on the amount of land the participant owns.

80. A participant may then, in his unbridled discretion and control, split the land into varying sizes and parcels, resell it to other participants and convey title, retain it, build upon it, restrict What can be built upon it, change the shape of the land, i.e. "terraform" it, rent it, lease it, and / or exclude all participants, or just some participants from trespassing upon it. While the land continues to exist and is not "deleted" or otherwise destroyed. It is unique, just like real land. ...

82. Participants access their personal account information, purchase "lindens" (the in game money), buy and sell lindens for U.S. currency, pay for land, and monitor their accounts via the Internet. A currency exchange is maintained that sets, just like any other currency exchange, the exchange rate between "lindens" and U.S. currency. Third parties also provide for additional currency exchanges between "lindens" and U.S. currency, including ebay.com. ...

MARC BRAGG IS INDUCED INTO "PARTICIPATING" IN THE SECOND LIFE WORLD

84. Plaintiff is an individual who signed up and paid Defendants to participate in Second Life in or about November / December 2005. ...

87. Plaintiff believed the representations made by Linden and Rosedale and justifiably relied upon them. Indeed, there was nothing to make Plaintiff suspect that the representations being made by Linden and Rosedale were false.

88. By promising Plaintiff that he would receive and retain all right, title, interest, copyright and intellectual property rights to the land, objects and virtual property Plaintiff purchased and/or created in Second Life, Defendants intended to and did in fact deceptively induce Plaintiff to invest thousands in US. Dollars via the wires and mails crossing state lines. ...

SECOND LIFE'S AUCTION OF LAND

91. Defendants generally sell their lands via auctions hosted on Defendants' website. ...

96. If a participant wanted to bid on an auction, Defendants provided unique auction pages for each piece of land being auctioned which allowed the participant to enter the amount they intended to bid, confirm the bid, advising the participant that any bid won constituted a "legal and binding contract," and then once bid, posting the amount bid on that auction page for anyone to review and bid against. ...

99. In all cases, the auction would then run for 48 or 72 hours at which time anyone else who was aware of the auction and wanted to bid on the land was free to do so.

100. Once auctions were won, participants were charged for the purchase of the land at the final bid price via their credit cards and/or PayPal accounts, or by deducting the U.S. currency in their accounts then held in trust by Defendants for such purposes. ...

105. Plaintiff deposited real world money with Linden to obtain the land. ...

107. Plaintiff trusted and believed that the money he deposited with Linden, as well as the money he invested in the virtual property, could not and would

not be converted or stolen by the Defendants. Further, Plaintiff trusted and believed that Linden's representations that Plaintiff would retain all of his intellectual property rights were true and that Defendants would not interfere in the use and/or exercise of those rights.

"[Y]ou Can't for Example Just Take Someone Else's Property in Second Life", (Philip Rosedale, July 20, 2006), i.e. Linden Steals Bragg's Property

108. In or about April, 2006, Bragg had significantly grown his real estate holdings as well as his own virtual goods, items and content that he had created and offered for sale. Indeed, not only had Bragg purchased numerous parcels of land from Defendants, but he had also created content such as "fireworks" that Plaintiff offered for sale and did sell to other participants. Plaintiff had also acquired numerous other virtual items from third-parties, independent of Defendants. ...

111. On or about April 30, 2006, Bragg bid on and subsequently won the bid on a piece of virtual land named "Taessot." Bragg paid Defendants $300.00 in U.S. currency for that land, which amount Defendants accepted per the terms of their "legally binding contract" and auction list reflecting the price paid.

112. On or about May 2, 2006 or May 3, 2006, however, Bragg received an e-mail from "Jack Linden," a Linden agent, employee and/or servant, advising Bragg that the Taessot land had been purchased using an "exploit" in the system, and accordingly, the land had been taken away from Bragg and further, that Bragg would receive his $300.00 U.S. currency refunded to him.

113. The statements of the Linden agent were a lie, however. While Defendants did remove Bragg's name from the title to the Taessot land, they failed and refused to return Bragg's $300 to him that they had agreed to refund.

114. Even worse and deceptive, Linden "froze" Bragg's account preventing him from accessing the account to use, cancel or modify it. In essence, Linden prevented Bragg from access any of his items, land or goods to which he had all rights, title and interest. Moreover, despite preventing Bragg access to his items, land and goods, Linden continued to charge Bragg a "tax" on the land he owned and, also, refused to release Bragg's credit card information.

115. In the ultimate act of deception and fraud, Linden, without any right to do so or any consent from Bragg, removed Bragg's name from all other land owned by Bragg ... .

121. With regard to the land owned by Bragg and wrongfully confiscated and taken by Linden, Defendants listed the property at auction and sold it to the highest bidder. ...

123. Thus, not only did Defendants "eject" Bragg from their "Disney World," but before doing so, they confiscated all the goods he had purchased at the stores, refused to refund his money for the purchases, re-listed the purchased goods for re-sale, resold the goods to third parties, did not provide the proceeds to Bragg (keeping it for themselves) and – to top it off – simply took his other possessions as well as his wallet (with all his U.S. currency in it) that Bragg had, evidently, made the serious mistake of bringing into the "park" with him. ...

[Bragg asserted causes of action based on fraud, breach of contract, and conversion.]

ANSWER AND COUNTERCLAIM
(filed Aug. 17, 2007)

PRELIMINARY STATEMENT

1. This Counterclaim arises from a fraudulent scheme perpetrated by Marc Bragg and persons acting in concert with him to obtain money through a scheme and artifice involving unauthorized access to Linden's proprietary computers that host the online digital platform, or virtual world, known as "Second Life."...

ALLEGATIONS COMMON TO ALL CLAIMS

6. Linden created and operates Second Life, a three-dimensional online digital "virtual world" in which users develop and create the content and experiences that exist in the world, and determine their own ways to interact with and explore the world, much like the way users create websites on the Internet and other users interact with and experience those websites. To participate in Second Life, a user must choose a user name, agree to the Second Life Terms of Service, create an account by registering as a user, and then download Linden's proprietary viewer software to his or her computer....

7. After agreeing to the Terms of Service, registering, choosing a user name, and downloading the Second Life software, a user creates an avatar, a three-dimensional character through which the user can travel throughout the Second Life environment, interact with other users (also called "residents"), and create and experience representations of objects such as clothing, automobiles, and jewelry, conduct business, and attend events and meetings. Linden does not claim intellectual property rights in the objects or other content users create in Second Life. ...

9. Second Life has a fully-integrated virtual economy designed to reward users' entrepreneurship, innovation, and craftsmanship. Because users retain whatever intellectual property rights exist in the objects they have created, subject to the Terms of Service and conditions the creators may impose, they may sell, transfer or gift them to other users within Second Life. Likewise, users may also sell services to other users, such as design, advertising, and development services, within Second Life.

10. Users engage in purchase and sale transactions within Second Life using an internal unit-of-trade called "Linden Dollars." Linden Dollars may be bought and sold for real currency on an exchange provided by Linden, and also on third-party exchanges.

11. Second Life users with "Premium" memberships (which require a monthly fee) may also purchase "virtual land," which enables them to create representations of buildings such as shops and homes, where they may display and store their virtual creations as well as host events and operate businesses.

12. What a user actually obtains as a result of purchasing "virtual land" in Second Life is a license to have their created environment hosted on a dedicated and designated portion of Linden's proprietary servers, storage space, bandwidth, memory allocation, and a portion of the computational re-

sources of the server. Each server contains two or more CPU cores, which each represent a particular amount of "virtual land."

13. A user who purchases "virtual land" does not obtain rights in or control over Linden's server software, which is Linden's intellectual property, or in Linden's server hardware.

14. Users may purchase newly created "virtual land" in the Second Life "mainland" from Linden by auction, and users may also purchase "islands" for a fixed fee. Linden creates new "virtual land" in response to user demand, and does so by adding additional servers to its computing network on which to host the "virtual land" and the activities that occur and the content that users create on it. Users also may purchase existing "virtual land" from other users, in essence transferring the right to be hosted on, and computational resources of, Linden's servers, though the server software itself is not transferred.

15. In order to hold "virtual land," a user must pay a monthly "land use fee," also called a "tier fee," based on the peak amount of "virtual land" the user "owned" during the previous 30 days. The tier fee is determined by the user's "ownership tier," which the user may increase or decrease to accommodate the amount of "virtual land" he or she desires to "own." The tier fee is a fee for the services Linden provides that comprise and host the experience of "virtual land."

16. "Virtual land" in Second Life is different from the objects and other content users create within Second Life. "Virtual land" is part of the Second Life service; Linden provides Second Life users a license to use the services associated with "virtual land" pursuant to the Terms of Service and as long as tier fees and any other charges are paid. Because the "virtual land" itself in Second Life is not content created by a user, but rather a graphical representation of server space in the form of land features that are produced by Linden, a user does not obtain or retain intellectual property rights in "virtual land." Rather, "virtual land" is analogous to a canvas or blank page on which one may create his or her own original content: the user could have intellectual property rights in what he or she creates on it, but not in the canvas – or "virtual land" – itself.

17. Only a minority of Second Life users own "virtual land." Most of those who own "virtual land" purchase it in order to build communities or businesses upon it. Some others purchase "virtual land" in order to subdivide it and sell it to other users at a profit.

18. Linden offers different-sized parcels of newly-created "virtual land" to Second Life users by auction. At all times relevant to these Counterclaims, Linden's procedure was to conduct auctions of specific, newly-available parcels of "land" as it added additional servers to its hosting networks. The auctions were published via listings on the main auction page of the Second Life web site. Once listed, the auctions would become visible to all Second Life users, so that all users with Premium memberships would have an opportunity to bid upon them. A user who was interested in bidding on a particular parcel would click on the listing for that parcel, and then would be taken by hyperlink to the specific auction detail page for that parcel, much like the way an auction on eBay works. Each auction would begin at a minimum bid set by Linden. Users would make their bids by entering them on the auction detail

page for the relevant parcel. Once an opening bid was entered, users would have 48 hours from that point to bid before the auction automatically closed and the parcel automatically went to the high bidder; again, much like an eBay auction.

19. At all times relevant to these Counterclaims, the largest size of mainland parcel that Linden offered by auction was called a "region," and also colloquially known as a "sim." Linden uniformly set the minimum bid for such parcels at U.S. $1,000.00.

20. Each new region or "sim" requires its own computer central processing unit or CPU core. As such, as Linden creates new regions of "virtual land," it must install new computer servers containing the CPU cores for those regions. Linden set the opening bid at U.S. $1,000.00 to cover the cost of obtaining and installing the computer hardware for each new region.

21. On or about December 7, 2005, Bragg opened an account and registered as a user of Second Life under the user name "Marc Woebegone" and agreed to the Terms of Service then in force.

22. During the process of registering as a Second Life user, Bragg reached a screen containing the Terms of Service, which stated "Please read the following Terms of Service carefully. To continue logging on to Second Life, you must accept the agreement." Bragg manifested his agreement to the Terms of Service by clicking a button on the screen containing the Terms of Service reading "I Agree to the Terms of Service."

23. As an attorney admitted to the practice of law in three states and experienced in contract law, Bragg understood that by clicking the button reading "I Agree to the Terms of Service," he was entering into a contract with Linden. On information and belief, he was also familiar with the standard and ubiquitous practice of Internet software and service providers requiring their potential customers to accept an online agreement in order to gain access to such software and services. Indeed, Linden relied on his reading and accepting its Terms of Service as a condition to allowing him to gain access to its servers and software.

24. The Terms of Service to which Bragg agreed provided, among other things, that: Bragg would:

  (a) not "take any action or upload, post, e-mail or otherwise transmit content that violates any law or regulation" (Section 5.1(iii)),

  (b) not "take any action that would violate any right or duty under any law or under contractual or fiduciary relationships" (Section 5.1(vi)),

  (c) not "interfere with or disrupt the [Second Life] Service or servers or networks connected to the Service, or disobey any requirements, procedures, policies, or regulations of networks connected to the Service" (Section 5.1(viii)),

  (d) "use the Service only as offered by Linden at its web site or partner websites and not through any other means" (Section 5.2), and

  (e) not "create or provide any other means through which the Service may be accessed or used, as through server emulators" (Section 5.2). ...

29. The only way Linden authorized users to bid on parcels of "virtual land" it had offered for sale by auction was by entering a bid on the Auction Details page for a parcel listed on the main auction page.

30. As such, any means of obtaining parcels of "virtual land" to be offered by Linden by auction other than by entering a bid on the Auction Details page for a parcel listed on the main auction page was a violation of section 5.2 of the Terms of Service and contrary to the Auction FAQs, and therefore not authorized by Linden.

31. After opening his Second Life account, Bragg began purchasing "virtual land" from Linden through its customary auction system, whereby parcels were listed on the main auction page and bids were entered on the published Auction Details page for each parcel listed on the main auction page.

32. For example, on or about February 27, 2006, Bragg was the successful bidder on a region or "sim" called Songi, for which the bidding started at U.S. $1,000.00 and his winning bid was U.S. $1,605.00. On or about March 19, 2006, he was the successful bidder on a region or "sim" called Shinjung, for which the bidding started at U.S. $1,000.00 and his winning bid was U.S. $1,798.00. On or about April 13, 2006, he was the successful bidder on a region or "sim" called Ho Su, for which the bidding started at U.S. $1,000.00 and his winning bid was U.S. $1,501.00. Bragg also purchased other parcels at auction in Second Life.

33. After purchasing his parcels of "virtual land," Bragg subdivided them and resold them to other Second Life users in order to make a profit. Bragg used some of the proceeds from his sales to purchase other parcels from Linden. Bragg converted some of the Linden dollars he earned from his transactions in Second Life into U.S. dollars.

34. In or about April 2006, however, Bragg learned of a scheme that, if successful, would allow him to make far more profit from his "virtual land" sales, at Linden's expense. Specifically Bragg learned that another user with whom he was acquainted, "User M.S.," had acquired one or more full regions or "sims" of "virtual land" for as low as one U.S. dollar, despite the fact that the minimum bid set by Linden for "sims" was U.S. $1,000.00.

35. On information and belief, Bragg realized that if he, too, could acquire "sims" for as little as one U.S. dollar, he could make much more money upon subdividing and reselling portions to other users than if he had to pay U.S. $1,000.00 or more for "sims," as he had done before in Linden's authorized auctions. ...

40. Essentially, the scheme User M.S. shared with Bragg and User D.S. involved surreptitiously and without authorization accessing auction detail information on Linden's computers for "sims" that Linden had not yet listed on the main auction page of the Second Life site, and before Linden had set the minimum opening bid of U.S. $1,000.00, in order to trick Linden's computer system into starting an auction that was not visible to those who were unaware of the scheme. As these parcels had not yet been listed for auction by Linden, no user could access the auction detail information by any method authorized by Linden. Therefore, the scheme required the use of an artifice or "exploit" to access the auction detail information in advance of the legitimately conducted auction, which User M.S. described to Bragg and User D.S.

41. As a result of this scheme, beginning on or about April 24, 2006, User M.S., employing a method that was not authorized by Linden, was able to cause Auction Detail pages to be dynamically generated from information on Linden's computers, for "sims" that Linden had not yet published for auction and that did not appear on the Second Life main auction page. These were not pages posted on the Internet by Linden, and the data necessary to generate these pages was not yet intended for user access. These "sims" were in a state of preparation for auction – the data associated with many of these "sims" was not yet complete as required for a legitimate auction. For example, the "sims" did not yet have the standard minimum bid of U.S. $1,000.00 associated with them.

42. User M.S. was able to enter bids on these dynamically-generated pages he caused to be created and thereby trick Linden's computer system into starting the auctions. User M.S. would enter a bid of as low as zero dollars, which was possible because Linden had not intended to start the auction at that time, and therefore had not yet set the U.S. $1,000.00 minimum opening bid. Entering a bid would automatically trigger the 48 hour term of the auction. However, on information and belief, User M.S. soon learned that the system would not recognize a zero dollar bid as a winning bid when the auction ended, and thus learned that he needed to bid at least $1.00 to win the unauthorized auctions. Because the parcel had not been published for auction by Linden, this unauthorized auction never appeared as a listing on the main auction page and no one else could bid on it – except someone who knew of the exploit. If no one else placed a bid, after 48 hours passed the computer system would automatically declare User M.S. the winner of the auction with a high bid of as little as U.S. $1.00. ...

59. On April 29, 2006, Bragg caused the 48-hour period to begin for an unauthorized auction for an entire region or "sim" known as "Pak," No. 0026198533, by making a bid of zero. About five minutes later, at Bragg's direction, User D.S. caused the 48-hour period to begin for an unauthorized auction for an entire region or "sim" known as "Taesot," No. 0026198533, by making a bid of zero. Neither auction ever appeared on the main auction page. Bragg subsequently entered bids of U.S. $5.00 for both "sims," and a bid for $25.00 for the Taesot "sim." For most of the auction periods for both "sims," the only bidders were Bragg and User D.S., working together. But with only minutes left in the auctions, User S.S. swooped in and began bidding. Bragg and User S.S. engaged in a last minute bidding war, visible only to those aware of the scheme. When the auction for "Pak" ended on May 1, 2006 at 1:00 p.m., User S.S. was the high bidder at $151.00. When the auction for "Taesot" ended five minutes later, Bragg won the auction with the high bid of U.S. $300.01. ...

64. As Bragg was the winning bidder in Auction No. 0026198533, his Second Life account was automatically charged U.S. $300.01 and he obtained the parcel known as Taesot.

65. On information and belief, based on Bragg's transaction history in Second Life and his statements to other participants in the scheme, Bragg would have subdivided the "sims" he purchased through the fraudulent auction scheme, sold them to other Second Life users, and converted the proceeds (to the extent they were in Linden Dollars) to U.S. dollars. ...

67. At about the time that Bragg and his confederates were engaging in their scheme, Linden personnel noticed certain anomalous auction transactions and began to investigate. Linden also received a complaint from another user who had discovered that User M.S. and User M.S.2 had won auctions for as little as $1. Linden promptly investigated this auction activity, and determined that Bragg and his confederates had used an exploit to access auction detail information they were not authorized to access and trick Linden's computers into allowing them to secretly bid on certain "sims" before Linden listed those "sims" for auction. Linden reasonably and necessarily incurred expenses in connection with this investigation and as a result of the fraudulent scheme, in an amount to be proven at trial.

68. Upon discovering the irregular auction activity, on May 1, 2006 Linden put Bragg's account under user name Marc Woebegone on "administrative hold," preventing Bragg from further transactions in Second Life pending further investigation. Linden also placed administrative holds on the other accounts associated with the irregular auctions. In addition, on May 1, 2006, Linden altered the code associated with its auction system to prevent future use of the exploit.

69. Linden also took back the Taesot "sim" from Bragg's account.

70. Once the relevant accounts had been placed on hold, Linden continued its investigation into the matters surrounding the exploited auctions in order to determine the nature and extent of users' participation in the exploit and the extent of any additional risk to the Second Life auction system. Linden conducted extensive investigation into the accounts and recent activity of the users known to have bid on the unpublished auctions. Linden reasonably and necessarily incurred expenses in connection with this investigation and as a result of the fraudulent scheme, in an amount to be proven at trial.

71. Linden was not able to recover most of the "virtual land" acquired by User M.S., User M.S.2, and User T.L. in the conspiracy, as it had been resold to other users, who, based on Linden's investigation into the transactions, did not appear to have been part of the scheme. Five of the "sims" User M.S. acquired in furtherance of the conspiracy were not recovered. Likewise, the two "sims" User T.L. acquired in furtherance of the conspiracy were not recovered.

72. As a result of the fraudulent scheme, Linden was damaged by, among other things, the loss of the revenue it would have received had those seven "sims" been sold in auctions as authorized by Linden, namely at least U.S. $1,000.00 per "sim." ...

79. At the time Bragg's account under the user name Marc Woebegone was placed on administrative hold on May 1, 2006, the account had a cash balance of U.S. $1,970.79, and that remains the balance in that account as of the date of this Counterclaim. This did not include the U.S. $300.01 that was deducted from his account for his fraudulent purchase of the Taesot parcel.

80. In addition, other "virtual land" that was in Bragg's account prior to engaging in the fraudulent scheme was sold by Linden to other users at auction on or about May 23, 2006, pursuant to Section 7.1 of the Terms of Service then in force and in an effort to mitigate its own damages, and yielded a total of U.S. $3,632.00.

81. The total of these three amounts is U.S. $5,902.80. Section 7.1 of the Terms of Service in force at the time Bragg perpetrated the fraudulent scheme, and at the time his account was placed on fraud hold, provided that in the event an account is suspended or terminated for material breach by the user, Linden would attempt to sell at auction any "virtual land" held by the user, and that any money received from such auctions would be applied to satisfy the user's existing obligations to Linden and others, and any money remaining from the sale of land after the repayment of the user's obligations and a $100 resale fee may be returned to the user. Section 7.1 also provided that "Notwithstanding the foregoing, no money will be returned to [the user] in the event that [the user's] Account is terminated due to suspicions of fraud, violations of other laws or regulations, or deliberate disruptions to or interference with the Service."

82. Linden has not returned any money to Bragg pending the litigation he initiated.

[Linden asserted causes of action based on fraud, breach of contract, and conversion.]

QUESTIONS

1. Is Taessot property? If so, is it real property or personal property? What are Linden Dollars?

2. Both sides seem quite comfortable using words like "own" and "sell" to describe virtual land in Second Life. Is that relevant?

3. What role do terms of service play in defining what is and isn't property? The World of Warcraft Terms of Use specify:

    > Blizzard owns ... all of the content that appears in the Game. You agree that you have no right or title in or to any such content, including without limitation the virtual goods or currency appearing or originating in the Game or any other attributes associated with any Account.

    Suppose that Greg and Dan are avid World of Warcraft players. Greg learns Dan's password, logs into Dan's account, and transfers a valuable Irontree Greatsword to his own account. Has Greg committed conversion? Theft?

4. Suppose that Linden is right about Bragg's wrongdoing in the auction system, but that Bragg is right that Second Life parcels are property. What then? Remember that Second Life auctioned off Bragg's other parcels after it froze his account, and that some of the parcels Bragg bought fraudulently were sold on to innocent buyers.

5. If Taessot is property, what happens if Linden wants to shut down Second Life? Must it reimburse the players?

NOTE ON BITCOIN

Bitcoin is simpler than it sounds. It is a "cryptocurrency" not because it is mysterious but because it is based on cryptography. To see how, let us consider what jobs a financial record-keeping system needs to do, and then see how Bitcoin does them.

The most intuitive way of talking about money is as a tangible thing: dollars are pieces of paper that you hold in your hand. On this view, the numbers in a bank account balance also represent a thing: the number of dollars "in" the account. So a bank, or an online substitute for one, needs to keep track of who has which things.

But another way of thinking about money is in terms of verbs, rather than nouns. What matters are the transactions in which it passes from hand to hand. When you deposit a $50 birthday check from your aunt in your bank account, that's a transaction in which your aunt gives you $50. You are now capable of engaging in transactions in which you give away up to $50. So you could write a $50 check to your aunt, or a $25 check to your dentist and a $25 check to your cousin. With credit cards and online payment systems like Paypal, the transactions are electronic rather than paper, but the idea is the same: keep track of who pays how much to whom and when.

In this example, the bank maintains a ledger of transactions involving your account. Your aunt's bank maintains a ledger of transactions involving her account. When you deposit her check, the two banks consult with each other, and then very carefully adjust both of their ledgers. Bitcoin is exactly the same, with three differences:

- The Bitcoin ledger, called the *blockchain*, keeps track of transactions involving everyone's Bitcoin accounts.

- Instead of being maintained by a centralized authority, the blockchain is maintained collectively, by everyone who uses Bitcoin.

- The blockchain is secured using public-key cryptography.

First, start with the blockchain. Suppose that Alice sends Bob two Bitcoins. (Perhaps he mowed her lawn, or perhaps he gave her some U.S. dollars in exchange.) Abstracting slightly from the technical details, this transaction could be represented as:

```
From: Alice         To: Bob         Amount:    2.000 BTC
```

Alice makes the transfer to Bob by appending this new transaction to the blockchain. Suppose that just before she does, the blockchain (ordered with the most recent transaction at the top) read:

```
From: Carol         To: Alice       Amount: 200.000 BTC
From: Sujit         To: Rajiv       Amount:    .500 BTC
From: Dave          To: Alice       Amount:   7.250 BTC
From: Carol         To: Alice       Amount:   5.250 BTC
[millions of previous transactions]
```

After Alice adds her transaction to Bob, the blockchain now reads:

```
From: Alice         To: Bob         Amount:    2.000 BTC
From: Carol         To: Alice       Amount: 200.000 BTC
From: Sujit         To: Rajiv       Amount:    .500 BTC
From: Dave          To: Alice       Amount:   7.250 BTC
From: Carol         To: Alice       Amount:   5.250 BTC
[millions of previous transactions]
```

What keeps Alice honest? It is only possible for Alice to make a transaction giving Bob Bitcoins if there are *previous* transactions giving Alice enough Bitcoins. Just as a bank will bounce a check drawn against an account without sufficient funds, other Bitcoin users will reject the transaction unless there are previous transactions already in the blockchain supplying the necessary Bitcoins.* But if Alice has the Bitcoins to spend, other Bitcoin users will agree to add the transaction to the blockchain. When Bob sees that the blockchain has been extended to include Alice's payment to him, he knows that the payment has succeeded.

Second, the blockchain is publicly maintained. The blockchain is just a large and growing file that lists every Bitcoin transaction ever since the start of time. Instead of a bank storing the file on its servers (with appropriate backups), many different Bitcoin users keep a copy of the blockchain. Every time a new "block" of transactions is added to the chain (hence the name), the user adding the block broadcasts it to other users, who add the new transactions to their own copy of the blockchain. It is this collective process of agreement on which transactions have taken place that most distinguishes Bitcoin from traditional payment systems. Bitcoin relies on a peer-to-peer process of consensus rather than on one authority with the power to say which transactions are valid and which are not. Anyone who wants to take part, or to check up on past Bitcoin transactions, can obtain a copy of the blockchain and examine it. In theory, at least, this makes Bitcoin less vulnerable to arbitrary exercises of power: no single person or government can arbitrarily create new Bitcoins or take them away from their owners.

Third, add security into the mix. Bitcoin uses digital signatures to guard against all of the obvious attacks, and a great many subtle ones as well. Every Bitcoin *address* (the source or destination of a transaction) has its own private-key/public-key pair. The "From: Alice" part of the transaction is a digital signature generated using the private key for Alice's address. If the signature matches, anyone examining the transaction can confirm that Alice authorized it; if the signature doesn't match, the transaction will be rejected. Thus, while it is easy to receive Bitcoins, only someone controlling the appropriate private key can spend them. (This also means that if you lose the private key for a Bitcoin address, the Bitcoins are gone forever; no one can spend them.)

Now we are ready to answer two questions hanging over the system: *Where do Bitcoins come from?* and *Why do Bitcoin users cooperate in maintaining the blockchain?* The answer is that there are rewards for participating. A new block of transactions is added to the blockchain roughly every ten minutes: the user who first adds it receives a reward of 25 Bitcoins.† Which user that is is chosen essentially at random through a digital version of a scratch-off lottery in which there is an immense supply of free tickets and scratching one off takes a little bit of work

---

* This checking process is substantially easier because each Bitcoin transaction explicitly identifies the previous transaction or transactions providing the necessary funds.

† As of 2014. The number will gradually decrease over time, and be replaced by transaction fees offered by the Alices of the world as an incentive to process their transactions.

and time.* Since whoever scratches off a winning number first wins, Bitcoin users have an incentive to devote their computers' time to "mining" Bitcoins, as the process is called. Each time someone proves that they have won the lottery by exhibiting the winning number for a block of transactions, everyone adds that block and immediately starts scratching off tickets in the next lottery for the next block. This scheme cleverly harnesses Bitcoin users' greed to get them to participate in keeping the system working.

Bitcoin is interesting for many regulatory reasons, as the materials below explore. But it also raises some interesting questions about anonymity. On the one hand, Bitcoin transactions are not identified with users' names, only with inscrutably opaque Bitcoin addresses like 16UwLL9Risc3QfPqBUvKofHmBQ7wMtjvM, so it can be hard to tell who is behind Bitcoin transactions. On the other hand, the blockchain is public, so anyone can scrutinize its history. It is easy to follow Bitcoins from one address to another, unlike cash, which can circulate in near-total secrecy.

UNITED STATES V. ULBRICHT
31 F. Supp. 3d 540 (S.D.N.Y. 2014)

Forrest, District Judge: ...

The Government alleges that Ross Ulbricht engaged in narcotics trafficking, computer hacking, and money laundering conspiracies by designing, launching, and administering a website called Silk Road ("Silk Road") as an online marketplace for illicit goods and services. ...

A conspiracy claim is premised on an agreement between two or more people to achieve an unlawful end. The Government alleges that by designing, launching, and administering Silk Road, Ulbricht conspired with narcotics traffickers and hackers to buy and sell illegal narcotics and malicious computer software and to launder the proceeds using Bitcoin. ...

The Government alleges that Silk Road was designed to operate like eBay: a seller would electronically post a good or service for sale; a buyer would electronically purchase the item; the seller would then ship or otherwise provide to the buyer the purchased item; the buyer would provide feedback; and the site operator (i.e., Ulbricht) would receive a portion of the seller's revenue as a commission. Ulbricht, as the alleged site designer, made the site available only to those using Tor, software and a network that allows for anonymous, untraceable Internet browsing; he allowed payment only via Bitcoin, an anonymous and untraceable form of payment.

Following the launch of Silk Road, the site was available to sellers and buyers for transactions. Thousands of transactions allegedly occurred over the course of

---

* To be a little more precise, Bitcoin miners are computing hash values. The winner is the one who finds a 32-bit number with a hash that is sufficiently close to zero. Since the hash function used by Bitcoin (SHA-256) produces outputs that are all but indistinguishable from random, there is no way to speed up the process other than to try one 32-bit number after another. The Bitcoin protocol automatically calibrates the difficulty of the hashing problem – i.e., the number of winning tickets in the lottery, or how close is "sufficiently close" to zero – so that someone will find a matching hash and add a block roughly every ten minutes. There is no way to save up winning numbers from one block to the next, since the details of the hashing depend on the transactions in the block.

nearly three years – sellers posted goods when available; buyers purchased goods when desired. As website administrator, Ulbricht may have had some direct contact with some users of the site, and none with most. This online marketplace thus allowed the alleged designer and operator (Ulbricht) to be anywhere in the world with an Internet connection (he was apprehended in California), the sellers and buyers to be anywhere, the activities to occur independently from one another on different days and at different times, and the transactions to occur anonymously. ...

VIII. COUNT FOUR

Count Four charges the defendant with participation in a money laundering conspiracy in violation of 18 U.S.C. § 1956(h). The Government has alleged the requisite statutory elements. First, the Government has alleged that a conspiracy existed between the defendant and one or more others, the object of which was to engage in money laundering. In paragraph 20, the Indictment recites the specific elements required for money laundering:

> It was a part and an object of the conspiracy that ... the defendant, and others known and unknown, ... knowing that the property involved in certain financial transactions represented proceeds of some form of unlawful activity, would and did conduct and attempt to conduct such financial transactions, which in fact involved the proceeds of specified unlawful activity, to wit, narcotics trafficking and computer hacking ... with the intent to promote the carrying on of such unspecified unlawful activity ....

The defendant argues that the factual allegation that Bitcoins constituted the exclusive "payment system that served to facilitate [ ] illegal commerce" on Silk Road cannot constitute the requisite "financial transaction." The Court disagrees.

As an initial matter, an allegation that Bitcoins are used as a payment system is insufficient in and of itself to state a claim for money laundering. The fact that Bitcoins allow for anonymous transactions does not ipso facto mean that those transactions relate to unlawful activities. The anonymity by itself is not a crime. Rather, Bitcoins are alleged here to be the medium of exchange – just as dollars or Euros could be – in financial transactions relating to the unlawful activities of narcotics trafficking and computer hacking. It is the system of payment designed specifically to shield the proceeds from third party discovery of their unlawful origin that forms the unlawful basis of the money laundering charge.

The money laundering statute defines a "financial transaction" as involving, inter alia, "the movement of funds by wire or other means, or [ ] involving one or more monetary instruments, [ ] or involving the transfer of title to any real property, vehicle, vessel, or aircraft." 18 U.S.C. § 1956(c)(4). The term "monetary instrument" is defined as the coin or currency of a country, personal checks, bank checks, and money orders, or investment securities or negotiable instruments. 18 U.S.C. § 1956(c)(5).

The defendant argues that because Bitcoins are not monetary instruments, transactions involving Bitcoins cannot form the basis for a money laundering conspiracy. He notes that the IRS has announced that it treats virtual currency as property and not as currency. The defendant argues that virtual currencies have some but not all of the attributes of currencies of national governments and that virtual currencies do not have legal tender status. In fact, neither the IRS nor FinCEN purport to amend the money laundering statute (nor could they). In any event, neither the IRS nor FinCEN has addressed the question of whether a "financial transaction" can occur with Bitcoins. This Court refers back to the money laundering statute itself and case law interpreting the statute.

It is clear from a plain reading of the statute that "financial transaction" is broadly defined. It captures all movements of "funds" by any means, or monetary instruments. "Funds" is not defined in the statute and is therefore given its ordinary meaning. "Funds" are defined as "money, often money for a specific purpose." See Cambridge Dictionaries Online, http://dictionary. cambridge.org/us/dictionary/american-english/funds?q=funds (last visited July 3, 2014). "Money" is an object used to buy things.

Put simply, "funds" can be used to pay for things in the colloquial sense. Bitcoins can be either used directly to pay for certain things or can act as a medium of exchange and be converted into a currency which can pay for things. See *Bitcoin*, https://bitcoin.org/en (last visited July 3, 2014); *8 Things You Can Buy With Bitcoins Right Now*, CNN Money, http://money.cnn. com/gallery/technology/2013/11/25/buy-with-bitcoin/ (last visited July 3, 2014). Indeed, the only value for Bitcoin lies in its ability to pay for things – it is digital and has no earthly form; it cannot be put on a shelf and looked at or collected in a nice display case. Its form is digital – bits and bytes that together constitute something of value. And they may be bought and sold using legal tender. See *How to Use Bitcoin*, https://bitcoin. org/en/getting-started (last visited July 3, 2014). Sellers using Silk Road are not alleged to have given their narcotics and malicious software away for free – they are alleged to have sold them.

The money laundering statute is broad enough to encompass use of Bitcoins in financial transactions. Any other reading would – in light of Bitcoins' sole raison d'etre – be nonsensical. Congress intended to prevent criminals from finding ways to wash the proceeds of criminal activity by transferring proceeds to other similar or different items that store significant value. With respect to this case, the Government has alleged that Bitcoins have a value which may be expressed in dollars. (Ind. ¶ 3 (alleging that Ulbricht "reaped commissions worth tens of millions of dollars, generated from the illicit sales conducted through the site").)

There is no doubt that if a narcotics transaction was paid for in cash, which was later exchanged for gold, and then converted back to cash, that would constitute a money laundering transaction.

One can money launder using Bitcoin. The defendant's motion as to Count Four is therefore denied.

QUESTIONS

1. Silk Road, the "Amazon.com of illegal drugs," was reachable only through the Tor network, which hides users' IP addresses. Buyers of obviously illegal substances like heroin or LSD paid sellers using Bitcoins. How secure was this approach?

2. In 2013, the FBI shut down Silk Road by arresting Ulbricht, a/k/a Dread Pirate Roberts, as he logged in from a public library. As part of the arrest, the FBI seized about 174,000 Bitcoins. What does that mean? How do you "seize" a Bitcoin? The government plans to auction them off under the asset forfeiture laws. What does that mean? How do you "auction" a Bitcoin?

ILLINOIS DEPT. OF FINANCIAL AND PROFESSIONAL REGULATION
DIGITAL CURRENCY REGULATORY GUIDANCE
2017

Digital currencies such as Bitcoin, Dogecoin, Ethereum, Litecoin, and ZCash have raised questions with respect to money transmission and exchange of currency. This guidance outlines the policy of the Illinois Department of Financial and Professional Regulation (the "Department") with regards to digital currencies. This guidance expresses the Department's interpretation of Illinois' Transmitters of Money Act ("TOMA") and its application to various activities involving digital currencies. This guidance seeks to establish the regulatory treatment of digital currencies under TOMA as it currently exists. ...

Whether or not an Illinois money transmitter license is required for an entity to engage in the transmission of decentralized digital currencies turns on the question of whether digital currency is considered "money" as defined in TOMA. Accordingly, Section 5 of TOMA defines a "[m]oney transmitter" as:

> [A] person who is located in or doing business in this State and who directly or through authorized sellers does any of the following in this State:
>
> 1) Sells or issues payment instruments
>
> 2) Engages in the business of receiving money for transmission or transmitting money.
>
> 3) Engages in the business of exchanging, for compensation, money of the United States Government or a foreign government to or from money of another government. ...

Section 5 of TOMA defines "[m]oney" as:

> [A] medium of exchange that is authorized or adopted by a domestic or foreign government as a part of its currency and that is customarily used and accepted as a medium of exchange in the country of issuance.

Accordingly, although digital currencies are a digital representation of value that is used as a medium of exchange, store of value, or unit of account, they are not considered money for the purposes of TOMA as digital currencies have not been "authorized or adopted by a domestic or foreign government as a part of its currency." A person or entity engaged in the transmission of solely digital currencies, as defined, would not be required to obtain a TOMA license. However, should transmission of digital currencies involve money in a transaction, that transaction may be considered money transmission depending on how the transaction is organized. ...

In order to provide further guidance and clarity on the application of digital currencies to TOMA, listed below are some examples of common types of digital currency transactions. Please note this is a non-exhaustive list.

Activities Generally Qualifying as Money Transmission

- Exchange involving both digital currency and money through a third party exchanger is generally considered to be money transmission. For example, some digital currency exchange sites facilitate exchanges by acting as an escrow-like intermediary. In a typical transaction, the buyer of digital currency sends money to the exchanger who holds the funds until it determines that the terms of the sale have been satisfied before transmitting the funds to the seller. Irrespective of its handling of the digital currency, the exchanger conducts money transmission by receiving the buyer's money in exchange for a promise to make it available to the seller.

- Exchange of digital currency for money through an automated machine is generally considered to be money transmission. For example, several companies have begun selling automated machines commonly called "Bitcoin ATMs" that facilitate contemporaneous exchanges of digital currency for money. Most such machines currently available, when operating in their default mode act as an intermediary between a buyer and seller, typically connecting through one of the established exchange sites. When a customer buys or sells digital currency through a machine configured this way, the operator of the machine receives the buyer's money and is engaging in the "business of receiving money for transmission or transmitting money."

    Some digital currency ATMs, however, can be configured to conduct transactions only between the customer and the machine's operator, with no third parties involved. If the machine never involves a third party, and only facilitates a sale or purchase of digital currency by the machine's operator directly with the customer, there is no money transmission because at no time is money received and neither party is engaging in the "business of receiving money for transmission or transmitting money."

Activities Not Qualifying as Money Transmission

- Exchange of digital currency for money directly between two parties does not qualify as money transmission. This is essentially a sale of goods between two parties. The seller gives units of digital currency to the buyer, who pays the seller directly with money. The seller does not receive money with the intent to transmit it to another entity or "engage in the business of exchanging, for compensation, money of the United States Government or a foreign government to or from money of another government."

- Transfer of digital currency by itself is not transmitting money. Because digital currency is not money, the receipt of it with the intent to transmit it to another entity is not "transmitting money." This includes intermediaries who receive digital currency for transfer to a third party, and entities who, akin to depositories (commonly referred to as wallets), hold digital currency on behalf of customers and can either unilaterally execute or prevent a digital currency transaction.

- Exchange of one digital currency for another digital currency is not money transmission.

- A merchant who accepts digital currency as payment for goods or services or an individual who pays for goods or services with digital currency are commonly referred to as "users" of digital currency. Regardless of how many parties are involved, no money is involved at any point in this transaction, so "transmitting money" does not occur.

- Miners do not receive money for verifying transactions. Instead, Miners receive digital currency as payment for verifying transactions, typically by contributing software, connectivity, or computing power to process transactions. Because money is not involved in the payment of this work, "transmitting money" does not occur.

- Blockchain 2.0 technologies refer to the use of a digital currency's decentralized or distributed ledger system for non-monetary purposes such as verifying ownership or authenticity in a digital capacity. This technology includes software innovations such as colored coins (i.e. coins that are marked specifically to represent a non-monetary asset), smart contracts (i.e. agreements implemented on a distributed ledger), and smart property (i.e. property that is titled using a decentralized distributed ledger). These uses for non- monetary purposes may use digital currency as a medium of exchange, but do not involve the exchange or transmission of money or the sale or issuance of a "payment instrument" and as a result "transmitting money" does not occur.

QUESTIONS

1. What is the difference between money *laundering* and money *transmission*?

2. Maura mines Bitcoins. Every few months, she uses the Erebor exchange to convert them into U.S. dollars. She also occasionally transfers some Bitcoins directly to Barrow Burgers to buy dinner. Is she required to register as a money transmitter? Should any of them have to pay income taxes on their Bitcoin transactions?

3. The Bank Secrecy Act and other federal laws require that money transmitters keep detailed records and report on suspicious transactions. These laws are designed to prevent tax evasion, money laundering, black markets, and other skulduggery. Does it make sense to extend them to Bitcoin transactions?

4. State money transmission laws go further. They require money transmitters to make numerous disclosures to consumers and maintain a sufficient reserve of assets, among many other things. Does it make sense to extend these laws to Bitcoin transactions?

5. There are many other kinds of financial regulation, each with its own complicated statutory scheme. There are "commodities," *see* 7 U.S.C. § 1a(9), "securit[ies]," *see* 15 U.S.C. § 77b, "banks," *see* 12 U.S.C. § 1813(a)(1), "negotiable instrument[s]," *see* U.C.C. § 3-104, and many more. With such a well-developed regulatory apparatus, why is it so hard to figure out how Bitcoins fit in?

6. Does Bitcoin raise any new jurisdictional issues?

SLOT MACHINE PROBLEM

A statute in the state of Campania prohibits possessing or offering to the public any "slot machine," which is defined as:

> a machine, apparatus, or device that is operated by insertion of a coin or other object or by any other means, and that by reason of any element of chance grants the user any thing of value

Your client, First Century, is the developer of Sword and Sandal, a massively popular massively multiplayer smartphone game. Players construct empires in a fantasy world vaguely reminiscent of ancient Rome, as filtered through Hollywood. Players can ally with or attack each other, making for massively massive battles. Sword and Sandal is free to play, but it is difficult to manage an empire larger than a "province" without spending more than 1,000 in-game "gold pieces" a day building fortifications and paying troops. All players receive 500 gold pieces daily and can purchase more at rates ranging from $1.99 for 2,000 gold pieces to $99.99 for 1,000,000. When two players have allied, they can give each other soldiers, gold, or other in-game resources like stone and wood.

Sword and Sandal also includes an in-game "Crassus's Casino." Players can spend 100 gold to wager on an animated spinning wheel. After each spin, the player receives a virtual prize of between 10 and 5,000 stone, wood, gold, or other resources. What the player receives, as well as how much, is randomly determined; smaller prizes are more common than large ones. Sword and Sandal's terms of service provide that "Virtual Currency and Virtual Goods may never be redeemed for 'real world' money, goods or other items of monetary value from First Century or any other person" and expressly prohibit "buying or selling any Virtual Currency or Virtual Goods outside the Services or in exchange for 'real world' money or items of value."

First Century has received a letter from the Campania attorney general seeking more information about Crassus's Casino and asserting that it may qualify as a prohibited slot machine. Advise the client on whether this is a risk it should be worried about, and if so, what to do.

POST.MORTEM PROBLEM

You have been approached by an entrepreneur, Susan Mortimer, who has an idea for what she calls an "email probate" service to be called Post.Mortem. Her plan is that estate attorneys drafting wills for their clients will specify that Post.Mortem will be responsible for processing their email accounts after they die. At the time the will is signed, the client will give Post.Mortem the password to his email account and a list of (secret) instructions. Every three months thereafter, Post.-Mortem will send him a reminder to give it the latest password. After the client's death, the executor will get in touch with Post.Mortem, which will then follow the client's written instructions as to which emails should be deleted and which should be turned over his heirs. Upon payment of its fee from the estate, Post.Mortem will take the remaining emails, burn then to CDs, give the CDs to the appropriate heirs, and then delete the email account.

Your first thought, when Mortimer told you her idea, was to check the terms of service for popular email services. As you suspected, some of them flatly prohibit sharing one's password with a third party. Mortimer is undeterred, however. "Aren't they *your* emails," she asked? "Shouldn't *you* be the one to decide what happens to them? How could they possibly stop you?"

What is your advice to Mortimer? Will her business model work? If there are legal problems with her plan, are there ways to solve them?

DAVY JONES PROBLEM

Davy Jones' Locker is a "file locker" service. Users pay $5 a month for each 100 gigabytes of space, to which they can upload files for online storage. Each file is given a URL, which the user can (if they wish) share with others to download the file. Moderate-speed downloads with ads are free; users can pay another $15/month for faster ad-free downloads.

Three weeks ago, the United States Attorney for the Eastern District of Virginia unsealed an indictment charging Davy Jones and its officers with massive criminal copyright infringement. According to the indictment, they had personal knowledge of numerous infringing files and actively solicited uploads of recent movies, music, software, and other obviously infringing content. In some cases, they were alleged to have personally discussed the upload of specific infringing files with users who then received large cash payments (of $1500 or more) for uploading them. The president and two other officers were arrested and have since been released on substantial bail.

Simultaneously with the unsealing of the indictment, the FBI executed a search warrant on the Virginia data center of Transylvania Hosting, which rented to Davy Jones over six hundred computer servers, along with supplying power and network connectivity. The FBI instructed Transylvania to disconnect the Davy Jones servers from the Internet, but to leave them otherwise powered on and connected. FBI technicians made complete digital copies of twelve of the servers and copied a few hundred individual files from other servers. The government also froze Davy Jones' bank accounts, containing a total of over $9 million.

Three days ago, Transylvania filed a motion with the court asking for permission to turn off the Davy Jones servers, which it claims are costing it over $4,000 a day to store. Davy Jones has been unable to pay the hosting bills since its accounts are frozen. In addition, a Davy Jones user, Anne Read, has filed a motion with the court demanding the return of her files from Davy Jones. She is a wedding videographer and used Davy Jones' locker to store 800GB of videos from recent weddings that she was in the process of editing for her clients. Read's motion calls for the Locker servers to be reconnected to the Internet so that she and other users can download their files. The government's response, delivered orally at a hearing yesterday, is that Davy Jones's bank accounts consist of the proceeds of illegal activity, and so cannot be unfrozen to pay for the hosting, and that reconnecting the servers to the Internet would enable the criminal activity to continue.

You are a court-appointed mediator; you have been asked by the District Judge to see if it is possible to broker a compromise. You will be meeting with the attorneys for Davy Jones, Transylvania, Read, and the U.S. Attorney's office in thirty minutes. What do you expect them to say, and do you see any potential room for flexibility in their positions? What could be done with the servers that would properly take into account the various property interests implicated by the case? Is there anything else you would need to know?

B. Defective Software

Ask any programmer: programming is hard. How should the legal system deal with the inevitable bugs and design mistakes?

QUESTION

Have you ever dealt with a customer service agent who couldn't help you because "the computer" wouldn't allow it? Have you ever been unable to buy something because the sales clerk couldn't get "the computer" to work? Why are computers so often associated with bureaucracy and frustration?

KENNISON V. DAIRE
High Court of Australia
[1986] HCA 4

Gibbs, Chief Justice:

The appellant was convicted of larceny. ... He was the holder of an Easybank card which enabled him to use the automatic teller machine of the Savings Bank of South Australia to withdraw money from his account with that bank. It was a condition of the use of the card that the customer's account could be drawn against to the extent of the funds available in that account. Before the date of the alleged offence, the appellant had closed his account and withdrawn the balance, but had not returned the card. On the occasion of the alleged offence, he used his card to withdraw $200 from the machine at the Adelaide branch of the bank. He was able to do so because the machine was off-line and was programmed to allow the withdrawal of up to $200 by any person who placed the card in the machine and gave the corresponding personal identification number. When off-line the machine was incapable of determining whether the card holder had any account which remained current, and if so, whether the account was in credit.

It is not in doubt that the appellant acted fraudulently with intent permanently to deprive the bank of $200. The appellant's submission is that the bank consented to the taking. It is submitted that the bank intended that the machine should operate within the terms of its programme, and that when it did so it gave effect to the intention of the bank.

In the course of an interesting argument, Mr Tilmouth pointed out that if a teller, having the general authority of the bank, pays out money on a cheque when the drawer's account is overdrawn, or on a forged order, the correct conclusion is that the bank intends that the property in the money should pass, and that the case is not one of larceny. ... He submitted that, in effect, the machine was invested with a similar authority and that if, within the instructions in its programme, it handed over the money, it should be held that the property in the money passed to the card holder with the consent of the bank.

With all respect we find it impossible to accept these arguments. The fact that the bank programmed the machine in a way that facilitated the commission of a fraud by a person holding a card did not mean that the bank consented to the withdrawal of money by a person who had no account with the bank. It is not suggested that any person, having the authority of the bank to consent to the particular transaction, did so. The machine could not give the bank's consent in fact and there is no principle of law that requires it to be treated as though it were a person with authority to decide and consent. The proper inference to be drawn from the facts is that the bank consented to the withdrawal of up to $200 by a card holder who presented his card and supplied his personal identification number, only if the card holder had an account which was current. It would be quite unreal to infer that the bank consented to the withdrawal by a card holder whose account had been closed. The conditions of use of the card supplied by the bank to its customers support the conclusion that no such inference can be drawn. It is unnecessary to consider what the position might have been if the account had remained current but had insufficient funds to its credit. ...

For these reasons ... the appeal should be dismissed.

POMPEII ESTATES, INC. V. CONSOLIDATED EDISON CO. OF N.Y., INC.

397 N.Y.S.2d 577 (Civ. Ct. N.Y.C. 1977)

Posner, Judge:

The "Dawn of the Age of Aquarius" has also ushered in the "Age of the Computer."

There is no question that the modern computer is as indispensable to big business as the washing machine is to the American household. To ask the American housewife to go back to washing clothes by hand is as unthinkable as asking Consolidated Edison to send out its monthly bills by any other method than the computer.

This is an action in negligence by a builder against a public utility for damages sustained as a result of the alleged "wrongful" termination of electricity at an unoccupied one-family house (that had recently been constructed by the plaintiff) at 200-15 Pompeii Rd., Holliswood. Sometime in October, 1975, the defendant had installed electric services to the plaintiff's property. On or about January 20, 1976, the defendant terminated such service because of two unpaid bills amounting to $25.11. Since the premises were unoccupied, the lack of electricity caused the motor which operated the heating unit to go off, which resulted in frozen water pipes, which burst and caused $1,030 of proven damages to the premises. ...

Defendant through the use of five witnesses, made out a good case proving that the notice to disconnect was probably mailed even though no witness had actual knowledge of mailing this specific notice. Obviously, it would be overly burdensome, if not impossible, to expect a utility mailing out thousands of disconnect notices a day to be able to prove that each one was individually mailed. ...

Accordingly, this court finds that the defendant did comply with the statutory requirement of mailing even though we are also convinced that the plaintiff had never received the notice because an expert witness from the U.S. Postal Department testified that the postal service does not leave mail at an unoccupied address. Unless a statute or the contract between the parties calls for actual notice proof of mailing is sufficient to prove notice, even though the notice was never received.

While the parties, at the trial and in their memoranda of law devoted considerable time to the issue of "notice", the court finds that this is not the main issue in this case. Let us say that this was a "procedural" hurdle which Consolidated Edison cleared successfully. However, the court has serious doubts as to whether the defendant has cleared the "substantive" hurdle – did it act reasonably or negligently in discontinuing plaintiff's electric service?

... The defendant's witnesses stated that a customer's file is opened when a new account is established and that all correspondence and other documents involving the customer are included in this file. Defendant's attorney admitted that he had found in such file the original letter from plaintiff requesting the opening of electrical current. This letter is reproduced in its entirety because of its significance to the case:

POMPEII ESTATES INC.
34-34 Bell Blvd.
Bayside, N.Y. 11361
212-631-4466

June 12, 1975

Con Edison
40-55 College Pt. Blvd.
Flushing, N.Y. 11354
Att: Mr. A. Vebeliunas – 670-6152

To Whom It May Concern:
   Please be advised that there have been no changes in the original Building Plans for the 2 Houses located at the following addresses:

House #1 – 200-15 Pompeii Rd., Holliswood, N.Y. – Lot #163
House #2 – 200-19 Pompeii Rd., Holliswood, N.Y. – Lot #160

Be further advised that the electrical load within the house will be:

6KW Lighting and 3 1/2 Horse Power Air-Conditioning
1/4 Horse Power Blowers
1.2 KW Dishwashers

There will be 1-150 AMP – 3 wire socket type electric meter for each house.

Sincerely yours,
        POMPEII ESTATES
    AT: SWR
    ALBANO TESTANI – PRESIDENT

Between the date of this letter (June 12, 1975) and the time service was installed (Oct. 24, 1975) four months elapsed. There was no other correspondence; but the plaintiff's witness (Testani) testified that he had numerous conversations with Mr. Vebeliunas on the phone and at the job site. Mr. Vebeliunas, defendant's employee never appeared in court, even though the case was tried on three separate occasions over a period of two weeks. Though Vebeliunas was defendant's field representative and the only contact plaintiff had with defendant, he was never consulted when the decision was made to discontinue service for the nonpayment of the first two months rent. The testimony of defendant's witnesses bore out the fact that said decision was a routine procedure activated by the computer and ordered by a Mr. Chris Hagan. Did defendant produce Mr. Hagan to testify what human input there was to the computer's order? No, like Mr. Vebeliunas, he never graced the courtroom scene. Failure to produce two key witnesses under the defendant's control can only lead to the inference that they would not contradict the plaintiff's contention that defendant acted unreasonably.

Negligence is lack of ordinary care. It is a failure to exercise that degree of care which a reasonably prudent person would have exercised under such circumstances. The statute only requires the notice of discontinuance to be sent to the premises where the service is provided; though, by regulation, the Public Service Commission has said that the customer may direct another address for mailing purposes. While the plaintiff's letter (*supra*) does not specifically direct that the mail be sent to 34-34 Bell Boulevard, any reasonably prudent person examining the letter would realize that this is a builder building new homes and that it is not customary for a builder to occupy the homes he builds. Certainly, any reasonably prudent person, if in doubt, would contact Mr. Vebeliunas to ascertain the facts. This is especially so when the termination of service is in the middle of winter and the foreseeable consequences to the heating system and the water pipes are apparent. Where there is a foreseeability of damage to another that may occur from one's acts, there arises a duty to use care. In this instance, a one-minute cursory glance at plaintiff's letter (*supra*) would have alerted Mr. Hagan to the fact that there was something unusual in this situation. To the contrary, the computer said, "terminate," and Mr. Hagan gave the order to terminate.

This court finds the defendant liable to the plaintiff for damages in the amount of $1,030, with interest and costs. While the computer is a useful instrument, it cannot serve as a shield to relieve Consolidated Edison of its obligation to exercise reasonable care when terminating service. The statute gives it the discretionary power to do so, and this discretion must be exercised by a human brain. Computers can only issue mandatory instructions – they are not programmed to exercise discretion.

QUESTIONS

1. *Kennison* implies that the result would have been different if the defendant had dealt with a human, rather than with a computer. Why? Would the result in *Pompeii Estates* have been different if the defendants there had dealt with a human, rather than a computer?

2. Does the law treat computers as people? Should it?

3. Who programmed the computer in *Kennison*? Who programmed the computer in *Pompeii Estates*? Did any of them make mistakes in what they programmed the computers to do?

4. Why did Easybank use a computer? Why did ConEd? What advantages does a computer provide? What are the disadvantages? Would society be better off if we prohibited the use of computers for these purposes altogether? If not, what safeguards do we need on their use?

5. If you receive some information from a computer, are you allowed to take the computer at its word? If you put information into a computer, are you now responsible for all the consequences? What about the person who provides the computer? The person who programmed it? Who, if anyone, *ought* to be held responsible?

ROSENBERG V. HARWOOD
No. 100916536, 2011 BL 333199 (Utah Dist. Ct. May 27, 2011)

Himonas, Judge:

INTRODUCTION

Plaintiff Lauren Rosenberg alleges that Defendant Google negligently provided her with walking directions that directed her to cross State Route 224 (SR 224), a rural highway with heavy traffic and no sidewalks, where she was seriously injured after being struck by an automobile that was negligently driven by Defendant Patrick Harwood. Google now brings this motion to dismiss Rosenberg's claims against it, on the ground that the Complaint fails to state a cause of action against Google. See Utah R. Civ. P. 12(b)(6). For the reasons discussed below, I GRANT the motion to dismiss Rosenberg's claims against Google.

ANALYSIS

The Complaint asserts four causes of action against Google: (1) General Negligence, (2) Failure to Warn, (3) Strict Liability-Defective Design, and (4) Strict Liability-Failure to Warn. In her memorandum opposing the motion to dismiss, Rosenberg consented to the dismissal of the third and fourth claims, which are based on a product liability theory. Therefore, my analysis of Google's motion to dismiss is limited to the remaining negligence claims. ...

I. Whether Google Owed Rosenberg a Duty

In the negligence context, a duty may be defined as an obligation, to which the law will give recognition and effect, to conform to a particular standard of conduct toward another. The determination of whether a legal duty exists falls to the court. It is a purely legal question, and since in the absence of a duty a plaintiff will not be entitled to a remedy, it is the first question to be answered. To determine whether a duty exists, courts analyze several factors, including "the legal relationship between the parties, the foreseeability of injury, the likelihood of injury, public policy as to which party can best bear the loss occasioned by the injury, and other general policy considerations." *Normandeau v. Hanson Equipment, Inc.*,

2009 UT 44, ¶ 9, 215 P.3d 152. The determination that a duty does or does not exist is an expression of the sum total of those considerations of policy which lead the law to say that the plaintiff is or is not entitled to protection.

Here, the Complaint alleges that Google owed Rosenberg two duties: (1) "to exercise reasonable care in providing reasonably safe directions," and (2) to warn of dangers that Google either knew or should have known about, such as the facts that SR 224 is "a rural highway with no sidewalks," and that vehicles "travel[] at a high rate of speed" along the road. Applying the *Normandeau* factors in this case, I conclude that Google did not owe Rosenberg the broad duties alleged in the Complaint.

A. The Legal Relationship Between Google and Rosenberg ...

In support of her claim that a duty exists, Rosenberg correctly states that service providers may be liable if they negligently provide services to their customers. However, a relationship that is highly attenuated is less likely to be accompanied by a duty. For example, where a publisher or other information provider publishes information to the general public, courts have regularly held that they owed no duty to the public at large. Therefore, the fact that Google provided the same information to Rosenberg that is available to limitless other users of the Google Maps service does not warrant imposing any heightened duty on Google. ...

B. The Foreseeability of Harm ...

In this case, Rosenberg claims that her injury was reasonably foreseeable based on the Complaint's allegations that Google directed her to walk along SR 224, a dangerous road that lacks sidewalks and is frequently used by vehicles traveling at a high rate of speed. Although the Complaint does not specifically state that those vehicles are negligently operated at high speeds, as Rosenberg alleges that Harwood's vehicle was, such a conclusion could be inferred from the facts alleged in the Complaint. These allegations do not necessarily contemplate the "specific mechanism of the harm" that occurred in Rosenberg's case, but the allegations are sufficient to establish that it was foreseeable that Rosenberg would be harmed as a result of following walking directions that led her along a dangerous road. *Normandeau*, 2009 UT 44, ¶ 20.

C. The Likelihood of Injury ...

Rosenberg claims that she "has alleged and will prove that th[e] route [at issue] made an accident far more likely." However, Rosenberg points to nothing in the Complaint that alleges that an accident is more likely along the route in question than any other route. Furthermore, as Google points out, it is unlikely that a pedestrian will be injured while crossing a road, as Rosenberg was here, unless the pedestrian breaches their own duty and disregards the risks to cross the road in front of oncoming traffic. The facts relating to any negligence on Rosenberg's part are not currently before the Court and are not considered in connection with the motion to dismiss, but it is clear that Google was not required to anticipate that a user of the Google Maps service would cross the road without looking for cars, and that, absent negligence on the user's part, an injury while crossing the road would be unlikely.

D. Policy Considerations

Before addressing the specific policy considerations, I first address Google's contention that it is a "publisher," albeit an electronic one, entitled to the protections the law affords the same. Rosenberg argues that Google is not a publisher because the Google Maps service "provide[s] one-on-one information about walking routes" that is not "published to the general public." ...

To claim that Google provided the information only to one individual, and therefore is not entitled to the protections afforded publishers, ignores the realities of modern society and technology. As Google notes, the Complaint itself states that the information provided on the Google Maps service "is readily available via the internet," and any individual who enters the same starting and ending points will obtain the same walking directions that were provided to Rosenberg. While a user of the service is able to customize the results of his or her search, the exact same information provided to Rosenberg is readily available to any individual who uses the same search terms as Rosenberg, and anyone who obtains those directions is free to disseminate the search terms and directions to others. Given these facts, it is difficult to imagine that information could be disseminated more broadly to the public. Therefore, Google is clearly a publisher because it makes all of the information on the Google Maps service available to the public worldwide, and the fact that a user of the Google Maps service obtains customized search results does not remove the protections afforded to any other publisher of information to the public.

Having established that Google is a publisher, it is apparent that the same policy considerations are present here as those in other cases that have rejected imposing a duty on publishers for providing faulty information. Chief among those considerations is the possibility that a publisher may be subject to liability to an unlimited number of individuals who may read or receive the information. Likewise, requiring Google to investigate its routes to ensure that every portion of the walking directions is safe would impose an onerous burden on Google. Indeed, as the United States Supreme Court has recognized, some errors are "inevitable" in the publishing business. *See Gertz v. Robert Welch, Inc.*, 418 U.S. 323, 340 (1974).

Rosenberg suggests that these burdens might be ameliorated if Google simply posted a statement that included a warning of dangers of which Google knows or should know along a potential route. However, for Google to warn users of such dangers, they would still be required to investigate each portion of the walking directions to determine what dangers might lie along a specific route. Indeed, the duty articulated in the Complaint includes no limits on the potential dangers of which Google would be required to warn against. Thus, under such a broad duty, Google might have to investigate and warn about any foreseeable risks along every route, which might include negligent drivers, drunk drivers, dangerous wildlife, sidewalks or roads in disrepair, lack of lighting, and other risks that may only exist during certain times of day. Such a duty would impose a burden that would clearly be difficult, if not impossible for Google to bear.

When these burdens are weighed against other factors, such as the high social utility of Google's information services and the accompanying First Amendment values, courts have placed more value on the societal benefits of information availability than on the rights of private persons who claim to have been harmed. I agree that such is the case here, where Google's activities have a high social value and the burdens associated with imposing the broad duties suggested by Rosenberg would be heavy, while the actual likelihood of injury is relatively low. Therefore, under this basic Hand Formula negligence analysis, I conclude that policy considerations weigh strongly against imposing the duties articulated in the Complaint.

QUESTIONS

1. Since Google owes Maps users no duty of care, is there anything to stop it from giving directions that send drivers crashing through walls and the wrong way up one-way streets?

2. Why did Rosenberg drop her product-liability claims? Is the problem perhaps that Google Maps isn't a physical "product"? Would the result have been different with a paper map?

3. The Google Maps terms of service state, "GOOGLE AND ITS LICENSORS ...MAKE NO REPRESENTATIONS OR WARRANTIES REGARDING THE ACCURACY OR COMPLETENESS OF ANY CONTENT OR THE PRODUCTS ... AND WILL NOT BE LIABLE FOR ANY DAMAGE OR LOSS RESULTING FROM YOUR USE OF THE CONTENT OR THE PRODUCTS." Should this term be enforceable?

4. The Powell Motors Canyonero has an "autopilot" feature that automatically speeds up or slows down to keep pace with other cars, and changes lanes as needed to avoid obstructions. Lance Murdock, proud Canyonero owner, is on a long car trip and turns on the autopilot. An uneventful hour later, Murdock is getting drowsy when a truck pulls out into an intersection in front of him. The truck is white, and the autopilot fails to distinguish it from the clouds in the sky behind it. Murdock hits the brakes, much too late, and is killed in the resulting crash. Can his estate recover against Powell Motors?

5. X Marks is a pirate-themed smartphone augmented reality game: it shows players a map of their area in the physical world overlaid with "enemy ships," "ports of call," and "buried treasure." One particularly valuable "buried treasure" is located in Elaine Marley's front yard. She's tired of having people trampling on her flowers and walking past her windows as they stare at their smartphone screens. Can she sue Big Whoop Software, the company that makes X Marks?

HOUSTON FEDERATION OF TEACHERS, LOCAL 2415 V. HOUSTON INDEPENDENT SCHOOL DISTRICT
— F. Supp. 3d. —, 2017 WL 1831106 (S.D. Tex. 2017)

Smith, Magistrate Judge:

This case presents a matter of first impression in this circuit—the use of privately developed algorithms to terminate public school teachers for ineffective performance. Of course, an employer's impulse to quantify employee performance is neither new nor inherently objectionable. The difficulty, as this case illustrates, is the tension between the understandable secrecy surrounding proprietary algorithms developed by private commercial enterprises, on the one hand, and the Fourteenth Amendment due process protections against substantively unfair or mistaken deprivations of life, liberty, or property, on the other.

BACKGROUND

In 2010, HISD began its transition to a "data driven" teacher appraisal system, with the goal of "having an effective teacher in every HISD classroom." ...

The basic idea behind the new appraisal system is that a teacher's impact on student performance, for better or worse, can appropriately be measured by student growth on standardized tests. This is generally referred to as the "value-added model" (VAM) for evaluating teacher effectiveness. Under HISD's new policy, student growth will whenever possible be calculated by a value-added statistical model called the Educational Value–Added Assessment System (EVAAS), developed by private software company SAS and licensed for use by HISD. The EVAAS system measures teacher effectiveness by attempting to track the teacher's impact on student test scores over time. The details are more complicated, but in general a teacher's EVAAS score is based on comparing the average test score growth of students taught by the teacher compared to the statewide average for students in that grade or course. ...

SAS's source codes and other information underlying the EVAAS statistical methodology are proprietary trade secrets unavailable to plaintiffs or HISD.

Plaintiffs challenge the use of EVAAS under various aspects of the Fourteenth Amendment, including [procedural due process, lack of a rational basis, vagueness, and equal protection].

HISD has moved for summary judgment on all counts. ...

ANALYSIS

1. Plaintiffs' protected property interests ...

The Fourteenth Amendment prohibits a state from depriving any person of life, liberty, or property without due process of law. ...

While HISD maintains that teachers were not terminated solely on the basis of low value-added scores, the record indicates otherwise. HFT president Zeph Capo, based on his review of HISD documents (including one labeled "Status of Low Three-year EVAAS Teachers"), identified 12 HFT members whose continuing contracts were terminated for low value-added scores between 2012–14. ...

2. Procedural due process

Once it is determined that the Due Process Clause applies, the question remains what type of process is due. The core requirement of procedural due process is the opportunity to be heard at a meaningful time and in a meaningful manner. *Mathews v. Eldridge*, 424 U.S. 319, 333, (1976). The Supreme Court has emphasized that procedural due process has two related but distinct goals:

> The purpose of this requirement is not only to ensure abstract fair play to the individual. Its purpose, more particularly, is to protect his use and possession of property from arbitrary encroachment—to minimize substantively unfair *or mistaken deprivations* of property ... For when a person has an opportunity to speak up in his own defense, and when the State must listen to what he has to say, substantively unfair *and simply mistaken* deprivations of property interests can be prevented.

Fuentes v. Shevin, 407 U.S. 67, 80–81 (1972) (emphasis added). In short, due process is designed to foster government decision-making that is both fair and accurate. ...

In the context of public school teacher terminations, the Fifth Circuit has long required "timely notice and an opportunity to answer charges so as to minimize the likelihood of an erroneous discharge." *Findeisen v. North East Independent School Dist.*, 749 F.2d 234, 239 (5th Cir. 1984). ... Within these boundaries the State has discretion to adopt the procedures it finds most appropriate. ...

HISD does not itself calculate the EVAAS score for any of its teachers. Instead, that task is delegated to its third party vendor, SAS. The scores are generated by complex algorithms, employing sophisticated software and many layers of calculations. SAS treats these algorithms and software as trade secrets, refusing to divulge them to either HISD or the teachers themselves. HISD has admitted that it does not itself verify or audit the EVAAS scores received from SAS, nor does it engage any contractor to do so. HISD further concedes that any effort by teachers to replicate their own scores, with the limited information available to them, will necessarily fail. This has been confirmed by plaintiffs' expert, who was unable to replicate the scores despite being given far greater access to the underlying computer codes than is available to an individual teacher.

The EVAAS score might be erroneously calculated for any number of reasons, ranging from data-entry mistakes to glitches in the computer code itself. Algorithms are human creations, and subject to error like any other human endeavor. HISD has acknowledged that mistakes can occur in calculating a teacher's EVAAS score; moreover, even when a mistake is found in a particular teacher's score, it will not be promptly corrected. As HISD candidly explained in response to a frequently asked question, "Why can't my value-added analysis be recalculated?":

> Once completed, any re-analysis can only occur at the system level. What this means is that if we change information for one teacher, we would have to re-run the analysis for the entire district, which has two effects: one, this would be very costly for the district, as the analysis itself would have to be paid for again; and two, this re-analysis has the potential to change all other teachers' reports.

The remarkable thing about this passage is not simply that cost considerations trump accuracy in teacher evaluations, troubling as that might be. Of greater concern is the house-of-cards fragility of the EVAAS system, where the wrong score of a single teacher could alter the scores of every other teacher in the district. This interconnectivity means that the accuracy of one score hinges upon the accuracy of all. Thus, without access to data supporting all teacher scores, any teacher facing discharge for a low value-added score will necessarily be unable to verify that her own score is error-free.

Value-added teacher evaluation systems such as EVAAS are a relatively recent development, and no Fifth Circuit case has addressed a procedural due process challenge to such a system. Plaintiffs rely most heavily upon *Banks v. Federal Aviation Admin.*, 687 F.2d 92 (5th Cir. 1982), in which two air traffic controllers challenged their dismissal for drug usage after their urine samples were destroyed and unavailable for independent testing on their behalf. The lab tests showed traces of cocaine, the only evidence of drug use in the record. The Fifth Circuit overturned their discharges, agreeing that the controllers were denied due process because their inability to evaluate the critical lab samples rendered the administrative hearings fundamentally unfair:

> The laboratory tests here were the only meaningful evidence resulting in the discharges. The accuracy of those tests, including the possibility that the samples were mixed-up, damaged, or even inaccurately tested, was the likely determinant of the entire case. Indeed, challenging the laboratory reports was probably the only way the controllers could succeed in their appeal.

Id. at 94. Mere description of the lab's general testing methods and results was not good enough, the court declared. "We hold that due process required an opportunity by the controllers to test on their own behalf to evaluate the accuracy of the government-sponsored tests." *Id.* at 96. Plaintiffs assert that *Banks* is controlling here, and that due process similarly requires an opportunity by teachers to test on their own behalf the accuracy of their HISD–sponsored value-added scores. The court agrees.

HISD's efforts to distinguish *Banks* fall wide of the mark. It is true that HISD provides some information about EVAAS to teachers—such as an overview of value-added growth as a measure of student learning, a general description of the EVAAS test methods and how they are applied in HISD, and how to read the EVAAS teacher value added report. A teacher is also provided a list of the students linked to that teacher and the percentage of their instruction for which the teacher was responsible. Contrary to HISD's claim, however, this information does not "surpass" the *Banks* standard. The controllers in *Banks* were similarly advised about the lab's general testing methods, and even had the opportunity to cross-examine the laboratory director. Yet, the Fifth Circuit held these measures fell short of due process, because without the test samples it was not possible to verify or replicate the controllers' particular test results. *Banks*, 687 F.2d at 94. The same is true here. HISD's own discovery responses and witnesses concede that an HISD teacher is unable to verify or replicate his EVAAS score based on the limited information provided by HISD.

HISD argues that *Banks* did not require access to proprietary information of the independent testing laboratory used by the FAA to perform the analysis. As defendant's brief correctly observes, "the Due Process Clause does not empower Plaintiffs to put SAS out of business" by requiring disclosure of its trade secrets. By the same token, SAS's trade secrets do not empower, much less compel, HISD to violate the constitutional rights of its employees. When a public agency adopts a policy of making high stakes employment decisions based on secret algorithms incompatible with minimum due process, the proper remedy is to overturn the policy, while leaving the trade secrets intact.

Moreover, in at least one respect the teachers' due process argument is stronger than the controllers in *Banks*. A drug test is a widely accepted, routine procedure to detect the presence of a physical substance in the body. By contrast, the EVAAS score purports to measure an intangible, job-related trait ("effectiveness") using a recently invented method that by HISD's own admission is the subject of vigorous academic debate. No similar controversy attends the detection of illicit drugs based on urine samples. Given the same urine sample, independent verification of a positive drug test is possible. But independent verification of a negative EVAAS score is impossible. According to the unrebutted testimony of plaintiffs' expert, without access to SAS's proprietary information—the value-added equations, computer source codes, decision rules, and assumptions—EVAAS scores will remain a mysterious "black box," impervious to challenge.

While conceding that a teacher's EVAAS score cannot be independently verified, HISD argues that the Constitution does not require the ability to replicate EVAAS scores "down to the last decimal point." But EVAAS scores are calculated to the second decimal place, so an error as small as one hundredth of a point could spell the difference between a positive or negative EVAAS effectiveness rating, with serious consequences for the affected teacher.

Finally, HISD contends that, unlike in *Banks* where the drug tests "controlled" the outcome of the hearings, the EVAAS score is merely "one factor the hearing officer might or might not consider." This argument casually elides the compelling summary judgment evidence recounted above, such as HISD's aggressive goal of "exiting" 85% of teachers with "ineffective" EVAAS ratings, as well as its amended policy adding low value-added scores as grounds for nonrenewal. ...

On this summary judgment record, HISD teachers have no meaningful way to ensure correct calculation of their EVAAS scores, and as a result are unfairly subject to mistaken deprivation of constitutionally protected property interests in their jobs. HISD is not entitled to summary judgment on this procedural due process claim.

3. Substantive due process: rational basis

A successful substantive due process claim requires evidence that the challenged law or practice is not a rational means of advancing a legitimate governmental purpose. Plaintiffs contend that EVAAS violates their rights to substantive due process because there is no rational relationship between EVAAS scores and HISD's stated "goal of having an effective teacher in every HISD classroom so that every HISD student is set up for success."

Rational basis scrutiny presents a very demanding standard for plaintiffs, and a very forgiving standard for policymakers. ...

Plaintiffs argue that EVAAS is not a rational evaluation tool "because it is sytematically biased against large categories of teachers on the basis of the type and size of classrooms they teach, is highly volatile, is highly variable on the basis of which models or tests are used, and is highly divergent from other measures of teacher effectiveness." As discussed above, it is also highly secretive and impossible to replicate.

HISD counters that 42 states and the District of Columbia use some measure of student performance in teacher evaluations, and value-added models have been throughly vetted and endorsed by much of the academic community. ...

The Eleventh Circuit considered a value added model based on student scores on the Florida Comprehensive Assessment Test (FCAT VAM) in *Cook v. Bennett*, 792 F.3d 1294 (11th Cir. 2015). ... The Eleventh Circuit affirmed the dismissal of plaintiffs' substantive due process and equal protection claims because "[w]hile the FCAT VAM may not be the best method—or may even be a poor one—for achieving [the government's goal of improving instruction], it is still rational to think that the challenged evaluation procedures would advance the government's stated purpose." *Id.* at 1301. ...

In *Wagner v. Haslam*, 112 F.Supp.3d 673 (M.D. Tenn. 2015), the court ... explained at length the extremely limited role a court has in applying the rational basis standard:

> [O]ne can conceive of performance metrics that would be truly irrational, such as basing a Tennessee teacher's evaluation on the test scores of students in Arizona, whether the Nashville Sounds baseball team had a winning season that school year, or the State of Tennessee's economy on evaluation day. It is inconceivable that a Tennessee teacher's 'value added' to a student's performance would bear any relationship to those metrics.

112 F. Supp. 3d at 696.

Most recently, in *Trout v. Knox Cty. Brd. of Educ.*, 163 F. Supp. 3d 492 (E.D. Tenn. 2016), teachers who did not receive annual performance bonuses asserted that use of TVAAS violated their constitutional rights to due process and equal protection. Although not the primary basis for its ruling, the court discussed plaintiffs' claims based on the statistical shortcomings of TVAAS. The court ruled as a matter of law that it is not irrational for the state to rely on a 68% confidence level in TVAAS results, stating "were this case to go to trial, its merits would be subject to a preponderance of the evidence standard. That is, the Court could make its decisions based on a 51% confidence level. Surely then, a 68% confidence level must pass rational basis review." *Id.* at 503. ... The court concluded that while TVAAS may be a "blunt tool," that is all the constitution requires. *Id.* at 505.

It is certainly disputed here whether EVAAS algorithms have been validated, and plaintiffs offer up numerous other ways in which EVAAS falls short. Even accepting plaintiffs' criticisms at face value, the loose constitutional standard of rationality allows governments to use blunt tools which may produce only marginal results. HISD's motion for summary judgment on this substantive due process claim is granted.

4. Substantive due process: vagueness

Plaintiffs' claim that EVAAS is unconstitutionally vague also arises from the Fourteenth Amendment's guarantee of substantive due process. The applicable test for unconstitutional vagueness requires plaintiffs to show that EVAAS "fail[s] to provide the kind of notice that will enable ordinary people to understand what conduct it prohibits" or "authorize[s] and even encourage[s] arbitrary and discriminatory enforcement." *City of Chicago v. Morales*, 527 U.S. 41, 56 (1999). ...

In *San Filippo v. Bongiovanni*, 961 F.2d 1125 (3d Cir. 1992). a tenured professor sued after being dismissed by Rutgers University for failure to maintain "standards of sound scholarship and competent teaching." The Third Circuit rejected San Filippo's argument that these regulations were unconstitutionally vague because they do not specify exactly what conduct is prohibited, holding that broad and general regulations are not necessarily vague. *Id.* at 1137. A vague standard is one that does not specify *any* standard at all, not one that merely proscribes a wide range of not-specifically-enumerated behaviors.

HISD teachers, like Rutgers professors, can "evaluate their behavior's conformity to the dismissal standard" provided by regulations implementing EVAAS. Teachers are advised that a low EVAAS score can lead to termination, and given general information about the EVAAS system and how it measures teacher effectiveness. While teachers may not be able to verify the accuracy of their EVAAS scores, a suitably definite rule or regulation is not rendered unconstitutionally vague simply because it may be unfair or prone to error. HISD's motion for summary judgment on plaintiffs' vagueness claim is granted.

5. Equal protection

To state a claim under the Equal Protection Clause, a § 1983 plaintiff must allege either that (a) a state actor intentionally discriminated against [him] because of membership in a protected class, or (b) he has been intentionally treated differently from others similarly situated and that there is no rational basis for the difference in treatment. Plaintiffs' claim is of the latter type. They allege that HISD wrongly classifies teachers according to their EVAAS scores, and then subjects them to different treatment based on the classification. ...

Plaintiffs' factual allegations simply do not fit the mold of an equal protection claim. ... The court has already determined that the EVAAS system satisfies rational basis review.

CONCLUSION

For these reasons, HISD's motion for summary judgment is denied with respect to the procedural due process claim, but granted on all other claims.

QUESTIONS

1. Suppose that HISD discloses all the details of the EVAAS-score algorithm and all of the data on which it is based. Would that end the matter?

2. Title VII of the Civil Rights Act of 1964 prohibits employment discrimination "because of [an] individual's race, color, religion, sex, or national origin." 42 U.S.C. § 2000e-2(1). Suppose that an independent statistical analysis found that female and African-American teachers were more likely to have lower EVAAS scores. Would HISD's continued use of EVAAS violate Title VII?

3. In *State v. Loomis*, 2016 WI 68, the plaintiff challenged Wisconsin's use of COMPAS "risk assessment scores" in sentencing. The COMPAS scores, which are calculated by a private entity using a a proprietary algorithm, purport to measure "the general likelihood that those with a similar history of offending are either less likely or more likely to commit another crime following release from custody." Courts consider the COMPAS scores as part of their overall sentencing decision, but are not required to follow it. In *Loomis*, the court upheld the use of the scores, reasoning that (1) COMPAS scores have been validated in scientific studies, (2) Loomis had access to general information about how his score was calculated and the data it was based on, and (3) sentencing courts "will exercise discretion when assessing a COMPAS risk score with respect to each individual defendant." Are *HFT v. HISD* and *Loomis* consistent?

4. If HISD were a private employer rather than a government agency, there would be no state action, and the plaintiffs would have no Fourteenth Amendment due process rights. What do you think about private employers' use of algorithmic scores in deciding whom to hire, promote, and fire? How about credit scores? Pricing algorithms that pick the optimal price for each customer? Where else is algorithmic scoring already being used?

5. Would this opinion be more or less persuasive if you did a search and replace to change "algorithm" to "wizard" everywhere it appears?

NCIC CONFIDENTIAL PROBLEM

You represent Archibald Buttle, a resident of Carrollton, Michigan, who has repeatedly been arrested for crimes he didn't commit. In October 2009, Buttle saw a neighbor preparing to cut a tree from his, Buttle's, land. The two of them got into a heated argument, with the neighbor claiming that the tree was a danger in case of a storm. Someone called the police, and Patrolman Jack Vincennes of the Carrollton Township Police Department responded to the call. Patrolman Vincennes broke up the fight, then put Buttle's name into the National Crime Information Center (NCIC) computer network run by the FBI. The NCIC network reported that there was an outstanding warrant for his arrest in California on charges of robbery and murder.

Buttle spent four days in jail while the Carrollton police contacted the Los Angeles Police Department (LAPD) about the warrant. Sergeant Ed Exley of the LAPD reported that an "Archibald Buttle" had been arrested in Los Angeles in July 2008 on suspicion of murder. He had been released several days later, but additional evidence discovered in early August 2008 had convinced the LAPD that Buttle was their man. By that time, however, he had disappeared, and so Lieutenant Dudley Smith of the LAPD had a warrant issued for Buttle's arrest and entered the warrant into the NCIC's computer network.

On being informed of this, your client loudly protested that there must have been a mistake, that he hadn't been to California in over a decade. On the fourth day of his confinement, a comparison of his fingerprints and physical description with the LAPD's files definitively showed that your client was not the man wanted in California, who had several distinctive scars and tattoos. Buttle was released. Further investigation by Patrolman Vincennes revealed that one Rollo Tomasi, an escapee from an Alabama prison, had obtained a copy of your client's birth certificate and used it to obtain a California driver's license in the name of "Archibald Buttle."

When your client was arrested, the entry for the warrant was automatically purged from the NCIC system. In November 2009, Lieutenant Smith reentered the arrest warrant in Buttle's name in the NCIC system. Each entry in the NCIC system has, in addition to name, charges, warrant number, and issuing jurisdiction, a "miscellaneous" field that allows for the entry of up to 121 characters. Lieutenant Smith did not enter any information in that field.

In March 2010, Buttle was driving when he was stopped by Bay County sheriff's deputy Bud White outside of Saginaw, Michigan, for failure to use a turn signal. Deputy White took Buttle's driver's license and checked the name against the NCIC system, turning up the California warrant. As a result, Deputy White ordered Buttle out of the car at gunpoint, then searched, handcuffed, and arrested him. He was released after about two hours, when Deputy White had made phone calls to the Saginaw Police and the LAPD.

Buttle has been arrested three more times, twice at gunpoint, by police in Michigan and Texas. Each time, he was released after his true identity was confirmed. He sought the assistance of the FBI, who confirmed that the NCIC contained a murder warrant in his name, but informed Buttle that "only the originating state agency (i.e. the LAPD) could delete, amend, or correct the computer warrant entry."

Buttle has come to you for legal advice. He would like to stop being arrested for crimes he didn't commit and, if possible, recover damages for the past arrests. What, if anything, can he do?

C. Litigation

Computers' effects are being felt beyond just "Internet" cases. Even in ordinary commercial disputes or slip-and-fall personal injury cases, the parties, their lawyers, judges, and jurors all have access to computers and the Internet. Everything from service of process to the execution of judgments is potentially up for grabs. This section briefly considers some of the ways that litigation might (or might not) be changing, with special attention to anonymous defendants and social media.

ARISTA RECORDS, LLC, V. DOES 1–19
551 F. Supp. 2d 1 (D.D.C. 2008)

Kollar-Kotelly, District Judge:

This is a copyright infringement case in which Plaintiffs, ten music and recording entities, allege that nineteen unidentified "John Doe" Defendants infringed their copyrighted recordings by downloading and/or distributing the recordings using an online media distribution system. Simultaneous with the filing of their Complaint, Plaintiffs filed an *ex parte* Motion for Leave to Take Immediate Discovery by serving a subpoena on non-party Internet Service Provider, The George Washington University ("GW"), to obtain identifying information for each Defendant. The Court initially granted the Motion for Leave and Plaintiffs served a subpoena on GW. Prior to GW's response, Counsel for John Doe # 3 filed a Motion with the Court seeking to (i) vacate the Court's Order granting leave to take immediate discovery, (ii) quash Plaintiffs' subpoena, and (iii) dismiss Plaintiffs' Complaint. ...

I. BACKGROUND

Plaintiffs filed their Complaint on September 19, 2007, alleging that "each Defendant, without the permission or consent of Plaintiffs, has continuously used, and continues to use, an online media distribution system to download and/or distribute to the public certain" musical recordings. ... Plaintiffs' Complaint identifies each Defendant by an Internet Protocol ("IP") address, and includes corresponding lists of the recordings allegedly infringed by each Defendant.

Simultaneous with the filing of their Complaint on September 19, 2007, Plaintiffs filed an *ex parte* Motion for Leave to Take Immediate Discovery. The Motion explained that Plaintiffs had identified each Defendant by an IP address assigned on the date and the time of each Defendant's allegedly infringing conduct. The Motion also explained that Plaintiffs gathered evidence of each Defendant's infringing activities, including evidence of "every file (at times numbering in the thousands) that each Defendant illegally distributed to the public." Without the ability to serve immediate discovery on the Internet Service Provider ("ISP"), however, Plaintiffs indicated that they were unable to ascertain the true identities of the Defendants. Accordingly, the Motion sought leave of Court to serve a subpoena on GW, the ISP, to obtain identifying information for each Defendant. ...

II. LEGAL STANDARDS AND DISCUSSION ...

Equally unavailing is Defendant's argument that Plaintiffs should not be permitted to serve their subpoena because the information possessed by GW is unreliable (e.g., GW student IDs and passwords may be lost or stolen) and that Plaintiffs must show a "real evidentiary basis" that Defendants have "engaged in wrongful conduct" prior to being allowed to conduct discovery. Defendant attaches the Declaration of Thomas J. Swanton who provides various explanations as to why Defendants may not be liable for the conduct alleged in Plaintiffs' Complaint. The Court declines to review Defendant's factual and technical arguments based on Mr. Swanton's declaration because they are unrelated to any appropriate inquiry associated with a motion to quash. *See* [Fed. R. Civ. P. 45(d)(3)] (describing grounds for quashing a subpoena). "If Defendant believes that he or she has been improperly identified by the ISP, Defendant may raise, at the appropriate time, any and all defenses, and may seek discovery in support of its defenses." *Fonovisa, Inc v. Does 1–9*, Civ. A. No. 07–1515, 2008 WL 91970, *8, 2008 U.S. Dist. LEXIS 27170 at *28, (W.D. Pa. Apr. 3, 2008).

Defendant's final argument with respect to Plaintiffs' subpoena is that file sharing is protected speech under the First Amendment and that Defendants have the right to speak anonymously. Accordingly, Defendant invites the Court to quash Plaintiffs' subpoena based on "the multi-part test" adopted by the Arizona Court of Appeals in *Mobilisa, Inc. v. John Doe* 1, 217 Ariz. 103, 170 P.3d 712 (2007) (setting forth a multipart test requiring a plaintiff to show, among other elements, that its claims could survive a motion for summary judgment). The Court declines Defendant's invitation because Mobilisa, Inc. involved *actual* speech. See *Mobilisa, Inc.*, 170 P.3d at 715 (describing an intimate email sent from plaintiff's protected computer system that was the focus of the lawsuit's trespass to chattels claim). The "speech" at issue in this case is Defendant's alleged infringement of Plaintiffs' copyrights. Not surprisingly, courts have routinely held that a defendant's First Amendment privacy interests are exceedingly small where the "speech" is the alleged infringement of copyrights. See *Fonovisa, Inc.*, 2008 WL 919701, *9, 2008 U.S. Dist. LEXIS 27170 at * 32 ("a Doe Defendant, who allegedly used the internet to unlawfully download and disseminate copyrighted sound recordings, has a minimal expectation of privacy in remaining anonymous"); *Sony Music Entm't Inc.*, 326 F. Supp. 2d at 567 (examining defendant's First Amendment claims on facts materially similar to the present and concluding that "defendants' First Amendment right to remain anonymous must give way to plaintiffs' right to use the judicial process to pursue what appear to be meritorious copyright infringement claims"); *Arista Records LLC v. Does 1–11*, Civ. A. No. 07–568 (W.D. Okla. Nov. 14, 2007) (Order holding that "[t]he Doe Defendants' First Amendment rights are not implicated because the information sought by the subpoena does not infringe their rights to engage in protected speech"). In fact, the *Mobilisa, Inc.* court even recognized that the right to speak anonymously is not absolute, and there are situations that require lesser degrees of First Amendment protection, citing Sony Music Entertainment, Inc. Consistent with *Sony Music Entertainment, Inc.* and the other cases cited by the Court above, the Court finds that Plaintiffs' need for disclosure outweighs any First Amendment interest claimed by Defendant.[8]

For these reasons, the Court denies Defendant's Motion insofar as it seeks to quash Plaintiffs' subpoena. ...

B. MOTION TO DISMISS ...

In the present case, Plaintiffs' Complaint alleges that "each Defendant, without the permission or consent of Plaintiffs, has continuously used, and continues to use, an online media distribution system to download and/or distribute to the public certain" musical recordings. The Complaint further alleges that each Plaintiff is a "copyright owner[ ] or licensee[ ] of exclusive rights" of the recordings, and that each of the recordings is "the subject of a valid Certificate of Registration issued by the Register of Copyrights to each Plaintiff." Plaintiffs' Complaint identifies each Defendant by IP address, and includes a corresponding list of recordings allegedly infringed by each Defendant. At this early stage of the case, these allegations (taken as true) are more than sufficient to find that Plaintiffs' right to relief rises

---

8 ... Defendant asks the Court to take into account that Doe # 3 is a university student who has a high expectation of privacy, that he must spend time defending this lawsuit rather than focusing on his studies, that Plaintiffs have not employed other means to obtain Defendant's identity, and that the IP address information obtained by Plaintiffs may not be reliable. ... Nevertheless, the Court notes that Defendant's privacy interest as a student does not allow him to infringe others' intellectual property, and that, if Plaintiffs' allegations are correct, Defendant has already taken time away from his studies by infringing on Plaintiffs' copyrights. Defendant also fails to explain how Plaintiffs could otherwise obtain Defendant's identity and why that would even matter in the context of Defendant's First Amendment rights. Finally, whether or not the information supplied by GW is reliable is an area into which Defendant may inquire at the appropriate time in discovery.

"above the speculative level" described in *Bell Atlantic v. Twombly* [550 U.S. 544 (2007)].[11]

IN RE BITTORRENT ADULT FILM COPYRIGHT INFRINGEMENT CASES
Nos. 11-3995(DRH)(GRB) et al.
2012 U.S. Dist. LEXIS 61447, 2012 WL 1570765 (E.D.N.Y. May 1, 2012)

Brown, Magistrate Judge:

These actions are part of a nationwide blizzard of civil actions brought by purveyors of pornographic films alleging copyright infringement by individuals utilizing a computer protocol known as BitTorrent. The putative defendants are identified only by Internet Protocol ("IP") addresses. These four civil actions involve more than 80 John Doe defendants; these same plaintiffs have filed another nineteen cases in this district involving more than thrice that number of defendants. One media outlet reports that more than 220,000 individuals have been sued since mid–2010 in mass BitTorrent lawsuits, many of them based upon alleged downloading of pornographic works.

This Order addresses (1) applications by plaintiffs in three of these actions for immediate discovery, consisting of Rule 45 subpoenas directed at non-party Internet Service Providers ("ISPs") to obtain identifying information about subscribers to the named IP addresses and (2) motions to quash similar subpoenas by several putative John Doe defendants in the remaining action. ...

BACKGROUND
1. Allegations in the Complaints

The four complaints that are subject to this Order are nearly identical, though each involves a different pornographic film, to wit: *Gang Bang Virgins, Veronica Wet Orgasm, Maryjane Young Love* and *Gangbanged*. ... Each defendant is identified only by an IP address purportedly corresponding to a physical address in this district, defined in the complaint as "a number that is assigned by an ISP to devices, such as computers, that are connected to the Internet." The Complaints further allege that "[t]he ISP to which each Defendant subscribes can correlate the Defendant's IP address to the Defendant's true identity."

The complaints describe, in some detail, a peer-to-peer filing sharing protocol known as BitTorrent ... . [Refer to *Columbia Pictures v. Fung* in Section 2.A for the technical details.] BitTorrent also uses a "tracker" computer that tracks the pieces of the files as those pieces are shared among various computers. This tracking feature allows the plaintiffs to identify the IP addresses from which the films

---

11 Defendant repeatedly highlights the fact that Plaintiffs have identified several of the same IP addresses as different John Doe Defendants. According to Defendant, "[t]his discrepancy calls into question both Plaintiffs' modus operandi and bona fides." Def.'s Reply at 6. The Court finds that it does neither, as Plaintiffs explain that the same Defendant may have engaged in multiple acts of infringement or the same IP address may have been issued to different individuals at different date and times. The fact remains that this inquiry is an appropriate one after Defendants have been identified and once such arguments may be explored using actual facts and not speculation. *See Arista Records LLC v. Does 1–11*, Civ. A. No. 07–568 (W.D. Okla. Nov. 14, 2007) ("[i]f [defendants] claim someone else used their computers without their knowledge, that is a matter for their defense. But the Plaintiffs do not have to prove the merits of their case to obtain the discovery sought.").

were downloaded, the subscribers to which have become the defendants in these actions. ...

4. Additional Facts

a. Factual Defenses Raised by the Moving John Doe Defendants

The factual defenses presented are vastly different and highly individualized. One movant – John Doe # 16 – has stated that he was at work at the time of the alleged download. John Doe # 2 states under oath that he closed the subject Earthlink account, which had been compromised by a hacker, before the alleged download. John Doe # 29's counsel represents that his client is an octogenarian with neither the wherewithal nor the interest in using BitTorrent to download *Gang Bang Virgins*. John Doe # 10 represents that downloading a copy of this film is contrary to her "religious, moral, ethical and personal views." Equally important, she notes that her wireless router was not secured and she lives near a municipal parking lot, thus providing access to countless neighbors and passersby.[3]

b. The Use of IP Address to Identify the Alleged Infringers

The complaints assert that the defendants – identified only by IP address – were the individuals who downloaded the subject "work" and participated in the BitTorrent swarm. However, the assumption that the person who pays for Internet access at a given location is the same individual who allegedly downloaded a single sexually explicit film is tenuous, and one that has grown more so over time. An IP address provides only the location at which one of any number of computer devices may be deployed, much like a telephone number can be used for any number of telephones. ...

Thus, it is no more likely that the subscriber to an IP address carried out a particular computer function – here the purported illegal downloading of a single pornographic film – than to say an individual who pays the telephone bill made a specific telephone call.

Indeed, due to the increasingly popularity of wireless routers, it much less likely. While a decade ago, home wireless networks were nearly non-existent, 61% of U.S. homes now have wireless access. Several of the ISPs at issue in this case provide a complimentary wireless router as part of Internet service. As a result, a single IP address usually supports multiple computer devices – which unlike traditional telephones can be operated simultaneously by different individuals. Different family members, or even visitors, could have performed the alleged downloads. Unless the wireless router has been appropriately secured (and in some cases, even if it has been secured), neighbors or passersby could access the Internet using the IP address assigned to a particular subscriber and download the plaintiff's film. ...

Some of these IP addresses could belong to businesses or entities which provide access to its employees, customers and sometimes (such as is common in libraries or coffee shops) members of the public.

These developments cast doubt on plaintiffs' assertions that "[t]he ISP to which each Defendant subscribes can correlate the Defendant's IP address to the Defendant's true identity." or that the subscribers to the IP addresses listed were

---

3 While Plaintiffs claim that they can amend their complaints to allege negligence against the owner of a WiFi router who failed to password-protect the device which was then used by an intruder to infringe its copyright, this assertion flies in the face of common sense.

actually the individuals who carried out the complained of acts. As one judge observed:

> The Court is concerned about the possibility that many of the names and addresses produced in response to Plaintiff's discovery request will not in fact be those of the individuals who downloaded "My Little Panties # 2." The risk is not purely speculative; **Plaintiff's counsel estimated that 30% of the names turned over by ISPs are not those of individuals who actually downloaded or shared copyrighted material.** Counsel stated that the true offender is often the "teenaged son . . . or the boyfriend if it's a lady." Alternatively, the perpetrator might turn out to be a neighbor in an apartment building that uses shared IP addresses or a dormitory that uses shared wireless networks. This risk of false positives gives rise to the potential for coercing unjust settlements from innocent defendants such as individuals who want to avoid the embarrassment of having their names publicly associated with allegations of illegally downloading "My Little Panties # 2."

Digital Sin, Inc. v. Does 1–176, __ F.R.D. __, 2012 WL 263491, at *3 (S.D.N.Y. Jan. 30, 2012). Another court noted:

> the ISP subscriber to whom a certain IP address was assigned may not be the same person who used the Internet connection for illicit purposes . . . By defining Doe Defendants as ISP subscribers who were assigned certain IP addresses, instead of the actual Internet users who allegedly engaged in infringing activity, Plaintiff's sought-after discovery has the potential to draw numerous innocent internet users into the litigation, placing a burden upon them that weighs against allowing the discovery as designed.

SBO Pictures, Inc. v. Does 1–3036, 2011 WL 6002620, at *3 (N.D .Cal. Nov. 30, 2011).

In sum, although the complaints state that IP addresses are assigned to "devices" and thus by discovering the individual associated with that IP address will reveal "defendants' true identity," this is unlikely to be the case. Most, if not all, of the IP addresses will actually reflect a wireless router or other networking device, meaning that while the ISPs will provide the name of its subscriber, the alleged infringer could be the subscriber, a member of his or her family, an employee, invitee, neighbor or interloper.

c. Indicia of Unfair Litigation Tactics

One moving defendant has provided concrete evidence of improper litigation tactics employed by K–Beech. In a sworn declaration, John Doe # 16 states the following:

> Upon receipt of the Complaint, I reached out to Plaintiff and spoke to a self-described "Negotiator" in an effort to see if I could prove to them (without the need for publicly tying my name to the Complaint) that I had nothing to do with the alleged copyright infringements. **The Negotiator was offered unfettered access to my computer, my employment records, and any other discovery they may need to show that I was not the culpable party.** Instead, the Negotiator refused and was only willing to settle the Complaint for thousands of dollars. While the Negotiator said on October 24, 2011 that he would

check to see if he could come down from the thousands of dollar settlement amount, the Negotiator has not responded to two voice mails
that were left on October 25, 2011. Notably, the Negotiator justified
the settlement amount because, in part, I would incur legal fees in
hiring an attorney.

Significantly, since plaintiff has not yet been provided with the identities of the
moving John Does, this record exists only because John Doe # 16 proactively contacted counsel for K–Beech (who is also representing Patrick Collins, Inc. in another matter), rather than await a determination by the Court. John Doe # 16's
experience directly mirrors that of defendants in a separate action by plaintiff K–
Beech regarding *Gang Bang Virgins,* as well as another action filed by Patrick
Collins, Inc. relating to a film entitled *Cuties.*

Remarkably, plaintiff's opposition to John Doe # 16's motion, encompassing 62
pages of material,[7] does not provide any evidentiary response to these sworn assertions of improper conduct. Rather, counsel attempts to dismiss this evidence as
"mere denials", and unabashedly argues that "[d]efendant's] assertion that the
negotiations between him and Plaintiff have ended further supports the need for
litigation." Moreover, K–Beech has filed "Notices of Settlement and Voluntary
Dismissal" as to three of the John Does in this action. "This course of conduct indicates that the plaintiffs have used the offices of the Court as an inexpensive
means to gain the Doe defendants' personal information and coerce payment from
them. The plaintiffs seemingly have no interest in actually litigating the cases, but
rather simply have used the Court and its subpoena powers to obtain sufficient
information to shake down the John Does." *Raw Films,* 2011 WL 6182025, at *2.

In a similar case by plaintiff Patrick Collins filed in this district, after being
granted discovery of the IP subscribers, counsel for that entity described in motion
papers the intended approach to the John Doe defendants:

Plaintiff requested and was granted additional time within which to
effectuate service upon the Doe Defendants to accommodate Plaintiff's need for obtaining their identifying information, as well as its
further settlement and litigation strategy. The latter involves Plaintiff
contacting Doe Defendants once their identities are known and attempting to reach a settlement with them. In cases where a settlement
cannot be reached, Plaintiff would then consider the feasibility of filing suit, and proceed with service upon those Doe Defendants against
whom it chooses to proceed.

On a cold record, this overview could be viewed as a reasoned approach. However,
when viewed against undisputed experience of John Doe # 16, described above,

---

7 Plaintiff K–Beech's rambling motion papers often lapse into the farcical. In its papers, counsel for K–Beech equate its difficulties with alleged piracy of its adult films
with those faced by the producers of the Harry Potter books, Beatles songs and Microsoft software, and compare its efforts to collect from alleged infringers of its rights
to the efforts of the FBI to combat child pornography. In an ironic turn, the purveyors of such works as Gang Bang Virgins, explain how its efforts in this matter will
help empower parents to prevent minors from watching "movies that are not age
appropriate" by ensuring that viewers must pay for plaintiffs products, and thereby
effectively notify parents of such activity because "many parents would surely notice
if they showed up on billing statements." It is difficult to accord the plaintiff, which
features "Teen" pornography on its website, the moral high-ground in this regard.

and findings by other courts, this suggests an approach that is highly inappropriate.

DISCUSSION

The Legal Standard

Federal Rule of Civil Procedure 26(d)(1) forbids a party from seeking discovery "from any source before the parties have conferred as required by Rule 26(f) except as "authorized . . . by court order." Fed. R. Civ. P. 26(d)(1). This is generally viewed as requiring a showing of good cause. Plaintiffs rely principally upon the five factor *Sony Music* test, adopted by the Second Circuit, which requires the Court to weigh:

> (1) [the] concrete[ness of the plaintiff's] showing of a prima facie claim of actionable harm, . . . (2)[the] specificity of the discovery request, . . . (3) the absence of alternative means to obtain the subpoenaed information, . . . (4)[the] need for the subpoenaed information to advance the claim, . . . and (5) the [objecting] party's expectation of privacy.

Arista Records, LLC v. Doe 3, 604 F.3d 110, 119 (2d Cir. 2010) (citing *Sony Music Entm't Inc. v. Does 1–40*, 326 F. Supp. 2d 556, 564–65 (S.D.N.Y. 2004)). This test, articulated in the context of evaluating a motion to quash, frames the inquiry in evaluating defendants' motions in *K–Beech*. Additionally, plaintiffs correctly note that the test is also instructive in evaluating the motions for early discovery. ...

Element 1: Prima Facie Claim of Actionable Harm

[The court held that three of the four plaintiffs had sufficiently made out prima facie cases of copyright infringement.]

Element[ ] 2: The Specificity of the Discovery Requests

With respect to the specificity of discovery requests, the *Sony Music* court explained that this factor requires that "Plaintiffs' discovery request is also sufficiently specific to establish a reasonable likelihood that the discovery request would lead to identifying information that would make possible service upon particular defendants who could be sued in federal court." *Sony Music, 326* F. Supp. 2d at 566. While the discovery propounded by plaintiffs is specific, for the reasons discussed above, it does not establish a reasonable likelihood it will lead to the identity of defendants who could be sued. *See Pacific Century Int'l Ltd. v. Does*, 2011 WL 5117424, at *2 (N.D. Cal. Oct. 27, 2011) ("Plaintiff must go beyond the 'limited discovery' that it earlier asserted would lead to Defendants' identities . . . [p]resumably, every desktop, laptop, smartphone, and tablet in the subscriber's residence, and perhaps any residence of any neighbor, houseguest or other sharing his internet access, would be fair game. Beyond such an inspection, [the plaintiff] might require still more discovery, including interrogatories, document requests and even depositions.").

In this regard, the instant matter is factually distinguishable from the *Arista Records* decision.[*] In that case, the sought after discovery involved an Internet service provider located at a university. Based on that setting, and at that time, it was almost certain that the end user at an IP address was a particular individual, rather than a wireless network. The instant case involves broadband Internet ser-

---

[*] [Ed: This is a different infringement lawsuit brought by Arista Records against anonymous defendants, not the one excerpted *supra*.]

vice in a largely residential suburban area at a time when wireless is widely available. Furthermore, it is alleged that each John Doe in the instant case downloaded only a single pornographic film. By contrast, in *Arista Records,* the plaintiff alleged that a file sharing folder located at the IP address in question contained 236 audio files, containing at least a half-dozen copyrighted songs owned by the plaintiff. *Arista Records,* 604 F.3d at 122. In fact, in that case, plaintiffs' investigator was able to "download[ ] music files from the user's computer," which is not the case here. *Arista Records LLC v. Does* 1–16, 2009 WL 414060, at *1 (N.D.N.Y. Feb. 18, 2009) aff'd 604 F.3d 110 (2d Cir. 2010). Clearly, the level of activity in *Arista Records* made it far more likely that the subscriber to the IP address would have conducted or at least been aware of the illegal downloading. In sum, it is not clear that plaintiffs have satisfied this factor. ...

Element 3: The Absence of Alternative Means

As one court observed, "[b]ecause the transactions in question occurred online, the defendants have been elusive and the IP addresses and ISP are the only available identifying information. Without the requested discovery, there are no other measures Plaintiff can take to identify the personal information for the Doe defendants." *Raw Films, Ltd. v. Does 1–11,* 2012 WL 684763, at *2 (S.D. Cal. Mar. 2, 2012). Plaintiffs retained a company that provides forensic investigation services including the identification of IP addresses using BitTorrent protocol. Since plaintiffs have only been able to identify IP addresses used for potential infringement, they have established to the satisfaction of the Court that there are not alternative means available to identify the alleged infringers.

Element 4: The Need for Subpoenaed Information to Advance the Claim

Plaintiffs clearly need identification of the putative John Does in order to serve process on them and prosecute their claims. However, not all the information sought is required to advance the claim. For example, in addition to names and addresses, plaintiffs seek both the home telephone numbers and email addresses of the putative John Does, information which is clearly not required to proceed with this action. In particular, obtaining the home telephone numbers seems calculated to further plaintiffs' settlement strategies, discussed above, rather than advancing their claims by allowing them to effect service.

Element 5: Defendants' Expectation of Privacy

In *Arista Records,* the John Doe defendant, conceding that he had engaged in the alleged improper downloading, sought to quash the subpoena on First Amendment grounds. While recognizing the protected nature of anonymous speech, the Court rejected the challenge, concluding that the "First Amendment does not . . . provide a license for copyright infringement." *Arista Records,* 604 F.3d at 118. In examining this factor, the *Sony Music* court noted "defendants have little expectation of privacy in downloading and distributing copyrighted songs without permission." *Sony Music,* 326 F. Supp. 2d at 566–67. Here it is uncertain – indeed, it may be unlikely – that the subscribers sought to be identified downloaded the plaintiffs' copyrighted works. *Cf. Pacific Century,* 2011 WL 5117424, at *2 (denying discovery to protect "innocent internet users"). Thus, this Court cannot conclude with any reasonable certainty that plaintiffs have overcome the expectation of privacy by putative defendants.

Abusive Litigation Tactics Employed by the Plaintiffs

The most persuasive argument against permitting plaintiffs to proceed with early discovery arises from the clear indicia, both in this case and in related matters, that plaintiffs have employed abusive litigations tactics to extract settlements from John Doe defendants. Indeed, this may be the principal purpose of these actions, and these tactics distinguish these plaintiffs from other copyright holders with whom they repeatedly compare themselves (arguing that this decision "will affect the rights of intellectual property holders across all segments of society"). While not formally one of the *Sony Music* factors, these facts could be viewed as a heightened basis for protecting the privacy of the putative defendants, or simply grounds to deny the requested discovery on the basis of fundamental fairness. ...

It would be unrealistic to ignore the nature of plaintiffs' allegations – to wit: the theft of pornographic films – which distinguish these cases from garden variety copyright actions. Concern with being publicly charged with downloading pornographic films is, understandably, a common theme among the moving defendants. As one woman noted in *K–Beech*, "having my name or identifying or personal information further associated with the work is embarrassing, damaging to my reputation in the community at large and in my religious community." ... This consideration is not present in infringement actions involving, for example, popular music downloads. *See Arista Records*, 604 F.3d at 122, ("Teenagers and young adults who have access to the Internet like to swap computer files containing popular music . . . The swappers . . . are ignorant or more commonly disdainful of copyright.").

The Federal Rules direct the Court to deny discovery "to protect a party or person from annoyance, embarrassment, oppression, or undue burden or expense." Fed. R. Civ. P. 26(c)(1). This situation cries out for such relief. ...

CONCLUSION ...

For all of the reasons set forth herein, the Court is not inclined to grant the broad early discovery sought by Malibu and Patrick Collins. At the same time, these plaintiffs are allegedly the owners of copyrighted works who should not be left without any remedy. Given the record in this case, however, this must be done in a fashion that will ensure that the rights of all parties are adequately protected. Thus, the Court is prepared to grant these plaintiffs limited early discovery, to wit: the names and addresses (**not** email addresses or phone numbers) of **only** the subscribers designated as John Doe 1 in *Malibu 26, Malibu 11, and Patrick Collins*. Following service of subpoenas, under the terms and conditions set forth below, the identifying information will be provided to plaintiffs at a status conference, with each John Doe 1 present, giving them an opportunity to be heard, to obtain counsel and, if appropriate, request appointment of counsel from this Court's *pro bono* panel. ...

QUESTIONS

1. What explains the divergent results in *Bittorrent Adult Film* and *Arista*?

2. What's so "abusive" about extending settlement offers to people who appear to have downloaded your copyrighted work without permission?

3. Compare the plaintiffs here to Raanan Katz from *Katz v. Google*, who didn't take the photo of himself and isn't trying to make money distributing or licensing it. Which of these plaintiffs is it fair to describe as "copyright trolls?"

4. Should the subscriber to an Internet connection be held legally responsible for any use of it? Should she be required to secure her WiFi router to prevent strangers from using it?

5. All three cases in this section involve multiple John Doe defendants. Is this a proper use of joinder, or should the plaintiffs have been required to sue each defendant individually? What difference does it make? Some copyright holders in file-sharing cases have named hundreds or thousands of defendants in a single lawsuit, arguing that they have infringed the same work in the same way and helped each other to do so. Is this a proper use of joinder? If not, would turning the case into a class action against "all persons who have downloaded [plaintiff's work] using the BitTorrent file-sharing protocol" fix the problem?

6. Suing anonymous defendants has its risks. Consider Brianna LaHara, Gertrude Walton, and Sarah Seabury Ward, all named as defendants in RIAA lawsuits. LaHara was 12 at the time; Walton was deceased; Ward was a "computer neophyte" grandmother accused of downloading gangster rap. All three suits were quickly withdrawn or settled. How did the RIAA end up suing them? If you were in charge of a copyright owner's litigation against individual file-sharers, whom would you try to target?

BAIDOO V. BLOOD-DZRAKU
5 N.Y.S.3d 709 (Sup Ct. 2015)

Cooper, Justice:

As recently as ten years ago, it was considered a cutting edge development in civil practice for a court to allow the service of a summons by email. Since then, email has all but replaced ordinary mail as a means of written communication. And while the legislature has yet to make email a statutorily authorized method for the service of process, courts are now routinely permitting it as a form of alternative service.

The past decade has also seen the advent and ascendency of social media, with websites such as Facebook and Twitter occupying a central place in the lives of so many people. Thus, it would appear that the next frontier in the developing law of the service of process over the internet is the use of social media sites as forums through which a summons can be delivered. In this matrimonial action, the issue before the court, by way of plaintiff-wife's ex parte application, is whether she may serve defendant-husband with the divorce summons solely by sending it through Facebook by private message to his account.

The standard method – or perhaps better stated, the method of first resort – for serving the summons in a divorce action is personal delivery to a defendant. New York Domestic Relations Law [DRL] § 232[a]. This reflects the great emphasis that this state places on insuring that a person who is being sued for divorce – a proceeding that can have immeasurable financial and familial consequences – be made aware of and afforded the opportunity to appear in the action. The problem with personal service, of course, is that in order for it to be accomplished, a plaintiff must be able to locate the defendant. Even where a defendant's whereabouts are known, there are times when it is logistically difficult, if not impossible, for a process server to gain the close proximity necessary for personal delivery.

Fortunately, the Domestic Relations Law provides a remedy for a person who is seeking a divorce but faces the prospect of being unable to effect personal service. DRL § 232 permits plaintiffs to request permission to utilize one of the alternative methods allowed under the Civil Practice Law and Rules (CPLR) that does not require "in-hand" delivery to the defendant. One such method, often referred to as "substitute service," involves delivering the summons to a person of "suitable age and discretion" at the defendant's "actual place of business, dwelling or usual place of abode." CPLR § 308[2]. Another method, known as "nail and mail" service, requires affixing the summons to the door of a defendant's "actual place of business, dwelling or usual place of abode," CPLR § 308[4], and then, as with "substitute service," mailing a copy to the defendant's "last known address" or "actual place of business." A third method is "publication service," where the summons is printed in a newspaper designated by the court and which can be granted upon a showing that "service cannot be made by another prescribed method with due diligence" CPLR § 315.

Additionally, pursuant to CPLR § 308(5), a court, upon a plaintiff's ex parte application, may direct the manner by which service is to be made. This allows a court to go beyond any of the specifically prescribed methods of service and devise a method that fits the particular circumstances of the case. An application for alternative service under CPLR § 308(5) can be granted only upon a sufficient showing that personal service, "substitute service," or "nail and mail" service would prove "impracticable." Case law, in accordance with well-established constitutional principles, further imposes the requirement that the method devised by the court be one that is "reasonably calculated, under all the circumstances, to apprise [the defendant] of the pendency of the action." *Mullane v. Cent. Hanover Bank & Trust Co.*, 339 U.S. 306, 314 (1950).

In the instant application, plaintiff asks the court to find that service of the divorce summons via a social media site, in this case Facebook, constitutes an appropriate form of alternative service under CPLR § 308(5). Moreover, contending that she has no other way to reach defendant, she requests that this judicially-crafted method of service be designated the only means by which notice of the divorce action is given. ...

Plaintiff has easily met the requirement of demonstrating that she will be unable to effect personal service on defendant. Although the parties married in 2009, they never resided together, and the last address plaintiff has for defendant is an apartment that he vacated in 2011.* Plaintiff has spoken with defendant by telephone on occasion and he has told her that he has no fixed address and no place of employment. He has also refused to make himself available to be served with divorce papers. As detailed in her attorney's affirmation, the investigative firms that plaintiff hired to assist in locating defendant have all been unsuccessful in their efforts, the post office has no forwarding address for him, there is no billing address linked to his pre-paid cell phone, and the Department of Motor Vehicles has no record of him. Inasmuch as plaintiff is unable to find defendant, personal delivery of the summons to him is an impossibility.

Similarly, plaintiff has shown that it would be an exercise in futility to attempt the two alternative service methods provided for by CPLR 308. Both "substitute service" and "nail and mail" service require knowledge of the defendant's "actual place of business, dwelling or usual place of abode." The record establishes that

* ["[Baidoo] and Blood-Dzraku tied the knot back in a civil ceremony back in 2009, but their relationship crumbled when Blood-Dzraku reneged on his promise to have a traditional Ghanaian wedding ceremony as well ... ." Barbara Ross & Dareh Gregorian, *EXCLUSIVE: Judge says Brooklyn Woman Can Use Facebook to Serve Divorce Papers*, N.Y. DAILY NEWS, Apr. 6, 2015.]

plaintiff has been unsuccessful in obtaining either a business or home address for defendant, even though she has diligently sought that information. As a result, she has met her burden of demonstrating that it would be impracticable to attempt to serve defendant by either of these methods.

Having demonstrated a sound basis for seeking alternative service pursuant to CPLR 308(5), plaintiff must now show that the method she proposes is one that the court can endorse as being reasonably calculated to apprise defendant that he is being sued for divorce. ... If the summons for divorce is sent to what plaintiff represents to be defendant's Facebook account, is there a good chance he will receive it?

In order for the question to be answered in the affirmative, plaintiff must address a number of this court's concerns. The first is that the Facebook account that plaintiff believes is defendant's might not actually belong to him. As is well known, the Facebook profile somebody views online may very well belong to someone other than whom the profile purports it to be. ... As a result, this court required plaintiff to submit a supplemental affidavit to verify that the Facebook account she references is indeed that of the defendant. Plaintiff submitted such an affidavit, to which she annexed copies of the exchanges that took place between her and defendant when she contacted him through his Facebook page, and in which she identified defendant as the subject of the photographs that appear on that page. While it is true that plaintiff's statements are not absolute proof that the account belongs to defendant – it being conceivable that if plaintiff herself or someone at her behest created defendant's page, she could fabricate exchanges and post photographs – plaintiff has nevertheless persuaded the court that the account in question does indeed belong to defendant.

The second concern is that if defendant is not diligent in logging on to his Facebook account, he runs the risk of not seeing the summons until the time to respond has passed. Here too, plaintiff's affidavit has successfully addressed the issue. Her exchanges with defendant via Facebook show that he regularly logs on to his account. In addition, because plaintiff has a mobile phone number for defendant, both she and her attorney can speak to him or leave a voicemail message, or else send him a text message alerting him that a divorce action has been commenced and that he should check his account.

The third concern is whether a backup means of service is required under the circumstances. ... Here, plaintiff does not have an email address for defendant and has no way of finding one. Nor does she have a street address for defendant that could constitute a viable "last known address;" defendant's last known address dates back at least four years and the post office confirmed that defendant no longer resides there and he has left no forwarding address. Thus, plaintiff has a compelling reason to make Facebook the sole, rather than the supplemental, means of service, with the court satisfied that it is a method reasonably calculated to give defendant notice that he is being sued for divorce.

[The court next considered service by publication.] After all, publication is not only expressly sanctioned by the CPLR, but it is a means of service of process that has been used in New York in one form or another since colonial times. Even today, it is probably the method of service most often permitted in divorce actions when the defendant cannot be served by other means.

The problem, however, with publication service is that it is almost guaranteed *not* to provide a defendant with notice of the action for divorce, or any other law suit for that matter. In divorce cases brought in New York County, plaintiffs are often granted permission to publish the summons in such newspapers as the *New York Law Journal* or the *Irish Echo*. If that were to be done here, the chances of defendant, who is neither a lawyer nor Irish, ever seeing the summons in print, either in those particular newspapers or in any other, are slim to none. The dangers of allowing somebody to be divorced and not know it are simply too great to allow notice to be given by publication, a form of service that, while neither novel or unorthodox, is essentially statutorily authorized non-service. This is especially so when, as here, there is a readily available means of service that stands a very good chance of letting defendant know that he is being sued.

Moreover, the court will not require publication in any newspaper even as a backup method to Facebook. Although a more widely circulated newspaper, like the *New York Post* or the *Daily News*, might reach more readers, the cost, which approaches $1,000 for running the notice for a week, is substantial, and the chances of it being by seen by defendant, buried in an obscure section of the paper and printed in small type, are still infinitesimal.

Under the circumstance presented here, service by Facebook, albeit novel and non-traditional, is the form of service that most comports with the constitutional standards of due process. Not only is it reasonably calculated to provide defendant with notice that he is being sued for divorce, but every indication is that it will achieve what should be the goal of every method of service: actually delivering the summons to him.

In light of the foregoing, plaintiff is granted permission to serve defendant with the divorce summons using a private message through Facebook. Specifically, because litigants are prohibited from serving other litigants, plaintiff's attorney shall log into plaintiff's Facebook account and message the defendant by first identifying himself, and then including either a web address of the summons or attaching an image of the summons. This transmittal shall be repeated by plaintiff's attorney to defendant once a week for three consecutive weeks or until acknowledged by the defendant. Additionally, after the initial transmittal, plaintiff and her attorney are to call and text message defendant to inform him that the summons for divorce has been sent to him via Facebook.

QUESTIONS

1. Are you convinced that it would not violate the defendant's Due Process rights to serve him via Facebook? Would it violate his Due Process rights *not* to use Facebook now that it is available?

2. Some courts have allowed service of process by email. What happens if the email is caught in a spam filter and never seen by the defendant?

3. If the defendant can be served on Facebook, should he be able to enter an appearance on Facebook as well? Is there still a reason to have physical courthouses in a digital age?

4. Should court records be available online?

GRIFFIN V. STATE
419 Md. 343 (2011)

Battaglia, Judge:

In this case, we are tasked with determining the appropriate way to authenticate, for evidential purposes, electronically stored information printed from a social networking website, in particular, MySpace.

Antoine Levar Griffin, Petitioner, seeks reversal of his convictions in the Circuit Court for Cecil County, contending that the trial judge abused his discretion in admitting, without proper authentication, what the State alleged were several pages printed from Griffin's girlfriend's MySpace profile. ...

Griffin was charged in numerous counts with the shooting death, on April 24, 2005, of Darvell Guest at Ferrari's Bar in Perryville, in Cecil County. During his trial, the State sought to introduce Griffin's girlfriend's, Jessica Barber's, MySpace profile to demonstrate that, prior to trial, Ms. Barber had allegedly threatened another witness called by the State. The printed pages contained a MySpace profile in the name of "Sistasouljah," describing a 23 year-old female from Port Deposit, listing her birthday as "10/02/1983" and containing a photograph of an embracing couple. The printed pages also contained the following blurb:

FREE BOOZY!!!! JUST REMEMBER SNITCHES GET STITCHES!!
U KNOW WHO YOU ARE!!

When Ms. Barber had taken the stand after being called by the State, she was not questioned about the pages allegedly printed from her MySpace profile.

Instead, the State attempted to authenticate the pages, as belonging to Ms. Barber, through the testimony of Sergeant John Cook, the lead investigator in the case. Defense counsel objected to the admission of the pages allegedly printed from Ms. Barber's MySpace profile, because the State could not sufficiently establish a "connection" between the profile and posting and Ms. Barber ...

Whether the MySpace printout represents that which it purports to be, not only a MySpace profile created by Ms. Barber, but also upon which she had posted, "FREE BOOZY!!!! JUST REMEMBER SNITCHES GET STITCHES!! U KNOW WHO YOU ARE!!," is the issue before us.

Anyone can create a MySpace profile at no cost, as long as that person has an email address and claims to be over the age of fourteen ...

The identity of who generated the profile may be confounding ... because anyone can create a fictitious account and masquerade under another person's name or can gain access to another's account by obtaining the user's username and password ...

The potential for fabricating or tampering with electronically stored information on a social networking site, thus poses significant challenges from the standpoint of authentication of printouts of the site, as in the present case. Authentication, nevertheless, is generally governed by Maryland Rule 5–901, which provides:

(a) *GENERAL PROVISION.* – The requirement of authentication or identification as a condition precedent to admissibility is satisfied by evidence sufficient to support a finding that the matter in question is what its proponent claims.

Potential methods of authentication are illustrated in Rule 5–901(b). The most germane to the present inquiry are Rules 5–901(b)(1) and 5–901(b)(4), which state:

(b) *ILLUSTRATIONS.* – By way of illustration only, and not by way of limitation, the following are examples of authentication or identification conforming with the requirements of this Rule:

  (1) *TESTIMONY OF WITNESS WITH KNOWLEDGE.* – Testimony of a witness with knowledge that the offered evidence is what it is claimed to be. ...

  (4) *CIRCUMSTANTIAL EVIDENCE.* – Circumstantial evidence, such as appearance, contents, substance, internal patterns, location, or other

distinctive characteristics, that the offered evidence is what it is claimed to be.

... In the present case, Griffin argues that the State did not appropriately, for evidentiary purposes, authenticate the pages allegedly printed from Jessica Barber's MySpace profile, because the State failed to offer any extrinsic evidence describing MySpace, as well as indicating how Sergeant Cook obtained the pages in question and adequately linking both the profile and the "snitches get stitches" posting to Ms. Barber. The State counters that the photograph, personal information, and references to freeing "Boozy" were sufficient to enable the finder of fact to believe that the pages printed fromMySpace were indeed Ms. Barber's. ...

We agree with Griffin that the trial judge abused his discretion in admitting the MySpace evidence pursuant to Rule 5–901(b)(4), because the picture of Ms. Barber, coupled with her birth date and location, were not sufficient "distinctive characteristics" on a MySpace profile to authenticate its printout, given the prospect that someone other than Ms. Barber could have not only created the site, but also posted the "snitches get stitches" comment. The potential for abuse and manipulation of a social networking site by someone other than its purported creator and/or user leads to our conclusion that a printout of an image from such a site requires a greater degree of authentication than merely identifying the date of birth of the creator and her visage in a photograph on the site in order to reflect that Ms. Barber was its creator and the author of the "snitches get stitches" language.

... In *Commonwealth v. Williams*, 456 Mass. 857 (2010), the Supreme Judicial Court of Massachusetts considered the admission, over the defendant's objection, of instant messages a witness had received "at her account atMySpace." *Id.* at 1171. In the case, the defendant was convicted of the shooting death of Izaah Tucker, as well as other offenses. The witness, Ashlei Noyes, testified that she had spent the evening of the murder socializing with the defendant and that he had been carrying a handgun. She further testified that the defendant's brother had contacted her "four times on her MySpace account between February 9, 2007, and February 12, 2007," urging her "not to testify or to claim a lack of memory regarding the events of the night of the murder." *Id.* at 1172. At trial, Noyes testified that the defendant's brother, Jesse Williams, had a picture of himself on his MySpace account and that his MySpace screen name or pseudonym was "doit4it." She testified that she had received the messages from Williams, and the document printed from her MySpace account indicated that the messages were in fact sent by a user with the screen name "doit4it," depicting a picture of Williams. *Id.*

The Supreme Judicial Court of Massachusetts determined that there was an inadequate foundation laid to authenticate the MySpace messages, because the State failed to offer any evidence regarding who had access to the MySpace page and whether another author, other than Williams, could have virtually-penned the messages:

> Although it appears that the sender of the messages was using Williams's MySpace Web "page," there is no testimony (from Noyes or another) regarding how secure such a Web page is, who can access a MySpace Web page, whether codes are needed for such access, etc. Analogizing a MySpace [message] to a telephone call, a witness's testimony that he or she has received an incoming call from a person claiming to be "A," without more, is insufficient evidence to admit the call as a conversation with "A." Here, while the foundational testimony established that the messages were sent by someone with access to

> Williams's MySpace Web page, it did not identify the person who ac-
> tually sent the communication. Nor was there expert testimony that
> no one other than Williams could communicate from that Web page.
> Testimony regarding the contents of the messages should not have
> been admitted.

Id. at 1172–73. The court emphasized that the State failed to demonstrate a sufficient connection between the messages printed from Williams's alleged MySpace
account and Williams himself, with reference, for example, to Williams's use of an
exclusive username and password to which only he had access. ...

Similarly, in *People v. Lenihan*, 911 N.Y.S.2d 588 (Sup. Ct. 2010), Lenihan challenged his second degree murder conviction because he was not permitted to
cross-examine two witnesses called by the State on the basis of photographs his
mother had printed from MySpace, allegedly depicting the witnesses and the victim making hand gestures and wearing clothing that suggested an affiliation with
the "Crips" gang. The trial judge precluded Lenihan from confronting the witnesses with the MySpace photographs, reasoning that "[i]n light of the ability to 'photo
shop,' edit photographs on the computer," Lenihan could not adequately authenticate the photographs. *Id.* at 592. ...

The State refers us, however, to *In the Interest of F.P.*, 878 A.2d 91 (Pa. Super.
Ct.2005), in which the Pennsylvania intermediate appellate court considered
whether instant messages were properly authenticated pursuant to Pennsylvania
Rule of Evidence 901(b)(4), providing that a document may be authenticated by
distinctive characteristics or circumstantial evidence. In the case, involving an assault, the victim, Z.G., testified that the defendant had attacked him because he
believed that Z.G. had stolen a DVD from him. The hearing judge, over defendant's objection, admitted instant messages from a user with the screen name
"Icp4Life30" to and between "WHITEBOY Z 404." *Id.* at 94. Z.G. testified that his
screen name was "WHITEBOY Z 404" and that he had printed the instant messages from his computer. In the transcript of the instant messages, moreover, Z.G.
asked "who is this," and the defendant replied, using his first name. Throughout
the transcripts, the defendant threatened Z.G. with physical violence because Z.G.
"stole off [him]." *Id.* On appeal, the court determined that the instant messages
were properly authenticated through the testimony of Z.G. and also because
"Icp4Life30" had referred to himself by first name, repeatedly accused Z.G. of
stealing from him, and referenced the fact that Z.G. had told high school administrators about the threats, such that the instant messages contained distinctive
characteristics and content linking them to the defendant. *In the Interest of F.P.* is
unpersuasive in the context of a social networking site, because the authentication
of instant messages by the recipient who identifies his own "distinctive characteristics" and his having received the messages, is distinguishable from the authentication of a profile and posting printed from MySpace, by one who is neither a creator
nor user of the specific profile.

... It is clear, then, that the MySpace printout was a key component of the
State's case; the error in the admission of its printout requires reversal.

In so doing, we should not be heard to suggest that printouts from social networking sites should never be admitted. Possible avenues to explore to properly
authenticate a profile or posting printed from a social networking site, will, in all
probability, continue to develop as the efforts to evidentially utilize information
from the sites increases. A number of authentication opportunities come to mind,
however.

The first, and perhaps most obvious method would be to ask the purported creator if she indeed created the profile and also if she added the posting in question, i.e. "[t]estimony of a witness with knowledge that the offered evidence is what it is claimed to be." Rule 5–901(b)(1). The second option may be to search the computer of the person who allegedly created the profile and posting and examine the computer's internet history and hard drive to determine whether that computer was used to originate the social networking profile and posting in question. ...

A third method may be to obtain information directly from the social networking website that links the establishment of the profile to the person who allegedly created it and also links the posting sought to be introduced to the person who initiated it. ...

Harrell, Judge, dissenting: ...

[A] reasonable juror could conclude, based on the presence on the MySpace profile of (1) a picture of a person appearing to Sergeant Cook to be Ms. Barber posing with the defendant, her boyfriend; (2) a birth date matching Ms. Barber's; (3) a description of the purported creator of the MySpace profile as being a twenty-three year old from Port Deposit; and (4) references to freeing "Boozy" (a nickname for the defendant), that the redacted printed pages of theMySpace profile contained information posted by Ms. Barber.

I am not unmindful of the Majority Opinion's analysis relating to the concern that someone other than Ms. Barber could access or create the account and post the threatening message. The record, however, suggests no motive to do so. The technological heebie jeebies discussed in the Majority Opinion go, in my opinion, however, not to the admissibility of the print-outs under Rule 5–901, but rather to the weight to be given the evidence by the trier of fact. ...

QUESTIONS

1. Did Jessica Barber post "SNITCHES GET STITCHES" to her MySpace page?

2. The MySpace profile in question contained a photograph of the witness (Jessica Barber) and the defendant (Antoine Griffin) embracing. Is there any serious doubt that the photo is authentic? If it is authentic, how can there any question about who wrote "SNITCHES GET STITCHES?"

3. How would you authenticate an email message sent by your client to an opposing party? One sent to your client by an opposing party? What about the contents of your client's website as of 2010? The contents of your opponent's website?

4. *People v. Lenihan*, discussed in *Griffin*, held that that an online photograph seemingly of an individual flashing gang signs was not self-authenticating because it might have been Photoshopped. Does this mean that authenticating a digital photograph requires a full chain of custody starting with the camera? If so, most digital photographs are going to be inadmissible, aren't they?

5. How about discovery? You represent the plaintiff in a slip-and-fall personal injury lawsuit. The defendant plans to argue at trial that your client is exaggerating her injuries. Opposing counsel has just served you with a discovery request for "the complete contents of Plaintiff's Facebook, Twitter and other social media accounts." How should you respond?

6. Consider the Fitbit: a wristband that tracks the wearer's physical activity to help him mange his exercise routine. How would you obtain data from one? How would you authenticate it? Are there any privacy concerns here? Should you advise a client to throw away her Fitbit before opposing counsel subpoenas it?

7. Your client has been charged with reckless endangerment on the basis of two successive photographs from a red-light camera that appear to show her car traveling at 120 miles per hour through an intersection. You would like to argue that your client was actually driving only 60 miles per hour but the camera was miscalibrated or misprogrammed so that its internal clock was running two times as fast as it should have. Can you prevent the photographs from being introduced as evidence? If not, how can you respond?

CHACE V. LOISEL
2014 WL 258620 (Fla. Dist. Ct. App. Jan 24, 2014)

Cohen, District Judge:

Petitioner, Sandra Chace, seeks a writ of prohibition to quash the trial court's order denying her motion to disqualify [Linda Schoonover,] the trial judge presiding over her and Respondent Robert Loisel, Jr.'s dissolution of marriage case. Upon review, we conclude that the trial court erred in denying Petitioner's motion.

The following allegations formed the basis for Petitioner's motion to disqualify. Prior to entry of final judgment, the trial judge reached out to Petitioner, ex parte, in the form of a Facebook "friend" request. Upon advice of counsel, Petitioner decided not to respond to that invitation. Thereafter, the trial court entered a final judgment of dissolution, allegedly attributing most of the marital debt to Petitioner and providing Respondent with a disproportionately excessive alimony award. [Petitioner filed a motion to disqualify the trial judge, which the trial judge denied.]

If the grounds asserted in a motion for disqualification are legally sufficient to create a well-founded fear in the mind of a party that he or she will not receive a fair trial, it is incumbent upon a judge to disqualify herself. To determine whether the motion is legally sufficient, this Court must resolve whether the alleged facts, which, accepted as true, would prompt a reasonably prudent person to fear that she could not get a fair and impartial trial before that judge. An affiant's mere subjective fear is insufficient to form the basis for disqualification.

It seems clear that a judge's ex parte communication with a party presents a legally sufficient claim for disqualification, particularly in the case where the party's failure to respond to a Facebook "friend" request creates a reasonable fear of offending the solicitor. The "friend" request placed the litigant between the proverbial rock and a hard place: either engage in improper ex parte communications with the judge presiding over the case or risk offending the judge by not accepting the "friend" request.

In *Domville v. State*, 103 So.3d 184 (Fla. 4th Dist. Ct. App. 2012), rev. denied, *State v. Domville*, 110 So.3d 441 (Fla. 2013), the Fourth District addressed a Facebook issue with regard to judges "friending" *attorneys* through social media. That court determined that a judge's social networking "friendship" with the prosecutor of the underlying criminal case was sufficient to create a well-founded fear of not receiving a fair and impartial trial in a reasonably prudent person.

We have serious reservations about the court's rationale in *Domville*. The word "friend" on Facebook is a term of art. A number of words or phrases could more aptly describe the concept, including acquaintance and, sometimes, virtual stranger. A Facebook friendship does not necessarily signify the existence of a close relationship. Other than the public nature of the internet, there is no difference between a Facebook "friend" and any other friendship a judge might have. *Domville's* logic would require disqualification in cases involving an acquaintance of a judge. Particularly in smaller counties, where everyone in the legal community knows each other, this requirement is unworkable and unnecessary. Requiring disqualification in such cases does not reflect the true nature of a Facebook friendship and casts a large net in an effort to catch a minnow.

That said, *Domville* was the only Florida case that discussed the impact of a judge's social network activity and, as such, was binding upon the trial judge in this case. Although this case involves the "friending" of a party, rather than an attorney representing a party, for purpose of ruling on the motion to disqualify we find that the difference is inconsequential. In our view, the "friending" of a party in a pending case raises far more concern than a judge's Facebook friendship with a lawyer.

Beyond the fact that *Domville* required the trial court to grant the motion to disqualify, the motion to disqualify was sufficient on its face to warrant disqualification. The trial judge's efforts to initiate ex parte communications with a litigant is prohibited by the Code of Judicial Conduct and has the ability to undermine the confidence in a judge's neutrality. The appearance of partiality must be avoided. It is incumbent upon judges to place boundaries on their conduct in order to avoid situations such as the one presented in this case.

Because Petitioner has alleged facts that would create in a reasonably prudent person a well-founded fear of not receiving a fair and impartial trial, we quash the order denying the motion to disqualify and remand to the trial court for further proceedings consistent with this opinion. We trust that the issuance of a formal writ will be unnecessary.

QUESTIONS

1. What, precisely, was wrong with Judge Schoonover's friend request? What are the ethical implications if Judge Schoonover was Facebook friends with the plaintiff *before* the case was assigned to her?

2. Can attorneys ethically be Facebook friends with opposing counsel? Opposing parties? Witnesses? If the answer is, "it depends," on what does it depend?

FLORIDA STANDARD JURY INSTRUCTIONS
(Oct. 7, 2011 update)

§ 1.01 – *Preliminary Instruction ...*

You must decide this case only on the evidence presented during the trial in your presence, and in the presence of the respondent, the attorneys, and myself. You must not conduct any investigation of your own. This includes reading newspapers, watching television, listening to the radio, or using a computer, cell phone, the Internet, any electronic device, or any other means at all, to get information related to this case or the people and places involved in this case. This applies whether you are in the courthouse, at home, or anywhere else. Accordingly, you must not visit any of the places described in the evidence, or the scene of the occurrence that is the subject of the trial, or use the Internet to look at maps or pictures to see any place discussed during the trial, unless I direct you to view the scene.

Jurors must not have discussions of any sort with friends or family members about the case or the people and places involved. So, do not let even the closest family members make comments to you or ask questions about the trial. In this age of electronic communication, I want to stress again that just as you must not talk about this case face-to-face, you must not talk about this case by using an electronic device. You must not use phones, computers or other electronic devices to communicate. Do not send or accept any messages related to this case or your jury service. Do not discuss this case or ask for advice by any means at all, including posting information on an Internet website, chat room or blog.

2.08 – *Verdict and Submitting Case to Jury ...*

During deliberations, jurors must communicate about the case only with one another and only when all jurors are present in the jury room. You are not to communicate with any person outside the jury about this case. Until you have reached a verdict, you must not talk about this case in person or through the telephone, writing, or electronic communication, such as a blog, twitter, e-mail, text message, or any other means. Do not contact anyone to assist you during deliberations. These communications rules apply until I discharge you at the end of the case. If you become aware of any violation of these instructions or any other instruction I have given in this case, you must tell me by giving a note to the bailiff.

QUESTIONS

1. Why is it necessary to warn jurors not to discuss the case online? Wouldn't jurors understand that the rule against discussing the case applies online? Is a juror who does offline research or online research more likely to be caught?

2. In a world where anyone can call up the most detailed encyclopedia ever produced with just a few keystrokes, why should the legal system try to restrict jurors' out-of-court research? Won't they do a better job of finding the truth if they are free to consult the widest possible range of sources?

3. What about judicial notice? Is Wikipedia reliable enough for a court to take judicial notice of its contents? What about Google Maps driving times? Zillow home value estimates? Yelp reviews?

4. Can lawyers Google jurors and potential jurors to look for conflicts of interest or to help in making individually persuasive arguments? Can they send friend requests to jurors? How else might computers reshape jury selection?

COURTHOUSE TECHNOLOGY PROBLEM

You have been asked to consult with a committee of the Administrative Office of the Courts for the state of Nebraska, which is considering revising its rules on the use of computers and electronic devices in courthouses. Currently, each judge sets policies on the use of computers in his or her courtroom; the court security personnel at each courthouse set screening procedures for the courthouse; and the court systems' IT office supplies computers to judges for their chambers and courtrooms upon request. The result has been a chaotic patchwork of policies. Some judges encourage attorneys to use the Internet to give live demonstrations in court and to manage their case files. Others prohibit the use of all electronic devices entirely. Some courthouses require attorneys and visitors to check all cell phones when entering; others have no checkrooms and no restrictions on bringing devices in.

The AOC has asked for your help in designing a more reasonably uniform set of policies for the Nebraska courts. It would like to respect judges' autonomy about how to run their courtrooms while establishing good baselines on when attorneys should expect to find computers or bring their own, what kinds of features in-court computers should have, how security personnel will deal with various kinds of electronic devices, and so on. The AOC is particularly worried that there may be important questions that it is not even thinking to ask. What is your advice?

D. The Physical World

Throughout this book, we have drawn a contrast between the physical and the digital, and struggled to apply doctrines developed in the offline world to online activities. But maybe this distinction itself is overblown, or maybe the time has come to take lessons learned online and apply them offline. This section examines places in which laws governing physical things seem to be running into the same challenges as laws governing the Internet. Does our study of Internet law help at all in understanding those challenges – and maybe even in dealing with them?

ADAM THIERER AND ADAM MARCUS

GUNS, LIMBS, AND TOYS: WHAT FUTURE FOR 3D PRINTING?

17 Minn. J. Sci. & Tech. L. 805 (2016)

I. Background

A. How 3D Printing Works

3D printing, or what is more accurately labeled additive manufacturing, refers to technology that moves us away from the Henry Ford era mass production line, and will bring us to a new reality of customizable, one-off production. Working from digital blueprints, 3D printers let users fabricate or replicate almost any product imaginable using various materials. But unlike a milling machine which starts with a solid block of metal or wood and cuts away material until only the final form remains, 3D printers print objects layer-by-layer.

Think of a normal 2D inkjet printer like you may have on your desk right now. It works by spraying ink at a piece of paper. On most inkjet printers, the print heads move left to right and rollers move the paper forward and backwards below the print head. In other words, the printer prints in two dimensions: the head moves in the x-axis and the paper moves in the y-axis.

Many 3D printers work in a very similar fashion. To add the third dimension, instead of rolling a sheet of paper underneath the print head, the print head moves in two dimensions over a plate that can move up and down to add the third dimension.

Instead of ink, basic 3D printers use spools of plastic filament, not that much different from the filament used in a grass trimmer. 3D printers can also use wood, metal, ceramics, concrete, molecules for medicine, and even human cells. And some printers can use multiple materials at once, making it possible to print working circuits. Another major benefit of additive printing is that it is possible to print working mechanisms like gears in a single step. ...

III. POLICY FAULT LINES FOR 3D PRINTING ...

B. Firearms

In the United States, firearm production, distribution, and use are already governed by an extensive array of federal, state, and local laws and regulations. At the federal level, the Bureau of Alcohol, Tobacco, Firearms and Explosives (ATF) is responsible for firearm regulation ...

The ATF allows unlicensed manufacturing of firearms for personal use (i.e. not for resale or distribution). Manufacturers who want to sell or distribute arms must register for a license with the ATF, engrave and record identification numbers for each gun, and perform the necessary background checks.

Importantly, the Undetectable Firearms Act of 1988 (UFA) requires that all guns, whether made for personal or commercial use, contain trace amounts of metal that can be detected through screening. Senator Chuck Schumer and Representative Steve Israel have proposed revisions to the UFA that would expand the number of weapons controlled under the Act and more explicitly criminalize fully plastic weapons, including 3D-printed guns made of nothing but plastic. ...

Defense Distributed, a Texas-based non-profit advocacy organization, is focused on defending the rights of those engaged in the 3D printing of firearms. The organization, which was founded in 2012 by Cody Wilson, a former law student at the University of Texas, has attracted a great deal of media and policy attention. In 2012, Wilson was named by Wired magazine as one of "The 15 Most Dangerous People in the World." The Defense Distributed website lists as its mission to defend the human and civil right to keep and bear arms as guaranteed by the United States Constitution and collaboratively produce, publish, and distribute to the public without charge information and knowledge related to the digital manufacture of arms. In 2012, Defense Distributed launched its first effort to promote this vision, the Wiki Weapon Project, which aimed to collect the necessary schematics to build a 3D-printed gun and publish them online. ... On May 5, 2013, Defense Distributed released the schematics for the Liberator, a single-shot pistol, online for anyone to download and use.

The response to the Liberator was intense. The plans were downloaded over 100,000 times in only two days. The Department of Homeland Security issued a bulletin worrying that 3D-printed guns could be impossible to stop. And days after Defense Distributed published the Liberator schematics online, the Directorate of Defense Trade Controls (DDTC) of the U.S. State Department issued a cease and desist letter to Cody Wilson, citing the agency's International Traffic in Arms Regulations (ITAR). ...

By the State Departments logic, publishing 3D printing schematics qualifies as exporting arms secrets, in the same manner that exporting strong cryptography was targeted in the 1990s in the so-called Crypto Wars....

Following the State Departments letter, Wilson removed the schematics from his personally hosted website, but the designs remained online for months, garnering hundreds of thousands of downloads in the meantime.

In 2015, Defense Distributed launched a lawsuit against the DDTC, arguing a violation of Wilson's First Amendment speech rights. In another parallel to the Crypto Wars, Wilson's lawyers argued that source code for 3D-printed guns represents a form of speech (as *Bernstein v. U.S. State Department* successfully argued in the 1990s). In subsequent proceedings, Wilson has added Second and Fifth Amendment violations to his list of complaints. A few months after Wilson launched these lawsuits, the State Department proposed new regulations that would amend ITAR language to explicitly outlaw the publishing of such schematics. ...

C. Health Technology & Medical Devices

Health technology is another area likely to be impacted by 3D printers. As Brian Proffitt suggests, "[v]ery soon . . . the day will come when a patient in need of a custom medical device, such as a prosthesis or stent, can have such an object manufactured within minutes right at the healthcare facility, instead of waiting for days to get the device delivered from a factory." Brian Proffitt, *How We'll 3D-Print the Internet of Things*, READWRITE (Oct. 2, 2013), http://readwrite.com/2013/10/02/3d-printing-internet-of-things/.

In fact, 3D-printed medical devices are already being used to improve and even save lives. Researchers at the University of Michigan have 3D-printed splints to help children with a rare breathing disorder called tracheobronchomalacia. Splints are not the only such instance of 3D-printed medical devices being implanted into the human body. 3D printing is providing new solutions to a variety of medical problems: 3D-printed titanium meshes are used for cranial reconstruction, the layer-by-layer method of 3D printing to uniquely place active and inactive ingredients in ways that result in epilepsy pills with specialized disintegration times, 3D-printed titanium sternum and ribs substitute for a cancer patients own, and 3D-printed neonatal catheters help premature newborns.

Meanwhile, average citizens are using 3D printing to help others with various medical needs. Michael Balzer, a software engineer, used 3D imaging software and a 3D printer to create life-size replicas of his wife's skull in an attempt to seek less invasive approaches to her impending cranial surgery. And prosthetic hands and arms are being 3D-printed by volunteers to help victims of or children born with limb deficiencies.

Decentralized production of medical devices such as 3D-printed prosthetics could raise policy concerns at the U.S. Food and Drug Administration (FDA). How the FDAs convoluted regulatory regime for might apply to 3D-printed prosthetics remains unclear, as it will likely be difficult for regulators to stop bottom-up innovation of this sort given its highly decentralized and even non-commercial nature. ...

Prosthetics are medical devices in a traditional regulatory sense, but it does not appear that those parties who are currently creating new 3D-printed limbs are going to the FDA and asking for permission to do so. Instead, they are simply engaging in this sort of innovation without prior approval.

What are the difficulties for one who wishes to 3D print prosthetic legs, arms, or hands? Under federal regulations, owners and operators of establishments engaged in the manufacture or processing of medical devices are required to register their products with the FDA. Does this apply to an ordinary citizen that is 3D printing prosthetic body parts at their home? The FDA also requires keeping records of all medical devices manufactured and reporting complaints associated with the use of these devices. How much would compliance with these requirements cost for someone who charitably 3D prints arms for amputees? ...

D. INTELLECTUAL PROPERTY

Unlike firearms and medical devices, intellectual property cases are usually civil matters: when rights are infringed, its the rightsholders that must identify and file suit against the infringers. Many of the intellectual property issues likely to arise with 3D printing have been a fact of life since high-speed Internet access became ubiquitous. Rightsholders have developed strategies for dealing with infringement that should easily map to 3D printing.

3D printing is the trifecta of intellectual property infringement. Imagine a father uses his 3D scanner and 3D printer to make an identical copy of one of his sons action figures. The action figure is probably of a copyrighted character, marked with a trademarked company logo, and may contain a patented mechanism (e.g. a rocket-firing arm). That single 3D-printed object thus will infringe trademarks, patents, and copyrights. ...

QUESTIONS

1. Based on what you know about governments' success and failure in regulating the Internet, are they likely to succeed or fail in regulating 3D printing?

2. Does the Second Amendment protect your right to keep and bear a 3D-printed Liberator pistol? To keep and bear a 3D printer? To keep and bear the schematics for making a Liberator on a 3D printer? What about the First Amendment? Do the First Amendment and Second Amendment arguments support or undercut each other?

3. The FDA and the states closely regulate more than just medical devices. They also control the practice of medicine, the business of clinical laboratory testing, and the sale of drugs. Which of these regulatory regimes are at risk from the Internet? From 3D printing?

4. Is DRM for 3D printers a brilliant idea or a terrible idea?

ELIZABETH E. JOH
POLICING POLICE ROBOTS
64 UCLA L. Rev. Discourse 516 (2016)

In July 2016, Dallas police chief David Brown decided to end a violent standoff with Micah Johnson, who had fatally shot five officers and wounded several more, in an unusual way. As a makeshift solution, the police attached a pound of the plastic explosive C4 to a Remotec F-5, a robot designed for bomb disposal. The intentional detonation of the explosive killed Johnson, and was the first deliberate use by American police of a robot armed with deadly force. ...

Consider a future in which robots could supplement or replace some basic police functions. An autonomous police vehicle patrols a neighborhood and briefly detains a person deemed suspicious so that an officer at headquarters can subject him to questioning. During the detention, the vehicle dispatches a micro drone to obtain a DNA identification sample. Or consider the possibility of thousands of autonomous police drones the size of insects flying through a city without detection to conduct surveillance and carrying nano-chemicals to disable dangerous suspects. Or imagine social patrol robots that dispense advice to the lost, record surveillance data, and call in other robots to assist in unexpectedly hostile situations.

Rapid changes in technology result in big shifts as to how police perform their jobs. The squad car and the two-way radio provided the police with a geographic range and communication ability far superior to traditional foot patrol. Robots represent the next leap. Robot staff have already attended to guests at the Henn-na Hotel in Japan. Hotel robots deliver towels and coffee to guests, while other robot bartenders serve drinks and still others deliver pizza. Robot journalists create online content for Thomson Reuters and Yahoo. A novel co-written with an artificial intelligence (AI) program advanced to the first stage of a Japanese literary contest. Semiautonomous Predator and Reaper unmanned drones carry Hellfire missiles. In the near future, robots will probably serve as our delivery drivers and our garbage collectors. Robots like the Japanese Robear will probably provide eldercare to seniors. ...

Sophisticated and inexpensive robotics will be attractive to the police just as they have been to the military. The federal government is already spending significant amounts of money and attention on robotics research. These robotic applications will make their way to policing, and federal monies for robotics will become available to local law enforcement agencies just as they have in the case of recent technologies like body cameras, biometrics, and big data analysis. What is more, police departments will also likely raise the argument that they must be prepared for a robotics arms race, such as against criminals and terrorists who could 3D print an army of weaponized micro-drones. ...

A. What Is a Robot?

The definition of a police robot depends on the definition of the term robot itself. Popular depictions of robots going back to the 1920s suggest machines in humanoid form; think of the Maschinemensch in Fritz Lang's 1927 film *Metropolis*, or Rosie the maid robot in the *Jetsons*. Yet robots neither have to look like people or behave in any specific way. Robots can look like people, animals, or insects; they can provide information, fire upon an enemy, or engage in financial trades. Indeed, there is no single definition of a "robot."

An emerging consensus has suggested, however, that a robot be defined as any machine that can collect information, process it, and use it to act upon the world. These qualities vary widely from one robot to another. This sense-think-act model might describe anything from a "bot" that makes independent online purchases to an eldercare robot that provides emotional comfort or assists with lifting objects. In appearance, robots could take any form. Some military robots, for instance, may assume the shape of four legged centaurs to enhance stability. ...

That robots might look alive and act in unpredictable ways distinguishes them from other technologies. Indeed the special attributes of robots might counsel robot-specific policies. Robotics law scholar Ryan Calo has identified these qualities as "embodiment, emergence, and social valence." [Ryan Calo, *Robotics and the Lessons of Cyberlaw*, 103 CAL. L. REV. 513, 532 (2015).]

First, the physicality of robots enables them to translate their data analysis into action. Robots act upon the world: They can lift objects, transport people, create art, and engage in commerce. And unlike other robots that may cause real- world harm through accident, police robots – at least some of them – will be designed with the capacity to exercise deliberate coercive force. That physicality creates new operational possibilities for the police, but it also raises new types of concerns when autonomous machines may be able to harm people by design.

Second, robots with artificial intelligence will behave in ways that are not necessarily predictable to their human creators. Some robots may just replace human labor in jobs that are repetitive and dull, but others will be capable of adapting to their environment, learning from mistakes, and become increasingly skilled in their assigned tasks. At one end of the spectrum, a robot may be a glorified vacuum cleaner, designed to address the drudgery of housecleaning. At the other end, a robot's artificial intelligence may be designed not only to act upon processed information, but also to improve its performance over time by learning from past mistakes. Not all of this learning will be welcome. Microsoft quickly disabled its social chatbot Tay after it incorporated online responses and began spouting racist speech and called for genocide online. Since artificial intelligence would drive the behavior of robots, robots may behave in ways that we cannot predict, or even explain afterwards.

Artificial intelligence by itself is not unique to robotics. We can already feel the impact of big data-applying complex computer algorithms to massive sets of digitized data-in fields like finance, healthcare, and even policing. A number of police departments already use artificial intelligence in software that tries to identify future geographic locations where crime will occur, to predict which individuals may be at highest risk for violent crime commission or victimization, and to identify which among the billions of daily Internet posts amount to suspicious behavior. The police employ these big data tools, however, as guidance for human decision-making. Robots with artificial intelligence are distinct because they would be able to translate their analysis of data into physical action.

Third, robots are different from other technologies because they are in appearance somewhere between inanimate objects and humans. No robot today will fool a person into believing that it is alive, but many robots do not seem completely inert, either. Research suggests that we tend to approach robots as if they had human characteristics.so Exploiting the human-like nature of some robots could be useful. We could deliberately design caretaking robots to be physically cute (such as rounded shapes, humanoid faces) to maximize their benefits, whether for children or the elderly.

The ambivalence we feel toward robots might also counsel new legal characterizations particular to them. We may think that a person smashing his lawn mower merely has an ill temper, but that a person abusing a social robot is cruel.si If robots are designed to serve as pets, caregivers or friends, could robots be the victims of criminal assault, abuse, or even rape and murder? In this way, the law may need to extend some legal protections to robots, for some of the same reasons we criminalize animal cruelty. We prohibit the infliction of needless violence against some animals because such behavior reflects something depraved about the perpetrator. Though we may not mistake robots for humans yet, we may soon reach a point where machines endowed with artificial intelligence may need protection from human abuse.

QUESTIONS

1. Is a Remotec F-5 with a pound of C4 strapped to it dangerous because it is embodied? Because it is unpredictable? Because it is anthropomorphic? All in all, is it safer or more dangerous than a police sniper or a SWAT team? What about in more routine settings? If robots replaced human officers in traffic stops, would it be good or bad for public safety? If algorithms decided which leads to follow up on in investigations, would it be good or bad for justice?

2. If robots can be police, maybe they can also be criminals. The Swiss art group !Mediengruppe Bitnik created a shopping program they called the "Random Darknet Shopper." They programmed it to purchase a random item once a week from an online marketplace dedicated to illegal items. It bought "a Hungarian passport, Ecstasy pills, fake Diesel jeans, a Sprite can with a hole cut out in order to stash cash, Nike trainers, a baseball cap with a hidden camera, cigarettes and the 'Lord of the Rings' e-book collection." Arjun Kharpal, *Robot with $100 Bitcoin Buys Drugs, Gets Arrested*, CNBC

(Apr. 21, 2015), http://www.cnbc.com/2015/04/21/robot-with-100-bitcoin-buys-drugs-gets-arrested.html. Is the Random Darknet Shopper guilty of drug dealing? Are its programmers?

3. Darius Kazemi, a self-decribed "Internet artist," wrote @SortingBot , a program that posts to Twitter. According to his description of it, "If you follow it on Twitter, it adds you to a queue, and when it's your turn it gives you a short rhyming couplet sorting you into a Hogwarts house from the *Harry Potter* books." For example:

   - @Patthemaker The prowess of an ocelot, the stinging of a bug / Your future lies with Hufflepuff for you are rather smug

   - @kkharrypotter Your nose is wild, your fist insane, yet you are so forlorn / From this rewarding recipe, a Ravenclaw is born!

   Assuming that these tweets constitute copyrightable authorship, who if anyone ought to own the resulting copyrights?

4. Is it good for humans or bad for humans that robots are learning to do jobs – like policing – that previously only humans could do?

ANDY GREENBERG

HACKERS REMOTELY KILL A JEEP ON THE HIGHWAY – WITH ME IN IT
WIRED (July 21, 2015)
https://www.wired.com/2015/07/hackers-remotely-kill-jeep-highway/

I was driving 70 mph on the edge of downtown St. Louis when the exploit began to take hold.

Though I hadn't touched the dashboard, the vents in the Jeep Cherokee started blasting cold air at the maximum setting, chilling the sweat on my back through the in-seat climate control system. Next the radio switched to the local hip hop station and began blaring Skee-lo at full volume. I spun the control knob left and hit the power button, to no avail. Then the windshield wipers turned on, and wiper fluid blurred the glass.

As I tried to cope with all this, a picture of the two hackers performing these stunts appeared on the car's digital display: Charlie Miller and Chris Valasek, wearing their trademark track suits. A nice touch, I thought.

The Jeep's strange behavior wasn't entirely unexpected. I'd come to St. Louis to be Miller and Valasek's digital crash-test dummy, a willing subject on whom they could test the car-hacking research they'd been doing over the past year. The result of their work was a hacking technique – what the security industry calls a zero-day exploit – that can target Jeep Cherokees and give the attacker wireless control, via the Internet, to any of thousands of vehicles. Their code is an automaker's nightmare: software that lets hackers send commands through the Jeep's entertainment system to its dashboard functions, steering, brakes, and transmission, all from a laptop that may be across the country. ...

Miller and Valasek's full arsenal includes functions that at lower speeds fully kill the engine, abruptly engage the brakes, or disable them altogether. The most disturbing maneuver came when they cut the Jeep's brakes, leaving me frantically pumping the pedal as the 2-ton SUV slid uncontrollably into a ditch. The researchers say they're working on perfecting their steering control – for now they can only hijack the wheel when the Jeep is in reverse. Their hack enables surveillance too: They can track a targeted Jeep's GPS coordinates, measure its speed, and even drop pins on a map to trace its route.

All of this is possible only because Chrysler, like practically all carmakers, is doing its best to turn the modern automobile into a smartphone. Uconnect, an Internet-connected computer feature in hundreds of thousands of Fiat Chrysler cars, SUVs, and trucks, controls the vehicle's entertainment and navigation, enables phone calls, and even offers a Wi-Fi hot spot. ...

After the researchers reveal the details of their work ... , only two things will prevent their tool from enabling a wave of attacks on Jeeps around the world. First, they plan to leave out the part of the attack that rewrites the chip's firmware; hackers following in their footsteps will have to reverse-engineer that element, a process that took Miller and Valasek months. ...

Second, Miller and Valasek have been sharing their research with Chrysler for nearly nine months, enabling the company to quietly release a patch ... .

QUESTIONS

1. Exploits again! Is anything different about the stakes when people are hacking cars rather than "just" computers? Can the legal system do anything more about it?

2. If you buy a car, should you have the "freedom to tinker" with its internals, for example to put in a better sound system or to do your own scheduled maintenance? Does that include the ability to modify its emissions controls?

3. George and Jane, gadget enthusiasts, have a "smart home." They can turn the lights on and off from their laptops. Their baby monitor streams video and audio, so they can have it playing picture-in-picture in the corner while they watch TV. Using their smartphones, they can lock and unlock their doors. Sounds great, right? What could possibly go wrong?

ETHAN ZUCKERMAN
BEWARE THE LISTENING MACHINES
The Atlantic (June 17, 2015)
http://www.theatlantic.com/technology/archive/2015/06/listening-machines/396179/

... What's a listening machine? The example of everyone's lips [at a Listening Machines Summit held at Microsoft Research in New York City on June 11 and 12, 2015] was Hello Barbie, a version of the impossibly proportioned doll that will listen to your child speak and respond in kind. Here's how *The Washington Post* described the doll back in March: "At a recent New York toy fair, a Mattel representative introduced the newest version of Barbie by saying: 'Welcome to New York, Barbie.' The doll, named Hello Barbie, responded: 'I love New York! Don't you? Tell me, what's your favorite part about the city? The food, fashion, or the sights?'"

Barbie accomplishes this magic by recording your child's question, uploading it to a speech recognition server, identifying a recognizable keyword ("New York") and offering an appropriate synthesized response. The company behind Barbie's newfound voice, ToyTalk, uses your child's utterance to help tune their speech recognition, likely storing the voice file for future use.

And that's the trick with listening systems. If you can imagine reasons why you might not want Mattel maintaining a record of things your child says while talking to his or her doll, you should be able to imagine the possible harms that could come from use—abuse or interrogation of other listening systems. ("Siri, this is the police. Give us the last hundred searches Mr. Zuckerman asked you to conduct on Google. Has he ever searched for bomb-making instructions?")

As one of the speakers put it ... , listening machines trigger all three aspects of the surveillance holy trinity:

1. They're pervasive, starting to appear in all aspects of our lives.

2. They're persistent, capable of keeping records of what we've said indefinitely.

3. They process the data they collect, seeking to understand what people are saying and acting on what they're able to understand.

To reduce the creepy nature of their surveillant behavior, listening systems are often embedded in devices designed to be charming, cute, and delightful: toys, robots, and smooth-voiced personal assistants. Proponents of listening systems see them as a major way technology integrates itself more deeply into our lives, making it routine for computers to become our helpers, playmates, and confidants. A video of a robot designed to be a shared household companion sparked a great deal of debate, both about whether we would want to interact with a robot in the ways proposed by the product's designers, and how a sufficiently powerful companion robot should behave.

If a robot observes spousal abuse, should it call the police? If the robot is designed to be friend and confidant to everyone in the house, but was paid for by the mother, should we expect it to rat out one of the kids for smoking marijuana? (Underlying these questions is the assumption that the robot will inevitably be smart enough to understand and interpret complex phenomena. One of our best speakers made the case that robots are very far from having this level of understanding, but that well-designed robots were systems designed to deceive us into believing that they had these deeper levels of understanding.) ...

QUESTIONS

1. Is Hello Barbie an illegal wiretap device? Could hackers make it into one? What other things do you own that could spy on you?

2. Is it a good thing or a bad thing that Hello Barbie looks like a person and pretends to understand you? Where else have you encountered computers that try to trick you into thinking they're human?

3. Does Hello Barbie have First Amendment rights? It speaks, doesn't it?

FEDERAL AVIATION ADMINISTRATION
FACT SHEET – SMALL UNMANNED AIRCRAFT REGULATIONS
June 21, 2016

http://www.faa.gov/news/fact_sheets/news_story.cfm?newsId=20516

The new rules for non-hobbyist small unmanned aircraft (UAS) operations – Part 107 of the Federal Aviation Regulations – cover a broad spectrum of commercial uses for drones weighing less than 55 pounds. Here are the highlights of the new rule.

Operating Requirements

The small UAS operator manipulating the controls of a drone should always avoid manned aircraft and never operate in a careless or reckless manner. You must keep your drone within sight. Alternatively, if you use First Person View or similar technology, you must have a visual observer always keep your aircraft within unaided sight (for example, no binoculars). However, even if you use a visual observer, you must still keep your unmanned aircraft close enough to be able to see it if something unexpected happens. Neither you nor a visual observer can be responsible for more than one unmanned aircraft operation at a time.

You can fly during daylight or in twilight (30 minutes before official sunrise to 30 minutes after official sunset, local time) with appropriate anti-collision lighting. Minimum weather visibility is three miles from your control station. The maximum allowable altitude is 400 feet above the ground, and higher if your drone remains within 400 feet of a structure. The maximum speed is 100 mph (87 knots).

You can't fly a small UAS over anyone who is not directly participating in the operation, not under a covered structure, or not inside a covered stationary vehicle. No operations from a moving vehicle are allowed unless you are flying over a sparsely populated area.

Operations in Class G airspace are allowed without air traffic control permission. Operations in Class B, C, D and E airspace need ATC approval.

You can carry an external load if it is securely attached and does not adversely affect the flight characteristics or controllability of the aircraft. You also may transport property for compensation or hire within state boundaries provided the drone – including its attached systems, payload and cargo – weighs less than 55 pounds total and you obey the other flight rules. (Some exceptions apply to Hawaii and the District of Columbia. These are spelled out in Part 107.)

You can request a waiver of most operational restrictions if you can show that your proposed operation can be conducted safely under a waiver. The FAA will make an online portal available to apply for such waivers.

Pilot Certification

To operate the controls of a small UAS under Part 107, you need a remote pilot airman certificate with a small UAS rating, or be under the direct supervision of a person who holds such a certificate

You must be at least 16 years old to qualify for a remote pilot certificate, and you can obtain it in one of two ways:

- You may pass an initial aeronautical knowledge test at an FAA-approved knowledge testing center.

- If you already have a Part 61 pilot certificate, other than a student pilot certificate, you must have completed a flight review in the previous 24 months and you must take a small UAS online training course provided by the FAA.
  ...

If you have a non-student pilot Part 61 certificate, you will immediately receive a temporary remote pilot certificate when you apply for a permanent certificate. Other applicants will obtain a temporary remote pilot certificate upon successful completion of a security background check. We anticipate we will be able to issue temporary certificates within 10 business days after receiving a completed application.

UAS Certification

You are responsible for ensuring a drone is safe before flying, but the FAA does not require small UAS to comply with current agency airworthiness standards or obtain aircraft certification.Instead, the remote pilot will simply have to perform a preflight visual and operational check of the small UAS to ensure that safety-pertinent systems are functioning properly. This includes checking the communications link between the control station and the UAS. The UAS must also be registered.

Respecting Privacy

Although the new rule does not specifically deal with privacy issues in the use of drones, and the FAA does not regulate how UAS gather data on people or property, the FAA is acting to address privacy considerations in this area. The FAA strongly encourages all UAS pilots to check local and state laws before gathering information through remote sensing technology or photography.

As part of a privacy education campaign, the agency will provide all drone users with recommended privacy guidelines as part of the UAS registration process and through the FAA's B4UFly mobile app. The FAA also will educate all commercial drone pilots on privacy during their pilot certification process; and will issue new guidance to local and state governments on drone privacy issues. The FAA's effort builds on the privacy "best practices" the National Telecommunications and Information Administration published last month as the result of a year-long outreach initiative with privacy advocates and industry.

Other Requirements

If you are acting as pilot in command, you have to comply with several other provisions of the rule:

- You must make your drone available to the FAA for inspection or testing on request, and you must provide any associated records required to be kept under the rule.

- You must report to the FAA within 10 days any operation that results in serious injury, loss of consciousness, or property damage (to property other than the UAS) of at least $500.

QUESTIONS

1. Under the FAA's new rules, can Amazon deploy a fleet of delivery drones to bring you your packages by airdrop?

2. If your neighbor's drone hovers over your house at a height of 50 feet, is that a trespass? If there's a drone hovering over your house, can you shoot it down? If there's a drone hovering over your house, how can you tell whose drone it is?

3. Some places, like the White House, are "restricted airspace" where drone flights are strictly prohibited. Should drones be required to have GPS units that can detect when they are about to enter restricted airspace and prevent them from flying in?

4. Is there a First Amendment right to fly a drone with a camera on it to film police activity? To shoot an action movie? To get pictures for a real estate ad?

5. Could the police use a drone to tail a suspect? Does it matter how long the surveillance continues? Does it matter whether the drone is being actively monitored?

5THWHEEL PROBLEM

You are the general counsel to 5thWheel, a "peer-to-peer, crowdsourced, DIY, bottom-up, artisanal small-batch ride-sharing website." The 5thWheel website lets car owners post short descriptions of trips they're planning to make, including starting point and destination and approximate time. Users of the site can browse and search the list of trips. If they find a car owner who's going their way, they can "reserve a seat" by clicking a button and entering their credit-card details. The prices are automatically calculated by 5thWheel based on the distance and time of day. The driver gets 80% of the price; 5thWheel takes a 20% commission. If there is any dispute over no-shows, 5thWheel customer service agents get in touch with the driver and passenger to sort out what happened and issue a refund, if appropriate.

5thWheel posts drivers' descriptions of their trips exactly as submitted. It arranges them within a carefully-developed taxonomy to make for easy browsing. The site is first divided into different cities: so far, 5thWheel operates in 25 cities across the United States. The trips are then broken down by neighborhood, and then sorted by the time at which they will take place. 5thWheel determines which neighborhoods to classify a trip with by examining the start and end addresses supplied by the user, and it requires the user to select the starting time using a drop-down date-and-time widget.

5thWheel has received a cease-and-desist letter from the St. Louis Metropolitan Taxicab Commission (SLMTC), alleging that it is operating an unlicensed transportation service. Specifically, a local ordinance requires any person who "provides passenger transportation services for a fee or other valuable consideration" to have a license from the SLMTC. The SLMTC regulates drivers' working hours and pay rates, the safety and environmental impact of taxicabs, maximum and minimum legal fares, and passengers' remedies for being overcharged or mistreated. It is a misdemeanor punishable by up to three months' imprisonment and a fine of $500 per violation to sell rides without a license.

5thWheel's CEO has informed you, in an impassioned tirade, that it would be "impossible" to obtain licenses in every city for which 5thWheel has a ride board, let alone to comply with all of the SLMTC's rules. For one thing, she explains, local taxi and limousine companies would fight it tooth and nail to prevent the competition. For another, the administrative expense of satisfying dozens of cities' wildly diverse licensing rules would make 5thWheel's business model unprofitable unless it took a much larger commission – which, of course, would drive away drivers. The whole point of 5thWheel, she finished, is to "route around inefficient local bureaucracies and that obsolete stick-your-arm-out model of getting from point A to point B." She has asked you to draft a response letter to the SLMTC. What arguments will you make, what responses do you expect from the SLMTC, and how will you reply?

CODA

What if Internet law is no longer a "specialized area of law" because *all law is Internet law now*?

Made in the USA
Lexington, KY
23 August 2017